new dictionary of the history of ideas

EDITORIAL BOARD

new dictionary of the history of ideas

maryanne cline horowitz, editor in chief

volume 1

Abolitionism to Common Sense

CHARLES SCRIBNER'S SONS

An imprint of Thomson Gale, a part of The Thomson Corporation

THOMSON

GALE

Detroit • New York • San Francisco • San Diego • New Haven, Conn. • Waterville, Maine • London • Munich

New Dictionary of the History of Ideas
Maryanne Cline Horowitz, Editor in Chief

LIBRARY OF CONGRESS CATALOGING-IN-PUBLICATION DATA

New dictionary of the history of ideas / edited by Maryanne Cline Horowitz.
    p. cm.
  Includes bibliographical references and index.
  ISBN 0-684-31377-4 (set hardcover : alk. paper) — ISBN 0-684-31378-2 (v. 1) — ISBN 0-684-31379-0 (v. 2) — ISBN 0-684-31380-4 (v. 3) — ISBN 0-684-31381-2 (v. 4) — ISBN 0-684-31382-0 (v. 5) — ISBN 0-684-31383-9 (v. 6) — ISBN 0-684-31452-5 (e-book)
  1. Civilization—History—Dictionaries. 2. Intellectual life—History—Dictionaries.
  I. Horowitz, Maryanne Cline, 1945–

CB9.N49 2005
903—dc22   2004014731

This title is also available as an e-book.
ISBN 0-684-31452-5
Contact your Thomson Gale sales representative for ordering information.

Printed in the United States of America
10 9 8 7 6 5 4 3 2

CONTENTS

EDITORIAL AND PRODUCTION STAFF

Project Editors
Mark LaFlaur, Scot Peacock, Jennifer Wisinski

Editorial Support
Kelly Baiseley, Andrew Claps, Alja Collar, Mark Drouillard, Kenneth Mondschein, Sarah Turner, Ken Wachsberger, Rachel Widawsky, Christopher Verdesi

Art Editor
Scot Peacock

Chief Manuscript Editor
Georgia S. Maas

Manuscript Editors
Jonathan G. Aretakis, John Barclay, Sylvia Cannizzaro, Melissa A. Dobson, Ted Gilley, Gretchen Gordon, Ellen Hawley, Archibald Hobson, Elizabeth B. Inserra, Jean Fortune Kaplan, Christine Kelley, John Krol, Julia Penelope, Richard Rothschild, David E. Salamie, Linda Sanders, Alan Thwaits, Jane Marie Todd

Proofreaders
Beth Fhaner, Carol Holmes, Melodie Monahan, Laura Specht Patchkofsky, Hilary White

Cartographer
XNR Productions, Madison, Wisconsin

Caption Writer
Shannon Kelly

Indexer
Cynthia Crippen, AEIOU, Inc.

Design
Jennifer Wahi

Imaging
Dean Dauphinais, Lezlie Light, Mary Grimes

Permissions
Margaret Abendroth, Peggie Ashlevitz, Lori Hines

Compositor
GGS Information Services, York, Pennsylvania

Manager, Composition
Mary Beth Trimper

Assistant Manager, Composition
Evi Seoud

Manufacturing
Wendy Blurton

Senior Development Editor
Nathalie Duval

Editorial Director
John Fitzpatrick

Publisher
Frank Menchaca

LIST OF ARTICLES

LIST OF ARTICLES

PREFACE

Seeking to present a comprehensive work that discusses pivotal topics of human concern, the editors at Charles Scribner's Sons and a multidisciplinary editorial board of nineteen professors and two librarians designed the *New Dictionary of the History of Ideas* (*NDHI*) with an emphasis on the diverse perspectives of thinkers around the globe. This six-volume set, which contains all new and original entries, addresses topics in the fields of history, anthropology, and women's studies; philosophy and religion; politics, law and economics; area studies and ethnic studies; literature, performance, music, and the visual arts; communication studies and cultural studies; and science, engineering and medicine. The first *Dictionary of the History of Ideas* was published by Scribner's in 1973–1974 and swiftly became a landmark of scholarship on European thought primarily. The *NDHI* extends this legacy into the twenty-first century with entirely new content on Africa, Asia, Europe, Latin America, North America, and the Middle East. With many more articles than the original edition, hundreds of illustrations, as well as profusely illustrated visual entries, the *NDHI* provides an expansive cross-cultural and global outlook on the history of ideas.

The first *Dictionary of the History of Ideas* is known especially for the history of influential texts. Most significantly, while all articles of *NDHI* discuss influential texts and provide an up-to-date bibliography, there are very few articles in the *NDHI* that are primarily the history of texts. Articles may give evidence of oral communication, such as in a public debate of politicians or in a religious person sharing beliefs and sacred practices with another individual; furthermore, articles on contemporary culture analyze the impact of high technology communication such as the cinema and the Internet. Some authors evocatively describe a thinker's vision of an idea, while others reenact conversational philosophical exchanges. Articles may also depict the experiential expression of ideas in such practices as a social science survey of voter attitudes, patriotic ritual of flag-waving, or political protest.

The field of the history of ideas, in the mid-twentieth century, served as a trendsetter in establishing "interdisciplinarity" in academia, encouraging the pursuit of ideas across the borders of academic disciplines. Perhaps the greatest accomplishment of the *NDHI* is its focus on the most influential multidisciplinary practices, such as "Mysticism," "Mathematics," and "Reading," which have ancient origins, and "Representation: Mental Representation" and "Bioethics," which are creations of our own times. The *NDHI* aims to assist the reader to participate in a wide range of methods and practices of scholarly and popular inquiry.

The Organization of the *NDHI*

From "Abolitionism" and "Absolute Music" to "Zen" and "Zionism," the *NDHI* is arranged alphabetically. Following this introduction is an entry on global historiography that introduces the traditions of history-writing in specific geographical areas. The start of each volume also contains the multifaceted "Reader's Guide," a guide to help high school students, general readers, college and university students, and scholars organize their reading systematically according to their preferences: media of communication of ideas (whether visual images, oral traditions or high technology media, practices or rituals, or mainly texts), geographical area, chronological period, disciplinary or interdisciplinary field. For further reference there is an index at the close of the sixth volume.

Chronological Length and Area-Studies Breadth

The *NDHI* is designed to introduce a general audience to the main ideas and movements of global cultural history from antiquity to the twenty-first century. The chronological scope of the *NDHI* permits examination of a topic over centuries and millennia of development. For example, article range chronologically from ideas created by humanity several millennia ago, such as "Animism" and "Textiles and Fiber Arts as Catalysts for Ideas," to such contemporary concepts as "Computer Science," "Critical Race Theory," and "Media, History of." Articles also analyze newly conceived ideas, such as "Sexual Harassment," a recent label for an age-old phenomenon, as well ideas labeled long ago such as "Untouchability," "Yin and Yang," and "Cycles."

The *NDHI* focuses not only on the ideas themselves (as tends to be the case in companions, dictionaries, and encyclopedias of philosophy), but also on the cultural environments within which those ideas arose, on the transformations and intermingling of the ideas, and on their influence far in time or place from site of origin. The editorial board, which included specialists on Africa, Asia, Europe, Latin America, the Middle East, and North America, invited hundreds of distinguished scholars from around the globe to explore the impact of ideas from their particular areas of expertise. The editorial board also utilized a variety of rubrics to ensure that the alphabetically arranged volumes contain a balance of approaches to the exchange of ideas between individuals and between peoples.

Transformations in Communication

The *NDHI* aims to explore the oral, visual, participatory, and textual processes by which communities communicated, instilled, and ritualized their ideas. A cluster of articles by area specialists on "Communication of Ideas"—which appears in the Reader's Guide under the headings Geographical Areas and Communication of Ideas—introduces the changing means of communication across the centuries in Africa, the Americas, Asia, Europe, the Middle East, and Southeast Asia, respectively. The authors of these entries discuss the continuation of oral techniques after the emergence of literate elites, as well as the growing importance of the mass media today. The authors consider the impact of the printing press and of journalism on the distribution of ideas, and discuss the trade routes and electronic media that spread ideas from one continent to another. The cluster on "Communication of Ideas" describes the practices of religious leaders, educators, and governing officials who instill religious, disciplinary, and civic rituals and approaches into daily life. The Reader's Guide suggests "Cinema" and "Third Cinema" as well as the visual essay "Protest, Political" as articles for further reading on communication. The *NDHI* vividly narrates and illustrates the multiple ways in which cultures communicate ideas.

Eight authors contributed to a cluster on education, focusing on the role of diverse forms of education in the transmission and transformation of ideas in Asia, China, Japan, India, Europe, Islam, and North America, respectively; there is also an article on the contemporary movement to which the *NDHI* aims to contribute, "Global Education." One will find all these articles listed under Education in the Reader's Guide section on Liberal Arts Disciplines. For developments in higher education, "University: Overview" concentrates on Europe and "University: Postcolonial" on Africa. "Childhood and Child Rearing" discusses the history of childhood, the education of children, and the changing views of what it means to be a child. Two related articles on "Dialogue and Dialectics" focus on the methods for student learning taught by Greek "Socratic" education and by Jewish "Talmudic" education. The practices of evaluation are the focus of "Experiment" and "Examinations Systems, China." In "Pan-Africanism," "Pan-Arabism," "Pan-Asianism," "Pan-Islamism," and "Pan-Turkism," five experts explain the recent rapid development, across wide geographical areas, of unifying cultural and educational movements of identity politics.

Focus on a Geographical Area or Global Chronological Period

Readers may choose to focus on the cultural and intellectual history of a specific area of the globe. For this reason, articles are categorized by geographical focus in the Reader's Guide under the heading Geographical Areas.

Example of Area Studies. For the study of sub-Saharan Africa, the Reader's Guide recommends the entries "Communication of Ideas: Africa and its Influence" and "Communication of Ideas: Orality and the Advent of Writing." For anthropological approaches on sub-Saharan Africa, the reader is advised to turn to "Ethnography." The visual arts of Africa are discussed in "Arts: Africa" and "Architecture: Africa." For sacred texts and the practices that accompanied them, see "Islam: Africa" and "Religion and the State: Africa." Among contemporary movements, consider "Feminism: Africa and African Diaspora" and "Postcolonial Studies." For political philosophies and governmental practices, see "Socialisms, African" and "Democracy, Africa." "Philosophies:

African" is a text-based history of African philosophical ideas. For African responses to external influences, see "Westernization: Africa." For further influences of African thought on other continents, see "Black Atlantic," "Diasporas: African Diaspora," "Religion: African Diaspora," and "African-American Ideas." As one will find in looking into the index under "Africa," as well as in the Reader's Guide under "Africa," many of the global entries discuss African intellectual history.

Example of Period Studies. Readers choosing to focus on a chronological period are encouraged to consider the period globally. The category Chronological Periods in the Reader's Guide is divided into the broad periods Ancient, Dynastic, Early Modern, Modern, and Contemporary; the chronology at the back of Volume 6 shows events in the global history of ideas. For example, if one seeks out modern and contemporary intellectual discourse on politics, there are several clusters of articles by area studies specialists in the Modern and Contemporary categories. The series of articles on "Nationalism," "Empire and Imperialism," "Colonialism," and "Anticolonialism" provide a multifaceted introduction to the political and cultural turmoil of the nineteenth and twentieth centuries. To consider discourse on economics, see "Economics," "Scarcity and Abundance, Latin America," "Capitalism," "Consumerism," "Work," and the composite article "Globalization." For an introduction to postcolonial ideas from twentieth- and twenty-first-century authors around the globe, see "Postcolonial Theory and Literature."

Disciplines and Interdisciplinary Studies

The comprehensive entries on specific disciplines (e.g., "Historiography" and "Education") and interdisciplinary studies (e.g., "Ecology" and "Cultural Studies") provide cross-references to relevant articles on ideas, ideologies, movements, and methods in the A–Z volumes (the disciplines are listed in the Reader's Guide under Liberal Arts Disciplines). Let us consider the field of religious studies.

Organization of religious studies. The world religions receive an introductory composite entry in "Religion," which is organized globally and concerned with the transmission of religion by both text and oral tradition. Readers might consider also "Sacred Texts" and "Prophecy." One will find composite entries on "Christianity," "Judaism," and "Islam," as well as individual entries on "Buddhism," "Hinduism," "Jainism," and "Pre-Columbian Civilization." Relevant to philosophy, as well as to religion, are the articles on "Agnosticism," "Atheism," "Deism," and "Confucianism." For Asian religions, it is important to also look at "Chinese Thought," "Japanese Philosophy, Japanese Thought," and "Meditation, Eastern." The practices of religion are the focus of "Ritual: Religion," "Monasticism," and "Fundamentalism" and are also a concern of the six-part composite on "Mysticism." "Orthopraxy" explicitly focuses on strict rules for religious practices, in contrast to the focus on strict rules for religious belief in "Orthodoxy." The physical locations that provide a geographical center to religious rites are the focus of the visual essay "Sacred Places."

The reader thus might learn how religion in its multitude of variations has been spread orally, by text, by disciplined practices, and by sacred objects and sacred locations. The impact of cultural history, cultural studies, and anthropology on current practices in the history of ideas is very evident in many articles in this encyclopedia.

Oral, Visual, Experiential, and Textual Transmission of Ideas

The section titled "Communication of Ideas" in the Reader's Guide indicates articles about oral communication, articles showing visual expression, articles discussing the spread of ideas through practices and rituals, and articles based mainly on history of important texts. The aim of this categorization is to feature the main types of historical evidence the author used in the writing of the entry.

Oral ideas. For further exploration of oral communication, one might consider "Everyday Life," "Oral Traditions," and "Myth." The entry "Language, Linguistics, and Literacy" further enhances understanding of the oral traditions underlying language development. The entry "Wisdom, Human" focuses on global examples of popular wisdom traditions, in contrast to the entry "Knowledge," which highlights the learning of books. "Theater and Performance" and "Musicology" focus on those liberal arts that rely on communication by sound waves.

Visual ideas. People often express their thoughts and their ideas visually. There are more than 400 illustrations throughout the *NDHI* to make that point, to visibly show the correspondence between ideas expressed in images and ideas spoken or written. Readers are encouraged to thumb through the volumes and allow the images to pique their curiosity. In addition, there are fifteen special visual essays in which the images are the focus of the entry. The illustrations are offered with meaningful commentary to explain their context and analyze their content. For example, the visual essay "Gesture" shows human communication by hand and face, while the entry "Maps and the Ideas They Express" analyzes the conceptual mapping processes of diverse historical cultures. "Gender in Art" is one of several "gender" articles that together help the reader to see and understand the concerns of academic programs in Women's Studies and Gender Studies.

Experiential ideas. Practices are explored in articles on controversial and easily misunderstood topics, such as "Ancestor Worship" and "Jihad." Military and civic practices are discussed in "Bushido," "Cannibalism," "Terror," "Nihilism," "Civil Disobedience," and "Nonviolence." The political practices of "Apartheid" and "Segregation" contrast with those of "Diversity" and "Multiculturalism, Africa." Practices related to human exploration of nature and the power of humans to influence nature are considered in "Witchcraft," "Astrology," and "Alchemy," as well as in "Scientific Revolution" and "Physics." The experiential aspects of performance arts are discussed in "Masks," "Dance," "Theater and Performance," and "Tragedy and Comedy." Authors consider music from around the globe, with attention to both performer and audience, in "Music, Anthropology of" and in the visual essay "Musical Performance and Audiences." The experiential dimension of ideas ranges from the pain inferred in "Punishment" to the joy and reciprocity in "Gift."

The Reader's Guide category Communication of Ideas: Practices lists entries focused on practices and experiences, as well as on schools of thought, religions, and political movements. The combined listing encourages readers to consider how the practices overlap among those seeking to spread viewpoints and lifestyles. Schools of thought, such as "Stoicism," "Confucianism," and "Existentialism," are movements of ideas, generally in the humanities; many of these have premodern origins and educated disciples into particular schools of thought that adapted to new times. Schools of thought are in fact schools of thought and practices, which contend with religions. Focusing on the human relationship with the divine, religions tend to create popular movements as well as new schools of thought; scholars who emphasize the pantheism of the Stoics consider Stoicism to be a religion. Political movements such as "Temperance," "Anti-Semitism," and "Chicano Movement" are movements of ideas in the fine arts, humanities, and social sciences expressed in socioeconomic and political movements. These movements usually have modern developments associated with ideologies.

Textual ideas. Anyone looking at this six-volume encyclopedia in which every article has a bibliography would notice that the written word is one of the major sources for the authors' evidence and in some cases the exclusive source. Some authors selected primary source passages to quote in sidebars, which are set along side their articles. The bibliographies exhibit the primary sources— the historical texts, images, and transcriptions of oral communication—by which we become familiar with thought from ancient or faraway societies, or with the latest contemporary thought. The bibliographies also exhibit the secondary sources, recent authorities' accounts of the topic at hand. Many *NDHI* authors are among the authorities cited in the bibliographies of other authors.

Example of political philosophy. Political philosophy is a good example of a field that traditionally has relied on interpreting major texts of history, law, and philosophy. One may learn about political philosophy from the introductory articles "Political Science" and "Power." Or one might look at specific concepts that have been elaborated in texts for use by governments and citizens such as "Citizenship," "Democracy," "Sovereignty," "Utopia," "Liberty," and "Justice." Political movements that have involved personal experiential participation are well represented in "Fascism," "Capitalism," "Machiavellism," and "Volunteerism, U.S." Visual display and practices are important for "Ritual: Public Ritual," "Public Sphere," and "Resistance." Oratory abounds in "Liberation Theology."

Ideas and their accompanying practices that provoked controversies are enhanced by the cross-references in each article, guiding the reader to antonyms and to alternative scholars' viewpoints; for example, see "Terror" as well as "Human Rights," "Atheism" as well as "Religion," or "Evil" as well as "Good." Likewise, to treat independent developments, diffusion and differentiation of ideas, movements, and practices around the globe, we have provided composite articles for topics such as "Medicine" and "Marxism."

Reader's Guide to the Liberal Arts

The entries on specific disciplines and on interdisciplinary studies are intended to introduce the reader to a field of study. These introductions to the disciplines are listed for convenience under the university liberal arts classifications of divisions or schools of Fine Arts, Humanities, Social Sciences, and Sciences. In addition, there are listings under three professions: Medicine, Law, and Engineering. The divisions or schools of a university are historically based on the exploration of related topics, as well as an apprenticeship in distinctive crafts and methodologies. We live in an age of crossing "Borders, Borderlands, and Frontiers," yet it is helpful to recognize the whereabouts of the border one is crossing. Generally, fine arts is concerned with creative artistic production; it relies on both the philosophical field of aesthetics and apprenticeship in distinctive crafts. Humanities, increasingly influenced by studies of communication and language, evaluates the traditions and texts at the foundation of distinctive cultures and fosters the expression of philosophical, religious, and literary ideas. Social sciences (or, in recognition of its humanities traits in secondary education, "Social Studies") investigates human societies from the points of view of both observer and observed to find general societal patterns and variations, and contributes to such professions as law. The sciences, seeking to understand nature, have acquired many humanities topics considered in philosophical and religious texts. Scientists analyze aspects of nature (including human perception) through the tools of theory, experiment, and mathematics, and applications of science abound in engineering and in medicine.

Aside from the major differences of academic divisions, the *NDHI* attests to contemporary trends internalized within each discipline. These trends pervade inquiry at the beginning of the twenty-first century: respect for individual creativity, heart-and-mind concern for ethical issues of human and societal relations, and honest consideration of the specific societal position of the inquirer and the inquirer's impact on the investigation.

Combining Approaches of Fine Arts, Humanities, Social Sciences, and Sciences

The multiple sections of the Reader's Guide aim to prevent the reader from treating any listing location as rigid. Each article in the *NDHI* cross-references many other articles. The growth of interdisciplinary programs reflects the increasing overlap among topics listed under the labels of Fine Arts, Humanities, Social Sciences, and Sciences. Specific disciplinary practices include the very multifaceted approaches of biology and history and interdisciplinary programs that are even more difficult to classify in one of the four classifications, such as the earth sciences of ecology and geology or the performance studies exhibited in oratory, drama, ceremony, and dance.

The Liberal Arts Disciplines category has been designed with awareness that the relationship of disciplines to one another has changed over time, and that there is a benefit to studying a topic from several angles. To help encourage cross-fertilization in the fields of knowledge, articles are often listed under the several disciplines or interdisciplinary studies to which they contribute. An important development in the *NDHI* is the listing of entries that overlap the four divisions and of entries that overlap three or two divisions; these listings are designed to help the reader understand how scholars from diverse fields have problemetized subjects in new ways, contributed the results of their approaches, and thus added to the comprehension of a multifaceted topic of human concern. The reader will observe that all four divisions of Fine Arts, Humanities, Social Sciences, and Sciences are confronted with issues of "Objectivity" and "Subjectivism," topics within the rubric Multidisciplinary Practices in the Reader's Guide under Liberal Arts Disciplines and Professions.

Example of Interdisciplinary Discipline: History

We might consider the field of history, which utilizes methods of both social science and humanities and considers topics historically from all four classifications of the arts and sciences. For convenience, history is listed here as a discipline under the social sciences. As most of the articles in the *NDHI* are historical, the list of articles under the discipline history concerns historiography and interpretative methods. One will find terms such as "Hermeneutics" and "Volksgeist" and debates on historical periodization, as in "Periodization of the Arts," "Renaissance," and "Reformation," as well as "Modernity" and "Postmodernism." There are specific types of history, such as "Social History, U.S.," "Cultural History," "History, Idea of," "Iconography," and "Science, History of" ("Iconography" is also in "Visual Studies"). The discipline of the history of science appears in the Sciences, where it has numerous articles. The listing separates those articles in the

History of Science focused on the origins of modern or contemporary ideas in the physical, chemical, biological, mathematical, or earth sciences from articles focused on early ideas about nature and the human relationship with nature.

Listing of Each Article under Its Multiple Disciplines

The Liberal Arts Disciplines section of the Reader's Guide allows for duplication of entries in an attempt to provide the student with a full list of relevant articles for the discipline to which the student inquires. One would find "Narrative" and "Trope" under Literature as well as under History. The topic of "Family" is under Anthropology and Sociology and under Women's Studies and Gender Studies. The topic of "Virtual Reality" occurs under Visual Studies and Computer Science. The student and the public are encouraged to perform interdisciplinary inquiries and to freely examine ideas wherever they lead.

An Encyclopedia of, by, and for Humanity

The focus of the *NDHI* is the main ideas that humans have created, expressed, described, visualized, experienced, and proclaimed. What idea might be more important than the idea of "Humanity," yet only recently has a scholarship been accumulating on the history of the idea of "humanity" (rather than the idea of "man"). A cluster of articles treats the abstract idea and the visual imaging of "Humanity" and another cluster addresses the movements around the globe associated with the term "Humanism."

Nevertheless, there are numerous articles on movements that hierarchically categorized humans and deemphasized the commonality, as in the series of articles on "Ethnicity and Race" and on "Race and Racism," as well as in articles on "Ethnocentrism" and "Eurocentrism." Articles on "Sexuality," "Women's Studies," "Universalism," and "Essentialism" add further sophistication to inquiries into the idea of humanity (humans of diverse races, color, and ethnicities; sexes, sexualities, and gender; religions, cultures, and nationalities).

Entries on "Individualism," "Person, Idea of the," and "Personhood in African Thought" focus attention on self-definition. The bridge between studies of particularity and studies of humanity is represented in the series of articles on "Identity," particularly "Multiple Identity," brought about by trends of "Migration" and of "Globalization." The *NDHI*, available in print and electronic versions to readers of English around the globe, challenges readers within the multiplicity of their individual identities to personally identify with humanity and with humanity's more humanitarian ideals.

Charles Scribner's Sons: Continuity and Commitment

Charles Scribner's Sons published the *Dictionary of the History of Ideas: Studies of Selected Pivotal Ideas* (edited by Philip P. Wiener) in five volumes in 1973-1974 and in 2003 approved its free release online through a subsidy by the *Journal of the History of Ideas* to the University of Virginia Library Electronic Text Center (http://www.historyofideas.org). Readers are encouraged to utilize that resource for its outstanding entries by prominent historians of an earlier decade. In this brand-new sequel by leading contemporary scholars of cultural history, the title *Dictionary of the History of Ideas* has been retained. As in a dictionary, entries do typically begin with a definition or clarification of a concept, yet the heart of each article lies in the detailed contextual narrative of the changes of meaning over time. Each entry's bibliography further clarifies the discourse and debate concerning the concept. The treatment is therefore encyclopedic in the truest sense.

The *NDHI* is an entirely new publication with many more articles. Area specialists on Africa, the Middle East, Asia, Latin America, Europe, and North America, and specialists on women's studies and ethnic studies advised on the ideas most important to include. Seeking to present cross-cultural perspectives on the history of ideas, the new edition encourages scholarship that is gender-inclusive and global. It focuses on topics of interest today and features developments in scholarship since 1970; it appraises new thinking on some topics in the *NDHI* (communism, linguistics, physics), but mostly addresses entirely new topics (structuralism and poststructuralism, genetics, paradigm, queer theory, text/textuality). While the *DHI* entries were to a great extent the history of texts, the *NDHI* entries are generally the cultural history of ideas, utilizing the records of oral communication, visual communication, communication through practices, as well as the history of texts, in order to emphasize the impact of the idea on a wide variety of people. There are articles on disciplines and interdisciplinary studies, on multidisciplinary scholarly practices, on genres in the fine arts, on movements, on ideas and the controversies they provoked, and on ethnic traditions. The content is appropriate for assignment in class and for educating a general public. With its generous illustrations and lively entries, the *NDHI* visibly reaches out to communicate ideas.

Acknowledgments

I have greatly appreciated the enthusiasm for and commitment to this project of the publisher Frank Menchaca of Charles Scribner's Sons, an imprint that resides within the publishing offices of Thomson Gale. Nathalie Duval and Jennifer Wisinski supervised the editorial and production staff magnificently. Nathalie Duval, John Fitzpatrick, Mark LaFlaur, and Sarah Turner were instrumental in working with me and the first members of the editorial board on the design of the project at meetings held in New York City in November 2002 and at the American Historical Association in Chicago in January 2003. Jennifer Wisinski, assisted by Scot Peacock who arranged for the illustrations, produced the volumes in Farmington Hills, Michigan, at the main offices of Thomson Gale. I would like to thank also Kelly Baiseley and Kenneth Mondschein for their communication via email to prospective authors, as well as the numerous others noted on the editorial and production staff page.

Each faculty member listed on the editorial board page contributed expertise in area studies, in a historical specialty, and in specific other disciplines and interdisciplinary studies. I thank each of my eighteen colleagues, and their universities and colleges, for the commitment, intelligence, and attention they gave to writing scopes for articles, suggesting authors, and reviewing and improving article content. Occidental College also deserves our appreciation, not only for their encouragement of my commitment to history of ideas, and the *NDHI* in particular, but also for Occidental College graduate Lisa Griffin, assistant to the editorial board. At Occidental College I have experienced first-hand the importance of recruiting a diverse community of faculty and students in order to participate in and experience a multicultural, gender-inclusive global curriculum. My research into authors, images, and bibliography for the *NDHI* took place mainly in Los Angeles: at Occidental College, at the University of California, Los Angeles, at the Getty Research Institute, and in e-mail correspondence with the editorial board and with numerous authors.

I contracted for this project in August 2002, and thanks to a very hard-working editorial board of professors and librarians, excellent authors who fulfilled our invitations, and a very efficient publisher providing clear procedures and practices for a quality production, readers may now enjoy fresh, up-to-date entries on some of the major ideas that have concerned and influenced humanity. Might these volumes help contribute to the global liberal arts appropriate for the twenty-first century!

Maryanne Cline Horowitz

HISTORIOGRAPHY

Since very early times, human beings have had some sense of the past, both their own and that of their community or people. This is something that has distinguished us from other species. Having said that, historiography in the narrower sense of "intentional attempts to recover knowledge of and represent in writing true descriptions or narratives of past events" has had a rather briefer career throughout the world, though one more complex and variegated than most accounts allow. It is not possible in the space of a brief essay such as this to convey the entire richness of the human effort to recapture the past, but an effort must be made to summarize the historiographical traditions of many different regions.

At least three major (in terms of their international scope, longevity, and influence) and a variety of minor independent traditions of historical thought and writing can be identified. The major ones are the Western (descended jointly from the classical Greek and Roman and, via the Old Testament, from the Hebraic), the Islamic (originating in the seventh century C.E.), and the Chinese. Minor ones include the various indigenous traditions of thinking about the past (not all of which involved writing), including ancient Indian, precolonial Latin American, African, and those arising in certain parts of east and Southeast Asia. The Western form (which would include modern Marxist Chinese writing) has predominated for a century or more in most of the world, but it would be a mistake to see that as either inevitable or as based on an innate intellectual superiority of method. Its hegemony springs much more from the great influence of Western colonial powers in various parts of the world during the nineteenth and early twentieth centuries, and perhaps even more from the profound effect in the last hundred years of Western, and especially North American, cultural, linguistic, and economic influences.

A consequence of the global dominance of Western academic historical practices is that not just history, but historiography, has been "written by the victors." None of the major histories of historical writing produced in the last century addresses other historiographical traditions, undoubtedly in part owing to linguistic difficulties. This has produced a thoroughly decontextualized and celebratory grand narrative of the rise of modern method that has only been challenged in recent years. It is thus critical that any new survey of historical writing not only pay serious attention to non-Western types of historical writing (and indeed to nonliterary ways in which the past was recorded and transmitted), but that it also steer clear of assuming that these were simply inferior forms awaiting the enlightenment of modern European-American methodology.

Early Ideas of History in the Western Tradition

Arguments can certainly be made for a sense of the past in ancient Egypt, and in particular an effort to memorialize the successive dynasties of the Old, Middle, and New Kingdoms. An early specimen is the so-called Palermo stone, a fragmentary stele inscribed with king lists from predynastic times to the fifth dynasty (mid-third millennium B.C.E.); this was probably used by the much later Hellenized Egyptian Manetho in his own *Aegyptiaca*, very little of which has survived. The later Turin papyrus (c. 1300 B.C.E.) extends to the sixteenth century B.C.E. However, the lack of a written alphabet imposed limits on the capacity to convey the past; nor is it clear that Egyptian efforts at record keeping, though certainly serious, were deliberately aimed at constructing accounts of the past for the benefit of present and future generations. Elsewhere in the ancient Near East, various historical inscriptions and texts are attributable to the Hittites, Syrians, and Phoenicians. It is in Mesopotamia, however, that one finds the clearest early evidence of a deliberate human intention to write about the past.

The successive peoples that inhabited the land between the Tigris and Euphrates, especially the Sumerians, Akkadians, Babylonians, and Assyrians, generated the first type of writing in cuneiform and developed rudimentary forms for the representation of the past, such as king lists, annals, and chronicles. The oldest extant epic, that of the Uruk king Gilgamesh, though it recounts largely legendary episodes, probably has some connection to historicity. Closer to a recognizable historical document is the Sumerian King List probably initiated in the twenty-second century B.C.E., and existing in several recensions. It stretches back into mythical antiquity but goes beyond a mere list in later times to indicate inquisitive uncertainty about the historicity of some rulers expressed in the utterance "Who was king? Who was not king?" It is also a deliberate attempt to present the historical record in a particular light, necessitated by the circumstances of the author's own time. Various other forms of Sumero-Babylonian historical record exist, including building inscriptions, stele, and other durable media. Other genres, such as astronomical diaries, played a part in establishing a precise chronological grid against which to record events, and both the Babylonians of the second millennium and their neo-Babylonian or Chaldean successors of the middle of the first millennium were keen astronomers and devoted listmakers.

Other ancient peoples in the region authored historiographic documents of some variety. There are significant differences between these writings, but the focus of most was on maintaining a proper record of kings and their achievements—the Assyrian *Eponymous Chronicle,* for example, relays the annual military campaigns of its kings down to Sennacherib (r. 704–681 B.C.E.). While it would be foolish to impose modern Western standards of "objectivity" (themselves highly contested today) in assessing ancient forms of historical writing, subtle differences in this regard have been noted between Assyrian and Babylonian approaches. Assyrian royal annals are largely written in first-person bombastic prose, allegedly by the kings themselves. And whereas the *Synchronous History* of the Assyrians, in describing boundary disputes in the late second to early first millennium invariably blames the Babylonians, those accounts written by the Babylonians themselves are often more neutral. The neo-Babylonian and Chaldean periods produced further works such as the Babylonian Chronicle Series. The Persians, successors to Babylonian power in the sixth century B.C.E., would continue this historiographical activity, for instance in the multilingual Behistun Inscription erected by Darius I (r. 521–486 B.C.E.). The latest Babylonian work is that of Berossus, a contemporary of the Egyptian Manetho in the third century B.C.E.; nothing of Berossus's original work has survived though it was well known in Hellenistic and Roman times.

What truly puts these writings into the realm of the historical is the evidence that successive works had to be based on what we would now call research—the examination, selection from, and collation of multiple earlier sources—rather than on any tradition of continuous record keeping. Many went beyond that to aspire to provide advice, counsel, or cautionary tales, a recurring motive through much of the global history of historical writing. One of the best-known examples of early Mesopotamian history is the Old Babylonian *Weidner Chronicle,* reaching back to early times but largely devoted to the Sargonic dynasty of Akkad in the twenty-fourth century B.C.E. This is one of the first historical works clearly designed with a didactic purpose, to recover and preserve the past for the edification of present and future, with a lesson attached, in this case the propagation of the cult of the god Marduk. The *Weidner Chronicle*'s account of Sargon I and his grandson Naram-Sin contrasts the godliness of the former with the disobedience to Marduk of the latter, with the consequence of the downfall of Akkad at the hands of Gutian barbarians. The alternation of divine favor and punishment, another frequent theme in historical writing, thus had an early start. It turned up again in the early seventh century B.C.E. when the later Assyrian defeat of Babylon was ascribed to Marduk's displeasure at recent kings, and it appears frequently throughout the travails of the children of Israel at the hands of foreign hosts depicted in the Hebrew Bible.

The Israelites (or Jews as they later became) were the other major people in the ancient Near East to develop historiography. The Old Testament or Hebrew Bible is now known to have been the work of several hands, and much of it originates from later periods such as the Davidic kingship (tenth century B.C.E.) and the Babylonian Exile (late seventh–early sixth centuries B.C.E.). But in the early genealogies of Genesis and in the more chronological accounts of the Books of Samuel, Kings, and Chronicles, one finds both an effort to memorialize the past accurately as a written record and a strong sense of the divine destiny of the Israelites as a chosen people, a linear progress through which oscillates a recurrent cycle of triumph and misery as God chastises an erring people for disobedience, sin, or idolatry, and then delivers them from oppressors such as the Egyptians, Philistines, Assyrians, and Babylonians. The Hebrew-Judaic view of history and of time is one of the foundation stones of Christian historiography of the past two millennia. It is an achievement all the more striking when one contrasts it with the relative dearth of Jewish secular historical writing during the millennium-and-a-half of Diaspora between Flavius Josephus (c. 37–c. 100 C.E.) and the sixteenth century when Jews, still stateless, began to rediscover the formal study of the past.

Many Western accounts of historical writing begin with the ancient Greeks rather than the Mesopotamians or the Hebrews, in part because the very word *history* is itself of Hellenic origin. The Greeks developed several different genres of writing about the past, including genealogy or mythography; ethnography; history "proper" or a continuous narrative of sequential events with their causal connections; horography, the year-by-year history of a particular city; and chronography, a system of time-reckoning. Moreover, it is in fifth-century Athens that one first encounters both the word *history* and two historians whose works have survived largely intact and who are known to us by name. Herodotus (c. 484–c. 420 B.C.E.), the first of these, certainly had his predecessors. Among these are numbered the mythographers Hesiod (fl. c. 700 B.C.E.) and (contemporary with Herodotus himself) Hellanicus of Lesbos, who was notable for his attention to the problem of reconciling multiple chronologies; and the murky ninth-century figure of Homer (to whom are ascribed the great epics the *Odyssey* and *Iliad,* first written down several centuries after the heroic events they purport to relate). More directly, these precursors also included the Ionic writer Hecataeus of Miletus (fl. c. 500 B.C.E.), one of a group of geographical writers and recounters of stories collectively known as the "logographers." Borrowing from Hecataeus, who first distinguished between mythical, genealogical, and "historic" times, and using something of the poetic force of the Homeric epics, Herodotus linked ethnography with history, coining the term *historia* in the sense of "inquiry," "discovery," or, in some renderings, "inventory" (the Greek verb *historein* means "to investigate"). His focus was the recent events of the Persian Wars, the origins of which he sought to explain. Herodotus relied to a considerable degree on oral information (although the veracity of that has often been called into question from antiquity to modern times), and in his ethnographic attention to other, non-Greek peoples and their customs he is often held to be the West's "father" of history in its broader, more inclusive, and nonpolitical sense. Herodotus's younger contemporary Thucydides (d. c. 401 B.C.E.), in his account of a particular event over a shorter period, namely the thirty-year struggle between Athens and Sparta known as the Peloponnesian War (431–404 B.C.E.), can similarly be regarded as the progenitor of a narrower, politically focused history, though this dichotomy can be overemphasized. Thucydides also fully developed a device employed by Herodotus that would become a convention of much later historical writing, namely the semifictitious speech ascribed to a major figure (Pericles' funeral oration being a famous example). Zealous in his efforts to represent both sides in the conflict fairly and impartially, Thucydides' account of the arrogance and fall of Athens goes far beyond ascriptions to Olympian whims—it identifies actual and proximate causes of the Athenians' eventual humiliation by a city regarded as its cultural inferior; the arrogance of the Athenians, their flaw, is a more fundamental cause of their downfall drawn from Greek tragedy. Finally, unlike Herodotus, Thucydides proclaimed his own intention of writing for the edification of future ages as much as for those living in his own time.

For all the importance that we now assign to these two Greek masters, history did not enjoy a high stature in the Hellenic world, in part because the Greeks were philosophically rather less interested in the past per se than in the realms of nature, ethics, and the mind. Historians nonetheless there certainly were: the authors of *Hellenika* that followed Thucydides focused, like him, on contemporary or recent history. The list of later Greek historians includes Ephorus (c. 405–330 B.C.E.), the first writer of "universal history"; the memorialist Xenophon (c. 431–c. 352 B.C.E.); Theopompus (b. c. 380 B.C.E.); Dionysius of Halicarnassus (fl. c. 20 B.C.E.); and the highly regarded Polybius (c. 200–118 B.C.E.). A Romanized Greek, Polybius is especially significant for articulating a theory of predictable constitutional cycles among three pure and three corresponding perverted forms of government and for postulating the stability of "mixed" regimes consisting of all three pure forms. This was to prove a powerful tool of historical analysis in later centuries.

It was the Romans, however, who produced the next substantial corpus of European historical writing. They were initially much influenced by Greek models, turning such genres as the horography into official *annales* kept by the *pontifex maximus,* a religious figure. The earliest Roman historians such as Quintus Fabius Pictor (fl. 225 B.C.E.) were especially affected by Greek non-annalistic history, though eventually annalistic models were to predominate in a way that had not been true in Greece. The Romans would also introduce a close association of the act of history writing with the experienced politician or general. This became prized in later times (and was frequently used as an argument to exclude women from writing history), despite having been only sporadically evident (Thucydides and Xenophon) among the Greeks. It signaled the priority of rhetoric and experience over research, with the result that the Herodotean association of history with inquiry now slipped into a Latin notion of *historia* as a "story" in the sense of a narrative, true or not. The Romans also celebrated the laudatory and exemplary value of history, and especially the lives of great men, a concept largely absent among most of the early Greek historians.

Among mature Roman historians, the outstanding figures include Sallust (86–35 or 34 B.C.E.), who described the Catilinian conspiracy that had ominous consequences for the republic; Julius Caesar (c. 100–44 B.C.E.), memorialist of his own campaigns; and Livy (59 B.C.E.–17 C.E.), the great Augustan narrator of Rome's history from its legendary foundation—*ab urbe condita* (c. 753 B.C.E.). "Universal" history along Ephorus's lines, eventually an all-purpose model for many medieval and Reformation historians, would find practitioners in the Sicilian Greek Diodorus Siculus (c. 90–c. 21 B.C.E.) and, much later, the imperial pagan Ammianus Marcellinus (c. 330–395 C.E.). No extant Roman historian, however, has been more praised by subsequent ages than Cornelius Tacitus (c. 56 C.E.–120 C.E.), narrator of the reigns of the Julio-Claudian emperors in his *Annales* and of the troubles leading to the accession of the Flavians in his *Histories*. An admirer of German tribal simplicity, as compared in his *Germania* with the luxury and corruption of imperial Rome, Tacitus continued the moral-decay theme detectable in Polybius, Sallust, and Livy; he also established a common motif of later historiography, the juxtaposition of the virtuous and hardy barbarian with the decadent city-dweller. This, along with his terse style, political acuity and epigrammatic comments on events would make Tacitus's works very popular in much later centuries.

The Romans had a strong sense of the divine destiny of their city and its expanding empire, which provided a horizon for their history writing in the way that the known world as a whole had done for the Greeks. They also injected a teleological and progressive element that was lacking in Greek historiography. Where cycles of rise and fall and the random hand of *Tyche* (fortune) appear in many of the Greek historians, history becomes more purposeful and almost providential among the Romans: Livy, much of whose history has not survived, is both the celebrant of Rome's seemingly divine expansion and conquests over time, and among the mourners of the dissipation of its republican virtues and loss of liberty. Beginning in the first century B.C.E., a number of Romans also considered, as few Greeks had done, what we would call theoretical—or at least rhetorical—issues of historiography, including the question of what actually constituted history, what were its best models, and what pitfalls ought to be avoided in its composition. The great rhetorician and politician Marcus Tullius Cicero (106–43 B.C.E.), who had an enormous influence on the Renaissance fifteen centuries later, wrote in *De oratore* (55 B.C.E.) about the uses of history, stressing again its utilitarian function. Cicero was not himself a historian. Nor was Lucian (c. 129–after 180 C.E.), who two centuries later penned a tract on *How to Write History*, thereby initiating a historiographical-method genre that would reappear with vigor in the sixteenth century.

Early Chinese Historical Thought and Writing

The second major tradition of thinking and writing about the past is the Chinese. It has been neglected or at best patronized in many modern accounts of historical writing. Despite the triumph in the twentieth century of Western approaches to the past, Chinese historical writing has a longer continuous tradition, and it developed much earlier than the West a clear and consistent set of rules and practices for the recovery and representation of the past. History was a major category of knowledge (along with philosophy, literature, and the "classics") from as early as the fourth century C.E., a status it would not acquire in Europe before the late seventeenth century. With some important modifications, Chinese historiography was to influence the historical thought and writing of neighboring nations such as Japan, Vietnam, and Korea. Significant Chinese thinking about the past can be dated back to ancient canonical texts such as the *I Ching* (Book of changes), which reached a definitive form about the end of the second millennium B.C.E.

Earliest Chinese thought evinced the notion that there were discernible patterns in the flow of human affairs from which one could learn to govern oneself and navigate a world of continuous change. As this suggests, Chinese thought about the past was very quickly linked to philosophy and the search for the Dao (the "path" or moral order). The first significant independent work of history, the *Chunqiu* or *Spring and Autumn Annals,* is an account of events from 722 to 479 B.C.E. It is generally associated with the enormously influential philosopher Confucius or Master Kong (551–479 B.C.E.), though he may only have authored a commentary upon this work. Various collections such as the *Zuozhuan* and *Guoyu,* both sometimes attributed to a Confucian contemporary called Zuo Qiuming, drew on the *Chunqiu* and other early chronicles to present historical anecdotes and speeches in support of a Confucian outlook which, like the Buddhist, tended to a cyclical view of time that dominated Chinese historical thought until the nineteenth century. Other philosophical schools departed from the dominant Confucianism. The Daoists, pursuing harmony with nature and retreat from a world of cyclical but unpredictable change, did not accept that history had any discernible pattern or didactic value. The Mohists (followers of Mozi or Mo Di) and Legalists both saw discernible patterns of progress, though the latter, adherents of a totalitarian philosophy adopted by the brutal Qin dynasty (221–206 B.C.E.), asserted that such progress, enforced by state control over naturally evil individuals, made the past largely irrelevant.

The most important early figure in Chinese historical thought and writing, however, was the Han dynasty figure Sima Qian (145–86 B.C.E.). After the unification of various "Warring States" into a single empire by the violent but short-lived Qin (whose first emperor ordered an infamous book-burning and mass execution of scholars, virtually eliminating records of the conquered kingdoms), the succeeding Han emperors (206 B.C.E.–220 C.E.) created the stable conditions under which historiography could mature. Sima Qian, often known as the Grand Historian, did far more than write in his *Shiji* (Historical Records) a comprehensive account of Chinese history. He also evinced a clear sense of the historian's purpose: to record major and minor occurrences accurately in order to counsel the present and to bestow fame on the good and infamy on evildoers. Perhaps most important, his model for the compilation of facts about the past with its clearly worked out format, a combination of year-by-year annals and individual biographical treatments, influenced the next two millennia of Chinese historical writing. No Western historian, not even Herodotus or Thucydides, can claim that kind of influence, nor does Western historical writing display the continuity of a systematic and eventually institutionalized approach to the past that is exemplified by China. Sima Qian created various categories for the representation of the past that would be developed and augmented by subsequent writers. By the time he finished the *Shiji* that his father had begun, it was nearly four times the size of Thucydides' *Peloponnesian War.* The *Shiji* would come to be regarded as the first in a long series of twenty-four "Standard Histories" (*zhengshi*), the official history of a dynasty written under its successor dynasty. (The *Shiji* itself, since it covered both the Han and their predecessors, is an exception to the rule that Standard Histories cover only one dynasty and are written after its fall). Sima Qian would most immediately be followed by the historian of the Former or Western Han dynasty, Ban Gu (fl. 1st century C.E.) and his sister and successor, Ban Zhao; their *Hanshu* set the pattern for a history covering only a single dynasty, followed three centuries later by Fan Ye's *Hou-Hanshu* (History of the Later or Eastern Han), which was left unfinished at its author's beheading for political conspiracy in 445 C.E.

Over the course of the twelve centuries from the end of the Later Han to the advent of the Ming (the last indigenous Chinese dynasty) in 1368, the basic genres of historical writing were set. In addition to the Standard Histories, one finds that various works in the chronicle format (originated in the *Chunqiu*) or *Biannian shi,* and the Standard Histories themselves, following Sima Qian, continued to combine annalistic sections with biographical accounts, along with accompanying sections such as chronological tables to establish common years for events in different areas (a practice that soon spread to other parts of Asia). A particularly notable example of writing outside the *zhengshi* model is Sima Guang's (c. 1085 C.E.) *Zizhi tongjian* (Comprehensive mirror for aid in government), which recounts history from the late fifth century B.C.E. to the tenth century C.E., a work that in turn inspired numerous commentaries. Finally, universal histories (in the mode established by Sima Qian) were also compiled, in particular during the Song dynasty (960–1279 C.E.).

Exact analogies between Chinese and Western historiography should be drawn with a high degree of caution since certain fundamental assumptions were quite different. Chronology was based in frequently changed era names (the practice used in many Asian countries until the twentieth century) rather than the single chronology *ab orbe condito* (from the founding of the world), *ab urbe condita* (from the founding of the city), or (especially since the seventeenth century), B.C. (B.C.E.) and A.D. (C.E.)—this accounts for the much earlier development of synchronous chronological tables in China than in Europe. Moreover, where "annals" in the European tradition have usually been seen as the most rudimentary form of historical record, Chinese historiography regarded the annal as the highest form, the distillation of knowledge from other sources. Grant Hardy has further argued that the Western preference since the Renaissance for the single-voiced omniscient narrator and an internally self-consistent story fits ill with the multiple voices and often competing accounts of a single event included by Sima Qian in the *Shiji*. Perhaps most important, Western historiography places high value upon the independence of the historian from outside interference, though in fact that arms' length relationship has really only occurred in a minority of countries and in relatively recent times; official history, courtly history, and other variants have not fared well in the estimation of modern European-American historiographers.

Yet the Chinese experience testifies to the vigor and achievement of a historiographical enterprise under official sponsorship. Under the Tang dynasty (618–907), historiography became elaborately bureaucratized and even more closely linked to the official civil service; it was also "promoted" within the four categories of learning to second place, behind the classics and before philosophy and literature. Under the Tang, seven new Standard Histories were produced, and by the end of the dynasty the Bureau of Historiography had become virtually an independent arm of government, with a fully worked out system of compilation. From a set of court diaries kept during the reign of an incumbent emperor, a recording of his sayings and actions, and an administrative record, a set of "Veritable Records" (*shilu*) would be developed at the end of the reign. These in turn, after the final eclipse of the dynasty, would form the basis of the Standard History of that dynasty. The latter was intended, at least in theory, to be the official and unchallengeable truth, not subject to rival versions or interpretations. This strategy did not always succeed—a new history of the Mongol Yuan dynasty (1279–1368) was composed in 1920, over five centuries after Ming historians had written an earlier version. Some dynasties such as the Tang and "Five Dynasties" (907–960) each have two Standard Histories. It was customary to destroy the earlier sources once the Standard History had been composed, which accounts for the rarity of surviving examples of Veritable Records, those of the Ming being a notable exception. The writing of Standard Histories would continue for every dynasty up to the final composition of the *Draft History of Qing* in 1927 and its 1962 Taiwanese counterpart, which are sometimes counted as a twenty-fifth and twenty-sixth *zhengshi*. All share the annals-biography form first adumbrated by Sima Qian two millennia earlier, often accompanied (as in the *Shiji*) by other elements such as chronological tables and treatments of hereditary houses.

In addition to the Standard Histories and chronicles, a further major category of historical writing, closer to continuous narrative, was developed under the Song dynasty, the *Jishi benmo* (Histories of beginnings and ends of events). The first example, by Yuan Shu (1131–1205), was completed and published in 1174. This genre would later flourish under the Ming and Qing dynasties. Its specimens largely consisted of rearrangements of existing histories—Yuan's, for instance, built on Sima Guang's *Comprehensive Mirror*—but their attention to the cause and effect of particular occurrences was a significant development in Chinese thinking about the past.

The European Middle Ages

Following the foundation of the Eastern Roman Empire in the fourth century at Constantinople (the former Byzantium) and the establishment of Christianity as the official religion of Europe, western and eastern European historical writing evolved in rather different directions. The continuity of the Byzantine Empire for another millennium facilitated the further evolution of classical historiography written to a high standard of accuracy, primarily in Greek. It comprised both secular history—represented initially by Eutropius, Zosimus, and Procopius—and, beginning with Eusebius of Caesarea (c. 260–c. 339), ecclesiastical history.

The separation of ecclesiastical from secular history, though not absolute, proved fundamental to medieval and early modern historical writing and to later Renaissance divisions among historical genres. Late antique ecclesiastical writers, before the sixth century, included Socrates, Rufinus, Sozomen, Theodoret, and Evagrius and, as the religious inspiration suggests, their work was often highly polemical. But ecclesiastical history (borrowing wholesale the sense of divinely guided destiny immanent in Old Testament historiography and turning it into a more explicit eschatology) had a strong focus on the foundation, growth, and triumph of the Christian religion, and a steady eye toward the eventual return of Christ and the ultimate end of history. This helped its Byzantine writers to develop, quite early, an attention to precise chronology and periodization. Ecclesiastical history was also, significantly, generally devoid of set speeches, its authors preferring to insert original documents and letters, which had not been a characteristic of most classical histories. The parallel line of Byzantine political historians and chroniclers was just as significant, though it dried up temporarily in the seventh century. A significant revival occurred in the eleventh century with Michael Constantine Psellus's memoirs of court life, and Byzantine historiography is widely regarded to have peaked in the next quarter-millennium under the Komnenian and Palaiologan dynasties. Notable authors included Anna Comnena (1083–c. 1153), one of the first great female writers of history, who composed an account of the reign of her father, the fourteenth-century emperor John VI Cantacuzenus (1292–1383), and the scholars George Pachymeres (1242–c. 1310) and Nicephorus Gregoras (c. 1295–c. 1359); Pachymeres is also significant as the earliest historical source for the rise of the Ottomans in nearby Anatolia.

Historical writing developed much less smoothly elsewhere in Europe. The collapse of the Western Roman Empire and its displacement by various barbarian kingdoms strained and obscured, but did not wholly break, the continuity with ancient models: a writer like Gildas, who recounts the last days of Roman Britain, sounds like an Old Testament prophet or a latter-day Tacitus in his moralizing criticism of British kings. The so-called Dark Ages from the fifth to the ninth centuries were no historiographic vacuum, for historians wrote significant accounts about the various Germanic peoples. Each was quite different in scope and content and each transcended the limits of annals, variously drawing on Eusebius and certain Roman and Byzantine historians. The most important of these "barbarian" works included histories of the Goths (Jordanes, summarizing a lost history by Cassiodorus), the Franks (Gregory of Tours, whose work is more accurately described as a history of his own times), the Lombards (Paul the Deacon), and the Anglo-Saxons (the Latin *Ecclesiastical History of the English People* by the early-eighth-century monk, Bede). Among these, Bede (d. 735) was arguably the greatest historian of the period. The author of several other historical works, he is also credited with first introducing into historical writing the chronological scheme whereby events were dated *anno domini,* from the birth of Jesus Christ, a system previously developed in the form of "Easter Tables" by scholars such as the sixth-century monk Dionysius Exiguus.

Even more than in the Byzantine East, Christianity proved, despite internecine theological disputes, the closest thing to a unifying force in the development of a common vocabulary and shared set of standard themes for history-writing. Eusebius had been translated into Latin. Beginning with Saint Augustine of Hippo and his disciple Orosius (active 414–418), the author of a wide-ranging and much-read universal history, the *Seven Books of History against the Pagans,* a Western scheme emerged for narrating the unfolding of the divine will through history. Accompanying it was the Neoplatonic juxtaposition of "Two Cities," a heavenly and an earthly, a theme that would be revisited in the twelfth century by the pro-imperial Otto, bishop of Freising, (c. 1111–1158), who used it as the title of his major historical work. It was Otto who provided the classic formulation of a historical continuity argument in the *translatio imperii,* the thesis that the Roman empire had not, in fact fallen, but merely been "translated" from Rome to the Byzantine Greeks and thence, in 800, to the Frankish king Charlemagne, whose ultimate heirs were the Hohenstaufen emperors such as Otto's own nephew Frederick I, called Barbarossa. (The Ottoman conquerors of Constantinople would in turn appropriate this notion, stripped of its Christian association, in the fifteenth century).

There are several other types of medieval historical literature, of which the Norse (Norwegian and Icelandic) sagas of the twelfth to fourteenth centuries (initially an oral record but committed to writing after about 1150) present an especially interesting departure from the prose chronicle and form a link between the world of the annalist and that of the heroic poet; they are the major source for Norway's medieval past. Culminating in Snorri Sturluson's (1179–1241) compendious *Heimskringla* (History of the kings of Norway), itself a reference point for Norwegian national consciousness in much later centuries, the sagas existed alongside Latin prose works such as Saxo Grammaticus's (c. 1150–after 1216) *Gesta Danorum* (Deeds of the Danes), and vernacular chronicles such as Aelnoth's *Krönike* (c. 1120), and Sweden's series of rhymed royal chronicles. Ultimately, however, prose annals and chronicles, and the occasional verse chronicle, would prove the most common form of historical writing through much of the Middle Ages, with the constraints that year-by-year accounts (without the Chinese convention of accompanying biographies) impose on representing the past as a series of continuous events. A good vernacular instance of this would be the *Anglo-Saxon Chronicle,* initiated late in the ninth century and continued by successive writers until the mid-twelfth century.

This does not of course mean, as some later writers supposed, that historiography was simply frozen between classical antiquity and its Renaissance recovery. Historical writing matured considerably beyond simple annals during the twelfth and thirteenth centuries. Monasteries such as Saint Albans in England and Saint-Denis in France developed traditions of multigenerational continuous historical writing (the only Western analogy to the contemporary Chinese experience), in which a summary universal history was often affixed before a contemporary account, which in turn was extended forward by subsequent writers. A separate class of chronicles, more aristocratic in flavor, was influenced by earlier chivalric literature, especially the tales of King Arthur and the *chansons* of figures like Roland, and the biographical *gesta* of deeds of emperors and other rulers. The writing of aristocratic chronicles was stimulated by foreign events and especially by wars such as the ongoing Crusades in the Holy Land, generating such works as the history of the Fourth Crusade by Geoffroi de Villehardouin (c. 1150–c. 1213). Such writing appealed to both rulers and their fighting nobility and was often expressed in languages outside the learned Latin of clerical chronicles. Gabrielle Spiegel has even suggested that the aristocrats of thirteenth-century France, for instance, evolved a vernacular prose historiography in response to concerns about social change and the aggrandizement of royal power. Perhaps the most widely read aristocratic works both at that time and since have been the narrative by Jean Froissart (1333?–c. 1405) of the first phases of the Anglo-French Hundred Years' War (1337–1453) and the various vernacular Scots accounts, in verse and prose, of the Scottish wars of independence against the English. Finally, semifictional works in Latin providing elaborate accounts of the foundations of kingdoms and theories of racial descent were also produced, such as Simon of Kéza's (fl. late 13th century) *Gesta Hungarorum,* which celebrated the deeds of Attila and the supposedly ancestral Huns. The most notorious work of this sort was the *History of the Kings of Britain* by Geoffrey of Monmouth (c. 1100–1154), a major source for subsequent Arthurian literature, and already attacked as an imaginative fabrication by its author's younger contemporary, William of Newburgh (1136–c. 1198).

By the fifteenth century, in the context of the struggles of the French crown with English power and with Burgundian independence, one can discern a sharper political analysis in certain historians such as Thomas Basin (1412–1491) and especially Philippe de Commynes (c. 1447–1511), who anticipates in many ways the flavor of Renaissance humanist historiography already unfolding to the east in Italy. In an unrelated but parallel development, relatively late in the European Middle Ages, the growth of towns in Italy and in northern Europe (especially Germany, the Low Countries, and England) produced a distinct vernacular tradition of urban chronicle-writing. Often developing from lists of civic officials, and written by laity, these annals recorded local events in varying degrees of detail and were an important counterpart, for the emerging middling sort of merchants and townsmen, to the more learned Latin chronicles of the monastic and secular clergy, and the aristocratic works by the likes of Villehardouin and Froissart.

The Rise and Growth of Islamic Historiography

Mention of the Crusader chroniclers brings us directly to the third great independent historiographical tradition, the Islamic. There are indigenous examples of historiography, genealogy, and oral traditions among both Arabs and Persians, such as popular stories about battles (*Ayyam*); and Julie Scott Meisami points out that the Sasanian dynasty of Persia (224 C.E.–651 C.E.) is known to have had both royal and priestly historical narratives. Islamic historiography, a highly elaborate and systematic development of historical writing and thought about the past, begins in the seventh century, its first subject being the life and deeds or expeditions (*maghazi*) of Muhammad himself, whose *Hegira* to Medina in 622 C.E. provided a firm date on which to anchor an Islamic chronology. From the very beginning, a zealous effort to record only true statements about or by the Prophet from authoritative testimony, beginning with eyewitnesses, led to careful attention to the chain of transmission (*isnad*) whereby one successive authority passed information, often orally, down to the next: a hadith or report of the words of the Prophet generally consisted of an *isnad* followed by a *matn* (the actual text).

The earliest Muslim historians, many of whose works are only known to us fragmentarily or as part of subsequent works, include Ibn al-Zubayr and his successor, al-Zuhri (d. 742), who was probably the first to combine several accounts into one continuous narrative committed to writing. They were quickly followed by the first great and fully intact biography (*sira*) of the Prophet, by Ibn Ishaq (c. 704–767), and by the more critically and chronologically rigorous treatment of al-Waqidi (747–823), who also wrote several further works on Islamic history. In the early or "formative" period of Islamic historical writing (from the death of Muhammad to the early ninth century), one can identify subbranches respectively associated with the Western Arabian, Syrian, and Iraqi regions; the outstanding works of this period include the genealogical histories of al-Baladhuri (d. c. 892), the historical geography of al-Ya'qubi (d. 897) and especially the universal chronicle of al-Tabari (c. 839–923), *Ta'rikh al-Rusul wa al-Muluk* (History of prophets and kings), which was translated into Persian (the *lingua franca* in much of the region) during the mid-tenth century. By the advent of the Baghdad-based Abbasid dynasty in the mid-eighth century, terminology to express the idea of an account of the past had also developed. A *khabar* (plural, *akhbar,* literally "information") was an account of the past composed for historical interest rather than to shed light on Islamic law, and often devoted to the relation of a single event. The term *Ta'rikh,* which first appeared about 644 C.E. and is the modern Arabic word for history, was initially used to describe various sorts of writing organized chronologically (it literally means "dating") whether by annals or by the reigns of caliphs. Both terms were used, often interchangeably, up to the mid-nineteenth century.

By the ninth century, though Islamic history was still written principally in Arabic, the religion's learned language, Islam had ceased to be predominantly a religion of the Arabs alone. The classical period of Islamic historiography, from the tenth century to the fourteenth, would see a great deal of historical writing by ethnic Persians, particularly under the Ghaznavid dynasty of the eleventh and twelfth centuries. This succeeded a pre-Islamic Persian tradition of verse epic that culminated in the post-conquest *Shahnama* (Book of kings) by Firdawsi, which was completed in 1010 C.E. Persian Muslim historiography would also witness a departure from strict attention to the tradition of hadith and the adoption by many historians of rather more secular intellectual outlook characterized by *adab,* a moral and intellectual education for the elites beginning in the eighth century that is comparable in ambition to later European humanism. This proved liberating in the sense that it permitted departure from strict adherence to the narrowness of the *isnad,* which was never easily able to absorb foreign history; and histories written under the influence of *adab* provide more information as to the author's intentions in writing them. Historical thought was also influenced by philosophical concerns derived from the notion of *hikmah* (judgment or wisdom) and by a concept of research or inquiry (*bahth*). The work of the tenth-century historian al-Mas'udi reflects these tendencies and is notable both for its critical apparatus and its author's bald assertion of the superiority of history to all other sciences. The prolific scientist and polymath al-Biruni (973–1048), much of whose life was spent in India, deployed his mathematical and philological knowledge to the resolution of calendrical and chronological conflicts between the world's nations.

As Islam spread into other regions, including its Western European beachhead in Spain, as well as sub-Saharan Africa and India, Muslim-authored histories of those regions appeared; the earliest history of Islamic Spain dates from the tenth century and was followed by others over the next half-millennium. Muslims in this period produced a great quantity of historical writing, most of which compares very favorably with the best chroniclers of the West and exceeds it in attentiveness to detail and accuracy, for instance the great biographical dictionary of Ibn Khallikan (1211–1282) and the travel writings (themselves a major source for Muslim social history) of the peripatetic Ibn Battutah (1304–1368 or 1369). Like the European invaders, Arabs such as the Damascene mayor Ibn al Qalanisi (1073–1160) and Saladin's minister 'Imad al-Din (d. 1201) also wrote about the Crusades, though it has been observed that most did not regard them as anything other than the latest in a series of struggles against the infidel. Ibn al-Athir (1160–1233), another chronicler of the Crusades, wrote his world history, the *Al-Kamil fil-Ta'rikh* in the wake of the Mongol invasions of the Muslim world during the early 1220s, an event that had a significant impact on history-writing. Half a century later, another Islamic historian, the Persian 'Ala' al-Din 'Ata-Malik b. Muhammad Djuwayni (or al-Juvayni, 1226–1283) served in the capital of the Great Khan before returning to Baghdad as governor and composing an incomplete *History of the World Conqueror* about Genghis Khan. Rashid al-Din, a Persian converted from Judaism to Islam, also served Persia's Mongol rulers until his execution in 1318; his *Complete Collection of Histories* is a vast world history especially full of details on the Mongol regime. The Mongols, a nomadic and warlike non-Muslim people who came into conflict with Islam to the West and China to the East in the course of the thirteenth century, developed their own tradition of historical writing, which includes the thirteenth-century epic known as the *Secret History of the Mongols.* There is little sign of historical writing among them for three centuries following, during a period of great internecine turmoil and division among the various descendants of the Khan, but the early seventeenth century witnessed a revival and produced several specimens of chronicles. These included the *Altan Tobči* (Golden Summary) which begins with the death of Genghis Khan and continues to the early seventeenth century, and the collection of chronicles known as *Erdeni-yin Tobči* (Precious Summary).

At least one Muslim author, the fourteenth-century Tunisian Ibn Khaldun (1332–1406), stands as among the most significant historical thinkers of that or any age, and as the culmination of the philosophical tendencies previously observed in al-Mas'udi. Although he was the author of a long history, Ibn Khaldun has become better known for that work's prolegomenon or *Muqaddimah,* an ambitious attempt to work out the many factors underlying historical change including customs, manners, climate, and economics; it has often led to his being considered the first sociologist of history. "It should be known that history, in matter of fact, is information about human social organization, which itself is identical with world civilization." So begins the *Muqaddimah.* "It deals with such conditions affecting the nature of civilization as, for instance, savagery and sociability, group feelings, and the different ways by which one group of human beings achieves superiority over another." Ibn Khaldun's idea that individuals and groups that come to power are animated by a group spirit or *asabiyya* has counterparts in much later Western writers such as Johann Gottfried von Herder (1744–1803), while his belief that regimes once consolidated will almost inevitably become divided or corrupted and fall echoes the cyclical politics of the Greek Polybius.

Beginning in the early fifteenth century, the newly rising Islamic power, the Ottoman Turks, produced significant historical works, commencing with 'Abdu'l-vasi Celebi's (fl. 1414) account of the accession of Mehmed I, and continuing with chronicles by Asikpasazade or Asiki (1400–after 1484) and the obscure Nesri (d. c. 1520), who synthesized many of the sources up to his own time. These "chronicles of the house of Osman," many more of which remain anonymous, are distinguished by having largely been written by authors who lived through many of the events they described. The chronicles are supplemented and in some cases overlaid by other sources. These include royal calendars (starting in the 1440s) containing historical lists, and poems and oral traditional accounts reaching back to an earlier heroic age of Islamic warriors, which provide a backdrop of legend, folklore, and pseudohistory. Examples of such works include the *Iskender-name* by Ahmedi (c. 1334–1413), parts of which amount to a world history, the *Danismendname* and the later, more historically specific *Dusturname* (completed 1465 and attributed to one Enveri, about whom little is known). Sultan Bayezid II (r. 1481–1512) commissioned the first two histories devoted specifically to the Ottomans, one in Persian and the other in Turkish (Persian influences were especially potent on early Ottoman literature).

In an interesting parallel with China's mandarin-dominated historical writing, as well as with the civic courtly historiography of many contemporary Italian states, the major Turkish historical works produced for the next two centuries were sponsored by the Sultan or composed by ministers or functionaries such as the grand vizier Karamani Mehmed Pasha (d. 1481), the secretary Tursun Beg (fl. 1453–1499), the chancellor Mustafa Çelebi Celalzade (c. 1490–1567), the poet and tutor to Sultan Murad, Hoca Efendi (or Sa'duddin bin Hasan Can, 1535–1599), and the provincial functionary Ibrahim Peçevi (1574–1650). The Istanbul bureaucrat Mustafa Naima (1655–1716) wrote an important history of the empire in the first half of the seventeenth century, which remains today one of the most cited sources for that period.

Renaissance and Seventeenth-Century Europe

A recurring theme in several of the traditions we have discussed is that history should be a useful guide to behavior, the past itself a vast ocean of examples from which the present could fish, often without much attention to the water itself. In the West, the classic exposition of this idea came from the Roman orator Marcus Tullius Cicero (106–43 B.C.E.), who defined history as the *magistra vitae* or mistress of life. Cicero was among the classical authors known in part during the Middle Ages but rediscovered in full by the humanists of the Renaissance, who appropriated the authors of Greece and especially Rome as their models of style, genre, and suitable content. This was true across many areas of intellectual activity from the mid-fourteenth century on, but the rediscovery of classical texts and categories would have wide-ranging effects on historical thought and writing, not least because from the mid-fifteenth century, the advent of printing permitted the easy replication of texts in large numbers. Within two centuries this would create a larger reading public for historical writing than had ever existed previously anywhere in the world.

First, more generally, a sense of remoteness from classical times and an accompanying aspiration to reconnect with them bestowed a temporal perspective that was largely (though not as completely as is often supposed) absent from much medieval writing. This took longer to mature than is usually acknowledged, but by the early seventeenth century this "sense of anachronism" is regularly discernible in various media, for instance in art and in drama: it was increasingly difficult to conceive of Julius Caesar or Alexander the Great as medieval Crusaders or Renaissance *condottieri*. A more period-specific visual sense of the past was slower to develop, though archaeological discoveries, especially the ruins of Rome and of former Roman encampments across Europe soon stimulated this too. Much more quickly, however, there developed a sense of linguistic change. The humanists of the fifteenth century were devoted above all to the restoration of Latin to its classical form after centuries of "barbarism," though the notion that a "pure" language could be transplanted in frozen form on to a different era actually negated 1500 years of change and introduced a different sort of anachronism.

Second, the rediscovery of particular historians, and ebbs and flows in popularity among them (the notable rise of Tacitus's popularity at the end of the sixteenth century being a good illustration), served to restore the writing of biography and history as continuous narrative, in neoclassical Latin and vernacular languages, in place of the religious and secular chronicles, annalistically organized, that had dominated for the past millennium or more. Leonardo Bruni, the early-fifteenth-century chancellor of the Florentine Republic, was one member of a long line of learned civic officials who would combine public life with scholarly activity and in particular with the writing of history. His sixteenth-century successors, far too many to enumerate, included two who were also outstanding political thinkers, Francesco Guicciardini (1483–1540) and the more famous Niccolò Machiavelli (1469–1527), both of whom wrote full-length histories. Each also authored works of political wisdom, in Machiavelli's case drawing inspiration directly from Livy (and, more ambiguously, from Polybius and Tacitus), and yoking together examples from the recent and remote past in *The Prince* and *Discourses*. Guicciardini, his more pessimistic contemporary, had as a young man written a history of Florence; but he grew less interested than Machiavelli in pursuing the history of his city back to barbarian times than in narrating the unfolding of its and all Italy's current troubles (the invasions by French and Spanish armies and the erosion and collapse of republican independence). Perhaps as a consequence of this Thucydidean focus on the very recent past, he was more attentive to detail (in particular the complexity of contemporary international relations among states), and, unusually for his day, more skeptical about the capacity of past examples to serve the present, owing to variations of circumstance between superficially similar historical situations. This latter point is an important insight that anticipates much later thinking on the uniqueness of discrete historical events and the incommensurability of different historical epochs, and it is no coincidence that Guicciardini eventually found a modern disciple (albeit a critical one) in the great nineteenth-century German historian Leopold von Ranke.

Third, the above-mentioned discovery of physical ruins, statuary, coins, and buildings in Italy and elsewhere nurtured an ancillary branch of historical study often referred to by the generic title "antiquarianism." This took various forms in different countries, but beginning with Flavio Biondo (1392–1463) in the mid-fifteenth century and continuing through most of western Europe in the sixteenth and seventeenth, the antiquaries engaged in inquiries into what might be called the non-narrative past. Not bound by classical exemplars (there were no ancient antiquarian works extant except fragments of the late republican Roman Marcus Terentius Varro) they turned for a literary model to geography, as exemplified by Pliny the Elder (23–79 C.E.), rather than to history, and many of their works are thus organized by place rather than time. They were also considerably less concerned with using the past as a source of advice for the present, though a keen interest in great families and especially genealogy permitted many of these works to include extensive memorials of the great and their deeds. Among the most significant works in this genre outside Italy was William Camden's (1551–1623) *Britannia* (1586). This was a pathbreaking account, built on extensive personal travel around Britain (and on unpublished work by the early-sixteenth-century antiquary John Leland), of Roman and medieval British antiquities. Expanded and reprinted several times over the next century, *Britannia* became a virtual *vade mecum* for subsequent generations of antiquaries and for interested country squires. Bound by classical notions of form and genre, Camden was reluctant to consider such a descriptive, non-narrative survey as "history" (unlike the later *Annales* that he wrote about the reign of Queen Elizabeth), so he defined the *Britannia* as a "chorography," a term adopted by his many imitators in ensuing decades.

Not all of this erudite work was chorographical and peripatetic. In France, where the study of Roman legal tradition was especially sophisticated, philologists and antiquaries from Guillaume Budé in the early sixteenth century to Jacques Cujas and François Hotman a generation further on studied language and law, developing a "French school of historical study." There was a philosophical aspect to this too, in the belief of certain writers—contrary to the view of contemporary skeptics or "pyrrhonists" that the past could indeed be restored and represented accurately. One of these, Henri de la Popelinière, even wrote a complete "History of histories, with the idea of perfect history." Another, Jean Bodin (1530–1596), perhaps the most subtle of late-sixteenth-century European intellectuals, and a voice of secular moderation at a time of vicious religious warfare, wrote a widely read *Methodus* (Method) for the reading of history. This was intended to guide the reader through the thickets of past historians and in particular to dispel certain timeworn notions such as the "Four Monarchies" scheme of periodization, inherited from the Middle Ages and reappropriated by writers of apocalyptic literature (the notion that the return of Christ would follow the end of the four successive secular empires of Babylonians, Persians, Greeks, and Romans). Bodin was the most politically astute and philosophical among a number of writers determined to impose order on the proliferating species of writing about the past, which were threatening to bolt from their classical cages, and to offer guidance to bewildered readers. Describing the genres and forms of history according to well-defined categories, these late-sixteenth-century authors of *artes historicae* (arts of history) hearken back to Lucian's *How to Write History* in the second century.

Historical thought and scholarship was not, of course, invariably or even mainly devoted to the recovery of knowledge for its own sake. Propaganda has always been a significant part of historical writing, both in the sense of mining the past for evidence in support of current ideologies, practices, and regimes, and the use of formal accounts of the past to disseminate such support widely. As the anthropologist Arjun Appadurai has commented, the past can be regarded as a "scarce resource," control over which must be fought for or negotiated. We have seen a variant of this in the Chinese approach to establishing Standard Histories, and it was true in different ways in the West. Much medieval historical writing had been undertaken as propaganda for one side or the other in disputes such as the long-running papal-imperial or Anglo-French rivalries. Various Renaissance courts had employed humanists to write elegant Latin histories explicitly favorable to their regimes and intended to cast their achievements in the best possible light to ensure that their positive image would be passed down as fame to posterity. Protonationalist sentiments stimulated the propagation of elaborate national myths of descent from Trojans, Gauls and Scythians. (Making the wrong assertion about one of these peoples or their modern heirs could have serious consequences. In Sweden, newly independent of Denmark, Gustav I Vasa condemned the historian Olaus Petrei [Olof Petersson] for apparent criticism in the latter's *En Swensk Crönika* [Swedish Chronicle]; asserting French descent from Germanic Franks as opposed to Trojans landed Nicolas Fréret in prison in 1714). Spanish historians from the time of Ferdinand II of Aragon and Isabella I of Castile to the twentieth century have periodically sought a basis for Iberian solidarity in a remote and imagined Visigothic past. In central and eastern Europe, subject ethnic groups such as Hungarians, Bohemians, Moldavians, and Croats developed historical writing in an effort to preserve and promote a sense of national identity, for instance in István Szamosközy's (1565–1612) history of his native Transylvania, Miklós Istvánffy's (1538–1615) treatment of Habsburg-controlled Hungary in the fifteenth and sixteenth centuries, and Pavao Ritter Vitezović's Latin history of Dalmatia and Croatia (1666).

With the religious Reformation in Europe this polemical dimension of historical writing reached new levels as not just particular perspectives but the beginnings of what we would now call "ideology" began for the first time to splinter historical writing into conflicting camps, now able to conduct their campaigns with print, the powerful new weapon of mass instruction. Early Protestant reformers, needing to blacken the papacy and the medieval church generally as one long decline from apostolic purity, provided histories such as the *Magdeburg Centuries,* directed by the Croat reformer Matija Vlačic (Matthias Flacius), which recounted the survival of the true church over centuries of papist decay. While much of this work continued to be composed in Latin, historians were increasingly using local vernaculars in order to reach a wider domestic audience. Thus, notes P. K. Hämäläinen, sixteenth-century Finnish clerics, for instance, began for virtually the first time to write history in that tongue rather then the Latin or Swedish used in medieval annals and chronicles. The propaganda potential of such works, even an in era of restricted lay literacy, was enormous, and was maximized, in the age of religious persecution and intolerance, by a subset of historians who focused on collecting the stories of early and more recent martyrs, as did the Englishman John Foxe, Huguenot Jean Crespin, and the Dutchman Adrian Cornelis van Haemstede. Catholic Europe responded in kind, for instance in the *Ecclesiastical Annals* of Cardinal Cesare Baronio, intended as an antidote to the Protestant version of the past. Partisanship would become virtually routine in historical writing during the religious wars across Europe and Britain during the late sixteenth and seventeenth centuries, although any individual author continued to stress his own impartiality and the bias or falsity of his opponents.

While it is easy to look back at such works and recognize their obvious slant, it would be a gross error to dismiss them as the worthless detritus of religious bigotry. Although openly hostile to alternative views, and often naively supposing (in the manner of la Popelinière or, somewhat later, England's Francis Bacon), that a correct or "perfect" version of the past was achievable, the strength of their convictions led many of these authors to undertake careful research in order to buttress their cases. Nor were the battle lines exclusively confessional, since a broad Latin republic of letters connecting Catholics and Protestants would develop through the late sixteenth and seventeenth centuries. The savagery with which two Protestant chronologers, Thomas Lydiat and Joseph Scaliger, treated each other's works, or the scorn heaped by the great English lawyer and antiquary John Selden (1584–1654) on the Protestant critics of *Historie Tithes* (1618) illustrate this point well, as do the papacy's hostile reactions to the renegade Venetian priest Paolo Sarpi (1552–1623) for his critical *History of the Council of Trent*.

Moreover, ecclesiastical erudition in the cause of belief continued to drive some of the best scholarship of the late sixteenth and seventeenth centuries, as a defense against both alternative faiths and the potentially more serious threat posed by general "pyrrhonism" or skepticism towards the possibility of recovering the past. An intense search for a firm chronology for events before and since Christ climaxed in the sophisticated work of the French Huguenot philologer Joseph Scaliger (1540–1609) and his Jesuit successor, Denis Pétau (or Dionysius Petavius, 1583–1652), as well as in more notorious attempts to fix with certitude dates such as the first day of Creation—most famously assigned by the Irish archbishop James Ussher (1581–1656) to Sunday, 23 October 4004 B.C.E. Building on this chronological corpus, the Maurists, French Benedictines at Saint-Germain-des-Prés and other houses, produced editions of church fathers, based on original sources, but their principal contribution was in the development of systematic paleography (interpretation of historical scripts and hands) and diplomatic (knowledge of the structure, layout, and conventional formulae of documents) for the analysis of sources. This is best summed up by one of their leading figures, Jean Mabillon (1632–1707), in his treatise *De re diplomatica libri VI* (Six books on diplomatics), which focused on the authenticity of medieval charters. The Bollandists—Belgian Jesuits—commenced the *Acta Sanctorum* (Acts of the saints), organized as a month-by-month calendar of feast days, in order to set the lives and deeds of the historical saints on a sounder scholarly footing. Their project continues today and significantly improved the level of source editing then practiced.

Such tendencies in evidentiary criticism could have unintended consequences in nurturing unbelief. The same skepticism that appears in earlier antiquaries' doubts about such myths as the Trojan descent, or in Jean Bodin's dismissal of the Four Monarchies periodization, soon produced doubts about the literal truth of the Old Testament as a historical source, and deistic views of rational religion. The skeptical tendency first notable in the later sixteenth century produced in the seventeenth both reactive affirmations of received traditions (the *Discourse on Universal History*, Bishop Jacques-Bénigne Bossuet's splendid effort to rehabilitate medieval world history in a Christian context being a famous example), and more thoughtful attempts to address what was now an urgent problem, the very reliability of not just specific traditions, but of *any* historical knowledge. Some of these efforts had a secular focus: Francis Bacon's (1561–1626) empirical attempt to build truths from individually verified "facts" (it was in this period that the word "fact" acquired something like its modern meaning) applied in his judgment both to the realm of the past and the realm of nature, both of which were best represented by "histories"—echoes of the old Herodotean notion of a discovery or inventory can here be heard. Bacon also enumerated the various genres of history in a manner directly derived from the sixteenth-century *artes historicae* (although his only significant effort at history-writing, on the reign of England's King Henry VII (r. 1485-1509), was a rather conventional humanist "politic" history in the style of Tacitus and Machiavelli, intended to provide advice to the crown). The French philosopher René Descartes (1596-1650) addressed the problem of knowledge from the interior to the exterior world, through deduction, but his solution to pyrrhonism in areas like mathematics and religion did little to buttress confidence that knowledge of the past could be similarly verified. In ensuing decades, others (such as Bacon's fellow Englishmen, Edward, Lord Herbert of Cherbury, Joseph Glanvill, and William Chillingworth) sought to reaffirm the historical foundations of religious truth.

Skepticism about received knowledge, and the belief that reason (we might say "common sense") must take precedence over the revealed truth in Scripture, is perhaps most famously represented in the *Dictionnaire historique et critique* by the exiled French *érudit* Pierre Bayle (1647–1706). The *Dictionnaire,* which appeared in several editions beginning in 1697, was enormously influential in the eighteenth century, but Bayle was scarcely alone in his doubts, especially with respect to the status of scripture as a historical source. Another Frenchman, Isaac de la Peyrère, had anticipated this position in 1655 (the very time at which Archbishop Ussher was confidently working out the date of Creation), after concluding that the Old Testament chronologies were irreconcilable with the existence of non-biblical peoples. The Dutch philosopher Baruch or Benedict Spinoza (1632–1677) espoused the notion that the Pentateuch was the work not of Moses but of a much later, post-Exilic author. Churchmen were active participants in these discussions. The French priest Richard Simon (1638–1712) advanced Spinozan doubts as to Mosaic authorship in his *Histoire critique du Vieux Testament,* published at Paris in 1678 and soon seized by authorities. The English cleric Thomas Burnet (c. 1635–1715) authored works of criticism in a similar vein, two centuries of philological refinement having now been reinforced by the physical evidence of fossils, bones and other artifacts collected by the "curious," the virtuoso assemblers of cabinets of marvels during the previous century. When Burnet later suggested that Genesis could be read "metaphorically," he was quickly dismissed from the office he held at court.

Others, however, continued to build new foundations for historical knowledge (in some cases literally) from the ground up, using erudition as the key to decoding and verifying the obscurities of the past. This was not strictly a Christian perquisite. Jewish historical writing, largely a vacuum since the first century C.E., experienced its own renaissance in the sixteenth century with the Iberian exiles Solomon ibn Verga (1460–1554) of Seville and Samuel Usque (fl. 1540–1555) and the messianic world historian Joseph ha-Kohen. But it was the Mantuan-born Azariah de' Rossi (c. 1511–1578) who most resembled the great Christian antiquaries in his attention to the sources of ancient Jewish history. Azariah's *Me'or 'Einayim* (Enlightenment of the Eyes) was roundly rejected by contemporary rabbinical scholars, but it pointed ahead to the more secure revival of Jewish secular historiography in the early nineteenth century.

By 1700, there was considerable overlap between the study of the erudite side of the past (numismatics, epigraphy, papyrology, paleography, and chronology) and the natural philosophy and natural history of the day. Leading intellectuals in other arenas such as Sir Isaac Newton (1642–1727), who was keenly interested in chronology, and Gottfried Wilhelm von Leibniz (1646–1716) participated in these erudite activities and corresponded with the antiquarian *savants* of the day. The atmospheric pressure and velocity of knowledge is well captured in the letters between scholars, and in the interconnected activities of the great many European academies and societies that were founded at this time, as well as in the earliest journals that circulated knowledge in print. There was also intense activity in the area of source publication and criticism. This included both ancient materials and (with an interest not shown previously) those from the Middle Ages, such as the sources of French history begun by the Maurists as *Rerum Gallicarum et Franciscarum Scriptores,* or the scholarship in hagiography and imperial Roman history by Louis-Sébastien Le Nain de Tillemont (1637–1698). Perhaps the outstanding examples of this Baroque source publication are provided by the works of the Modenese Lodovico Antonio Muratori (1672–1750), including the *Rerum Italicarum Scriptores* and *Annali d'Italia.*

The tremors affecting thinking about the past, chronology, and history were undoubtedly magnified by two centuries of explorations overseas, for this was also the era of European expansion to the East and the West. The discovery of other peoples, especially primitive indigenous cultures, also complicated inherited schemes for the periodization of history and the Creation story, as la Peyrère had demonstrated. The conquistadors and the more learned clerical missionaries who followed them discovered advanced non-Christian civilizations in the Aztecs, Mayans, and Incas. Many of these had developed their own sense of the past and non-alphabetic means to represent it—the Incas used the *quipu* or knotted cords combined with memorized traditions, and Mayan glyphs record a dynastic history for the period 250–900 C.E. This was also the first period at which

Western modes of history began to spread outside their European confines and exercise influence elsewhere, as both natives and missionaries constructed chronicles of the preconquest and conquest eras. By the seventeenth century, an Indian, Felipe Guamán Poma de Ayala (fl. 1613), and a Mestizo, Garcilaso de la Vega, El Inca (1539–1616), both of whom were influenced by the Dominican Bartolomé de Las Casas (1474–1566), could be relatively comfortable writing history in the mode of the Spanish conquerors, as did the Texcocan Fernando de Alva Ixtlilxóchitl (1578–1650). European expansion also moved east, and other missionaries contributed histories of China and Japan in the late sixteenth and seventeenth centuries. They were uninfluenced by very different Chinese historical genres of the late Ming period. Nor, in contrast to their rapid subjugation of indigenous American traditions, did they exercise much immediate impact on the Chinese and Japanese. The great period of Western influence on Asian historical writing lay several centuries ahead.

India in the Pre-Islamic and Mughal Periods

Among indigenous forms of historical writing that differ from those of the West, none is as hard to grasp as, or more contentious than, those of pre-Islamic India. The values and style of Islamic and Chinese historiography differ from the European, but their products are nonetheless clearly recognizable as histories, and they share common concerns with matters such as chronology and the memorialization of particular facts about the past. For this reason, even the respect accorded to these traditions in most Western histories of history is often completely withheld from other modes of apprehending the past that seem much more remote. Early Indian historical writing is among these. India's very capacity to generate thought and writing about the past has often been rejected—al-Biruni commented on the Hindu lack of interest in "the historical order of things" as early as the 1020s; Edward Gibbon commented on general "Asiatic" lack of history in the eighteenth century; and the indictment was echoed by James Mill and by Georg Wilhelm Friedrich Hegel in the nineteenth century. This is a view that modern scholars of ancient India have fought hard to dispel, though from two very different directions. Some, like Romila Thapar, have argued that there is a historicity or at least historical consciousness in early Indian texts. More recently, scholars such as Vinay Lal have denied this but argued that the very notion of the importance of history is a Western imposition upon a colonized South Asia, an epistemological privileging of a category that should *not* be applied to other cultures such as the Indian. Certainly the complexity of ethnic groups and languages, and the rigidities of the caste system, did not permit anything like Western historiography to develop. Nor was there the central government apparatus that stimulated and systematized Chinese historiography, or the religious imperative underlying classical Islamic histories. It is arguable that Indian philosophy paid no special heed to history (though this was also true of the ancient Greeks) in part because the Hindu outlook is thought to have rejected the notion of individual causality and denied the significance of short-term events in favor of much longer epochs or periods. The most frequently cited exception, a twelfth-century text that actually resembles a chronological "history" is the Sanskrit-language *Rajtarangini* (c. 1148–1149) by Kalhana. This verse composition covered the history of Kashmir from remote antiquity to the author's own time and was derived from legends, oral traditions, written records, and inscriptions. Kalhana was followed by four other Sanskrit-language historians: Jonaraja (early fifteenth century), Srivara (later fifteenth century), Prajyabhatta (early sixteenth century), and Suka (early seventeenth century).

But historical forms *of some sort* assuredly did exist in ancient India, indicating a sense of the past quite different from that in the West, but scarcely the happy ignorance suggested by James Mill. Much more typical than Kalhana's work was the combined tradition known as *itihasa-purana*, which by the mid-first millennium C.E. had become an authoritative source for the ruling Brahman caste. *Itihasa* translates as "thus it was" while *purana* refers to "that which pertains to ancient times" or "old lore." Early Indian historical tradition contains origin myths and extensive genealogical material on the descents of major families (which generally do not place the figures chronologically). There are also some biographies of individual rulers, beginning in the seventh century C.E. and peaking from the tenth to thirteenth centuries, as well as chronicles of ruling families (*Vamsavalis*, literally, "path to succession") in inscription or textual form, of which Kalhana's text is the best example and the one most familiar in its use of multiple sources, critically evaluated. An additional category is the collection of historical narratives or *Prabandha,* which again have a biographical orientation.

Pre-Islamic India also developed other traditions of writing about the past, distinct from *itihasa-purana*, especially Buddhist and Jaina, both centered in monastic institutions; the Pali-language chronicles from Sri Lanka for instance focus on the history of a particular Buddhist order or monastery but also stray into secular history and the history of earlier times. Writings such as the *Rajavaliya*, compiled by several hands between the fourteenth and nineteenth centuries, and the *Mahavamsa*, a sixth-century work continued in the tripartite *Culavamsa* of the twelfth, fourteenth, and late eighteenth centuries, together represent a cumulative history of nearly two millennia. To India's north, in Tibet, Buddhist scholarship produced (in Tibetan and Sanskrit) the large history known as the *Deb-ther sngon–po* (*Blue Annals*, the work of the translator and compiler 'Gos lo-tsa-ba gzhon-nu-dpal (1392–1491) who used and frequently simply copied earlier sources such as *rnam-thar* (lives) by religious teachers, not all of which are still extant. The chronology of this work and the names of Tibetan rulers can be verified by comparison with events described in earlier Chinese annals from the Tang dynasty. Together with the slightly earlier "History of Buddhism" by Buston (composed c. 1322), the *Blue Annals* has become the source of information for most later histories of Tibet. Apart from language variations (Pali and Tibetan as opposed to Sanskrit), South Asian Buddhist historical writing parted from the Brahmanic in at least one important respect, its dating of events from a single point, the death of the Buddha c. 483 B.C.E. (a controverted date also used by some, but not all, Buddhist-influenced countries). There is an obvious analogy with Christian and Muslim dates A.D. and A.H., and the greater sense of time that one finds in a work like Kalhana's may well be attributable to Buddhist influences, though a comparably Buddhist "era" never achieved historiographical usage in either South or East Asia.

Various regions developed historiographic forms during India's "medieval" or Muslim-ruled period, which ended in the mid-eighteenth century. In the Rajput state, Mughal-inspired official chronicles or *khyats* (some of which contained information from earlier Hindu bardic literature) first appeared in the late sixteenth century. In the early eighteenth century a king of Assam, Siva Singha, ordered a history of his predecessors to be written, and a century later, Ramram Basu, at the behest of a British missionary, authored a vernacular history of the government of Bengal. There exists also a distinct tradition of historical writing among the Maratha people of Western India, including *bakhars* (chronicles and biographies) that continued to be written into the period of British imperial governance. While the reliability of some of these works as chronological sources for the periods they depict has been questioned by modern scholars, they nevertheless constitute intentional attempts to capture the past. It is thus important to recognize that the absence of the usual Western forms of historical writing through much of this period does not entail a lack of any such activity, much less the complete absence of historical *thinking*. However, European traditions would eventually prove effective in bringing the indigenous Indian tradition to a close, following its earlier encounters with Islamic historical thought introduced by Arabic and Persian visitors and Mughal conquerors.

These previous contacts date from the eleventh century, when al-Biruni had traveled into India and reported back on its culture. The newcomers brought with them what was by then a mature Muslim historiography, and in the fourteenth-century, the Bengali official Ziya'-ud-Din Barani would remark of historians that they must be truthful and provide insight into virtuous behavior but also inquire into the reasons underlying change in human affairs, injunctions that would not have arisen in the context of *itihasa-purana*. By the sixteenth century, when Mongol-descended Islamic rulers from Turkestan (the Mughals) ruled much of India, Islamic and especially Persian, cultural influences on historiography became more widespread: the Sanskrit-language Kashmir chronicles were superseded by Persian-language works such as the anonymous *Baharistan-i-Shahi* (1614), or the sixteenth-century autobiographical history of the Central Asian Mughals, *Tarikh-i-Rashidi* (comp. c. 1541–1544) by the warrior Mirza Muhammad Haidar (c. 1500–1551). The latter's cousin, the Mughal conqueror Zahir-ud-Din Muhammad, known as Babur (1483–1530), composed or dictated a detailed autobiographical history of his times, the *Baburnama*. Abu-'l Fazl 'Allami (1551–1602), the minister of Babur's grandson Akbar, authored the *Akbarnama*, which brought together a variety of sources; it also contains many interesting reflections on the nature of history, which he conceived of as both rational and as a source of solace for grief in the present. At precisely the same period that court-sponsored histories were in vogue in Renaissance Europe, the same feature can be observed in Mughal India, and Akbar inaugurated with Abu-l Fazl the Persian-influenced practice of having an official historiographer write the history of the empire, a practice that was maintained until the last great Mughal emperor, or Aurangzeb 'Alamgir, in the following century. During the next two hundred years, Islam continued to dominate historical writing in India, producing works on various regions and localities, such as Ali Muham-mad Khan's mid-eighteenth-century history of Gujrat over the previous seven hundred years.

Early Japanese and Korean Historical Thought

The story of Japanese historical writing begins with the influence of China and Korea and appears to have concluded in our own time with the impact of the West. History developed considerably later in Japan than in China, and then not in the same forms, despite the frequent use of Chinese as the language of composition. Historical writing can be found in the Japanese archipelago from the seventh century C.E. The emperor Temmu had ordered compilation of a chronicle in 681 in order to correct errors in and conflicts between imperial genealogies and the traditional origin tales of various great families The earliest extant texts are two official historical works, the *Kojiki* (Record of ancient matters, completed 712 C.E.) and *Nihon shoki* or *Nihongi* (Chronicles of Japan [Nihon], comp. 720 C.E.). These were both commissioned in 711, ostensibly by the empress Gemmei, as the preface to the *Kojiki* stated. Both texts relayed a powerful mythology of the creation of the world and the subsequent foundation of the empire by the first human monarch, Jimmu or Jinmu, a direct descendant of the sun goddess—belief in the emperor's divine ancestry would continue to be taught in twentieth-century Japanese schools. The *Nihon shoki* was composed in Chinese in an attempt to imitate Chinese historiography. The *Kojiki* was written in a commonly used mixture of Chinese and Japanese that grew unfamiliar to readers in later centuries, which led in part to the work's being neglected until the 1700s. By 901 C.E. the *Nihon shoki* had been augmented by five other Chinese-language works that with it form the Six National Histories (*Rikkokushi*).

In some ways, however, the Chinese system of historical writing, and in particular the use of the dynasty as the basic unit of the Standard History, was ill-suited to Japan. From the Japanese point of view, all emperors belonged to the same dynasty, being directly descended from the sun goddess via Jimmu—the *Kojiki* in particular stresses the continuity of the imperial line rather than the cycle of dynastic rise and decay immanent in the Chinese Standard Histories. This linealism, and a degree of resistance to Chinese cultural dominance in spite of the influence of Confucianism, ensured that while its language was initially borrowed, the edifice of Chinese historical writing was not reconstructed wholesale, even in officially sponsored chronicles such as the *Azuma kagami,* a late-thirteenth-century product of the first, Kamakura, shogunate or military government, which is presented as if it were a diary compiled as events occurred. Moreover, beginning in the eleventh century during the Heian period, a different type of history, written in Japanese, began to appear in the *Rekishi monogatari* or historical tales, which were composed by independent scholars and departed considerably from the national histories; at least one of these, the *Eiga monogatari* (c. 1100), was composed by a woman. Many works in this genre were biographically organized; a number, such as the *Gunki monogatari,* dealt principally with war and were often recited orally (not unlike the Homeric epics, which they resemble in military values) before being committed to writing. Examples include the fourteenth-century *Taiheiki* (Chronicle of great peace). Most widely read among medieval Japanese historical writings were the *Gukansho* by the priest Jien (c. 1220), the *Eiga monogatari* and the twelfth-century *Okagami* or Great Mirror.

Following several centuries of imperial decline, the Tokugawa Bakufu (1603–1868) was established whereby shoguns ruled the country on behalf of a figurehead emperor through regional *daimyo* or warlords. During this era, Japan was kept rigidly secluded from outside influences. Historical thinking achieved higher intellectual prominence to the extent that Ogyu Sorai (1667–1728) could confidently proclaim that history was "the ultimate form of scholarly knowledge." Official history-writing in the mode of the Six National Histories continued to flourish, often tied to a particular shogunal "domain" or feudal territory—the pro-imperial *Dai Nihon Shi* (Great history of Japan, begun in 1657 and only completed in 1906) was, for example, initiated in the Mito domain. Much of this work began to depart from the imperial mythology of Jimmu since it did nothing to support the case for shogunal primacy over a puppet emperor. Among shogunal officials, Arai Hakuseki (1657–1725) stands out for his *Tokushi yoron* (Essays on history), a series of lectures on the past intended to instruct the shogun through example while making use of a wide variety of sources and largely ignoring the early origin myths. Arai painted a progressive picture of Japanese history that validated noncentralized governance; it also subordinated individual action and choice to inevitable historical trends. Two generations earlier, Hayashi Razan (1583–1657), an unabashed admirer of Chinese historical texts, had set the stage for a Neo-Confucian philosophy of history strongly allied to the shogunate. A number of private scholars were also writing about the past, often from non-Confucian perspectives. Motoori Norinaga (1730–1801), an exponent of the "National Learning" school of history, rejected Chinese-influenced accounts of the past in favor of the earlier record of the *Kojiki,* which now achieved a status it had not enjoyed for a millennium. (Motoori conveniently overlooked the fact that it, too, was heavily indebted to Chinese histories).

Like Japan (which it in turn influenced), Korea was strongly affected by Chinese historiography through much of the premodern period. Unlike Japan, Korea had distinct dynasties, and the annals of each reign (*sillok*) are analogous to Chinese Veritable Records. The *chongsa* or dynastic histories of early Korea are similarly comparable to the Chinese Standard Histories (which in fact provide the earliest source material for Korean history). Historical records were maintained from the fourth century C.E., and a history was compiled in 600 C.E. by Yi Mun-jin of the Koguryo kingdom, but these have not survived; Korean writings may even have influenced the Japanese *Nihon shoki* in the eighth century. The earliest example still extant of Korean history-writing, compiled in the Koryo period, is Kim Pu-sik's *Samguk Sagi* (History of three kingdoms) (1145 C.E.); this used both now-lost Korean sources and Chinese writings, and is clearly modeled on Chinese Standard Histories. The Koryo dynasty (918–1392), following earlier Tang Chinese practice, established a History Office in the tenth century; this bureaucracy was considerably expanded during the ensuing Yi or Choson dynasty (1392–1910), and in the fifteenth century a group of scholars led by Chong In-ji (1418–1450) completed the *Koryosa* (a dynastic history of the Koryo). Choson historians would eventually produce a whole series of *sillok* for each reign covering nearly five centuries up to 1863. As with the Chinese Veritable Records, *sillok* were carefully guarded so that even the reigning monarch was denied access to them in order to protect against interference. Again as with China, the presence of an official bureaucracy could not prevent alternate or private interpretations of the past from being written. A more Korean-focused tradition of historical writing also sprang from this Confucianism, for instance the thirteenth-century monk Iryon's *Samguk Yusa* (Memorials of three kingdoms). In the eighteenth century, a school of "practical learning" or *sirhak* developed that produced such works as An Chong-bok's distillation and analysis of Korean history, *Tongsa kangmok,* one of the first histories to be written by a private scholar independent of government support. Beginning in the late nineteenth century, both Western and Meiji Japanese historical scholarship would displace Chinese influences in Korean historiography.

Enlightenment in the West

With the close of the era of religious wars that had marked the sixteenth and much of the seventeenth century, European historiography expanded its scope considerably beyond the political and ecclesiastical topics that had predominated since the Renaissance and Reformation. This does not mean that Enlightenment historiography was a radical departure from what came previously. To the contrary, it relied very heavily on many of the historiographical accomplishments of the previous two centuries, and in particular on the enormous corpus of erudite knowledge in the form of printed documents and texts, engravings of archaeological and architectural remains, and especially the study of different legal systems. Two centuries of travel and expansion also encouraged many of the historians of the late seventeenth and eighteenth centuries to undertake a comparative approach to the study of the past.

A major goal of Enlightenment historiography may be described as the search for a synthesis and balance between erudite knowledge and philosophy. Some of the best examples show a turn away from the narration and description of political events toward the consideration of civilization, customs, and especially *moeurs* (the French word for "manners"). Having said that, it should immediately be admitted that the term *Enlightenment* is itself loaded and complex, and there exists a wide range of views of history and historical writing among the historians who subscribed to its principles. Moreover, far from every historian during the Enlightenment can be described as a practitioner of what J. G. A. Pocock has referred to as "enlightened historiography."

Two significant Italian contemporaries stand out at the beginning. The younger, Pietro Giannone (1676–1748), was a Neapolitan jurist who authored a *Civil History of the Kingdom of Naples* (1723). This blended detailed knowledge of documents (often derived at second hand from the erudite works of earlier generations) with a focus on social history and a reform-minded and specifically antiecclesiastical outlook that would characterize much later Enlightenment thinking. The older and ultimately—though not immediately—more important was Giambattista Vico (1668–1744), like Giannone a jurist. The influence of Vico on subsequent European thought—

by no means limited to historiography—has been profound, though it was to fall on deaf ears for a century. Vico's *Scienza Nuova* (1725; New science), which has aptly been called a virtual Newton's *Principia* for history, espoused an erudite synthesis of the human past—including the non-Western. Vico erected this edifice on a postulated series of cycles of progress and decline, dividing the past into a series of recurring ages: of gods, of heroes, and of men (the historical age)—there had been two such cycles (*corso e ricorso*) up to his own time. Each age was characterized by distinctive modes of speech, thought, law, and government, and all unfolded against the imagined horizon of an "Ideal Eternal History." An admirer of Plato and Tacitus, of the empiricism of Francis Bacon and the legal scholarship of the Dutchman Hugo Grotius, Vico's application of philology and jurisprudence to the study of the past both echoes the Renaissance humanists and presages the work of later anthropologists, linguists, and comparative religion scholars. His ingenious insight that myths were an expression of an earlier mode of consciousness and of a language rooted in poetry, and that they needed to be understood metaphorically, was a powerful tool. It permitted him to embrace the biblical account of man's early history rather than dismiss or query it in the manner of French skeptics such as Bayle. He also provided an apparent answer to Cartesian skepticism in the notion that men *can* understand with certainty the things that they make, which include nations and their history. For Vico, *verum* (truth) was equivalent to *factum* (that which is made—or, we might add, *done*).

The anticlericalism that appears in Giannone would be taken up by one of the period's most well-known figures, Voltaire (the pseudonym of François-Marie Arouet, 1694–1778), whose *Essai sur les moeurs et l'esprit des nations* was an overview and critique of several centuries' worth of institutions and customs, including those of non-Western civilizations such as the Chinese. Less erudite than many other historians of the era, unsympathetically critical of the errors and folly of past ages, and at times positively hostile to "pedantic" scholarship and "useless obscurities," Voltaire praised features in other civilizations while still arriving at the conclusion that Western culture represented the triumph of human reason. He nevertheless contributed to public knowledge of other past societies, often employing contemporary travel accounts as sources; and in *Le siècle de Louis XIV* (1751) he offered a brilliant if uncritical analysis of civilization during the age of Louis XIV, which he aspired to establish as a benchmark for reform in his own time. The notion that there is a cumulative progress in human events had been a recurring theme in history for centuries, though typically ascribed to a divine plan as in the Judeo-Christian eschatological view of time. In the eighteenth century, progress as an organizing principle really came into its own, with the most optimistic views being espoused by the likes of Voltaire and especially his Revolutionary-era successor, Marie-Jean Caritat, marquis de Condorcet (1743–1794). The latter, an ill-fated aristocratic philosophe, left at his death the introduction to a *Sketch for a Historical Picture of the Progress of the Human Mind,* a book that adumbrated a nine-stage history of humanity's progress, with a culminating tenth stage of reason and achievement to follow the Revolution.

In Britain, Enlightenment historiography took a rather different turn. William Robertson (1721–1793) was influenced by Voltaire (though critical of the latter's errors) in his *History of Charles V.* His fellow Scot David Hume (1711–1776)—who was better known as a historian than as a philosopher in his own time—tried to apply his own skeptical theory of causation (and an admiration of ancient historians, especially Thucydides) to England's past. Hume's multivolume *History of England from the Invasion of Julius Caesar to the Abdication of James II* struck a chord with contemporary audiences, and he is also noteworthy for having developed a "sentimental" approach to historical writing that he hoped would appeal to female readers, who found much of historical writing dry and unappealing. The outstanding figure of British historiography during the period, still read frequently today, was Edward Gibbon (1737–1794), whose *The History of the Decline and Fall of the Roman Empire* (1776–1788) was a towering masterpiece synthesizing enormous erudition in literary, numismatic, and other antiquarian sources (albeit often at secondhand) with a philosophical and critical outlook. Gibbon was the late Enlightenment heir to two thousand years of thinking about historical problems such as the relationship between empire and liberty, virtue and power, citizenship and wealth, simplicity and luxury, and the nature and reasons underlying historical decline, themes that can be traced back, in different forms, through Renaissance humanists to post-Eusebian ecclesiastical history and beyond, back to Tacitus and Sallust. Gibbon was just as much the beneficiary of a hundred more recent years of enlightened history and erudition in the different modes of Tillemont, Muratori, Giannone, Voltaire, and Robertson. Though he was by no means an anticlerical in the style of Voltaire, Gibbon has become celebrated for his famous ascription of the fall of Rome to the triumph of "barbarism and religion," meaning, respectively, the various migratory tribes and the Christian Church. It is less widely recognized that the majority of his famous book in fact dealt with the Eastern, Byzantine half of the empire, and thus is properly considered a work of medieval, not ancient, history.

Eastern Europe first began to develop a substantive corpus of historiography at this time, often under foreign influence. The Hungarian-Slovak pastor Mátyás Bél (Matthias Belius; 1684–1749) established the first learned society in Austria while publishing an extensive collection of the sources of Hungarian history. Russia had produced a sporadic tradition of chronicle writing, including its *Primary Chronicle* (early twelfth century) since the later Middle Ages. Beginning with the late-seventeenth-century Westernization under Peter the Great, a new national historiography emerged, first with Vasilii Nikitich Tatischev's (1686–1750) compilation from older chronicles into a *Russian History from Most Ancient Times,* and then with two national histories by Mikhail Vasilyevich Lomonosov (1711–1765) on the earliest periods, and the seven-volume survey of Prince Mikhail Mikhailovich Shcherbatov (1733–1790). Eighteenth-century Russian historical writing reached its highest achievement just after the Napoleonic struggles in the multivolume synthesis, based on a wide variety of sources, of Nikolai Mikhailovich Karamzin (1766–1826). Western European philological scholarship had also arrived in Russia with two Germans, Gerhard Müller and his literary assistant August Schlözer, the latter of whom edited and published the *Primary Chronicle.*

The German *Aufklärung* contribution to historical thought and writing may have had the most profound and lasting effects on the next century. In contrast to the gentlemanly tradition of a Gibbon or the journalism of a Voltaire, German historical thought and writing was intimately linked to the educational system, and especially to universities such as Göttingen. The list of achievements is considerable. Schlözer (1735–1809) returned from Russia to Göttingen and a prolific career as a historian in 1767. Johann Christoph Gatterer (1727–1799) pursued the development of a "universal history" and promoted erudite scholarship at Göttingen. Elsewhere, at Halle, Friedrich August Wolf (1759–1824) revolutionized Homeric studies and created a new term for the interdisciplinary study of antiquity, *Altertumswissenschaft.* Others worked without university appointments. Johann Winckelmann (1717–1768), a librarian at Dresden, put art history, and especially the study of Greek sculpture, on a new footing, refocusing attention away from artists' biographies and on to changing styles and their periods. Johann Gottfried Herder (1744–1833), a schoolmaster and clerical official, anticipated the historicism and nationalism of the next century with his notion that a *Volk,* or people, exhibited cultural characteristics, the product of language, climate, and experience, that transcended political boundaries. His *Ideen zur Philosophie der Geschichte der Menschheit* (1784–1791), in some ways a synthesis of the previous century's work, nonetheless marked a significant departure from the standard early Enlightenment rationalist view of an unchanging nature common to all humans at all times. Herder directed attention away from political and military history (the edificatory value of which he doubted) toward the "inner life" of humans discernible from art, music, and literature, an approach that would ultimately evolve into the later German idea of *Kulturgeschichte.*

Chinese Scholarship under the Qing

Allowing for its very different circumstances, China under the late Ming and succeeding Qing dynasties experienced many of the same historiographical developments as the West. One leading authority on the period, Benjamin Elman, has characterized it as a transition "from philosophy to philology," as the Neo-Confucianism that had marked most of the previous half-millennium of Chinese historical writing, especially under the Song and Ming, was challenged and a new emphasis placed on evidentiary research—itself anticipated by many Song scholars centuries previously. Despite the strictures and quotas on civil service careers imposed by the Manchu Qing dynasty, which by and large adopted Chinese language and cultural practices, a higher degree of professionalization occurred in the eighteenth century. Philology and ancillary disciplines such as epigraphy, paleography, manuscript collation, and phonology were developed against the backdrop of an argument within Confucianism between Qing advocates of "Han Learning" (who had a preference for the texts and methods of Han-era scholars in studying the earlier Chinese classics) and their Neo-Confucian "Song Learning" opponents—an interesting if inexact analog to the slightly earlier European *querelle* of ancients and moderns. During this period, official academies supplanted the private schools of earlier years. Ming-era survivors such as Gu Yanwu (1613–1682) epitomized the careful attention to research among a wide range of sources of the physical as well as the textual, especially in his *Rizhilu* (Record of daily knowledge). As so often in historiography, contemporary issues proved a powerful stimulus for detailed and accurate research that could transcend polemical positions and, a century after Gu, Wang Mingsheng (1722–1798) would assert the responsibility of the historian to examine all available evidence. Together with Zhao Yi (1727–1814) and the respected teacher Qian Daxin (1728–1804), Wang was a member of a great trio of mid-Qing historical scholars who brought historical scholarship to a new level.

Western influences were increasingly felt during this period, albeit inconsistently, and indeed the parallels with Renaissance humanism three centuries earlier are striking, including the considerable expansion of woodblock printing that began late in the Ming era, the frequent exchange of correspondence among scholars, and the particularly high valuation of ancient learning. A consequence of this was that certain venerable texts were held up to the kind of critical scrutiny that Renaissance philologists had applied to forgeries like the Donation of Constantine or the pseudo-histories of Annius of Viterbo. And, as the humanism of the Renaissance had preceded the rationalist skepticism of the Enlightenment, so the Han Learning revival eventually produced a decline in the status of Confucianism. Methodologically, the "School of Evidentiary Research" (*kaozheng* or *k'ao-cheng*) as it is often called, is exemplified in works such as Yan Ruoqu's (1636–1704) exposure of selected chapters of the *Shujing* (the "Book of Documents," both a classic and a history) as a piece of later, post-Confucian authorship. This iconoclastic pursuit of truth had effected momentous changes in scholarship before the School itself declined in the nineteenth century. It would clear the way by the end of the Qing era in 1911 for Liang Qichao's (1873–1929) now Western-influenced call for a "new historiography" and for his associate Xia Zengyu's general history of China, itself affected by Western-style Japanese histories of China.

A number of other important genres of historical writing appeared during the period. Histories of institutions (*Zhi guan*), previously annexed to the Standard Histories and other works, were now presented as independent reference books. A preexisting form of local history or "gazetteer" dating back to the Song dynasty or earlier, the *Fangzhi* also proliferated, initially as a guide to local administrators who were often strangers to their region, intending to provide a complete history of all phenomena, natural and human, within a particular administrative area. Nearly one thousand Ming and five thousand Qing-era *Fangzhi* survive; although they have no exact Western counterpart, their local focus and emphasis on multiple sources bears comparison with the natural histories and "surveys" of late-seventeenth-century Britain, and, more remotely, with an outstanding German work of local history, Justus Möser's *History of Osnabrück* (1768).

Romanticism, Historicism, and Nationalism

Möser's *Osnabrückische Geschichte* has been praised by modern historians such as Friedrich Meinecke for its sensitivity to the uniqueness of the local community. When combined with Herder's understanding of the cultural differences among various peoples and the integrity of the *Volk*, and with the enormous influence of a cultural icon such as Johann Wolfgang von Goethe, late-Enlightenment Germans had anticipated a number of coming trends in European historical thought. In the political aftermath of the French Revolution and Napoleonic wars, and amid the intellectual wake of the Romantic reaction to Enlightenment rationalism, the nineteenth century saw a turn away from grand theories (philosophers such as Hegel being notable exceptions) and world histories and an increased focus on the individual—especially the heroic individual—and the nation. Early-nineteenth-century French historians such as François Guizot (1787–1874) and Adolphe Thiers (1797–1877) postulated a unified past for their nation, while the more radical Jules Michelet (1798–1874) directed readers to the history of *le peuple* (the common people). Both the interest in individuals and the intuitive sympathy for the unique and distinctive contributions of past ages to modernity (the latter traceable to Herder and as far back as Vico) are hallmarks of a mode of apprehending the past that subsequent ages have called "historicism" (or, following Meinecke, "historism").

But Romanticism had more immediate outcomes. Initially a conservative or even reactionary movement that privileged nature over reason and revalued neglected periods such as the Middle Ages, it proved adaptable for many in the next generations into a creed for the advancement of liberty and for the promotion of the rising tide of nationalism that threatened the stability of post-Napoleonic Europe. Romantic nationalism was often linked to a sense of identity built upon a shared sense of a people's ethnic or even political past—for an example one need only think of

Lord Byron's fatal sortie into the Greek war against the Turks in 1824. The impact of nationalist historical consciousness was magnified, following the revolutions of 1848 and the return of progressive ideas in liberal or even radical political clothing, by national unification movements such as the Italian Risorgimento, and in the emerging independence of former satellites in Europe from imperial rule (already anticipated in the American Revolution sixty years previously) and that of other former colonies in North and South America.

Though there had certainly been eminent historians in newly established kingdoms like Belgium prior to their independence, sovereignty or the drive toward it provided an urgent need to establish both the shape of a national past and the capacity to write about it. Even those regions such as Bohemia that did not achieve political autonomy during the period still celebrated their separate identity and marked out a distinctive past. Thus František Palacký's (1798–1876) five-volume history of the Czech nation from earliest times to the Habsburg union of 1526 espoused a highly romantic and nationalist view of the Czech heritage, celebrating the Hussite religious reformers of the fifteenth century, for instance, as exponents of Slavic liberty against Germanic authoritarianism. European Jews, after centuries of rabbinically dominated treatments of their past, acquired a modern national history for the first time in the successive works of Isaac Marcus Jost (1793–1860) and Heinrich Graetz (1817–1891). The latter was a German whose *Geschichte der Juden* put Jewish history on a firm archival and philological basis while not losing sight of the connecting theme of endurance through centuries of exiles, persecutions, and massacres.

The pattern is similar elsewhere. In Hungary, Romantic historians such as István Horvat (1784–1846) created a popular if highly fictionalized remote past for the Hungarian people. The unsuccessful revolt of 1848–1849 was followed by nationalist histories (often authored by exiled liberals such as Mihály Horváth [1809-1878]) and by the foundation of the Historical Commission of the Hungarian Academy of Sciences (1854) and the Hungarian Historical Association (1867), as well as by the extensive publication of source material in the *Monumenta Hungariae Historica* (initiated 1857). Polish aspirations for independence and political reform are likewise reflected in the great quantity of sources published in the early nineteenth century, and in the liberal, pro-peasant multivolume history of Poland by Joachim Lelewel (1786–1861). The proto-Romantic nationalism of the historian Father Paisiy of Hilendar (1722–1773) set his native Bulgaria on a century of historical nation-building leading up to independence in 1878, at first affirming in an uncritical manner the nation's Slavic affiliations and ancient descent from remote nomadic progenitors like the Scythians—a time-honored convention going back to medieval and Renaissance theories of mythical national descent from peoples like the Trojans. Romania, which achieved independence in 1877, established a national academy shortly thereafter, and history was introduced at its newly founded universities.

In northern Europe, Norway acquired a university in 1811, just prior to its establishment (1814) of a semi-independent state in union with Sweden. Most historical activity remained for a time the work of politicians, jurists and poets, such as Henrik Wegeland (1808-1845), author of *Norges Konstitutions Historie* (1841-1843). An academic historiography first emerged in the 1830s with Peter Andreas Munch (1810-1863) and Rudolf Keyser (1803-1864); it retained the romantic outlook of earlier writers, but made significant advances in source-editing. French liberal historiography (Michelet and Guizot) as well as Darwinian-Spencerian notions of progress introduced a more positivist climate in the next generation, which was dominated by the radical proponent of complete independence, Ernst Sars (1835-1917). In Finland, academic historiography had existed since the foundation of the University of Turku in 1640, and had flourished in the Enlightenment with historians such as Henrik Gabriel Porthan (1739-1804), who had mainly written in international Latin. The new nationalist impulse (Finland became an autonomous state in 1809) ensured that vernacular-language works eventually overtook in volume those written in Swedish; the first full-length Finnish-language history of Finland would be produced by Yrjö Sakari Yrjö-Koskinen (1830-1903). Historical consciousness was further stimulated by authors such as the journalist, educator, and novelist Zacharias Topelius (1818-1898), a Finnish Sir Walter Scott, while foreign-authored histories from the south were also widely read. As in Norway, positivist historiography found an audience: England's Henry Thomas Buckle would have one of his strongest followings in Finland.

South of Finland in the Baltic region, nationalist sentiments were much slower to develop. The history of Estonia and Latvia was written almost entirely by their Baltic German intellectual elites prior to their independence in 1918, national sentiments from the 1860s producing relatively little by way of historiography. Lithuanian historiography has been more fully documented thanks to Virgil Krapauskas, though its story is similar. Tied to Poland through much of the late medieval and early modern periods and dominated by Russia in the nineteenth century, Lithuania had actually lacked a written language prior to the late fourteenth century—early historical sources emanated from Russian, German, or Polish writers. Unlike other ethnic groups, Lithuanians thus had little by way of historiographical tradition prior to the romantic-era historian Simonas Daukantas (1793-1864), who wrote in Lithuanian and created a dubious pedigree for his people in a remote barbarian tribe. Earlier histories were rare. The "Bychovko chronicle," the long version of a pro-Lithuanian sixteenth-century text generally known as the *Lithuanian Chronicle* was not available till 1846, when it was published by Daukantas's contemporary, Teodor Narbutt (1784-1864). Another sixteenth-century Lithuanian chronicle, by Augustine Rotundus (c. 1520-1582), had long been lost. Daukantas had no immediate followers. As Krapauskas notes, between 1832, when the Russians closed the University of Vilnius, and the early twentieth century, Lithuania produced no academically trained historians of its own, though distinguished Poles such as Lelewel wrote about the Lithuanian past. The creation of a sense of national identity where none had existed fell to non-professionals: minor noblemen, poets and linguists, who were more interested in creating a heroic past than in following the canons of western historical scholarship; and the occasional part-time scholar like Bishop Motiejus Valančius (1801-75), whose historical work on his Samogitian diocese more closely approximates mainstream European critical historiography. Collectively, their work provided an essential ingredient for the establishment in 1918 of Lithuania's own short-lived independence. Beginning in 1883, with the publication of the nationalist newspaper *Auszra*, Lithuanian intellectuals increasingly took an anti-Polish tack. While they traced their linguistic and cultural heritage back, rather tenuously, to the remote centuries of the once-powerful Grand Duchy of Lithuania, they repudiated connections to that state's association with Poland in favor of a Herderian-style concept of the nation.

Russian historical writing continued to be influenced by Western European traditions in the late eighteenth and nineteenth centuries as it had in the time of Schlözer. As elsewhere, considerable activity was devoted in the post-Napoleonic era to the collection and publication of source materials, especially government documents, under the leadership of the Chancellor Nikolai P. Rumiantsev (1754–1826). An "Archeographic Commission" undertook a nationwide survey of archives and repositories analogous to Britain's Victorian-founded Historical Manuscripts Commission. Various other archaeological and historical societies were established, such as the Russian Historical Society of Petersburg, whose *Russian Biographical Dictionary* (publication of which was interrupted by the October Revolution in 1917 and the society's dissolution), is again a counterpart of a British publication, the *Dictionary of National Biography*. Influenced by the German classicist B. G. Niebuhr, M. T. Kachenovskii (1775–1842) adopted a highly skeptical approach to the early, Kievan period of Russian history. Hegel's philosophy of history and the works of Friedrich Wilhelm Joseph von Schelling (1775–1854) were widely read among the intelligentsia of the 1830s and 1840s, influencing a "slavophilic" school of historians, but the general trend was toward Westernization of practical historical methodology in a "scientific" vein. The two outstanding historians of the second half of the nineteenth century were S. M. Soloviev (1820–1879) and V. O. Kliuchevskii (1841–1911). Soloviev had traveled in the West and heard lectures by the German Leopold von Ranke (see further below), as well as by Guizot and Michelet; he was personally acquainted with the great Czech Palacký. Soloviev's prodigious *History of Russia since Ancient Times* appeared in twenty-nine annual volumes beginning in 1851, accompanied by numerous monographs. Rather like Ranke, he had a vision of history as a unified and continuous story of organic development. In the following generation Kliuchevskii, Soloviev's pupil and successor, assigned a new prominence to the analysis of economic and social history, which would establish the groundwork for post-revolutionary Marxist historiography.

In North America, the British colonies diverged historiographically following the American Revolution. The northern colonies—the future Canada—remained firmly within the British imperial orb (despite the existence of a distinctive Francophone Catholic majority within the colony of Lower Canada, subsequently Quebec). A consciousness of Canada as a nation, historically, did not begin to mature until Confederation (1867) brought political unity and semiautonomous status within the empire, and even then Francophone historiography remained apart from its Anglophone counterpart, with recurrent sovereignty movements still building today on the belief in a historically separate Quebecois nation awaiting its rightful autonomy. To the south, the experience was very different. The prototype for a nationalist historiography had been established in colonial-era writings that acknowledged the colonies' place in the empire but also celebrated aspects of their differences—for instance, in Puritan writings marking New England colonists as reformed "saints" who had voluntarily separated themselves from the ungodliness of the Old World. A distinctive nationalist historiography (admittedly fragmented by ideological and sectional differences for a century or more) thus emerged quite quickly following the independence of the new United States. Early postindependence American historians such as Mercy Otis Warren (1728–1814) provided a history of the Revolution emphasizing democratic values, while the biographers of major figures such as George Washington helped establish a pantheon of national heroes. Historical novels on the model of Britain's Sir Walter Scott were emulated by the likes of James Fenimore Cooper (1789–1851). Both American and world history were enormously popular among readers during the first half of the nineteenth century, but their writing remained the domain of gentlemen of leisure (and the occasional woman like Warren) or of journalists. Famous examples (both blind through most of their careers) include William Prescott (1796–1859), narrator of the Latin American conquests, and Francis Parkman (1823–1893), historian of the frontier. Internationally, the most widely recognized American historian was George Bancroft (1800–1891), a former professor turned diplomat and one of the first of his country to earn a Ph.D. from a German university, a trend that would increase in the second half of the century.

In Latin America, there had been a steady flow of historical writing in both Spanish and Portuguese areas since the conquests of the sixteenth century, a good deal of it by expatriate Spaniards such as the Jesuit historian of Paraguay, Pedro Lozano (1697–1752). The liberal values of the late Enlightenment dominated the writing of history during the nineteenth century, first in the form of constitutionalist historians who focused on the European-inherited legal institutions underlying independence, and later in a more independent and romantic kind of writing that, following Herder and Michelet, emphasized instead the importance of the spirit of the people itself in establishing well-functioning new societies in a postcolonial era: the Chilean Literary Society of the 1830s, for instance, had regular meetings in which selections from Herder and other eighteenth-century historians were read. A third and later group emulated the positivism of writers like Auguste Comte (1798–1857), Henry Thomas Buckle (1821–1862), and Herbert Spencer (1820–1903) to advocate a history that demonstrated the economic and scientific progress of the region along European industrial lines—knowledge of the past, said Vicente Fidel López in the 1840s, would allow planning for the future. The Chilean José Victorino Lastarria, who did not read Comte until the 1860s, nonetheless found in the Frenchman an endorsement of his own ideas from two decades earlier.

In Mexico, conquistadors and missionaries had documented the past since the sixteenth century, including the precolonial histories of the subjugated peoples, derived from native codices and oral information: the Franciscan Bernardino de Sahagún (d. 1590) presented his own survey in both Spanish and the Aztec Nahuatl tongue. Following independence from Spain in 1810, and during the political vicissitudes of the next hundred years, distinctive nationalist and liberal schools of history emerged. Portuguese Brazil, a nation of multiple ethnic groups, followed a similar pattern, as independence in 1822 produced a need for a national history. Early feeble efforts in this direction were transformed in 1838 by the foundation of the Instituto Histórico e Geográfico Brasileiro, which staged a competition in 1840 on the theme of how best to write a Brazilian history—a contest ironically won by the German naturalist Karl Friedrich Philip von Martius. The acknowledged founder of modern Brazilian history during this period was Francisco Adolfo de Varnhagen (1816–1878). Author of both a *General History of Brazil* and a history of Brazilian independence, Varnhagen made pioneering use of documents in European archives and opened up unstudied new subject areas, such as the relationship between Portuguese and native populations. Elsewhere in South America, as Allen Woll has shown, an intense debate concerning the proper method of history-writing followed the publication of Claude Gay's (1800–1873) political history of Chile. Gay, a French botanist, was commissioned by the Chilean government to write this work, and despite its endorsement by the respected Latin American academic and man of letters Andrès Bello, younger writers (including Bello's own one-time pupil, Lastarria) found its recitation of facts without a search for meaning unsatisfactory. Finally, there were those who sought meaning and instruction in the patriots of the South American past, drawing literary inspiration from across the Atlantic. Bartolomé Mitre (1821–1906), for instance, was initially enamored of H. T. Buckle's erudition. In the end, he gravitated toward Thomas Carlyle's "great man" interpretation of history, and Mitre's account of Argentine independence focused on the careers of its leaders, the revolutionary heroes Manuel Belgrano and José de San Martín.

The "Professionalization" of History

If the first half of the West's nineteenth century is characterized by literary historical writing in a romantic and nationalist vein, the second half may be noted for a rapid growth in what may, with due caution, be loosely called "professionalization." Although this too has nationalist origins, it is associated less with the "nation" in any ethnic, linguistic, or cultural sense than with the political "state" and its bureaucratic apparatus. The romantic liberalism of national independence and unity rapidly transformed itself in much of Europe into the institutional conservatism of preservation and social stability. Changes were signaled by a number of developments: the expansion of university systems and the turning of many of them by the century's end to advanced training in historical scholarship; the systematization of public record systems in many countries; the advent of several new professional associations, frequently accompanied by a new style of high-standard periodical or journal; a further development of the longstanding trend to publish archival documents, often under government sponsorship and now with a considerably higher standard of accuracy than previously applied; and the systematic convergence of the erudite skills evolved over the previous three centuries (paleography, diplomatic, numismatics, and epigraphy) within an overarching science of the criticism of sources, for which the German term *Quellenkritik* provides the best shorthand descriptor. This is also significant as the period during which Western-style historiography first began seriously to have a lasting effect on its rival traditions in the Orient and the Middle East, starting it down a road to eventual hegemony in the twentieth-century world.

Any account of nineteenth-century professionalization must begin with a colossus: the imposing figure of the German Leopold von Ranke (1795–1886). Initially a student of ancient history and philology (which were themselves making considerable advances under the older contemporary whom Ranke admired, the philologist Barthold Georg Niebuhr), Ranke wrote a doctoral dissertation on Thucydides. He quickly expanded his interests to include the medieval and modern history of much of the world, beginning in *The Histories of the Latin and Germanic Peoples from 1494 to 1514* with the period tackled by Francesco Guicciardini three centuries earlier. Subsequent works traced the emergence of the European state system that this good German public servant much admired as the source of modern civilization and individual freedom; and with a gaze wandering steadily outward in expanding circles, his life closed with an unfinished multivolume *Weltgeschichte*. Staggeringly prolific as he was, however, Ranke is less important for any of his individual histories than for what he came to symbolize. Over his long career at the University of Berlin, which had displaced Göttingen as the epicenter of German scholarship, he thoroughly transformed the training of young historians (many of them foreigners), by focusing his research seminars on primary sources and their criticism. Among his pupils and associates, Ranke could include many of the great names of the mid- to late nineteenth century, such as Georg Waitz (1813–1886) and Heinrich von Sybel (1817–1895); the latter deserves much of the credit for having converted Ranke's ideas into institutional form throughout Prussia and then Germany as a whole. Some of Ranke's students, to be sure, departed from the master's model. The Swiss historian Jacob Burckhardt (1818–1897), for instance, was an unusual apprentice whose great *Kulturgeschichte, The Civilization of the Renaissance in Italy* (1860) remains one of the most-read historical works of the entire century and is a forerunner of modern cultural history. The conservative Heinrich von Treitschke (1834–1896), who was not a student of Ranke but succeeded him in the chair of history at the University of Berlin (an opportunity Burckhardt had declined), deviated in a different direction. Treitschke's multivolume history of early-nineteenth-century Germany (1879–1894) provided a celebration of the Bismarckian state and a script for later German imperialism—a development that Ranke, a European rather than a strict nationalist, would not have embraced.

Willingness to subject to criticism documents and texts, and the received notions that derive from them, has often been taken as a sign of secularism or impiety by contemporary critics and later admirers alike: one recalls John Selden's experience in seventeenth-century England and the reaction to the Han Learning scholars of early Qing China, discussed above. The adulation now paid to earlier critics of Old Testament texts such as Richard Simon and Baruch Spinoza as heralds of modern secularism is not necessarily more accurate than the scorn heaped upon those scholars by conservatives of their own day. With Ranke we find a devoutly religious man, with intellectual debts to German idealist philosophers such as Johann Gottlieb Fichte, attempting to find God's handiwork in history, as had so many historians before him, but with a focus on the mechanics of human action on the earthly stage to the degree that these could be recovered through careful criticism of sources. Ranke had a strong belief in divinely dictated progress, but also in the distinctive value and contribution of each historical era and people, all "equal before God." He promoted a historiography that as far as possible could tell the story of the past *wie es eigentlich gewesen.* This famous phrase translates most accurately as "the past as it essentially was"—not, as some later students thought, "the past as it actually happened." Later admirers wrongly believed that this meant the complete avoidance of anything not based on a specific fact and the absolute repudiation of conjecture or interpretation, thereby ignoring the moral and philosophical side of Ranke's work.

Thanks to Ranke, his immediate disciples, and the celebrated German university seminar environment, German scholarship loomed large over many of Europe's nations in the second half of the nineteenth century and beyond; the Sorbonne historian Ernest Lavisse (1842-1922) was so impressed by Ranke's successes that he introduced the historical seminar into French higher education. In truth, many of the methodological practices were already practiced elsewhere in Europe. The real appeal of the German approach to historiography was its emphasis on the historian's calling as a professional (with the high status that it accorded in German society) rather than an amateur or "gentleman scholar."

If anything, German influence was stronger outside western and central Europe than within. To the east, for instance, several generations of early-twentieth-century Romanian historians derived inspiration from Germany, including the archaeologist Vasile Pârvan (1882–1927) and the methodologist Alexandru Xenopol (1847–1920). To the north, the Dane Kristian Erslev (1852–1930) and the Norwegian Gustav Storm (1845–1903) both spent extended periods in German seminars. Although some British and French historians trained in Germany (Lord Acton [1834–1902], for instance, with the Catholic scholar Johann Joseph Ignaz von Döllinger), it was American students who most frequently flocked to Germany, returning home to staff departments of history and new graduate schools at U.S. universities. Of those historians working at American universities in the 1880s and 1890s, roughly half had spent some period of time studying in Germany, though frequently too short a period to permit them really to absorb German historical method—much less the whole philosophy behind it—in detail. The "objectivity" mantra chanted in American historiography for many decades may be ascribed in large measure to the importation of a naïve version of Rankeanism that upheld Ranke himself as an idol while largely misunderstanding the more subtle aspects of his thought. Indeed, the myth of Ranke was far more influential in America than his methods, and Gabriele Lingelbach has argued persuasively that the concrete influence of German historiography among U.S. historians at this time has been overstated. Many American scholars, such as Henry Adams, who introduced a seminar at Harvard, even held the German university system in low esteem. Again, it was the aura of the "professional" that was most appealing. Professional standards that upheld a creed of "scientific history" were policed by influential academics like J. Franklin Jameson (1859–1937), editor of the *American Historical Review* (est. 1895) and upheld by the newly founded (1884) American Historical Association. The brief assault on the supremacy of political history by James Harvey Robinson (1863–1936) and the "New Historians" before and after World War I, and the work of the Progressive historians such as Carl Becker (1873–1945) and Charles Beard (1874–1948), did not endure, but it opened the door to the advent of social history in the 1960s. Becker and Beard's "relativist" doubts about objectivity were also rejected in the conservative search for certainties after World War II. The arrival of postmodernism has given them a new relevance in recent decades, though probably not one that either man would have welcomed.

European methods began to penetrate elsewhere in the world. Late Victorian notions of "scientific history" migrated into India during the first third of the twentieth century through British-trained Indian historians returning home to teach. In part owing to the influence of scholars such as the Sanskrit philologist Sir R. G. Bhandarkar (1837–1925), his son, D. R. Bhandarkar (1875–1950, an epigrapher and numismatist), and the Mughal-period scholar Sir Jadunath Sarkar (1870–1958), the institutional apparatus of Western historiography gradually emerged, beginning with the Historical Records Commission of 1919 and the Indian History Congress established in 1937–1938. Early attempts at multivolume histories of India were aborted, but advocates such as the novelist Kanaiyalal Maneklal Munshi promoted Hindu rediscovery of their ancestral, pre-Islamic past. Following independence in 1947, Munshi called for a new history of India which, on this occasion, under the direction of the prolific historian Ramesh Chandra Majumdar, resulted in *The History and Culture of the Indian People* (11 vols., 1951–1969). In recent decades, India has continued to produce outstanding scholars of international reputation such as the historian of early India, Romila Thapar (b. 1931), and the social historian Sumit Sarkar (b. 1939).

Perhaps the most interesting example of direct importation from the West and the profound change it could occasion is provided by Japan. Long closed to the West during the Tokugawa era, Japan rapidly opened up to international influence in the years running up to and following the Meiji Restoration of 1868, which brought an end to the age of the Bakufu. History had enjoyed considerable popularity through much of the nineteenth century, and the new regime established an official department of history and then, in 1875, an expanded Office of Historiography. Its initial purpose was to organize the compilation of the *Dainihon hennenshi,* a new history along the lines of the Six National Histories, and from a pro-Imperial perspective. A rival official history, the *Taisei Kiyo* (Outline of the Imperial Rule), to be written in Japanese, was also initiated by more conservative members of the new regime.

Following a series of renamings and reorganizations, the Office of Historiography was transferred to the Tokyo Imperial University in 1888, and a department of Japanese history founded there in the following year. Closed in 1893 when the government disapproved of its research agenda, the Historiographical Institute, as it had become, was briefly closed. It reopened in 1895, by which time the plans to write a new national history had been all but abandoned: attention now focused on the narrower mandate of recovering and publishing documents.

Any residual Chinese traditional influences on historiography were soon overwhelmed by Western scholarship, for in the meantime, the director of the office, Shigeno Yasutsugu (1827–1910) had arranged for one of Ranke's later disciples, the German Jew Ludwig Riess (1861–1928), to come to Japan in 1887 and teach at Tokyo Imperial University; he remained there until 1902. At the same time, reform-minded and pro-Western scholars such as Fukuzawa Yukichi (1835–1901), a reader of Alexis de Tocqueville, Buckle, Spencer, and Guizot, formulated a theory of civilization espousing the superiority of the West and the need for Japan to catch up with the rest of the world after centuries of isolation. Others practiced the equivalent of British "Whig history," describing the restoration as a major milestone on the road to progress. The popular historian Taguchi Ukichi, another admirer of Western liberals and social theorists, epitomized this outlook in his multivolume *Nihon kaika shoshi* (Brief history of Japanese civilization, 1877–1882). As in Europe, not everyone accepted the value of academic historiography: Yamaji Aizan (1864–1917), an outsider and popular historian highly critical of the sterility of scholarship at Tokyo Imperial, and of "dead history." Moreover, the consequences of the kind of source criticism that Riess's Japanese friends espoused were by no means always welcome, especially among conservative nationalists determined to maintain the tradition of a social and moral function in historiography. Shigeno (who was also president of the Historical Society established in 1889) was himself reviled as "Dr. Obliterator" for his attacks on historical verities. Another historian, Kume Kunitake (1839–1931) was forced to resign from his position in 1892 for using scholarly methods to undermine the historical basis of Shinto and thereby calling into question the historicity of the early myths; this in part occasioned the temporary closing of the Institute in the following year. In her authoritative study of the period, Margaret Mehl has argued (Mehl, p. 14) that in comparison with their German counterparts, scholars at the Historiographical Institute had scant influence on the national interpretation of the Japanese past.

By the end of the nineteenth century, Japanese historians had divided themselves into three formal fields: national (Japanese) history (*kokushi* or *Nihonshi*), oriental history (*Toyoshi*), and Western history (*Seiyoshi*). As the Kume affair illustrates, there was an uneasy tension in the application of what the Japanese themselves called "scientific history" to the construction of a national and Imperial-focused account of the past; in the decade leading up to World War II, the so-called "Imperial view of history" seriously constricted freedom of interpretation. Though actual incidents of government interference were not numerous, they have become well-known: for instance, the historian Tsuda Sokichi (1873–1961) was convicted in 1942 for undermining the still-revered national mythology of the *Kojiki* in work he had published nearly three decades earlier on the ancient imperial court. His doubts about the historicity of Jimmu and his immediate successors were entirely unacceptable in an aggressively militaristic state that had marked the founding emperor's 2600th anniversary in 1940 with national celebrations.

History as Philosophy and as Science
Although the general thrust of nineteenth-century historiography was toward critical scholarship and away from philosophical speculation, the period nevertheless gave birth to a number of schemes for the explanation of all of history, often by nonhistorians. Many of these had origins in German

idealism, especially Hegel's philosophy of history as the gradual self-realization of mind in history through a process of "dialectic." His views, while distinctive, had roots in earlier Enlightenment thinkers, but Hegel firmly rejected—as Herder had earlier questioned—the longstanding classical notion that history was "philosophy teaching by examples." For Hegel, history was a process and simultaneously a coherent narrative of that process, rather than a well from which useful guides to morality and behavior could endlessly be drawn.

The most significant consequence of Hegel's philosophy of history and its dialectic engine was its inversion by the socialist Karl Marx (1818–1883) into a historical materialist philosophy of economic and social change leading from primitive times, through feudal and capitalist phases, to the triumph of the proletariat. With less obvious debts to the philosophy of Ludwig Feuerbach (whom he severely criticized), the scientific positivism of Auguste Comte (whom he viewed with contempt), and more remotely to such a theorist as Vico, Marx developed his views of history piecemeal through several theoretical works, beginning with *The German Ideology* (1846). He wrote at least one work that can be considered a political history, the *18th Brumaire of Louis Napoleon* (1852). Without exception, no theory of history in modern times has had more influence, in terms of sheer numbers of adherents, especially among Marx's Soviet, Eastern European, and Chinese admirers, and the citizens of their states.

Germany also produced other versions of thought about the unfolding of history, and about the nature of the historical discipline. The historian turned theoretician Johann Gustav Droysen (1838–1908), though a believer in the possibility of improved historical knowledge, argued in his *Grundriss der Historik* and elsewhere for a less naive view of the historian's relationship to sources. Droysen placed particular emphasis on the creative role of interpretation as guided by present-day circumstances and values and the need for firm and consistent methodological rules. He was just as hard on historical positivists like Britain's H. T. Buckle for their reduction of human actions and institutions to the categories of the natural world. A further late-nineteenth-century turning away from the post-Rankean fetish of the document can be seen in Wilhelm Dilthey's (1833–1911) assertion that history is a mental act of understanding (*Verstehen*) whereby the meaning of events must be intuited from our own inner experience, not simply narrowly read from the sources. Like Droysen's, Dilthey's position was antipositivist because it assumed historical acts could be apprehended in a way that did not apply to the natural world of science, owing to our essential human similarity with historical figures. Wilhelm Windelband (1848–1915) similarly poured doubt on the modish tendency across Western Europe to see history as a "science" (in a positivist mode that went well beyond anything that Ranke would have advocated) by defending its status as an "ideographic" (representative of the unique and singular) rather than a "nomothetic" (law-generating) practice.

The notorious *Methodenstreit* or "dispute about method" set off in 1891 by Karl Lamprecht (1856–1915) presaged some of the uncertainties of the twentieth century. Critical of the neo-Rankeans of his day, but more sympathetic to positivism than Droysen or Dilthey, Lamprecht cast doubt on the usefulness of history conceived as the account of leaders and particular events, as opposed to larger groups, and invoked the need for an alliance with the incipient social sciences, including psychology. Though roundly denounced at the time, Lamprecht was not without adherents. His students included the leading Romanian historian of the next generation, Nicolae Iorga (1871–1940), and he was seen by a number of East German historians, following World War II, as having provided an "alternative to Ranke" (Chickering, p. xiii). At the same time, Lamprecht's historically minded contemporaries, the philosopher Georg Simmel (1858–1918), the political economist Max Weber (1864–1920), and a French former history student, Émile Durkheim (1858–1917), were pushing the study of the past toward the emerging discipline of sociology, which has enjoyed a steady if troubled relationship with its parent discipline in the century since.

German philosophy and German practice were powerful, and traveled well, but were not in the end omnipotent. The great French ancient historian of the mid-nineteenth century, Numa Denis Fustel de Coulanges (1830–1889), remained quite immune to Niebuhrian *Altertumswissenschaft*. In Britain, which has never highly valued speculative history (Arnold Toynbee being a notable, and oft-criticized, twentieth-century exception), little attention was paid to the philosophy of history. More surprisingly, even the reception of German scholarship and pedagogy was at best mixed. It was perhaps most influential in the area of the history of law, which enjoyed its closest association with history since the days of John Selden in the seventeenth century. The legal historical scholarship of earlier jurists such as Friedrich Carl von Savigny (1779–1861) on Roman civil law proved useful in the historical debate at the turn of the century regarding the origins of English law and of medieval land-holding practices. Lawyers played a similar role in Germany, Britain, and the United States in related arguments about the degree to which medieval villeinage (and by extension, more modern Anglo-American institutions) was descended principally from Roman colonial origins, as suggested by the lawyer Frederic Seebohm (1833–1912), in pioneering work on agrarian and economic history, or from Anglo-Saxon freemen whose liberties were disrupted before and after the Norman Conquest, as maintained by another lawyer-historian, the émigré Russian Sir Paul Vinogradoff (1854–1925). This was an old debate, going back to the seventeenth century, but it was now investigated through a much wider array of sources. Perhaps the greatest British historian of the beginning of the twentieth century was also a lawyer. The Cambridge scholar Frederic William Maitland (1850–1906), who in 1887 founded the Selden Society to publish medieval legal documents, held a professorship of law rather than history, continuing the long connection between those disciplines that had produced the sixteenth-century French *érudits,* Vico, and Maitland's immediate model, Savigny.

In other contexts, German practices were less influential. England evolved independently a system for training historians (still based on the individual tutorial and without, as yet, the American emphasis on the Ph.D.), a professional journal in the *English Historical Review,* and a series of systematic publications or calendarings of documents such as the *State Papers* and the *Rolls Series* of chronicles, the last-mentioned essentially a counterpart to the German *Monumenta Germaniae Historica.* The most widely read historians, however, remained those of a more literary bent, outside the universities, such as Thomas Babington Macaulay (1800–1859) and the positivist speculator on the history of civilization, Buckle. Despite the eventual impact of educational reformers such as Cambridge's Sir John Seeley (1834–1895) on the curriculum, the British university until near the end of the century occupied a much less important role in historical scholarship than in either Germany or the United States. Celebrated historians such as the medievalist William Stubbs (1825–1901), the exponent of Teutonism Edward Augustus Freeman (1823–1892), and the Reformation historian James Anthony Froude (1818–1894), spent significant periods of their careers in church, journalism, or government rather than in a university setting (Stubbs resigned the Regius professorship of history at Oxford to become a bishop; Freeman became his successor after several unsuccessful attempts at a chair; Froude abandoned the university early in his career and only returned as Freeman's successor late in life, after most of his work had been written). The author of scholarly and popular works on this history of the English people, John Richard Green (1837–1883), was a sickly parish curate turned Episcopal librarian, and never held a university appointment at all.

German historical thought was under duress from other directions in the years leading up to World War I. The historical agency of "spirit," "providence," "mind," and even God, so important for Hegel's or Ranke's predecessors and contemporaries, was fading fast in the age of the iconoclastic philosopher Friedrich Nietzsche (1844–1900), of Marxism, and of modern science. The nineteenth century ended on a quasi-positivist or at least "scientific" note with a variety of "method" books. Ernst Bernheim's (1850–1942) massive *Lehrbuch der historischen Methode: Mit Nachweis der wichtigsten Quellen und Hülfsmittel zum Studium der Geschichte* (1889), which was quickly translated into languages such as Japanese, confidently avowed that many facts of history could be known with certainty, though he conceived that others could only be surmised as "probable." This trend toward a rather narrow preoccupation with method was also observable in fin-de-siècle France. Earlier French historians such as Jules Michelet and Edgar Quinet (1803–1875) had indeed been affected by speculative philosophy, the latter by Herder and the former by Vico (for whose rediscovery Michelet was largely responsible); the Hebraist and religious scholar Ernest Renan (1823–1892), who developed his own Herderesque theory of nationhood as a "spirit," also flirted with materialism as a substitute for shaken faith. But as in Germany, this was increasingly a minority position. The apparatus of modern French historiography was established with the founding of the famous graduate research center, the École pratique des Hautes Études, in 1868 and of the major journal, *Revue historique* in 1876. Perhaps the most naïve expression of the evidentiary positivism at the root of scientific history—a belief in the methodological improvability and rock-solid documentary foundation of historical knowledge, without the Comtean reduction of all human knowledge to the natural sciences—can be found in a more concise French counterpart to Bernheim. A hugely successful manual on method, the *Introduction aux études historiques*

(1897) by Charles Victor Langlois (1863–1929) and Charles Seignobos (1854–1942) was soon translated or adapted into several other languages. The apparent confidence of some historians in the canons of historical method—soon to be seriously shaken—is best captured in the famous declaration of the Cambridge professor J. B. Bury (1861–1927) that history was a "science . . . nothing more and nothing less."

The later nineteenth century also witnessed something else not seen before historiographically, namely the far greater involvement of women in historical writing in Europe and North America. Women had been readers of history for three centuries or more, and there had been a handful of notable female historians such as Ban Zhao, Anna Comnena, Catharine Sawbridge Macaulay (1731–1791), and Mercy Otis Warren, as well as numerous women authors of popular histories and biographies such as England's Agnes Strickland (1796–1874) in the mid-1800s; Germaine de Staël (1766–1817) offered an iconic figure of female "genius" and historical imagination outside the realm of scholarly research. J. R. Green's widow and collaborator, Alice Stopford Green (1847–1929), outlived her husband by nearly half a century, during which time she published several works on Irish history in her own right. Mary Anne Everett Wood (later Green; 1818–1895) abandoned an early career as a Strickland-like biographer of princesses to spend her life as a full-time editor of documents at England's Public Record Office. With their admission to some universities women began to make even more significant contributions to scholarship: one of the most formidable economic historians of the first half of the twentieth century, Eileen Power (1889–1940) would proceed from Girton (a women's college at Cambridge) to postgraduate study at the École des Chartes. In the United States, late-nineteenth-century feminists such as Elizabeth Cady Stanton, Susan B. Anthony, and Matilda Joslyn Gage compiled a *History of Woman Suffrage,* while Mary Ritter Beard (1876–1958) published what became the most important English-language survey of female agency and power, *Woman as Force in History* (1946). With all that, the career barriers to women in academic historiography remained daunting until at least the 1970s; the American Historical Association elected only one female president in its first hundred years of existence, although a number have been chosen since then.

Twentieth-Century Developments and New Paths

Historiography has changed enormously during the past hundred years, in ways that merit much fuller treatment than can be afforded here. This final section will be devoted to exploring some of these, including significant transformations in European-American and East Asian historical writing, and developments in other parts of the globe (for instance Africa and Southeast Asia) not treated in earlier sections. It is not the case—contrary to views once confidently held—that these regions had no forms of historiography prior to the arrival of Western imperial powers (any more than this is true of China or Japan). For convenience, however, the earlier history of historical writing in these understudied areas is included in the present section.

The African Past. In order to appreciate twentieth-century African historiography, it is first necessary to examine earlier forms of history on the continent. It was once commonplace to assert that Africa had no past prior to colonial times—it was one of those regions, like the New World or India, that Hegel dismissed as "without history," a pronouncement that the late Hugh Trevor-Roper (1914–2003) notoriously repeated in the 1960s. In recent decades, this myth has been exploded, largely owing to the considerable efforts of historians to recover and compare oral traditions and to establish reasonably reliable chronologies of events, but also because of growing knowledge of the existence of writing outside Islamic North Africa before the arrival of Europeans. Poetry and folk tales from many regions have been demonstrated to possess a sense of the past and of historical events, with or without the presence of literacy. The oral tales of the Dinka of southern Sudan, for example, frequently begin with the standard assertion, "This is an ancient event." In some regions hieroglyphics also preserved a record of the early past. Writing was introduced not by European colonizers, but by Arab and Berber invaders in the centuries following the rise of Islam, and a number of west African non-Arabic writing systems appeared in later centuries.

The Islamic influence was especially strong in the north, the region known as Maghreb, Ibn Khaldun's *Muqaddimah* being its most famous historiographical product. Many indigenous tongues were represented with Arabic script (a practice known as *adjami*), for instance those of the Hausa of Sudan and the nomadic Fulani who conquered much of the Hausa territory in the nineteenth century. Historiographically, the Hausa were especially influenced by the *Ta'rikh al-*

khulafa (History of the caliphs) by the prolific Jalal al-Din al-Suyuti (1445–1505): as late as the early twentieth century, for instance, Abubakar dan Atiku's *Chronicle of Sokoto* imitated the form and style of al-Suyuti. The Hausa also evolved a courtly tradition of contemporary historical writing, exemplified in Ahmad b. Fartua of Bornu's chronicle of the reign of the Sultan Idris III (1570–1602). In more recent times, Hausa communities have developed local chronicles written in either Hausa or Arabic and have focused on maintaining chronological lists of rulers; that of the town of Kano, to give one example, goes back to a legendary founder and ends with a late-nineteenth-century emir, Mahammadu Bello.

In East Africa, *Kitāb al-Sulwa fi-akhbar Kilwa* (The history of the town of Kilwa, in modern Tanzania) was recounted in an anonymous early-sixteenth-century work commissioned by the Sultan Muhammad b. al-Husayn. Royal chronicles in the ancient Ethiopian Ge'ez tongue first appear in the thirteenth century (at the very same time that secular chronicle writing was increasing in medieval Europe) and continue (sometimes in Amharic) into the twentieth. Other Ethiopian historical literature in Amharic appears in the sixteenth century, such as the *History of the Galla,* composed in the 1590s. Further south, the language of Swahili includes a preponderance of narrative poems (*utendi*), of which the earliest written example, *Utendi wa Tambuk* (1728), is a historical epic set during the life of Muhammed. At the other end of the Sahara, west African kingdoms developed an Arabic-language historical literature, such as the *Ta'rikh-as-Sudan* (Chronicle of the blacks) by 'Abd al-Rahman al-Sa'di (fl. 1596–1656) and *Ta'rikh al-Fattash* (Chronicle of the researcher), initiated by Mahmud al-Ka'ti of Timbuktu, which was completed by a descendant about 1665.

Modern Western-style historical writing per se appears first in nineteenth-century colonial times—not a great deal later than its establishment in Europe. Initially, Western historical writing was largely the domain of the colonizers, especially missionaries, who were concerned to integrate African schoolchildren into a Christian and European past. There were some notable indigenous exceptions, such as Samuel Johnson (1846–1901), the Yoruba son of a Sierra Leone freedman who returned to his parents' home in Nigeria as a missionary. Johnson, strongly affected by classical historians such as Xenophon, authored a *History of the Yorubas from the Earliest Times to the Beginning of the British Protectorate* (published posthumously in 1921). This was based largely on Yorubaland oral historical narratives (*itàn*) and eyewitness accounts, in addition to colonial documents; Johnson's purpose, as he announced at the start of his book, was to ensure "that the history of our fatherland might not be lost in oblivion, especially as our old sires are fast dying out." Carl Christian Reindorf (1834–1917), another African cleric, used both oral and written evidence for his 1895 *History of the Gold Coast and Asante,* and the Buganda (part of Uganda) politician Sir Apolo Kagwa (c. 1869–1927) provided an orally based history of *The Kings of Buganda* (1901). In the West Central African territory of the Bamum (modern Cameroon), its local sultan, Njoya (c. 1880–1933), created his own ideographic script, modeled on European writing, and then commissioned the writing of a 548-page manuscript on the history and customs of his people.

All of these works were ethnically based, that is devoted to recovering and telling the past of a particular tribe. Unsurprisingly, given the clerical careers of most authors except Kagwa, they were also Christian-influenced, and most were heavily reliant on European sources, as was the somewhat later work of the Xhosa missionary John H. Soga, *The Southeastern Bantu* (1930). In the areas colonized by Germans, such as Tanganyika (part of modern Tanzania), Swahili historical works in Roman script, as well as verse chronicles in *adjami* appeared in the early twentieth century, beginning with Abdallah bin Hemedi 'lAjjemy's (c. 1835–1912) *Habari za Wakilindi* (Chronicles of the Kilindi, completed in 1906); this was an extensive record of the Kilindi dynasty that ruled the area in the nineteenth century, derived from oral traditions of the Shambala, a non–Swahili-speaking tribe. A reminder that the traffic between spoken tradition and written history can run in both directions is provided by Kenya's *Chronicle of the Kings of Pate.* The original manuscript of this work, which covers the town's history from the thirteenth to the late nineteenth century, was destroyed in 1890, but knowledge of its contents was so vivid that several writers were able to produce new written versions in the decades thereafter.

In South Africa, an indigenous black African oral tradition included Xhosa oral narratives, a subset of which, *amibali* (sing. *ibali*), dealt specifically with historical events and genealogical details. These were marginalized in the late nineteenth century by the "Settler School" of white historians and by white imperially focused historians (principally British though including the occasional Afrikaner like Henry Cloete). Both of these groups advanced a negative view of the subordinated black culture. The earliest examples of colonial historical writing, in English, Dutch, or Afrikaans, appeared in the first third of the nineteenth century, but the Settler School really only consolidated with the work of the Canadian-born George McCall Theal (1837–1919), who, ironically, had compiled one of the earliest collections of Xhosa narratives. Although criticized for defects of scholarship such as a refusal to cite his sources and a reluctance to do more than recount events without analysis—like many of his contemporaries, he was not a professional historian— Theal proved hugely influential on subsequent historiography. The racist theme of European supremacy in his eleven-volume *History of South Africa* would be accentuated in the distinctive Afrikaner nationalist tradition after 1910, albeit with the center of gravity provided by events such as the Great Trek (the 1830s migration northward of Afrikaners in search of freedom from British Cape colony rule) rather than British imperial expansion.

The almost total neglect or disparagement of the black population continued into the apartheid era. Liberal historians such as W. M. Macmillan and C. W. de Kiewiet, beginning in the 1920s, began to integrate black and white experience, and to attend to social and economic history; they evinced concern for the treatment of indigenous blacks while maintaining the assumption of European civilized superiority. The writing of missionary-trained black historians, such as Soga, of the first half of the century, was notably inclined to a favorable view of the British. In the 1970s, however, more radical scholars, many of them Marxists, advanced a more serious attack on past historiography, likening colonialism and its apartheid aftermath to the class system. The works of British Marxist historians such as Eric Hobsbawm and E. P. Thompson and of the American Eugene Genovese seemed transplantable to Africa. Social theories such as André Gunder-Frank's "underdevelopment" thesis (originally developed with Latin America in mind) were similarly adapted by Africanists.

European-American historiography on Africa began in the nineteenth century—the celebrated American historian and civil rights activist W. E. B. DuBois (1868–1963) had provided inspiration for an early generation of black American scholars. Most early efforts were devoted to countering racist assumptions about the inferiority of Africans. These in turn were often derived from the so-called "Hamitic hypothesis" (the Bible-derived view that Africans were descended from Ham, son of Noah, or alternatively that only the "civilized" cultures of Egypt and North Africa sprung from European peoples such as the Phoenicians). It was not until after World War II, however, that the subject began to make its way, slowly, on to mainstream history curricula. Beginning in the late 1940s with the retreat of the European colonial powers and the establishment of independent nations in ensuing decades, a deeper interest in exploring their own past quickly emerged among African populations, stimulated by reaction to decades of education in an alien imperial historiography. With this came an urgent need to recast the historical record and to recover evidence of many lost precolonial civilizations. At the same time, European intellectuals' (especially British, Belgian, and French) own discomfort with the Eurocentrism of previous scholarship provided for the intensive academic study of African history, an innovation that had spread to North America by the 1960s. Foundational research was done at the School of Oriental and African Studies (SOAS) in London by scholars such as Roland Oliver (cofounder in 1960 of the *Journal of African History*), by the American economic historian Philip Curtin, and by the Belgian Jan Vansina (an authority on oral tradition). Francophone scholars have been as influential as Anglophones, in particular the Parisian social historian, Catherine Coquery-Vidrovitch (b. 1935). But African historiography has not been the sole creation of interested Europeans. African universities have, despite the instabilities of politics and civil war in many areas, trained their own scholars and sent many others overseas for doctoral training (South Africa has been rather exceptional in having a number of powerful research-intensive universities). The pioneering Nigerian historian Kenneth Onwuka Dike (1917–1983) studied at Durham, Aberdeen, and London, and SOAS alone has produced several African-born scholars, including the Ghanaian Albert Adu Boahen (b. 1932). Boahen in turn participated in the important early summary work of postcolonial historical writing, the UNESCO *General History of Africa,* directed by a "scientific committee" two-thirds of whom were Africans and written by over three hundred authors including the Kenyans Ali Mazrui (b. 1933) and Bethwell Allan Ogot (b. 1933), Joseph Ki-Zerbo (b. 1922) of Burkina Faso (formerly Upper Volta), and the Nigerian J. F. A. Ajayi (b. 1929). Francophone African historians had until recently an especially close relationship with French universities, notes Matthias Middell, though African history generally is less prominent within France than in the English-speaking world.

African historiography has also proved a fertile field for the application of various interdisciplinary approaches, including archaeology and linguistics. In particular, it has welcomed the application of social science theories such as "modernization," "dependency," and the above-mentioned "underdevelopment." It has also provided a forum for Marxist concepts such as "modes of production" and "capital"; the work of Walter Rodney (a black radical historian assassinated in Guyana in 1980) has been especially significant in this regard. At the same time, the early focus on political history and the establishment of chronology has been displaced to a considerable degree by an interest in social, economic, and cultural issues, reflecting historiographic trends elsewhere in the world. In recent decades, "Africa" has proved too unwieldy an umbrella term, and the field has segmented into thematic subfields such as slavery and gender; postmodernism has also begun to make itself felt as the colonial and early postcolonial periods are revisited by a fresh generation. The popularity of African history has waned somewhat among North American students, but it remains firmly established as an area of research, sometimes conjoined with Afro-American studies.

China, Japan, and Korea. Western historiographical practices, often derived at second hand via Japan, began to influence late Qing scholars by the end of the nineteenth century. Chinese historical analysis had long been inclined to cyclical views of history as a series of alternating periods of order and disorder, throughout which individual dynasties rose and fell. In the face of rapid change, historians would turn instead to an explanation of the past as linear development over a series of periods. Liang Qichao, as Luke Kwong has shown, built on the previous generation's works and on the thought of Britain's Thomas Huxley in developing a five-stage, progressive theory of history (though he would express doubts as to progress and insist on the need for both cyclical and linear views). Liang and Zhang Taiyan advocated a general history *(tongshi)* based on Western practices (largely absorbed through Japanese and Chinese translations). Liang's own *Xin shixue* (New history) appeared in 1902, citing Edward Gibbon as an exemplary model. A few years further on, in the wake of the republican overthrow of the Qing, and the "May Fourth" New Culture movement that began in 1919, American-style academic history arrived with the translation of the Columbia University historian James Harvey Robinson's (1863–1936) *The New History* (advocating a broader inquiry into the past that went beyond politics) into Chinese by one of his admirers, He Bingsong (1890–1946). He, who had studied at Wisconsin and Princeton, also adapted Langlois and Seignobos into Chinese as a work on the writing of general history, *Tongshi xinyi* (1928). Another American-trained historian, Hu Shi (1891–1962) authored a history of Chinese philosophy, while Gu Jiegang (1895–1980) published a popular school textbook situating China in world history. At the same time, other Chinese scholars who were German-trained were introducing the very Rankean type of historical writing of which Robinson's New Historians had been critical, a fine distinction that seems to have mattered little to the Chinese readers of both.

The early twentieth century would see some extensive reconsideration of the Chinese past. Archaeology produced alternative sources such as oracle bone inscriptions for the study of the most ancient dynasties, especially the Shang. Gu Jiegang authored a fundamental revaluation of ancient Chinese history that was so strong in its dismissal of some received myths that his works were declared unsuitable for students in the late 1920s. In the 1930s an extensive debate arose over the periodization of Chinese history; the outcome of this "Social History Controversy" was the adaptation of the Chinese past into European and especially Marxist period categories such as "feudalism." Even more than May Fourth scholarship, early Chinese Marxist historical thought, initially derived from Russian sources, produced a fundamental break with the Confucian didactic and moralizing practices that had dominated two-and-a-half millennia of history writing.

With the advent of the People's Republic after the chaotic period of the Japanese occupation and the ensuing Communist-Nationalist civil war, Marxist historiography became state-sponsored orthodoxy. Fan Wenlan (1893–1969), whose *Zhongguo Tongshi* (General history of China) is a landmark of Chinese Marxist history, had been a Communist since the 1920s and was eventually appointed to head the Institute of Modern History—his close relationship with Chairman Mao Zedong probably saved his life during the Cultural Revolution. Early historiographical efforts were often Soviet-inspired, with textbooks translated directly from Russian. Beginning in the early 1950s and continuing into the 1970s, the focus of scholarship was the history of the peasantry and of capitalism, with the triumph of Communism depicted as inevitable. "Party" historiography became a significant subject in its own right, the texts produced by scholars carefully controlled and orchestrated from above in a manner that makes the bureaucrat-historians of the Tang era seem positively independent by comparison.

Since 1949, historians at various times have suffered persecution for heterodox statements, while within the Communist Party itself, different factions have sought historical support for contending political positions. The Great Leap Forward (1959–1961) opened a rift among older and younger Marxist scholars and pressured academic historians toward a militant repudiation of "feudal" or "bourgeois" dynastic history, along with the construction of general histories on Marxist principles, and purged of reference to former dynasties, emperors, and events. This was accompanied by directives to subordinate past to present, history to theory, in a simplistic manner resisted by moderate academics such as Beijing University's Jian Bozan (1898–1968). The Cultural Revolution had an even more terrible impact a few years later, virtually beginning with an attack on the respected historian of the Ming era, Wu Han (1909–1969), who would die in prison. Wu was the first of many historians whose careers were destroyed in these years, including Jian Bozan, who was hounded into suicide (both Jian's and Wu's reputations were subsequently rehabilitated under Deng Xiaoping). Following Mao's death in 1976, the extremist Gang of Four even appealed to the memory of the despotic first Qin emperor in support of autocracy, while liberal critics looked to the ancient Zhou dynasty (eleventh to third centuries B.C.E.) for a model of democratic city-states along the lines of fifth-century Athens. Since the 1980s, entire eras have been rehabilitated, though a Party resolution of 1981 attempted to cut off ongoing historical discussions of the Maoist period in the name of unity. In the last quarter of the twentieth century, Chinese historiography opened up again to the West, and many Chinese academicians have been trained in Western graduate schools and Western books translated into Chinese. This liberalization has largely continued, despite brief setbacks such as the 1989 Tiananmen Square reaction.

The Westernization of Japanese historiography in the late nineteenth century has been recounted above. The early twentieth century saw a considerable expansion of this trend after World War I, with Marxist and social science influences gathering momentum in the 1920s and 1930s; economic history of Japan was practiced by scholars such as Honjo Eijiro (1888–1973) and Otsuka Hisao (1907–1996), and local history by Yanagita Kunio (1875–1962). Extensive publication of sources also occurred. As we have seen, the period of the late 1930s and the war years marked a disastrous period for historiography, either silencing or co-opting those on the left. During the American occupation and after, Marxist interpretations would rebound, and an enormous effort was directed in the first postwar decades to the support of democracy by identifying the historic weaknesses in the imperial system that had brought the country to the brink of destruction: Maruyama Masao's (1914–1996) studies of Japanese political thought, for instance, exposed the roots of "ultranationalism" and fascism. The 1960s would see a reaction against "elitist" history (including the Marxist version) and the creation of a "people's history" (*Minsushi*). Although national devotion to the imperial past has never disappeared entirely, much of postwar Japanese scholarship reflects historiographical trends elsewhere, including the awareness of Eurocentrism. Since the 1970s, the same multiplication of subfields experienced in the West has also occurred in Japan.

Modern Korean historiography acquired a Western face through the intermediary of Meiji Japan, and Japanese scholarship dominated the study of Korea in the early twentieth century, during the period of occupation (1910–1945). One of the early consequences was a reactive rewriting of early Korean history on liberal, progressivist, and nationalist rather than dynastic lines by historians such as Sin Ch'ae-ho (1880–1936) and Ch'oe Nam-sŏn (1890–1957). Beginning in the 1930s and culminating in his acquisition of political influence in the north following World War II, the Marxist Paek Nam-un (1895–1974) featured prominently in the construction of a historical materialist past that integrated Korea within Marxist periodization. When Soviet de-Stalinization spread to allied countries in the mid-1950s, strictly deterministic materialism began to fall from favor among a younger generation of historians; beginning in the late 1960s, traditional international Marxism was largely abandoned in favor of a nationalist historiography of "self-reliance" (*Juch'e*) devoted especially to celebration of the personality and family of Kim Il Sung. To the south, in the Republic of Korea, a central thrust of historiography since World War II has been to dispel foreign and especially Japanese views of Korea as backward and servile. The most influential recent members of the nationalist school have been specialists on ancient history, who have used archaeology as well as history to promote the notion of the Koreans as an independent and homogeneous ethnic group (*minjok*). According to this view, which continues to be taught in school curricula, the Korean people and state can be traced back over four millennia to a mythic ancestor and state founder, Tan'gun (whose importance was first championed by Sin Ch'ae-ho in the 1930s), their unity having successfully endured generations of suffering from Chinese and Japanese oppressors. The various parallels with the oppression theme of European Romantic-era nationalist historical writing (Poland's Lelewel and Bulgaria's Paisiy, for instance), with modern Jewish historiography since Heinrich Graetz, and with the earlier foundation myths of late medieval and Renaissance Europe, would be worth further exploration.

Southeast Asia.   Our account has so far neglected much of Asia outside India, the Middle East, China, and Japan. Yet there exists a variety of historiographical traditions in other parts of the continent that deserve mention and which for ease of reference are summarized here in one section devoted to Southeast Asia. The region as a whole has been studied extensively by Western scholars (in particular Dutch, British, and French) since colonial times, but we will address our attention to select indigenous forms of history writing, and to those authors the Thai-American historian Thongchai Winichakul usefully calls "home" scholars. In nearly every part of Southeast Asia, local forms of history have arisen, most of which have been influenced at some point by Islamic, Chinese, or Western ideas. The perceptions of the past in most Southeast Asian countries are complicated by the multitude of languages and by the thorny heritage of regional conquests and foreign colonization; they are virtually invisible in standard histories of historical writing, even those that pay heed to China and Islam.

From the perspective of the West, it is often easy to lump subregions such as Indochina together and assume that proximity will have produced similar cultural developments. This can be a mistake, as the examples of Cambodia and Vietnam illustrate. Cambodia, despite over a millennium of literacy, developed relatively little that could be called historiography prior to the establishment of French colonial rule since the *pangsavatar* (sometimes rendered as *bangsavatar*), or chronicle texts of the medieval period, did not survive; there are a few specimens from the nineteenth century such as the 1818 *Nong Chronicle*, which covers the years 1414–1800 and refers to an earlier chronicle that had by then been lost. Late exemplars of this form survive from the end of the colonial regime, under King Sisowath Monivong (d. 1941) and his grandson Noradom Sihanouk. Such histories or palace chronicles (*rajabangsavatar*) as did exist were generally deemed unpublishable regalia, and the royal monopoly discouraged scholarship prior to the country's independence. Much of the earlier material they contain is of questionable accuracy and may in fact have been copied wholesale from Thai chronicles. The major work from the early twentieth century is the *Tiounn Chronicle* (so-named for Monivong's principal minister, who directed its compilation) composed from 1903 to 1907 and then from 1928 to 1934, which was based on a range of earlier materials. Under the French, European methods were introduced, but Cambodian history was given low curricular priority; the brief and terrible rule of the Khmer Rouge in the late 1970s would pronounce an "end to 2000 years of history."

In contrast, Vietnam has a much longer and richer experience of historical writing dating back nearly a millennium, with a great deal of genealogical activity occurring at the family level from the fifteenth century. Much of the early historical writing was Chinese-influenced (either Confucian or Buddhist) and written in now-archaic Sino-Vietnamese characters. Although successive Chinese invasions and domestic struggles are thought to have destroyed many early sources, an interest in the past extended down to local communities and clans that scrupulously maintained genealogical and biographical information (*gia pha*). Chinese-style dynastic histories or imperial annals, the *Chanh-Su'*, record major events reign by reign, and were intended to celebrate the current ruling house, often at the expense of its predecessor. Vietnamese kings strenuously enforced an "authentic history" during the precolonial period. The most noteworthy distinctive historical texts include the *Viet su luoc* (Historical annals of Viet) from the fourteenth century, itself based on a thirteenth-century text by Le Van Hu'u, and the 1479 *Dai Viet su ky toan thu'* (Complete historical annals of Great Viet) by Ngo Si Lien.

The eighteenth and nineteenth centuries also produced major historical works, such as Le Quy Don's (c. 1726–1784) *Dai Viet thong su* (Complete history of Dai Viet, also known as the complete history of the Le Dynasty). Traditional Vietnamese historiography would survive the advent of Europeans, especially the French, from the mid-nineteenth century, although it was subject to official censorship: a popular general history was Tran Tron Kim's (1882–1953) *Viet-nam su-luoc* (1929–1930). However, French scholars working on the area (and French-educated Vietnamese returning home) gradually succeeded in introducing Western models of historiography during the 1900s, along with potent concepts such as nationalism and Marxism, with formidable effects on the country's subsequent development. The advent of the printing press in turn gave history a much wider public currency. Patriotic and anti-French historians like Phan Boi Chau (1867–1940), one of many Vietnamese intellectuals either jailed or exiled from 1908 until the 1920s, abandoned dynastic history and adopted Western historical categories, together with a concept of progress and social development derived from Sino-Japanese interpreters of Darwin and Spencer. The flurry of publishing in the 1920s, 1930s, and 1940s included a significant proportion of historical and biographical books and pamphlets, and Ho Chi Minh himself, after his 1941 return to Vietnam, authored a poetic history of the country. New histories, written by Vietnamese, followed the French withdrawal in the 1950s and signaled a further turn in scholarly historiography in the partitioned country. During the extended period of war prior to 1975, state-enforced Marxist interpretations in the north were met with equally fervent anticommunist historiography in the south, seriously constraining the range of topics that could be addressed. Since the introduction of an official policy of "renovation" in the late 1980s, some liberalization has occurred, including better exchanges of information with the rest of the world. However, an official history, subordinate to political ends, is still conveyed in textbooks, and certain subjects remain proscribed.

Myanmar (Burma before 1989) and Thailand (Siam prior to 1939) also have distinctive historiographies although there are some common points in Tai-language areas of Burma. The study of Burmese historiography is complicated by the powerful influence of myths and stories upon historical writing during relatively recent times rather than in older indigenous sources. Research by Michael Aung-Thwin has demonstrated that a number of so-called historical events rest not on primary sources but on "retroactive myths" or misinterpretations, principally of modern and colonial rather than ancient and indigenous creation. Early Burmese sources include nonroyal historical records, generally concerning particular kingdoms, places, or towns and known as *thamaing*, which is also the modern Burmese word for history. Monastic chronicles such as the *Padaeng Chronicle* recount the arrival of Theravada Buddhism in the Shan states bordering on Siam and Laos during the fifteenth century and the establishment of the Padaeng Vat (Red Forest monastery) itself. The *Jengtung State Chronicle* begins with a legendary or semilegendary section before covering the history of that Shan state from the fourteenth to the early twentieth centuries. Much Burmese historical writing is devoted to specific dynasties and particular kings, in particular the prose chronicles collectively called *Yazawin* (literally, "genealogies of kings"), which are based on written and oral sources and employ literary devices not unlike the classical set speech. According to Aung-Thwin, the *Yazawin* date back at least as far as 1520, when the monk Shin Thilawuntha produced his *Yazawinkyaw* (Celebrated chronicle of kings); only a few such chronicles are extant.

The great age of Burmese historical writing was the eighteenth century, beginning with the *Mahayazawingyi* written by the wealthy independent author U Kala (the first Burmese history thought to be sole-authored) during the first quarter of the eighteenth century. U Kala was followed in the late eighteenth century by an anonymous work, probably by a monk, the *New Pagan Chronicle,* devoted to the Pagan dynasty (1044 C.E.–1287 C.E.). The *Twinthin Myanma Yazawinthit* (The new history of Myanma, or Burma), written at the end of the eighteenth century by Twinthintaikwun Mahasithu, was the first to use inscriptions to verify facts in earlier chronicles such as U Kala's and to expand the meaning of *Yazawin* beyond the deeds of kings. This practice was not maintained in a series of nineteenth-century writings, generally under official sponsorship, which reverted to the older meaning. These included the *Hmannan Mahayazawindawgyi* (Great royal chronicle of the Glass Palace, so named after the meeting place of its authors), the collective work of a group of selected intellectuals. Essentially an updated version of U Kala's *Mahayazawingy,* the Glass Palace chronicle was extended in subsequent chronicles up to 1905. These works focused almost entirely on royalty and were intended to present a clear and uncontested record of events accompanied by moral lessons—the *Maniyadanabon* of the late-eighteenth-century monk Shin Sandalinka is a repository of historical examples illustrating pragmatic political principles worthy of Machiavelli.

From 1947 to the 1960s, nationalist histories predominated in Burmese writing, accompanied by a few scholarly local histories and by an increase in biographical writing. The Burma Historical Commission was created in 1955, but has yet to generate the official national history with which it was charged. As Ni Ni Myint observes, *thamaing* displaced *yazawin* as the preferred term for a new kind of non-dynastic history in the years following World War II.

To the southeast, in Thailand, the premodern Siamese elite, who valued history from a very early period, produced historical poetry (for example, the fifteenth-century *Yuan Pâi* or "Defeat of the Yuan"), and generated an extensive series of chronicles in various forms. The Buddhist-oriented *tamnan* (stories or legends), often written in Pali, the learned language of South Asian Buddhist culture, were composed from the fifteenth to the twentieth century. Thai-language *phong-sawadan* (annals or dynastic chronicles) superseded them in the seventeenth century. The earliest and best, if briefest, example of the latter—which are more secular in interest though they still reflect Buddhist values—is the *Luang Prasert* (also spelled *Prasoet*) chronicle of Ayutthaya (or Ayud-hya), the Siamese capital and associated dynasty destroyed by the Burmese in 1767. This work covers Siamese history from the fourteenth century and was composed about 1680; its name derives not from its author, who is unknown, but from its manuscript owner. Subsequent recensions of the chronicles of Ayutthaya, written in the late eighteenth century, extend its history to that time. Chronicle-writing was at its peak during a prolonged period of struggles with Siam's neighbors, especially Burma, from 1760 to 1828.

The kings of the Chakri dynasty continued to support historical writing. King Rama I (d. 1809) commanded the revision of a number of *phongsawadan,* and his famous later successor, the Buddhist monk-turned-monarch Rama IV or Mongkut ([d. 1868] of *Anna and the King of Siam*) authorized the definitive Royal Autograph edition of the chronicles of Ayutthaya. Keenly interested in history, Mongkut also pursued the study of epigraphy. He and his heir, Rama V (d. 1910), commissioned the last in this tradition, a series of chronicles of his four Chakri predecessors by their long-serving administrator Chaophraya Thiphakorawong (1813–1870). Outside Bangkok, a particularly vigorous tradition of local chronicle-writing developed in northern Thai communities and subsidiary kingdoms. That of Chiang Mai (capital of the old kingdom of Lan Na), the work of an anonymous author who borrowed selectively and carefully from earlier sources, recounts its history from the thirteenth to the nineteenth century. Usually written on palm-leaf manuscripts or bark-paper, these chronicles peaked in the early nineteenth century, although there are well-known later examples such as the *Nan Chronicle,* compiled in 1894 by Saenluang Ratchasom-phan, an official of the Nan king. Similar chronicles were written in Tai-language regions of Burma and what is now Laos.

Western non-chronicle histories and school textbooks first began to appear in the late 1920s. At the same time, the introduction of printing expanded the circulation of historical works, including many from abroad, among the Thai learned class. History-teaching at a university level also commenced in the 1920s, at which time a Westernized Thai historiography (*prawatsat*) emerged. A tradition of royalist-nationalist historiography was established by Mongkut's younger son Prince Damrong Rajanubhab (1862–1943). A prolific author and educational reformer, Dam-rong was also an admirer of Ranke and Western scholarship in general. His historical work embodied a use of source criticism while retaining the dynastic focus of the older *phongsawadan.* The long-serving Thai official Luang Wichit Wathakan (1898–1962) developed the nationalist view of the past in a twelve-volume history, *Prawattisat Sakon,* which appeared opportunely in 1931, just before the overthrow of the monarchy. This veered away from dynastic history in favor of an account of the Thai nation. At the other end of the ideological spectrum, left-wing historiography has been represented in recent decades by a number of economic historians who have built on a seminal study of Thai "feudalism" by Jit Phumisak (1930–1966), a Marxist who was killed while fighting with a guerilla movement. The 1973 overthrow of Thailand's military regime, and the recurrent instability of the next two decades, opened up historical scholarship to a range of new interpretations and to sources far beyond the traditional chronicles. Although the royalist-nationalist tradition established by Damrong has remained intact (especially in school textbooks), it has been challenged in recent years by scholars such as Nidhi Eoseewong, in works of local history, and through mass media such as television and magazines.

Malay-language historical genres, long influenced by Indian, Persian, and Arabic sources, have been well studied though most of their exemplars remain in manuscript. Originating in oral traditions, the first Malay writings about the past tended to be a mix of history and fiction intended principally for didactic purposes and to be orally performed rather than read in silence. The earliest surviving historical work is the *Hikayat Raja-Raja Pasai,* which dates from the later fourteenth to the very early sixteenth centuries and begins with the reign of a thirteenth-century Sumatran ruler, Malik al-Sâlih. The quantity of verifiable material proliferates somewhat after the seventeenth century. Islamic ideas of historiography, present from two centuries earlier, can be observed more clearly from that point on. The chronological fixity and sense of causality in histories after this date distinguish them from other varieties of Malay literature, though these too contain historical material, most of which is of courtly origin and is organized around dynasties, often beginning with an origin myth. The best-known Malay historical work is the *Sulalat'us-Salatin* (Genealogy of kings) which exists in plural versions, the earliest of which dates from 1612 and which may be a revision of a sixteenth-century text. It is most often attributed to an early editor, the obscure prime minister of the kingdom of Johor, Tun Seri Lanang, and was extended forward by subsequent writers. This work is more often known by the title *Sejarah Melayu* (rendered rather misleadingly as "Malay Annals") and reaches back several centuries. As with other such "palace" chronicles, its function is not to establish accurate dates in the Western style but to make a case, in this instance for the descent of the fifteenth-century Malaccan sultanate, predecessor of the Johor empire, from Iskandar Zulkarnain (Alexander the Great). The *Hikayat Marong Mahawangsa* (or *Kedah Annals*), from the Thai-influenced northwest Malay peninsula, is a didactic text relaying the arrival and triumph of Islam in that area, and its events are much less verifiable from external sources than those in the *Sejarah Melayu*. Other *Hikayats* vary considerably in the degree to which they contain verifiable historical events as opposed to myths and legends, and modern Malay scholars such as Sir Richard Winstedt subdivided them formally into historical and romance categories. (This now seems an artificial division, and we must once again guard against applying modern Western divisions of fact and fiction to other cultures' perceptions of their pasts. The anthropologist Shelly Errington has even commented that genres like the *hikayat* ought not be considered history at all since they appear not to arise from "an impulse to write history," cannot be assumed to relate events in chronological order, and rarely contain events that can be explicitly identified as having occurred). Examples include an anonymous eighteenth-century chronicle, the *Hikayat Negeri Johor,* which covers events in parts of the Malay peninsula since 1672, and the *Hikayat Bandjar,* a product of the south Borneo coastal Malay kingdom of Bandjar.

Modern Malay historical writing began in the early twentieth century, when *tawarikh* (a modern, Muslim-derived term for history) was introduced into schools and a distinction made between it and the more literary content of the *hikayats* (though it maintained the preoccupation with dynasties and political elites). Abdul Hadi bin Haji Hasan published the three-volume *Sejarah Alam Melayu,* the first modern national history, during the 1920s, and a significant number of state and local histories appeared in the years leading up to and following Malaysia's acquisition of statehood in 1957. More recently, academic historiography has expanded considerably in Malaysia owing to the mandatory study of history in secondary schools since 1987.

Though it shares the Malay language with Malaysia as its modern lingua franca, the case of Indonesia is especially complex, because of its many constituent peoples and languages. Javanese historiographical forms, for instance, include the genre known as *babad,* historical poems generally relating the foundation and subsequent history of Java, or the relation of a particular event, usually a war. These *babad,* also featured in the literature of Java's neighbor, Bali, were often composed by court poets. They are generally of recent (eighteenth-century and after) origin, and scholars differ on the degree to which they may be relied upon for factual accuracy—though it has been argued that the Western dichotomy between fact and fiction is simply irrelevant since the concept of fiction does not exist, only a notion of degrees of veracity. Examples include the *Babad Tanah Jawi* (Chronicle of the land of Java), a group of texts covering the era from mythical times to the late eighteenth century, *Babad ing Sakhala* (written 1738), a two-thousand-line verse chronicle running from 1478 to 1720, and *Babad Jaka Tingkir,* a mid-nineteenth-century account in seven thousand lines of events that occurred in the sixteenth history, drawn in part from Dutch texts. There are also much earlier Javanese works like the fourteenth-century poem by Mpu Prapanca, the *Desawarnana* and the fifteenth-century (approx.) *Pararaton* (Book of kings), which covers thirteenth-century events.

In northern Sumatra, historical narratives imported from Malay and other languages circulated orally before being written down in verse forms; the eighteenth-century Acehnese-language epic *Hikajat Pòtjoet Moehamat* describes an earlier civil war, and provides an indigenous history quite in contrast to the official versions of successive Dutch and Indonesian rulers. Oral traditional historical narratives, or *tutui teteek* ("true tales"), circulated widely on the southeast Indonesian island of Roti, as did oral dynastic genealogies of the Rotinese lord or *manek*; many of these traditions have been independently verified by reference to Dutch colonial documents. On Sulawesi, Bugis, and Makasar, historical works date from the seventeenth century and include chronicles or narratives called *attoriolong* (Bugis for "that which concerns people of the past") which use lengths of reigns and elapsed times rather than dates to fix chronology.

As these few examples illustrate, a proper survey of Indonesia's historiography must examine several distinctive literatures and traditions. The construction of a national sense of the past in the face of multiple ethnicities has been no less daunting than the establishment of the nation itself. In the first half of the twentieth century, Dutch-trained Indonesian historians concentrated on providing a background to support aspirations for Indonesian national independence. With the backing of Japanese occupiers at war with Western colonial powers, a nationalist-anticolonial historiography was introduced during the early 1940s. This was largely the work of the nationalist leader and future president Sukarno, the textbook writer Sanusi Pane (1905–1968), and especially the lawyer Muhammad Yamin (1903–1962). Yamin, an admirer of the Malay Tun Seri Lanang and a reader of the French historian Ernest Renan, popularized a romantic vision of history centered on Java. A number of academics such as Muhammad Ali criticized the nationalist bent in historiography in the late 1950s and early 1960s, but it acquired new teeth with the advent of the Suharto regime after 1965. A more militaristic official nationalist history emerged under the direction of the historian, soldier, and minister of education, Nugroho Notosusanto; a virulently anticommunist and "patriotic" multivolume history of Indonesia prepared in the 1970s, *Sejarah Nasional Indonesia,* was an uneasy amalgam of official history with the work of university-based historians. During Suharto's "New Order," the nationalist tradition was strictly enforced on schools, even in outlying and problematic territories such as East Timor. Since Suharto's 1998 resignation, nationalist historiography has been openly challenged by a number of alternative visions of the past, including those representing different localities and submerged ethnic groups such as the Acehnese.

To the northeast of Borneo lie the Philippine islands. Long under Spanish and then American rule, the peoples of the Philippines adapted early on to the historical interests of the conquerors, to the great detriment of pre-existing historical memory. Tagalog *awits* or metrical poems include the *Historia famosa ni Bernardo Carpio,* a romance derived from older stories of medieval Spanish-Moorish conflict. Having largely eradicated precolonial forms of literature, Spanish missionaries used the awit as a tool of colonization; the *awits* became so familiar in both written and oral form that, Reynaldo C. Ileto notes, the average Filipino by the nineteenth century "knew more about Emperor Charlemagne, the Seven Peers of France and the destruction of Troy than of pre-Spanish Philippine rajahs and the destruction of Manila by the conquistadores" (Ileto in Reid and Marr, p. 381). Ironically, the chivalric and heroic figures in the *awits* would prove inspirational to Tagalogs dreaming of emancipation from Spanish rule at the end of the nineteenth century, as they transformed the legendary Spaniard Bernardo into a nationalist hero.

According to John N. Schumacher, there appears not to have been any formal historiography in the Philippines prior to the Spanish, despite the existence of writing. The first post-Conquest example is the *Sucesos de las Islas Filipinas,* written by the Spanish official and unsuccessful warrior Antonio de Morga (1559–1636) and published in Mexico in 1609—the only early history to be written by a layman. Throughout the seventeenth and eighteenth centuries, the various resident religious orders produced chronicles largely focused on their own missionary activities. As with the *awits,* however, western histories proved eventually an incitement to nationalism, particularly in the hands of young Filipino secular priests sent back to Europe for higher education in the 1860s. Published work on Filipino folklore and customs began to appear, along with previously unpublished chronicles put out in the *Biblioteca Historica Filipina* series in the 1880s; the journalist Isabelo de los Reyes would establish a Filipino identity in a number of historically-oriented newspaper articles and books. A more sophisticated appeal to history would emerge from José Rizal (1861–1896), who had visited Germany and become aware of western historical methods. During an exile in London in 1887–1888, he provided a carefully annotated edition of Morga's work, stressing the achievements of pre-Spanish Filipinos and their moral decline under foreign rule. In this form, Rizal's views would both contribute to revolutionary sentiment following his execution, and ultimately to the continuation of historical study through the ensuing decades of American rule.

This very short survey of a small selection of Southeast Asian historical traditions is far from exhaustive (we have said nothing of the South Sea Islands, for example, where a great deal of ethnographic work on historical memory has been done in recent years by anthropologists), but it provides a warning against assuming that history is exclusively the perquisite of Western nations, or even of highly bureaucratized Asian countries like Imperial China. It is perhaps worth offering the further cautionary observation that the types of recent political repression of historians, and attempts by governments to enforce a particular perspective on the past, are conversely not restricted to Indochinese totalitarian regimes or island military dictatorships (nor to older authorities like the Catholic Church and the ancient Qin emperors). In the world's largest democracy, India, the advent in 1998 of the BJP-led government (defeated in elections as this essay was going to press) posed a serious threat to historiography and historical pedagogy as the Hindu nationalist regime undertook measures that included the excision of material in school textbooks (a measure publicly condemned by historians such as Sumit Sarkar) and the encouragement of attacks upon distinguished scholars such as Romila Thapar who were deemed to hold disloyal views of the nation's past. Other examples can be found in the West, such as the controversy in the United States in 1995 over an exhibition to commemorate the fiftieth anniversary of the dropping of the Hiroshima atomic bomb, the virulent public reaction in Canada to a 1991 television series perceived as critical of the Canadian forces during World War II, or the ongoing "history wars" in Australia, turning in 2004 on sharp right-left disagreements over the past treatment of the aboriginal population by colonists and imperial authorities. Even more odious monthly additions to the list of historians suffering persecution of one sort or another across the globe make for uncomfortable reading.

The Middle East.   After an eighteenth-century decline in Ottoman historical writing, and the temporary displacement of Arabic by Turkish as the dominant elite language of much of the Islamic world, Islamic historiography written in Arabic began to recover in the mid-nineteenth century. This occurred in the wake both of European expansion into the Middle East and Africa and of reforms within the Ottoman Empire itself, which gave rise to incipient Arab nationalism. Many areas had enjoyed some autonomy from Istanbul for a century, with the result that there were already some examples of Arabic-language histories focused on pan-Arab national identity. This was true in Tunisia and Lebanon as well as in Morocco, which historically lay outside Ottoman control. Arab intellectuals in the second half of the nineteenth century began to write histories as continuous narratives, rather than annals, devoted to establishing national pasts, which now also included the pre-Islamic periods. Older pan-Islamic cultural and religious impulses remained as important as newer Arab nationalism, as Muslims confronted the dilemma of how to coexist with Western infidel powers, and as modern Islamic thought, influenced by Western science and technology, itself began to take shape in the hands of activist-reformers like Sayyid Jamal al-Din Afghani (1838–1897), the author of a history of Afghanistan.

During this period, efforts were made to print historical sources, and a number of learned societies were founded with historical interests. The Egyptian 'Abd al-Rahman al-Djabarti (1753–1825) anticipated this revival of historiography with his compelling account of the French occupation of Egypt, and a philosophy of history that echoed Ibn Khaldun's. Al-Djabarti's countryman Rifa'ah Rafi' al-Tahtawi (1801–1873), who had spent five years in Paris, became the channel through which modern European historiography began to enter the Arab world. He translated several French works into Arabic and authored a history of ancient Egypt that consciously emulated modern rather than classical Islamic historical forms; he was also instrumental in reforming the Egyptian school curriculum, which by the 1870s routinely included history. During the era of British rule in Egypt, the influential politician Mustafa Kamil further encouraged nationalist views of his country's past; this trend cut across and in many ways contradicted the Islamic views of most historical writing in the previous millennium.

Most of the historians in this period tended to be non-academics: the Syrian Ilyas Matar (1857–1910) was an Ottoman official, physician, and lawyer, and his compatriot Jurji Yanni (1856–1941) an Orthodox Christian journalist and intellectual. The Lebanese-Egyptian Jurji Zaydan (1861–1914) was a journalist and a prolific author of historical novels in addition to a multivolume history of Islamic civilization (1902–1906). Academic historiography began slowly in the post-Ottoman era starting in the 1920s, initially in the hands of North American- and European-trained scholars, thus extending the dominance of Western-style academic history over the Islamic world's long distinct historiographic traditions. Asad Rustum, a historian of Syria, published an Arabic-language manual on Western historical method in 1939, largely drawn from Langlois and Seignobos's famous textbook, a work that was already fast losing ground in its homeland in the face of the emerging *Annaliste* (see below) historical revolution. A Lebanese Maronite, Philip Hitti, published a survey of *Lebanon in History* in 1957; more recently, Kamal Salibi (b. 1929) has revised the history of Lebanon and made a close study of its earlier, medieval historiography.

In Turkey itself, the collapse of the Ottoman regime and the institution of Kemal Atatürk's republic in 1923 occasioned a significant rupture with the recent past and with the longer tradition of Ottoman official historiography whose last great representative, Ahmed Cevdet Pasa (1822–1895), a remote disciple of Ibn Khaldun, had produced an enormous annalistic account of events from 1774 to 1826 (continued by Cevdet Pasa's successor Ahmed Lutfi up to the 1860s). Western scholarly methods had, however, begun to appear in Turkey, along with European texts, in the mid-nineteenth century; at the same time, new historical genres such as memoirs also appeared. The study of numismatics and sigillography arrived in Turkey about the same time, and the newer methods began to influence reference books, school texts, and popular histories. The Faculty of Letters at the University of Istanbul, established in 1900, became a training ground for historians, and institutions such as the Imperial Museum of Antiquities (1891, now the Archaeological Museums) provided the infrastructure.

These developments provided a backdrop to the writings of the first generation of republican historians. Unsympathetic to the decay of the later Ottoman Empire in the previous two hundred years, the republicans nevertheless embraced the successes of the empire's glory days from the thirteenth to the seventeenth centuries. As Cemal Kafadar notes, the founder of modern Turkish historiography, Mehmet Fuat Köprülü (1890–1966), began to articulate this vision in the 1930s in a series of lectures at the Sorbonne, soon published as *The Origins of the Ottoman Empire* in French and Turkish. Köprülü focused on Osman (the eponymous founder of the Ottoman house) and the rise of the Turks in thirteenth-century Anatolia; his theories would be elaborated and revised by the Austrian Paul Wittek (1894–1978). The task of this generation of historians, sorting out legend from fact, and balancing ethnicity, religion, and other influences, is in some ways redolent of the romantic nationalist historiographies of the early and middle years of the nineteenth century and, more remotely, of Renaissance debates about national origins, albeit now approached with the tools of modern scholarship. The new work, to which non-Turks such as Wittek and the Greek George Arnakis (a severe critic of Köprülü) contributed, was carried out against a long-standing Western European historiography of the Ottomans dating back to the Englishmen Richard Knolles (c. 1550–1610) and Paul Rycaut (1628–1700) and including more recently the early-nineteenth-century Viennese Joseph von Hammer-Purgstall (1774–1856), and the American Herbert Gibbons (1880–1934). The opening of Ottoman archives in the 1940s redirected scholarship in newer directions of social and economic history, and since the mid-twentieth century, Turkey has continued to produce academic historians such as the left-leaning economic historian Mustafa Akdağ (1913–1972) and his critic, the distinguished historian Halil Inalcik (b. 1916), a student of Köprülü.

As in other regions, since the 1960s social and economic history have emerged in the Middle East as serious rivals to an older, politically focused narrative history. Islamic-focused women's history (which can be traced back to entries on women in an older form, the biographical dictionary or *tabaqat*) has also developed, with newer feminist approaches strongest in Egypt; the male-oriented and restrictive practices of the Muslim fundamentalist regimes have themselves become the subject of study. As Judith E. Tucker notes, recent feminist historians of Islam, some working outside the region, have restored women to roles of significant influence in the longer Muslim past, for instance in Leila Ahmed's *Women and Gender in Islam* and numerous works by the Moroccan sociologist Fatima Mernissi, such as *Women and Islam* (1991). Recent collections of essays such as Guity Nashat and Lois Beck's *Women in Iran from the Rise of Islam to 1800* have also explored the historical place of women in Islamic societies from very early times.

Europe and the Americas. The myriad developments of Western historiography over the past century could easily merit an article in their own right, but since they are readily accessible in other works, the principal developments will only be summarized briefly here. Broadly speaking, the trends outlined for the nineteenth century continued into the first half of the twentieth, though the Einstein-Planck challenges to Newtonian physics, closely followed by the horrors of World War I and the end of the old empires, severely shook whatever remained of the late-nineteenth-century faith in progress and in science. The pessimism following the war's unprecedented slaughter produced some gems of *Kulturgeschichte,* built on the themes of civilization's decadence and decline, such as the Dutch historian Johan Huizinga's (1872–1945) brilliant and Burckhardtian aesthetic excavation of *The Autumn of the Middle Ages* (1919), which could be read as an allegory for pre-war cultural decadence. A longer and much less subtle example is the German Oswald Spengler's (1880–1936) multivolume speculative analysis of distinctive cultures through history. Hearkening back to Nietzsche, and at least superficially anticipatory of Nazism, *The Decline of the West* was a work of reactionary generalization and extreme intellectual relativism; largely completed before the beginning of World War I, it appeared to great fanfare just at its end. Among other things, Spengler's *Decline* would help to inspire the very different (if equally speculative and relativist) British take on comparative civilizations, Arnold Toynbee's (1889–1975) *A Study of History* (12 vols., 1934–1961), which its author began in earnest in 1920, after reading Spengler.

Meanwhile, academic reactions to strict scientific history in the more narrow, positivist sense, echoing Dilthey's earlier qualifications, can be seen in the enormously influential Italian philosopher and historian, Benedetto Croce (1866–1952). Like Dilthey, Croce rejected both Rankean historical method and scientific positivism, arguing instead the autonomy of history from science, and the inseparability of history and life—records and documents only have significance insofar as living humans can reflect upon them and, indeed, relive them; conversely, we only make sense of life by thinking historically. A pronounced antifascist, he also held to a view of "history as the story of liberty." Croce's views appealed to many, including his younger British contemporary, the archaeologist turned philosopher R. G. Collingwood (1889–1943). Collingwood's posthumously published *The Idea of History* advanced the notion that "all history—is the history of thought" and suggested that the historian must empathize with his or her subjects, enter into the "interior" of a historical event (the thought of the agent behind the event), and mentally "re-enact" it in order to retell it. His book remains very widely read, and its concept of historical imagination has come back into vogue with the advent of postmodernism in the past twenty years. The Brazilian-born Spanish literary scholar and historian, Américo Castro (1885–1972) echoed both Collingwood and the American Carl Becker in his assertion that "To write history demands a historian willing (and able) to enter into the living consciousness of others through the door of his own life and consciousness" (p. 305). Castro, who fled to the United States following the Spanish Civil War further reflected historicist sentiments in his views upon the inseparability of a people and its history, and of the relationship between individual and general histories. In a very different focus on the human interior, the later works of Sigmund Freud, especially *Moses and Monotheism* (1939), applied his own psychoanalytic theories and clinical experience to the "diagnosis" of history. The process of civilization Freud envisaged as an endless struggle of love and hate, sex and death, arising from primal patricide, and carried forward by leader-figures such as Moses in conflict with the mobs whom they dominated—the irony of the similarity in this regard between a Viennese Jew and aspects of the thought of both Nietzsche and Hitler is difficult to escape. The European scholarly tradition had without doubt put some distance between itself and Ranke's history *wie es eigentlich gewesen*.

If irrationalism, skepticism, and pessimism were the dominant chords struck in Western Europe and, to a lesser degree, in North America, the dissonant sound from further east came in the form of Marxism. Just prior to the Bolshevik Revolution, Kliuchevskii's former pupil, Mikhail Nikolaevich Pokrovskii (1868–1932), developed a Marxist version of Russian history in his multivolume study *History of Russia from the Earliest Times to the Rise of Commercial Capitalism* (1910–1914; English trans. 1931). This was endorsed by Lenin and for a time Pokrovskii was the dominant force in early Soviet historiography; after his death, however, he was condemned by Stalin and abandoned by Party historians for his lack of nationalist sentiment. Initial tolerance of intellectual autonomy in the 1920s gave way to rigid Party control in the 1930s, and the state would have an overbearing influence on history-writing from the purges of scholars in the 1930s to the collapse of the Soviet Union seven decades later. This control spread far beyond the borders of the USSR to include the various Soviet satellite states and Warsaw Pact allies in Romania, Poland, Bulgaria, East Germany, Hungary and Czechoslovakia.

Without state sanctions to support it, academic Marxism never attained a dominant position in the West, but had a profound influence nonetheless through the 1980s. Marxist, socialist, or left-leaning historiography began to appear in the Western democracies relatively early in the twentieth century; the leading Norwegian historian of the first half of the twentieth century, Halvdan Koht (1873–1965), for instance was an early self-avowed Marxist. The attraction of Marxism increased in the aftermath of the financial collapse of 1929 and the ensuing Great Depression, which seemed to bear out Marx's views of the inevitable collapse of capitalism. The dalliance of many interwar British and some American intellectuals with communism provided the earliest examples of historiography that, in the 1960s, would evolve into Labor history, "radical history," and what is sometimes called "history from below." Several classics of late twentieth-century historical writing such as E. P. Thompson's (1924–1993) *The Making of the English Working Class* (1963) and Georges Lefebvre's (1874–1959) many books on the French revolution were written from an explicitly Marxist, albeit more humanistic, perspective that emphasized the daily lives of the history's underclasses. A modified version of Marxism articulated by the Italian socialist Antonio Gramsci (1891–1937), with its concept of cultural "hegemony," has retained an influence in much non-Marxist historical scholarship and literary history.

A very different creation of the interwar period was what has become known as the *Annales* school in France, so called after the journal that began publication in 1929 at the University of Strasbourg under the guidance of Marc Bloch (1886–1944) and Lucien Febvre (1878–1956), two French scholars much influenced by the earlier work of the sociologist Durkheim and the geographer Henri Berr, and with close ties to the Belgian medievalist Henri Pirenne (1862–1935). The journal and the "school" (rather a misnomer, albeit useful as a shorthand) have evolved considerably through successive generations but remain an influential force in France and much admired elsewhere, particularly in North America. The *Annalistes'* repudiation of the political history of previous decades—Febvre condemned Charles Seignobos for an obsession with events—in favor of an *histoire totale* that examined geography, climate, economy, and agricultural and trade patterns, as well as manners, still seems fresh after seventy-five years. It is, however, a further reminder of the recurrent swing of the pendulum of European historiographical taste between the social and the political, the broad and the particular, dating back to the Enlightenment—and beyond, as far back as Herodotus and Thucydides.

The Annales historians also advocated a new modus vivendi between history and the social sciences, with Fernand Braudel (1902–1985) calling for the subjugation of *histoire événementielle* (short-term human actions, for instance in the political world) to the study of longer periods of social, material, and economic *conjonctures* and the much slower geographical and climatalogical changes that occurred over the *longue durée* of centuries; the classic expression of this layered periodization is Braudel's own study of *The Mediterranean and the Mediterranean World in the Age of Philip II* . The statistical tendencies of many members of Braudel's generation of *Annalistes* are most clearly evident in the work of Pierre Chaunu (whose history of Seville and the Atlantic established a subgenre often called "serial history" because of its attention to establishing continuous series of historical data on such matters as food prices). Intellectual historians such as Robert Mandrou and François Furet pioneered a quantitative approach to the history of *mentalités,* opening up what has since evolved into *histoire du livre,* the history of the book. In more recent decades, however, the Annales historians have veered away from quantification to the study of *mentalités* in Bloch and Febvre's mode, with considerably more emphasis being placed on individual and collective beliefs, and on life experienced in local settings. The "microhistory" genre of the late 1970s, 1980s, and 1990s, including works like Emmanuel Le Roy Ladurie's *Montaillou: The Promised Land of Error* (a study of a medieval Cathar village) and Carlo Ginzburg's *The Cheese and the Worms: The Cosmos of a Sixteenth Century Miller,* has proved highly saleable in the academic and even popular book market and has spawned numerous European and North American imitators.

If any word most characterizes twentieth-century and especially post-1945 historiography, it would have to be *fragmentation* (a more optimistic descriptor might be *diversity*). Historians are now political, military, family, gender, women's, economic, social, environmental, intellectual or cultural, and the expansion of university history departments especially in the 1960s has encouraged a high degree of subspecialization, together with a proliferation of journals and book series (which the relatively recent introduction of the Internet shows no sign of slowing down given its capacity to offer cheap alternatives to conventional print). Although Marxism has by and large faded from most North American history departments, social history has been maintained, albeit now often dissolved into various components. Among these, women's history and its offshoot, the history of gender (now including masculinity studies) have perhaps been the most successful in reshaping the recent agenda of the entire discipline. The history of particular ethnicities and religions or sexual orientations has also become more firmly established in departments and often in specialty journals. Interdisciplinary approaches to history began seriously in the 1960s with historians looking to the social sciences, especially sociology and economics, for the theoretical underpinnings that appeared to be lacking from history itself (it is remarkable how often in the history of historical writing a great cataclysm has been followed by a search for new certitudes, a pronounced skepticism toward old ones, or both in combination). Among the more interesting if controversial experiments one must include psychohistory (best represented by Erik H. Erikson). Equally debatable has been the use of "counterfactuals" (the supposition that events in history occurred in ways other than they actually did, and the attempt to model mathematically a hypothetical projected course of events from that alternate starting point), especially in the "Cliometric" or New Economic History of American academics such as Robert W. Fogel. In the 1980s and 1990s, as the stock of sociology and economics began to fall in the judgment of historians, many turned instead to the work of cultural anthropologists such as Clifford Geertz, Marshall Sahlins, and Victor Turner. (In contrast, social scientists, as Eric H. Monkkonen and others have argued, maintain a steadfast claim to the appropriation of history across their various disciplines, without necessarily intending by "history" the discipline that historians actually practice). Meanwhile, the "history of ideas" has been transformed at one end into cultural history (including most recently the history of the book), and at the other into the pursuit of the meaning of terms and of texts in their linguistic and/or social contexts. The latter stream is in turn divisible into a so-called Cambridge School of the history of political thought, associated with Quentin Skinner in Britain and J. G. A. Pocock in the United States, the *Begriffsgeschichte* (history of political and social concepts) approach associated with the German Reinhart Koselleck, and the "New Historicist" and "cultural materialist" movements in literary criticism

One trend that began in the mid-1970s but has roots in literary theory and in continental philosophy (especially the French figures Michel Foucault and Jacques Derrida, and the Germans Hans-Georg Gadamer, Martin Heidegger and, more remotely, Friedrich Nietzsche) is the so-called linguistic turn in historiography, often identified with the broader theoretical shift known as postmodernism. Influenced by cultural theorists such as Roland Barthes, Foucault, Jacques Lacan, and Paul Ricoeur, and by the prewar German intellectual Walter Benjamin, postmodernism also draws extensively, if often superficially, from cultural anthropology. The thrust of this has been seriously to challenge conventional boundaries between history and literature, leading American exponents of this view being the Americans Hayden White and Dominick LaCapra. It has also, as the historical theorist F. R. Ankersmit suggests, had the effect of "de-disciplining" and "privatizing" history—restoring the individual author, as opposed to the institutional structures erected in the nineteenth and twentieth centuries, to the center of historical writing. In its most extreme version (which is articulated less frequently than postmodernism's most severe critics would have us believe), it hearkens back to Renaissance pyrrhonism in its radical denial of the fixity of any historical meaning, the existence of any external reality beyond language (there are only infinite floating "signifiers," and no definable or recoverable "signifieds"), and the impossibility of making "true" statements about the past. The position derived from this—that any version of history is no more or less valid than another—while seemingly liberal, also opens the door to the legitimation of morally repugnant positions such as Holocaust denial. This issue has come to the fore in recent years through a number of celebrated cases, most notoriously the 1990s libel suit brought by Holocaust denier David Irving against the American historian Deborah Lipstadt, who had charged him with gross fabrication and distortion of evidence to support his theories. A spectacle followed around the globe. The trial involved the historian Richard Evans and a team of graduate students scrutinizing David Irving's research intensively, the consequences of which were the utter demolition of his arguments and an overwhelming legal victory in the year 2000 for Lipstadt and her publisher.

It is tempting to dismiss much postmodern theorizing, historiographically, as chaotic and intellectually anarchistic nonsense, perhaps even a sign of fin-de-siècle cultural decadence. There has recently been an extreme conservative reaction to it, epitomized in the work of the late British historian Sir Geoffrey Elton, and in the critiques of those who lament the loss of any sense of master-narrative. But the postmodern trend has been highly influential in academic settings (especially literature departments); and, while still a minority influence in history departments, it has found a receptive audience among historians of gender and many social and cultural historians for whom it has provided a set of codes and categories to replace those once derived from Marxism. While some of its arguments are virtually self-discrediting, postmodernism has at least provided a salutary reminder to all historians (if one were really needed) that, Ranke notwithstanding, documents and texts never "speak for themselves" but are interpreted by historians, and, more important, that even the most "neutral" document was ultimately the creation of a human being driven by the assumptions, social pressures, and linguistic conventions of his or her own time.

Few historians would now endorse the French ancient historian Fustel de Coulanges' optimistic admonition to group of applauding students that it was not he who spoke to them but "history, who speaks through me."

A related variant, postcolonial studies, often associated with the literary theorists Edward Said (1935–2003), Gayatri Spivak, and Homi K. Bhabha, has refocused scholarship concerned with former colonies such as India on the subjected masses rather than on the imperial rulers and their indigenous elite allies or political successors. The Subaltern School of Indian historiography (the term derives from Marx and from Antonio Gramsci's theory of hegemony) founded by Ranajit Guha is a prominent example, the academic foundation against which it rebels having been established with the rapid increase of university history departments following independence in 1947, and the development of social-science–influenced South Asian studies. Guha in particular has argued that the Renaissance assignment of non-Europeans to the realm of "peoples without history" was compounded by the subsequent imposition of Enlightenment ideas upon the various colonized areas of the world, in particular the notion that statehood, as well as writing, was essential for a people to achieve historical standing. The colonizers, using their control of language, education, and writing, subjected the Indian past, for example, to Western (and especially Hegelian) notions of "world-history," limited by European standards of chronology and narrative. In other words, they imposed a kind of imperial "dominance without hegemony" over a nation's true sense of its own history. "History" in the Western sense (projected backwards onto indigenous *itihasa* in an effort to make these seem protohistorical) thus permanently completed the displacement, commenced by the Persian-influenced histories of the Mughal era, of the ancient tradition and "old lore," as well as the sense of everyday experience, embodied in the poetic myths contained in *purana* and in epics such as the Ramayana. Vinay Lal, a critic of Subaltern Studies has adopted an even more radical position, asserting that the accommodation of Indian scholars to the very value of history, not simply adoption of its Western forms, is an acceptance of servitude. Sumit Sarkar, an early participant in the Subaltern project, has criticized it for a growing loss of focus on the very groups it was designed to rescue from oblivion and for its swing in the direction of cultural studies, while endorsing a microhistorical approach analogous to the practice of Europeans such as Carlo Ginzburg.

The Latin American experience reflects both European and, more recently, North American trends, while some of its historical concerns have for decades anticipated the very issues raised in the 1960s by European Marxists such as E. P. Thompson and Eric Hobsbawm, and more recently in South Asia by Subaltern scholars. Academic historiography was firmly established with the foundation of public archives at the end of the nineteenth century, and the creation of history departments at universities. The longest-standing graduate programs date back to the 1950s and include El Colegio de México, Universidad Nacional Autónoma de México, Universidad San Marcos in Lima, and the Universidad de Chile, but a significant proportion of academics with doctorates have acquired them abroad at European (especially Oxford, Cambridge, and Madrid) and major American universities, many of which (the University of Texas and the University of California, Berkeley, for example) have first-rate library collections and strong graduate programs in Latin American studies.

By the end of the nineteenth century, the liberalism and positivism that had marked the first decades of postindependence historiography were under duress, in part owing to a growing alienation from America and Europe. The Mexican Revolution of 1910–1920, with its populist and agrarian origins, suggested that the historical role of Latin American masses and especially indigenous and mestizo populations had been seriously underestimated; moreover, the political and economic success of many of the liberal states had been mixed at best. Efforts turned to revisiting the history of Central and South America from a less Eurocentric perspective. Historians and ethnohistorians began to pay special attention to the role of the indigenous peoples and to the ethnic intermixture of populations that had produced a distinctive set of postcolonial societies. The kinds of anthropological excavation of native perceptions of the past applied in the South Pacific have also been employed in Latin America in recent decades. Some of the features of African historiography can also be observed here, in particular the application of Marxist and social science paradigms such as "dependency" and "modernization" theory. And, as with India, an anti-imperialist scholarship has developed (encouraged by the ideologically controversial five hundredth anniversary celebrations of Columbus's 1492 expedition) that insists on the role of European and especially Iberian colonizers in the "invention" of historical categories such as "America."

Conclusion

This article has necessarily been selective, summary, and in places even cursory, in its treatment of the history of history around the planet. While the differences between various forms of historical writing—and different traditions—have deliberately been emphasized, some connecting points also exist. There has been a close relationship between the historical record and the exercise of power for much of the past four thousand years, power being taken in the ethnic, social, and economic as well as narrowly political sense. This is perhaps another way of putting the old saw, mentioned at the very beginning of the essay, that "history is written by the victors," although in fact it has just as often been written by the losers (consider Thucydides, the Indian Felipe Guamán Poma de Ayala, or the poet and historian John Milton, a failed revolutionary) and those bewildered by the specter of sudden or unwelcome change. There has been an ongoing, dialectic, and much-changing relationship between literature, legend, myth, and history, and firm and categorical divisions between these are by no means the hallmark of all historical cultures. One may also observe the recurrent influence of various forms of present-day self-identification in the construction of pasts, ranging from the Greek city-states through Renaissance debates about racial origins, through Spanish discussions of Visigothic foundations, to the competing global nationalisms of the nineteenth and twentieth centuries. Now as then, current problems and perspectives often drive the most intense and searching investigation of the past: Where French and Spanish invasions of Italy drove Machiavelli and Guicciardini to the past for explanation, similar calamities inspired many of the chroniclers of Burma and Thailand in the late eighteenth and early nineteenth centuries. Where the Reformation ignited a European debate over the history of the church, modern German historians have had to wrestle since 1945 with the problem of the country's aggressive twentieth-century past and the horror of the Holocaust.

At the start of the twenty-first century, there is a high degree of disintegration and remarkably little consensus as to what a "proper" historical method is, what phenomena constitute legitimate subjects of historical inquiry or whether any historical narrative merits "privileging" (a favored term of literary criticism) as true—or at least more true—over any other. But in facing our own postmodern confusion, we would be entirely wrong to project a nostalgic, supposititious, and comfortable uniformity of opinion onto the historical thought of earlier times. Let us in closing recall the differences between Babylonian, Assyrian, and Hebrew historical writing; Thucydides' quick departure from the model established by Herodotus; the contemporary medieval critics of Geoffrey of Monmouth's invented British past; the Qing evidentiary debates; the pyrrhonist challenge to historical knowledge in early modern Europe; and the German quarrels about method in the late nineteenth century. These are but a few reminders that there have always been many mansions in the house of history and an almost infinite number of windows, each providing a fresh perspective on to the past.

BIBLIOGRAPHY

GENERAL AND COMPARATIVE

Appadurai, Arjun. "The Past as a Scarce Resource." *Man* 16, no. 2 (1981): 201–219.

Black, Jeremy. *Maps and History: Constructing Images of the Past.* New Haven and London: Yale University Press, 1997. Valuable study of maps and atlases, and their role in the shaping of perceptions of history.

Breisach, Ernst. *Historiography: Ancient, Medieval, and Modern.* 2nd ed. Chicago: University of Chicago Press, 1994. Useful survey, confined to western traditions, but full of shrewd judgments and connections.

Brown, Donald E. *Hierarchy, History, and Human Nature: The Social Origins of Historical Consciousness.* Tucson: University of Arizona Press, 1988. Perceptive commentary on a variety of world traditions, regrettably marred by author's Eurocentric assumption that there are "sound" historiographies against which others fall short.

Burke, Peter. *History and Social Theory.* Ithaca, N.Y.: Cornell University Press, 1993.

Butterfield, Herbert. *Man on his Past: The Study of the History of Historical Scholarship.* Cambridge, U.K.: Cambridge University Press, 1955.

Castro, Américo. *An Idea of History: Selected Essays of Américo Castro.* Translated and edited by Stephen Gilman and Edmund L. King. Columbus: Ohio State University Press, 1977.

Collingwood, R. G. *The Idea of History.* Oxford: Oxford University Press, 1946. Classic exposition of philosophy of history also contains a good history of western historical thought.

Elton, G. R. *Return to Essentials: Some Reflections on the Present State of Historical Study.* Cambridge, U.K., and New York: Cambridge University Press, 1991.

Kelley, Donald R. *Faces of History: Historical Enquiry from Herodotus to Herder.* New Haven: Yale University Press, 1998. Excellent interpretive chapters on major aspects of European historiography.

Kochan, Lionel. *The Jew and His History.* London: Macmillan, 1977.

Lefebvre, Georges. *La naissance de l'historiographie moderne.* Paris: Flammarion 1971.

Lorenz, Chris. "Comparative Historiography: Problems and Perspectives." *History and Theory* 38 (1999): 25–39.

Maciu, Vasile, et al. *Outline of Rumanian Historiography until the Beginning of the Twentieth Century.* Bucharest: Academy of the Rumanian People's Republic, 1964.

Monkkonnen, Eric H., ed. *Engaging the Past: The Uses of History across the Social Sciences.* Durham, N.C.: Duke University Press, 1994.

Orr, Linda. "The Revenge of Literature: A History of History." *New Literary History* 18 (1986–1987): 1–21.

Sato, Masayuki. "Comparative Ideas of Chronology." *History and Theory* 30 (1991): 275–301.

Woolf, D. R., ed. *A Global Encyclopedia of Historical Writing.* 2 vols. New York: Garland, 1998. Covers most regions and traditions of the world. See especially articles by Romila Thapar, David K. Wyatt, David Chandler, Anthony Reid, Judith Tucker, Shawn McHale, Ian Copland, Stuart Robson, Ulrich Kratz, and Somkiat Wanthana on less accessible areas such as Southeast Asia, early India, and Islamic women's history, as well as Toivo U. Raun, Andrejs Plakans and P. K. Hämäläinen on understudied European countries such as Estonia, Latvia, and Finland. All have provided information used in the present account.

Zagorin, Perez. "History, the Referent, and Narrative: Reflections on Postmodernism Now." *History and Theory,* 38 (1999): 1–24. A recent critique of the relevance of postmodernism to historiography.

EARLIEST FORMS OF HISTORICAL WRITING

Brundage, Burr C. "Historiographic Traditions: The Birth of Clio: A Résumé and Interpretation of Ancient Near Eastern Historiography." In *Teachers of History: Essays in Honor of Laurence Bradford Packard,* edited by H. Stuart Hughes. Ithaca, N.Y.: Cornell University Press, 1954.

Cogan, Mordechai, and Israel Eph'al, eds. *Ah, Assyria . . . Studies in Assyrian History and Ancient Near Eastern Historiography Presented to Hayim Tadmor.* Vol. 33 of *Scripta Hierosolymitana.* Jerusalem: Magnes Press, Hebrew University, 1991.

Dentan, Robert, ed. *The Idea of History in the Ancient Near East.* New Haven: Yale University Press, 1955.

Grayson, A. K. *Assyrian and Babylonian Chronicles.* Locust Valley, New York: J. J. Augustin, 1975.

Kraus, Christina Shuttleworth. *The Limits of Historiography: Genre and Narrative in Ancient Historical Texts.* Leiden: Brill, 1999.

Pocock, J. G. A. "The Origins of Study of the Past: A Comparative Approach." *Comparative Studies in Society and History* 4 (1961–1962): 209–246.

Van Seters, John. *In Search of History: Historiography in the Ancient World and the Origins of Biblical History.* New Haven and London: Yale University Press, 1983. Detailed comparative analysis of various Mesopotamian and Jewish historical texts; not for the beginner.

AFRICA

Fage, J. D., ed. *Africa Discovers her Past.* London: Oxford University Press, 1970.

Falola, Toyin, ed. *African Historiography: Essays in Honour of Jacob Ade Ajayi.* Harlow: Longman, 1993.

Gérard, Albert S. *African Language Literatures.* Washington, D.C.: Three Continents Press, 1981.

Harneit-Sievers, Axel, ed. *A Place in the World: New Local Historiographies from Africa and South-Asia.* Leiden: Brill, 2002.

Henige, David. *The Chronology of Oral Tradition: The Quest for a Chimera.* Oxford: Clarendon, 1974.

Hiskett, Mervyn. *A History of Hausa Islamic Verse.* London: School of Oriental and African Studies, University of London, 1975.

History in Africa: A Journal of Method. Contains many useful articles on aspects of African historiography, both indigenous and Western.

Jewsiewicki, Bogumil and David S. Newbury, eds. *African Historiographies: What History for Which Africa?* Beverly Hills, Calif.: Sage, 1986.

Middell, Matthias. "Transfer and Interaction: France and Francophone African Historiography." In *Across Cultural Borders: Historiography in Global Perspective,* edited by Eckhardt Fuchs and Benedikt Stuchtey, 163–182. Lanham, Md.: Rowman and Littlefield, 2002.

Miller, Joseph C. "History and Africa/Africa and History." *American Historical Review* 104, no. 1 (February 1999): 1–32. Useful excursus into the beginnings and major developments within African historiography.

Pankhurst, Richard K. P., ed. *The Ethiopian Royal Chronicles [Extracts].* Addis Ababa: Oxford University Press, 1967.

Prins, Adrian. "On Swahili Historiography." *Journal of the East African Swahili Committee* 28 (1958): 26–40.

Saunders, Christopher. *The Making of the South African Past: Major Historians on Race and Class.* Capetown and Johannesburg: David Philip, 1988.

Scheub, Harold. "Xhosa Oral and Literary Traditions." In B. W. Andrzejewski, S. Piłaszewicz, and W. Tyloch, eds. *Literatures in African Languages: Theoretical Issues and Sample Surveys.* Warsaw: Cambridge University Press, 1985, 529–609.

Smith, Ken. *The Changing Past: Trends in South African Historical Writing.* Athens, Ohio: Ohio University Press, 1988.

Van Jaarsveld, Floris Albertus. *The Afrikaner's Interpretation of South African History.* Capetown: Simondium Publishers, 1964. Dated account that should be read in conjunction with more recent studies by Smith, Saunders, and Wright listed above and below.

Vansina, Jan, Raymond Mauny, and L. V. Thomas. *The Historian in Tropical Africa: Studies Presented and Discussed.* London: Oxford University Press, 1964.

Vansina, Jan. *Oral Tradition as History.* Madison: University of Wisconsin Press, 1985.

Wright, Harrison M. *The Burden of the Present: Liberal-Radical Controversy over Southern African History.* Cape Town: David Philip, 1977.

EAST ASIA

Beasley, W. G., and E. G. Pulleyblank. *Historians of China and Japan.* London: Oxford University Press, 1961.

Brownlee, John S. *Japanese Historians and the National Myths, 1600–1945: The Age of the Gods and Emperor Jinmu.* Vancouver: UBC Press; Tokyo: University of Tokyo Press, 1997.

Brownlee, John S., ed. *History in the Service of the Japanese Nation.* Toronto: University of Toronto-York University Joint Centre on Modern East Asia, 1983.

Ch'oe Yŏng-ho. "An Outline History of Korean Historiography." *Korean Studies* 4 (1980): 1–28.

Dirlik, Arif. *Revolution and History: the Origins of Marxist Historiography in China, 1919–1937.* Berkeley: University of California Press, 1978. Especially good on pre-1949 materialist historiography.

Duus, Peter. "Whig History, Japanese Style: The Min'yūsha Historians and the Meiji Restoration." *Journal of Asian Studies* 33 (1974): 415–436.

Edmunds, Clifford. "The Politics of Historiography: Jian Bozan's Historicism." In *China's Intellectuals and the State: In Search of a New Relationship,* edited by Merle Goldman, 65–106. Cambridge, Mass: Harvard University Press, 1987.

Elman, Benjamin A. *From Philosophy to Philology: Intellectual and Social Aspects of Change in Late Imperial China.* Cambridge, Mass.: Harvard University Press, 1984.

Feuerwerker, Albert, ed. *History in Communist China.* Cambridge, Mass: MIT Press, 1968.

Gardner, Charles S. *Chinese Traditional Historiography.* Cambridge, Mass: Harvard University Press, 1938. Should be read in concert with more recent studies in Unger, 1993, below and Dirlik, 1978, above.

Hardy, Grant. "Can an Ancient Chinese Historian Contribute to Modern Western Theory? The Multiple Narratives of Ssu-ma Ch'ien." *History and Theory* 33 (1994): 20–38.

Kwong, Luke S. K. "The Rise of the Lineard Perspective on History and Time in Late Qing China." *Past and Present* 173 (2001): 157–190.

Leslie, Donald D., Colin Mackerras, and Wang Gungwu, eds. *Essays on the Sources for Chinese History.* Canberra: Australian National University Press, 1973.

Mass, Jeffrey P. *Antiquity and Anachronism in Japanese History.* Stanford: Stanford University Press, 1992.

Mehl, Margaret. *History and the State in Nineteenth-Century Japan.* Basingstoke: Macmillan, 1998. Excellent study of its subject.

Najita, Tesua. "History and Nature in Eighteenth-Century Tokugawa Thought." In *The Cambridge History of Japan.* Vol. 4: *Early Modern Japan,* edited by John W. Hall et al., 596–659. Cambridge, U.K.: Cambridge University Press, 1988–1999.

Pai, Hyung Il. *Constructing "Korean" Origins: A Critical Review of Archaeology, Historiography, and Racial Myth in Korean State-Formation Theories.* Cambridge, Mass: Harvard University Press, 2000.

Petrov, Leonid A. "North Korean Historiography in Crisis (1956–1967)." In *Korean Studies at the Dawn of the Millennium: Proceedings of the Second Bienniel Conference, Korean Studies Association of Australia,* edited by Young-A Cho, 374–383. Monash: Monash University, 2002.

Schaberg, David. *A Patterned Past: Form and Thought in Early Chinese Historiography.* Cambridge, Mass., and London: Harvard University Press for Harvard University Asia Center, 2001.

Schwartz, Benjamin. "History in Chinese Culture: Some Comparative Reflections." *History and Theory* 35 (1996): 23–33.

Tanaka, Stefan. "Alternative National Histories in Japan: Yamaji Aizan and Academic Historiography." In *Across Cultural Borders: Historiography in Global Perspective,* edited by Eckhardt Fuchs and Benedikt Stuchtey, 119–138. Lanham, Md.: Rowman and Littlefield, 2002.

——. *Japan's Orient: Rendering Pasts into History.* Berkeley: University of California Press, 1993.

Twitchett, Denis Crispin. *The Writing of Official History under the T'ang.* Cambridge, U.K., and New York: Cambridge University Press, 1992.

Unger, Jonathan, ed. *Using the Past to Serve the Present: Historiography and Politics in Contemporary China.* Armonk, N.Y.: M. E. Sharpe, 1993. See especially chapters by Lawrence R. Sullivan, Geremie Barmé, and Tom Fisher.

Wang, Q. Edward. *Inventing China through History: The May Fourth Approach to Historiography.* Albany: State University of New York Press, 2001.

EUROPE: ANCIENT AND MEDIEVAL

Archambault, Paul. *Seven French Chroniclers: Witnesses to History.* Syracuse, N.Y.: Syracuse University Press, 1974.

Dalven, Rae. *Anna Comnena.* New York: Twayne, 1972.

Dorey, T. A., ed. *Latin Historians: Chapters by E. A. Thompson [and Others].* London: Routledge and Kegan Paul, 1966.

Fornara, Charles W. *The Nature of History in Ancient Greece and Rome.* Berkeley: University of California Press, 1983.

Goffart, Walter A. *The Narrators of Barbarian History (AD 550–800: Jordanes, Gregory of Tours, Bede, and Paul the Deacon).* Princeton: Princeton University Press, 1988.

Gransden, Antonia. *Historical Writing in England.* 2 vols. Ithaca, N.Y.: Cornell University Press, 1974–1982.

Hartog, François. "The Invention of History: The Pre-History of a Concept from Homer to Herodotus." *History and Theory* 39 (2000): 384–395.

Hay, Denys. *Annalists and Historians.* London: Methuen, 1977.

Hillgarth, J. N. "Spanish Historiography and Iberian Reality." *History and Theory* 24 (1985): 23–43.

Linehan, Peter. *History and the Historians of Medieval Spain.* Oxford: Clarendon, 1993. Long and definitive treatment of its subject.

Momigliano, Arnaldo. *The Classical Foundations of Modern Historiography.* Berkeley: University of California Press, 1990.

——. *Essays in Ancient and Modern Historiography.* Middletown, Conn.: Wesleyan University Press, 1977.

Rohrbacher, David. *The Historians of Late Antiquity.* London and New York: Routledge, 2002.

Smalley, Beryl. *Historians in the Middle Ages.* London: Thames and Hudson, 1974.

Spiegel, Gabrielle. *Romancing the Past: The Rise of Vernacular Prose Historiography in Thirteenth-Century France.* Berkeley: University of California Press, 1993.

Syme, Ronald. *Tacitus.* 2 vols. 1958. Reprint, Oxford: Clarendon, 1989.

EUROPE: RENAISSANCE THROUGH EIGHTEENTH CENTURY

Allan, David. *Virtue, Learning and the Scottish Enlightenment.* Edinburgh: Edinburgh University Press, 1993.

Barret-Kriegel, Blandine. *Les historiens et la monarchie.* 4 vols. Paris: Presses universitaires de France, 1988.

Burke, Peter. *The Renaissance Sense of the Past.* London: Edward Arnold, 1969.

Cochrane, Eric. *Historians and Historiography in the Italian Renaissance.* Chicago: University of Chicago Press, 1981.

Chickering, Roger. *Karl Lamprecht: a German Academic Life (1856–1915).* Atlantic Highlands, N.J.: Humanities Press, 1993.

Huppert, George. *The Idea of Perfect History: Historical Erudition and Historical Philosophy in Renaissance France.* Urbana: University of Illinois Press, 1970.

Johannesson, Kurt. *The Renaissance of the Goths in Sixteenth-Century Sweden: Johannes and Olaus Magnus as Politicians and Historians.* Translated and edited by James Larson. Berkeley: University of California Press, 1991.

Kelley, Donald R. *Foundations of Modern Historical Scholarship: Language, Law, and History in the French Renaissance.* New York: Columbia University Press, 1970.

Knowles, David. *Great Historical Enterprises: Problems in Monastic History.* London: Nelson, 1963.

O'Brien, Karen. *Narratives of Enlightenment: Cosmopolitan History from Voltaire to Gibbon.* Cambridge, U.K., and New York: Cambridge University Press, 1997.

Pocock, J. G. A. *The Ancient Constitution and the Feudal Law: A Study of English Historical Thought in the Seventeenth Century: A Reissue with a Retrospect.* Cambridge, U.K.: Cambridge University Press, 1987.

Pocock, J. G. A. *Barbarism and Religion.* 3 vols. to date. Cambridge, U.K.: Cambridge University Press, 1999–. Brilliant exposition of Gibbon's intellectual environment; far wider-ranging than the title suggests. Vol. 3 is especially good as an interpretive history of European historiography and key concepts such as "decline and fall."

Segal, Lester A. *Historical Consciousness and Religious Tradition in Azariah de' Rossi's Me'or 'Einayim.* Philadelphia, New York, and Jerusalem: Jewish Publication Society, 1989.

Skovgaard-Petersen, Karen. *Historiography at the Court of Christian IV (1588–1648): Studies in the Latin Histories of Johannes Portanus and Johannes Meursius.* Copenhagen: Museum Tusculanum Press, 2002.

Wilcox, Donald. *The Development of Florentine Humanist Historiography in the Fifteenth Century.* Cambridge, Mass.: Harvard University Press, 1969.

Woolf, D. R. *The Social Circulation of the Past: English Historical Culture 1500–1730.* Oxford: Oxford University Press, 2003.

EUROPE AND NORTH AMERICA: NINETEENTH AND TWENTIETH CENTURIES

Ahokas, Jaakko. *A History of Finnish Literature.* Bloomington: Indiana University Press, 1973.

Ankersmit, F. R. "The Postmodernist Privatization of the Past." In the author's *Historical Representation,* 149-175. Stanford, Calif.: Stanford University Press, 2001.

Baets, Antoon de. *Censorship of Historical Thought: A World Guide, 1945–2000.* Westport, Conn.: Greenwood Press, 2002.

Bromke, Adam. *The Meaning and Uses of Polish History.* Boulder, Colo.: East European Monographs, 1987.

Burke, Peter. *The French Historical Revolution: The Annales School, 1929–1989.* Stanford, Calif.: Stanford University Press, 1990.

Burrow, J. W. *A Liberal Descent: Victorian Historians and the English Past.* Cambridge, U.K.: Cambridge University Press, 1981.

Dorpalen, Andreas. *German History in Marxist Perspective: The East German Approach.* Detroit, Mich.: Wayne State University Press, 1985.

Enteen, George M. *The Soviet Scholar-Bureaucrat: M. N. Pokrovskii and the Society of Marxist Historians.* University Park, Pa.: Penn State University Press, 1978.

Evans, Richard J. *Telling Lies about Hitler: The Holocaust, History and the David Irving Trial.* London: Verso, 2002.

Gooch, G. P. *History and Historians in the Nineteenth Century.* 2nd ed., revised. London and New York: Longmans, Green, 1952. First published in 1913 and revised by its author, an Acton-influenced historian, in 1952; though dated, it remains useful as an index of pre-World War I attitudes to the nineteenth century's historiographic achievements.

Hasquin, Hervé, ed. *Histoire et historiens depuis 1830 en Belgique.* Brussels: Éditions de l'Université de Bruxelles, 1981.

Herbst, Jurgen. *The German Historical School in American Scholarship: A Study in the Transfer of Culture.* Ithaca, N.Y.: Cornell University Press, 1965.

Hiemstra, Paul A. *Alexandru D. Xenopol and the Development of Romanian Historiography.* New York and London: Garland, 1987.

Hofstadter, Richard. *The Progressive Historians: Turner, Beard, Parrington.* Reprint of 1968 edition. Chicago: University of Chicago Press, 1979.

Hubbard, William H., et al., eds. *Making a Historical Culture: Historiography in Norway.* Oslo: Scandinavian University Press, 1995.

Iggers, Georg G. *The German Conception of History: The National Tradition of Historical Thought from Herder to the Present.* Rev. ed. Middletown, Conn.: Wesleyan University Press, 1983.

Iggers, Georg G., and James M. Powell, eds. *Leopold von Ranke and the Shaping of the Historical Discipline.* Syracuse: Syracuse University Press, 1990.

Jacobitti, Edmund E. *Revolutionary Humanism and Historicism in Modern Italy.* New Haven: Yale University Press, 1981.

Krapauskas, Virgil. *Nationalism and Historiography: The Case of Nineteenth-Century Lithuanian Historicism.* Boulder, Colo.: East European Monographs, 2000.

Krieger, Leonard. *Ranke: The Meaning of History.* Chicago: University of Chicago Press, 1977.

Lehmann, Hartmut, and James Van Horn Melton, eds. *Paths of Continuity: Central European Historiography from the 1930s to the 1950s.* Washington, D.C.: German Historical Institute and Cambridge, U.K.: Cambridge University Press, 1994.

Linenthal, Edward Tabor, and Tom Engelhardt, eds. *History Wars: The Enola Gay and Other Battles for the American Past.* New York: Metropolitan Books, 1996.

Lingelbach, Gabriele. "The Historical Discipline in the United States: Following the German Model?" In *Across Cultural Borders: Historiography in Global Perspective,* edited by Eckhardt Fuchs and Benedikt Stuchtey, 182–204. Lanham, Md.: Rowman and Littlefield, 2002.

Mazlish, Bruce. *The Riddle of History: The Great Speculators from Vico to Freud.* New York and London: Harper and Row, 1966. A still useful and entertaining general introduction to select thinkers, somewhat prone to judgmental criticism.

Mazour, Anatole G. *Modern Russian Historiography.* Rev. ed. Westport, Conn.: Greenwood Press, 1975.

Meinecke, Friedrich. *Historism: The Rise of a New Historical Outlook.* Translated by J. E. Anderson. Translation revised by H. D. Schmidt. 2nd ed. London: Routledge. 1972.

Novick, Peter. *That Noble Dream: The "Objectivity" Question and the American Historical Profession.* Cambridge, U.K.: Cambridge University Press, 1988.

Pók, Attila. "Scholarly and Non-Scholarly Functions of Historical Research Institutes: An Outline of the Case of Hungary in International Context." In *History-Making: The Intellectual and Social Formation of a Discipline. Proceedings of an International Conference, Uppsala, September, 1994,* edited by Rolf Torstendahl and Irmline Veit-Brause, 169–177. Stockholm: Kungl. Vitterhets, historie och antikvitets akademien, 1996.

Raphael, Lutz. "Organizational Frameworks of University Life and their Impact on Historiographical Practice." In *History-Making: The Intellectual and Social Formation of a Discipline. Proceedings of an International Conference, Uppsala, September, 1994,* edited by Rolf Torstendahl and Irmline Veit-Brause, 151–167. Stockholm: Kungl. Vitterhets, historie och antikvitets akademien, 1996.

Riis, Carsten. *Religion, Politics, and Historiography in Bulgaria.* Boulder, Colo.: East European Monographs, 2002.

Shelton, Anita K. *The Democratic Idea in Polish History and Historiography: Franciszek Bujak (1875–1953).* Boulder, Colo.: East European Monographs, 1989.

Shteppa, Konstantin F. *Russian Historians and the Soviet State.* New Brunswick, N.J.: Rutgers University Press, 1962.

Smith, Bonnie G. *The Gender of History: Men, Women, and Historical Practice.* Cambridge, Mass: Harvard University Press, 1998.

Smith, Leslie F. *Modern Norwegian Historiography.* Oslo: Norwegian Universities Press, 1962.

Stieg, Margaret F. *The Origin and Development of Scholarly Historical Periodicals.* University: University of Alabama Press, 1986.

Taylor, M. Brook. *Promoters, Patriots, and Partisans: Historiography in Nineteenth-Century English Canada.* Toronto and Buffalo: University of Toronto Press, 1989.

Torstendahl, Rolf, ed. *An Assessment of Twentieth-Century Historiography: Professionalism, Methodologies, Writings.* Stockholm: Kungl. Vitterhets, historie och antikvitets akademien, 2000.

———. "Fact, Truth, and Text: The Quest for a Firm Basis for Historical Knowledge around 1900." *History and Theory* 42 (2003): 305–331. Interesting evaluation of nineteenth-century methodology treatises, demonstrating significant differences among a number of them.

Vardy, Steven Bela. *Modern Hungarian Historiography.* Boulder, Colo: East European Monographs, 1976.

Vernadsky, George. *Russian Historiography: A History.* Edited by Sergei Pushkarev. Translated by Nickolas Lupinin. Belmont, Mass.: Norland Publishing, 1978.

White, Hayden. *Metahistory: The Historical Imagination in Nineteenth-Century Europe.* Baltimore: Johns Hopkins University Press, 1973.

LATIN AMERICA

Adorno, Rolena. *Guaman Poma: Writing and Resistance in Colonial Peru.* 2nd ed. Austin: University of Texas Press, 1986.

Burns, E. Bradford, ed. *Perspectives on Brazilian History.* New York and London: Columbia University Press, 1967.

Carey, David, Jr. *Our Elders Teach Us: Maya-Kaqchikel Historical Perspectives.* Tuscaloosa: University of Alabama Press, 2001. Fascinating analysis of indigenous Guatemalan oral traditions and memories, by a historian rather than an anthropologist.

Cline, Howard F., ed. *Latin American History: Essays on its Study and Teaching, 1898–1965.* 2 vols. Austin: University of Texas Press, 1967. Somewhat dated but still useful collection of essays, principally on U.S. approaches rather than indigenous ones.

Cormier, Loretta. "Decolonizing History: Ritual Transformation of the Past among the Guajá of Eastern Amazonia." In *Histories and Historicities in Amazonia,* edited by Neil L. Whitehead, 123–139. Lincoln and London: University of Nebraska Press, 2003. Recent example of the ethnohistorical approach (informed by postcolonial discourse) to one variety of the Latin American sense of the past, among indigenous peoples.

Griffin, Charles C., ed. *Latin America: A Guide to the Historical Literature.* Austin: University of Texas Press, 1971.

Hill, Jonathan D., ed. *Rethinking History and Myth: Indigenous South American Perspectives on the Past.* Urbana: University of Illinois Press, 1988. Relations between myth, legend, history, and consciousness among various native populations.

Robinson, John L. *Bartolomé Mitre: Historian of the Americas.* Washington, D.C.: University Press of America, 1982.

Rabasa, José. *Inventing America: Spanish Historiography and the Formation of Eurocentrism.* Norman and London: University of Oklahoma Press, 1993.

Thomas, Jack Ray. *Biographical Dictionary of Latin American Historians and Historiography.* Westport, Conn.: Greenwood Press, 1984. Brief entries; useful as a reference tool.

Wilgus, A. Curtis. *The Historiography of Latin America: A Guide to Historical Writing, 1500-1800.* Metuchen, N.J.: Scarecrow Press, 1975.

Woll, Allen. *A Functional Past: The Uses of History in Nineteenth-Century Chile.* Baton Rouge and London: Louisiana State University Press, 1982. Excellent study of relations between history and politics in a newly-independent nation.

THE OTTOMAN EMPIRE AND THE MIDDLE EAST

Ahmed, Leila. *Women and Gender in Islam: Historical Roots of a Modern Debate.* New Haven, Conn.: Yale University Press, 1992.

Chejne, Anwar G. "The Concept of History in the Modern Arab World." *Studies in Islam: Quarterly Journal of Indian Institute of Islamic Studies* 4 (1967): 1–31.

Choueiri, Youssef M. *Arab History and the Nation-State: A Study in Modern Arab Historiography 1820-1980.* London and New York: Routledge, 1989.

Crabbs, Jack A., Jr. *The Writing of History in Nineteenth-Century Egypt.* Detroit: Wayne State University Press; Cairo: American University in Cairo Press, 1984.

Dengler, Ian C. "Turkish Women in the Ottoman Empire: the Classical Age." In *Women in the Muslim World,* edited by Lois Beck and Nikki Keddie, 229-244. Cambridge, Mass.: Harvard University Press, 1978.

Duri, A. A. *The Rise of Historical Writing Among the Arabs.* Edited and translated by Lawrence I. Conrad. Introduction by Fred M. Donner. Princeton: Princeton University Press, 1983.

Kafadar, Cemal. *Between Two Worlds: The Construction of the Ottoman State.* Berkeley: University of California Press, 1995. Useful summary of the sources and modern historiography of the empire.

Keddie, Nikki R., and Beth Baron. *Women in Middle Eastern History: Shifting Boundaries in Sex and Gender.* New Haven, Conn.: Yale University Press, 1991. See especially introduction by Keddie.

Khalidi, Tarif. *Arab Historical Thought in the Classical Period.* Cambridge, U.K., and New York: Cambridge University Press, 1994.

———. *Islamic Historiography: The Histories of Mas'ūdī.* Albany: SUNY Press, 1975.

Lewis, Bernard, and P. M. Holt, eds. *Historians of the Middle East.* London: Oxford University Press, 1962.

Mahdi, Muhsin. *Ibn Khaldûn's Philosophy of History: A Study in the Philosophic Foundation of the Science of Culture.* Chicago: University of Chicago Press, 1964.

Meisami, Julie Scott. *Persian Historiography to the End of the Twelfth Century.* Edinburgh: Edinburgh University Press, 1999.

Mernissi, Fatima. *Women and Islam: An Historical and Theological Enquiry.* Translated by Mary Jo Lakeland. Oxford: Basil Blackwell, 1991.

Nashat, Guity, and Lois Beck, eds. *Women in Iran from the Rise of Islam to 1800.* Urbana: University of Illinois Press, 2003.

Robinson, Chase F. *Islamic Historiography.* Cambridge, U.K., and New York: Cambridge University Press, 2003. Invaluable introduction with useful glossary of terms.

Rosenthal, Franz. *A History of Muslim Historiography.* 2nd rev. ed. Leiden, Netherlands: Brill, 1968.

Taher, Mohamed, ed. *Medieval Muslim Historiography.* Vol. 5 of *Encyclopaedic Survey of Islamic Culture.* New Delhi: Anmol Publications, 1997.

SOUTH AND CENTRAL ASIA

Bahāristān-i-Shāhī: A Chronicle of Mediaeval Kashmir. Translated and edited by K. N. Pandit. Calcutta: Firma KLM, 1991.

Ganguly, Dilip Kumar. *History and Historians in Ancient India.* New Delhi: Abhinav Publications, 1984.

Guha, Ranajit. *History at the Limit of World-History.* New York: Columbia University Press, 2002.

———. *An Indian Historiography of India: A Nineteenth-Century Agenda and Its Implications.* Calcutta and New Delhi: K. P. Bagchi, 1988.

Hardy, Peter. *Historians of Medieval India: Studies in Indo-Muslim Historical Writing.* London: Luzac and Co., 1960.

Hasan, Mohibbul, and Muhammad Mujeeb, eds. *Historians of Medieval India.* Meerut: Meenakshi Prakashan, 1968.

Lal, Vinay. *The History of History: Politics and Scholarship in Modern India.* Oxford and New Delhi: Oxford University Press, 2003. See especially chapter 1 on "the history of ahistoricity."

Pargiter, F. E. *Ancient Indian Historical Tradition.* London: Oxford University Press, 1922. Reprint, Delhi: M. Banarsidass, 1962.

Perrett, Roy W. "History, Time, and Knowledge in Ancient India." *History and Theory* 38 (1999): 307–321.

Philips, C. H., ed. *Historians of India, Pakistan, and Ceylon.* London and New York: Oxford University Press, 1961.

Prakash, Buddha. "The Hindu Philosophy of History." *Journal of the History of Ideas* 16 (1955): 494–505.

Sarkar, Jagadish Narayan. *History of History-writing in Medieval India: Contemporary Historians: An Introduction to Medieval Indian Historiography.* Calcutta: Ratna Prakashan, 1977.

Sarkar, Sumit. "The Decline of the Subaltern in Subaltern Studies." In his *Writing Social History.* New Delhi: Oxford University Press, 1997.

Sen, S. P., ed. *Historians and Historiography in Modern India.* Calcutta: Institute of Historical Studies, 1973.

Singh, G. P. *Ancient Indian Historiography: Sources and Interpretations.* New Delhi: D.K. Printworld, 2003.

Thapar, Romila. *History and Beyond.* New York and New Delhi: Oxford University Press, 2000.

———. "Some Reflections on Early Indian Historical Thinking." In *Western Historical Thinking: an Intercultural Debate,* edited by Jörn Rüsen. New York and Oxford: Bergahn Books, 2002.

Warder, A. K. *An Introduction to Indian Historiography.* Bombay: Popular Prakshan, 1972.

Waseem, Shah Mohammed, ed. *Development of Persian Historiography in India from the Second Half of the Seventeenth Century to the First Half of the Eighteenth Century.* New Delhi: Iran Culture House, 2003.

Žamcarano, C. Ž. *The Mongol Chronicles of the Seventeenth Century.* Translated by Rudolf Loewenthal. Wiesbaden: Otto Harrassowitz, 1955.

SOUTHEAST ASIA, PACIFIC ISLANDS, AND AUSTRALASIA

Ahmad, Abu Talid, and Tan Liok Ee, eds., *New Terrains in Southeast Asian History.* Athens, Ohio: Ohio University Press; Singapore: Singapore National University Press, 2003. Excellent collection; see especially essays by Ni Ni Myint on Burma/Myanmar, and Kobkua Suwannathat-Pian for an introduction to several southeast Asian historical genres and comparison of Thai and Malay writings.

Aung-Thwin, Michael. "The 'Classical' in Southeast Asia: the Present in the Past." *Journal of Southeast Asian Studies* 26, no. 1 (1995): 75–91.

———. *Myth and History in the Historiography of Early Burma: Paradigms, Primary Sources, and Prejudices.* Athens, Ohio: Ohio University Press; Singapore: Singapore National University Press, 1998.

Cowan, C. D., and O. W. Wolters, eds. *Southeast Asian History and Historiography: Essays Presented to D. G. E. Hall.* Ithaca, N.Y., and London: Cornell University Press, 1976.

Errington, Shelly. "Some Comments on Style in the Meanings of the Past." *Journal of Asian Studies* 38, no. 2 (1979): 231–244.

Florida, Nancy K. *Writing the Past, Inscribing the Future: History as Prophecy in Colonial Java.* Durham, N.C., and London: Duke University Press, 1995.

Hall, D. G. E., ed. *Historians of South East Asia.* London: Oxford University Press, 1961.

Jory, Patrick. "Problems in Contemporary Thai Nationalist Historiography." *Kyoto Review of Southeast Asia* 3 (March 2003). Available at http://kyotoreview.cseas.kyoto-u.ac.jp/issue/issue4/index.html.

Larkin, John A., ed. *Perspectives on Philippine Historiography: A Symposium.* New Haven, Conn.: Yale University Southeast Asian Studies, 1979.

Macintyre, Stuart, and Anna Clark. *The History Wars.* Carlton, Australia: Melbourne University Press, 2003.

Marr, David. "Vietnamese Historiography, Past and Present." *Nordic Newsletter of Asian Studies* 4 (2002): 1–3. Available at http://eurasia.nias.ku.dk/activities/publications/niasnytt/2002-4/vietnamese.htm.

Moses, John A., ed. *Historical Disciplines and Culture in Australasia: An Assessment.* St. Lucia, Queensland: University of Queensland Press, 1979. Valuable collection of essays covering New Zealand and Papua New Guinea as well as Australia.

Nguyên Thê Anh. "Historical Research in Vietnam: A Tentative Survey." *Journal of Southeast Asian Studies* 26, no. 1 (1995): 121–132.

Pascoe, Rob. *The Manufacture of Australian History.* Melbourne and Oxford: Oxford University Press, 1979.

Pelley, Patricia M. *Postcolonial Vietnam: New Histories of the National Past.* Durham and London: Duke University Press, 2002.

Ras, J. J., ed. and trans. *Hikajat Bandjar: A Study in Malay Historiography.* The Hague: Nijhoff, 1968.

Reid, Anthony and David Marr, eds. *Perceptions of the Past in Southeast Asia.* Singapore: Published for the Asian Studies Association of Australia by Heinemann Educational Books, 1979. See in particular R. C. Ileto and John N. Schumacher, S.J., on Philippine historiography, which is relatively understudied within the region. A useful appendix lists extant writings by southeast Asians about their own past, including those discussed in the present essay.

Ricklefs, M. C. *Modern Javanese Historical Tradition: A Study of an Original Kartasura Chronicle and Related Materials.* London: School of Oriental and African Studies, University of London, 1978.

Sao Sāimöng Mangrāi, ed. *The Pādaeng Chronicle and the Jengtung State Chronicle Translated.* Ann Arbor: University of Michigan Center for South and Southeast Asian Studies, paper no. 19, 1981.

Siegel, James. *Shadow and Sound: The Historical Thought of a Sumatran People.* Chicago: University of Chicago Press, 1979.

Soedjatmoko, et al. eds. *An Introduction to Indonesian Historiography.* Ithaca, New York: Cornell University Press, 1965.

Thongchai Winichakul. "The Changing Landscape of the Past: New Histories in Thailand since 1973." *Journal of Southeast Asian Studies* 26, no.1 (1995): 99–120.

Van Klinken, Gerry. "The Battle for History after Suharto: Beyond Sacred Dates, Great Men, and Legal Milestones." *Critical Asian Studies,* 33:3 (2001): 323–350.

Vickers, Adrian, "Balinese Texts and Historiography." *History and Theory* 29 (1990): 158–178.

Winstedt, Richard. *A History of Classical Malay Literature.* 2nd ed. Kuala Lumpur, Oxford, and New York: Oxford University Press, 1961. Reprint, 1969.

Wyatt, David K., ed. and trans. *The Nan Chronicle.* Ithaca, N.Y.: Cornell University Southeast Asia program, 1994. Valuable introduction and edition.

Daniel Woolf

READER'S GUIDE

This Reader's Guide was compiled by the editors to provide a systematic outline of the contents of the New Dictionary of the History of Ideas, *thereby offering teachers, scholars, and the general reader a way to organize their reading according to their preferences. The Reader's Guide is divided into four sections: Communication of Ideas, Geographical Areas, Chronological Periods, and Liberal Arts Disciplines and Professions, as indicated in the outline below.*

COMMUNICATION OF IDEAS

Introduction to History of Communication of Ideas

Communication Media

GEOGRAPHICAL AREAS

Global Entries

Africa

Asia

Europe

Middle East

North America

Latin and South America

CHRONOLOGICAL PERIODS

Ancient

Dynastic (400 C.E.–1400 C.E.)

Early Modern (1400–1800 C.E.)

Modern (1800–1945)

Contemporary

LIBERAL ARTS DISCIPLINES AND PROFESSIONS

Fine Arts

Humanities

Social Sciences

Sciences

Professions

Multidisciplinary Practices

Especially Interdisciplinary Entries

COMMUNICATION OF IDEAS

This category is the newest aspect of the *New Dictionary of the History of Ideas*; cultural studies, communications studies, and cultural history are moving the disciplines in this direction.

Introduction to History of Communication of Ideas

The following entries focus on the media humans have used to communicate with one another.

Absolute Music
Aesthetics: Asia
Architecture: Overview
Architecture: Asia
Arts: Overview
Astronomy, Pre-Columbian and Latin American
Bilingualism and Multilingualism
Borders, Borderlands, and Frontiers, Global
Calendar
Cinema
City, The: The City as a Cultural Center
City, The: The City as Political Center
Communication of Ideas: Africa and Its Influence
Communication of Ideas: Asia and Its Influence
Communication of Ideas: Europe and Its Influence
Communication of Ideas: Middle East and Abroad
Communication of Ideas: Orality and Advent of Writing
Communication of Ideas: Southeast Asia
Communication of Ideas: The Americas and Their Influence
Consumerism
Cultural Revivals
Cultural Studies
Dance
Diffusion, Cultural
Dress
Dualism
Education: Asia, Traditional and Modern
Education: Global Education
Emotions
Experiment
Garden
Gesture
Humor
Iconography
Images, Icons, and Idols
Japanese Philosophy, Japanese Thought
Language and Linguistics
Language, Linguistics, and Literacy
Learning and Memory, Contemporary Views
Mathematics
Media, History of
Metaphor
Migration: United States
Modernity: Africa
Museums
Music, Anthropology of

Communication Media

This is a listing of the types of historical evidence the author used in writing the entry. While entries in the original Dictionary of the History of Ideas were to a great extent the history of texts, the entries in the New Dictionary of the History of Ideas are generally the cultural history of ideas, making use of the records of oral communication, visual communication, and communication through practices, as well as the history of texts, in order to show the impact of the idea on a wide variety of people.

ORAL

The selective list below contains the entries that give the most coverage to historical examples of the oral transmission and transformation of ideas.

COMMUNICATION THROUGH HIGH TECHNOLOGY MEDIA (radio, television, film, computer, etc.)

VISUAL

Each of the following entries in the *NDHI* either evocatively describes ideas, includes a visual image of an idea, or provides historical examples of societies visually transmitting and transforming ideas.

PRACTICES

Most of the entries in the *NDHI* discuss how specific societies habituated people to specific ideas. This selective list includes the entries on schools of thought and practice, religions, and political movements, as well as the entries on distinctive practices.

TEXTUAL

Every entry in the *New Dictionary of the History of Ideas* used texts. The following is a list of entries that focused mainly on the history of a succession of texts. Each academic discipline has a succession of major authors with whom later practitioners of the discipline build upon and respond to creatively. The historian of a discipline—such as the history of political philosophy, literary history, or the history of science—considers the responses of thinkers and practitioners of a discipline to the major earlier texts in the discipline. In tracing the origin, development, and transformation of an idea, the historian of ideas considers thinkers' responses to texts from a variety of disciplines.

GEOGRAPHICAL AREAS

Global Entries

ENTRIES ON AT LEAST THREE GEOGRAPHIC
AREAS OR A GLOBAL TOPIC

Ritual: Religion
Sacred and Profane
Sage Philosophy
Segregation
Slavery
State, The: The Postcolonial State
Syncretism
Temperance
Third Cinema
Third World
Third World Literature
Time: Traditional and Utilitarian
Toleration
Totems
Treaty
Tribalism, Middle East
University: Postcolonial
Untouchability: Menstrual Taboos
Victorianism
War
Wisdom, Human
Witchcraft
Womanism
Women's Studies
Work
World Systems Theory, Latin America

Asia

ENTRIES FOCUSING ON ASIA
Aesthetics: Asia
Alchemy: China
Anticolonialism: Southeast Asia
Architecture: Asia
Authoritarianism: East Asia
Buddhism
Causation in East Asian and Southeast Asian Philosophy
Chinese Thought
Chinese Warlordism
Christianity: Asia
Colonialism: Southeast Asia
Communication of Ideas: Asia and Its Influence
Communication of Ideas: Southeast Asia and Its Influence
Confucianism
Consciousness: Chinese Thought
Consciousness: Indian Thought
Cosmology: Asia
Daoism
Education: Asia, Traditional and Modern
Education: China
Education: India
Education: Japan
Empire and Imperialism: Asia
Examination Systems, China
Globalization: Asia
Heaven and Hell (Asian Focus)
Hinduism
Humanism: Chinese Conception of
Humanity: Asian Thought
Islam: Southeast Asia
Jainism
Japanese Philosophy, Japanese Thought
Justice: Justice in East Asian Thought
Landscape in the Arts

Legalism, Ancient China
Literature: Overview
Maoism
Marxism: Asia
Medicine: China
Medicine: India
Meditation: Eastern Meditation
Modernity: East Asia
Mysticism: Chinese Mysticism
Mysticism: Islamic Mysticism in Asia
Orthopraxy: Asia
Pan-Asianism
Pan-Turkism
Philosophy: Historical Overview and Recent Developments
Race and Racism: Asia
Religion: East and Southeast Asia
Sacred Texts: Asia
Science: East Asia
Time: China
Time: India
Westernization: Southeast Asia
Women's History: Asia
ENTRIES THAT CONSIDER ASIA
Algebras
Ancestor Worship
Anthropology
Anticolonialism: Africa
Architecture: Overview
Arts: Overview
Asceticism: Hindu and Buddhist Asceticism
Asian-American Ideas (Cultural Migration)
Astrology: China
Astronomy, Pre-Columbian and Latin American
Atheism
Autobiography
Barbarism and Civilization
Beauty and Ugliness
Bilingualism and Multilingualism
Biography
Body, The
Borders, Borderlands, and Frontiers, Global
Bushido
Calculation and Computation
Cannibalism
Censorship
Childhood and Child Rearing
Christianity: Overview
Cinema
Civil Disobedience
Civil Society: Responses in Africa and the Middle East
Communication of Ideas: Middle East and Abroad
Communication of Ideas: Orality and the Advent of Writing
Constitutionalism
Cosmopolitanism
Creativity in the Arts and Sciences
Critical Theory
Cultural Revivals
Cycles
Dance
Deism
Demography
Demonology
Dependency

CHRONOLOGICAL PERIODS

This section is divided according to five periods in world history: Ancient, Dynastic, Early Modern, Modern, and Contemporary. Use this section together with the section on Geographical Areas.

Ancient (before 400 C.E.)
ENTRIES FOCUSED ON THE PERIOD
Buddhism
Consciousness: Chinese Thought
Consciousness: Indian Thought
Democracy
Dialogue and Dialectics: Socratic
Epicureanism
Gnosticism
Greek Science
Hinduism
Justice: Justice in East Asian Thought
Language, Linguistics, and Literacy
Microcosm and Macrocosm
Orthopraxy: Asia
Orthopraxy: Western Orthopraxy
Poetry and Poetics
Sacred Places
Sacred Texts: Asia
Sophists, The
Textiles and Fiber Arts as Catalysts for Ideas
Time: China
Time: India
Yin and Yang

ENTRIES WITH EXAMPLES FROM BEFORE 400 C.E.

Generally the examples in this category are from the ancient Middle East, Europe, or Asia.

Aesthetics: Asia
Aesthetics: Europe and the Americas
Africa, Idea of
Alchemy: China
Alchemy: Europe and the Middle East
Algebras
Ambiguity
Anarchism
Anthropology
Anti-Semitism: Overview
Architecture: Overview

New Dictionary of the History of Ideas

ENTRIES WITH EXAMPLES FROM THE PERIOD
1800–1945

Contemporary

ENTRIES FOCUSED ON THE PERIOD

Jihad
Liberation Theology
Liberty
Life
Linguistic Turn
Literary History
Logic and Philosophy of Mathematics, Modern
Maoism
Marxism: Overview
Marxism: Asia
Marxism: Latin America
Media, History of
Modernization
Modernization Theory
Nationalism: Overview
Nationalism: Africa
Nationalism: Cultural Nationalism
Nationalism: Middle East
Neocolonialism
Neoliberalism
Nuclear Age
Orientalism: African and Black Orientalism
Pan-Africanism
Pan-Arabism
Pan-Asianism
Pan-Islamism
Pan-Turkism
Paradigm
Parties, Political
Personhood in African Thought
Phenomenology
Philosophies: Feminist, Twentieth-Century
Poetry and Poetics
Populism: Latin America
Populism: United States
Positivism
Postcolonial Studies
Postcolonial Theory and Literature
Postmodernism
Pragmatism
Presentism
Privatization
Protest, Political
Psychoanalysis
Psychology and Psychiatry
Quantum
Queer Theory
Realism: Africa
Relativism
Relativity
Science Fiction
Segregation
Sexual Harassment
Sexuality: Sexual Orientation
Sociability in African Thought
Social Darwinism
Socialisms, African
Structuralism and Poststructuralism: Overview
Structuralism and Poststructuralism: Anthropology
Subjectivism
Technology
Terrorism, Middle East
Text/Textuality
Theater and Performance
Third Cinema

Third World
Totalitarianism
Virtual Reality
Virtue Ethics
War
Westernization: Africa
Westernization: Southeast Asia
Witchcraft
Womanism
Women and Femininity in U.S. Popular Culture
Women's Studies
Zionism

ENTRIES WITH EXAMPLES FROM THE PERIOD SINCE 1945 (especially since the 1970s)

Absolute Music
Aesthetics: Africa
Aesthetics: Asia
Aesthetics: Europe and the Americas
Africa, Idea of
Afrocentricity
Afropessimism
Agnosticism
Algebras
Alienation
Altruism
Ambiguity
America
Analytical Philosophy
Anarchism
Animism
Anthropology
Antifeminism
Anti-Semitism: Overview
Architecture: Overview
Architecture: Africa
Arts: Overview
Arts: Africa
Asceticism: Western Asceticism
Asian-American Ideas (Cultural Migration)
Assimilation
Atheism
Authenticity: Africa
Authoritarianism: Overview
Authoritarianism: East Asia
Authoritarianism: Latin America
Authority
Autobiography
Autonomy
Avant-Garde: Overview
Aztlán
Barbarism and Civilization
Beauty and Ugliness
Behaviorism
Bilingualism and Multilingualism
Biography
Biology
Body, The
Bushido
Calculation and Computation
Cannibalism
Capitalism: Overview
Cartesianism
Casuistry
Causality
Causation

Privacy
Probability
Progress, Idea of
Propaganda
Property
Pseudoscience
Public Sphere
Punishment
Race and Racism: Overview
Race and Racism: Asia
Race and Racism: Europe
Race and Racism: United States
Radicals/Radicalism
Rational Choice
Reading
Reason, Practical and Theoretical
Reflexivity
Reform: Europe and the United States
Reform: Islamic Reform
Regions and Regionalism, Eastern Europe
Religion: Africa
Religion: African Diaspora
Religion: Indigenous Peoples' View, South America
Religion: Latin America
Religion: Middle East
Religion and Science
Religion and the State: Africa
Religion and the State: Latin America
Religion and the State: Middle East
Religion and the State: United States
Renaissance
Representation: Mental Representation
Representation: Political Representation
Resistance
Resistance and Accommodation
Responsibility
Ritual: Public Ritual
Ritual: Religion
Sacred Places
Sacred Texts: Koran
Sage Philosophy
Science: Overview
Science: East Asia
Science, History of
Scientific Revolution
Secularization and Secularism
Sexuality: Overview
Sexuality: Islamic Views
Shinto
Skepticism
Slavery
Social Capital
Social Contract
Social History, U.S.
Society
Sophists, The
Sovereignty
Sport
State, The: Overview
State, The: The Postcolonial State
State of Nature
Superstition
Surrealism
Symbolism
Syncretism

Taste
Terror
Third World Literature
Toleration
Totems
Trade
Tradition
Translation
Treaty
Tribalism, Middle East
Trope
Truth
Universalism
University: Overview
University: Postcolonial
Untouchability: Overview
Untouchability: Menstrual Taboos
Untouchability: Taboos
Utilitarianism
Utopia
Visual Culture
Visual Order to Organizing Collections
War and Peace in the Arts
Wealth
Wildlife
Wisdom, Human
Witchcraft, African Studies of
Women's History: Africa
Women's History: Asia
Work
World Systems Theory, Latin America

LIBERAL ARTS DISCIPLINES AND PROFESSIONS

This section is in accord with the university divisions of the Liberal Arts into Fine Arts, Humanities, Social Sciences, and Sciences and the graduate programs of the professions of Law, Medicine, and Engineering. The sample of Interdisciplinary Programs are listed under their most common university grouping. For example, Fine Arts includes Performance Arts; Social Sciences includes Women's Studies and Gender Studies, as well as Ethnic Studies; Sciences includes Ecology and Geology, as well as Computer Sciences; Humanities includes programs of Communication, Language, and Linguistics. Meanwhile, the growth of interdisciplinary programs reflects the increasing overlap between studies listed under the labels of Fine Arts, Humanities, Social Sciences, and Sciences. A discipline or interdisciplinary program only appears once, but an entry may appear under the several disciplines and interdisciplinary programs that influenced the scholarship of the article. Titles that appear in bold indicate entries that are especially suited as a introduction to the discipline.

Under the category Multidisciplinary Practices, there are entries on the many methods, techniques, theories, and approaches that have spread across the disciplines. The Multidisciplinary Practices help explain the contemporary trend of interdisciplinarity for which the history of ideas has long been known. At the end of this Reader's Guide is a listing of a number of entries that overlap three of the four divisions and a listing of entries that overlap all four divisions.

Fine Arts
  VISUAL STUDIES
    Absolute Music
    Aesthetics: Africa
    Aesthetics: Asia
    Aesthetics: Europe and the Americas
    Ambiguity
    Anthropology
    Architecture: Overview
    Architecture: Africa
    Architecture: Asia
    Arts: Overview
    Arts: Africa
    Asceticism: Hindu and Buddhist Asceticism
    Asceticism: Western Asceticism
    Avant-Garde: Overview
    Avant-Garde: Militancy
    Aztlán
    Beauty and Ugliness
    Body, The
    Buddhism
    Change
    Chinese Thought
    Cinema
    City, The: Latin America
    City, The: The City as a Cultural Center
    City, The: The Islamic and Byzantine City
    Classicism
    Classification of Arts and Sciences, Early Modern
    Communication of Ideas: Asia and Its Influence
    Composition, Musical
    Consumerism
    Context
    Cosmopolitanism
    Creativity in the Arts and Sciences
    Cultural History
    Dada
    Death
    Dream
    Dress
    Dystopia
    Environmental Ethics
    Environmental History
    Everyday Life
    Expressionism
    Extirpation
    Fascism
    Fetishism: Overview
    Garden
    Gay Studies
    Gender in Art
    Genre
    Geography
    Geometry
    Gesture
    Ghetto
    Globalization: Asia
    Heaven and Hell (Asian Focus)
    Hinduism
    History, Idea of
    Humanity: European Thought
    Humanity in the Arts
    Humor
    Iconography
    Ideas, History of

Images, Icons, and Idols
Imagination
Impressionism
Islamic Science
Kantianism
Knowledge
Landscape in the Arts
Life Cycle: Overview
Literary History
Literature: Overview
Maps and the Ideas They Express
Masks
Matriarchy
Media, History of
Medicine: Europe and the United States
Mestizaje
Modernism: Overview
Modernism: Latin America
Modernity: Africa
Modernity: East Asia
Monarchy: Overview
Motherhood and Maternity
Museums
Musical Performance and Audiences
Musicology
Mysticism: Chinese Mysticism
Mysticism: Christian Mysticism
Naturalism in Art and Literature
Negritude
Nude, The
Occidentalism
Organicism
Pan-Africanism
Paradise on Earth
Periodization of the Arts
Perspective
Philosophy: Historical Overview and Recent Developments
Political Protest, U.S.
Postmodernism
Pre-Columbian Civilization
Protest, Political
Psychoanalysis
Pythagoreanism
Realism
Realism: Africa
Religion: Africa
Renaissance
Representation: Mental Representation
Ritual: Public Ritual
Sacred Places
Sacred Texts: Asia
Science: East Asia
Science, History of
Science Fiction
Social History, U.S.
Sport
Surrealism
Symbolism
Syncretism
Taste
Text/Textuality
Textiles and Fiber Arts as Catalysts for Ideas
Third Cinema
Victorianism

Humanities

COMMUNICATION, LANGUAGE, AND LINGUISTICS

Neoplatonism
Newtonianism
Nuclear Age
Nude, The
Objectivity
Occidentalism
Oral Traditions: Overview
Organicism
Orientalism: Overview
Orthodoxy
Pan-Arabism
Pan-Asianism
Paradigm
Periodization of the Arts
Philosophies: American
Philosophies: Feminist, Twentieth-Century
Philosophies: Islamic
Philosophy: Historical Overview and Recent Developments
Philosophy, History of
Philosophy, Moral: Ancient
Philosophy, Moral: Medieval and Renaissance
Philosophy, Moral: Modern
Philosophy of Mind: Ancient and Medieval
Physics
Platonism
Political Protest, U.S.
Population
Populism: United States
Practices
Pragmatism
Prejudice
Privacy
Propaganda
Protest, Political
Pseudoscience
Psychoanalysis
Punishment
Queer Theory
Reading
Realism: Africa
Reason, Practical and Theoretical
Reflexivity
Reform: Islamic Reform
Reformation
Relativism
Religion: East and Southeast Asia
Religion: Middle East
Religion and the State: Europe
Religion and the State: Latin America
Religion and the State: Middle East
Religion and the State: United States
Renaissance
Representation: Political Representation
Republicanism: Republic
Resistance
Rhetoric: Overview
Rhetoric: Ancient and Medieval
Ritual: Public Ritual
Sacred Places
Sacred Texts: Asia
Sage Philosophy
Scholasticism
Science: East Asia
Segregation

Sexuality: Overview
Skepticism
Slavery
Sociability in African Thought
Social Capital
Social History, U.S.
Sophists, The
Sport
State, The: Overview
Stoicism
Subjectivism
Sufism
Superstition
Temperance
Theater and Performance
Third Cinema
Third World Literature
Time: China
Totalitarianism
Tragedy and Comedy
University: Overview
University: Postcolonial
Untouchability: Menstrual Taboos
Untouchability: Taboos
Utilitarianism
Utopia
Victorianism
Visual Order to Organizing Collections
Volunteerism, U.S.
War and Peace in the Arts
Westernization: Africa
Westernization: Middle East
Westernization: Southeast Asia
Wisdom, Human
Women's History: Africa
Women's Studies
Yoga
Zen

Social Sciences
WOMEN'S STUDIES AND GENDER STUDIES
Abolitionism
Aesthetics: Asia
African-American Ideas
Anarchism
Anthropology
Antifeminism
Asceticism: Western Asceticism
Autobiography
Beauty and Ugliness
Biography
Black Atlantic
Body, The
Capitalism: Africa
Censorship
Chicano Movement
Childhood and Child Rearing
Christianity: Overview
Cinema
Class
Colonialism: Africa
Colonialism: Southeast Asia
Communication of Ideas: Southeast Asia
Composition, Musical
Confucianism

Sciences

New Dictionary of the History of Ideas

Multidisciplinary Practices

The *New Dictionary of the History of Ideas* has many entries that discuss the methods by which scholars and researchers pursue knowledge. The entries below discuss approaches, methods, and practices that have influenced many disciplines.

ENTRIES ON MULTIDISCIPLINARY PRACTICES
THAT ORIGINATED IN ANCIENT TIMES

Especially Interdisciplinary Entries

The most interdisciplinary entries synthesized knowledge by using the methods and focusing on the topics of practitioners of several disciplines. Very few entries listed below are in only one division. Common pairs for the history of ideas are social sciences and humanities, social sciences and sciences, and humanities and sciences. In the early twenty-first century there is generally a recognition of the common overlap of the social sciences with the humanities; social scientists may take ethical and literary factors into consideration and humanists may incorporate societal contexts into their work. The presence of psychology in the sciences, as well as the quantitative nature of some social sciences work, creates an overlap of social sciences with sciences. Another interesting overlap is between humanities and sciences—topics that in antiquity were treated as philosophy or religion are now investigated by those following scientific methods.

SOCIAL SCIENCES, SCIENCES, AND FINE ARTS
   Architecture: Africa
   Geography
   Phrenology
   Virtual Reality
SCIENCES, FINE ARTS, AND HUMANITIES
   Enlightenment
   Epistemology: Early Modern
   Feminism: Third World U.S. Movement
   Field Theories
   Geometry
   Globalization: Asia
   Text/Textuality
FINE ARTS, HUMANITIES, AND SOCIAL SCIENCES
   Aesthetics: Africa
   Alienation
   Americanization, U.S.
   Anticolonialism: Africa
   Arts: Overview
   Arts: Africa
   Authenticity: Africa
   Autobiography
   Avant-Garde: Overview
   Aztlán
   Censorship
   Chinese Thought
   City, The: The Islamic and Byzantine City
   Civil Disobedience
   Civil Society: Europe and the United States
   Colonialism: Southeast Asia
   Communication of Ideas: Africa and Its Influence
   Communication of Ideas: The Americas and Their Influence

A

ABOLITIONISM. Historical studies of the ideas that gave rise to abolitionism, whether in the Caribbean, Latin and South America, Africa, or the United States, have provided analyses that are variously political, economic, social, demographic, or religious in focus. This entry examines the political, religious, and economic ideas surrounding abolitionism to illustrate that these factors were often intertwined. The role of ideas, ideologies, movements, tactics, and personalities are examined to demonstrate the complexity of this social movement in terms of gender, race, socioeconomic background of the participants, and time and location of the movement.

Political Ideas

The early abolitionist movement in the United States and Great Britain during the late eighteenth century was guided by the ideas of the Age of Enlightenment, the French and American revolutions, and Christian morality. The concept that individuals were created equal and had the right to life, liberty, and the pursuit of happiness led them to advocate abolitionism. The slave revolt in Saint-Domingue (Haiti) in 1791 led by Toussaint Louverture was based on these ideas of universal liberty and freedom. The importance of the Haitian revolution to the idea of abolitionism is important because it demonstrated that slavery could be abolished quickly and violently and that a gradual approach using persuasion and rationality might not be the answer. Moreover, the revolution radically transformed this former French possession, providing the slaves with full emancipation and political control. Although a visible antislavery movement did not emerge in Brazil until 1850, the political movement for abolitionism there can be traced to the early nineteenth century, infused with ideas from the Haitian, American, and French revolutions. The abolition of slavery in the British West Indies during the nineteenth century grew out of a liberal political reform agenda that sought to provide better treatment for slaves with the view that emancipation would occur gradually. Slave uprisings in Martinique, Cuba, Tortola, Trinidad, Grenada, and Dominica convinced colonial authorities that slavery needed to be reevaluated. For example, in Barbados, after slavery was abolished in 1834 the government instituted an apprenticeship program of six (unpaid) years for field workers and four years for household servants. Jamaica freed its slaves in 1833, and Antigua and Bermuda provided slaves with full emancipation in 1834; as in Barbados, apprenticeship programs served as a transitional institution for several years after emancipation. However, colonial offices throughout the Caribbean dealt with the former slaves in a harsh manner, inflicting punishment for various minor offenses, extending the apprenticeship period, and sending house servants into the fields to labor.

Colonization

The ideas of abolitionism were linked to missionary, colonial, and commercial motives and ideologies of the French, British, and Americans. Quakers in the antislavery movement in the United States worked to settle slaves in Africa based on religious beliefs that slaves had the right to be free and that these political ideas only could be achieved through colonization in Liberia and Sierra Leone. The political ideas of justice, equality before the law, liberty, and the rule of law were meant to serve as the foundations of the colonies. It was equally important politically to utilize former slaves and re-captives in this endeavor to prove that people of African descent were capable of understanding laws, social responsibility, and the dignity of labor. The belief that people of African descent were inherently inferior to whites and could not be assimilated into a white society led many to advocate colonization. The connection between French abolitionism and colonization on the African continent were intimately linked according to some scholars. It has been argued that when the French government abolished slavery in 1848, it was merely replaced with colonization, starting with Algeria; therefore the master-slave relationship continued to leave the African in an inferior, subordinate position, and the French continued to gain from its economic exploitation of land and labor. The same argument can be made for Great Britain following its abolition of slavery, especially in Sierra Leone. Former slaves and recaptured Africans who ended up in Sierra Leone, along with indigenous Africans, were not viewed as having the same claim to citizenship and sovereignty as the British—otherwise the former slaves and recaptured Africans would not have been colonized. In sum, some Europeans advocated abolitionism, but they did not support full citizenship, equality, and freedom for Africans, and whenever and wherever the slave trade ended, missionaries and commercial enterprises entered the African continent with the backing of the colonial state.

Religious Ideas

The religious ideas that fueled abolitionism in the eighteenth and nineteenth centuries, especially in the United States and Great Britain, were firmly rooted in the Christian belief that all people are equal in the eyes of God; therefore, the practice of one person owning another was against Christianity. The doctrine of a divine sovereignty that made people accountable only to God was utilized. Under slavery, the slave was accountable to her or his owner and not to God. Another religious idea that served as a catalyst during the 1820s and 1830s included evangelicalism and revivalism, which supported the belief that slave owners and others associated with slavery and its institutions could

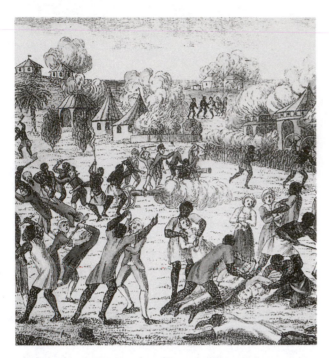

Engraving of slave revolt, Saint-Domingue, from a contemporary German report. The 1791 uprising resulted in personal freedom and political control for Haiti's slave population and paved the way for subsequent abolitionist and reform movements in other countries. THE GRANGER COLLECTION

experience personal salvation through instant conversion. The idea of "come-outism" is important in evangelicalism and abolitionism, adopted by American abolitionists who publicly took a stand against slavery by withdrawing from any institution, especially churches, that did not recognize the sinfulness of slavery.

Economic Ideas

Although religious ideas were important to abolitionism in the United States and Great Britain and for colonization, they were not as significant in South American, Latin American, and Caribbean abolitionism, which contained more economic and political ideas. This could be due to the fact that abolitionism operated in these regions within the colonial framework, and abolitionists were often fighting on several fronts—to achieve independence, achieve freedom for the slaves, and achieve citizenship and other rights for free people of African descent. Throughout most of the nineteenth century, abolitionism in Cuba and Puerto Rico was hampered by the civil war and the revolution in Spain. Abolitionists had to contend with the economic interests of Spain, Cuba, and Puerto Rico—mainly wealthy slave owners who were vehemently opposed to the abolition of slavery, especially in Cuba, which had a large slave population vital to its sugar industry in the western part of the island. Puerto Rico had a much smaller slave population, and by 1835 slavery was virtually nonexistent. In addition, the United States had significant economic investments that it wanted to protect in Cuba and Puerto Rico. But at the same time, there were American abolitionists who demanded an end to slavery in colonies controlled by Spain.

The debate among modern historians between the role of economics and the role of humanitarianism in abolishing slavery in British slaveholding colonies in the Caribbean was sparked by Eric Williams's *Capitalism and Slavery* (1944). According to Williams, capitalism, and not Christian humanitarianism, was the driving force to end slavery because the emerging capitalist system that evolved from the Industrial Revolution demanded free trade and more productive labor than slaves provided. Rational business practices were needed, including a literate workforce. The failing British West Indian plantation economies could not compete with industrial capitalism. This deviated sharply from the British imperial historiography that placed moral humanitarianism as the catalyst for abolitionism. However, Williams's analysis of abolitionism was subsequently rejected by several historians, most notably Roger Anstey and Seymour Drescher, who argued that slavery continued to be economically viable in the United States and Brazil, along with capitalism. They contended that in the late eighteenth century slavery and the slave trade were important to the British economy at the same time that abolitionism began. Still others have contended that abolitionism was a social movement that involved a variety of actors and organizations all grounded in the popular culture and trends of the time in their respective societies. Within the American context, this changing historiography over time includes: historians who supported the humanitarian view of abolitionists (that is, the belief that they were guided by moral and religious values); historians who downplayed the moral aspect and emphasized economic factors; historians who viewed abolitionists as one-sided fanatics who led the country into a needless civil war; and, during the 1960s, historians who again portrayed abolitionists in a more positive light as people who were committed to a just and social cause. Additionally, other scholars—most prominently W. E. B. Du Bois, Eugene Genovese, and Herbert Aptheker—have given agency to the slaves themselves in bringing about emancipation.

The idea of free labor was another economic idea behind abolitionism in the Caribbean, South America, and Latin America, primarily the commercialization of agriculture, which made slave labor economically outdated. The urban-based abolitionist movement in Brazil responded to economic changes that included greater integration into the global economy, an increase in the urban population, expansion of its infrastructure, and creation of new industries and businesses in both rural and urban areas. As a result of these changes, a more liberal form of economics developed that supported free labor instead of slave labor. Moreover, as people became urbanized, traveled outside the country, and learned more about world developments, the institution of slavery seemed backward and made Brazilians appear uncivilized and out of step with a world that was developing new ideas based on science and rationality. Abolitionism in Puerto Rico, Brazil, Cuba, and other Caribbean islands did not mean immediate emancipation accompanied by full citizenship rights; rather, as outlined above, the practice of apprenticeships was employed to compensate slave owners. It was feared that ex-slaves would not be willing to work for wages, the economies would plummet, and a race war would ensue. The aim was to make a gradual transition from slavery to freedom that would not destabilize society.

Tactics, Organizations, and Individuals in the Americas

In discussing abolitionism in the United States and Great Britain, it is important to divide the movement into periods because the tactics, organizations, and individuals the movement attracted evolved in response to changing religious and political ideas. Following the Revolutionary War, the Quakers in Pennsylvania were in the forefront of the abolitionist movement; their tactics and organizations reflected the elite status of their members (wealthy white men) and their belief in gradual abolitionism. They believed that slavery could be gradually abolished by pressuring government representatives to enact laws and statutes against slavery, providing legal aid to runaway slaves, petitioning the federal government to end the importation of slaves and halt the westward expansion of slavery, and pressuring state governments to grant slaves rights.

The Quakers were active in Great Britain as well. In 1783 they formed the London Committee to Abolish the Slave Trade. In 1787 they joined the Evangelical Christians led by William Wilberforce and Thomas Clarkson to form the Society for the Abolition of the Slave Trade. They led petition drives and lobbied the government, and in 1807 the British slave trade was abolished. The goal in Britain now shifted to gradual abolition and then to immediate abolition. In 1823 Clarkson, Wilberforce, and Thomas Fowell Buxton formed the British Anti-Slavery Society after British West Indian plantation owners were reluctant to abolish slavery, and in 1833 the Emancipation Act (which applied to the British colonies but not to Great Britain itself) was passed. In France, Jacques-Pierre Brissot formed the Society of the Friends of Blacks in 1788, and in 1834 the French Society for the Abolition of Slavery was established. In the Netherlands, the Réveil movement associated with the Dutch Reform Church was formed in the 1840s after British Quakers convinced them that slavery was against the Bible. The Spanish Abolition Society was founded in Madrid in 1865. The major actors in abolitionism throughout the Caribbean and Latin and South America were the slaves and free people of African descent who staged revolts, work stoppages, and insurrections, and ran away. Significant slave uprisings occurred in the nineteenth century in Brazil in Bahia, Minas Gerais, Espírito Santo, Rio de Janeiro, and São Paulo. Slave revolts and desertions from the plantations led to the emergence of immediatism and the formation in 1880 of the Brazilian Anti-Slavery Society (Joaquim Nabuco was elected president), which started as a small group of abolitionists based in major urban areas. This movement grew in size to include people from various educational and social backgrounds. Other antislavery organizations in Brazil included the Cearense Liberator Society, Bahian Liberator Society, and Abolitionist Confederation.

People of African descent played a critical role in U.S. abolitionism before and after the movement became integrated; some of these include Richard Allen, Prince Hall, James Forten, Harriet Jacobs, and Mary Shadd Carey. Upstate New York had a major community of activists who believed in immediatism, among them Frederick Douglass, Sojourner Truth, Harriet Tubman, Austin Steward, and Thomas James. Because they were kept out of the first wave of abolitionism, they were forced to establish their own organizations, newspapers,

educational institutions, and churches. They realized early on the importance of using moralism and emotionalism as tactics, and the print media served as the vehicle. Some of those who had escaped slavery wrote and published their narratives, lectured, and helped slaves to escape, and many traveled to Europe to gain support (Frederick Douglass, Nathaniel Paul, Robert Purvis, William Wells Brown, Alexander Crummell, and Ellen and William Craft). People of African descent in both abolitionist periods advocated full emancipation and rights for the enslaved and free.

The role of women of African descent in the abolitionist movement was important and different because they had to deal with issues of race, sex, and class within the antislavery movement and the white women's movement. These women included Grace Bustill Douglass, an educator and founder of the Philadelphia Female Anti-Slavery Society, and her daughter Sarah Douglass; Frances Ellen Watkins Harper, who was a teacher and poet; Maria Miller Stewart, Sarah Forten, and Eliza Dixon Day. These woman helped to recruit members to the movement, gave public lectures, raised funds, and organized rallies and events.

Abolitionism and Feminism

The history of feminism in the United States is very directly linked to the abolitionist movement. Black and white women in northern cities in the United States were very active in various religious and benevolent organizations before they joined the abolitionist movement in the 1830s. The administrative and leadership skills and experience they had gained in these organizations were then utilized in the abolitionist movement. It is clear why black women were involved in the struggle to end slavery; however, white women from the working class to the upper middle class saw a correlation between the oppression of slaves and their oppression as women in terms of their legal status, which defined them as the property of their husbands and as their inferiors in society. Women found an outlet in the abolitionist movement for expressing their ideas toward marriage, divorce, and domestic violence. Men made up most of the leadership in abolitionist organizations, and their treatment of female members convinced many of these women that both slaves and women needed to be emancipated. Some abolitionist organizations did not allow African-Americans to join, while others curtailed the participation of women, especially in public speaking, voting, and business decisions. Many of these women continued their efforts to transform society through social movements by working on women's rights in the campaign for suffrage and property rights, along with the rights to file lawsuits, obtain a divorce, and obtain custody of children. The intersection of abolitionism and women's rights influenced the ideas and work of Sarah and Angelina Grimké, Abigail Kelley Foster, Lucretia Mott, and Elizabeth Cady Stanton. The Grimké sisters, who were Quakers, believed they had been called to do God's work in the antislavery movement. Moreover, the linkages between abolition and women's rights in the work of black women abolitionists such as Sojourner Truth cannot be overstated. They were fighting for a double victory—one to end slavery and the other to end discrimination based on gender.

Sojourner Truth (c. 1797–1883). Born into slavery in upstate New York, Isabella Van Wagener gained her freedom when the state abolished the practice in 1827. In the early 1840s she took the name Sojourner Truth and began touring the country to advocate abolition. ARCHIVE PHOTOS, INC.

Tactics, Organizations, and Individuals in Africa

Following the end of the Revolutionary War, many slaves and free people of African descent, as well as some American and British whites, began to question the slaves' future, especially in terms of achieving full citizenship rights and economic independence. Colonization was used as a strategy to end slavery, and Freetown in Sierra Leone was established as a colony in 1787. The American Colonization Society was formed in 1816, followed by the colonization of Liberia in 1847. Individuals of African descent who advocated colonization included Paul Cuffee, who was independently wealthy and free. He made two trips to Sierra Leone with financial backing from the British government—one in 1811 to inquire about the feasibility of African emigration and another in 1815 when he took thirty-eight free Africans with him. Others who shared these beliefs included Joseph Brown Russwurm, Martin Delany, Edward Blyden, and Thomas Peters from Nova Scotia, Canada, who petitioned the British government for assistance. They believed that human dignity, justice, hard work, and the rule of law could be put into practice in the new settlements and that this would prove that these outcasts and marginalized individuals could be given a second chance in life. These philosophical ideas were often intertwined with religious ideas that appealed to ex-slaves because they espoused the importance of God's authority and individual freedom that allowed them to employ petitions, preaching, and the print media as tactics. In addition, a number of Africans, people of African descent, Europeans, and Americans believed that worldwide emancipation would not be

achieved as long as there remained a supply and demand for slaves. Therefore, to contain slavery at its source, the campaign against slavery had to shift from the West to the African continent. To do this, Africans, former slaves, and re-captives were mobilized to advance the idea that if slavery were to end, the antislavery movement had to be based on the African continent and Africans and people of African descent on the continent had to be in the forefront of the antislavery movement.

*See also **Capitalism; Liberty; Resistance; Resistance and Accommodation; Slavery.***

BIBLIOGRAPHY

Azevedo, Celia M. *Abolitionism in the United States and Brazil: A Comparative Perspective.* New York and London: Garland, 1995.

Baronov, David. *The Abolition of Slavery in Brazil: The "Liberation" of Africans through the Emancipation of Capital.* Westport, Conn.: Greenwood Press, 2000.

Bender, Thomas, ed. *The Antislavery Debate: Capitalism and Abolitionism as a Problem in Historical Interpretation.* Berkeley: University of California Press, 1992.

Corwin, Arthur F. *Spain and the Abolition of Slavery in Cuba, 1817–1886.* Austin: University of Texas Press, 1967.

Eudell, Demetrius L. *The Political Languages of Emancipation in the British Caribbean and the U.S. South.* Chapel Hill: University of North Carolina Press, 2002.

Newman, Richard S. *The Transformation of American Abolitionism: Fighting Slavery in the Early Republic.* Chapel Hill: University of North Carolina Press, 2002.

Oostindie, Gert, ed. *Fifty Years Later: Antislavery, Capitalism, and Modernity in the Dutch Orbit.* Pittsburgh: University of Pittsburgh Press, 1996.

Sanneh, Lamin. *Abolitionists Abroad: American Blacks and the Making of Modern West Africa.* Cambridge, Mass.: Harvard University Press, 1999.

Schmidt-Nowara, Christopher. *Empire and Antislavery: Spain, Cuba, and Puerto Rico, 1833–1874.* Pittsburgh: University of Pittsburgh Press, 1999.

Sernett, Milton C. *North Star Country: Upstate New York and the Crusade for African American Freedom.* Syracuse, N.Y.: Syracuse University Press, 2002.

Temperley, Howard, ed. *After Slavery: Emancipation and Its Discontents.* London: Frank Cass, 2002.

Williams, Eric. *Capitalism and Slavery.* 1944. Reprint, Chapel Hill: University of North Carolina Press, 1994.

Cassandra R. Veney

ABSOLUTE MUSIC. "Absolute music" is an idea that took root in the writings of early German Romantics such as Wilhelm Heinrich Wackenroder (1773–1798), Ludwig Tieck (1773–1853), and E. T. A. Hoffmann (1776–1822) beginning at the turn of the nineteenth century, and came to dominate musical aesthetics over much of the next two centuries, frequently invoked to argue for music's elevation to a position above the other arts. The term is often allied with such terms as "abstract music," referring to the separation of music from other considerations, and "formalism," referring to the logic

Ludwig van Beethoven (1770–1827). During the eighteenth and nineteenth centuries, the concept of absolute music—exemplified by the works of composers such as Beethoven—played an important role in the development of a nationalistic movement in Germany. THE LIBRARY OF CONGRESS

whereby music makes sense without any accompanying words, drama, or dance. It is most often contrasted with "program music," whose full sense and purpose depend on a variety of narrative, literary, pictorial, dramatic, or other explanatory bases. In truth, however, the term is much richer, and historically more significant, than these associations would indicate.

The elevation of music to the highest of the arts entailed a shift in the perceived relationship of art to the world around us. As "art for art's sake" and similar sentiments gained ground in the nineteenth century, music became prized for its very separation from the real world, its lack of precise representational meaning. The symphony became the focal point for a new valorization of music, especially as it developed in the German lands at the hands of Haydn, Mozart, and Beethoven. Beyond its presumed purity, music's removal from the here and now made it seem a perfect vehicle for expressing the Romantics' sense of "infinite longing," which Hoffmann, in an 1810 essay on Beethoven's Fifth Symphony (1808), called the "essence of Romanticism." Within this formulation, music could be allied with the sublime, the unattainable, the infinite, and the ineffable, while at the same time expressing and probing profound inner states. Through music, one's soul could connect, through "longing" or some other deep feeling, to something beyond the everyday world. In this way, as the German musicologist Carl Dahlhaus argues, music could be understood as "absolute" in

two senses, both through its purity, its "absolute" separateness from the reality we can see and touch, and through its capacity to connect us to the "absolute" in the philosophical sense, after Georg Wilhelm Friedrich Hegel (1770–1831).

Beethoven and German Influence

The evolution of the concept proceeded in conjunction with the German Idealist philosophical tradition and figured prominently in the development of German nationalism, as well. Immanuel Kant and Hegel provided the underpinnings, and Arthur Schopenhauer (1788–1860), Richard Wagner (1813–1883), and Friedrich Nietzsche (1844–1900) developed a more specifically musico-philosophical edifice. Ironically, however, while it was Wagner who coined the term "absolute music" around mid-century and thereby embedded it securely within Idealist philosophy, he did so in order to argue against its validity, claiming that music, which he equated with "woman" (thus, essentially sensuous and inchoate), could not flourish in isolation, needing the masculine "poet" (by nature seminal and rational) to thrive. Already, Beethoven's works, especially his symphonies, were being touted in the second quarter of the century as both the best representative of pure music and the cornerstone of a German musical tradition that represented the highest expression within the highest of the arts, an emblem and indispensable part of what it meant to be German. This elevation of Beethoven was accomplished largely through the writings of Adolf Bernhard Marx (1795–1866), who laid much of the groundwork for formal analysis through his descriptions of sonata form, the basic formal principle for not only Beethoven's instrumental music, but also of his immediate forebears and principal descendants.

In his landmark *On the Musically Beautiful* (1853), Eduard Hanslick (1825–1904), without using the term "absolute music," attempted to refute Wagner's arguments against pure music, arguing that music's form was identical to its content (thereby effectively divorcing music even from emotion) and claiming for it an eminently masculine rationality based on formalist musical logic. A variety of methods for analyzing music were developed over the century or so following Hanslick's short book, most notably by Hugo Riemann (1849–1919), an advocate of functional harmonic analysis and phrase-structure analysis; Heinrich Schenker (1868–1935), who introduced layered reductive voice-leading analysis; and Rudolph Réti (1885–1957), who relied on motivic analysis. Since all these systems were developed in large part to validate the logic of Beethoven's instrumental music, and since Beethoven had become both the figurehead of German music and a supposed universal, the concept of "absolute music" that these methods helped reinforce consolidated the position of German music as the standard of musical value.

Crosscurrents: Program Music and Modernism

From the beginning, there was much resistance to the idea that music is best understood as separate from what soon became known as the "extramusical." Opera and similar forms, of course, balanced musical logic with and against dramatic necessities (although Wagner argued that Italian opera was essentially "absolute" in its dependence on musical formula). Songs of various types were intimately tied to their texts. Most significantly opposed to the new concept was the idea of "program music"—instrumental music that relied on a programmatic explanation to orient an audience to its meanings—launched by Hector Berlioz (1803–1869) in the years following Beethoven's death in 1827. The tradition of program music, to some extent also rooted in Beethoven (especially in his Sixth Symphony, known as the "Pastoral" Symphony, 1808), was continued by Franz Liszt (1811–1886) in his symphonic poems and programmatic symphonies, implicitly disavowed by Johannes Brahms (1833–1897) and Anton Bruckner (1824–1896), but taken up again by both Gustav Mahler (1860–1911) in his first symphonies and Richard Strauss (1864–1949) in his tone poems and programmatic symphonies, beginning in the mid-1880s and continuing through the turn of the twentieth century. Nevertheless, although programmatic music is most readily identified, in musical terms, according to its departures from "musical logic," there is substantial overlap in the two categories as well, so that they should not simply be viewed as opposite types. Thus, even a programmatic work had to make musical sense and could depend on an underlying sense of music's absoluteness, while many "absolute" works conveyed implicit programmatic content through their engagement with familiar musical gestures and topics.

During the twentieth century, especially with the advent of high modernism, music's separateness from other discourses became in some cases more pronounced (by the insistence on sometimes arcane musical logic over what most audiences still perceive as "natural") and in others virtually eliminated (as when programmatic rationales demanded extreme expressive or descriptive modes at the expense of musical logic). While the latter possibility played a large part in the development of musical modernism, it also led at each turn to the development of new "systems," such as the concept of *Klangfarbenmelodie* (tone-color melody) proposed by Arnold Schoenberg (1874–1951) in 1911 and the twelve-tone system that he created ten years after that (also known as serialism, which was later developed further by applying it to other elements besides pitch, such as rhythm, meter, and dynamics). In consequence, the former possibility, advancing the principle of music's absoluteness, was often seen as more fundamental. Thus, in the Soviet Union during the 1930s and 1940s, the charge of "formalism" was used against composers such as Dmitry Shostakovich (1906–1975) when their music was perceived to be too modern. While this charge has been described as little more than a tool for exercising political control, its basis has much in common with Wagner's insistence on music's subordination to an exterior logic, and it is based in part on the premise that musical modernism extends the idea of "absolute" music.

Late Twentieth- and Early Twenty-First-Century Perspectives

The last few decades of the twentieth century and the start of the twenty-first century have seen renewed and often highly skeptical interest in the claims of music's absoluteness alongside an increasingly entrenched advocacy, the latter reinforced by the growth of musical analysis as a discipline. Carl Dahlhaus has historicized the concept, grounding it in Germanic philosophical and musical thought. Many have argued persuasively that the idea is fundamentally a fiction, that music is always referential to a variety of contexts, some historical and others acquired through reception. Most of these arguments have focused either on a consideration of musical narrative (i.e., the way that music may be understood to tell stories (Anthony Newcomb, Lawrence Kramer, and Susan McClary) or on musical semiotics, of how music has continued to develop an evolving system of referential gestures redolent of the older "doctrine of the affections" (Jean-Jacques Nattiez, Leonard Ratner, and Wye Allanbrook). If "absolute music" has indeed been a fiction, it has been a useful one from many perspectives, helping to enable the experience of music as a uniquely powerful art medium. Under the aegis of its absoluteness, which renders its shapes and gestures officially neutral, music has been capable of reinforcing—but with full deniability— a full array of values and ideas, and of projecting, within its "meaningless" interplay of definiteness and vagueness, phantasmal versions of a re-imagined reality.

See also **Composition, Musical; Harmony; Idealism; Sacred and Profane.**

BIBLIOGRAPHY

Bent, Ian. *Analysis.* New York: Norton; Basingstoke, U.K.: Macmillan Press, 1987.

Dahlhaus, Carl. *The Idea of Absolute Music.* Translated by Roger Lustig. Chicago: University of Chicago Press, 1989.

Hanslick, Eduard. *On the Musically Beautiful: A Contribution towards the Revision of the Aesthetics of Music.* Translated and edited by Geoffrey Payzant. Indianapolis: Hackett Publishing, 1986.

Kramer, Lawrence. *Musical Meaning: Toward a Critical History.* Berkeley and Los Angeles: University of California Press, 2002.

McClary, Susan. "Narrative Agendas in 'Absolute' Music: Identity and Difference in Brahms's Third Symphony." In *Musicology and Difference: Gender and Sexuality in Music Scholarship,* edited by Ruth A. Solie, 326–344. Berkeley and Los Angeles: University of California Press, 1993.

Newcomb, Anthony. "Once More between Absolute and Program Music: Schumann's Second Symphony." *19th-Century Music* 7, no. 3 (April 1984): 233–250.

Treitler, Leo. "Mozart and the Idea of Absolute Music." In Treitler, *Music and the Historical Imagination,* 176–214. Cambridge, Mass., and London: Harvard University Press, 1989.

Raymond Knapp

AESTHETICS.

This entry includes three subentries:

Africa
Asia
Europe and the Americas

AFRICA

Africa has more than two thousand languages, representing several thousand cultures, each with its own system of logic. No single aesthetic philosophy characterizes the continent, and any concept of a coherent "Africa" is arbitrary, given such extraordinary diversity. Furthermore, a given culture may possess several aesthetic discourses, as may any artistic genre. Globalization complicates matters even more, for one cannot discuss the aesthetics of contemporary African artists without considering transnational paradigms and hybrid visions.

Given such complexities, how can one propose any comprehensive notion of African aesthetics? One may consider key aesthetic concepts of a particular group, such as the Yoruba peoples of Nigeria, to demonstrate the specificity of aesthetics. Other revealing themes are aesthetic experiences crossing the boundaries of "traditional" African societies; the efficacy, concealment, and revelations of African arts; a common aesthetic of accumulation and process; and the performativity and polysemy of African expression. Finally, colonial and postcolonial aesthetic encounters are relevant to a discussion of how changing aesthetics shape present concerns.

Aesthetic Discourse

Aesthetics comes from the Greek word for "sense of perception" and can be defined only within particular cultural systems. Cultural insiders must be consulted to ascertain how and why aesthetic concepts come to hold value. African aesthetic concepts reach into moral and spiritual realms. Linguistic exploration of African aesthetic terms finds that words for beauty and goodness often intersect, as Susan Vogel has noted among the Baule peoples of Côte d'Ivoire and others have discerned among the Lega and Songye of the Congo and the Igbo, Edo, and Ibibio of Nigeria, among others. External perfection and internal moral excellence are linked, as are physical perfection and ideal social order. An anti-aesthetic is also common, as in certain satirical masquerades among the Mende of Sierra Leone and the beauty-beast performances of the Igbo and Ibibio of Nigeria.

Most Western knowledge of African aesthetics is derived from research by African scholars and the few ethnographic studies that have carefully examined aesthetic discourse. The most profound knowledge concerns the Yoruba peoples of Nigeria. Yoruba philosophy reveals how and why their varied arts look and do things the ways they do. A compelling concept of Yoruba aesthetics is *ashe,* or life force, possessed and conveyed by all art forms, from visual to narrative to performative. Furthermore, *ashe* provides a tangible contact with the Orisha deities of the Yoruba spiritual pantheon.

Ashe is intrinsically related to the essential nature of creativity called *iwa,* perceptible to those who have "walked with the ancestors" and thus acquired critical and discerning eyes. Important to *iwa* are *oju-inu,* an "inner eye" or the artist's insight, and *oju-ona,* the external harmony of artworks. For the Yoruba, the beauty of objects, performances, or texts lies not only in what catches the eye but also in the *ashe* derived from the work's completeness. From these elements one can then discern the artwork's *iwa,* or essential nature, and finally its *ewa,* or beauty.

Another critical concept of Yoruba aesthetics is *ara,* the "evocative power" of visual, verbal, musical, and performance

arts associated with the ability to amaze (Roberts and Roberts, p. 27). *Ara* bespeaks creativity through departure from norms. Yoruba artists are explorers, and their works reflect new understandings. As the Yoruba philosopher Olabiyi Yai states, art is always "unfinished and generative" (p. 107). Yoruba visual and verbal arts are also linked through *ori,* individuality, and *iyato,* difference and originality, and Yai argues for a definition of art that is "an invitation to infinite . . . difference and departure, and not a summation for sameness and imitation" (p. 113). The tradition-creativity binary posed for so many cultures is thereby dissolved, and "innovation is implied in the Yoruba idea of tradition" (p. 113).

Cross-Cultural Thematics

Through *ashe,* Yoruba arts are highly efficacious—that is, objects *work* and transform peoples' lives. For many African cultures, how an object looks is related to the way it works, according to strict aesthetic specifications, for protection, healing, communication, mediation, or empowerment. Like aesthetics more generally, each culture has its own concepts of efficacy. For Bantu-speaking peoples of central, eastern, and southern Africa, a power called *nkisi* is manifest in sculpture and other expression, while for Mande-speaking peoples of western Africa, secret and instrumental knowledge is called *nyama.* For African Muslim mystics, *baraka* is a blessing energy emanating from saintly tombs, written and spoken verses, and visual forms. All these terms imply a power-knowledge relationship inhering in works of art, enabling their effectiveness and capacity.

As is true for many other African philosophies, Yoruba aesthetics also privilege knowledge that is allusive, indirect, and enigmatic. Patterns in textiles and scarification; designs on ceramics, houses, and sculpture; graphic inscriptions on walls, masks, and the body; and verbal arts such as proverbs, epics, and songs communicate messages of cultural significance. These can be highly esoteric and understood only by the initiated. For example, geometric patterns on Bamana *bogolanfini* textiles from Mali encode women's herbal medicinal recipes. In other cases, patterns connote resistance, as did the surreptitious painting of African National Congress colors on homes by southern African women during apartheid.

Another characteristic of many African aesthetic systems is that objects, narratives, songs, and performances are interpreted by audiences in many different ways through intentional semantic variability. African artworks are semantically loaded texts abounding in exegetic richness. For example, among Luba peoples of the southeastern Democratic Republic of the Congo, thrones and staffs embody beauty and royal authority but are also mnemonic devices stimulating the making of history. Polysemy is also the product of a processual and accumulative aesthetic. The process of making art is often more valuable than the final products, and such dynamism is the essence of aesthetic experience. Once created, objects may have ephemeral usage before being destroyed or progressing to the next phases in layered histories.

Aesthetics on the Move

Recent study of African aesthetics includes two critically important thrusts: popular urban arts and diasporic art forms of the black Atlantic, and an Indian Ocean world linking eastern Africa with South Asia. Again, aesthetic principles of urban arts are contingent upon local use and intent. For instance, urban paintings by the late Congolese artist Tshibumba Kanda Matulu reflect an aesthetic inspired by European comic books while addressing issues of critical historical and political importance. Ghanaian urban arts reflect a vibrant immediacy stemming from subjects of daily life—from soccer to hairstyles to music and film—whereas arts of urban Senegal conform to the aesthetics of a very particular mystical Islam realized through mass-produced images and inspired by photography. As Karin Barber notes, African popular arts fall between the cracks of "traditional" and "elite" or "modern" art. The hybridized forms of Africa's dynamic popular urban arts reflect not only constant absorption of ideas from the outside but also long-standing adaptive processes through which Africans have always been innovative players in world forums.

Similar dynamism can be witnessed in Africa's diasporic traditions. Much research, in particular that of Robert Farris Thompson, has shown that some of the most powerful aesthetic carryovers from west Africa to the black Atlantic are based on deeply embedded linguistic concepts such as an "aesthetic of the cool." Thompson illuminates the origins of slang, gestures, and attitudes by demonstrating how certain aesthetic categories in the African Americas merge moral philosophy, right living, and artistic quality.

One cannot discuss African aesthetics without addressing the effects of colonialism and postcolonialism and modernist and postmodernist expressive trends of the last century. Encounters and entanglements fostered by the colonial experience in Africa have produced complex issues of appropriation and commodification: compelling research reveals close association between aesthetic norms and capitalist incentives (Phillips and Steiner). This has been noticeable since the colonial conquests of the nineteenth century but earlier as well in Portuguese influence upon the late-fifteenth-century kingdoms of Benin in Nigeria and Kongo in Angola and the impact of Christianity in Ethiopia from the fourth century C.E. African styles were adapted to meet changing economic and political circumstances, with a most compelling case among the Mangbetu people of the northeastern Democratic Republic of the Congo and Zaire, whose aesthetics shifted to a European "naturalism" to meet foreign expectations.

Similar dynamics are found on a global scale in the early twenty-first century. Those who study contemporary African arts define modernisms both discrepant from and overlapping with European models. In the early twentieth century, expatriate teachers opened fine arts schools in a number of African cities, introducing new techniques and aesthetics. Often these synthesized existing frameworks produced hybrid forms, as in the workshop of Ulli Beier in Nigeria.

It is safe to say, though, that the most exciting time to study African aesthetics may be the present, for artistic landscapes are extending in many new ways. Scholar-curators such as Okwui Enwezor, artistic director of Documenta 11 in 2002 and the Second Johannesburg Biennale in 1997, and Salah Hassan, editor of *Nka: Journal of Contemporary African Art,*

are transcending the boundaries of aesthetic discourse by introducing riveting work of emerging artists. Africa is a continent of richness, resilience, and diasporic energies because of how its traditions adapt to new circumstances. Whether in the domains of the most traditional rural art forms, such as masquerade or shrines, or in tourist arts, colonial encounters, early workshops, and art movements, African arts defy easy categorization; they simply do not sit still, nor have they ever. Across their huge diversities, African aesthetics can only be appreciated for their very multiplicity and systems of representation that they uphold, accommodate, and transform.

See also **Arts: Africa; Literature: African Literature.**

BIBLIOGRAPHY
Abiodun, Rowland, Henry John Drewal, and John Pemberton III. *Yoruba: Art and Aesthetics.* Edited by Lorenz Homberger. New York and Zurich: The Center for African Art and Rietberg Museum, 1991.
Barber, Karin, ed. *Readings in African Popular Culture.* Bloomington: International African Institute, in association with Indiana University Press, 1997.
Berlo, Janet Catherine, and Lee Anne Wilson, eds. *Arts of Africa, Oceania, and the Americas: Selected Readings.* Englewood Cliffs, N.J.: Prentice Hall, 1993.
Hallen, Barry. "Some Observations about Philosophy, Postmodernism, and Art in Contemporary African Studies." *African Studies Review* 38, no. 1 (April 1995): 69–80.
Mudimbe, V. Y. *The Invention of Africa: Gnosis, Philosophy, and the Order of Knowledge.* Bloomington: Indiana University Press, 1988.
Nooter, Mary H. *Secrecy: African Art that Conceals and Reveals.* New York: The Museum for African Art, 1993.
Oguibe, Olu, and Okwui Enwezor, eds. *Reading the Contemporary: African Art from Theory to Marketplace.* Cambridge, Mass.: MIT Press, 1999.
Phillips, Ruth B., and Christopher B. Steiner, eds. *Unpacking Culture: Art and Commodity in Colonial and Postcolonial Worlds.* Berkeley: University of California Press, 1999.
Roberts, Mary Nooter, and Allen F. Roberts. *A Sense of Wonder: African Art from the Faletti Family Collection.* Phoenix, Ariz.: Phoenix Art Museum, 1997.
Rubin, Arnold. *African Accumulative Sculpture: Power and Display.* New York: Pace Gallery, 1974.
Thompson, Robert Farris. *African Art in Motion: Icon and Act in the Collection of Katherine Coryton White.* Los Angeles: University of California Press, 1974.
Viredu, K. "On Defining African Philosophy." In *Postkoloniales Philosophieren: Afrika,* edited by N. Nagl-Docekal and F. M. Wimmer, 40–62. Vienna and Munich: R. Oldenbourg Verlag.
Vogel, Susan Mullin. *African Aesthetics: The Carlo Monzino Collection.* Photographs by Mario Carrieri. New York: Center for African Art, 1986.
Yai, Olabiyi Babalola. "In Praise of Metonymy: The Concepts of 'Tradition' and 'Creativity' in the Transmission of Yoruba Artistry over Time and Space." In *The Yoruba Artist: New Theoretical Perspectives on African Arts,* edited by Rowland Abiodun, Henry J. Drewal, and John Pemberton III. Washington and London: Smithsonian Institution Press, 1994.

Mary Nooter Roberts

ASIA

Culturally, Asia encompasses an enormous range of cultural diversity, with philosophical traditions going back 2,500 years. And aesthetics is the philosophical study of art and the elaboration of criteria of value in arts and in nature, as well as how these two notions overlap with the study of nature and being human. In many Asian traditions value focuses on human well-being. In Daoism and Shintoism—and arguably Buddhism and Confucianism—divinity is not transcendent but immanent. Here human beings are at one with divinity and/or the natural world. The division of the various intellectual disciplines is the product of human histories; they developed differently in Asia. For example, throughout Asia there is little dichotomization of mind and body, of spiritual and material. As a result, aesthetic ideas and practices operate very differently, overlapping with the religious in India, helping to constitute the ethical and sociopolitical in East Asia.

Philosophy in the West is thinking, and thinking is done in language. Not so in Asia, where in every tradition the arts are as important as language in grasping ideas. The Japanese Buddhist priest Kukai (774–835) summed up the teachings of his Chinese master Huiguo thus:

> The abbot informed me that the Esoteric scriptures are so abstruse that their meaning cannot be conveyed except through art. For this reason he ordered the court artist Li Chen and about a dozen other painters to execute ten scrolls of the Womb and Diamond Mandalas. . . . He also ordered the bronzesmith Chao Wu to cast fifteen ritual implements." (Tsunoda, p. 141)

Understanding Asian aesthetics thus presupposes bodily experience. For this reason, direct experience with aesthetic values—whether through Japanese tea ceremony or in a Japanese garden—is as crucial to wisdom in the Asian sense as intellectual mastery. This means that for any discussion to do full justice to Asian aesthetics, it must take into consideration the contributions of the arts.

Asian aesthetics has begun to influence European-American philosophy, and both have begun to recognize the importance of situating aesthetics historically and within the contexts of colonialism, cultural hegemony, "race" studies, economics, power, gender politics, and the diasporas.

Buddhism

Early Theravada Buddhism records the importance of aesthetic (Pali, *Samvega*) and distinguishes different kinds of reactions to beauty analogous to reactions to diversity. The Lotus Sutra of Mahayana Buddhism introduced the idea of paradise and encouraged the production of visuals and sounds in honor of the Buddha as meritorious; this later developed into the ideas that art could clarify reality and could make such abstract concepts more concrete. It also provides the earliest example of taking children's art seriously. Thus began the interest of Mahayana Buddhism in art.

The Japanese priest Kukai (774–835) brought the Shingon Sect of esoteric Buddhism to Japan. Shingon recognized four main categories of art: (1) painting and sculpture, including mandala painting; (2) music and literature; (3) gestures and acts, including hand positions called *mudras,* ritual, and dance (much of which was ritual); and (4) the implements of civilization and religion.

Kukai was the first Japanese to develop the theoretical dimensions of the visual arts. "For Kukai whatever was beautiful partook of the nature of Buddha. Nature, art and religion were one" (De Bary, 1958, p. 138). This was true of other Japanese Buddhists as well. Summarizing the Shingon view of art, Kukai wrote, "In truth, the esoteric doctrines are so profound as to defy their enunciation in writing. With the help of painting, however, their obscurities may be understood" (Tsunoda, pp. 137–138).

Pure Land Buddhism (10th–13th century) brought enlightenment to the masses through chanting, dancing and singing, and paintings of paradise and hell—practices reflecting new views on enlightenment and who could attain it. The priest Ippen (1239–1289) insisted that the grace of Amida was not confined to the Pure Land Sect or even to Buddhist temples but was everywhere, even in Shinto shrines. Along with this popularization of religion occurred a concurrent popularization of Buddhist art.

The Zen Sect has the most influential aesthetic tradition of all the Buddhist sects. Zen arts attest to the central values of "simplicity, the spirituality of the ordinary, and genuineness of heart," focusing on the maker's mind and the process rather than a final product (Kasulis, 1998, pp. 357–371; Suzuki). Painters with a few rough brush strokes convey the mind of the monk and enlightenment itself. In flower arrangement, oddly shaped twigs (only odd numbers are used) convey the simple beauty of the uniquely ordinary. The haiku poet uses a few words to evoke an idea that the reader completes. The gardener helps the rocks find where they want to be and where they fit naturally. In calligraphy, misshapen, oddly arranged characters convey with apparently childlike simplicity a renewed childlike view of the world. In cooking, the Abbot Dogen (1200–1253) insisted monks present the freshest foods beautifully to make meatless menus enticing. Zen arts set up relationships among artist(s), audience, materials, and the environment, as well as express and provoke enlightened mind (Bullen; Kasulis). Zen also countered any distinction between "fine" and "applied" arts and aesthetics, and strengthened, especially for Samurai warriors, the intimate relationship between the arts and martial training.

China

China has a diverse and ancient tradition in aesthetics. Early in the tradition, art was integrally related with metaphysics, social and political philosophy, and ethics. At this stage in the tradition, aesthetics had primacy over rational discourse (Hall and Ames, 1987).

For Confucius (551–479 B.C.E.), ceremony and music, "conducted with style like an artistic performance," define the behavior of the Confucian gentleman (Graham, p. 11). Music (*yue*) comprises instrumental music, song, and dance, primarily those of the sacred rites and ceremony (*li*). They both arise from and produce harmony, and, by transforming the heart, transform human relations—and therefore government. For Confucius, "all government can be reduced to ceremony" (Graham, p. 13). The Mohists, in contrast, "condemned music . . . (reconstruing morality) as a set of abstract principles" (Graham, p. 259). Xunzi (300–237 B.C.E.) and his followers developed Confucius's idea that music was beneficial (or harmful if the wrong kind) into a general theory of the moral efficacy of music. Xunzi was the first to elaborate on the relation between music and ceremony. His "Discourse on Music" begins, "Music is joy, what the authentic man inevitably refuses to do without" (Graham, p. 260). Training in music, therefore, was crucial to education and government. On this view, the sovereign could use music and ritual to enlighten his people and thereby govern well. Yet by 530 C.E. poet-critic Xiao Tong liberated aesthetics from ethics, writing that his selection for his literary anthology had been guided only by aesthetic merit, not moral considerations.

From the fifth century to the present aesthetics was dominated by the arts of the literati class—calligraphy, painting, and poetry, set in the context of natural landscapes or gardens—appreciated in the setting of natural landscapes and gardens. Three characteristics define literati arts: its amateur status as the product of scholar-officials, its function as an expressive outlet, and its style (Bush, 1971, p. 1).

The transition from political-ceremonial aesthetics to literati aesthetics of personal expression is seen in an essay attributed to the scholar Wang Wei (c. 415–443), who situated landscape painting in relation to ceremony and the cosmos:

[According to Wang Wei,] Paintings must correspond to the *ba gua* [the eight trigrams of geomancy], meaning that just as the *ba gua* are a symbolic diagram of the workings of the universe, so must landscape painting be a symbolic language through which the painter may express not a relative, particularized aspect of nature seen at a given moment from a given view point, but a general truth, beyond time and place. Though Wang Wei . . . is full of wonder at the artist's mysterious power of pictorial compression, he insists that painting is more than the exercise of skill; "the spirit must also exercise control over it; for this is the essence of painting." (Sullivan, p. 97)

Slightly later, Xie He (fl. 479–501) outlined six principles for judging paintings and painters that have never been superceded: (1) animation through spirit consonance (*qi yun*), (2) structural method (literally *bone means*) in the use of the brush, (3) fidelity to the object in portraying forms, (4) conformity to kind in applying colors, (5) proper planning in placing elements, (6) in copying, perpetuating the ancient models (Soper; Sakanishi; Sullivan, p. 95; Wen). Although Chinese interpretations of principles 3 to 6 diverge, they are roughly equivalent to naturalism, coloring, composition, and training.

Michael Sullivan (p. 96) explains principle 1 as follows:

Qi is that cosmic spirit (literally, breath or vapor) that vitalizes all things, that gives life and growth to the trees,

movement to the water, energy to human beings, and that is exhaled by the mountains as clouds and mist. The artist must attune himself to this cosmic spirit and let it infuse him with energy so that in a moment of inspiration—and no word could be more appropriate—he may become the vehicle for its expression. *Qi* infuses all things, [with] no distinction between animate and inanimate. Seen in this light, the third, fourth and fifth principles involve more than mere visual accuracy; for, as the living forms of nature are the visible manifestations of the workings of the *qi*, only by representing them faithfully can the artist express his awareness of the cosmic principle in action. (Sullivan, 1999, p. 96; Wen, 1963)

During the Southern Song Dynasty (1127–1279), philosophers undertook an intellectual defense of Confucianism against the challenges of Buddhism and Daoism in the Song Synthesis. In the field of aesthetics, this culminated in a synthesis integrating literati arts with ethics, mysticism, and education in the classics that continued till the end of the Qing Dynasty in 1911 (Chan; De Bary, 1960, chaps. 17–19; Koller and Koller, chaps. 21–22; Black).

Mao Zedong (1893–1976) overturned the elitist literati emphasis on the classics and the value of the past. During the Republican Period (1912–1949), Lu Xun (1881–1936)—writer, activist, and founder of the Creative Print Movement—had urged artists to use art in the service of revolution (based on European ideologies). In his 1942 *Talks at the Yan'an Conference on Literature and Art* (the foundation for Communist Chinese aesthetics until 1979), Mao adapted Lu's thinking to his revolution, acknowledging Lu as a source. Mao argued that the history of art was a product of political-economic structures that must be rejected: Bronze Age art was the product of a slave-based society, while from Han (140 B.C.E.–220 C.E.) to the twentieth century China was feudally unified under an emperor, from whom all value stemmed (McDougall). Yet Mao Zedong adapted aspects of literati aesthetics to revolutionary Communist purposes, including the use of images and texts to teach virtues and a belief in the power of art to transform the human heart and thereby political reality. In 1958 a print by Niu Wen integrated poetry into visual art—a literati concept dating from at least the Song—and peasants were adding poetry to their village murals. By the early 1960s even landscape painting in traditional media (*guo hua*) was adapted to Communist purposes: Huang Peimo's landscape print *A Distant Source and a Long Stream* (1973) incorporates the deliberate literati archaism and treatment of "empty" space literati aesthetics.

But Mao focused on the masses—both as audience and as agents of their own transformation. This required the masses to be "the sole and inexhaustible source" of subject matter, and it required a new style depicting the masses as inspiring heroes, not as agonized victims (as in Lu Xun's writings). During this time, setting the framework for aesthetic understanding and debate were praise and criticism in government-published reviews of artworks that the government established as models of art; deviation was dangerous. The impact of Jiang Qing

(1914?–1991), Mao's wife and deputy director of the Cultural Revolution (1966–1976), is seen in her principles for "model operas" (1961–1965), codified to reform opera and all the visual arts, and in the feminist content of visual art during the Cultural Revolution (1966–1976).

In 1953 Zhou Yang iterated Mao's advocacy of socialist realism, but declared the enrichment of Chinese tradition to be the objective of using foreign art and aesthetics. He concluded by advocating "free competition of various artistic forms" (Soviet and Chinese) and stated that Mao Zedong's guiding principle was "Let a hundred flowers bloom and a hundred schools contend."

The debates over retention of traditional aesthetics and the inclusion of foreign components within Chinese arts continue in the early twenty-first century. Debates focus on the Chinese appropriation and critique of universalizing Euro-American paradigms and meta-narratives, "culture as leisure," and the resurgence of Mao fever and neo-nationalism.

India

Despite the philosophical diversity within India, there is a surprising degree of consensus about the nature and importance of aesthetics and aesthetic pleasure (*rasa*). Like truth and goodness, *rasa* belongs to reason (*buddhi*); its relation to truth remains a major vein of speculation. Although the specific role that *rasa* plays in the human psyche depends on the metaphysical premises of a given philosophy—whether dualistic or nondualistic, etc.—*rasa* is a highly valued, central part of human experience. It encompasses sexuality, but also takes its place among the spiritual disciplines.

The second basic concept of Indian aesthetics is *kama,* the pursuit of love and enjoyment. *Kama* includes refined aesthetic pleasure, sexual pleasure, and love of the divine (the human search for transcendence). The epitome of *kama* is found in the love of the divine Krishna and Radha, his consort, and in their dance, called the *rasa-lila* (the "playful dance of the god")—a recurring theme in painting, poetry, and drama. The most famous text of the science of *kama,* Vatsyayana's *Kama Sutra* (Aphorisms of love) lists sixty-four arts and sciences in which a cultured person or courtesan was educated (Embree, p. 256).

Bharata Muni's *Natya Sastra* (Treatise on dramaturgy) (written sometime between the 2nd century B.C.E. and the 2nd century C.E.), the first written theory of drama, claims that when humanity began to suffer from pride and the joyful life became full of suffering, the god Brahma created drama—with its attendants music, poetry, and dance—to uplift humanity morally and spiritually by means of aesthetics (*rasa*) (Bharata, 2003).

From Bharata on, emotion (*rasa,* meaning "flavor" or "relish") is recognized as the heart of drama and all art. *Rasa* thus came to mean the feeling that a poet conveys to a sympathetic reader, aesthetic taste, or aesthetic rapture (Gupta). *Rasa,* the aesthetic rapture accompanying the appreciation of dance and drama, is mentioned in the Upanishads, and some claim that it is even comparable to "the realization of ultimate reality"

(Tripurari, p. 10). The differences between aesthetic *rasa* and Brahman realization of the form of the Absolute became important philosophical issues. Krishna's *rasa-lila* (his love dance with Radha) provides one answer to these problems and leads to philosophical development of kinds of love (Tipurari, p. 37). This dance, first described in the *Bhagavata Purana* (tenth century?) and set in verse in the twelfth century, inspires poetry and paintings (together called *ragamala*); it forms the kernal for the devotional aesthetic called *bhakti rasa* popular in Vedanti [Tripurari].

Dating from the thirteenth century, the *ragamala* (garland of *ragas*) are painting albums, often with poems, based on *ragas,* the secular musical modes associated with particular feelings/flavors (*rasa*). The paintings depict male or female human heroes or divinities, identified by name and an emblem, in love scenes coordinated with time of day, season, and aesthetic mode, and sometimes a color, deity, planet, or animal. Although conceived within the framework of Hinduism, the *rasa-lila* reaches well beyond it: the Moghuls, who were Muslim, also commissioned pictures of the *rasa-lila.*

Music in India has a similarly long aesthetic tradition. The *Samaveda* treats it as a divine art. Indian philosophers have been particularly interested in the aesthetics of sound (Malik), music and dance (Mittal; Iravati), and chant and storytelling (Kaushal).

Japan

Japanese aesthetics is unique among non-Western traditions in the degree to which it has permeated international awareness. It did this not only through the arts but also by introducing its extensive aesthetic vocabulary—*wabi* (a taste for the simple), *sabi* (quiet simplicity), *shibui* (subdued), *iki* (stylish, elegant), *yugen* (rich or deep beauty), etc. (for explanations, see Miner et al., pt. 4). Saito has reinterpreted *sabi* and *wabi* in terms of an "aesthetics of insufficiency." This vocabulary has often been interpreted as referring to an "eternal" Japanese spirit, but in fact it has undergone continuous expansion and reinterpretation since medieval times. The political uses served by both the aesthetics and their mythologizing interpretations comprises an important part of Japanese aesthetics in the early twenty-first century. Saito, for instance, reinterprets *sabi* and *wabi* in terms of an "aesthetics of insufficiency." Perhaps the most important area of current Japanese aesthetics develops the implications of the experience of being bombed and its aftermath(s), which seems to demand utterly new ways of "understanding."

Several dichotomies are used to organize thinking about the arts in Japan, including the polarities between feminine and masculine, and between native and foreign (originally Chinese; since 1868, American or Western). The earliest Japanese writing on aesthetics, by Kukai (774–835), was deliberately permeated by Chinese Buddhist philosophy. But a native Shinto aesthetic was evident a century earlier in the *Manyoshu* (Collection of ten thousand leaves), an anthology of folk songs and poems. Within the anthology, poems by Kakinomoto no Hitomaro (c. 658–c. 708) exemplify a Shinto aesthetic in which there is a "total unity of world and people, time and nature, public and private motivations" (Miner et al., p. 176). Concern over what constitutes as Shinto or native aesthetic, often phrased in terms of what is "uniquely Japanese," continues through Kamo no Mabuchi (1697–1769) and Motoori Norinaga (1730–1801) to the novelists Tanizaki Jun'ichiro and Kawabata Kasunari in the twentieth century, and Emiko Ohunki-Tierney in the twenty-first.

The single most influential figure in the history of Japanese aesthetics (according to Japanese specialists from the twelfth century on) was undoubtedly the Heian poet and diarist Murasaki Shikibu (c. 973–c. 1014). Her explications of the philosophy of literature and painting in her novel *The Tale of Genji* became famous (Tsunoda, vol. 1, pp. 176–179). *Genji* discusses the aesthetics of gardens, calligraphy, nature (especially the moon and the seasons), paper and wrapping, incense, color, fashion, and music; it presents the aesthetic concepts *miyabi* (courtly elegance) and *mono no aware* (awareness of the pathos of things). It exemplifies quintessential Japanese values including the "aesthetics of indirection," ambiguity, elusiveness, allusion and it developed Buddhist impermanence into an aesthetic virtue.

Subsequent critics extolled *Genji*. An ability to comment intelligently on it became necessary for establishing cultural credentials, although as a woman Murasaki also provoked anxiety. The literary and national-learning scholar Motoori Norinaga (1730–1801) developed the political and social dimensions of the expression frequently found in *Genji* of "the pathos of things" (*mono no aware*) and identified it as fundamental to Japanese culture and national identity (Miner, pp. 95–96; Nishimura). Heian women writers possessed a distinctive sensibility because they wrote in the vernacular rather than Chinese as men did; this allowed them to create their work within a native aesthetic distinct from that of male writers writing in Chinese (Keene).

Murasaki's contemporary Sei Shonagon (b. c. 967) presented an aesthetics of everyday life (as well as discoursing on more standard topics) in her *Pillow Book,* one of the three great "prose miscellanies" (*zuihitsu*). Her format was used by other medieval aesthetic recluses, notably Kamo no Chomei (1153–1216), *waka* poet and man of letters. His *Hojoki* (Account of my hut) displays an aesthetic distance that typifies this genre.

Fujiwara Shunzei (1114–1204) and Fujiwara Teika (1162–1241)—father and son poets, critics, and anthologists—devised new conceptions of literature and were the first to discern a history of poetry in Japan (Miner et al.). They assessed such matters as the temporalities of *The Tale of Genji* and ways of handling allusion. Shunzei advocated the aesthetic concepts *yugen* and *sabi*, relating them to Buddhist and Shinto values, and outlined a theory of effect in poetry that utilizes the poem's general configuration (*sugata*), diction (*kotoba*), and spirit (*kokoro*). Teika also wrote instructions to inspire poets.

Saigyo (1118–1190), a poet from a warrior family who became a Shingon priest, wrote a travel diary, a collection with poems on war, and another with poems on Yoshino's cherry blossoms that "assisted in the gradual shift from the plum to the cherry as the ideal Japanese flower" (Miner et al., p. 223). He helped popularize the aesthetic recluse's ideal of seclusion from the world, poetry, and travel. Matsuo Basho (1644–1695)—poet, critic, diarist, and traveler—brought the lowly and the commonplace into the subject matter and vocabulary for poetry and introduced new elements of humor (Tsunoda).

In theater, Zeami (1363–1443), playwright and theater critic, established a critical vocabulary and aesthetics for No: *yugen, monomane* (imitation), *ka* or *hana* (flower)—an allusion both to the transmission of his father's art and to the traditional aesthetics of Japanese poetry. Chikamatsu Monzaemon (1653–1725), a puppet-theater playwright whose works were adapted for the Kabuki stage, addressed the problem of realism in theater (Tsunoda). Kabuki (like most Asian theater) aims at presentation of an explicitly theatrical reality, unlike Western theater, which aims at representation of everyday life.

Tea ceremony aesthetics of simplicity and austerity creates an appreciation of the ordinary and alternative modes of sociality. Based on Zen, it introduces mindfulness into everyday life.

Several genres of gardens developed distinct aesthetics, specializing in allusion and reference (*katsura*); Zen-like mindfulness, simplicity and austerity, and/or relationships to nature, especially to the seasons, to natural landscape.

By the early twentieth century novelists such as Natsume Soseki, Tanizaki Junichiro, and Kawabata Yasunari explored through fiction ideas from Western aesthetics, such as Kant's disinterest. Akutagawa's famous short story "The Hell Screen" (1973) is an instantiation—and an exploration of the ramifications for human life—of the view that realism must be based on experience; the artist can only paint what he or she knows.

Korea

Korea's contributions to aesthetics and the arts have often been misascribed to China and Japan. The best known are the Choson-Dynasty (1392–1910) debates based on Confucian literati aesthetics (and ethics) that led to the abandonment of elaborate Koryo-period (918–1392) incised and inlaid ceramics in favor of simpler forms. Current studies attend especially to the distinctive aesthetics of the many native and folk traditions.

See also **Aesthetics: Africa; Aesthetics: Europe and the Americas; Architecture: Asia; Arts.**

BIBLIOGRAPHY

Akutagawa, Ryunosuke. "The Hell Screen." In *The World of Japanese Fiction,* edited by Yoshinobu Hakutani and Arthur O. Lewis. New York: Dutton, 1973.

Anesaki, Masaharu. *Art, Life, and Nature in Japan.* New York: Japan Society, 1933; Rutland, Vt., and Tokyo: Charles E. Tuttle Co., 1973.

Bharata Muni. *Natya Sastra* (Treatise on dramaturgy). Edited by Kapila Katsyayan. New Delhi: Sahitya Akademi, 1996.

Bush, Susan. *The Chinese Literati on Painting: Su Shih (1037–1101) to Tung Ch'i-ch'ang (1555–1636).* Cambridge, Mass.: Harvard University Press, 1971.

Callicott, J. Baird, and Roger T. Ames, eds. *Nature in Asian Traditions of Thought: Essays in Environmental Philosophy.* Albany: State University of New York Press, 1989.

Chan, Wing-tsit, ed. *Chu Hsi and Neo-Confucianism.* Honolulu: University of Hawaii Press, 1986.

Chang, Chung-yuan. *Creativity and Taoism: A Study of Chinese Philosophy, Art, and Poetry.* New York: Julian Press, 1963; Harper Colophon Books, 1970.

Davis, Darrell William. *Picturing Japaneseness: Monumental Style, National Identity, Japanese Film.* New York: Columbia University Press, 1996.

De Bary, Wm. Theodore, Wing-tsit Chan, and Burton Watson. *Sources of Chinese Tradition.* 2 vols. New York: Columbia University Press, 1960.

De Bary, Wm. Theodore, et al., eds. *Sources of Japanese Tradition.* 2 vols. New York: Columbia University Press, 1958.

Embree, Ainslie T. *Sources of Indian Tradition.* Vol. 1: *From the Beginning to 1800.* 2nd ed. New York: Columbia University Press, 1988.

Gupta, Shyamala. *Art, Beauty, and Creativity: Indian and Western Aesthetics.* New Delhi: D. K. Printworld, 1999.

Hall, David L., and Roger T. Ames. *Thinking through Confucius.* Albany: State University of New York Press, 1987.

Iravati. *Performing Artists in Ancient India.* New Delhi: D. K. Printworld, 2003.

Kamo no Chomei. *Hojoki: Visions of a Torn World.* Translated by Yasuhiko Moriguchi and David Jenkins. Berkeley, Calif.: Stone Bridge Press, 1996.

Kasulis, Thomas P. "Zen and Artistry." In *Self as Image in Asian Theory and Practice,* edited by Roger T. Ames with Thomas P. Kasulis and Wimal Dissanayake, 357–372. Albany: State University of New York Press, 1998.

Keene, Donald. "Feminine Sensibility in the Heian Era." In *Japanese Aesthetics and Culture: A Reader,* edited by Nancy G. Hume, 109–123. Albany: State University of New York Press, 1995.

Ki no Tsurayuki. *Kokin Wakashu: The First Imperial Anthology of Japanese Poetry.* Translated by Helen Craig McCullough. Stanford, Calif.: Stanford University Press, 1985.

Malik, S. C. *Dhvani: Nature and Culture of Sound.* New Delhi: D. K. Printworld, 1999.

McDougall, Bonnie S., trans. and ed. *Mao Zedong's "Talks at the Yan'an Conference on Literature and Art": A Translation of the 1943 Text with Commentary.* Ann Arbor: University of Michigan, 1980.

Miner, Earl, Hiroko Odagiri, and Robert E. Morrell. *The Princeton Companion to Classical Japanese Literature.* Princeton, N.J.: Princeton University Press, 1985.

Mittal, Anjali. *Hindustani Music and the Aesthetic Concept of Form.* New Delhi: D. K. Printworld, 2000.

Murasaki Shikibu. *The Tale of Genji.* Translated by Edward G. Seidensticker. New York: Vintage Books, 1976.

Ohnuki-Tierney, Emiko. *Kamikaze, Cherry Blossoms, and Nationalisms: The Militarization of Aesthetics in Japanese History.* Chicago: University of Chicago Press, 2002.

Reinhold, Christiana. "Okakura Kakuzo and the Production of the Japan Discourse in the Early Twentieth-Century United States." In *Essays in History,* edited by the Corcoran Department of History at the University of Virginia, vol. 39. Charlottesville: Corcoran Department of History, University of Virginia, 1997.

Saito, Yuriko. "The Japanese Appreciation of Nature." *British Journal of Aesthetics 23,* no. 3 (1985): 239–251.

Sei Shonagon. *The Pillow-Book of Sei Shonagon.* Translated by Arthur Waley. London: George Allen and Unwin, 1928.

Sullivan, Michael. *The Arts of China.* 4th ed. Berkeley and Los Angeles: University of California Press, 1999.

Teng Gu. *Tang Song huihua shi* (A history of painting during the Tang and Song dynasties). Beijing: Zhongguo gudian yishu chubanshe, 1958.

Tripurari, B. V. *Aesthetic Vedanta: The Sacred Path of Passionate Love.* Eugene, Oreg.: Mandala Publishing Group, 1998.

Tsunoda, Ryusaku, William Theodore de Bary, and Donald Keene, eds. *Sources of Japanese Tradition.* 2 vols. New York: Columbia University Press, 1958.

Wen Fong. "On Hsieh Ho's *Liu-fa.*" *Oriental Art* (new series) 9, no. 4 (1963): 3–6.

Zhou Yang. Report delivered to the Second Congress of Literary and Art Workers, September 1953.

Mara Miller

EUROPE AND THE AMERICAS

Aesthetics is a branch of philosophy concerned with aesthetic experience and the fundamental principles of art and criticism. It is distinct from the history of art and the practice of art criticism, although its own history follows a path parallel to both. It is not an empirical study of the psychology or sociology of art, nor is it the same as *aestheticism,* which names a particular attitude to aesthetic matters, exemplified by the fin-de-siècle "art for art's sake" movement. There is no need to be an "aesthete" to engage in aesthetics. In what follows, a brief history of the subject will be outlined from its eighteenth-century foundations, back through earlier anticipations from the classical period, and on to the modern legacy. Then an analytical survey of contemporary trends and current issues will be offered.

Eighteenth-Century Foundations

Aesthetics in the European tradition, conceived as philosophical inquiry into the experience of beauty, acquired its name and essential nature in the eighteenth century, even though cognate concerns had been debated in Europe for two millennia before that. The term *aesthetics,* from the Greek *aesthēsis* (perception), was coined, in roughly its modern sense, in 1735 by Alexander Baumgarten (1714–1762), a German philosopher who sought to develop a "science of sensitive cognition." Baumgarten's unfinished book *Aesthetica* was the first to bear this new term in its title. In fact the term took some time to catch on and was not established in Great Britain, for example, until the 1830s. Immanuel Kant (1724–1804), perhaps the most influential of all aestheticians, was slow to adopt the new usage, remarking in the second edition of his *Critique of Pure Reason* (1787) that "The Germans are the only people who currently make use of the word 'aesthetic' in order to signify what others call the critique of taste." In that same passage Kant lambastes what he describes as "the abortive attempt made by Baumgarten . . . to bring the critical treatment of the beautiful under rational principles." But whatever its name— *aesthetics* or *critique of taste*—a distinctive inquiry gathered pace through the eighteenth century and came to define what is now universally acknowledged as the field of aesthetics. What are the characteristics of this new inquiry?

Judgments of taste. Several developments in the eighteenth century form the foundations of modern European aesthetics.

One is a growing interest in judgments of taste, notably how attributions of beauty are grounded. Is beauty an objective quality of nature itself or is it merely a projection of the mind? An important impetus for this debate was the writing of Anthony Ashley Cooper (1671–1713), third earl of Shaftesbury, whose Neoplatonist work *Characteristics of Men, Manners, Opinions, Times* (1711) presents the view that beauty, like goodness, resides in the harmony of the natural world, as created by God, and that humans can immediately discern such beauty (or goodness) by an "inward eye" or "moral sense." Furthermore, the enjoyment of beauty has a disinterested quality distinct from the desire of possession. The Scottish philosopher Francis Hutcheson (1694–1746), in *An Inquiry into the Original of Our Ideas of Beauty and Virtue* (1725), adopted the notion of "moral sense," including the concomitant sense of beauty, and sought in detail to show how beauty, grounded in "uniformity amidst variety," could be the object of intersubjectively valid judgments. David Hume's (1711–1776) influential essay "Of the Standard of Taste," first published in his *Four Dissertations* (1757), gives explicit focus to "taste" as a capacity for judging beauty, and while emphasizing that beauty "is no quality in things themselves," nevertheless finds a "standard of taste" in the joint verdict of qualified judges. Hume's focus is on taste in cultural matters, especially poetry, rather than natural beauty, but judgments about art and nature were seldom at this stage differentiated. In Kant's definitive contribution to aesthetics, the first part of his *Critique of Judgment* (1790), we find many of the threads of the previous debates subtly interwoven. Kant proposes, in contrast to Shaftesbury and Hutcheson, a clear divide between moral and aesthetic judgments, highlighting the role of disinterestedness in the latter; he steers a path between the avowed subjectivity of beauty and the justifiable aspiration of universality in judgments about beauty; and he distinguishes natural beauty from the beauty of art. For Kant a "pure judgment of taste" rests on a universally communicable, disinterested pleasure in the appearance of an object apart from any conceptualization of that object.

The sublime. A second feature that characterizes the birth of modern aesthetics in the eighteenth century is also closely associated with Kant. This is the interest given to the sublime in addition to the beautiful. Kant's account of the sublime, in the *Critique of Judgment,* as well as in *Observations on the Feeling of the Beautiful and Sublime* (1763), is again definitive. The sublime rests on the vastness and overwhelming power of nature and the awe that these inspire in humans. Thunder and lightning, hurricanes and volcanoes, towering mountains and crashing waterfalls are judged sublime and induce a mix of fear and pleasure. Kant's own discussion is complex, distinguishing the "mathematical sublime" (vastness) and the "dynamical sublime" (power), and relating response to the sublime with reflection on the greatness of reason as "a faculty of the mind surpassing every standard of Sense." The pleasure of the sublime derives from awareness that, in spite of physical frailty in the face of terrifying nature, humans remain superior as rational and moral beings. Interest in the sublime did not originate in the eighteenth century, and discussions often referred back to the literary treatise *On the Sublime,* attributed to "Longinus" from the first century C.E., although the principal focus in that work is not the awesomeness of nature so much as the sublime style in rhetoric. Edmund Burke's (1729–1797) *Philosophical Enquiry into the Origin of Our Ideas of the Sublime and Beautiful* (1757) was an important precursor to Kant's discussion and developed the idea that aesthetic responses stemmed from universal predispositions in human nature.

Fine arts. A third relevant factor in the foundations of aesthetics was the emergence of a conception of the fine arts (*beaux arts*) as belonging to a single category. The seminal work was *Les beaux arts réduits à un même principe* (1746; Fine arts reduced to a single principle) by Abbé Charles Batteux (1713–1780). This work listed the fine arts, whose aim is pleasure, as music, poetry, painting, sculpture, and dance. In another category, those arts that combine pleasure and usefulness, he puts eloquence and architecture, while theater is deemed a combination of all the arts. The "single principle" is "the imitation of beautiful nature." Few followed Batteux in stressing imitation as the definitive element in art, but by the time of Kant's discussion in the *Critique of Judgment,* the notion of the fine arts was taken for granted. Kant himself offered a quite different common principle of fine art—that of genius—anticipating an aesthetic conception associated with Romanticism. Genius, for Kant, is "a talent for producing that for which no definite rule can be given" and fine art, he insists, "is only possible as a product of genius."

Conditions in eighteenth-century Europe seemed entirely conducive to the flourishing of aesthetics as an inquiry into the principles of beauty and the fine arts. Marxist historians offer a partial explanation in terms of the rise of a confident and prosperous middle class with the time and inclination to indulge a love of beauty and the display of "sensibility," "refinement," and taste. Notions of individuality and subjectivity, central to Enlightenment thought, developed in this century, as did notions of a common human nature on which universal judgments of value might be grounded. It should be emphasized, though, that many aspects of aesthetic inquiry long predate the eighteenth century. A summary survey of these is necessary to map out any adequate history of aesthetics, prior to exploring the legacy of the nineteenth and twentieth centuries.

Classical Anticipations

Both Plato (c. 428–348 or 347 B.C.E.) and Aristotle (384–322 B.C.E.) have extensive and influential discussions of art and beauty, and there is a clear sense that in many cases they were contributing to debates already well established in ancient Greek culture. Plato, for example, famously refers to the "ancient quarrel" between poetry and philosophy. When Batteux, as we have seen, uses the term *imitation* to characterize a feature common to the fine arts he is self-consciously evoking the notion of *mimesis,* central to ancient Greek thought about the arts. The precise meaning of *mimesis,* sometimes translated as "imitation," sometimes "representation," is disputed. Undoubtedly Plato often uses the term with negative connotations, as when, in the *Timaeus,* he refers to poets as a "tribe of imitators." In book ten of the *Republic,* Plato gives an unflattering account of a painter, whose picture of a bed is twice removed from reality being a mere "imitation" of a carpenter's bed, which itself is a copy of an ideal form. Plato's constant worry about mimetic art, especially poetry, was that it dealt in appearance or illusion, thus being both epistemologically and morally suspect. It was the Neoplatonist Plotinus (205–270 C.E.), writing over five hundred years later, in the *Enneads,* who showed how Plato's metaphysics of forms could be reconciled with a positive conception of artistic mimesis. Plotinus argued that art, by directly imitating the forms themselves, could aspire to an even greater beauty than that found in nature and thus achieve the highest truthfulness.

This debate about the truth of art resonates through the centuries. Plato's pupil Aristotle addressed the matter in his treatise *Poetics,* a discussion of the nature and status of poetic tragedy that has become one of the seminal texts in Western aesthetics. For Aristotle the desire to imitate is both natural and a source of pleasure. Tragedy is an imitation of action and attains, according to Aristotle, thereby contradicting Plato, a status somewhat akin to philosophy in presenting universal truths about what "such and such a kind of man will probably or necessarily say or do." Aristotle went on to argue that mimesis in tragedy had other values as well, including the pleasurable stirring of emotion, notably pity and fear, leading to an ultimate purgation (*katharsis*) or cleansing. The perplexing problem of what makes the viewing of tragedy a pleasurable experience is the subject of a subtle essay by David Hume, "Of Tragedy" (1757).

Although the ancient Greek philosophers had much to say about each of the individual art forms—drama, poetry, music, painting, and sculpture—it seems they possessed no concept equivalent to *fine art.* The term *technē* is sometimes translated as "art" but is closer to "craft" in the modern sense, denoting a specialized skill. For Plato the highest "art" is the statecraft taught to the young guardians in the Republic, which intriguingly he sometimes compares to painting, coloring sculpture, or writing a tragedy. Perhaps, though, the main reason for locating the origins of modern aesthetics in the eighteenth century rather than in ancient Greek philosophy is that there is no systematic attempt in the latter to address interconnected issues about the role of beauty and the arts in human experience. Both Plato and Aristotle write about beauty (*to kalon*) and, although disagreeing on its metaphysical status, broadly agree on the marks of beauty: "measure and proportion" (Plato), "order and symmetry and definiteness" (Aristotle). But such observations are integrated into more general discussions, and neither philosopher felt the need for a distinctive branch of philosophy given over to aesthetic concerns.

In subsequent centuries, up to the eighteenth century, a similar story could be told of isolated, sometimes brilliant, sometimes hugely influential, contributions, but there was no sustained attempt (as epitomized by Kant's *Critique of Judgment*) to establish a philosophy of the beautiful. Often the legacy of debates from the Greeks is in evidence, few more so than Plato's attack on poetry. A deep ambivalence is manifest throughout the history of the Christian Church from the early church fathers through the Middle Ages toward secular poetry and in particular drama. Plato's concerns about the falsehood

and seductiveness of poetry and its antipathy to reason found an analogue in Christian thought in the profane and the sacred. Periodic defenses of poetry were not uncommon. Sir Philip Sidney's (1554–1586) *Defense of Poesie* (1595) takes on the Puritans and is an eloquent argument for the educative and edificatory benefits of poetry. Curiously, in spite of the extraordinary flourishing of the arts in the European Renaissance, the two hundred years between 1400 and 1600 saw little sustained philosophical debate about the arts or beauty. Treatises on individual arts by the likes of Leon Battista Alberti (1404–1472), Leonardo da Vinci (1452–1519), and Albrecht Dürer (1471–1528) were concerned more with theoretical questions about aim and technique than with abstract philosophical investigation. These would not standardly be classified as works in aesthetics, in the stricter sense that emerged after Baumgarten.

The Growth of Modern Aesthetics

A striking development in aesthetics after the eighteenth century was a gradual shift of interest from inquiries into beauty per se and "judgments of taste" to specifically the philosophy of art. Nineteenth- (and late-eighteenth-) century aesthetics was largely dominated by German philosophers, including Johann Christoph Friedrich von Schiller (1759–1805), Friedrich Wilhelm Joseph von Schelling (1775–1854), and Arthur Schopenhauer (1788–1860). A way of writing about art developed that was distinctively philosophical and that contrasted with explorations of art, however theoretical, by artists themselves. Nowhere is this better exemplified than in the magisterial *Lectures on Fine Art,* given in the 1820s by the paramount German aesthetician Georg Friedrich Wilhelm Hegel (1770–1831), a work comparable in importance and influence to Kant's *Critique of Judgment.* Hegel afforded art a central place in his metaphysical system of absolute idealism, locating it, along with religion and philosophy, as one of the modes of "absolute spirit" whereby the mind comes to know itself. Hegel retold the history of art in terms of changing relations between spiritual content (idea) and sensuous medium: in symbolic art, characterized by Egyptian and Indian art, the medium dominates the idea; in classical art, from ancient Greece, idea and medium are in perfect balance; in romantic art, from Christian art onward, the idea reaches its ascendancy, manifesting "infinite subjectivity." Hegel proposed a hierarchy of individual arts, from architecture to poetry, and suggested, somewhat obscurely, that the capacity for further development had been exhausted (the "death of art").

Hegel showed par excellence how a philosophy of art could be fully integrated into wider philosophical speculation, and increasingly in the history of aesthetics theories of the arts (or of beauty more generally) would come to be discriminated in terms of the philosophical frameworks within which they are couched. Idealism, either Kantian or Hegelian, had a major impact well into the twentieth century, notably in works like the Italian Benedetto Croce's *Estetica come scienze dell' espressione e linguistica generale* (1902; Aesthetics as science of expression and general linguistics) and the English Robin George Collingwood's *Principles of Art* (1937). Both Collingwood and Croce identified the true work of art not with its physical manifestation but with an inner state of mind seeking expression. Other philosophical outlooks produced their own distinctive aesthetic theories. Phenomenologists, such as Roman Ingarden (1893–1970) and Mikel Dufrenne (1910–1995), give attention to the properties of an "aesthetic object" in relation to the acts of consciousness of artist and audience. John Dewey (1859–1952), the American pragmatist philosopher, in one of the most important contributions to twentieth-century aesthetics, *Art As Experience* (1934), stresses the origin of art in the everyday world of human action. For Marxist aestheticians, the context in which art must be explained is social and economic, a complete rejection of the premises of the idealist. Contemporary analytical aesthetics, that is, aesthetics influenced by the developments of logic and conceptual analysis in the early to middle parts of the twentieth century, gives less focus to the social or psychological aspects of art as to questions about what kind of entities art works are and what kinds of properties they possess.

Contemporary Trends and Issues

Increasingly from the latter half of the twentieth century into the twenty-first century aesthetics grew in stature as an established branch of philosophy in both the Anglo-American (analytic) and European (Continental) schools of philosophy. The subject was widely taught in universities and learned societies devoted to the subject—the American Society for Aesthetics and societies from the individual European nations—had strong support. Aesthetics was well integrated into mainstream philosophical inquiry with aestheticians drawing on work in, for example, philosophy of language, philosophy of mind, ethics, epistemology, and metaphysics. Indeed the borrowings go both ways, as sometimes technical work in aesthetics—on fictionality, aesthetic properties, ontology of art, interpretation, narrative—has contributed to an advance of understanding in other philosophical fields.

Twenty-first-century concerns in aesthetics might be seen as falling into two broad areas: philosophy of art, on the one hand, and on the other the investigation of aesthetic experience more generally, including experience of the natural world. Philosophy of art encompasses theoretical questions about the nature of art itself, how works of art are distinguished from other artifacts, what values art embodies, and also the special qualities of individual art forms, not only the traditional "fine arts" but other arts such as film, photography, and "mass art." Inquiries into aesthetic experience go beyond the experience of art and investigate human responses to beauty and other aesthetic qualities wherever they are manifested.

Philosophy of art. When analytic philosophers began to turn their attention to aesthetics in the 1940s, one of their early concerns was to analyze the concept of *art* itself. The idea of providing a definition of art, one that covered all art forms, had not been a central preoccupation of aesthetics in previous centuries. Leo Tolstoy in *What Is Art?* (1898) had proposed that art involves the transmission of feeling from artist to audience; and other kinds of "expression" views, ultimately deriving from romantic conceptions of art, were developed by Croce and Collingwood. More often than not, those who sought an "essence" for art had, implicitly if not explicitly, one particular art form in mind, for example, painting or poetry. Thus the

idea that art is essentially a "representation," a descendent of classical "mimetic" theories, foundered on "nonrepresentational" arts, including music and all abstract art. Clive Bell's claim in *Art* (1914) that what is essential to art is "significant form" and the arousing of "aesthetic emotion" was more convincing about modernist painting, which he championed, than about the realist novel. Analytic philosophers felt the need to go back to basics. Could there be any property that all forms of art—painting, music, literature, sculpture, dance, drama—had in common, a property possession of which was both necessary and sufficient for something to be art?

Initially many philosophers were skeptical that art has such an "essence" and indeed that the concept of art lent itself to strict definition. In an influential paper from 1956, "The Role of Theory in Aesthetics," Morris Weitz (1916–1981) argued that there could be no definition of art because "art" is an "open concept," allowing for radically new kinds of instantiation. Weitz was one of the first philosophers to recognize the difficulty posed for philosophy of art by the rapid proliferation of art movements in the twentieth century, from modernism to dadaism. If the "readymades" (a urinal, a snow shovel, a bottle rack, etc.) of the avant-garde artist Marcel Duchamp (1887–1968) could count as art, then traditional conceptions would have to be revised. Weitz proposed that all that binds together the disparate products called "art" are loosely connected "family resemblances," a notion drawn from Ludwig Wittgenstein's *Philosophical Investigations* (1953).

However, not all philosophers agreed with Weitz's anti-essentialism, and a swing back toward essentialist accounts was evident in the final quarter of the twentieth century. What is distinctive about these developments is that rather than seeking some *intrinsic* property shared by all works of art—such as "beauty," "form," "representation," "expression"—they highlighted *extrinsic* or *relational* properties of a social, historical, or "institutional" kind. The American philosopher Arthur Danto (b. 1924) was one of the first to develop this line of thought, suggesting that what makes something art is not what it *looks* like but what role it plays in an "artworld." This is a striking repudiation of a long-standing premise that art must engage aesthetic perception. Following Danto, "institutional" definitions were proposed whereby an object becomes art only by virtue of having that status conferred on it by an institution or artworld or "art circle," consisting of a loose-knit community of artists, critics, and art appreciators. There is no suggestion that each putative work comes before a panel of experts for authentication but only that there is an essentially social aspect to the existence of art. A related species of art theory makes explicit a historical dimension to art. According to these accounts, to acquire the status of art, an object must be connected in some way with works previously accepted as art: for example, they must be intended to be regarded in ways that earlier works were regarded, or there must be some narrative that links the present with the past.

The immense variety of art forms poses a problem not just for definition but for the more metaphysical question of what *kinds* of entities art works are. It is common to postulate a deep divide between those works that are unique physical objects, like paintings, carved sculptures, or buildings, and those that allow for multiple instances, like musical and literary works, films, prints, and photographs. While a painting can be destroyed in a fire, it is less easy to see how a symphony might be destroyed (it could, for example, survive the loss of the original score). There is considerable philosophical interest in pursuing the right "ontology" for art, that is, the mode of existence for different kinds of works. Some philosophers are anxious to present a unitary view, in contrast to the binary one just outlined, and it has been suggested that a painting might in principle also be a "type" with multiple instances, the original canvas being no more significant than an original score. Others have argued that the true identity of any work rests not in the final product but in the complex performance that brought it about. This theory recognizes that facts about a work's provenance are vitally relevant both to what the work is and how it should be appreciated.

A significant trend in contemporary philosophy of art has been to focus on particular art forms. There are recognized branches of aesthetics now labeled philosophy of music, philosophy of literature, philosophy of film, and so on. This tendency has brought aesthetics closer to critics and practitioners within the arts. Often, distinctive issues arise within these more narrowly defined areas. For example, philosophers of music have asked how music can express emotion; whether profundity is possible in music; whether musical works are created or discovered; and what it is to understand music, without assuming that musical understanding is the same as understanding literature or painting. In an important book, *The Aesthetics of Music* (1997), Roger Scruton has argued that music is nonrepresentational, requires a special kind of "intentional" understanding, and yields in its essential musical features only to metaphorical description.

In the philosophy of literature much attention has been given to fictionality, drawing on work in the philosophy of language. How is fictional discourse distinct from nonfictional? Can works of imaginative or fictional literature be bearers of truth (a question familiar from Plato and Aristotle)? One especially persistent problem concerns emotional responses to fiction: on the assumption that to feel, for example, fear and pity, one must believe that the objects of the emotions are real, how can an audience respond in this way (as Aristotle requires for tragedy) when it is known that the objects are mere fictions? Yet another important debate about literature—which extends to all the arts—concerns criteria for interpretation. Is the critic's role to recover an artist's intention or is meaning a product of cultural and literary convention?

In the philosophy of the visual arts, a fundamental question is how depiction in two dimensions can represent three-dimensional objects in space. The preliminary thought that pictures must resemble their subject in order to depict them is both difficult to make precise (in some respects anything resembles anything) and open to counterexamples, in the form of caricatures, cubist portraits, and symbolic representations (for example, Christ depicted as a lamb). Some philosophers reject resemblance altogether as an explanation of pictures, preferring to stress the conventional, quasi-linguistic nature of

representation. Kendall Walton, in his influential *Mimesis As Make-Believe* (1990), argues that viewers of pictures play a "game of make-believe" in which they make believe they see objects depicted when in fact they see only paint and canvas. Others have followed Richard Wollheim in supposing that depiction can be explained as a species of "seeing-in" or "seeing-as." Philosophical explorations of the visual arts have extended to include film and photography, and developments in the aesthetics of film have challenged theoretical approaches based on Marxism and psychoanalysis.

Across all the arts, the issue of what makes art in itself valuable and what criteria are available for evaluating particular works has posed a perennial conundrum. Some aestheticians see value judgments as relative, culture-bound, or "ideological" and have sought to play down their significance. Others have connected the value of art with the very conception of art itself. If art is mimesis, then good art is judged for how well it holds a "mirror to nature," but if art is expression then it is judged for the depth and sincerity of the artist's vision. In a subtle treatment of the question, *Values of Art* (1995), Malcolm Budd argues that the value of a work of art as a work of art is the intrinsic value of the experience the work offers. This is a noninstrumental value, and "experience" is left sufficiently wide to include traditional cognitive values such as moral insight.

There are important currents of thought in contemporary aesthetics that are different from, even opposed to, those based in analytic philosophy. The notion of the "death of the author," promoted by Roland Barthes (1915–1980) and Michel Foucault (1926–1984), has been influential not merely for its impact on literary criticism but also as part of a general poststructuralist skepticism about meaning and subjectivity. In rejecting the notion of a unified autonomous self as the origin of meaning and emphasizing "intertextuality" and the priority of writing over speaking, poststructuralists like Jacques Derrida (b. 1930) present a direct challenge to what they view as the "logocentrism," or focus on logic and reasoning, of analytic philosophers. Another challenge to core assumptions of traditional aesthetics comes from feminist aesthetics, a growing and influential development in the subject. There are many different, sometimes conflicting, strands to feminist approaches, but central ideas include a reshaping of the artistic canon to include more works by women; an emphasis on gendered responses to art in opposition to notions of universal aesthetic experience; a relocating of art production into its social and personal contexts and a tendency to downplay formalist approaches and concomitant conceptions like "disinterestness"; and the promotion of revised criteria for art evaluation. Marxists, like feminists, roundly reject the notion that art exists in a realm of pure experience or pleasure. Aestheticians like Theodor Adorno (1903–1969), of the Frankfurt School, follow general Marxist precepts in attributing to art deeply social meanings, either reinforcing or resisting prevailing ideologies. Aesthetics itself has been challenged as a set of interests and values inescapably imbued with (bourgeois) ideology.

Aesthetic Experience and Aesthetic Qualities

Aesthetics, as noted earlier, is not always concerned with art. The core of Kant's theory of aesthetic judgment had little to do with art but rather with the special kind of pleasure taken in the appearance of things (of any kind). There are longstanding debates over whether there exists a distinctive "aesthetic attitude" or "aesthetic experience" associated with contemplating an object "for its own sake," without interest or desire. The psychologist Edward Bullough (1880–1934) introduced the idea of *psychical distance* to explain aesthetic response, giving the illustration of someone fogbound at sea enraptured by the beauty of the swirling fog quite apart from the imminent dangers it presents. While recognizing some such phenomenon, philosophers have challenged the idea of an aesthetic attitude either as too narrow to do justice to the many interests, including moral and political ones, properly brought to art appreciation, or even as a "myth," reducible to other factors.

Setting aside difficulties in how to characterize the psychology of aesthetic appreciation, philosophers have raised questions about the kind of qualities sought in aesthetic experience. Are there distinctive aesthetic qualities? If so, what makes them different from nonaesthetic, physical, structural, or perceptual qualities? The English philosopher Frank Sibley (1923–1996) initiated the contemporary debate and was one of the first to broaden the scope of the inquiry beyond the limited focus on qualities like beauty and the sublime. Words that identify aesthetic qualities, he suggested, include: *unified, balanced, integrated, lifeless, serene, somber, dynamic, powerful, vivid, delicate, moving, trite, sentimental, tragic,* and many more. Some are purely evaluative, some have a descriptive element. Such qualities "emerge" from, but are not logically determined by, nonaesthetic properties like color, configuration, or material constitution. They require "taste" for their apprehension and might be missed by nondiscerning perceivers. A revived form of eighteenth-century debates about the objectivity of beauty addresses the question whether a "realist" or "antirealist" theory of aesthetic qualities is most apt. Those defending the former often postulate specially qualified observers whose judgments are normative.

The most striking reaffirmation that there is more to aesthetics than just philosophy of art comes in the recent renewed interest in the aesthetics of nature and its offshoot "environmental aesthetics." The dominance of philosophy of art in aesthetics (since Hegel) had distorting effects on philosophical understanding of the appreciation of nature. For one thing, art had become a paradigm for all aesthetic experience, and natural objects or landscapes were viewed as essentially *like* works of art. Even in the eighteenth century there is evidence of such a conception with the pleasure taken in landscaped gardens, scenic views, "prospects," the "picturesque." Pioneers in the new aesthetics of nature, including Ronald Hepburn and Allen Carlson, insist that appreciation of nature is sui generis. Nature, after all, does not come "framed" or designed by an artist, nor is it static. For Carlson a "true" or appropriate appreciation of the natural world, as it is in itself, does not rest on a merely intuitive response or "innocent eye" but should be informed by knowledge—drawn from geology, biology, and ecology—about the natural processes that brought about the objects perceived. What gives a mountain range its distinctive appearance? Why do landscapes look as they do? To explain our response to the appearance we must go deeper than mere

appearance. The advantage of Carlson's view is that it relates aesthetics to practical and informed decisions about environmental planning, and it connects to ethical concerns about ecological preservation. But other philosophers prefer a more subjectivist conception and dismiss as too prescriptive the idea of "appropriate" or "inappropriate" responses to nature.

Of course not all environments are "natural," just as not all "nature" is void of human intervention. Environmental aesthetics goes beyond the aesthetics of nature by considering environments of all kinds, man-made or wilderness, urban or rural. It is hard to see how norms for aesthetic appreciation for such a variety of environments might be established, although extensions of Carlson's "cognitive" approach have been proposed. Also, it is not clear exactly where the bounds lie between a genuinely aesthetic response to an environment and other more or less pleasurable responses, such as "feeling at home" or sensing a relaxed atmosphere.

Aesthetics has an immensely broad scope both in the objects of its inquiry—from the fine arts to a forest wilderness—and in its methods and underlying principles. A concern for beauty resides deeply in human nature, and inquiring into its sources and characteristics occupies a central place in philosophy. There is, as briefly outlined, a long and rich tradition of debate in Western intellectual history that seeks to explore and clarify the aesthetic dimension of human experience. That tradition continues strongly to this day.

See also **Analytical Philosophy; Essentialism; Kantianism; Music, Anthropology of; Musicology; Neoplatonism; Periodization of the Arts; Platonism; Pragmatism.**

BIBLIOGRAPHY

Aristotle. *The Poetics of Aristotle.* Translated by Stephen Halliwell. Chapel Hill: University of North Carolina Press, 1987.

Beardsley, Monroe C. *Aesthetics: Problems in the Philosophy of Criticism.* 2nd ed. Indianapolis: Hackett, 1981.

Brand, Peggy, and Carolyn Kormeyer, eds. *Feminism and Tradition in Aesthetics.* University Park: Pennsylvania State University Press, 1995. Useful anthology on feminist responses to historical and contemporary issues in aesthetics.

Budd, Malcolm. *Values of Art: Pictures, Poetry and Music.* London: Penguin, 1995.

Carlson, Allen. *Aesthetics and the Environment: The Appreciation of Nature, Art, and Architecture.* London: Routledge, 2000.

Carroll, Noël. *A Philosophy of Mass Art.* New York: Oxford University Press, 1998.

Collingwood, Robin George. *The Principles of Art.* Oxford: Oxford University Press, 1938.

Danto, Arthur. *The Transfiguration of the Commonplace.* Cambridge, Mass.: Harvard University Press, 1981.

Davies, Stephen. *Definitions of Art.* Ithaca, N.Y.: Cornell University Press, 1991. Useful survey and evaluation of attempts to define art.

Dewey, John. *Art As Experience.* New York: Putnam, 1934.

Goodman, Nelson. *Languages of Art.* 2nd ed. Indianapolis: Hackett, 1976.

Hegel, Georg Wilhelm Friedrich. *Aesthetics: Lectures on Fine Art.* (1835–1838), translated by T. M. Knox. Oxford: Clarendon, 1975.

Hume, David. "Of the Standard of Taste," "Of Tragedy." (1757). In *Essays, Moral, Political, and Literary,* edited by Eugene Miller. Indianapolis: Liberty Classics, 1985.

Kant, Immanuel. *Critique of Judgment* (1790). Translated by Werner S. Pluhar. Indianapolis: Hackett, 1987.

Kearney, Richard, and David Rasmussen, eds. *Continental Aesthetics: Romanticism to Postmodernism: An Anthology.* Malden, Mass.: Blackwell, 2001. Contains important selections from Schiller, Schelling, Schopenhauer, Croce, Heidegger, Adorno, Barthes, Derrida, and others.

Kelly, Michael, ed. *Encyclopedia of Aesthetics.* 4 vols. Oxford: Oxford University Press, 1998. Contributions by contemporary authors on a wide-ranging array of topics and writers in aesthetics.

Lamarque, Peter, and Stein Haugom Olsen, eds. *Aesthetics and the Philosophy of Art: The Analytic Tradition: An Anthology.* Malden, Mass.: Blackwell, 2004. Contains important articles from analytic philosophers, including Budd, Carlson, Currie, Danto, Dickie, Hepburn, Kivy, Levinson, Scruton, Sibley, Walton, Weitz, Wollheim, and others.

Scruton, Roger. *The Aesthetics of Music.* Oxford: Clarendon, 1997.

Sibley, Frank. *Approach to Aesthetics: Collected Papers on Philosophical Aesthetics.* Edited by John Benson, Betty Redfern, and Jeremy Roxbee Cox. Oxford: Oxford University Press, 2001.

Walton, Kendall L. *Mimesis As Make-Believe: On the Foundations of the Representational Arts.* Cambridge, Mass.: Harvard University Press, 1990.

Wollheim, Richard. *Art and Its Objects: With Six Supplementary Essays.* Cambridge, U.K.: Cambridge University Press, 1980.

Peter Lamarque

AFRICA, IDEA OF. The idea of "Africa" is an exceedingly complex one with multiple genealogies and meanings, which make any extrapolations of "African" identity in the singular or plural, any explorations of what makes Africa "Africa," quite difficult. Both Africans and non-Africans have conceived "Africa" differently in various historical and geographical contexts, especially in contemporary times. The descriptions, meanings, images, and discourses of Africa have changed over time as the continent's boundaries—geographical, historical, cultural, and representational—have shifted according to the prevailing conceptions and configurations of global racial identities and power, and African nationalism, including Pan-Africanism. At the beginning of the twenty-first century, the maps and meanings of "Africa" and "Africanness" are being reconfigured by both the processes of contemporary globalization and the projects of African integration.

Discourses about the "idea of Africa" can be framed in various ways. One common approach is to distinguish between Eurocentric and Afrocentric paradigms, between ideas and conceptions of what constitutes "Africa" derived from European as opposed to African perspectives. The difficulty with this method is that it assumes homogeneity within each paradigm and it inscribes an epistemic division between the two approaches that are otherwise deeply implicated with each other. There are other possible typological or taxonomic descriptions of Africa. One can think of religious, ecological, linguistic, and even ethnic taxonomies. This article has chosen four typologies that seem best able to capture a wide range of constructions of Africa: the racial, representational, geographic, and historical conceptions. As with the Eurocentric–Afrocentric dichotomy, there are no discursive Chinese walls separating the four typologies, nor do they exhaust other possible categorizations, but they do have heuristic value.

Origins of the Name *Africa*

The historical origins of the name *Africa* are in dispute. At least seven origins have been suggested: (1) it is a Roman name for what the Greeks called "Libya," itself perhaps a Latinization of the name of the Berber tribe Aourigha (perhaps pronounced "Afarika"); (2) it is derived from two Phoenician terms either referring to corn or fruit (*pharika*), meaning land of corn or fruit; (3) it comes from a Phoenician root *faraqa,* meaning separation or diaspora; a similar root is apparently found in some African languages such as Bambara; (4) it is drawn from the Latin adjective *aprica* (sunny) or the Greek *aprikē* (free from cold); (5) it might even stem from Sanskrit and Hindi in which the root *Apara* or *Africa* denotes that which, in geographical terms, comes "after"—to the west—in which case Africa is the western continent; (6) it is the name of a Yemenite chief named Africus who invaded North Africa in the second millennium B.C.E. and founded a town called Afrikyah; or (7) it springs from "Afer" who was a grandson of Abraham and a companion of Hercules (Ki-Zerbo; Spivak).

Clearly, there is little agreement on the sources and original meanings of the word *Africa.* The foreignness of the name once prompted Wole Soyinka to demand that it be dropped, and as an act of self-definition he proposed the adoption of terms for *Africa* and *African* rooted in an indigenous language, preferably *Abibirim* and *Abibiman* from Akan. It appears the term *Africa* was used widely from Roman times to refer initially to North Africa, originally called by the Greek or Egyptian word *Libya,* before it was extended to the whole continent from the end of the first century of the common era. The Arabic term *Ifriqiya* most probably represents a transliteration of the word *Africa.* In this sense, then, Africa was a European construct—as much as Europe itself was a construct inflicted by the idea of Africa (and Asia)—whose cartographic application was both gradual and contradictory in that as the name embraced the rest of the continent it increasingly came to be divorced from its original North African coding and became increasingly confined to the regions referred to in Eurocentric and sometimes Afrocentric conceptual mapping as "sub-Saharan Africa," seen as the pristine locus of the "real" Africa or what the German philosopher Georg Wilhelm Friedrich Hegel (1770–1831) called "Africa proper."

The divorce of North Africa may have started with the Arab invasions of the region in the seventh century, but got its epistemic and ideological imprimatur with the emergence of Eurocentrism following the rise of modern Europe, which for Africa entailed, initially and destructively, the Atlantic slave trade, out of which came the forced migration—the largest in human history—of millions of Africans and the formation of African diasporas in the Americas, diasporas that appropriated and popularized the name Africa and through whom Africa became increasingly racialized. For example, the adoption of "black" as the preferred name of African-Americans from the 1960s, in place of "Negro," simply reinforced the relabeling of Africa as "black," a tag that simultaneously rejected and reinscribed the old pejorative appellation of the "dark continent." For the French, *Afrique noire* served to distinguish the west and central African colonies from the fictive overseas provinces of metropolitan France in North Africa, especially Algeria.

Far less clear is when the appropriation of Africa, as a self-defining identity, occurred in the various regions and among the innumerable societies that make up this vast continent, the second largest in the world. Such an archaeological project has not been undertaken, partly because it is a daunting task to untangle the interpellations and intersections of political and cultural identities for Africa's peoples—ethnic, national, continental, and global—and partly because African intellectuals, whether nationalist or postcolonial, have been preoccupied with denouncing or deconstructing Eurocentrism.

The Racialization of Africa

The conflation of Africa with "sub-Saharan Africa," "Africa south of the Sahara" or "Black Africa" so common in discourses about Africa, within and without the continent, ultimately offers us a racialized view of Africa, Africa as the "black" continent. It rests on the metaphysics of difference, a quest for the civilizational and cultural ontology of blackness. For Georg Wilhelm Friedrich Hegel (1770–1831) and his descendants, as Olufemi Taiwo calls purveyors of contemporary Eurocentrism, Africa is the ultimate "undeveloped, unhistorical" other of Europe. Hegel's "Africa proper" is, in his words, the "land of childhood," from which North Africa and especially Egypt is excised and attached to Europe, and where history, philosophy, and culture are "enveloped in the dark mantle of night" because its inhabitants, "the Negro exhibits the natural man in his completely wild and untamed state" (Hegel, pp. 91, 93).

Hegel's ghost still stalks African studies and definitions of Africa. According to some this fragmentation of Africa in African studies has been unproductive intellectually, leaving aside its ideological motivations and effects. To quote John Hunwick:

> The compartmentalization of Africa into zones that are treated as 'Middle East' and 'Africa' is a legacy of Orientalism and colonialism. North Africa, including Egypt, is usually seen as forming part of the Middle East, though Middle East experts are not generally keen to venture farther west than the confines of Egypt. Northwestern Africa—the Maghreb—is generally regarded as peripheral to Middle Eastern Studies and extraneous to African studies. Even the Sahara has been generally viewed as something of a no-go area (especially among anglophone scholars), while the Sudan and Mauritania (which are impossible to label as either 'sub-Saharan' or 'Middle Eastern') remain in limbo. Northwestern Africa (from Morocco to Libya), despite the area's close and enduring relationship with West Africa, has been excluded from the concerns of most Africanists. (p. xiii)

This truncated characterization and racialization of Africa is of course not confined to Western scholars. Many African scholars also subscribe to it, as is so evident from their publications on Africa that often omit North Africa. Unlike Hegel and the Eurocentrists, however, African scholars seek to invest, not divest, sub-Saharan Africa with history and intellectual agency. The epistemological fixation with black Africa is so insidious that few remark on it, and when they do they tend to invoke cultural unity for sub-Saharan Africa in which "culture" largely serves as a proxy for race given the fact of cultural diversities within sub-Saharan Africa itself and the cultural affinities between some societies in this region, say the Sahel, with those of North Africa. Take language and religion, two critical attributes of culture: historically the Hausa of West Africa had more in common with their Berber and Arab neighbors to the North than with the Zulu of South Africa. The former traded with each other for centuries, shared religion (Islam) and a script (Arabic), and their languages are part of the Afro-Asiatic family. But this familiar material, moral, and mental universe does not count in the ontology of Africanness confined to the sub-Saharan region.

The separation of North Africa is sometimes based on the question of consciousness and self-representation. It is said people in North Africa perceive themselves to be part of the Arab world and therefore should not be considered a part of Africa. This ignores the simple fact that the vast majority of Arabs actually live in Africa, so that at a minimum Africa has to be considered an Afro-Arab continent. There is no doubt that North Africans have multiple identities and extracontinental affiliations, but so do people in so-called sub-Saharan Africa—ethnic, national, religious, gender, sexual, racial, and so on—in which the identity "African" may not be the primary one. Indeed, the African diaspora was African long before the communities they left behind on the continent developed a consciousness of being African.

Behind these conflicting definitions of Africa, about which regions to include and exclude, lie complex ideological and historical processes that need to be taken into account, for example, the relative decline from the sixteenth century of the trans-Saharan economy following the rise of the Atlantic economy. Another powerful development setting North and West Africa apart, it has been suggested, was the development of an autonomous Sufi Saharan/Sahelian Islam, independent from the North African impulse. Even more crucial, for our purposes, is the need to distinguish between historical knowledge on the one hand, and ideas or imaginings of Africa as intellectual and ideological projects on the other and to ask: who is defining Africa and for what purpose, whose ideas and imaginings predominate, and why? In this regard, it is important to underline the role of institutions from academic institutions to international organizations in this endeavor, to examine both scholarly and popular ideas of Africa and their discursive, spatial, and temporal articulations.

Adebayo Olukoshi and Francis Nyamnjoh remind us that to most ordinary people in Africa, to be African goes beyond making ontological, let alone epistemological, claims. It is a complex and constantly changing and challenging existential and ethical reality.

For the masses of Africans, Africa is above all a lived reality, one that is constantly shaped and reshaped by their toil and sweat as subjected and devalued humanity, even as they struggle to live in dignity and to transform their societies progressively. For these people, the fact of their Africanity is neither in question nor a question. And the least they would expect from concerned scholars is to refrain from adding onto their burdens in the name of a type of scholarship which, in being ahistorical, also trivializes their collective experiences and memories (pp. 1–2).

Representational Discourses of Africa

The notion that there is no racial essence that characterizes Africa and Africans because identities are socially constructed or invented and constantly changing has been the central message of scholars using postcolonial theory. V. Y. Mudimbe's seminal work has sought to map out this discursive process. In *The Invention of Africa* (1988), he interrogates the construction of Africa through Eurocentric categories and conceptual systems, from anthropology and missionary discourses to philosophy, an order of knowledge constituted in the sociohistorical context of colonialism, which produced enduring dichotomies between Europe and Africa, investing the latter's societies, cultures, and bodies with the representational marginalities or even pathologies of alterity (otherness).

In *The Idea of Africa* (1994), he seeks to demonstrate that conquering Western narratives, beginning with Greek stories about Africa, through the colonial library to contemporary postmodernist discourses, have radically silenced or converted African discourses. African intellectuals, he argues, have been reacting to this ethnocentric epistemological order, itself subject to the mutations of Western material, methodological, and moral grids, with varying degrees of epistemic domestication and defiance, in the process of which Africa's identity and difference have been affirmed, denied, inverted, and reconstituted.

For some thinkers one of the most important aspects of Africa's representation lies not in its invention per se, a phenomenon that is by no means confined to the continent, but in the fact that Africa is always represented and performed as a reality or a fiction in relation to something else, mostly Europe (white); Africa is always the Dark Continent (black). The question is precisely what makes the representation of Africa so distinctive and different from the representation of other continents: it is that Africa is always represented and imagined, in ways that Asia, for example, is not necessarily, in relation to master references—Europe, whiteness, Christianity, literacy, development, technology (the comparative and colonizing tropes mutate continuously)—mirrors that reflect, indeed refract Africa in peculiar ways, reducing the continent to particular (negative) images of "lack" and "becoming," lacking and becoming "Europe." In short, Africa more than any other continent is the quintessential representational other of Europe; from the moment (historically understood) that the two continents became entangled with each other, the grammar of their self-definitions became distorted mirror images of the other.

From this angle it can be seen why Eurocentric and Afrocentric representations of Africa are so deeply implicated with each other, why the inclusion or exclusion of North Africa is so crucial to both of them, why their discursive possessiveness centers on Egypt. At stake is the civilizing authority and antiquity of Africa. The contemporary debate about the Africanness, and for some the "blackness," of ancient Egypt was launched by Cheikh Anta Diop's provocative book, *The African Origin of Civilization: Myth or Reality* (1974). Afrocentric scholars in the United States led by African American scholar Molefi Asante, who coined the term *Afrocentricity*, picked up and popularized Diop's ideas.

But it was not until a European American scholar, Martin Bernal, published his tome *Black Athena* (1987, 1991), affirming the "blackness" of the ancient Egyptians and their enormous contributions to Greek civilization—the cradle of Western civilization—that Afrocentric claims received attention in the mainstream American and international academic media. Among those who were outraged was the classicist Mary Lefkowitz who vehemently attacked Bernal and the Afrocentric movement as a whole for its alleged "myths."

For many African scholars the debate about the race of the ancient Egyptians seemed rooted more in American preoccupations with race than African history as such. To some of them blackness is less about race and more about representation, a sign not of submission to the Hegelian and colonialist schema of inferior difference, but of subversion and struggle against it. They see black identity as the result of political, social, and cultural negotiations, cooperation, transactions, differences between self and the other that goes beyond skin color; it is about the common experience of pain, exploitation, and suffering shared by an oppressed people and is deployed as a powerful symbol of subversion, struggle, and self-affirmation. It was in this sense that the term *black* was extended to "coloreds" (people of mixed race, Indians, and people of Asian descent) in South Africa in the 1970s and 1980s, and used to refer to people of African and Asian descent in Britain.

Others denounce the use of *race* altogether as a biological determinism that should have no place in Africanist scholarship while affirming the possibilities of (forging) a common African identity. Kwame Anthony Appiah is perhaps the most renowned proponent of this critique in his book *In My Father's House* (1992). Appiah is unsparing in his attack on the dangerous fictions of race and racialist thinking and takes direct aim at some of the icons of Pan-Africanism, including W. E. B. Dubois (1868–1963). He seeks to demolish essentialist conceptions of Africa and demonstrate that Africa is not a primordial fixture, but an invented reality, and Africans are not molded from the same clay of racial and cultural homogeneity. This is a celebration of the diversity, complexity, richness, hybridity, and contingency of African identities and social and cultural life, mounted to challenge the totalizing narratives of both African nationalism and European imperialism with their dualistic and polarized representations of Africa and African identities and culture.

Critics of Appiah and Mudimbe and other postcolonial and postmodern African scholars such as Achille Mbembe, who also dismiss "nationalist" or what they sometimes refer to as "nativist" definitions of African identities, have pointed out that despite these writers' celebratory analyses of the plurality and social construction of African identities, their work is not always sufficiently historicized and is trapped in the "colonial library"—Western episteme—and virtually ignores the "Islamic library"—African writings in Arabic and Arabic script—which would radically shift their conceptions of African thought and ideas of self-representation.

These shortcomings are readily evident in Appiah's book, for example, when he compares the different roles of religion and the modes of thought in what he calls the traditional oral cultures of Africa and the industrialized literate cultures of the West. The comparisons drip with a fundamental tension rooted in a binary conception of African "orality" and European "literacy." This is a problematic formulation, not only because he draws his African examples largely from one culture, Asante, but the conflation of orality with Africa and literacy with Europe is simply false if the "Islamic library" is taken into account. Also, the framing of "traditional" Africa versus "modern" Europe locks both Africa and Europe in a temporal binary that effectively dehistoricizes each. The irony, then, is that despite his best intentions Appiah ends up with an essentialized Africa with an ontological essence—lacking the supposedly European attributes of literacy—and a racialized one as well in that his analysis is confined to sub-Saharan Africa.

Geographical Conceptions of Africa

If we dispense with the racial conceptions of Africa, we are left with geographical and historical notions, Africa as a spatio-temporal construct that is at once a process, product, and a project of a complex and contradictory historical geography. The concept of historical geography, sitting at the intersection of two disciplines, has allowed scholars to combine the spatial and temporal interests of geography and history, to understand that the physical environment and human agency are mutually constitutive, that people's creativity and thought produce places as much as places produce people's cultures and identities, in short, that landscapes are not only important aspects of culture, they are products of historical processes.

Whereas nobody denies that a geographical entity called "Africa" exists, for some this is merely a cartographic reality not a cultural one, an exercise in mapping devoid of experiential meaning for the peoples that have lived within the continent's porous borders. They would be right, some contend, if the argument were that Africa's peoples have always been conscious of living in a place called "Africa." Clearly, they have not, no more than people who in the twenty-first century are called "Asians" or "Europeans" have always had such a spatial consciousness. Historically, local spatial identities, encapsulated and articulated in ethnic, regional, and national terms, have been far more important, while broader (continental) spatial imaginaries have tended to develop as the processes of globalization, understood here to mean the expanding circuits of transregional connectedness, have grown in extensity and intensity.

Thus, in Africa, as elsewhere in the world, there is a hierarchy of spatial identities that are interwoven and interactive in complex ways engendering multiple cultural identities. Space and the spatial stage contextualize cultures, economies,

and politics, and invent and inscribe places and landscapes with ethical, symbolic, and aesthetic meanings. "'Space' is created," argues Doreen Massey, "out of the vast intricacies, the incredible complexities, of the interlocking and the non-interlocking, and the networks of relations at every scale from local to global" (pp. 155–156). Space, then, is not a static and passive template of social existence, but an active, constitutive force of the social's very composition and construction.

Seen in this way, then, the multiple mappings of Africa are indeed to be expected. The numerous peoples and societies that have carved out a place of their own across this vast continent have, in a sense, been creating their little Africas, each laying their bricks of African identity across the huge and intricate cartographic, cognitive, and cultural construct known as "Africa." Therefore, a geographical conception of Africa does not need the existence of racial solidarity or the invention of cultural homogeneity. But this is not an empty cartographic vessel either in so far as the diverse cultures and identities that have emerged and have yet to emerge have been and will continue to be shaped by the mapping and materiality of Africa as an ever changing spatial entity and social construct.

The map of Africa, as with all maps, entails many things. Maps are not simply representations of the geographical world. A map is, as David Woodward and Malcom Lewis argue in their massive global history of cartography, simultaneously a cognitive system, a material culture, and a social construction. They speak of "cognitive or mental cartography," "performance or ritual cartography," and "material or artifactual cartography." Recent studies on indigenous cartography in Africa demonstrate that all three have been employed by Africa's various peoples to map, name, and claim their landscapes, stretched over varying scales of expansiveness.

In the nineteenth century, many European explorers solicited and used some of these maps to produce their own maps, which shows cross-cultural intelligibility between African and European maps. To quote Thomas Bassett: "Notwithstanding broad epistemological divides separating Europeans from various African cultural groups, it appears Europeans had little difficulty in reading these maps. Solicited maps demonstrate that Africans had the spatial competence and requisite sign systems to produce maps spontaneously. . . . Indeed, there is evidence that [these] maps were influential in shaping the form and content of European maps of the continent" (p. 37).

Quite clearly African maps influenced European mapmaking in the nineteenth and twentieth centuries in several ways. They enabled European explorers to construct or correct their maps, and were essential for topological determinations, and place-names, which were widely transcribed onto European maps. In turn, European influences also became increasingly discernible in African mapmaking in terms of the materials used, the northerly orientation of some maps (e.g., Ras Makonnen's famous map of Ethiopia of 1899), and the methods employed in their construction (e.g., Cameroonian King Njoya's topographic survey from 1912 to 1916).

For more than fifteen hundred years maps of Africa produced in northern Africa, southern Europe, and western Asia had reproduced the maps made by Ptolemy in Alexandria in the second century B.C.E., only "altering them slightly to suit their needs" (Mbodji, p. 44). The creation of new and more accurate maps of continental Africa began with the emergence of "scientific" cartography and the beginnings of European global voyages and conquests in the fifteenth and sixteenth centuries, although it was not until the mid-nineteenth century that the broad external and internal contours of the continent were finally filled out as we know them today. The European mapping of Africa was implicated with imperialism both directly and indirectly, directly in that mapmaking facilitated the voyages of exploration and colonization, and indirectly insofar as it was part of the ideological architecture of inscribing European nationalisms at home and forging collective European grandeur globally: from Gerardus Mercator's (1512–1594) projection, still widely used in the twenty-first century, tiny Europe was inflated in size and massive Africa was dwarfed. It was almost as if Africa's civilizational diminution had to be accompanied by a cartographic one.

Upon this shriveled "blank darkness" Europe sought to write its cartographic and epistemic will by dividing the continent into colonies, themselves further splintered into allegedly primordial and antagonistic ethnic enclaves, a cognitive mapping sanctioned by the structuralist-functionalist paradigms of anthropology, the premier colonial science. But against the "tribalization" of Africa and African cultures and identities by the colonial administration and colonial anthropology, which were contested by local circuits of exchange, movement, and interaction so that borders served not simply as points of separation and struggle but often as places of convocation and conviviality, there emerged the countervailing elite paradigms, politics and projections of Pan-Africanism, the progenitor of the numerous territorial nationalisms in Africa.

As an ideological, intellectual, and institutional formation Pan-Africanism embodied within itself conflicting tendencies and imaginaries of Africa, premised on racial, spatial, and ideological constructs. While there always existed different versions of Pan-Africanism premised on diverse spatial conceptions of Africa (for example, trans-Atlantic Pan-Africanism embraced the African diaspora in the Americas), the one that received lasting institutional expression for independent African states was continental Pan-Africanism, which was sanctified in 1963 with the formation of the Organization of African Unity (OAU). In 2001 the African Union (AU), a more ambitious project of continental unification, succeeded the OAU.

The formation of the OAU and later the AU entailed a remapping of Africa, the creation and consumption of new national, regional, and continental maps that were produced, performed, and internalized everywhere from schools, the media, and academic and political conferences, to international forums where regional blocs assumed representational identities. In short, "Africa" the map and the place was becoming increasingly "Africa" the idea and the consciousness, buttressed by an intricate web of hundreds of continental institutions covering an ever expanding range of spheres from politics, the economy, environment, health, education, and culture, to technical cooperation and the prosaic world of leisure involving competitive games and sports and forms of popular entertainment.

By the beginning of the twenty-first century, "Africa" was perhaps more "African" than it had ever been in its history, that is to say, more interconnected through licit and illicit flows of commodities, capital, ideas, and people, not to mention multilateral conflicts and ecological and health panics, and more conscious of its collective identity in the global panorama and hierarchy of regional identities. The historical geography of Africa had been stretched and deepened despite, on the one hand the centrifugal push of spatial and social identities within the continent itself (some of which degenerated into destructive conflicts including civil wars, massive migrations, and state collapse), and on the other the centripetal pull of contemporary globalization and its "glocalization" effects—its tendency to simultaneously internationalize and localize identities and cultures—and the enduring seductions of extracontinental alliances for some regions and countries.

Historical Conceptions of Africa

From the discussion above it is evident that Africa and African identities can be conceived both as states of being and of becoming. In other words, "Africa" is a dynamic historical process, a messy spatio-temporal configuration of agency, structure, and contextuality that is subject to change, which is not always easy to perceive or predict. Africa, in this sense, has emerged out of the complex histories of the continent's peoples. Indeed, African historians have been in the forefront of constructing Africa as a coherent and complex object of study, investing the continent with a distinctive civilizational identity. They were among the first to take up the Eurocentric lie that Africa was a continent and Africans were a people "without history," an indictment intended to devalue their humanity.

The pivotal and central role of historians is precisely to propose a space, an axis to locate and make sense of the human experience, politically, socially, culturally, and economically. Needless to say, there are different types of African historians in terms of their training and institutional locations and methodological and theoretical orientations. Academic historians compete with "traditional" and popular historians in public historical discourse, so that there are continuous contestations about space, communities, and histories. But academic historians have tended to dominate in the production of the history of the postcolonial nation and the continental imaginary called Africa.

Once the dominant tendency was to produce linear and celebratory narratives of the nation and the continent, in which colonialism was reduced to a parenthesis or an episode, then the various subalterns wearing the identities of class, gender, or generation joined the historians' parade, before the postal turn (poststructural, postmodern, and postcolonial theories) that sought to reveal the fictionality of the whole enterprise, that the past is largely imagined, constructed, or invented. The better historians had always seen and constructed history as a series of messy, multiple, complex, and often conflicting processes and discourses about the past, produced simultaneously at local, national, and transnational levels, themselves connected and constructed in intricate and contradictory and ever changing ways.

By the end of the twentieth century, academic historians had produced a phenomenal amount of scholarship, invented and refined methodologies of research, and excavated the histories of African polities, societies, economies, cultures, and environments from the onerous weight of Eurocentric derision and Afrocentric romanticism. The publication of the UNESCO (1981–1993) and Cambridge (1977–1985) histories of Africa marked the apotheosis of this spectacular scholarly achievement. To be sure, there is much one can criticize about African historiography methodologically and theoretically, but the fact remains historians have written extensively on the development and invention of African cultural traditions and identities over time that make it possible to research, write, and teach about "African" history as a distinctive field, even if complexly connected to other histories, especially of "Europe."

Despite their prodigious production since independence, African historians, not to mention scholars from other disciplines, have not generally been anxious to propose the defining characteristics of Africa, the essential elements that constitute its development as an idea and a historical geography. The most renowned model is the one proposed by Ali Mazrui, the notion of the "triple heritage," that the African world is constituted by the confluence of three civilizations: the indigenous (traditional), Western (Christianity), and Arabic (Islam).

The three forces apparently exhibit enormous variations in their spatial and temporal manifestations, some are more dominant in certain regions, countries, and societies, and one could add here among certain classes and genders and at certain times, than in others. But the journey in Mazrui's gnosis seems not to be toward the harmonious and universal synthesis of the Negritude writers and philosophers, who posited a duality between Africa and Europe, reason and emotion, materialism and morality, humanity and nature, out of whose dialectical encounters and reconciliation a universal civilization would be forged. Rather it is toward a triumphant resurgence and reclamation of Africa's cultural spaces by tradition and Islam.

Mazrui did not invent the trilateralist view of Africa and its cultures and identities, that contemporary Africa contained an allegedly uneasy mixture of traditional, Western, and Islamic values and practices. The idea can be traced back to the 1887 work of Edward Blyden (1832–1912), the great nineteenth-century Liberian intellectual, for whom the modern "African personality," as he called it, was formed and would flourish out of the organic integration of the best elements from indigenous culture, Islam, and European science and Christianity. Kwame Nkrumah (1909–1972), the Pan-African activist and intellectual and Ghana's first president, elaborated on Blyden's notion of the "African personality" in his concept of conscientism, a cultural and cognitive synthesis between the humanistic and socialist ethos of "traditional" Africa, the acquisitive capitalist values and redemptive Christian hopes of the "West," and the holistic secular and spiritual precepts of Islam. Forged out of this crucible, the "African personality"

would emerge, modern, assured, and liberated, ready to take its rightful place in the world.

Nkrumah has been faulted for not giving the traditional and Islamic legacies the kind of serious analysis accorded the Western one in his book *Consciencism* (1964). Part of some critics' unease with Nkrumah's schema is based on doubts that there indeed exists an exclusive and distinctive African traditional culture or a homogeneous African cultural universe. The same critique has been leveled against Mazrui, who has been attacked for what some regard as his evident partiality to Islam as the more benevolent force than the European-Christian and indigenous parts of the triad. In his withering critique of Mazrui's television series, *The Africans: A Triple Heritage,* Soyinka accused Mazrui of denigrating indigenous religions and cultures, a charge Mazrui vigorously denied (Mazrui and Mutunga).

The Mazrui-Soyinka debate over Mazrui's television series underscores the unresolved issues and stakes in contemporary definitions of Africa and Africanness. As noted with reference to Appiah above, both Soyinka and Mazrui do not historicize the moral, societal, and cultural values that constitute African identities. Their ethnographic notions of tradition are problematic; they ignore the sedimentations of exchanges, adaptations, inventions, and changes that the traditions in question, whether seen positively or negatively, have undergone. Often forgotten in these debates are several basic questions, such as how foreign, indeed, are Christianity and Islam to Africa, if we can restrict ourselves to the religious dimensions of the triple heritage for a moment. As histories of both religions clearly indicate, Christianity and Islam were implanted in certain parts of Africa almost at their inception and Africans made significant doctrinal contributions to both religions long before they were introduced to many parts of Europe and Asia where they are considered "indigenous," "traditional," or at least their "foreign" pedigree is not always emphasized.

This is to suggest that while the notion of the "triple heritage" highlights the diverse sources of African identities and cultures and seeks to clarify the complex streams that have flowed into their making, it flirts with an essentialized and almost ahistorical notion of a primordial Africa, a "real Africa," that somehow exists alongside external cultural diffusions, a narrative that is quite reminiscent of the misguided searches for a Hegelian "Africa proper." The inadequacies of the Blyden-Nkrumah-Mazrui cultural typologies do not mean that all attempts at creating such schemas are mistaken or doomed. Typologies or conceptual categories are essential to intellectual analysis; they are intended to clarify complex social phenomena. Difficulties often arise when the categories cease to be explanatory devices sensitive to human agency, social structure, and spatiotemporal contexts and begin to wallow in their own transcendental magnificence.

Conclusion

It is quite evident that there is no agreement on what "Africa" means, let alone how to define African identities beyond what can only be provisional and partial conceptualizations and categorizations. Yet, we all believe we know what "Africa" is, what it must be, but when we think we have finally seen it, felt it, touched it, captured and tamed it with our terms of endearment, aversion, or indifference it suddenly melts away into a mirage beyond the assured and unilateral classifications of race, representation, geography, or history. Perhaps wisdom lies in accepting the simple proposition that Africa is indeed many things, a mélange of peoples, places, practices, processes, projects, and possibilities that are both unique and common in their configuration over time and space.

Africa is, in short, a critical site of the human drama, the original homeland, as modern archaeology and genetics tell us, of humanity and it continues to be the continent that hundreds of millions of people in all their marvelous and sometimes bewildering complexities, colors, and cultures still call home. Who can claim the right to divine who belongs or does not belong to its porous boundaries and the histories and memories etched on and eked out of its variegated landscapes? The idea of "Africa," it would seem, will continue to elude any definitive conceptualization that is premised on exclusive claims of race, geography, or history because it is a phenomenon that is always in a state of becoming.

See also **Afrocentricity; Afropessimism; Authenticity: Africa; Ethnicity and Race; Ethnocentrism; Eurocentrism; Europe, Idea of; Maps and The Ideas They Express; Multiculturalism, Africa; Other, The, European Views of; Pan-Africanism.**

BIBLIOGRAPHY

Amin, Samir. *Eurocentricism.* Translated by Russell Moore. New York: Monthly Press, 1989.

Appiah, Kwame Anthony. *In My Father's House. Africa in the Philosophy of Culture.* New York: Oxford University Press, 1992.

Asante, Molefi Kete. *The Afrocentric Idea.* Philadelphia: Temple University Press, 1987.

———. *Afrocentricity: The Theory of Social Change.* Rev. ed. Trenton, N.J.: Africa World Press, 1988.

Bassett, Thomas J. "Indigenous Mapmaking in Intertropical Africa." In *The History of Cartography: Cartography in the Traditional African, American, Arctic, Australian, and Pacific Societies,* edited by David Woodward and G. Malcolm Lewis, 24–48. Vol. 2, Book 3. Chicago and London: University of Chicago Press, 1998.

Bernal, Martin. *Black Athena: The Afroasiatic Roots of Classical Civilization.* 2 vols. New Brunswick, N.J.: Rutgers University Press, 1987–1991.

Blyden, Edward Wilmot. *Christianity, Islam and the Negro Race.* 1887. Reprint, Edinburgh: Edinburgh University Press, 1967.

Curtin, Philip D. *The Image of Africa: British Ideas and Action, 1780–1850.* Madison: University of Wisconsin Press, 1964.

Diop, Cheikh Anta. *The African Origin of Civilization: Myth or Reality.* Translated by Mercer Cook. Chicago: L. Hill, 1974.

Fage, J. D., and Roland Olivier, eds. *Cambridge History of Africa.* Cambridge, U.K., and New York: Cambridge University Press, 1977–1985.

Falola, Toyin, and Christian Jennings, eds. *Africanizing Knowledge: African Studies Across the Disciplines.* New Brunswick, N.J.: Transaction, 2002.

Gyekye, Kwame. *Tradition and Modernity: Philosophical reflections on the African Experience.* New York: Oxford University Press, 1997.

Hansberry, William Leo. *Africa and Africans as Seen by Classical Writers.* Edited by Joseph E. Harris. Washington, D.C.: Howard University Press, 1977.

Hegel, G. W. F. *The Philosophy of History.* Translated by S. Sibree. New York: Dover, 1956.

Hunwick, John. "The Same But Different: Africans in Slavery in the Mediterranean Muslim World." In *The African Diaspora in the Mediterranean Lands of Islam,* edited by John Hunwick and Eve Trout Powell, ix–xxiv. Princeton, N.J.: Markus Wiener, 2002.

Ki-Zerbo, Joseph. "General Introduction." In *General History of Africa,* edited by J. Ki-Zerbo. Vol. 1: *Methodology and African Prehistory.* London: Heinemann, 1981.

Lefkowitz, Mary. *Not Out of Africa: How Afrocentrism became an Excuse to Teach Myth as History.* New York: Basic Books, 1996.

Massey, Doreen. "Politics and Space/Time." In *Place and the Politics of Identity,* edited by Michael Keith and Steve Pile. London and New York: Routledge, 1993.

Mazrui, Alamin M., and Willy M. Mutunga. *Debating the African Condition: Ali Mazrui and His Critics.* Vol. 1. Trenton, N.J.: Africa World Press, 2003.

Mazrui, Ali A. *The Africans: A Triple Heritage.* Boston: Little, Brown, 1986.

Mbembe, Achille. *On the Postcolony.* Berkeley: University of California Press, 2001.

Mbodji, Mohammed. "'Sop Geographers in Africa Maps with Savage Pictures Fill Their Gaps': Representing Africa in Maps." In *Contested Terrains and Constructed Categories: Contemporary Africa in Focus,* edited by George Clement Bond and Nigel C. Gibson, 37–58. Boulder, Colo., and Oxford: Westview: 2002.

Miller, Joseph C. "History and Africa/Africa and History." *The American Historical Review* 104, no. 1 (1999): 1–32.

Mudimbe, V. Y. *The Idea of Africa.* Bloomington and Indianapolis: Indiana University Press, 1994.

———. *The Invention of Africa: Gnosis, Philosophy, and the Order of Knowledge.* Bloomington: Indiana University Press, 1988.

Nkrumah, Kwame. *Consciencism: Philosophy and Ideology for Decolonization with Particular Reference to the African Revolution.* New York: Monthly Review Press, 1964.

Olukoshi, Adebayo, and Francis Nyamnjoh. "Editorial." *CODESRIA Bulletin* nos. 1–2 (2004): 1–2.

Said, Edward W. *Orientalism.* New York: Pantheon, 1978.

Soyinka, Wole. "The Scholar in African Society." In *Second World Black and African Festival of the Arts and Culture. Colloquium on Black Civilization and Education. Colloquium Proceedings,* edited by A. U. Iwara and E. Mveng, 44–53. Vol. 1. Lagos: Federal Government of Nigeria, 1977.

Spivak, Gayatri. "Theory in the Margin: Coetzee's *Foe* Reading Defoe's *Crusoe/Roxana.* In *Consequences of Theory,* edited by Jonathan Arac and Barbara Johnson. Baltimore: Johns Hopkins University Press, 1991.

Taiwo, Olufemi. "Exorcizing Hegel's Ghost: Africa's Challenge to Philosophy." *African Studies Quarterly* 1, no. 4 (1997). Available on the Internet at *http://web.africa.ufl.edu/asq/.*

UNESCO General History of Africa. Vols. 1–8. London: Heinemann, 1981–1993.

Woodward, David, and G. Malcolm Lewis. "Introduction." In *Cartography in the Traditional African, American, Arctic,*

Australian, and Pacific Societies, edited by David Woodward and G. Malcolm Lewis, 1–10. Vol. 2, Book 3. Chicago and London: University of Chicago Press, 1988.

Zeleza, Paul Tiyambe. *Manufacturing African Studies and Crises.* Dakar, Senegal: Codesria Book Series, 1997.

Paul Tiyambe Zeleza

AFRICAN-AMERICAN IDEAS. For four hundred years, African-Americans have been engaged in a fierce struggle, a struggle for freedom, justice and equality, empowerment and self-determination, or social transformation, depending on one's ideology and its discourses. The lived African-American experience, in its class, gender, generational, and regional specificity, and the struggle against black racial oppression in the form of black social movements, are the soil from which African-American political and social thought are produced. Different social movements—abolition, the nineteenth-century Great Black March West (1879–1910), the protective leagues during the nadir (1877–1917), the New Negro Movement of the early 1900s, the Depression-era struggles, and the civil rights and black power movements of the 1960s—have developed distinct goals and objectives and consequently have evolved quite different strategies, ideologies, and discourses. Contrary to popular opinion, African-American political thought has always been a roiling sea of competing ideological currents. Political scientist Robert C. Smith described ideology as "the enduring dilemma of black politics" because of its variety and vibrancy. The tradition of viewing African-American history through the lens of historical debate underscores the diverse and dynamic character of African-American political discourse. For instance, it is popular to compare and contrast the ideas of Frederick Douglass (1817–1895) and Martin R. Delany (1812–1885), W. E. B. DuBois (1868–1963) and Booker T. Washington (1856–1915), and Marcus Garvey (1887–1940), Ida Wells-Barrett (1862–1931) and Margaret Murray Washington (1863–1953) or, more recently, Martin Luther King (1929–1968) and Malcolm X (1925–1965).

In the popular imagination, African-American political thought has been reduced to two ideological streams, black nationalism and integrationism. Harold Cruse, author of the influential but flawed *Crisis of the Negro Intellectual,* crystallized this binary framework into a Manichean perspective that characterized African-American history as primarily a conflict between proponents of these two ideologies. Cruse did not invent this conceptualization—August Meier had previously asserted it—but he made it the dominant interpretative schema in black political philosophy.

The binary framework has been challenged on two fundamental premises. One group has sought to complicate the categories of black ideologies. Anthropologist Leith Mullings, historian Manning Marable, and political scientists Robert C. Smith and Michael C. Dawson, among others, have offered more comprehensive frameworks. Adding radicalism to nationalism and integrationism, Smith conceives of three major African-American ideologies: black nationalism, integrationism, and radicalism. Mullings and Marable discern three "strategic

visions" in black political thought, which they term *inclusion, black nationalism,* and *transformation.* Interestingly, Mullings, Marable, and Smith would acknowledge conservatism as a distinct political perspective; yet, because they do not view it as politically salient before the 1990s, they have not conceptualized it as a major ideology among African-Americans. Dawson's framework, in contrast, includes black conservatism among the six "historically important" black ideologies he identifies: black nationalism, black liberalism, including three streams, black feminism, and black radicalism.

Taking a very different approach, sociologist John Brown Childs eschews the conventional debates over ideology to identify two worldviews, which he argues constitute the "coherent systematic approach" that undergirds political ideologies. Seeking to uncover the "conceptual currents" beneath strategic conflicts among social justice activists, Childs identifies two irreconcilable worldviews, the vanguard and mutuality perspectives. According to Childs, vanguard approaches posit an elite that possesses knowledge of the "way," which they bestow upon the ignorant and impose on the defiant. In contrast, mutuality approaches advocate praxis built on sociohistorical correspondence, communication, diversity, cooperation, (self-) transformation, and openness, and reject notions of a leading group. Despite the potency of Brown's insights, most scholars of black history and politics have continued to chart African-American social movements and individual activist intellectuals via their ideologies, rather than their worldview or organizing approach.

African-American Ideologies

Several ideologies salient among African-Americans require explication. Here, *ideology* is considered as a systematic theory of society composed of a relatively coherent set of interdependent concepts and values that adherents construct into historical narratives and contemporary discourses to articulate their interpretation of a social groups' economic, political, social interests, and cultural beliefs to rationalize particular public policies. The emergence and salience of African-American ideologies are conditioned by three broad factors: the sociohistorical context, the contemporary discursive matrix, and the black intellectual tradition. It is important to contextualize African-American ideologies historically because they develop during particular historical moments, and their discourses are designed to resolve or, at least, to respond to historically specific problems. Moreover, sociohistorical context not only shapes the emergence of specific ideologies, it also conditions the form and salience an ideology takes at a particular moment. African-American history can usefully be considered as a succession of different racial formations. Black racial formations represent African-Americans' distinct position within the U.S. political economy, polity, and civil society during particular historical periods.

African-American history can be divided into four periods: (1) slavery, 1619–1865; (2) the plantation economy, 1865–1960s; (3) proletarian and urbanization, 1940s–1979; and (4) the new nadir, from 1980 on.

Within the realm of ideation, African-American political thought evidences the dynamic interplay between African-American discourses and the dominant and emergent ideas circulating during particular historical periods. Contemporary events and discourses present in the United States and the world establish the contemporary examples and discursive matrix with which these African-American ideological discourses engage. Perhaps more pertinent, however, is knowledge of past debates among the black counterpublic and how previous black intellectual traditions have influenced historically specific policy formulations.

Because racial oppression is a system constructed around a matrix of domination, discrimination, and degradation, an appraisal of African-American political and social thought reveals that black activist intellectuals have mainly engaged two issue clusters: those that revolve around questions of *identity* and those concerning questions of *liberation:* "Who are we?" and "What is our present situation, and what should be done about it?" During slavery, the system of racial oppression attempted to destroy African identities, ethnic memories and cultural practices, and the collective and personal identities that derived from them. Since slavery it has sought to make African-Americans nonpersons, requiring, therefore, the search for and (re)assertion of new identities woven from the residue of African survivals and self-interested adaptations, a process that transcends the limits of what is derisively called "identity politics." Identity questions for oppressed racialized communities are fundamental to the pursuit of liberation. These overarching questions about identity, the present situation, and what should be done to create conditions of freedom, self-determination, and social transformation have elicited different answers from different groups of black activist intellectuals.

Allowing for terminological differences, most scholars of black history and politics would agree that African-American activist intellectuals have justified their political action via an interpretative repertoire drawn from one of the following five interrelated ideological approaches: (1) autonomic, (2) incorporative, (3) black conservatism, (4) black radicalism, and (5) black feminism.

Black Nationalist Ideologies

Black nationalist, or *autonomic,* strategies are the oldest ideological approaches developed by African-Americans. The slave revolts, especially those before the nineteenth century, that aimed to create maroon societies modeled after remembrances of African social organizational patterns perhaps best reflect the anteriority of black nationalism among African-American ideologies. Autonomic approaches are also the most varied and complicated of African-American ideologies, but they can be divided into two broad categories: *protonationalism* and *separatism.* Protonationalism refers to strategic visions that emphasize autonomy in the realm of civil society, the desire to reside in semiautonomous towns and regions, and the preference for preserving distinct cultural practices. Richard Allen's (1760–1831) creation of the African Episcopal Methodist Church in 1794 and W. E. B. DuBois's call for blacks to build on their group strengths in the 1930s or the 1960s era campaigns for "community control" of African-American communities are examples of protonationalism.

Separatism has a more delimited terrain, encompassing emigration and efforts to create an independent African-American

nation-state within the United States, such as Martin R. Delany's and others' proposals to emigrate to Africa, Canada, or South America during the 1840s and 1850s; Marcus Garvey's 1920s plan to repatriate to Liberia; or the Republic of New Africa's 1960s desire to create an African-American nation-state in the U.S. South.

Autonomic discourses are shaped by their sociohistorical context; they tend to surge and ebb in relationship to the economic and political position of blacks in U.S. society. As a rule, black nationalism swells during sustained economic downturns. Autonomic philosophies are also sensitive to the interplay of dominant and emerging ideologies. This is particularly true regarding questions of cultural difference. For instance, between 1850 and 1925, the era historian Wilson Moses terms the golden age of black nationalism, nationalists were ambivalent toward African culture and rejected Africanisms or cultural carryovers. Like the social Darwinists of the day, they often viewed Africans and African-Americans as "underdeveloped" or even "backward," although they usually ascribed environmental or religious, rather than genetic, causes. Consequently, they preferred European-American high culture. To a large extent, black power, the protonationalism that developed during the "turbulent sixties" (1955–1975) was predicated on *Africanization,* the adoption of actual or imagined African cultural values and practices.

Evidence from several years of the National Black Politics Study from 1979 to 1992 suggests that proto–black nationalism remained the predominant perspective of the majority of African-American people in the late twentieth century. For instance, political scientists Darren W. Davis and Ronald Brown discovered that 84 percent of African-Americans believed blacks should buy from black-owned businesses; 83.3 percent believed blacks should be self-reliant; 73.8 percent wanted blacks to control their communities' economics; and 68.3 percent believed blacks should govern their communities. Another 70.7 percent thought black children should learn an African language, and 56.5 percent advocated participating only in all-black organizations.

African-American Liberalism

Liberalism is the second oldest black ideology. Scholars often insert "liberal" as an adjective to describe the political values associated with the incorporativist perspective in order to distinguish this set of discourses from conservative and radical approaches, which also advocate incorporation into U.S. society, albeit for radicals into a fundamentally transformed society. And some variants of nationalism and feminism are decidedly liberal in their political social perspectives. Here *incorporative* should be understood as synonymous with *liberal pluralism.*

Smith has argued that liberalism, or incorporativism, is not so much an ideology as a strategy. Applying the logic Anthony Bogues used regarding Quobna Cugoano's *Thoughts and Sentiments on the Evil of Slavery* to the work of Douglass, DuBois, Charles Johnson, Alain LeRoy Locke (1886–1954), Martin Luther King, Jr., Thurgood Marshall (1908–1993), Mary Frances Berry (b. 1938), and Lani Guiner (b. 1950), among others, illuminates how their critiques of U.S. society stretched the boundaries of liberal pluralism and provided alternative theories of American democracy.

Incorporative approaches advocate structural integration into the U.S. state and political economy, arguing that the inclusion of African-Americans in traditionally white institutions *in and of itself* constitutes a significant transformation. This is the view that undergirded the legal strategy Charles Hamilton Houston (1895–1950) designed for the National Association for the Advancement of Colored People (NAACP) during the 1930s and of the civil rights movement of the 1960s.

Incorporativists are more ambivalent toward inclusion in European-American civil society: they tend to oppose restrictions barring access to traditionally white institutions, but usually oppose dismantling African-American institutions. For instance, Martin Luther King, Jr. never imagined the dissolution of the black church. Historically a few incorporativists, such as Frederick Douglass, have advocated biological assimilation as well as structural integration. Incorporative approaches generally encourage acceptance of bourgeois European-American cultural values and practices, viewing them as quintessentially "modern," even though privately many incorporativists often continue to practice the styles and idioms of African-American culture.

While tension exists between the core components of white liberalism and black incorporativism, particularly regarding individualism and notions of equality—equal opportunity versus equality of results—incorporativists generally share their white colleagues' views on the power of knowledge, the value of diversity, and economic enterprise. Incorporativists are also skeptical of American liberalism's assertions of pluralism, especially the assertion that the U.S. state is neutral regarding racial and ethnic disputes. Although incorporativists are often critical of the practice of American liberalism, they tend to accept most of its values.

African-American Radicalism

Perhaps more than any other ideology, black radicalism is sensitive to the sociohistorical context. During the slavery period, the radical black perspective advocated the immediate destruction of slavery and the extension of full civil rights to black people. After slavery, as most African-Americans were being incorporated into the semicapitalist plantation economy, things became more complex. Confronting sharecropping, black radicalism required more than the advocacy of black landownership. Circumstances required that black radicals develop a critique of the capitalist system that maintained the plantation economy. Whereas during slavery Frederick Douglass and Martin R. Delany were radicals, during Reconstruction and the first nadir (1877–1917) Douglass became the quintessential black liberal while Delany descended into conservatism. This hypersensitivity to sociohistorical context derives from the general premises of radicalism: transformation of the fundamental structural and ideological elements of a society. Black radicalism has consisted of philosophies and practices that sought the essential transformation of the system of racial oppression and the social system that institutionalized it.

Peter H. Clark, the first modern black radical, joined the Socialist Party in 1877, during the first nadir. Ironically, Clark's reasons for leaving the socialists probably affected the construction of black radicalism more than his reasons for joining. (Clark left the Socialist Party because it did not confront the specificity of race and racial oppression, preferring to view race as subordinate to class.) The outlines of a distinct black radical perspective, however, did not appear until after World War I, after Hubert H. Harrison (1900–1945), Cyril V. Briggs (1888–1966), and the African Blood Brotherhood (c. 1920s) examined the state of African peoples and the relationship of black and white radicals in the United States. Black radicalism was a unique effort to merge and remake classical Marxist theory and black nationalism into a race-conscious socialist theory. Although Ralph Bunche (1904–1971) and Abram Harris (1899–1963) were radical blacks during the 1930s, unlike W. E. B. DuBois, Langston Hughes (1902–1967), Claudia Jones (1915–1964), and C. L. R. James (1901–1989), their ideas might be too orthodox to be considered foundational for black radicalism. Black radicals, according to Anthony Bogues, are either *heretics* or *prophets*.

Heretics, usually highly educated in European-American radicalism, use subjugated knowledge from black experiences to challenge white radical orthodoxies and to rework them into theories that can accommodate black experiences and perspectives. Bogues's prophets come from the realm of religion. They are often undereducated by U.S. standards. They tap subjugated knowledge from sources outside the mainstream academy: the Bible, the Koran, particularly esoteric interpretations of both. In addition to derived religious sources, prophets articulate, in Hobsbawm's terms, an *inherent* ideology, one drawn from the murkier repositories of African survivals and popular culture. Noble Drew Ali (1866–1929) and the Moorish Science Temple, Elijah Muhammad (1897–1975) and the Nation of Islam, and Prince Asiel Ben Israel and the Original Black Hebrew Israelite Nation represent this type of black radicalism. (Note that, by this author's criterion—opposition to the dominant mode of production—they would not be considered black radicals.)

In more recent times, Huey P. Newton (1942–1989) and the Black Panther Party (1960s), especially their theory of intercommunialism, the Revolutionary Action Movement (late 1960s), and the League of Revolutionary Black Workers (late 1960s) have represented the black radical perspective. Since the late twentieth century, the Black Radical Congress has represented this ideological tendency.

Black Feminism

Like modern black radicalism, black feminism is of comparatively recent origins, although its roots reach back into the nineteenth century. The earliest foreshadowings of this ideology are found in the slave-era speeches and writings of Maria Stewart (1803–1879), Sojouner Truth (c. 1797–1883), and Frances Ellen Watkins (1825–1911). The ideas that would ultimately become the ideology of black feminism developed to a large extent during the first nadir through the speeches, writing, and practices of Ida Wells-Barnett, Mary Church Terrell (1863–1954), and Anna Julia Cooper (1859–1964). While black women activists, especially women associated with the U.S. Communist Party, such as Esther Cooper Jackson and Claudia Jones, engaged in practices and advocated philosophies that amounted to black feminism, the theory was not formally visible until the 1960s.

According to Linda Burnham, contemporary black feminism, with its emphasis on the simultaneity of overlapping oppressions—race, class, gender, sexuality—is a product of the transition from the civil rights to the black power movement. She locates the origin of this iteration of black feminism with the Student Nonviolent Coordinating Committee's (SNCC) Black Women's Liberation Committee and later the Third World Women's Alliance, in both of which Frances Beal (1900–1987) played a leading role. This stream of black feminism has become a core component of contemporary black radicalism. It can be sharply contrasted with another stream of black feminism, *womanism,* as articulated by Clenora Hudson-Weems, which is more correctly viewed as a tributary of conservative black nationalism.

African-American Conservatism

Black conservatism has a long history and includes a large number of prominent African-Americans. Nevertheless, it has never become a salient ideology for a significant number. Jupiter Hammond (1711–c. 1800) during the slave period, William Hooper Council (1848–1909) during the first nadir, George Schuyler (1895–1977) during the 1940s and 1950s, as well as A. G. Gaston (1892–1996) during the 1960s, represented conservative ideologies. However, none of these individuals shared the virulent antiblack positions of contemporary black conservatives. Black neoconservatives differ from previous generations of black conservatives in that they are often alienated from the black community and divorced from its institutional networks, especially political organizations.

Black conservatism articulates better with its mainstream equivalent than do the other black ideologies. Conservative approaches are premised on white American cultural values, particularly notions of individualism, which advocate *colorblind* individual incorporation into the U.S. political economy, polity, and mainstream white civil society. According to psychologist William Cross, Jr., race and the history and continuing practice of racial oppression are either denied or viewed as not salient by black neoconservatives in constructing their identities. Twenty-first-century black neoconservatives, Thelma Duggin, Clarence Thomas, Gwen Daye Richardson, and Ward Connerly, share the assumptions, interpretations, and goals of the leading white neoconservatives. Black neoconservatives blame the dislocations endemic to poverty on welfare and government subsidies. They claim the Great Society programs, instituted in the 1960s by President Lyndon Johnson, created a "culture of dependency" among the black poor. According to this perspective, instead of providing a social safety net, the Great Society created dependent personalities and an antiachievement culture in the black community. Perhaps more fundamental than the adoption of European-American cultural values is their reduction of African-American culture to a composite of pathological behaviors. Conservatives, including autonomic conservatives, generally reject the African cultural survival thesis.

Summary

The five major ideological expressions of social thought by which African-Americans have sought to reconstruct their racial/ethnic identity, to contemplate the structures, ideologies, and functions of racial oppression, and to envision a future free from that oppression constitute an extraordinarily complex body of evolving political theory. All are shaped by dynamic interaction with their sociohistorical experiences and the dominant and emerging ideologies and discourses in U.S. society and the world, especially pan-African ideas and the black intellectual tradition.

See also **Afrocentricity; Assimilation; Black Consciousness; Civil Disobedience; Class; Conservatism; Critical Race Theory; Diasporas: African Diaspora; Discrimination; Diversity; Equality: Racial Equality; Feminism: Africa and African Diaspora; Liberalism; Negritude; Pan-Africanism; Philosophies: Feminist, Twentieth-Century; Political Protest, U.S.; Segregation; Slavery; Womanism.**

BIBLIOGRAPHY

Allen, Robert L. *Black Awakening in Capitalist America: An Analytic History.* New York: Doubleday, 1969.

Bracey, John H., Jr., August Meier, and Elliott Rudwick, eds. *Black Nationalism in America.* Indianapolis: Bobbs-Merrill, 1970.

Bogues, Anthony. *Black Heretics, Black Prophets: Radical Political Intellectuals.* New York: Routledge, 2003.

Burnham, Linda. "The Wellspring of Black Feminist Theory." *Southern University Law Review* 28, no. 3 (2001): 265–270.

Bush, Rod. *We Are Not What We Seem: Black Nationalism and Class Struggle in the American Century.* New York: New York University Press, 1999.

Cha-Jua, Sundiata Keita. *America's First Black Town: Brooklyn, Illinois, 1830–1915.* Urbana: University of Illinois Press, 2000.

———. "Racial Formation and Transformation: Toward a Theory of Black Racial Oppression." *Souls: A Critical Journal of Black Politics, Culture, and Society* 3 (winter 2001): 25–60.

Cha-Jua, Sundiata Keita, and Clarence Lang. "Providence, Patriarchy, Pathology: The Rise and Decline of Louis Farrakhan." *New Politics* 8 (winter 1997): 47–71.

Childs, John Brown. *Leadership, Conflict, and Cooperation in Afro-American Social Thought.* Philadelphia: Temple University Press, 1989.

Collins, Patricia Hill. *Black Feminist Thought: Knowledge, Consciousness, and the Politics of Empowerment.* Boston: Unwin Hyman, 1990.

Cross, Jr., William E. *Shades of Black: Diversity in African-American Identity.* Philadelphia: Temple University Press, 1991.

Cruse, Harold. *The Crisis of the Negro Intellectual.* New York: Quill, 1984.

Davis, Darren W., and Ronald E. Brown. "The Antipathy of Black Nationalism: Behavioral and Attitudinal Implications of an African-American Ideology." *American Journal of Political Science* 46, no. 2 (2002): 239–252.

Dillard, Angela. *Guess Who's Coming to Dinner Now?: Multicultural Conservatism in America.* New York: New York University Press, 2001.

Glaude, Eddie S., Jr., ed. *Is It Nation Time?: Contemporary Essays on Black Power and Black Nationalism.* Chicago: University of Chicago Press, 2002.

Grimshaw, Anna, ed. *The C. L. R. James Reader.* Cambridge, Mass.: Blackwell, 1992.

Harding, Vincent. *There Is a River: The Black Struggle for Freedom in America.* New York: Harcourt Brace Jovanovich, 1981.

Hudson-Weems, Clenora. *Africana Womanism: Reclaiming Ourselves.* Troy, Mich.: Bedford, 1993.

Jeffries, Judson L. *Huey P. Newton: The Radical Theorist.* Jackson: University Press of Mississippi, 2002.

Marable, Manning, and Leith Mullings. "The Divided Mind of Black America: Race, Ideology, and Politics in the Post-Civil Rights Era." *Race and Class* 36, no. 1 (1994): 61–72.

McCartney, John T. *Black Power Ideologies: An Essay in African-American Political Thought.* Philadelphia: Temple University Press, 1992.

Meier, August. *Negro Thought in America, 1880–1915: Racial Ideologies in the Age of Booker T. Washington.* Ann Arbor: University of Michigan Press, 1969.

Neville, Helen A., and Jennifer Hamer. "'We Make Freedom': An Exploration of Revolutionary Black Feminism." *Journal of Black Studies* 31, no. 4 (March 2001): 437–461.

Richardson, Marilyn, ed. *Maria W. Stewart, America's First Black Woman Political Writer: Essays and Speeches.* Bloomington: Indiana University Press, 1987.

Robinson, Cedric. *Black Marxism: The Making of the Black Radical Tradition.* London: Zed, 1983.

Smith, Robert C. "Ideology as the Enduring Dilemma of Black Politics." In *Dilemmas of Black Politics: Issues of Leadership and Strategy,* edited by Georgia Anne Persons, 200–215. New York: HarperCollins, 1993.

Stuckey, Sterling. *Slave Culture: Nationalist Theory and the Foundations of Black America.* New York: Oxford University Press, 1987.

Sundiata Keita Cha-Jua

AFROCENTRICITY.

Afrocentricity is a theory that emerged in the early 1980s in the United States within the academic context of African-American studies. Afrocentricity was articulated by Molefi Kete Asante, a professor of African-American studies at Temple University and creator of the first Ph.D. program in African-American studies in the nation, in three major essays published between 1980 and 1990.

Like most theories, Afrocentricity has come to be associated with different thrusts, some of which may even be contradictory or incompatible with the original definition of Afrocentricity. However, at its core, Afrocentricity is a theory concerned with African epistemological relevance, also referred to as centeredness or location. The ultimate goal of Afrocentricity is the liberation of African people from the grips of Eurocentrism. The primary and indispensable mechanism to achieve this goal is the fostering of African intellectual agency.

Historical and Intellectual Context

African-American studies academic units came into existence as a result of great political pressure on European institutions of higher learning in a demand for space for the African voice and experience in the late 1960s, during the Black Power movement. No longer satisfied to be culturally disenfranchised and to feel alienated from the classroom (Asante, 1990),

African-American students and community activists brought to the fore of the discussion the question of educational relevance for black people, arguing for a culturally inclusive and sensitive curriculum apt to produce scholars in tune with and committed to the betterment of their communities (Karenga). One of the major characteristics of black studies, therefore, has been a dual concern for academic matters and the life conditions of African-Americans, with African-American studies scholars expected to be scholar-activists.

However, if the political mandate of African-American scholars is clear, their intellectual mission has, on the other hand, been clouded with conceptual confusion since the very beginning. Particularly vexing has been the issue of the relationship between African-American studies and the Western academe, with much debate over the status of African-American studies as a full-fledged independent discipline, or rather a field of studies, devoted to the Black experience and yet operating within the confines of Western intellectual thought. At the core of this issue, however, lies the question of Eurocentrism, with the degree to which one seems willing to challenge European intellectual hegemony determining one's position in the debate over the intellectual status of African-American studies.

Eurocentrism is understood as the interpretation of all reality from the Western perspective, especially as it emerged during the European Age of the Enlightenment. That perspective developed both internally, with the development of a metaparadigm specific and relevant to Europe; and externally, in opposition to "others," especially African people. Hence there are at least four assumptions of that European metaparadigm that have played a major and negative role as far as black people are concerned: (1) all human beings evolve along the same line; (2) the European experience is universal; (3) Europeans are superior; and (4) "others" are defined by their experiences with Europeans. In other words, the European metaparadigm rests among other things on the belief in the superiority and universality of the European experience.

Indeed, in that linear and evolutionary schema of thought, the West claims that when it talks about itself, it is also ipso facto talking about all human beings. The history of all women, men, and children in the world supposedly naturally coincides with that of Europeans. The latter are thus implicitly or explicitly held to be the universal norm by which African intellectual, cultural, and social "progress" will be evaluated. However, if all human beings share a common essence, it is also obvious that they have not all reached the same stage of development. Indeed, it is rather clear, from reading European writers, that Europe precedes the rest of humankind, and time after time it is suggested that Africans must emulate Europeans in order to put an end to their inferior condition.

The expected outcome of such emulation has been a process of mental *conversion* (Mudimbe, 1988), predicated upon the belief that only through a careful imitation of Europeans would Africans improve their lot. While the ontological reduction of the colonized had been well understood as a necessary part of colonialism, the implications of the conversion process, on the other hand, had not been fully appreciated. This may be precisely because the early African critiques of European colonialism (e.g., Frantz Fanon) still functioned within a fundamentally European conceptual framework, such as Marxism. Hence what was challenged was not Western modernity per se, but its abusive practices. Europe's tacit advancement of its own culture as some "no-man's cultural land"—its implicit claims to cultural neutrality and universality—was rarely questioned for it was not construed as problematic.

Such an approach, which was to be expected during those early days, would not allow one to understand the colonization process as the systematic imposition of the European worldview, grounded in a specific time and place yet parading as universal, on people whose cultural and historical experiences were quite different.

Afrocentric Organizing Principle and Concepts

Europe's attempted occupation of practically all human space resulted in Africans being considerably removed from their own cultural base to be relegated to footnote status, to the periphery, the margin of the European experience and consciousness. This mental disenfranchisement is held responsible for Africans often not existing on their own cultural and historical terms but on borrowed European ones. Africans are *dislocated* and, having lost sight of themselves in the midst of social decay, find it exceedingly difficult to orient themselves in a positive and constructive manner, a most difficult plight. *Relocation* is the remedy suggested by Afrocentricity. Only when Africans become *centered*, that is, when they consciously and systematically adopt ways, attitudes, and behaviors that are germane to their own cultural traditions and historical reality, can they hope to achieve freedom. In other words, African freedom is predicated upon the conscious activation of one's Africanness, that is, ultimately, with the exercise by African people of their own *agency*.

Afrocentricity further stresses agency as an African cultural imperative. Indeed, in African culture, ancestral traditions must be preserved and transmitted out of respect for one's personal and collective ancestors. Asante therefore defines Afrocentricity as "a frame of reference" generated by Africans themselves, based on African cosmology, axiology, aesthetic, and epistemology: "Afrocentricity is the study of the ideas and events from the standpoint of Africans as the key players rather than victims. This theory becomes, by virtue of an authentic relationship to the centrality of our own reality, a fundamentally empirical project" (1991, p. 172). Asante further insists that while one may argue over the meaning of Africanness, one cannot argue, as an Afrocentrist, over "the centrality of African ideals and values" for African people (1990, p. 6), thus identifying the notion of cultural, and more specifically, epistemological centeredness as *the* Afrocentric organizing principle. In addition to this major principle, Afrocentricity includes a set of unquestioned propositions that it inherited from its intellectual and ideological antecedents, namely, Garveyism, the negritude movement, Fanonism, Kawaida, and Cheikh Anta Diop's historiography. Those propositions can be listed as follows: African people must be conceived as agents and victors; a Pan-African perspective is essential; a deep commitment to African people and Africa is necessary; there exists an African cultural matrix common to all African people with different

surface manifestations; culture is primary and all-inclusive; Africans must reconnect with African culture for genuine African freedom to be; African cultural rebirth is necessary; the colonizer within the African psyche must be killed; and finally, Nile Valley civilizations (in particular, ancient Egypt, or Kemet) are the foundation of African culture and will serve as a model upon which to elaborate new bodies of thought and action relevant to African contemporary needs. Those principles, which are primary both chronologically and logically, function very much as Afrocentricity's premises.

Afrocentricity as the African-American Studies Metaparadigm

The implications of Afrocentricity for African-American studies have been considerable. Indeed, Asante argues that only when African-American studies scholars center themselves mentally and intellectually in the African cultural and historical experience will genuine African-American studies come into existence. Until then, Asante maintains, Eurocentric studies of African people and phenomena will continue to parade as African-American studies, with the latter existing only as a subfield of European studies. First, Afrocentricity insists, it must be realized that any idea, concept, or theory, no matter how "neutral" it claims to be, is nonetheless a product of a particular cultural and historical matrix. As such, it carries specific cultural assumptions, often of a metaphysical nature. Hence to embrace a European theory or idea is not as innocent an academic exercise as it may seem. In fact, it is Afrocentricity's contention that unless African scholars are willing to reexamine the process of their own intellectual conversion, which takes place under the guise of "formal education," they will continue to be the easy prey of European intellectual hegemony. What is suggested, instead, is that African intellectuals must consciously and systematically relocate themselves in their own cultural and historical matrix, from which they must draw the criteria by which they evaluate the African experience. Their work must be informed by "centrism," that is, "the groundedness of observation and behavior in one's own historical experiences" (Asante, 1990, p. 12). *Africology* is the discipline to which those who study African people and phenomena from an Afrocentric perspective belong.

Thus it can be said that Afrocentricity emerged as a new paradigm to challenge the Eurocentric paradigm responsible for the intellectual disenfranchisement and the making invisible of African people, even to themselves in many cases.

In that respect, Afrocentricity therefore presents itself as *the* African-American studies metaparadigm. As such, it includes three major aspects: cognitive, structural, and functional. The cognitive aspect involves the metaphysical foundations—such as the organizing principle and set of presuppositions that were outlined above, a methodology, methods, concepts, and theories. The structural aspect refers to the existence of an Afrocentric intellectual community, such as is found at Temple University. Finally, the structural aspect of the Afrocentric paradigm refers to the ability of the latter to activate African people's consciousness and to bring them closer to freedom, the ultimate goal of Afrocentricity. Hence Asante concludes that what can be called *the* discipline of African-American studies itself is intimately linked to the development of Afrocentricity and the establishment in the late eighties of the Temple doctoral program, the first Ph.D. program in African-American studies in the United States.

The Temple Ph.D. program in Africology was immediately successful, as hundreds of national and international applicants sought admission in order to be a part of the Afrocentric epistemological watershed. Although the program has suffered serious setbacks since its inception, there can be little doubt about its influence on African-American studies. Over four hundred dissertations employing the Afrocentric paradigm have been defended, at Temple and at other institutions. Indeed, the Temple Ph.D. program opened the path for the creation of other African-American studies Ph.D. programs in the United States in subsequent years.

Afrocentricity and Its Critics

As could be expected, however, Afrocentricity's growing paradigmatic ascendancy over African-American studies also prompted serious critiques, which fall within five broad categories. First, critics have disagreed with some of Afrocentricity's premises, in particular the notion of an African essence that undergirds the notion of *center*. This criticism is often heard in poststructuralist circles, since the very idea of a *center* is antithetical to the poststructuralist paradigm. Often associated with this criticism is the additional claim that in its search for Africanness, Afrocentricity does not allow for cultural change. In fact, some argue, Afrocentricity's inability to deal adequately with cultural change prevents it from understanding that being African today also means being at least partly European as a result of colonization and widespread Westernization. Afrocentricity, then, is perceived as too restrictive and incapable of grasping the dialectical complexity of modern African identities. While he denies being an "immutabilist," Asante's response has been that Africans need a place to stand in order to challenge oppressive White structures and systems of knowledge and therefore cannot afford postmodern, evanescent, fluid selves. In any case, any discourse on identity is necessarily essentialist. Afrocentrists also point out that far from denying the Westernization of many Africans' consciousness, they recognize it as a destructive force that must be circumvented.

Second, some have taken issue with Afrocentricity's main category, culture. black feminists and black neo-Marxists advance gender and social class, respectively, as the primary contradiction in African-American life. With regard to feminism, however, Afrocentric scholars who tackle gender issues question the relevance of feminist philosophical and political assumptions for African people, including African women. Concerning the question of class, while it is quite feasible and necessary to articulate an Afrocentric economic theory, Afrocentricity maintains that race/culture remains the most socially relevant category in American society.

Third, Afrocentricity has also been criticized for making untenable historical claims, especially in relation to ancient Egypt. This argument, probably the most publicized, has stemmed from European classicists who, having subscribed to the Greek Miracle theory, became disturbed by two related developments associated with the spread of Afrocentricity: first,

credit was being taken away from Europe for the great civilizations of the Nile Valley (in particular, Egypt); and second, as a consequence the original intellectual achievements of Greece itself were revisited and diminished. For instance, it was pointed out that many Greek philosophers had studied for long periods of time in ancient Africa, and were in reality indebted to their African teachers for many of their ideas. Therefore many European scholars in the United States and Europe proceeded to refute those "Afrocentric" claims. However, it must be noted that the debate over the racial identity of the early Egyptians predates the emergence of Afrocentricity by several decades and is not, therefore, an issue germane to Afrocentricity per se. It must be more correctly understood within the context of Diopian historiography, which places Egypt at the beginning, both chronologically and conceptually, of African civilization. In fact, several of the scholars associated with this thrust, such as Martin Bernal, have never claimed to be Afrocentric.

Fourth, Afrocentricity has also been criticized for intellectual bad faith because of wrong attributions and associations. For instance, Afrocentricity has been associated with biological-deterministic arguments (such as that around melanin) that were never part of its premises.

Finally, criticism of an ideological nature has been voiced. In one instance, Afrocentricity has been blamed as reversed Eurocentrism. Some scholars contend that Afrocentricity merely seeks to replace one geopolitical hegemonic center, Europe, with another hegemonic one, Africa. However, as even a cursory reading of Asante's texts would reveal, Afrocentricity is fundamentally nonhegemonic and welcomes the existence of a multiplicity of cultural centers. It is precisely that position that allowed Afrocentricity to challenge Eurocentrism in the first place. Some have also contended that Afrocentricity undermines the very fabric of American society. By emphasizing the Africans' prerogative to be *human as Africans,* Afrocentricity is said to threaten the unity of American society, including the American academe. However, Afrocentrists remark that the unspoken fear is not so much about a shattered national unity (which, given racism, could have never truly existed) but about the threat that Afrocentricity poses to Europe's self-serving monopoly over reason.

While Afrocentricity continues to exercise a significant influence in the United States, it has also been receiving increased attention in Europe and Africa, where a vigorous intellectual movement has emerged informed by Afrocentric tenets and referred to as the "African Renaissance," thus creating the possibility for Afrocentricity to be transformed into a Pan-African school of thought in the years to come.

See also **Black Atlantic; Black Consciousness; Eurocentrism; Negritude; Orientalism: African and Black Orientalism; Pan-Africanism; Philosophies: African.**

BIBLIOGRAPHY

Asante, Molefi Kete. *Afrocentricity.* Rev. ed. Trenton, N.J.: Africa World Press, 1988.
———. *Kemet, Afrocentricity, and Knowledge.* Trenton, N.J.: Africa World Press, 1990.

———. *The Afrocentric Idea*. Rev. and expanded ed. Philadelphia: Temple University Press, 1998.

———. "The Afrocentric Idea in Education." *Journal of Negro Education* 60 (1991): 170–179.

Conyers, James L., Jr. ed. *Afrocentricity and the Academy*. London: McFarland, 2000.

Fanon, Frantz. *A Dying Colonialism*. New York: Grove Press, 1967.

Gray, Cecil Conteen. *Afrocentric Thought and Praxis: An Intellectual History*. Trenton, N.J.: Africa World Press, 2001.

Karenga, Maulana. *Introduction to Black Studies*. Inglewood, Calif.: Kawaida Publications, 1982.

Lemelle, Sydney J. "The Politics of Cultural Existence: Pan Africanism, Historical Materialism, and Afrocentricity." In *Imagining Home: Class, Culture and Nationalism in the African Diaspora*, edited by Sidney J. Lemelle and Robin D. G. Kelley. New York: Verso, 1994. A Marxist critique of Afrocentricity.

Mazama, Ama, ed. *The Afrocentric Paradigm*. Trenton, N.J.: Africa World Press, 2002.

Mudimbe, V. Y. *The Invention of Africa: Gnosis, Philosophy, and the Order of Knowledge*. Bloomington: Indiana University Press, 1988.

Okafor, Victor Oguejiofor. *Towards an Understanding of Africology*. Dubuque, Iowa: Kendall/Hunt, 2002.

Ama Mazama

AFROPESSIMISM.   Afropessimism refers to the perception of sub-Saharan Africa as a region too riddled with problems for good governance and economic development. The term gained currency in the 1980s, when many Africanists in Western creditor countries believed that there was no hope for consolidating democracy and achieving sustainable economic development in the region. The earliest use in print of the word was in a 1988 article from the Xinhua News Agency in which Michel Aurillac, France's minister of cooperation, criticized the prevailing pessimism in the West about Africa's economic development and cautioned against what he referred to as an "Afro-pessimism" on the part of some creditors.

Depiction

Many writers have given different expressions to the phenomenon of Afropessimism. Attempts to explain the concept include both cogent studies (Ayittey, 1992, 1998; Jackson and Rosberg; Kaplan, 1994) and polemical and shallow travelogues (Richburg). In general, one virtue of Afropessimist writings is that they do not whitewash Africa's problems. Further, they correctly refuse to excuse the outrages of some African dictators on the basis of political ideology or racial identity. In particular they refuse to use colonial exploitation to mask postcolonial kleptocracy, the personalization of state power, and the politics of prebendalism. The writers mentioned above (excepting Richburg and Kaplan) do not reject the hope that Africa can develop or that it is capable of overcoming its political and economic problems. In this sense they are not themselves pessimistic about the future of Africa but rather are simply describing the phenomenon of Afropessimism. The real Afropessimists are writers who call for abandoning, or worse,

recolonizing the continent (Johnson; Kaplan, 1992, 1994; Michaels; Hitchens). While generally the writers in the first group merely denounce postcolonial African leadership by pointing out its weaknesses, those in the latter tend to conclude that Africans are incapable of self-rule.

However, a common characteristic of the two modes of Afropessimist writings is imbalance. They all tend to highlight the horrors of a few African countries and ignore the advances of many other countries at various times. The unscientific establishment of doomsday conclusions about Africa characteristic of studies in this genre (see, in particular, Richberg) are usually not warranted by the limited sample of African countries discussed in the narratives. The unintended result is that Africa is given a blanket negative portrayal. (There are, by contrast, prominent works that for the most part decry Africa's image in the West—see, for instance, Hammond and Jablow; Hawk.) The resultant foreboding and ominous image in Western media and the academy weakens the continent in the global competition for foreign investment and tourism (see Onwudiwe, 1996). This is an economic effect of Afropessimism.

African Rebirth

Still, the conditions that merit pessimism for the future of Africa are not manufactured by Afropessimists; such conditions are empirically verifiable. Since the end of the Cold War, important African leaders such as Presidents Thabo Mbeki of South Africa, Olusegun Obasanjo of Nigeria, and Maître Abdoulaye Wade of Senegal have come to recognize this and have resolved to do something about it. As a result, there has been an honest effort on the continent to address the important issues of good political, economic, and corporate governance and the professionalization of the army in order to diminish chances for destabilizing military coups. These efforts had led the Organization of African Unity (OAU) to found a new institution, the New Partnership for Africa's Development (NEPAD), charged with the responsibility to provide a vision and strategic framework for Africa's renewal. NEPAD attempts to provide African interventions with regard to issues of relative underdevelopment and marginalization. NEPAD's formation and other historic African transformative actions have been referred to as African renaissance.

Impact

In the donor countries of the West in the 1980s, Afropessimists were found in the government, media, and academia. The prevailing view that votes for Africa's stabilization and development were a waste of scarce resources was fanned by conservative politicians, bureaucrats, journalists, and scholars. This quickly led to an era of strained relationships between Western donor countries and African recipient countries in the late 1980s and early 1990s. Donor countries complained that progress was being slowed by bad governance, corruption, and mismanagement of funds, creating disillusionment and donor (or aid) fatigue. African countries in turn complained of unfulfilled promises and unwarranted intrusiveness in domestic policies by donors. The net result was a reduction in the volume of development aid from Western to African countries.

Explanations

Two explanations have been put forth for the conditions that produced the phenomenon of Afropessimism. One is the apparent inability of postcolonial African leaders to practice good governance. Since the 1960s, when most countries in Africa south of the Sahara regained political independence from European colonialists, the standard of living in Africa has fallen below expectations. The achievement of political self-rule naturally came with raised expectations of the good life for Africans who had been subjected to exploitation and subjugation by colonial tyranny. In the exuberance of the freedom moment, the new indigenous leaders of Africa promised their fellow citizens a brighter future. However, by the 1980s, more than twenty years after independence, the African condition (especially for the masses) had fallen far below the continent's potential. For the most part, bad leadership was responsible for the disappointing performance. Independence ushered in an era of political instability, military dictatorships, and gross mismanagement of natural resources by very corrupt African leaders. By the 1980s all these conspired to drive down the standard of living in most African countries, forcing an otherwise resource-rich continent to become severely dependent on foreign aid and foreign debt.

Another school of thought locates the source of Africa's social and economic downfall on the international political environment. According to this school, Africa regained self-rule during the era of the Cold War, when the relationship between the countries in the Eastern bloc led by the Soviet Union and countries of the Western bloc led by the United States was marked by a state of military competition and political tension. The rivalry stopped short of actual war between the two superpowers, but it forced Africa to become a surrogate terrain for the hot war between the two camps. In the process, African countries, most of them weak and dependent on the Western or Eastern ideological blocs, became little more than client states. Under this new dispensation, Africans lost the power to choose their own leaders. Africa's dependent dictators owed their offices to the economic and military support of Cold War powers. For the most part they put the interests of the foreign powers on which they were dependent ahead of their own national interests. This situation, which was as exploitative and impoverishing as colonialism, became known as neocolonialism and is blamed for the postcolonial impoverishment of Africans that fueled the fires of Afropessimism in the 1980s. Consequently, with the end of the Cold War, some Africanists came to believe that if the detrimental international conditions it imposed were ultimately reversed, then conditions in Africa would improve through good governance. Those who believe in this are known as Afro-optimists. Challenging the view that sub-Saharan Africa has only regressed since independence, they advance examples of postcolonial triumphs achieved by Africa's political leadership despite the prevailing problems identified by Afropessimists. They argue that the energy and perseverance of African peoples portend hope for the future of the continent.

A Middle Ground

The truth about Africa's impoverishment lies somewhere between the analyses of Afropessimists and Afro-optimists. There is no doubt that corrupt and uncourageous leadership has been the bane of socioeconomic development of sub-Saharan Africa in the postcolonial period. These leaders stunted democratic processes with force in order to preserve a system of one-person rule with no accountability. They awarded overpriced contracts to foreign companies in exchange for large kickbacks deposited in personal accounts in foreign banks. Their conspicuous consumption, cult of personality, nepotism, and naked abuse of political power encouraged a culture of greed, military coups, and instability, which reduced Africa's competitiveness for foreign investment. Governments borrowed billions in the name of the nation and cronies squandered the money, thereby saddling the people with debt.

It is also true that in the same period, global political and economic policies reinforced the legacy of colonialism and exacerbated Africa's problems of self-rule. Apartheid South Africa sponsored destabilizing wars in the southern African region, and a cycle of Cold War–surrogate wars and conflicts ravaged Angola and Mozambique. These wars claimed millions of African lives and devastated the economies of the warring countries. Economic adjustment policies of the World Bank forced African countries to cut spending in health, education, and infrastructure in order to save money to service foreign debts. Low international prices of commodities produced by Africans caused African countries to lose about $50 billion in the 1980s and early 1990s, the same period of the most virulent Afropessimism. These externally induced problems combined with internal inefficiencies to stunt Africa's political and economic growth and give rise to Afropessimism. However, by the turn of the twenty-first century sub-Saharan Africa's fortunes seemed to have turned markedly for the better.

See also **Africa, Idea of; Anticolonialism: Africa; Capitalism: Africa; Colonialism: Africa; Postcolonial Studies; Postcolonial Theory and Literature; Westernization: Africa.**

BIBLIOGRAPHY

Ayittey, George B. N. *Africa Betrayed.* New York: St. Martin's Press, 1992.

———. *Africa In Chaos.* New York: St. Martin's Press, 1998.

Hammond, Dorothy, and Alta Jablow. *The Africa That Never Was: Four Centuries of British Writing about Africa.* New York: Twayne, 1970.

Hawk, Beverly G., ed. *Africa's Media Image.* New York: Praeger, 1992.

Hitchens, Christopher. "Africa without Pity." *Vanity Fair* (November 1994): 43–52.

Jackson, Robert H., and Carl G. Rosberg. *Personal Rule in Black Africa: Prince, Autocrat, Prophet, Tyrant.* Berkeley: University of California Press, 1982.

Johnson, Paul. "Colonialism's Back—and Not a Moment Too Soon." *New York Times Magazine* (18 April 1993): 22

Kaplan, Robert. "The Coming Anarchy." *Atlantic Monthly* (February 1994): 44–76.

———. "Continental Drift." *New Republic* (28 December 1992): 15.

Michaels, Marguerite. "Retreat From Africa." *Foreign Affairs* 72, no. 1 (winter 1993): 93–108.

Onwudiwe, Ebere, "Africa's Other Story." *Current History* 101 (2002): 225–228.

———. "Image and Development: An Exploratory Discussion." *Journal of African Policy Studies* 1, no. 3 (1995): 85–97.

Onwudiwe, Ebere, and Minabere Ibelema, eds. *Afro-Optimism: Perspectives on Africa's Advances.* Westport, Conn., and London: Praeger, 2003.

Joseph, Richard A. *Democracy and Prebendal Politics in Nigeria: The Rise and Fall of the Second Republic.* New York: Cambridge University Press, 1987.

Richburg, Keith B. *Out of America: A Black Man Confronts Africa.* New York: Basic Books, 1997.

Rieff, David. "In Defense of Afropessimism." *World Policy Journal* 15, no. 4 (winter 1998–1999): 10–22. Also available at http://www.worldpolicy.org/journal/rieff.html

Xinhua News Agency. "France: Creditors Should Do More for Africa's Debt Problem." Paris, March 27, 1988, item no. 0327019.

Ebere Onwudiwe

AGNOSTICISM. The heyday of agnosticism was in Victorian Britain between the 1860s and the 1890s. Its leading exponents were Herbert Spencer (1820–1903), Thomas Henry Huxley (1825–1895) (who coined the term), Leslie Stephen (1832–1904), John Tyndall (1820–1893), and William Kingdon Clifford (1845–1879). This group all shared a disillusionment with orthodox Christianity; an opposition to the dominance of British science and education by the Anglican establishment; belief in the theory of evolution and in the importance of science more broadly; and an aspiration to replace dogmatism and superstition with a freethinking, scientific, and ethical religion (see Lightman, 1987, 1989, 2002; Pyle; Turner, 1974, 1993). While agnosticism may have been an antitheological and secularist movement, it was certainly not antireligious. The Victorian agnostics were intensely moralistic people who had a deep sense of the spiritual, especially as evoked by the wonders of the natural world.

The Philosophical Sources of Agnosticism

The term *agnosticism,* as it is used in common parlance, normally refers to a neutral or undecided position on the question of the existence of God. It is shorthand for a rejection of religious faith on the one hand and of outright atheism on the other. The philosophical sources and Victorian expositions of agnosticism, however, reveal it to signify a much broader set of arguments about the limits of human knowledge, whether religious or scientific.

Bernard Lightman's definitive study, *The Origins of Agnosticism* (1987), places particular emphasis on the concept's Kantian origins. It is true that Kantian views about the limits of speculative reason, the relativity of knowledge, and the active role of the categories of the mind in constituting that knowledge formed an important part of agnosticism. Lightman argues convincingly for the influence of two writers in particular—William Hamilton (1788–1856) and Henry Longueville Mansel (1820–1871)—on later Victorian agnostics. Hamilton was a Scottish metaphysician who, as well as seeing himself as a defender of the Scottish "common sense" philosophy of Thomas Reid (1710–1796) and Dugald Stewart (1753–1828), was probably the most

important expositor of Kantian philosophy in Britain in the first half of the nineteenth century.

Mansel drew heavily on Hamilton's particular version of Kantianism in his controversial 1858 Bampton Lectures, entitled *The Limits of Religious Thought.* In these lectures, Mansel argued that speculative reason on its own led to all sorts of contradictions if allowed free rein in the area of theology. His conclusion was that only relative knowledge was possible and that the absolute (or the *unconditioned,* to use Hamilton's term) was not knowable through the faculties of sense and reason. Mansel's conclusion was that in the realm of theology, final authority must rest with revelation rather than reason. While Mansel believed that he had used Kant's philosophy constructively—to demonstrate the necessity of revelation and the authority of the Bible—critics from all sides felt that his arguments constituted, in effect, a complete capitulation in the face of rationalism and modern science and a retreat into an extreme form of fideism.

The idea that Kantian philosophy was at the heart of agnosticism needs to be qualified in a couple of ways (as Lightman himself acknowledges). First, Hamilton and Mansel were far from being simply followers of Kant. They tried to make use of his ideas for their own polemical purposes and certainly did not agree with or reproduce his entire system. The attempt to use philosophy to undermine reason in the realm of theology and establish the necessity and authority of revelation is certainly not "Kantian" in the sense of being a teaching of Kant. Second, a recognition of the influence of Kant on Victorian agnostics should not obscure the very important contributions of David Hume (1711–1776), to whom Kant himself famously acknowledged an important debt, and of other philosophers in the Scottish tradition. These included Reid and Stewart, in whose footsteps Hamilton was following, as well as Hamilton's principal philosophical antagonist, the empiricist John Stuart Mill (1806–1873). The agnostic philosophy of Thomas Huxley, for instance, was based on a teaching central to the Scottish school, namely that "mind" and "matter" were merely shorthand terms for unknown realities that underlie the world of experience (which is the only domain in which we can have knowledge).

Victorian Agnosticism

Herbert Spencer's *First Principles* (1862) laid the groundwork for the hugely ambitious, multivolume *Synthetic Philosophy,* finally completed in 1896, which articulated Spencer's vision of how philosophy, biology, sociology, ethics, religion, and society itself needed to be reconceptualized and transformed in the light of the doctrine of evolution (see Peel). The first part of the *First Principles,* entitled "The Unknowable," was considered the Bible of agnosticism for the rest of the Victorian period. Spencer argued that science and religion could be reconciled if they recognized that both, ultimately, were concerned with realities whose foundations were beyond the grasp of human knowledge. However, while science could get on with measuring, analyzing, and interpreting observable phenomena, nothing was left for theologians but total silence in the face of the unknowable. There was no role for revelation in Spencer's proposed scientific and agnostic religion, and Mansel's conservative critics saw

THOMAS HUXLEY AND THE COINING OF *AGNOSTIC*

Thomas Henry Huxley (1825–1895) rose to prominence in Victorian Britain as a man of science and a brilliant and combative essayist. His polemical defenses of the theory of evolution against its theological detractors, especially in a legendary debate with Samuel Wilberforce (1805–1873), the bishop of Oxford, in 1860, earned him the nickname "Darwin's Bulldog." His writings covered topics in philosophy and politics as well as natural science—he was a passionate advocate of better and more widely accessible state education, especially in the sciences. His writings, which included a book on the philosophy of Hume, also reveal the depth and breadth of his learning in the areas of philosophy, religion, and theology. The following excerpt from his 1889 essay "Agnosticism" is Huxley's own account of how and why he had come to coin the term *agnostic* some twenty years earlier.

> When I reached intellectual maturity and began to ask myself whether I was an atheist, a theist, or a pantheist; a materialist or an idealist; Christian or a freethinker; I found that the more I learned and reflected, the less ready was the answer; until, at last, I came to the conclusion that I had neither art nor part with any of these denominations, except the last. The one thing in which most of these good people were agreed was the one thing in which I differed from them. They were quite sure they had attained a certain "gnosis,"—had, more or less successfully, solved the problem of existence; while I was quite sure I had not, and had a pretty strong conviction that the problem was insoluble. And, with Hume and Kant on my side, I could not think myself presumptuous in holding fast by that opinion. Like Dante,
>
> Nel mezzo del cammin di nostra vita
> Mi ritrovai per una selva oscura,
> but, unlike Dante, I cannot add,
> Che la diritta via era smarrita.
>
> On the contrary, I had, and have, the firmest conviction that I never left the "verace via"—the straight road; and that this road led nowhere else but into the dark depths of a wild and tangled forest. And though I have found leopards and lions in the path; though I have made abundant acquaintance with the hungry wolf, that "with privy paw devours apace and nothing said," as another great poet says of the ravening beast; and though no friendly spectre has even yet offered his guidance, I was, and am, minded to go straight on, until I either come out on the other side of the wood, or find there is no other side to it, at least, none attainable by me.
>
> This was my situation when I had the good fortune to find a place among the members of that remarkable confraternity of antagonists, long since deceased, but of green and pious memory, the Metaphysical Society. Every variety of philosophical and theological opinion was represented there, and expressed itself with entire openness; most of my colleagues were *-ists* of one sort or another; and, however kind and friendly they might be, I, the man without a rag of a label to cover himself with, could not fail to have some of the uneasy feelings which must have beset the historical fox when, after leaving the trap in which his tail remained, he presented himself to his normally elongated companions. So I took thought, and invented what I conceived to be the appropriate title of "agnostic." It came into my head as suggestively antithetic to the "gnostic" of Church history, who professed to know so much about the very things of which I was ignorant; and I took the earliest opportunity of parading it at our Society, to show that I, too, had a tail, like the other foxes. To my great satisfaction, the term took; and when the *Spectator* had stood godfather to it, any suspicion in the minds of respectable people, that a knowledge of its parentage might have awakened was, of course, completely lulled.

SOURCE: Thomas Huxley, "Agnosticism," in his *Collected Essays,* 9 vols. (London: Macmillan, 1893–1894), pp. 237–239.

in Spencer's system exactly the conclusions they had feared would follow from Mansel's teachings on the impotence of human reason in the theological realm.

Although Spencer was later generally considered to be the leading representative of agnosticism, the terms *agnostic* and *agnosticism* did not themselves come into use until about ten years after the publication of the *First Principles*. The terms gained currency through their use by Spencer but also by the theologian and journalist R. H. Hutton, the editor of the *Spectator* in the 1870s, and the lapsed Anglican minister Leslie Stephen, who, after leaving the Church of England, wrote *An Agnostic's Apology* (1876).

Although he made some use of the term in his writings from the 1870s onward, it was only in 1889 that Thomas Huxley revealed himself as the inventor of the terms *agnostic* and *agnosticism* and explained how and why he had come to coin them (Lightman, 2002). One of Huxley's earlier essays that gained him much attention (and much criticism) was entitled "On the Physical Basis of Life" (reprinted in *Collected Essays,* vol. 1). This essay, based on a lecture delivered in Edinburgh in 1868, just a year before he coined the term *agnostic,* is one of the most helpful illustrations of the essence of Huxley's agnosticism. Although the essay was criticized for espousing a materialistic view of life (the idea that all living things are made up of the same substance—"protoplasm"), in fact it defended a nescient or radically empiricist understanding of science as producing nothing more than a set of symbols with which to describe and organize observable phenomena. Huxley rejected materialism on the grounds that it was impossible for empirical science to determine anything at all about the nature of any putative substance or substances underlying the phenomena or of any supposed laws or causes. "In itself," Huxley said, "it is of little moment whether we express the phænomena of matter in terms of spirit; or the phænomena of spirit in terms of matter: matter may be regarded as a form of thought, thought may be regarded as a property of matter—each statement has a certain relative truth" (1893–1894, vol. 1, p. 164). (The materialistic terminology was to be preferred, however, for the pragmatic reason that it connected with other areas of scientific investigation, which were expressed in the same terms, and for the reason that spiritualistic terminology was entirely barren.) Huxley denied that this was a "new philosophy" and especially that it was the invention of the positivist Auguste Comte (1798–1857), as some supposed. Comte, he said, lacked entirely "the vigour of thought and the exquisite clearness of style" of the true author of this philosophy, "the man whom I make bold to term the most acute thinker of the eighteenth century—even though that century produced Kant" (1893–1894, vol. 1, p. 158). The man Huxley had in mind, of course, was Hume.

The closing pages of "On the Physical Basis of Life," then, show several important things about Huxley's agnosticism. They show that Huxley felt the need for a new label—*agnostic*—not in order to distance himself from Christianity (everyone already knew he was an opponent of theological orthodoxy) but primarily in order to repudiate the labels *materialist, atheist,* and *positivist.* They also show that Huxley considered Hume to be at least as important as Kant, if not more

important, in the historical pedigree of agnosticism. And finally, they show that agnosticism involved admitting ignorance about the fundamental nature of the physical universe as well as about the existence and attributes of the divine.

Agnosticism in the Twentieth Century

The scientific and religious creed of agnosticism died with Leslie Stephen in 1904. However, the philosophical and theological questions around which it was based, especially about the relationship between the observable and the unobservable, persisted into the twentieth century (although not generally under the banner of agnosticism).

The logical positivism of the earlier twentieth century, along with more recent antirealist philosophies of science (such as Bas van Fraassen's "constructive empiricism" as developed in his 1980 book, *The Scientific Image*), have contained some of the radically empiricist elements of agnosticism as endorsed by Huxley (and derived from Hume and Mill). These philosophers have insisted that all true knowledge must be grounded in experience and that since we cannot have direct experience of unobservable substances, entities, laws, or causes, we must treat them as, at best, useful fictions that serve as shorthand for empirical generalizations. Logical positivists dismissed all "metaphysical" discourse, which claimed to describe underlying realities, as meaningless. In this they agreed both with Comtean positivists and with agnostics.

In the realm of religion and theology, the problems that were central to the agnostics—especially the difficulty of reconciling religion and morality with a scientific worldview—continued to occupy religious thinkers (see Dixon). Some, such as Thomas Huxley's grandson Julian Sorell Huxley (1887–1975), put forward "evolutionary humanism" as a scientific religion based on reason and morality but without revelation. Others took a similar approach but while remaining within the Christian tradition. Don Cupitt, for instance, in books such as *Taking Leave of God* (1980) and *The Sea of Faith* (1984), adopted a "nonrealist" metaphysics and articulated a post-theological version of the Christian religion. For Cupitt, himself a minister in the Church of England, the claims of Christian theology should not be taken to refer to unseen supernatural realities, such as a personal God, but to be expressions of human values and aspirations.

So scientists seeking to give expression to a religious impulse while retaining their intellectual integrity along with theologians looking for an interpretation of the gospel that will resonate in a secular and scientific world have both continued the religious project that the Victorian agnostics had begun.

See also **Atheism; Christianity; Gnosticism; Skepticism.**

BIBLIOGRAPHY

PRIMARY SOURCES

Blinderman, Charles, and David Joyce, eds. "The Huxley File." Available at http://aleph0.clarku.edu/huxley. This is an invaluable online resource at Clark University, providing information on Huxley's life and works and access to hundreds of Huxley's published and unpublished writings.

Cupitt, Don. *Taking Leave of God.* London: SCM, 1980.

Huxley, Thomas H. "Agnosticism," "Agnosticism: A Rejoinder," and "Agnosticism and Christianity." *Nineteenth Century* 25 (1889): 169–194, 481–504, 937–964. Reprinted in Thomas H. Huxley, *Collected Essays*, vol. 5: *Science and Christian Tradition.* London: Macmillan, 1894.

———. *Collected Essays.* 9 vols. London: Macmillan, 1893–1894.

Pyle, Andrew, ed. *Agnosticism: Contemporary Responses to Spencer and Huxley.* Bristol: Thoemmes, 1995.

Spencer, Herbert. *First Principles.* London: Williams and Norgate, 1862. Especially pt. 1.

Van Fraassen, Bas. *The Scientific Image.* Oxford: Clarendon, 1980.

SECONDARY SOURCES

Budd, Susan. *Varieties of Unbelief: Atheists and Agnostics in English Society, 1850–1960.* London: Heinemann, 1977.

Cockshut, A. O. J. *The Unbelievers: English Agnostic Thought, 1840–1890.* London: Collins, 1964.

Desmond, Adrian. *Huxley: From Devil's Disciple to Evolution's High Priest.* London: Penguin, 1998.

Dixon, Thomas. "Scientific Atheism as a Faith Tradition." *Studies in History and Philosophy of Biological and Biomedical Sciences* 33 (2002): 337–359.

Helmstadter, Richard J., and Bernard Lightman, eds. *Victorian Faith in Crisis: Essays on Continuity and Change in Nineteenth-Century Religious Belief.* Stanford, Calif.: Stanford University Press, 1990.

Lightman, Bernard. "Huxley and Scientific Agnosticism: The Strange History of a Failed Rhetorical Strategy." *British Journal for the History of Science* 35 (2002): 271–289.

———. "Ideology, Evolution, and Late-Victorian Agnostic Popularizers." In *History, Humanity, and Evolution: Essays for John C. Greene*, edited by James Moore. Cambridge, U.K.: Cambridge University Press, 1989.

———. *The Origins of Agnosticism: Victorian Unbelief and the Limits of Knowledge.* Baltimore: Johns Hopkins University Press, 1987.

Peel, J. D. Y. *Herbert Spencer: The Evolution of a Sociologist.* New York: Basic Books, 1971.

Turner, Frank M. *Between Science and Religion: The Reaction to Scientific Naturalism in Late Victorian England.* New Haven, Conn.: Yale University Press, 1974.

———. *Contesting Cultural Authority: Essays in Victorian Intellectual Life.* Cambridge, U.K.: Cambridge University Press, 1993.

White, Paul. *Thomas Huxley: Making the "Man of Science."* Cambridge, U.K.: Cambridge University Press, 2003.

Thomas Dixon

ALCHEMY.

This entry includes two subentries:

China
Europe and the Middle East

CHINA

Chinese alchemy is based on doctrinal principles, first set out in the founding texts of Daoism, concerning the relation between the domains of the Absolute and the relative, or the Dao and the "ten thousand things" (*wanwu*). Its teachings and practices focus on the idea of the elixir, frequently referred to as the Golden Elixir (*jindan*), the Reverted Elixir (*huandan*), or the Medicine (*yao*). Lexical analysis shows that the semantic field of the term *dan* (elixir) evolves from a root-meaning of "essence"; its connotations include the reality, principle, or true nature of an entity, or its most basic and significant element or property. The purport of alchemy as a doctrine is to illustrate the nature of this underlying "authentic principle" and to explicate its relation to change and multiplicity.

In the associated practices, compounding the elixir has two primary meanings. In the first sense, the elixir is obtained by heating its ingredients in a crucible. This practice, as well as the branch of alchemy that is associated with it, is known as *waidan*, or "external alchemy" (literally, "outer elixir"). In the second sense, the ingredients of the elixir are the primary components of the cosmos and the human being, and the entire process takes place within the practitioner. This second form of practice (which incorporates some aspects of Daoist meditation methods and of physiological techniques of self-cultivation), as well as the corresponding branch of the alchemical tradition, is known as *neidan*, or "inner alchemy" (literally, "inner elixir"). The Chinese alchemical tradition has therefore three main aspects, namely a doctrinal level and two paradigmatic forms of practice, respectively based on the refining of an "outer" or an "inner" elixir.

The Elixir in External Alchemy

Although the first allusions to alchemy in China date from the second century B.C.E., the combination of doctrines and practices involving the compounding of an elixir, which is necessary to define alchemy as such and to distinguish it from proto-chemistry, is not clearly attested to in extant sources until the third century C.E. The first identifiable tradition, known as Taiqing (Great Clarity; Pregadio, 2005), developed from that time in Jiangnan, the region south of the lower Yangzi River that was also crucial for the history of Daoism during the Six Dynasties (third to sixth centuries). The Taiqing scriptures consist of descriptions of methods for compounding elixirs and of benefits gained from their performance and contain virtually no statements regarding their doctrinal foundations. The emphasis given to certain aspects of the practice and the terminology used in those descriptions, however, show that the central act of the alchemical process consists in causing matter to revert to its state of "essence" (*jing*), or *prima materia*. The main role in this task is played by the crucible, whose function is to provide a medium equivalent to the inchoate state (*hundun*) prior to the formation of the cosmos. In that medium, under the action of fire, the ingredients of the elixir are transmuted, or "reverted" (*huan*), to their original state. A seventh-century commentary to one of the Taiqing scriptures equates this refined matter with the "essence" that, as stated in the *Daode jing* (Scripture of the Way and Its Virtue), gives birth to the world of multiplicity: "Indistinct! Vague! But within it there is something. Dark! Obscure! But within it there is an essence."

In the Taiqing texts, compounding the elixir constitutes the central part of a larger process consisting of several stages, each of which is marked by the performance of rites and ceremonies.

Receiving the scriptures and the oral instructions, building the laboratory, kindling the fire, and ingesting the elixir all require offering pledges to one's master and to the gods, observing rules on seclusion and purification, performing ceremonies to delimit and protect the ritual area, and making invocations to the highest deities. Ingesting the elixir is said to confer transcendence and admission into the celestial bureaucracy. Additionally the elixir grants healing from illnesses and protection from demons, spirits, and several other disturbances. To provide these supplementary benefits, the elixir does not need to be ingested and may simply be kept in one's hand or carried at one's belt as a powerful apotropaic talisman.

The methods of the Taiqing texts are characterized by the use of a large number of ingredients. Sources attached to later *waidan* traditions instead describe different varieties of a single exemplary method, consisting of the refining of mercury (Yin) from cinnabar (Yang), its addition to sulfur (Yang), and its further refining. This process, typically repeated seven or nine times, yields an elixir that is deemed to embody the qualities of pure Yang (*chunyang*)—that is, the state of oneness before its differentiation into Yin and Yang.

Role of Cosmology

The doctrinal aspects of alchemy are the main focus of many sources dating from the Tang period (seventh to tenth centuries) onward. These sources formulate their teachings and practices by borrowing the language and the abstract emblems of correlative cosmology, a comprehensive system designed to explicate the nature and properties of different domains—primarily the cosmos and the human being—and the relations that occur among them. The main work that reflects these changes and provides them with textual authority is the *Zhouyi cantong qi* (Token of the Agreement of the Three According to the *Book of Changes*; the "three" mentioned in the title are, according to some commentaries, Daoism, cosmology, and alchemy). Virtually the entire alchemical tradition from the Tang period onward acknowledges this text as its most important scriptural source. Despite this, the *Cantong qi* does not primarily deal with either *waidan* or *neidan* and only occasionally alludes to both of them. Its main purpose is to illustrate the nonduality of the Dao and the cosmos; the task of explicating the details of this doctrinal view, and of applying it to *waidan* and *neidan*, is left to the commentaries and to a large number of related texts.

The emblems of correlative cosmology—typically arranged in patterns that include Yin and Yang, the five agents (*wuxing*), the eight trigrams and the sixty-four hexagrams of the *Book of Changes* (*Yijing*), and so forth—play two main roles closely related to each other. First, they illustrate the relation between unity, duality, and the various other stages of the propagation of Original Pneuma (*yuanqi*) into the "ten thousand things." In this function, cosmological emblems serve to show how space, time, multiplicity, and change are related to the spacelessness, timelessness, nonduality, and constancy of the Dao. For instance, the *Cantong qi* describes the five agents (which define, in particular, the main spatial and temporal coordinates of the cosmos) as unfolding from the center, which contains them all, runs through them, and "endows them with its efficacy." In their second role, the emblems of the cosmological system are used to formulate the relation of the alchemical practice to the doctrinal principles. For instance, the trigrams of the *Book of Changes* illustrate how the alchemical process consists in extracting the pre-cosmic Real Yin (*zhenyin*) and Real Yang (*zhenyang*) from Yang and Yin as they appear in the cosmos, respectively, and in joining them to produce an elixir that represents their original oneness (Pregadio, 2000, pp. 182–184).

In the traditions based on the *Cantong qi*, alchemy is primarily a figurative language to represent doctrinal principles. The *waidan* process loses its ritual features, and the compounding of the elixir is based on two emblematic metals, mercury and lead. The refined states of these metals—respectively obtained from cinnabar and from native lead—represent Yin and Yang in their original, pre-cosmic state, and their conjunction produces an elixir whose properties are said to be equivalent to Pure Yang. The central role played by cosmology in these *waidan* traditions is reflected in two works related to the *Cantong qi*, which respectively state that "compounding the Great Elixir is not a matter of ingredients, but always of the Five Agents," and even that "you do not use ingredients, you use the Five Agents."

Doctrines and Practices of Inner Alchemy

Besides a new variety of *waidan*, the *Cantong qi* also influenced the formation of *neidan* (Robinet, 1989, 1995), whose earliest extant texts date from the first half of the eighth century. The authors of several *neidan* treatises refer to their teachings as the Way of the Golden Elixir (*jindan zhi dao*). Their doctrines essentially consist of a reformulation of those enunciated in the early Daoist texts, integrated with language and images drawn from the system of correlative cosmology according to the model provided by the *Cantong qi*. The respective functions of these two major components of the alchemical discourse are clearly distinguished in the doctrinal treatises. Their authors point out that the alchemical teachings can only be understood in the light of those of the *Daode jing* (which they consider to be "the origin of the Way of the Golden Elixir") and that correlative cosmology provides "images" (*xiang*) that serve, as stated by Li Daochun (fl. 1288–1292), "to give form to the Formless by the word, and thus manifest the authentic and absolute Dao" (*Zhonghe ji*, chapter 3; see Robinet, 1995, p. 75). The alchemical discourse therefore has its roots in metaphysical principles; it uses the language and images of correlative cosmology to explicate the nature of the cosmos and its ultimate unity with the absolute principle that generates and regulates it. Its final purpose, however, is to transcend the cosmic domain, so that the use of images and metaphors involves explaining their relative value and temporary function.

The status attributed to doctrines and practices reflects this view. Some authors emphasize that the inner elixir is possessed by every human being and is a representation of one's own innate realized state. Liu Yiming (1737–1821) expresses this notion as follows:

> Human beings receive this Golden Elixir from Heaven.
> . . . Golden Elixir is another name for one's fundamental
> nature, formed out of primeval inchoateness [*huncheng*,
> a term derived from the *Daode jing*]. There is no other

Golden Elixir outside one's fundamental nature. Every human being has this Golden Elixir complete in oneself: it is entirely achieved in everybody. It is neither more in a sage, nor less in an ordinary person. It is the seed of Immortals and Buddhas, and the root of worthies and sages. (*Wuzhen zhizhi,* chapter 1)

Borrowing terms from the *Cantong qi,* which in turn draws them from the *Daode jing,* Liu Yiming calls "superior virtue" (*shangde*) the immediate realization of the original "celestial reality" (*tianzhen*), which is never affected by the change and impermanence that dominate in the cosmos, and "inferior virtue" (*xiade*), the performance of the alchemical process in order to "return to the Dao." He states, however, that the latter way, when it achieves fruition, "becomes a road leading to the same goal as superior virtue" (*Cantong zhizhi,* "Jing," chapter 2).

While the *neidan* practices are codified in ways that differ, sometimes noticeably, from each other, the notion of "inversion" (*ni*) is common to all of them (Robinet, 1992). In the most common codification, the practice is framed as the reintegration of each of the primary components of being, namely essence, pneuma, and spirit (*jing, qi,* and *shen*), into the one that precedes it in the ontological hierarchy, culminating in the "reversion" (*huan*) to the state of nonbeing (*wu*) or emptiness (*kong*). The typical formulation of this process is "refining essence and transmuting it into pneuma," "refining pneuma and transmuting it into spirit," and "refining spirit and returning to Emptiness." Li Daochun relates these stages to the passage of the *Daode jing* that states: "The Dao generates the One, the One generates the Two, the Two generate the Three, the Three generate the ten thousand things." According to this passage, the Dao first generates Oneness, which harbors the complementary principles of Yin and Yang. After Yin and Yang differentiate from each other, they rejoin and generate the "Three," which represents the One at the level of the particular entities. The "ten thousand things" are the totality of the entities produced by the continuous reiteration of this process. In Li Daochun's explication, the three stages of the *neidan* practice consist in reverting from the "ten thousand things" to emptiness, or the Dao. In this way, the gradual process that characterizes inner alchemy as a practice is equivalent to the instantaneous realization of the nonduality of the Absolute and the relative.

Just as *waidan* draws many of its basic methods from pharmacology, so *neidan* too shares a significant portion of its notions and methods with classical Chinese medicine and with other bodies of practices, such as meditation and the methods for "nourishing life" (*yangsheng*). What distinguishes alchemy from these related traditions is its unique view of the elixir and a material or immaterial entity that represents the original state of being and the attainment of that state.

See also **Alchemy: Europe and the Middle East; Medicine: China.**

BIBLIOGRAPHY

Needham, Joseph. *Science and Civilisation in China.* Vol. 5, *Chemistry and Chemical Technology,* parts 2–5. Cambridge, U.K.: Cambridge University Press, 1974–1983. Broad overview of the Chinese alchemical tradition, partly superseded by later studies.

Pregadio, Fabrizio. "Elixirs and Alchemy." In *Daoism Handbook,* edited by Livia Kohn. Leiden: E. J. Brill, 2000. Surveys the history, texts, doctrines, and practices of *waidan.*

———. *Great Clarity: Daoism and Alchemy in Early Medieval China.* Stanford, Calif.: Stanford University Press, 2005. Study of the Taiqing tradition of *waidan* and its relation to Daoism; includes translations of early sources.

Pregadio, Fabrizio, and Lowell Skar. "Inner Alchemy (*Neidan*)." In *Daoism Handbook,* edited by Livia Kohn. Leiden: E. J. Brill, 2000. Survey of history, texts, doctrines, and practices.

Robinet, Isabelle. *Introduction à l'alchimie intérieure taoïste: De l'unité et de la multiplicité. Avec une traduction commentée des Versets de l'éveil à la Vérité.* Paris: Les Éditions du Cerf, 1995. Collection of articles reflecting the best understanding of *neidan* among Western-language studies; includes a translation of a major *neidan* text.

———. "Le monde à l'envers dans l'alchimie intérieure taoïste." *Revue de l'Histoire des Religions* 209 (1992): 239–257. On the notion of "inversion" in *neidan.*

———. "Original Contributions of *Neidan* to Taoism and Chinese Thought." In *Taoist Meditation and Longevity Techniques,* edited by Livia Kohn in cooperation with Yoshinobu Sakade. Ann Arbor: Center for Chinese Studies, University of Michigan, 1989. Focuses on the notions and linguistic expedients used in texts of "inner alchemy" to formulate their doctrines.

Sivin, Nathan. *Chinese Alchemy: Preliminary Studies.* Cambridge, Mass.: Harvard University Press, 1968. Translation of a seventh-century text, with an extensive introduction on *waidan* seen as a branch of the history of Chinese science.

Sivin, Nathan. 1980. "The Theoretical Background of Elixir Alchemy." In Joseph Needham, *Science and Civilisation in China.* Vol. 5, *Chemistry and Chemical Technology,* part 4, *Apparatus, Theories and Gifts.* Cambridge, U.K.: Cambridge University Press. On the role of time in *waidan* and the cosmic correspondences embodied in the apparatus.

Fabrizio Pregadio

EUROPE AND THE MIDDLE EAST

To a modern observer, *alchemy* likely connotes only the transmutation of base metals into gold, or perhaps a more metaphorical transformation of the soul. In its roughly two-thousand-year history, however, alchemy's practices and ideas have ranged much more broadly, encompassing everything from the production of dyes, medicines, precious metals, and gemstones to assaying techniques, matter theory, and spiritual practices linking the manipulation of matter to changes in the alchemist's soul. Although all of these dimensions were present from alchemy's beginnings, practitioners have chosen to highlight particular facets of their art at different times. Any definition of alchemy, therefore, must be both sensitive to its historical permutations and broad enough to include each of its chemical, pharmacological, metallurgical, and spiritual components. To be more precise, one may speak of technical or practical alchemy, spiritual alchemy, natural philosophical alchemy, transmutational alchemy, and medical alchemy (often referred to as iatrochemistry or *chimiatria*). This essay offers an overview of alchemy's changing meaning over its rich and long history.

Practical Origins in Hellenistic Egypt

Although alchemy's roots undoubtedly extend as far back as metallurgy itself, the textual record dates to the first centuries C.E. in the Egyptian city of Alexandria. Immersed in an extraordinary mix of cultures and traditions, Alexandrian alchemists blended Greek matter theory and philosophy, Neoplatonism, Gnosticism, Babylonian astrology, Egyptian mythology, mystery cults, and craft recipes for making cosmetics, beer, precious stones, and gold. Because the few extant texts from this period were written in Greek, this initial period is typically known as Greek alchemy.

The oldest text documenting early alchemy is the *Physika kai mystika* (Of natural and mystical things), purportedly written by the Greek natural philosopher Democritus but likely written by Bolos of Mendes (third century B.C.E.). The *Physika kai mystika* and other similar texts (such as two anonymous Egyptian papyri known as the Leiden Papyrus X and the Stockholm Papyrus) focus on the kind of practical knowledge that would continue to engage alchemists for centuries, providing instructions for how to manufacture and "multiply" gold and silver, as well as how to produce chemically other valuable gemstones, pearls, and dyes. The works of a female alchemist from Hellenistic Egypt named Maria the Jewess (fl. 250 C.E.) contain the oldest descriptions of some of alchemy's most important apparatus, namely alchemical furnaces and stills.

Theoretical Foundations in Antiquity

Such practical alchemical work received theoretical justification in part from Greek natural philosophy. Although Aristotle (384–322 B.C.E) did not write about alchemy per se, he provided a theory of matter that made it possible to conceptualize the transmutation of metals. Aristotle posited the notion that all things were composed of the same formless, passive matter (*materia prima*), which was then transformed into a specific substance by an active, shaping form. For alchemical theory, Aristotle's crucial notion was that, because the four elements—earth, fire, water, and air—were composed of the same basic matter, they could be transmuted into one another by altering their forms. Through the application of heat, for example, water could be transmuted into "air" (steam). From this, alchemists developed the idea of isolating the *materia prima* in metals and transmuting one into another through the use of an agent known as the philosophers' stone or elixir.

The rich cultural resources of the Hellenistic world further developed alchemy's theoretical foundations. From Stoic matter theory, pneuma, or spirits, replaced Aristotelian forms as the active defining force of matter. From Babylonian astrological traditions alchemists adopted the identification of the seven metals (gold, silver, mercury, copper, iron, tin, and lead) with the seven planets (sun, moon, Mercury, Venus, Mars, Jupiter, and Saturn) and the division of both metals and planets into male and female. Finally, the central transmutational process of reducing metals to their *materia prima* before recreating them as gold or silver drew on ideas presented in the Egyptian myth of Isis and Osiris, in which Osiris was killed and dismembered before Isis brought him back to life.

A collection of texts written in the first centuries C.E. known as the *Hermetica* were attributed to Hermes Trismegistos, a figure identified with the Egyptian god Thoth, the mythical creator of the arts and sciences. Although alchemy was only one topic among many in the *Hermetica,* in the European Middle Ages Hermes came to be known as the legendary first alchemist and alchemy as the "hermetic art." The *Hermetica* ranged in content from medical, astrological, and magical treatises to much more theosophical ruminations on the redemption of the spirit through gnosis.

This association in the *Hermetica* between practical alchemy and spiritual gnosis found its way into alchemical theory through later authors. The link between spiritual and practical goals of transmutational alchemy is particularly evident in the work of the Alexandrian Zosimos of Panopolis (fl. 300 C.E.; later Latinized as Rosinius). In his compilation of older alchemical writings known as the *Cheirokmeta,* Zosimos wove his practical alchemy into a mystical theoretical framework that would prove just as enduring as alchemy's more technical concerns. Full of secretive language, dream sequences, and allegories, Zosimos's texts describe alchemical processes metaphorically—as sexual generation, for instance—and highlight the role of spirits in transforming matter. With a clear debt to Gnosticism, Zosimos established an enduring connection between practical laboratory work and spiritual perfection.

Medieval Arabic Alchemy

When Islamic empires expanded into centers of Hellenistic culture in the seventh century, Muslim natural philosophers and physicians inherited the Greek alchemical tradition. From the eighth to the tenth centuries, scholars in intellectual centers like Baghdad synthesized the basic elements of the Greek alchemical tradition. The anonymous editor of the *Turba philosophorum* (Crowd of philosophers; c. 900), for instance, assembled excerpts from various Greek alchemical authors into a virtual conversation. Alchemists writing in Arabic also elaborated on the Greek theoretical foundation, contributing a number of key concepts to alchemical matter theory and medicine. The word *alchemy,* a combination of the Arabic definite article *al* with the Greek word *chemeia,* or *chymeia* (likely derived from the word for smelting metals, *cheein*), represents this fusion of Greek and Arabic scholarship, while continued use of Arabic alchemical terms such as *alkalai, alcohol, alembic,* and *elixir* (*al-iksir*) highlights the legacy of Arabic scholarship.

The translation of Greek alchemical texts into Arabic also underscores a central problem in the history of alchemy: pseudonymous texts. In the first centuries C.E., alchemical texts appeared purportedly authored by figures such as Plato, Socrates, Aristotle, and Cleopatra. Because Arabic and later European translators did not identify these pseudonyms as such, these prominent ancient figures entered the alchemical corpus as legitimate alchemical authors. The authorship of Arabic texts has been equally difficult for scholars to decipher. One of the more influential medieval Arabic texts, for instance, contains a dialogue between King Khalid ibn Yazid (c. 660–704) and a Christian hermit living in Jerusalem, Morienus. Although it is unclear whether Khalid and Morienus actually wrote this text, both figures remained prominent personages in the medieval alchemical tradition.

A collection of thousands of texts dating to the eighth and tenth centuries known in Latin as the *Corpus Gabirianum* and attributed to Jabir ibn Hayaan (c. 721–c. 815) contained fundamental contributions to the medieval Arabic alchemical corpus. Among the innovations of the *Corpus* was the concept of a tripartite division of all things into soul, spirit, and body, a division that would play a central role in European alchemical thought of the sixteenth century. The *Corpus* also introduced the sulfur-mercury theory, which its author had adopted from the ninth-century author Balinus (pseudo-Apollonius of Tyana). This variation on Aristotle's forms and the Stoic pneuma stated that all matter was formed by two qualities, sulfur and mercury, the balance of which existed in varying degrees in different metals. Using the elixir (or philosophers' stone) to shift the balance between these two principles, the alchemist could transmute one metal into another. The *Corpus* also posited that the elixir could be made of plant or animal substances as well as mineral, and that it could be used both as a panacea in medicine and in transmutation. Just as the elixir "cured" base metals of their impurities by transmuting them into silver or gold, so too could it "cure" sick people of their illnesses.

The Persian physician and philosopher Abu Bakr Muhammad ibn Zachariya al-Razi, known in Latin as Rhazes (c. 865–between 923 and 935) is best known for setting out a systematic summary of the "state of the field" of alchemy. Al-Razi added a third quality, salt, to the sulfur-mercury theory, and divided the chemical world into animal, vegetable, and mineral realms. Al-Razi's texts show that he was clearly a practicing alchemist, describing experiments, apparatus, and ingredients, as well as the standard steps of the "great work" of making the elixir.

Although both al-Razi and the *Corpus Gabirianum* provided theoretical justifications of the notion of transmutation, not all Arabic-speaking philosophers supported this idea. The physician Abdallah ibn Sina (Latinized as Avicenna; 980–1037) famously inveighed against the possibility of transmutation in his *Kitab al-shifa* (Book of the remedy), articulating an argument that would prove widely influential in the Latin Middle Ages.

The Latin Middle Ages

In the twelfth century, Europeans such as Gerard of Cremona, Daniel of Morley, and Robert of Ketton began to translate more than seventy Arabic texts into Latin, introducing Europeans for the first time to the alchemical corpus and the Arabic term *al-kimiya*, which became the Latin *alquimia, alkimia, alchimia,* or *alchemia*. By the end of the century, translations from Morienus, the *Corpus Gabirianum,* and al-Razi, as well as a host of other spurious alchemical texts, acquainted Europeans with the central figures, techniques, and ideas of the Greek and Arabic alchemical traditions. A vibrant European technical literature emerged, dealing with alchemical techniques for dye-making, distilling, metallurgy, mineralogy, and, of course, the transmutation of metals.

Alongside this practical literature, European alchemists writing in Latin also continued to develop the theoretical foundations of their art. Around 1250 the prominent philosopher Albertus Magnus (c. 1200–1280) legitimated scholarly interest in alchemy when he praised alchemists' ability to imitate nature in his *De mineralibus* (On minerals). The late-thirteenth-century *Summa perfectionis magisterii* of Pseudo-Geber (or "the Latin Geber," likely the Italian Franciscan Paul of Taranto) replaced the mercury-sulfur theory with the "mercury alone" theory, which stated that mercury was the fundamental component of metals, while sulfur was a pollutant. Drawing on Aristotle, medieval natural philosophy, and medical theory, Pseudo-Geber also articulated a corpuscular theory of matter, positing that all matter is composed of small particles.

In the thirteenth century a debate emerged around alchemy's legitimacy and its relationship to other fields of knowledge. The central issue was whether alchemy, as a form of human art or technology, was capable of successfully imitating or even surpassing nature. Responding initially to ibn Sina's famous rejection of transmutation (often given greater authority by its erroneous attribution to Aristotle), scholars such as Roger Bacon (c. 1220–1292) and Paul of Taranto forcefully argued that true alchemists could indeed use their knowledge of metals to affect real transmutations. In the late thirteenth and fourteenth centuries Thomas Aquinas, Giles of Rome (Aegidius Romanus), and the inquisitor Nicholas Eymeric formulated theological objections to alchemy, arguing that the power to transmute species was reserved for God alone. This religious critique reached its peak around 1317 with Pope John XXII's condemnation of those alchemists who "promise that which they do not produce." Although this papal bull's primary target was alchemical counterfeiting of metals, it sanctioned the increasingly vociferous backlash against alchemists' claims of power over nature. Still, alchemy continued to flourish in the fourteenth century, as evidenced by the popularity of the Fransciscan Johannes de Rupescissa's treatise on the quintessence, or inner essence, of all matter, and a spate of alchemical texts spuriously propagated in the fourteenth century under the name of the thirteenth-century Catalan physician Ramon Lull.

Renaissance Europe

The fifteenth-century rediscovery of the ancient Hermetic corpus and a concurrent revival of Neoplatonism introduced learned Europeans to ancient connections among alchemy, gnosis, and magic. Alchemy's renewed associations with magic and nature's occult forces broadened the primarily technical and natural philosophical discussions of alchemy of the Middle Ages. Hermetic philosophers began to reenvision themselves as operators who might use knowledge of nature to manipulate their world.

At the same time, alchemy's practical utility gained prominence in the sixteenth century, primarily through the work of the Swiss physician and alchemist Paracelsus (1493–1541) and his followers. Although he did not deny the possibility of alchemical transmutation, Paracelsus focused mainly on alchemy's medical applications, advocating a new kind of alchemical medicine, known as *chimiatria* or iatrochemistry, in which practitioners used alchemical distillation and extraction to isolate the quintessence of matter for medicinal purposes. These powerful (and often controversial) new alchemical drugs were designed to attack the specific disease, in contrast to traditional humoral medicine, which sought to treat the balance of humors within the body as a whole. On the theoretical level, Paracelsus also offered a new understanding of matter, complementing the ancient four elements with the *tria principia* or *tria prima,* adding salt to the two medieval principles of matter (sulfur and mercury). By refining alchemical matter theory and re-situating medicine on a new foundation of alchemy, Paracelsus and his followers gave the ancient art a new prominence both in the study of nature and in the practice of medicine.

Transmutation remained a prominent goal for many alchemists, particularly the consumers of a burgeoning trade in printed alchemical books. By the sixteenth century, alchemy had burst the bounds of the world of scholarship and found a much wider audience in Europe. In particular, alchemy's central image of purification and ennoblement resonated with religious reformers such as Desiderius Erasmus, Martin Luther, and the German mystic Jakob Böhme, all of whom drew on alchemical metaphors and imagery in their writings. Alchemical authors also made explicit connections between alchemy and Christianity. Heinrich Khunrath (1560–1605), for instance, specifically articulated such connections, comparing the healing power of the philosophers' stone to the redemptive powers of Christ in the *Ampitheatrum sapientiae aeternae solis verae* of 1595.

Urban readers, literate artisans, and learned ladies also took an interest in alchemy, consuming popular vernacular alchemical literature that tended to focus on the practical benefits of the art, particularly the production of precious metals, gemstones, and medicines. Many self-trained alchemists ultimately found employment among Europe's courts, where many princes generously supported practical and theoretical alchemical work. Faced with an increasingly crowded field of practitioners and no traditional markers of authority such as university degrees, licenses, or guilds, those who consumed alchemical knowledge and products struggled to make their own decisions about what constituted legitimate alchemy. With such a wide variety of people both seeking out knowledge and claiming to be alchemists, new debates emerged in the sixteenth century about what true alchemy was and who could legitimately claim to practice it.

The Scientific Revolution and Beyond

Although it has been assumed that alchemy was inconsistent with new ideas about nature associated with the scientific revolution or that the promoters of the "new science" rejected alchemy, historians now refuse simple narratives associating the scientific revolution with the decline of alchemy. During the seventeenth century, alchemy continued to be a vibrant field of natural philosophical inquiry; most prominent natural philosophers took a mixed view of it. Francis Bacon (1561–1626), for instance, condemned alchemists' tendency toward secrecy, contrasting it with the openness and cooperation that he advocated in reforming the pursuit of natural knowledge. Still, he looked to alchemy as an important source of knowledge about matter and medicine.

Historians have shown that Robert Boyle (1627–1691) and Isaac Newton (1642–1727) were both deeply involved with alchemy both in theory and practice, often in startlingly productive ways. Boyle, for instance, believed in the possibility of transmutation and worked on it for decades, seeking out the knowledge and skills of numerous adepts. Boyle's corpuscular matter theory, for which he is often hailed as a crucial figure in the history of chemistry, bolstered his belief in transmutation and the philosophers' stone. Scholars have shown that Isaac Newton was an avid student of alchemy as well, likely devoting more time to alchemical study and experiments in his lifetime than to physics. Although historians still have a great deal to understand about the exact purpose of Newton's alchemical studies, they clearly played a crucial role in his larger project of understanding God and nature.

By the end of the seventeenth century, alchemy was associated with new medicines, natural magic, ancient wisdom, and popular recipes for making gold as well as the innovations of the scientific revolution. Over the course of the eighteenth century, however, the alchemist's purview came to be more limited. Influenced by Antoine Lavoisier's (1743–1794) efforts to resituate chemical natural philosophy on a foundation of quantitative analysis of matter, a new kind of chemist emerged. Whereas the terms *alchemy* and *chemistry* were used synonymously until the end of the seventeenth century, in the eighteenth century scholars increasingly sought to separate the two, restricting *alchemy* to gold making and spiritual alchemy (activities that natural philosophers began to exclude from science), while also redefining alchemy's scientific and technical dimensions as *chemistry.* As a result, alchemy increasingly lost its long-standing association with science in the eighteenth century, retaining only its ancient links to mysticism and transmutation.

Alchemy continued to flourish among communities of occultists and Romantic natural philosophers in the late eighteenth, nineteenth, and twentieth centuries. Johann Wolfgang von Goethe (1749–1832), for instance, had an enduring interest in alchemy, viewing it as a secret key to the relationships between humans, God, and the cosmos. Nineteenth-century occultists picked up a theosophical thread in the writings of earlier authors such as Paracelsus, Valentin Weigel (1533–1588), Jakob Böhme (1575–1624), and Emanuel Swedenborg (1688–1772), incorporating alchemical study and images into the activities of secret societies. Finally, in the early twentieth century, the psychologist Carl Gustav Jung identified similarities between alchemical symbols and the dreams of his patients, positing that alchemists' descriptions of transmutation were a metaphor for the development of the individual. This view of alchemy, which interprets alchemy as a symbol for deeper psychological processes, has endured in the popular imagination into the twenty-first century.

See also **Chemistry; Magic; Medicine: Islamic Medicine; Neoplatonism; Pseudoscience; Science, History of.**

BIBLIOGRAPHY

Baldwin, Martha. "Alchemy and the Society of Jesus in the Seventeenth Century: Strange Bedfellows?" *Ambix* 40 (1993): 41–64.

Dobbs, Betty Jo Teeter. *The Janus Faces of Genius: The Role of Alchemy in Newton's Thought.* Cambridge, U.K., and New York: Cambridge University Press, 1991.

Eamon, William. *Science and the Secrets of Nature: Books of Secrets in Medieval and Early Modern Culture.* Princeton, N.J.: Princeton University Press, 1994.

Harkness, Deborah E. *John Dee's Conversations with Angels: Cabala, Alchemy, and the End of Nature.* Cambridge, U.K., and New York: Cambridge University Press, 1999.

Lindsay, Jack. *The Origins of Alchemy in Graeco-Roman Egypt.* London and New York: Muller, 1970.

Moran, Bruce. *The Alchemical World of the German Court: Occult Philosophy and Chemical Medicine in the Circle of Moritz of Hessen (1572–1632).* Stuttgart, Germany: F. Steiner, 1991.

Multhauf, Robert P. *The Origins of Chemistry.* Langhorne, Pa.: Gordon and Breach Science Publishers, 1993.

Newman, William R. *Gehennical Fire: The Lives of George Starkey, an American Alchemist in the Scientific Revolution.* Cambridge, Mass.: Harvard University Press, 1994.

———, ed. *The Summa Perfectionis of Pseudo-Geber: A Critical Edition, Translation, and Study.* Leiden, Netherlands, and New York: Brill, 1991.

Newman, William R., and Lawrence M. Principe. "Alchemy vs. Chemistry: The Etymological Origins of a Historiographic Mistake." *Early Science and Medicine* 3 (1998): 32–65.

Patai, Raphael. "Maria the Jewess—Founding Mother of Alchemy." *Ambix* 29, no. 3 (November 1982): 177–197.

Principe, Lawrence M. *The Aspiring Adept: Robert Boyle and His Alchemical Quest.* Princeton, N.J.: Princeton University Press, 1998.

Principe, Lawrence M., and William R. Newman. "Some Problems with the Historiography of Alchemy." In *Secrets of Nature: Astrology and Alchemy in Early Modern Europe,* edited by William R. Newman and Anthony Grafton, 385–431. Cambridge, Mass.: MIT Press, 2001.

Rattansi, Piyo, and Antonio Clericuzio, eds. *Alchemy and Chemistry in the Sixteenth and Seventeenth Centuries.* Dordrecht, Netherlands: Kluwer, 1994.

Smith, Pamela H. *The Business of Alchemy: Science and Culture in the Holy Roman Empire.* Princeton, N.J.: Princeton University Press, 1994.

Yates, Frances A. *Giordano Bruno and the Hermetic Tradition.* Chicago: University of Chicago Press, 1964.

Tara E. Nummedal

ALGEBRAS. The word *algebra* refers to a theory, usually mathematical, which is dominated by the use of words (often abbreviated), signs, and symbols to represent the objects under study (such as numbers), means of their combination (such as addition), and relationships between them (such as inequalities or equations). An algebra cannot be characterized solely as the determination of unknowns, for then most mathematics is algebra.

For a long time the only known algebra, which was and is widely taught at school, represented numbers and/or geometrical magnitudes, and was principally concerned with solving polynomial equations; this might be called "common algebra."

But especially during the nineteenth century other algebras were developed.

The discussion below uses a distinction between three modes of algebraic mathematics that was made in 1837 by the great nineteenth-century Irish algebraist W. R. Hamilton (1805–1865): (1) The "practical" is an algebra of some kind, but it only provides a useful set of abbreviations or signs for quantities and operations; (2) In the "theological" mode the algebra furnishes the epistemological basis for the theory involved, which may belong to another branch of mathematics (for example, mechanics); (3) In the "philological" mode the algebra furnishes in some essential way the formal language of the theory.

Lack of space prevents much discussion of the motivations and applications of algebras. The most important were geometries, the differential and integral calculus, and algebraic number theory.

Not Distant Origins?

Several branches of mathematics must have primeval, unknown, origins: for example, arithmetic, geometry, trigonometry, and mechanics. But algebra is not one of them. While Mesopotamian and other ancient cultures show evidence of methods of determining numerical quantities, the means required need only arithmetical calculations; no symbolism is evident, or needed. Concerning the Greeks, the *Elements* of Euclid (fourth century B.C.E.), a discourse on plane and solid geometry with some arithmetic, was often regarded as "geometric algebra"; that is, the theories thought out in algebraic terms. While it can easily be so rendered, this reading has been discredited as historical. For one reason among many, in algebra one takes the square on length *a* to be *a* times *a* but Euclid worked with geometrical magnitudes such as lines, and never multiplied them together. The only extant Greek case of algebraization is the number theory of Diophantus of Alexandria (fl. c. 250 C.E.), who did use symbols for unknowns and means of their combination; however, others did not take up his system.

A similar judgment applies to ancient Chinese ways of solving systems of linear equations. While their brilliant collection of rules can be rendered in terms of the modern manipulation of matrices, they did not create matrix theory.

The Arabic Innovations

Common algebra is a theory of manipulating symbols representing constant and unknown numbers and geometrical magnitudes, and especially of expressing polynomial equations and finding roots by an algorithm that produces a formula. Its founders were the Arabs (that is, mathematicians usually writing in Arabic) from the ninth century, the main culture of the world outside the Far East. Some of the inspiration came from interpreting various Greek or Indian authors, including Euclid. The pioneer was Al-Khwarizmi (fl. c. 800–847) with his work *Al-jabr wa'l-muqabala,* known in English as the *Algebra,* and over the next five centuries followers elaborated his theory.

The problems often came from elsewhere, such as commerce or geometry; solutions usually involved the roots of

Postage stamp bearing the likeness of Al-Khwarizmi. The early-ninth-century Arab librarian and astronomer was a pioneer in the field of mathematics, setting forth theories that were expanded upon for centuries. The term *algebra* was first derived from his groundbreaking work *Al-jabr wa'l-muqabala.* Keith Bauman, TNA Associates, Franklin, Michigan

polynomial equations. Algebra was seen as an extension of arithmetic, working with unknowns in the same way as arithmetic works with knowns. The Arabic manner of expression was verbal: the word *shay* denoted the unknown, *mal* its square, *ka'b* its cube, *mal mal* for the fourth power, and so on. Arabs also adopted and adapted the Indian place-value system of numerals, including 0 for zero, that is called Hindu-Arabic. They were suspicious of negative numbers, as not being pukka quantities.

European Developments to the Seventeenth Century

Common algebra came into an awakening Europe during the thirteenth century. Among the various sources involved, Latin translations of some Arab authors were important. A significant homegrown source was the Italian Leonardo Fibonacci, who rendered the theory into Latin, with *res, census,* and *cubus* denoting the unknown and its powers. He and some translators of Arabic texts also adopted the Indian system of numerals. Communities developed, initially of Italian *abbacists* and later of German *Rechenmeister,* practicing arithmetic and common algebra with applications—some for a living.

The title of al-Khwarizmi's book included the word *al-jabr,* which named the operation of adding terms to each side of an equation when necessary so that all of them were positive. Maybe following his successor Thabit ibn Qurra (836–901), in the sixteenth century Europeans took this word to refer to the entire subject. Its theoretical side principally tackled properties of polynomial equations, especially finding their roots. An early authority was Girolano Cardano (1501–1576), with his *Ars magna* (1545); successors include François Viète (1540–1601) with *In artem analyticem isagoge* (1591), who applied algebra to both geometry and trigonometry. The Europeans gradually replaced the words for unknowns, their powers, means of combination (including taking roots), and relationships by symbols, either letters of the alphabet or special signs. Apart from the finally chosen symbols for the arithmetic numerals, no system became definitive.

In his book *Algebra* (1572), Rafael Bombelli (1526–1572) gave an extensive treatment on the theory of equations as then known, and puzzled over the mystery that the formula for the (positive) roots of a cubic equation with real coefficients could use complex numbers to determine them even if they were real; for example (one of his), given

$$x^3 = 15x + 4 \ / \ \text{root } x = (2 + \sqrt{-1}) + (2 - \sqrt{-1}) = 4.$$

The formula involved had been found early in the century by Scipione del Ferro (1465–1526), and controversially published later by Cardano. It could be adapted to solve the quartic equation, but no formula was found for the quintic.

Developments with Equations from Descartes to Abel

René Descartes's (1596–1650) *Géométrie* (1637) was an important publication in the history algebra. While its title shows his main concern, in it he introduced analytic geometry, representing constants and also variable geometric magnitudes by letters. He even found an algebraic means of determining the normal to a curve. Both this method and the representation of variables were to help in the creation of the calculus by Isaac Newton (1642–1727) in the 1660s and Gottfried Wilhelm Leibniz (1647–1716) a decade later.

During the seventeenth century algebra came to be a staple part of mathematics, with textbooks beginning to be published. The binomial theorem was studied, with Newton extending it to non-integral exponents; and functions were given algebraic expression, including as power series. Algebraic number theory developed further, especially with Pierre de Fermat (1601–1665). Negative and complex numbers found friends, including Newton and Leonhard Euler (1707–1783); but some anxiety continued, especially in Britain.

The theory of polynomial equations and their roots remained prominent. In particular, in Descartes's time "the fundamental theorem of algebra" (a later name) was recognized though not proved: that for any positive integer n a polynomial equation of degree n has n roots, real and/or complex. The Italian mathematician J. L. Lagrange (1736–1813) and others tried to prove it during the eighteenth century, but the real breakthrough came from 1799 by the (young) C. F. Gauss (1777–1855), who was to produce three more difficult and not always rigorous proofs in 1816 and 1850. He and others also interpreted complex numbers geometrically instead of algebraically, a reading that gradually became popular.

Another major question concerning equations was finding the roots of a quintic: Lagrange tried various procedures, some elaborated by his compatriot Italian Paolo Ruffini (1765–1822). The suspicion developed that there was no algebraic formula for the roots: the young Norwegian Niels Henrik Abel (1802–1829) showed its correctness in 1826 with a proof that was independent of Lagrange's procedures.

Lagrange was the leading algebrist of the time: from the 1770s he not only worked on problems in algebra but also tried philologically to algebraize other branches of mathematics. He based the calculus upon an infinite power series (the Taylor series); however, his assumption was to be refuted by Augustin-Louis Cauchy (1789–1857) and W. R. Hamilton (1805–1865). He also grounded mechanics upon principles such as that of "least action" because they could be formulated exclusively in algebraic terms: while much mechanics was encompassed, Newtonian and energy mechanics were more pliable in many contexts.

The Nineteenth Century: From Algebra to Algebras

Lagrange's algebraic ambitions inspired some new algebras from the late eighteenth century onward. The names used below are modern.

Firstly, in differential operators, the process of differentiating a function in the calculus was symbolized by D, with the converse operation of integration taken as $1/D$, with 1 denoting the identity operation; similarly, finite differencing was symbolized by Δ, with summation taken as $1/\Delta$. Much success followed, especially in solving differential and difference equations, though the workings of the method remained mysterious. One earnest practitioner from the 1840s was George Boole (1815–1864), who then imitated it to form another one, today called Boolean algebra, to found logic.

Secondly, in functional equations, the "object" was the function f itself ("sine of," say) rather than its values. In this context F.-J. Servois (1767–1847) individuated two properties in 1814: "commutative" ($fg = gf$) and "distributive" ($f(g + h) = fg + fh$); they were to be important also in several other algebras.

As part of his effort to extend Lagrange's algebraization of applied mathematics, Hamilton introduced another new algebra in 1843. He enlarged complex numbers into quaternions q with four units 1, i, j and k:

$$q := a + ib + jc + kd, \text{ where } i2 = j2 = k2 = ijk = -1;$$
$$\text{and } ij = k \text{ and } ji = -k$$

and similar properties. He also individuated the property of associativity (his word), where $i(jk) = (ij)k$.

At that time the German Hermann Grassmann (1809–1877) published *Ausdehnungslehre* (1844), a very general algebra for expressing relationships between geometrical magnitudes. It was capable of several other readings also; for example, later

his brother Robert adapted it to rediscover parts of Boolean algebra. Reception of the Grassmanns was much slower than for Hamilton; but by the 1880s their theories were gaining much attention, with quaternions extended to, for example, the eight-unit "octaves," and boasting a supporting "International Association." However, the American J. W. Gibbs (1839–1903) was decomposing quaternions into separate theories of vector algebra and of vector analysis, and this revision came to prevail among mathematicians and physicists.

Another collection of algebras developed to refine means of handling systems of linear equations. The first step (1840s) was to introduce determinants, especially to express the formulae for the roots of systems of linear equations. The more profound move of inventing matrices as a manner of expressing and manipulating systems themselves dates from the 1860s. The Englishmen J. J. Sylvester (1814–1897) and Arthur Cayley (1821–1895) played important roles in developing matrices (Sylvester's word). An important inspiration was their study of quantics, homogeneous polynomials of some degree in any finite number of variables: the task was to find algebraic expressions that preserved their form under linear transformation of those variables. They and other figures also contributed to the important theory of the "latent roots and vectors" (Sylvester again) of matrices. Determinants and matrices together are known today as linear algebra; the analysis of quantics is part of invariant theory.

On polynomial equations, Lagrange's study of properties of functions of their roots led especially from the 1840s to a theory of substitution groups with Cauchy and others, where the operation of replacing one root by another one was treated as new algebra. Abel's even younger French contemporary Évariste Galois (1811–1832) found some remarkable properties of substitutions around 1830.

This theory of substitutions gradually generalized to group theory. In its abstract form, as pioneered by the German Richard Dedekind (1831–1916) in the 1850s, the theory was based upon a given collection of laws obeyed by objects that were not specified: substitutions provided one interpretation, but many others were found, such as their philological intrusion into projective and (non-)Euclidean geometries. The steady accumulation of these applications increased the importance of group theory.

Other algebras also appeared; for example, one to express the basic properties of probability theory. In analysis the Norwegian Sophus Lie (1842–1899) developed in the 1880s a theory of "infinitesimal transformations" as linear differential operators on functions, and formed it as an algebra that is now named after him, including a group version; it has become an important subject in its own right.

Consolidation and Extensions in the Twentieth Century

At the end of the nineteenth century some major review works appeared. The German David Hilbert (1862–1943) published in 1897 a long report on algebraic number theory. The next year the Englishman Alfred North Whitehead (1861–1947) put out a detailed summary of several of them in his large book *A Treatise on Universal Algebra,* inspired by Grassmann but covering also Boole's logic, aspects of geometries, linear algebra, vectors, and parts of applied mathematics; an abandoned sequel was to have included quaternions. His title, taken from Sylvester, was not happy: no algebra is universal in the sense of embracing all others, and Whitehead did not offer one.

Elsewhere, group theory rose further in status, to be joined by other abstract algebras, such as rings, fields (already recognized by Abel and Galois in their studies of polynomial equations), ideals, integral domains, and lattices, each inspired by applications. German-speaking mathematicians were especially prominent, as was the rising new mathematical nationality, the Americans. Building upon the teaching of Emmy Noether (1882–1935) and Emil Artin (1898–1962), B. L. van der Waerden's (1903–1996) book *Modern Algebra* became a standard text for abstract algebras and several applications, from the first (1930–1931) of its many editions.

This abstract approach solved the mystery of the need for complex numbers when finding real roots of real polynomial equations. The key notion is closure: an algebra A is closed relative to an operation O on its objects a, or to a means of combining a and b, if Oa and $a \cdot b$ always belong to A. Now finding roots involved the operations of taking square, cube, . . . roots and complex but not real numbers are closed relative to them.

One of the most striking features of mathematics in the twentieth century was the massive development of topology. Algebraic topology and topological groups are two of its parts, and algebras of various kinds have informed several others. Both (abstract) algebras and topology featured strongly in the formalization of pure mathematics expounded mainly after World War II by a team of French mathematicians writing under the collective name "Bourbaki."

Reflections

The proliferation of algebras has been nonstop: the classification of mathematics in the early twenty-first century devotes twelve of its sixty-three sections of mathematics to algebras, and they are also present in many other branches, including computer science and cryptography. The presence or absence in an algebra of properties such as commutativity, distributivity, and associativity is routinely emphasized, and (dis)analogies between algebras noted. Meta-properties such as duality (given a theorem about + and ·, say, there is also one about · and +) have long been exploited, and theologically imitated elsewhere in mathematics. A massive project, recently completed, is the complete classification of finite simple groups. Textbooks abound, especially on linear and abstract algebras.

Abstract algebras bring out the importance of structures in mathematics. A notable metamathematical elaboration, due among others to the American Saunders MacLane (b. 1909), is category theory: a category is a collection of mathematical objects (such as fields or sets) with mappings (such as ismorphisms) between them, and different kinds of category are studied and compared.

Yet this story of widespread success should be somewhat tempered. For example, linear algebra is one of the most widely taught branches of mathematics at undergraduate level; yet such teaching developed appreciably only from the 1930s, and textbooks date in quantity from twenty years later. Further, algebras have not always established their own theological foundations. In particular, operator algebras have been grounded elsewhere in mathematics: even Boole never fixed the foundations of the D-operator algebra, and a similar one proposed from the 1880s by the Englishman Oliver Heaviside (1850–1925) came to be based by others in the Laplace transform, which belongs to complex-variable analysis. However, a revised version of it was proposed in 1950 by the Polish theorist Jan Mikusinski (1913–1987), drawing upon ring theory—that is, one algebra helped another. Algebras have many fans.

See also **Logic; Logic and Philosophy of Mathematics, Modern; Mathematics.**

BIBLIOGRAPHY

Corry, Leo. *Modern Algebra and the Rise of Mathematical Structures.* Basel, Switzerland, and Boston: Birkhäuser, 1996.

Cournot, Antoine Augustin. *De l'origine et des limites da la correspondance entre l'algèbre et la géométrie.* Paris and Algiers: Hachette, 1847.

Crowe, Michael J. *A History of Vector Analysis: The Evolution of the Idea of a Vertical System.* Notre Dame and London: Notre Dame University Press, 1967. Reprint, New York: Dover, 1987.

Dieudonné, Jean. *A History of Algebraic and Differential Topology 1900–1960.* Basel, Switzerland, Birkhäuser, 1989.

Grattan-Guinness, I., ed. *Companion Encyclopedia of the History and Philosophy of the Mathematical Sciences.* 2 vols. London: Routledge, 1994. Reprint, Baltimore: Johns Hopkins University Press, 2003. See especially Part 6.

Hawkins, Thomas W. *Emergence of Lie's Theory of Groups: An Essay in the History of Mathematics, 1869–1926.* Berlin: Springer, 2002.

Høyrup, Jens. *Lengths, Widths, Surfaces: A Portrait of Old Babylonian Algebra and Its Kin.* Berlin and New York: Springer, 2002.

Hutton, Charles. "A History of Algebra." In vol. 2 of his *Tracts on Mathematical and Philosophical Subjects.* London: F. C. and R. Rivington, 1812.

Klein, J. *Greek Mathematical Thought and the Origins of Algebra.* Cambridge, Mass.: MIT Press, 1968.

Lam, Lay Yong, and T. S. Ang. *Fleeting Footsteps: Tracing the Conception of Arithmetic and Algebra in Ancient China.* Singapore: World Scientific Publishing, 1992.

Mehrtens, Herbert. *Die Entstehung der Verbandstheorie.* Hildesheim, Germany: Gerstenberg, 1979.

Nesselmann, G. H. F. *Versuch einer kritischen Geschichte der Algebra.* Reprint, Frankfurt, Germany: Minerva, 1969.

Novy, Lubos. *The Origins of Modern Algebra.* Translated by Jaroslav Taner. Prague: Academia, 1973.

Pycior, Helena M. *Symbols, Impossible Numbers, and Geometric Entanglements: British Algebra through the Commentaries on Newton's Universal Arithmetick.* Cambridge, U.K., and New York: Cambridge University Press, 1997.

Scholz, Erhard, ed. *Geschichte der Algebra: Eine Ausführung.* Mannheim: Wissenschaftsverlag, 1990. Up to Noether, but no algebraic logic, differential operators, or functional equations.

Sinaceur, Hourya. *Corps et modèles: Essai sur l'histoire de l'algèbra réele*. Paris: Vrin, 1991. English translation Basel, Switzerland: Birkh.

Stedall, Jacqueline A. *A Discourse Concerning Algebra: English Algebra to 1685*. Oxford, and New York: Oxford University Press, 2002.

van der Waerden, B. L. *A History of Algebra: From al-Khwarizmi to Emmy Noether*. Berlin: Springer, 1985. See the remark above on Scholz.

Vercelloni, Luca. *Filosofia delle strutture*. Florence, Italy: La Nuova Italia, 1988.

Vuillemin, Jules. *La philosophie de l'algèbre*. Paris: Presses Universitaires de France, 1992.

Wallis, John. *Treatise of Algebra, Both Historical and Practical. . . .* London: Printed by J. Playford, for R. Davis, 1685. And not a little corrigible.

Wussing, Hans. *The Genesis of the Abstract Group Concept: A Contribution to the History of the Origin of Abstract Group Theory*. Translated by Abe Shenitzer. Cambridge, Mass.: MIT Press, 1984. German original, Berlin, 1969.

Zeuthen, H. *Die Lehre von den Kegelschnitten im Altertum*. Copenhagen: Høst, 1886. Influential source on the supposed Greek geometric algebra.

I. Grattan-Guinness

ALIENATION. The notion of alienation is a very unusual one because it is at once an attempt to explain a widespread feeling—a very subjective, somewhat indefinable feeling—and a critique of the nature of any society that regularly produces it.

This was not always so. The feeling that one is not at home in the world, the sense of estrangement from one's surrounding, oneself, and other people, appears to be as old as history; for most world religions (Buddhism, most strains of Christianity and Daoism, Sufi strands in Islam) this feeling was seen mainly as reflecting a profound insight into the truth of the human condition. Hermits, monks, and meditators often actively valued or cultivated feelings of alienation as a way to something higher. Calvinism came closer to the modern conception in seeing feelings of isolation and emptiness as a sign of humanity's fall from grace, but it was really only in the nineteenth century that the modern understanding of the term came into being. This conception was closely tied to the experience of living in a vast, impersonal, industrial city. Feelings of alienation were particularly prone to strike those who in earlier generations might have been considered likely victims of melancholia: intellectuals, artists, and youth. The effects were much the same: depression, anxiety, hopelessness, suicide.

One might distinguish two main strains in the modern alienation literature: one that stressed the experience itself as an unavoidable (though possibly ameliorable) effect of the impersonal, bureaucratized nature of modern life, entailing the loss of any ability to use that experience to attain some deeper, more genuine truth about the world—since with the death of God and traditional structures of authority, most of these truths were considered definitively lost. The other, drawing on older theological traditions, saw alienation as the key to the true, hidden nature of the modern (i.e., capitalist, industrial) order itself, showing it to be an intolerable situation that could be resolved only by overthrowing that order and replacing it with something profoundly different.

The first tradition can be found in social thinkers such as Alexis de Tocqueville, Émile Durkheim, or Max Weber; novelists such as Fyodor Dostoyevsky or Franz Kafka; and philosophers such as Søren Kierkegaard or Friedrich Nietzsche. Here alienation is the darker underside of all the positive values of modernity, the experience of those sundered from all previous sources of meaning: community, hierarchy, the sacred. It is the point where individualism becomes isolation, freedom becomes rootlessness, egalitarianism becomes the destruction of all value, rationality, an iron cage.

Probably the most famous formulation within this genre was Émile Durkheim's (1858–1917) notion of anomie. Observing that suicide rates tend to go up during times of both economic boom and economic collapse, Durkheim concluded that this could only be because both booms and busts threw ordinary people's expectations so completely in disarray that they ended up in a state of lacking norms, unable to determine what they had a right to expect or even want from life and unable to imagine a time when they could. This kind of analysis could lead either to a resigned pessimism, the assumption (favored by social conservatives) that public life in modern society can never really be anything but alienated, or to a liberal approach that saw alienation as a form of deviance or lack of proper integration that policymakers should ideally be able to ameliorate or even overcome.

The other tradition can be traced to Georg Wilhelm Friedrich Hegel (1770–1831), who drew heavily on theological sources. For Hegel, "alienation" was a technical term, a necessary moment in the process whereby Spirit (which for Hegel was simultaneously God, Mind, Spirit, and Human Self-Consciousness) would achieve true self-knowledge. Human history involved the same story: Mind would project itself out into the world, creating, say, Law, or Art, or Science, or Government; it would then confront its creations as something alien to it and strange; then, finally, coming to understand that these alienated forms are really aspects of itself, would reincorporate them and come to a richer self-conception as a result.

Karl Marx (1818–1883) remained true to this dialectical approach but concentrated on the material creativity of work, emphasizing that under capitalism, not only the products of one's labor but one's labor itself, one's very capacity to create—and for Marx, this is one's very humanity—becomes a commodity that can be bought and sold and hence appears to the worker as an "alien force." Insofar as Marx shares Hegel's optimism, and sees this dilemma as opening the way to a new, revolutionary society, all this is much in line with the older, theological conception in which alienation, however painful, is a realization about the truth of one's relation to the world, so that understanding this becomes the key to transcending it. Twentieth-century Marxists, though, have not been so uniformly optimistic.

While Marxist regimes officially claimed to have eliminated the problem of alienation in their own societies, Western

Marxism, starting with György Lukács (1885–1971) and climaxing with the Frankfurt School, forced to explain the lack of revolutionary change in industrial democracies, gradually became a prolonged meditation on the varied forms of alienation (reification, objectification, fetishism, etc.) in modern life. This emphasis set the tone for an outpouring of literature on the subject in the mid-twentieth century, not all of it Marxist.

France in the 1950s and early 1960s saw the emergence of a particularly rich body of alienation theory, ranging from the Existentialism of Jean-Paul Sartre and Albert Camus, which attempted to formulate an ethics for the isolated individual, to a variety of Marxist approaches, of which the most extravagant—and influential—was developed by the Situationist International, whose members saw modern consumer society as a gigantic "spectacle," a vast apparatus composed of not only media images but market logic, the rule of experts, and the nature of the commodity form, all combining together to render individuals passive and isolated spectators of their own lives. Like many of the radical art movements from which they emerged, the Situationists were dedicated to imagining ways to revolutionize everyday life itself as a way of overcoming the "living death" of capitalist alienation.

After the failed insurrection of May 1968 in France, this literature on alienation rapidly disappeared in the face of post-structuralist critiques that argued it was impossible to talk about a human subject alienated from society or from itself because the subject was itself an effect of discourse and hence a social construct. Over the course of the 1970s and 1980s, these critiques spread outside France and the theme of alienation has, as a result, largely disappeared from intellectual debate in the early twenty-first century.

There are two main exceptions. First, in its radical, redemptive form, the idea of alienation has remained alive in artistic and revolutionary circles largely outside the academy. Situationism, for example, is still very much at the center of the (increasingly international) anarchist and punk scenes, both of which are largely rebellions against the meaninglessness and alienation of "mainstream" urban, industrial, or postindustrial life. These themes have suddenly reemerged to public attention with the rise of the "antiglobalization" movement, though they have still found almost no echo in the academy.

Second, in its more liberal, ameliorative form, the idea of alienation became ensconced in certain branches of sociology and hence reemerged in what is increasingly called "postmodern" alienation theory. When American sociologists started taking up the theme of alienation systematically in the 1950s and 1960s, they began by making it into a factor that could be quantified. Various questionnaires and techniques of tabulating an individual's degree of alienation were developed; surveys then revealed, not entirely surprisingly, that aside from students, those who scored highest for alienation were, precisely, aliens, immigrants, or else members of minority groups already defined as marginal to mainstream American life. Over the course of the 1990s and the early twenty-first century, this sociological work has converged with an interest in identity and identity-based social movements to yield a new, "postmodern" body of alienation theory.

On the individual level, alienation is said to occur when there is a clash between one's own self-definition and the identity assigned one by a larger society. Alienation thus becomes the subjective manner in which various forms of oppression (racism, sexism, ageism, etc.) are actually experienced and internalized by their victims. As a result, where the older revolutionary conception sees alienation as essential to the fundamentally violent, antihuman nature of "the mainstream," postmodern theories now once again see alienation as a measure of exclusion from the mainstream. On the social level, the postmodern conception of alienation is said to be caused by a surfeit rather than a lack of freedom; a notion that appears almost impossible to distinguish from what were, in the late nineteenth century, called "modern" concepts of alienation. So far, these two traditions have barely come into contact with each other—except, perhaps, in recent environmentalist ideas about "alienation from nature." How or whether they will make contact remains an open question.

See also **Existentialism; Identity; Person, Idea of the; Society.**

BIBLIOGRAPHY

Geyer, Felix, ed. *Alienation, Ethnicity, and Postmodernism.* London and Westport, Conn.: Greenwood Press, 1996.

Ollman, Bertell. *Alienation: Marx's Conception of Man in Capitalist Society.* Cambridge, U.K., and New York: Cambridge University Press, 1976.

Schmitt, Richard, and Thomas E. Moody, eds. *Alienation and Social Criticism.* Atlantic Highlands, N.J.: Humanities Press, 1994.

Schweitzer, David, and Felix Geyer, eds. *Alienation Theories and De-Alienation Strategies: Comparative Perspectives in Philosophy and the Social Sciences.* London: Science Reviews, 1989.

David Graeber

ALTRUISM. The term *altruism* was coined by the French philosopher and sociologist Auguste Comte (1798–1857). Derived from the Italian word *altrui,* meaning "to others" or "of others," "altruism" was introduced as an antonym for "egoism" to refer to the totality of other-regarding instincts in humans. The new terms *altruism, altruist,* and *altruistic* provided nineteenth-century thinkers with a controversial new conceptual framework within which to discuss ancient philosophical, religious, and ethical questions. In the earlier idiom of Enlightenment moralism, these had been expressed as questions about the relationship between particular self-serving passions and benevolent moral sentiments or between the principle of self-love and the authority of the conscience. It was in this earlier idiom that writers such as Thomas Hobbes and Bernard Mandeville expressed their view that all human action was ultimately driven by self-interest and that their critics, including Francis Hutcheson and Joseph Butler, expressed the contrary view that benevolence was as fundamental a principle of human action as self-interest. The conceptual history of "altruism" proper began in the 1850s and has generated its own particular set of scientific, religious, and philosophical questions.

"Altruism" and "altruistic" have been used to refer to at least three different sorts of things: intentions, actions, and ideologies. These three sorts of usage can be grouped under the headings of "psychological altruism," "behavioral altruism," and "ethical altruism." Psychological altruism is any set of inclinations or intentional motivation to help others for their own sakes. Behavioral altruism is defined in terms of consequences rather than intentions: it refers to any action that benefits others (normally with the additional condition that there is some cost to the agent). "Evolutionary altruism" or "biological altruism" is a form of behavioral altruism, since it is defined solely in terms of consequences rather than intentions: it refers to any behavior that reduces the fitness of the organism performing it and increases the fitness of another organism (see Dawkins; Sober and Wilson). Finally, ethical altruism is an ideology stating that the happiness of others should be the principal goal of one's actions. (Ethical egoism, by contrast, states that what the individual should seek above all else is his or her own happiness.)

A frequent cause of confusion has been equivocation between the first two of these three possible meanings—between claims about psychology and claims about behavior. The claim that there is no such thing as true altruism, for example, might be intended to convey the view that, psychologically, no one's motives are ever entirely forgetful of self, since we know that we will receive approval and pleasure as a result of our charitable actions. The reply might be that true altruism certainly exists because many people engage in charitable activities at a cost to themselves, but by shifting from the psychological to the behavioral perspective on altruism, this reply fails to rebut the initial claim. Such conceptual confusion and disagreement over the meaning of altruism marked discussions of it from the outset and persist to this day. (Blum provides one useful and concise discussion of some of the definitional and conceptual issues.)

Discussions of altruism also have revolved around fundamental empirical, ethical, and political questions. What are the real roots of human altruism? Are they biological, psychological, social, or cultural? Is altruism really the highest moral good? Are we morally obliged to extend our altruism to strangers just as much as to family and friends? Should we even behave altruistically toward nonhuman animals? In what ways can societies be arranged in order to maximize the amount of altruism? Are the best societies, in any case, really those in which altruism is maximized?

Comte and Sociology

The term *altruism* was coined, in French *(altruisme),* by Auguste Comte (1798–1857) in the first volume of his *Système de politique positive* (1851–1854; System of positive polity). The first uses in English followed in the 1850s and 1860s in works by British thinkers sympathetic to Comte, including George Eliot, G. H. Lewes, and John Stuart Mill (see Dixon, 2005). In the Comtean system, "altruism" stood for the totality of other-regarding sentiments. The new cerebral science of phrenology, Comte said, proved that altruistic sentiments were innate. He heralded this as one of the most important discoveries of modern science and contrasted it with what he presented as the Christian view, namely that human beings

are, by nature, entirely selfish (because of the taint of original sin). Comte's hope was that through the institution of a new humanistic religion based on a scientific understanding of human nature and society, civilized nations would develop to a stage where altruistic sentiments prevailed over egoistic ones. Working out how to bring such a society about, Comte taught, was the greatest problem facing humanity. In his view, one of the keys to increased altruism was a recognition of the fact that women, because of their maternal instincts, were more altruistic than men. They therefore should have supreme moral and religious authority (although only within the domestic sphere). Thus the Religion of Humanity, as he called it, encouraged a particular emphasis on feminine moral virtues and the great sanctity of motherhood (see Wright).

Another important Comtean coinage with which altruism was initially closely associated was "sociology"—the new science of society. Two of the most significant nineteenth-century theoretical treatments of altruism, other than Comte's own, were also produced by pioneering sociologists, namely Herbert Spencer (1820–1903) and Émile Durkheim (1858–1917). Durkheim, who drew on the sociological theories of both Comte and Spencer while making much greater and more sophisticated use of empirical data than either of them, made a distinction between egoistic, altruistic, and anomic types of suicide in his 1897 study of the subject. Egoistic suicide was most widespread in developed, Western nations (especially strongly Protestant ones), Durkheim said, as a result of the highly developed sense of individual autonomy such nations encouraged. Altruistic suicide, on the other hand, was particularly prevalent among primitive peoples, who had an excessive sense of social integration. The main sorts of altruistic suicide with which Durkheim was concerned were the suicides of men on the threshold of old age or stricken with sickness, suicides of women on their husbands' deaths, and the suicides of followers or servants on the death of their chief (Durkheim, book 2, chapter 4).

Darwin, Spencer, and Evolution

Charles Darwin did not use the term "altruism," preferring to use older terms with which he was familiar from his reading of moral philosophy in the 1830s and 1840s, such as "benevolence," "sympathy," and "moral sense" (see Darwin; Richards). In his *Descent of Man* (1871), Darwin famously developed a group-selection explanation for the apparent self-sacrificing behavior of neuter insects. According to this view, communities of insects that happen to contain self-sacrificers benefit in the struggle for existence at the expense of communities made up of more selfish individuals with which they are in competition. As a result, contrary to the popular caricature of Darwinian nature as dominated by selfishness and competition, Darwin actually argued that benevolence and cooperation are entirely natural—that they are deeply embedded in our biology. The problem of how to account for altruistic behavior, especially in insects, continued to puzzle biologists (see Lustig) and became a central topic in the new discipline of "sociobiology" founded by the entomologist E. O. Wilson in the 1970s.

In the English-speaking world of the later nineteenth century, however, it was Herbert Spencer (1820–1903) rather than Charles Darwin (1809–1882) who was celebrated as the leading exponent of the philosophy of evolution. Spencer was also one of the writers most responsible for the spread of the language of altruism (and sociology) from the 1870s onward (see Dixon, 2004). Spencer acknowledged that he had borrowed these terms from Comte. In his *Principles of Psychology* (second edition of 1870–1872) and *Data of Ethics* (1879), he developed his theory of how altruistic instincts could evolve and be inherited and how they would increase as social evolution progressed. He denied, however, that by doing so he endorsed Comte's views on philosophy, science, or religion. Indeed, although Spencer agreed with Comte that altruism would increase as societies evolved further, his vision of the ideal future society was in many ways the opposite of the Comtean vision. Whereas Comte envisaged a hierarchical and, in effect, totalitarian society in which individuals sacrificed personal freedom in the interests of order and progress, Spencer hoped for a society in which individual freedoms (and responsibilities) were maximized (see Richards). Spencer's hope was that people would increasingly act in altruistic ways spontaneously and voluntarily, without state intervention. Although Spencer had a very elevated reputation and a wide sphere of influence in Britain and America in the 1860s and 1870s, the scientific rejection of his belief in the heritability of acquired moral and intellectual characteristics, along with the rise of a political consensus in favor of some kind of state provision of welfare, rendered much of his thought untenable by the early twentieth century.

Utilitarianism

Utilitarianism, as discussed by its most distinguished nineteenth-century advocate, John Stuart Mill (1806–1873), was based on the view that a good act was one that would increase the general prevalence of pleasure over pain in the whole of society. It could thus be construed as a form of ethical altruism. In *Auguste Comte and Positivism* (1865), however, Mill made clear that his utilitarianism did not imply a one-sided commitment to altruism. He believed that a commitment to the general happiness was quite consistent with each individual living a happy life, and he criticized Comte for advocating an extreme sort of altruism. According to Mill's utilitarian principles, Comte's idea of happiness for all, procured by the painful self-sacrifice of each, was a contradiction; a sufficient gratification of "egoistic propensities" was a necessary part of a happy life and was even favorable to the development of benevolent affections toward others. Later in the nineteenth century Henry Sidgwick further developed the utilitarian tradition of philosophical ethics (see Schneewind). In his celebrated *Methods of Ethics* (1874 and several subsequent editions), Sidgwick tried to establish the proper extent of individual altruism and to show how such behavior could be encouraged while also recognizing the legitimate, independent demands of self-interest.

Christianity and Unbelief

At its inception, the concept of altruism resonated widely in a Victorian culture saturated with moral and religious earnestness (see Collini). Some were attracted to Comtean positivism and its worship of humanity as an eminently respectable form of unbelief, one that combined a commitment to the sciences

with a continuing religious sense and with the strong social conscience that the positivist ideology of altruism involved (see Wright). On the other hand, some who were committed to a Christian view of morality and society saw in Comtean altruism a concept of the love of others that was detached both from an understanding of appropriate self-love and from the necessity of a love of God. There were also those who saw in humanistic celebrations of altruism simply a secularized version of the Christian ideology of service to others (see Dixon, 2004, 2005). This last view was held by both proponents and opponents of Christianity. Among the latter, one of the most trenchant was Friedrich Nietzsche (1844–1900). In Nietzsche's vision, Christianity was at the root of all ideologies of altruism, self-sacrifice, and pity—in short, of the "slave morality" that was the exact opposite of the assertive and aristocratic ideals he celebrated (see Nietzsche and the introduction by Ansell-Pearson).

From the twentieth century onward, once the origins of altruism in Comte's atheistic philosophy had largely been forgotten, it was much more common to encounter the assumption that altruism was a term that encapsulated the heart of Christian teaching. The French philosopher Jacques Maritain (1882–1973), however, continued to press the point that Comte's extreme and atheistical concept of altruism differed significantly from Christian love, whether human or divine. The difference between Christian love and altruism that Maritain insisted upon could be summarized as the difference between loving one's neighbor *as* oneself and loving one's neighbor *instead of* oneself (see Maritain). Nonetheless, some Christian writers still consider altruism to be virtually identical to Christian love, or agape.

Socialism and Economics

The 1880s saw a downturn in the economic prosperity of Britain and its empire. The results of this included waning confidence in the inevitability of social and economic progress and increased public awareness of the plight of the urban poor. The economic orthodoxy of laissez-faire, which emphasized the freedom and autonomy of the individual and had accompanied the optimism and success of the earlier Victorian period, also increasingly came into question. A renewed interest in altruism was now evident, not only in philosophy and religion but also in economics. A central assumption of classical political economy was that man had benevolent as well as selfish instincts, but when it came to economic activity, the rigorous application of self-interest was the most rational principle. This assumption was now subjected to more serious examination (see Pearson). Altruism became associated with political creeds of cooperation and collectivism. One commune in the United States was even named "Altruria" in recognition of the importance of altruism to this new movement. The concept of altruism was thus redefined as an ideology, in a way that brought it closer to communism than either the Comtean positivism or the Spencerian individualism with which it had earlier been associated. Altruism, for these groups, was a radical and universal denial of self in the pursuit of harmonious and egalitarian community living. In the later twentieth century, the viability of the assumption of self-interest in economics would again be called into question (see Mansbridge; Monroe).

First Half of the Twentieth Century

The closing decades of the nineteenth century, as well as seeing a new interest in "altruism" as an economic and political doctrine, witnessed an accelerated professionalization of intellectual discussions of the subject. Whereas writers like Lewes, Eliot, Mill, and Spencer had pursued their intellectual projects outside the universities (they were, to use Collini's phrase, "public moralists"), it was increasingly the case by the turn of the twentieth century that rigorous academic discussions of moral philosophy, economics, psychology, and sociology were conducted by university-based experts. The resultant discussions were thus both more detached from public political life and more fragmented. In the first half of the twentieth century the influence of the ethos of logical positivism meant that those working in the human and social sciences were inclined to avoid or even to deny the meaningfulness of questions with ethical and religious overtones. G. E. Moore claimed (in his 1903 work *Principia ethica*) that any system of ethics that tried to draw moral conclusions on the basis of a scientific account of human nature and society (as the systems of both Comte and Spencer had done) committed the "naturalistic fallacy." (See Maienschein and Ruse's collection of essays investigating the possibility of founding ethics on biology.) Finally, the success of the neo-Darwinian synthesis in biology and the rejection of the doctrine of the inheritance of acquired characteristics seemed to undermine earlier theories of the gradual evolution of greater altruism. All that was left was a starkly amoral vision of nature as the domain of competition and natural selection. All of these factors meant that even though philosophers, sociologists, and economists continued to discuss concepts of altruism, the first fifty or sixty years of the twentieth century saw a reduction of academic interest in the subject.

Social Psychology, Sociobiology, and Altruism since the 1960s

Scientific research into altruism has markedly increased since the 1960s. During the 1970s, "helping behavior" and the problem of the "unresponsive bystander" were among the most popular topics in social psychology (see Howard and Pilliavin; Latané and Darley; Wispé). Later C. Daniel Batson stimulated considerable discussion among social psychologists with a series of experiments trying to establish the genuinely altruistic motivation of some helping behavior, explaining it as the product of empathy (see Batson). Others have preferred more egoistic hypotheses, such as the theory that helping behavior is undertaken in order to alleviate the helper's own distress at the suffering of the person to be helped.

In the field of evolutionary biology, 1975 saw the publication of E. O. Wilson's controversial *Sociobiology,* which set out to explain all social phenomena in terms of underlying biological mechanisms. The following year Richard Dawkins's highly successful popular science book *The Selfish Gene* was published. It was based on mathematical models developed by William D. Hamilton to explain altruistic behaviors in terms of their benefits to genetically related individuals. Absolutely central to both these books was the puzzle of how self-sacrificing individuals could ever have been successful in the merciless struggle for existence. In short, how could Darwinian evolution produce altruism? Dawkins's straightforward answer was that it could not. According to Dawkins, human beings and other animals are blind robots programmed by their "selfish genes," and any actions that on the surface seem to be examples of "altruism" are in fact driven by the interests of the genes. The existence of apparently altruistic impulses could thus be explained by the fact that an individual who acts in the interests of close relatives (who have many of the same genes) is increasing the chances of copies of the individual's genes persisting into the next generation. Since there is no genuine altruism in nature, Dawkins concluded, the most we can do is to try to teach our children altruism in the hope that they can succeed in rebelling against their genetic inheritance.

Scientific, philosophical, and theological critiques of Dawkins's ideas have been abundant. Some have argued that the idea that genes can have "interests" or be described as "selfish" is misleadingly anthropomorphic. Dawkins has replied that these are only metaphors, but ones that help to communicate the fact that the real business of evolution goes on at the genetic level. But others have questioned whether it has really been established that selection operates exclusively, or even primarily, at the genetic level rather than at the level of individuals, groups, or species (see Sober and Wilson). And many commentators have found the view of human nature implicit in *The Selfish Gene* to be unacceptably cynical, fatalistic, and pessimistic.

Since the 1990s, although academic discussions have now moved on from the agenda set by sociobiology and *The Selfish Gene,* the topic of "altruism" has continued to attract a great deal of attention from a wide range of disciplines, including theology, philosophy, evolutionary biology, economics, social psychology, and sociology (see Batson; Mansbridge; Monroe; and for a particularly helpful collection, Post et al.). The same central questions about what science, religion, and philosophy each have to contribute to an understanding of human altruism, and about their ethical and political implications, continue to be vigorously debated.

See also **Christianity: Overview; Good; Moral Sense; Philanthropy; Utilitarianism.**

BIBLIOGRAPHY

PRIMARY SOURCES

Batson, C. Daniel. *The Altruism Question: Toward a Social-Psychological Answer.* Hillsdale, N.J.: Erlbaum, 1991.

Comte, Auguste. *System of Positive Polity; or, Treatise on Sociology, Instituting the Religion of Humanity.* Translated by Edward Spencer Beesly et al. 4 vols. London: Longmans, Green, 1875–1877.

Darwin, Charles. *The Descent of Man, and Selection in Relation to Sex.* 1871. Edited and with an introduction by James Moore and Adrian Desmond. London: Penguin, 2004.

Dawkins, Richard. *The Selfish Gene.* Oxford: Oxford University Press, 1976.

Durkheim, Emile. *Suicide: A Study in Sociology,* 1897. Translated by John A. Spaulding and George Simpson, edited with an introduction by George Simpson. London: Routledge and Kegan Paul, 1952.

Latané, Bibb, and John M. Darley. *The Unresponsive Bystander: Why Doesn't He Help?* New York: Appleton-Century Crofts, 1970.

Mill, John Stuart. *Auguste Comte and Positivism.* London: Trübner, 1865.

Nietzsche, Friedrich. *On the Genealogy of Morality,* 1887. Translated by Carol Diethe, edited with an introduction by Keith Ansell-Pearson. Cambridge, U.K.: Cambridge University Press, 1994.

Sober, Elliott, and David Sloan Wilson. *Unto Others: The Evolution and Psychology of Unselfish Behaviour.* Cambridge, Mass., and London: Harvard University Press, 1998.

Wispé, Lauren, ed. *Altruism, Sympathy, and Helping: Psychological and Sociological Principles.* New York and London: Academic Press, 1978.

SECONDARY SOURCES

Blum, Lawrence. "Altruism." In *Encyclopedia of Ethics,* edited by Lawrence C. Becker and Charlotte B. Becker. New York and London: Routledge, 2001.

Collini, Stefan. "The Culture of Altruism." In *Public Moralists: Political Thought and Intellectual Life in Britain, 1850–1930.* Oxford: Clarendon Press, 1991.

Dixon, Thomas. "Herbert Spencer and Altruism: The Sternness and Kindness of a Victorian Moralist." In *Herbert Spencer, 1820–1903: Founding Father of Modern Sociology,* edited by Greta Jones. London: Galton Institute, 2004.

———. "The Invention of Altruism: Auguste Comte's *Positive Polity* and Respectable Unbelief in Victorian Britain." In *Science and Beliefs: From Natural Philosophy to Natural Science, 1700–1900,* edited by David Knight and Matthew Eddy. Aldershot, U.K.: Ashgate, 2005.

Lustig, Abigail. "Ants and the Nature of Nature in Auguste Forel, Erich Wasmann, and William Morton Wheeler." In *The Moral Authority of Nature,* edited by Lorraine Daston and Fernando Vidal. Chicago: University of Chicago Press, 2004.

Maienschein, Jane, and Michael Ruse, eds. *Biology and the Foundation of Ethics.* Cambridge, U.K., and New York: Cambridge University Press, 1999.

Mansbridge, Jane, ed. *Beyond Self-Interest.* Chicago: University of Chicago Press, 1990.

Maritain, Jacques. *Moral Philosophy: An Historical and Critical Survey of the Great Systems.* London: Geoffrey Bles, 1964. Chapters 11, 12.

Monroe, Kristen Renwick. "A Fat Lady in a Corset: Altruism and Social Theory." *American Journal of Political Science* 38 (1994): 861–893.

Pearson, Heath. "Economics and Altruism at the *Fin de Siècle.*" In *Worlds of Political Economy,* edited by Martin J. Daunton and Frank Trentmann. Basingstoke, U.K.: Palgrave Macmillan, 2004.

Post, Stephen G., et al., eds. *Altruism and Altruistic Love: Science, Philosophy, and Religion in Dialogue.* Oxford and New York: Oxford University Press, 2002.

Richards, Robert. *Darwin and the Emergence of Evolutionary Theories of Mind and Behavior.* Chicago: University of Chicago Press, 1987. Especially chapters 4–7.

Schneewind, J. B. *Sidgwick's Ethics and Victorian Moral Philosophy.* Oxford: Clarendon Press, 1977.

Spencer, Herbert. *The Data of Ethics.* London: Williams and Norgate, 1879.

Wright, Terence R. *The Religion of Humanity: The Impact of Comtean Positivism on Victorian Britain.* Cambridge, U.K.: Cambridge University Press, 1986.

Thomas Dixon

AMBIGUITY. By instinct humans yearn for reassurance and certainties and dream of an orderly universe where the reasoning process corresponds to external reality. This attitude is reflected by the assumption, authoritatively legitimized by Aristotle (384–322 B.C.E.), that no responsible statement can exhibit internal contradictions. In his *Categories,* Aristotle states that the essential character of a substance seems to be its ability to host opposites. At any instant, however, one can assign either a quality or its opposite to a substance: According to Aristotle, "Nobody can be simultaneously sick and healthy. Similarly, nothing is at the same time white and black. No object exists simultaneously hosting opposites." No alternatives exist besides these two; any third possibility is excluded: *tertium non datur.*

Ambiguity

According to Aristotle, the substitution of opposite qualities hosted by a substance during a transformation has a discontinuous character. His logic seems to imply a step-by-step flow of time and rules out the intervention of a critical situation where opposite qualities can smoothly cooperate and compete together in the same substance. This schematizes evolution as a quasi-static change of objects rather than a continuous course of events.

Aristotle's conception is reflected in the rigid aesthetic canons of the art of antiquity. For instance, in Myron's *Discobolus* (The discus thrower), fifth century B.C.E., Museo nazionale, Rome, time seems to be frozen in the act of launching the discus. Furthermore, throughout two millennia, the *tertium non datur* has influenced Mediterranean culture.

It is only during the twentieth century that, thanks to an attentive evaluation of the nature of time and the adoption of a probabilistic approach to the evolution of natural systems, ambiguity, meaning the coexistence or confluence of two or more incompatible aspects in the same reality, has acquired a non-negative connotation in the Western world.

Probability, Uncertainty, and the Arrow of Time

In the 1680s Isaac Newton's concept of absolute, mathematical time depicted a uniform flow deprived of any psychological aspect, including a propensity to flow only toward the future. In the 1700s Pierre-Simon Laplace's rigid, deterministic viewpoint left no space to uncertainties and contradictions.

In the 1820s, however, Nicolas-Léonard-Sadi Carnot's second principle of thermodynamics and Rudolf Clausius's principle of the increase of entropy or disorder in isolated systems attached a directional arrow to time from past to future. In the 1900s Albert Einstein's theory of relativity assigned time an additional role in the fourth dimension of physical space known as the space-time continuum. In the 1920s the

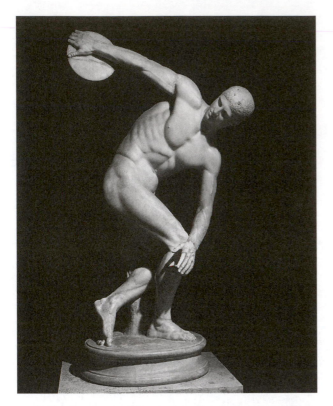

Roman copy of *Discobolus* by Myron, created 2nd century B.C.E. The concept of arrested motion, as seen in Myron's sculpture of a discus thrower, illustrates the substitution of opposite qualities that can sometimes characterize ambiguity. © DAGLI ORTI/CORBIS

probabilistic approach and Werner Karl Heisenberg's uncertainty principle of quantum mechanics brought an end to certainties. In the 1960s, the irreversible thermodynamics of nonlinear systems removed from equilibrium by fluxes of energy, matter, and information regarded time as the creator of spatial, temporal, or functional structural order. These systems include the mind.

Most likely the above breakthroughs in the *Weltanschauung* (worldview), relevant for an analysis ennobling ambiguity, played a role in focusing the attention of eminent philosophers—Immanuel Kant, Georg Wilhelm Friedrich Hegel, Arthur Schopenhauer, Friedrich Nietzsche, Henri-Louis Bergson, and Jean-Paul Sartre, among them—on the dynamics of the processes of transformation rather than on Aristotle's statics of the objects.

Even closer correlations can be conjectured between the scientific and artistic milieus. Look at, for example, Claude Monet's *Waterloo Bridge, Effect of Fog* (1903, Hermitage State Museum). While looking at this painting, the observer, driven by curiosity, correlates his or her sensory stimuli, assembling them in an interiorized pattern. While this mental pattern develops, the fog on the Thames seems to lift slowly, until a critical state is reached where the bridge, the boats on the river, and the urban background merge into the meaning of the painting. This critical state, at a boundary sharing foggy

and meaningless scenery and, at the same time, a meaningful picture, is loaded with ambiguity.

The mental process just described can be viewed as a metaphor of Jean Piaget's statement, "The intelligence organizes the world while it organizes itself." This aphorism leads to self-referentiality. Contextually, ambiguity sneaks in: "Concerning what one cannot talk about, it's necessary to be silent," Ludwig Wittgenstein writes, and yet he talks—and is "silent"—at the same time.

Should one agree in interpreting ambiguity as equivocalness, self-referentiality would make the language totally ambiguous. Rome? A city, a town, and a four-letter word. Again with reference to the above breakthroughs, think of a cubist portrait by Picasso. Its perception lends itself ambiguously to several reconstructions of percepts—front figure, profile, and so forth—and recalls the process of measurement of a quantum structure: a process whose result allows us to access, with different probabilities, the several possible basic modes of being (or behaving) characteristic of the structure.

Similar considerations hold for the ambiguous representation of the fourth dimension on a two-dimensional canvas, seen in several futurist de-structured paintings and in Marcel Duchamp's *Nude Descending a Staircase, No. 2* (1912, Philadelphia Museum of Art), an organization of kinetic elements expressing the space-time continuum through the abstract representation of movement.

The Dynamics of Ambiguity

Open systems, far removed from (thermodynamic) equilibrium by intense fluxes of resources—such as matter, energy, and information—exceeding certain critical thresholds, undergo dynamic instabilities resulting in the emergence of spatial, temporal, or functional order. These instabilities exhibit a critical region where the transformation has not yet occurred and yet, at the same time, has already occurred. This region hosts ambiguity, an ambiguity that can be captured at the critical state marking the onset of convective motions in an initially still fluid heated from below (for example, think to the critical state of the formation of the Giants Causeway, the hexagonal volcanic rocks of Northern Ireland), at the starting of a chromatic chemical clock during the Belousov-Zhabotinsky autocatalytic reactions, or at the arising of a synchronized, ordered applause from a stochastic clapping when the audience in an auditorium, driven by enthusiasm, demands an encore from the soloist.

Dynamic instabilities occur under special critical conditions in nature and in society. They also occur during perception, not seldom but continuously and systematically. Their outcome, at the critical state of the perceptive process, is the emergence of visual thinking.

Vivid examples of ambiguity in the mind can be experienced while looking at an ambiguous structure such as *Fragment of Psychoplastic Structure* (1963, collection of the author). This figure may be conceived as a visual metaphor for a diatomic hydrogen molecule formed by two identical atoms. It helps to visualize both the two lower energy modes of being three-dimensional space and assign its central region to the right- or to the left-hand cubic modulus. Thereafter, visual thinking cannot get stuck in either of these positions: soon an endless sequence of approximately periodic perceptive alternations of right/left/right prospects sets in.

As anticipated, the process of perception, leading to the dynamics of visual thinking, turns out to resemble closely the process of measurement of a homonuclear diatomic molecule according to quantum mechanics. Both processes share ambiguity.

Ambiguity as a Permanent Cultural Value

In conclusion, complex concepts of quantum physics and the structure of matter are intimately connected with optical illusions, paradoxes, and ambiguity, features usually attributed to the world of art rather than to science. Both art and science are produced, emotionally and rationally, by our thinking. And our thinking proceeds chaotically, on the jagged watershed of a permanent cultural value: ambiguity.

See also **Authority; Metaphor; Perspective; Quantum.**

BIBLIOGRAPHY

Arnheim, Rudolf. *Visual Thinking*. Berkeley: University of California Press, 1969.

Caglioti, Giuseppe. *The Dynamics of Ambiguity*. Berlin: Springer, 1992.

———. "Perception of Ambiguous Figures: A Qualitative Model Based on Synergetics and Quantum Mechanics." In *Ambiguity in Mind and Nature: Multistable Cognitive Phenomena*, edited by Peter Kruse and Michael Stadler. Berlin: Springer, 1995. Psychologists, physicists, neurologists, and chemists analyze multistability in perception.

Empson, William. *Seven Types of Ambiguity*. London: Chatto and Windus, 1953.

Haken, Hermann. *Synergetics, an Introduction: Nonequilibrium Phase Transitions and Self-organization in Physics, Chemistry, and Biology*. 2nd ed. Berlin: Springer, 1983.

Hoffmann, Roald. *The Same and Not the Same*. New York: Columbia University Press, 1995.

Piaget, Jean. *La construction du réel chez l'enfant*. Neuchâtel, France: Delachaux and Niestlé, 1937.

Prigogine, Ilya. *La fin des certitudes: temps, chaos et les lois de la nature*. Paris: O. Jacob, 1996.

Wittgenstein, Ludwig. *Tractatus logico philosophicus*. New York: Harcourt Brace, 1922.

Giuseppe Caglioti

Nude Descending a Staircase (No. 2) **(1912) by Marcel Duchamp. Oil on canvas.** Fourth-dimensional representations of an object on a two-dimensional surface, such as Duchamp's painting, can lead to ambiguous perceptions of the object's features. THE PHILADELPHIA MUSEUM OF ART / ART RESOURCE, NY. © 2004 ARTISTS RIGHTS SOCIETY (ARS), NEW YORK / ADAGP, PARIS / SUCCESSION MARCEL DUCHAMP

(the so-called stationary states) of this molecule and its resonant behavior during a spectroscopic observation of it.

At first this figure, by construction, could be envisaged superficially as a two-dimensional structure exhibiting a center of symmetry. Keep looking at it as passively as possible. Its central region around the center of symmetry could be described in two ways: (1) as belonging 50 percent to the modulus at left and 50 percent to the modulus at right and, paradoxically, (2) as belonging neither to the modulus at left nor to the modulus at right. These two descriptions, though quite acceptable if considered separately, are incompatible if attributed to the same reality simultaneously, as they should be in this case. Indeed, we react instinctively to the absurdity of the situation and hasten to remove the ambiguity built into the figure by letting the two-dimensional figure invade the

AMERICA. America is one of the greatest political-philosophical symbols in world history. It is equal in importance to Athens representing philosophy, Jerusalem representing biblical religion, Rome representing both its pagan and Catholic manifestations, and Mecca representing the home of Islam. But what is meant by *America?* When people refer to it are they signifying the precise measurements of the landmass that incorporates the territory from Canada's Ellesmere Island above the magnetic pole in the north to Tierra del Fuego off the tip of Argentina in the south? Do they want to call attention to the area that in the year 2000 was home to forty-five countries and territories with 900 million people, where dozens of languages are spoken, and where can be found people of almost every ethnic origin, religion, and social and economic class? It is unlikely that they are referring to these basic facts. Facts and figures do not begin to touch what *America* represents symbolically. Throughout its history, *America* has stood for two different, almost opposite, things. First, it stands for natural man, the Indians, who are said to represent the world's beginning. Second, it stands for the United States, the great political experiment based on natural rights, which has evoked inspiration and fear and envy. It inspires such strong feelings because the United States is often perceived as the world's future. *America* thus represents both the world's origins and its endpoint. This essay attempts to shed light on the "idea" of *America* by tracing its genealogy from America's discovery by Western man until the twenty-first century.

The Indians

From 1492 until the American Revolution, and in some sense continuing into the twenty-first century, *America* evoked the image of Indians. Archaeologists believe that the American continent was first inhabited by human beings who walked from Siberia to Alaska over the Bering Strait on a frozen land bridge about 30,000 to 40,000 years ago. However, what the Indians represent in the global imagination is a fairly static image informed by media portrayals that starkly depict the Indians either as barbaric savages or as noble stewards of the land living in harmony with nature. These images have a long genealogy.

First attempts to explain America. Although the Americas were undoubtedly visited by the Vikings around the year 1000, the "discovery" of America is attributed to Christopher Columbus, whose voyage to America in 1492 captured the European imagination. Ironically, to Columbus's dying day, he insisted that what he had found was part of Asia. Thus, perceptions of America have been mistaken from the very beginning. (Sixteenth-century mapmakers, recognizing Columbus's mistake, named the New World not after him, but after Amerigo Vespucci—hence the name *America*—whom they credited as the first to realize that the New World was its own continent.)

The Indians of America were misrepresented from the very beginning and ever since their discovery. Not only did Columbus believe America was someplace else—hence the name Indians—but his description of its inhabitants was fanciful, too. He claimed to discover cannibals, Cyclopes, Amazons, Sirens, dog-faced peoples, people with no hair, and people with tails. These bizarre claims were suggested to him by centuries of fanciful tales passed on through medieval times by supposedly reliable authorities. In short, Columbus claimed to find what he was looking for. This began a pattern of preformed opinions dictating what is supposedly found in America. He saw the land as potential wealth and its people as possible converts or slaves. For him, as for most of the early conquistadores and missionaries, the Indians had no independent status, no integrity of their own. They were just to be used.

The Spanish Renaissance philosophers who first reflected on the discovery of the Indians did little better in appreciating them. Two positions dominated the Spanish debates. The first position, arguing that the Indians did not possess the faculty of reason, went so far as to argue that the Indians were the concrete embodiment of Aristotle's natural slave. According to this view, the Indians could be incorporated into Europe's traditional Christian-Aristotelian worldview but only in its lowest place. God created the Indians as naturally inferior, the argument went, so it was just and right that the Spanish subjugate them. The second view saw the Indians as rational—as evidenced by their languages, economics, and politics—but as underdeveloped and needing Spanish tutelage. Because they were human, the Indians had to be governed by consent—not their formal, explicit consent, but rather what they would consent to after they came to understand the natural law, which of course the Spanish thought they possessed. In short, because the Spanish were so confident in their worldview, it never occurred to them that they might be incorrect or possess only a partial truth. Their cultural confidence led them to reject the Americans as barbaric.

America as the home of natural man. In 1580 the French philosopher Michel de Montaigne (1533–1592) began a pathbreaking new way of thinking about the Indians. A skeptic and a keen observer of human diversity, Montaigne argued that "each man calls barbarism whatever is not his own practice; for indeed it seems we have no other test of truth and reason than the example and pattern of the opinions and customs of the country we live in." Unlike the Spanish, Montaigne doubts the standards of his own place and time. In his famous essay "Of Cannibals" (*Essays*) he describes Indian society as the best society that ever was, real or imagined, because they are "still very close to their original naturalness" and thus live in a "state of purity" according to "*les loix naturelles.*" He claims their society, held together with "little artifice and human solder," is as pure and natural as a society can be. His account claims that these Indians do fight and eat their captives, but he says they do so not for economic gain but as a kind of aristocratic struggle for mastery. He describes their warfare as "wholly noble" and "as excusable and beautiful as this human disease can be." This is the origin of the image of the noble savage.

Montaigne knows, however, that his account of the Indians' tranquility and bliss is fictitious. He concedes the barbarous horror of some of their actions, writing, "I am not sorry that we notice the barbarous horror of [their] acts, but I am heartily sorry that, judging their faults rightly, we should be so blind to our own." Here Montaigne reveals his true intentions in describing the Indians: he uses them as an image with which to expose the horrors and cruelty of his own world. This usage of the Indians as a countercultural marker was to become the norm. While Montaigne's account of the Indians is in the end neither anthropologically accurate nor fully desirable, he is the first to misrepresent the Indians in a positive fashion.

After Montaigne, no major philosopher in Europe doubted the Indians' naturalness. To the contrary, the Indians came to represent natural man par excellence. From Montaigne until the end of the Enlightenment, every major philosopher agreed with John Locke's (1632–1704) famous statement that "in the beginning all the world was America" (*Second Treatise of Government*). America represented Europe's past. In ending one debate, however, Montaigne began a new one. While every major thinker agreed that the Indians represented mankind's natural state, debate arose over the interpretation of the natural state: was it a brutishness to overcome or an innocence to recapture?

Among these philosophers the debate evolved in a single direction. Thomas Hobbes (1588–1679) first argued that mankind's natural state is a horrible state of war to be avoided at all costs. Locke and Charles-Louis de Secondat, baron de Montesquieu (1689–1755), countered that the state of nature is pacific but undesirable. Jean-Jacques Rousseau (1712–1778), François Marie Arouet de Voltaire (1694–1778), and Denis Diderot (1713–1784) later praised the Indians as naturally good and happy, in contrast to European artificiality and corruption. These varied representations, it should be noted, do not correspond to any changes in Indian societies, nor do they respond to new information about the Indians. In truth, the available evidence was barely consulted at all by any of the great thinkers. Rather, these philosophers clearly used their descriptions of the Indians as support for their own ends. As dissatisfaction with Europe increased, so did praise of the Indians grow as an alternative, more desirable and more natural, way of living.

In sum, contemporaneous representations of the American Indians really reflect Europe's own debates, not the reality of America. They have left the legacies of brutishness and of the noble savage, which remain in the twenty-first century. But there is another legacy of these debates. In using the Indians of America to promote their own visions of freedom and legitimate institutions, the philosophers set in motion a train of thought and actions that would lead to revolution. The first of these revolutions took place in America and led to the founding of the United States.

The United States

When people speak about America, they usually are referring not to the Indians, nor to the hemisphere as a whole, but to the United States of America (USA), the world's most powerful nation since World War II. The global obsession with American power revolves around four axes: cultural, economic, political, and military. American popular culture (e.g., blue jeans, rock and roll and jazz music, cinema and television programming, McDonald's restaurants, and Disneyland) is both highly prized for its energy, ease, accessibility, and speed and condemned as an unwanted cultural intrusion that threatens to swamp indigenous ways. Economically, America has for centuries represented the possibility of riches beyond belief ("streets paved with gold"), and as such has been the goal of tens and tens of millions of immigrants. But since the United States became the world's dominant economic power, its material wealth has become both envied and resented. Politically, America has been lauded as a uniquely favorable place (what the American colonist John Winthrop called a "city on a hill") for the promise of freedom that it offers, and it has been condemned, as in the eyes of the Iranian revolutionary, the Ayatollah Khomeini, as

"the great Satan" for what are perceived to be its heathen and materialistic ways. Militarily, the United States has since World War II been the strongest country on earth, and since the collapse of the Soviet Union, it is universally cited as the world's only superpower. This power is sometimes feared and envied by those without it. Moreover, people throughout the globe paradoxically call for the United States to use its power when they want it to do something and condemn the United States as arrogant when it uses it for a cause of which they disapprove.

These perceptions of the United States are neither new nor unmediated reactions to perceived facts. Each of these praises and complaints can be traced back almost to the founding of the United States itself. Thus, they cannot be explained merely as a reaction to a particular political administration or to the rise of American power. Deeper phenomena are at play.

First reactions to the United States. The United States was formed in a rebellion from England in 1776. Its revolution was the first successful modern revolution in that it was inspired and justified (at least in part) by philosophical doctrine. The United States' Declaration of Independence invokes philosophy when it argues that "all men are created equal" and endowed with "inalienable rights" such as the rights to "life, liberty, and the pursuit of happiness." Government exists only to secure these rights, and any government that does not secure them is deemed illegitimate. The founders of the United States wrote a Constitution to secure these rights based on limited government and the separation of public and private spheres. At a time when no country on earth was based on the consent of the governed, the success of American democracy proved to the modern world that democratic and representative government could exist.

The relationship between the Old and New Worlds (and the two images of America) is intertwined and reciprocal. The American Revolution marked the first major step in the collapse of the European empires founded after Columbus discovered the New World. This revolution was inspired in part by the European philosophical doctrines based on natural rights, which had themselves been partly inspired by the original inhabitants of America. Ironically, the political experiment in the name of natural rights then helped destroy the "natural" people who helped inspire the United States' philosophical forefathers. The American Revolution then helped inspire the French Revolutionaries and other lovers of liberty throughout the world. The complex nature of this relationship is seen in the following quotation from the essay "On the Influence of the American Revolution on Europe" by the French philosopher Marie-Jean Caritat, marquis de Condorcet (1743–1794):

> "The human race had lost its rights. Montesquieu found them and restored them to us" (Voltaire). It is not enough, however, that these rights be written in the philosophers' works and engraved in the heart of virtuous men. It is also necessary that the ignorant or feeble man be able to read them in the example of a great people.
>
> America has given us this example. Its Declaration of Independence is a simple and sublime exposition of

these rights, so sacred and so long forgotten. Among no nation have they been so well known, or preserved in such perfect integrity.

The reciprocal relationship is evident: it moves from Montesquieu and Voltaire, who had been partially inspired by America's original inhabitants, to the Declaration of Independence then back to Condorcet, who authored France's Constitution of 1793.

Condorcet's praise of America was typical of the Enlightenment philosophes. Immediate reaction to the American Revolution by Enlightenment thinkers was one of enthusiastic praise. In his popular pamphlet entitled "Observations on the Importance of the American Revolution and the Means of Making it a Benefit of the World," Richard Price (1723–1791) writes, "I see the revolution in favor of universal liberty which has taken place in America; a revolution which opens a new prospect in human affairs, and begins a new era in the history of mankind." Given the unprecedented liberties guaranteed in America, Price is hopeful, nay certain, that liberty will soon spread throughout the world, if unchecked by tyrannical governments. He says the revolution will "raise the species higher" and compares its effect to "opening a new sense." Indeed, he goes so far as to suggest that "next to the introduction of Christianity among mankind, the American revolution may prove the most important step in the progressive course of human improvement." So many hopes has he pinned on America that "perhaps there never existed a people on whose wisdom and virtue more depended; or to whom a station of more importance in the plan of Providence has been assigned." Similarly, Anne-Robert-Jacques Turgot (1727–1781), whose brief stint as finance minister in France marked the last serious attempt at reform before the French Revolution, says in a "Letter to Price" that America is "the *hope* of the world" and should "become a *model* to it."

The Enlightenment thinkers did not think America was perfect. Slavery was America's greatest flaw. They understood the difficulties in eradicating this execrable institution and argued that America would be judged by the manner of eliminating it as circumstances allowed.

The great strengths of America, however, more than outweighed its imperfections. Enlightenment leaders praised the numerous liberties in the United States, including freedom of the press, speech, conscience, and religion. Moreover, America was seen as an inspiration for the world. As Condorcet writes, it is an example "so useful to all the nations who can contemplate it"; "it teaches them that these rights are everywhere the same"; "the example of a free people submitting peacefully to military, as to civil, laws will doubtless have the power to cure us." Europe developed these Enlightenment ideas, but due to its powerfully entrenched institutions, it could not act on them. The Enlightenment philosophes, however, thought that the example of America would inspire the deeds that their words could not. In fact, they were right. The American Revolution inspired the French Revolutionaries in 1789, and it has continued to inspire revolutionaries throughout the world.

Nineteenth-century views of the United States.

Nineteenth-century views of the United States are seen through the lens of the French Revolution. After the French Revolution devolved into terror, anarchy, and despotism, no major thinker ever again unqualifiedly praised the American Revolution. This is peculiar. Thinkers might have said that the French got it wrong, the Americans right, so let us praise the Americans and further intensify the study of it. Instead, they let the horrors of the French Revolution color their understanding of the American. This shows once again how the perceptions of America were based more on European dynamics than on the reality of America itself.

Despite the failure of the French Revolution, the existence of the United States, coupled with the Enlightenment belief in progress, led to a general feeling that the United States was the future. If the French proved that the path to the future was not simple and smooth, the perception of what the future was to be like, as embodied in the United States, was also ambivalent. Interest in the United States was heightened because everyone had a stake in the future, which the United States seemed to represent.

In the aftermath of the French Revolution, criticism arose about the United States. The substance of this criticism was similar across the ideological spectrum of the nineteenth century and is familiar to anyone aware of contemporary critiques of the United States. What America had become and what critics thought Europe would become—democratic—was regarded as a mixed blessing. The greatest representative of this ambivalence is Alexis de Tocqueville (1805–1859), the great French thinker and statesman. According to Tocqueville, democratic government is inefficient, meandering, and petty. But it has its advantages. It gets more done by energizing the people to do things themselves: "it does that which the most skillful government often cannot do: it spreads throughout the body social a restless activity, superabundant force, and energy never found elsewhere, which, however little favored by circumstance, can do wonders. Those are its true advantages" (*Democracy in America*). Democracy is not conducive, however, to refinement, elevated manners, poetry, glory, or heroic virtues. All of the main political theorists of the nineteenth century agreed with this ambivalent assessment of America—and of the budding liberalism of Europe.

America was seen as epitomizing the self-interested individualism of the new commercial society and as representing the centralization of power by the new middle-class regime. As such, four criticisms were repeatedly leveled at it. First, America was said to embody the disorder caused by collapsing institutions. The authority of all previous standards—experience, age, birth, genius, talent, and virtue—was undercut in America. Second, America represented a growing obsession with money. It was because of this that all other standards of human value were ignored. Third, America represented unchecked equality. The new type of man preferred equality to liberty, as Tocqueville and John Stuart Mill (1806–1873) warned. Finally, the new form of government represented the power of the majority, the "tyranny of the majority" in Tocqueville's famous phrase. This stifled creativity and individuality. It guaranteed that society would be geared to the mediocre middle at the expense of individual refinement, the cultivation of culture, and the emergence of spiritual sublimity and greatness. These are essentially the same charges leveled against the United States in the late twentieth and early twenty-first centuries by traditional authorities in Africa, Asia, and the Middle East, by the educated elites in Europe and elsewhere, and by the antimodern radicals, such as the Ayatollah Khomeini, Hizbollah, and Al Qaeda.

Twentieth-century views of the United States. The main twentieth-century critiques of America, such as those by Oswald Spengler (1880–1936) and Martin Heidegger (1889–1976) on the right and by the Frankfurt School on the left, argue that America is overly technological and materialistic. Thus, America, once described as the home of nature, became the place where nature is most obscured. Twentieth-century thinkers did not agree on the origins of America's technological morass. For example, the Frankfurt School saw technology as the result of capitalism, whereas Heidegger attributed it to a particular metaphysical way of being. The characteristics that they lamented in America's overtechnicalization, however, are similar. They lament the mechanization of society and the way it alienates human beings from their deeper essences. They deplored the monotonization and leveling of the world and the resulting loss of individuality. They decried the way technology kills the spirit and prevents the attainment of the highest human developments. In short, their substantive list of complaints is very similar to those made during the nineteenth century; but whereas the nineteenth-century thinkers attributed the problems to an array of social, political, and economic factors, twentieth-century thinkers blamed them on technology.

Beyond the technological blame, there is another important divergence between nineteenth- and twentieth-century thinkers' assessments of America. Whereas nineteenth-century thinkers like Tocqueville saw Russia, as well as the United States, as an emerging power, they almost all greatly preferred the American model to the Russian. This was not true in the twentieth century. Many figures on the left, such as Jean-Paul Sartre (1905–1980) and Simone de Beauvoir (1908–1986), ideologically committed to communism, lauded Soviet approaches and condemned American ones. Even among the anticommunist right, many considered the United States and the Soviet Union to be equally bad. Heidegger, for example, says that America and Russia "are metaphysically the same." An abstraction from politics that allows such comparisons is regrettable, but in Heidegger's case it is even worse. While formally arguing that the United States and Russia are the same, when he needs a shorthand label for the phenomena that he describes as a "*Katastrophe,*" he calls it "Americanization," not Russianization, implying that the former is closer to the core of the problem.

Critical Reflections

According to its representations, *America* has moved from representing Europe's past to representing Europe's future and from the epitome of nature to the epitome of technology, polar opposite views. Four points might be noted, however, that

raise questions about the validity of these representations. First, descriptions of America have been fantastical from the beginning. They are inaccurate and often intentionally so. Second, although twentieth-century thinkers blame the United States for the technologization of the world, it is apparent that the technological attitude long predates the founding of the United States. Columbus and the conquistadores neither saw the New World for what it was nor had any desire to do so. Rather, they sought to exploit resources and people, and this is the essence of the technological attitude, the attitude that some claim began only with the United States. Third, twentieth-century thinkers miss the mark in blaming America for problems that have to do with modernity itself. Because the United States was created from scratch by colonists with minimal feudal baggage, the United States emerged as perhaps the purest embodiment of modern values. But there are multinational corporations in Europe and other countries around the world, and most people wherever they live in the world desire the standard of living and freedom that the United States—and many modern countries—have. So while there is a certain justification for seeing the United States as embodying modernity, it is not modernity's sole embodiment.

Fourth, there is a fundamental continuity in the views about America. The Indians have been described as on the one hand, naïve, innocent, childlike, and simple, and on the other as brutish, vulgar, shallow, stupid, and lacking spirituality. These are essentially the same charges that Europe and the world leveled at the United States throughout the nineteenth and twentieth centuries. The United States might be all of these things, although probably not more than most countries and possibly less so than many. But the fact that ways of life as opposite as those of the Indians and the United States are described in fundamentally the same terms indicates a problem in the substantive nature of the representations.

As an epilogue, it is worth noting briefly a postmodern view of America. Postmodern thinkers reject the idea of there being any humanly knowable truth and choose to play with images, which they claim is all we are left with. The French postmodern thinker Jean Baudrillard has done this with the United States. In a book entitled *America* (1986; English translation published in 1988), Baudrillard writes contradictorally, "For me there is no truth of America" and, "I knew all about this nuclear form, this future catastrophe when I was still in Paris, of course." He also mixes all of the main images of America, describing the United States both as "the original version of Modernity" and as "the only remaining primitive society." For him, America is the "Primitive society of the future." He combines five hundred years of images of America in a clever fashion.

See also **Enlightenment; Europe, Idea of; Individualism; Natural Law.**

BIBLIOGRAPHY
Beichman, Arnold. *Anti-American Myths: Their Causes and Consequences.* Rev. ed. New Brunswick, N.J.: Transaction, 1993.
Ceaser, James W. *Reconstructing America: The Symbol of America in Modern Thought.* New Haven, Conn.: Yale University Press, 1997.

Chiappelli, Fredi, Michael J. B. Allen, and Robert L. Benson, eds. *First Images of America: The Impact of the New World on the Old.* 2 vols. Berkeley: University of California Press, 1976.

Chinard, Gilbert. *L'exotisme américain dans la littérature française au XVI siècle.* Geneva: Slatkine Reprints, 1970.

Dudley, Edward, and Maximillian E. Novak, eds. *The Wild Man Within: An Image in Western Thought from the Renaissance to Romanticism.* Pittsburgh: University of Pittsburgh Press, 1972.

Echeverria, Durand. *Mirage in the West: A History of the French Image of American Society to 1815.* Princeton, N.J.: Princeton University Press, 1957.

Elliott, John H. *The Old World and the New: 1492–1650.* Cambridge, U.K.: Cambridge University Press, 1970.

Gerbi, Antonello. *The Dispute of the New World: The History of a Polemic, 1750–1900.* Rev. and enl. ed. Translated by Jeremy Moyle. Pittsburgh: University of Pittsburgh Press, 1973.

Hollander, Paul. *Anti-Americanism: Critiques at Home and Abroad, 1965–1990.* New York: Oxford University Press, 1992.

O'Gorman, Edmundo. *The Invention of America: An Inquiry into the Historical Nature of the New World and the Meaning of Its History.* Bloomington: Indiana University Press, 1961.

Pagden, Anthony. *The Fall of Natural Man: The American Indian and the Origins of Comparative Ethnology.* New York: Cambridge University Press, 1982.

Revel, Jean-François. *Anti-Americanism.* Translated by Diarmid Cammell. San Francisco: Encounter Books, 2003.

Roger, Philippe. *L'ennemi américain: Généalogie de l'antiaméricanisme français.* Paris: Seuil, 2002.

Rubinstein, Alvin Z., and Donald E. Smith, eds. *Anti-Americanism in the Third World: Implications for U.S. Foreign Policy.* New York: Praeger, 1985.

Todorov, Tzvetan. *The Conquest of America: The Question of the Other.* Translated by Richard Howard. Norman: University of Oklahoma Press, 1999.

Woodward, C. Vann. *The Old World's New World.* New York: Oxford University Press, 1991.

Alan Mitchell Levine

AMERICANIZATION, U.S.

AMERICANIZATION, U.S. *Americanization* refers to processes of "becoming American," and to organized efforts to encourage the transformation of immigrants into "Americans." The term was in informal use in the United States in the mid-nineteenth century, but it is most prominently associated with the movement of that name during the 1910s and early 1920s. The term is often used interchangeably with *assimilation.*

The "problem" of Americanization arises because American national identity must be constructed in the absence of primordial ethnic mythology, and in the face of exceptional diversity. There is general recognition that the United States is a "civic nation," rather than an "ethnic nation," in which devotion to "founding principles" is the source of national identity and community. The creedal nature of American identity carries the implication that anyone may "become American" by committing himself or herself to the nation's founding principles, and to their expression in distinctively American symbols and ways of living. However, the propositional nature of American identity carries with it the question of who is capable of the necessary understanding of, and commitment to, American principles, and to the ways of living that they are taken to imply. That seed of doubt has led Americans to scrutinize cultural differences, ethnic consociation, and race as potential indicators of the lack of qualification for trusted membership in the polity, and to insist on outward demonstrations of Americanization by those considered for membership.

American National Identity and Ideologies of Americanization

The definition of American identity in ideological terms was elaborated in the early postindependence period. While the extent to which a new American people would emerge from the fusion of diverse strands of Europeans, as Michel-Guillaume-Jean de Crevecoeur's (1735–1813) famous "Letter from an American Farmer" rhapsodized, was questionable, what was firmly established was the association of American identity with individual "transformation."

Americanization in the nineteenth century. Nineteenth-century Americans expected life in the United States to transform European newcomers into culturally compatible neighbors. While not directing specific "Americanization" efforts toward immigrants, American communities placed faith, in particular, in the common schools to be "culture factories" in which to inculcate principles of republican virtue, and to cultivate American habits and identities. A general pattern of acceptance of diversity and confidence in the workings of America's natural "melting pot" was not obtained until the 1890s.

The 1890s represent a crucial turning point that intensified the salience of ethnicity as an element of national identity, gave rise to the "Americanization movement," and, ultimately, resulted in long-lasting restrictions on immigration. A massive influx of new immigrants, primarily from southern and eastern Europe, combined with the perception of the frontier having closed, accelerated industrialization, rural emigration, recurring economic distress, perceptions of urban disorder and disorganization, labor conflict, and radical political agitation diminished Americans' faith in the naturally absorptive powers of American life and in a laissez-faire approach to immigrant absorption. So, too, did the development of a distinctively racialist ideology that identified Anglo-Saxon descent with authentic American identity and placed the new immigrants into inferior classifications.

Americanization in the first quarter of the twentieth century. The resulting effort to "Americanize" immigrant newcomers was part of the Progressive movement's broader efforts to construct a modern and cohesive social order, and also part of a new purifying national effort to cultivate patriotism among all Americans. As World War I approached, the priorities of immigrant adjustment would yield to the priority of coercively assuring loyalty through insistence on naturalization, quick acquisition and sole use of English, and adherence to "American" cultural norms.

Well before the official birth of the "Americanization movement" in 1915, educators began to grapple with what they determined were the needs of the increasing number of foreign-born adults and their children. Settlement houses and other agencies

Immigrants in Americanization class. In the early 1900s, citizenship classes such as those conducted by the U.S. Bureau of Naturalization often sought to teach immigrants not only basic civic facts about America, but also how the newcomers could be more "American" in their everyday life. © CORBIS

like the YMCA initiated programs and activities intended to familiarize immigrants with the language and cultural practices of the United States and to smooth the transition from "immigrant" to "American." Public schools began to adopt distinctive curricular, extracurricular, and disciplinary innovations intended to "Americanize" the children of immigrants. These included, among other measures, kindergartens, instruction in hygiene, manners, and the conduct of daily life, home visitations, and special classes for teaching English. During this phase of "humanitarian" Americanization, professionals sought to integrate immigrants into American life without harshly and rapidly stripping them of their homeland ties and concerns or of their culturally distinct languages, values, beliefs, and customary ways.

The Americanization movement that followed was multifaceted and involved professional, popular, and political elements. Its participants were not of one mind, and some shifted their viewpoints and priorities over time. It is the coercive and strident activities of campaigns of the World War I period against "hyphenation," and, then, for "100 Percent Americanism" that have left the lasting image of the Americanization movement, and account for its repudiation in the 1920s.

According to John Higham, the Americanization movement represented "nothing less than an alteration in the whole texture of nationalist thought." One-Hundred Percent Americanism demanded "universal conformity organized through total national loyalty." The new spirit of nationalism required complete identification with country so as to "permeate and stabilize the rest of [the individual's] thinking and behavior" (1970, pp. 204–205). In this vein, citizenship classes included lessons not only on civic duties like voting, but also on "American" ways of performing routine tasks like cooking and cleaning, child rearing, and personal hygiene. "Becoming an American, immigrants were taught, involved making yourself over entirely" (McClymer, p. 109).

Perhaps highest on the Americanizers' agendas for remaking immigrants into Americans was conversion by immigrants from home-language to the use of English. For the most extreme among the "English First" crusaders, language was foremost a matter of loyalty. Professional Americanizers, however, emphasized that only a common language could guarantee the "community of interest" required for national unity. Among professional Americanizers, English was deemed necessary to facilitate the widespread social intercourse and participation that they so ardently championed.

Historians have not often been kind to the Americanization movement of the 1890–1925 period. Robert Carlson has labeled the Americanization movement a "Quest for Conformity" that demanded an unfair exchange, and, in general, was psychologically damaging to its putative beneficiaries. Gary Gerstle identifies the Americanization movement with coercive nation-building that almost destroyed German Americans as an ethnic group, limited the identities that Americans could adopt, and hardened the racial color-line. John Higham, while recognizing the mixed impulses of the movement, interprets the movement as fundamentally an episode in American nativism.

Not all historians, however, have viewed the Americanization movement in unrelentingly negative terms. The circumstances to which the Americanizers were responding were, given their perspectives, threatening and challenging. In the face of the massive immigration from parts of the world that heretofore had not been large sources of emigration to America, worries over whether democracy could function in the absence of a common language, common culture, and common commitment, were, in Robert Wiebe's judgment, reasonable. Stephan Brumberg is critical of academic critics of the Americanization movement who fail to appreciate the immigrant's real needs for structure and direction in an alien, threatening, perplexing, and dehumanizing environment. Moreover, the vocabulary of Americanization, with its proclamations of American symbols and ideals celebrating liberty, democracy, and equal opportunity, could be adopted by immigrant and American workers alike, to help forge an American working-class consciousness in opposition to the rule of capitalist elites.

While most historians have evaluated the Americanization movement by what it did to immigrants, Michael Olneck has questioned the proximate effects of Americanization and has argued that perhaps the largest significance of the movement was to create new "public meanings" rather than to have changed immigrants. Most significantly, the Americanization movement defined subsidiary identities as incompatible with "American" identity, delegitimated collective identities, relegated ethnic identities to the "background," and demarcated a supraethnic, shared public terrain of "American life" into which all were expected to "enter," as well as symbolically represented the abstract autonomous individual as the constitutive element of American society.

Americanization between 1930 and 1965.

During the 1920s occasional voices were raised against the project of a homogeneous America, and by the 1930s an ideology of "cultural pluralism" gained currency. With the rise of fascism in Europe, concerns over ethnic, racial, and religious tensions in the United States, the ongoing social and political incorporation of second-generation Americans, scholarly discovery of persistent ethnicity in the cities, and anthropological refutations of racialist doctrines, ideas of America as encompassing a potentially harmonious diversity consistent with assimilation took hold, and were reinforced during the mass mobilization for World War II. Cultural diversity would be tolerated within the context of shared national ideas and sentiments that

ensured civic harmony and cooperation. Cultural pluralism in this form represented a powerful reaffirmation of American ideology as a basis of national identity.

Pluralism in the 1950s was "predicated on consensus around the American value system despite seeming to place a premium verbally on diversity" (Gleason, p. 62). Subsequently, American universalistic egalitarian and individualistic civic ideals appeared to triumph in passage of the Civil Rights Act of 1964 and the Immigration Reform Act and Voting Rights Act of 1965. The triumph, in the view of some, was short-lived.

Americanization after 1965.

The emergence and legitimacy of Black Power and other ethnic nationalisms in the mid-1960s, anti–Vietnam War critiques and mass protests, and the adoption of policies encouraging ethnic identification, recognition, and rights, was seen by some to have replaced civic nationalism with a strong version of cultural pluralism, later to be termed *multiculturalism*. In the process, *assimilation* joined the already discredited term *Americanization* as a term of opprobrium.

However, reactions against multiculturalism have occasioned calls for the revival of a civic ideology of American identity, and some have attempted to revive a modern ideal of Americanization. Significantly, academic and journalistic critics of multiculturalism rarely claim to seek a return to the demands for homogeneity characteristic of the Americanization movement period, nor do they urge an end to ethnicity. John Higham advocates "pluralistic integration," in which individual rights and needs for group solidarity are balanced, as are universalistic principles and particularistic needs. David Hollinger propounds a model of "postethnic cosmopolitanism," which prefers voluntary to prescribed affiliations, appreciates multiple identities and communities of broad scope, and accepts the formation of new groups as part of the normal life of a democratic society. Peter Salins commends "Assimilation, American Style" that requires citizens to accept English as the national language, take pride in American identity, and believe in America's liberal and democratic egalitarian principles, and to live by a Protestant ethic of self-reliance, hard work, and moral rectitude, but does not demand cultural homogeneity. Even John Miller, who protests "The Unmaking of Americans" and the undermining of an earlier assimilation ethic by multiculturalism, argues not that racial and ethnic identities should be suppressed, but only that their expression remain confined to the private sphere. In its 1997 recommendations, the United States Commission on Immigration Reform recommended "taking back" the word *Americanization*, since it is "our word" that was "stolen" by racists and xenophobes in the 1920s. The Commission defined *Americanization* in ways that are consistent with the ideal of civic nationality. "Americanization," the Commission wrote, " is the process of integration by which immigrants become part of our communities and by which our communities and the nation learn from and adapt to their presence," and is "the cultivation of a shared commitment to the American values of liberty, democracy and equal opportunity" (p. 26). "The United States," the Commission continued,

> is a nation founded on the proposition that each individual is born with certain rights and that the purpose

of government is to secure these rights. The United States admits immigrants as individuals. . . . As long as the United States continues to emphasize the rights of individuals over those of groups, we need not fear that the diversity brought by immigrants will lead to ethnic division or disunity. (pp. 28–29)

Whether or not subsequent government action is as attentive as the Commission tried to be to the "cosmopolitan" elements in defining American identity is debatable, but government policies certainly evidence an ongoing commitment to Americanization. In 2001 the Congress replaced the Bilingual Education Act with the English Language Acquisition Act, which included replacing the United States Department of Education's Office of Bilingual Education and Minority Language Affairs with an Office of English Language Acquisition. In 2003 Congress established the "Office of Citizenship" in the United States Department of Homeland Security. The Office of Citizenship is meant to work to revive and emphasize "the common civic identity and shared values that are essential to citizenship," according to a government fact sheet. And, despite apparent commitments to multiculturalism in the pubic schools, actual formal and informal practices, particularly those emphasizing the rapid acquisition of English, suggest that schools continue to regard "Americanization" as a priority, even if they do not use that term. What remains absent from the schools is the civics education component of Americanization that predominated during the 1910s.

Conclusion

At the juncture of the early twenty-first century, those made uneasy by America's increasing ethnic and linguistic diversity called, through such efforts as attempting to legislate an "official" status for English, for a kind of revived Americanization movement. While a majority supported proposals to make English the "official" language, acceptance of diversity nevertheless appeared embedded in expressed attitudes, and public-opinion studies strongly supported the conclusion that Americans' ". . . preference for an inclusive nationalism coexists with the widespread acceptance of pluralism in cultural practices" (Citrin et al., p. 266). A "cosmopolitan liberal" view of American identity and polity appeared to predominate over either a multiculturalist or nativist view, and so we would expect coercive Americanization crusades to remain a thing of the past.

See also **Assimilation; Diversity; Ethnicity and Race; Identity: Personal and Social Identity**

BIBLIOGRAPHY

Carlson, Robert A. *The Americanization Syndrome: A Quest for Conformity.* New York: St. Martin's, 1987.

Citrin, Jack, et al. "Multiculturalism in American Public Opinion." *British Journal of Political Science* 31 (2001): 247–274.

Gleason, Philip. *Speaking of Diversity: Language and Ethnicity in Twentieth-Century America.* Baltimore: Johns Hopkins University Press, 1992.

Higham, John. *Send These to Me: Jews and Other Immigrants in Urban America.* New York: Atheneum, 1975.

———. *Strangers in the Land: Patterns of American Nativism, 1860–1925.* 1955. Reprint, New York: Atheneum, 1970.

Hollinger, David A. *Postethnic America: Beyond Multiculturalism.* New York: Basic Books, 2000.

McClymer, John F. "The Americanization Movement and the Education of the Foreign-born Adult, 1914–1925." In *American Education and the European Immigrant, 1840–1940,* edited by Bernard J. Weis, 96–116. Urbana: University of Illinois Press, 1982.

Miller, John J. *The Unmaking of Americans: How Multiculturalism Has Undermined the Assimilation Ethic.* New York: Free Press, 1998.

Olneck, Michael R. "Americanization and the Education of Immigrants, 1900–1925: An Analysis of Symbolic Action." *American Journal of Education* 97 (1989): 398–423.

Salins, Peter D. *Assimilation, American Style.* New York: Basic Books, 1997.

Schultz, Stanley K. *The Culture Factory: Boston Public Schools, 1789–1860.* New York: Oxford University Press, 1973.

United States Commission on Immigration Reform. *Becoming an American: Immigration and Immigrant Policy: 1997 Report to Congress.* Washington, D.C.: United States Commission on Immigrant Reform, 1997.

Michael R. Olneck

ANALYTICAL PHILOSOPHY.

It was only in the 1960s that the phrase "analytical philosophy" came into frequent use as a way of describing the kind of philosophy characteristic of much English-language philosophy of the twentieth century. But occasional references to "analytical" (or "analytic") philosophy as a new kind of philosophy can be found much earlier, where it is primarily used to introduce a contrast with "speculative philosophy." The thought here is that whereas traditional philosophers have attempted by means of speculative arguments to provide knowledge of a kind that is not otherwise possible, "analytic" philosophers aim to use methods of philosophical analysis to deepen the understanding of things that are already known—for example, concerning the past or concerning mathematics. In doing so analytic philosophers will seek to clarify the significance of essentially uncontentious historical or mathematical truths and to explain the possibility of our knowledge of them. This program does not require that analytic philosophers deny the possibility of speculative philosophy; but many did so, most famously those associated with the Vienna Circle such as Rudolph Carnap (1891–1970), who held that "all statements whatever that assert something are of an empirical nature and belong to factual science" and went to claim that, for philosophy, "What remains is not statements, nor a theory, nor a system, but only a method: the method of logical analysis" (1932; 1959, p. 77).

Methods of philosophical analysis are in fact as old as philosophy, as in Socrates' dialectic. The method was especially prominent in the theory of ideas characteristic of seventeenth- and eighteenth-century philosophy, which involved the analysis of complex ideas into simple ones. One of Immanuel Kant's (1724–1804) insights was to recognize the priority of complete judgments over ideas, or concepts, and this led him to hold that analytic methods of inquiry were subordinate to the elucidation of synthetic unities, such as the unity of consciousness. Kant's successors in the tradition of German idealism took this subordination much further as they sought to articulate the internal relations that hold together ever more encompassing "organic wholes" such as the state and the universe. For them, analysis was only ever a preliminary stage of inquiry, a kind of falsification to be transcended once a relevant organic whole and its relationships had been identified.

Moore

A good place to mark the start of analytical philosophy is therefore with the young G. E. Moore's (1873–1958) emphatic denunciation of this idealist philosophy. Moore rejected internal relations and organic wholes, and in their place he gives priority to individual judgments, or propositions, and their constituent concepts. Since he holds that true propositions are real structures that do not represent facts, but constitute them, it follows that an analysis of a proposition into its constituent concepts is equally an analysis of a fact into its elements: as he puts it "A thing becomes intelligible first when it is analysed into its constituent concepts" (1899; 1993, p. 8). Thus in Moore's early work a method of conceptual analysis is employed to identify the basic properties of things. This is manifest in Moore's *Principia Ethica* (1903), where Moore famously argues that goodness is the basic ethical property and thus that ethical theory is the theory of the good. It should be observed, however, that Moore's method of analysis does not specify the content of his theory of the good, even though this is also supposed to be a priori. Moore's method of metaethical analysis is therefore combined with an appeal to intuitive reflection concerning synthetic a priori ethical truths; and one of the issues that has remained a matter of debate is just what contribution conceptual analysis has to offer to ethical theory.

Russell, Frege, Wittgenstein

The decisive development that gave a distinctive character to analytical philosophy was that whereby the young Bertrand Russell (1872–1970), freshly converted from idealism by Moore, used his new logical theories to enhance the possibilities for philosophical analysis. For what is special about analytical philosophy is the preeminence given to logical analysis. In Russell's early work this development is manifest in his "theory of descriptions," whereby he uses his logical theory to provide an analysis of propositions in which particular things are described. Russell argued that he was thereby able to resolve long-standing metaphysical puzzles about existence and identity, and equally to show how it is possible for us to have knowledge ("by description") of things of which we have no direct experience. Indeed as Russell became increasingly adept at developing and applying his logical theory, he came to think that its use was really the only proper way of doing philosophy. Thus in 1914 he gave some lectures that included one with the title "Logic as the Essence of Philosophy," and he here declares: "every philosophical problem, when it is subjected to the necessary analysis and purification, is found either to be not really philosophical at all, or else to be, in the sense in which we are using the word, logical" (1914, p. 33).

Russell here describes his method as "the logical-analytic method of philosophy" (p. v) and he goes on to add that the first clear example of this method is provided by Gottlob Frege's (1848–1925) writings. Russell has in mind here Frege's development in 1879 of a radically new logical theory (first order predicate logic, as we would now call it) in his *Begriffsschrift* ("Concept-script"). Although Frege does not here apply his logic to philosophical debates, he does offer it as "a useful tool for the philosopher" who seeks to "break the domination of the word over the human spirit by laying bare the misconceptions that through the use of language almost unavoidably arise concerning the relations between concepts" (1879; 1970, p. 7). This contrast between the new logical "concept-script" and the apparent structure of ordinary language brings to the surface a concern with the proper understanding of language that is characteristic of analytical philosophy. The relationship between logic and ordinary language remains a contested matter, but the identification of "logical form" is one enduring strand of analytical philosophy, as in Donald Davidson's theories of action and causation.

As indicated, Russell looked back to Frege when describing his "logical-analytic method of philosophy"; but in truth Russell's philosophy also contained much more besides, in particular a problematic emphasis on the priority of the things that are presented in experience, the things that we "know by acquaintance." One of the achievements of Ludwig Wittgenstein (1889–1951), who had studied with Russell and through him made contact with Frege, was to set aside this aspect of Russell's philosophy and present a purified logical-analytic method in his *Tractatus Logico-Philosophicus* (1922). Wittgenstein maintains here that "Philosophy is not one of the natural sciences"; instead "Philosophy aims at the logical clarification of thoughts. Philosophy is not a body of doctrine but an activity" (4.111–112). There is a sharp disagreement here with Russell, whose philosophy certainly does offer "a body of doctrine" based on his theory of knowledge by acquaintance. By contrast Wittgenstein holds that one should be able to demonstrate to anyone who seeks to advance a philosophical proposition that in doing so they have fallen into talking nonsense (6.53).

The Vienna Circle

Whether Wittgenstein altogether succeeds in explaining his own position without convicting himself of nonsense remains debated. But there is a different element in his position that requires attention: the thesis that logic has a special a priori status because it articulates the rules that make language possible. This thesis is often associated with the claim that logic is "analytic" because logical truth depends only on the definition of logical vocabulary. In fact there is a distinction here: it is one thing to hold that logic is a priori because it is integral to language, it is another to hold that logic is "analytic" in the sense that it is just true by definition. But this distinction was not drawn by the members of the Vienna Circle whose "logical empiricism" constitutes the next phase in the development of analytical philosophy. As indicated by the passage cited earlier from Carnap, a leading member of this group, their starting point was an empiricist presumption that the understanding of language is rooted in perceptual experience; but they recognized that ordinary experience does not exhibit the complex laws and structures of which the natural sciences speak. So they invoked logic to make the connections between observation and theory. In order to remain true to their empiricism, therefore, they emphasized the "analyticity" of logic, such that logic was not to be thought of as a body of abstract nonempirical doctrine but simply a way of working out the conventions of language.

Ordinary Language Philosophy

Although there was much disagreement among the logical empiricists their position constituted an immensely influential antimetaphysical paradigm for mid-twentieth-century philosophers, especially after the rise of the Nazis had led to the emigration of the leading philosophers of the group from Central Europe to the United States. While traditional philosophers complained, quite rightly, that the antimetaphysical rhetoric of the position concealed its own metaphysical assumptions, two other lines of criticism were especially important for the subsequent development of analytical philosophy. In Britain, especially after 1945, the logical empiricists' emphasis on logical analysis was felt to be excessively restrictive. It was argued by the defenders of "ordinary language philosophy" such as J. L. Austin and Peter Strawson that formal logic does not adequately capture the complex conceptual structures of our thought and language, and thus that a much more heterogeneous and informal approach to conceptual analysis is required. This work led to the development of a variety of approaches to the study of language, especially speech act theory, which treats speech as a kind of action and therefore conceives of its meaning in the light of the things speakers *do* by means of their speech acts (for example, making a promise or naming a child). At much the same time Wittgenstein's later *Philosophical Investigations* (1953) were published, with a similar emphasis on the need to understand our ordinary "language-games" instead of relying on formal logic to capture the structure of thought. One of the most challenging features of Wittgenstein's later investigations was his critical discussion of psychological concepts, and this, together with other work, has helped to direct recent analytical philosophers at least as much to the philosophy of mind as to the philosophy of language.

Quine

The other main criticism of logical empiricism came from the American philosopher Willard Van Orman Quine (1908–2000), who argued that the logical empiricists had been mistaken in regarding logic as "analytic"—that is, true by definition. Quine argued that logic is of the same type as other beliefs: it is an element of the web of belief through which we make sense of our experience as experience of an objective world. Hence logic is not analytic, since it concerns the world, and it is not a priori, since it is revisable in the light of experience. Quine's arguments remain disputed, but his work has certainly helped to encourage philosophers to address broader disputes in the natural sciences and other areas. There is no enclosed domain for a priori logical and conceptual analysis. Some critics, most notably Richard Rorty, argue that it follows that there is now nothing worth calling "analytical philosophy." But these claims are exaggerated. Although Quine was a critic of the analyticity of logic, he was a distinguished logician and used logical analysis throughout his philosophy; so his practice shows that analytical philosophy does not depend on the analyticity of logic. Second, although Quine's arguments call into question the "linguistic" conception of the a priori as analyticity it is widely accepted that some distinction between the a priori and the empirical has to be made if we are to be able to reason coherently; and as long as that distinction is in place, analytical philosophers can draw on it to characterize the significance of their conclusions. Analytical philosophy today, therefore, continues the tradition captured by Russell and Wittgenstein at the beginning of the twentieth century. It is not "a body of doctrine," it is a "method," typically "logical-analytic," but often informal, of using reasoning to capture and criticize conceptual structures. As such one finds it regularly employed across the whole spectrum of contemporary philosophical debate, by feminists and political philosophers as much as by metaphysicians and epistemologists.

Analytical and Continental Philosophy

Throughout much of the twentieth century analytical philosophy was very different from the approach to philosophy characteristic of "continental" philosophers such as Edmund Husserl, Martin Heidegger, Jean-Paul Sartre, and Maurice Merleau-Ponty. One reason for this was simply their ignorance of logic, which excluded them from any serious understanding of analytical philosophy. Conversely analytical philosophers, by and large, remained uncomprehending of the phenomenological project of recovering the basic structures of intentionality. By the end of the twentieth century, however, with translations of all the main works involved into the relevant languages, a much greater degree of mutual comprehension has been achieved. As a result, while continental philosophers such as Jacques Derrida have sought to appropriate analytical techniques such as speech-act analysis, analytical philosophers have turned their attention to the theme of intentionality, though sometimes with conclusions far removed from those of continental philosophers. Thus the situation is now one of dialogue despite profound disagreements.

See also **Continental Philosophy; Idealism; Language, Philosophy of: Modern; Philosophy of Religion; Positivism.**

BIBLIOGRAPHY

Analysis (1933–). A journal founded to promote analytical philosophy. See the statement in vol. 1, which remains a characteristic expression of this kind of philosophy.

Austin, John Langshaw. *How to Do Things with Words.* Oxford: Clarendon Press, 1962. Austin here begins to develop speech-act theory.

Ayer, Alfred J. *Language, Truth, and Logic.* London: Gollancz, 1936. A brilliant statement of the logical empiricist position.

———, ed. *Logical Positivism.* Glencoe, Ill.: Free Press, 1959. An excellent collection of papers.

Baldwin, Thomas. *Contemporary Philosophy: Philosophy in English since 1945.* Oxford and New York: Oxford University Press, 2001. A book in which the author of this entry discusses the main themes of analytical philosophy since 1945.

Butler, R. J., ed. *Analytical Philosophy.* 2 vols. Oxford: Blackwell, 1962–1965. Two collections of papers characteristic of mid-twentieth century analytical philosophy.

Carnap, Rudolph. "The Elimination of Metaphysics through Logical Analysis of Language." 1932. In *Logical Positivism,* edited by A. J. Ayer, 60–81. Glencoe, Ill.: Free Press, 1959. Originally published in German as "Uberwindung der Metaphysik durch logische Analyse der Sprache," this is Carnap's classic statement of his logical empiricism.

———. "Empiricism, Semantics and Ontology." *Revue Internationale de Philosophie* 4 (1950): 20–40. Reprinted in *The Linguistic Turn: Recent Essays in Philosophical Methods,* edited by Richard Rorty. Chicago: University of Chicago Press, 1967. 2nd ed., 1992. Carnap here introduces a distinction between "internal" and "external" questions to clarify his defense of analyticity. Rorty's collection is a useful resource, and the 2nd ed. contains two interesting skeptical retrospective essays.

Cohen, G. A. *Karl Marx's Theory of History: A Defence.* Oxford: Clarendon Press, 1978. A work showing how analytical philosophy can be applied to the study of Marxism; the starting point of "analytical Marxism."

Davidson, Donald. *Essays on Actions and Events.* Oxford: Clarendon Press, 1980. This collection includes Davidson's discussions of "logical form."

Derrida, Jacques. "Signature, Event, Context." In his *Margins of Philosophy.* Translated by Alan Bass. Chicago: University of Chicago Press, 1982. Derrida's critical discussion of Austin.

Frege, Gottlob. *Begriffsschrift.* 1879. In *Frege and Godel: Two Fundamental Texts in Mathematical Logic,* edited by J. van Heijenoort. Translated by S. Bauer-Mengelberg. Cambridge, Mass.: Harvard University Press, 1970. Frege's revolutionary new logical theory.

Fricker, Miranda, and Jennifer Hornsby. *The Cambridge Companion to Feminism in Philosophy.* Cambridge, U.K., and New York: Cambridge University Press, 2000. A collection of papers showing how issues in feminist philosophy are addressed by analytical philosophers.

Montefiore, Alan, and Bernard Williams. *British Analytical Philosophy.* London: Routledge, 1966. A useful collection in which the British conception of analytical philosophy is expounded and discussed.

Moore, G. E. "The Nature of Judgment." 1899. In *G. E. Moore: Selected Writings,* edited by Thomas Baldwin, 1–19. London and New York: Routledge, 1993. Moore's early rejection of the idealist theory of judgment.

———. *Principia Ethica.* Cambridge, U.K.: Cambridge University Press, 1903. Rev. ed., edited by Thomas Baldwin. Cambridge, U.K.: Cambridge University Press, 1993. Moore's classic presentation of his analytical ethics.

Quine, Willard van Orman. *From a Logical Point of View: 9 Logico-Philosophical Essays.* Cambridge, Mass.: Harvard University Press, 1953. A collection which includes some of Quine's early papers, especially "Two Dogmas of Empiricism" in which he launches his critique of analyticity.

———. *Ways of Paradox.* New York: Random House, 1966. A collection that includes two of his main papers on logical empiricism, "Truth by Convention" and "Carnap on Logical Truth."

Rorty, Richard. *Philosophy and the Mirror of Nature.* Princeton, N.J.: Princeton University Press, 1979. Rorty here sets out his skeptical critique of analytical philosophy.

Russell, Bertrand. "On Denoting Mind." 1905. In *Logic and Knowledge: Essays, 1901–1950,* edited by R. Marsh, 41–56. London: G. Allen and Unwin, 1956. Russell's presentation of his theory of descriptions.

———. *Our Knowledge of the External World as a Field for Scientific Method in Philosophy.* Chicago, Ill.: Open Court, 1914. Russell's presentation of his logical-analytic method in philosophy.

Strawson, P. F. *Logico-Linguistic Papers.* London: Methuen, 1971. A collection that includes Strawson's early criticisms of Russell's logic and his later reflections on logic and language.

Wisdom, John. *Problems of Mind and Matter.* Cambridge, U.K.: Cambridge University Press, 1934. An early example of an exposition of "analytic" philosophy as such.

Wittgenstein, Ludwig. *Philosophical Investigations.* Translated by G. E. M. Anscombe. Oxford: Blackwell, 1953. Wittgenstein's later discussion of language-games, rule-following, and psychological concepts.

———. *Tractatus Logico-Philosophicus.* Translated by C. K. Ogden. London: K. Paul, Trench, Trubner and Co., 1922. Wittgenstein's early attempt to present philosophy as logical analysis.

Thomas Baldwin

ANARCHISM. The term *anarchy* comes from an ancient Greek word meaning "without a leader or ruler." However, proponents of anarchism have most often used the term to refer to a natural state of society in which people are not governed by submission to human-made laws or to any external authority. Anarchism is above all a moral doctrine concerned with maximizing the personal freedom of individuals in society. To achieve this end, leading anarchist social theorists have tended to offer critical analyses of (1) the state and its institutional framework; (2) economics; and (3) religion. Anarchist hostility to the state is reflected in the rejection of the view popularized by contract theorists that a government's sovereignty is legitimated by the consent of its subjects. Anarchists contend that no contractual arrangement among human beings justifies the establishment of a ruling body (government) that subordinates individuals to its authority. From their observations of the historical development of the state, anarchist thinkers such as Pierre-Joseph Proudhon (1809–1865) and Peter Kropotkin (1842–1921) concluded that all forms of government have been used as instruments for establishing monopolies that favor the propertied and privileged. Anarchists also argue that the all-encompassing authority of the state allows it to exercise undue influence over the lives of its citizens. It is further maintained by anarchists that the state, using laws and the organs of power at its disposal, can control not only citizens' public and private behavior but also their economic lives. As such, the state, in all its forms, is condemned as an unnecessary evil.

From an economic standpoint, most anarchists have identified themselves as members of the anticapitalist socialist movement. In common with socialists, anarchists see capitalism as a system ruled by elites, one that exploits the working or productive members of society economically and represses them culturally and spiritually. Accordingly, anarchists argue that the emancipation of the worker will only be achieved by completely destroying the pillars of capitalism.

Anarchists differ as to what form of economic arrangements should replace capitalism. Collectivists and mutualists insist that private ownership of the fruits of individuals' labor is desirable, while anarchist communists maintain that individual freedom can only be achieved in a society where all material goods and natural resources are placed under common ownership. Still another group of anarchists known as individualists have advocated a system of "labor for labor" exchange, which they believe could operate in accordance with natural market forces.

Anticlericalism is another important dimension of anarchist thinking. Though most anarchists are materialists, they are not opposed to spirituality per se: indeed anarcho-pacifists such as Leo Tolstoy (1828–1910) were self-identified as Christians. Rather, anarchists condemn organized religion, which they see as an agent of cultural repression. They have, for example, attacked the Catholic Church among other religious institutions on the grounds that it has historically served as a means of empowering church government and not of enriching the spiritual lives of its adherents. Anarchists further contend that the church has consistently acted as an ally of secular governments and therefore forms part of the general system of state repression that operates against the common person.

Because the heyday of anarchism as an ideological movement was during the nineteenth and early twentieth centuries, the focus here will be on the core beliefs of key anarchist theorists in this period. Thus a discussion of other, less historically significant anarchist strands such as pacifism and individualism will be mentioned only in passing. The impact that classical anarchist theory has had on recent political and social movements will be summarized in the concluding section.

Anarchist Principles in Context

The ideas associated with modern anarchism can be traced to the period of the French Revolution (1789–1799), although they did not crystallize into a formal political doctrine until the middle part of the nineteenth century. The first book that offered the clearest intimation of the anarchist conception of society was William Godwin's *An Enquiry concerning Political Justice and Its Influence upon General Virtue and Happiness* (London, 1793). In this, Godwin identifies the state as the main source of all social ills. In order for humans to live freely and harmoniously, Godwin advocates the establishment of a stateless society in which individuals are no longer subject to the economic exploitation of others. Despite its antistatist message, the ideas found in Godwin's magnum opus belong to a tradition of British political radicalism that cannot be classified as anarchist. In fact his work had its greatest influence on the liberal thinkers of his age as well as on Robert Owen, John Gray, and other early socialist reformers.

Of far greater significance to the development of modern anarchist ideology is the French social philosopher Pierre-Joseph Proudhon, whose indictment of private property under capitalism was made famous in his book *What is Property?* (1840). Proudhon's main contributions to the anarchist view of society lay in his theories of mutualism and federalism. In the former he argued that the exploitative capitalist system could be undermined by creating economic organizations such as the People's Bank, an institution of mutual credit meant to restore the equilibrium between what individuals produce and what they consume. Because he believed that concentrating political power in the hands of the state militated against the economic forms he was proposing, Proudhon argued for a society in which power radiated from the bottom upward and was distributed along federal or regional lines.

Though he himself never belonged to any party or political organization, Proudhon's writings inspired a substantial following among freethinkers, liberal intellectuals, and workers across Europe, particularly in France and Spain. One of his most famous disciples was the Russian anarchist Mikhail Bakunin (1814–1876). Like Proudhon, Bakunin was an eclectic thinker who was constantly revising and reformulating his views on society. More so than Proudhon, who did not believe that the transition to an anarchist society demanded violent and sweeping changes, Bakunin gave both physical and ideological expression to the view that revolutionary upheaval was a necessary and unavoidable process of social development, a view summed up in his oft-quoted dictum, "The urge to destroy is also a creative urge." At the core of his creed was collectivism, by which he meant that the land and means of production should be collectively owned and that future society should be organized around voluntary associations—such as peasant communes or trade unions—that were not regulated or controlled by any form of government. Too impatient to set forth a systematic exegesis of his antiauthoritarian beliefs, Bakunin tended to express his concepts in tracts that could be used by revolutionary bodies (for example, the Alliance of Social Democracy) with which he was associated. Indeed Bakunin's most enduring legacy to anarchism resides in his conception of revolutionary transformation. According to him, the dispossessed and most repressed elements of society—particularly the working classes and peasantry in economically backward countries such as Spain, Italy, and Russia—were by nature revolutionary and only needed proper leadership to rise up against their oppressors. Because he adamantly rejected the Marxian notion that conquering political power was a precondition for overthrowing capitalism, Bakunin was convinced that the exploited masses should be led into revolt by a small and dedicated group of individuals who were acting in their interests. It was his belief that revolution could not be achieved until the state was completely abolished, which brought him into conflict with Karl Marx and his followers, who insisted that a "dictatorship of the proletariat" was a necessary phase in the transition to a stateless society (communism).

Bakunin's antipolitical conception of revolutionary change as well as his forceful repudiation of the authoritarian communist principles embodied in the Marxism of his day drove a wedge between his adherents in the First International (1864–1876) and those of Karl Marx, thus establishing a divide in the European socialist movement that would never be bridged.

However, not all anarchists were hostile toward the idea of communism. Another Russian aristocrat turned revolutionary, Peter Kropotkin, developed over the course of his lifetime a sociological theory of anarchism that combined the antiauthoritarian beliefs espoused by his predecessors in the anarchist movement with those of communism. Unlike Proudhon and Bakunin, both of whom believed in the right of individual possession of products produced from one's labor, Kropotkin advocated an economic system based on the communal ownership of all goods and services that operated on the socialist principle "from each according to his abilities, to each according to his needs." By distributing society's wealth and resources in this way, Kropotkin and other anarchist communists believed that everyone, including those who were unproductive, would be able to live in relative abundance.

Kropotkin's greatest contributions to anarchist theory, however, were his attempts to present anarchism as an empirically verifiable worldview, one that was based on "a mechanical explanation of world phenomena, embracing the whole of nature." Following in the positivist tradition laid down by Auguste Comte (1798–1857), Herbert Spencer (1820–1903), and other forerunners of modern social science, Kropotkin believed that the study of society was analogous to that of the world of nature. In *Modern Science and Anarchism* (1912), for example, Kropotkin contends that the anarchist method of sociological enquiry is that of the exact natural sciences. "Its aim," he says, "is to construct a synthetic philosophy comprehending in one generalization all the phenomena of nature—and therefore also the life of societies." In developing his views on human nature, Kropotkin went farther in extending the analogy between society and the natural world. Like the Social Darwinists of his era, Kropotkin maintained that all human behavior was a reflection of our biological condition. But while most Social Darwinists argued that a "tooth and nail" impulse in the struggle for existence was the dominant natural law governing the evolution of human behavior, Kropotkin insisted that the instinct of cooperation was an even more important factor in this process. According to him, it is the species in nature that shows the greatest tendency toward mutual aid—not cutthroat competition—that is the one most likely to survive and flourish over time. By arguing in this way, Kropotkin was attempting to demonstrate that anarchism was a highly evolved state of human nature but one that could not be obtained until the state and other coercive institutions were completely abolished.

The relationship between anarchism and violence.

The efforts of Kropotkin and other anarchist thinkers to define anarchism as a rational and practicable doctrine were overshadowed by the negative publicity generated by the violence-prone elements of the movement. Beginning with the assassination of Tsar Alexander II in 1881 and continuing up to the turn of the century, when the American president William McKinley was murdered in 1901 by a lone gunman, anarchists everywhere were viewed as sociopaths who terrorized society by throwing bombs and assassinating heads of state. The fact that not all of these public outrages were committed by anarchists (Alexander II was killed by nihilists) or individuals who were representative of the movement as a whole did little to dispel the exceedingly negative image of anarchists that was being projected by the popular press and government authorities.

The violent practices that were now associated with anarchism were largely the product of an ill-defined tactic known as "propaganda by the deed," a direct-action policy advocated by some anarchists from the late 1870s on. That violent and even criminal deeds were necessary to advance the anarchist movement appealed especially to a small number of disaffected idealists who were convinced that the only way to intimidate the ruling classes and overturn the capitalist system was to disrupt the daily routines of bourgeois society. Killing public figures close to the centers of political and religious power was one way of doing this. Bombing cafés, robbing banks, and destroying churches and similar hierarchical institutions were also seen as justifiable means to a revolutionary end.

A number of the perpetrators of "propaganda by the deed" were influenced by a highly individualistic strain of anarchist thought that became popular among déclassé intellectuals and artists around the turn of the twentieth century. A seminal figure in the individualist branch of anarchist thinking was the German philosopher Max Stirner (1806–1856). In his *The Ego and His Own* (1845), Stirner espoused a philosophy that was premised on the belief that all freedom is essentially derived from self-liberation. Because he identified the "ego" or "self" as the sole moral compass of humankind, he condemned government, religion, and any other formal institution that threatened one's personal freedom. It was his abiding concern with the individual's uniqueness and not his views as a social reformer that made Stirner attractive to certain segments of the anarchist community at the end of the nineteenth century. This was particularly true not just of the devotees of violence in Europe but also of the nonrevolutionary individualist anarchists in the United States. For example, the foremost representative of this strand of anarchism in the United States, Benjamin R. Tucker (1854–1939), took from Stirner's philosophy the view that self-interest or egoistic desire was needed to preserve the "sovereignty of the individual."

Spiritual anarchism and anarcho-syndicalism.

Parallel to the terrorist acts committed at this time, the Christian pacifist Leo Tolstoy (1828–1910) was developing an antiauthoritarian current of thinking that, in its broadest sense, can be regarded as belonging to the anarchist tradition. Tolstoy promoted a form of religious anarchism that was based on the "law of supreme love" as defined by his personal (anti-doctrinal) reading of the Scriptures. Though he did not see himself as an anarchist, he nevertheless believed that in order for men and women to live in a morally coherent world it was necessary to destroy the state and its institutions. Because of his rejection of the use of force and violence, Tolstoy and his followers advocated civil disobedience, or nonviolent resistance, as a means of achieving the stateless and communally based society they envisioned.

It was also around this time that anarchist doctrine experienced another significant metamorphosis. From the late 1890s until the 1930s, anarchist activity was increasingly centered in working-class cultural and economic organizations, and the tactics and strategy of the movement were grounded in the theory of revolutionary syndicalism. While not wholly abandoning the use of violence, the anarcho-syndicalists believed that, against the organized forces of big government and monopoly capitalism, the revolutionary élan of the workers could be most effectively channeled through trade union organizations. Using tactics such as the general strike, which was meant to paralyze the economy by linking shutdowns in different industries, the anarcho-syndicalists believed that it would be possible to create the general conditions for a complete collapse of capitalism and the state. Anarcho-syndicalism became an important force in the labor movements in parts of Latin America (Mexico, Argentina) and in European countries such as Italy, France, and Spain. Its greatest impact was felt in Spain. During the Second Republic (1931–1936) and continuing through the civil war period (1936–1939), anarcho-syndicalism developed into a powerful mass movement. At its peak the anarcho-syndicalist organizations known as the CNT-FAI (National Confederation of Workers and Federation of Iberian Anarchists) counted more than 1.5 million adherents. Their influence over the course of events during the civil war was most dramatically illustrated by the fact that they set up and ran thousands of industrial and agricultural collectives throughout the Republican zone. The triumph of Franco's Nationalist forces in 1939, followed by the outbreak of another global world war that same year, sounded the death knell for anarcho-syndicalism not only in Spain but in other Western European countries as well.

It deserves mention here that, by the time World War II began, anarchism's reach extended across the globe. Besides taking root in the Americas, the doctrine had penetrated parts of East Asia and even the subcontinent. In both China and Japan, for example, Western anarchist ideas influenced leading social thinkers such as Mao Zedong and labor organizers who were seeking to establish socialism in those countries. However, the emergence of authoritarian and totalitarian regimes of both the right and left in the 1930s and late 1940s effectively quashed the libertarian tendencies that had been developing up to then. It would take another forty years before anarchist ideas would be resurrected by tiny protest groups (mostly in Japan) that wanted to express their cultural and intellectual dissatisfaction with the status quo.

Contemporary Anarchism

While the Spanish Civil War, World War II (1939–1945), and the rise of totalitarian communist regimes after 1949 were events that effectively ended the further development of the historical anarchist movement, anarchist ideas and sensibilities were not as easily repressed. The political and cultural protest movements of the 1960s and 1970s in Europe and the Americas saw a resurgence of interest in anarchism. Feminists, ecologists, student radicals, pacifists, and others who were eager to question the prevailing social and moral preconceptions of modern society held by both the left and the right were drawn above all to the doctrine's iconoclasm. At this time, elements from a variety of nonlibertarian groups—the Situationists in France, for example—freely borrowed anarchist ideas in developing their own ideological positions.

Anarchism has also been enriched by the thinking of some of the twentieth century's leading philosophers, political activists, artists, and intellectuals. Bertrand Russell, Herbert Read, Mahatma Gandhi, Martin Buber, Albert Camus, Michel Foucault, Paul Goodman, Lewis Mumford, and Noam Chomsky are among the notable figures who have been associated with anarchist beliefs and values.

From the late twentieth century on, anarchism has continued to branch out in different directions. Anarchist ideas have been influential in the development of radical feminism and the Green and antiglobalist movements that have spread across Europe and the Americas. Contemporary anarcho-feminism has its roots in the writings and activism of historically important figures like Emma Goldman, Voltairine de Cleyre, and Federica Montseny. Goldman was among the first female anarchists to emphasize that the emancipation of women in society must begin with psychological change within women themselves. By calling on women to struggle against the repressive and hierarchical structures that dominated their personal lives, Goldman anticipated late-twentieth-century anarcho-feminists, who have insisted that the "personal is political" and have developed a radical critique of everyday life. Anarchist principles also have been adopted by some of the more radical ecological movements of postindustrial societies. Libertarian social ecologists such as Murray Bookchin have attempted to extend the traditional anarchist demand to emancipate society from government rule to our natural environment, calling for an end to human beings' dominating and exploitative relationship with nature.

Perhaps because of its shock value in an age crowded by political neologisms, the anarchist label has also been applied to groups that do not properly belong to the anarchist tradition. For example, the term "anarcho-capitalism" is sometimes used to refer to libertarian economic and social thinkers such as Ayn Rand, David Friedman, and other pro-capitalists who hold strong antistatist views. But even though they share the anarchist's contempt for state authority, their commitment to free enterprise and laissez-faire principles places them completely at odds with classical anarchist thinking and practice.

Ever since the Cold War ended in 1991, small groups of anarchists around the world have been in the forefront of the antiglobalization movement. Like their predecessors, modern anarchist activists seek to expose the adverse power relationships that affect our daily lives. They are particularly concerned with the impact that the global expansion of corporate leviathans has had on society, not least because of the seemingly unlimited ways in which this advanced form of capitalism can manipulate and control the lives of individuals. While a few anarchist groups still resort to direct-action methods to get their revolutionary message across, a growing number are turning to advanced technologies like the Internet to promote their cause. In short, whether one admires or abhors anarchist principles, it cannot be denied that anarchism offers a critical perspective of authority that appears to be endlessly relevant to those who want to sharpen their awareness of the boundaries of personal freedom.

See also **Communism; Feminism; Marxism; Protest, Political; Social Darwinism; Socialism.**

BIBLIOGRAPHY

PRIMARY SOURCES

Bakunin, Mikhail. *Michael Bakunin: Selected Writings.* Edited by Arthur Lehning. Translated by Steven Cox and Olive Stevens. New York: Grove Press, 1973.

Bookchin, Murray. *Post-Scarcity Anarchism.* 1971. 3rd ed., Oakland, Calif.: AK Press, 2004.

Chomsky, Noam. *Radical Priorities.* 1981. Edited and introduced by Carlos Otero. Exp. 3rd ed. Edinburgh and Oakland, Calif.: AK Press, 2003.

Cohn-Bendit, Daniel, and Gabriel Cohn-Bendit. *Obsolete Communism: The Leftwing Alternative.* Translated by Arnold Pomerans. Harmondsworth, U.K.: Penguin, 1968.

Debord, Guy. *The Society of the Spectacle.* 1973. Reprint, New York: Zone Books, 1994.

De Cleyre, Voltairine. *Anarchism and American Traditions.* Chicago: n.p., 1932.

Goldman, Emma.. *Anarchism, and Other Essays.* 1910. Reprint, with a new introduction by Richard Drinnon, New York: Dover, 1969.

Goodman, Paul. *Growing Up Absurd.* New York: Random House, 1960.

Kropotkin, Peter. *The Conquest of Bread.* 1906. In *The Conquest of Bread and Other Writings,* edited by Marshall Shatz. Cambridge, U.K., and New York: Cambridge University Press, 1995.

———. *Modern Science and Anarchism.* Translated from the Russian by David A. Modell. Philadelphia: The Social Club of Philadelphia, 1903. 2nd ed., London: Freedom Press, 1923.

———. *Mutual Aid: A Factor of Evolution.* London: Heinemann, 1902.

Proudhon, Pierre-Joseph. *What Is Property: An Inquiry into the Principle of Right and Government.* 1890. Translated by Donald R. Kelley and Bonnie G. Smith. Cambridge, U.K.: Cambridge University Press, 1994.

Puente, Isaac. *Libertarian Communism.* 1932. Sydney: Monty Miller Press, 1985.

Reclus, Élisée. *An Anarchist on Anarchy.* London: Liberty Press, 1897.

Rocker, Rudolf. *Anarchosyndicalism.* London: Secker and Warburg, 1938.

Stirner, Max. *The Ego and His Own.* Translated by Steven T. Byington. New York: Benj. R. Tucker, 1907.

Tolstoy, Leo. *What I Believe.* Translated by Constantine Popoff. London: Elliot Stock, 1885.

Tucker, Benjamin J. *Instead of a Book.* 1893. Reprint, New York: Arno Press, 1972.

SECONDARY SOURCES

Guérin, Daniel. *Anarchism.* Translated by Mary Klopper. New York: Monthly Review Press, 1970.

Joll, James. *The Anarchists.* 2nd ed. Cambridge, Mass.: Harvard University Press, 1980.

Marshall, Peter H. *Demanding the Impossible.* London: Fontana, 1991.

Miller, David. *Anarchism.* London: Dent, 1984.

Pennock, J. Roland, and John W. Chapman, eds. *Anarchism.* New York: New York University Press, 1978.

Sonn, Richard D. *Anarchism.* New York: Twayne, 1992.

Woodcock, George. *Anarchism.* New ed. Harmondsworth, U.K.: Penguin.

George Esenwein

ANCESTOR WORSHIP. Ancestor worship is the reverent devotion expressed by descendants for their deceased forebears through a culturally prescribed set of rituals and observances. The prominence of ancestors as a focus of worship within a broader religious tradition is common in many parts of the world, including Asia, Africa, and Native America, but there are few unifying characteristics cross-culturally. Commonalities include:

> Only those deceased of appropriate relationship to the living and who have undergone the necessary *rites de passage* are worshiped.

> Those that are worshiped usually are recognized by name or title, often a special posthumous one.

> Services to the ancestors frequently include offerings and libations.

That ancestor worship is related to the animistic belief in a spirit or soul surviving the body after death, as proposed by early anthropologist Edward Burnett Tylor (1832–1917), is reasonable, since it is this spirit essence of the ancestor that is believed to continue its relationship with descendants. That ancestor worship is related to the earliest stage of religious expression among humans, however, as Tylor's theory further suggested, is certainly debatable. Other controversies in the study of ancestor worship include whether practices in honor of the deceased constitute actual worship; the extent to which linear versus collateral relatives comprise the worshiping group; the ways in which the living are influenced by the dead; and the individual, family, kin group, or regional variability in practice that can be present in a single cultural tradition.

Ancestors in Africa and Asia

In his work among the Tallensi of Ghana, Meyer Fortes emphasizes the significance of ancestor worship to patrilineage unification and lineage or segment differentiation. In particular, the father–oldest surviving son relationship is emphasized, the latter having the primary responsibility for performing the appropriate rituals and service. In general, placement of an African ancestral shrine and the performance of its services can also relate to and influence descendants' genealogical position and seniority.

In China, Daoist, Confucian, Buddhist, and folk concepts have contributed to the practice of ancestor worship in which heads of patrilineages are emphasized but other patrilineal relatives are included. There are three prominent sites for ancestor worship: family shrines, lineage halls, and tombs or graveyards of relatives. Proper placement and orientation of the latter will take geomancy (*feng-shui*) into account. Physical remains of the deceased are laid to rest in the tomb/graveyard, which serves as the site of public rituals; ancestral tablets represent the deceased in shrine and temple, in which their spirits are housed, and for which more private and personal observances are made. While the ancestors wield significant authority and influence in the lives of their living descendants, the latter care for and look after their ancestors—for example, by burning paper money at New Year's to contribute to their ancestors' bounty or prosperity.

Man with mummified remains of ancestor. In certain cultures, ancestors are seen as intermediaries between people and the gods, and it is believed that their involvement in the day-to-day happenings of the family does not end with death. © CHRIS RAINIER/CORBIS

Japanese ancestors are also emphasized on the father's side, and their worship is primarily related to Buddhist beliefs and practices. The deceased receive a posthumous or "Buddhist" name, which is written on a tablet and kept in the family's *butsudan* or Buddhist altar; Buddhist funerary services help purify the corpse from the polluting influences of death. Other services include "death day" memorial services for up to fifty years, New Year's and Bon (or Obon) celebrations, and household prayers. While tradition maintains a differentiation between stem and branch families and a main ancestral altar in the stem house, more modern practice has individual families establishing their own *butsudan* with the death of a household member. Proper care for the ancestors and observance of appropriate services, offerings, and prayers are believed not only to help the ancestors be restful and in peace, but also to result in blessings and good fortune for the descendants.

Among the Inca

In his early chronicle of Inca customs, Felipe Guaman Poma de Ayala pictures a mummy with feathered headdress and fine raiment carried on a litter as illustration of November or *aya marcay quilla* (Quechua for "the month of the dead"). He describes how during the holiday of the dead the deceased were removed from their crypts, adorned with clothing and feathers, given food—through burnt offerings—and drink, and carried dancing and walking through the streets and plazas, then laid to rest with various offerings. Such activities occurred

primarily in the worship of royal mummies, as an extension of the concept of the divine nature of the Inca king. While Inca beliefs included the departure of the soul from the body at death, royal bodies were mummified, served burnt offerings and drinks, and cared for by official attendants. Royal ancestors participated in affairs of state—counseling living rulers and contributing to their decision making, and, either in the guise of their mummified remains or as idols making formal appearances and visitations, receiving obeisance from their living subjects. Such beliefs were common in the Andes, as ancestral idols of subject peoples were held in Cuzco, the Inca capital, as a control mechanism.

Andean and Inca ancestor worship extended beyond that of royalty, and was probably common among all classes in the pre-Columbian era. Padre Bernabé Cobo attests that when the soul departed from the body, members of the deceased's *ayllu* (a corporate kin group) and family took and cared for the body, providing the veneration and care that was possible according to the family's means and status. The bodies were kept in relatives' houses, tombs, or shrines and were regularly paid tribute through sacrifice and prayer. This nonroyal worship was performed only by those descended in a direct line, and usually only by the children and possibly grandchildren of the deceased. Such worship was held to directly affect descendants' vitality and fortune, while its lack or disrespect to the ancestors could result in ill health or other maladies.

Ancestral Ambivalence

Ancestor worship is most likely to be practiced in a society with strong lineages or other consanguineal corporate groups whose continuity, standing, and control of resources extends over generations, and one in which there are strong beliefs in an active spirit world. In such contexts the appropriately related and ritually defined deceased continue to be interactive lineage and family members, cared for and reverenced by the living and in turn contributing to the prosperity of their succeeding generations as sources of or mediators with divine power. In general, ancestors who are worshiped are perceived as guardian or authority figures who are difficult to please, whose degree of influence on the living usually decreases with increasing genealogical distance from descendants. The power of the ancestors is therefore ambivalent: as likely to punish as to reward, they offer security and comfort while also contributing to uncertainty in an equivocal cosmos.

See also **Animism; Religion.**

BIBLIOGRAPHY

Cobo, Bernabé. *Historia del nuevo mundo.* 1653. Madrid: Biblioteca de Autores Españoles, 1964.

D'Altroy, Terence N. *The Incas.* Malden, Mass.: Blackwell, 2002.

Fortes, Meyer. *Oedipus and Job in West African Religion.* Cambridge, U.K.: Cambridge University Press, 1959.

Guaman Poma de Ayala, Felipe. *Nueva corónica y buen gobierno.* 1615. Paris: Institut d'ethnologie, 1936.

Hsu, Francis L. K. *Under the Ancestors' Shadow: Kinship, Personality, and Social Mobility in China.* Stanford, Calif.: Stanford University Press, 1971.

Newell, William H., ed. *Ancestors.* The Hague: Mouton, 1976.

Smith, Robert J. *Ancestor Worship in Contemporary Japan*. Stanford, Calif.: Stanford University Press, 1974.

Stephen M. Fabian

ANIMISM. Animism has had a long and important history in anthropology and outside it, as an intellectual concept with important implications not only for the study of religion, but also for the political struggles of indigenous peoples around the world. The anthropological study of animism has been a two-edged sword for indigenous people. It has brought their religious concepts, and thus their rich intellectual and spiritual lives, to the attention of the world, demonstrating the intrinsic value of their cultures. But to the extent that the apparent contrast between monotheistic and animistic religions has been exaggerated and used to create an artificial hierarchy of religious thought, it has also been used against them, to denigrate their beliefs and their intellectual capacities, and thus to deny them full equality with their colonizers.

Concepts

The concept of animism first appeared explicitly in Victorian British anthropology in *Primitive Culture* (1871), by Sir Edward Burnett Tylor (later published as *Religion in Primitive Culture,* 1958). His writings are preceded historically by those of the Greek Lucretius (c. 96–c. 55 B.C.E.) and the Roman Marcus Tullius Cicero (106–43 B.C.E.), among many others. "The doctrine of human and other souls" or "the doctrine of spiritual beings" constitutes the essence of Tylor's theory. The doctrine of souls is based on the foundational doctrine of "psychic unity," which affirms that all people, everywhere, for all time (or at least the past fifty thousand years or so), have the same capacity to comprehend all phenomena in the known, observed, and imagined universe by use of their own cultural symbols and languages. Tylor regards *Spiritualism* as a modern cult that lacks panhuman motivations of animism.

The idea of animism is that in all cultural systems people experience phenomena—such as dreams, visions, sudden insights, out-of-body experiences, near-death experiences, and trances—that simultaneously conjoin perceptions of being "elsewhere" with the knowledge of being "here." Some thinkers explain this experience through a belief in the human soul, which they envision as distinct from but inextricably attached to the body until death do they part, so that animistic belief in the soul becomes part of every cultural system.

Robert Ranulph Marett (1866–1943), Tylor's successor at Oxford, introduced the concept of *animatism* to that of *animism,* extending the idea of an animating spirit similar to the soul to include many different forces in nature and culture (*The Threshold of Religion,* 1909). Such force is what makes a tree grow from a seed, the rain fall, or the sun shine—that which brings fertility and fecundity to the earth. Loss of such force results in death. People are in awe of such forces as manifest in volcanoes and earthquakes and especially in inert corpses. Out of the observations and awe of force in nature comes the universality of the sacral basis for religious experience, which Marett argued was prior to animism. Animism

African man beside animist figure (sculpted from mud and bone and covered with feathers), Burkina Faso, c. 1979. Many indigenous cultures believe in spiritual beings, a concept first defined as animism by Sir Edward Burnett Tylor in 1871. Tylor proposed that animism derived from an attempt to explain certain phenomenon such as trances, dreams, and visions. © CHARLES LENARS/CORBIS

and animatism are often not clearly distinguished, as many of Marett's ideas have been blended through time in philosophical and religious literature with those of Tylor and many others.

The Canelos Quichua native people of Amazonian Ecuador illustrate concepts of animism and animatism. Souls and spirits are ubiquitous and even spirits have souls. Those who interact intensively with the souls are the male shamans and the female potters, both of whom influence the conceptual system of one another through mutual symbol revelation. For example, when a shaman in trance dimly "sees" an approaching colorful, noisy spirit, a woman quietly, from the darkened recesses of the room, clarifies his emerging vision and names the actual spirit.

Human souls are acquired through both mother and father. Spirit essences are hierarchized into four essential tiers, easily represented as spheres encompassing one another. Sungui, the master spirit of the rain forest and hydrosphere, is the apotheosis of androgynous power. This male and female spirit takes many corporeal forms, the most prominent being the giant anaconda. This spiritual superpower must be controlled or it will overwhelm and inundate the world; Amasanga, master spirit of the rain forest, controls the power of Sungui. The corporeal representative of this androgynous being is the great black jaguar. In turn, rainforest dynamics are controlled by Nungüi, a strictly feminine spirit, master of garden soil and pottery clay, whose corporeality is manifest in the deadly black coral snake with a mouth too small to bite humans. The inner sphere is the human household, wherein the souls and spirits come together in a special system of human knowledge, vision, and imagery. Power flows downward through the spheres, and control of power is exercised upward from inner to outer spheres.

Cultural Implications

In Tylor's original formulation, animism was an argument for the universality of human intellectual and spiritual worlds. The universality of concepts of souls, and hence the universality of religion, is a major contribution of Tylor, one that endures into the twenty-first century. Like the Canelos Quichua, humans everywhere, in one way or another, and with very great differences, conceptualize into cultural systems the spiritual dimensions of life, as well as the corporeal aspects of quotidian existence. With this concept of universalism of fundamental religious thought, Victorian England and the rest of the English-lettered world was exposed to cultural relativism.

What constitutes human difference in economy, society, psychology, and religion, then, is cultural, not biological. Although people are very "different" from one another, across space and through time, their mental capacities—cognitive, emotional, and imaginative—are not. As Clifford Geertz puts it: "The doctrine of the psychic unity of mankind, which so far as I am aware, is not seriously questioned by any reputable anthropologist, is but the direct contradictory of the primitive mentality argument" (p. 62).

Tylor, however, very much the Victorian gentleman, began his quest for the bases of animism with what he called the "lower races," whom he also labeled "savages," "rude, non-religious tribes," and "tribes very low in the scale of humanity," among other such figures of speech that link evolutionary biology and culture, thereby enforcing the "primitive mentality argument" later expanded by Lucien Lévi-Bruhl in *Les fonctions mentales dans les sociétés inférieures* (1910; translated in 1996 as *How Natives Think*). The Victorian contradiction of enlightened cultural relativity, attached to a scalar view of humans as evolving from the "lower races" to the "civilized nations," leads to the racist paradox that a few civilizations evolved while the rest of the world's people "remained" animist. Animism, by this reasoning, is evidence of low-level "relics." This contradiction became canonized by the sixteenth century through the emergence of Western modernity and mercantilist capitalism and remains strong in twenty-first-century Western cosmology.

It is, however, a fallacy. Every religious system, including the monotheistic religions such as Christianity and Islam, include representations of the supernatural with strong animistic dimensions. Despite religious scholars' assertions to the contrary, members of monotheistic religions nonetheless act at times as though there are spiritual beings detached from corporeal beings, manifest concern over the fate of their immortal souls, and make these beliefs part of their traditions, such as the jinn of Middle Eastern folklore, or of the dominant religion itself.

Nonetheless, the enduring Victorian contradiction between cultural relativity and social evolution continues to cast a shadow over the religious beliefs of indigenous peoples, leading many of the world's people with rich beliefs in spirits and noncorporeal essences of animate and inanimate things—but without a "high god" organizer—to resent the concept *animist* because of its connotation of savagery. Among the Canelos Quichua, for example, spokespeople to the outside world often express considerable resentment at the use of the word.

By the same token, animist symbolism does more than establish a template for understanding quotidian life and the universe. It also undergirds the ideological struggles of indigenous people to establish a place and space in nation-state life. In Amazonian Ecuador, for example, animistic concepts were utilized during political uprisings in 1990 and 1992, and again in 2000, when indigenous people rose up as one mighty body to claim—in part successfully—their territory and their rights. Animism as a concept is very powerful in its relativistic dimensions, but is destructive when used to place people in a universal or particular evolutionary scheme that ranges from primitive to civilized.

See also **Polytheism; Religion: Indigenous Peoples' View, South America; Sacred and Profane.**

BIBLIOGRAPHY

Geertz, Clifford. *The Interpretation of Culture.* New York: Basic Books, 1973.
Honigmann, John J. *The Development of Anthropological Ideas.* Homewood, Ill.: Dorsey, 1976.
Stocking, George W., Jr. *After Tylor: British Social Anthropology, 1888–1951.* Madison: University of Wisconsin Press, 1995.
———. *Victorian Anthropology.* New York: Free Press, 1987.
Swanson, Guy E. *The Birth of the Gods: The Origin of Primitive Beliefs.* Ann Arbor: University of Michigan Press, 1960.

Norman E. Whitten Jr.

ANTHROPOLOGY.

As an academic discipline, anthropology is somewhat less than two centuries old, but speculations, if not rigorous scientific theories, about where we human beings came from and how to account for the physical and cultural differences that distinguish our communities and nations from one another probably began during prehistory.

In the United States (but not in most other academic settings, for example, in Europe or Asia), the discipline is conventionally divided into four main subfields: biological (or physical) anthropology, archaeology, linguistics, and sociocultural anthropology. The history and current state of each subfield will be discussed in this entry, as well as how they have influenced one another during the last two-hundred-odd years. Although they will be described separately, the four subfields form the *logos* of *anthropos,* the broad science that studies the human species.

The concept that unites these four subfields is *culture.* The earliest systematic formulation of the anthropological concept of culture was articulated by Sir Edward Burnett Tylor (1832–1917) in the first sentence of his pioneering book, *Primitive Culture* (1871): "Culture, or Civilization, taken in its wide ethnographic sense, is that complex whole which includes knowledge, belief, art, morals, law custom, and any other capabilities and habits acquired by man as a member of society." This entry will use an updated version of Tylor's definition put forth by Daniel G. Bates and Elliot M. Fratkin: "Culture, broadly defined, is a system of shared beliefs, values, customs, and material objects that members of a society use to cope with their world and with one another, and that are transmitted from generation to generation through learning" (1999, p. 5). The work of biological anthropologists seeks—among other things—to discover how, when, and why our remote ancestors evolved the physiological capacity for culture; archaeologists attempt to trace the evolution of culture and seek to reconstruct the nature of prehistoric (as well as historic and contemporary) cultures from the material objects they left behind; linguists describe the principal symbolic system—language—through which cultural learning occurs; and sociocultural anthropologists are concerned with the nature of culture per se and the myriad factors that shaped (and continue to shape) its contemporary manifestations.

Biological Anthropology

The advent of geology and the study of fossil sequences in the late eighteenth and early nineteenth centuries by pioneer geologists such as James Hutton (1726–1797) and Sir Charles Lyell (1797–1875) who laid the groundwork for the study of human evolution. Two major events in the 1850s loom large in the history of this most basic of the subfields: (1) the accidental discovery in 1856 of the first premodern human being, the prototype of the Neanderthals, in a quarry near Düsseldorf, Germany, and (2) Charles Darwin's (1809–1882) theory of "natural selection," articulated in *On the Origin of Species* (1859). This theory gave scholars who wanted to study the course of human evolution systematically a theoretical framework for determining how one species evolved over time into another.

The human fossil evidence in Europe, and eventually throughout the Old World, from Africa to China and Indonesia, mounted rapidly, and by the early twentieth century anthropologists had developed several models of human evolution. At first, there appeared to have been two successive species of genus *Homo: Homo sapiens,* including all modern human beings as well as our immediate precursors, the Neanderthals, and the far older *Pithecanthropus erectus,* the earliest example of which was found near Solo on the island of Java in 1895. It had become clear that the human species was at least several hundred thousand years old. As the twentieth century unfolded, new and even older hominid fossils were discovered, primarily in Southern and Eastern Africa, and both

the dates and descriptions of hominid evolution changed markedly. The 1925 discovery of *Australopithecus africanus* in South Africa by Raymond Dart (1893–1988) pushed the origin of the hominids back at least a million years and added a new, pre-*Homo* genus, *Australopithecus,* or "Southern Ape-Man."

It is impossible here to outline the sequence of major fossil discoveries in Africa and elsewhere that have been made since 1925. The names of anthropologists responsible for these finds include the late Louis S. B. Leakey (1903–1972) and Mary Leakey (1913–1996), who, in the late 1950s and early 1960s, discovered a number of extremely important protohominids at Olduvai Gorge in northeast Tanzania. In 1974 Donald Johanson discovered "Lucy," an extremely early Australopithecine that lived in what is now southeastern Ethiopia around 3.1 million years ago, the prototype of *Australopithecus afarensis.* In 1994 fossil evidence of an even older genus and species of protohominids, *Ardipithecus ramidus,* more than a million years older than "Lucy" (c. 4.5 million years old), was found in the same region of Africa, and in the last several years fossil fragments found in East Africa push the origin of hominids even farther back, perhaps as much as 5.5 million years. Moreover, it is now suspected that hominid bipedalism evolved as early as 4.5 to 5 million years ago; by freeing our forelimbs, it affected the evolution of the capacity for culture profoundly by enabling our ancestors to use and make tools.

Of course, this did not happen overnight. The earliest evidence for the presence of crude tools, again in East Africa, dates from around 2.5 million years ago. By this time, the earliest species of our genus, *Homo habilis,* had evolved, followed by *Homo ergaster* (c. 1.9–1.5 million years ago), and then *Homo erectus,* which dominated the Old World from c. 1.5 million to about 200,000 years ago, when it began to be replaced, at least in Europe—*Homo erectus* appears to have lingered longer in parts of Asia—by the Neanderthals. They, in turn, were eventually displaced by our own immediate ancestors, anatomically modern hominids (*Homo sapiens*), who are now thought to have evolved around 130,000 years ago near the southern tip of Africa. By 27,000 years ago, *Homo sapiens* had replaced all other hominid species everywhere. Some biological anthropologists still subscribe to the "multiregional hypothesis" that human beings became "modern" simultaneously in several parts of the Old World, from Africa to Europe and East Asia about 40,000 to 50,000 years ago, but consensus in the profession supports the "out of Africa" model, strengthened by the absence of any evidence that Neanderthal mitochondrial DNA exists in modern European populations.

A significant element in this evolutionary journey was the development of our brains to the point that we were able not only to make crude stone tools but to envelope ourselves and the world around us in what cultural anthropologist Clifford Geertz has called "webs of significance," the capacity for culture. At the same time, it has become abundantly clear that, since the emergence of anatomically modern hominids, no appreciable differences in the capacity for culture have emerged among the several modern human physical types, what are still sometimes erroneously called "races," and that the behavioral and technological differences that separate contemporary human communities are cultural rather than biological. One of the most important contributions of biological anthropology to general knowledge has been to dispel the pernicious myths of racial superiority and inferiority.

In addition to tracing the course of human evolution, many biological anthropologists specialize in the comparative study of chimpanzees (e.g., Jane Goodall), gorillas (e.g., the late Dian Fossey [1932–1985]), and other nonhuman primates, hoping to throw additional light on human behavior and the extent to which it is grounded in our primate heritage. Such studies provide a better understanding of the profound biological changes in our ancestors during the last five million years, changes that culminated in *Homo sapiens*.

While biological anthropology is best known for the study of ancient humans and other primates, other branches of the field also make significant contributions. Forensic anthropologists assist law enforcement agencies in gathering and interpreting evidence in cases of homicide, massacres, and genocides; other biological anthropologists study the interaction of culture and biology as it affects our health, longevity, and well-being. Such researchers work on a range of topics including the spread of AIDS (autoimmune deficiency syndrome) and other communicable diseases; the relationship between health and social problems such as poverty, racism, and inequality; stress and rapid social change; diet and maternal well-being; and the long-term effects of violence and warfare. There is a close relationship between this type of biologically focused anthropology and the work of medical anthropologists, cultural anthropologists who study the social contexts of medical practice.

Archaeology

Archaeology's roots lie in the early eighteenth century, when the landed gentry in Britain and elsewhere in Europe began to acquire stone, bronze, and iron implements for display, but it was not until late in that century that serious excavations began, largely inspired by discoveries at Pompeii and Herculaneum.

Two major events in the 1830s moved the fledgling discipline of archaeology to a new level. One was Jacques Boucher de Perthes's (1788–1868) discovery in 1838, near Abbeville, France, of a crude lithic (stone) technology that predated the gentlemen's displayed objects by well over 100,000 years. The second was the Danish scholar Christian Thomsen's (1788–1865) articulation of the "three-age system"—still a fundamental archaeological concept: the Stone, Bronze, and Iron Ages, which appeared in 1836 in the Catalogue of the Danish National Museum's collection (Thomsen was its first curator). Because stone artifacts typically came from the lowest levels of a trench or pit, while bronze objects came from the middle levels, and iron objects were typically found closest to the surface, Thomsen realized that this reflected a universal temporal sequence.

A generation later, in another important book, *Prehistoric Times* (1865), Sir John Lubbock (1834–1913), later Lord

Avebury, not only coined the term *prehistory*, but also divided Thomsen's Stone Age into two successive stages, the Paleolithic, or Old Stone Age, and the Neolithic, or New Stone Age. Subsequent archaeologists added the term *Mesolithic* to refer to the transitional period at the end of the Ice Age between the Paleolithic and the Neolithic, which saw the beginnings of settled life, agriculture, and animal husbandry.

By the early twentieth century, archaeology was an established scholarly discipline. In subsequent decades, archaeologists sought to discover sequences, or stages, in the evolution of culture per se and to reconstruct the trajectory of cultural development in specific regions, such as the ancient Near East, Mexico, the American Southwest, Peru, Africa, India, Oceania, East Asia, and Southeast Asia. In the late twentieth and early twenty-first centuries, a split occurred between *processual* and *postprocessual* archaeologists. Processual archaeology starts from the assumption that all human communities are themselves systems, and need to be viewed as such. Processual archaeologists are primarily concerned with the processes whereby ancient peoples adapted to their ecosystems, and how these processes changed over time as the ecosystems changed. Postprocessual archaeology, on the other hand, focuses on reconstructing the daily lives of the people who lived in prehistoric communities, how their societies were organized, the nature of their religious beliefs and worldviews, their socioeconomic hierarchies, and other elements of culture that sociocultural anthropologists study in living communities. Postprocessualists, for the most part, see themselves as cultural anthropologists who work with artifacts rather than living informants.

Out of processual and postprocessual archaeology have developed branches of contemporary archaeology: urban archaeology, which looks at the nature of urban life in premodern cities, and industrial archaeology, which attempts to reconstruct what life was like for the majority of people in early industrial towns in the Midlands of England, parts of New England, and elsewhere in the emerging industrial regions of Europe and America in the late eighteenth and early nineteenth centuries. A similar approach has been applied to reconstructing the lives of enslaved Africans and African-Americans on antebellum plantations in the Caribbean and the American South, as well as of African-Americans in the urban northeast.

Other trends in contemporary archaeology include a focus on the lives of women, ordinary people, and the poor, rather than the "great men" of history. Scientific developments that make it possible to recover detailed data about diet, farming systems, and other aspects of everyday life have provided the technical impetus for these new research areas. While the study of the most ancient manifestations of human culture, such as the rise of agriculture or the state, remains important to archaeologists, an increasing number have turned to historical projects in which documents and archives and working with historians complement the material remains retrieved during excavations. Such projects promise new insights into many aspects of human history, including medieval Europe, colonial Latin America, and early settlements in the United States.

Linguistics

Linguists study the primary medium by which culture is transmitted, language. The discipline of linguistics—at first called philology—dates from approximately the same period that biological anthropology and archaeology began, the late eighteenth century. Sir William Jones (1746–1794), a jurist and student of Asian languages assigned to the British East India Company's outpost at modern-day Calcutta, is generally credited with founding the discipline. In 1786, in the course of a speech to the Bengal Asiatic Society, of which he was the founder and president, Jones outlined, for the first time, the family-tree model of linguistic relationships, focusing on what would soon be called the Indo-European language family.

Within a generation, comparative philology (now called historical, or diachronic, linguistics) was an established discipline. Scholars such as Jacob Grimm (1785–1863), Franz Bopp (1791–1867), and August Schleicher (1821–1868) had reconstructed what appeared to be the Proto-Indo-European lexicon. Eventually, other language families, such as Sino-Tibetan (Chinese, Tibetan, Thai, Burmese, etc.) and Hamito-Semtic (Ancient Egyptian, Hebrew, Babylonian, Arabic, and other Near Eastern languages), also began to be studied from this perspective. Franz Boas (1858–1942), in addition to being a pioneer sociocultural anthropologist, was also among the first to apply the comparative method to the study of Native American languages.

In the early decades of that century, thanks primarily to the efforts of a brilliant Swiss linguist, Ferdinand de Saussure (1857–1913), a new structural approach to the study of language emerged, one that emphasized synchronic studies rather than the historical focus that had dominated during the previous century. De Saussure made a basic distinction between what he called *la langue,* the basic rules that govern the grammar of a given language, and *la parole,* the specific speech patterns that occur at any given instant. The linguist's job is to elicit the nature of *la langue* by recording and analyzing examples of *la parole.* This approach soon led to two concepts that still dominate anthropological linguistics: the *phoneme* and *morpheme.* A phoneme is a minimal sound feature of a language that signals a difference in meaning; a morpheme is an ordered arrangement of such speech sounds that carries an indivisible meaning. Thus, the sounds represented by the English letters *d, o,* and *g* are phonemes, while the word *dog* is a morpheme. Combining the same phonemes in reverse order produces a wholly different morpheme, *god.* Structural linguists are also concerned with syntax, the arrangement of morphemes into phrases and sentences, and semantics, how meanings are structured by morphemes and their forms and their position and function in sentences. *Grammar* is the entirety of a language's phonological, morphological, syntactic, and semantic rules that enable humans to communicate and transmit culture.

In the course of the last few decades, linguists have debated the extent to which there are universal, innate features that form the fundamental structure of all human languages. The U.S. linguist Noam Chomsky has argued in favor of this proposition. In *Syntactic Structures* (1957), Chomsky suggested that all human beings have the innate ability to generate every possible sentence in their language. This approach to the study of language is called transformational-generative grammar (TG). However, not all linguists accept this model. A great many hold that, like culture, language is infinitely variable and that there are no proven universal features.

The relationship between language and culture has also been a major concern among linguists, especially anthropological linguists. Two pioneers in the study of this relationship were Edward Sapir (1884–1939) and his student Benjamin Lee Whorf (1897–1941), who suggested that there was an intrinsic connection between the fundamental features of a culture and the structure of its language. For example, as Whorf pointed out, the Hopi Indian language does not mark verb tense, a feature that Whorf said is reflected in the absence of a linear time concept in Hope culture. All events are intrinsically linked to one another, and life simply unfolds. Although by no means universally accepted by contemporary anthropologists—some critics object that his approach is tautological and that there is no evidence to support the priority of language over culture—the Sapir-Whorf Hypothesis continues to influence anthropological thinking.

Early in the twentieth century, after the publication of books such as Sapir's *Language* (1921) and Leonard Bloomfield's (1887–1949) book of the same title (1933), linguistics developed into a separate discipline dedicated to the scientific study of language, with connections to the related fields of cognitive science and cognitive psychology, as well as some aspects of computer science (artificial intelligence, machine translation), after the publication of Chomsky's *Syntactic Structures.* The development of TG grammar produced an explosion of research in both synchronic and diachronic linguistics that continues to extend our understanding of language and mind and how we communicate.

Anthropological linguistics exists as a separate but related discipline that emphasizes the relationship between language and culture, but adopts a more holistic and, often, humanistic approach than, for example, cognitive psychology. Anthropological linguists study a variety of language practices, ranging from the relationship between language and music within specific cultures to children's use of language in play. A major focus that distinguishes linguistic anthropology from other branches of linguistics is its focus on questions of politics, power, and social inequality, as these aspects of culture affect language. The study of language ideologies emphasizes the different statuses of certain language practices, in contexts ranging from a bank officer turning down a loan applicant, to political speeches, to bilingual and bicultural contexts (for example, the study of "Spanglish," forms of language developed by Americans who speak both Spanish and English), to the controversies about varieties of English spoken by African Americans.

Sociocultural Anthropology

Sociocultural anthropology, the subfield concerned with culture per se, especially in its many contemporary ethnographic manifestations, commands the attention of the majority of professional anthropologists. Although there are some excellent examples of ethnographic description in antiquity—Herodotus's (484?–425 B.C.E.) account of the ancient Scythians in Book 4 of his *History* (c. 440 B.C.E.) and Cornelius Tacitus's (55? B.C.E.–after 117 C.E.) detailed account of ancient Germanic-speaking culture, *Germania* (c. 98 C.E.)—like the other principal subfields of anthropology, sociocultural anthropology began to take shape in the early nineteenth century and is closely linked to colonialism. As Europeans (or people of European heritage) expanded into India, Southeast Asia, Africa, and Oceania, as well as across North America, they found themselves confronting—and eventually dominating—what they called "primitive" cultures. These encounters led to two fundamental questions that dominate anthropology: (1) Why do cultures differ? and (2) Why are some cultures technologically "simple" societies, while others developed more complex, technologically sophisticated societies? Accounting for the differences found among cultures is problematic. For example, while, in some regions, humans live in small-scale societies with very basic technologies and low population densities—what early anthropologists, influenced by colonialism and scientific racism, called "primitive"—in other places, such as the Valley of Mexico, people began millennia ago to develop complex, energy-intensive agricultural technologies that enabled them to congregate in great numbers, build enormous cities and finance the construction of elaborate buildings and works of art, and, in general, to develop what are called "civilizations."

This second question has especially been the province of archaeologists, but it underlies cultural anthropology as well. At its best, cultural anthropology has steadfastly argued for the value of the small-scale and the more environmentally wise "primitive" as culturally significant. At its worst, it has functioned as the "handmaiden of imperialism," either overtly, as when British anthropologists worked for the colonial enterprise in Africa, or indirectly, as purveyors of "exotica" that reinforce the prejudices of urbanites and racial elites regarding the "savagery" of foreigners or of native populations and minorities closer to home.

It is thus no accident that the first great theoretical paradigm in sociocultural anthropology was *unilineal evolutionism,* the idea that all cultures can be ranked along a grand scale that culminated, of course, with nineteenth-century European and American industrial civilization, the "best of all possible worlds." Darwin's *The Origin of Species* reinforced this approach to the assessment of cultural differences, in particular the concept of "natural selection." Unilineal evolutionism was predicated on two fundamental axioms: (1) the idea of *progress,* that the direction of cultural evolution is everywhere from "primitive" to "civilized" and (2) the idea of *psychic unity,* that all human beings, irrespective of their environment or specific history, will necessarily think the same thoughts and, therefore, progress through the *same* series of evolutionary stages. Sir Edward Burnett Tylor, who was the first anthropologist to define the concept of culture, was a major contributor to unilineal evolutionism, suggesting a three-stage model for the evolution of religion: animism (a belief that all phenomena are "animated" by unique spirit beings), polytheism, and monotheism, which, he held, is a prime characteristic of advanced civilizations.

The most influential unilineal evolutionist was Lewis Henry Morgan (1818–1881), a successful American lawyer who practiced anthropology as an avocation. In *Ancient Society* (1877), Morgan posited a three-stage model for the evolution of culture: savagery, barbarism, and civilization. The first two stages, which he labeled, collectively, *societas* (society), as opposed to *civitas* (civilization), were each subdivided into three successive substages: lower, middle, and upper. His prime criterion for assigning cultures to one or another of these stages was the character and complexity of their technology. Because they lacked the bow and arrow, a prime technological criterion, Morgan assigned the ancient Hawaiians to "Middle Savagery," despite the fact that they practiced agriculture and had a highly complex social organization.

Although Morgan's emphasis on material culture—tools, weapons, and other artifacts—had a significant influence on a later school of sociocultural anthropology, cultural materialism, he also pioneered the study of kinship systems. By the 1890s, however, the unilineal evolutionists' rigid adherence to paradigms based on incomplete and questionable ethnographic data (largely collected by missionaries, traders, colonial administrators, and so forth) was called into question by a new generation of anthropologists who had spent time in the field. (Most of the unilineal evolutionists were "armchair scholars," although both Tylor and Morgan did have some field experience in their youth, the former in Mexico and the latter among the Seneca, an Iroquois tribe that lived near his home in upstate New York.)

In the United States, the chief critic of what was then called the comparative method in anthropology was Franz Boas, the most influential American anthropologist. A rigorous, scientifically trained German-born scholar, he later switched to anthropology and did extensive fieldwork among the Baffin Island (Canada) Eskimo (or Inuit), as well as the Native Americans of British Columbia. He and other critics of the unilineal approach, many of whom were his students, such as Alfred Louis Kroeber (1876–1960) and Robert Lowie (1883–1957), also called into question unilinealism's fundamental axioms, seriously questioning whether "progress" was in fact universal or lineal and whether it was possible to rank all human cultures according to a *single* evolutionary scheme. Finally, the Boasians attacked the concept of "psychic unity," suggesting that all cultures are inherently different from one another and that they should be assessed on their own merits and not comparatively. This approach, which stressed empirical field research over "armchair" theorizing, came to be known as historical particularism, and emphasized cultural relativism and diffusion rather than rigid evolutionary sequences. Anthropologists were enjoined to reconstruct the culture-history of particular tribes and societies, but *not* the evolution of culture per se. Emphasis was also placed on what has been called "salvage ethnography," gathering ethnographic data before the simpler cultures of the world were overwhelmed by Western culture.

Boas left another important legacy: his work as a public intellectual who used his scholarly knowledge to educate the American public about racial equality. For Boas, who had experienced anti-Semitism in his native Germany, this kind of work on the part of intellectuals was crucial if America was to realize its democratic ideals. He inspired many of his students, including Ruth Benedict (1887–1948) and Margaret Mead (1901–1978), to their own forms of public work by his example. He also influenced several important African and Native American intellectuals who left anthropology for other pursuits, most notably the novelist Zora Neale Hurston (1891–1960), as well as the Brazilian sociologist Gilberto Freyre (1900–1987), who credits Boas's influence in the preface to his controversial books on race in Brazilian culture.

In Britain, the empirical reaction to Morgan, Tylor, and their colleagues took a different turn. Most early-twentieth-century British anthropologists, such as Bronislaw K. Malinowski (1884–1942), a Polish scholar who immigrated to England to complete his studies, and A. R. Radcliffe-Brown (1881–1955), were largely ahistorical; that is, they advocated a structural–functional, rather than historical, approach to the study of cultures. Their emphasis was primarily, if not in some cases wholly, on the here and now, on the social organization of living human communities and how the elements thereof were functionally interrelated to form integrated wholes. Malinowski, who spent four years (1915–1918) studying the culture of the Trobriand Islanders (near New Guinea), also focused on how social institutions function to serve basic human needs, such as shelter, reproduction, and nourishment. Radcliffe-Brown, who did field work in the Andaman Islands, South Africa, and Australia, drew liberally on the ideas of the French sociologist Émile Durkheim (1858–1917) in his attempts to discover what he called the "social laws" and "structural principles" that govern social organization everywhere. Among them, Boas, Malinowski, and Radcliffe-Brown trained or influenced at least two generations of sociocultural anthropologists on both sides of the Atlantic, from the early 1900s to the threshold of World War II, and, in Radcliffe-Brown's case, for a decade afterward as well.

However, beginning in the late 1930s, a reaction to the essentially antitheoretical stance of the Boasians began to take shape, based on the assumption that all cultures are necessarily adapted to the ecological circumstances in which they exist. The leading advocate of "cultural ecology" was Julian H. Steward (1902–1972), whose book *Theory of Culture Change* (1955) had a major impact on the discipline. Other scholars, such as Leslie A. White (1900–1975) and British archaeologist V. Gordon Childe (1892–1957), drawing on the Marxist assumption that the "means of production" is everywhere crucial in determining the nature of society, emphasized the primacy of material culture. (Indeed, White consistently described himself as a disciple of Lewis Henry Morgan, whose work had, in turn, influenced Marx's collaborator Friedrich Engels [1820–1895].) These early "neo-evolutionists" of the mid-twentieth century all acknowledged a debt to Marx, but the new materialism in anthropology soon split into two camps: one that emphasized historical materialism, political economy, and the study of imperialism and inequality, and another that repudiated Marx and focused on questions of ecological adaptation and evolution. The former include Eric Wolf, Sidney Mintz, Eleanor Leacock, and John Murra. Mintz's study of the history of sugar and Wolf's timely

comparative project on *Peasant Wars of the Twentieth Century* (1999), published in response to U.S. involvement in Vietnam, remain two classic studies from this school. Among the anti-Marxists, the best-known is the late Marvin R. Harris, whose provocative books for the general public argue that apparently "irrational" religious behavior, such as the Hindu refusal to eat meat or Jewish dietary law, can be attributed to biological needs unknown to practitioners.

Neo-evolutionism was not the only post-Boasian development in sociocultural anthropology. Also in the late 1930s, a number of American anthropologists, among them Margaret Mead, Ruth Benedict, and Ralph Linton, drew selectively on Freud and other early twentieth-century psychologists and developed the "culture and personality" school, which emphasized the interface among individual personalities and the cultures they share, as well as the "infant disciplines"—weaning and toilet training—and their effects on both the formation of individual personality structures and the nature of particular cultures. Early and harsh toilet training was held to produce "anal" personalities and authoritarian cultures, whereas relaxed attitudes toward sphincter control and related processes produce relaxed social systems. At the start of the twenty-first century this school has few proponents, but psychological anthropology remains a recognized branch of sociocultural anthropology.

In the 1950s, linguistics began to influence an increasing number of anthropologists. If the cultural ecologists and materialists had come to conceive of culture as essentially an adaptive system, their linguistically oriented colleagues were concerned with cognitive systems and shared symbols, with how people attach meaning to the world around them. Initially known as "ethnoscience," this approach has come to be called "cognitive anthropology." Closely related to it are two other approaches also concerned with meaning. One of them, closely identified with the eminent French anthropologist Claude Lévi-Strauss, is *structuralism*. Extremely influential outside of anthropology, especially in France, this school focused on underlying structures of thought based on binary oppositions, like the binary mathematical code used by computers. From simple pairs such as *hot/cold* or *up/down*, cultures construct elaborate systems of myth and meaning that shape everything from cooking to kinship, as well as providing answers to questions about life and death. When initially published, his partially autobiographical *Tristes tropiques* (1955; The sad tropics) in which he recounts his flight from Nazi Germany to find refuge among the tribes of Amazonian Brazil, was perhaps more influential than his dense and difficult works of structural analysis. Later, however, it was criticized for its portrayal of Native Americans as seemingly "outside of history."

In America, a different school of anthropology, "symbolic anthropology," would ultimately prove more influential than structuralism. This approach, which draws on the same linguistic and cognitive models as structuralism, emphasizes emotion and affect in addition to cognition, and looks back to traditional anthropological studies of magico-religious belief systems, especially Durkheim's work. Among the more important contributors to symbolic anthropology have been the British scholars Victor W. Turner and Mary Douglas, and the American anthropologist Clifford Geertz. Turner's study of the multivalent symbolic meanings of the "milk-tree" in the life of the Ndembu of northwestern Zambia—its milklike sap stands for everything from semen to mothers' milk—remains a classic. In it, he borrows from Arnold van Gennep's (1873–1957) classic work, *Les rites de passage* (1909; The Rites of Passage), the concept of the "transition" stage in a rite of passage, which Turner rechristened "liminality." Douglas studied the symbolic opposition between what she calls "purity and danger," as exemplified in her brilliant analysis of the food taboos in the Old Testament, which, she argues, reflect a fear of anomalous animals, like the pig, which is neither a browser nor a ruminant. Geertz, who has done extensive fieldwork in Indonesia and Morocco, is famous for his in-depth analysis of the symbolism of cockfighting in Bali, as well as for the concept of "webs of significance," the idea that all human beings are necessarily bound together by intricate symbolic "webs" in terms of which they collectively confront external reality.

In the last two decades, sociocultural anthropology has seen the emergence of the "post-isms": postcolonialism, which examines the impact of neoliberal capitalism on recently decolonized states; poststructuralism, which critiques the work of Lévi-Strauss and other classic structuralists; and, most importantly, postmodernism, a manifestation of a broader intellectual movement in architecture, literature, cinema, and the arts predicated in fair measure on the theories of French scholars Jacques Derrida and Michel Foucault. Postmodernists question the validity of externally imposed orders, as well as linear analysis and "essentialist" interpretations, and assert that anthropologists should "deconstruct" the cultures they are attempting to understand. Moreover, postmodern ethnographies often focus as much on the ethnographers as they do the communities they have studied, as any cultural account must necessarily include the impact of the investigator on the investigated, and vice versa. This element in postmodernism has been criticized a great deal, especially by materialists such as Sidney Mintz. Among the more prominent postmodernist anthropologists are Stephen A. Tyler, Vincent Crapanzano, and James A. Boon.

In recent years, sociocultural anthropologists—from a variety of perspectives—have been concerned with globalization, transnational communities, such as the African, Indian, and Chinese diasporas, and borderlands, in which the inhabitants freely share culture traits that are otherwise, for the most part, extremely different and seemingly contradictory and integrate them into new, "hybrid" cultures. There has also been increased concern with feminism, especially what has been labeled "third-wave feminism," and with the heretofore often neglected roles women play in shaping cultural norms, as well as the inequality that persists almost everywhere between the sexes. Finally, gay and lesbian, as well as transsexual, studies form a significant element of contemporary sociocultural anthropology, leading to a major reassessment of the concept of "gender" and the extent to which it is socially constructed rather than innate.

This brief overview of the history and current state of the discipline of anthropology, primarily in the United States, has necessarily omitted mention of many specific developments and schools of thought, for example, the *Kulturkreis,* or "culture-circle" school, centered on Father Wilhelm Schmidt (1868–1954), that took shape in Vienna in the early years of the last century; the impact of Sir James G. Frazer's (1854–1941) *The Golden Bough* (1890), which seduced Malinowski into completing his studies in England; and the single-diffusionist ideas of G. Elliot Smith (1871–1937). A great many important contributors, to say nothing of specific topical and regional specialties, such as urban anthropology, esthetic anthropology, East Asian anthropology, African anthropology, and so on, have been slighted. Nevertheless, this discussion provides a general description of what anthropology, in its several major dimensions, is about, how it got that way, and the overwhelming importance of the concept of culture to the discipline.

See also **Diffusion, Cultural; Ethnography; Eurocentrism; Gender Studies: Anthropology; Interdisciplinarity; Kinship; Language and Linguistics; Oral Traditions; Prehistory, Rise of; Structuralism and Poststructuralism: Anthropology.**

BIBLIOGRAPHY

Bates, Daniel G., and Elliot M. Fratkin. *Cultural Anthropology.* 2nd ed. Boston: Allyn and Bacon, 1999.

Benedict, Ruth. *Patterns of Culture.* 1934. Reprint, New York: New American Library, 1959.

Bloomfield, Leonard. *Language.* 1933. Reprint, New York: Holt, Rinehart and Winston, 1961.

Boas, Franz. "The Limitations of the Comparative Method of Anthropology." In *High Points in Anthropology,* edited by Paul Bohannan and Mark Glazer, 2nd ed., 81–93. New York: Knopf, 1988. Originally published in 1896.

———. *The Mind of Primitive Man.* 1911. Reprint, New York: Free Press, 1963.

Boon, James A. *Other Tribes, Other Scribes: Symbolic Anthropology in the Comparative Study of Cultures, Histories, Religions, and Texts.* New York: Cambridge University Press, 1982.

Bopp, Franz. *A Comparative Grammar of the Sanskrit, Zend, Greek, Latin, Lithuanian, Gothic, German, and Slavonic Languages.* Translated principally by Lieutenant Eastwick. London: Madden and Malcolm, 1845–1856, 1867.

Brandewie, Ernest. *When Giants Walked the Earth: The Life and Times of Wilhelm Schmidt, SVD.* Fribourg, Switzerland: University Press, 1990.

Campbell, Bernard G., ed. *Humankind Emerging.* New York: HarperCollins, 1992.

Childe, V. Gordon. *Man Makes Himself.* 1936. Reprint, New York: New American Library, 1951.

Chomsky, Noam. *Syntactic Structures.* 2nd ed. New York: Mouton de Gruyter, 2002. Originally published in 1957.

Crapanzano, Vincent. *Hermes' Dilemma and Hamlet's Desire: On the Epistemology of Interpretation.* Cambridge, Mass.: Harvard University Press, 1992.

Daniel, Glyn. *The Idea of Prehistory.* Harmondsworth, U.K.: Penguin, 1964.

Darwin, Charles. *On the Origin of Species.* New York: Modern Library, 1936. Originally published in 1859.

De Saussure, Ferdinand. *Course in General Linguistics.* Translated and annotated by Roy Harris. London: G. Duckworth, 1983. Originally published in 1907.

Derrida, Jacques. *The Derrida Reader: Writing Performances.* Translated and edited by Julian Wolfreys. Edinburgh: Edinburgh University Press, 1998.

Douglas, Mary. *Purity and Danger: An Analysis of the Concepts of Pollution and Taboo.* London: Routledge and Kegan Paul, 1966.

Durkheim, Émile. *The Elementary Forms of the Religious Life.* Translated by Joseph Ward Swain. New York: Collier, 1961. Originally published in 1915.

Fagan, Brian M. *Archaeology: A Brief Introduction.* 4th ed. New York: HarperCollins, 1991.

Fossey, Dian. *Gorillas in the Mist.* Boston: Houghton Mifflin, 1983.

Foucault, Michel. *The Essential Works of Michel Foucault, 1954–1984.* Translated by Robert Hurley, et al. New York: New Press, 1997–2000.

Frazer, Sir James G. *The Golden Bough: A Study in Magic and Religion.* Abridged ed. New York: Macmillan, 1922.

Geertz, Clifford. *The Interpretation of Cultures: Selected Essays.* New York: Basic Books, 1973.

Gennep, Arnold van. *Les rites de passage.* 1909. Reprint, Paris: A. and J. Picard, 1981.

Goodall, Jane. *Through a Window: My Thirty Years with the Chimpanzees of Gombe.* Boston: Houghton Mifflin, 1990.

Grimm, Jacob. *On the Origin of Language.* Translated by Raymond A. Wiley. Leiden, Netherlands: E. J. Brill, 1984. Originally published in 1851.

Harris, Marvin R. *The Rise of Anthropological Theory: A History of Theories of Culture.* New York: Crowell, 1968.

Herodotus. *The Histories.* Translated by Robin Waterfield. New York: Oxford University Press, 1998.

Johanson, Donald C., and Maitland A. Edey. *Lucy, the Beginnings of Humankind.* New York: Simon and Schuster, 1990.

Kroeber, A. L. *The Nature of Culture.* 1952. Reprint, Chicago: University of Chicago Press, 1965.

Leach, Edmund R. *Claude Lévi-Strauss.* New York: Viking, 1970.

Lévi-Strauss, Claude. *Structural Anthropology.* Translated by Claire Jacobson and Brooke Grundfest Schoepf. New York: Basic Books, 1963. Originally published in 1958.

Linton, Ralph. *The Cultural Background of Personality.* New York: Appleton-Century, 1945.

Littleton, C. Scott. "Anthropology's Moral Cosmos: Reinventing Heisenberg's Wheel and the Need for a Postmodern-Materialist Agenda." *Cosmos* 15 (1999): 111–127.

Lowie, Robert H. *The Crow Indians.* 1935. Reprint, New York: Holt, Rinehart and Winston, 1956.

Lubbock, Sir John (Lord Avebury). *Prehistoric Times as Illustrated by Ancient Remains and the Manners and Customs of Modern Savages.* 7th ed. New York: Holt, 1913. Originally published in 1865.

Malinowski, Bronislaw. *Argonauts of the Western Pacific: An Account of Native Enterprise and Adventure in the Archipelagoes of Melanesian New Guinea.* 1922. Reprint, Prospect Heights, Ill.: Waveland, 1984.

———. *A Scientific Theory of Culture and Other Essays.* 1944. Reprint, New York: Oxford University Press, 1960.

Mead, Margaret. *Coming of Age in Samoa: A Psychological Study of Primitive Youth for Western Civilization.* 1928. Reprint, New York: Morrow, 1961.

Mintz, Sydney W. *Sweetness and Power: The Place of Sugar in Modern History.* New York: Viking, 1985.

More, Jerry D. *Visions of Culture: An Introduction to Anthropological Theories and Theorists.* Walnut Creek, Calif.: Altamira, 1997.

Morgan, Lewis Henry. *Ancient Society, or Researches in the Lines of Human Progress from Savagery through Barbarism to Civilization.* Chicago: C. H. Kerr, 1877.

———. *Systems of Consanguinity and Affinity of the Human Family.* Washington, D.C.: Smithsonian, 1970.

Pedersen, Holger. *The Discovery of Language: Linguistic Science in the Nineteenth Century.* Translated by John Webster Spargo. Bloomington: Indiana University Press, 1962. Originally published in 1959.

Radcliffe-Brown, A. R. *Structure and Function in Primitive Society: Essays and Addresses.* 1952. Reprint, Glencoe, Ill.: Free Press, 1962.

Sapir, Edward. *Language: An Introduction to the Study of Speech.* 1921. Reprint, New York: Harcourt, Brace, 1957.

Service, Elman R. *Origins of the State and Civilization: The Process of Cultural Evolution.* New York: Norton, 1975.

Smith, G. Eliot. *The Diffusion of Culture.* London: Watts, 1933.

Steward, Julian H. *Theory of Culture Change: The Methodology of Multilinear Evolution.* Urbana: University of Illinois Press, 1972.

Stocking, George W., Jr. *The Ethnographer's Magic and Other Essays in the History of Anthropology.* Madison: University of Wisconsin Press, 1992.

Stringer, Chris. *African Exodus: The Origins of Modern Humanity.* New York: Holt, 1997.

Tacitus, Cornelius. *The Germania of Tacitus.* Translated by Rodney Potter Robinson. Middletown, Conn.: American Philological Association, 1935.

Turner, Victor W. *The Forest of Symbols: Aspects of Ndembu Ritual.* Ithaca, N.Y.: Cornell University Press, 1967.

Tyler, Stephen A. "Post-Modern Ethnography: From Document of the Occult to Occult Document." In *Writing Culture: The Poetics and Politics of Ethnography,* edited by James Clifford and George E. Marcus, 122–140. Berkeley: University of California Press, 1986.

Tylor, Sir Edward Burnett. *Primitive Culture: Researches into the Development of Mythology, Philosophy, Religion, Art, and Custom.* 2 vols. London: John Murray, 1871.

White, Leslie A. *The Science of Culture: A Study of Man and Civilization.* New York: Grove, 1949.

Whorf, Benjamin Lee. *Language, Thought, and Reality: Selected Writings.* Edited by John B. Carroll. Cambridge, Mass.: MIT Press, 1956.

C. Scott Littleton

ANTICOLONIALISM.

This entry includes four subentries:

Africa
Latin America
Middle East
Southeast Asia

AFRICA

In post–World War II history, *decolonization* is a term generally employed to describe and explain the struggle for, and attainment of, freedom from colonial rule by most countries in Asia and Africa. This attainment was marked by a transfer of power; national political elites assumed the administrative responsibilities and duties previously discharged by the colonial authorities. Thus, new sovereign nations were born.

Steadfast struggle through political parties and related movements, in the pursuit of decolonization, marked the era of nationalism in Africa. Nationalism was the indispensable vehicle utilized to achieve the desired goal of decolonization.

It is important to point out that the study and analysis of nationalism in Asia and Africa has been affected by the scholarly and ideological controversies that still surround the "national question," nationality, and nationalism. While the power and influence of nationalism is undisputed, Benedict Anderson points out that the terms *nation, nationality,* and *nationalism* have all "proved notoriously difficult to define, let alone to analyze." Many scholars, especially in the West, have continued to look at nationalism as an anachronism and therefore as a concept that is not a revealing tool of analysis. Part of the explanation for this scholarly disillusionment is the ill repute nationalism acquired during the era of Nazism and fascism in Europe, when it came to be associated with intolerance and a reactionary chauvinism that was "at odds with the proper destiny of man."

The study of nationalism has also been a source of intellectual and ideological frustration to Marxists, who have traditionally been troubled by its "chameleon qualities." Nationalism "takes many different forms, is supported by many different groups and has different political effects." Unlike Marxism, which places much emphasis on a society's class structure, economics, and "form of economic organization," nationalism is basically political and cultural. This explains in part why Marxism and nationalism have had a "difficult dialogue" over the years.

In Asia and Africa, post–World War II nationalism was, above all, a "revolt against the West" (Barraclough), its chief characteristic "resistance to alien domination." This resistance, which led to decolonization, ultimately created a multitude of nations out of lands that had had "little or no national consciousness." It is fair to conclude that in order to comprehend the centrality and diversity of nationalism in postwar Asian and African history, "European modalities" may not be strictly relevant.

Aims and Objectives

Political freedom from colonial rule was viewed by nationalists and their supporters as the instrument to redress the economic and social neglect and injustices of the colonial era. Kwame Nkrumah of Ghana urged fellow nationalists throughout Africa to "seek first the political kingdom and all else would be added unto" them. There could be no meaningful social and economic progress without political independence. Nationalist activists and their followers expected an improvement in their living conditions. This desire and expectation to live in dignity partly explains the political support given by the masses to the nationalists and nationalism.

In India, Jawaharlal Nehru (1889–1964) argued emphatically that without political freedom, Indians would have no

power to shape their destiny. They would remain "hopeless victims of external forces" that oppressed and exploited them.

In semicolonial China, Mao Zedong (1893–1976) also saw the critical value of national political freedom from external domination. Without this freedom, there could be no advancement of his revolutionary social and economic program. It would have been futile to dream of building a communist society without a nation in which to construct it.

Nationalism identified exploitation as the primary economic mission of colonialism—exploitation of the colonized people and their labor and resources. In Africa, the expansion of cash crop production, land alienation, mineral exploitation, and even limited manufacturing toward the end of colonial rule enriched the Western capitalist countries, and not Africans. In the struggle for decolonization, there was a general outcry by the nationalists against this exploitation. The colonial economic record in Asia, and especially in India, provided nationalists with rich evidence of exploitation. There was the familiar example of British investment in railways that remained quite profitable to the investors but did little for Indian economic advancement. Colonialism had deemphasized the production of food crops while actively promoting the growing of cotton, jute, indigo, and opium, which fetched high prices overseas. The profits that accrued from these exports and other British capital were, to a large extent, invested in "white settler countries," such as Canada, Australia, and New Zealand, and not in India. In addition, European powers did not encourage, nor support, the industrialization of their colonies. In India, this aggravated economic and social problems on the eve of decolonization.

Socially and culturally, colonialism was a racist system. The era of "modern" nineteenth-century imperialism was also the era of scientific racism. Colonialism, mediated through racism and racist policies, limited and even forbade meaningful cross-cultural dialogue between colonizer and colonized. Throughout most of Africa and Asia, racism was "not an incidental detail, but . . . a consubstantial part of colonialism." Harsh, brutal, and deliberately discriminatory treatment at the hands of European colonizers was the constant, painful reminder to Africans and Asians that they were a colonized and humiliated people. All nationalists, irrespective of ideological differences, were generally agreed that such treatment was indefensible; it must be ended.

The Development of Nationalism

The development of nationalism was not uniform throughout the countries of Asia and Africa. The majority of nationalist movements, however, roughly followed a distinct pattern. First, there were local protest movements; some were culturally based, while others were created by the local elite to protest against local and specific grievances, usually economic. Second, there was the crucial period of mass nationalism. In most countries of Asia and Africa, this occurred after World War II. In Africa, this rough pattern applies to all the countries that attained their political independence before 1975. The same is true in Asia, except for those countries that secured their freedom after protracted armed struggle led by communist parties.

This constitutes what can be characterized as the first and dominant phase of African and Asian nationalism.

The second phase applies in Africa to the former Portuguese colonies of Guinea-Bissau, Angola, and Mozambique, in addition to Zimbabwe, South Africa, and Namibia. In Asia, it applies to China and Vietnam, even though their wars of liberation had achieved key victories before 1975. In almost every case, political independence in the second phase was achieved after protracted guerrilla warfare. Liberation movements in China, Vietnam, and former Portuguese colonies in Africa moved to be more precise in their definition of national liberation and societal development. Further, they adopted a Marxist ideology as a guide to their struggle, much more deliberately and consistently than had the majority of the nationalist movements in the first phase. Although the nationalist movements in the second phase did not undertake to pursue identical policies, they nonetheless embarked on a far more detailed socioeconomic analysis of colonial and imperial domination.

In Africa, these Marxist-leaning movements were influenced by the revolutionary thought of Frantz Fanon (1925–1961). In his most famous book, *The Wretched of the Earth* (*Les damnés de la terre,* 1961; Eng. trans., 1963), Fanon argued passionately that true decolonization must be the product of violence. Colonialism, "created and maintained by violence," could be truly uprooted only through "mass participation in violent decolonization." This violence was to be the product of an organized revolutionary movement composed of urban intellectuals and peasants. Fanon also argued that revolutionary violence against the colonialists was "a cleansing force" for individual participants: "it frees the native from his inferiority complex and his despair and inaction." The meaning and implications of this observation continue to generate ideological and intellectual controversy. Still, it should be said that Fanon's formulation was not a "lyrical celebration of violence" (see L. Adele Jinadu) but rather a strategy to be employed by the colonized in pursuit of true liberation.

After World War II, European powers were not eager to liquidate their empires in Asia and Africa. Although drastically weakened by the war, neither Britain nor France (the major imperial powers) seemed anxious to grant political independence to their colonies. Indeed, the dominant postcolonial policies seemed to favor reassertion of imperial authority. To this end, France fought costly wars in Vietnam and Algeria as it tried unsuccessfully to suppress nationalism. Britain fought against a determined anticolonial movement in Malaya, as well as against the Mau Mau nationalist peasant revolt in Kenya. Even in those colonies where there was little or no armed resistance, European powers were quick to employ brutal force to try to stem the tide of nationalism.

Colonial administrators routinely dismissed the legitimacy of Asian and African nationalism. Any stirring of nationalism was seen as an alien, artificial, almost inappropriate creation, imposed by Asian or African elites on unwilling or otherwise ignorant masses. This was a disastrously mistaken claim and belief. It would have been impossible for nationalist activists to achieve any success without the sustained and spirited support of those masses. The ideological strife of the Cold War, however, led many colonial administrators to mistakenly view nationalist agitation as the unfolding of a global communist conspiracy.

In the end, imperial maneuvers, brutal force, and concessions failed to derail the drive toward decolonization. In the political climate of the postwar years, imperial powers were forced to see that there could be no compromise between direct imperial domination and the basic, nonnegotiable demands of nationalism.

On balance, it is fair to conclude that internal factors in each colony proved the chief determinant in the nature of the struggle for, and attainment of, political independence. Nationalist and revolutionary movements were essentially local in inspiration and objectives. These movements were not "exportable commodities," says Amilcar Cabral, but rather were "determined and conditioned by the historical reality of each people." This underscores the vitality and integrity of Asian and African nationalism and amply demonstrates (in Geoffrey Barraclough's words) that "the will, the courage, the determination, and the deep human motivation" that propelled it forward "owed little, if anything, to Western example."

After Political Independence: The Struggle Continues

The attainment of political independence by Asian and African countries left several questions unresolved. There was the question of ideology in the postcolonial period. In many countries, successful nationalist movements were essentially coalition parties, representing several ideological positions and tendencies. In Indonesia, President Sukarno (1901–1970) argued that the nationalist movement must be inclusive, and hence he saw "nothing to prevent Nationalists from working together with Moslems and Marxists." This expedient inclusiveness began to unravel in the postcolonial period. On this matter, it is vital to remember that these ideological questions were debated against the backdrop of the Cold War, which had an indelible impact not only on the texture of decolonization the imperial powers were willing to entertain but also on internal postcolonial ideological tensions.

Closely related is that decolonization did not lead to economic freedom or even sustained economic growth and development in most Asian and African countries. What happened? Asian and African countries rarely, if ever, inherited vibrant, varied, and integrated national economies. What they inherited, says Basil Davidson (1974), was a colonial economic system that for centuries had "developed little save the raw materials needed in the Atlantic world." In Africa, the imperial powers both before and after independence imposed "an institutionalized relationship between Africans and Europeans," which facilitated the exploitation of Africans and their resources. As in Asian countries, this system has proved to be very difficult to change. The consequences have been economic stagnation, often regression, and widespread poverty.

These economic problems have seriously compromised the essence of the political freedom won after so much sacrifice and determination. Yet in many of these countries, as in Latin America, the ruling elite lead opulent lifestyles amid grinding and widespread poverty. This cannot be taken as an indicator of economic development and social progress; it is the product of corruption, patronage, and oppression. Only "true decolonization," according to Fanon, could prevent the rise of an African national bourgeois eager to strike a self-serving compromise with Western imperialism. The critical point to remember is that in Africa, as in Asia, the inherited "economies remained externally oriented" and did not "provide the basis for a strong national economy."

The essence of decolonization has also been frequently compromised by the demands and expectations of foreign aid. For Asian and African countries, such aid has been an almost permanent feature of postcolonial history, but has not led to economic independence and progress; quite often, poverty and economic stagnation have persisted. Since the 1950s, aid from the West to African, Asian, and other developing countries has been guided by shifting political and economic paradigms. These have included import substitution, population control, and expansion of exports. "Structural adjustment" in support of globalization is the paradigm that currently guides the dispensation of Western aid. Still, poverty and poor economic performance have persisted in most Asian and African countries.

The formulation and implementation of these development fashions clearly indicate that a conscious effort has been made to sidestep tackling the fundamental and exploitative relationship between imperial powers and former colonies. The result, as described by Mahbub ul-Haq, is that a "poverty curtain" now exists, dividing the world into "two unequal humanities—one embarrassingly rich and the other desperately poor."

The struggle also continues in cultural affairs—a struggle over respect for Asian and African cultures. Culture is intricately linked to dignity and identity. Dignity, and with it cultural pride, are especially important for a people whose past has been dominated by alien rule and culture, and colonialism was hostile to the vibrant growth and assertion of local culture. This hostility was clearly evident in the propagation of racial stereotypes demeaning to Asians and Africans, characterizations and beliefs that are, sadly, not yet dead. A matter of critical importance to the people in former colonies is the survival of their cultures in the age of globalization, which has facilitated the rapidly expanding marketing of Western entertainment. Films, music, and general attitudes toward lifestyle promote a sort of global homogenization that is Western-derived and -controlled. This has not stimulated the survival or growth of local cultures and values. World culture is thought to be threatened if diversity is lost.

In the postcolonial period, culture has once again been invoked in the West as lying behind the poverty of developing countries. The cultures, values, and attitudes of most Asian, African, and Latin American countries, not their colonial legacy or even their underdevelopment by the West, are said to be at the root of their poverty; their traditional cultures are seen to inescapably impede progress. This is in contrast to Western societies, whose cultural values both inspire and facilitate progress. In the United States, key proponents of this "cultural factor" include Samuel P. Huntington and Lawrence E. Harrison.

The principal contentions advanced in arguing the cultural factor are not new. They formed an integral part of imperialism's theory and practice in Asia and Africa in the nineteenth century. They now mark the resurrection of a theory of development that has a distinct imperial lineage—cultural imperialism. As in the past, this theory avoids embracing history in its formulation and analysis. Perhaps even more crucial, it avoids discussing the origin and management of the current Western-dominated international political economy. There is no serious attempt made to analyze how this economy makes it particularly difficult for the majority of Asian and African countries to reap the economic and social benefits of decolonization.

The controversial and emotional question of language has emerged as critical in discussions of decolonization. What should be the language of creativity in African and Asian countries newly liberated from Western imperial rule? Many writers in these societies have agonized over this matter, concerned that the continued use of European tongues in literature and sometimes as the national language constitutes "linguistic imperialism."

In Africa, the foremost critic of what is called linguistic imperialism is Ngugi wa Thiong'o, Kenya's most eminent writer. In a 1991 interview, Ngugi emphasized the reality that a "very tiny minority, the tip of every nationality, speak French or English or Portuguese." Since most Africans speak their native languages, an African author who writes in a European language (rather than creating literature in an African language, which would then be translated into other African languages) essentially shuts off the huge majority and instead addresses fellow members of the elite. This is inherently undemocratic and is unlikely to serve as the cornerstone of a national literary tradition. Further, Ngugi holds that "African thought, literary thought, is imprisoned in foreign languages" and that African thinkers and writers, "even at their most radical, even at their most revolutionary are alienated from the majority." To Ngugi and his supporters, the language question, "is the key, not the only one, but definitely a very, very important key to the decolonization process."

See also **Colonialism: Africa; Nationalism: Africa; Neocolonialism.**

BIBLIOGRAPHY

Anderson, Benedict. *Imagined Communities: Reflections on the Origin and Spread of Nationalism.* London and New York: Verso, 1991.

Barnet, Richard, and John Cavanagh. "Homogenization of Global Culture." In *The Case against the Global Economy,* edited by Jery Mander and Edward Goldsmith. San Francisco: Sierra Club Books, 1996.

Barraclough, Geoffrey. *An Introduction to Contemporary History.* New York: Basic Books, 1965.

Cabral, Amilcar. *Unity and Struggle.* Translated by Michael Wolfers. New York: Monthly Review Press, 1979. Originally published in Portuguese, 1977.

Cooper, Frederick. *Africa since 1940: The Past of the Present.* Cambridge, U.K., and New York: Cambridge University Press, 2002.

Das, Manmath N. *The Political Philosophy of Jawaharlal Nehru.* New York: John Day, 1961.

Davidson, Basil. *Can Africa Survive?* Boston: Little, Brown, 1974.

———. *Which Way Africa? The Search for a New Society.* Baltimore: Penguin, 1964.

Davis, Horace B. *Toward a Marxist Theory of Nationalism.* New York: Monthly Review Press, 1978.

Fairchild, Halford H. "Frantz Fanon's *The Wretched of the Earth* in Contemporary Perspective." *Journal of Black Studies* 25, no. 2 (December 1994): 191–199.

Fanon, Frantz. *The Wretched of the Earth.* New York: Grove Press, 1968.

Gopal, Sarvepalli, ed. *Jawaharlal Nehru: An Anthology.* New Delhi: Oxford University Press, 1980.

Han, Suyin. *The Morning Deluge: Mao Tsetung and the Chinese Revolution, 1893–1954.* Boston: Little, Brown, 1972.

Haq, Mahbub ul-. *The Poverty Curtain.* New York: Columbia University Press, 1976.

Hargreaves, John D. *Decolonization in Africa.* 2nd ed. London and New York: Longman, 1996.

Harrison, Lawrence E., and Samuel P. Huntington. *Culture Matters: How Values Shape Human Progress.* New York: Basic Books, 2000.

Kohn, Hans, and Wallace Sokolsky. *African Nationalism in the Twentieth Century.* Princeton, N. J.: Van Nostrand, 1965.

Jinadu, L. Adele. "Some Aspects of the Political Philosophy of Frantz Fanon." *African Studies Review* 16, no. 2 (September 1973): 255–289.

Jussawalla, Feroza. "The Language of Struggle." *Transition* 54 (1991): 142–154.

Maloba, W. O. "Decolonization: A Theoretical Perspective." In *Decolonization and Independence in Kenya,* edited by B. A. Ogot and W. R. Ochieng. London: J. Currey; Athens: Ohio University Press; Nairobi, Kenya: East African Educational Publishers, 1995.

Memmi, Albert. *The Colonizer and the Colonized.* 2nd ed. Boston: Beacon, 1991.

Ngugi wa Thiong'o. *Decolonising the Mind: The Politics of Language in African Literature.* London: J. Currey, 1986.

———. "The Language of Struggle." Interview with Feroza Jussawalla. *Transition,* no 54 (fall 1991): 142–154.

———. *Moving the Centre: The Struggle for Cultural Freedoms.* London: J. Currey, 1993.

Soekarno, Achmed. *Nationalism, Islam and Marxism.* Translated by Karel H. Warouw and Peter D. Weldon. Ithaca, N. Y.: Cornell University, Modern Indonesia Project, 1970.

W. O. Maloba

LATIN AMERICA

Over the past five hundred years, Latin America has experienced three and possibly four periods of colonization, all of which gave rise to anticolonial movements. The first period symbolically began with Christopher Columbus's arrival in the Americas on 12 October 1492, launching three centuries of Spanish, Portuguese, and British colonial control over the hemisphere, with the French, Dutch, Danish, and other European powers competing for slices of the action in the Caribbean. In most of Latin America, this period came to an end with the wars of independence from about 1810 to 1825. Political independence ushered in a second period (known as neocolonialism), in which the countries of Latin America were still subject to foreign economic control—this time largely by the British. During the third period, corresponding to the twentieth century, this economic dependency shifted from the British to the United States, and anticolonial responses increasingly assumed anti-imperialistic characteristics. The twenty-first century arguably introduced a fourth period of neocolonialism, in which Latin America has become subject to control through the maquiladora system to transnational capital not necessarily rooted in one country and in which the export commodity is labor rather than raw materials.

Independence

The Latin American movement most closely associated with anticolonialism corresponds to the period at the beginning of the nineteenth century during which most of the region gained its political independence from European colonial powers. This "postcolonial era began before many territories became colonial," Robert Young notes, and "before some European imperial powers, such as Germany and Italy, had even become nations themselves" (p. 193). As in the United States, independence represented a shift of economic wealth and political power from a colonial elite to a domestic elite. In Latin America, this was expressed as a struggle between *peninsulares* (those born on the Iberian peninsula, i.e., Spain and Portugal) and *creoles* (those born in the New World). Independence did not result in any corresponding shift in social relations, nor did it result in the abolition of slavery or more rights for women. In fact, without the paternalistic protection of the European crowns the position of peasants and Indians actually worsened.

The 1780 Tupac Amaru uprising in the South American Andes is one of the largest, earliest, and most significant anticolonial movements in the history of Latin America. The leader of this uprising, José Gabriel Condorcanqui (d. 1781), a descendant of the Incas, first attempted to petition for the rights of his people through legal channels. When legal attempts failed, he took the name of the last Inca ruler (Tupac Amaru) and led an uprising that quickly spread throughout the southern Andes. The insurgents sacked Spanish haciendas and *obrajes* (textile mills), driven by messianic dreams of a renewed Inca empire that would free the indigenous peoples from hunger, injustice, oppression, and exploitation. The Spanish captured Tupac Amaru and other leaders of the uprising six months later and executed them in Cuzco, the former capital of the Inca empire. This did not end the rebellion but shifted its focus south to Bolivia, where under the leadership of Aymara people it entered a more radical, violent, and explicitly anticolonial phase. In this phase, the insurgents captured and held the city of La Paz for several months and threatened the silver mines at Potosí—a direct challenge to Spanish wealth and power. The Spanish finally captured and executed the leaders and the uprising eventually collapsed. This revolt has sometimes been seen as a forward-looking antecedent to the successful creole independence movements that came forty years later and sometimes as a reactionary messianic movement that sought to return to the time of the Inca empire. Sinclair Thomson positions these uprisings in the context of local struggles against abusive colonial practices and for self-determination

Christopher Columbus coming ashore at San Salvador. Columbus's arrival in the New World in 1492 gave rise to the first period of colonization of Latin America. Spain, Portugal, and Britain proceeded to control the region, which didn't achieve independence until the early nineteenth century. © BETTMANN/CORBIS

and equality. Although the uprising ultimately failed, it reveals a widening gap between the colonial elites and the subaltern masses, as well as a refusal of indigenous peoples to passively accept their marginalized role in society.

The Haitian slave revolt provides another stark contrast to the creole independence movements and in essence underscores the lack of a compelling anticolonial discourse in those events. Haiti was a French colony, and its production of sugar, cotton, and indigo made it one of the most important colonies in the world. Soaring sugar profits for French planters in the eighteenth century led to a dramatic increase in the number of African slaves they imported to work the plantations. By the end of the century, about 80 percent of the Haitian people were overworked and underfed slaves. Nevertheless, Haitian independence movements began in 1789 not as a slave revolt but from the small elite class of planters, who had been influenced by the French Revolution's rhetoric of "liberty, equality, fraternity." For the planters, liberty meant home rule and freedom from French tariff structures. The whites armed the slaves to fight the French, but instead, under the leadership of Toussaint L'Ouverture (1743–1803), slaves took advantage of the opportunity to revolt and destroyed the old society. The result was perhaps one of the few true social revolutions the world has ever seen, in which members of a mass movement completely obliterated the *ancien régime* and claimed power for itself. By the time Jean-Jacques Dessalines declared Haitian independence in 1804, the sugar economy had disappeared, having been displaced by subsistence agriculture. The example of a black slave republic sent a terrifying chill through creole elites, which had begun to agitate for independence elsewhere in Latin America. The only other independent country in the hemisphere, the United States, refused to recognize the Haitian government. The dangers exemplified by the first successful anticolonial movement in Latin America put the brakes on other independence movements, delaying their completion by perhaps a generation.

Neocolonialism

By the 1820s, most of Latin America had gained political independence from its colonial masters. With Iberian mercantile restrictions gone, northern European (and particularly British) capital flooded the region. As critics have noted, a legacy of colonization was a blocking of moves toward industrialization, which would have represented little gain for colonial powers. This trend continued with the British (and later the United States) extracting raw materials from and importing finished goods into the region. The infrastructure, such as the railroad systems, was designed to transport products from mines and plantations to seaports rather than to integrate a country. The economic benefits of this trade accrued to foreign powers, with wages and living standards remaining depressed as resources were drained away from the domestic economy. Neocolonialism also led to cultural shifts. For example, predominantly Catholic Latin American countries implemented freedom of religion in order to encourage foreign investment from Protestant powers. Despite formal independence, external economic forces determined many of the domestic policies in Latin America. This irony has come to be known as neocolonialism.

Nineteenth-century examples of neocolonialism include the export of Peruvian guano and Chilean nitrates, which fueled an agricultural boom in Europe. Neocolonialism, and Latin America's subsequent falling behind relative to economic growth in northern industrial economies, was not inevitable nor was it the only possible option. In *The Poverty of Progress*, E. Bradford Burns points to Paraguay as a viable example of autonomous economic development. The country's leaders eliminated large estates and emphasized domestic food production, and they restricted foreign penetration of the economy. Rapid economic development without outside foreign development alarmed the elitist governments in the neighboring countries of Argentina, Brazil, and Uruguay, who feared the model Paraguay offered to the poor in their own countries. Their opposition led to the War of the Triple Alliance (1864–1870), which devastated Paraguay and destroyed this alternative model to neocolonialism.

The concept of formally independent countries that remained economically dependent on outside powers first was articulated in Marxist circles in the 1920s, though the term *neocolonialism* was not introduced until the 1960s. It has always been closely associated with anti-imperialism, as was demonstrated at the 1966 Tricontinental Conference in Havana, Cuba, which linked anticolonial struggles in Asia, Africa, and Latin America. Although U.S. neocolonial control is largely a twentieth-century phenomenon, it is rooted in the 1823 Monroe Doctrine, which declared Latin America to be part of the U.S. imperial sphere of influence.

Anti-Imperialism

When the Haitian sugar economy collapsed with the slave revolt at the end of the eighteenth century, much of this production shifted to the neighboring island of Cuba. As a result, while other colonial economies stagnated, leading to elite discontent with European rule, the Cuban economy took off, undercutting any impetus for a serious anticolonial movement. As a result, the island remained a Spanish colony until the end of the nineteenth century. José Martí (1853–1895) perhaps best represents Cuban anticolonial movements. Born to *peninsular* parents (his father was a Spanish official), he was a teenage rebel who was exiled to Spain for his political activities and later

worked in the United States as a journalist. He was killed in battle on 19 May 1895, when he returned to the island to join the anticolonial struggle. Much of Martí's ideology emerged out of the context of nineteenth-century liberalism, but his contact with radical movements in the United States also imbued his anticolonialism with aspects of social revolution. Rather than seeking to merely change one elite for another, as had happened when colonialism ended in most other American republics, he wanted true social changes. He was an anti-imperialist and a revolutionary nationalist who worked against economic dependency as well as for political independence. Martí, like Venezuelan independence leader Simón Bolívar (1783–1830) before him and Argentine-born guerrilla leader Ernesto "Che" Guevara (1928–1967) after him, called for a unified America to confront the common problems left by a legacy of European colonization.

After Martí's death, with Cuba on the verge of gaining its independence in 1898, the United States intervened in order to control the economic wealth of the colony for its own benefit and to prevent the establishment of another black republic on the Haitian model. Disguising its efforts as altruism, the U.S. Senate passed the Teller Amendment, which declared that the United States would not recolonize the island. Although this legislation thwarted the imperial intent of the United States to annex the island, the 1901 Platt Amendment declared "that the government of Cuba consents that the United States may exercise the right to intervene for the preservation of Cuban independence, the maintenance of a government adequate for the protection of life, property and individual liberty" (Bevans, pp. 116–117). This led to a unique colonial situation, in which Cuba had a civilian government but not one that could be called a democracy. The island became an extension of Miami, and U.S. intervention promoted and perpetuated corruption, violence, and economic stagnation. This set the stage for the successful 1959 Cuban Revolution, which freed the country from economic colonization, much as independence in 1898 had freed it from Spain's political colonization. After the triumph of the revolution, Cuba became a global leader in postcolonial anti-imperialist struggles.

Although the Teller Amendment prohibited the annexation of Cuba to the United States, the legislation stood mute on Spain's few remaining colonial possessions in the Caribbean. Most importantly, this led the United States to occupy the island of Puerto Rico, a territory it continues to hold in the twenty-first century. In fact, after Namibia was freed from South African control in the 1980s, Puerto Rico became the sole remaining item on the agenda of the United Nations's decolonization committee, although anticolonial struggles continue elsewhere, notably in French Polynesia. For the United States, Puerto Rico remains an unresolved and seemingly irresolvable colonial question. In the early twenty-first century the island is an *Estado Libre Asociado* (literally, Associated Free State, but defined by the United States as a commonwealth), which means that it is an unincorporated territory that belongs to, but is not part of, the United States. This leaves Puerto Rico subject to the whims of the United States, and its residents with few legal avenues through which to address offenses committed against them. As an example of the colonial relationship, residents on the island were made

U.S. citizens during World War I so that they could be drafted to fight in Europe, but even in the early twenty-first century they do not have the right to political representation in Washington. However, the economic advantages of their status, including the ability to migrate freely to the United States to work, create a situation where only a small percentage of Puerto Ricans favor independence for the island, but resentment at the island's colonial status is nonetheless widespread and deeply felt.

Anticolonial sentiments in Puerto Rico flourished during the second half of the twentieth century, and in part gained a focus around political campaigns to halt U.S. naval bombing practice at Vieques Island. In 1941, with World War II on the horizon, the United States military acquired most of the land at Vieques as an extension of the Roosevelt Roads Naval Station in order to develop a base like Pearl Harbor for its Atlantic fleet. Noise from bombs and low-flying airplanes engaged in practice maneuvers disturbed inhabitants and disrupted the fishing economy. The later use of napalm, depleted uranium, and other experimental weapons left the area heavily contaminated. The imperialist nature of the military's occupation of Vieques quickly gave rise to popular sentiments against the navy's presence and calls for them to leave. Finally, on 19 April 1999, two off-target bombs destroyed an observation post, killing David Sanes Rodríguez, a local civilian employee. This triggered a massive civil disobedience campaign that finally forced the navy to leave Vieques on 1 May 2003. Independence leaders such as Pedro Albizu Campos and Rubén Berríos Martínez provided leadership to the campaigns, seeing Vieques as an important part of an anticolonial and anti-imperialist struggle. Their slogan became "Today Vieques, tomorrow Puerto Rico."

Non-Spanish Caribbean

European colonization of the Caribbean began with Colombus's arrival in 1492, and the region was so highly valued that it remained under the control of various European empires longer than any other part of the hemisphere. Spain maintained—and then lost—control over the largest and most populous islands of Cuba, Hispaniola, and Puerto Rico, known as the Greater Antilles. Other European powers, including the British, French, and Dutch, intruded into the Spanish domain and established a significant presence, particularly on the smaller islands, known as the Lesser Antilles, where descendants of African slaves and Asian indentured workers imported to replace the decimated indigenous population led many of the anticolonial movements.

As they did in Africa and Asia, modern nationalist anticolonial movements in much of the Caribbean emerged in the aftermath of World War II, with its emphasis on the values of democracy and self-determination. As Cary Fraser argues, independence movements in the Caribbean must be understood in the context of these broader decolonization efforts. During the second half of the twentieth century, some of the islands gained their independence, although the British, French, and Dutch still retained colonial control over several smaller islands. Many of the residents benefited economically from access to European welfare systems, which dampened anticolonial agitation.

Even after independence, many of the colonies maintained close relationships with their mother countries, leaving imprints on their political culture that marked them as significantly different from Latin America. For example, the former British colonies remained part of the Commonwealth and retained the British queen as their monarch.

As the European empires collapsed, U.S. economic, political, and ideological interests gained increased hegemony over the Caribbean. Tourism and providing tax havens for foreign banks and corporations became the area's primary roles in the global economy. An example of the United States' ambiguous commitment to self-determination and its growing neocolonial control was its successful efforts to unseat Cheddi Jagan and his People's Progressive Party from the presidency of British Guiana in the early 1960s. United States opposition to Jagan, who was influenced by Marxist ideology and maintained friendly ties with the communist world, indicated that the Caribbean (as well as Latin America in general) would remain within the U.S. sphere of influence.

See also **Anticolonialism: Africa; Anticolonialism: Middle East; Anticolonialism: Southeast Asia; Colonialism; Neocolonialism.**

BIBLIOGRAPHY

Barreto, Amílcar Antonio. *Vieques, the Navy, and Puerto Rican Politics.* Gainesville: University Press of Florida, 2002.

Bevans, C. I., ed. *Treaties and Other International Agreements of the United States of America, 1776–1949.* Vol. 8. Washington, D.C.: U.S. Government Printing Office, 1971.

Burns, E. Bradford. *The Poverty of Progress: Latin America in the Nineteenth Century.* Berkeley: University of California Press, 1980.

Fraser, Cary. *Ambivalent Anti-colonialism: The United States and the Genesis of West Indian Independence, 1940–1964.* Westport, Conn.: Greenwood, 1994.

Geggus, David Patrick, ed. *The Impact of the Haitian Revolution in the Atlantic World.* Columbia: University of South Carolina, 2001.

Pérez, Louis A. *The War of 1898: The United States and Cuba in History and Historiography.* Chapel Hill: University of North Carolina Press, 1998.

Thomson, Sinclair. *We Alone Will Rule: Native Andean Politics in the Age of Insurgency.* Madison: University of Wisconsin Press, 2002.

Young, Robert J. C. *Postcolonialism: An Historical Introduction.* Oxford and Malden, Mass.: Blackwell, 2001.

Marc Becker

MIDDLE EAST

Between the early nineteenth century and the outbreak of World War I, much of the area between Morocco and what is now Turkey came under different forms of European colonial rule. Thus France began the conquest of Algeria in 1830, took over Tunisia in 1881, and (in partnership with Spain) took over Morocco in 1912. Britain occupied Egypt in 1882, formalizing the occupation by the declaration of a protectorate in 1914, and Italy began its conquest of Libya in 1911.

Ottoman Empire and the Mandate System

With the exception of Morocco, the entire region either had been or still was in the early twentieth century at least nominally part of the Ottoman Empire, a multiethnic geopolitical unit that had been in existence since the late thirteenth century and that came to an end in the 1920s. Although it is misleading to regard the Ottomans as an imperial power, it is nevertheless the case that in spite of the Tanzimat reforms of the nineteenth century, which were generally intended to extend full citizenship to all subjects of the empire, the largely Christian provinces in southeastern Europe had become independent states in the course of the nineteenth century as a consequence of more or less bitter struggles to assert their various ethnolinguistic identities. In contrast, regardless of their ethnicity, the overwhelmingly Muslim population of the Arab provinces continued to regard the (Turkish) Ottomans as the natural defenders of Islam, with the result that most of the Middle East was barely affected by Arab nationalism until the early twentieth century.

On the coasts of the Arabian Peninsula, Britain's concern with keeping the route to India safe and open led to a series of treaties with various local rulers between the 1820s and 1916, under which the rulers generally agreed not to grant or dispose of any part of their territories to any power except Britain. In 1839, Britain annexed Aden and turned it into a naval base. Exclusive treaties were signed with the tribal rulers of the interior, and in 1937 the area was divided into the port and its immediate hinterland (Aden Colony) and the more remote rural/tribal areas (Aden Protectorate). Principally because of their remoteness and their apparent lack of strategic importance, central Arabia and northern Yemen were never colonized.

After the collapse of the Ottoman Empire at the end of the First World War, the empire's remaining Arab provinces were assigned by the newly created League of Nations to Britain and France as mandates, with Britain taking responsibility for Iraq, Palestine, and Transjordan, and France taking responsibility for Lebanon and Syria. The guiding principle of the mandate system was that the states concerned should remain under the tutelage of the mandatory power until such time as they were able to "stand alone," a period that, although not specified, was still understood to be finite. The mandate period was relatively short-lived, ending with the creation of Israel from the former Palestine mandate in 1948.

Islam and Anticolonialism

A number of factors are crucial to understanding the various manifestations of anticolonialism in the Arab world in the nineteenth and twentieth centuries. In the first place, the colonial period coincided with several movements of Islamic renewal; the same phenomenon can also be observed in the Indian subcontinent, West Africa, Central Asia, and Southeast Asia. Some movements clearly were, or became, reactions to colonialism, but one of the most influential, the Wahhabis in the center of the Arabian peninsula, both predated colonialism in the region and originated in an area relatively distant from any direct colonial activity. In the late eighteenth and nineteenth centuries, such renewal or reform movements spread out over a wide geographical area. Some, such as the Sanusi jihad, based in Saharan Libya, later the backbone of resistance to Italian colonization, exhibited an organizational structure similar to that of the Sufi orders, based on a network of lodges; others were urban-based, often around traditional centers of Islamic learning, while yet others were millenarian. Thus in the 1880s, the Sudanese Mahdi preached that he was the divinely appointed regenerator of Islam and consciously imitated the life and career of the Prophet. The renewal movements were by no means always sympathetic to, or even tolerant of, one another. Muhammad al-Mahdi al-Sanusi (1844–1902), for example, was at pains to point out that the Mahdi was not entitled to claim either the leadership of the universal Islamic community or a transcendental relationship with the Prophet Muhammad, and Wahhabism (if not checked by more prudent political considerations) has often exhibited considerable intolerance toward other manifestations of Islam.

The reform movements fed into anticolonialism in a number of ways. One of their effects was to draw a battle line between those rulers and elites in the Islamic world who were prepared to make accommodations to European colonizers and those sections of the community who were not. Thus 'Abd al-Qadir (1808–1883), the early leader of the resistance to the French, was quick to make use of a fatwa (legal opinion) obtained from the Mufti of Fez stating that those Muslims who cooperated with non-Muslims against other Muslims could be considered apostate and thus could be killed or enslaved if captured. Later in the nineteenth century, Ba Ahmad, the chamberlain of the Moroccan sultan 'Abd al-'Aziz (r. 1894–1908), believed his only recourse was to buy off or otherwise accommodate the French, who were making incursions into southern Morocco from both Algeria and Senegal. This policy alienated many influential religious and tribal leaders, who were bitterly opposed to the Commander of the Faithful giving up "the lands of Islam" to foreign invaders; some of them considered that this made him illegitimate and transferred their allegiance to a more combative leader.

The Economic Impact of Colonialism

An important effect of colonialism was to hasten the disintegration of long-established social and economic relations and to substitute the often harsher dictates of the market. The precolonial world was no egalitarian paradise, but, for example, the confiscation or purchase of land in colonial Algeria and mandatory Palestine and the formation of large landed estates in Syria and Iraq as a result of the establishment of regimes of private property under the mandates often resulted in cultivators either being driven off the land or being reduced from free peasants to serfs. Being far more incorporated into the world market than they had been before, with the concomitant pressure to cultivate cash crops, forced peasant households to migrate to slum settlements on the edges of the major cities where they faced an uncertain and often near-destitute existence.

Resistance to Colonialism

Twentieth-century resistance to colonialism inevitably partook of the general experience of its time, including assertions of national and ethnic identity, which were given added meaning and purpose in the face of alien colonizing. The press, the radio, and political parties and clubs provided new opportunities for disseminating the ideologies of anticolonialism. To these must be added the example first of Germany in the 1930s—a previously fragmented state that had turned its recent unification into a means of challenging the old colonizers, Britain and France; and for much of the 1940s, 1950s, and 1960s the Soviet Union as a new form of social and economic organization, under which a previously feudal regime was being transformed into an egalitarian welfare state. Such visions were especially attractive to those who had not experienced the realities of daily life under such regimes.

Algeria

Provided a certain flexibility is adopted, it is possible to identify the major templates of anticolonial resistance, which vary according to the nature of the colonizing process. The Algerian case is probably the most extreme because of the extent of the devastation caused by the colonization process over a period of some 130 years. In the months after the conquest of the city of Algiers in July 1830, the French military began to encourage the settlement of French *colons* in the city's rural hinterland. At the time, Algeria was, if only nominally, an Ottoman province and had no developed political structures. Local leaders in the west of the country turned first to the Moroccan sultan, but the French warned him not to interfere. The leaders then turned to the Sufi orders, the only bodies with an organizational structure, and Muhi al-Din, the leader of the Qadiriyya order, and his shrewd and energetic son 'Abd al-Qadir were asked to lead a tribal jihad against the French.

Between 1832 and 1844 'Abd al-Qadir managed to keep the French at bay with an army of about ten thousand. Initially, he achieved this by making agreements with the French recognizing his authority over certain parts of the country, but by the 1840s the French had decided on a policy of total subjugation and 'Abd al-Qadir, defeated at Isly in 1844, eventually surrendered in 1847. By this time the European population had reached over 100,000, living mostly in the larger towns. In the 1840s, the French had begun a policy of wholesale land confiscation and appropriation, and a number of local risings took place in protest. The settlers had influential allies in Paris, and throughout the nineteenth century the indigenous population faced the gradual erosion of most of their rights. The last major act of resistance until the war of 1954 to 1962 was the rebellion in Kabylia in 1870 to 1871, led by Muhammad al-Muqrani. For a while, al-Muqrani's army of some 200,000 controlled much of eastern Algeria, but it was no match for the better equipped French troops. After the defeat of al-Muqrani's rebellion (he was killed in battle in May 1871) the local communities involved were fined heavily and lost most of their tribal lands.

The Algerian national movement was slow to develop in the twentieth century. The tribal aristocracy had been defeated and no former indigenous governing class or emerging business bourgeoisie existed (as they did in, for example, Morocco, Tunisia, Syria, and Lebanon). Some Algerians felt that France had brought them into the modern world and wanted to become more French—that is, to enjoy the same rights as the

French in Algeria without having to give up their Islamic identity. This tendency, generally called assimilationist, was represented by Ferhat Abbas, who sought to become a member of the French Chamber of Deputies. The first strictly nationalist movement, the Étoile Nord-Africaine (later the Parti du Peuple Algérien), which initially had links to the French Communist Party, was founded by Messali Hadj in 1926, recruiting among Algerian workers in France. Yet another tendency was represented by Ahmad Ibn Badis (1889–1940), who sought to reform Algerian popular Islam through the Association of 'Ulama', asserting the Muslim nature of Algeria.

From the 1930s onwards, rapid urbanization fuelled Algerian resistance to France. By the end of World War II there was some hope on the part of moderates both in France and Algeria that compromises could be worked out that might deflect violent nationalism, but the Algerian European community's dogged insistence on maintaining its privileges meant that these hopes soon evaporated. Ferhat Abbas's movement soon became insignificant. Ibn Badis's death meant that the Association of 'Ulama' lacked influence, leaving Messali Hadj dominating the field, with supporters among Algerian workers in France as well as in Algeria. However, his organization was regarded as too moderate, and a splinter group, the Organisation Secrète, seceded from it in the mid-1940s. Its members included such major revolutionary figures as Ahmed Ben Bella, Ait Ahmad, Murad Didouche, Mohammed Boudiaf, and Belkacem Krim. This group subsequently launched the Algerian Revolution, or war of national liberation, on 1 November 1954. The war lasted until 1962, when Algeria became independent; over the eight years, between 1 million and 1.5 million Algerians and 27,000 French were killed. The war proved intensely divisive, especially as more Algerian Muslims fought as soldiers or *harkis* on the French side than in the Algerian army.

Tunisia, Egypt, and Morocco

In the case of Tunisia, Egypt, and Morocco, the decision of Britain and France to take over the reins of government (in 1881, 1882, and 1912) was at least partly precipitated by local opposition to the draconian financial measures that the European powers had forced local governments to impose in order to repay the debts they had contracted on the various European money markets. The ruler of Tunisia, Ahmad Bey (1837–1855), made strenuous efforts both to modernize Tunisia and to assert its independence from Istanbul, and he had been substantially aided by France in the latter objective. By the time of his death, Tunisia had a modern army and a modern navy; the Bey's brother-in-law, who survived him by nearly twenty years, was a modernizing finance minister and prime minister, and an Italian family provided the state's foreign ministers until 1878. In 1861, much to the discomfiture of Muhammad al-Sadiq Bey (1859–1882), Tunisia adopted a constitution and a modern (that is, generally secular) legal system under which the Bey's prerogatives were quite limited.

These reforms were better received in the outside world and among the sizeable local European community than within Tunisia, where a rural rising against the new legal system and the new taxes was put down with considerable brutality in 1864.

As happened in Egypt at much the same time, the contracting of substantial foreign debts (generally used to build the infrastructures that made the reforms possible or to pay the European consultants—officers, engineers, and so forth—in charge of putting them into effect) and the general mismanagement and corruption associated with the loans meant that the country found itself increasingly at the mercy of its foreign creditors. Tunisia declared bankruptcy in 1869 and Egypt in 1876. The sterling efforts of the reformer Khayr al-Din (c. 1825–1889) to balance the budget were no match for French colonial ambitions, which eventually forced the Bey to accept a protectorate under the terms of the Treaty of Bardo in May 1881. By 1892, four-fifths of cultivated lands were in French hands.

The situation in Egypt was similar; the additional taxes imposed as a result of British and French administration of the public debt, initiated in 1876 essentially to ensure that the bond-holders got their money back, eventually gave rise to a nationalist movement. Many of its members had the additional grievance that the government of Egypt was conducted by foreigners, that is, a Turco-Circassian aristocracy consisting of the descendants of the viceroy Muhammad 'Ali (1780–1848) and their courtiers, in which native Egyptians constantly encountered a glass ceiling. Another interesting component of the rebellion led by Ahmad 'Urabi (1839–1911) between 1879 and 1882 was the emphasis on restoring Egypt fully to the Ottoman Empire. Although relatively large numbers of foreigners resided in Egypt, they were generally neither settlers nor *colons* in the French North African sense: most were not bureaucrats or farmers and had not lived there for generations; they resided mostly in the cities and engaged in commerce or in service occupations. In addition, most of them were not citizens of the occupying power.

In spite of a succession of strong rulers for much of the nineteenth century, Morocco was also unable to avoid colonial penetration, first economic (imports of tea, sugar, candles, and cotton cloth; exports of wool, cereals, and ostrich feathers) and then military. The first major confrontation between locals and Europeans occurred in 1859 to 1860, when Spain besieged Tetouan. A month later, Spain demanded an indemnity as the price of withdrawal, and although the terms were punitive half the indemnity was paid within two years. This involved great hardship, particularly the imposition of nontraditional agricultural taxation, which caused considerable unrest. A massive devaluation of the currency took place, as did a near-universal switch to foreign coinage. Like Tunisia and Egypt, Morocco gradually moved from a state of general economic self-sufficiency to dependence on the world market. Morocco gradually became dependent on foreign loans and declared bankrupcty in 1903. Largely to preempt German colonial efforts, France and Britain signed the Entente Cordiale in 1904, under which Britain recognized France's preeminence in Morocco and France formally accepted the British occupation of Egypt. Franco-Spanish occupation of Morocco was formalized in 1912.

Independence

Some of the anticolonial movements of the twentieth century were urban-based mass movements, often led by charismatic leaders, perhaps most notably Habib Bourguiba of Tunisia, who led the Neo-Destour Party between 1954 and Tunisian independence in 1956 and who remained his country's leader until 1987. Allal al-Fassi, leader of the Istiqlal party, might have played a similar role in the history of Morocco. However, in 1953 the French exiled the sultan, Muhammad V, to Madagascar, and as a result the rallying cry of the national movement became the sultan's return from exile, which led in its turn to the sultan/king retaining his position as ruler after Morocco's independence in October 1956 and the virtual eclipse of the secular political parties.

In Egypt, a kind of independence was achieved in 1936, but the national movement went through two stages. In the first stage, some but not all powers were handed over to local elites. This arrangement involved some form of power-sharing with the former colonial power, which became increasingly intolerable to wide sections of the population. However, given the balance of forces, it was not possible to break these links by democratic means—that is, by voting in a political party or coalition that would be able to end the relationship. Thus a second stage was necessary, in which a determined group within the military seized power, destroying in the process the fairly rudimentary institutions of parliamentary government that the colonial powers had put in place. In this way, first General Mohamad Neguib (1901–1984) and then Gamel Abdel-Nasser (1918–1970) took power in 1952. Iraq went through a similar process, and 'Abd al-Karim Qasim took power in 1958. A similar but more complex process took place in Syria, although the old social classes still ruling in 1961 had long severed any links they may have had with France.

Palestine

The final and highly anomalous case of anticolonialism in the Middle East is Palestine, unique among its neighbors in that it was a settler state. The text of the Palestine mandate included the terms of the Balfour Declaration (1917), in which Britain as mandatory power undertook to facilitate the setting up of a "national home for the Jewish people." In 1922, there were 93,000 Jews in Palestine and about 700,000 Arabs; in 1936, there were 380,000 Jews and 983,000 Arabs; and in 1946, about 600,000 Jews and 1.3 million Arabs; thus the Jewish population increased from 13 percent to 31 percent over a period of twenty-four years. Anticolonialism took different forms, principally through opposition by both Arabs and Zionists to British policy, which they tried to combat in different ways, and Arab opposition to Zionism. The Palestine rebellion of 1936 to 1939 was mostly a peasant insurrection against colonial rule and the settlers; in 1947 to 1948, the Zionists fought and won against an assortment of Arab armies and the poorly organized Palestinian resistance forces; the colonial power had long indicated that it would withdraw.

Opposition to colonial rule and colonial settlement was fairly widespread throughout the nineteenth and twentieth centuries and took a variety of different forms, rural and urban, organized and spontaneous, religious and political, showing greater or lesser degrees of coherence. In any colonial situation, a wide spectrum of responses existed, with resistance at one end, acquiescence in the middle, and collaboration at the other end. Some members of the colonized population rebelled and some collaborated, but the majority acquiesced, at least for most of the time. In the nationalist historiography of the colonial period, the struggle for colonial freedom or national independence is often characterized in a way that shows the brave freedom fighters ranged against the brutal colonial authorities. The "achievements" of colonialism have long been open to question, and the divisions and chaos of the postcolonial world make the value of the legacy more questionable as time passes. Nevertheless, it is also important to understand the complexity and multifaceted nature of anticolonialism: the intrigues; the competing and often warring factions; the venality and corruption of many of them. For national maturity, and increasingly for national reconciliation, it will be necessary that such uncomfortable truths are boldly confronted rather than wilfully ignored.

See also **Anticolonialism: Africa; Anticolonialism: Latin America; Anticolonialism: Southeast Asia; Empire and Imperialism: Middle East.**

BIBLIOGRAPHY

Anderson, Lisa. *The State and Social Transformation in Tunisia and Libya, 1830–1980.* Princeton, N.J.: Princeton University Press, 1986.

Batatu, Hanna. *The Old Social Classes and the Revolutionary Movements of Iraq: A Study of Iraq's Old Landed Classes and Its Communists, Ba'thists, and Free Officers.* Princeton, N.J.: Princeton University Press, 1978.

Botman, Selma. *Egypt from Independence to Revolution, 1919–1952.* Syracuse, N.Y.: Syracuse University Press, 1991.

Khoury, Philip S. *Syria and the French Mandate: The Politics of Arab Nationalism, 1920–1946.* Princeton, N.J.: Princeton University Press, 1987.

Morris, Benny. *Righteous Victims: A History of the Zionist-Arab Conflict, 1881–2001.* New York, Vintage, 2001.

Morsy, Magali. *North Africa 1800–1900: A Survey from the Nile Valley to the Atlantic.* London and New York: Longman, 1984.

Prochaska, David. *Making Algeria French: Colonialism in Bône, 1870–1920.* Cambridge, U.K.: Cambridge University Press, 1990.

Sluglett, Peter. *Britain in Iraq, 1914–1932.* London: Ithaca Press, for the Middle East Centre, 1976.

———. "Formal and Informal Empire in the Middle East." In *Historiography.* Vol. 5 of *The Oxford History of the British Empire,* edited by Robin W. Winks, 416–436. Oxford: Oxford University Press, 1999.

Peter Sluglett

SOUTHEAST ASIA

Anticolonialism in Southeast Asia has been considered from a wide range of perspectives, resulting in deliberation over its character and place in the region's history. Generally, anticolonialism refers to one type of Southeast Asian response to the encounter with Euro-American colonialism. One might then describe anticolonialism as including everything from the personalities, institutions, and resistance movements that arose in direct response to the establishment of colonies in Southeast Asia, to the growth of literary expressions, rituals, history,

and popular culture that emerged within that historical context. More specifically, anticolonialism has also come to represent the ways in which colonized peoples protested, resisted, or expressed dissatisfaction with changes imposed by colonial authorities.

Because of the nature and history of colonialism in Southeast Asia (which occurred over four centuries involving different actors, intensities, locations, and agendas), expressions of anticolonialism in the region tend to reflect the circumstances and characteristics particular to each locality. So the study of anticolonial movements in the Spanish colonies was understood in the context of a "Philippine history" that was different from the historical context in which colonialism (and anticolonialism) would be examined in the case of nineteenth-century Myanmar (then known as Burma), whose history and colonial experience under the British had unfolded in quite a different manner. At the same time, scholars have also done extensive comparative work, demonstrating similarities in the way Southeast Asians articulated protest. In this regard, scholars have concentrated on the different forms of anticolonial expression in order to demonstrate variation and coherency in Southeast Asian cultural history. As a result, a distinctive and uniform "Southeast Asian" response to colonialism has yet to be clearly defined.

Categories and Features of Anticolonialism

In order to make sense of the variety of ways in which Southeast Asians responded to colonialism, expressions of protest and resistance might be approached under three general categories: traditional, synthesis, and radical movements. Although problematic in terminology, traditional movements represent those initial "knee-jerk" reactions to the immediate military and pacification operations of the colonial powers that preceded the establishment of administrative governments. These movements were generally led by elites of the traditional order, using the vocabulary and symbols of leadership to which their followers would associate with precolonial authority. Designed to resurrect the institutions and social networks that were dismantled by the encroaching Europeans, ex-princes, ministers, and priests (or monks) rallied their immediate followers to resist colonial encroachment at locations of significant religious, political, and cultural importance. Because these movements were based on patron–client, village, and locally defined networks of relations, these outbreaks of resistance were limited in scale. These types of responses were generally found throughout the region but were more locally oriented and unsuccessful in realizing the return of precolonial sociopolitical orders.

The second category of anticolonialism, which includes those expressions that exemplify a synthesis of indigenous and European ideals, refers generally to the types of programs championed by educated indigenous elites who wanted to initiate change and reform through the colonial system, using the vocabulary and procedures adopted from European education. These forms of protest were undertaken after colonial administrative and social institutions had already been entrenched in local soil, producing a generation of social reformers who saw the means for change within the apparatus and mechanics of the colonial system but who hoped to localize Western ideals of civil society and individualism through traditional symbols and belief systems. Unlike earlier responses that aimed to return to precolonial orders, these programs sought to initiate social reform within the parameters of colonial law and convention. Many who initiated such reforms were challenged by the inability to connect with rural populations, whose concerns, experiences, and conceptions of the world were much different from their more urbanized, Western-educated counterparts.

The third type of anticolonial response, which were more radical than the earlier "East-West" attempts to synthesize, describes the initiatives of younger, educated urban students and activists who sought complete independence from colonial authorities using the organizational and sometimes ideological blueprints inherited from Europe, Japan, and America. In contrast to the generation of educated elites who hoped to initiate social reform through the system, the leaders of these movements aimed to uproot the colonial powers using the language of anticolonial nationalism in order to replace the system. Based in cities but able to penetrate the countryside, these movements attempted to bridge the rural–urban gap by making the colonial experience itself the common inspiration to launch popular movements toward independence.

These three categories of analysis offer a preliminary structure to distinguish the different types of social and political protest that might be considered "anticolonial," while they also take into account the sociopolitical changes that occurred within Southeast Asian colonial society during the late nineteenth and early twentieth centuries as it affected local populations and communities. While anticolonial sentiment developed along these general lines, differences in the methods and natures of the colonial administrations, and the periods in which they were implemented, account for the variations and departures from the stages within this scheme.

One common feature that binds the scholarly understanding of anticolonialism in the region is that it was mainly directed toward institutions, individuals, and policies that had come to represent the way in which colonial authority threatened or affected the lifestyle, worldviews, or identities of local peoples. Symbols of the colonial state (such as infrastructural edifices, district offices, and administrators) were common targets for anticolonial protest, though local indigenous elites who were deemed collaborators or at least sympathetic to the colonial authorities were often subjected to distrust, scorn, and sometimes violence as well. Attacks on local headmen outnumbered attacks on British officials during the initial outbreak of the Saya San Rebellion in Burma in 1930, as these British-appointed headmen were perceived as acting on behalf of the newly formed British village administration.

While rebellions, riots, marches, and boycotts are all illustrative of more obvious forms of resistance, anticolonialism was expressed in a variety of other modes, harnessing local forms of public expression and media to articulate displeasure or disagreement with policies and pressures imposed by the colonial state. The growth of print culture alongside local theater, religious festivals, and other cultural outlets enabled anticolonialism to be articulated in a wide range of forms, much of which contributed to the scholarly understanding of culture, peasants, and nationalism in Southeast Asia. While these contexts represent more recent scholarly approaches to thinking about anticolonialism, the earliest versions of the idea can be found in the writings of colonial scholar-officials.

Colonial Origins of the Idea

The earliest traces of "anticolonialism" can be found in the documents compiled by scholar-officials working within the various colonial administrations. Specifically, political officers who accompanied the initial military campaigns of conquest and later those within the civil service were among the first to interpret and write about the wide range of responses to colonial operations in the region. Many of these accounts speak of anticolonial resistance as brief interludes or disturbances, mere interruptions to the social order established by the authorities. Within official reports, gazetteers, manuals, and censuses, administrators organized, defined, and made sense of these outbreaks, thereby creating the very categories and perspectives under which "resistance" and "anticolonialism" would eventually be considered. Throughout the region, officials identified key cultural markers such as protective tattooing, charms, and astronomical symbols as part of the "traditional" uniform of resistance, which combined superstitious beliefs and religion in order to appeal to the masses who participated in these movements. Other features included the rebuilding of royal palaces and religious edifices in mountain strongholds that were said to represent cosmological and spiritual power. Case studies demonstrate these similarities in the early *minlaung* (prince) movements of Burma (1885–1890s), the "save-the-emperor" movements of northern Vietnam (1885–1896), and the Java War (1825–1830). Characteristics of anticolonial resistance were first identified, labeled, and codified by officials whose jobs were to affirm colonial policies as much as they were supposed to collect and interpret the societies they were charged with administering.

More importantly, colonial officials were interested in establishing the causal factors for these disturbances and wrote their reports accordingly, influencing scholars who would later use these sources, their approaches, and their descriptions for their own studies. Reports often stated that these brief instances of violence resulted from irrationality, superstition, gullibility, false prophets, religious fanaticism, and other inherent cultural traits that predictably would endure if not for colonial intervention. It was no surprise that initial pockets of resistance that faced the Dutch in Java, the British in Lower Burma, and the French in Vietnam would be considered akin both in character and origin to the anticolonial rebellions in the early twentieth century, though the circumstances would be considerably different. Thus, officials were charged with finding and naming examples of what was "anticolonial" in Southeast Asia partly in hopes of establishing the difference between traditional Asia and modern Europe. In this manner, the idea of anticolonialism began to take shape along a binary framing that placed Southeast Asians and Europeans at opposite ends, structuring the way in which protest, resistance, and revolt would be studied in the years to come.

Nationalism and the Idea of Anticolonialism

With the exception of the Vietnamese and to a lesser extent the Indonesians (who had to endure the return of the colonial powers following World War II), the eventual exit of the European powers from the political scene created an important intellectual vacuum within which scholars of the former colonies could operate. Many of these "home" scholars sought to repair, renovate, or even remove the histories produced under colonial tutelage. Heeding the needs of nationhood, Southeast Asian scholars, many of whom were trained in European schools, began redressing the histories that were written for them by colonial historians by writing from the perspective of the nation. Where rebels, political activists, and influential religious figures were once marginalized and condemned by colonial historians, they were now transformed into "national" heroes who contributed to the fruition and emergence of the nation-state. Figures such as Java's Dipanagoro (c. 1785–1855), the Philippines' José Rizal (1861–1896), Burma's Saya San (d. 1931), and Vietnam's Tran Van Tra (1918–1996) became part of a common history of the nation and struggle that contributed to the imagining of the nation. Moreover, the rebellions and incidents first identified by colonial officials as being important were appropriated by home scholars for their narratives, intent on recasting the perspective in which they had originally been presented. So "anticolonial" movements became seen as independence movements, affecting the way in which protest and resistance was interpreted. For instance, the tone of the scholarship and the analysis of the movements were sympathetic rather than critical, shifting the movements' role and importance in history to demonstrate a national consciousness that was growing during colonial rule. Earlier elements of resistance that colonial writers had highlighted in order to establish the "backward" nature of political expression (such as tattooing, religious symbols, and language) were played down by nationalist historians in favor of more "objective" economic and political origins, although the interest and focus in causal factors as prescribed by colonial documents was nevertheless maintained. Local conceptions of protest and revolt were unintentionally deemed irrelevant, because nationalist scholars were keen on writing a modern narrative of the new nation. The shape and scope of anticolonialism had not changed, only its interpretation and coloring.

While these adjustments were being made by home scholars writing through the lens of the nation, scholars in the West began to reconsider anticolonialism within the context of nation as well, choosing to consider indigenous expressions of protest and revolt (which were ironically being played down by their counterparts in Southeast Asia) as evidence of proto-nationalism. As a result, the major rebellions and revolts (which continued to dominate the attention of scholars) that had taken on a religious or culturally specific character were deemed important to study under the rubric of "Asian" nationalism, which seemed to make these once dismissed ideological influences important and relevant to scholarly study. Consequently, disturbances and outbreaks of violence that demonstrated religious overtones drew attention on the grounds that they were early expressions of nationalism and therefore warranted closer scrutiny. The Saya San Rebellion (1930–1932) in Burma, which made use of Buddhist ideas in its program, was now being considered as a "Buddhist" protonationalist movement,

suggesting that religion and other Southeast Asian ideological sources were important to understanding the growth and expression of Asian nationalism. Similarly, Dipanogoro's rebellion in Java represented an Islamic nationalism that would precede movements in the twentieth century, while the Filipino revolt launched in 1896 by Andres Bonifacio (1863–1897), which alluded to Christian ideas, seemed to forecast the origins of a national consciousness.

Autonomous History and the Idea of Anticolonialism

In the early 1960s, shifts within Southeast Asian studies began promoting research that sought an alternative approach to the ways in which Southeast Asian culture and history had been conceptualized by earlier scholars. Following the call of John Smail to produce histories of Southeast Asia that were not bound to the European narratives, chronologies, and categories of analysis, scholars began directing their attention to writing about and studying what they perceived as indigenous history, which had finally attained its "autonomy" from the priorities and perspective of European-centered history. This trend affected the way in which anticolonialism came to be understood, in that Southeast Asian conceptions of resistance and protest were now being studied for what they revealed about the region's cultural heritage and conceptions of the world. Where scholars might have considered how revolts inspired by Islamic, Buddhist, or Christian ideas operated under the rubric of nationalism, emphasis was now directed toward understanding how these mentalities revealed something about the very nature of Southeast Asian culture.

This new direction in thinking led scholars to write some of the most important works about anticolonialism and Southeast Asian culture. For example, Reynaldo C. Ileto, author of the seminal work *Payson and Revolution,* studied the ways in which Filipino-Catholic conceptions of rebellion were articulated through the imagery, scenes, and narratives associated with the Passion story of Christ. It inspired a new interest in millenarianism, or the idea of the coming millennium (or end of the world/cycle), and its relation to religious anticolonial movements. Historians such as Emanuel Sarkisyanz demonstrated how Buddhist conceptions about the end of the world framed the way Burmese made sense of the rapid social and economic changes occurring around them and how the notion of a future Buddha was associated with leaders promising a return to precolonial social norms. Michael Adas would take this paradigm and extend it comparatively within the region and beyond, showing in his *Prophets of Rebellion* that anticolonial movements were forged by the charismatic leadership of men who used religious notions of the millennium in order to gain popular support among the peasantry. Most importantly, these studies and many others began using the idea of anticolonialism in order to flesh out what were perceived as indigenous conceptions of the Southeast Asian world.

Peasant Studies and the Idea of Anticolonialism

With the shift toward an "autonomous" reading of anticolonialism came a connected interest in focusing on peasant society and consciousness. Pathbreaking works, such as James C. Scott's *The Moral Economy of the Peasant,* applied models for studying peasants to the anticolonial movements of the 1930s (the Saya San Rebellion in British Burma and the Nghe-Tinh Uprising in French Vietnam) in order to understand not just how "Southeast Asians" might have articulated and understood revolt but also in what specific ways peasants would have expressed and made sense of the new colonial order. The work of Scott and others suggested that the economic conditions of the 1930s directly challenged the peasantry's locally defined threshold for subsistence, resulting in the widespread rebellions and resistance that occurred throughout the region. Peasant studies tended to also concentrate on economic causal factors, leading scholars to suggest possible connections between the anticolonial rhetoric and new communist influences that were slowly becoming a part of these and other nationalist movements to come. Yet peasant studies also led to the emerging interest in "everyday" forms of resistance and "avoidance" protest that focused on how peasants and communities may have expressed anticolonial sentiment on a daily basis as opposed to the larger and less frequent rebellions that officials and scholars had grown accustomed to study. Anticolonial behavior could be expressed by sabotage, flight, the dragging of one's feet, and other forms of self-preservation and protest that were directed against authority and/or the colonial state. In a fundamental way, the influence of peasant studies upon the idea of anticolonialism challenged for the first time some of the categories and foci of colonial officials by momentarily shifting attention away from the major rebellions and revolts to the everyday behavior of Southeast Asians. The breadth of scholarship generated by this focus continues to influence the field in the early twenty-first century, by which time the focus on the peasantry had broadened to include minority groups, women, and ethnicities involved in challenges to the state and its apparatus.

Postcolonial Studies and Anticolonialism

Scholars in the early twenty-first century have returned to the idea of anticolonialism, armed with new perspectives and interdisciplinary approaches. As colonialism continues to challenge scholars, many in the academe have been inspired by suggestions that "knowledge" and "power" are closely connected, which have resulted in studies attempting to show how "knowledge" about Southeast Asia reveals something about the contexts in which it was produced. Invariably, attention has returned to those early colonial official-scholars who first began collecting, cataloguing, inventorying, and labeling what they considered Southeast Asia to be. Following Edward Said's critique of Oriental knowledge production, scholars have demonstrated not only that this construction of Southeast Asian culture by colonial administrators represented European images of the "Orient" but that it also represented an underlying "power" to say what was and what was not "Southeast Asia." Applying these approaches to the study of resistance and protest, it has become clear that the very categories that define resistance, the rebel, the criminal, and anticolonialism itself were produced in particular contexts that reveal as much about the colonizer as they reveal something about the perceptions of anticolonialism. Research directed at prisons, anticolonial legislation/law, and criminality have become the focus of study in order to demonstrate how colonial administrations

defined Southeast Asian anticolonialism to fit, serve, and respond to the needs of counterinsurgency policies and the maintenance of colonial order. Where once anticolonialism shed light on forms of Southeast Asian culture, it is now redirected to the forms of colonial knowledge and counterinsurgency.

See also **Colonialism: Southeast Asia; Empire and Imperialism: Asia; Nationalism; Westernization: Southeast Asia.**

BIBLIOGRAPHY

Adas, Michael. *Prophets of Rebellion: Millenarian Protest Movements against the European Colonial Order.* Chapel Hill: University of North Carolina Press, 1979.

Cooper, Frederick, and Ann Laura Stoler, eds. *Tensions of Empire: Colonial Cultures in a Bourgeois World.* Berkeley and Los Angeles: University of California Press, 1997.

Dirks, Nicholas B., ed. *Colonialism and Culture.* Ann Arbor: University of Michigan Press, 1992.

Ileto, Reynaldo C. *Payson and Revolution: Popular Movements in the Philippines, 1840–1910.* Quezon City, Philippines: Ateneo de Manila University Press, 1979.

McHale, Shawn Frederick. *Print and Power: Confucianism, Communism, and Buddhism in the Making of Modern Vietnam.* Honolulu: University of Hawaii Press, 2004.

Mrázek, Rudolf. *Engineers of Happy Land: Technology and Nationalism in a Colony.* Princeton, N.J.: Princeton University Press, 2002.

Rafael, Vicente L., ed. *Figures of Criminality in Indonesia, the Philippines, and Colonial Vietnam.* Ithaca, N.Y.: Cornell University, Southeast Asia Program, 1999.

Reid, Anthony. *Southeast Asia in the Age of Commerce, 1450–1680,* Vol. 1: *The Lands below the Winds.* New Haven, Conn.: Yale University Press, 1988.

Scott, James C. *The Moral Economy of the Peasant: Rebellion and Subsistence in Southeast Asia.* New Haven, Conn.: Yale University Press, 1976.

Sears, Laurie J. *Shadows of Empire: Colonial Discourse and Javanese Tales.* Durham, N.C.: Duke University Press, 1996.

Steinberg, David Joel, ed. *In Search of Southeast Asia: A Modern History.* Rev. ed. Honolulu: University of Hawaii Press, 1987.

Stoler, Ann Laura. *Capitalism and Confrontation in Sumatra's Plantation Belt, 1870–1979.* 2nd ed. Ann Arbor: University of Michigan Press, 1995.

Tarling, Nicholas, ed. *The Cambridge History of Southeast Asia,* Vol. 2: *The Nineteenth and Twentieth Centuries.* Cambridge, U.K.: Cambridge University Press, 1992.

Zinoman, Peter. *The Colonial Bastille: A History of Imprisonment in Vietnam, 1862–1940.* Berkeley and Los Angeles: University of California Press, 2001.

Maitrii Aung-Thwin

ANTIFEMINISM. Since they became widely used in the late nineteenth century, both *feminism* and *antifeminism* have been hotly contested words, an indication of their politically charged complexity. Activists and thinkers in both camps have sought to control the field of discourse by defining their opponents, while resisting definition themselves. Each camp has adapted to circumstances that change with each victory or setback. The increasing global exchange of ideas and strategies has produced new local feminisms and antifeminisms. The problem of definition is further complicated by retrospective debates about the relative feminism and antifeminism of historical figures and traditions. Even among self-proclaimed feminists and antifeminists at any given time and place, great philosophical and programmatic diversity is the rule. Under these circumstances, all definitions must be provisional.

Defining Feminism and Antifeminism

Historically and conceptually, feminism precedes antifeminism, which arises as a reaction against and repudiation of feminism and can only be defined on that basis. The definition of *feminism* offered by the historian Linda Gordon has the requisite balance of precision and suppleness to serve as a starting point: "Feminism is a critique of male supremacy, formed and offered in the light of a will to change it, which in turn assumes a conviction that it is changeable" (quoted in Cott, pp. 4–5). Antifeminism, then, repudiates critiques of male supremacy and resists efforts to eliminate it (often accompanied by dismissal of the idea that change is possible). Note that this definition of *antifeminism* limits its reference to reactions against critiques of gender-based hierarchies and efforts to relieve the oppression of women. In this way, antifeminism is distinguished from the related concepts of male chauvinism, sexism, misogyny, patriarchy, and androcentrism, all of which can exist in the absence of feminism.

The origins of modern feminism and antifeminism are primarily found in the European Enlightenment. Among the earliest and most influential works of Enlightenment feminism was Mary Wollstonecraft's (1759–1797) *A Vindication of the Rights of Women* (1792). Her innovation was to include women in the Enlightenment ideal of autonomous individualism and to extend the critique of rule by divine right to men's subordination of women. Initially, *A Vindication of the Rights of Women* was praised in the majority of publications that took notice and largely ignored by more conservative journals. The disclosure of Wollstonecraft's transgressive sexual history in a memoir posthumously published by her husband then brought increased attention from conservative commentators who, in their denunciations, pioneered a common tactic of antifeminist discourse by linking her ideas to her behavior and then labeling both "immoral."

In a pattern that continues to the present, much of early antifeminism was both an authentic manifestation of opposition to the dismantling of male supremacy and an effective weapon against women and men seeking larger transformations in social, religious, moral, economic, and political relations. Wollstonecraft and the generations of feminists she inspired have most often been affiliated with radical movements such as abolition, free love, Jacobinism, Perfectionism, Communism, temperance, transcendentalism, antimilitarism, and other less-than-popular causes. These associations have provoked and shaped antifeminist reactions. For example, the anticommunist movements following the world wars utilized often tenuous connections between feminists and communists to condemn both. Near the end of the twentieth century, the U.S. radio personality Rush Limbaugh created the term *feminazi* as an all-encompassing epithet to discredit liberal activist

women. In practice, the two functions of antifeminism, as a means and as an end, have complemented and enhanced one another.

Feminism, Antifeminism, and Difference

At the core of the antifeminist program is the preservation (or reestablishment) of social, economic, and political differences based on gender. The most basic tenet of antifeminism is that the differences between men and women are such that inequalities of treatment and status are desirable or necessary. While the antifeminist position has been clear, feminists have been divided in their approaches to the nature and ramifications of gender differences. Individualist, liberal, or equality feminists have asserted an androgynous view of society and have sought to banish gender differentiation from social, political, and economic structures. In this view, equality is achieved by equal treatment without regard to gender. Difference, social, or relational feminists recognize gender differences (both biological and socially constructed) as of continuing significance, and base their claims for equity (in part) on these differences. The argument from difference emphasizes that utility and justice demand that, because men and women are different, women's interests cannot be represented by men and, therefore, women need to have the opportunity to participate fully in society. Difference feminists have been open, to varying degrees, to differential treatment of men and women in cases where gendered physical or other characteristics are such that equivalence appears more tenable than absolute equality. In practice, many feminists have employed both approaches, basing their opposition to male supremacy on universal human rights as well as uniquely female characteristics or experiences.

Equality feminism and difference feminism have aroused overlapping versions of antifeminism. The antifeminist reactions to equality feminism have mostly been of two types: exclusion and ridicule. By appealing to religion, tradition, science, and nature, antifeminists sought to exclude women from the Enlightenment category of autonomous individuals who should be granted rights. In this view, women lacked the rational capacity and independent nature required of members of society. As the mounting evidence of women's accomplishments and capabilities has made it increasingly difficult to directly dispute women's intelligence and rationality, opponents of equality feminism have turned to the other approach: exaggeration and ridicule. In one example, opponents of the Equal Rights Amendment in the United States equated equal rights for women with mandatory unisex toilet facilities in their successful campaign against ratification.

Ridicule has also been employed against difference feminism, often as part of a larger critique of the "feminization" of society. Because antifeminists and difference feminists share a belief in gender differentiation, their disagreements have centered on the nature of this differentiation, claims to superiority of one gender or the other, and appropriate spheres of participation. Although there is a strain of antifeminism that associates women with dangerous, uncontrolled sexuality, most antifeminists and difference feminists have held a common vision of women as more nurturing and less aggressive than men. Extreme antifeminists have presented this difference as absolute and unalterable, not a matter of degree or environment. On this basis, they have asserted that women are unfit for professions and pursuits demanding an aggressive intellect or personality and, more generally, for the rough-and-tumble of the public spheres of politics and business.

Equality feminists and some difference feminists have countered that gender characteristics vary greatly within each sex, are largely the product of education and opportunity, and that differences will lessen if males and females are treated equally. Other difference feminists, especially those associated with maternalist versions of feminism, have diagnosed the failings of the public sphere as symptoms of aggressive male dominance and prescribed female activism and influence as the cure. Expanded female influence has brought backlash protests against "momism" and the "softening" of individuals, institutions, and cultures informing the men's movement activities of Robert Bly (b. 1926) and others. Complaints about momism and "feminization" expose the antifeminist dimensions of ideas such as republican or national motherhood that celebrate women's abilities and contributions within the circumscribed private realm of the family, simultaneously seeking to limit women's participation in the larger society. When these boundaries have been stretched or broken, the reactionary ridicule has been based on the supposed inappropriateness of female-identified qualities in a shifting array of arenas ranging from education, governance, and the law (primarily in the late nineteenth and early twentieth centuries), to (in the twentieth century) science, police work, and the military.

Nature, Science, Religion, and Antifeminism

Antifeminists have appealed to both religious and scientific authority in defending male supremacy as "natural." The Abrahamic monotheisms (Judaism, Christianity, and Islam), like many of the world's religions, contain contradictions: they grew from liberatory roots but were shaped by the hierarchical and patriarchal environments of the societies they matured in. This is manifested in restrictions on women's actions, movement, contacts, dress, and worship as well as general dictates mandating female obedience. Feminists, ranging from the United States' Matilda Joslyn Gage (1826–1898) in the nineteenth century to Morocco's Fatima Mernissi (b. 1940) in the twenty-first, have identified established religion as a primary source of women's oppression while simultaneously providing feminist interpretations of cardinal religious texts to claim the liberatory traditions for women.

Established religions tend toward antifeminism because they have a vested interest in preserving the status quo. In contrast, religious fundamentalists are generally reactionary outsiders, opposing secular authority as well as conservative and liberal religious practices. Although much scholarship and most popular images portray fundamentalist movements as inherently antifeminist, other scholars and women within these movements have identified ways in which women have used fundamentalism to increase their power and freedom, if not actually to overthrow the male supremacy deeply encoded in most religious traditions. The historical record reveals that fundamentalist regimes, from Puritan Massachusetts to Afghanistan under the Taliban, have imposed severe restrictions on women,

indicating that the feminist potential of religious fundamentalism is limited in practice.

As religion has aided antifeminist appeals to tradition, science and social science have provided more modern justifications for the subjection of women. Scientific antifeminism begins and ends with the assertion that "biology is destiny." Charles Darwin (1809–1882), the pioneer of evolutionary theory, believed that the female's primary role and the focus of her evolutionary adaptations was reproduction. The influential nineteenth-century social philosopher and social scientist Herbert Spencer (1820–1903) held an even dimmer view of women's evolution, asserting that women had not taken part of the final step in human development, the acquisition of the ability to reason. Other scientists and pseudoscientists measured brain size, head bumps, musculature, and other characteristics to delineate women's supposed inferiority.

The belief that women had primarily (if not exclusively) evolved for reproduction was used to caution against their education and participation in almost all activities not directly connected to procreation and nurture. In this view, women who pursued other avenues were going against their nature, risking serious illness and damage to their reproductive capacity. At a time when "race suicide" anxiety was common among Northern and Western Europeans and the colonial project was underway, antifeminists depicted women's neglect of their reproductive nature as a selfish betrayal of their race and nation. The common diagnoses of "hysteria" given to a variety of mental, emotional, and physical symptoms drew on this analysis in that the "disease" was confined to women's childbearing years and was often portrayed as a product of women's inferior, childlike nature. Sigmund Freud (1856–1939), the founder of psychology, extended the (pseudo)scientific discourse on female inferiority by positing a phallocentric view of human nature. These versions of scientific antifeminism have fallen from favor, although echoes of them can still be discerned in discussions of gender difference. More common early in the twenty-first century are utilitarian social science arguments, offering anecdotal and statistical evidence that women who choose not to be wives and mothers are unhappy, that the children of working mothers are damaged, and that society suffers when women pursue any path but motherhood. Intellectual antifeminism in academia ranges from wholesale dismissal of feminist work to less obvious discrimination in publishing and career advancement.

Antifeminism, Patriarchy, Reproduction, and Sexuality

Feminists and antifeminists have staked claims to a range of positions on sexuality and reproduction. It is important to begin with the observation that control of female reproductive labor was the historic object of the establishment of patriarchal forms of male superiority around the globe. In the vast majority of societies, feminism has targeted some form of patriarchal relations, or their vestiges in industrial or industrializing societies. For this reason, control of female reproduction and sexuality have been major antifeminist themes and goals. Patriarchal practices as varied as patrilineal inheritance of property and female genital mutilation have been targeted by feminists and defended by antifeminists. Early feminist activists challenged direct legal manifestations of patriarchy by agitating for married women's property laws, maternal guardianship rights, and the liberalization of divorce statutes. Feminist success, real and perceived, led to a counter "men's rights" movement in the late twentieth century, largely concerned with the divorce-related issues of alimony, child support, and paternal custody rights.

Although not directly addressing reproductive issues, the struggle for political rights and educational and vocational opportunities sought to provide women with alternatives to patriarchal dependency. In each of these cases, antifeminists claimed that the resulting reforms would render women physically and temperamentally unfit for reproduction and motherhood. In the late nineteenth century, Margaret Sanger (1883–1966) and other birth-control advocates addressed reproduction directly in their promotion of contraception as a means to increase women's autonomy. The battles over access to contraception, like the continuing conflicts over abortion rights, divided women's rights advocates to some degree. At base, contraception and abortion are about control of reproduction, but a complex mélange of issues including religion, freedom of speech, medical authority, and female sexual pleasure have shaped the debates.

In these and other contexts, the antifeminist depictions of female sexuality have been multifaceted. Early feminists were often said to be *unsexed*. The exact meaning of this term varies greatly, but it was never used in a positive manner. The related concept of the "masculine woman" is clearer and equally negative in intent. The rhetoric associating feminists with lesbians—accurately and inaccurately—has been a mainstay of antifeminism. This trope has long coexisted with other conflicting stereotypes of feminists as antisex prudes and free-loving (heterosexual) libertines. Although all three have been present throughout the history of antifeminism, their relative popularity has gone through cycles. Perhaps due to the influence of Wollstonecraft, the depiction of feminism as a gateway to sexual license enjoyed an early popularity, but most feminists of the late nineteenth and early twentieth centuries actively espoused respectability. This, in concert with their involvement in the temperance movement and campaigns for social purity, inspired caricatures of feminists as antisexual. The emergence of the "New Woman" and the flapper ideals in the early twentieth century brought back complaints about the loose (heterosexual and homosexual) morals of feminists. The visibility of lesbians in the women's liberation movements of the 1970s inspired new attacks on feminists as sexually deviant "man-haters." In the late twentieth and early twenty-first centuries all three antifeminist tactics have been common. Prominent women with progressive politics are regularly the subjects of whispering campaigns about their homosexuality. In works such as Katie Roiphe's best-selling *The Morning After*, feminism is blamed for creating a puritanical climate of sexual fear, yet it is commonplace for religious activists to condemn feminists for "undermining" the morals of society. Leading antifeminist Phyllis Schlafly has exploited all three: equating feminism with lesbianism, blaming feminists for creating an overly sexualized culture, and taking them to task for their work against rape and pornography. The inconsistency in the antifeminist stance on sexuality is both a reflection of the diversity of feminism and a product of political expediency.

Colonialism, Anticolonialism, and Globalization

The colonial project of the eighteenth, nineteenth, and twentieth centuries was freighted with gender ideologies. One important aspect involved attempts to remake the gender relations of the colonized peoples in the image of Western male supremacy. The diverse societies subjected to colonization had developed unique systems of gender, some more egalitarian than Western norms, some less so. An unintended consequence of the colonial project was the contradictory spread of Western feminist ideas. Just as the official policies were based on a lack of understanding of the traditions and needs of the colonized people, Western feminism betrayed a narrowness of vision and arrogance that created distrust, even among those women who were the intended beneficiaries. This distrust and these misunderstandings continue to plague relations among feminists, creating schisms that have been exploited by antifeminists.

Anticolonial movements provided new but often fleeting opportunities for feminists. In many nations, the flux of revolutionary times combined with the need for the widest possible support created revolutionary nationalist movements open to expansive roles for women, if not always feminist ideas. Women's labor and leadership were celebrated, but in a manner that reinforced traditional images of women as wives and mothers, not as revolutionaries on their own terms, and the success of nationalist movements has often brought a backlash against the feminist women who were once comrades-in-arms. In strategic appeals, former revolutionaries and other local authorities have branded feminism as a Western influence. Feminists in the developing world have increasingly rejected Western models in order to create their own ideologies that are both truer to their experiences and less vulnerable to condemnation on nationalistic and anti-Western grounds.

See also **Discrimination; Diversity; Enlightenment; Equality: Gender Equality; Feminism; Gender; Gender Studies: Anthropology; Human Rights: Women's Rights; Identity: Personal and Social Identity; Motherhood and Maternity; Philosophies: Feminist, Twentieth-Century; Power; Sexuality; Untouchability: Menstrual Taboos; Witchcraft; Women and Femininity in U.S. Popular Culture; Women's Studies.**

BIBLIOGRAPHY

Chafeta, Janet Saltzman, and Anthony Gary Dworkin. "In the Face of Threat: Organized Antifeminism in a Comparative Perspective." *Gender and Society* 1, no. 1 (March 1987): 33–60.

Cott, Nancy F. *The Grounding of Modern Feminism.* London and New Haven, Conn.: Yale University Press, 1987.

Faludi, Susan. *Backlash: The Undeclared War against American Women.* New York: Crown, 1981.

Freedman, Estelle B. *No Turning Back: The History of Feminism and the Future of Women.* New York: Ballantine, 2002.

Gordon, Linda. "What's New in Women's History." In *Feminist Studies/Critical Studies,* edited by Teresa de Lauretis, 20–30. Bloomington: Indiana University Press, 1986.

Howard, Angela, and Sasha Ranae-Adams Tarrant, eds. *Antifeminism in America: A Collection of Readings from the Literature of the Opponents to U.S. Feminism, 1848 to the Present.* 3 vols. New York and London: Garland, 1997.

Kinnard, Cynthia D. *Antifeminism in American Thought: An Annotated Bibliography.* Boston: G. K. Hall, 1986.

Morgan, Robin, ed. *Sisterhood Is Global: The International Women's Movement Anthology.* New York: Feminist Press of the City University of New York, 1996.

Roiphe, Katie. *The Morning After: Sex, Fear, and Feminism on Campus.* New York, Toronto, and London: Little, Brown, 1993.

Schlafly, Phyllis. *Feminist Fantasies.* Dallas: Spence, 2003.

Sommers, Christina Hoff. *Who Stole Feminism: How Women Have Betrayed Women.* New York: Touchstone, 1995.

Thomas J. Mertz

ANTI-SEMITISM.

This entry includes two subentries:

Overview
Islamic Anti-Semitism

OVERVIEW

Anti-Semitism is that hatred of the Jews that defines them as a threat to humankind. The most important contemporary quarrel about anti-Semitism is the issue of its very nature. While some scholars have been insisting for decades that there is no continuing phenomenon of anti-Semitism, arguing on the contrary that "Jew hatred" has reinvented itself many times, others adhere to the contrary opinion, seeing a direct line connecting pre-Christian to modern forms of anti-Semitism.

Origins

Throughout the ages, many peoples have fought one another in the hope of conquering the wealth and land of others, but the antagonists do not usually declare that the existence of their enemy is a danger to the future of all of humankind. Anti-Semitism began in the third century before the beginning of the Christian era. It was defined by Manetho (3rd century B.C.E.), an Egyptian priest who had been substantially influenced by Hellenistic culture. Manetho asserted that the Jews are the enemies of the human race and that it is necessary to remove the Jews from human society. Indeed, a line may be drawn straight from this pre-Christian anti-Semitism of Manetho through the Christian anti-Semitism of ancient and medieval times, to the modern era, when the hatred of Jews was redefined but not essentially changed by secular ideologies.

Manetho's main contention, an obvious rebuttal to the biblical account of the exodus of the Jews from Egypt, is that the Jews did not leave Egypt as the victors in a revolt against the pharaoh who oppressed them. On the contrary, the Jews were expelled from Egypt because they were lepers and, on the side, engaged in nefarious and destructive acts. The Egyptians threw them out into the desert because the Jews endangered the existing civilization of Egypt. They were, in fact, a threat to all

other civilizations, as well. The Jews were therefore not like the Hittites, a powerful enemy with whom the Egyptians kept fighting but who were never regarded as a unique and fundamental threat to society. According to Manetho, the Jews ought to be expelled into the desert or quarantined wherever they appeared or, if these means failed, society as a whole had the right to defend itself by destroying the Jews. Thus, Manetho's "Jew hatred" was not a simple justification of a violent and vehement conflict.

There is a fundamental parallel between some anti-Semitic assessments of the Jews and the angriest descriptions in the Bible of the dangers posed by idolatry. This competing faith must be totally isolated and the idol worshipers must be walled off from the Jewish society, or utterly destroyed. So, in earliest times, the enemies of the Jews had no monopoly on the idea that a competing faith or way of life might be defined as so dangerous as not to merit the right to survive.

The Roman Empire

The basic "Jew hatred" as defined by Manetho was expanded by a number of Greek or Roman writers, historians, and statesmen. To be sure, not all Hellenistic literature in its two languages, Greek and Latin, was dominated by anti-Semitism. Some writers admired the steadfastness of the Jews and their continuing search for righteousness and social justice—but the majority of the Hellenistic creative forces were arrayed against the Jews.

Within a century or so, the issues came to a head over the large number of Gentiles who became converts, or who wanted to become converts, to Judaism. The Pharisees insisted that all converts to Judaism were joining "a new and godly commonwealth" (Baron, 1983, vol. 1, p. 181). This definition offered by Philo Judaeus (c. 13 B.C.E.–between 45 and 50 C.E.), the leading Jewish intellectual figure of the first century B.C.E., was accepted to mean that a new convert was classified as a child who was now newly born as a Jew. This conversion meant that he disavowed his previous family, for according to Philo, such proselytes "have left their country, their kinfolk and their friends and their relations for sacred virtue and holiness" (Baron, 1983, vol. 1, p. 181). A generation later Cornelius Tacitus (c. 56–c. 120 C.E.) made the same point but he expressed it in the language of a pronounced distemper with the Jews. Once they became converts to Judaism, they "despised the gods, disowned their own country and regard their parents, children and brothers as of little account" (Baron, 1983, vol. 5, p. 182). As the Jews became more numerous and more powerful throughout the Roman Empire, Tacitus considered the Jews as subversive because they were the enemies of the three main pillars of society: religion, country, and family (Baron, 1983, vol. 5, p. 194).

In this outlook Tacitus was following the Stoic philosopher Lucius Annaeus Seneca (14 B.C.E.?–65 C.E.): "The customs of that most criminal nation have gained such strength that they are now received in all lands. The conquered have given laws to the conquerors" (Baron, 1983, vol. 5, p. 191; quoted from *De superstitione* by Augustine in his *City of God,* 6:11). The same point had been argued by Marcus Tullius Cicero

(106–43 B.C.E.), the supreme orator of Rome, a generation earlier:

> Even while Jerusalem was standing and the Jews were at peace with us, the practice of their sacred rites was at variance with the glory of our empire, the dignity of our name, the customs of our ancestors. But now it is even more so, when that nation by its armed resistance has shown what it thinks of our rule. (Baron, 1983, vol. 5, p. 192: quoting Cicero's defense in *Pro Flacco*, 28:69)

But the best summary of the anti-Semitism that recurs in major Hellenistic figures is present in the Book of Esther, the biblical account of the victory of the Jews over Haman, their archenemy in the Persian Court. This book was probably composed in the third century B.C.E. or perhaps even a bit later. Haman's arguments against the Jews are addressed to King Ahasuerus:

> "There is a certain people, scattered and dispersed among the other peoples in all the provinces of your realm, whose laws are different from those of any other people and who do not obey the king's laws; and it is not in Your Majesty's interest to tolerate them. If it please Your Majesty, let an edict be drawn for their destruction, and I will pay ten thousand talents of silver to the stewards for deposit in the royal treasury." Thereupon the king removed his signet ring from his hand and gave it to Haman son of Hammedatha the Agagite, the foe of the Jews. (Esther 3:8–10)

In these brief verses the essential, classic doctrine of anti-Semitism is summarized: the Jews are different from everybody else; their very existence is an assault on the accepted standards of religion and good conduct. It would be best for the Persian Empire if the Jews were utterly removed. Anti-Semitism has now been defined as the doctrine by which all of the rest of human society can defend itself against the arrogance of Jewish monotheism.

Nonetheless, the question remained very much alive in the consciousness of the Roman Empire in the first century: What is one to do with the Jews? Clearly they would not obey the laws that Rome imposed on all of its own people. Jews refused to participate in civic celebrations because these invariably required worship of the gods and especially of the Roman emperors as gods. The Roman rulers in Alexandria, and even more in Judea, made allowances for the peculiar stubbornness of the Jews, but there were recurring clashes between Jews and the Roman authorities. These issues could not be resolved through negotiation between Jews and imperial officials. On the contrary, the Jews themselves had to find room for living in the larger society. So their traditions had to be changed.

By the middle of the second century after the suppression of the last great Jewish revolt under Bar Kokhba (131–135), the leading rabbis no longer expected a restoration of the Temple in Jerusalem and of Jewish sovereignty in the Holy Land. They made peace with the notion that the Messiah would come at some future date and redeem the Jews from exile and powerlessness, but the date was unknown and unpredictable. The Jews had to make peace with the notion that they would live as a minority among other religions.

The capital of Palestine was de facto in Caesarea, the port city from which the Roman Empire controlled all of its various subjects in Palestine. Rabbinic Judaism also had its headquarters in Caesarea, where the court of its religious leadership, headed by the descendants of Hillel, was situated. The leader in the last years of the first century and the beginning years of the second century C.E. was Rabban Gamaliel II. He regularly made use of the public bathhouse in Acre, even though entering that building required that he walk under an arch that was adorned at its apex by an image of the goddess Aphrodite. Gamaliel's critics regarded his use of the bathhouse as a form of worship of the pagan goddess. He responded that, of course, he intended no such conduct. The image of the goddess served a purely civic function at the entrance of the bathhouse, which was a facility that belonged equally to all the citizens of the region, including Jews.

Rabban Gamaliel II defended his conduct as religiously neutral, but soon those who defined rabbinic law went further. Later rabbis ruled that Jews were commanded to visit the sick even among the idolaters, to bury their dead together with the Jewish dead, and to support their poor among the Jewish poor. In the Middle Ages, these rabbinic rules were summarized by Moses Ben Maimon (Maimonides; 1135–1204) in his *Code of Jewish Law,* in the section on political law in what is written in the Hilkhot Melakhim (10:12). All of this was to be done "for the sake of peace" because it was written in Scripture that "God is good to everyone and His mercy extended to all of His creatures." It was said further that "its ways [that is, the ways of Torah] are the ways of grace and all its paths are peace." To be sure, these are not the only rabbinic opinions. There are many counterviews in the Talmud that Jews must maintain distance from non-Jews, but the more giving rulings suggest that Jews were looking for ways of accommodating themselves to a society that they had little hope of controlling or of converting to the Jewish faith.

Nonetheless, despite the rulings of the more liberal rabbis, the distance between Jews and non-Jews remained. These descendants of the Pharisees could never give up the notion that their religion was God's true teaching and that, at some unpredictable moment, the whole world would come to Mount Zion to be received and converted to the one true faith, the monotheism that Abraham had once proclaimed.

Christianity and Anti-Semitism

How could the Jewish religion be redefined so that it became a possible and even quickly accessible faith for all of humankind? The answer was devised by the first two or three generations of those who had adhered to the person and teaching of an itinerant Jewish preacher, Jesus of Nazareth. Despite centuries of thought and scholarly research, what Jesus himself believed is still not clear. The weight of the evidence is that Jesus regarded himself as a Jew who had come to wrest the leadership of his people from the priests who dominated in the affairs of the Temple and the Pharisees who had seized the initiative in defining the laws by which Jews were urged to live. In a few decades after his crucifixion, the religious leadership passed to a much more radical Jewish thinker, Saul of Tarsus (St. Paul; d. between 62 and 68 C.E.), who opened Judaism to all the non-Jews of the world without requiring that they accept the rituals and all the many restrictions that the rabbis had defined.

In its very beginnings Christianity could not choose the path that had been suggested by Manetho and elaborated by the pagan Hellenists, that Jews were by their very nature beyond redemption. On the contrary, Saul of Tarsus asserted in Romans 9 that Christianity was a shoot grafted on to the tree of Jesse, that is, that Christianity was the true offshoot of Judaism—if only the Jews would accept the truth of their religion as it was now being expounded by those of them who had become Christian believers.

Even more fundamentally, Christianity could not present itself as a universal religion that was setting out to convert the whole world. It demanded only that those who joined it should include themselves in the transforming faith in Jesus, who had died for sins of humankind. How could anyone be excluded from this transforming faith and the salvation that it offered each individual? And yet, as the church fathers saw with bitter dismay, the Jews did not behave according to the Christian theological plan. Jesus had been born among them, but the Jews were obdurate. Their majority refused to accept the truth that appeared among them. To the church fathers, it was unthinkable that the divine message was unclear or, worse still, that the Jews understood the message but rejected it.

By the middle of the second century, church fathers such as Saint Justin (Justin Martyr, c. 100–c. 165), writing in Greek, and half a century later, Tertullian (c. 155 or 160–after 220 C.E.), writing in Latin, were critical of the Jews for not having accepted Christ. Within a hundred years, especially after Emperor Constantine (ruled 306–337) proclaimed Christianity the state religion of Rome, later church fathers were offering an explanation for the obduracy of the Jews: they were too strongly in the grip of Satan, who had commandeered the synagogues and instructed the rabbis; the Jews could not see the truth of Christianity because they were now led by the enemy of God, the supreme anti-Christ. They were referred to as the "Synagogue of Satan" in *Revelations* 2:9 and 3:9. Two things could be done: Jews could be persecuted as the enemies of truth or the effort to convert them could be redoubled, over and over again, to persuade them to abandon their wrongheadedness. In this very early Christian explanation that the Jews were now "the synagogue of Satan" their otherness was explained, and the path was prepared that could lead to pronouncing the Jews to be totally dangerous to the rest of humankind—and all of this on the basis of Christian theology. Manetho had decided that the Jews were dangerous to the health of humankind because they were lepers; the earliest church fathers defined a different metaphor—the Jews were a threat to the souls of men and women because they were Satan's disciples in leading them away from divine truth. Thus,

the Christian relationship to Jews was defined as a paradox: the culmination of the triumph of the new faith would be in its conversion of the Jews, but the tasks of achieving this glorious time would be enormously difficult, because it involved direct war with Satan himself.

Early Christianity found a compromise between the two alternatives—that the Jews had to survive until they accepted Jesus and that they were by their very nature the hopelessly wicked "synagogue of Satan"—by asserting both alternatives: the Jews could not be totally obliterated, for there would be no one left to represent them at the end of days when they would finally accept the Christian truth, but society had to be defended against the Jews or it would be hopelessly corrupted. Further elucidations of this basic paradox included the permission to keep Jews alive by allowing them to perform pariah tasks that were forbidden to Christians, such as lending money at interest, but the notion that those who had condemned Christ deserved the most severe punishment was never abandoned.

Since living Jews were the enemies of truth, they could be blamed for everything that went wrong in society. So, early in the fifteenth century, when Europe was swept by the Black Plague, which killed perhaps a quarter of the population, it seemed self-evident that this scourge was brought on the Christian majority by the small Jewish minority, which was full of hate and anger. It also seemed self-evident that the possessions of the Jews had been acquired by deception and by stealing from the Christians. It was, therefore, logical and even lawful to treat them like a kind of sponge; whatever possessions they had could be confiscated by the ruling power. In the course of the Middle Ages, there was hardly a place in Europe that had not expelled the Jews and forced them to leave without any resources with which to live. Nonetheless, the myth remained that in the divine plan Jews or at least some of them needed to be kept alive so their acceptance of the true Christianity would be the dramatic act that would point to the end of days. Some historians call this medieval version of hatred of Jews "anti-Judaism" rather than "anti-Semitism." It was only late in the Middle Ages that Christian anti-Semitism came close to completing its ideological journey by asserting that the Jews were hopelessly dangerous always, even after they might convert to Christianity.

Conversos

The largest Jewish community in Europe in the fourteenth and fifteenth centuries existed on the Iberian Peninsula, the southern half of which was then controlled and ruled by Muslim states and the central and northern half by Christians. Jews were a significant minority in both these regions of Spain. They were especially important to the Christians who wanted to force them to convert and thus strengthen the Christian majority in the region. At the end of the fourteenth century, the Christians did succeed in forcing Jews to convert by the tens of thousands. In a century or so, the number of such converts grew until the climax in 1492, when the combined kingdom of Aragon and Castile, under the joint rule of Ferdinand and Isabella, confronted the Jews with a stark choice: either convert to Christianity or leave the land of their Christian majesties. A quarter million Jews then still remained in all the lands of Christian Spain; the larger half accepted conversion, and the rest left, hoping to find some refuge in places where Jews were allowed to live openly, or semiopenly, as Jews.

There were many forces that led to this decree of conversion or expulsion, but the economic motive was dominant. Many of the Jews in Spain had made their way into the middle class and even beyond, so their Christian competitors presumed that the increasingly prominent Jewish role in Iberian commerce could be ended by forcing them to become Christians. The Jews would redistribute themselves in such fashion that they would no longer be dominant in trade and commerce. None of this happened. On the contrary, the "new Christians" used their new privileges to become not only more major figures in banking and the ownership of land; they also intermarried, quite rapidly, with high figures in the nobility and rose to predominant positions in the state, the army, and even in the Church. Some Jews thought it would be safer to move to the Spanish colonies in the New World. In the middle of the seventeenth century, Spain had developed its rule in South America through the viceroyalty of Lima in Peru. At one moment in those years the viceroy and the archbishop were both descendants, at least in part, of "new Christians," and so, Lima was known mockingly as *La Juderia*. The Inquisition redoubled its efforts in Peru and Mexico, the main centers of Spanish rule, to suppress Marranos (that is, new Christians who actually or supposedly practiced Judaism in secret).

But the "new Christians" remained powerful. The way had to be found to make these converts from Judaism into second-class citizens or worse. At the beginning of the fifteenth century the doctrine was invented of *Limpieza de Sangre* (purity of blood). It first became law in Toledo in 1449 and restrictions were widely adopted: those who could not prove that all four of their grandparents were "old Christians" were denied roles in government or in the Church. The taint that Jewish blood now brought with it was not different from Manetho's insistence nearly two thousand years earlier that Jews were lepers and thus infectious beings. Anti-Semitism had changed on the surface, but its basic thrust had remained the same. The Jews are a lasting danger to the majority.

Modern Anti-Semitism

The major shift in the definition of anti-Semitism occurred in the eighteenth and nineteenth centuries, when Christianity was largely pushed aside among educated Europeans by the doctrines of the Enlightenment. The dominant cliché since the eighteenth century has been that the Enlightenment ushered in the age of equality of all religions and ethnic identities. This is largely true, but the most ideological wing of the Enlightenment asserted its own version of *Limpieza de Sangre*. The dominant figure in European letters in the second half of the eighteenth century was Voltaire (1694–1778). He paid some lip service to the notion that all people could be perfected including perhaps even the hardest case of all, some Jews, but his basic position was that the Jews were born with fanaticism in their hearts as Bretons were born with blond hair. It was not strange for Voltaire to assert such a view because he had

Le Petit Journal **illustration of Alfred Dreyfus being stripped of his rank (1895).** Dreyfus, a French army captain of Jewish descent, was accused of selling military secrets to the Germans. He was not exonerated and released from incarceration until 1906. © LEONARD DE SELVA/CORBIS

himself defined negroes as not human beings; they were an intermediate stage between humans and monkeys. Voltaire and those who followed after him, such as Paul-Henri-Dietrich d'Holbach (1723–1789) and, to some degree, Denis Diderot (1713–1784), thus solved the problem of what to do about the Jews by declaring it to be a question of how to defend the bulk of humanity against a dangerous infection that was carried by people who looked human but really were alien.

This notion appeared during the debates of the era of the French Revolution in the writings and decisions of the most radical Jacobins who asserted, both in Paris and in eastern France, that giving the Jews equality was simply to make it more possible for them to realize their nefarious plots under more respectable cover. In the next half century or so, after the revolutionary era, some of the greatest figures of the European left (such as Pierre-Joseph Proudhon, Charles Fourier, and even Karl Marx) argued, often quoting Voltaire, that the Jews were a danger and that the Jews themselves had to be saved from their Jewish identity for their own sake and for the sake of humankind.

Jewish man forced by Nazis to ride in open cart, c. 1935. Under Hitler, Jews were legally classified as a separate race and forced to endure many types of public humiliation, such as wearing a yellow Star of David for identification purposes. © HULTON-DEUTSCH COLLECTION/CORBIS

This doctrine of many of the radical Enlightenment thinkers was appropriated by the nationalists who took over European literature and political thought in the middle years of the nineteenth century. Their image of a nation was that it represented the purity of an older culture, and therefore, aliens who had not shared in that history had no role. Jews were certainly viewed as aliens from Asia who did not belong within any of the European nations. With variations, this doctrine became part of the thinking of the pan-Germans and the pan-Slavs, and of other European nationalists.

Toward the end of the nineteenth century at least three versions of anti-Semitism were very virulent in Europe. In tsarist Russia where some six million Jews, at least half of those in the world at the time, lived, the dominant form of anti-Semitism was based on many centuries of Christian hatred. In the last fifty years of its existence, the absolute rule of the tsars found it useful to deflect the angers of the poor by blaming the Jews as the source of all the troubles in Russia. In 1881–1882, pogroms swept through the realm and a mass migration of Jews fled the kingdom. Most of these refugees went west to America, but some were the first founders of the new Zionist settlement in Palestine. But even in tsarist Russia, where the ruling class and especially the tsars themselves were believing Christians of the old school, other, more modern forms of anti-Semitism contributed to the persecution of the Jews. Many of the archenemies of the tsarist regime nonetheless blamed the Jews. The new revolutionaries saw the uprising of the poor against the Jews as a movement to be supported because the Jews—so the revolutionaries argued—were the capitalist oppressors of the poor of Russia. By the last decades of the nineteenth century, pan-Slavism was also gaining strength and importance in eastern Europe and especially in Russia. The essential doctrine of this movement was that the Slavs had been chosen by history, and probably by God himself, to be the superior people of all of humankind. Obviously, the ancient Jewish claim to closeness had long been nullified, and those who would maintain this claim were troublemakers, or worse.

These various assaults on the Jews were given prominence, and special bitterness, in the last years of the century by the appearance of the book *The Protocols of the Elders of Zion*. This book was, of course, a forgery that was concocted by agents of the tsarist secret police probably working in Paris, which was then the intellectual capital of Europe. In the *Protocols* all the forms of anti-Semitism were combined: Jewish capitalists and Jewish revolutionaries were actually engaged—so the authors of the *Protocols* maintained—in a joint endeavor to undermine the civilization and culture of the European majority. The capitalist, Lord Rothschild, and the socialist Jews, who were trying to assassinate the tsar, pretended to hate each other, but this was not the truth. They were really partners in the immemorial Jewish enterprise, to undermine society in order to control it. The ultimate battle in the world was between those who would defend the majority culture and their immemorial enemies, the Jews. The *Protocols* have been repeatedly discredited as a fantasy, but this book has been reprinted in a variety of languages and continues to be read and believed by anti-Semites all over the world, including the newest recruits to the "great hatred" in the Muslim world and in Japan.

The essence of post-Christian anti-Semitism was a restatement of pre-Christian Hellenistic Jew hatred. In the middle of the eighteenth century, a second-level scholar and leader of the Enlightenment in France, the Count Jean-Baptiste de Mirabaud, had published a book of citations from Greek and Latin authors (*Opinion des anciens sur les Juifs,* 1769) in which the Jews were denounced as alien to European society and a danger to its future. This theme was carried forward in the next century and the one thereafter, to naturalize anti-Semitism in the rhetoric of both pre-Christian and post-Christian times. To be sure these attacks also derived some nourishment from Christian theology but this was not the essence of modern anti-Semitism. It was not necessary to denounce the Jews as Christ-killers; the charge of leprosy in various permutations was more than enough.

Nazi Anti-Semitism

The heyday of anti-Semitism, its ultimate climax, came with the rise of Nazism. Adolf Hitler and those who followed him were certain that they were engaged in a great and unavoidable task, the defense of European civilization against all forms of subversion by the Jews. Hitler's ultimate vision of the world was that it was poised on the verge of an ultimate war in which the Jews had to be destroyed. There was no longer any pretense that some Jews might be redeemable: this was now a war to the death. The results are well known. The overwhelming majority of the Jewish population of Europe, to the number of six million men, women, and children, were systematically murdered. The rest were saved only because Hitler and his allies lost the war. Nonetheless, the Nazis did not entirely lose their fierce war with the Jews.

The assault in the 1940s destroyed the most creative elements of the world Jewish community in the middle of the twentieth century. It changed the face of Europe, which was no longer a main center of Jewish life and creativity. More subtly, the emphasis within Jewish life has for the last half century been more on fighting off the attempt to destroy the Jews than it has centered on recreating the religious and cultural values that were destroyed. In the early twenty-first century those concerns were only beginning to be at the center of Jewish endeavors. Thus, Hitler's greatest success was to make of the Jews a people much more frightened for its future than it had been in the previous century.

After the victory in 1945 in World War II, Jews—and people of good will everywhere—thought that anti-Semitism would fade away. But anti-Semitism has not disappeared and in some parts of the world it is even more powerful than ever before. Society as a whole has not yet accepted the idea that those who will not play by its conventional rules are nonetheless entitled to a life of freedom and dignity. The question that was posed more than three thousand years ago, whether the Jews had a right to survive in a society that did not agree with the premises on which much of Jewish religion and culture is based, is still very much open. Will the societies that remember their pasts as Christians and Muslims make room for Jews? We cannot yet be sure.

See also **Christianity; Judaism; Prejudice; Toleration.**

BIBLIOGRAPHY

Baron, Salo W. *The Russian Jew under Tsars and Soviets.* 2nd edition, rev. and enl. New York: Schocken, 1987.

———. *A Social and Religious History of the Jews.* 8 vols. 2nd edition, rev. and enl. New York: Columbia University Press, 1983.

Gager, John G.. *The Origins of Anti-Semitism: Attitudes toward Judaism in Pagan and Christian Antiquity.* New York: Oxford University Press, 1983.

Hertzberg, Arthur: *The French Enlightenment and the Jews.* New York: Columbia University Press, 1968.

Katz, Jacob. *Exclusiveness and Tolerance: Studies in Jewish-Gentile Relations in Medieval and Modern Times.* 1961. Reprint, Westport, Conn.: Greenwood Press, 1980.

Langmuir, Gavin I. *History, Religion, and Antisemitism.* Berkeley: University of California Press, 1990.

Parkes, James. *The Conflict of the Church and Synagogue.* 1934. Reprint, New York: Hermon Press, 1974.

Poliakov, León. *The History of Anti-Semitism.* 4 vols. Philadelphia: University of Pennsylvania Press, 2003.

Pultzer, Peter G. J. *The Rise of Political Anti-Semitism in Germany and Austria.* New York: Wiley, 1964.

Tcherikover, Victor. *Hellenistic Civilization and the Jews.* 1959. Translated by S. Applebaum. Reprint, Peabody, Mass.: Hendrickson, 1999.

Trachtenberg, Joshua. *The Devil and the Jews: The Medieval Conception of the Jew and its Relation to Modern Antisemitism.* 1943. Reprint, Philadelphia: Jewish Publication Society, 1993.

Zimmerman, Moshe. *Wilhelm Marr, the Patriarch of Antisemitism.* New York: Oxford University Press, 1986.

Arthur Hertzberg

ISLAMIC ANTI-SEMITISM

Anti-Semitism became in the late twentieth century an integral part of Islamic and, particularly, Arab cultural discourse. Like other modern intellectual and political movements, such as nationalism, socialism, and fascism, anti-Semitism is a European import of fairly recent vintage into the Muslim world.

Traditional Islamic Attitudes

As in the case of Christianity, fundamental Islamic attitudes toward Jews and Judaism go back to the historical circumstances surrounding the founding of the new faith and are sanctioned by scripture and tradition. Jews figure into traditional Islam's theological worldview, and Jews lived as a subject population under Muslim rule, sometimes under better, sometimes under worse conditions. However, because Islam did not begin as a sect within Judaism or claim to be *verus* Israel (or the "true" Israel), as did Christianity, the Koran and later theological writings (with the exception of the Sira, or canonical biography of the Prophet Muhammad) do not exhibit anything comparable to the overwhelming preoccupation with the Jews that one finds in the New Testament, patristic literature, and later Christian theological writings.

Traditional Islamic thought had its own store of negative stereotypes of Jews. According to the Koran (Sura 2:61), "wretchedness and baseness were stamped upon them, and they were visited with wrath from Allah." The Koran, exegetical,

Edition of *Mein Kampf* translated into Arabic. In the late nineteenth century, anti-Semitic tracts and books began to appear, many of which were translations of existing works. Adolf Hitler's *Mein Kampf* was translated into Arabic in 1935, after careful editing removed the anti-Arabic sentiments within. © HULTON-DEUTSCH COLLECTION/CORBIS

and hagiographic literature brand the Jews of Medina as having been the principal opponents of the Prophet along with the idolaters and as a treacherous lot. But they were also people who had received a genuine divine revelation, like the Christians and Zoroastrians, and like the latter deserved tolerance as long as they accepted the status of humble tributary *dhimmis* ("protected peoples"). Though the image of Jews was on the whole even more negative and condescending than that of Christians, they shared the same legal status within the traditional Islamic social system, and throughout most of the fourteen hundred years of Islamic history were rarely singled out for greater discrimination than other non-Muslims. The relatively rare instances of specifically anti-Jewish violence often occurred when a Jew was perceived to have egregiously transgressed the boundaries of proper conduct by rising too high in the bureaucracy. Anti-Jewish rioting only became a more frequent phenomenon in the twentieth century in the Arab parts of the Muslim world with the anti-Jewish sentiments generated by Zionism and European colonialism.

Introduction of European Anti-Semitic Ideas in the Nineteenth Century

Modern anti-Semitic ideas made their first appearance in the Middle East among the Arabic-speaking Christians of Syria, who maintained commercial, educational, and cultural ties with the European nations making ever stronger inroads into the region during the nineteenth century. French merchants and missionaries seem to have played a principal role in this process. The classic European notion of the blood libel gained widespread circulation in the Levant after the notorious Damascus Affair of 1840 when the French consul, Count Benoît Ulysse de Ratti-Menton, accused the Damascene Jewish community of having kidnapped and murdered a Capuchin friar for the Passover ritual. The case became an international cause célèbre, and for several months Ratti-Menton received support

from the local Muslim authorities. The memory of the Damascus Affair was preserved by local Christians, but for a long time thereafter, anti-Semitic ideas, whether of the medieval or modern, post-Enlightenment varieties, made little or no headway among the vast majority of Arab and non-Arab Muslims. Anti-Semitic articles appeared occasionally in the late-nineteenth-century Syrian and Egyptian Arabic press in which Christians were prominent. Arabic anti-Semitic books and pamphlets also made their appearance at this time. Again, these were mainly by Christian authors and were frequently translations or adaptations of European works such as August Rohling's *The Talmudic Jew,* which was published in Egypt in 1899 under the title *al-Kanz al-Marsud fi Qawàid al-Talmud* (The guarded treasure of the principles of the Talmud). These early works laid the foundations for a very extensive literature in the twentieth century when the attitudes of the Muslim majority toward Jews became radically altered. Rohling's *The Talmudic Jew* has enjoyed enduring popularity in Arabic, has been reprinted a number of times, and has inspired numerous other books, as for example, Muhammad abri's *al-Talmud: Shari'at al-Yahud* (The Talmud: The religious law of the Jews).

Evolution of Islamic Anti-Semitism in the Twentieth Century

The Axis gained widespread sympathy in the Islamic world during the 1930s and 1940s because they were the enemies of the Western colonial powers and Western democratic values. Turkish, Arab, and Iranian nationalists admired German militarism. Nazi and Fascist propaganda helped familiarize educated Muslims with the vocabulary of modern anti-Semitism. *Mein Kampf* appeared in an Arabic translation in 1935 with its anti-Arab statements expunged. However, most of the Arabic literature that imitates Nazi Jew-baiting tracts dates from the postwar period.

No work has had a more profound impact upon modern Muslim anti-Semitism than the *Protocols of the Elders of Zion,* written in Paris at the end of the nineteenth century for the tsarist secret police and allegedly the secret minutes of a Jewish conspiracy for world domination. Although it was already being cited by Arab nationalists in Iraq and Palestine in the early 1920s, the complete text first appeared in Cairo in 1925 as *Mu'amarat al-yahudiyya 'ala'l-Shu'ub* (The Jewish conspiracy against the nations), translated by Antun Yamin, a Lebanese Maronite. This was the first of a long line of Arabic editions and translations, and the book has been a continual bestseller throughout the entire Arab and Muslim world. The *Protocols* have been quoted, praised, and recommended by politicians, academics, and religious leaders. The principal idea of the *Protocols* about an international Zionist-Jewish conspiracy is repeated in everything from television series to religious literature and has become a fundamental tenet of the Islamic fundamentalist worldview, both Sunni and Shiite. Ayatollah Khomeini, for example, writes in his *Vilayet-i Faqih: Hokumati Islami* (1971; The trusteeship of the jurisconsult: Islamic governance) that the true aim of the Jews "is to establish a world Jewish government." This and other notions from the *Protocols* may be found in the writings of Moroccan Islamist Sheikh Abdessalam Yassine, the Tunisian theologian Rached

Ghannouchi, and in the publications of the Muslim Brotherhood, Hamas, Hizbollah, al-Jama'a al-Islamiyya, and Al Qaeda.

Contemporary Islamists cite proof texts from the Koran and hadith to corroborate the *Protocols*. The widely disseminated writings of the Egyptian philosopher Sayyid Qub probably played an influential role in the spread of this harmonization of the *Protocols* and Islamic traditional texts.

The numerous humiliating defeats of Arab armies at the hands of tiny Israel, the strong relationship between the Jewish State and the United States, and the general social, technological, and political weakness of the Islamic world as a whole, despite the great oil wealth of some Islamic nations, have all contributed to the credence given by many Muslims to the notion of the invisible hand of a Zionist-Jewish cabal as depicted in the *Protocols*.

Though less a general belief among contemporary Muslims than the Jewish conspiracy for world domination, the blood libel has come to have wide circulation in the late twentieth and early twenty-first centuries, especially in the Arab world. Even ostensibly scholarly treatments of Judaism such as 'Ala 'Abd al-Wahid Wafi's *al-Yahudiyya wa'l-Yahud* (1970; Judaism and the Jews) and Hasan Zaza in his *al-Fikr al-Dini al-Isra'ili: At-waruhu wa Madhahibuhu* (1971; Israelite religious thought: Its phases and schools) present the blood libel as fact. Zaza devotes a learned discussion to the blood libel observing that such a practice is forbidden by Jewish law, but then notes that the accusation has followed the Jews throughout history, that people often act contrarily to their religious teachings, and finally cites the confessions of one of the accused murderers in the Damascus Affair as proof of the veracity of charge. Blood libel stories appear from time to time in the mainstream Arabic press as both features and news items. Syrian defense minister Mustafa Tlas has written one of the best selling books promoting the blood libel, *Fatir Sahyun* (The matzah of Zion). The book went into eight editions between 1983 and 2002, with the last alone selling over twenty thousand copies. As with the conspiracy of the *Protocols*, blood libel stories have been featured in Arabic television dramatizations during the nights of Ramadan in 2003.

See also **Anti-Semitism: Overview; Fundamentalism; Jihad; Law, Islamic.**

BIBLIOGRAPHY

Kepel, Gilles. *Muslim Extremism in Egypt: The Prophet and Pharoah.* Translated by Jon Rothschild. Berkeley and Los Angeles: University of California Press, 1985.

Lewis, Bernard, *Semites and Anti-Semites: An Inquiry into Conflict and Prejudice.* New York and London: Norton, 1986.

Stillman, Norman A. "Antisemitism in the Contemporary Arab World." In *Antisemitism in the Contemporary World,* edited by Michael Curtis. Boulder, Colo., and London: Westview Press, 1986.

———. *The Jews of Arab Lands: A History and Source Book.* Philadelphia: The Jewish Publication Society, 1979.

———. *The Jews of Arab Lands in Modern Times.* Philadelphia: The Jewish Publication Society, 1991.

Norman A. Stillman

APARTHEID. *Apartheid,* an Afrikaans word meaning "apartness," describes an ideology of racial segregation that served as the basis for white domination of the South African state from 1948 to 1994. Apartheid represented the codification of the racial segregation that had been practiced in South Africa from the time of the Cape Colony's founding by the Dutch East India Company in 1652. Its emergence in 1948 was antithetical to the decolonization process begun in sub-Saharan Africa after World War II. Widely perceived internationally as one of the most abhorrent human rights issues from the 1970s to the 1990s, apartheid conjured up images of white privilege and black marginalization implemented by a police state that strictly enforced black subordination.

Historical Background

The Dutch East India Company occupied the Cape Colony uninterruptedly from 1652 until the British takeover in 1795. The company's conflict with the indigenous Khoisan was exacerbated by its granting of farmland to company members who had completed their term of service. The Khoisan, who became indentured servants, were landless by the time of the British occupation. Slaves were imported from Asia and elsewhere in Africa throughout the eighteenth century. Briefly restored to Dutch rule in 1803, the colony was again brought under British control in 1806. Two events to which Dutch settlers reacted negatively were the British abolition of the slave trade in 1806 and of slavery in 1833. The latter precipitated the Great Trek, in which many Dutch (Afrikaner) farmers migrated outside the Cape Colony.

A "mineral revolution," financed by British capital, began in South Africa with the discovery of diamonds in Kimberley in 1868 and gold in Johannesburg in 1886. Later the British victory in the Boer War (1899–1902) brought the Transvaal and the Orange Free State under British rule. Natal was already a British colony. Collectively the four colonies formed the Union of South Africa in 1910.

Afrikaners, who suffered military defeat in the war, displayed intense anti-British sentiment as many of their farms were destroyed and their wives and children placed in concentration camps, resulting in a high mortality rate. Their efforts to increase their population contributed to proletarianization, precipitating their migration to cities for employment. They often became squatters alongside poor blacks. In 1928–1932 the Carnegie Corporation conducted a study of the "poor white problem" and made recommendations for improving the status of working-class Afrikaners. During that period, Afrikaans, a Dutch variant, became a written language. Members of the emerging Afrikaner bourgeoisie opened the first Afrikaner bank and insurance company.

Rise of Afrikaner Nationalism

After the Boer War, two Afrikaner generals, Jan Smuts and Louis Botha, sought conciliation with the British in forming the South African Party. Supporters also included enfranchised blacks. The South African Party defeated the Unionist Party in the 1910 elections. Cognizant of eroding political rights, members of the black educated elite formed the South African Native National Congress (later the African National Congress) in 1912. Racist legislation enacted during this period of "fusion" included the

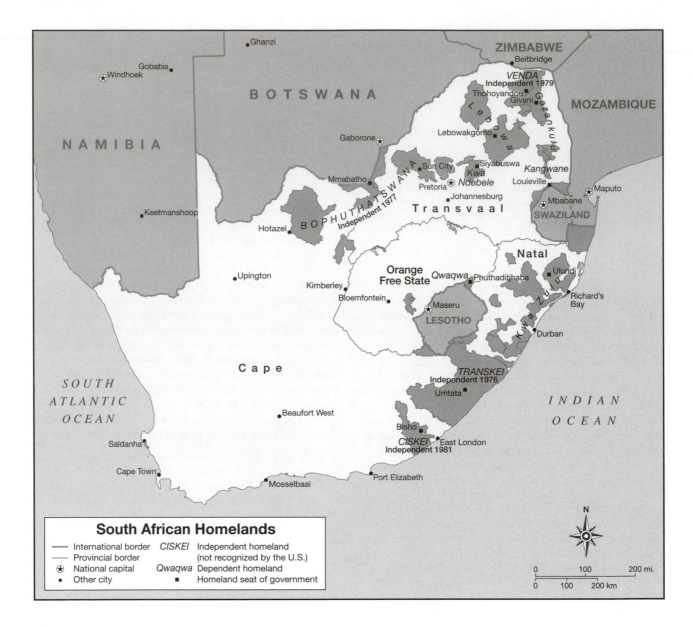

South African Homelands

— International border
— Provincial border
⊛ National capital
• Other city

CISKEI Independent homeland (not recognized by the U.S.)
Qwaqwa Dependent homeland
■ Homeland seat of government

1913 Land Act, which prohibited a type of sharecropping called farming-on-the-half, in which black sharecroppers negotiated with white farmers to farm part of the latter's land. Furthermore, blacks could not own land outside of designated areas.

Another Afrikaner general, J. B. M. Hertzog, led dissidents against a South African alliance with the British in World War I. A schism developed between Smuts and Hertzog over South African involvement in World War II, signaling the end of fusion. It was then that Hertzog advocated a South African republic outside the British Commonwealth. Further racist legislation included:

The Urban Areas Act of 1923, which legislated urban racial segregation, discouraging blacks from becoming town-rooted.

The Industrial Reconciliation Act of 1926, which introduced job protections for poor whites.

The 1936 Land Act, which reinforced the 1913 Land Act and designated homelands as areas for African land ownership.

A 1936 decree that struck Africans in the Cape Province from the common voters' roll.

The historian T. Dunbar Moodie has suggested that Afrikaner nationalism was a civil religion representing the integration of key symbolic elements. These include major events in Afrikaner history, the Afrikaans language, and Dutch Calvinism. From Moodie's perspective, Afrikaners viewed their history in terms of a repeating suffering-and-death cycle at the hands of the British through major events such as the Great Trek and the Boer War. The Broederbond, a secret society composed of Afrikaner professionals, formed the Federation of Afrikaner Cultural Organizations (FAK), affiliating cultural and language associations as well as church councils, youth groups, and scientific study circles in 1929.

Segregated bathrooms in Johannesburg, South Africa, 1984.
When the National Party came to power in 1948, many laws were
passed to segregate the population, one of which banned blacks
and Indians from using the same public facilities as whites. ©
IAN BERRY/MAGNUM PHOTOS

Black Resistance

Black activism increased after World War II in South Africa
as elsewhere in Africa. When A. B. Xuma became president-
general of the African National Congress (ANC) in 1940, he
attempted to unify the organization ideologically, regulate its
finances, and conduct a propaganda campaign. A major schism
developed when Xuma and a few middle-class members advocated negotiation through African representative bodies,
while more militant members leaned toward the Communist
Party and more assertive political activism.

In the mid-1940s a group of young professionals, including Nelson Mandela and Robert Sobukwe, banded together to
form the ANC Youth League. They made overtures to
Coloured and Indian political organizations in their call for
majority rule. Coloureds were descendants of "miscegenation"
that occurred in the Cape after the Dutch East India Company's occupation. Indians were recruited as indentured servants to work on Natal's sugar plantations in the 1860s.

Apartheid Legislation

After the National Party victory in 1948, a battery of laws was
enacted to strictly segregate South African society by race, eth-
nicity, and class. The Prohibition of Mixed Marriages Act of
1949 outlawed marriages between whites and blacks. The
Population Registration Act of 1950 required that each adult
South African be classified by ethnic group as follows: white
(Afrikaners and English), Coloured (mixed race, Asian [mostly
Indian]), and African (Xhosa, Zulu, Ndebele, Swazi, Basotho,
Batswana, Bapedi, Venda, and Tsonga). In 1951 South
Africa's "African" population was approximately 8.5 million,
nearly four-fifths of the entire population.

The Group Areas Act of 1950 enforced the residential segregation of Coloureds and Indians. These groups could not
use public facilities outside residential boundaries.

The Suppression of Communism Act of 1950 forced the
disbandment of the South African Communist Party and a

diplomatic break with the Soviet Union. The Bantu Authorities Act of 1951 abolished the Natives Representative Council, replacing it with indirect rule. The Natives (Abolition of
Passes and Coordination of Documents) Act of 1952 required
the assignment of detailed reference books to all pass holders
detailing their background, employment, and residential rights
outside the reserves.

Parliament also passed the Bantu Education Act of 1953,
providing for state control of African schools, which had
mostly been founded by missionary societies, at the primary,
secondary, and tertiary levels. The Ministry of Native Affairs
planned a curriculum to prepare the "Bantu" (South African
blacks) to occupy a servile position in South African society.
Undocumented Africans were removed from urban areas to
rural homelands under the provisions of the Native Resettlement Act of 1954. Cape Coloureds were removed from the
common voters' roll in the Cape Province in 1956.

When Hendrik F. Verwoerd, minister of native affairs from
1950, became prime minister in 1958, he continued to initiate apartheid legislation compatible with his views regarding
"separate development." The Promotion of Bantu Self-
Government Act of 1959 provided for the creation of eight
national units for African self-government supposedly reflective of African ethnic groupings. Since urban blacks had no
political representation, it devolved upon chiefs to act as rov-
ing ambassadors between African subjects in the urban areas
and those resident in homelands. Homelands or reserve areas
represented 13.7 percent of the land.

The Bantu Homelands Act of 1970 required that all
Africans be given exclusive citizenship in a homeland, disregarding place of birth and current residence. In 1972
Zululand and Bophuthatswana were granted self-governing
status, while Transkei, self-governing since 1963, was given
more autonomy as the model homeland. Transkei's "independence" in 1976 was followed by Bophuthatswana in 1977,
Venda in 1979, and Ciskei in 1981.

The Western Cape was declared a Coloured labor preference area in the 1950s. Indians, granted citizenship in 1963,
experienced racial discrimination in residential and trading
rights.

Gender Issues

Helen Suzman (1993), a long-term antiapartheid member of
parliament (MP), observed that in 1953, her first year, there
were actually four women in parliament. Two were fellow
United Party members, and one was a member of the Liberal
Party. Suzman, a liberal, dealt primarily with racial issues, although she also advocated equal rights for women regarding
marriage, divorce, abortion, and employment. White women
had been enfranchised in 1930 to counter the nonwhite male
vote. In general racial and gender issues were not intertwined.
However, in 1955 liberal white women founded the Black Sash
to protest the proposed disenfranchisement of Coloured men.
Members argued for respect for the South African constitution. In the 1970s the Black Sash set up "advice offices" in
major cities to assist blacks with problems regarding "influx

NELSON MANDELA

Nelson Mandela. Mandela was elected South Africa's first black president in 1994 after having spent over twenty years in prison. A well-known political activist, Mandela was arrested in 1962 and charged shortly thereafter with sabotage and conspiring against the government. © DAVID TURNLEY/CORBIS

Nelson Rolihlahla Mandela, South Africa's first black president, was born on 18 July 1918, to Chief Gadla Henry Mphakanyiswa, of Thembu royalty, and Noselkeni Fanny in the Eastern Cape village of Mveso, Transkei. After his father's death when Mandela was nine, the acting tribal chief, Jongintaba, assumed Mandela's guardianship. Mandela had access to the best education a black youth could have, attending Clarkesbury Boarding Institute, Healdtown College, and University College of Fort Hare. He eventually left Transkei to avoid an arranged marriage and moved to Johannesburg.

Mandela became politicized while living in Alexandra Township by attending African National Congress (ANC) and South African Communist Party (SACP) meetings. After receiving his B.A. in 1942, he entered law school at the University of Witwatersrand. His autobiography, *Long Walk to Freedom,* includes many names famous in the antiapartheid struggle—Walter Sisulu, A. B. Xuma, George Bizos, Bram Fischer, Robert Sobukwe, Joe Slovo, Ruth First, Oliver Tambo, and Z. K. Matthews.

Viewing the ANC leadership as too conservative, Mandela in 1943 became a founding member of the ANC Youth League, which sought to motivate the leadership to action. Shocked by the National Party victory in 1948, he and other leaders of the ANC organized a "defiance campaign," employing a variety of passive-resistance tactics against apartheid legislation. Because of these activities, ANC activists were put under government surveillance, and Mandela was eventually served with a two-year banning order (1953–1955). A banning order restricted an individual to a magisterial district. He or she was expected to report regularly to the police and was under constant police surveillance. A banned individual could not be quoted in the press, could

(continued on the next page)

NELSON MANDELA

(continued from previous page)

not work, and could not meet with more than one person at a time.

Mandela and 155 other ANC leaders were arrested during the defiance campaign. In 1956 ninety-one people were accused, and sixty-one charges were dropped due to lack of evidence (Saunders; Davenport). Thirty people were tried for treason, and all but one were acquitted, including Mandela, in 1961.

After the treason trial and the banning of the ANC and PAC, Mandela went underground in the newly formed military wing of the ANC, Umkhonto we Sizwe (Spear of the Nation), as chair of the high command. This office planned sabotage, guerrilla warfare, and open revolution. Mandela based his underground operations at a farm in the Johannesburg suburb of Rivonia. Upon his return from the Pan-African Freedom Movement of East and Central Africa meeting in Ethiopia, he was arrested near Pietermaritzburg and charged with inciting a strike and leaving the country without a passport. He received a three-year prison sentence for the former charge and a two-year sentence for the latter. While in prison, he discovered that many members of the ANC high command were arrested in Rivonia in July 1963. They were charged under the Sabotage Act of 1962, with the onus being on the accused to prove their innocence. The state had requested the death penalty. The accused were given life imprisonment on 12 June 1964. International pressure had a great impact on sparing their lives. The nine-month trial ended in June 1963 with Mandela sentenced to life imprisonment. Mandela was incarcerated on Robben Island, off Cape Town, for nearly three decades. In his autobiography he wrote of this experience, remarking about the degree to which apartheid permeated every aspect of life in South Africa, even for those in prison, where clothing and food were differentiated according to a prisoner's race.

There were a number of attempts to free Mandela, including a major campaign in 1980. He was transferred to Pollsmoor Prison in 1982 and to Victor Vester Prison in Paarl in 1988. During this time he was allowed increasing contact with his wife, Winnie Mandela, and their two daughters. Mandela began negotiations with the South African government for his freedom and the end of apartheid while at Pollsmoor. That continued in earnest at Victor Vester Prison in May 1988. Government representatives preferred to negotiate with Mandela alone and vetoed his request to discuss the first meeting with his ANC comrades. Mandela outlined the negotiated issues as "the armed struggle, the ANC's alliance with the Communist Party, the goal of majority rule, and the idea of racial reconciliation." The government representatives were concerned that the ANC might attempt "blanket nationalization of the South African economy" as stated in the ANC's Freedom Charter. The secret talks occurred against the backdrop of internal protests by the United Democratic Alliance and the Mass Democratic Movement, a state of emergency, and international economic sanctions.

The ANC, PAC, and SACP were legalized on 2 February 1990, and Nelson Mandela was released from Victor Vester Prison on 11 February 1990. When elected president in 1994, Mandela sought to create a "Rainbow Nation," and the ANC collaborated with other political parties to form a "Government of National Unity."

---

control, unemployment, contracts, housing, and pensions" (Saunders).

Black women were particularly discriminated against with influx control and pass laws, extended to women in 1956. Influx control was a policy designed to direct the flow of black labor to "white" urban areas for employment and to rural farms. With the Nationalist victory in 1948, influx control regulations were enhanced. Pass laws regulated document requirements for black people. Jacklyn Cock examined their status as domestic servants in suburban white households. In *Maids and Madams,* Cock reports on a study of 800,000 black domestic servants. She examines their status as workers and mothers and their dependency relationships with their white

HENDRIK FRENSCH VERWOERD

Hendrik Frensch Verwoerd, often considered the architect of apartheid, was born in Amsterdam on 8 September 1901, six months before his parents moved to Wynberg, near Cape Town, South Africa. As a lay missionary in South Africa, Verwoerd's father received an assignment in Bulawayo, Zimbabwe, where the family lived for five years. Young Verwoerd performed well academically there and in Brandfort, Free State, South Africa, his next home. Developing a strongly anti-British political orientation in Zimbabwe, he immersed himself in Afrikaner life in Brandfort. Verwoerd completed secondary school in 1918 and proceeded to the University of Stellenbosch.

At Stellenbosch, Verwoerd was elected chair of the Students' Representative Council in 1923. He majored in sociology, psychology, and logic. After receiving his B.A., he was appointed to a position in the Psychology Department, completing his master's in 1923 and his doctorate in 1924. In 1925 Verwoerd traveled to Germany for study at Leipzig, Hamburg, and Berlin. In 1927 he and his wife, Betsie Verwoerd, returned to Stellenbosch, where he assumed a position as professor of applied sociology. Becoming chair of the Department of Sociology and Social Work in 1933 at Stellenbosch, he began to work with social welfare organizations and undertook a committee assignment on housing and unemployment focusing on the plight of poor Afrikaner whites.

Verwoerd joined the Purified Nationalist Party in 1935 as Afrikaners were attempting to unite politically and also became a member of the nativist Broederbond. He left academia to establish the Nationalist paper *Die Transvaler* in 1937. The major objective of *Die Transvaler* was to lure Afrikaners away from the British-oriented United Party and foster the idea of a Christian-National republic. During World War II, *Die Transvaler* adopted a pro-German stance and was opposed to South African involvement with the Allies. That stance became more explicitly anti-Semitic when Nationalists sought to limit Jewish immigration, deny Jewish citizens party membership, and discourage support for their businesses.

Despite the party's national victory in parliament, Verwoerd lost his local election by a narrow margin in 1948. However, the new prime minister, Daniel F. Malan, appointed him to the senate, and in 1950 Verwoerd became minister of native affairs. In this role, which he described to his wife as the "Great Induna," or great chief, Verwoerd reviewed and restructured the entire ministry, considered the most important in the South African cabinet, and formulated a body of apartheid legislation. On the death of J. G. Strijdom, Malan's successor, Verwoerd became prime minister in 1958.

After organizing a successful whites-only referendum to create a South African republic, Verwoerd attended the Commonwealth Prime Ministers' Conference in London in 1961. There he explored the possibility of South Africa remaining a member of the British Commonwealth. Although rebuffed by the British, Canadians, and Afro-Asian bloc because of apartheid, the prime minister received a hero's welcome when he returned to South Africa in early 1961. He had hoped for commonwealth approval of South Africa's apartheid policy given the pro-British sentiment of English-speakers in the white electorate. Afrikaner Nationalists applauded South Africa's removal from the commonwealth.

Verwoerd was assassinated on 6 September 1966, before a parliamentary session in the presence of about four hundred people. The assassin, Demetrio Tsafendas, was later tried and incarcerated in mental institutions until his death in 1999. Officially classified white, he had been born in Mozambique to a Greek father and a Coloured mother. In a 2001 book Henk van Woerden argued convincingly that the assassination was politically motivated.

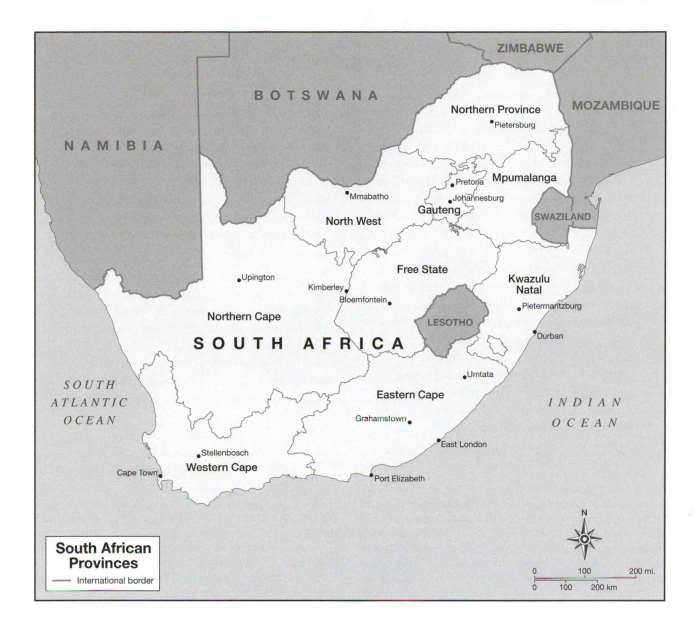

South African Provinces
International border

madams. Black domestic workers neglected their own families to be at the beck and call of the white madams and often lived in servants' quarters near the madams' houses. This enabled the madam to engage in leisure activities or to pursue employment to enhance her family's income. Cock illuminates gradations of female exploitation in the South African context in focusing on the relationship between maid and madam.

Increasing Black Nationalism

In 1952 the African National Congress, whose membership was estimated at 100,000, organized a campaign of defiance to protest racially discriminatory laws, burning passes and defying regulations concerning segregated facilities. Eighty-five hundred people were arrested during the four-month campaign, which resulted in a treason trial and the eventual acquittal of the accused. In 1955 the African National Congress and similar political organizations met and drafted the Freedom Charter, which embraced the tenets of a nonracial,

democratic society in which major capitalist enterprises would be nationalized.

Ideological differences within the ANC resulted in Robert Sobukwe breaking away to form the Pan-Africanist Congress (PAC) in 1959. In 1960 the PAC organized a campaign to protest pass laws and low wages. At Sharpeville, near Johannesburg, in March 1960, police opened fire on a crowd of demonstrators, killing 69 and injuring some 180. The government declared a state of emergency and arrested 1,600 people. The massacre precipitated international condemnation of the South African government, diminished investor confidence, and threw the economy into recession.

After Sharpeville, the ANC and PAC were banned, initiating underground political activity. Nelson Mandela, who had already been imprisoned on other charges, and his compatriots, taken into custody at a farm in the Johannesburg suburb of Rivonia, site of the ANC's underground headquarters, were

HELEN GAVRONSKY

Helen Gavronsky was born to Lithuanian Jewish immigrant parents near Johannesburg in 1917. She married Moses Suzman in 1937 and had two daughters. Later she returned to the University of the Witwatersrand to complete her B.A. Then she was hired as a lecturer in economic history. The United Party invited her to run for a seat in Houghton, a northern suburb of Johannesburg, in 1952. With the support of her husband, she successfully ran for the seat, which required her absence from her family while residing in Cape Town half a year. In parliament Suzman was a proponent of racial equality, South Africa's return to the commonwealth, rule of law, and the administration of justice. During her tenure in parliament she visited prisons, townships, and "resettlement areas" in the rural homelands. She was in parliament when Hendrik Verwoerd was assassinated and visited Nelson Mandela on Robben Island and in Pollsmoor Prison.

Often at odds with the United Party over apartheid legislation, she formed the Progressive Party in 1959 and became its sole representative. After fourteen years, six colleagues joined her in 1974. Although it was unpopular to participate in an increasingly oppressive apartheid parliament, Suzman was a vigorous advocate of racial equality. Despite their admiration, many black South Africans were critical of her antisanctions stance in the 1980s.

Suzman received many international honors, including honorary degrees from Oxford, Cambridge, and Harvard; the United Nations Human Rights Award (1978) and Medallion of Heroism (1980); and the Liberal International Prize for Freedom (2002). Suzman left parliament in 1989 but continued her activities in the Helen Suzman Foundation, which is devoted to liberal causes.

charged with sabotage and conspiracy to overthrow the government. In 1964 all but one of the codefendants were sentenced to life imprisonment. The Rivonia trial signaled the cessation of black nationalist resistance in South Africa. Many members of banned organizations sought refuge in other countries. Neighboring colonies provided South Africa a protective buffer against guerrilla insurgency, investor confidence was restored, and the country embarked on a period of economic prosperity. Meanwhile, after an all-white referendum, South Africa was declared a republic outside the commonwealth in 1961.

Dismantling of Apartheid

The outbreak of the Soweto riots in 1976 marked the denouement in the South African struggle. Students in the Johannesburg township rioted when the government made Afrikaans the language of school instruction in science subjects. Combating police bullets with sticks and stones, hundreds of students were killed. Others fled the country. The ANC set up recruitment stations in Mozambique from which refugees were transferred for military training. Coloured students in Cape Town intensified their activism. Unrest continued around the country and lasted well into 1977, having a deleterious effect on the economy. Refugees, both male and female, began to infiltrate the country to conduct acts of sabotage.

South Africa's protective buffers began to erode in 1975 with the independence of Angola and Mozambique, followed by that of Zimbabwe in 1980, allowing for increasing guerrilla infiltration into the country. After the Muldergate information

scandal, P. W. Botha, minister of defense, became prime minister in 1978. Muldergate was an information scandal in which substantial sums of money allocated to buy international media support for apartheid was funneled to the *Citizen,* a progovernment newspaper in Johannesburg (Saunders, p. 116). The disclosure and attempted cover-up precipitated dissension within the ranks of the National Party. Botha's total strategy combined militarism and reform.

Recognizing the potential for a racial bloodbath, the Nationalists sought a "consociational democracy" in which no racial group would dominate. In an effort to bring legitimate leaders to the negotiating table, a campaign began to free the long-imprisoned ANC leader Nelson Mandela in the early 1980s. The president (formerly prime minister) proposed a tricameral parliament with chambers for Asians, Coloureds, and whites. The exclusion of those classified African led to the formation of the United Democratic Front to coordinate activism within the country.

In the mid-1980s major Western powers initiated econ-omic sanctions against apartheid South Africa. Governmental negotiations began in 1990, when Mandela was released from prison. The ANC and other liberation organizations were "unbanned," or legitimized. An interim constitution was written, and elections were held in 1994. The ANC was victorious nationally.

Conclusion

When South Africa celebrated its first decade of postapartheid government, it had rejoined the commonwealth and a number of international bodies. The ANC was returned to power for a third term in April 2004 with 70 percent of the vote. Some progress had been made toward racial equality despite inequities in the distribution of wealth. However, South Africa continued to grapple with the legacy of apartheid—high unemployment, low literacy rates, inadequate housing, the HIV/AIDS pandemic, and the dynamics of globalization. In the early twenty-first century the unemployment rate was estimated at 38 to 40 percent. According to the South African Survey 1999, one-third of South Africans needed adequate housing. The HIV rate in prenatal clinics was 22.8 percent in 1998.

South Africa is not viewed as competitive in global production due to high labor costs. A number of mining and manufacturing enterprises have established branches in other African countries. The government seeks to attract new investment and to enhance the skills of its black labor force. With regard to the Internet, in the early twenty-first century South Africa was the best-wired country in Africa.

See also **Prejudice; Race and Racism; Segregation.**

BIBLIOGRAPHY

Adam, Heribert. *Modernizing Racial Domination: South Africa's Political Dynamics.* Berkeley: University of California Press, 1971.

Ballinger, Margaret. *From Union to Apartheid: A Trek to Isolation.* Cape Town: Juta, 1969.

Bernstein, Hilda. *For Their Triumphs and for Their Tears: Conditions and Resistance of Women in Apartheid South Africa.* London: International Defence and Aid Fund, 1978.

Biko, Steve. *I Write What I Like.* Edited by Aelred Stubbs. New York: Harper and Row, 1979.

Cock, Jacklyn. *Maids and Madams: A Study in the Politics of Exploitation.* Johannesburg: Ravan, 1980.

Davenport, T. R. H, and Christopher Saunders. *South Africa: A Modern History.* 5th ed. New York: St. Martin's, 2000.

Davis, Stephen M. *Apartheid's Rebels: Inside South Africa's Hidden War.* New Haven, Conn.: Yale University Press, 1987.

De Klerk, F. W. *The Last Trek: A New Beginning.* London: Macmillan, 1998.

Desmond, Cosmos. *The Discarded People: An Account of African Resettlement in South Africa.* Harmondsworth, U.K.: Penguin, 1970.

Doxey, G. V. *The Industrial Colour Bar in South Africa.* Cape Town and New York: Oxford University Press, 1961.

Forgey, Herma, et al. *South African Survey 1999/2000.* Johannesburg: South African Institute of Race Relations, 2000.

Gregory, T. E. *Ernest Oppenheimer and the Economic Development of Southern Africa.* Cape Town and New York: Oxford University Press, 1962.

Hepple, Alexander. *Verwoerd.* Harmondsworth, U.K.: Penguin, 1967.

Hirson, Baruch. *Year of Fire, Year of Ash: The Soweto Revolt, Roots of a Revolution?* London: Zed, 1979.

James, Wilmot G., ed. *The State of Apartheid.* Boulder, Colo.: L. Rienner, 1987.

Johnstone, Frederick A. *Class, Race, and Gold: A Study of Class Relations and Racial Discrimination in South Africa.* London and Boston: Routledge and Kegan Paul, 1976.

Kadalie, Clements. *My Life and the ICU: The Autobiography of a Black Trade Unionist in South Africa.* New York: Humanities, 1970.

Kuzwayo, Ellen. *Call Me Woman.* San Francisco: Spinster's Ink, 1985.

La Guma, Alex, ed. *Apartheid: A Collection of Writings on South African Racism by South Africans.* New York: International, 1971.

Lambley, Peter. *The Psychology of Apartheid.* Athens: University of Georgia Press, 1980.

Le May, G. H. L. *Black and White in South Africa: The Politics of Survival.* New York: American Heritage, 1971.

Lerumo, A. *Fifty Fighting Years: The Communist Party of South Africa, 1921–1971.* London: Inkululeko, 1971.

Luthuli, A. J. *Let My People Go.* New York: McGraw-Hill, 1962.

Magubane, Bernard. *The Political Economy of Race and Class in South Africa.* New York: Monthly Review, 1979.

Mandela, Nelson. *Long Walk to Freedom: The Autobiography of Nelson Mandela.* Boston: Little, Brown, 1994.

———. *No Easy Walk to Freedom: Articles, Speeches, and Trial Addresses of Nelson Mandela.* London: Heinemann, 1973.

Mbeki, Govan. *South Africa: The Peasants' Revolt.* Baltimore: Penguin, 1964.

Michelman, Cherry. *The Black Sash of South Africa: A Case Study in Liberalism.* Oxford and New York: Oxford University Press, 1975.

Moodie, T. Dunbar. *The Rise of Afrikanerdom: Power, Apartheid, and the Afrikaner Civil Religion.* Berkeley: University of California Press, 1975.

Murray, Martin. *South Africa: Time of Agony, Time of Destiny: The Upsurge of Popular Protest.* London: Verso, 1987.

Nkomo, Mokubung. *Student Culture and Activism in Black South African Universities: The Roots of Resistance.* Westport, Conn.: Greenwood, 1984.

Ramphele, Mamphela. *A Bed Called Home: Life in the Migrant Labour Hostels of Cape Town.* Cape Town: David Philip; Athens: Ohio University Press, 1993.

Rees, Mervyn, and Chris Day. *Muldergate: The Story of the Info Scandal.* Johannesburg: Macmillan, 1980.

Saunders, Christopher. *Historical Dictionary of South Africa.* Metuchen, N.J., and London: Scarecrow Press, 1983.

Seidman, Ann, and Neva Seidman. *South Africa and U.S. Multinational Corporations.* Westport, Conn.: L. Hill, 1978.

Shimoni, Gideon. *Jews and Zionism: The South African Experience (1910–1967).* Cape Town: Oxford University Press, 1980.

Slabbert, F. van Zyl, and David Welsh. *South Africa's Options: Strategies for Sharing Power.* New York: St. Martin's, 1979.

Stultz, Newell M. *Afrikaner Politics in South Africa, 1934–1948.* Berkeley: University of California Press, 1974.

Suzman, Helen. *In No Uncertain Terms: A South African Memoir.* New York: Knopf, 1993.

Thompson, Leonard. *The Political Mythology of Apartheid.* New Haven, Conn.: Yale University Press, 1985.

Troup, Freda. *Forbidden Pastures: Education under Apartheid.* London: International Defence and Aid Fund, 1976.

Tutu, Desmond. *Crying in the Wilderness: The Struggle for Justice in South Africa.* Grand Rapids, Mich.: W. B. Eerdmans, 1982.

Walshe, Peter. *The Rise of African Nationalism in South Africa: The African National Congress, 1912–1952.* Berkeley: University of California Press, 1971.

Wilson, Frances. "Farming 1866–1966." In *The Oxford History of South Africa,* vol. 2, edited by Monica Wilson and Leonard Thompson. New York: Oxford University Press, 1971.

Woerden, Henk van. *The Assassin: A Story of Race and Rage in the Land of Apartheid.* New York: Metropolitan, 2001.

Betty J. Harris

APOCALYPSE. *See* **Dystopia; Eschatology; Nuclear Age.**

APPEARANCE AND REALITY. *See* **Metaphysics.**

ARCHITECTURE.

This entry includes three subentries:

Overview
Africa
Asia

OVERVIEW

Architecture is the crystallization of ideas. Architecture has been defined many ways—as shelter in the form of art, as a blossoming in stone and a flowering of geometry (Ralph Waldo Emerson), as frozen music (Johann Wolfgang von Goethe), man's triumph over gravitation and his will to power (Friedrich Nietzsche), the will of an epoch translated into space (architect Mies van der Rohe), the magnificent play of forms in light (architect Le Corbusier), a cultural instrument (architect Louis I. Kahn), or inhabited sculpture (sculptor Constantin Brancusi). The architectural critic Ada Louise Huxtable framed a rather clinical definition, saying architecture is a "balance of structural science and aesthetic expression for the satisfaction of needs far beyond the utilitarian." Most people in the early twenty-first century—users, that is, as opposed to designers and critics—seldom think of architecture as anything more than a mute utilitarian container. Yet architecture is a form of nonverbal communication, as was recognized by many builders in centuries past. Architecture speaks volumes about the values and priorities of the designer or architect, and of those who built it. This view of architecture has been voiced by many commentators but was expressed particularly well by the nineteenth-century critic John Ruskin, who pointed out in his preface to *St. Mark's Rest* (1877) that nations "write their autobiographies in three manuscripts—the book of their deeds, the book of their words, and the book of their art. Not one of these books can be understood unless we read the other two; but of the three, the only quite trustworthy one is the last."

Accounts of military exploits and written expressions of theory and practice are records of ideas often subtly worded to shade the values of a time and culture; architecture, in contrast, is fundamentally driven by the most essential economic pressures. Architecture therefore is a truly revealing cultural artifact. In contrast to all the other durable visual arts, architecture comes into being only through the coordinated efforts of client, architect, builder, and scores of workers, and therefore—since it requires such a formidable financial investment—caprice and personal whimsy are normally restricted, replaced by the pressures of what is truly important in the culture of client, architect, and builder. Architecture is a "bottom line" art form. Moreover, who people are and what they do is influenced, if not determined, by the architecture around them. As Winston Churchill suggested in speaking to Parliament in 1944, "we shape our buildings, and afterwards our buildings shape us."

Early Humans in Europe

Buildings or shelters were being constructed by early human ancestors as early as 400,000 to 300,000 years ago, judging from the traces found at a site called Terra Amata, near Nice, France. The remains of the oldest human dwellings found so far do not suggest anything other than protection from the elements, but that must have changed with the rise of thinking in terms of symbols and metaphors between 50,000 and 30,000 years ago among Neanderthal people in Europe and certainly their Cro-Magnon *homo sapiens* successors. How symbolic thinking may have found expression in shelters so far has been impossible to determine, for all that survives from the infancy of modern humans are nonorganic materials; whatever else they may have built of timbers and hides, or carved in wood, long ago disappeared. The tantalizing evidence that does endure is found in the skilled paintings of animals and cryptic symbols created deep in the caves of Spain and France, in Australia, and at other locations.

Also suggesting a complex system of spiritual belief is the evidence of careful and thoughtful burial given some Neanderthal individuals, which became more customary for the Cro-Magnon. Reverence and respect for the remains of the dead as departed members of the human community seems to have developed about 250,000 years ago, along with ideas concerning some persistence of life after death, or at least the notion that the remains of dead parents, elders, and children merited care and reverence. Megalithic stone burial chambers were built in France and Ireland as early as 6,700 years ago (4700 B.C.E.). Cut into the limestone hill of Hal Saflieni, Malta, is a tomb called the "hypogeum," carved perhaps 5,500 years ago (3500 B.C.E.). Because it was excavated long ago, much of its chronological evidence was destroyed, but another semisubterranean burial site on the Maltese island of Gozo, called the Brochtorff Circle, was excavated in the 1990s and more accurately dated as having been built roughly 6,000 years ago.

Built evidence suggests that around 5,500 years ago the notion of time as a continual cycle of recurring celestial events was well developed in northern Europe, as the technically sophisticated construction of such sites as the Newgrange tomb in the Boyne Valley of Ireland (constructed 5,200 years ago) and the first phases of construction at Stonehenge in the plain of Salisbury, Wiltshire, England (started about 4,950 years ago) demonstrate. The enormous well-known megalithic stones at Stonehenge were put in place much later, between 4,000 and 3,500 years ago. These sites were carefully constructed to mark critical points in the cycle of the year, such as the day of the winter solstice sunrise and the summer solstice sunrise and sunset.

Antiquity: Egypt, Greece, Rome

Egypt. In ancient Egypt, Greece, and Rome architecture reflected the worldviews and underlying concepts of each society itself. The culture of ancient Egypt was rooted in chronometric concepts—the cycle of the year, the notion of time extending endlessly from the past toward an unfathomable future, the human spirit continuing in existence into this future. As Herodotus (c. 484–c. 420 B.C.E.) observed in his *Histories,*

Aerial view of Stonehenge, Wiltshire, England. Some early constructions, such as that of Stonehenge, which was constructed in three phases between 2950–1500 B.C.E., were dedicated to marking time and the cycle of seasons throughout the year. © JASON HAWKES/ CORBIS

Egypt is the gift of the Nile, a long linear oasis extending from the south to the north, where the river expands into its delta and empties into the Mediterranean. Across this south-north line lies the east-west path of the sun. These two orthogonal lines and the cycles of what define them—the daily passage of the sun and the yearly rising flood and lowering of the river— also define the human life cycles of ancient Egypt. Geometry and symmetry were fundamental to this life, both in remeasuring the fields after inundation and in laying out the ancient temples, the houses of the gods where endless ceremonies were carried out during the course of the year. The linear, rigorously ordered grid of the temple layout exemplified the idea of *ma'at,* a concept that combines the ideas of truth, justice, order, stability, security, harmony—the total of the right order of things that was established by the gods at the creation of the world.

For artisans, scribes, officials, and others who served the bureaucracies, life could be very pleasant in the valley of the Nile, at least during the politically settled periods that lasted hundreds of years. So the ancient Egyptians came to think that following death, an individual's soul passed into an afterlife where—properly provided for with a preserved physical body and stores of food and drink, and assisted by statue-substitute servants—life could be enjoyed forever. It was for this reason that so much of the Egyptians' creative effort and energies went into the building of their temples, tombs, and (for the Pharaoh god-kings) the pyramids that were their ascent stairs to join the gods. Their focus was on the life to come.

Greece. The Greeks, for whom daily life was a much more arduous and risky affair, focused not on an unverifiable spiritual life after death but on achieving knowable excellence of human achievement in this world. Their term for this was *aretē,* that quality of excellence that comes from studied refinement, skill, and testing, demonstrated by achievement through valor in war or athletic competition or contest, *agōn.* Excellence could be

Columns at the Hypostyle Hall of The Temple of Amon, Al Karnak, Egypt. Constructed c. 1315–1235 B.C.E. Ancient Egyptian society gradually came to ascribe special significance to the afterlife, and thus much care and detail was given to the design of temples and tombs. © ROYALTY-FREE/CORBIS

represented in poetry, music, and athletic skill—all of which were the subject of contests—as well as in sculpture and architecture. Through such contests individuals learned their abilities and limitations, what the priests of Apollo meant when they said "know thyself." In all things the ancient Greeks sought *logos,* a concept that encompasses reason, logic, generating idea, conception, a natural order that existed in the world, the opposite of *chaos.* The Greeks strove to realize this ideal of balance and symmetry (from *symmetria,* meaning "of like measure"). Heracleitus (c. 540– c. 480 B.C.E.) described this concept of symmetry, saying "measure and logos are firm in a changing world," and describing how cold is balanced by hot, day by night, health by disease. The risk was that such mental constructs might venture into the realm of mystic speculation, as was somewhat the case with Pythagoras of Samos (c. 580–c. 500 B.C.E.), who asserted that the universe was governed by a symmetry of numbers, demonstrated by the harmonic sounds created by vibrating strings of proportional lengths. Out of this theorizing, however, came such highly useful mathematical demonstrations as the Pythagorean theory describing how the areas of the squares drawn on the two sides of a right triangle are together equal to the area of the larger square drawn on the side of the connecting side, or hypotenuse.

This perfection of mathematical proportions and excellence in construction was embodied in the Greek temples, buildings erected in durable permanent materials such as marble, with

blocks having sides ground to perfect planes that fitted together so tightly that a knife blade could not be inserted between them. In particular, the temple dedicated to Athena Parthenos (the Parthenon), built atop the Athenian acropolis in 447–438 B.C.E., in addition to having this precision of assembly, also incorporated in its design numerous interrelated proportional systems governing such dimensions as the ratio of building length to width to height, and the thickness and spacing of the outer ring of marble columns, among many other dimensions and relationships. Moreover, it incorporated a subtle inward slant to the columns, especially a diagonal inward slant to the corner columns, as well as optical corrections, such as the upward swelling curvature of the base repeated in the upward curve of all the parallel horizontal lines of the building. These nearly imperceptible optical corrections make the building appear to be straighter and lighter, more perfect, than is physically the case. What the eye actually sees, then, and what the mind expects to see, are not in exact agreement. The result is that the building constantly shimmers and shifts in the viewer's perception between these two subtly conflicting mental activities, giving it a visual stimulation that has excited comment since the time of its construction.

Rome. Greek architecture is not particularly concerned with the enclosure of interior public spaces. Most activities in the Greek city-state polis took place in outdoor spaces such as the agora (marketplace) or the open precincts around temples. The Romans, however, developed numerous kinds of public buildings to house groups of people—law courts (basilicas), markets, and baths, among others—as cities across their empire grew in size and density of population. To certain abstract constructs of Greek culture and learning, the Romans added a practical mind-set that enabled them to solve technical problems such as supplying water to their cities and carrying away waste products. They adopted arch and vault construction for a wide variety of buildings. To this they added the use of readily available volcanically modified materials to make a form of natural concrete. Using this concrete enabled Romans to vault spans of unprecedented size in their public buildings.

All these social programs and architectural developments come together in the Roman public baths, versions of which were built in cities the length and breadth of the empire, including Bath, in England, and Paris among countless other settlements. Aqueducts, carried aloft on stacked arches, brought water into the baths, where it was heated and distributed to the various bathing areas, with cold, tepid, and warm pools. In the warm bath areas the rooms themselves were heated by means of hollow passages under the floor and running up through the walls, acting as so many chimney flues for fires kept burning in side furnaces. In the early 2000s the great public baths of the city of Rome stand, mostly in fragmented unroofed portions, as testaments to the engineering skill of the Romans, but a better sense of the majesty of these vast spaces can still be glimpsed in the church of Santa Maria degli Angeli, originally the baths built by the emperor Diocletian in 298–306 C.E., but sufficiently intact to be converted into a huge church with monastery by Michelangelo in the mid-sixteenth century.

Romans, for the most part, were concerned with the here and now. During the republican period Romans embraced the

The Parthenon (Temple of Athena Parthenos), Athens, Greece. The focus of ancient Greek architecture was symmetry and harmonious proportions. The design of the Parthenon, which was constructed 447–438 B.C.E., displays the precision and exacting detail to construction common to the period. © HECTOR WILLIAMS

quality of *gravitas,* a sense of the importance of matters at hand, combined with ingrained discipline, patriotic responsibility, and seriousness of purpose, austerity, conservatism, and a deep respect for tradition. A good Roman citizen upheld a rigid morality, served the state, maintained unimpeachable honor, and strove for a physical and spiritual asceticism—all qualities discernable in the first Roman emperor, Augustus (r. 27 B.C.E.–14 C.E.) himself. It is all too easy to think of Romans comporting themselves as commonly depicted in novels and films, devoted to depravity and sensual excess, but this was more the case during the later empire. The goal of many earnest Romans in the first centuries after Augustus was to reestablish the moral standards of the republican past. In many ways, the best representative of the Roman personal values of probity and self-discipline can be found in the emperor Marcus Aurelius (r. 161–180), trained in the tradition of the Greek Stoics. His *Meditations,* intended for his personal reflection—with their repeated admonitions to uphold personal honor because of its basic practicality—are a tribute to the persistence of republican virtues.

Middle Ages

Even around 175 C.E., as Marcus Aurelius was writing his *Meditations,* Christianity was spreading across the empire. Of the various cults and religions that vied for converts during the early years of what has come to be called the common era,

Christianity was the most persuasive for several reasons. Unlike the impersonal state religion of Rome, with its removed and depersonalized rituals to placate Jupiter and the deified emperors, Christianity offered direct communication with a personalized deity, embodied in the crucified Christ. The present world, with all of its shortcomings and disappointments, was seen as only the preparation ground for a subsequent eternal life. The classical focus on the practicalities of the here and now faded in importance. In the West, the old Roman Empire was transformed, through invasion after invasion from the north and east, as well as through the rise of Christianity, whose strong vertical bureaucratic structure took on much of the character of the fading Roman government. The old position of the Roman emperor as chief priest (*pontifex maximus*) was taken over by the bishop of Rome as head of all bishops, and therefore head of the church.

Although Christianity maintained that all humans are born in original sin, and are destined to persist in this fallen state, doomed to spend eternity in Hell, doctrine held out the hope of Heaven. This consuming aspiration, directed away from the present world in favor of the next, is embodied in the abundant and mutually reinforcing vertical motifs in Gothic architecture, developed in France and other areas of Europe around 1150. Every line of the Gothic cathedral seems to point toward heaven. Moreover, the architecture is covered across its entire

Baths of Diocletian, Rome, Italy (built 298–306 B.C.E.), refurbished as the Church of Santa Maria degli Angeli (interior). In ancient Rome, the use of modified concrete led to buildings that were large and spacious, as can be seen in this church, which was converted in the mid-sixteenth century from a public bath house. © ELIO CIOL/CORBIS

surface with sculpted images drawn from Scripture and the lives of the saints. Influenced by the writings of the abbé Suger of St.-Denis, architects opened up ever larger clerestory windows in the upper ranges of the churches and cathedrals. The windows were filled with highly colorful stained glass, an allegory of divine light, with images amplifying the stories told in the stone carvings. The churches became veritable Bibles in stone and colored glass, inculcating scriptural lessons in the faithful.

The later High Gothic urban cathedrals, for the most part dedicated to the Virgin Mother—Our Lady, or Notre Dame,

in French-speaking regions—were not only ecclesiastical buildings commissioned and paid for in part by the church, but also municipal undertakings raised to celebrate the status and power of the cities. Often the naves of these cathedrals were owned by the city, while the transept and crossing area as well as the choir were church property.

Renaissance. The culture of the so-called Middle Ages in Europe, focused on the life of the church, was bolstered by Scholasticism and the infusion of Aristotelian logic through the writing of St. Thomas Aquinas (c. 1224–1274). By the

Cathedral of Saint-Pierre, Beauvais, France. Constructed 1125–1548. The architecture of cathedrals built during the Gothic period focused on soaring lines and arches. Light was abundant, and facades were decorated with religious imagery. © PAUL ALMASY/CORBIS

fourteenth century, with the growth of merchant cities in Italy and the development of banking, wealthy merchants began to underwrite the new scholarly study of Roman and Greek literature and history, not so much to augment religious doctrine but for its own inherent merit and political implications. In fact, in Florence, where the powerful and enormously wealthy Medici family supported scholars and artists, the qualities of humanism were seen as demonstrating how the self-governing Florentines were superior to the autocratic rulers of other Italian states. Thus was set in motion a rebirth of ancient classical learning, a Renaissance.

The challenge of the time was to link humanist study with religious doctrine, to uncover how the knowledge of the ancients paralleled and thus supported church doctrine; the means for this was a reinvigorated Neoplatonism. Just as Scripture maintained that Adam had been made in the physical image of an all-perfect god, so too did the pagan Roman architect Vitruvius (1st cent. B.C.E.) declare that within the form of the human body could be found the modules of the most perfect geometric forms, the circle and the square. His written description was beautifully depicted in the well-known drawing by Renaissance artist/architect Leonardo da Vinci, planned as

Santa Maria delle Carceri Church, Prato, Italy. Constructed 1485–1506. In Italy during the Middle Ages, most religious architecture was simple and clean in design, comprised of balanced combinations of circles and squares. © DENNIS MARSICO/ CORBIS

an illustration for a new edition of Vitruvius's *Ten Books on Architecture*: a man with outstretched arms just touches the edges of a circle and square.

The circle and square became the measure of perfect architectural form as well in scores of new churches and chapels built in Italy. Of the many examples, the small church of Santa Maria delle Carceri in Prato, designed by Giuliano da Sangalloin in 1485, shows this modular perfection well. Its basic plan is a square of about 38 feet, extended upward to the top of the main cornice to form a cube. Short half-square arms project on the four sides. Atop the internal cube span four semicircular arches (half the height of the cube), and these define four curved pendentives that carry the topmost dome, circular in plan and nearly a perfect hemisphere in section. Circles and squares, and their three-dimensional counterparts, define the edges and perimeters of this idealized building.

The Renaissance emphasis on the ability of the human mind to grasp the rational structure of the universe led Martin Luther (1483–1546) to analyze the New Testament in search of support of papal practices, particularly the sale of indulgences. Instead, Luther uncovered in the letters of St. Paul the assertion that salvation was God's gift through faith and repentance, not something to be parceled out by, much less purchased from, an established church and clerical hierarchy. Coupled with the desire of numerous German princes to shed the political yoke imposed by the Roman Church, Luther's church reforms led to a splintering of the church universal. Delayed in reacting to this attack, the Roman Church convened the Council of Trent (1545–1563) to draft responses to the Reformation split in the church. Whereas the Reformationists, to varying degrees, shunned the use of sensory aids in worship—and in certain

regions of Northern Europe engaged in the wholesale destruction of paintings and statuary—the Council of Trent decreed that, on the contrary, the ordinary worshiper can only grasp the mysteries of faith with difficulty and so highly evocative painted and sculpted imagery were to be emphatically employed. A superb illustration of this dictum can be found in the highly emotive and mysteriously illuminated sculpted figure of St. Theresa found at the end of the right transept arm of the church of Santa Maria della Vittoria, Rome, built by Gian Lorenzo Bernini in 1645–1652. Here in a total work of art, fusing painting, sculpture, and architectural enframement, the ecstatic divine experience of St. Theresa is shown to the common worshiper in terms of seemingly carnal ecstasy, an analogy easily understood. Architecture, merged with painting and sculpture, was to serve as an instrument of propaganda in bringing the strayed faithful back into the protective arms of Mother Church (exactly the image Bernini said he was after in the curved encircling colonnade of his new piazza in front of the huge basilica of St. Peter's in Rome).

Modern Era

The emphasis on the place of human understanding and reason, on rational analysis, initiated by the Renaissance and Reformation, reemerged in the eighteenth century.

Enlightenment. During the so-called Age of Reason, or Age of Enlightenment, scientific analysis of the structural forces at work in a building began to be modeled mathematically, and the strength of building materials such as different woods and stones were tested and recorded in statistical tables. A good example in which the Age of Faith and the Age of Reason overlap can be seen in the Church of Saint Geneviève in Paris, begun in 1755 by architect Jacques-Germain Soufflot. Returning to the perfected forms of the Renaissance, Soufflot used a plan based on a Greek cross, with four arms of equal length extending from a central rotunda capped with a dome. Heavily influenced by what he had learned on a recent trip to southern Italy to inspect and study the ruined Greek temples at Paestum, near Naples, Soufflot used rows of structural Corinthian columns inside the church, balancing the weight of the smaller domes over the arms of the building directly on these columns. Seldom in the preceding three centuries had free-standing columns been used—as in ancient Greek architecture—for true structural support. Moreover, the great central dome was supported by slender piers. Using his knowledge of the strength of materials, Soufflot made the entire building much more delicate and lighter in appearance than had been the accepted norm. When cracks began to appear in the dome piers, construction was ordered halted while Soufflot's computations were subjected to scrutiny. Overall, Soufflot's calculations were proven to be correct, although some strengthening of the building took place. The building was finished in 1790 after Soufflot's death, but such was the shift in ideology and patronage in those tumultuous years of the French Revolution that the church was desacralized and converted to become the Panthéon, a memorial to great deceased French military and literary heroes.

United States. The nascent utilitarianism incorporated into the design of the Panthéon was carried to the newly formed

Nineteenth-century drawing of the Panthéon (originally Church of Saint Geneviève), Paris, France. Constructed 1755–1790. During the Age of Enlightenment, attention began to be paid to different methods of structural support, one example being the freestanding columns Jacques-Germain Soufflot used in his design for the Panthéon. © ARCHIVO ICONOGRAFICO, S.A./CORBIS

United States of America where the demands of commerce became the driving cultural force. The greatest and most innovative achievements made by American architects were not in churches, nor even in buildings to house representative government; in these they borrowed heavily from Greek and Roman and even Renaissance models. Instead their most innovative achievements were made in the design of the free-standing single family residence (as in the work of McKim, Mead & White in their early years, and in the career of Frank Lloyd Wright) but most recognizably in soaring office sky-scraper towers. The first accomplishments were made in Chicago in the 1880s and 1890s in ten- and twenty-story office towers, but the lead soon passed to New York architects, who piled floor upon floor to create spires of forty and fifty stories. In an effort to attach a measure of culture and time-honored respectability to his world headquarters, Frank W. Woolworth instructed his architect Cass Gilbert to model his new fifty-five-story office building, to be named the Woolworth Building, on northern Gothic European guild halls. Although a marvel of applied engineering—from its massive caisson foundations extending to bedrock, to its steel frame clad in terra

cotta panels, to its innovative elevator system, among scores of other technical innovations—externally the building is Gothic in style, artfully composed, like Gothic churches, with every line straining heavenward. Here, however, the aspiration is not for heaven, but for self-advertisement, aggrandizement, and profits. Woolworth called it a "Cathedral of Commerce." The apotheosis of the American office tower was reached in the soaring 102-story Empire State Building, 1929–1931, begun just months before the onset of the Great Depression. The tallest building in the world, it was not surpassed in height for thirty years.

American office skyscrapers became ever taller by the mid-twentieth century—sixty, eighty, and finally a hundred stories. These were proud towers, often showing little real concern on the part of patrons or architects for the impact on urban scale. They became symbols of American enterprise, and were first exported by American corporations around the world, and then embraced by developing countries around the globe in the late twentieth century. Even where the concentration of activities into narrow soaring towers made no practical sense—most

The Empire State Building, New York City. Constructed 1929–1931. In the United States, most advancements in architecture were based on the societal need for copious office space, leading to structures that reached over a hundred stories into the air. The Empire State Building held the record for world's tallest office building for thirty years. © BETTMANN/CORBIS

MBF Tower, Penang, Malaysia. Constructed 1990–1993. In designing the MBF Tower, architect Ken Yeang utilized construction methods that allowed for natural light and ventilation, a technique seen more and more frequently in the twenty-first century. PABLO ZIEGLER / EMPORIS.COM

notably in the twin Petronas towers designed for Kuala Lampur, Malaysia, in 1996, by the American architect Cesar Pelli, to rise 1,476 feet or 450 meters—towers they became nonetheless, as symbols of national power and pride. Such dramatic symbols, proud, standing free in the open air, inescapable emblems of American cultural imperialism (in some viewers' eyes), proved irresistible targets for terrorists at the dawn of the twenty-first century. Damaged in 1993 by a bomb, the twin World Trade Center towers (1,368 ft., 417 m) were brought crashing to the ground on 11 September 2001, after terrorists used commercial aircraft as flying bombs. For the terrorists, the ideas represented by the towers were too loathsome to let stand.

Postmodernism

As the twenty-first century opened, new architectural paradigms emerged. One building type that gained new cachet as the embodiment of urban identity and cultural striving was the art museum. Such commissions came to represent the pinnacle of an architect's career, particularly after Frank Gehry made the small city of Bilbao, Spain, a cultural destination with his Guggenheim Museum on the waterfront there.

Gehry's free-form undulating buildings are only one representation of postmodernism, a multifaceted philosophical and artistic expression derived from literary analysis. In many instances the drive of late-twentieth-century architects to break the strictures of conventional mid-twentieth-century modernism rendered their efforts both disjointed and self-absorbed. The counterpart to this kind of postmodernism is found in so-called developing countries around the globe. Since roughly 1950 there has been a growing reawakening in these areas to long-standing regional building cultures and building methods. This "critical regionalism" encourages architects to draw once again on the wisdom gained in centuries of construction in their regions, in preference to the imported European and American building forms and methods, with the accompanying reliance on high energy consumption for lighting, heating, and cooling buildings. This regionalism began with the work of Hasan Fathy in Egypt and his advocacy of adobe brick in vaulted and domed construction, a time-honored building method in that land, and one that used building materials available at minimal cost. More recently in Egypt, Saudi Arabia, numerous Middle Eastern countries, and generally in the Third World nations, there has been a return to traditional building forms (but often using twentieth-century materials) for various public buildings but especially for mosques because of their strong symbolic importance. In Sri Lanka, architect Geoffrey Bawa drew on imagery associated with traditional small-scale village meeting houses for his expansive Sri Lanka

Parliament of Sri Lanka, Kotte (near Colombo). Constructed 1980–1983. Beginning in the mid-twentieth century, some architects advocated a return to traditional designs that drew upon the resources readily available in the area. Drawing internally on the British House of Commons, the external forms are inspired by ancestral local buildings of assembly. © 2004 LANDOV LLC. ALL RIGHTS RESERVED. REPRODUCED BY PERMISSION

Parliament building complex; its recognizable broad overhanging eaves and open pavilion-like structures providing shade and free movement of air in this tropical country.

Around the globe, as the twenty-first century began there was rising interest in sustainable building design and construction, in using materials in ways that minimize toxic production methods, and in using natural sunlight for energy and natural air movement and water for cooling. In this way, over time, the impact of such architecture on public resources will be limited and the total social and economic cost minimized. Among many late-twentieth-century architects who drew on this design philosophy, one whose work is particularly interesting is Ken Yeang of Malaysia. His thirty-two-story MBF Tower in Penang employs the skyscraper tower form, a symbol of progressive modernity, but also uses traditional ideas such as curved external terraces and separation of elements to promote natural ventilation in place of massive cooling machinery.

These examples demonstrate that there need be no elemental conflict between the use of modern materials such as concrete, glass, steel, and aluminum in the creation of traditional forms that reflect long-established ways of living and also make accommodation to local climatic conditions.

See also **Aesthetics; Arts; Modernism; Postmodernism; Sacred Places.**

BIBLIOGRAPHY

Bergdoll, Barry. *European Architecture, 1750–1890.* New York: Oxford University Press, 2000.

Bony, Jean. *French Gothic Architecture of the Twelfth and Thirteenth Centuries.* Berkeley: University of California Press, 1983.

Braham, Allan. *The Architecture of the French Enlightenment.* Berkeley: University of California Press, 1980.

Burenhult, Gören, ed. *People of the Past: The Epic Story of Human Origins and Development.* San Francisco: Fog City, 2003. A global treatment of human origins and the earliest cultures, drawing on the expertise of scores of expert contributors and the results of recent archaeological discoveries.

Collins, Peter. *Changing Ideals in Modern Architecture, 1750–1950.* 2nd ed. Montreal: McGill-Queens University Press, 1998.

Curtis, William J. R. *Modern Architecture since 1900.* 3rd ed. Upper Saddle River, N.J.: Prentice Hall, 1996.

Heydenreich, Ludwig Heinrich. *Architecture in Italy, 1400–1600.* 2 vols. 1903. Reprint, New Haven, Conn.: Yale University Press, 1995–1996.

Hurwit, Jeffrey M. *The Athenian Acropolis: History, Mythology, and Archaeology from the Neolithic Era to the Present.* New York: Cambridge University Press, 1999.

Jencks, Charles. *The Language of Post-Modern Architecture.* 6th ed. New York: Rizzoli, 1991.

Kalnein, Wend von. *Architecture in France in the Eighteenth Century.* New Haven, Conn.: Yale University Press, 1995.

Klotz, Heinrich. *The History of Postmodern Architecture.* Cambridge, Mass.: MIT Press, 1988.

Lewis-Williams, David. *The Mind in the Cave: Consciousness and The Origins of Art.* London and New York: Thames and Hudson, 2002.

Moffett, Marian, Michael Fazio, and Lawrence Wodehouse. *Buildings across Time: An Introduction to World Architecture.* Boston: McGraw-Hill, 2004.

Rhodes, Robin F. *Architecture and Meaning on the Athenian Acropolis.* Cambridge, U.K.: Cambridge University Press, 1995.

Roth, Leland M. *American Architecture: A History.* Boulder, Colo.: Westview Press, 2001.

———. *Understanding Architecture: Its Elements, History, and Meaning.* New York: Icon Editions, 1993.

Smith, William S. *The Art and Architecture of Ancient Egypt.* 3rd ed., rev. New Haven, Conn.: Yale University Press, 1998.

Steele, James. *Architecture Today.* London: Phaidon, 1997.

Trachtenberg, Marvin, and Isabelle Hyman. *Architecture from Prehistory to Postmodernity.* 2nd ed. New York: Abrams, 2002.

Ward-Perkins, J. B. *Roman Imperial Architecture.* Harmondsworth, U.K.: Penguin, 1981

Wittkower, Rudolf. *Architectural Principles in the Age of Humanism.* 4th ed. London: St. Martin's, 1988.

Leland M. Roth

AFRICA

Sketching a comprehensive history of African architecture remains a daunting task because of the enormous size of the continent, the thousands of distinct ethnic groups that inhabit the vast lands, the differences in climate, and the various colonial, economic, political, and religious experiences. Yet, African geography, characterized by the large size of the continent, which encompasses multiple population and cultural distributions, can provide the methodological and temporal means for studying and understanding the continent's architectural history, practices, and scholarship.

The "Triple Heritage" Architectural Concept

Looking at the floor plan of a family dwelling in Africa, one needs to ask: Who lives there? Is it a Muslim family, a Christian family, or a family that believes in ancestor worship? Is there an extended family ancestors' shrine? Is the dwelling laid out as an extended family compound or as a single-family bungalow in an exclusive wealthy section of the city? When examining the tectonics—that is, the construction methods by which the structures of the house, the styles of decorations on the façade and elevations (fronts), roof, openings, and columns, are held together in harmony—of a built object in Africa, one is bound to reflect on what the walls are made of. Are they constructed from grass, branches of trees, reeds, raffia palm fronds, timber, coral shells and sands, clay, or stones? Regarding more recently built structures, one must ask: Are the walls built with concrete materials, zinc, plywood, synthetic materials, engineered wood, or cardboard boxes? What about climatic control and protection from the elements such as the sun and rain? Is the roof of the dwelling high-pitched, low-pitched, sloping to one side, or flat? What material(s) is it made of? Slate, zinc, shingles, clay, thatch, or grass? How are cooling, heating, and humidity controlled? Furthermore, because one of the most important aspects of buildings is the elevation, and many traditional African compounds have portals, one is bound to ask questions regarding the relationships between the portals and the elevations of the houses in the compound, such as: What styles and motifs articulate the portal's surrounding elements, and how are the doors and windows decorated? Are they painted with clay or other pigments? Do they display specific symbols that can be recognized by the members of the community? These are questions that can be addressed with a clear understanding of Africa's geography.

The distribution of climatic zones and vegetation types, along with the availability of building materials, influences the manner in which people build in different parts of the continent. While the coastal tips of northern and southern Africa are covered by Mediterranean vegetation, further inland one encounters semiarid wooded steppe lands that border the deserts—the Sahara Desert in the North, the Kalahari Desert in the South. Both regions are buffered by vast Sahel and savanna grasslands and forests that stretch to West Africa and parts of East Africa. Heading north from the West African Atlantic, mangrove forests, dense tropical rain forests, and evergreen forests gradually transition into Sahel and savanna woodlands and then into the desert proper—the Sahara.

The distribution of cultural groups and political experiences across different parts of the continent from ancient times through the present also underscores the importance of understanding the geography of the continent when studying its architectural heritage. The northern parts of the continent, comprised of the countries of Morocco, Algeria, Tunisia, Libya, and Egypt, are inhabited by populations that are predominantly Muslim, and certain cultural buildings and edifices from the past and present reflect this way of life. The Muslim population in northern Africa extends to West Africa in countries such as Mauritania, Senegal, Guinea, Mali, Burkina Faso, Niger, and Chad, although these nations contain pockets of Christian communities. Similarly, building techniques reflect these religious cultural affinities as well as responses to specific regional, vernacular, and climatic needs.

Moving eastward toward the Atlantic coast from the northwestern African coastal countries, a great change in religious affiliations and cultural identifications can be observed among citizens of the same country. For example, in Sierra Leon, Liberia, Côte d'Ivoire, Ghana, Togo, Benin, Nigeria, and Cameroon, the populations in the northern parts of these countries are predominantly Muslim, whereas the southern populations are predominantly Christian. The middle parts, often identified as middle belts, seem to have balanced numbers of Christians and Muslims. In the Central African Republic, Gabon, the Democratic Republic of Congo (formerly Zaire), and Angola, large Catholic and other Christian denominations reside side by side with large Muslim populations. With the exception of Ethiopia, a Christian country with a predominantly Coptic sect as well as a minority Muslim population, many East African countries are predominantly populated by Muslims with fairly large number of citizens affiliated with the Christian faith. The Republic of Sudan, Djibouti, Somalia, Kenya, Uganda, and Tanzania have large Muslim and minority Christian populations. As in West Africa, northern Sudan is predominantly Muslim, whereas the southern part is principally Christian. Mozambique, Zambia, Zimbabwe, Namibia, Botswana, and the Republic of South Africa are inhabited by populations that are predominantly Christian with significant populations of Muslims. Once again, the architecture of these regions of Africa reflects the cultural and climatic variations.

It is important to emphasize that the West did not introduce Christianity to all parts of Africa. Certain North African territories and East African countries such as Ethiopia adopted the Christian faith in the middle of the fourth century C.E.—that is, about the same time that Imperial Rome adopted Christianity as its official state religion. One cannot ignore, however, the proselytization of the Christian faith to Africans by later colonizing European missionaries. Also, keeping in mind that the Islamic religion began to spread on the continent in the seventh century C.E., one is left with the inevitable question: What form(s) of cultural affiliations were on the African continent before the coming of Islam and Christianity? The answer is that there has always been indigenous African culture; in fact, one has to speak in the plural by stating that there have always been indigenous cultures that were generated and propagated by the peoples of the continent and that varied greatly from place to place. Indigenous African cultures have had the greatest impact on the continent's architecture(s).

When discussing African architectural practices, the most important thing to keep in mind about the indigenous, Western, and Islamic aspects of African cultures is that they are broad concepts that vary from place to place and region to region. Nevertheless, these concepts lay solid foundations for studying the continent's architecture across time and space in different regions of the continent. For that reason, Nnamdi Elleh, in his book *African Architecture: Evolution and Transformation* (1997), summed up the original sources of African architecture as indigenous, Western, and Islamic in what he called the "triple heritage architectural concept." The formation of this theory followed years of research exploring the works of architectural historians such as Udo Kultermann, Peter Garlake, Susan Denyer, and Susan B. Aradeon, and it took into consideration the geography, anthropology, sociology, history, and political systems of Africa, especially as reflected in the works of such scholars as Ali A. Mazrui, who first coined the phrase "triple heritage" in his book titled *The Africans: A Triple Heritage* (1986).

It is obvious that for a continent as large as Africa, such a sweeping proposition can be problematic. The triple heritage concept needs to be clarified, because when examined from cultural, functional, stylistic, and tectonic perspectives, there are gray areas in which it is difficult to separate indigenous from Western architectural motifs, or indigenous from Islamic architecture. Conversely, there are several cases in which motifs that help identify Western and Islamic architecture cannot be completely isolated from one another. Issues of regionalism and vernacular articulations that are inspired by climatic necessities and available building technologies can compound this problem. This is where history and archaeology can help sort out how these three large building cultures came together and provided the continent its architectural heritage. The aim in

Ruins of a conical stone tower of a convent in Zimbabwe. The religion of a region and other cultural variations can play an important role in African architecture, affecting such choices as elevation, construction style, building materials, and decoration or ornamentation. © CHARLES & JOSETTE LENARS/CORBIS

adopting this historical approach is not necessarily to achieve a total level of cultural separation asserting in absolute terms that this is indigenous, that is Western, and that is Islamic—as desirable as that may be; it would be hard to reach a level of absolute certainty regarding which tectonic and stylistic motifs could be identified and separated from one another in all cases. Nevertheless, understanding the mechanisms in which architectural fusion took place among the three cultures places one in a better position to determine the functions, styles, and systems of the continent's architectural practices. Hence, the next three sections provide synopses of the indigenous, Western, and Islamic aspects of the triple heritage architectural concept.

The Roots of Indigenous African Architecture

The most challenging task for scholars of African architecture is determining its historical sources. This task is compounded by the nuances of intellectual historiography that bifurcate the continent into two parts comprising an "uncivilized" black Africa occupying sub-Saharan regions and an Arab North Africa fairly "civilized" because of its proximity to the Western civilizations of the Mediterranean region and southern Europe. Gaining currency from the middle of the eighteenth century, the early history of Africa, which was constructed primarily by European explorers, has been an obstacle to scholars who work on the architectural history of the continent because it favors the advancement of the concept of a "primitive" architecture for sub-Saharan Africa in opposition to a mature Islamic architectural civilization for northern Africa. As such, when looking at the history of sub-Saharan African architecture, early scholars of the subject ignored its historical, geographical, and regional variations. Often, the published titles on African architectural history were classified under "primitive" architecture. This method of exploring African history has a major consequence because it denies the reality that Africans also produced monumental architecture during ancient times.

The evidence from archaeological sites in different parts of the continent contradicts the notion that Africans were unable to produce monumental architecture. So far, there are only two main texts that ground traditional African architecture in antiquity and make a strong case for exploring what the archaeological evidence reveals about the continent's architectural history: Elleh's aforementioned *African Architecture* and Labelle Prussin's *African Nomadic Architecture: Space, Place, and Gender* (1995). Both books strongly argue that scholars should look at the archaeological records in the Sahara, especially from the regions of Tassili and Fezzan, in order to gain insights into how different architectural elements evolved on the continent. Prussin's contribution is particularly interesting in that it traces the origins of the tent structure and the role of women in its construction and perpetuation from prehistoric to contemporary times. Prussin's propositions help buttress Elleh's concept of the triple heritage when it comes to the relationships between ancient Egyptian architecture and traditional architecture in sub-Saharan Africa. In *Art History in Africa: An Introduction to Method* (1984), Jan Vansina makes the point that ancient Egyptian art and architecture cannot be fully understood without recognizing that it inherited most of its traditions from the Saharan cultures that predate it by more than three thousand years.

Usually, when people think of ancient Egyptian architecture the image that comes to mind is great pyramids and temples that were built by people whose skin color was lighter than the complexion of people who reside in sub-Saharan Africa. The implication is that, culturally speaking, these people with lighter skin color are entirely distinct from those with very dark skin, and, as such, those with very dark skin produced nothing in antiquity. On the contrary, and backed by strong archaeological evidence, Elleh argues that early Egyptian dynasties and their monumental architecture were built by ancient African kings. Thus, indigenous African architecture includes pyramids, temples, clay (adobe) structures, tent structures, huts made of grass and reeds, and a combination of multiple building materials, and the tectonics of each structure depended on its geographical location and the time in which it was conceived and produced.

For example, Elleh emphasizes that monumental architecture such as the pyramids did not just develop in ancient Egypt overnight. It evolved slowly following the desiccation of the

Sahara Desert, whereupon certain building traditions from the Sahara were transferred to the newly founded kingdom of Egypt by Menes (fl. c. 2925 B.C.E.), the pharaoh whom archeologists identify as Narmer. By the third and fourth dynasties, when Djoser's Step Pyramid and the Great Pyramid of Khufu (Cheops) were built, the pharaohs were African kings, and their monumental productions were indigenous African productions. This proposition could be extended to the Middle Kingdom (2000–1786 B.C.E.) when most of the powerful pharaohs ruled Egypt. The evolution of ancient Egyptian dynastic architecture shows that long before the conquest of Egypt by Alexander the Great, king of Macedonia, in 332 B.C.E., the Assyrians had taken over around 670 B.C.E., followed by the Persians in 525 B.C.E. This leads one to recognize that the early structures built before the invasions were all proposed and constructed by indigenous African monarchs. J. C. Moughtin's book *Hausa Architecture* (1985) sheds light on the relationships between certain ancient Egyptian architectural motifs and the motifs that are used by Hausa adobe builders. The relationships between Hausa building traditions and Islamic building traditions within the West African region was studied by Prussin in *Hatumere: Islamic Design in West Africa* (1986). Also important are Peter Garlake's contributions on the architecture of Great Zimbabwe, the site of ruins within Zimbabwe dating from as early as the eleventh century C.E.

Western (European Colonial) Influences on African Architecture

It has been suggested that the relationships among the three strands of the African architectural heritage cannot be completely isolated from one another in many cases because the cultures have intermixed over time. Yet there are two clearly defined phases during which Western-inspired architectural styles were imported into Africa. The first phase began with the Roman conquest of the North African city-state of Carthage in 146 B.C.E. at the end of the Third Punic War. This conquest brought with it Roman building cultures and architectural traditions that can be found throughout most of North Africa, especially in sites such as El Djem, Tunisia, where a Roman coliseum dating to 300 C.E. can be found.

The second phase began much later, during the fifteenth century, when European explorers began to look for a sea route to the Orient. Pioneered by the Spaniards and the Portuguese, who sailed around the West African Atlantic coasts on their journey to India and the Far East, numerous trading fortresses began to dot the West African coastal landscapes as trade between Europe, Africa, and the Orient became more lucrative. These large structures also heralded the arrival of people from other European countries, such as the Belgians, Dutch, English, French, and Germans, who began to settle along the African coastal territories. Among the first and largest of the European structures was Fort Elmina, built by Diogo d'Azambuja, a Portuguese captain, in 1482, in what was then called the Gold Coast (today's Ghana). The booming trade between Africa, Europe, and the Orient expanded to the Americas as the slave trade brought from Europe new seekers of treasures in Africa.

In 1820 about five thousand English settlers moved to the Cape in southern Africa. In 1830 France invaded and occu-

The Great Mosque in Djenne, Mali. Built in the thirteenth and fourteenth centuries, the mud-brick mosque at Djenne is an example of the influence of Islamic tradition upon African architecture. The Djenne mosque is the largest mud structure in the world. © ROBERT VAN DER HILST/CORBIS

pied Algiers. In 1867 the availability of diamonds in the Griqualand West region of southern Africa was brought to the attention of the European settlers. Likewise, gold was brought to the attention of Europeans at Lydenberg, in Transvaal, in 1873. The Berlin Conference of 1884–1885 set in motion the "Scramble for Africa" in which the European powers subdivided the continent into spheres of influences. Cecil Rhodes, who would become prime minister of the Cape Colony in 1890, founded De Beers Consolidated Mines in 1888 and the British South Africa Company one year later. This synopsis of nineteenth-century colonial African history mirrors the manner in which Western architecture was spread on the continent from the turn of the nineteenth century through most of the twentieth century. Because of the manner in which the continent was settled by later European economic immigrants, it is not surprising that South Africa was the area most greatly influenced by Western architecture.

The Arrival and the Sources of Islamic Architecture in Africa

Coupled with Islamic architectural influence in Africa are the processes of Arabization in northern Africa spawned by migrating and conquering Muslims who were spreading the faith and the new forms of political leadership that Islam inspired from the early part of the seventh century C.E. The religion founded by the prophet Muhammad (c. 570–632 C.E.) spread rapidly throughout most of the Arabian Peninsula into northern Africa. By 641 Egypt had fallen to the Muslim conquerors, and it was only a matter of time before the remaining parts of Byzantine North Africa fell. The rapid spread of Islam and its new building traditions, which incorporated traditions from Byzantine Rome, helped inspire various styles of Islamic architecture in northern Africa. The Great Mosque of Kairouan, Tunisia, started around 670 and completed in the ninth century, is one of the great mosques that set the pace for the new building traditions that emerged in northern Africa. The evidence that Islam had spread to most of West and East Africa before the tenth century is abundant, and Islamic-inspired architectural structures dating to the fourteenth century can be located in Mali, such as the Great Mosque of Djinguere Ber, and Tanzania, such as the Palace of Husuni Kubwa at Kilwa. It is important to keep in mind that the styles of Islamic architecture varied greatly between northern, western, and eastern Africa.

Conclusion

While the triple heritage concept is an important starting point for understanding African architectural history, scholars have to look beyond the traditional sources by exploring the influences of late-twentieth-century capitalism in order to understand the forces that are propelling contemporary African architectural practices. Following the independence movements of the 1960s, leaders of the newly independent African states sent many students to Europe and the Americas to study architecture. Also, a number of schools of architecture were established in Africa, and several postcolonial cities, such as Dodoma, Tanzania; Yamoussoukro, Côte d'Ivoire; and Abuja, Nigeria's new federal capital, which was designed for three million inhabitants, were built. These twentieth-century modernist projects remain to be studied and documented.

See also **Architecture: Overview; Arts: Africa.**

BIBLIOGRAPHY

Aradeon, Susan B. "Al-Sahili: The Historians' Myth of Architectural Technology Transfer from North Africa." *Journal des Africanistes* 59, nos. 1–2 (1989): 99–131.

Davidson, Basil. *African Civilization Revisited: From Antiquity to Modern Times.* Trenton, N.J.: African World Press, 1991.

Denyer, Susan. *African Traditional Architecture: An Historical and Geographical Perspective.* London: Heinemann, 1978.

Elleh, Nnamdi. *African Architecture: Evolution and Transformation.* New York: McGraw-Hill, 1997.

Garlake, Peter. *Early Art and Architecture of Africa.* Oxford: Oxford University Press, 2002.

———. *Great Zimbabwe.* London: Thames and Hudson, 1973.

Hoag, John D. *Islamic Architecture.* New York: Harry N. Abrams, 1977.

Kultermann, Udo. *New Architecture in Africa.* Translated by Ernst Flesch. New York: Universe Books, 1963.

———. *New Directions in African Architecture.* Translated by John Maass. New York: George Braziller, 1969.

Mazrui, Ali A. *The Africans: A Triple Heritage.* Boston: Little, Brown, 1986.

Moughtin, J. C. *Hausa Architecture.* London: Ethnographica, 1985.

Prussin, Labelle. *African Nomadic Architecture: Space, Place, and Gender.* Washington, D.C.: Smithsonian Institution Press, 1995.

———. *Hatumere: Islamic Design in West Africa.* Berkeley and Los Angeles: University of California Press, 1986.

Vansina, Jan. *Art History in Africa: An Introduction to Method.* New York: Longman, 1984.

Nnamdi Elleh

ASIA

Parallel to cultural developments in the West during the centuries around the start of the common era—and in essential isolation from the West—completely separate developments were occurring in southern and eastern Asia, shaping civilizations and cultures that continue to this day, and whose fundamental philosophical views continue with little change, despite long contact with the West.

Indian Architecture

The first of these cultures to be treated, and in some ways those that had the most important influence on other Asian cultures, were those that developed in what is now India. As early as 5,000 years ago several cities flourished along the Indus River in northeastern India, producing remarkable artwork and forms of writing still debated as to methods of decipherment. A native Dravidian religion later developed in this area, with emphasis on male and female fertility imagery. About 3,500 years ago groups of Aryan invaders moved in from the north, bringing more ascetic religious practices. These two ancient belief systems underlie Indian temple architecture to this day, combining abstract diagrammatic and symbolic plan arrangements overlaid with a profusion of luxuriant carvings portraying the numerous gods, shown in episodes from their many stories, including depictions of transcendental male and female physical union.

Around 2,600 years ago three major religions developed in India—Hinduism, Jainism, and Buddhism—each with a variant belief in the transmigration of souls, reborn in new bodily form after death. In Hinduism, with its pantheon of numerous deities largely associated with natural elements and events, the ancient emphasis on the individual and the universal, male and female, the phallic *lingam* form and the corresponding female *yoni* imagery, was strongly developed. Hinduism, with its many elaborate rituals carried out by Brahmin priests, was rejected by Jainism, and also by Buddhism, started by Siddhartha Gautama (c. 563–c. 483 B.C.E.), who, through meditation directed at release from human desire, achieved the state of "enlightened one," or Buddha. Spread throughout India and far beyond by disciples and monks who emulated the Buddha's example, Buddhism rejected the elaborate Hindu rituals in favor of seeking release from self with the extinction of desire, leading ultimately to a state of *nirvana*.

Hindu architecture. In Hindu belief the primordial world floated in a vast ocean, with a sacred mountain at its center consisting of five or six ascending levels or terraces. From this idea developed the concept of the gods residing in the mountains or in sacred caves; this led to the creation of temples as caves carved into the solid rock of cliff sides, the carved elements of the shaped space inside recalling more ancient forms once carved in wood. A good example is the Vishnu cave-temple carved out in the sixth century at Badami in Karnataka, southern India, a hall with many square columnar piers, oriented on a north-facing axis.

Two axes typically govern Hindu temple architecture: a horizontal ground-plane axial system oriented to the cardinal directions, most often facing east; and a towering mass marking a vertical axis. This vertical mass, the *shikhara*, represents the sacred mountain, and rises in massed layers, gently rounded at the top. The enormously thick masonry walls of the base enclose a small internal chamber, the sacred cave-womb space, *garbhagriha*. Leading up to the *garbhagriha* are several chambers, aligned on the principal east-facing axis, surrounded by columnar porches, the entire complex set on a tall plinth or base, the *mandapa*. The type of the northern Indian temple is well represented by the Khandariya Mahadeva temple at Khajuraho, built about 1030 in the Madhya Pradesh region of north central India, whose rising, slightly parabolically curved *shikhara,* in the quintessential mountain profile, is composed of bundled layers.

Buddhist architecture. Ironically, Buddhist architecture in India is comparatively rare, surviving better in examples based on Indian prototypes but built in places to which Buddhism was carried, such as Sri Lanka and Cambodia, and in wooden framed temples built in China and Japan. The building type mostly closely related to Indian sources is the *stupa.* Following the Buddha's death, his ashes were divided into ten parts, which were carried to places associated with his life and teaching. These portions of his remains were buried in mounds inspired by the small mounded village memorials or *chaityas* traditionally built over the remains of deceased leaders. The Buddhist stupa, a large domed mound covered with stone, represents the dome of heaven; it is enclosed by circular walkways for meditation, and defined by encircling stone fences punctuated by large gates in the cardinal directions representing the winds. A splendid example (remaining in India) is the Great Stupa at Sanchi in the Madhya Pradesh, begun by the Indian ruler Asoka sometime between 273 and 236 B.C.E. The broad dome, 120 feet (36.5 meters) in diameter and rising 54 feet (16.5 meters) in height, is capped with a square railing (*harmika*) and a spire-like form (*chatra*) resembling superimposed umbrellas representing the stages of enlightenment achieved by Buddha as well as symbolizing the bodhi tree under which he achieved his final enlightenment. As Buddhism spread eastward, this *chatra* form is believed to have inspired the development of the Chinese pagoda tower (the name for which derives from the Sanskrit *dagoba* for stupa).

Islamic Architecture

The religious landscape of India, and indeed large portions of southeast Asia, was dramatically changed with the spread of

India's Taj Mahal. The Taj Mahal in Agra, Uttar Pradesh, represents a shining example of Asian architecture during the Mughal dynasty. Constructed as a tomb to honor Shah Jahan's deceased wife, the building displays harmonious proportions and a purity of design. © SUSAN D. ROCK

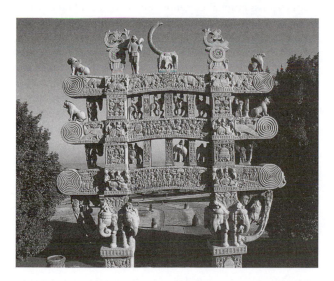

Detail of the sculptured gate of the Great Stupa at Sanchi, India. Constructed sometime between 273 and 236 B.C.E., the Great Stupa is one of the few surviving examples of original Buddhist architecture. Stupas were built to commemorate the deeds of Buddha, and some are said to enshrine his mortal remains. © ARCHIVO ICONOGRAFICO, S.A./CORBIS

Islam from the west. Islamic armies of the Turks and Afghans conquered northern India in the late twelfth century, and an independent Islamic state was declared there in 1206. Mosque building now took the place of temple building, revealing a fundamental difference in the concept of the religious building. Whereas the Hindu temple was a vertical point marker in space, its interior densely enclosed, dark, mysteriously introvert, the mosque in contrast (inspired by the court of the prophet Muhammad's house in Mecca) was open to the sky, a public gathering place for prayer, extrovert. The introduction of Islam in Hindu India set up a fundamental conflict that still continues, after eight centuries, to generate intense clashes and to cause bloodshed.

By about 1500 this Islamic empire was enlarged by Babur, founder of the Mughal dynasty, to extend from Afghanistan to Bengal. By this time a distinctive north Indian Islamic culture had emerged, with Islam established as the official religion, but with later Mughal emperors such as Akbar and Shah Jahan fostering a broader cultural tolerance. Where the teaching of Islam held firm, however, was in the elimination of figural sculpture from sacred buildings (although figural painting was practiced separately). Gardens, mirroring the Koranic descriptions of paradise, became a design specialty of the Mughals.

For many observers, the pinnacle of Mughal architecture was reached with the creation of a striking white marble tomb, the Taj Mahal, built by the bereft emperor Shah Jahan on the banks of Jumna River near Agra, Uttar Pradesh, to honor his beloved wife Mumtaz Mahal, who died in childbirth. Begun around 1631, the building itself was finished in six years, while the garden and adjoining buildings were completed in 1643. Bounded by a wall punctuated by a large entry gate on the southern edge is a broad square garden laid out in a precise grid, with channels of water on the axes (symbolic of the rivers of paradise) converging on a slightly elevated pool in the center. Lawns and planted beds fill the four quadrangles; originally intended to have different plants producing flowers continuously during the cycle of the seasons, the flower beds were framed by fruit trees. No literate Mughal entering the garden could fail to appreciate the images of paradise that informed every aspect of the design, for over the entry gate, written out in black marble inlay in a white marble band, is this passage from the Koran:

> But Oh thou soul at peace,
> Return thou unto thy Lord, well-pleased, and well-pleasing unto Him,
> Enter thou among thy servants,
> And enter thou My paradise.

At the northern edge, on a raised platform is the white domed tomb, a masterwork conceived by the Shah's architects, Ustad Ahmed Lahori and 'Ahb al-Karim Ma'mur Kahn, aided by the court calligrapher Amanat Khan. The square mass of the central building is a symbol of calm and harmony, for it is exactly as high as it is wide, and the height of the dome is exactly the same as that of the arched entry block. The white marble mass of the building is embellished everywhere with representations of the flowers of paradise, crafted of inlays of jade, lapis, amber, carnelian, jasper, amethyst, agate, heliotrope, and green beryl. In addition to the flower and geometrical ornamental inlays, black marble inlay everywhere presents passages from the Koran that relate to paradise on the Day of Judgment. In its purity of material and its balance of proportions, the Taj Mahal serves as a fitting representation of paradise.

Chinese Temples and Residences

Buddhism was introduced to China around the first century B.C.E. Buddhist temples there were built in the wood-frame tradition that had developed in China around the second millennium B.C.E. A good example, because constrained in size, is one of the oldest surviving wood buildings in China, the Nanchan Temple on Wutai Mountain in Shaanxi province, begun 782 C.E. Stupas in China were replaced by pagodas, inspired not only by the multilevel *chatra* but also drawing on the tradition of local watchtowers. The horizontal layers of the stacked parasols were modified as encircling projecting roof bands (as in the brick pagoda of the Song Yue temples at Song Mountain, Henan province, built in 523). From this evolved the timber-framed pagoda, with superimposed broad eaves carried by the densely stacked brackets, as seen in the Fogong temple at Yingxian, Shaanxi province, built in 1056.

Before the onslaught of Western influence in the nineteenth century, China's social structure had long been shaped by two philosophical systems resulting from the writings of two sages of the fifth century B.C.E.—Laozi and Confucius (Kong fuzi). These two systems fit nicely with the Chinese concept of *yin* and *yang*, the necessary presence of basic dualities or polarities in the universe, such as male and female. The system of Laozi, called Daoism (from *Dao,* "the way"), in comparison with Confucianism, is nonrational or naturalistic, and nonauthoritarian, embracing the spontaneous variation of nature. Confucianism, in contrast, originally developed as a system to ensure logical orderly governance, was rooted in a sense of underlying order, obedience to authority, veneration of ancestors, and respect for one's elders. These two philosophical systems were brought into alignment with the religious tenets of Buddhism, which flourished in China (prior to the Communist Revolution in the mid-twentieth century).

Confucian ideas of an orderly system intended to promote and maintain social order are well illustrated by one of the oldest manuscripts to survive in China, *Kao gong ji* (The artificer's record), from the fifth century. This remarkable document is a guide for laying out cities, outlining general principles that hold true in large measure for modest residential compounds as well as for the sprawling complex of the imperial household and governmental center of Ming and Qing China—the Forbidden City, Beijing. Chinese culture is about containment—the nation is bounded by a wall (the Great Wall to keep out the barbarians); the city is bounded by a wall (indeed, the word for city and wall is the same, *cheng*); and the individual household compound is bounded by a closed wall. The *Kao gong ji* instructs that a capital city should be a square 4,000 feet to a side, oriented to the cardinal directions, with three gates to a side. The main gate should face south, and the principal street runs north-south, leading to the governmental center. Each of the cardinal axes and directions is associated with one of the five elements, with attributes and colors associated with each of the cardinal directions. East is linked with spring, wood, and the color green. South is associated with summer, fire, and red. West is associated with autumn, metal (in particular gold), and white. North is connected with winter, night, and the color black. Where the axes of the city intersect in the center, *zhong,* is the location of the ruler's residence and place of administration, associated with a vertical *axis mundi,* earth, and the royal color yellow (the central imperial palace buildings—and only these buildings—were covered with yellow glazed roof tiles). There, in a room facing southward toward a court sat the emperor, likewise facing south, at the center of all things.

Residences were walled family compounds, ruled by the male master, with lesser authority associated with his wife and several consorts. The walled house was made up of a series of inward-focused courtyards, and the "good wife" was one who never ventured outside the walls. Ideally laid out on a north-south axis, the house had a simple door opening to the street,

Entrance to Phoenix Hall, Byōdōin Temple, Honshū, Japan. Previously the site of aristocrat Fujiwara Yorimichi's country villa, Byōdōin was converted into a Buddhist monastery in the mid-eleventh century. Phoenix Hall was built at the time of this conversion and was named for its resemblance to the outstretched wings of the mythical bird. © Archivo Iconografico, S.A./Corbis

leading to a first inner service court, lined by kitchen and service rooms to the south, with children's and guest rooms east and west. A door in the northern wall of this court led to a second inner court, lined with children's suites east and west, but on the axis on the north side of this court would be the parents' suite of rooms, often in the very center of which was a large room, the ancestral hall, with an altar on its north side for the veneration of ancestors and the gods.

In contrast to this ordered regularity and the straight axial lines of the house itself was the studied and felicitous irregularity of the adjoining garden in compounds of the more well-to-do. In a *yin* (feminine) and *yang* (male) balance, the house was seen as Confucian while the garden was Daoist. While some gardens could be large, such as the famous ones in Suzhou, even a small court could be made a symbol of nature by the adroit use of a small lagoon or pond, a few selected trees, a selected unusually irregular rock. Paths were made of curved or broken and bent lines, since inauspicious or malevolent spirits could only move along straight lines. Gardens were considered more difficult to design than houses, and they were intended to look as if they had grown entirely out of nature. Hence, the intellectual study of garden design and the making of gardens was a discipline associated with highly educated

poets, philosophers, and men who had distinguished themselves in government service.

Japanese Architecture and Gardens

Japanese architecture, like Japanese culture, is distinct and unique but at the same time incorporates elements imported from China, notably Buddhism. The native religion of Japan, Shinto, is described as a form of nature's idealization, and was largely responsible (some scholars have suggested) for Japan's being able to retain a distinct cultural identity in the face of the strong Chinese influence. The "way of the gods" (the literal meaning of *Shinto*) is based on deep respect for *kami,* an eternal superconsciousness believed to be inherent throughout nature, in ancient trees, in remarkable boulders, in streams, and other natural manifestations, provoking profound awe. Shinto as a religion is itself unique, having neither dogma, scriptures, nor form. The religious content of Shinto, reflected in a native focus on purity of form, material, and construction in objects and architecture, is thought to have been formulated during the Yayoi period (c. 300 B.C.E. to c. 300 C.E.). *Kami* is considered present also in human constructions of utmost simplicity of form and purity of construction. This is demonstrated by the ritual reconstruction, every twenty years, of the most sacred Shinto shrines, as at the Ise Jingu precinct or shrine on the eastern coast. There, since the reign of Emperor Temmu (672–686), now some sixty times, on identical adjoining sites, the complex of buildings has been meticulously duplicated and rebuilt with new carefully prepared cypress timbers and thick perfectly trimmed thatch roofs, leaving only the most sacred central pole covered and protected on the adjoining site, awaiting the next rebuilding.

Beauty as a principle pervading all nature and, ideally human construction, reshaped Buddhist architecture, introduced from China after 552 C.E. Factions of the imperial family, early converts to Buddhism, strongly endorsed this new religion that was seemingly so contradictory to native Shinto, and supported the building of a temple and monastery complex that became the Horuji temple complex, marked by its tall five-storied pagoda. Other larger temple and monastery compounds followed elsewhere, but perhaps the perfection of Sino-Nipponese Buddhist architecture was reached in a private residential compound converted by its owner, Fujiwara Yorimichi (994–1074) into a realization of the Pure Land Buddhist Paradise as illustrated in the Taima Mandala brought from China in the late ninth century. Built in 1053 in Uji, near Kyoto, the Byodoin contains the regent's private chapel, the Amida Hall, called the Hodo (Phoenix Hall) because its plan with central tail and outstretched wings is said to resemble the phoenix, and also because of the ceramic phoenix images crowning its roof. Reflected in the waters of the lake, the outstretched wings might be seen to suggest flight. Inside sits a gilded wooden image of the Buddha, seated on an open lotus, hands serenely folded in meditation.

An exceptionally ascetic form of Buddhism—Chan (Zen) Buddhism—was introduced from China around 1200. Emphasizing pragmatism while shunning elaborate external rituals, Zen Buddhism held strong appeal for the ruling samurai warriors. Replacing perfunctory ritual with highly focused meditation and stern self-discipline, Zen Buddhism proposed a different path to enlightenment, and its reduction to pure essence is well illustrated by the austere meditative rock gardens of Zen monasteries, most notably in the rock garden at Ryoanji, built in the 1480s in Kyoto. Within this temple courtyard, five groups of judiciously placed rocks are set into a broad bed of carefully raked white pebbles, presenting an image resembling islands in a shimmering sea or mountain tops poking through layers of clouds.

A fine residential example showing the Zen Buddhist focus on essentials and on refinement of detail can be found in the Katsura Villa, built from c. 1616 to 1660 in stages by Prince Hachijo Toshihito and his son Noritada on the Katsura River southwest of Kyoto. The plain-frame construction of now-darkened unlacquered cedar, contrasted with white plastered walls and white paper screens, the studied angles of its gentle gable roofs, and its internal spaces governed in their proportions by the standardized *tatami* floor mats measuring roughly 3 by 6 feet, perfectly realize Zen ideals. But as part of the villa complex itself, the purest manifestation of Zen artlessness, painstaking attention to detail, and careful balance of differing textures in building materials and garden elements is found in the five dispersed teahouses placed with subtle precision in the surrounding garden. With absolute simplicity of building materials and intimate human scale, the Japanese teahouse is the perfect setting for the austere, stylized, slowly choreographed quasi-religious tea ceremony in which partaking a beverage can be considered a Zen meditation.

See also **Aesthetics: Asia; Buddhism; Confucianism; Daoism; Garden; Religion: East and Southeast Asia; Sacred Places; Shinto.**

BIBLIOGRAPHY

Boyd, Andrew. *Chinese Architecture and Town Planning, 1500 B.C.–A.D. 1911.* Chicago: University of Chicago Press, 1962.

Chinese Academy of Sciences, Institute of the History of Natural Sciences. *History and Development of Ancient Chinese Architecture.* Beijing: Science, 1986.

Dehejia, Vidya. *Indian Art.* London: Phaidon, 1997.

Huntington, Susan L. *The Art of Ancient India: Buddhist, Hindu, Jain.* New York: Weatherhill, 1985.

Isozaki, Arata. *Katsura Villa: Space and Form.* New York: Rizzoli, 1987.

Liu, Laurence G. *Chinese Architecture.* New York: Rizzoli, 1989.

Mason, Penelope. *History of Japanese Art.* New York: Abrams, 1993.

Michell, George. *Hindu Art and Architecture.* London and New York: Thames and Hudson, 2000.

———. *The Hindu Temple: An Introduction to Its Meaning and Forms.* 2nd ed. Chicago: University of Chicago Press, 1988.

Rowland, Benjamin. *The Art and Architecture of India: Buddhist, Hindu, Jain.* 3rd ed. Baltimore: Penguin, 1967.

Stanley-Baker, Joan. *Japanese Art.* London and New York: Thames and Hudson, 2000.

Tange, Kenzo, and Nooru Kawazoe. *Ise: Prototype of Japanese Architecture.* Cambridge, Mass.: MIT Press, 1965.

Leland M. Roth

ARISTOTELIANISM. Aristotelianism is the tradition that stressed the theoretical "sciences" rather than the practical disciplines in Aristotle's encyclopedia of the disciplines, and within the theoretical disciplines the systematic presentation of "true and certain" knowledge rather than the inductive search for its principles.

Greek Aristotelianism

The edition of Aristotle's works made by Andronicus of Rhodes (fl. c. 70–c. 50 B.C.E.) established the knowledge of a comprehensive, structured body of demonstrated conclusions as Aristotle's ideal of science. The works of Alexander of Aphrodisias (fl. c. 200), the first great commentator on Aristotle, complemented this view of the philosopher's scientific corpus. The Neoplatonic movement attempted to harmonize the thought of Plato and Aristotle as the two great representatives of the Greek tradition. The tradition of commentary on Aristotle as an introduction to the higher wisdom of Plato was represented at Athens by two works that transformed Aristotle's encyclopedia into an idealistic system. The *Elementatio theologica* (Rudiments of theology) and the *Elementatio physica* (Rudiments of physics) of Proclus (410?–485) exhibit all forms of substance as deriving from a single first principle, the Platonic One.

Alexandrian exegesis of Aristotle's text, following Ammonius Hermiae, a pagan (fl. c.550), was more independent. John Philoponus, a Christian (fl. c. 529), even contested various Aristotelian notions. His introduction of the Judeo-Christian idea of creation into philosophy rendered Proclus's entire system questionable. These Alexandrian developments determined, in large measure, the approach to Aristotle's philosophy in the Byzantine world. Plato and Aristotle were regarded as representatives of "Hellenic philosophy," as part of a pagan tradition, generally opposed to "our (Christian) philosophy." The interest of Christian theologians in Aristotle was mostly limited to the parts of his logic necessary in theology, although under the dynasty of the Komnenoi (11th–12th century), Aristotle's practical philosophy enjoyed a rebirth with the commentary on the *Ethics* put together by Eustratius of Nicaea (1054–c. 1117). After the fall of Constantinople to the Crusaders in 1204, the necessity of answering the challenge of an increasingly sophisticated Latin theology led to the composition of compendia of Aristotelian doctrine, although the debate regarding Aristotelian methods of proof continued.

Arabic Aristotelianism

By the ninth century practically the entire corpus of Aristotle's works, together with those of his Greek commentators, had been made available in Islam. Aristotle's classification of the natural sciences supplied the structure for an encyclopedia in which classical authors like Hippocrates (c. 460–c. 377 B.C.E.) and Galen (129–c. 199), Euclid (fl. c. 300 B.C.E.) and Ptolemy (second century C.E.) also found a place. The understanding of science as a body of strictly demonstrated conclusions was decisive for Islamic Aristotelianism. In their commentaries on this enormous body of new doctrine, Arabic philosophers tended to comment on the logic, metaphysics, and natural philosophy as parts of a philosophical encyclopedia; few commentaries on the practical philosophy were written. Muslim thinkers opposed studies concerned with their own way of life, called the "Arabic or traditional sciences" (the Koran; traditions; kalam, or dialectical theology; and the like), to the "Greek or rational sciences," associated for the most part with Aristotle's name. Kalam's task was to supply the faithful with logical proofs for their belief, but its methods of proof forced the Aristotelian philosophers to refine their idea of scientific methodology.

In his *Catalogue of the Sciences,* the Persian philosopher, al-Farabi (c. 878–c. 950) attempted to fit the "traditional sciences of the Arabs" into the Aristotelian division of the sciences. The doctrine of God is taken up under the theoretical science of metaphysics, whereas kalam is regarded as a part of politics, with the function of defending the articles of faith. Al-Farabi demanded that the theologians provide strict demonstrations in defense of Muslim doctrine. About a century later, another Persian philosopher, the famous physician Avicenna (980–1037), undertook to reform kalam in accordance with the Aristotelian theory of demonstrative science and understood kalam not as a part of politics, but rather as metaphysics. Through the Persian theologian al-Ghazali (1058–1111),

Avicenna's conception of logical proof was influential in Muslim theology. Averroës (1126–1198), writing in Muslim Spain, also confronted the theologians with Aristotle's idea of demonstrative science, stressing the truth and certainty of Aristotle's presentation of theoretical science.

Medieval Jewish Materialism

Medieval Judaism also needed Aristotelian science and the logic that went with it. Where conflicts between philosophy and the Jewish faith appeared, some thinkers—of whom Moses Maimonides (1135–1204) was the most significant—held that philosophical speculation must proceed according to the theory of demonstrative science, without regard for theological doctrine. Only when the philosophical and theological doctrines have been clearly defined can one ask how the two realms are related. In spite of this view, an increasingly critical evaluation of Aristotle's doctrines in the light of the Jewish faith appeared in the fourteenth century.

Medieval Latin Aristotelianism

The works of Aristotle were made available in the Latin West in three clearly distinguishable stages. The first stage opened in the sixth century with Boethius's (c. 480–c. 524) translations of Aristotle's treatises on logic, along with some notions transmitted by Cicero (106–43 B.C.E.). Such works had but little effect upon the monastic life of the early Middle Ages. The second stage began in the twelfth century with the gradual translation of the entire corpus of Aristotle's works. Working in the tradition of the *concordia discordantium* (reconciliation of disagreements), Scholastic teachers made the epoch-making decision not to try to separate—as the Byzantines and Muslims before them had done—their own religious disciplines from the profane sciences inherited from the ancients. They attempted rather to situate theological teaching within the Aristotelian classification of the sciences. The masters were guided at first by Boethius and then by Euclid. In his *De hebdomadibus* (Concerning the weekly conferences), Boethius described the organization of scientific knowledge much as Aristotle had done, and early authors sought to develop a general theory of scientific method from it. Gilbert de La Porrée (1076–1154) maintained, for example, that first principles can be established for all the liberal arts and in the same way for theology itself. Nicholas of Amiens (fl. c. 1190) in his *Ars fidei catholicae* (Art of the Catholic faith) attempted to present theological doctrine in accordance with Euclid's geometrical model.

The condemnation in 1210 and 1215 of Aristotle's *libri naturales* (books of natural philosophy) at Paris was followed by an intense effort to axiomatize the quadrivial sciences. The attempt was most successful in the science of optics, a science subalternate to geometry. But the philosophers also turned their attention to Aristotle's theory of science. Robert Grosseteste (c. 1175–1253) commented on Aristotle's *Posterior Analytics,* explaining that "science" means true and certain knowledge derived by syllogistic demonstration from first principles. Accordingly, the theologians undertook to transform their discipline into an Aristotelian science. In his *Summa aurea* (Golden compendium), William of Auxerre (c. 1150–1231) proposed taking the articles of faith as the principles of theological demonstration, on the basis of which Catholic theology could be presented as a structured body of strictly demonstrated conclusions. This lead was followed in particular by the Dominican theologians of the early part of the century.

By about 1230 the Latins had at their disposal the complete body of Aristotelian teaching together with Averroës's commentaries. The Aristotelian paradigm for science was established institutionally in the year 1255, when Aristotle's works were prescribed for the lectures in the Paris arts faculty. Working within this paradigm, the Latins made, in the course of the next two centuries, enormous progress not only in mathematics and the physical sciences, but also in the Aristotelian practical philosophy, following new translations of the *Ethics* and *Politics.* Albert the Great (c. 1200–1280) was among the first to turn his attention to the complete Aristotelian encyclopedia. His paraphrases of all of the fundamental works in Aristotle's encyclopedia prepared the way for the vast commentatory literature through which the Middle Ages assimilated Aristotelian science.

The Aristotelian paradigm was also taken up by the theologians, most prominently by Thomas Aquinas (1225–1274). At this period the theologians were faced with the same problem as that which confronted the masters of arts—the systematic presentation of a body of traditional knowledge. In Thomas's view, theology should present the teaching of Scripture and the church fathers deductively, taking its departure from the indemonstrable, but to the Christian evident, articles of faith. Thomas sought to establish a concord between Aristotle's conclusions and revealed doctrine. While Christian doctrines could not be proved, their acceptance was thought to be able to be shown at least reasonable because congruent with basic philosophical conclusions that Aristotle was thought to have demonstrated.

Anomalies in this paradigm appeared even in the thirteenth century. About the year 1250, as Averroës's real position on the immortality of the human soul became known, the Latins came increasingly to distinguish between the teaching of Aristotle and that of Averroës. But in the year 1277 the bishop of Paris condemned 219 propositions—of which the majority represented Aristotelian positions—because they entailed consequences contrary to revealed doctrine. In the light of the condemnation, John Duns Scotus (1266?–1308) proposed a new conception of the theoretical sciences. His claim that the first object of the intellect is not sensible reality, but, rather, being as such, made it possible to study corporeal reality in a metaphysical way in contradistinction to the corporeal reality studied by the Aristotelian physics. The fact that many of Aristotle's doctrines were in apparent conflict with Christian teaching helped the philosophers to adjust the metaphysical assumptions that lay behind many of his positions, especially in astronomy. Aided by the Aristotelian idea that the individual sciences are autonomous in their own realm, philosophers like John Buridan (c. 1295–c. 1358) were able to develop theories in physics that were independent of Aristotle's treatment, while mathematicians like Nicole d'Oresme (c. 1325–1382) turned to areas that Aristotle had neglected.

Renaissance Aristotelianisms

During the third and final stage in the evolution of Latin Aristotelianism, the traditional conception of the Aristotelian encyclopedia of the sciences became increasingly untenable. This period began in the year 1438 with the arrival of the Greeks at the Council of Florence. The aged philosopher George Gemistus Plethon (c. 1355–1450 or 1455) charged the Latins not only with being unacquainted with Platonic philosophy, but also with misunderstanding Aristotle's teaching. These misunderstandings arose because the Latins had been misled by Averroës to believe that the philosopher's works contained a demonstrative summary of scientific truth. Nevertheless, the Renaissance witnessed a vast increase in the literature of commentary on Aristotle's works. But at the same time Aristotelianism became but one among many philosophies, with Platonism, Stoicism, and Epicureanism also claiming attention. And the hierarchically unified worldview offered by Scholastic Aristotelianism had by the sixteenth century broken down, so that we must speak, in this period, not of one, but of several Aristotelianisms.

Catholic Aristotelianism. The encounter of the Christian Aristotelianism adumbrated by Thomas Aquinas with a secular Aristotelianism that had arisen in the Italian medical faculties resulted in the radical transformation of the Aristotelian speculative sciences in the sixteenth century. The Scholastic understanding of Aristotle's science of human nature was challenged in particular by Pietro Pomponazzi (1462–1525), who maintained that according to Aristotle the doctrine of the soul belongs to physics as a part of the doctrine dealing with *corpus animatum* (animated physical bodies). Because the soul is a material form, it is impossible to prove its immortality. The proponents of Christian Aristotelianism took up this challenge. They sought to retain Aristotle's deductive theory of science but were forced to modify radically Aristotle's ideas of the subject matter of natural philosophy. Their efforts were based on the search for metaphysical rather than physical proofs for the soul's immortality. Dominicans like Tommaso de Vio (Cajetan, 1469–1534) and Crisostomo Javelli (d. c. 1538) and Jesuits like Benito Perera (c. 1535–1610) and Francisco Suárez (1548–1617) constructed a new science of metaphysics based on the revealed idea of creation. The high point of this development was reached with the publication of Suárez's *Disputationes metaphysicae* (Metaphysical disputations) at Salamanca in 1597. Suárez retained the Aristotelian–Scholastic understanding of science and used the Scotist distinction of reality into *ens infinitum, ens creatum immateriale,* and *ens creatum materiale* (infinite being, immaterial created being, and material created being) to render the growing crisis of the Aristotelian physics as the science of *corpus mobile* (changeable physical bodies) irrelevant to Scholastics.

Italian secular Aristotelianism. Constrained by the immense amount of scientific material that the Renaissance had recovered, Aristotelian authors in Italy wrote increasingly during the sixteenth century about the teaching of this new body of doctrine and sought to situate Aristotle's theory of science within a broader context. Jacopo Zabarella (1533–1589), professor at Padua, was the author who brought these developments together most successfully in his tract *De methodis* (On method) of 1578. He distinguished scientific "method" from "orders" of presentation. There are two "methods" of discovery: (1) the compositive or synthetic method, which is the demonstrative method of "science," as Aristotle had conceived it; and (2) the resolutive or analytic method belonging to the operative disciplines or "arts," which begin with the end of an action and seek to discover the means and principles by which this end may be attained. "Orders" of presentation are simply ways of presenting the available material clearly. There are two "orders" corresponding to the two "methods" described above.

Lutheran Aristotelianism. Despite Luther's rejection of Aristotle, the Aristotelian conception of science gained a central place in Protestant universities. Lutheran authors of the late sixteenth century tended to regard theology as a practical science and, following Zabarella, came to think that theological doctrine should be presented according to the analytic "order." In his *Epitome theologiae* (Epitome of theology) of 1619, Georg Calixt (1586–1656) first applied Zabarella's idea of the analytic method to theology. But the *Formula concordiae* (Formula of concord) of 1577 established a Lutheran orthodoxy, and philosophical textbooks, like the *Exercitationes metaphysicae* (1603–1604; Metaphysical exercises) of the Wittenberg professor Jacob Martini (1570–1649) and the *Metaphysica commentatio* (1605; A metaphysical commentary) of Cornelius Martini (1568–1621) of Helmstedt, turned to the metaphysics proposed by Suárez, which all those who admitted the idea of creation could accept. Their understanding of the relationship between philosophy and theology opened the way for the free development in Lutheranism of a natural theology as a theoretical science, presented in accordance with Zabarella's synthetic order. The first independent treatise on *Theologia naturalis* (Natural theology) was published by Christoph Scheibler (1589–1653) at Giessen in 1621.

Calvinist Aristotelianism. Reformed theologians of the early seventeenth century regarded their science as essentially theoretical. In the works of authors like Bartholomew Keckermann (1571/73–1609) of Heidelberg and Danzig, Clemens Timpler (1567–1624) of Heidelberg and Steinfurt, and Johann Heinrich Alsted (1588–1638) of Herborn, the idea of a synthetic presentation of doctrine was maintained, but the encyclopedia of the disciplines was enlarged and transformed by a theory of the arts, a "technology." Reformed theologians began to use the term "system" for ordered compilations of Christian teaching. For the Marburg professor Rudolph Goclenius (1547–1628), who used the word for the first time in his *Lexicon philosophicum* (1613; A philosophical lexicon), "ontology" has the role of assigning to each of the scientific disciplines its proper place in this new encyclopedia of the practical, productive disciplines.

Neo-Scholasticism. The last edition of the Latin text of Aristotle's works was published by the Jesuit Silvester Maurus (1619–1687) in the year 1668. After the Thirty Years' War, Protestant Aristotelianism generally disappeared. But Catholic Scholasticism continued to enjoy a shadowy existence in the seminaries decreed by the Council of Trent (1545–1563). A new literary form appeared, the *cursus philosophicus,* a summary of Scholastic teaching in philosophy, generally written in the form of disputations on the works of Aristotle. The purpose of the *cursus* was to provide the basic philosophical knowledge necessary for the study of Catholic theology, and it tended

increasingly to return to the teaching of one of the great thirteenth-century doctors, like Thomas Aquinas (Thomism) and Duns Scotus (Scotism).

Modern Study of Aristotle

The Neo-Scholasticism of the nineteenth century thought of Aristotle's philosophy as a response to the Enlightenment's rejection of a worldview in which revelation appeared necessary and its acceptance reasonable. The *cursus* found the support of the Catholic Church in Pope Leo XIII's encyclical *Aeterni Patris* of 1879 and various pieces of legislation concerning the instruction in seminaries. The Dominican and Jesuit orders followed the doctrine of Thomas Aquinas, while the Franciscan order followed that of Duns Scotus, both emphasizing Aristotle's metaphysics, even for cosmological and psychological questions.

The publication by the Berlin Academy of the *Aristotelis opera* between 1831 and 1870 and of the *Commentaria in Aristotelem graeca* between 1882 and 1909 has supplied the basis for the modern study of Aristotle and the Greek tradition of his philosophy. The *Aristoteles latinus,* undertaken by the Union Académique Internationale in 1939 for the edition of the medieval Latin translations, two collections of the Latin translations of the Greek commentaries, as well as a series of English translations of them, have contributed to a new understanding of Aristotelianism in the twentieth century.

See also **Greek Science; Islamic Science; Logic; Metaphysics; Natural History; Natural Law; Natural Theology; Philosophy and Religion in Western Thought; Platonism; Scholasticism.**

BIBLIOGRAPHY

Gottschalk, Hans B. "Aristotelian Philosophy in the Roman World from the Time of Cicero to the End of the Second Century AD." In *Aufstieg und Niedergang der römischen Welt,* edited by W. Haase. Berlin: Walter de Gruyter, 1987.

Lohr, Charles H. *Latin Aristotle Commentaries: II. Renaissance Authors.* Florence, Italy: Olschki, 1988.

———. "Medieval Latin Aristotle Commentaries." *Traditio* 23–30 (1967–1974).

———. "Metaphysics." In *The Cambridge History of Renaissance Philosophy,* edited by C. B. Schmitt et al., 535–638. Cambridge, U.K.: Cambridge University Press, 1988.

———, ed. *Commentaria in Aristotelem graeca: Versiones latinae temporis resuscitatarum litterarum.* 12 vols. Frankfurt, Germany: Minerva, and Stuttgart, Germany: Frommann-Holzboog, 1978.

Mikkeli, Heikki. *An Aristotelian Response to Renaissance Humanism: Jacopo Zabarella on the Nature of Arts and Sciences.* Helsinki: Finnish Historical Society, 1992.

Peters, F. E. *Aristoteles arabus: The Oriental Translations and Commentaries on the Aristotelian Corpus.* Leiden, Netherlands: Brill, 1968.

Schmitt, Charles B. *Aristotle and the Renaissance.* Cambridge, Mass.: Harvard University Press, 1983.

Sorabji, Richard, ed. *The Ancient Commentators on Aristotle: A Series of English Translations.* London and Ithaca, N.Y.: Duckworth, 1987.

———. *Aristotle Transformed: The Ancient Commentators and Their Influence.* London: Duckworth, 1990.

Verbeke, Gerard, et al., eds. *Corpus latinum commentariorum in Aristotelem graecorum.* 12 vols. Louvain, Belgium: University of Louvain, 1957; Leiden, Netherlands: Brill, 1973–1981.

Charles H. Lohr

ARTIFICIAL INTELLIGENCE. *See* Computer Science.

ARTS.

This entry includes two subentries:

Overview
Africa

OVERVIEW

While people have always made objects that are rightly considered works of art, the *idea* of the arts is a separate category of human endeavor—distinct, that is, from other kinds of human activity such as hunting or food gathering or making in general—is a relatively modern construction.

The "Era of Art"

In the forward to his monumental study of the medieval icon, *Bild und Kult,* translated *Likeness and Presence* in the American edition, Hans Belting explains the book's rather curious subtitle—*A History of the Image before the Era of Art*—in terms that immediately focus on the issues surrounding the idea of the visual arts, especially just what they are and how they function in culture as a whole:

> Art, as it is studied by the discipline of Art History today, existed in the Middle Ages no less than it did afterwards. After the Middle Ages, however, art took on a different meaning and became acknowledged for its own sake—art as invented by a famous artist and defined by a proper theory. While the images from olden times were destroyed by iconoclasts in the Reformation period, images of a new kind began to fill the art collections which were just then being formed. The era of art, which is rooted in these events, lasts until this present day. From the very beginning, it has been characterized by a particular kind of historiography which, although called the history of art, in fact deals with the history of artists. (p. xxi)

The historiography to which Belting refers is exemplified by the work of Giorgio Vasari (1511–1574). A painter in his own right, he was by all accounts the first serious collector of drawings—he believed that they revealed the very moment of artistic inspiration. His passion for drawing also led him to found the Accademia del Disegno (Academy of Design) in Florence in 1562. He theorized that *disegno* (meaning both "drawing" and "design") was superior to *colorito* ("painting in color") because the former was an exercise of the intellect, while the latter appealed only to the sensual appetites. At the

Reliquary effigy of St. Foy (gold and silver over a wooden core, studded with precious stones and cameos), mostly 983–1013, with later additions. Created to contain the skull of a martyred child who was put to death for refuting pagan worship, the artistic power of the effigy lies not in its resemblance to the actual child, but in its purpose as the vessel that houses the sacred remains. © GIRAUDON / ART RESOURCE, NY

Accademia he encouraged artists to develop their talents unfettered by the constraints of tradition and convention, arguing that genius was most readily realized in invention.

All of Vasari's preoccupations are reflected in his *Lives of the Most Eminent Painters, Sculptors, and Architects,* first published in 1550 and then greatly revised and expanded in 1568.

Vasari's book marks the historical moment when what people today so readily think of as the visual arts were transformed from objects reflecting the manual skills of the individual craftsman to reflections of the intellectual and creative powers of the artist. Before the "era of art," the image, however artistically made, served specific cultural, religious, or political functions. It was required, quite literally, to perform. As Belting puts it, "Authentic images seemed capable of action, seemed to possess *dynamis,* or supernatural power" (p. 6). They performed miracles, warded off danger, and healed the sick. If in the "era of art" images lost this power, they gained a considerable expressive dimension. They became the medium through which artists—in the era of art, they are called "artists"—express their own ideas and feelings and make manifest their own individual talent or genius.

The difference between the image before the era of art and the image after is readily apparent if we compare the reliquary effigy of St. Foy at Conques in France and Leonardo da Vinci's (1452–1519) famous *Mona Lisa.* St. Foy was a pilgrimage church built in 1050–1120 to accommodate pilgrims on their way to Santiago de Campostela, in the northwest corner of present-day Spain, a favorite pilgrimage destination because the body of the apostle St. James the Greater, which lay at rest there, had a reputation for repeated miracles. St. Foy housed the relics of St. Foy ("Saint Faith" in English), a child who was martyred when she was burned to death in 303 for refusing to worship pagan gods. Her skull was contained in this elaborate jeweled reliquary, which stood in the choir of the church where pilgrims could view it from the ambulatory that circles the space. The head of the reliquary was salvaged from a late Roman face guard and parade helmet and reused here. Many of the precious stones that decorate the reliquary were the gifts of pilgrims themselves. The saint's actual skull was housed in a recess carved into the back of the reliquary, and below it, on the back of her throne, was an engraving of the Crucifixion, indicating the connection between St. Foy's martyrdom and Christ's own.

Now, the St. Foy effigy, fashioned out of the antique Roman mask, bears no real resemblance to the saint herself. Its value resides not in any likeness, but in its contiguity with the skull housed within. It literally "touches" the physical remains of a child burned to death, at least symbolically, by the soldier whose face this mask once guarded. The Roman artifact has thus been completely transformed—from the pagan to the Christian, from male ornament symbolic of war to a female form symbolic of faith. And it symbolizes, further, the transformation that awaits the faithful, from the physical confines of the body to the spiritual realm of the soul. Pilgrims decorated the reliquary not merely in penitence for their sins but because they felt, in its presence, the need to sacrifice their material wealth in symbolic repetition of the saint's sacrifice of her person. In one of the most important first-hand accounts of the relationship between the cult statue and the pilgrims who came to venerate it, Bernard of Angers, who made three trips to Conques beginning in 1013, describes how he was at first skeptical of the reliquary's power: "I looked with a mocking smile at [his companion] Bernier, since so many people were thoughtlessly directing their prayers at an object

without language or soul, . . . and their senseless talk did not come from an enlightened mind." But he soon changed his mind:

> Today I regret my foolishness toward this friend of God. . . . Her image is not an impure idol but a holy momento that invites pious devotion. . . . To be more precise, it is nothing but a casket that holds the venerable relics of the virgin. The goldsmith has given it a human form in his own way. The statue is as famous as once was the ark of the covenant but has a still more precious content in the form of the complete skull of the martyr. This is one of the finest pearls in the heavenly Jerusalem, and like no other person in our century it brings about the most astonishing miracles through its intercession with God.

It is as if, he says, "the people could read from the luster of these eyes whether their pleas had been heard" (pp. 536–537). It is the efficacy of the relics within that the people read into the statue's outward gaze.

The relationship between the image and its beholder is entirely different in Leonardo's *Mona Lisa* (1503–1506). In the first place, the image is, above all, a likeness. Vasari was the first to use the name by which the painting is now known, leading to speculation that the sitter is Lisa Gherardini, who married the Florentine merchant Francesco Bartolomeo del Giocondo in 1495, but other testimony contradicts this thesis, and her identity remains a mystery. This mystery, of course, lends the painting much of its fame, for without any relevant biographical knowledge, any clues as to what she might be thinking are pure speculation. As David Summers put it in his important contribution to global and intercultural art history, *Real Spaces* (2003), "She is the individual mask of her own inwardness, of the mind and heart suggested to us by her famous smile." Leonardo's purpose, Summers reminds us, was to make "the invisible (the movements of the soul) visible in the movements of the body," even in such a small movement as the upward turn of the sitter's lips. But Leonardo himself recognized

> that artists run the risk of making images look like themselves because the same individual soul that shaped the artist's physical appearance also judges the beauty and rightness of the figures the artist makes. Leonardo recommended that artists study proportion, which will give them the means to counteract this distorting narcissistic tendency. His argument assumes coincidence between individual appearance and individual soul, outwardness and inwardness. It also suggests the difficulty of distinguishing the perception of another from oneself. (p. 331)

Thus the enduring myth that *Mona Lisa* is in fact a self-portrait, Leonardo's revelation of his "feminine side." But more important, Summers makes clear here the way in which the visual arts, in the era of art, are removed from the cultural dynamic that informs the medieval icon. Just as surely as the meaning of the reliquary statue at St. Foy resides "inside" its mask, so the meaning of the *Mona Lisa* resides beneath her

Mona Lisa (1503–1506) by Leonardo da Vinci. Oil on wood. Da Vinci's masterpiece is a study in inwardness and what exists just below the surface, and admirers have spent centuries trying to decipher the subtle clues in the subject's face for an indication of what thoughts are in her head. © THE BETTMANN ARCHIVE

superficial appearance. But her meaning is private, personal, immaterial. She is forever meditative, forever a mystery, a self-reflective soul. People visit the Louvre in the early twenty-first century, in a procession not so unlike that of the medieval pilgrims, because, in the space between image and beholder, the self-reflection that the image portrays is recreated in one's reflections upon it. As Denis Donoghue has put it, "The mysteriousness of art is in all art; . . . it suffuses the space between the image and its reference" (p. 32).

From *Ars* to *Arte* to *Beaux-Arts*

The transformation of the image from an efficacious to a reflective space is coincident with the rise of the very idea of the "arts." Before the era of art, the word *art* had much broader meaning than it does today. The Latin *ars* (and the Greek *technē*) referred to almost any branch of human endeavor—the work of the farmer, the shipwright, the military commander, the magician, the cobbler, the poet, the flute player, the vase painter, all were included in the general category of the "arts" so long as their endeavors were executed with a certain

degree of skill. In the *Ethics* (book 6), Aristotle distinguished between two spheres of action— *praxis,* doing, or moral or political conduct, and *poiesis,* making, producing, or performing. The intellectual virtue attendant to *poiesis* is *techne*—art, technique, skill, and know-how—"the trained ability of making something under the guidance of rational thought" (1140.9–10). Aristotle further distinguishes between the liberal and servile arts. The liberal arts are those that work with the intellect, including the verbal arts of grammar and rhetoric and the mathematical arts of arithmetic, geometry, astronomy, and music. The servile arts are those associated with physical labor and, generally, work for pay. Thus the work of the farmer and the cook were more or less equivalent to that of the architect, the sculptor, and the painter. As John Boardman puts it in his *Greek Art,* "'Art for Art's sake' was virtually an unknown concept; there was neither a real Art Market nor Collectors; all art had a function and artists were suppliers of a commodity on a par with shoemakers" (p. 16).

Even by Vasari's time, things had hardly changed. He does not use the Italian *artista* to refer to "the artist," but rather *artifice,* "artificer." "What a happy age we live in!" he wrote, reacting to the sight of Michelangelo's Sistine Chapel frescoes. "And how fortunate are our artists [*artifice*] who have been given light and vision by Michelangelo and whose difficulties have been smoothed away by this marvelous and incomparable artist [*artifice*]." Indeed, the word *artista* was more generally used to refer to those who studied the more intellectual liberal arts, particularly rhetoricians. Furthermore, the Italian word *arte,* which in modern usage means simply "art," was in medieval times and throughout the Renaissance, the word for "guild," including, in Florence, the *Arte della Lana,* the wool guild; the *Arte di Seta,* the silk guild; and the *Arte di Calimala,* the cloth merchants' guild. Thus *art* remained simply making, skill, and know-how. The bankers had their *arte,* and so did the lawyers—perhaps because of their rhetorical skill the lawyers' was the most prestigious of all.

Not until the middle of the eighteenth century did the arts separate themselves off from other fields of endeavor into their own exclusive area of expertise. In what is one of the best surveys of the history of the *arts* as an idea, Larry Shiner points to two crucial texts—Charles Batteux's *Les beaux arts réduit à un même principe* (The fine arts reduced to a single principle), published in 1746 in France and translated into English three years later as *The Polite Arts; or, A Dissertation on Poetry, Painting, Musick, Architecture, and Eloquence,* and the 1751 edition of Denis Diderot and Jean Le Rond d'Alembert's *Encylopédie.*

Batteux claimed there are actually three classes of arts: those that simply minister to our needs (the mechanical arts); those whose aim is pleasure (the beaux-arts par excellence); and those that combine utility and pleasure (eloquence and architecture). Batteux also used two other criteria for separating the beaux-arts from the rest: genius, which he calls "the father of the arts," because it imitates beautiful nature, and taste, which judges how well beautiful nature has been imitated. . . . The *Encyclopédie* now grouped all five fine arts (poetry, painting, sculpture, engraving, and music) under the faculty of

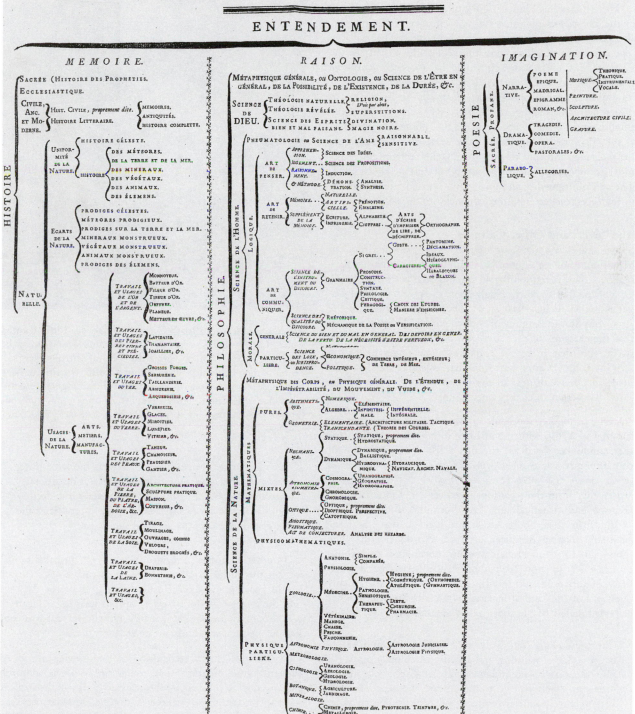

Système Figuré des Connoissances Humaines (Table of Human Knowledge; 1751), a diagram of the arts by Denis Diderot and Jean le Rond d'Alembert. Researchers did not begin to classify the arts into their own separate field of study until the eighteenth century, when several groundbreaking texts on the subject were published. ANNENBERG RARE BOOK AND MANUSCRIPT LIBRARY, UNIVERSITY OF PENNSYLVANIA imagination as one of three main divisions of knowledge, splendidly isolated from all other arts, disciplines, and sciences. (pp. 83–84)

Nevertheless, as Shiner points out, Diderot's article "Art" in the *Encyclopédie* ignores the new category of "beaux-arts" altogether and concentrates exclusively on the mechanical arts, representations of which constitute almost the entirety of the *Encyclopédie*'s illustrations. It would be another twenty-five years before an article on the "beaux-arts" would finally find its way into a supplement to the *Encyclopédie*. According to d'Alembert, the category of the *beaux-arts*—the term that the English world would translate first as the "polite arts" and then as the "fine arts"—consisted of any works that have pleasure for their aim and that rely on the imagination (inventive genius) as opposed to memory (history) or reason (philosophy). The cult of originality and imagination inaugurated by Vasari in his *Lives* reached its ultimate conclusion here.

The "Arts" and Other Cultures

Shiner makes a convincing case that the arts are a modern invention, "not an essence or a fate but something we have made . . . [an] invention barely two hundred years old" (p. 3). One of the first to convincingly argue the point was Paul Oskar Kristeller in his 1950 essay "The Modern System of the Arts," but Shiner's argument is distinguished by its awareness that the category of the "arts" is a markedly European construct, one that in recent years has come under increasing scrutiny as the (Western) art world has "opened" itself to works made in other cultures. In the process, the very idea of the "arts" has begun to change once again.

One of the key moments in this process happened in the summer of 1989, with the opening of an exhibition in Paris that announced itself as "the first world-wide exhibition of contemporary art." Called *Magiciens de la terre,* or *Magicians of the Earth,* the show consisted of works by one hundred artists, fifty from the traditional "centers" of Western culture (Europe and America) and fifty from the so-called Third World, from Asia, South America, Australia, Africa, and, incidentally, Native American art from North America. The show's curator, Jean-Hubert Martin, conceived of the exhibition as a way to show the real differences between and specificity of different cultures. But the exhibition raised many questions of the kind articulated by Eleanor Heartney in her extended review of the show in *Art in America*:

> Can there really, one wonders, be any continuum between a Kiefer painting and a Benin ceremonial mask? How does one make judgments of "quality" about objects completely foreign to our culture and experience? Is there any "politically correct" way to present artifacts from another culture, or does the museological enterprise inevitably smack of cultural exploitation? Wary of the tendency to romanticize the lost purity of vanished worlds, the organizers have emphasized societies in transition, in many cases choosing Western and non-Western artists who represent an exchange of influences between their respective cultures. Still, one wonders if

Kwakiutl mask from British Columbia, Canada, 1887. Painted wood. The Kwakiutls, a native American tribe found along the northwest coast of Canada, utilized masks for virtually every occasion in their culture. William Rubin, director emeritus of New York's Museum of Modern Art, attempted to compare Kwakiutl art to that of Picasso to prove that abstraction is a universal concept. © BILDARCHIV PREUSSISCHER KULTURBESITZ / ART RESOURCE, NY

such exchanges are really equivalent. Is the same thing going on when an artisan from Madagascar incorporates airplanes and buses within the traditional tomb decorations of Madagascar and Mario Merz appropriates the igloo or hut form into his sculptures? (pp. 91–92)

In order to treat all the show's exhibitors on equal terms, the curators included only the names of each work's creator and its geographical origin in identifying the pieces. As a result, the average Western viewer was encouraged, as Heartley says, "to apply preexisting Western esthetic standards to objects where such standards are irrelevant" (p. 92).

Nevertheless, in its recognition of the growing impact of Western culture and modern technology on "evolving" cultures, and its refusal to romanticize the originary purity of the artifacts on display, the show marked a distinct advance over the Museum of Modern Art's 1984 exhibition *'Primitivism' in 20th-century Art: Affinity of the Tribal and Modern.* Curator William S. Rubin tried to show that abstraction was a universal language by comparing, for instance, Pablo Picasso's *Girl before a Mirror* to a Kwakiutl mask from British Columbia the likes of which Picasso had almost certainly never seen and arguing that what "led artists to be receptive to tribal art" in the twentieth century

The greatest gifts are often seen, in the course of nature, rained by celestial influences on human creatures; and sometimes, in supernatural fashion, beauty, grace, and talent are united beyond measure in one single person, in a manner that to whatever such a one turns his attention, his every action is so divine, that, surpassing all other men, it makes itself clearly known as a thing bestowed by God (as it is), and not acquired by human art. This was seen by all mankind in Leonardo da Vinci, in whom, besides a beauty of body never sufficiently extolled, there was an infinite grace in all his actions; and so great was his genius, and such its growth, that to whatever difficulties he turned his mind, he solved them with ease. . . . In learning and in the rudiments of letters he would have made great proficience, if he had not been so variable and unstable, for he set himself to learn many things, and then, after having begun them, abandoned them. Thus, in arithmetic, during the few months that he studied it, he made so much progress, that, by continually suggesting doubts and difficulties to the master who was teaching him, he would very often bewilder him. He gave some little attention to music, and quickly resolved to learn to play the lyre, as one who had by nature a spirit most lofty and full of refinement: wherefore he sang divinely to that instrument, improvising upon it. . . . He practised not one branch of art only, but all those in which drawing played a part; and having an intellect so divine and marvellous that he was also an excellent geometrician, he not only worked in sculpture, making in his youth, in clay, some heads of women that are smiling, of which plaster casts are still taken, and likewise some heads of boys which appeared to have issued from the hand of a master; but in architecture, also, he made many drawings both of ground-plans and of other designs of buildings; and he was the first, although but a youth, who suggested the plan of reducing the river Arno to a navigable canal from Pisa to Florence. . . . And there was infused in that brain such grace from God, and a power of expression in such sublime accord with the intellect and memory that served it, and he knew so well how to express his conceptions by draughtmanship, that he vanquished with his discourse, and confuted with his reasoning, every valiant wit. . . . It is clear that Leonardo, through his comprehension of art, began many things and never finished one of them, since it seemed to him that the hand was not able to attain to the perfection of art in carrying out the things which he imagined; for the reason that he conceived in idea difficulties so subtle and so marvellous, that they could never be expressed by the hands, be they ever so excellent.

SOURCE: Giorgio Vasari, "Life of Leonardo Da Vinci: Painter and Sculptor of Florence." In *The Lives of the Most Eminent Painters, Sculptors, and Architects*, pp. 89–92.

had "to do with a fundamental shift in the nature of most vanguard art from styles rooted in visual perception to others based on conception"—that is, abstraction (p. 11). The reaction to Rubin's show was dramatic—and negative. Many critics believed that Rubin unwittingly outlined the terms by which so-called tribal cultures had traditionally been appropriated—that is, colonized and consumed—by Western culture. Others pointed out that Rubin's so-called tribal art was not, to the cultures that produced it, art at all. In a particularly severe review in *Artforum*, Thomas McEvilley took Rubin to task for insisting that the specific function and significance of each of the objects in the show was irrelevant. "But it is also true," McEvilley points out, "that he attributes a general function to all the objects together, namely, the esthetic function, the function of giving esthetic satisfaction. In other words, the function of Modernist works is tacitly but constantly attributed to the primitive works. . . . Religious objects . . . are misleadingly presented as art objects" (pp. 58–59).

In other words, most of the works in this exhibition were produced before their particular cultures had entered the "era of art," and Rubin proceeded as if Western historiography determines global historiography. There was long-standing precedent for Rubin's position, one of the most notable of which was Paul Guillaume and Thomas Munro's groundbreaking *Primitive Negro Sculpture,* first published in 1926 but still current enough in 1968 to be reprinted by Hacker Art Books. As Christa Clarke has summarized the book's ground-breaking principles: "*Primitive Negro Sculpture* . . . differs from earlier publications in providing clearly developed aesthetic criteria for an evaluation of African sculpture. The text not only makes distinctions between 'art' and 'artifact,' but also specifies ideal formal properties and delineates cultural 'style regions' based on shared stylistic characteristics" (p. 41). All the illustrations in the book were from the collection of the Barnes Foundation, collected by Albert C. Barnes in order to demonstrate his own aesthetic theory,

Girl before a Mirror (1932) by Pablo Picasso. Oil on canvas. The parallels William Rubin attempted to draw between tribal art and the abstract works of artists such as Picasso drew negative commentary from many critics, including some who argued that much tribal art wasn't considered art at all by its creators. DIGITAL IMAGE © THE MUSEUM OF MODERN ART / LICENSED BY SCALA / ART RESOURCE, NY. © 2004 ESTATE OF PABLO PICASSO / ARTIST RIGHTS SOCIETY (ARS), NEW YORK

Quetzal feather headdress of Aztec emperor Montezuma II, c. 1520. Fashioned from beads, shells, and over four hundred iridescent quetzal feathers, this elaborate headdress was presented to Holy Roman Emperor Charles V by Cortés. Quetzals were considered sacred by the Aztecs, who believed the birds represented wisdom and peace. © ERICH LESSING / ART RESOURCE, NY

which was founded on the belief in ideal form. In Clark's summary:

> Great art does not imitate nature but interprets the experience of seeing nature through "plastic means"— that is, through color, line, light, and space. This exclusive focus on "plastic form" provided a critical framework that encompassed all visual material, regardless of cultural origin or subject matter. Barnes's aesthetic studies led him to consider African sculpture as the purest expression of three-dimensional form. (pp. 42–43)

Thus Guillaume and Munro, working at Barnes's behest, not only differentiate African "art"—sculptures and masks (i.e., religious objects and fetishes)—from African "artifacts"— cups, utensils, musical instruments—but they emphasize the formal qualities of the "art" in particular:

> To the eye, to the hand, to both together moving over the surface, the statue is like music in its succession of repeated and contrasting sensuous forms, its continuities and subtle alterations of a theme. Or rather it is the material for music that one may compose at will,

proceeding always in a new order from line to line and mass to mass, singling out and reorganizing the elements, perceiving always some new relationship that had never presented itself before. (p. 33)

Guillaume and Munro may as well be writing about the art of Picasso or Henri Matisse (1869–1954), both of whose work, of course, Barnes admired and collected.

In fact, one of the most notable aspects of modern art historiography in the West is its refusal to see the artifacts of other cultures in terms other than the formalist aesthetic of modernism. McEvilley underscores the fact with a telling example:

> In New Guinea in the '30s, Western food containers were highly prized as clothing ornaments—a Kellogg's cereal box became a hat, a tin can ornamented a belt, and so on. Passed down to us in photographs, the practice looks not only absurd but pathetic. We know that the tribal people have done something so inappropriate as to be absurd, and without even beginning to realize it. Our sense of the smallness and quirkiness of their world view encourages our sense of the larger scope and greater clarity of ours. Yet the way Westerners have related to the primitive objects that have floated through their consciousness

would look to the tribal peoples much the way their use of our food containers looks to us: they would perceive at once that we had done something childishly inappropriate and ignorant, and without even realizing it. Many primitive groups, when they have used an object ritually (sometimes only once) desacralize it and discard it as garbage. We then show it in our museums. In other words: our garbage is their art, their garbage is our art. (p. 59)

In sum, the category "art" is by no means universal.

In *The Invention of Art,* Larry Shiner points out that "the Japanese language had no collective noun for 'art' in our sense until the nineteenth century" nor before the nineteenth century had anyone in China "grouped painting, sculpture, ceramics, and calligraphy together as objects" sharing any qualities in common (p. 15). Indeed, there is, among non-Western peoples and those cultures that exist on Western culture's margins, a growing antipathy to the appropriation of their "crafts" into the art context. Shiner cites a statement by Michael Lacapa, an "artisan" of mixed Apache, Hopi, and Tewa heritage, that he encountered at the Museum of Indian Arts and Culture in Santa Fe in 1997:

What do we call a piece of work created by the hands of my family? In my home we call it pottery painted with designs to tell us a story. In my mother's house, we call it a wedding basket to hold blue corn meal for the groom's family. In my grandma's place we call it a Kachina doll, a carved image of a life force that holds the Hopi world in place. We make pieces of life to see, touch, and feel. Shall we call it "Art?" I hope not. It may lose its soul. Its life. Its people. (p. 273)

Quite clearly, the process that would transform Lacapa's pottery, basket, or Kachina doll is not so much their appearance in the Museum of Indian Arts and Culture (where they apparently fall on the "culture" side of things), but the fact that they were to be purchased, collected, and commodified by agencies outside the culture and "life" in which they were produced.

Homi Bhaba, one of the great students of contemporary "global" culture, has reminded us of the "artifactual" consequences of Western colonization. "The great remains of the Inca or Aztec world are the debris," he writes, "of the Culture of Discovery. Their presence in the museum should reflect the devastation that has turned them from being signs in a powerful cultural system to becoming the symbols of a destroyed culture"(p. 321). The headdress of Montezuma II (in Nahuatl, Motecuhzoma; r. 1502–1520), presented to the Habsburg emperor Charles V (r. 1519–1556) by Hernán Cortés and now in the Museum of Ethnology in Vienna, is a case in point. Consisting of 450 green tail feathers of the quetzal bird, blue feathers from the cotinga bird, beads, and gold, it is a treasure of extraordinary beauty. But the historical moment is being approached, if not already here, when such objects will be allowed to give up their status as "art," except insofar, perhaps, the recognition that the "arts" are a historically constructed phenomenon that conveniently serves to mask social history. "It seems appropriate," Homi Bhaba says, "[to make] present in the

display of art what is so often rendered unrepresentable or left unrepresented—violence, trauma, dispossession" (p. 321). It seems likewise appropriate to let the arts, which in the early twenty-first century have neither pleasure nor the revelation of genius as their principal aims, represent these things.

See also **Aesthetics; Classification of Arts and Sciences, Early Modern; Creativity in the Arts and Sciences; Gender in Art; Humanity in the Arts; Landscape in the Arts; Periodization of the Arts; War and Peace in the Arts.**

BIBLIOGRAPHY

Belting, Hans. *Likeness and Presence: A History of the Image before the Era of Art.* Translated by Edmund Jephcott. Chicago: University of Chicago Press, 1994.

Bernard of Angers. *Book of the Miracles of St. Faith (Liber miraculorum S. Fides).* Text 34 in the "Appendix: Texts on the History and Use of Images and Relics," in Belting, *Likeness and Presence,* pp. 536–537. Chicago: University of Chicago Press, 1994.

Bhabha, Homi K. "Postmodernism/Postcolonialism." In *Critical Terms for Art History,* edited by Robert S. Nelson and Richard Shiff. Chicago and London: University of Chicago Press, 1966.

Boardman, John. *Greek Art.* London: Thames and Hudson, 1996.

Clarke, Christa. "Defining African Art: Primitive Negro Sculpture and the Aesthetic Philosophy of Albert Barnes." *African Arts* 36, no. 1 (spring 2003): 40–51, 92–93.

Donoghue, Denis. *The Arts without Mystery.* Boston: Little, Brown, 1983. Contrary to the sense of its title, Donoghue's book is a meditation on the place of mystery in the arts widely defined to include painting, sculpture, literature, music, dance, and theater.

Guillaume, Paul, and Thomas Munro. *Primitive Negro Sculpture.* New York: Harcourt Brace, 1926.

Heartney, Eleanor. "The Whole Earth Show: Part II." *Art in America* 77, no. 7 (July 1989): 90–97.

McEvilley, Thomas. "Doctor Lawyer Indian Chief: *Primitivism in Twentieth-Century Art* at the Museum of Modern Art." *Artforum* 23, no. 3 (November 1984): 54–61.

Rubin, William S. *"Primitivism" in Twentieth-Century Art: Affinity of the Tribal and the Modern.* New York: Museum of Modern Art, 1984.

Shiner, Larry. *The Invention of Art: A Cultural History.* Chicago: University of Chicago Press, 2001.

Summers, David. *Real Spaces: World Art History and the Rise of Western Modernism.* New York: Phaidon, 2003.

Vasari, Giorgio. *The Lives of the Most Eminent Painters, Sculptors, and Architects.* 2 vols. Translated by Gaston du C. de Vere. New York: Knopf, Everyman's Library, 1996.

Henry M. Sayre

AFRICA

Between 1520 and 1521, the famous German painter and engraver Albrecht Dürer (1471–1528) purchased two African ivory carvings in the Netherlands. He was so impressed by their craftsmanship that he noted in his diary:

all sorts of marvelous objects for human use much more beautiful to behold than things spoken of in fairy tales.

. . . And in all the days of my life, I have seen nothing which rejoiced my heart as these things—for I saw among them wondrous artful things and I wondered over the subtle genius of these men in strange countries. (Fagg, p. 9)

The Myth of Primitivism

Although stylized carvings from the kingdoms of Sapi, Benin, and Kongo were popular in Europe in the sixteenth century, scholarly interest in African art in general did not begin until the nineteenth century, when European colonization of Africa increased the number of examples arriving in European museums. But by this time the European attitude to the arts of other cultures had changed drastically, having been influenced by ideas of Enlightenment and evolution. Both ideas placed European culture at the apex of human development, using its naturalistic representations as the benchmark for the arts of other cultures. And since most of the sculptures and masks from Africa were stylized or conceptual in form, European scholars looked down on them as "primitive" and a failed attempt to imitate nature.

Although naturalistic representation turned up as early as 1910 in Africa, such as the terra cotta and brass figures of Ife, Nigeria, they were dismissed as the works of foreigners. In fact, Leo Frobenius, the German anthropologist who first brought Ife art to world attention, attributed the portraits to the ancient Greeks, who, he speculated, might have settled among the Yoruba before the Christian era. According to him, if a full figure in the Ife style were to be found, it would almost certainly reflect a proportion similar to that of classical Greek art. Fortunately, a full figure has been found and dated to the twelfth and sixteenth centuries of the Christian era. Contrary to expectation, its proportion is completely different from that of Greek art but closer to what is found in the generality of African figure sculpture—the head being about a quarter of the whole body, notwithstanding the naturalistic treatment of body parts.

By and large the myth of primitivism is no longer taken seriously. First, its assumption that naturalism was a late stage in the progressive evolution of art from the conceptual to the lifelike has been debunked by the occurrence of naturalistic images in the prehistoric rock art of Africa, Europe, and Australia. Some of the examples from Africa were created about twenty-five thousand years ago. Second, from a close study it is now known that the disregard for naturalism in African art is deliberate, not the result of a technical deficiency. It has been influenced by different cosmologies that not only trace the origin of art to supernatural beings but also identify the human body as a piece of sculpture animated by a vital force or soul. In other words, art makes the spirit manifest in the physical world. The time-honored ritual still associated with the creation of sculptures and masks today clearly shows that art in precolonial Africa was not so much concerned with imitating reality as with evoking its essence. Thus stylization hints at the interrelatedness of the physical and metaphysical. Ironically, the same so-called primitive art of Africa contributed significantly to the birth of modern European art at the beginning of the twentieth century, inspiring prominent artists such as André Derain, Maurice Vlamnick, and Pablo Picasso, among others, to abandon naturalism in favor of stylization and abstraction.

Functionalism, Structuralism, and "One Tribe, One Style"

The pre-nineteenth-century European distinction between "art" (the nonutilitarian) and "craft" (the utilitarian) also contributed to the prejudice against African art, given its use in ritual ceremonies. This distinction turned African sculptures and masks into ethnological specimens and a gold mine for anthropologists interested in the relationship between art and society. Some applied the functional theory developed in the 1920s by the French sociologist Émile Durkheim (1858–1917) and his followers, emphasizing the interconnection of ritual, religion, language, social practices, and symbolic expressions. Others employed the structuralist model popularized in the 1950s and 1960s by Claude Lévi-Strauss (b. 1908) to search for deeper meanings or a concealed order in symbolic or language systems. In both approaches—often combined in the same study—art was treated as part of an organic whole and as an aspect of myth, religion, or kinship system. Little attention was paid to aesthetic factors, individual creativity, and the historical factors affecting form and style (for a comprehensive review of the literature, see Gerbrands).

Between 1935 and 1946, the Museum of Modern Art in New York organized major exhibitions of African and Oceanic art to familiarize the public with their influence on European and American modernism. By the 1950s some American art historians such as Robert Goldwater (New York University) and Paul Wingert (Columbia University) had started offering courses in African art. The emergence of many newly independent African states from the 1960s onward resulted in a worldwide increase of scholarly interest in African affairs.

Most of the early surveys of African art focused on style areas, inaugurating what Sidney Kasfir (1984) calls the "one tribe, one style" conceptual model. Its underlying assumption was that the styles and iconographical elements that define the art of a given group had been fixed for centuries, untouched by outside influences. It thus encouraged the study of African art in the "ethnographic present." A sea change occurred in the late 1960s and early 1970s with the arrival in the field of new scholars who combined art-historical and anthropological methods in a more critical way. Apart from focusing on the art of specific African cultures, they took cognizance of individual and regional variations within a major style area. In addition, they documented artistic exchanges between contiguous and distant groups due to military conquest or centuries of trade, migration, and/or social interaction.

Unlike their predecessors, who focused mainly on art objects and ignored the artists who created them, the new scholars and their students recorded names of artists, possible dates of objects, and contexts of use, among other data. Since then there has been a shift from an emphasis on the religious significance of art to its implications in the realm of politics, psychology, gender, mass communication, and performance. Such was the involvement of art in all phases of life in precolonial

Africa that scholars began to use the term *art for life's sake* to distinguish African art from the European idea of art for art's sake.

In the early twenty-first century the more rigorous approach of a new generation of scholars is shedding new light on old problems and assumptions. For example, previous scholars paid little attention to the interaction between Islam and African art or simply concluded that Islam had had a totally negative impact on African sculpture, given its injunction against image-making. Late twentieth and early twenty-first century scholarship provides evidence to the contrary. Field studies by René Bravmann (1974), Labelle Prussin, Frederick Lamp, and other scholars demonstrate that Muslims in some areas of West Africa have not totally abandoned their ancestral art and religion. By emphasizing the recreational function of African masking, they have succeeded in preserving it in an Islamic context. It is therefore not unusual (among the Baga of Guinea and the Dyula of Mali, Côte d'Ivoire, and Ghana) to see masked performers in the early twenty-first century during important Islamic holiday celebrations, such as the end of Ramadan or the birthday of Prophet Mohammed. Non-Muslims are also known to attach Islamic talismans to altar sculptures so as to make them more efficacious. Arabesque motifs also abound in masks, wood carvings, and fabrics all over Africa. Thus the idea of "tradition" in African art has been modified. Whereas it was once regarded as a strict conformity to forms handed down from the past, in the early twenty-first century the idea is understood as a process of continuity and change (for an overview of the major paradigms in the study of African art up to the 1980s, see *African Art Studies* [1987], Adams, and Ben-Amos).

Beyond Sub-Saharan African Art

Admittedly, the influence of African sculpture on modern art has virtually eliminated the evolutionist prejudice against its conceptual form. Yet it has encouraged a scholarly bias for figure sculpture and masks from West, Central, and Equatorial Africa, marginalizing the equally significant artistic expressions in other media within and outside the region. Until the turn of the twenty-first century, this bias isolated the study of sub-Saharan African art from those of northern, northeastern, and southern parts of the continent, where the decorative arts predominate.

It is gratifying to note, however, that in the early twenty-first century scholars are beginning to correct this anomaly. Surveys cover not only the entire continent (including Ancient Egypt, Nubia, and the Swahili civilizations of East Africa) but also previously neglected art forms such as body adornment, weaving, pottery, calabash decoration, leatherwork, beadwork, and architecture. Thanks to new data from archaeology, prehistoric rock art, various eyewitness accounts by Arab and European visitors to the continent between the eleventh and nineteenth centuries, and works of African origin that found their way to Europe from the fifteenth century onward, it has become possible to attempt a more comprehensive and reliable overview of the artistic developments in the continent from the earliest times to the present, though there are still gaps in knowledge.

The Paradox of Modernism

As is well known, European colonization of a good part of Africa between the late nineteenth century and the mid-1970s resulted in the imposition of European values. It also disrupted the social order, precipitating metamorphic changes. Having discredited African art as "primitive" and as "fetishes," colonial administrators introduced a new art education program, stressing naturalism and art for art's sake. At first talented Africans were encouraged to go to Europe for further training, but by the late 1930s European-type art departments had been established at Achimota College, Gold Coast (now Ghana), and Makarere College, Uganda. Others were introduced in the 1940s and 1950s in Senegal, Nigeria, Republic of Sudan, and Congo-Leopoldville (now the Democratic Republic of Congo). The paradox is that colonialism foisted European-type naturalism on Africa, touting it as "modern art" at the same time as the leading modern European artists were being inspired by African stylization. Conversely, "modernism" had different implications in Africa and Europe during the colonial period, denoting naturalism in the former and stylization/abstraction in the latter.

Dissatisfied with this paradox, some European expatriates in Africa initiated an alternative modernism—a conceptual art that would evoke the spirit of African art without necessarily imitating its forms. They established informal art workshops where individuals without previous art training could create freely, emphasizing genre and folkloric themes. These workshops include L'Academie de l'Art Populaire Congolais, Elizabethville (now Lubumbashi), Democratic Republic of Congo (founded in 1946 by Pierre Romain Desfosses); the Poto-Poto School of Art, Brazzaville, Peoples Republic of Congo (founded in 1951 by Pierre Lods); the Central African Workshop, Salisbury, Southern Rhodesia (now Zimbabwe) (founded in the late 1950s by Frank McEwen); the Lourenço Marques Workshop, Mozambique (founded in 1960 by Amancio Guedes); and the Oshogbo Workshop, Oshogbo, Nigeria (founded in 1962 by Ulli Beier). The graduates of these workshops created images ranging from the realistic and surrealistic to the expressionistic and abstract. Some were very original while others were derivative, reflecting influences from European modernism, or what Marshall Mount describes as "a rather condescending Western stereotype of what African painting should be" (p. 75).

The Traditional, Neotraditional, and Authentic

As mentioned above, many Africans have not totally abandoned their cultural heritage despite conversion to Islam. This is also the case with Christianity. During the colonial period, many converts venerated their ancestors secretly. Those living in the urban areas frequently returned to their villages to participate in initiation ceremonies and annual festivals featuring masks. Thus artists trained in the traditional or the so-called classical styles continued to receive commissions, though the number of their local clients had declined considerably.

However, these artists found new clients in the international market created by the interest in African sculptures and masks as a result of their influence on modern European art. The huge demand led some artists to move from rural to urban areas, forming cooperatives such as those of the Bamana (Bamako, Mali), Senufo (Abidjan, Côte d'Ivoire), Edo (Benin City and Lagos, Nigeria), Ibibio (Ikot Ekpene, Nigeria), Okavango (Rundu, Namibia), Wakamba (Nairobi, Kenya), and Makonde (Dar es Salaam, Tanzania). These cooperatives were still flourishing in the early twenty-first century, creating what is popularly known as "neotraditional," "tourist," or "souvenir" art. They specialize in copying and mass-producing the art of the ethnic groups to which they belong, in addition to occasionally replicating popular images in exhibition catalogs from other groups. Their products are sold wholesale to traders who then distribute them across Africa and overseas, making them available at hotel lobbies, supermarkets, boutiques, and duty-free shops in local and international airports. Other artists specialize in beadwork, leatherwork, jewelry, weaving, dyeing, pottery, and calabash decoration, among other arts.

This revival of interest in African art during the colonial period encouraged the Catholic Church in Nigeria to explore the possibility of adapting the art to a Christian context. So between 1947 and 1953 the church established an experimental art workshop in the Yoruba town of Oye Ekiti, Western Nigeria, where it employed the services of Yoruba artists. Two young British priests, Kevin Carroll and Sean O'Mahoney, supervised the project. They supplied the themes and encouraged the artists to render biblical characters in the Yoruba style, though without the rituals that sometimes preceded or accompanied the production of images destined for local shrines. The workshop produced madonnas, crucifixes, nativity sets, altarpieces, baptismal fonts, carved doors, and other works with Christian motifs. The finished objects replaced imported artworks in Catholic churches within and outside Oye Ekiti. The reception of the images, however, varied; it was positive in some areas but so negative in others that they had to be removed because they reminded some Yoruba Catholics of the "pagan" shrines of their ancestors (Carroll; Picton, 2002, pp. 100–101).

Thus a distinction is now made between "traditional" and "neotraditional" African art. The former refers to a work in the so-called classical style originally created for and actually used in private rituals or public ceremonies by the same society to which the artist belongs. The "neotraditional," on the other hand, refers to a similar work created outside its time-honored context for the tourist/souvenir market or to function as "art for art's sake." And because most Western scholars and curators regard the used image as "authentic" and the unused as "fake," the carving cooperatives in the urban and rural areas have devised various ways of artificially aging replicas to enable them to make the grade. In fact, such is the demand in the early 2000s for "old" or "authentic" art that a well-executed contemporary work may be passed over in favor of a damaged mediocre piece if the latter appears to be much older.

Sidney Kasfir (1992) has criticized this Western "antiquarianist mind-set" because it tends to ignore formal quality, an important yardstick for judging a work of art. According to Christopher Steiner, because "authenticity" is defined by Western patrons, those who sell both ancient and recent African art "are not only moving a set of objects through the world economic system, they are also exchanging information—mediating, modifying, and commenting on a broad spectrum of cultural knowledge" (Steiner, p. 2).

Pan-Africanism, Negritude, Decolonization, and the Search for a New Identity

It is easy to understand why art historians ignored modern and contemporary African art for a long time. First, they were preoccupied with the so-called classical African art, which had influenced the birth of modern European art. Second, some of them assumed that the belief system that inspired the best of African creativity was on the wane due to the negative impact of colonialism, Western education, industrialization, urbanization, and mass conversion to Islam and Christianity. That African creativity has not only recovered from the ordeals of colonialism but has in fact been rejuvenated is apparent in the early-twenty-first-century rise in the number of mainstream museums and galleries collecting contemporary African art as well as in the spate of publications on it.

Although it is customary to trace the beginnings of this recovery to the period after World War II when the products of the colonial art schools used their art to critique the colonialism as part of local agitation for political independence, the roots lie much deeper in the Pan-African movement of the nineteenth century. Spearheaded by George Padmore (1902–1959) and Henry Sylvester Williams (1869–1911) of Trinidad, Edward Wilmot Blyden (1832–1912) of the Danish West Indies, and W. E. B. DuBois (1868–1963) of the United States, among others, the movement organized a number of international conferences of black leaders from Africa and the Americas between the early 1900s and the 1940s. There were two principal objectives. The first was to inspire all blacks within and outside Africa to be proud of their color, history, and cultural heritage; and the second, to unite all blacks in their struggle against racial discrimination and toward the decolonization of Africa.

These conferences—along with Marcus Garvey's (1887–1940) ideology of "Africa for Africans," which promoted a millennial vision of decolonized Africa as a future superpower—generated many debates and publications on different aspects of black history and culture as well as the political, economic, and creative potentials of blacks. In the United States, the quest for a distinct black identity in the arts gave birth to the Harlem Renaissance of the 1920s and 1930s during which African-American artists, writers, musicians, dancers, and intellectuals experimented with their African heritage. In France, Pan-Africanism, along with the Harlem Renaissance, inspired the Negritude movement in the 1930s among a group of African and Caribbean students.

Apart from celebrating the richness of their African past in their works, the Negritude writers and poets also questioned the "civilizing mission" of Europe in Africa, in view of the impact of African art on European modernism. Besides, they claimed that black people all over the world share certain cultural and emotional characteristics that constitute the essence of blackness and called on artists to capture this essence in their creations. The journal *Presence Africaine* was founded in Paris in 1947 to serve as an organ for disseminating the Negritude manifesto to the black world.

In short, these black-consciousness movements culminated in the political agitation that spread across Africa after World War II, motivating artists to explore the potentials of their African heritage and synthesize them with Western elements. The situation varied from one country to another, however, depending on the degree of the artistic commitment of the political leadership. For example, when Ghana gained political independence from Britain in 1957, Kwame Nkrumah (1909–1972), an active member of the Pan-African movement, became its first prime minister and, later, president. He urged contemporary Ghanaian artists to research into their ancestral legacy and to cultivate an "African personality" in their works. To this end, he made funds available for public art projects.

Léopold Sédar Senghor (1906–2001), one of the founders of negritude along with Aimé Césaire of Martinique and Léon Damas of Guyana, became the first Senegalese president when Senegal became independent from France in 1960. During his twenty years in office, he promoted negritude as a national artistic philosophy, becoming the patron of the "École de Dakar," a group of artists manifesting this philosophy in their works. Having been influenced by negritude while studying in Europe, the Nigerian artist Ben Enwonwu (1921–1994) returned home to become his country's flag bearer in the search for a national identity in the visual arts, especially after Nigeria gained independence from Britain in 1960. As the special art adviser to the government, he received a lot of commissions to decorate public buildings.

However, the most significant attempt to decolonize the visual arts in the country was initiated by the Zaria Art Society formed in 1958 by a group of students at the Nigerian College of Arts, Science and Technology in Zaria, whose art department was dominated by expatriate art teachers. To counter the naturalism being forced upon them by their teachers, these students (now known as the "Zaria Rebels") organized private sessions to formulate strategies for evolving a Nigerian identity in their works. Space limitations will not allow a survey of artistic developments in all African countries. Suffice it to say that political independence inspired a cultural and artistic reawakening throughout sub-Saharan Africa. It led to a drastic review of the colonial art education program. New art schools, museums, and national galleries have since been created to promote an African consciousness in the arts, although not everybody agrees with the premise of Negritude that all black people share a common emotional characteristic.

There were similar post-emancipation reactions in northern and northeastern Africa (Mauritania, Morocco, Algeria, Tunisia, Libya and Egypt, and the Republic of Sudan) where there are large Arab populations, although Egypt and Libya attained political independence before World War II. The academic realism introduced to these countries during the colonial period has been modified. In the early twenty-first century, their contemporary artists experiment with different materials, forms, and ideas, seeking inspiration from diverse sources ranging from Islamic calligraphy and crafts to Pan-Africanism and different Euro-American styles. In Egypt some artists also draw on ancient Egyptian and Coptic sources in an attempt to relate the past to the present.

While Ethiopia has been exposed to Orthodox Christianity since the fourth century, it was never colonized except for a brief period of Italian occupation between 1936 and 1941. For a long time, the Ethiopian Church was the chief patron of the arts, commissioning metal crosses, illuminated manuscripts, paintings, and murals. Most of the artists were priests trained to work in the Coptic-Byzantine or modified Italian Renaissance style. But in the early nineteenth century, the nobility and members of the royal family started commissioning secular paintings from freelance artists. Modernization commenced in the 1920s with the introduction of European-type art education. Some Ethiopians later studied in Europe, returning in the 1930s to popularize new forms and styles. A school of fine arts was created in 1958; initially the school encouraged students to focus on Ethiopian history, culture, and political aspiration, but by the start of the twenty-first century the school's program stressed experimentation and individual creativity.

South Africa became a Dutch colony in the seventeenth century. The British took it over in the nineteenth century, granting it political independence under white minority rule in 1910. The notorious apartheid system that disenfranchised the black majority was introduced in 1948. Until recently, most of the well-equipped and state-sponsored art institutions were reserved for whites. Blacks had to be content with informal art workshops or craft centers run by churches and philanthropists. Black art focused mainly on black suffering under the oppressive apartheid regime between 1948 and 1994. Much of white South African art, in contrast, reflected the prevailing trends in Europe. However, by the 1980s some concerned white artists, no longer willing to be silent while the rest of the world condemned apartheid, had started using their art overtly or covertly to critique it. Since the end of the apartheid system in 1994, contemporary South African art has been charting a new course, reflecting on the past and projecting the collective aspirations of a new nation now ruled by a black majority.

The Postcolonial, Postmodern, and Transnational

In the early twenty-first century contemporary African art is no longer confined to the works of black artists; it now includes those produced by artists of European, Arab, and Asian descent. That it has come of age is evident in the creative ways it often combines ancient African elements with new and frequently Western materials, forms, and techniques to reflect the peculiarity of the continent's history and the complexity of its encounters with other cultures. No wonder that contemporary African artists have been receiving more invitations to participate in international exhibitions and biennials. Africa itself has become the site of major expositions such as the Cairo International Biennial in Egypt, first held in 1984; the Dakar Biennial (Dak'Art) in Senegal, first held in 1992; and the Johannesburg Biennale, South Africa, first held in 1995.

The strong visibility of contemporary African art on the world stage was reflected in the inclusion for the first time in a 1996 major textbook on world art (Stokstad) the works of two contemporary African artists, Magdalene Odundo of Kenya and Ouattara of Côte d'Ivoire. In 1998 curator Okwui Enwezor of Nigeria, the founder of *Nka: Journal of Contemporary African Art*, was appointed the artistic director of

Documenta 11 in Kassel, Germany—the first time an African would be trusted with such a major responsibility. A year later, the Egyptian artist Ghada Amer won the UNESCO Prize at the Forty-Eighth Venice Biennial in Italy. As Barbara Pollack aptly observes in the April 2001 issue of *Art News:* "While the political upheavals in . . . [African] . . . countries serve as a backdrop to their work, many of these artists struggle to make individual statements that transcend politics and nationality. By so doing, they are transforming our very definition of African art" (p. 124).

As the postcolonial period in Africa coincided with the postmodernist deconstruction of the Eurocentric hegemony in the visual arts, the question has been raised as to whether the two phenomena are related. They are, insofar as the multiculturalism promoted by the postmodern movement has opened new doors for contemporary African art, enabling it show the world that the creativity formerly associated with its past has been rejuvenated. Yet, and as Kwame Anthony Appiah points out, much of the so-called postcolonial African art is not as independent as implied in the rhetoric of decolonization. For despite an increase in local patronage, contemporary African art still depends largely on the European-American market, which in turn exerts a considerable influence on its materials, techniques, form, and content as well as on what is produced and where it is exhibited overseas. In other words, elements of the colonial—now neocolonial—still lurk in the postcolonial like an old masquerade in a new costume. No wonder some critics see a kind of "neoprimitivism" in the emphasis on self-taught art in major exhibitions such as "Magiciens de la Terre," organized in 1989 by the Centre Pompidou in Paris, and "Africa Explores," organized in 1991 by the Center for African Art and the New Museum of Contemporary Art in New York (Oguibe and Enwezor, p. 9; Picton, 1999, pp. 120–125; Hassan, 1999, pp. 218–219).

Lastly, it is significant to note that many African artists have been living permanently abroad wince the middle of the twentieth century, if not earlier. Many have become naturalized English, French, Belgian, or American citizens, yet they retained strong ties with Africa. This has produced a "double consciousness" that often resonates in their work, transcending racial, geographical, and national boundaries while at the same time identifying the black self in a largely Caucasian ambience—a new home away from home in the global village that the world has become.

See also **Aesthetics: Africa; Ancestor Worship; Masks; Modernism; Negritude; Pan-Africanism.**

BIBLIOGRAPHY

Adams, Monni. "African Visual Arts from an Art Historical Perspective." *African Studies Review* 32, no. 2 (1989): 55–103. A comprehensive overview of the literature up to the 1980s.

African Art Studies: The State of the Discipline. Papers Presented at a Symposium Organized by the National Museum of African Art, Smithsonian Institution. Washington, D.C.: National Museum of African Art, 1990.

Appiah, Kwame A. "Is the Post- in Postmodern the Post- in Postcolonial?" *Critical Inquiry* 17 (1991): 336–357.

Ben-Amos, Paula. "African Visual Arts from a Social Perspective." *African Studies Review* 32, no. 2 (1989): 1–53. A review of anthropological literature.

Bravmann, René A. *Islam and Tribal Art in West Africa.* Cambridge, U.K., and New York: Cambridge University Press, 1974.

———. *Open Frontiers: The Mobility of Art in Black Africa.* Seattle: University of Washington Press, 1973.

Carroll, Kevin. *Yoruba Religious Carving: Pagan and Christian Sculpture in Nigeria and Dahomey.* Foreword by William Fagg. London and Dublin: G. Chapman, 1967.

Deliss, Clémentine, gen. ed., and Jane Havell, ed. *Seven Stories about Modern Art in Africa.* London: Whitechapel, 1995.

Enwezor, Okwui, ed. *The Short Century: Independence and Liberation Movements in Africa, 1945–1994.* Munich and New York: Prestel, 2001.

Fagg, William. *African Majesty: From Grassland and Forest: The Barbara and Murray Frum Collection, May 22–July 12, 1981.* Introduction by Alan G. Wilkinson. Toronto: Art Gallery of Ontario, 1981.

Fall, N'Goné, and Jean Loup Pivin, eds. *An Anthology of African Art: The Twentieth Century.* New York: Distributed Art Publishers, 2002. A collection on the transition from traditional to contemporary African Art.

Geiss, Imanuel. *The Pan-African Movement: A History of Pan-Africanism in America, Europe, and Africa.* Translated by Ann Keep. New York: Africana, 1974.

Gerbrands, A. A. *Art as an Element of Culture, Especially in Negro-Africa.* Leiden, Netherlands: Brill, 1957.

Hassan, Salah M. "The Khartoum and Addis Connections." In *Seven Stories about Modern Art in Africa,* edited by Jane Havell; general editor Clémentine Deliss, 105–125. London: Whitechapel, 1995.

———. "The Modernist Experience in African Art: Visual Expressions of the Self and Cross-Cultural Aesthetics." In *Reading the Contemporary: African Art from Theory to the Marketplace,* edited by Olu Oguibe and Okwui Enwezor Oguibe, 215–235. London: Institute of International Visual Arts, 1999.

Hassan, Salah M., and Achamyeleh Debela. "Addis Connections: The Making of Modern Ethiopian Art Movement." In *Seven Stories about Modern Art in Africa,* edited by Jane Havell, general editor Clémentine Deliss, 127–139. London: Whitechapel, 1995.

Kasfir, Sidney L. "African Art and Authenticity: A Text with a Shadow." *African Arts* 25, no. 2 (1992): 41–53, 96–97.

———. "One Tribe, One Style: Paradigms in the Historiography of African Art." *History in Africa* 11 (1984): 163–193.

Lamp, Frederick. *Art of the Baga: A Drama of Cultural Invention.* Forewords by Simon Ottenberg and Djibril Tamsir Niane. New York: Museum for African Art, 1996.

Mount, Marshall W. *African Art: The Years since 1920.* Bloomington: Indiana University Press, 1973. Reviews contemporary art schools, workshops, and styles up to the early 1970s.

Oguibe, Olu, and Okwui Enwezor, eds. *Reading the Contemporary: African Art from Theory to the Marketplace.* London: Institute of International Visual Arts, 1999.

Perani, Judith, and Fred T. Smith. *The Visual Arts of Africa: Gender, Power, and Life Cycle Rituals.* Upper Saddle River, N.J.: Prentice-Hall, 1998.

Phillips, Tom, ed. *Africa: The Art of a Continent.* New York: Prestel, 1995.

Picton, John. "In Vogue, or The Flavour of the Month: The New Way to Wear Black." In *Reading the Contemporary: African Art from Theory to the Marketplace,* edited by Olu Oguibe and Okwui Enwezor, 115–126. London: International Institute of Visual Arts, 1999.

———. "Neo-Traditional Sculpture in Nigeria." In *An Anthology of African Art: The Twentieth Century,* edited by N'Goné Fall and Jean Loup Pivin, 98–101. New York: Distributed Art Publishers, 2002.

Pollack, Barbara. "The Newest Avant-Garde." *Art News* 100, no. 4 (2001): 124–129.

Prussin, Labelle. *Hatumere: Islamic Design in West Africa.* Berkeley: University of California Press, 1986.

Sieber, Roy, and Arnold Rubin. *Sculpture of Black Africa: The Paul Tishman Collection.* Los Angeles: Los Angeles County Museum of Art, 1968.

Steiner, Christopher B. *African Art in Transit.* Cambridge, U.K., and New York: Cambridge University Press, 1994.

Visonà, Monica Blackmun, Robin Poynor, Herbert M. Cole, and Michael D. Harris. *A History of Art in Africa.* New York: Harry N. Abrams, 2001.

Williamson, Sue. *Resistance Art in South Africa.* New York: St. Martin's Press, 1989.

Babatunde Lawal

ARTS, PERIODIZATION OF. *See* **Periodization of the Arts.**

ASCETICISM.

This entry includes two subentries:

Hindu and Buddhist Asceticism
Western Asceticism

HINDU AND BUDDHIST ASCETICISM

The English term *asceticism* derives from the Greek *askesis,* originally meaning "to train" or "to exercise," specifically in the sense of the training and self-denial that an athlete undergoes to attain physical skill and mastery over the body. The Stoics adapted the word to refer to the moral discipline of the sage who learns, through self-mastery, how to act freely—how to choose or refuse a desired object or an act of physical pleasure at will and how to control the emotions with reason. Plato and the neo-Platonic philosophers also used the term in the sense of the denial of "lower" sensual desires in order to cultivate "higher" spiritual traits.

The word was then passed on from the Greeks to early Christians in this sense of self-control over physical and psychological desires in favor of spiritual ideals or goals. Asceticism has come to function cross-culturally to refer to a whole host of activities in the religions of the world. Most religions have at least some practices that can be deemed ascetic: fasting, celibacy, seclusion, voluntary infliction of pain, bodily mutilation, temperance or complete abstinence from intoxicants, renunciation of worldly goods and possessions, and, in some cases, religious suicide. Asceticism can also include the cultivation of moral qualities requiring self-restraint and discipline, such as patience and forbearance. One sometimes reads of an "inner asceticism," which involves various practices where one learns to be "in the world, but not of it."

Ascetic practices are engaged in for a variety of ends. Many traditions encourage or demand asceticism at periodic or designated times of the religious calendar, usually for purification or preparation for a significant ritual event. Fasting and celibacy are particularly common practices used to this end. Most rites of passage or life-cycle rites also require some form of self-denial and self-discipline on the part of the person undergoing the ritual. Ascetic practices as forms of penance are also very frequently prescribed for expiation of sin or impurity. In some cases, ascetic practices are employed as a sort of sacrifice to the deity or powers one is trying to influence to obtain fulfillment of a request, while in other instances asceticism is seen as meritorious in general, leading to or ensuring a good result in this world or the next.

Many religions have within them an elite group of specialists, renouncers or monastics, who maintain an ascetic lifestyle more or less continuously. These "permanent" ascetics may be marked by their special appearance (distinctive clothes or robes, or no clothes at all; long, uncut hair or heads completely shorn of hair; the possession of certain characteristic implements or items, such as a begging bowl or staff; or in some extreme cases, signs in the form of physical mutilation, such as castration). They may be associated with particular locales (monasteries or other isolated and secluded areas, such as forests, deserts, jungles, or caves; or a mandate to wander homeless) to further indicate that they have separated themselves from ordinary society. Ascetic techniques in many traditions are said to bring magical or supernatural powers.

While asceticism is a feature of virtually every religion, it plays an especially prominent role in the three principal Indian religions: Hinduism, Buddhism, and Jainism. All three of these traditions originated at more or less the same time and out of the same religious and philosophical milieu. In the middle centuries of the first millennium B.C.E., many individuals and groups known collectively as "wanderers" (*shramanas*) arose in India to oppose certain features of the older Vedic religion and to advocate new ideas, methods, and goals. Most wanderer groups—especially those responsible for the formation of the new religions of Hinduism, Buddhism, and Jainism—shared the belief that this world has suffering and potentially endless rebirth. This negative evaluation of the world came to be called *samsara.* All three religions also posited the new religious goal of an escape or release from this cycle, variously called *moksha* ("liberation"), *nirvana* ("extinguishing" of suffering and rebirth), or *kevala* ("isolation" or "perfection").

Samsara is believed to be perpetuated by desire, *karma,* and worldly life in general. The quest for liberation from *samsara* thus entailed asceticism and renunciation, and such practices became central to all three of these Indian religions. Meditation techniques, yoga, austerities of various sorts all were developed to further the end of disengaging from the world of sensual desires, and this in turn led to the final goal of release.

Asceticism in Hinduism

Asceticism in the form of yoga and meditation possibly goes back to the earliest period of Indian history. Seals depicting a figure sitting in what looks like a yogic pose have been found at sites of the Indus Valley Civilization dating to the second millennium B.C.E. In the texts of the early Vedas (c. 1500–c. 1000 B.C.E.), ascetic practices appear in a variety of contexts. References are made to long-haired silent sages (*munis*), clad in soiled yellow garments or naked, who are depicted as having supernatural powers, acquired perhaps as a result of their ascetic practices. The early texts also tell of the shadowy wandering ascetics (*vratyas*), who seem to have also practiced physical austerities.

The Vedas in some places say that the deities gained their status, or even created the entire universe, through the power of their inner, ascetic heat (*tapas*), acquired through the rigorous practice of physical and spiritual self-discipline and mortification of the body. The term *tapas* derives from a Sanskrit root meaning to heat up or burn, and refers to any one of a variety of ascetic methods for achieving religious power. In the Rig Veda, Indra is said to have achieved his divine place through the practice of asceticism and the generation of this powerful "heat," while elsewhere in that ancient work are encountered cosmogonic hymns that attribute the origins of the universe to the Primal One who creates by "heating up ascetic heat." The metaphysical qualities of both truth and order are said to have derived from ascetic heat, and the ancient Indian seers (*rishis*) also were supposed to have achieved their powers through ascetic heat.

This notion of ascetic heat as a creative, or even coercive, religious force was to persist in Indian religious thinking through subsequent centuries to the present. One may gain ascetic heat through a variety of ascetic techniques, including fasting, chastity, and various yogic techniques such as breath control (*pranayama*), and through it the adept can procure tremendous supernatural powers and even the status of a god. In the Upanishads, epics, and other Sanskrit texts one often learns of various ascetics who force their way into heaven and become gods through the power of their ascetic heat. Deities such as Shiva were especially associated with this power of ascetic heat, derived from proficiency in yoga, meditation, and extreme austerities.

Various classes of ascetics (*tapasvins*, "specialists in the practice of *tapas*") eventually arose in Hindu India and are sometimes enumerated. They are mainly differentiated by the form of austerities they engage in. Some ascetics, for example, stay totally stationary for years at a time or remain standing or in water for weeks on end. Some ascetics subsist solely on fruits, wild plants, and roots, or they live only on grain left in the fields. Among the most famous are ascetics who practice the "five fires" ritual (building four fires around themselves, with the sun as the fifth) and "spike-lying" ascetics who sleep on beds of nails.

A second strand of asceticism within the Hindu tradition might better be termed "renunciation." Such renunciation can be either *tyaga* (relinquishing a desire for actions to produce effects) or *samnyasa* (abandoning family, social, economic life, and the ritual activity associated with the householder's way of life), in order to pursue single-mindedly the ultimate goals of religion. World renouncers seem to have been a feature of Indian religious life since very early times. Already mentioned above are the silent sages and wandering ascetics discussed in the Vedas. Later texts depict a wide variety of renouncers, hermits, and ascetic "orders" living in the jungles and forests.

Among such ascetics were those who, with or without their wives, live on wild fruits and plants and maintain a ritual sacrificial fire; those who are "god-possessed" but perform the Vedic rituals; those with matted hair who wear bark clothing; those who sleep on the ground, eat only what drops from trees and plants, and regulate their meals according to the waxing and waning of the moon; those who wander from one monastery to another, eating only eight mouthfuls of food per day; those who remain naked, live under trees or in graveyards, and remain indifferent to what they eat or receive from others; renouncers who wear red and beg only at the homes of high-caste Brahmins; and radical ascetics who do not remain more than a day in any one place and live on cow urine and feces.

Renunciation (and the values and practices associated with it, especially nonviolence [*ahimsa*], vegetarianism, lack of possessions, and begging for a living) came to play an enormously influential role in Hinduism from the time of the Upanishads onwards. Not only were there dedicated ascetics and renunciates who committed their lives to this kind of religious practice; even those who chose to remain householders were influenced by renunciatory values. From a very early date, then, Hinduism was shaped by asceticism and renunciation.

Yet the Hindu tradition also had dissenting voices. The religion was somewhat divided about the value and necessity of asceticism and the renunciatory lifestyle. Some ancient texts condemn renunciation in general. (In the Hindu epic *Mahabharata*, one of the heroes of the epic goes so far as to say that renunciation is only for those who have failed in worldly affairs.) More often, texts condemn renunciation by householders—those with families to support and occupations to fulfill.

Indeed, Hindu texts written in the wake of the wanderer movement often extolled the householder's life of marriage, reproducing, and raising children. In the *Dharma Sutras* the householder stage is sometimes said to be the only legitimate or best stage of life—better even than the stage of pursuing the ultimate religious goal of final liberation from rebirth. Those in all other stages of life (the student, forest dweller, and world renouncer) depend on the householder, in part because it is the householder who feeds or donates to them when they beg from him:

> A householder alone offers sacrifices. A householder afflicts himself with austerities. Of the four stages of life, therefore, the householder is the best. As all rivers and rivulets ultimately end up in the ocean, so people of all stages of life ultimately end up with the householder. As all creatures depend on their mothers for their survival, so all mendicants depend on householders for their survival. (*Vasishtha Dharma Sutra*, 10.14–16, quoted in Olivelle, p. 93)

As another text puts it, when "carried out with zeal," the householder stage of life procures both happiness in this life and heaven in the next:

> Just as all living creatures depend on air in order to live, so do members of the other stages of life subsist by depending on householders. Since people in the other

three stages of life are supported every day by the knowledge and food of the householder, therefore the householder stage of life is the best. It must be carried out with zeal by the man who wants to win an incorruptible heaven [after death] and endless happiness here on earth. (*Manu*, 3.77–79)

Nevertheless, one also finds ascetic and renunciatory values—especially nonviolence (*ahimsa*), but also nonpossession and ascetic heat—included in ethical lists that seem generally applicable to all, no matter what stage of life they are in. Indeed, even the householder's life came to include certain kinds of austerities, especially as a way of penance and cleansing one's conscience: "If his mind-and-heart is heavy because of some act that he has committed, he should generate the inner heat [*tapas*] [prescribed] for it until he is satisfied. . . . Those who have committed major crimes and all the rest who have done what should not be done are freed from that guilt by well-generated inner heat" (*Manu*, 11.234, 240).

From an early age in the history of Hinduism there was also a recognition that one could live two basic kinds of religious lives within the boundaries of the religion: a life of engagement and a life of disengagement. Both were usually regarded as legitimate (although some texts do weight one or the other more heavily), and both were accorded Vedic authority and pedigree. Both were also generally regarded as efficacious—according to the following text, engagement leading to a state of equality with the gods, and disengagement to a transcendent condition beyond the world of *samsara*:

There are two kinds of Vedic activity: the one that brings about engagement [in worldly action] and the rise of happiness, and the one that brings about disengagement [from worldly action] and the supreme good. The activity of engagement is said to be driven by desire in this world and the world beyond; but the activity of disengagement is said to be free of desire and motivated by knowledge. The man who is thoroughly dedicated to the activity of engagement becomes equal to the gods; but the man who is dedicated to disengagement passes beyond the five elements. (*Manu*, 12.88–90)

Reconciling these two apparently different modes of religious life was not always easy, however. On the face of it, the life of engagement and the life of disengagement appear to be incompatible—the one involved in the world of activity and *karma*, and the other attempting to renounce such activity and free oneself of *karma*.

One of the principal methods for synthesizing the two was the system of the four stages of life (*ashramas*)—perpetual student, householder, forest dweller, and world renouncer—developed especially in the *Dharma Sutras*. In some texts the four states of life seem to have been regarded as four different types of life that a student could pursue after study with a teacher. In other cases, however, the early authorities insisted that there is only one legitimate stage of life, that of the householder. Finally, however, the tradition settled into conceptualizing the system of stages of life as progressive and more or less incumbent upon all upper-caste Hindus. This framework of stages of life could then be used to affirm life in the world (by emphasizing that all must pass through the householder stage of life before renunciation) while still incorporating the values and practices of asceticism into the ideal life of the Hindu practitioner. Three of the four classical stages of life emphasized ascetic practices, as will be seen, while the system also validated, and indeed insisted upon, the legitimacy of and need for the nonrenunciatory householder stage.

In the ideal structure laid out in Hindu texts, the first stage of life is that of a student. A young boy is given over to a teacher (*guru*), whom he lives with and serves for many years while studying the sacred Vedas under the teacher's guidance. The lifestyle assigned to this stage of life is one of austerity, asceticism, and discipline. Not only should the student remain chaste for the duration of this period; he should also observe a variety of other restraints and avoidances:

The chaste student of the Veda who lives with his guru should obey these restraints, completely restraining the cluster of his sensory powers to increase his own inner heat. . . . He should avoid honey, meat perfume, garlands, spices, women, anything that has gone sour, and violence to creatures that have the breath of life; anointing [his body with oil], putting make-up on his eyes, wearing shoes, and carrying an umbrella; desire, anger, and greed; dancing, singing, and playing musical instruments; gambling, group arguments, gossip, telling lies, looking at women or touching them, and striking another person. He should always sleep alone and never shed his semen, for by shedding his semen out of lust he breaks his vow. (*Manu*, 2.175–80)

Another text gives a slightly different list of observances, vows, and practices, but similarly emphasizes the importance of an austere life dedicated to self-restraint, the cultivation of virtue, and obedience to the teacher:

Now the rules for the studentship. He shall obey his teacher, except when ordered to commit crimes which cause loss of caste. He shall do what is serviceable to his teacher, he shall not contradict him. He shall always occupy a couch or seat lower than that of his teacher. He shall not eat food offered at a sacrifice to the gods or the ancestors, nor pungent condiments, salt, honey, or meat. He shall not sleep in the daytime. He shall not use perfumes. He shall preserve chastity. He shall not embellish himself by using ointments and the like. He shall not wash his body with hot water for pleasure. But, if it is soiled by unclean things, he shall clean it with earth or water, in a place where he is not seen by a guru. Let him not sport in the water whilst bathing; let him swim motionless like a stick. . . . Let him not look at dancing. Let him not go to assemblies for gambling, etc., nor to crowds assembled at festivals. Let him not be addicted to gossiping. Let him be discreet. Let him not do anything for his own pleasure in places which his teacher frequents. Let him talk with women so much only as his purpose requires. Let him be forgiving. Let him restrain his organs from seeking illicit objects. Let him be untired in fulfilling his duties; modest; possessed of self-command; energetic; free from anger; and free from envy. (*Apastamba Dharma Sutra,* quoted in Embree, pp. 84–86)

Also among the duties laid out for those in the student stage of life is begging for a living—more precisely, begging and then turning over the proceeds to the teacher. Begging, for the religious student and other renunciates who legitimately live by such means, was said to be like fasting:

He should fetch a pot of water, flowers, cow dung, clay, and sacrificial grass, as much as are needed, and go begging every day. A chaste student of the Veda, purified, should beg every day from the houses of people who do not fail to perform Vedic sacrifices and who are approved of for carrying out their own innate activities. He should not beg from his guru's family nor from the relatives of his mother or father, but if he cannot get to the houses of others he should avoid each of these more than the one that precedes it. And if there are none of the people mentioned above, he should beg from the whole village, purified and restrained in his speech, but he should avoid those who have been indicted. . . . When he is under the vow [of a chaste student] he should make his living by begging, nor should he eat the food of just one person; when begging is the livelihood of a person under a vow it is traditionally regarded as equal to fasting. (*Manu,* 2.182–85, 188)

When the student reaches marriageable age, he should take a wife and start a family, eschewing, by and large, renunciatory and ascetic practices in favor of the pursuit of private gain (*artha*)—understood as material prosperity, self-interest, political advantage, and in general getting ahead in the world. Hinduism thus recognizes making a good living (in an acceptable occupation) and taking care of one's family as important and indeed religiously enjoined goals of life. Private gain is listed as one of the three "ends of life" in Hindu texts, the other two being the pursuit of religious duty (*dharma*) and the pursuit of pleasure (*kama*). And while following the dictates of religious duty is obviously of great importance for one's spiritual well-being and can involve certain ascetic practices, especially for purification and penance, the pursuit of pleasure and creature comforts is to be fully embraced in the householder stage of life. In some texts, private gain is in fact the most important of these ends of life: "Of the three ends of human life, material gain is truly the most important. . . . For the realization of religious duty and pleasure depend on material gain" (*Artha Sastra,* 1.7).

But, according to the scheme of the ideal stages of life, when the householder has completed this stage of life (upon the birth of grandchildren), he should begin to withdraw from the world and once more cultivate a more ascetic lifestyle. After finishing the life of a student and after marrying and raising a family as a householder, a man may enter the third stage of life, that of the forest dweller. This stage of life, like that of the student, is characterized by ascetic practices and detachment from the world, including the renunciation of cultivated food (in favor of wild food that grows in the jungle) and of all possessions:

After he has lived in the householder's stage of life in accordance with the rules in this way, a twice-born Vedic graduate should live in the forest, properly restrained and with his sensory powers conquered. But when a householder sees that he is wrinkled and gray, and [when he sees] the children of his children, then he should take himself to the wilderness. Renouncing all food cultivated in the village and all possessions, he should hand his wife over to his sons and go to the forest—or take her along. . . . He should eat vegetables that grow on land or in water, flowers, roots, and fruits, the products of pure trees, and the oils from fruits. . . . He should not eat anything grown from land tilled with a plough, even if someone has thrown it out, nor roots and fruits grown in a village, even if he is in distress [from hunger]. (*Manu,* 6.1–3, 13, 16)

Subsistence on gathered food that grows naturally and spontaneously in the wild can be supplemented with food obtained by begging. The begged food, however, should be only enough for "bare subsistence" and should be obtained from the right donors:

He should get food for bare subsistence by begging from priests who are ascetics themselves, from householders, and from other twice-born forest-dwellers. Or a man who lives in the forest may get [food] from a village, receiving it in the hollow of a leaf or in his hand or in a broken clay dish, and eat [only] eight mouthfuls of it. To perfect himself, a priest who lives in the forest must follow these and other preparations for consecration, as well as the various revealed canonical texts of the Upanishads, and those that sages and priestly householders have followed, to increase learning and inner heat and to clean the body. (Manu, 6.27–30)

The final stage of life is that of the world renouncer, who continues and furthers the ascetic practices of the forest dweller: "And when he has spent the third part of his lifespan in the forests in this way, he may abandon all attachments and wander as an ascetic for the fourth part of his lifespan" (*Manu,* 6.33). In this stage, the renouncer sends his wife away to live with his sons and performs a ceremony equivalent to his own funeral, stating that from this time on "no one belongs to me, and I belong to no one." Dying to his social persona, the wandering hermit from this time forth may no longer return to his previous home and should live entirely detached from the things of this world, owning nothing, alone and without companions, perfectly content and indifferent. He should beg but once a day, and he should not be "addicted to food" or hope for lots of alms or be disappointed should he receive nothing.

He should always go all alone, with no companion, to achieve success; realizing that success is for the man who is alone, he neither deserts nor is deserted. The hermit should have no fire and no home, but should go to a village to get food, silent, indifferent, unwavering and deep in concentration. A skull-bowl, the roots of trees, poor clothing, no companionship, and equanimity to everything—this is the distinguishing mark of one who is Freed. He should not welcome dying, nor should he welcome living, but wait for the right time as a servant waits for orders. . . . He should live here on earth seated in ecstatic contemplation of the soul, indifferent, without any carnal desires, with the soul as his only companion and happiness as his goal . . . . He should go begging once a day and not be eager to get a great quantity, for an ascetic who is addicted to food becomes attached to sensory objects, too. . . . He should not be sad when he does not get anything nor delighted when he gets something, but take only what will daily sustain his vital breath, transcending any attachment to material things. (*Manu*, 6.42–45, 49, 55, 57)

The system of stages of life was the principal way in which Hinduism reconciled the apparently contradictory pulls of its life-affirming and world-renouncing strains. But there was also another way of reconciling the householder and renunciatory ways of life in the classical texts of Hinduism. This is the yoga of action (*karma yoga*) in the *Bhagavad Gita*. As opposed to the renunciation *of* action characteristic of ascetics and world renouncers, the *Bhagavad Gita* advocates a renunciation *in* action: one performs one's duties in society but dedicates the fruits of all action to God.

Asceticism in Buddhism

According to Buddhist texts, Siddhartha Gautama (c. 563–c. 483 B.C.E.), the founder of Buddhism, was born into a royal family and raised in the lap of luxury. Upon learning of the true nature of the world outside his insulated life—a world full of suffering, sickness, old age, and death—Gautama immediately renounced his privileged life, left his family, and joined a group of ascetics in the jungle.

The time of the Buddha seems to have been one in which many different renunciatory groups in the uninhabited regions of north India experimented with various techniques—ascetic, yogic, philosophical, and meditational—to attain release from suffering and rebirth. Early Buddhist texts are replete with references to ascetics of various types. One such text depicts the typical ascetic (*tapasvin*) of the time as one who

goes naked, is of certain loose habits, licks his hands, respects no approach nor stop; accepts nothing expressly brought, nor expressly prepared, nor any invitations. . . . He takes food once a day, or once every two days, or once every seven days. . . . He feeds on herbs, or on the powder of rice husks, on rice-scum, on flour of oil seeds, on grasses, on cowdung, or on fruits and roots from the woods. . . . He wears coarse hempen cloths, discarded corpse cloths, discarded rags, or antelope hide, or bark garments. (*Digha Nikaya*, quoted in Bhagat, p. 151)

According to hagiographies of the life of the Buddha, Gautama hooked up with such a group and practiced and

mastered the radical ascetic regimen they advocated, to such an extent that he ate virtually nothing and shriveled to nothing more than skin and bones. Finding that he had not achieved his goal through such austerities, Gautama rejected the ascetic path and pursued what he called the "middle way" between the poles of sensuality and asceticism: "There are two extremes, O monks, which he who has given up the world ought to avoid. What are these two extremes? A life given to pleasure, devoted to pleasures and lust; this is degrading, sensual, vulgar, ignoble and profitless. And a life given to mortifications; this is painful, ignoble and profitless" (*Mahavagga*, quoted in Bhagat, p. 161).

Buddhism in its origins is thus somewhat ambivalent about the usefulness of asceticism. On the one hand, it rejects the extreme forms of physical abnegation and self-torture that appear in the other Indian religions it grew up with. Buddhism denies that such physical asceticism alone can procure for the practitioner the highest spiritual goals. On the other hand, however, there can be no question that Buddhism requires its more serious practitioners not only to renounce worldly life but also to train diligently in self-discipline and self-control through the "eightfold path" (right views, intention, speech, action, livelihood, effort, mindfulness, and concentration). Attaining the permanent peace and happiness known as *nirvana* also requires the elimination of desire and aversion through ascetic self-discipline and abnegation. If one can eliminate desire, selfishness, and egotism by more moderate means, the more radical physical austerities are unnecessary: "All mortification is vain so long as selfishness leads to lust after pleasures in this world or in another world. But he in whom egotism has become extinct is free from lust; he will desire neither worldly nor heavenly pleasures, and the satisfaction of his natural wants will not defile him. He may eat and drink to satisfy the needs of life" (*Mahavagga*, quoted in Bhagat, p. 162).

While the Buddha rejected the extreme forms of physical asceticism recommended by others, he did allow for a number of ascetic practices called the *dhutangas*. These practices are said not to be the path itself but only preparatory for the path; they help the seeker eliminate all forms of attachment. The *dhutangas* include wearing only monastic robes made from discarded fabric, living only on alms begged for indiscriminately, eating only once a day, living in the forest or at the foot of a tree or in a cemetery, and sleeping only while sitting upright (and never while lying down).

The main form that asceticism took in Buddhism was monastic renunciation of the world. In stark contrast to the Hindu system of the four stages of life, in which renunciation was relegated to the end of life after the householder stage, Buddhists insisted that as soon as one recognized that this world is like a "house on fire," one should give up the worldly life and join the monastery. There, in the company of other monks or nuns, one could pursue a regulated life of study, meditation, and self-discipline similar to the monastic lifestyle pursued in other religious traditions.

Asceticism in Jainism

The founder of the religion of Jainism was, like the Buddha, a world renouncer. Unlike the Buddha, however, Mahavira (599–527 B.C.E.) embraced a program of extreme austerities to reach his religious goal. Having left the social world, Mahavira adopted the life of a naked wandering mendicant and for twelve years practiced the most severe of physical austerities until he reached perfection.

The life of Mahavira set the tone for the development of the Jain tradition. Jainism is perhaps the most ascetically oriented of all the world's religions. Most Jains are and have always been householders, but even householders are urged to live lives of self-restraint and especially nonviolence. Jain monks pursue lives of even greater austerities, following the five "great vows" (no killing living beings, truthfulness, no stealing, chastity, and renunciation of possessions) and, in some sects, not wearing any clothing. Jains seek ascetic heat in both its "external" and "internal" forms—the former entailing fasting, begging, and mortification of the body; the latter requiring penance, modesty, service to others, study, meditation, and nonattachment to the body. The epitome of asceticism is found in the Jain tradition of religious suicide by starvation.

Conclusion

While renunciation of the world and asceticism have had a huge influence on Indian religions, it must be remembered that the more extreme practices have always been limited to the very few, the religious virtuosi. Also, these world-denying and self-abnegating practices have always coexisted with equally or more powerful strains in these traditions valorizing a worldly life and, to some extent, material goals. The ascetic quality of Indian religions has often been exaggerated, even caricatured, at the expense of a more realistic portrait—one that admits the impact of asceticism on these traditions while contextualizing such practices and values within what have always been complex and varied religious traditions.

See also **Asceticism: Western Asceticism; Buddhism; Hinduism.**

BIBLIOGRAPHY
Bhagat, M. G. *Ancient Indian Asceticism.* New Delhi: Munshiram Manoharlal, 1976.
Bronkhorst, Johannes. *The Two Sources of Indian Asceticism.* New York: Peter Lang, 1993.
Chakraborti, Haripada. *Asceticism in Ancient India in Brahmanical, Buddhist, Jaina, and Ajivika Societies, from the Earliest Times to the Period of Śankarāchārya.* Calcutta: Punthi Pusak, 1973.
Doniger, Wendy. *Asceticism and Eroticism in the Mythology of Siva.* New York: Oxford University Press, 1973.
Dutt, Sukumar. *Buddhist Monks and Monasteries of India: Their History and Their Contribution to Indian Culture.* London: George Allen and Unwin, 1962.
Eliade, Mircea. *Yoga: Immortality and Freedom.* 2nd ed. Princeton, N.J.: Princeton University Press, 1969.
Embree, Ainslie T., ed. *The Hindu Tradition: Readings in Oriental Thought.* New York: Vintage, 1972.
Manu. *The Laws of Manu.* Translated by Wendy Doniger, with Brian K. Smith. London: Penguin Books, 1991.
Olivelle, Patrick. *The Āśrama System: The History and Hermeneutics of a Religious Institution.* New York: Oxford University Press, 1993.

Brian Smith

WESTERN ASCETICISM

Asceticism, defined for our purposes within the context of the premodern tradition, refers to specific passive and active practices that are engaged in out of ideological motives: on the one hand, abstinence from nourishment, sleep, sexuality, social communication, and social ties—thus from natural human expression—and from other components of civilization, such as bodily cleanliness; on the other hand, the active cultivation of physical revulsion, whether through intentional exhaustion or bloody self-mutilation. As long as the passive practice is performed in a balanced manner, it may bring positive physical and spiritual results. More common, however, are examples wherein this sort of practice leads to abiding physical and spiritual damage; with the active sort this is generally the case. While technically similar, certain therapeutic practices, engaged in for medical reasons, are not to be considered asceticism in this context. Asceticism, although grounded in metaphysical motivations, is decidedly a concept concerned with practical realization; thus the following will discuss both theory and practice.

The Ancients

The ancient Greek word *askesis* referred at first to the physical practices of soldiers and athletes, and only later to intellectual exercises such as philosophizing, training of the will, or morality. Religious asceticism only played a role with small groups (cultish chastity of the priestesses of the Roman goddess Vesta, castration of the priests of the Egyptian god Attis), or during specific times (yearly abstinence for several days in honor of Ceres) or activities (especially magic).

The main arguments for asceticism lay, on the one hand, in the realm of a cult's purity codes and, on the other, in the philosopher's requirement for ethical strengthening of will and nonattachment: marriage and children would only disrupt the thinker's conduct of life. Thus retreat from the world was recommended by philosophers such as Plato, and many wise men, like Apollonius of Tyana in the first century C.E., took vows of chastity. Related is the philosophical ideal of imperviousness to all earthly circumstances (apathy, ataraxy). Within Orphicism, Pythagoreanism, Stoicism, and Cynicism there were strains that viewed the physical as far inferior to the spiritual. The essential ancient conception (the *soma sema* doctrine, for example, in Plato's *Gorgias*) was that the soul, caught in the "grave" of the body, should be liberated through a weakening of precisely this body. Examples of this idea occurred in the Eleusian fasts, in Neoplatonism, and—most clearly delineated—in Manichaeism. Passive asceticism was considered the best means to attain this liberation. Ascetic tendencies supported, furthermore, a strand of ancient medicine that energetically recommended abstinence from sexuality, as the discharge of semen was thought to weaken the body and soul of both men and women.

In Old Testament Judaism, asceticism only appeared in the form of cultish abstention, or fasting, as practiced by the Nazareans or John the Baptist, or more strictly in sects such as the Therapeutae. The Celts utilized fasting as a coercive method for deciding disputes: they fasted at their enemy's door, thereby compelling him to fast as well, on pain of loss of honor.

Early Christianity

The most important early Christian ascetic forms were fasting and sexual abstinence. The former, as habitual practice, cannot be traced back to Jesus—his disciples did not even fast on the Sabbath. He said of himself, "The son of man came eating and drinking," wherefore he was criticized as a "glutton and drunkard" (Matt. 11:19). His apparently exceptional forty-day fast in the desert (like Moses and Elias) became, nevertheless, the paradigm whereby this practice later became part of the permanent *imitatio Christi*. The basis for the ideal of chastity was in Jesus's saying "And there are eunuchs who have made themselves eunuchs for the kingdom of heaven's sake" (Matt. 19:12). Yet this was practiced very rarely (according to the most important theologian of the third century, Origen of Alexandria), in order to avoid comparison with the priests of Attis. Paul was more influential, teaching, in the face of the imminent coming of the end of the world, that he who has a wife shall behave as if he has none (1 Cor. 7:29). He only allowed for physical love reluctantly, as a concession; it was far preferable that all believers would be as chaste as he. For how else could one concentrate oneself entirely upon Christ? The doctors of the church built upon these elements enthusiastically and combined them with misogynist components of the Judaic creation doctrine and ancient philosophy. St. Jerome (c. 347–419 or 420), who devalued marriage in favor of chastity, and St. Augustine (354–430), who argued that original sin is reenacted through the sex act, laid the foundations of the Christian sexual ethic that are still with us today. Doubts about the eschatological salvation of married people (as in the ascetic sect of the Encratites) were, however, consistently refuted as heresies.

Christian asceticism, as a movement that truly shaped the conduct of life, found its most emphatic expression in the monastic fathers in the deserts of Egypt and Syria, who were also paradigms for the ideal of *contemptus mundi* and self-mortification. The spread of asceticism throughout the Western world paralleled that of monasticism, which based itself consistently upon vows of chastity, poverty, and obedience. The following aspects contributed to its ideological background:

1. The wish to imitate the religious founder (*imitatio Christi*), a consequence of a (hardly authentic) saying of Jesus, "And anyone who does not take up his cross and follow me is unworthy of me" (Matt. 10:38).

2. The reception of the pagan *soma sema* doctrine: spiritualized, this led to the commandment, in harmony with a dualistic belief system, to "leave" all pleasurable earthly things in order not to sully oneself with material goods (*contemptus mundi*).

3. The monastic ideal of the *angelikos bios,* the angelic life, which implied wakefulness, fasting, and sexual abstinence, since angels neither sleep, nor eat, nor love.

4. Self-punishment during earthly existence in order to avoid the incomparably more horrific divine revenge in the beyond; also, taking on penance for another's sins (with the same intention) as atonement toward the Godhead.

5. Presentation of an immaterial oblation.

6. Weakening of the body with the aim of rendering it less susceptible to sinful practices.

The Middle Ages

The high and late Middle Ages were the epochs of the widest proliferation of ascetic ideals in European history. Up to the turn of the first century, self-mortification was almost exclusively the duty of the "virtuosos" of this religion, the monks; it was only after the church reform of the high Middle Ages that an outbreak of lay piety initiated this ideal for every truly engaged Christian in the world. A maxim of St. Bartholomew of Farne (d. 1193) can be taken as paradigmatic of the wide proliferation of the *soma sema* doctrine: "We must inflict our body with all kinds of adversity if we want to deliver it to perfect purity of soul!" The mendicant orders, founded in the thirteenth century, were especially important for the spread of ascetic ideals among the laity. Their basic tenets, grounded in asceticism, were traditional: contempt of the world as well as weakening and chastisement of the body as an instrument of sin. In addition to these goals of self-salvation, and in contrast to older monasticism, the goal of brotherly love fostered the attempt to atone for the sins of other believers, both living and deceased. The founders of the Minorites and the preaching orders created a precedent as well. St. Francis of Assisi (1181 or 1182–1226) taught, "I have no greater enemy than my body," arguing that "We should feel hatred towards our body for its vices and sinning!" For St. Francis this attitude entailed fasting and self-flagellation for the disciplining of the body, which he called "brother donkey." This metaphor, beloved by the ascetics, expresses the idea of the body as a beast of burden that, according to *Legenda maior,* the life of St. Francis by St. Bonaventure (c. 1217–1274), "should be weighed down by hard work, often scourged with the whip, and nourished with poor fodder." As for St. Dominic (c. 1170–1221), aside from the usual waking and fasting, three times every night he would "whip himself with an iron chain: once for himself, once for the sinners in the world, and one for the sinners who are suffering in purgatory."

The most common ascetic practices of the Middle Ages and the early modern period were poverty, self-flagellation, fasting, waking, hunger, and other works of penitence.

Self-flagellation (*disciplina*),previously rare, spread first with the teachings of the doctor of the church Pier Damiani (1007–1072): he recommended that one flagellate oneself for the duration of forty psalms daily, on high holy days one-half more again. His treatise *De laude flagellorum* (In praise of flagellation) established this idea: participation in the sufferings of Christ promises a part in his glory (self-punishment and reward). Many saints of the late Middle Ages individually practiced similar self-punishments; as a collective practice, self-flagellation was institutionalized in convents such as those of the Dominicans in southern Germany. This ascetic act was practiced collectively by the laity as well, at least since the advent of the many flagellant movements from 1260 to 1348, which were reactions against plague and apocalyptic fears; there sprang up, in Italy above all, numerous penitential brotherhoods (*penitenti*) with the popular name Battuti. A practice initially developed as a reaction against a particularly terrifying crisis situation became thereby an abiding institution that existed into modern times. Self-flagellation was, as a rule, practiced along with meditations on the Passion, with the aim of imitating Christ's sufferings. Ludolf of Saxony (c. 1295–1377), for example, demanded in his widely read *Vita Christi* that the reader should whip himself, at least in his imagination, to perfect the scourging, and should stretch his arms out in the form of a cross, to imitate the Crucifixion.

Genuflection (*veniae*) was one of the most common methods of prayer, practiced already in ancient times. The prayer position became, in the ancient church, a penitential practice and, at least from the high Middle Ages on, an ascetic achievement: St. Maria of Oignies (c. 1177–1213), for example, managed up to six hundred genuflections without interruption.

Wakefulness (*vigiliae*) found its theological justification in Luke 6:12, when Jesus kept a vigil before calling the twelve apostles. Here too the monks of the Middle Ages attempted to outdo their religious leader: some, for example, such as the beatified Benevenuta of Bojanis, bathed their eyes in vinegar. Sleep deprivation was a given in any case, since sleep was constantly interrupted by the cloister's prayer rhythm; it was further assured by hard beds.

Penitential robes (*cilicium*) and girdles (*cingulum, catena*) were often worn by those living in the world, even under everyday clothing. The beatified father confessor Wilbirg of St. Florian (c. 1230–1289), who chastised himself with an iron girdle that inflamed the skin egregiously, outlined their typical rationale: "In this way I have afflicted my flesh hardily and through this affliction have I won a reward which is not small."

Fasting (*ieiunum*) was not only prescribed during certain times in the church year (Holy Week) but was, beyond this, the most frequently practiced ascetic achievement. The two female doctors of the church, St. Catherine of Siena (1347–1380) and St. Teresa of Avila (1515–1582), followed this practice: in order to force themselves to regurgitate, they inserted, amid great pain, plant stems or branches down their throats to their stomachs. Catherine called this act "retribution" and introduced it with the words "And now we will deliver retribution to this most wretched sinner!" In 1380 she died of thirst, following an ascetic trial. According to themselves and the reports of their contemporaries, many late medieval ascetics took their holy anorexia to the point that they were able to live entirely without nourishment: these included Benevenuta of Bojanis, Elsbeth Achlerin, St. Lidwina of Schiedam, and the Swiss national saint, Nicholas of Flüe.

Total chastity (*castimonia*), in accordance with the above-mentioned ideal of Paul and the church fathers, was a matter of course for all who took their priestly role or monasticism seriously. It is not surprising that numerous visions by celibate men and women have come down to us that openly or subliminally incorporate sexuality, be it in the form of sadistic punishment fantasies in purgatory or hell or as the mystical love union of bride and Christ. As many married lay people began, following the eleventh- and twelfth-century church reforms, to strive for monastic ideals, the problem of accommodating asceticism and the *debitum maritum* came sharply to the fore. Some couples, like the count and countess St. Eleazar and St. Delphina of Sabran (fourteenth century), carried on a chaste marriage. Women with less pious husbands, like St. Dorothy of Montau (1347–1394) or St. Francesca of Rome (1384–1440), made every sexual coupling into a torture through self-mutilation.

Ascetic practices of this kind were not generally intended to be private matters; they were supposed to be public, as part of a contemporary worldview that saw the ascetic's suffering body as a sign written for God—a visible demonstration of election and an exhortation to imitation. The contemporary paintings and sculptures of, for example, St. Bernardino of Siena, John of Capistrano, and Nicholas of Flüe, document this clearly.

Asceticism gained, from the high Middle Ages on, a further function that had not previously been present—the mystical inducement of trancelike or ecstatic states. In this function—which fully parallels the preparation for the soul's journey of shamanism, excepting that Christianity does not employ drugs—asceticism was practiced by almost all experiential mystics from the late Middle Ages to the present, although it evoked criticism from some theoretical mystics, such as Meister Eckehart (c. 1260–?1327).

Extreme ascetic trials were often demanded as tests of obedience or as punishments by father confessors or cloister leaders; the disciplining of the individual therefore served the interests of the churchly authority's exercise of power. The internalization of asceticism as an ideal could also, seen from a sociological perspective, subconsciously serve this same goal.

Western Christianity did not consist only of Catholics, of course, but included, with increasing frequency toward the turn of the first millennium, alternative sects as well. Heresies, developed as a result of intensive theological and philosophical reflection, such as Amalric of Bena's doctrines in the late twelfth and early thirteenth centuries, but also, in time, Protestantism, show a particular tendency toward asceticism. Sects that leaned toward libertine ideas, however, such as the Adamites, the Free Spirit Brotherhood, and the Luciferians, were naturally opposed to asceticism. Asceticism, however, took on an enormous significance in the dualistic heresy of the Manichaean tradition. According to its teachings, the material world was evil, especially anything that was related to sexuality and its accompanying animal satisfactions. The "light soul" needed to be freed from the prison of "dark materiality." Thus the Cathars (Albigensians) fasted three days in every week and an additional forty days every year. Marriage was forbidden. An extreme form of nutritional deprivation, the *endura,* was practiced as well, whereby terribly ill sect members would fast themselves to death; sick babies would be deprived of their milk, a practice that was called "preparing a good end." The intensification of Catholic asceticism since the twelfth century was, to a large extent, a reaction to these practices, an attempt, in other words, to outdo these heretical dualists.

The Early Modern Period

In Catholic lands the medieval ascetic forms were continued in principle, especially in the Latinate countries, aided by the development of a thorough theoretical collection of texts on asceticism and mysticism systematizing the abovementioned theological foundations. St. Veronica Giuliani (1660–1727), who, among other things, used her tongue to lick half of her cloister clean of dust and spiders, may be taken as a practical example; the most widespread theoretical example of a *direttio ascetico* (ascetic instruction) was the *Direttorio ascetico* by the Jesuit Giovanni Scaramelli (1687–1752).

Sects like the Jansenists had strands who practiced extreme forms of asceticism: in Paris, after 1730, there appeared the female Convultionists, who swallowed burning coals or pebbles, suffered under the body weight of other members, and voluntarily underwent crucifixion for hours at a time. This was a mass movement that spread through the energy of group dynamics and evolved during communal religious services.

Twiggy modeling a dress, 1968. By the mid-twentieth century, asceticism had been diluted to a concept practiced primarily by those seeking to attain personal satisfaction in sports, political or financial gain, or, as in the case of a fashion model, a desirable physical appearance. © BETTMANN/CORBIS

The Protestant reformers, more emphatically even than the humanists, rejected the asceticism that had previously been quite well known because they counted it as an act of "good works" and a mark of monasticism. With the exception of Methodists and Anglicans, Protestant piety recognized retreat from the world but no active asceticism. Max Weber and Ernst Troeltsch have seen this attitude as a strict work ethic and a denial of the earned pleasures of an upwardly mobile life of production and consumption; in other words, Calvinism is an "internal asceticism," or a secularized equivalent of monastic asceticism (implying, naturally, a considerable expansion of the term's meaning). To the Enlightenment philosophers, asceticism was no longer comprehensible and became merely a cause to mock Catholicism.

Modernity

Since the Enlightenment, even the Catholic Church has come, more and more, to reject the above-described ascetic forms—at a distance from an approximately eighteen-hundred-year tradition—as aberrations and "exaggerations." In the early twenty-first century, Catholic theologians of this denomination define asceticism as balanced, consisting of harmless penances like moderation in alcohol and nicotine intake or separation from the entertainment industry, as components of a lifetime of striving for perfection. In twenty-first-century monastic life, ascetic achievements are limited to a daily practice regulated by prayer times and reduced to a mild fast before the holy days. Often asceticism is just a synonym for morality—practices that manifest a striving toward God (avoidance of sin, practice of the virtues, or concentration on God). Even Pope Pius XII's teaching that a Christian should wish to seek physical pain in order to take part in the sufferings of Christ, should reject sensual satisfaction and debase his flesh, has not altered the general watering down of the ascetic ideal. That ideal has more in common now with the (Protestant) philosophy of the eighteenth and nineteenth centuries, which reached back to the original meaning of the word: Immanuel Kant saw in asceticism a cheerful fulfillment of duty, Friedrich Nietzsche an exercise of the will. In the modern age, asceticism, thus secularized, is practiced for purely personal purposes: in sports (painful training and sexual abstinence in order to attain ultimate achievement), for the realization of aesthetic norms (fasting to attain an ideal figure, sometimes to the extent of a striving for gauntness), or for the attainment of social and lucrative ends. In 2004, for example, the English television station Channel 4 aired a reality show in which the contestants competed to see who could go without sleep the longest—a week of sleep deprivation brought the winner 140,000 euros.

Another ascetic form, grounded in subjective ethics—not religious as a rule—is fasting for the implementation of an ideological stance (as in ancient Ireland). In modern times it has become a common method (hunger strike) to appeal through the media for the sympathy of the public.

Conclusion

As a widespread phenomenon, asceticism was historically significant only within the religious realm. Self-discipline and self-infliction of pain, as voluntary practices of piety, primarily functioned as part of a predetermined contract with the God-head in the sense of a religious *do ut* (principle of reciprocity) that anticipated a reward in this and the other world. Asceticism was therefore always commonly seen as a means to an end, although it may have been, for those with corresponding psychosomatic dispositions, a goal in itself. Remarkably, no other religion besides Christianity so positively values suffering and pain. This value begins with voluntary participation in the Passion of the religious leader, attains a decided accent with Paul, the martyrs, and monasticism, and reaches its high point in the era between the thirteenth and the eighteenth centuries. And Christianity alone uses, as its most important symbol, a physical body that has been pierced with nails to an instrument of torture and left there to die. In the third chapter of her major work, *Il dialogo,* Catherine of Siena emphasizes the foundations of Catholic asceticism: "For God, who is infinite, wants infinite love—and infinite suffering."

With the advent of Protestantism and, above all, through the Catholic Church's own reception of the Enlightenment, such roads to the heavenly realm became obsolete. Behind this change was also a fundamental transformation of the historical perspective on the body, which manifested itself in law with the elimination of torture and capital punishment. From a social psychology perspective, asceticism is defined as an elite organization of conduct of life that critically rejects the general cultural values of the "masses"; psychologically, asceticism is seen as a socially accepted and rewarded overcompensation for guilt feelings, as in masochism and the death instinct. In the Western world of the early twenty-first century, traditional Christian asceticism, with very few exceptions, no longer exists; asceticism only exists in purely personal, secularized, analogous forms, which inspire more criticism than admiration.

See also **Body, The; Christianity; Enlightenment; Manichaeism; Monasticism; Neoplatonism.**

BIBLIOGRAPHY
Auer, Albert. *Die philosophischen Grundlagen der Askese.* Salzburg, Austria: Jgonta, 1946.
Deth, Ron van, and Walter Vandereycken. *From Fasting Saints to Anorexic Girls.* New York: New York University Press, 1994.
Dinzelbacher, Peter. "Über die Körperlichkeit in der mittelalterlichen Frömmigkeit." In *Bild und Abbild vom Menschen im Mittelalter,* edited by Elisabeth Vavra, 49–87. Klagenfurt, Austria: Wieser, 1999.
Gougaud, Louis. *Devotional and Ascetic Practices in the Middle Ages.* Translated by G. G. Bateman. London: Burns, Oates and Washbourne, 1927.
Lehmann, Hartmut. "Asketischer Protestantismus und ökonomischer Rationalismus." In *Max Webers Sicht des okzidentalen Christentums,* edited by Wolfgang Schluchter, 529–553. Frankfurt, Germany: Suhrkamp, 1988.
Ranke-Heinemann, Uta. *Eunuchs for the Kingdom of Heaven.* Translated by Peter Heinegg. New York: Penguin, 1991.
Schjelderup, Kristian. *Die Askese.* Berlin: de Gruyter, 1928.
Vaage, Leif E., and Vincent L. Wimbush, eds. *Asceticism and the New Testament.* New York: Routledge, 1999.
Viller, Marcel, ed. *Dictionnaire de spiritualité ascétique et mystique.* 16 vols. Paris: Beauchesne, 1932–.
Viller, Marcel, and Karl Rahner. *Aszese und Mystik in der Väterzeit.* 2nd ed. Freiburg, Germany: Herder, 1990.
Wimbush, Vincent L., and Richard Valantasis, eds. *Asceticism.* New York: Oxford University Press, 1995.
Zöckler, Otto. *Askese und Mönchtum.* Frankfurt, Germany: Heyder and Zimmer, 1897.

Peter Dinzelbacher

ASIAN-AMERICAN IDEAS (CULTURAL MIGRATION).

Asian migration to the United States is a trans-Pacific flow of people, social networks, and cultural values. Asian immigrants arrived in America with their own lifestyles, labor and vocational skills, business expertise and capital, family rituals and traditions, religious and philosophical beliefs. As Asians have adapted to American society, some of their home cultures have remained, others have disappeared, and still others have changed. Migration is often a process of negotiation over cultures during which Asian immigrants and their descendants construct new identities, community structure, and cultural sensibilities. Race and ethnicity play important roles in such processes. The formation of Asian-American culture is not a simple blending of Western and Asian cultures. (This entry will not cover immigrants from South Asia.)

The Migration of Values: Religion and Education

Asian experience in America illustrates how cultural values are transplanted, transformed, and developed. In Asia, Confucianism, Buddhism, and Daoism play important roles in people's spiritual life. Confucianism is a philosophical doctrine that guides Asians in human relationships, such as the relationship between the rulers and the ruled or between parents and children. Although Buddhism is a religion, Buddhist teaching is more psychological than theological. When monks pray for deceased family members at a funeral, they help people relieve pain. Daoism advises people to live a simple life and to pursue tranquility and harmony with nature. Those belief systems accompanied Asian immigrants to America. The respect for elders and filial piety advocated by Confucianism have influenced family relationships in both early and contemporary Chinese-American families. Family and district associations of early Chinese communities made sure that a joss house for ancestry worship was available for immigrants and sometimes built temples for prayers. Hsi Lai Temple, completed in 1988 in Hacienda Heights, Los Angeles County, is the largest Buddhist temple in North America. A high percentage of early Japanese immigrants were Buddhists as well, since the Jodo Shinshu (True Pure Land) branches of Amida Buddhism were prevalent in the southwestern part of Japan where immigrants came from. Once rooted in American society, Asian cultural institutions have adapted themselves to local settings. In the early twentieth century, Japanese Buddhist priests often prayed in both Japanese and English, referred to their temples as "churches," installed pews in the temples, and even used hymnals in prayer activities.

Influenced by Confucianism in China, education is the most important social mobility path in Asia. Asian immigrants have brought their belief in the value of education to the United States. Children are expected to compete vigorously at school and earn good grades, and parents often feel obliged to see children through college. Ethnic-language schools have existed in Asian communities since the nineteenth century. Asian children often go to ethnic-language school after attending regular American public schools, though many of them dislike the arrangement. However, language class is only part of the curriculum, as ethnic-language schools often provide Asian cultural classes as well as classes supplementary to public school education. Ethnic-language schools in the early Japanese community offered English-language classes to assist the second generation to do well at American public schools. Contemporary Chinese-language schools often provide SAT or other college entrance preparation classes. Education is an important agenda in the Asian-American family. The value of education has been transmitted to the second generation as Asian parents send their children to attend ethnic-language schools.

Media and Festivals

Other cultural components of Asian-American communities include ethnic-language newspapers, journals, and Web sites, as well as radio and TV stations. Ethnic mass media are instrumental in allowing immigrants to receive news about both America and their home country and to obtain information on job and business opportunities. It also gives them a sense of community. Ethnic festival celebrations are the most visible community events to provide Asian-Americans with a collective cultural identity. Nisei Week in Los Angeles is the largest ethnic festival for Japanese-Americans. Created in the 1930s, the Nisei Week festival aimed to rejuvenate Little Tokyo's economy and reach out to mainstream American society. More importantly, the issei (immigrant) generation was concerned about rapid assimilation of the nisei (second) generation and wanted to use this occasion to promote ethnic pride among the American-born Japanese. Nisei were often advised that buying in Little Tokyo demonstrated their loyalty to Japanese culture. During Nisei Week, stores were colorfully decorated, fashion and talent shows were performed, and a grand parade was organized. The Nisei Week queen often rode together with local government officials in the parade. Under the festival atmosphere, however, lay conflicts between generations, racial tensions, and the struggle of Asian small-business owners.

Lunar New Year is the most important festival for Chinese-Americans. In China, it is essentially a family celebration. Family members clean the house, pay off debts, cook a rich family dinner, give red envelopes containing money to children, and use firecrackers to scare away evil spirits. In America, however, it becomes a public event. Chinese community organizations sponsor the Lunar New Year banquet, organize a dragon or lion dance parade, and decorate the community with red lanterns and bright banners. Before the Chinese Exclusion Acts were repealed in 1943, many Chinese immigrants were separated from their wives and children in China. Clan association banquets replaced the family feast in order to give the single males a sense of family life. Merchants allowed their employees a couple of days off from work to express ethnic solidarity. The Lunar New Year festival was also an occasion to reach

out to mainstream America. While most stores were closed in China during the holidays, decorated Chinatown welcomed visitors as merchants commercialized it to attract tourists. Modeled after the Rose Bowl Parade on New Year's Day in Los Angeles, the Golden Dragon Parade tradition originated in the San Francisco Chinese community in the 1950s. Local celebrities, government officials, famous Chinese professionals and artists, and Miss Chinatown U.S.A. all rode on the floats during the parade. As the Chinese take this occasion to show their ethnic pride, the Lunar New Year gains new meanings in America.

Influences on Mainstream Society

Asian-American culture has influenced American society at large. Grocery chains such as 99 Ranch Market attract both Asian and non-Asian clients. Many Americans consult acupuncture specialists or feng shui masters. Asian food is probably the most visible transplanted culture in America. Wherever they went, immigrants brought their cookery with them. A business directory in 1856 listed five restaurants and thirty-eight grocery stores among eighty-eight Chinese businesses in San Francisco. Obviously Chinese immigrants cooked their own meals and visited Chinese restaurants during their leisure time. However, as racial discrimination gradually forced the Chinese out of other occupations and channeled them into menial service jobs such as the restaurant or laundry business, many Chinese picked up cooking skills and worked as professional cooks. With numerous Chinese restaurants and laundry shops in metropolitan areas during the exclusion years, cooking and laundry became an ethnic label for Chinese-Americans. To adapt Chinese cuisine to American society, Chinese immigrants created "sweet and sour pork" or "chop suey" as "authentic" Chinese dishes in America and invented the "fortune cookie" as an additional incentive to American customers. Restaurants in China had no such thing as a "fortune cookie." Original "chop suey" consisted of intestines and giblets, as ordinary Chinese did not want to waste any part of butchered livestock. Hundreds of "chop suey houses" appeared in New York, Boston, Washington, Philadelphia, and Chicago in the 1900s after Li Hongzhang, a senior Chinese official, visited the United States in 1896. Chinese restaurant operators capitalized on the visit and marketed "chop suey" as Li's favorite dish. Being an authentic Chinese food in America, chop suey is defined in Webster's dictionary as "a dish prepared chiefly from bean sprouts, bamboo shoots, water chestnuts, onions, mushrooms, and meat or fish and served with rice and soy sauce." While the Chinese restaurant has become popular in America society, cooking is a false trademark of Chinese ethnicity.

Herbal medicine, on the other hand, is a true ethnic skill of the Chinese. Like Chinese restaurants, herbal stores began to appear as soon as the Chinese arrived in America. With the growth of Chinese immigrants, more and more herbal doctors arrived to serve the needs of the community. Soon the herbalists began to serve non-Chinese patients as well. By the 1930s, many Chinese herbal doctors had more Caucasian patients than Chinese. Unlike Chinese cuisine, herbal medicine could not change its ingredients, flavor, or dispensation to suit the taste of mainstream Americans. As a transplanted culture, it had to remain distinctively Chinese for its effectiveness. Herbal medicinal formulations were made from hundreds of indigenous herbs gathered in the mountains and valleys of China. The supply of medicine relied on the constant importation of herbs from China. In their efforts to bypass unfair restrictions and cross ethnic boundaries to serve a larger community, Chinese herbalists developed and expanded an ethnic career and business in a Western society where most of their patients were not familiar with Chinese culture and where the medical profession was becoming increasingly standardized and regulated. Acceptance of and respect for Chinese herbal medicine demonstrate how mainstream American patients adapted themselves to an Asian medical therapy. The history of Chinese herbal medicine is a case of reverse assimilation and an expression of ethnic resilience in cultural migration.

See also **Confucianism; Identity, Multiple: Asian-Americans; Race and Racism: Reception of Asians to the United States; Religion: East and Southeast Asia.**

BIBLIOGRAPHY

Chan, Sucheng. *Asian Americans: An Interpretive History.* Boston: Twayne, 1991.

Ichioka, Yuji. *The Issei: The World of the First Generation Japanese Immigrants, 1885–1924.* New York: Free Press, 1988.

Kurashige, Lon. *Japanese American Celebration and Conflict: A History of Ethnic Identity and Festival in Los Angeles, 1934–1990.* Berkeley: University of California Press, 2002.

Liu, Haiming. "The Resilience of Ethnic Culture: Chinese Herbalists in the American Medical Profession." *Journal of Asian American Studies* 1, no. 2 (June 1998): 173–191.

Takaki, Ronald. *Strangers from a Different Shore: A History of Asian Americans.* Rev. ed. Boston: Little, Brown, 1998.

Tong, Benson. *The Chinese Americans.* Rev. ed. Boulder: University of Colorado Press, 2003.

Tsai, Shih-shan Henry. *The Chinese Experience in America.* Bloomington: Indiana University Press, 1986.

Yin, Xiao-huang. *Chinese American Literature since the 1850s.* Urbana: University of Illinois Press, 2000.

Yu, Renqiu. "Chop Suey: From Chinese Food to Chinese American Food." *Chinese America: History and Perspectives* 1 (1987): 87–100.

Zhou, Min. *Chinatown: The Socioeconomic Potential of an Urban Enclave.* Philadelphia: Temple University Press, 1992.

Haiming Liu

ASSIMILATION. In 1964 Milton M. Gordon (b. 1918) produced a groundbreaking book called *Assimilation in American Life.* He informed readers that three different theories of assimilation existed in the United States: "Anglo-Conformity," the "Melting Pot," and "Cultural Pluralism." Gordon acknowledged, though, that Anglo-Conformity was "the most prevalent ideology of assimilation in America throughout the nation's history" (p. 89). The other two theories, proposed by members of minority groups who wanted to "fit in" but who were unwilling to accept the cultural demands of the dominant society, suggested that all people who came to the United States ultimately mixed together and formed a "new American," or

that individuals could "assimilate" while maintaining aspects of their own culture. History has shown, however, as Gordon himself noted, that to be accepted by others as an American, one had to conform totally to the values of Anglos in the United States. ("Anglo" values are sometimes referred to as WASP—white, Anglo-Saxon, Protestant—characteristics.)

Colonial Period

No one questions, of course, that the United States, and the British colonies before the formation of the American government, almost always welcomed European Caucasians as future citizens. In the colonial era there was an incessant call for additional laborers. And although much of the need was filled by black Africans, white people had no desire to intermingle with them socially or on an equal basis. Since the way to assimilate in American society requires marriage with a member of the dominant culture, and adoption of the folkways and mores of that culture, any non-Caucasian could not be considered. Nonwhites could not become white, and prejudice prevented most white people from marrying people of any other skin color.

Starting in colonial America, however, the standards for assimilation included adoption of the religion and language of the community. Most of the Pilgrims, Puritans, and others who traveled to the southern part of what is now the United States were Protestants. Catholics were feared because they were viewed as subject to the "tyrannical dictates" of the pope in Rome. The epithet "Jews, Turks, and Infidels" assumed inferiority, non-Protestant faiths, and lack of the attitudes and characteristics required of all Americans.

These views did not prevent Catholics and Jews from coming to the colonies, but these groups were rarely accepted as equals by members of the dominant culture. It is true, also, that some Protestant denominations, such as Quakers and Huguenots (French Protestants), were also looked down upon. Once they changed their denominations, however, they had the option of blending with members of the dominant culture. Some accepted the colonial demand for assimilation into a more mainstream Protestant denomination. This choice, however, was usually made by their children or grandchildren. Moreover, other European immigrants could either conform to American values or choose to remain with people of similar backgrounds. The latter was not acceptable to the colonists; it concerned members of the dominant culture. Benjamin Franklin (1706–1790) warned fellow Pennsylvanians in the eighteenth century about the Germans in their midst:

> Why should the *Palentine Boors* be suffered to swarm into our Settlements, and by herding together, establish their Language and Manners, to the Exclusion of ours? Why should *Pennsylvania*, founded by the *English*, become a Colony of *Aliens*, who will shortly be so numerous as to Germanize us instead of our Anglyfying them? (Dinnerstein et al., 1999, p. 7)

Franklin's thoughts reflect not only the values of people of his own time but also those of Americans throughout the centuries. As a result of their anxiety about maintaining the dominant culture, colonists feared new immigrants who might undermine it with their own preferences. Often individuals, some of whom had been here perhaps for less than one generation, expressed the most hostile feelings about the new immigrants. Subsequent generations in the United States also frowned on newcomers with different backgrounds. Only foreign-born Protestants who spoke English were easily accepted without criticism by Americans.

From the colonial era stereotypical impressions of almost every group became part of the thought and expression of members of the Anglo-American culture. Descendants of the English regarded Germans as fat, stupid, and drunk; Jews and Quakers as clever and wealthy; Scots-Irish as violent and drunk; and French, Spaniards, and other "papists" as "hot-blooded lovers" and "slaves" of tyrannical rulers in the Catholic Church. Nineteenth- and twentieth-century immigrants like the Irish, the Poles, and the Jews were similarly branded with epithets Americans fantasized.

Responses to Crisis

Whenever a crisis occurred in American society, some ethnic group was usually targeted as the culprit. In the 1790s, at the time that the English and French were battling for control of the Atlantic Ocean, French "radicalism" supposedly undermined American society. Fears of the French led to the passage in 1798 of the Alien and Sedition Acts, which gave the president unilateral power to jail and/or force people back to where they came from if they criticized the government. During World War I, Americans denounced people of German ancestry; during World War II, the U.S. government incarcerated Japanese-Americans; and after the attack on the World Trade Center and the Pentagon, on September 11, 2001, legislation quickly passed through Congress calling for the "registration" of Muslims from several Middle Eastern and Asian nations. In each of these periods, most other Americans regarded members of these groups as threats to the security of the nation.

Throughout American history, once crises had passed, Caucasians could engage in whichever economic endeavors they chose. Members of society who had not married people of the dominant culture, however, had a more difficult time functioning in the United States. Some, who were even prohibited from having equality by state laws or customs, such as Asians and Mexican-Americans, nonetheless found their niche in a variety of endeavors. The Irish, in the nineteenth and twentieth centuries, could buy saloons, join the army, or attend law school. Civil-service positions were generally open to them as well as to others of different backgrounds who passed qualifying examinations. Through the middle of the twentieth century many political "bosses" were of Irish ancestry. Given the opportunities for independent entrepreneurships, Jews as well as Japanese rose in society. After World War II, where educational opportunity existed, everyone who partook of it fully moved up a notch or two on the socioeconomic scale.

Nonetheless, many newcomers and their children still retained traditional values and refused to marry outside of their cultures. Although almost everyone acculturated in stages, that

is, adopted the characteristics, attributes, and behavior of members of American society, it sometimes took three or four generations before they actually assimilated. For these people and their descendants, "success," but not total acceptance, was also possible. Thus, in tracing the evolution of people in American history, one notes that while wealth or accomplishments were always signs of having succeeded in the dominant culture, such attributes were not enough to be considered "one of us." An athlete or an entertainer might be extremely skillful, popular, and appealing in his or her field of endeavor, but still not accepted as an "equal" by members of the dominant culture. At one time a Jewish actor or an Italian baseball player might be universally applauded, but that did not make Jews or Italians part of the mainstream.

In general, Americans welcomed all Caucasian immigrants until approximately the 1920s. There were always concerns, though, that non-Protestants could not fit into American society. Thus, when the tide of European immigration turned overwhelmingly Catholic and Jewish in the late nineteenth and early twentieth centuries, Congress passed laws curbing their influx. In the 1920s new immigration legislation favored people whose compatriots had predominated in the settlement of the United States. Laws establishing quotas for different nationalities passed in 1921 and 1924, respectively. These bills set low quotas for southern and eastern Europeans but much more generous ones for the British, Germans, and Irish. In the 1930s American consular officials placed more stringent restrictions on Jewish people trying to emigrate from Germany than they did on non-Jews. Similarly, after World War II, legislation to bring in displaced persons from Europe favored non-Jews over Jews, and former fascists over Communists. Not until 1965 did Congress pass immigration legislation favoring family unification.

The opportunities for assimilation in American society have always been greater for Caucasian Protestants than for people of other backgrounds. Before World War II sociologists noted that people of different national heritages had begun marrying members of other ethnic groups who shared their religion. In the 1960s, the nation witnessed a rise in the rates of intermarriage by people of European descent who had had different religious and ethnic backgrounds. The United States Supreme Court then declared, in *Loving v. Virginia* (1967), that states could not ban interracial marriage. Immediately the prohibition of interracial marriage, which still existed in twenty-two states, mostly in the South and the West, ceased.

Since that time, Americans of all stripes have witnessed increasing numbers of marriages based on individual choices and characteristics. Demographers and statisticians, moreover, have concluded that more than 50 percent of all Americans have chosen life partners based on individual characteristics rather than religious, ethnic, or legal considerations. As one boy put it in 1993, "I'm half Italian, half Japanese, and all American."

Class, rather than any other factor in the twenty-first century, should be examined before making assessments about intermarriage as well as ease of assimilation. In the twenty-first century, in countries such as Germany and England, both class and heritage play a more significant aspect in acceptance than they do in the United States. But unlike the United States, where place of birth determines citizenship, in some European countries—for example, Switzerland—one is never automatically a citizen, regardless of birthplace.

See also **Americanization, U.S.; Asian-American Ideas (Cultural Migration); Identity, Multiple; Loyalties, Dual; Migration.**

BIBLIOGRAPHY

Alba, Richard. *Remaking the American Mainstream: Assimilation and Contemporary Immigration.* Cambridge, Mass.: Harvard University Press, 2003.

Dinnerstein, Leonard, Roger L. Nichols, and David M. Reimers. *Ethnic Americans: A History of Immigration.* 4th ed. New York: Columbia University Press, 1999.

———. *Natives and Strangers: A Multicultural History of Americans.* 4th ed. New York: Oxford University Press, 2003.

Gordon, Milton M. *Assimilation in American Life: The Role of Race, Religion, and National Origins.* New York: Oxford University Press, 1964.

Jacoby, Tamar. *Reinventing the Melting Pot: The New Immigrants and What It Means to Be American.* New York: Basic Books, 2003.

Portes, Alejandro, and Rubén A. Rumbaut. *Legacies: The Story of the Immigrant Second Generation.* Berkeley: University of California Press, 2001.

Leonard Dinnerstein

ASTROLOGY.

This entry includes two subentries:

Overview
China

OVERVIEW

Astrology, the effort to relate earthly occurrences to the stars and planets, is one of the oldest known intellectual endeavors. The oldest evidence for the Western tradition of astrology comes from Mesopotamia in the late third millennium B.C.E. Mesopotamian astronomical documents correlated celestial phenomena like eclipses with public events, including political changes and natural catastrophes. The first surviving "natal" horoscope, recounting the position of the planets at an individual's birth, is also Mesopotamian and dates from the late fifth century B.C.E. One Mesopotamian people, the Babylonians or Chaldeans, long remained famed for their astrological ability. Astrologers generally were called Chaldeans as early as the first century B.C.E. in Rome.

Greek interest in astrology began in the Hellenistic period, as Alexander the Great's (r. 336–323) conquests exposed Greek thinkers to Mesopotamian culture. The Greeks put astronomy in a cosmological framework, emphasizing the motions of the planets rather than static correlations. Hellenistic Alexandria was a center of astrology, and the Hermetic texts that originated there incorporated astrology into their magical and religious system. The Hellenistic period also saw the first evidence

of Jews embracing astrology, a practice traditional Judaism condemned.

The Roman upper classes also initially condemned astrology, which they associated with popular divination and superstition. This position is reflected in Marcus Tullius Cicero's (106–43 B.C.E.) *On Divination*. Following the Roman conquest of the Hellenistic east in the first century B.C.E., Roman interest in astrology increased. The earliest evidence for Roman astrologers dates from this period. The Stoic school of philosophy, popular among the Roman elite, endorsed astrology along with other forms of divination. (The Epicureans, great rivals of the Stoics, condemned it.) Astrology became particularly prominent in the Roman Empire, as Augustus Caesar (63 B.C.E.–14 C.E.) employed it in his propaganda, subsequent emperors employed court astrologers, and rebels and aspirants to the imperial throne consulted astrologers to estimate their chances for success.

The imperial period saw the first surviving Latin astrological work, the Roman poet Manlius's Stoic-influenced *Astronomica*. Manlius had little astronomical or mathematical skill, however, and the most important astrological writer in the Roman Empire was the Greek astronomer Claudius Ptolemy (2nd century C.E.), author of the most influential ancient astrological book, *Tetrabiblios*. Ptolemy, more a codifier than an innovator in astrology, defended it as a science of the influence of the stars on the terrestial world based on conjecture rather than certainty. The early Christians attacked astrology, associating it with determinism and Gnosticism. St. Augustine of Hippo's (354–430) denunciation of astrology in *The City of God* was particularly influential in the Latin West. The Christian Roman Empire included astrology in its strong antidivination laws, which were however only sporadically enforced.

Medieval Astrology

During the early Middle Ages, astrology, like many ancient disciplines, languished in the Latin West less because of the church's condemnation than because few Westerners were able to draw an astrological chart or read Greek astrological works. The most important theoreticians and practitioners in the early Middle Ages were Arabic speakers in the Islamic world. Arabs developed several astrological ideas later accepted in the West, such as the correlation of patterns in human history with the conjunctions of Jupiter and Saturn, the so-called great conjunctions. Greek and Arabic works of astrological theory were translated into Latin only in the twelfth and thirteenth centuries. Medieval intellectuals like Albertus Magnus (c. 1200–1280) and Roger Bacon (c. 1220–1292) endorsed astrology but faced the problem of reconciling astrological determinism with the Christian doctrine of free will. They claimed that the stars influenced only the body, and not the soul. St. Thomas Aquinas (c. 1224–1274) conceded that the stars influenced human passions, and that many astrological predictions were correct because most people were ruled by their passions. He claimed, however, that the wise man could resist his passions, and thus the stars could not determine his actions. The medieval emphasis on the power of the stars over the body helped astrology become closely allied with medicine. Charles V of France (r. 1364–1380), whose library contained many books

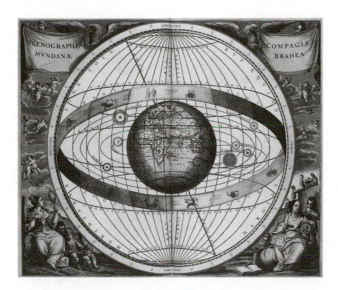

Map of Tycho Brahe's system of planetary orbits around the earth, with signs of the horoscope (1660–1661), by Andreas Cellarius. Danish astronomer Brahe, who calculated the measurements of the solar system in the sixteenth century, was one of the last major Western astronomers to practice astrology. © STAPLETON COLLECTION/CORBIS

on astrology, contributed to the foundation of a college of astrological medicine in the 1360s.

Not all late medieval intellectuals accepted the new astrology. Six propositions of Bishop Étienne Tempier's famous prohibition of 1277 condemned astrology, mostly on the grounds of its determinism. The Scholastic philosopher Nicole d'Oresme (c. 1325–1382) vigorously opposed astrology. He reiterated the Christian attack on astrological determinism and added a new argument, that the velocities of the heavenly bodies were mathematically irrational and incommeasurable, and thus it was impossible to know them exactly enough for astrology to work.

Astrology in the Renaissance and Reformation

As in other ancient sciences, Renaissance humanists claimed to be recovering the true, ancient astronomy from corruption by Arab and medieval Latin writers (although Arab-derived great conjunction theory remained very popular.) Renaissance philosophers, particularly those influenced by Neoplatonism, also extended the discipline's scope. The third book of Marsilio Ficino's (1433–1499) *Three Books on Life* (1489) treated the planets as a guide to all aspects of human life. Girolamo Cardano (1501–1576), who wrote a commentary on the *Tetrabiblios,* scandalized many by drawing a natal horoscope of Jesus Christ. While Martin Luther (1483–1546) and John Calvin (1509–1564) both condemned astrology, many of their Protestant followers (including Philipp Melanchthon; 1497–1560) practiced it. Protestant astrologers were particularly interested in reconciling astrology with the apocalyptic interpretation of the Bible, using the stars and great conjunctions to help predict the date of the end of the world.

Astrology was an important support for professional astronomers in the late Middle Ages and Renaissance, as many

patrons were interested in astronomical data principally for its astrological uses. The leaders of the scientific revolution differed in their opinions of astrology. The last major Western astronomers to seriously practice astrology were Tycho Brahe (1546–1601) and Johannes Kepler (1571–1630), both of whom drew horoscopes for the monarchs they served. Mechanical philosophers like Marin Mersenne (1588–1648) and the "Christian Epicurean" Pierre Gassendi (1592–1655) denied the doctrine of the influence of the stars on the Earth that astrology was based on, as it had no mechanical explanation. Although several of the founding members of the Royal Society practiced astrology, it lost its central intellectual role in the late seventeenth century. Astronomers increasingly justified their science as useful in navigation and cartography rather than astrology. Copernican astronomy did not "disprove" astrology, but the shift from an earth-centered to a sun-centered cosmos did call into question traditional geocentric astrological interpretation. Astrology also suffered from the general decline of magical thinking as Europe entered the eighteenth century. Although many ordinary people continued to believe in astrology, it was not taken seriously by most scientists and intellectuals.

See also **Magic; Pseudoscience; Science.**

BIBLIOGRAPHY

Barton, Tamsyn. *Ancient Astrology.* New York: Routledge, 1994.

Grafton, Anthony. *Cardano's Cosmos: The Worlds and Works of a Renaissance Astrologer.* Cambridge, Mass.: Harvard University Press, 1999.

Tester, S. Jim. *A History of Western Astrology.* Woodbridge, Suffolk, U.K.: Boydell, 1987.

Zambelli, Paola, ed. *"Astrologi Hallucinati": Stars and the End of the World in Luther's Time.* New York: de Gruyter, 1986.

William E. Burns

CHINA

In China, coordination of human activity with the sun, moon, and stars, including the cardinal orientation of structures in the landscape, can be traced back to the Neolithic cultures of the fifth millennium B.C.E. In the words of Sima Qian (fl. 100 B.C.E.), "Ever since the people have existed, when have successive rulers not systematically followed the movements of sun, moon, stars, and asterisms?" By the early Bronze Age, around the beginning of the second millennium, attention had already begun to focus on the circumpolar region as the abode of the sky god *di,* and from this time forward the North Pole increasingly became a locus of practical and spiritual significance. The polar-equatorial emphasis of Chinese astronomy began to take shape, which meant that the ancient Chinese remained largely indifferent to heliacal phenomena and the ecliptic (the sun's apparent path through the skies). A prominent feature of this polar focus was the use of the handle of the constellation Northern Dipper (Ursa Major) as a celestial clock-hand and the identification of certain cardinal constellations with the seasons and their unique characteristics—the green dragon with spring, the red bird with summer, the white tiger with autumn, the dark turtle with winter. As Sima Qian would later say: "The 28 lunar lodges govern the 12 provinces, and the handle of the Dipper seconds them; the origin [of these conceptions] is ancient." Massings of the five planets, *di*'s "Minister-Regulators," solar and lunar eclipses, and other astronomical and atmospheric phenomena were seen as portents of imminent, usually ominous events. Astronomical records are not abundant in the earliest written documents, the oracle-bone divinations of the late Shang dynasty (c. 13th to mid-11th B.C.E.); however, a theory of reciprocity prefiguring later Chinese astrological thinking is already in evidence. What transpired in the heavens could and did profoundly influence human affairs, and conversely, human behavior could and did provoke a response from the numinous realm beyond the limits of human perception. Astral divination was reactive and opportunistic and, as elsewhere, never focused on individuals beyond the royal person, but only on affairs of state such as the sacrifices to the royal ancestors, the harvest, warfare, and the like.

By the late Zhou dynasty (1046–256 B.C.E.) *tianwen*, "sky-pattern reading" or astrological prognostication, took as its frame of reference the twenty-eight lunar mansions or equatorial hour-angle segments into which the sky was by then divided. In classical "field allocation" astrology of mid to late Zhou, these twenty-eight segments of uneven angular dimensions were correlated with terrestrial domains according to different schemes. Allocated among the astral fields for purposes of prognostication were either the nine provinces into which China proper was traditionally thought to have been divided, or the twelve warring kingdoms of the late Zhou, whose successive annihilation by Qin led to the establishment of the unified empire in 221 B.C.E. The classical job description of the post of astrologer royal is found in the third century B.C.E. canonical text *The Rites of Zhou*:

> [The *Bao zhang shi*] concerns himself with the stars in the heavens, keeping a record of the changes and movements of the stars and planets, sun and moon, in order to discern [corresponding] trends in the terrestrial world, with the object of distinguishing (prognosticating) good and bad fortune. He divides the territories of the nine regions of the empire in accordance with their dependence on particular celestial bodies; all the fiefs and territories are connected with distinct stars, based on which their prosperity or misfortune can be ascertained. He makes prognostications, according to the twelve years [of the Jupiter cycle], of good and evil in the terrestrial world. (trans. Needham, p. 190; modified by the author)

In this scheme, movements of the sun, moon, and planets formed the basis of prognostication, taking also into account their correlations with the five elemental phases (Mercury-Water; Venus-Metal; Mars-Fire; Jupiter-Wood; Saturn-Earth), as well as *yin* and *yang*. While sparsely documented in contemporary sources, probably as a result of the hermetic nature of the practice, evidence suggests the influence of astrological considerations was pervasive. As a common aphorism put it not long after the founding of the empire, "astute though the Son of Heaven may be, one must still see where Mars is located." Although Babylonian influence on Chinese astrology has occasionally been claimed, and a few suggestive parallels between specific late planetary prognostications (c. 100 B.C.E.) have been drawn, on the whole the evidence in favor is unpersuasive. Ancient Chinese cosmology and astrology are distinctive in essential respects, and any parallels are so circumstantial that it is more likely that throughout its formative period Chinese astrology developed in isolation from significant external influences. When it comes to China's immediate neighbors, the flow of ideas has been overwhelmingly outward from the center.

Early Imperial Period

In the early imperial period, Han dynasty (206 B.C.E.–220 C.E.) cosmologists amalgamated field-allocation astrology with hemerological concepts (lucky and unlucky days for various activities), yin-yang and five phases correlative cosmology, as well as the symbolic trigrams of the *Book of Changes*, to develop the systematic and highly complex method of divination embodied in the *shi* or diviner's board so representative of that period. Examples of the latter excavated from Han tombs typically consist of a round heaven plate with the Northern Dipper inscribed at the center as if seen from above, and with the twenty-eight lunar mansions, months of the year, or solar chronograms inscribed in bands around the circumference. The pivot of the heaven plate is conventionally placed in or near the handle of the Dipper in recognition of its symbolic centrality and numinous power, while the square earth plate underneath is graduated around its exposed perimeter in concentric bands showing the twenty-eight lunar mansions, the twelve earthly branches and ten heavenly stems marking the cardinal and intercardinal directions, the twenty-four seasonal nodes, and so on. Some examples substitute for the heaven plate an actual ladle fashioned from magnetic lodestone and designed to rotate within a highly polished circular enclosure representing the circumpolar region.

As originally conceived, the twenty-eight lunar mansions did not technically constitute a zodiac, since, with the exception of comets, novae, and the like, the sun, moon, and planets did not actually appear among their constituent stars: many of the latter in ancient times actually lay closer to the equator than to the ecliptic. Rather, astronomical phenomena occurring within a given astral field were connected with noteworthy events in the corresponding terrestrial region. In terms of classical resonance theory this was because the astral and terrestrial realms were continuous and composed of the same quasi-matter, quasi-*pneuma* called *qi*. Theory held that disequilibrium at any point in the system could potentially provoke imbalance throughout by a mysterious process somewhat analogous to magnetism or sympathetic resonance. In case of disruption it was essential to identify the cause and to take corrective action, based on yin-yang and five phases phenomenological correlations, to remedy the situation and restore harmony to the system. Unlike the Ptolemaic scheme, which has aptly been dubbed "astrological ethnology," despite modifications designed to take account of historical changes in political boundaries and the relative balance of power between the empire and its non-Chinese neighbors, from the outset field-allocation astrology was resolutely sinocentric. The non-Chinese world remained essentially unrepresented in the heavens and in astrology except as a reflex of Chinese concerns.

Though individualized horoscopic astrology did not figure in the repertoire, the increasing complexity of astrological theory in Han times was accompanied by a proliferation of prognostication methods and devotions directed toward astral deities. The ancient cult of Tai yi, the supreme ultimate or numinous cosmic force resident at the pole, rose to prominence even in the imperial sacrifices, being imaginatively linked in contemporary iconography with the image of the celestial thearch driving his astral carriage (Ursa Major) around the pole.

> The Dipper is the Celestial Thearch di's carriage. It revolves about the center, visiting and regulating each of the four regions. It divides yin from yang, establishes the four seasons, equalizes the Five Elemental Phases, deploys the seasonal junctures and angular measures, and determines the various periodicities: all these are tied to the Dipper. (Sima Qian, Shi ji, "Treatise on the Heavenly Offices")

The protection of Tai yi and lesser astral spirits was invoked both in local cults led by magicians and by imperial officials, in the latter case especially before initiating major military campaigns, when

> a banner decorated with images of the sun, moon, Northern Dipper, and rampant dragons was mounted on a shaft made from the wood of the thorn tree, to symbolize the Supreme Ultimate and its three stars. . . . The banner was called 'Numinous Flag.' When one prayed for military success, the Astrologer Royal would hold it aloft and point in the direction of the country to be attacked. (Sima Qian, Shi ji, "Basic Annals 12: The Filial and Martial Emperor")

Prognostication based on the appearance of the stars of the Dipper appeared, as well as that based on the color, brightness, movements, and so forth, of comets, "guest stars" or supernovae, eclipses, occultations of planets by the moon, and a variety of atmospheric phenomena. Ancient precedent dating from the Three Dynasties (Xia, Shang, Zhou) of the Bronze Age in the second millennium led to the establishment by Han times of certain astrological resonance periods, especially dense clusters of the five visible planets at roughly 500-year intervals, as the preeminent sign of Heaven's conferral of the "mandate" to rule on the new dynasty. Other alignments of the five planets, or simply their simultaneous appearance in the sky, were popularly held to be "beneficial for China," in an indirect allusion to the existence of a non-Chinese world. Not surprisingly, given the close theoretical link in Han imperial ideology between portents, anomalies, and the conduct of state affairs, the popularization of prognostication by omens led to a politicization of astrology, and the fabrication of all manner of portents for political ends, especially during succession

crises, reached a level unmatched in later imperial history. Because of the connection between astrological omens and state security, in time only imperial officials were allowed to make observations and study the records, and by imperial decree unauthorized dabbling in astrological matters became a capital offense.

Six Dynasties Period and After

Along with the gradual spread of Buddhism in the centuries following the collapse of the Han dynasty, efforts were made by Buddhist writers during the Three Kingdoms and Six Dynasties period (220–589 C.E.) to integrate Indian Buddhist cosmological and astrological concepts and to reconcile incommensurate numerological categories—for example, matching the Buddhist mahābhūtas (four elements) with the Chinese five phases. Subsequently, attempts were made to establish even more complex correspondences between Chinese and Indian astrological sets such as the twenty-eight lunar mansions with the twelve Indian zodiacal signs derived from Hellenistic astrology, the nine planets of Indian astronomy with the seven astral deities of the Northern Dipper, and so on. During the Six Dynasties era and the early Tang dynasty (618–906) in particular, China's most influential translators of Buddhist astrological works and compilers of astrological treatises were Indians such as Qutan Xida (Gautama Siddhārta, fl. 718), author of the Kaiyuan zhanjing (Kaiyuan reign-period treatise on astrology), the greatest compendium of ancient and medieval Chinese astrological fragments. On the whole, however, these efforts at syncretism exerted surprisingly little influence on long-established Chinese astrological theory, especially given the drastic decline of Buddhism following the Tang dynasty proscriptions in the mid-ninth century and the subsequent resurgence of Neo-Confucianism. Assimilation was also hindered by the difficulty of rendering the foreign concepts and terminology into Chinese, which was often accomplished by means of bizarre or idiosyncratic transliterations.

At the popular level Chinese astrology continued to absorb influences (Iranian, Islamic, Sogdian) via the Central Asian trade routes, and although certain Western numerological categories (such as the seven-day week) are represented in the enormously popular and widely circulated lishu or almanacs (documented from the ninth century), and individualized horoscopic astrology appears in later horoscopes (from the fourteenth century), Hellenistic concepts apparently had little discernible impact on the practice of astrology at the imperial court. Until modern times the most common popular forms of divination employed ancient prognostication techniques connected with lucky and unlucky denary and duodenary cyclical characters (paired to generate the sequence of sixty unique designations used to enumerate the days since at least the Shang dynasty), fate-calculation based on the eight characters bazi designating the exact time of birth, and so forth.

During the Song dynasty (960–1279) astrology entered a period of routinization and gradual decline, in part as a result of overexploitation by sycophants and careerists as a means of enhancing their status or prospects at court, and in part because of the resurgence of Neo-Confucianism and a return to a more anthropocentric outlook. Along with an increasing emphasis on human affairs and moral self-cultivation, which was philosophically antithetical to superstition, the archaic belief in an interventionist Heaven that communicated by means of signs in the heavens faded into the background, and *tianwen* or "sky-pattern reading" shifted focus from the ever-precarious genre of prediction to a safer and more manageable interpretive mode. As a consequence, the objective status of natural phenomena declined, and the practice of astrology by imperial officials on the whole reverted to routine observing and recording of observations, focusing on the anomalous.

Henceforth, the interpretation of "sky-patterns" was Confucianized—one might even say domesticated—and only isolated instances of inductive generalization from observation are to be found, rather than interpretation more or less tendentiously based on historical precedent. Given its subservience to the state ideology, Chinese astrology was incapable of growing into an independent body of learning or science of the heavens, but remained throughout imperial history the handmaiden of politics when not dismissed as mere superstition, which humble status is confirmed by the traditionally low rank of the post of court astrologer.

See also **Astrology: Overview; Cosmology.**

BIBLIOGRAPHY

Henderson, John B. *The Development and Decline of Chinese Cosmology.* New York: Columbia University Press, 1984.

Major, John S. *Heaven and Earth in Early Han Thought: Chapters Three, Four, and Five of the Huainanzi.* Albany: State University of New York Press, 1993.

Needham, Joseph, et al. *Science and Civilisation in China.* Vol. 2: *History of Scientific Thought.* Cambridge, U.K.: Cambridge University Press, 1956.

———. *Science and Civilisation in China.* Vol. 3: *Mathematics and the Sciences of the Heavens and the Earth.* Cambridge, U.K.: Cambridge University Press, 1959.

Pankenier, David W. "Applied Field Allocation Astrology in Zhou China: Duke Wen of Jin and the Battle of Chengpu (632 B.C.E.)." *Journal of the American Oriental Society* (1999): 261–279.

———. "The Cosmo-Political Background to Heaven's Mandate." *Early China* 20 (1995): 121–176.

———. "Popular Astrology and Border Affairs in Early Imperial China: An Archaeological Confirmation." *Sino-Platonic Papers* 104 (July 2000): 1–19.

Schafer, Edward H. *Pacing the Void: T'ang Approaches to the Stars.* Berkeley: University of California Press, 1977.

Wu, Yiyi. "Auspicious Omens and Their Consequences: Zhen-Ren (1006–1066) Literati's Perception of Astral Anomalies." Ph.D. dissertation, Princeton University, 1990.

David W. Pankenier

ASTRONOMY, PRE-COLUMBIAN AND LATIN AMERICAN.

The sun and the moon, the planets and the stars are the same the world over. One might hypothesize, therefore, that diverse cultures of the world would think the same of them. The two American continents, having been cut off from the Old World from the time of the Asian migration across the Bering land bridge more than ten thousand years ago up to European contact in the fifteenth century, provide an excellent laboratory to test such a hypothesis. One does find some remarkable Old–New World parallels. For example, ancient Maya divisions of the movement of the planet Venus inscribed on bark paper are practically identical to those written in cuneiform by the Babylonians. Moreover, in both of these highly urbanized cultures, planetary sightings were employed to the same end by a class of astronomer-astrologers situated very close to royalty: to cast omens.

This essay is divided into two parts. It begins by reviewing the astronomies of the so-called high cultures of the New World: the Maya, the Aztecs, and the Incas, those must often compared with the classical world, Egypt, and the Middle East, from whom are inherited the roots of modern scientific astronomy. Then follows a brief examination of astronomical practices by less complex societies of North and South America.

"High Cultures" of the New World

Of all the Pre-Columbian civilizations none has received as much attention both by scholars and the media as the ancient Maya. The reason is very simple: at its pinnacle, between 200 and 900 C.E., the classical Maya civilization created great art, sculpture, and architecture; they devised a complex religious pantheon; and they developed syllabic writing and numerical systems on a par with the West.

Maya. Maya math was directed largely toward timekeeping (indeed the priest in charge of the calendar was—and still is—called the keeper of the day, *ah kin*). They counted their days in a base-20 system. Like the Babylonians (who used a different base) they dealt with time uniquely, by changing the scheme so as to identify the third position with 360 (18×20 rather than 20×20). Here was a way of handily reckoning the approximate length of the year. By the beginning of the Christian era they were writing inscriptions in "long count" that reckoned the number of days lapsed since the most recent cycle of creation. Maya mathematicians fixed the great event, which we would transcribe as 0.0.0.0.0 on their temporal odometer, to a date that corresponds in the Christian calendar to 12 August 3114 B.C.E. Though the reasons why they did so remain elusive, this deep-time setting of the commencement of creation is relatively common in highly stratified societies. But Maya time was enmeshed with other cycles that suggest a belief in a sensate universe, with all of its components interconnected—a universe that did not operate apart from human concern.

A shorter cycle, called the *tzol kin* (count of days), which the Maya still employ in the early 2000s, predated the long count by several centuries. Widespread throughout Mesoamerica yet unknown in the Old World, this 260-day round consisted of a series of twenty day-names preceded by numerical coefficients ranging from one to thirteen. Thirteen was the number of layers of heaven in Maya cosmology, while the bodily origin of twenty already is obvious. But other reasons may underlie the popularity of the number 260. In contemporary

Guatemala, there is evidence linking this basic time cycle to the human gestation period. This convenient round number approximates nine lunar months (265.77 days) in the same way that 360 approximates the length of the seasonal year (365.2422 days). The *tzol kin* is also a close approximation to the mean interval of appearance of Venus as evening or morning star, and it beats harmoniously in the ratio of 2:3 with the eclipse reckoning period of 173.32 days. Such approximations offer the advantage to the calendar keeper of assigning particular sets of dates in the *tzol kin* to eclipse or Venus warnings.

Astronomers, along with the mathematicians and scribes who worked with them during the Classic period (c. 200–900 C.E.), were members of a courtly class. Excavations of an eighth-century elite burial at the Maya ruins of Copán, Honduras, revealed the remains of a scribe, his paint pot and brushes still intact. These specialists were required to know with meticulous accuracy every celestial cycle that might conceivably guide human destiny. Control over these time periods by the Maya lords, their superiors, enabled them to appropriately schedule their own affairs as well as those of the state. As in China, such court professionals advised the ruler about the proper time to make decisions. When should they enter into armed conflict, set a date for a royal marriage, or an ascent to the throne? When ought they to conduct a ritual, or make an offering to pay the debt to the gods for their assistance in producing a good crop or a healthy newborn child? One can imagine royal appointees going from town to town, their codices filled with detailed planetary calculations and agricultural almanacs tucked under their arms, ready and willing to advise the local rulers on such issues. Likewise can be imagined their subordinates advising commoners in the marketplace.

Inscriptions on carved monuments (*stelae*) at the Maya ruins of Copán, Yaxchilán, Palenque, and elsewhere connect seminal events in the lives of the rulers with key sky events such as eclipses and planetary conjunctions. These suggest that the ruler may have achieved cosmic status, there being an implied descent of royalty from ancestor deities who resided in the sky. Outdoor rites held in the open spaces that front the temples served to legitimize heaven-ordained actions by the ruler. Cosmic hierophanies, the interplay of timed light and shadow to manifest the sacred, were likely staged in the architecture of Palenque and Yaxchilán. The shadow of a descending serpent on Chichén Itzá's largest pyramid is still witnessed today on the spring equinox.

There exists little evidence regarding Mesoamerican observational technology. Pictographs from Central Mexican codices depict men peering over what could be sighting devices that consist of pairs of crossed sticks. Often these characters are portrayed in the recesses of temples, which suggests that such edifices might have been preferentially aligned toward events that took place at the local horizon. A few oddly skewed misshapen structures and buildings with narrow slots or windows do seem to align astronomically. For example, the cylindrically shaped Caracol of Chichén Itzá, Yucatan, possesses built-in sighting shafts oriented to key positions of Venus, the Mayan god representing the recycling of creation.

Aztecs. At the time of European contact, the Aztecs controlled a vast empire centered on their capital of Tenochtítlan on the site of modern Mexico City. While their well-described practice of human sacrifice might tend to divert one's attention from pursuits so esoteric as astronomy, it must be remembered that the Aztecs offered the blood of their captives to the sun god Tonatiuh to keep the heavens in motion, lest eternal darkness befall them. Politically such a policy may be thought of as a mechanism of control and domination exerted by the Aztec rulers over their newly conquered tributaries all around the lake basin that surrounded their island capital. But from a religious perspective these sacrificial acts might be better regarded as mandatory rites of renewal of cyclic time in the life of the Aztec city paired with its dedication to cosmically sanctioned military conquest. The shape of Aztec time is also manifest in their documents. The Aztec historical record is rife with pictorialized events of nature, among them eclipses and smoking stars (comets and/or meteors). These books tell the reader that the sky is very much a part of civic life, for the pictures are juxtaposed alongside events of social importance, such as deaths, conquests, and accessions.

The Templo Mayor, largest of all Aztec buildings, exhibits a celestial alignment. One informant told a sixteenth-century Spanish friar that a certain festival took place at the temple when the equinox sun stood at its midpoint, but because it was a bit misaligned, Moctezuma needed to pull the temple down and straighten it. The temple's orientation is just what it would have had to be to permit the rising equinox sun to fall into the notch between the twin temples that once surmounted the flat-topped forty-meter-high pyramid. When the sun arrived there, Spanish chroniclers relate, a royal observer situated in the plaza fronting the bottom of the stairs carefully watched it. Like a town crier he would signal the time to begin the ritual of human sacrifice that attended that particular month of the year. The Aztec 52-year calendar round (the meshing of 260- and 365-day cycles) was cosmically timed as well. It began with the precise sighting of the Pleiades in the overhead position at midnight. When the time approached, one chronicler says, the priests ascended the Hill of the Star to affirm that the movements of the heavens had not ceased and that the end of the world was not imminent. Thus, one thinks of the sky as part of the background set for the effective performance of religious rites.

Inca. The Inca, whose even larger empire thrived in the Andes while the Aztecs ruled much of Mesoamerica, embedded the sky in a unique scheme that united ideas about religion, social organization, and hydrology. The *ceque* system was conceived as a giant mnemonic map built into the capital city Cuzco's natural and artificial topography. Likely used elsewhere, the system is best known from descriptions by Spanish chroniclers, who state that ceques were imaginary radial lines grouped like spokes on a wheel, dividing the city into sections much like a pie graph. The wheel's hub was the Coricancha, the navel of the world and the temple of ancestor worship.

Each of the Cuzco's forty-one *ceques* was traced by a line of *huacas,* or sacred shrines, that extended outward along irrigation canals and natural water sources across the landscape.

The Inca believed the 328 *huacas* to be openings in the mountain body of Pachamama, or Mother Earth, and there specific Xin groups left her offerings at specified times of the year. Some huacas were temples, others intricately carved rock formations, natural springs, and other landscape features. Still others were astronomical markers involved with the establishment of a calendar.

While not all investigators agree on the precise placement of astronomical *huacas,* it seems clear that they were part of a horizon-based solar calendar. In one instance, the northernmost pillar of a set of four on a hillside overlooking the capital served as a warning device. When the sun reached there the planting season in the Cuzco valley was approaching. People who cultivated crops at higher altitudes, where growth occurred at a slower pace, therefore would be allowed sufficient additional time to sow their seeds before planting commenced in lower levels of the valley. These dates were marked by the other pillars. The *ceque* system also indicated the various kin and ethnic groups that made up the population by designating certain *huacas* to their care. In this sense the order of worship of the *ceques* and their *huacas* constituted a mnemonic scheme that incorporated information, including astronomy, considered vital to the operation of the state.

Less Complex Societies

Other great indigenous cities of the Americas also used the pristine order evident in the sky to establish social order on earth. For example, the same general kind of sky symmetry found in Cuzco is apparent at Cahokia, located near where the Mississippi and Missouri Rivers join. Built one thousand years ago, Cahokia was truly a significant economic and political center of great proportions: it controlled the distribution of maize and exotic trade items over a very wide area. Though no chroniclers ever wrote about it and no indigenous writing system survives it, its axis of orientation is cardinal, and mound alignments imply that the sun was a major object of attention. Following and marking out the annual solar path along the horizon, rulers of this economic hub regulated the seasonal flow of goods and services and scheduled the holidays. Their accompanying solar rituals would take place when the local populace and the tributaries of the state turned out in the plaza in front of the great Monks Mound. The same can be said of Ohio's Hopewell, who erected large geometrical earthworks in the first millennium C.E. The axes of these structures, the interior spaces of which, like Great Britain's Stonehenge, were used as places of assembly, are aligned to the solstices and possibly to the stationary points of the moon at the horizon.

North America's Hopi of Arizona were among the many Native American skywatchers. The Hopi marked the solstices, which the elders referred to as "houses" where the sun stops in his travels along the horizon. At these places along the high mesa the priests erected small shrines. There a sun priest in charge of the calendar would deposit prayer sticks as offerings to welcome the sun and to encourage him along on his celestial journey. Some of these shrines have special openings that allow shafts of sunlight to penetrate particular directions, thus serving as another way to mark time. Sometimes the sun priest would gesture to the sun, whirling a shield on which was painted a sun

design, to imitate the sun's turning motion, hastening away any malevolent spirits who might impede the great luminary.

Though archaeoastronomers and historians of pre-Columbian astronomy suffer a lack of data relative to their Old World counterparts (the entire corpus of pre-Columbian Mesoamerican texts can easily be accommodated by a coffee table), they are offered some distinct advantages. First, some cultures survive and remain isolated enough from the domination of the West, so that authentic astronomical customs and beliefs can still be retrieved. Second, these living cultures are not so distant in time from their predecessors. Data from these cultures offer inroads into understanding the more complex systems of the past. For example, present-day Quechua-speaking people of South America still chart constellations that date all the way back to Inca times, if not earlier. They still call the Pleiades *collca,* or "storehouse," as the Inca named them; and alpha and beta Centauri, which are among the few bright stars that may figure in alignments tied to the *huacas* of Cuzco's *ceque* system, represent the "Eyes of the Llama." They are part of a parade of dark cloud animal constellations that, along with star-to-star constellations like our own, comprise the Milky Way, which is so much more prominent in the southern than in the northern hemisphere.

What once was a cosmic temple lives on in the early twenty-first century's cosmic house. The Pawnee lodge of the Midwest United States has a smoke-hole through which can be observed certain groups of stars used in storytelling. Likewise, the bell-shaped quarters of the Warao of Venezuela's Orinoco Delta consist of a zenith pole marked out with a yearly calendar calibrated by following the ascension of the solar image at noon. The difference between house and city is but one of size and social complexity. If the home incorporates a design for life and the calendar regulates activity, it is easy to understand why cities such as Cuzco and Tenochtítlan would have been imbued with similar cosmic imagery.

Whether ancient or contemporary, what is striking about pre-Columbian astronomy is that, in stark contrast with the West, all of the sky observations seem to have been acquired with either low technology or no technology. These societies used neither wheel nor gear, and few of them employed metals. Moreover, their mental devices diverge from those of Western astronomy. One hears mention neither of fractions nor of Euclidean geometry. Nor did indigenous Americans raise questions about the rotundity of the earth, or speculate on whether the Sun or any distant celestial body might lie at the center of the universe. This is because the spatial view of the universe—the concept of orbits, maps, deep space—is one of the gifts of the Greeks. Such concepts are culture-bound, and one ought not anticipate that pre-Columbian people would have entertained questions that appear to be common sense to the Westerner. This does not mean that Native Americans did not philosophize or theorize about the world around them. Their speculations were basically human centered. Theirs was not a mechanistic universe that operated as an entity apart from what is thought of as human consciousness.

In sum, studying pre-Columbian skies helps enable a realization of the uniqueness, rather than superiority, of the

Western worldview. The sky offered Native Americans a means of solving some of life's basic problems: how to regulate human activity, how to understand and worship the gods, and above all how to know what it means to be a member of society.

See also **Calendar; Cosmology; Philosophies: American.**

BIBLIOGRAPHY
Aventi, Anthony. *Ancient Astronomers.* Washington, D.C.: Smithsonian Books, 1993.
———. *Stairways to the Stars: Skywatching in Three Great Ancient Cultures.* New York: Wiley, 1997.
Bauer, Brian, and David Dearborn. *Astronomy and Empire in the Ancient Andes.* Austin: University of Texas Press, 1995.
Krupp, Edwin. *Skywatchers, Shamans, and Kings: Astronomy and the Archaeology of Power.* New York: Wiley, 1997.
Ruggles, Clive, and Nicholas Saunders, eds. *Astronomies and Cultures: Papers Derived from the Third "Oxford" International Symposium on Archaeoastronomy.* Niwot: University Press of Colorado, 1993.
Tedlock, Barbara. *Time and the Highland Maya.* Alberquerque: University of New Mexico Press, 1992.
Urton, Gary. *At the Crossroads of the Earth and the Sky: An Andean Cosmology.* Austin: University of Texas Press, 1981.
Williamson, Ray A. *Living the Sky: The Cosmos of the American Indian.* Boston: Houghton-Mifflin, 1984.

Anthony F. Aveni

ATHEISM. The term *atheism* usually refers to the belief that there is no God or are no gods. This position has been called *positive atheism,* since it involves an actual belief and not just the absence of belief. In contrast, *negative atheism* involves the absence of belief in a God or gods. Atheism is typically contrasted with agnosticism, the view that one cannot know if a deity exists. Negative atheism, however, is compatible with agnosticism, for in the name of rationality one who does not know if God exists should suspend belief in God.

In Western and Near Eastern societies the term *atheism* has sometimes been used narrowly to refer to the denial of theism, in particular Judeo-Christian and Islamic theism. According to theism, God is a personal being, an all-powerful, all-knowing, and all-good creator of the universe who takes an active interest in human concerns and guides creatures by revelation. Positive atheists disbelieve that this God exists and reject concomitants including an afterlife, a cosmic destiny, the supernatural origin of the universe, an immortal soul, the revealed nature of texts such as the Bible and the Koran, and a religious foundation of morality. Negative atheists, in the narrow sense, simply do not have a belief in the theistic God and what that entails.

Theism is not a characteristic of all religions, however. For example, although the theistic tradition is found in Hinduism in the Bhagavad Gita, the earlier Upanishads teach that ultimate reality, Brahma, is an impersonal and pantheistic god. Positive atheism in its broadest sense would advocate disbelief in the pantheistic as well as the theistic aspects of Hinduism. Indeed, there are skeptical and atheistic schools of thought

within the Hindu tradition itself. Theravada Buddhism and Jainism are commonly believed to be atheistic, but this interpretation holds only for the narrow sense of disbelieving in a creator God. For although these religions reject a theistic creator God, they accept numerous lesser deities.

In the Western world, nonbelief in the existence of God is a pervasive phenomenon with a long and illustrious history. Ancient philosophers such as Lucretius were nonbelievers, and important thinkers of the Enlightenment such as the Baron d' Holbach (1723–1789) and Denis Diderot (1713–1784) were outspoken atheists. In the nineteenth century the most articulate and best-known atheists and critics of religion were Ludwig Feuerbach, Karl Marx, Arthur Schopenhauer, and Friedrich Nietzsche. Bertrand Russell, Sigmund Freud, and Jean-Paul Sartre were among the twentieth century's most influential atheists. In contemporary philosophical thought atheism has been defended by, among others, Paul Edwards, Antony Flew, Paul Kurtz, John Mackie, Michael Martin, Kai Nielsen, Michael Scriven, and J. J. C. Smart. In the United States, many contemporary atheists are also self-identified as humanists, secular humanists, or rationalists.

At the beginning of the twenty-first century atheism can be found from the Netherlands to New Zealand, from Canada to China, from Spain to South America. State atheism prevailed in the U.S.S.R. until the breakup of the Soviet Union. It was estimated in the 2002 *New York Times Almanac* that there are in the world about 222 million atheists (4 percent of the total population) and 887 million agnostics (negative atheists).

Popular misunderstandings of atheism abound. Thus, for example, it has been claimed that atheists are immoral, that morality cannot be justified without belief in God, and that life has no meaning without belief in God. There are, however, no grounds for supposing that atheists are any less moral than believers; many ethical systems have been developed that do not assume the existence of supernatural beings, and the meaning of life can be based on secular purposes such as the betterment of humankind.

Philosophically, atheism has been justified in differing ways. Negative atheists attempt to establish their position either by showing that the standard arguments for the existence of God—for instance the argument from first cause, the argument from design, the ontological argument, and the argument from religious experience—are unsound, or by demonstrating that statements about God are meaningless. Positive atheists argue in turn that the concept of God is inconsistent and that the existence of evil makes the existence of God improbable.

In particular, positive atheists have maintained that theism does not provide an adequate explanation of the existence of seemingly gratuitous evil such as the suffering of innocent children. Rejecting the standard defenses given by theists, they argue that justifications in terms of human free will leave unexplained why, for example, children suffer because of genetic diseases. Positive atheists hold that arguments that God allows much pain and suffering in order to build human character fail, in turn, to explain why there was suffering among animals before human beings ever evolved and why human character could not be developed with less suffering than in fact there is. They argue that an explanation of evil better than the explanation that God has given us free will or the chance to develop character is that God does not exist.

Atheism has wide-ranging implications for the human condition. Among other things it entails that ethical goals must be determined by secular aims and concerns, that human beings must take charge of their own destiny, and that death is the end of human existence.

Although it is sometimes associated with materialism, communism, rationalism, existentialism, or anarchism, there is no necessary relation between atheism and any of these other positions. Some atheists, for example the objectivist writer Ayn Rand (1905–1982), have been opposed to communism, and some—for example, Bertrand Russell—have rejected materialism. Although all contemporary materialists are atheists, the ancient materialist Epicurus believed that the gods were made of atoms. And although rationalists such as René Descartes have believed in God, many contemporary atheists consider themselves rationalists. Jean-Paul Sartre was an atheist and an existentialist; Søren Kierkegaard was an existentialist who accepted God. In turn, Karl Marx was an atheist who rejected anarchism, but Leo Tolstoy was a Christian who embraced it.

In sum, atheism is a complex phenomenon with a rich history, brilliant defenders, and a wide following. It is often unjustly maligned and confused with other positions.

See also **Agnosticism; Creationism; Evil; Religion; Religion and the State.**

BIBLIOGRAPHY

Hiorth, Finngeir. *Atheism in India.* Mumbai, India: Indian Secular Society, 1998.

———. *Atheism in the World.* Oslo, Norway: Human-Etisk Forbund, 2003.

Joshi, S. T., ed. *Atheism: A Reader.* New York: Prometheus Books, 2000.

Martin, Michael. *Atheism: A Philosophical Justification.* Philadelphia: Temple University Press, 1990.

Michael Martin

AUTHENTICITY, AFRICA. Ideologies of authenticity within African thought are self-affirming and counterideological positions adopted by individuals, groups, and communities of resistance who have all had their identities traumatically impacted upon or disrupted by forces of imperialism and conquest—namely slavery, colonialism, and neocolonialism. African authenticity is in this sense fundamentally an ongoing cultural, socioeconomic, and political process of self-definition. Particularly noteworthy are the theoretical and philosophical commonalities between these discourses, which enable their collective identification and characterization as movements seeking self-affirmation and self-legitimation as part of a vital project of self-rehabilitation.

The African oral tradition, a very significant part of African epistemology and knowledge production, has been vital to this project. One thinks immediately, for example, of the Jamaican-Caribbean–West Indian reggae group Culture, which, espousing the old "Back to Africa" philosophy and vision of Marcus Mosiah Garvey (1887–1940), consistently critiques and confronts "the West," or Babylon (a historical and geographical referent for England and other imperial powers), in its music as a way of combating the dominance and hegemony of an ever-pervasive Western imperialism. The powerful and invigorating lyrics of Culture and the melodious spiritual chanting of Rastafari worldviews are deployed as a critical counterdiscursive ideology that continually reminds Africans and black people generally of the "agony and pain" of slavery, whose effects, as is constantly affirmed, are being felt even in the early twenty-first century.

Culture espouses an ideology of authenticity—nostalgically articulated around the idea of Africa as "home," or the homeland to which all black people must return one day. With this recurrent theme, the world-famous group not only connects Caribbean cultural identity with Africa but also blames the dispersal of Africans in the diaspora on an inhumane imperialist system, the oppressive entity of Babylon, which from the days of slavery until the present has bequeathed a debilitating legacy of brutal racist exploitation on Africans and peoples of African descent. As a sign that Africa (as against the Caribbean or the New World) remains the authentic home for Black people, the members of Culture indict the slave master and sing of "travelling from home to Jamaica" (in the track "Still Rest My Heart," of the album *Three Sides to My Story*) while yearning for liberation and affirming black humanity. African displacement and dispersal within the diaspora therefore become emblematic of a historical abnormality necessitating redress. Retribution is envisaged in the form of "fire," which the prophetic voice of lead vocalist Joseph Hill calls upon to "burn" Babylon or the West as a means of ensuring restitution.

African authenticity would also be unimaginable without Cheik Anta Diop's *The African Origin of Civilization,* a classic work with an interdisciplinary fusion of historical, anthropological, sociological, and linguistic material that, together with such accompanying texts as *Precolonial Black Africa* and *Civilization or Barbarism,* redefines the historical contribution of black people to world civilization by staking a claim for perceiving Ethiopia-Nubia and ancient Egypt as historical sources of present-day civilization. Diop's comprehensive assemblage of evidence on the black race contests the epistemological dominance of Western civilization in contemporary knowledge production by contending that European civilization, which posits itself as evolutionarily and universally superior and as a global model, is derived from Greek civilization, which in turn "stole," or borrowed, largely from black Egyptian and African civilization.

In literature, authenticity has found expression in *Muntu* and *Two Thousand Seasons,* two historical narratives by Ghanaians Joe de Graft (1924–1978), a playwright and theater practitioner, and Ayi Kwei Armah (b. 1939), a novelist and critic. Reconstructing precolonial African history, *Muntu* proposes that Africans inhabited a state of innocence devoid of materialistic greed, exploitation, and corruption before the advent of European colonialism and the transatlantic slave trade. The nostalgic precolonial world of *Two Thousand Seasons* similarly narrativizes the vicissitudes of a pan-African community whose hospitality before the dawn of Arab and Western slavery and colonialism was encapsulated in a humane philosophy articulated simply as "the way." The gruesome images of imperialist gluttony and excess and the portrait of the corruption of precolonial traditional institutions of governance in Africa in both works also, however, encode a rhetorical idealism that has led to accusations of racial essentialism, a critical charge indiscriminately applied to other discourses of African authenticity.

Relevant in this regard is Negritude, the literary movement of the 1930s developed by French-educated African and Caribbean students and intellectuals in France and founded upon a politics of racial solidarity among mutually oppressed African, Caribbean, and other black people in response to the alienating and suffocating ambience of French colonialism and culture. Led by poets Aimé Césaire (b. 1913) of Martinique and Léopold Sédar Senghor (1906–2001) of Senegal, Negritude harked back to an old and authentic Africa whose identity Negritudinists identified with in the face of the inequalities they experienced within the failed French colonial policy of assimilation. Although the racialist discourse of Negritude was justifiable, it did not always state its case properly.

Similarly, *Toward the Decolonization of African Literature,* a work that claims to be exorcising African literature of domination by aesthetic and critical Eurocentrism, has come to be equated with a deeply conservative endeavor to retain a purist form of African identity in an impractical and regressive manner. In this polemical work of soul-searching that advocates a return to African sources within literature and cultural theory and clamors for deep immersion in African aesthetics as central to the project of reinventing an authentic African identity in the aftermath of colonialism, authors Chinweizu (b. 1943), Onwuchekwa Jemie (b. 1940), and Ihechukwu Madubuike (b. 1943) also present exoticized notions of African culture and African tradition, thereby diminishing the force of their argument. Critics have, however, never addressed the deeper question of Eurocentrism that Chinweizu and colleagues raise and have instead gleefully exploited the glaring simplification of African identity in *Toward the Decolonization.* However, the prevailing contradictions in no way invalidate the urgent need for a counterdiscursive and oppositional critique of the Western aesthetic and critical domination of African literature.

The ideological project of African authenticity is in the final event a critical counterculture that self-consciously contests all oppressive ideologies. Such a project informs *I Write What I Like,* the radical and defiant work by the famous political activist and black South African Steve Biko (1946–1977), whose resistance to the vicious and inhuman system of apartheid in South Africa led to his incarceration, brutalization, and subsequent murder. While Biko's text has been acclaimed as the definitive work of the black consciousness movement, which he founded and led, it is also an individuated work locatable outside the strict parameters and confines of the black consciousness movement.

Biko's quest for authentic liberation for black people was unique in contending that self-emancipation derived foremost from within a person's psychological makeup. Biko was the first singularly and vociferously to contend that liberation from the structures and strictures of apartheid could in no proper sense be spearheaded by, for example, the white liberal establishment in South Africa. Biko therefore encouraged black South Africans as an oppressed group to adopt a strategy of liberation in which their self-worth necessitated a calculated disavowal of the patronizing contribution of members of the oppressor group.

Reactionary and reductionist attempts to deny the historical realities that works of African authenticity speak about have often engendered some willfully gross misinterpretations and simplistic trivializations of what are essentially and in reality existentially rooted quests for freedom and liberation. While African authenticity is often misconceptualized as a puritanist discourse, it is an ambivalent creative process and a miscellaneous philosophy or approach to life that inevitably closely relate to other forms of African thought and practice. Thus one might, for instance, find the concept being expressed in different kinds of material artifacts that may simultaneously be referred to as African art, African culture, and so on.

See also **Africa, Idea of; Afrocentricity; Black Consciousness; Negritude; Philosophies: African.**

BIBLIOGRAPHY

Arham, Ayi Kwe. *Two Thousand Seasons.* Nairobi: East African Publishing House, 1973.

Biko, Steve. *I Write What I Like: A Selection of His Writings.* Edited with a personal memoir by Aelred Stubbs. London: Bowerdean Press, 1978.

Césaire, Aimé. *Notebook of a Return to My Native Land.* Translated by Mireille Rosello with Annie Pritchard; introduction by Mireille Rosello. Newcastle upon Tyne, U.K.: Bloodaxe, 1995.

Chinweizu, Onwuchekwa Jemie, and Ihechukwu Madubuike. *Toward the Decolonization of African Literature.* Vol. 1: *African Fiction and Poetry and Their Critics.* Enugu, Nigeria: Fourth Dimension, 1980.

Culture. "Rolling Stone." In the album *Humble African.* Jamaica, N.Y.: Heartbeat, 2000.

———. *Three Sides to My Story.* New York: Shanachie Records, 1991.

de Graft, Joe. *Muntu.* Nairobi: Heinemann Educational Books, 1977.

Diop, Cheikh Anta. *The African Origin of Civilization: Myth or Reality.* Translated by Mercer Cook. New York: Lawrence Hill, 1974.

———. *Civilization or Barbarism: An Authentic Anthropology.* Translated by Yaa-Lengi Meema Ngemi, edited by Harold J. Salemson and Marjolijn de Jager. Brooklyn, N.Y.: Lawrence Hill, 1981.

———. *Precolonial Black Africa: A Comparative Study of the Political and Social Systems of Europe and Black Africa from Antiquity to the Formation of Modern States.* Translated by Harold J. Salemson. Westport, Conn.: Lawrence Hill, 1987.

Irele, Abiola, ed. *Selected Poems of Léopold Sédar Senghor.* Cambridge, U.K., and New York: Cambridge University Press, 1977.

Jack, Belinda Elizabeth. *Negritude and Literary Criticism: The History and Theory of "Negro-African" Literature in French*. Westport, Conn.: Greenwood Press, 1996.

Kesteloot, Lilyan. *Black Writers in French: A Literary History of Negritude*. Translated by Ellen Conroy Kennedy. Washington, D.C.: Howard University Press, 1991.

wa Thiong'o, Ngugi. *Decolonising the Mind: The Politics of Language in African Literature*. London: Currey, 1986.

Kwadwo Osei-Nyame Jr.

AUTHORITARIANISM.

This entry includes three subentries:

Overview

East Asia

Latin America

OVERVIEW

The term *authoritarianism* can be applied to a great variety of contexts. It can refer to authoritarian behavior, leadership styles, or personality types in families, industrial enterprises, bureaucracies, and other forms of organizations. Here, it refers to political regimes that fall under this broad label. The major characteristics of authoritarian regimes include a limited political pluralism with restrictions on the activities of interest groups and parties, a low level of social mobilization and popular political participation, a dominantly "subject" or "parochial" political culture, and usually a personalized form of leadership.

The term came into use in the nineteenth and twentieth centuries when it became necessary to distinguish hierarchically structured, traditional monarchical or more recent "bonapartist" autocratic regimes from liberal democracies, on the one hand, and all-encompassing "totalitarian" systems, on the other. Liberal democracies can be defined with regard to three major dimensions: an open and competitive political pluralism (usually in a multiparty system), a high level of political participation (as in fair and free elections, referenda, etc.), and political institutions that guarantee a certain separation of powers, the rule of law, and basic human rights (such as freedom of expression, information, organization, religion, etc.). Totalitarian systems, at the other extreme, are characterized by monistic, all-encompassing social and political organizations (such as a single party; dependent unions; organizations for women, youth, etc.), a high level of social mobilization (as in political rallies, high election turnouts), an explicit, monolithic, absolutist ideology, and a strong repressive apparatus. In fact, however, these distinctions cannot always be drawn precisely and some "gray" areas exist between these types. In common usage, all nondemocratic systems are lumped together as "dictatorships." Whereas the original use of this term in the Roman republic referred to emergency powers for a limited period, today it implies all kinds of arbitrary rule and political repression. Nevertheless, important qualitative differences can be found among such nondemocratic regimes.

Dominant Characteristics of Political Systems

Among the most important dimensions of political systems are the basis of legitimacy, the party system, the pattern of recruitment of the executive, the actual power structure, the scope of political control, the ideological orientation of the system, and the formal vertical and horizontal separations of power. Legitimacy can be based on strong attachment to a political leader (charismatic), on elective procedures (legal-rational), or on a customary or informal acceptance (traditional) of political incumbents or a regime. Party systems are distinguished according to their degree of competitiveness, ranging from one-party states without any competitive elements, through semicompetitive single-party structures and restricted multiparty systems, to fully competitive ones. The recruitment of the executive can be achieved by inheritance, direct election by the population, a majority vote by parliament, or through forceful usurpation. The actual power structure within the executive can be strongly personalized and clientelistic or have a small collective group at its base (e.g., a military junta or a politburo of a centralized party), or it can be broadly composed to incorporate the most important plural elements of society.

The scope of control can range from limited to totalitarian. Ideological orientation is considered in relation to its respective social basis. This can consist of a "communalistic" (e.g., ethnic or religious) group, or of the lower, middle, or upper classes of society, corresponding to the political continuum of "left," "center," and "right." Finally, in a constitutional sense, the vertical separation of power can be viewed as complete, as limited but with an independent judiciary, or as nonexistent. Similarly, the horizontal separation of power can be federal or centralized. These dimensions and their discrete expressions are listed on the left-hand side in Table 1.

Specific Forms of Authoritarian Rule

Based on the characteristics outlined above, we can differentiate six forms of authoritarian rule.

Authoritarian monarchy. The most traditional political system in the world today is the authoritarian monarchy. Its basis of legitimacy is customary and is often linked to mythical assumptions regarding the foundation of the respective dynasty. Examples of this type are Ethiopia (until 1974) and Saudi Arabia. Accession to the throne is generally regulated by heredity, and there is little, if any, open political competition. Formal separation of powers is nonexistent, the power structures are personalistic and reinforced by an aristocratic upper-class ideology. In former times, most regimes of this kind were built upon feudal agrarian structures. Today they tend to have centralized and absolutist characteristics.

"Old" oligarchy. Another type of authoritarianism, which has been prevalent in Latin America, is the "old" oligarchy or, to use Howard J. Wiarda's term, the *traditional-authoritarian* regime. Such a regime receives its support from feudalistic or "neofeudalistic" rural structures and, since the late twentieth century, from segments of the urban upper classes. In the old oligarchy's extreme forms (e.g., in Nicaragua until 1979), a small number of leading families exercise almost exclusive control over political and economic life. In this system, a leader may be replaced relatively easily by another, sometimes through holding manipulated elections that do not alter the power structure.

Table 1. Dominant characteristics of political system types

Characteristics:	Authoritarian Monarchy	"Old" Oligarchy	"New" Oligarchy	Semicompetitive	Personalistic military	Corporatistic military	Socialistic military	Socialist	Communist	Fascist	Theocratic	Democracy
Legitimacy:												
weak or none		X	X	(X)	X	X	X	X	X			
traditional or customary	X							(X)	(X)		X	
personalistic (charismatic)				(X)			(X)	(X)	(X)	X	(X)	
elective (legal-rational)				X								X
Party System:												
no party	X	X			X	X					X	
one party without competitive elements			X				X	X	X	X		
one party with competitive elements or restricted multiparty		(X)		X		(X)		(X)				
multiparty												X
Head of Executive:												
monarch	X											
president or prime minister		X	X	X				X	X	X		X
military ruler					X	X	X					
religious leader											X	
Power Structure:												
personalistic	X	X	X	X	X		(X)			X	(X)	
collective group						X	X	X	X		(X)	
representative				(X)								X
Ideological Orientation Toward:												
communalistic groups			(X)	(X)	(X)					(X)	X	
"old" upper classes	X	X				X						
"new" upper classes				X	X	X						
lower classes							X	X	X			
middle classes or broader social basis										X		X
Scope of Power:												
partial	X	X	X	X	X	X	X					X
all-encompassing								X	X	X		
Vertical Separation of Power:												
none	X	X	X	(X)	X	X	X	X	X	X	X	
limited with independent judiciary				X								X
full												(X)
Horizontal Separation of Power:												
centralized	X	X	X	X	X	X	X	X	X	X	X	X
federal						(X)			(X)			(X)

Note: Marks in brackets indicate the possibility of certain variations among subtypes.

SOURCE: Courtesy of the author

Political leadership in these states has been connected with the traditional elements of the Catholic Church and the military. Antonio de Oliveira Salazar's (1889–1970) Portugal, and to some extent Francisco Franco's (1917–1989) Spain, also can be placed in this category. Political activities and the media are usually controlled by the regime's repressive apparatus. Other elements that constitute a separation of powers, such as an independent judiciary or a federal structure, are equally lacking.

"New" oligarchy. The "new" oligarchy receives its support from the dominant urban groups in a contemporary context. In this "hegemonic" regime, open competition for public office does not occur. Usually, there is a single-party structure, which, however, is predominantly formal and not very effective. Instead, great emphasis is placed on the bureaucracy. Public opinion and the media are controlled, while leadership is centralized and highly personalistic. In this respect, some charismatic elements of legitimacy may exist. Compliance is established either in terms of passive acceptance or by repressive measures. Both the social base and "inclusiveness" vary in ethnic and class terms. In a majority of cases, a relatively wide ethnic base is combined with more restricted class interests that favor the prosperous groups in society. Countries such as Cameroon, Tunisia, and the Philippines (under Ferdinand Marcos; 1917–1989) are cases in point.

Semicompetitive authoritarianism. Another type can be termed "semicompetitive." In Latin America this system was also based on the traditionally dominant classes, but there is a greater balance between the rural and urban elements. This type also comes close to what Wiarda calls an "open corporatist" system. The contending elements are often institutionalized in "conservative" and "liberal" parties such as those found in nineteenth-century Chile, Colombia, or Uruguay. The "dominant one-party" system in postrevolutionary Mexico is a special case in point. Active participation remains restricted to the middle and upper segments of the population, while mass mobilization is largely prevented or restricted to more symbolic functions. In a different social context, one-party systems embodying competitive elements (e.g., that of Kenya until 1992) and states in which "regulated competition" prevails (e.g., Singapore, Lebanon until 1975) can also be subsumed under this category. Semicompetitive regimes tend to follow established constitutional rules within a presidential or parliamentary system. Regular transfers of power occur within the set framework. They are generally less repressive than "oligarchic" systems. The media often enjoy greater freedom as well.

Socialist authoritarianism. "Socialist" regimes reveal another pattern. They are characterized by an effective single-party organization, a centralized system of government, and an ideology directed toward an egalitarian social order and a "noncapitalist" and "self-reliant" development. Freedom of expression and pluralistic forms of organization are curtailed. There is, however, a great deal of variation. One group (e.g., Tanzania and Guinea after independence) attempted to found their specific type of socialism upon their societies' egalitarian traditions and culture. Another group (e.g., Algeria, Mozambique) advocated a Marxist-oriented "scientific" brand of socialism. In both groups, there may exist some semicompetitive elements in the intraparty and parliamentary spheres. Socialist regimes must be distinguished from their totalitarian "communist" counterparts, if only because of their generally "underdeveloped" condition and the relative lack of effective social control.

Military regimes. In addition to civilian regimes, there are systems that are controlled by "men on horseback" (Janowitz). These military rulers come to power through a coup d'état after the previous civilian institutions fail. In the absence of significant countervailing powers, the military's monopoly over the physical means of coercion makes less efficient civilian governments an easy prey for armed groups. The social bases of these regimes are usually rather narrow. Some military rulers act as temporary caretakers and make genuine attempts to return their countries to civilian rule (as Olusegun Obasanjo in Nigeria in 1980). Others, on the contrary, seek to establish their power permanently. Three subtypes can be distinguished.

The first is personal military authoritarianism. These regimes center around a "strong man" and his most immediate following. Because there are few, if any, formalized input structures, they rely heavily on their centralized output apparatus. In many Latin American countries, this type of rule was exercised by the characteristic "caudillo" in the nineteenth century. Although the caudillo's ascent to power was largely due to his personal qualities (i.e., his military prowess and perhaps charismatic appeal), his rule cannot be understood without reference to the established landed oligarchy. The large haciendas remained one of the stable elements in turbulent times, and caudillos often were (or became) *haciendados* as well. In cases where a caudillo managed to establish a durable regime, this was often accomplished through a system of regional and local subpatrons, the "caciques." Since this type of rule is highly personalistic, it remained inherently unstable. Caudillos were often overthrown by successful rivals.

A second subtype is corporate military authoritarianism. In the 1960s some Latin American states, such as Brazil and Argentina, witnessed the emergence of more "modern" military regimes. In these countries, power had been assumed by the military on a corporate basis. Within the leading ranks of the armed forces, a certain institutionalized transfer of power was established. Although the political orientation of these regimes was "national" and favorable to "modernization," they nonetheless

have left older social structures essentially intact. Formal interest groups and parties were strongly regulated, and the repressive nature of the regime was often particularly blatant.

A third subtype is that of socialist military authoritarianism, which establishes its authority on a permanent basis through the creation of a single-party system. In contrast to the other forms of military rule, these regimes have a socialist and lower-class orientation. In such cases (e.g., Gamal Abdel Nasser's Egypt, or Peru after 1968), the power of the military was directed toward social reforms. The long-term success of such reforms depends, however, upon the government's ability to secure participation from below. If these efforts fail, a shift to a semicompetitive type of regime (e.g., Anwar as-Sadat's Egypt), a polyarchic system (in Peru after 1980), or a return to personalistic military rule may take place.

Outlook

After the dramatic events in Eastern Europe in 1989–1990 and their repercussions in other parts of the world, many of these authoritarian regimes disappeared. To a large extent, they were replaced by liberal democracies. Nevertheless, in some regions, most conspicuously in the Middle East, nondemocratic regimes persisted (e.g., the monarchies and sheikdoms in the Arabian peninsula, the personalistic military dictatorships in Iraq, Lybia, and Syria, or the "semicompetitive" systems in Egypt and Tunisia). In other areas, as in parts of the former Soviet Union, communist regimes were transformed into "post-totalitarian" but still harshly authoritarian and personalistic "new oligarchic" or "sultanistic" ones, In other cases, the newly established democratic forms of government remained defective with respect to important aspects such as truly "free and fair" elections, meaningful popular participation, and the guarantee of the rule of law and basic human rights. Some authors termed these regimes purely "electoral," "illiberal," or "delegative" democracies. In most cases, they resemble the former "semicompetitive" or even "new oligarchic" types.

Thus, at the beginning of the twenty-first century authoritarianism has been on the decline and at least the worst totalitarian forms of rule, with the possible exception of some fundamentalist "theocratic" ones, seem to be over. New variants, however, may yet occur and there remain certain authoritarian and populist dangers in some of the longer-established democracies as well.

See also **Communism; Democracy; Socialism; Totalitarianism.**

BIBLIOGRAPHY

Altemeyer, Bob. *Right-Wing Authoritarianism.* Winnipeg: University of Manitoba Press, 1981.

Berg-Schlosser, Dirk. "Typologies of Third World Political Systems." In *Contemporary Political Systems: Classification and Typologies,* edited by Anton Bebler and Jim Seroka, 173–201. Boulder, Colo.: Lynne Rienner, 1990.

Chehabi, Houchang E., and Juan J. Linz. *Sultanistic Regimes.* Baltimore: Johns Hopkins University Press, 1998.

Collier, David, ed. *The New Authoritarianism in Latin America.* Princeton, N.J.: Princeton University Press, 1979.

Dahl, Robert A. *Polyarchy: Participation and Opposition.* New Haven, Conn.: Yale University Press, 1971.

Hermet, Guy, Richard Rose, and Alain Rouquié, eds. *Elections without Choice.* New York: Macmillan, 1978.

Linz, Juan J. "Totalitarian and Authoritarian Regimes." In *Handbook of Political Science,* vol. 3: *Macropolitical Theory,* edited by Fred I. Greenstein and Nelson W. Polsby. Reading, Mass.: Addison-Wesley, 1975.

Linz, Juan J., and Alfred C. Stepan. *Problems of Democratic Transition and Consolidation: Southern Europe, South America, and Post-Communist Europe.* Baltimore: Johns Hopkins University Press, 1996.

O'Donnell, Guillermo A. *Modernization and Bureaucratic-Authoritarianism: Studies in South American Politics.* Berkeley: Institute of International Studies, University of California, 1973.

Rosberg, Carl G., and Thomas M. Callaghy, eds. *Socialism in Sub-Saharan Africa.* Berkeley: Institute of International Studies, University of California, 1979.

Wiarda, Howard J. "The Political Systems of Latin America: Developmental Models and a Typology of Regimes." In *Latin America,* edited by J. W. Hopkins. New York: Holmes and Meier, 1985.

Dirk Berg-Schlosser

EAST ASIA

Grand claims have been made about the superiority and inevitability of liberal democracy. Do they hold true for East Asian countries? According to typologies in political science, most East Asian countries are considered authoritarian. Japan, Philippines, Taiwan, Thailand, and South Korea are considered democracies; Indonesia is considered ambiguous while all other East Asian governments (Brunei, Cambodia, China, Laos, Malaysia, Myanmar, North Korea, Singapore, and Vietnam) are seen as authoritarian. While this way of organizing and talking about the world is dominant in political, academic, and even popular discourses, its persuasiveness is often compromised upon closer scrutiny.

First, this classification system is confusing because its analytical categories are heavily infused with normative overtones; not only do governments involve scholars in their international programs (e.g., Alliance For Progress), students of politics are also often politically invested and concerned with social change. This conflation of the scientific and the ideological has been criticized by Jeanne Kirkpatrick. She observed that regimes were not classified only by their political form (e.g., regular elections, civil and political liberties) but by their ideologies and economic organization. Totalitarian regimes were exclusively communist regimes with command economies while authoritarian regimes were typically market-driven and seen as more benign despite being equally repressive.

Second, mediating the dichotomous categories of democratic/authoritarian are various theories of democratization whose predictions about East Asian regimes are, at best, as often inaccurate as they are accurate. Democratization and its absence were explained by a variety of factors tied to modernization, such as, in order of theoretical importance, socioeconomic development (measured by the Human Development Index), the rate of pop-

Southeast Asian countries	Freedom House rating (2000)	Average annual GDP per capital (1975–2000)
Un-free countries	(Rating 5.5–7)	
Myanmar	7.7	1.3%
Vietnam	7.7	4.8%
Laos	7.6	3.2%
Brunei	7.5	unavailable
Cambodia	6.6	1.9%
Partly free countries	(Rating 3–5.5)	
Malaysia	5.5	4.1%
Singapore	5.5	5.2%
Indonesia	4.4	4.4%
Free countries	(Rating 1–2.5)	
Philippines	2.3	0.1%
Thailand	2.3	5.5%

SOURCE: freedomhouse.org, nationmaster.com

ulation growth, and the vigor of civil society. Conversely, it was believed that with economic and social development, or modernization, authoritarian regimes would transition to democracy. The strongest formulation of this modernization theory is perhaps Francis Fukuyama's "end of history" thesis, in which he predicted the triumph of liberal democracy over all other political forms in late capitalism through increasing institutional and ideological convergence globally.

Among East Asian countries, evidence against the thesis outweighs evidence for it. In Northeast Asia, economic development in Japan, Taiwan, and South Korea appeared to have triggered a transition to democracy while its absence in Mongolia and North Korea correctly predicts nondemocratization. With the exception of China, which remains staunchly nondemocratic despite impressive economic growth (8.1 percent average annual GDP per capita from 1975 to 2000), the thesis appears to hold true.

In Southeast Asia, there are ample instances where economic growth induces the reverse. As a region, despite the fact that Southeast Asia has a higher average income than South Asia (considered "partly free"), it is rated as the least free region in Asia by Freedom House and remains the only region in the world that has not established a regional system of human rights.

Among the five Southeast Asian countries rated as "unfree," only three support the thesis that economic stagnation inhibits democratization. In prosperous Brunei and in Vietnam (which has the second highest average annual GDP among the ten countries), there appears to be no correlation between economic development and democracy.

The most significant counterevidence to the theory comes from the "free" and "partly free" countries, with Singapore and the Philippines being especially significant counterevidence to the thesis. Singapore was able to forestall democratization despite impressive economic development (considering the devastation of the recent Asian economic crisis that significantly lowered these figures). Singapore's average annual GDP per capita from 1965 to 1990 was a stunning 6.5 percent. In the case of the Philippines, the absence of economic development did not appear to handicap political development; it is the most free despite being worst off economically.

Empirically, the reality of political regimes in East Asia offers mixed evidence to the thesis that economic growth would trigger democratization. In trying to understand why and how they are perpetuated, we obviously need more than modernization theory. Modernization theorists themselves are cognizant of the problems and have attempted to repair the theory without relinquishing the essential paradigm, its dichotomies, or categories.

Revised Modernization Theories

Concerned with the persistence of authoritarianism despite strong and sustained economic growth in East Asia, revised modernization theorists began to argue that authoritarianism was necessary for late-industrializing countries to kick-start their economies, but continue to subscribe to the transition paradigm by pointing out that after the initial phase of growth, contradictions between authoritarianism and capitalism would trigger what is seen as the natural evolution to democracy. In this sense, revised modernization theorists merely redefine authoritarianism as a necessary evil and as a steppingstone; they do not deviate significantly from the modernist view of authoritarianism as transitory and democracy as the end point.

Another revisionist group criticized the economic determinism of modernization theorists but continues to frame the question of authoritarianism within the transition paradigm. For instance, O'Donnell, Schmitter, and Whitehead turned to more voluntaristic explanations by focusing on the role of civil society in triggering a transition to democracy. Theorizing about political opposition in East Asia, Rodan criticized these approaches for romanticizing civil society as "the locus of free-minded and mutually cooperative groups and individuals beyond the state's purvey" (p. 3). Because civil societies cannot exist as alternatives to states but only in relation to them, the notion of civil society not only presupposes the state, but its autonomy crucially depends on and can only be guaranteed by the state. In East Asia, the relationship between civil society (if it exists) and the state is often one of co-option. Depending on how scholars perceive the state, studies of East Asian societies often refer to this political arrangement as paternalistic or guardian states if authority is perceived to be benevolent, or clientalist or nepotist states if authority is deemed corrupt.

A third attempt at revising modernization theory clusters around the concept of "modern authoritarianism." Within modernization theory, authoritarianism had been understood as a premodern phase, and it was believed that with modernization, societies develop into either totalitarian or democratic polities. Rejecting this typology, Linz elaborated on regimes that were authoritarian and modern and proposed a definition of authoritarianism that has become classic:

> Authoritarian regimes are political systems with limited, not responsible, political pluralism; without elaborate and guiding ideology (but with distinctive mentalities); without intensive nor extensive political mobilization (except some points in their developments); and in which a leader (or occasionally a small group) exercises

power within formally ill-defined limits but actually quite predictable ones. (p. 255)

The applicability of this theory to East Asia should be obvious, even if actual empirical studies were few and far between. While much of theorization on authoritarianism focused on Spain and Latin American countries, it should be recalled that among developing countries, few regions were modernizing (and leaving feudalism behind) as quickly as East Asia.

As with other revisionist attempts, this theory continues to operate within the modernization paradigm. First, it continues to subscribe to the authoritarian-democratic dichotomy; liberal democracy remains the point of reference while authoritarianism appears to be a residual category into which all nondemocratic countries are shoveled. Because authoritarianism is seen as a crisis of governance within a democracy, it continues to be seen as unstable and lacking in legitimacy.

Second, what (revised) modernization cannot afford to acknowledge (without having to undergo a paradigm shift) is that even in the most coercive of states, authoritarian governments have always attempted to justify their policies and to acquire legitimacy for their governance. Especially with the global hegemony of democratic values, authoritarian governments in East Asia are devoting more and more attention to the articulation of national ideologies and are less willing to rely on sporadic justifications or sheer coercion. From Vietnam's exhortation to citizens to become "cultural soldiers" to Indonesia's Pancasila democracy to the variants of Asian Values discourse articulated by Cambodia, China, Malaysia, Myanmar, and Singapore, the reality in East Asia challenged the "modern authoritarianism" thesis that regards authoritarianism regimes as ideologically weak, unable to secure consent, and thus illegitimate and unstable.

Legitimate(d) Authoritarianism

While (revised) modernization theorists focused on the transitory nature of authoritarianism, there were other theorists who were interested in the internal logic and staying power of authoritarianism in East Asia. Focused on the question of legitimacy, these approaches typically developed in dialogue with Max Weber's (1864–1920) theory of the three modes of legitimacy (traditional, charismatic, legal-rational). We will review Karl Wittfogel's (1896–1988) exploration of bureaucratic centralization (legal-rational legitimacy) and Lucian and Mary Pye's investigation of Asian culture (traditional legitimacy) before considering how recent theoretical developments such as hegemony theory may contribute to the further understanding of authoritarianism in East Asia.

Wittfogel's *Oriental Despotism* argues that water control and distribution (especially the management of extensive system of canals) spawned hydraulic civilizations with authoritarian centralized empires and sprawling bureaucracies both deeply hostile to change. Critiques of this thesis range from observations that irrigation is often organized locally rather than by centralized bureaucracies to highlights of counterevidence from the West such as the rise and fall of ancient Greece and the chronic backwardness of eastern Europe.

Resonating with other studies of the cultural-psychological studies of authoritarianism (such as studies of fascism in Germany), the Pyes' study of cultural psychology focused on values of frugality, hard work, family values, respect for authority, and Asians' understanding of power. Critiquing the imposition of Western notions of power in understanding Asian societies, they argued that power should not be understood as "participation in the making of significant decisions" or in terms of choice but as status and, indeed, the freedom from having to decide at all. To the Pyes, this Asian sense of power generates authoritarian regimes: "When power implies the security of status, there can be no political process. Contention and strife cease" (p. 22). Insofar as power derives from morality, any challenge to the system or democratic competition is necessarily an affront to the leader and is thus responded to with a heavy hand.

This thesis has been criticized for its culturalism (using culture as an explanation rather than as something to be explained), which in this case generates the tautological thesis that "authoritarian cultures produce authoritarianism." Exactly what is Asian or Confucian culture, and is culture destiny? While the Pyes focused on hierarchical features, others rediscover alternative trajectories to argue that Asian cultures have democratic roots. For instance, William Theodore de Bary and Wei-ming Tu demonstrate the affinities between Confucianism and liberalism while Chu and Winberg Chai argue that current authoritarian regimes distort Confucian values and that if implemented correctly, Confucianism would produce democracy. Furthermore, even if there is agreement on the nature of Asia's values and historical roots, its future—what to preserve and what to change—remains something hotly debated by East Asian leaders (e.g., Singapore's Lee Kwan-Yew versus South Korea's Kim Dae-Jung).

Whatever the mode of legitimacy—legal-rational, charismatic, or traditional—contemporary theorists are increasingly acknowledging that authoritarianism can be legitimate(d) and that the distinction between democracy and authoritarianism is more blurred than modernization theories suggest. Given the problems with modernization theories, the question of why authoritarianism in East Asia is sometimes seen as legitimate by its subjects and the question of why it endures despite development need to be broached from the perspective of legitimacy rather than in terms of modernization. Because legitimacy is a subjective concept pegged to the perceptions of the ruled, the question of why authoritarian regimes (especially prosperous ones) endure is necessarily a question of ideology and research in this direction necessitates close examination of cultural and historical conditions within a regime rather than the broad socioeconomic comparisons associated with modernization theory.

One useful perspective comes from cultural studies, especially the concepts of hegemony and popular authoritarianism. Instead of the dichotomy of democratic/authoritarianism, Antonio Gramsci (1891–1937) postulated the categories of consent/coercion—the latter categories do not correspond

with the former because they are not mutually exclusive. Following Weber's definition of the state as an organ with a legitimate monopoly over coercion, Gramsci distinguished between this "outer ditch" of coercion and an "inner ditch" of consensus and commonsense. To the extent that there is consensus, it becomes unnecessary to mobilize repressive state apparatuses to discipline society; political alternatives are sufficiently de-legitimized through the molding of commonsense. Since the 1990s, some applications of this theory to Asia have included John Girling's analysis of middle-class hegemony in Thailand, John Hilley's analysis of Mahathirism in Malaysia, and Soek-Fang Sim's analysis of the Asian Values project in Singapore.

The various theories outlined here can combine to offer a sophisticated understanding of authoritarianism in East Asia. Modernization theory, although flawed, offers effective descriptions of the democratization pressures confronted by rapidly developing countries. What it fails to do, and what is advantageous about localized theories, is the focus on how history, geography, culture, and ideology can come together to engender countervailing forces that stabilize the regime and arrest the drift toward democracy.

See also **Authority; Democracy; Pluralism.**

BIBLIOGRAPHY

Chai, Chu, and Winberg Chai. *Confucianism.* Woodbury, N.Y.: Barron's, 1973.

De Bary, Wm. Theodore. *The Liberal Tradition in China.* New York: Columbia University Press, 1983.

Diamond, Larry. "Thinking about Hybrid Regimes." *Journal of Democracy* 13, no. 2 (2002): 5–21.

Fukuyama, Francis. *The End of History and the Last Man.* New York: The Free Press, 1992.

Girling, John. *Interpreting Development: Capitalism, Democracy, and the Middle Class in Thailand.* Ithaca, N.Y.: Cornell University Press, 1996.

Gramsci, Antonio. *Selections from the Prison Notebooks.* Edited and translated by Quinton Hoare and Geoffrey Nowell Smith. London: Lawrence and Wishart, 1971.

Hilley, John. *Malaysia: Mahathirism, Hegemony and the New Opposition.* London and New York: Zed Books, 2001.

Kirkpatrick, Jeanne. "Dictatorships and Double Standards." *Commentary* 68, no. 2 (1979): 34–35.

Linz, Juan J. "An Authoritarian Regime: The Case of Spain." In *Mass Politics: Studies in Political Sociology,* edited by Erik Allardt and Stein Rokkan. New York: Free Press, 1970.

Lipset, Seymour Martin. "Some Social Requisites of Democracy." *American Political Science Review* 53, no. 1 (1959): 69–105.

O'Donnell, Guillermo, Phillipe Schmitter, and Laurence Whitehead. *Transitions from Authoritarian Rule: Latin America.* Baltimore: John Hopkins University Press, 1986.

Pye, Lucian W., and Mary W. Pye. *Asian Power and Politics: The Cultural Dimensions of Authority.* London: Belknap Press, 1985.

Rodan, Garry. "Theorizing Political Opposition in East and Southeast Asia." In *Political Oppositions in Industrializing Asia,* edited by Garry Rodan. London and New York: Routledge, 1996.

Sim, Soek-Fang. "Asian Values, Authoritarianism and Capitalism." *The Public* 8, no. 2 (2001): 45–66.

New Dictionary of the History of Ideas

Tu, Wei-ming. *Way, Learning and Politics: Essays on the Confucian Intellectual.* Albany: State University of New York, 1993.

Wittfogel, Karl. *Oriental Despotism: A Comparative Study of Total Power.* New Haven, Conn.: Yale University Press, 1957.

Soek-Fang Sim

LATIN AMERICA

Traditional interpretations of authoritarianism in Latin America root this phenomenon in the style of Iberian colonization in the region. The Hispanic world, this argument alleges, was naturally more authoritarian than Anglo-Saxon cultures. Furthermore, the cultures they encountered in the New World (particularly the Aztec and Inca Empires) were themselves very hierarchical, which further facilitated authoritarian forms of governance. Subsequent interpretations have generally rejected the racist implications of these theories in favor of more sophisticated and nuanced explanations. Nevertheless, debates continued on how best to confront authoritarian tendencies.

Authoritarianism is related to, but distinct from, dictatorship and totalitarianism. Unlike totalitarianism, authoritarian regimes sometimes allow limited political pluralism (though, unlike in a democracy, that opposition is limited and often not legitimate). In addition, authoritarianism lacks a defined ideology, which characterizes totalitarian regimes. Furthermore, authoritarianism tends to rely on apathy rather than a mobilized and engaged population. George Philip notes how rising inequality under democratic government leads to disenchantment, with significant minorities preferring authoritarian over democratic leadership. Some scholars contend that democratic systems can be strengthened through a reformation of political institutions, such as political parties and electoral processes. Others maintain that prolonged socioeconomic crises are a larger threat to stability and that economic growth is necessary to prevent a lapse back into authoritarianism. These economic policies, however, often take the form of neoliberal reforms that are profoundly antidemocratic and lead back to an authoritarian style of governance.

Caudillos

During the nineteenth century, authoritarian political structures were expressed in the form of caudillo styles of leadership. A lack of a functioning democratic system that allowed for peaceful transfers of power from one civilian government to another led to a series of palace coups and military governments. Facing a power vacuum after the disappearance of patriarchal monarchies at independence, leaders sought legitimacy through charisma and appeals to tradition rather than expressing a coherent ideology. A caudillo, which broadly means a "strongman," style of government represents the use of charisma rather than military force to keep political forces under control through promotion of allegiance to a central leader. These caudillos were not necessarily of a specific ideological orientation, could be associated with liberal or conservative politicians, and could take a military or civilian form; in addition, they might be rooted in either urban or rural populations and be oriented toward either modernizing or traditional forces. Perhaps the most common unifying thread among caudillos was their appeal to nationalism. Caudillos sometimes relied on legal means, including elections and plebiscites, to legitimate their control but once in office tolerated no dissent to their authority. Representative of this in Mexico are both Benito Juárez (r. 1861–1872) and Porfirio Díaz (r. 1877–1880; 1884–1911) who came into power claiming to support freely contested elections but then became deeply entrenched in power. Both caudillos were liberals from the poor and largely indigenous southern state of Oaxaca. They relied on this home base of support to maintain themselves in power even as their policies increasingly served elite interests. Juárez is commonly regarded as Mexico's first "Indian" president though he implemented legislation that took land away from rural villages. Díaz ruled using the strategy of *pan o palo* (carrot or the stick) to reward lavishly his supporters and repress brutally his opponents. It took the Mexican Revolution (1910–1920) to remove Díaz from power after thirty-four years, one of the longest-running dictatorships in the history of Latin America.

One of the most noted and resilient examples of Latin American authoritarian regimes is that of General Antonio López de Santa Anna (1794–1876) during the first half century after Mexico's independence in 1821. Santa Anna held power eleven different times with catastrophic results perhaps unequaled in Latin America's history, including the loss of half of Mexico's territory to the United States. Seemingly contradictory ideological principles, including adhering to federalism, centralism, liberalism, conservatism, and even monarchism, characterized his different times in office. When liberals held the upper hand, he ruled Mexico as a liberal. Later Santa Anna became a conservative and passed some of the most reactionary legislation in Mexico's history. Historians often point to his charisma and political opportunism as explaining his success in holding onto (or, more accurately, repeatedly returning to) power. Will Fowler, however, finds such interpretations to be unsatisfactorily simplistic in explaining Santa Anna's resilience. Rather, his success is a result of elite support, motivated by the desire to preserve hegemonic class interests. Santa Anna's promises to deliver political stability and prevent social dissolution were more important than differences in ideology. A subsequent long tradition of casting the ruler as a villain is what has made it "difficult to understand why he was so successful" (Fowler, p. 13). Santa Anna perhaps was no worse or no more opportunistic a leader than his contemporaries, just perhaps more successful in riding out political changes. In Fowler's assessment, his commitment to elite privilege and detachment from partisan politics ultimately made him an arbitrator of competing ideological interests. Whichever group currently held the upper hand courted his support in order to consolidate its control over the country.

Caudillos were not necessarily a negative force and have sometimes been divided into the categories of "cultured caudillos" and "barbarous caudillos" (Hamill, p. 5). Mariano Malgarejo from Bolivia is often considered to be a classic representation of the later. He abrogated land titles of Indian peasants and sold off large slices of Bolivian territory as if it were

Tanks in Santiago during the Chilean coup. In 1973 Chilean military forces overthrew the democratic government of President Salvador Allende, supplanting it with a dictatorship that widely repressed basic human rights and banned any political opposition. © HORACIO VILLALOBOS/CORBIS

his own personal property in order to generate funds to put down chronic revolts against his government. As a result, Bolivia lost to neighboring countries half of its territory as well as its outlet to the sea. Like Santa Anna, Malgarejo was perhaps no worse than any other caudillo but just more active and successful at this style of government.

Corporatism

Traditional interpretations of authoritarianism argue that after independence in the early nineteenth century, the Latin American republics had difficulties in shaking their Iberian heritage. Although they drafted constitutions that borrowed heavily on liberal ideals and institutions, leaders proved ineffective at governing. As a result, many Latin American countries soon shifted to dictatorial forms of government, marked with elite rule, political instability, militarism, and authoritarianism. This led some leaders to argue that the new republics needed strong, centralized governments more than social and economic equality. Fowler points to these as common reasons throughout Latin American history for the "longevity, resilience, and endurance" of authoritarian regimes, including "the consummate political skills of the dictators, their pragmatism, flexibility and timely opportunism, their use of clientelism, patronage and cooption, their personalist politics, prestige or charisma, and effective repression." Authoritarian leaders supplemented these characteristics with the use of military forces, a manipulation of political parties, and expression of "a certain ideological vagueness" (Fowler, p. xiii). This au-

thoritarian tradition hindered the emergence of Western-style democratic forms of government.

Corporatist theories, which gained popularity in the 1950s, emphasized this Iberian heritage of authoritarianism to explain underdevelopment in Latin America. This authoritarianism expressed itself politically through a patriarchal monarchy, economically in feudalistic landholding systems, militarily with elitist structures, and religiously with the Catholic hierarchy. During its colonization of the Americas, Iberia transferred these authoritarian institutions to the New World. Corporatist interpretations blamed a failure of democracy and economic development on the persistence of hierarchical structures in modern institutions, with power flowing vertically from the top down. Jan Knippers Black summarized corporatist theories as "blaming the Iberians" (p. 4). Critics of corporatist theories have noted that countries like Chile that were subject to authoritarian military rule toward the end of the twentieth century were on the fringes of Spanish colonization and emerged out of a long democratic tradition. Given this reality, many aspects of corporatist theories begin to break down, as do interpretations that place blame on the legacy of hereditary absolute monarchies for the persistence of strong, centralized authoritarian structures.

Bureaucratic Authoritarianism

In the second half of the twentieth century, personalist dictators such as Manuel Noriega (r. 1983–1989) in Panama gave way to authoritarian military regimes, particularly in the South American countries of Argentina, Chile, Brazil, and Uruguay. These authoritarian regimes were unparalleled in their brutality and suppression of civil society and political movements. Fearing a rising leftist threat, both from electoral coalitions as well as armed guerrilla movements, these authoritarian regimes sought to redraw the structure of their countries along more traditional lines. Rather than relying on the personal power of an individual dictator, these regimes used military institutions to maintain control over society. The resulting bureaucratic-authoritarian regimes fundamentally restructured political and economic institutions to remake their countries along neoliberal lines that dramatically widened the gap between the rich and the poor. Critics claimed that these economic reforms were so unpopular that they could only be imposed through undemocratic means. Popular reactions to structural adjustments that sharply reduced living standards led authoritarian regimes to crack down even more viciously on their opponents.

The Argentine political scientist Guillermo O'Donnell introduced the concept of *bureaucratic authoritarianism* to describe institutional dictatorships that were not a legacy of Iberian rule but used coercion to respond to what they viewed as threats to the capitalist system. While the revolutionary left condemned these dictatorships as fascist and turned to armed struggle as a means to overthrow them, O'Donnell argued "that the appropriate way to oppose them was through an unconditional commitment to democracy" (O'Donnell, p. xiii). These regimes resulted from a failure of democracy to extend the protections of citizenship to an entire population. A notable gap between liberal principles and exclusionary economic practices led to what O'Donnell terms "low-intensity citizenship" (p. 143). Unfortunately, economic inequalities persisted and even grew as part of neoliberal policies that were retained even after O'Donnell's long-desired return to democratic governance in Latin America.

Alberto Fujimori's (r. 1990–2000) government in Peru in the 1990s provides another important variation on the authoritarian tradition in Latin America. In what came to be known as an *autogolpe* (self-coup) or "fujicoup," Fujimori launched a coup against himself in April 1992 to shut down the congress and rewrite the country's constitution. Using what George Philip calls "semi-authoritarianism," Fujimori realized some significant policy achievements, including stopping inflation and ending the bloody Shining Path guerrilla insurgency (p. 169). More significantly, his violation of Peru's constitutional order did not lead to a fall in his popularity. Rather, many people believed that the country's crisis legitimized authoritarian measures. By 2000, however, the crisis had passed, and public opinion swung away from support for his abuses of power. His fall from power was neither a triumph of democracy nor a blow against authoritarianism but a result of popular responses to a changing political situation.

In an interesting twist on condemnations of authoritarian traditions in Latin America, James F. Petras and Frank T. Fitzgerald argue that sometimes democratic governments are not authoritarian enough to defend positive social reforms. Pointing specifically to Salvador Allende's (r. 1970–1973) gov-

ernment in Chile in the early 1970s and the Sandinista government in Nicaragua in the 1980s, they note that the ruling classes do not give up their elite privileges without a struggle. This argument contrasts these failed attempts at social, economic, and political transformation to that of Cuba. If the Cuban government had not taken the drastic authoritarian measures that it did in the early 1960s, the revolution's attempts to redistribute wealth to the lower classes and extend education and health care throughout the country would have failed. Because the bourgeoisie and their international allies are not ideologically committed to democratic rule, they do not hesitate to use whatever tactics might be necessary to undermine social reforms when they are implemented through democratic means. Ironically, Petras and Fitzgerald argue, social reformers need to utilize authoritarian tactics to defend democratic processes or risk total failure.

The fall of Salvador Allende's government in Chile is the most noted example in Latin America of a fall of a democratic government to an authoritarian regime. Rooted in a long history of civilian institutions, Allende pledged to put the country on a "Chilean Road to Socialism" that would utilize existing democratic structures to redistribute wealth in an attempt to end extreme economic and social inequalities. When his reforms led to nationalization of U.S.-owned copper mines and other industries, the U.S. Central Intelligence Agency (CIA) helped engineer a bloody military coup on 11 September 1973 that overthrew his government. General Augusto Pinochet (r. 1974–1990) then implemented one of the most savage military dictatorships in the history of Latin America. A country that had one of the longest democratic traditions in Latin America now became a prime example of an authoritarian regime that suppressed the basic principles of liberal democracy, including values of individual freedom, civil liberties, social and economic equality, and free elections. At the same time, these regimes embraced laissez-faire economic systems that critics subsequently termed "savage capitalism." As a type of dictatorship, they outlawed political opposition and greatly restricted individual freedoms.

As relations with the Pinochet dictatorship illustrate, the U.S. government "supported authoritarian regimes that promised stability, anticommunism, and economic trade and investment opportunities." David F. Schmitz notes how this policy conflicted with a theoretical embrace of the principles of liberal democracy and human rights. U.S. officials viewed Latin Americans as racially inferior and strong authoritarian leadership as necessary to maintain order, prevent social and political chaos, and implement neoliberal policies necessary for economic modernization (Schmitz, p. 304). Rather than fostering democratic institutions, U.S. support for authoritarian regimes often led to political polarization, instability, and radical nationalist movements. Critics constantly charge that such support conflicts with U.S. interests, virtually no matter how those interests are conceptualized. "Equating dictators with freedom," Schmitz maintained, "blinded American leaders to the contradictions and failures of their policy" (p. 7). Authoritarian regimes often performed poorly in terms of economic development and, together with extensive human rights violations, lost legitimacy internally. Democracy emerged and economies grew in Latin America in spite of, rather than because of, U.S. policies.

By the end of the twentieth century, with a reemergence of democratic governments throughout Latin America, authoritarianism appeared to be safely buried in the past. Nevertheless, Leigh Payne points to the persistence of an authoritarian tradition in right-wing threats to democratic structures. These "uncivil movements" that use political violence to promote exclusionary objectives do not necessarily seek to overthrow democratic systems, but nevertheless they are able to shape the discourse and practices of democratic institutions. A search for social justice and equality all too often continues to be an elusive goal. In subtle, and sometimes not so subtle, ways, authoritarianism is still a force to be reckoned with in Latin America.

See also **Democracy; Dictatorship in Latin America; Nationalism; Pluralism; Populism; Totalitarianism.**

BIBLIOGRAPHY

Black, Jan Knippers. "Introduction: The Evolution of Latin American Studies." In *Latin America, Its Problems and Its Promise: A Multidisciplinary Introduction,* 3rd ed., edited by Jan Knippers Black, 1–17. Boulder, Colo.: Westview, 1998.

Domínguez, Jorge I., ed. *Authoritarian and Democratic Regimes in Latin America.* New York: Garland, 1994.

Fowler, Will, ed. *Authoritarianism in Latin America since Independence.* Westport, Conn: Greenwood, 1996.

Hamill, Hugh M., ed. *Caudillos: Dictators in Spanish America.* Norman: University of Oklahoma Press, 1992.

Mainwaring, Scott, and Arturo Valenzuela, eds. *Politics, Society, and Democracy: Latin America.* Boulder, Colo.: Westview, 1998.

O'Donnell, Guillermo A. *Counterpoints: Selected Essays on Authoritarianism and Democratization.* Notre Dame, Ind.: University of Notre Dame Press, 1999.

Payne, Leigh A. *Uncivil Movements: The Armed Right Wing and Democracy in Latin America.* Baltimore: Johns Hopkins University Press, 2000.

Petras, James F., and Frank T. Fitzgerald. "Authoritarianism and Democracy in the Transition to Socialism." *Latin American Perspectives* 15, no. 1 (winter 1988): 93–111.

Philip, George. *Democracy in Latin America: Surviving Conflict and Crisis?* Malden, Mass.: Polity, 2003.

Schmitz, David F. *Thank God They're on Our Side: The United States and Right-Wing Dictatorships, 1921–1965.* Chapel Hill: University of North Carolina Press, 1999.

Marc Becker

AUTHORITY. The conceptual history of *authority* reveals it to be an essentially contested concept because of the many debates about its sources, purposes, and limits, as well as its proximity to the concept of power.

Since Plato's critique of Athenian democracy, physical force and rhetorical persuasion have been viewed as types of power but not authority. Hannah Arendt observes that "[i]f author-

ity is to be defined at all, then it must be in contradistinction to both coercion by force and persuasion through arguments" (p. 93). Indeed, it is only when authority fails that force or persuasion is used to elicit compliance. This distinction is reflected in Jean-Jacques Rousseau's (1712–1778) discussion of what a legislator must do to form a political community guided by the general will:

> Since, then, the legislator can use neither force nor argument, he must, of necessity, have recourse to authority of a different kind which can lead without violence and persuade without convincing. That is why, in all periods, the Fathers of their country have been driven to seek the intervention of Heaven, attributing to the Gods a Wisdom that was really their own. (pp. 207–208)

In this passage, religious authority is so widely accepted and unquestioned by the people that, if it is appealed to, no force or persuasion is necessary.

Rousseau's legislator, however, might be engaging in deception by invoking religious authority as a proxy. To be authoritative, the legislator's statement should be accepted or rejected on its merits. As Richard Friedman states, "[i]f there is no way of telling whether an utterance is authoritative, except by evaluating its contents to see whether it deserves to be accepted in its own right, then the distinction between an authoritative utterance and advice or rational persuasion will have collapsed" (p. 132). Deference toward authority may not be automatic, as those affected by it evaluate its statements to judge whether they are, in fact, authoritative.

Given this, it may be said that if power is the ability of some individual, group, or institution to control, coerce, or regulate others, authority is the recognition of the right of that individual, group, or institution to exercise power. In short, those over whom power is exercised recognize that whoever or whatever is exercising that power is doing so legitimately. There is an element of trust, faith, and recognition on the part of those following authority that the person exercising it possesses some quality (for example, wisdom, expertise, or the fact that the person was elected by the people) that ought to be deferred to. If this is the case, then authority, rather than simple power, exists and must be followed, adhered to, and, within limits, obeyed.

The Sources of Authority

One approach to authority focuses on the question of who has a right to rule, and on what this right rests. Early notions of authority based it on the right of the strongest, the many, or the wisest to make laws. For example, while Pericles (c. 495–429 B.C.E.) praises Athenian democracy as the rule of the many according to the rule of law, Plato (c. 428–348 or 347 B.C.E.) views it as an unstable form of government that rests on the opinion and force of the majority. Instead, he prefers authority be given to those who possess reason and wisdom. Also, from antiquity to the Middle Ages, authority is often related to the divine, with rulers seen as "gods" themselves or as receiving authority from a divine power. In the European Middle Ages, the notion of civil and religious authority was clearly tied to the Catholic Church. For example, papalism asserted that the pope had final authority over both ecclesiastical and civil realms. Also, the notion of divine right monarchy, promoted by Robert Filmer (c. 1588–1653), asserted that the absolute authority of monarchs rests on Adam's patriarchal authority in the Garden of Eden.

In the latter part of the Middle Ages, the intellectual flourishing of the Renaissance led to the rediscovery of the notion of self-government in the form of republican city-states such as Florence, Italy. In turn, this influenced the emergence of the social-contract theory of John Locke (1632–1704) and Rousseau that rests legitimate government on the consent of the citizens of a political community. Locke's theory of consent and the right to revolt helped shape the Declaration of Independence and the republican character of the U.S. Constitution. However, the social-contract theory was criticized as resting on abstract notions of consent, reason, equality, and liberty. Edmund Burke (1729–1797), for instance, favored moderate reforms of existing institutions, and stressed that members of each generation must respect their entailed inheritance that obliged them to follow traditions established by previous generations. Furthermore, Joseph-Marie de Maistre (1753–1821) saw the abstract ideas that inspired the French Revolution as undermining the "throne and altar," which were the traditional authorities that held society together.

Authority and Legitimacy

Another approach to authority focuses more on the question of whether those who are ruled accept authority as legitimate regardless of its source. This approach originated with Max Weber (1864–1920), who distinguished three ideal types of authority: traditional authority that rests on history and tradition; charismatic authority that rests on the personality of the leader; and legal-rational authority that rests on impersonal rules and powers and is associated with the office rather than the personal characteristics of the office holder. If those affected think that power is exercised legitimately, then any of these three types of authority is legitimate, regardless of its moral justification.

Weber suggested that as societies modernize, authority transforms from traditional, to charismatic, to legal-rational. This implies that only one type of authority exists at a time, or that authority is a linear sequence from traditional to charismatic to legal-rational. Clearly, these three types of authority coexist. This is illustrated by distinguishing between the notions of "an authority" and "in authority." For example, the U.S. Congress possesses legal-rational authority, and representatives and senators have certain powers that derive from their office. Representatives and senators are "in authority" but are often influenced by individuals called to testify before committee hearings who, because of their charisma or expertise, are "an authority."

The Purposes of Authority

The purposes of political authority are as contested as its sources. For some, authority should promote a virtuous society. The desired virtues differ depending on whether one looks to Aristotle's (384–322 B.C.E.) discussion of the golden mean, Niccolò Machiavelli's (1469–1527) discussion of republican

virtue, religiously inspired notions of Christian or Islamic virtue, or the emphasis on character as evident in Bill Bennett's *Book of Virtues*. For some, authority should promote a just society. Similarly, the definition of justice differs depending on whether one looks to Plato's ideal republic or John Rawls's (1921–2002) view that justice is the fair distribution of resources and opportunities in a society. And for some, authority is needed to provide stability and order. Here too are found differences ranging from Thomas Hobbes's (1588–1679) emphasis on an absolutist government created by the consent of the people who simply desire protection and order, or the republican tradition that suggests that stability comes from dividing authority among different branches of government that check and balance each other.

Since authority is valued but exists in tension with other social values, there is a debate about its limits. Some, like Filmer and Jean Bodin (1530–1596), defend absolute authority in the hands of one person, and oppose the separation of its powers, on grounds that absolutism alone can provide stability and order. Others, such as Locke and James Madison (1751–1836), suggest that absolute authority in the hands of one person or group of persons inevitably leads to arbitrary and excessive power that squelches political and civil liberties. Thus, authority must be divided among separate branches that can check and balance each other, and operate within certain constitutionally prescribed limits such as the Bill of Rights. Furthermore, the authority of government can conflict with the demands of conscience or standards of justice that transcend government. Thus, civil disobedience, as Henry David Thoreau (1817–1862) suggests, can be justified on grounds that individuals should not be coerced into supporting an evil they otherwise oppose.

Several controversies continue to surround authority in the early 2000s. Issues such as identifying the origin of the social-contract tradition and delineating the limits of obedience continued to attract scholarly attention. Other debates are both scholarly and politically important. For example, the proper relationship between religious and secular authority remains controversial in the United States, France, and in some predominately Islamic countries debating democratic reforms. There are also ongoing concerns that all types of authority are not respected or deferred to as much as in the past. Cultural conservatives in the United States especially bemoan the loss of respect for and faith in authority, and point to a culture that promotes relativism, cynicism, and irony as the culprit. Finally, the U.S. government's reaction to the terrorist attacks of September 11, 2001, the invasions of Afghanistan and Iraq, and the Patriot Act have each, in different ways, sparked controversy. For example, there continues a global discussion about the appropriate use of unilateral or multilateral military force. And, within the United States, the tension between governmental authority and civil liberties remains controversial. From these examples, one can see that the historical debates regarding the sources, purposes, and limits of authority remain important in this era.

See also **Civil Disobedience; Democracy; Liberty; Power; Republicanism: Republic.**

SOME DEFINITIONS OF AUTOBIOGRAPHY

Philippe Lejeune: "A retrospective account in prose that a real person makes of his own existence stressing his individual life and especially the history of his personality" ("The Autobiographical Pact").

Sidonie Smith and Julia Watson: "Our working definition of autobiographical or life narrative, rather than specifying its rules as a genre or form, understands it as a historically situated practice of self-representation. In such texts, narrators selectively engage their lived experience through personal storytelling" (*Reading Autobiography*).

Leigh Gilmore: "As a genre, autobiography is characterized less by a set of formal elements than by a rhetorical setting in which a person places herself or himself within testimonial contexts as seemingly diverse as the Christian confession, the scandalous memoirs of the rogue, and the coming-out story in order to achieve as proximate a relation as possible to what constitutes truth in that discourse" (*The Limits of Autobiography*).

BIBLIOGRAPHY

Arendt, Hannah. "What Is Authority?" In *Between Past and Future: Eight Exercises in Political Thought*. Enl. ed. New York: Penguin, 1977.

Friedman, Richard. "On the Concept of Authority in Political Philosophy." In *Concepts in Social and Political Philosophy*, edited by Richard Flathman. New York: Macmillan, 1973.

Rousseau, Jean-Jacques. "The Social Contract." In *Social Contract: Essays by Locke, Hume, and Rousseau*, edited by Sir Ernest Barker. London: Oxford University Press, 1947.

Gregory W. Streich

AUTOBIOGRAPHY. Growing scholarly interest in the relationship between truth and fiction, along with popular interest in personal life-narratives and the "culture of confession," have brought new prominence to the genre of autobiography. Indeed, according to Leigh Gilmore, the number of English-language autobiographies and memoirs roughly tripled from the 1940s to the 1990s (p. 1, n. 1), and scholarly attention to life writing has followed this trend. Paradoxically, however, as interest in autobiography has risen, debates over the nature and definition of the genre have become increasingly prevalent. Etymologically the word "autobiography" is a compound of the Greek terms *autos* (self), *bios* (life), and *graphe* (writing). At its simplest, then, autobiography can be defined as "self-life-writing." But, as illustrated by debates over what counts as autobiography—and indeed, over what counts as "truth" in the postmodern world—the apparently simple act of writing one's own life is much more complex than this definition suggests. In fact, autobiography is as diverse and as protean as any literary genre, and attempts to define it have always been troubled.

Scholars of autobiography have long theorized the genre not as a discrete set of characteristics but as a literary and cultural practice informed by diverse cultural, rhetorical, and institutional contexts (see especially Bruss; Butterfield; Eakin; Egan; Gilmore; Hesford; Lionnet; Smith and Watson). This way of thinking resonates with postmodern theories of language, subjectivity, identity, and power that have reshaped how we think about autobiography and other "true" stories. "Self-life-writing," then, involves more than simply writing or reading a life story; it also requires attention to the rhetorical situation in which that story is embedded and to the cultural narratives that shape what counts as "truth" in a particular time and place.

Culture and Identity: Narrative Strategies

Contemporary philosophers and cultural critics have convincingly argued that identity and experience are themselves socially constructed, shifting according to historical and cultural ideas about personhood and everyday life. Despite this postmodern turn to thinking about how identity is made, not born, scholars of autobiography nevertheless insist on the materiality of identity in theorizing life writing, particularly the material consequences of race, ethnicity, class, gender, sexuality, and ability, and how autobiographical narratives are affected by culturally available identity categories and narratives. From Sei Shōnagon's *The Pillow Book* (Japan, c. 1000 C.E.) to Margery Kempe's *The Book of Margery Kempe* (England, 1436) to Benjamin Franklin's *The Autobiography of Benjamin Franklin* (United States, 1771–1789) to Richard Rodriguez's immigration memoir *Hunger of Memory* (United States, 1982), identity and narrative provide key frames through which autobiographers negotiate their life stories. For example, Shōnagon's notebooks, containing observations, poems, and stories written by a tenth-century Japanese woman, differ in many ways from

AUTOBIOGRAPHY AND TRAUMA

Given the culture of confession that infuses contemporary life in the United States, it may not come as a surprise that trauma memoirs have become remarkably popular with both autobiographers and audiences alike. Trauma memoirs often narrate state-sponsored and human rights violations, such as Elie Wiesel's *Night* (1960) and Loung Ung's *First They Killed My Father: A Daughter of Cambodia Remembers* (2000), but they also often narrate acts of individual violence, such as rape, domestic violence, and incest, such as Mary Karr's *The Liar's Club* (1995) and Michael Ryan's *Secret Life* (1995). Autobiographies that attempt to narrate traumatic experiences, such as child abuse, rape, and war, are caught within a paradox: trauma is often understood to be defined by a radical unrepresentability, since it is that which shatters the self and makes language and narrative impossible. In this context, narrative, argues Arthur W. Frank in *The Wounded Storyteller: Body, Illness, and Ethics* (1995), is an ethical as well as an aesthetic imperative, testifying to the narrator's continuing presence in the world in spite of injury, illness, and even imminent death. Indeed contemporary scholars of trauma autobiographies have become increasingly interested in the process and the politics of articulating pain and injury through life narrative. For example, Marianne Hirsch's *Family Frames: Photography, Narrative, and Postmemory* (1997), Annette Kuhn's *Family Secrets: Acts of Memory and Imagination* (1995), and Nancy Miller and Jason Tougaw's collection *Extremities: Trauma, Testimony, and Community* (2002), explore the difficulty of representing trauma. Significantly Leigh Gilmore's *The Limits of Autobiography: Trauma and Testimony* argues that trauma is a key site at which to deconstruct the generic boundaries between fiction and nonfiction, the imagined and the real. Many authors of trauma narratives, such as Mikal Gilmore, Dorothy Allison, and Jamaica Kincaid, strategically choose to turn away from the autobiographical label and instead to embrace fiction as a genre that can achieve the project of self-representation without putting the author in the position of being scrutinized and judged by readers and critics. As these theorists suggest, turning one's life into a story is laden with difficult representational and political choices concerning which stories to tell, which culturally available narratives to draw upon, and which generic categories to affix to the final product.

Franklin's archetypal autobiography, which reveals his investment in white male privilege in the early U.S. republic. Nevertheless both autobiographies show that "self-life-writing" is a process that is historically and culturally situated, and through which identity and experience are negotiated, materialized, and refashioned.

Significantly Franklin's *Autobiography* relies on a larger cultural narrative, the bildungsroman, which has widely accepted currency in the United States. The bildungsroman follows a classic narrative trajectory of conversion in which the individual hero embarks on a long journey that ends with his resolution with the larger social community—in Franklin's case, the national community as represented by Philadelphia. The bildungsroman provides narrative shape and truth-value to a wide range of mainstream and marginal autobiographies published in the United States, from Franklin's to Mary Antin's *The Promised Land* (1912), Jade Snow Wong's *Fifth Chinese Daughter* (1950), Malcolm X and Alex Haley's *The Autobiography of Malcolm X* (1965), and Rodriguez's *Hunger of Memory*. The fact that several immigrant, ethnic, and women autobiographers have relied on the bildungsroman to give their stories a recognizable trajectory and broad cultural currency is no accident. Indeed many autobiographers have used this form deliberately and strategically in order to persuade their readers that they too deserve a place of privilege in the United States and that their achievement of the "American Dream" is a result of individual hard work and intelligence. Therefore many autobiographies that are shaped by the bildungsroman narrative downplay structural inequities such as gender, ethnicity, race, class, sexuality, and ability. Wong and Rodriguez, for example, openly dispute the assumption that gender or ethnicity has served as a barrier in their lives, even when their autobiographies clearly show otherwise. The bildungsroman, then, is a form that both enables and constrains the kinds of life stories that can be told by particular autobiographers.

Narratives of mobility and/or immobility structure a wide variety of autobiographies that bring into view questions concerning the representation of the racialized, gendered, and classed body. Unlike the heroic journey narrative of the bildungsroman, which relies on an individualized story of social mobility, many autobiographical narratives of mobility and immobility engage questions of community, belonging, and citizenship and their relationship to how the freedoms of particular bodies are granted or restricted. For example, the slave narrative articulates the broad cultural, economic, and historical forces that compelled racialized subjects into slavery in the United States, Britain, and the British colonies. Frederick Douglass's *The Narrative of the Life of Frederick Douglass, an American Slave* (1845) gained wide influence in the United States in the nineteenth century for its indictment of white slave owners whose personal and political freedom depended upon the forced servitude of an entire class of people. Slave narratives by female slaves, such as Harriet Jacobs's *Incidents in the Life of a Slave Girl* (1861) and Mary Prince's *The History of Mary Prince, a West Indian Slave* (1831), added to this an exploration of how gender also operated to the advantage of white men in the slave economy. An examination of slave narratives, then, exposes the abstract narrative of individual social mobility in bildungsroman narratives to be a patent fiction and shows instead how race, gender, and class privilege operate to enable or constrain particular bodies and particular life narratives.

Likewise other autobiographical narratives structured by the dynamics of immobility or restricted mobility provide key insights into how society is constructed around gender, race, ethnicity, class, sexuality, and ability. For example, early American captivity narratives told the story of American Indians' supposed savagery and white women's supposed civility. For example, Mary Rowlandson's *A True History of the Captivity and Restoration of Mrs. Mary Rowlandson* (1682), perhaps the most famous of the captivity narratives, creates a solid opposition between white settlers and native "savages," arguing in the process that the settlers, not the natives, have God-given authority over the American wilderness. In contrast, prison memoirs and Japanese-American internment narratives illustrate the racial and class dynamics that constrain the movement of individuals who are deemed by the state to be a danger to the citizenry. In one of the most famous internment narratives, Jeanne Wakatsuki Houston and James D. Houston's *Farewell to Manzanar* (1973), the narrator describes the racialization process by which Japanese immigrants and citizens were reconstructed as enemies of the state solely on the basis of their ethnicity and without regard to their citizenship status or national loyalties. Similarly prison memoirs such as Alexander Berkman's *Prison Memoirs of an Anarchist* (1912) and *Against All Hope: The Prison Memoirs of Armando Valladares* (1986) expose how race and class factor into a supposedly impartial criminal justice system. As these autobiographies illustrate, mobility and immobility are intricately tied to social constructions of race, ethnicity, class, gender, and citizenship status and differ radically depending upon one's privilege or lack thereof. The choice to write an autobiography shaped by the form of the slave narrative, the captivity narrative, the prison narrative, or the internment narrative is likewise a choice with a range of political and rhetorical effects and is not simply a neutral or self-evident choice. Likewise immigration narratives provide a culturally intelligible form for many autobiographies and call attention to the ways in which "citizen," "alien," and "immigrant" are shifting and socially constructed categories. Immigration narratives sometimes draw on other culturally available narratives such as the bildungsroman, as we have seen with Jade Snow Wong and Richard Rodriguez. But other immigration autobiographies resist the individualist trajectory of the bildungsroman by explicitly challenging the terms by which the nation-state defines "citizen" and "Other." For example, in Judith Ortiz Cofer's *Silent Dancing: A Partial Remembrance of a Puerto Rican Childhood* (1990), the concept of *La Tristeza,* "the sadness that only place induces and only place cures" (p. 14), functions as a poignant way to theorize the pain of immigration and displacement. In Ernesto Galarza's *Barrio Boy: The Story of a Boy's Acculturation* (1971), the narrator constructs his life as a series of lessons in coming to gender, ethnic, and class consciousness. Self-consciously portraying his life as historically and psychologically representative of all Mexican immigrants to the United States, Galarza resists the psychological characterization of Chicanos as lacking "self-image" (p. 2) and insists that his identity, like his autobiography, is profoundly affected both by his childhood in Jalcocotán and by his participation in the U.S. Chicano labor movement of the 1960s.

The case of immigrant and ethnic autobiography brings up another issue that informs the study of self-life-writing: namely, the question of who can speak for whom. The politics of collaboration, editing, and translation inform much ethnic life writing throughout U.S. history as well as earlier and non-U.S. autobiographies such as Margery Kempe's *Book,* over which questions about the author's literacy continue to throw her status as autobiographer into doubt. In the U.S. context, a primary example of the politics of who can speak for whom is the history of nineteenth- and early-twentieth-century Native-American autobiographies, many of which were produced collaboratively between the native subject and a white ethnographer. For example, *The Life of Ma-ka-tai-me-she-kia-kiak, or Black Hawk* (1833), transcribed and edited by J. B. Patterson, and *Black Elk Speaks* (1932), transcribed and edited by John G. Neihardt, are both as-told-to autobiographies that call attention to the politics of cross-cultural representation, translation, and authorial agency. But the collaborative autobiography continues into the late twentieth century and on to the present day with classics such as *The Autobiography of Malcolm X* and the contemporary *testimonio* of Rigoberta Menchú, *I, Rigoberta Menchú: An Indian Woman in Guatemala* (1984), transcribed and edited by Elisabeth Burgos-Debray.

Menchú's *testimonio,* published and circulated in North America, calls for attention to the contemporary politics of globalization and the transnational production, circulation, and reception of life narratives in the "First World" about "Third World" subjects. But *testimonio* also differs from conventional autobiography. As Doris Sommer argues, whereas autobiography generally tells the story of an individualized "I" and its unique experiences, in *testimonio* the "I" becomes plural and stands in for a community of people who share a common identity and representative, rather than unique, experiences. In Menchú's case, this plural "I" has renewed public and scholarly interest in the question of "truth" in autobiography, as she has been accused of misrepresenting "her" experiences for aesthetic and political gain.

"Outlaw" Genres

Debates such as these over the slipperiness of autobiography as a genre have led contemporary scholars to turn to the increasingly complex production and reception of autobiographical "outlaw genres," which call attention to how generic distinctions have always been troubled, fluid, and contestable. In "Resisting Autobiography: Out-Law Genres and Transnational Feminist Subjects" (1992), Caren Kaplan argues that hybrid autobiographical forms constitute strategic political moves for women, ethnic, and immigrant authors who do not wish to write their lives according to culturally available scripts. Moreover, Sidonie Smith and Julia Watson's edited collection *Getting a Life: Everyday Uses of Autobiography* (1996), broadens conceptions of autobiography past purely written forms into everyday cultural practices that are in fact identity practices. These scholars point out that contemporary "autobiographical" texts call into question the generic boundaries between fiction, autobiography, biography, ethnography, myth, and performance. Authors are increasingly labeling their works "biomythography" (Audre Lorde's *Zami: A New Spelling of My Name*, 1982), "fictional autobioethnography" (Norma Elia Cantú's *Canícula: Snapshots of a Girlhood en la Frontera*, 1995), and other generic hybrids, and many authors are combining text with images and drawings that call attention to the visual as a self-representational practice. For example, Art Spiegelman's two-volume *Maus: A Survivor's Tale* (1986 and 1991) uses a comic book or "graphic novel" form in order to explore Spiegelman's troubled relationship with his father, a survivor of Auschwitz, and his life story. Cherríe Moraga's *Loving in the War Years: lo que nunca pasó por sus labios* (1983) and Gloria Anzaldúa's *Borderlands/La Frontera: The New Mestiza* (1987) combine personal essays and poems with history and feminist theory in English and Spanish to create hybrid forms that are both autobiographical and academic. And Theresa Hak Kyung Cha's multimedia *Dictee* (1982) draws on autobiography, biography, photographs, drawings, and cinema in order to explore the challenges of immigration for the Korean-American narrator and her mother.

Outlaw genres suggest that autobiography is moving from a generally textual narrative form into a range of complex oral, textual, visual, and performative cultural practices that explore the challenges of identity and self-representation in diverse ways and through diverse media. Coco Fusco and Guillermo Gómez-Peña's autobiographical performance art is one striking example of contemporary attempts to expand self-representation beyond textual forms. In *Year of the White Bear: Two Undiscovered Amerindians Visit the West* (1992), Fusco and Gómez-Peña, dressed up as exotic tribal figures from an unnamed and "undiscovered" island, displayed themselves in a cage in London, Madrid, and New York. Counting on their audiences' familiarity with the colonial practice of putting native peoples on display for Western audiences, Fusco and Gómez-Peña were surprised by the extent to which their performance, intended as a satire of popular nineteenth-century cultural expositions that presented cultural tribes as specimens, was taken literally and as truth by audiences. This ironic performance of racialized identity goes to the heart of questions of truth, authenticity, and audience expectations in "nonfictional" self-representational acts. It also illustrates the continuing need for autobiography to be theorized complexly and rhetorically, especially in the contemporary global landscape in which texts cross national, cultural, and language boundaries with ever-increasing frequency.

See also **Biography; Identity; Memory; Narrative; Person, Idea of the; Representation.**

BIBLIOGRAPHY

Bruss, Elizabeth W. *Autobiographical Acts: The Changing Situation of a Literary Genre.* Baltimore and London: Johns Hopkins University Press, 1976.

Butterfield, Stephen. *Black Autobiography in America.* Amherst: University of Massachusetts Press, 1974.

Eakin, Paul John. *How Our Lives Become Stories: Making Selves.* Ithaca, N.Y.: Cornell University Press, 1999.

Gilmore, Leigh. *The Limits of Autobiography: Trauma and Testimony.* Ithaca, N.Y.: Cornell University Press, 2001.

Hesford, Wendy S. *Framing Identities: Autobiography and the Politics of Pedagogy.* Minneapolis: University of Minnesota Press, 1999.

Kaplan, Caren. "Resisting Autobiography: Out-law Genres and Transnational Feminist Subjects." In *De/Colonizing the Subject: The Politics of Gender in Women's Autobiography,* edited by Sidonie Smith and Julia Watson, 115–138. Minneapolis: University of Minnesota Press, 1992.

Lejeune, Philippe. "The Autobiographical Pact." In *On Autobiography,* edited by Paul John Eakin. Translated by Katherine Leary. Minneapolis: University of Minnesota Press, 1989.

Lionnet, Françoise. *Autobiographical Voices: Race, Gender, Self-Portraiture.* Ithaca, N.Y.: Cornell University Press, 1989.

Smith, Sidonie, and Julia Watson. *Getting a Life: Everyday Uses of Autobiography.* Minneapolis: University of Minnesota Press, 1996.

———. *Reading Autobiography: A Guide to Interpreting Life Narratives.* Minneapolis: University of Minnesota Press, 2001.

Sommer, Doris. "'Not Just a Personal Story': Women's *Testimonios* and the Plural Self." In *Life Lines: Theorizing Women's Autobiography,* edited by Bella Brodzki and Celeste Schenck, 107–130. Ithaca, N.Y.: Cornell University Press, 1988.

Theresa A. Kulbaga
Wendy S. Hesford

AUTONOMY. *Autonomy* was first used by the ancient Greeks to describe city-states that had the power to legislate their own laws and direct the course of their own affairs. The etymology (*auto* [self] + *nomos* [law]) suggests self-governance or the imposition of law on oneself. The original implication of autonomy was pejorative when applied to the individual. When, for example, in Sophocles' tragedy, the chorus uses the word *autonomos* to describe the actions of Antigone, the audience is meant to understand that she has placed her own judgments above the laws of the city—a clear violation of Greek norms.

By the seventeenth or eighteenth century, however, people as well as governments came to be viewed as autonomous agents. If human reason is able to discern the difference between right and wrong, each person can formulate his or her own conception of how to live without relying on religious or secular authorities.

This idea had a decisive impact on liberal political philosophies, which claimed that each person is sovereign over himself, so that the only way governments can exercise control over their citizens is on the basis of consent, implicit or actual. In this way, authority flows not from the ruler downwards but from the citizens—conceived as free rational agents with an equal share in society—upwards. Along these lines, Jean-Jacques Rousseau (1712–1778) argues that freedom for the individual consists in obedience to self-imposed law, and the sovereignty of the state derives from laws that the people, as expressed in the general will, impose on themselves.

It is generally agreed that the classic formulation of the doctrine of autonomy occurs in Immanuel Kant (1724–1804). While God or a national leader can command certain actions and threaten punishment if we do not obey, each person is responsible for the actions he performs. In fact, Kant took this idea to its logical conclusion: every moral agent is both an end *in* itself and a being capable of legislating morality *for* itself.

Suppose God or a political leader orders us to do something. Why should we obey? No one doubts that life will be uncomfortable if we do not. But the question is not "What is it in our interest to do?" but "What are we obliged to do?" Kant's point is that obligation must derive from within: no external source can create obligation *for* us. Rather than say, "Do this" and "Don't do that," a person in authority must allow us to see for ourselves what is right. Not to do so is patronizing or degrading.

Kant therefore proclaims: "The will is thus not merely subject to the law but is subject in such a way that it must be regarded also as legislating for itself and only on this account as being subject to the law, of which it can regard itself as the author" (p. 38). Once we can regard ourselves as authors, reward and punishment no longer matter. The only thing that matters is whether we are convinced our action is right.

Even for as vocal a critic of Kant as John Stuart Mill (1806–1873), autonomy plays a central role. The best way to maximize the happiness of the greatest segment of society is to restrict the authority society can exercise over the individual and grant the individual sovereignty over his thought and person. The only warrant society has for interfering with this sovereignty is if the actions of one person impinge on the rights of another. Barring that, each person has the right to pursue his own happiness in whatever way he judges best.

Finally, one can find the doctrine of autonomy in the thought of John Rawls (1921–2002), for whom a just society is one which free and equal agents would choose for themselves if they had to take a place in that society but did not know what place they would be assigned—rich or poor, gifted or challenged, religious believer or atheist. This is simply a modern way of expressing the idea of implicit consent and saying that each person has the right to formulate and pursue his or her own conception of the good life.

Common Misconceptions

It is worth noting that, for Kant, autonomy does not permit me to do as I please. If it is degrading for someone to deny me the status of a moral agent, it is equally degrading to deny someone else that status. In Kant's view, the only law I can impose on myself in a coherent fashion is one that simultaneously upholds the dignity of others.

A second misconception concerns authorship. To say that I must *regard* myself as the author of something is not to say that I am the author in fact. Consider the Fifth Amendment to the U.S. Constitution. Although I was not present when the founders drafted it, by prohibiting torture it articulates a principle to which I am strongly committed. So I can take responsibility for it even if I had to learn about it in a civics class.

Finally, there is the question of scope. Although Kant defines autonomy as rational self-legislation, this does not mean it is based on an intelligence test. By rationality he simply means the ability to recognize that moral agents have obligations; as such, autonomy applies to all of humanity regardless of education or social standing.

Objections

Though it is often said that Kant's conception of autonomy leads to atheism, there is no reason why this has to be so. I can obey God as long as my reason for doing so is that the commandment to obey is morally valid; what I cannot do is obey blindly. The same is true of the government. Rather than urging obedience to legitimate authority, autonomy rejects the claim that legitimacy is irrelevant to authority: "Right or wrong, it's my country, my religion, my family, and so on."

Another objection claims that emphasizing individual sovereignty undermines virtues like trust, friendship, and cooperation. It does—if that means it is possible, in principle, for one person to be right and the rest of society wrong. But it hardly follows that one should go through life disregarding the advice of others and avoiding intimate relationships. To say that I should take responsibility for my actions is not to say that I must become a citadel. To live up to my obligations and fulfill myself as a person, I need the help of family, friends, and a host of institutions. All autonomy demands is that these groups or institutions respect my dignity as a free and rational agent (as well as respecting the dignity of others). At bottom, what autonomy denies is any form of political, religious, or moral tyranny.

See also **Enlightenment; Kantianism; Reason, Practical and Theoretical; Responsibility.**

BIBLIOGRAPHY

Allison, Henry E. *Kant's Theory of Freedom.* Cambridge, U.K.: Cambridge University Press, 1990.

Dworkin, Gerald. *The Theory and Practice of Autonomy.* Cambridge, U.K.: Cambridge University Press, 1988.

Kant, Immanuel. *Grounding for the Metaphysics of Morals.* 3rd ed. Translated by James W. Ellington. Indianapolis: Hackett, 1993.

Korsgaard, Christine M. *The Sources of Normativity.* Cambridge, U.K.: Cambridge University Press, 1996.

Mill, John Stuart. *On Liberty*. Indianapolis: Hackett, 1978.

Rousseau, Jean-Jacques. *Discourse on Political Economy and the Social Contract*. Translated by Christopher Betts. Oxford and New York: Oxford University Press, 1994.

Schneewind, J. B. *The Invention of Autonomy*. Cambridge, U.K.: Cambridge University Press, 1998.

Kenneth Seeskin

AVANT-GARDE.

This entry includes two subentries:

Overview
Militancy

OVERVIEW

Beginning in the nineteenth century, the term *avant-garde* has been applied to a wide range of social activities, from military to political to artistic. Since the early twentieth century, however, it has most commonly been used to designate those artists who, in making works of art, knowingly transgress aesthetic and social norms, seeking thus to scandalize, to disrupt established canons of taste, and to criticize the limits of society and project utopian alternatives.

In the common viewer or reader, avant-garde art often provokes indignation, uproar, outrage, puzzlement, or even violent rejection. Still, these audience responses, which have accompanied the artistic avant-garde throughout its history, do not lead back to a common set of stylistic and attitudinal traits that would allow for a clear, exhaustive conceptual analysis of avant-gardism. As an art-criticism term, *avant-garde* has been applied equally to the extremist subjectivism of the expressionists and the geometrical rationalism of Russian suprematism and constructivism; in music, to the serialism of Karlheinz Stockhausen (b. 1928) and the chance-operational compositions of John Cage (1912–1992); in literature, to the "transrational" pure-sound poetry of the Russian futurists, the densely allusive modernist epic of Ezra Pound (1885–1972), and the graphic and grammatical minimalism of concrete poets; in film, to the lush romanticism of Stan Brakhage's (1933–2003) handmade films and to the self-reflexive, analytical bent of Malcolm Le Grice (b. 1940); in architecture, to the exuberant utopianism of El Lissitzky (1890–1941) and the icy rationality of Mies van der Rohe (1886–1969); and in performance, to the minimalist, disciplined stage images of Samuel Beckett (1906–1989) and the Dionysian spontaneity of the Living Theater. Similarly, the political affiliations of the avant-garde offer no unitary picture: ranging from the tormented anarchism of the early expressionists to the studied political indifference of Marcel Duchamp (1887–1968), from the fascist partisanship of Italian futurism to the communist and Trotskyite engagements of the surrealists, from John Cage's playful antiauthoritarianism to the more regimented left-wing politics of many American artists of the later 1960s and the 1970s.

The term's conceptual blurriness, however, has hardly hampered its successful career in the arts. On the contrary, its indeterminate content and constantly shifting, constantly expanding application points to essential features of "avant-garde" dynamics in the art world. Less a coherent concept than a highly effective ideological metaphor, the term and the ideas surrounding it have proven a convenient vehicle for unsettling artistic conventions and canons of value, for proliferating technical innovations from one medium to another, and for communicating new aesthetic ideas across disciplinary as well as national borders.

Avant-Garde as Ideological Metaphor

The ideological components of avant-garde as a metaphor can be grouped under three headings: political, formal, and temporal-historical. The avant-garde artist, often a self-conscious member of a sectarian group or movement, creates artworks that at once lay claim to formal innovativeness and to their effective quality as social criticism. "Avant-garde" connotes precisely this implication of social criticism in acts of formal innovation and the artist's corollary struggle to find new artistic expressions—new figures and forms—to probe imaginatively beyond the strictures of a given social order. But this conflation of form and political meaning carries only two dimensions of avant-garde as metaphor. A further, temporal dimension gives that ideology its peculiar depth. "Avant-garde" also suggests an historical measure that lies in the future, a goal toward which artists are leading, while others merely follow. Through its artistic practice and products, the avant-garde adumbrates this end toward which the whole of a society is—or at least *should be*—heading. Where the avant-garde was, it is implied, there the social mainstream must inevitably find itself.

At first glance, the ideology is patently absurd. How could an abstract painting, a dadaist collage, an aleatory musical composition, or a film composed of mere patches of light and color be an anticipation of a new social norm, when it cannot even appeal to the present taste or understanding of a majority of citizens? At this point, however, the political and formal dimensions of the metaphor come to the ideological rescue of the avant-garde artist, by investing this estrangement of the artist from the audience with a paradoxical surplus value. The interpretative gap between the artist and his or her audience is taken by the artist (or by his or her critical champions) to represent the difference between the transfigured future, which the artist anticipates figurally, and the unredeemed present, which the audience literally embodies and from which the artist must break free. The audience's lack of understanding with respect to the avant-garde work thus in no way discredits or devalues the work in the artist's eyes. On the contrary, from the perspective of the avant-garde, this incomprehension indicates that the artist has authentically broken with the present and now stands in secret league with the future. The audience must be directed, perhaps even forced to catch up over time, to that which the artist has already discovered freely, through acts of artistic intuition and creation. But of course by that time the artist will have already moved on to new terrain, in perpetual revolt even against those utopian orders that presently can hardly be imagined.

Theories and Historiographies of the Avant-Garde

Theories and historiographies of the avant-garde have tended to emphasize one of the three dimensions of this basic ideological metaphor—political, formal, and temporal-historical—while downplaying or even excluding the others.

Examples of important formally-based theories and histories include the work of the art critic Clement Greenberg, who conceived of avant-gardism as the intensified focus of artworks on the essential properties of their media and attacked prominent avant-garde multimedial experimentation (such as minimalist sculpture) as leading to a bad theatricality akin to kitsch; Umberto Eco, who in his study *The Open Work* discussed the avant-garde's construction of works that require participatory completion by performers and audience; Julia Kristeva, who in *Revolution in Poetic Language,* sought to show how avant-garde poets such as Rimbaud and Mallarmé disrupted the grammatical means by which language functions as a vehicle of normal communication and ideology; and Marjorie Perloff, who traced out in a series of books the landmarks of a "poetics of indeterminacy," a futurist legacy, and a Wittgensteinian poetics.

Theorists of particular importance for the illumination of the political dimension of the avant-garde include Peter Bürger, whose *Theory of the Avant-Garde* focuses on the institutional status of art as autonomous from social life and the avant-garde's attempt to break down that autonomy and return art to its effective place in society; the urban historian Manfredo Tafuri, who considers the unanticipated role that avant-garde radicalism played in subordinating modern architecture and urbanism to big business, socialist planning, or the capitalist state; Fredric Jameson, who views the avant-garde as an intense site in which the contradictions of late capitalism were given aesthetic and experiential form; and the poststructuralist philosophers Jean-François Lyotard and Gilles Deleuze, who interpret avant-garde art as postconceptual models of embodied thinking in which mind, body, and technology merge in novel, free ways.

Theories focused on the temporal and historiographic dimension of the avant-garde are rarer than the other two, more dominant orientations, but these include the writings of the Frankfurt school philosopher Theodor Adorno, especially in his studies of modern music; the poet Octavio Paz's Harvard lectures, *Children of the Mire: Modern Poetry from Romanticism to the Avant-Garde*; Peter Osborne's *The Politics of Time: Modernity and Avant-Garde*; and Fredric Jameson's *A Singular Modernity*.

In the early years of the twenty-first century, however, a theory that accounts holistically for the interactions of all three dimensions of the avant-garde's basic metaphor—its constitutive identification of the formal with the political and the temporal-historical—had yet to appear.

See also **Arts: Overview; Avant-Garde: Militancy; Dada.**

BIBLIOGRAPHY

Adorno, Theodor W. *Philosophy of Modern Music.* Translated by Anne G. Mitchell and Wesley V. Blomster. New York: Continuum, 2003.

Bürger, Peter. *Theory of the Avant-Garde.* Translated by Michael Shaw. Minneapolis: University of Minnesota Press, 1984.

Deleuze, Gilles. *Francis Bacon: The Logic of Sensation.* Translated by Daniel W. Smith. Minneapolis: University of Minnesota Press, 2003.

Eco, Umberto. *The Open Work.* Translated by Anna Cancogni. Cambridge, Mass.: Harvard University Press, 1989.

Greenberg, Clement. "Avant-Garde and Kitsch." *Partisan Review* 6, no. 5 (1939): 34–49.

———. "Toward a Newer Laocoon." *Partisan Review* 7, no. 4 (1940): 296–310.

Jameson, Fredric. *Postmodernism; or, The Cultural Logic of Late Capitalism.* Durham, N.C.: Duke University Press, 1991.

———. *A Singular Modernity: Essay on the Ontology of the Present.* London and New York: Verso, 2002.

Kristeva, Julia. *Revolution in Poetic Language.* Translated by Margaret Waller. New York: Columbia University Press, 1984.

Lyotard, Jean-François. *Duchamp's Trans/formers.* Translated by Ian MacLeod. Venice, Calif.: Lapis, 1990.

Osborne, Peter. *The Politics of Time: Modernity and Avant-Garde.* London and New York: Verso, 1995.

Paz, Octavio. *Children of the Mire: Modern Poetry from Romanticism to the Avant-Garde.* Translated by Rachel Phillips. Cambridge, Mass.: Harvard University Press, 1974.

Perloff, Marjorie. *The Futurist Moment: Avant-Garde, Avant-Guerre, and the Language of Rupture.* Chicago: University of Chicago Press, 1986.

———. *The Poetics of Indeterminacy: Rimbaud to Cage.* Princeton, N.J.: Princeton University Press, 1981.

———. *Wittgenstein's Ladder: Poetic Language and the Strangeness of the Ordinary.* Chicago: University of Chicago Press, 1996.

Tafuri, Manfredo. *Architecture and Utopia: Design and Capitalist Development.* Translated by Barbara Luigia La Penta. Cambridge, Mass.: MIT Press, 1976.

———. *The Sphere and the Labyrinth: Avant-Gardes and Architecture from Piranesi to the 1970s.* Translated by Pellegrino d'Acierno and Robert Connolly. Cambridge, Mass.: MIT Press, 1987.

Tyrus Miller

MILITANCY

Gustave Courbet (1819–1877) was the first artist to assume the mantle of the avant-garde, savoring its military associations from within his outpost in the Pavillon du Réalisme he had constructed to exhibit his paintings that had been rejected by the official salon of the 1855 World's Fair. While the largest of these works—*Studio of the Painter: A Real Allegory* (1855)—could be thought to constitute a manifesto of Courbet's beliefs, he issued a written manifesto as well, in which he stated his determination to be "nothing but a painter."

Courbet's rejection from officialdom was institutionalized in 1863 by the Salon des Réfusés, which France had been forced to set up next to the recognized salon in the Palais des Beaux-Arts. It was to this salon of the refused artists that Édouard Manet (1832–1883) was consigned, showing his *Déjeuner sur l'herbe* and *Olympia* to the shrieks of laughter of the scandalized visitors. Indeed, it was Manet's own determination to be "nothing but a painter" that incensed his viewers,

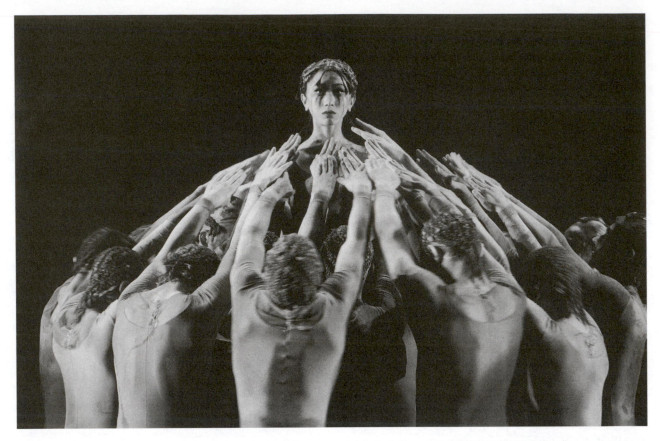

Dancers perform *The Rite of Spring,* **English National Ballet, 2003.** At the ballet's premiere in Paris in 1913, Igor Stravinsky's dissonant composition and the distinctly unusual choreography sparked outrage in the audience, which raised such an uproar that the dancers were unable to hear the music. © ROBBIE JACK/CORBIS

since his maintenance of the painterly qualities of his works led him to suppress the half-tones of representational shading and to flaunt wide expanses of percussive white paint in the eyes of his audience. "Nothing but a painter" was soon endowed with the epithet "*l'art pour l'art*" or art for art's sake, another mantle willingly assumed by the growing numbers of the self-professed avant-garde.

It is the position of Peter Bürger, whose *Theory of the Avant-Garde* (1984) remains the best treatment of this subject, that the withdrawal of the artist into the sanctuary of art for art's sake was the necessary condition for the formation of what he terms the "historical avant-garde," or the first wave of intensely militant activity that characterized the movements of futurism, cubism, dada, and surrealism during the opening decades of the twentieth century. Because their militancy was aimed at breaking down the barriers separating art from the life around it, it was necessary, Bürger maintains, that these barriers really existed. By incorporating the columns they cut from their daily newspapers into works now called *collage* (or gluing), the cubists transgressed the sanctity of the special province of the work of art. This same principle of transgression was practiced by the dada *photomonteurs,* such as John Heartfield and Hannah Hoch, who extended the collage technique to include photographic reproductions from illustrated magazines in order to wage political battle against the mounting powers of fascism.

Another obvious example of this avant-garde indifference to the separation of art and life is the readymade, introduced by Marcel Duchamp (1887–1963) in the form of the urinal he entered into the New York Salon des Independents in 1917. For Bürger, these transgressive modes of operation constituted specific paradigms of avant-garde attack against the boundaries of *l'art pour l'art*. Further, he argued, after the historic avant-garde had come to an end during World War II, the postwar avant-garde had no ground on which to maneuver except that of repeating the already-explored paradigms of the earlier avant-garde: the readymade, the photo-montage, the monochrome painting, the assemblage. Bürger's designation for this state of affairs and the artists consigned to it is "neo-avant-garde," which would include the photo-montage canvases of Robert Rauschenberg (b. 1925), the readymades of Andy Warhol 1928–1987), the monochromes of Lucio Fontana (1899–1968), and so forth.

The cries of rage that greeted Manet's *Olympia* soon became the hallmark of the avant-garde as each new transgression elicited it own storm of protest, such as the audience that stormed out of the theater during Igor Stravinsky's (1882–1971) *Rite of*

Spring or the thunder of catcalls hurled at *Parade,* scored by Erik Satie (1866–1925) for typewriters and other machines.

The philosopher Stanley Cavell posits that these expressions of anger, triggered by the fear of being hoodwinked by a fraudulent work, are what characterizes modernism itself, such that "the dangers of fraudulence, and of trust, are essential to the experience of art" (pp. 188–189). In relation to the avant-garde, he writes, "What looks like 'breaking with tradition,' in the successions of art is not really that; or is that only after the fact, looking historically or critically; or is that only as a result not as a motive: the unheard of appearance of the modern in art is an effort not to break, but to keep faith with tradition. It is perhaps fully true of Pop Art that its motive is to break with the tradition of painting and sculpture; and the result is not that the tradition is broken, but that these works are irrelevant to that tradition, i.e., they are not paintings, whatever their pleasures" (pp. 206–207).

The scholar and critic Leo Steinberg has also emphasized this problem of fraudulence dogging the most important works of modernism and striking not just the outsider or layperson, but the inner circle of artists as well. In "Contemporary Art and the Plight of Its Public," he reports Henri Matisse's anger at Pablo Picasso's *Les Demoiselles d'Avignon* (1907), which he called "Picasso's hoax," and Georges Braque's refusal of the picture with: "It is as though we were supposed to exchange our usual diet for one of tow and paraffin."

Two important essays by the critic Clement Greenberg analyze the relation between the avant-garde and modernism: "Avant-Garde and Kitsch" (1939) and "Modernist Painting" (1960). As Greenberg defines it, in the 1939 essay, "Kitsch is a product of the industrial revolution which urbanized the masses of Western Europe and America and established what is called universal literacy" (1986, p. 11). He gives as its examples: "popular, commercial art and literature with their chromeotypes, magazine covers, illustrations, ads, slick and pulp fiction, comics, Tin Pan Alley music tap dancing, Hollywood movies, etc., etc." (p. 11). If, as he puts it, "Kitsch is vicarious experience and faked sensations" (p. 12), there were artists who felt the need to resist this fraudulence. These, to which are given the name "avant-garde," "sought to maintain the high level of [their] art by both narrowing it and raising it to the expectation of an absolute in which all relationships would be either resolved or beside the point. 'Art for art's sake' and 'pure poetry' appear, and subject matter or content becomes something to be avoided like a plague" (p. 8). In order to pursue this "purity" the avant-garde artist detaches himself from bourgeois society to which he is nonetheless attached, as Greenberg puts it, "by an umbilical cord of gold."

"Modernist Painting," assuming the existence of the avant-garde, gives an account of how the "narrowing and raising" of a given art began historically, and what its new logic consists of. Defining modernism as an Enlightenment phenomenon, Greenberg locates its onset with Kant who "used logic to establish the limits of logic" (1993, p. 85). What then follows is that "the essence of Modernism lies . . . in the use of characteristic methods of a discipline to criticize the discipline itself, not in order to subvert it but in order to entrench it more firmly

in its area of competence" (p. 85). What each art sought, Greenberg argued, was to exhibit "not only that which was unique and irreducible in art in general, but also that which was unique and irreducible in each particular art" (p. 86). What follows from this is that "the enterprise of self-criticism in the arts become one of self-definition with a vengeance" (p. 86).

For painting itself, self-criticism produced as defining features: the flat surface, the shape of the support, and the properties of the pigment, all of which needed, under Modernism, to be acknowledged openly. "Manet's," Greenberg explains, "became the first Modernist pictures by virtue of the frankness with which they declared the flat surfaces on which they were painted" (1993, p. 86).

Greenberg's avant-garde continues through the twentieth century, picking up ever-new strength and certainty. For him, Bürger's "neo-avant-garde" could only be a version of Kitsch, the triumph of not-art in place of the real thing.

See also **Avant-Garde: Overview; Dada; Modernism; Surrealism.**

BIBLIOGRAPHY

Bürger, Peter. *Theory of the Avant-Garde.* Translated by Michael Shaw. Minneapolis: University of Minnesota Press, 1984.
Cavell, Stanley. "Music Discomposed." In his *Must We Mean What We Say? A Book of Essays.* New York: Scribners, 1969.
Greenberg, Clement. *The Collected Essays and Criticism.* Edited by John O'Brian. Vol. 1. Chicago: University of Chicago Press, 1986.
———. *The Collected Essays and Criticism.* Edited by John O'Brian. Vol. 4. Chicago: University of Chicago Press, 1993.
Poggioli, Renato. *The Theory of the Avant-Garde.* Translated by Michael Shaw. Minneapolis: University of Minnesota Press, 1984.
Steinberg, Leo. "Contemporary Art and the Plight of Its Public." In his *Other Criteria: Confrontations with Twentieth-Century Art.* New York: Oxford University Press, 1972.

Rosalind Krauss

AZTLÁN. As a region in mythical geography, Aztlán (the land of the [white] herons) has a long history. According to the Náhuatl myth, the Aztecs (whose name is derived from Aztlán) were the last remaining tribe of seven, and they were advised by their god Huitzilopochtli to leave Aztlán in search of the promised land, which they would know by an eagle sitting on a cactus, devouring a serpent. They found it, and there they built Tenochtitlan, now Mexico City. Later the Aztecs remembered the region of their origin as an earthly paradise. Wanting to know more about it, Moctezuma Ilhuicamina (r. 1440–1469) sent his priests in search of Aztlán. They found it and gave the ruler a hyperbolic description of the place, as told by Diego Durán (1537–1588) in his *Historia de las Indias de Nueva-España y Islas de Tierra Firme,* a work finished in 1581 and translated into English in 1964 as *The Aztecs.* Although other early historians mention Aztlán, Durán presents the most elaborated description of the utopian nature of the city.

With few exceptions, the topic of mythical Aztlán was forgotten until the 1960s, when the rebirth of the myth flourished in Chicano thought. The cultural nationalists—one of the most important branches of the Chicano movement—appropriated the term *Aztlán* to establish the indigenous nature of their culture, a characteristic central to their philosophy. The appropriation of the myth took place during the "Crusade for Justice Youth Conference," held in Denver in March 1969. It was there that for the first time the myth of Aztlán was mentioned in a Chicano document, "El Plan Espiritual de Aztlán."

"El Plan," which owes its creation to the poet Alurista, became the cultural nationalists' manifesto. First, it establishes the unique nature of Chicano culture, since La Raza (the Bronze race) has an Aztec origin. The Spanish word *raza* means "the people," and *raza de bronce* means "the brown people," who claim to be descendants of the Aztecs. Second, it identifies Aztlán as the Mexican territory ceded to the United States in 1848—that is, present-day California, Arizona, New Mexico, and parts of Colorado. Third, following one of the basic ideas of the Mexican Revolution, it recognizes that the land belongs to those who work it. And fourth, it identifies the Chicano nation with Aztlán.

Aztlán became the symbol most used by Chicanos and Chicanas—activists as well as authors—writing about the history, the culture, or the destiny of their people. In April 1969 a group of concerned activists met in Santa Barbara and drafted *El Plan de Santa Barbara: A Chicano Plan for Higher Education*. Recommendation number nine deals with students' organizations: "The various students groups, MAYA, MASC, UMAS, adopt a united name as symbol and promise; such as CAUSA (Chicano Alliance for United Student Action) or MECHA (Movimiento Estudiantil Chicano de Azatlán)" (p. 22). The name MECHA was adopted and is much in the news, as during the 2003 elections for governor of California one of the candidates, Cruz Bustamante, was attacked for having belonged to MECHA during his student days.

During the spring of 1970 the first number of the journal *Aztlán* (still in existence) was published, and in it the plan was reproduced in both English and Spanish. The prologue consists of a piece by the Chicano poet Alurista (b. 1947), "Poem in Lieu of Preface," in which he unites the mythical Aztec past with the present. From that year on books based on the concept of Aztlán multiplied. The myth of Aztlán was popular not only among academics, but also among the common people. According to Michael Pina:

> A cultural renaicense inspired by the powerful ideological thrust of cultural nationalism swept through the barrios of the Southwest. . . . Chicanos turned to pre-Hispanic myths and symbols. . . . The most outstanding example of this practice is illustrated by the vital role that the Aztec myth of Aztlán played in the development of Chicano nationalism. (Anaya and Lomelí, p. 40)

Artists and dramatists also took up the concept. In 1971 Luis Valdez (b. 1940), who had helped César Chávez organize the farm workers, published his collection *Actos* (one-act plays). In the preliminary piece, "Notes on Chicano Theater," Valdez states, "The concept for a national theatre for La Raza is intimately related to our evolving nationalism in Aztlán" (p. 3).

The myth has been utilized with advantage for political purposes. The novels of Miguel Méndez (b. 1930) and Rudolfo Anaya (b. 1937) are examples representative of two aspects of cultural nationalism based on the concept of Aztlán. In *Peregrinos de Aztlán* (1974) Méndez depicts the plight of the Yaqui Indians of the border in their peregrination back to Aztlán. The narrator, the old Yaqui Loreto Maldonado, tormented by the memories of his fallen and abused people, wants to take them back to Aztlán, the lost paradise.

Anaya's *Heart of Aztlán* (1976) is also a novel about the search for Aztlán. Clemente Chávez, a man of some years, goes to the mountains, guided by the blind minstrel Crispín, on a truly imaginary pilgrimage: "They walked to the land where the sun rises, and . . . they found new signs, and the signs pointed them back to the center, back to Aztlán" (Anaya, pp. 129–130). For Anaya, Aztlán is not a political concept but a personal one. Clemente finds Aztlán in his own heart. "Time stood still, and in that enduring moment he felt the rhythm of the heart of Aztlán beat to the measure of his own heart. . . . A joyful power coursed from the dark womb-heart of the earth into his soul and he cried out I AM AZTLAN!" (Anaya, p. 131). This spiritual interpretation of Aztlán has been criticized by writers who believe that Chicano literature should be social, that literature of this type "didn't contribute to that movement, or to bettering the life of the people in any way" (Johnson and Apodaca, p. 424).

For Clemente the search for Aztlán has ended. In a similar way it has also ended for the followers of cultural nationalism, as the movement—like the social movements of other ethnic groups—came to an end in the early 1980s. Even Alurista, the creator of the nationalist concept of Aztlán, in an interview with Wolfgang Binder agreed about the danger of idealizing the Aztecs and their myths. "Yes, without question, and I see it now" he said in 1981. "At the moment we are talking of a period during which the call of arms was the cry for self determination. So it was very important to be proud of everything we had been" (p. 4). In the early 2000s younger Chicanos and Chicanas considered the idealization of Aztec mythology as belonging to a romantic period in the history of their culture. While the symbolism of Aztlán still resonated in the literature, art, and political legacies that it helped inspire, few idealized that aspect of their historical past.

See also **Chicano Movement; Nationalism: Cultural Nationalism.**

BIBLIOGRAPHY

Anaya, Rudolfo. *Heart of Aztlán*. Berkeley, Calif.: Justa, 1976.
Anaya, Rudolfo, and Francisco Lomelí, eds. *Aztlán: Essays on the Chicano Homeland*. Albuquerque, N. Mex.: El Norte, 1989. See especially Michael Pina, "The Archaic, Historical, and Mythicized Dimensions of Aztlán," 14–48, and "El Plan Espiritual de Aztlán," 1–5.

Binder, Wolfgang, ed. *Partial Autobiographies: Interviews with Twenty Chicano Poets.* Erlangen, Germany: Palm and Enke, 1985.

Johnson, David, and David Apodaca. "Myth and the Writer: A Conversation with Rudolfo Anaya." In *Rudolfo A. Anaya: Focus on Criticism,* edited by César A. Gonzalez, 414–438. La Jolla, Calif.: Lalo, 1990.

Plan de Santa Barbara: A Chicano Plan for Higher Education. Oakland, Calif.: La Causa Publications, 1969.

Valdez, Luis. *Actos: By Luis Valdez y El Teatro Campesino.* San Juan Bautista, Calif.: Cucaracha, 1971.

Luis Leal

B

BARBARISM AND CIVILIZATION. Barbarism and civilization are salt and pepper concepts that are inextricably interlinked. In the Western world, "barbarism" is derived from the classical Greek word *barbaros* (barbarian) that referred originally to foreigners who did not speak Greek. In the modern world, barbarism carries a negative connotation of unrefined and savage. "Civilization" is derived from the Latin word *civis* (citizen) that referred originally to those living in a Roman city. In the modern world, civilization carries a positive connotation of education and sophistication.

Although "barbarians" and "barbarism" come from the ancient world, "civilization" does not. Fernand Braudel maintains that "civilization" first appeared in 1732 in regard to French jurisprudence that "denoted an act of justice or a judgement which turned a criminal trial into civil proceedings" (p. 3). In 1752 the statesman Anne Robert Jacques Turgot used "civilization" to describe a process of being civilized. "Civilization" stood firmly against its opposite of "barbarism." By 1772 "civilization" and its mate "culture" replaced "civility" in England and fostered *Zivilization* (civilization) alongside the older *Bildung* (culture) in Germany (see Braudel, p. 4).

Friedrich Engels: Barbarism and Civilization
Against this backdrop, the dual concepts of barbarism and civilization emerged in the works of Friedrich Engels (1820–1895), who was influenced by Lewis H. Morgan's (1818–1881) pathbreaking study *Ancient Society* (1878). Engels writes: "Barbarism—the period during which man learns to breed domestic animals and to practice agriculture, and acquires methods of increasing the supply of natural products by human activity. Civilization—the period in which man learns a more advanced application of work to the products of nature, the period of industry and of art" (1972, p. 93). Homeric Greeks, native Italian tribes, Germanic tribes of Caesar's time, and the Vikings represent the upper stages of barbarism. Citing descriptions in Homer's *Iliad*, Engels continues: "Fully developed iron tools, the bellows, the hand mill, the potter's wheel, the making of oil and wine, metal work . . . the wagon and the war chariot, shipbuilding with beams and planks, the beginnings of architecture as art, walled cities with towers and battlements, the Homeric epic and a complete mythology—these are the chief legacy brought by the Greeks from barbarism into civilization" (p. 92).

It is evident that modern Western ideas of barbarism and civilization have a hierarchy built in. On the one hand, barbarians are seen as belligerent precursors of civilization. On the other hand, civilization is considered a culturally advanced stage of human development. Many of these ideas begin in ancient Greece.

Herodotus and the Barbarians
The Greek historian Herodotus (c. 484–420 B.C.E.) divides the world into those who speak Greek and those who do not. Barbarians are the latter. Herodotus writes: "But the Greek stock, since ever it was, has always used the Greek language, in my judgment. But though it was weak when it split off from the Pelasgians [originary Greek tribes], it has grown from something small to be a multitude of peoples by the accretion chiefly of the Pelasgians but of many other barbarian peoples as well" (p. 57). Herodotus further punctuates the Greek language: "But before that, it seems to me, the Pelasgian people, so long as it spoke a language other than Greek, never grew great anywhere" (p. 57). The Greeks saw the barbarians as fascinating enemies whose "natural status" was that of the slave (see Harrison, p. 3). Herodotus scrutinizes two "barbarian" cultures on the opposite ends of the spectrum: the Egyptians and the Scythians. In Egypt, the sky rarely rains while the river always rises when others fall; in Scythia, the sky rains in summer but not in winter while the river never changes; in Egypt, the Nile unites the land while in Scythia, the Danube divides the land into many districts; in Egypt there is one king while in Scythia there are many; in Egypt, they believe themselves to be the oldest of peoples while the Scythians believe themselves to be the youngest; in Egypt, culture is marked by strict religious rituals that rarely change while the Scythian culture illustrates constant change and varying rituals (see Herodotus, pp. 138–290, cf. Redfield, pp. 35–37). As Herodotus claims, the Egyptians know many things while the Scythians know one great thing, "how no invader who comes against them can ever escape and how none can catch them if they do not wish to be caught. For this people has no cities or settled forts; they carry their houses with them and shoot with bows from horseback; they live off herds of cattle, not from tillage, and their dwellings are on their wagons" (p. 298). At the time of Alexander the Great (356–323 B.C.E.), the Persians were the main barbarian adversaries. Fighting his way through Asia, he arrived at Maracanda (Samarkand, Uzbekistan) in Sogdiana, the first meeting point of Eastern and Western civilizations (see Arrian, pp. 351–537). Although Alexander occupied the fortified citadel, he was unable to secure it because of counterattacks by Scythian coalitions. A major city on the Silk Road, Samarkand was the site for Chinese paper mills established in the early eighth century (see Gernet, p. 288) and the center of a Turkic-Mongol empire under Tamerlane in the fourteenth century (see Nicolle). Tamerlane's grandson, Ulugh-Beg (1394–1449), was an astronomer who built

Attila Burning Townships during the Invasion of Italy, **woodcut, c. 19th century.** Embodying the barbarian threat to Western civilization, Attila the Hun (406?–453) conquered much of Central Europe. Although tribes such as the Huns were all overthrown by stronger forces of civilization, they represented what Arnold J. Toynbee termed a barbarian "heroic age." © BETTMANN/CORBIS

an observatory at Samarkand and was the first since Ptolemy to compile a star chart.

Toynbee's Rhythm of History

Paying close attention to the ancient Greeks and Romans, Arnold Toynbee did not subscribe to a linear, hierarchical view of civilization. Even Karl Marx and Friedrich Engels's dialectical approach to history resulted in successive stages of development toward a desired end (see Marx and Engels, pp. 23–40). Although Toynbee's own vision of human history was nostalgic for the lost past and pessimistic for the future, his comparative theory of civilizations (East and West) was linked to an acute understanding of Greek philosophy and an essentialist view of Chinese philosophy. Toynbee concentrates on the idea of a "rhythm" of history. On the one hand, Empedocles' ancient Greek philosophy sees the universe caught in the ebb and flow of a rhythmic alternation of the "integrating force" of love and the "disintegrating force" of hate, a unity arising from plurality and a plurality arising from unity (see Toynbee, 1935, pp. 200–201). On the other hand, Chinese philosophy sees the universe caught in the ebb and flow of a rhythmic alternation of the "shadow" force of yin and the "sunshine" force of yang: "Each in turn comes into

the ascendant at the other's expense; yet even at the high tide of its expansion it never quite submerges the other, so that, when its tide ebbs, as it always does after reaching high-water mark, there is still a nucleus of the other element left free to expand, as its perpetual rival and partner contracts" (p. 202). Toynbee's assessment of the growth and breakdown of civilizations is a yin-yang beating out of "the song of creation" through challenge and response, withdrawal and return, and rout and rally (Toynbee, 1939, p. 324).

Through this rhythm of history, tensions between state and church are disrupted by an interregnum of barbarians that Toynbee calls collectively the *Völkerwanderung* (the wandering peoples). In the Western world, this refers to Germanic and Slavic tribes from the north on the borders of the Greco-Roman civilization as well as Sarmatians and Huns from the Steppes of Eastern Europe. Although they were all overthrown by stronger forces of civilization, these wandering tribes represent a barbarian "heroic age" (Toynbee, 1939). The Vandals and Ostrogoths were destroyed by Roman counteroffensives, while Visigoths succumbed to both Frankish and Arabian assaults. In the long run, Toynbee felt the barbarians had little impact on Western civilization because the church was more powerful in regard to cultural and philosophical transmissions (see 1935, pp. 58–63, cf. Bury, pp. 177–230).

Toynbee could not apply his yin-yang theory of history in any great detail to China itself. In *Reconsiderations,* he laments the lack of a classical Chinese upbringing: "I should, of course, have taken Chinese, not Hellenic, history as my model, and I should have seen Chinese history as a series of successive realizations of the ideal of a universal state, punctuated by intermediate lapses into disunion and disorder . . . the Yin-Yang rhythm would be cyclical without having any regular periodicity" (1960, p. 188).

China's Yin-Yang Polarities

A closer look at China validates Toynbee's suspicions. China had ancient words for both "civilization" and "barbarism" that are still in use today. *Wenming* refers literally to a bright and clear culture that possesses writing, art, and literature. In China's classical world, the most used term for barbarian was *hu* (beard), which gave rise to expressions such as *huche* (talk nonsense) (see Wilkinson, p. 724). The Chinese word for barbarian combined both the Roman idea of *barbarus* ("the bearded one") and the Greek idea of *barbar* ("talk nonsense"). The Han dynasty expression *yiyi gong yi* ("use barbarians to attack barbarians") (see Wilkinson, p. 723) is reminiscent of Julius Caesar's deployment of subdued Germanic and Gallic cavalry at Alesia against Vercingetorix's Gallic horsemen (see Caesar, pp. 186, 218, 221).

Although the Greeks, Romans, and Japanese share a centralized view of their own respective civilizations, it is only the Chinese who name theirs as such. In the Wei and Jin periods (220–420 C.E.), Zhongguo (Middle Kingdom) and Huaxia (Cathay) were syncopated into Zhonghua (Central Cultural Florescence) (see Smith, p. 3), making civilization both a geographic and cultural entity for all under heaven. Even today, the term for "middle kingdom" is retained in the name of the People's

Republic of China (*Zhonghua renmin gongheguo*). As Richard Smith, a renowned historian of China, maintains: "Barbarian conquest affirmed and reinforced this Sinocentric world view rather than shattering it" (p. 3). Like Toynbee, Smith sees every aspect of Chinese civilization, including barbarian intrusion, as following the polarities of yin and yang. He writes: "Yin and yang were, then (1) cosmic forces that produced and animated all natural phenomena; (2) terms used to identify recurrent, cyclical patterns of rise and decline, waxing and waning; (3) comparative categories, describing dualistic relationships that were inherently unequal but almost invariably complementary" (p. 4). Hence, yin and yang are mutually conditioning linked opposites that are co-constitutive of Chinese cosmology. When Smith writes that "the boundaries of China waxed and waned in response to periodic bursts of either Chinese expansion or 'barbarian' invasion" (p. 11), he echoes Toynbee's universal rhythm for civilizations as "the perpetual alternation of a Yin state of quiescence with a Yang burst of activity" (1960, p. 188).

Mongols and Manchu Emperors

Non-Han peoples as "outsiders" were "dynamically and inextricably intertwined" with Chinese civilization (Smith, p. 11). Confucians felt that barbarians could adopt Chinese culture and become Chinese (see Ebrey, p. 179). Therefore, the history of China is the history of barbarian withdrawal and return. The pressure of the Ruzhen (Jurchen descendants of the Xiongnu) invasion in the Jin dynasty and the Mongol attacks of the thirteenth century forced the southern courts to establish strict civil service examinations. As the Mongols Genghis Khan (c. 1162–1227) and his grandson Kublai Khan (r. 1260–1294) adapted to Chinese culture, Confucian-style civil service examinations were reestablished. In 1313 the commentaries of the neo-Confucian Zhu Xi were included in these examinations, where they lasted until 1904 (see Smith, p. 37). The overthrow of the Mongols by Chinese patriots in the Ming dynasty saw the reinstatement of a Qin-Han structure of civil, military, and despotic reign. In turn, the Ming were ousted by the Manchu (Tungusic descendants of the Ruzhen), who marked the beginning of the Qing dynasty. The Manchu were organized under banners or civil-military units distinguished by colored flags. Before 1644, their administrative units for conscription and taxation recruited Chinese and Mongols. By 1648, the "multi-ethnic army" of bannermen included less than 16 percent Manchu (see Naquin and Rawski, pp. 4–5). Like the Mongols, the Manchu adopted Chinese culture, allowing for a renaissance of ancient philosophy and literature (see Goulding). While the first emperor of China burned most of the books in the known world, the Manchu established the largest known library that included literature and philosophy of China's classical age (see Smith, p. 3; cf. Wilkinson, pp. 273–277, 485). Although censorship saw the destruction of many Ming books, the Complete Library of the Four Treasuries (1772–1782) resulted in seven sets of thirty-six thousand volumes (see Naquin and Rawski, p. 66). Whereas the Western world annihilated barbarians in a quest for civilization, the Eastern world accommodated them as co-constitutive elements of its yin-yang cosmology.

See also **Confucianism; History, Idea of; Marxism; Yin and Yang.**

BIBLIOGRAPHY

Arrian. *History of Alexander and Indica.* Vol. 1. Translated by P. A. Brunt. Cambridge, Mass.: Harvard University Press, 1976.

Braudel, Fernand. *A History of Civilizations.* Translated by Richard Mayne. New York: Penguin Books, 1995.

Bury, J. B. *The Invasion of Europe by the Barbarians.* New York: W. W. Norton and Company, 2000. First published in 1928.

Caesar, Julius. *The Conquest of Gaul.* Translated by S. A. Handford. London: Penguin Books, 1951.

Curtin, Jeremiah. *The Mongols: A History.* Boston: Little, Brown, 1908. Reprint, Cambridge, Mass.: Da Capo Press, 2003.

Ebrey, Patricia Buckley. *Cambridge Illustrated History of China.* Cambridge, U.K.: Cambridge University Press, 1999.

Engels, Friedrich. *The Origin of the Family, Private Property, and the State.* Edited by Eleanor Burke Leacock. Translated by Alec West. New York: International Publishers, 1972.

Gernet, Jacques. *A History of Chinese Civilization.* 2nd ed. Translated by J. R. Foster and Charles Hartman. Cambridge, U.K.: Cambridge University Press, 1996.

Goulding, Jay. "'Three Teachings Are One': The Ethical Intertwinings of Buddhism, Confucianism, and Daoism." In *The Examined Life—Chinese Perspectives: Essays on Chinese Ethical Traditions,* edited by Xinyan Jiang. Binghamton, N.Y.: Global Academic Publishing, Binghamton University, 2002.

Harrison, Thomas. "General Introduction." In *Greeks and Barbarians,* edited by Thomas Harrison. London: Routledge, 2002.

Herodotus. *The History.* Translated by David Grene. Chicago: University of Chicago Press, 1987.

Marx, Karl, and Friedrich Engels. *The Communist Manifesto.* Edited by Samuel H. Beer. Northbrook, Ill.: AHM Publishing, 1955.

Morgan, David. *The Mongols.* Oxford, and New York: Blackwell, 1986.

Morgan, Lewis Henry. *Ancient Society.* New York: Henry Holt, 1878. Reprint, Tucson: University of Arizona Press, 1985.

Naquin, Susan, and Evelyn S. Rawski. *Chinese Society in the Eighteenth Century.* New Haven, Conn.: Yale University Press, 1987.

Nicolle, David. *The Age of Tamerlane.* Oxford: Osprey Publishing, 1990.

Redfield, James, "Herodotus the Tourist." In *Greeks and Barbarians,* edited by Thomas Harrison. London: Routledge, 2002.

Smith, Richard J. *China's Cultural Heritage: The Qing Dynasty, 1644–1912.* 2nd ed. Boulder, Colo.: Westview Press, 1994.

Toynbee, Arnold J. *A Study of History.* Vol. 1. 2nd ed. London: Oxford University Press, 1935.

———. *A Study of History.* Vol. 6. London: Oxford University Press, 1939.

———. *A Study of History.* Vol. 12: *Reconsiderations.* London: Oxford University Press, 1960.

Wilkinson, Endymion. *Chinese History: A Manual.* Rev. and enlarged. Cambridge, Mass.: Harvard University Asia Center, 2000.

Jay Goulding

BAROQUE. *See* **Periodization of the Arts.**

BELIEF. *See* **Religion.**

BEAUTY AND UGLINESS. Beauty is a vital and central element of human experience. It is associated with pleasure, which influences personal choices and cultural developments. Poets praise it, artists strive to capture it in their works, moralists warn against its deceiving influence, scientists seek to uncover its secrets, and philosophers reflect on its illusive nature. Expressions of the vitality of beauty in its role in everyday life are found in any culture. The attraction of beauty, the desire to be beautiful and obtain beautiful objects, is universal, although the manifestations of this desire vary across cultures and ages. Classical Western philosophy has regarded beauty as one of the three fundamental concepts of human understanding: truth (and falsehood), good (and evil), beauty (and ugliness). However, in the seventeenth century beauty was considered a marginal concept, while in the twentieth century it came to be regarded as dispensable altogether.

Beauty is typically related to the visual field, but is not limited to it. The Hebrew Bible attributes beauty mainly to human appearance and natural scenery, but also to the voice (Ezekiel, 33:32), to wisdom (Ezekiel, 28:7), and to God (Psalms, 50:2). The ancient Greeks ascribed beauty to things that are morally good, appropriate, and pleasing, be they natural objects or artifacts, tangible and concrete or abstract, personal deeds, or social institutions. In China beauty refers to wealth, longevity, talent, good reputation, and behavior. There appears to be a cross-cultural agreement that beauty is relevant to all aspects of life, but the nature of the concept and its actual applications are a matter of constant dispute. The variety of tastes and their suppleness, the difficulties in justifying judgments of beauty (and in determining their common ground) indicate that the idea of beauty is far more complicated than the way it appears in everyday experience.

Theories of beauty typically focus on two aspects: defining beauty, and determining its function and significance.

Definitions of Beauty

In the *Greater Hippias,* Plato (c. 428–348 or 347 B.C.E.) ascribes to Socrates the viewpoint that knowledge of beauty is a prerequisite for actual applications: one cannot properly distinguish between beautiful and ugly objects without knowing what beauty is. On the other hand, in the *Symposium,* Plato has Diotima argue that knowledge of beauty begins with direct experience of particular cases and knowledge of the abstract form of beauty is the highest and final stage, distilled from everyday experience.

Direct experience, Socrates claims, is unreliable. It reveals a complex of contradicting qualities that cohabit in the same object: any beautiful object is at the same time not beautiful when compared with a higher beauty. Appearance can be misleading. A person may appear beautiful when wearing suitable clothes, although he is not truly beautiful. Socrates in fact dismisses all expressions of physical beauty as untrustworthy. The ultimate beauty that contains no contradicting elements is beyond earthly experience. Plato portrays such absolute beauty in the *Phaedo,* where Socrates sees its heavenly form. Socrates rejects further the idea that beauty is that which functions properly: an object may function well, but if its purpose is evil, the object is not beautiful. He also disagrees that beauty should be defined as a cause of delight. The good, Socrates argues, also causes delight, and the two should be kept distinct.

Socrates concludes in the *Greater Hippias* that beauty is difficult to define. Voltaire (1694–1778) goes further to argue that beauty, due to its relativist nature, is not just difficult but impossible to define. In his *Philosophical Dictionary* (1764) Voltaire writes that the toad sees beauty in large round eyes and a flat snout, and the devil sees beauty in a pair of horns and four claws. Epicharmus (c. 530–c. 440 B.C.E.), the comic dramatist, similarly remarks that a dog considers a dog the most beautiful creature, and equally an ox prefers an ox, a donkey a donkey, and a pig a pig. Realizing that beauty has no common core, Voltaire believes that one had better save oneself the trouble of attempting to study its nature.

Neither the difficulties presented by Socrates nor Voltaire's reservations have discouraged philosophers, artists, critics, and scientists from reflecting upon the nature of beauty throughout the centuries. Attempts to define beauty can be divided into two main groups: theories that regard beauty as a form of order and theories that regard beauty as a kind of pleasure. Theories of beauty may be divided further according to the logical status assigned to beauty: objective, subjective, relative, and relational. The objective approach asserts that beauty inheres in the object, and that judgments of beauty have objective validity. The subjective approach maintains that beauty is not a quality of the object but rather a creation of the mind. Relativism tends to associate beauty with cultural values, and the relational approach regards beauty as a product of both the object and the contemplative mind.

Beauty as a form of order. The Pythagoreans believed that beauty is a manifestation of harmonious, mathematical relations such as the golden section. In this proportion a straight line, *c,* is divided by two unequal parts, *a* and *b,* in such a way that the ratio of the smaller, *a,* to the greater part, *b,* is the same as that of the greater part, *b,* to the whole, *c.* Ugliness is the expression of disorder and a lack of rational proportions. Beauty was thus considered an objective expression of cosmic truth. The ancient Egyptians were probably the first to use the golden section in the design of the Pyramids, but it was Pythagoras of Samos (c. 580–c. 500 B.C.E.) who first presented its mathematical formulation.

Many have followed the Pythagorean notion of order. Plato writes that proportions constitute beauty (*Philebus*). Aristotle (384–322 B.C.E.) associates beauty with order and size in *Poetics,* and with symmetry and definiteness in *Metaphysics.* St. Augustine of Hippo (354–430) holds that beauty is based on numbers (*De libero arbitrio*). St. Thomas Aquinas (c. 1224–1274) mentions proportion and harmony among the three requirements of beauty (*Summa theologica*). Gottfried Wilhelm von Leibniz (1646–1716) describes beauty as an obscure, sensual perception of mathematical configurations (*Principles of Nature and Grace Based on Reason,* 1714), and the painter William Hogarth (1697–1764) formulates principles of beauty applicable to art (*The Analysis of Beauty,* 1753). Many other authors expressed similar views.

Plotinus (205–270) is an exception. In *Enneades* (I, 6) he rejects the idea that beauty consists of order and proportion. His main points are: (1) Proportions, order, symmetry, and harmony apply to compound objects, while beauty is also found in simple elements like sunlight or gold. (2) The parts of a beautiful object must be beautiful, too, because beauty cannot consist of ugly elements. However, the parts themselves are simple and cannot convey order. (3) A beautiful face may look ugly when it expresses anger or wickedness, yet its proportions are the same. (4) Physical beauty is a reflection of the divine beauty, which unifies the formless multiplicity of matter. Thus, unity, not complexity, is essential to beauty.

Notwithstanding Plotinus's criticism, the Pythagorean notion of beauty became influential in Western philosophy for two principal reasons: The association of beauty with order was appealing to the rational mind, and experience suggests that the parts of a beautiful object are well situated, complement each other, and create a unified whole. This understanding generated the notion of unity in variety: Beauty resides in complexity that is unified by order. Accepting the fact that order is the key concept for understanding beauty, the question arises whether there are unifying laws of beauty that apply to all cases of beautiful objects, in the same way that the laws of nature apply to all physical phenomena.

Alexander Baumgarten (1714–1762) believed that the laws of beauty, like the laws of nature, could be uncovered by systematic, empirical investigations. He called for the establishment of a new science, which he named *aesthetics*. This science was intended to investigate direct perception in which particular representations are combined into a whole. Baumgarten was not influential among philosophers, but psychologists and mathematicians from the nineteenth century onward pursued his vision, seeking to translate the traditional formula—unity in variety—into measurable variables. In the field of psychology, the investigation of beauty is associated mainly with Gestalt theory and experimental aesthetics. Ernst H. Weber (1795–1878) and Gustav T. Fechner (1801–1887) investigated sensual perceptions and the relation between the intensity of the stimulus and the responsive sensation it causes. Fechner founded experimental aesthetics and made it a branch of psychology. Max Wertheimer (1880–1943), Wolfgang Köhler (1887–1967), and Kurt Koffka (1886–1941) defined the principles of the "good gestalt" (*Prägnanz*) and examined its application in various fields. A good gestalt expresses order, regularity, simplicity, stability, and continuity. According to Hans J. Eysenck (1916–1997), the fundamental law of aesthetics derives from the law of the good gestalt while, conversely, the law of aesthetics determines the properties of the good gestalt (1942).

In the mathematical realm we find George D. Birkhoff (1884–1944), who analyzed polygons and vases in order to formulate a concept of beauty. Birkhoff's conclusion is that the pleasure derived from any work of art or object of beauty depends on two variables: order (O), which expresses the unity of the object, and complexity (C), or the diversity exhibited by the object. The resulting measure of the aesthetic pleasure (M) derived from an object is then expressed mathematically:

Statue head of Queen Nefertiti, Egypt, 14th century B.C.E. Beauty has long been considered by many to play a prominent role in sexual selection among both animals and humans. Noted feminist Camille Paglia believes this theory can be traced back as far as ancient Egypt. © CORBIS-BETTMANN

$M = O/C$—that is, aesthetic pleasure is equal to the ratio of order to complexity (*Aesthetic Measure*, 1933).

From a different perspective, information theory inspired the idea that beauty is a measurable informative value. This theory offers a mathematical apparatus that describes, analyzes, and measures the transmission of information in communication systems. A clear message—namely, a highly ordered message—is a message of low informative value, high redundancy, and high predictability. Since the elements of a beautiful object are obviously neither redundant nor predictable, beauty in this context is regarded not as a form of high order, but rather as a happy medium, a balance between high order and disorder. Sir Fran-

The Parthenon on the Acropolis, Athens, Greece. One of the many definitions of beauty focuses on order and symmetry. Philosophers such as Plato, Aristotle, and the Pythagoreans considered harmonious proportions—often based on mathematical formulas—as an indication of beauty. © BETTMANN/CORBIS

cis Galton (1822–1911) demonstrates this idea of averages by superimposing photographs of convicted murderers and distilling a single photograph out of the many images. According to the viewers who examined the photos, this composite photograph was the best-looking face of all the original ones. Galton concluded that the average (composite) face is free from the irregularities that variously blemish each of the individual faces (1878).

Daniel E. Berlyne (1924–1976), one of the leading figures of experimental aesthetics in the twentieth century, sets the idea of happy medium in a psychological perspective. He describes the pleasure derived from beauty and good art as a reduction of arousal. The complexity of the object generates arousal in tension, and subsequently, when the unified whole is perceived, tension is reduced. According to Berlyne, experiments tend to confirm that some intermediate degree of complexity produces the most pleasing effect and that extremes of simplicity or complexity are distasteful (*Conflict, Arousal, and Curiosity*, 1960).

Monroe C. Beardsley (1915–1985), one of the most influential aestheticians of the last century, criticizes attempts to render beauty or good art in terms of a happy medium or an average. He maintains that the identification of complexity with disorder fails to explain the fact that complexity is a relevant ground for praise, and that the degree of informative value is not high enough to establish the aesthetic worth of an object. Beardsley agrees that beauty is a form of order, but argues that the beauty formula inspired by information theory leads to absurdities. Aesthetic order, according to Beardsley, escapes mechanical patterns and is marked by freedom, diversity, and uniqueness (1968). Abraham Moles (1920–1992) similarly acknowledges the limitations of information theory. He distinguishes between semantic information and aesthetic information. Semantic information has a universal logic and can be expressed in different languages. Aesthetic information cannot be translated into any other language or system of logic; it refers to particular objects apprehended by particular spectators (1966).

The notion of organic form or an organic whole suggests that beauty expresses a nonmechanical order consisting of inner forces or structures. In an organic form the whole precedes the differentiation of the parts, and the various parts are interdependent. Plato is the first to offer a formulation of art as an organic form (*Phaedrus*) in relation to literary works of art. Samuel T. Coleridge (1772–1834) turns to organic form in his defense of Shakespeare's works against the claim that they are formless. He emphasizes the harmony required in such works, not only between parts but also between matter and form. George E. Moore (1873–1958) adds that the value of an organic whole is different from the sum of its parts (*Principia Ethica*, 1903). Harold Osborne (1905–1987) defines aesthetic order in terms of an organic whole that cannot be reduced to its parts and is, therefore, directly apprehended as a whole. Beauty is an emergent property of a whole that reflects upon the parts, although each of the parts on its own is aesthetically neutral (1982). Heinrich Wölfflin (1864–1945), an influential art historian, describes good art as an organism in which nothing could be changed or moved from its place, but in which all must be as it is (*Principles of Art History,* 1915). Ruth Lorand, however, argues that the concept of an organic whole ignores, in most of its variants, the quantitative aspect of beauty. Some objects are more beautiful than others, and absolute beauty of the kind described by Wölfflin and others is hardly ever found. Aesthetic order, according to Lorand, is quantitative, highly informative, unpredictable, and, paradoxically, an order without laws (2000).

Beauty as a kind of pleasure. The immediate connection between beauty and feeling, and the difficulties inherent in defining beauty as a quality of the object, have given rise to the idea that beauty is not a quality of the object, but rather an emotion evoked by the object. St. Augustine asks whether an object is beautiful because it pleases or pleases because it is beautiful, and answers that the object pleases because it is beautiful. That is, beauty is the cause of pleasure and not identical with it (*De vera religione*). By contrast, Thomas Aquinas does not separate beauty from pleasure; he calls that beautiful whose apprehension pleases us. The definition of beauty as an expression of emotion usually renders judgments of beauty individual and subjective. René Descartes (1596–1650) regards beauty as totally subjective and dependent on individual conditions (letter to Marin Mersenne, 1630). Baruch Spinoza (1632–1677) dismisses beauty as mere sensual content. He mocks those who believe that beauty is objective, and that God, too, finds delight in beautiful things. (*Ethics,* I, appendix, 1667).

Empiricists of the eighteenth century, however, regarded this subjective aspect of beauty as an informative indication of human nature. Taste, the capacity for appreciating beauty, became a key concept. Francis Hutcheson (1694–1746) defines beauty as a source of pleasure that indicates not only qualities found in the object, but also the character of the spectator's sense of beauty (*Inquiry into the Original of Our Ideas of Beauty and Virtue,* 1725). Joseph Addison (1672–1719) writes that perhaps there is no real beauty, only certain modifications of matter that the mind pronounces beautiful (*The Spectator,* 1712). In his *Essays on the Intellectual Powers of Man* (1785), Thomas Reid (1710–1796) describes beauty as an occult quality: we know how it affects our senses, but not what it is in itself. According to Edmund Burke (1729–1797), beauty is the quality that causes love or passion and is not an objective quality like proportion (*A Philosophical Enquiry into the Origin of Our Ideas on the Sublime and Beautiful,* 1757). Archibald

Woman with tattooed face, China, c. 1900. The concept of beauty often varies from culture to culture. Physical enhancements such as tattoos, elaborate piercings, and facial hair may be considered beautiful among some societies but ugly among others. © MICHAEL MASLAN HISTORIC PHOTOGRAPHS/CORBIS

Alison (1757–1839) goes further, arguing that it is impossible to imagine an object of taste that is not an object of emotion (*Essays on the Nature and Principles of Taste,* 1790).

David Hume (1711–1776) writes in the same spirit that Euclid did not mention the beauty of the circle in any of the relevant propositions because beauty belongs to the sentiment of the spectator and is not a quality of the circle (*Enquiry Concerning the Principles of Morals,* 1751). He defines beauty as an expression of a subjective order that reflects our nature, customs, or capricious inclinations (*A Treatise of Human Nature,* 1739). In his influential essay *Of the Standard of Taste* (1757), Hume observes that different spectators equally praising the beauty of the same object does not necessarily indicate that they refer to the same features, or that they find delight for the same reasons.

Immanuel Kant (1724–1804), regarded as the most influential figure in modern philosophy, sought to bridge the gap between rationalism and empiricism. His account of beauty in *Critique of Judgment* (1790) is the first systematic analysis of the aesthetic phenomenon in modern philosophy. Kant rejects Baumgarten's vision of aesthetics as a science and holds that genuine judgments of beauty do not convey knowledge; they are individual judgments that cannot be generalized. Like Burke, he distinguishes between the beautiful and the sublime: Beauty

New Dictionary of the History of Ideas

Illustration from *Beauty and the Beast* (1874) by Walter Crane. Freud believed that humans found beauty in that which inspired sexual feelings. Darwin concurred with this theory, claiming that beauty played a role in the courting habits of many diverse cultures. © HISTORICAL PICTURE ARCHIVE/CORBIS

pleases through the free play of imagination and understanding and sustains the mind in restful contemplation. The sublime presents a disharmony between sensual capacities and reason. Thus, the feeling of the sublime carries with it a mental agitation: it is a pleasure compounded with displeasure. Kant defines beauty in terms of a peculiar kind of pleasure that consists in paradoxical features. He formulates four elements of the pleasure evoked by beauty: (1) Unlike the pleasures of the good and the pleasant, the pleasure of the beautiful is devoid of all interest. It is a disinterested pleasure. (2) Unlike other pleasures, the pleasure of the beautiful is not based on concepts. It is a nonconceptual pleasure. (3) The pleasure of the beautiful is a form of purposiveness without the presentation of a purpose. That is, the beautiful object demonstrates an inner order that is not subordinated to any external purpose. (4) The pleasure of the beautiful raises expectations for universal agreement. It is cognized as the object of a necessary liking. The necessity of universal assent that we associate with judgment of taste is a subjective necessity that we present as objective by presupposing a common sense. Kant, therefore, defines beauty as subjective-objective.

Many authors after Kant, however, preferred to deny the objective aspect of beauty and defined it as essentially subjective. Edgar Allan Poe (1809–1849) writes in *The Philosophy of Composition* (1846) that when men speak of beauty, they do not mean a quality but an affect—an intense and pure elevation of the soul. George Santayana (1863–1952) follows Hume by stating that beauty is not a property of an object. It is an emotion, a pleasure that is erroneously regarded as a quality of the object, such as color, proportion, or size. In this view, beauty is a value that reflects the beholder's position, and therefore is entirely subjective. The tendency to relate beauty to objects and expect other people to experience the same beauty is, according to Santayana, a strange psychological phenomenon that calls for psychological investigation (*The Sense of Beauty,* 1896).

However, not all of those who explain beauty in terms of pleasure consider it subjective. Clarence I. Lewis (1883–1964), for instance, regards all evaluations, including aesthetic evaluation, as forms of empirical knowledge. In *An Analysis of Knowledge and Valuation* (1946), he states that all forms of empirical knowledge are relational—that is, they depend equally on both the qualities of the object in question and the contribution of the contemplating mind. Viewing beauty as a relational quality bypasses the subjective-objective conflict and draws similarities between perception of beauty and relational perception of other qualities. Samuel Alexander (1859–1938) maintains that beauty is a kind of illusion that depends on the viewer's perspective. The perceived beauty is a result of a mutual contribution of the genuine qualities of the object as well as the mind that apprehends it (*Space, Time and Deity,* 1920).

John Locke (1632–1704) differentiates between objective and relational qualities. The former are primary qualities independent of the spectator's apprehension; the latter are secondary and tertiary qualities that reflect sensual perceptions and emotional reactions (*An Essay Concerning Human Understanding,* 1690). Following this understanding, David W. Prall (1886–1940) maintains that beauty is constituted in pleasurable apprehension and is therefore a tertiary quality that reflects the spectator's reaction to the object's qualities (*Aesthetic Judgment,* 1929). Beauty, as a tertiary quality, is most sensitive to individual differences among spectators. Individuality is also central in Mary Mothersill's definition of beauty. According to Mothersill, an object is beautiful if it causes pleasure by virtue of its aesthetic properties. Aesthetic properties are the properties that define the individuality of the object and distinguish it from others. The measure of beauty, so Mothersill holds, demands a reliable affect theory, since the measure of beauty is in fact the measure of the emotion it causes (1983).

Opposites of beauty. Examining the opposites of beauty illuminates the nature of beauty from a different angle. Although ugliness seems to be the immediate opposite of beauty, the complexity and peculiarity of the concept generates more than one opposite, each contrasting beauty in a different way.

The ugly. George E. Moore defines beauty in terms of the good—that of which the admiring contemplation is good in itself—and, accordingly, ugliness in terms of evil—that of which the admiring contemplation is evil in itself (1903). Understanding beauty in terms of order renders ugliness as a form of disorder. Rudolf Arnheim defines it as a struggle of conflicting, uncoordinated orders (1966). Conflicts express trends and values and therefore ugliness, like beauty, is a matter of cultural conceptions. For example, in the 1939 film *Gone with the Wind,* hair dyed shocking red is associated with prostitution and is thus considered ugly; it created a conflict with the prevailing standards of decency. Contemporary Western notions of decency are different; as a result, the sight of colored hair is no longer shocking or perceived as irregular, as it used to be.

The boring. Boredom indicates a failure to maintain a sufficient degree of novelty or a failure to deal with materials that interest the observer. This may partly explain the phenomenon of fashion: an oft-repeated style gradually loses its charm and fails to evoke the pleasure it generated before. When set in opposition to beauty, boredom indicates that beauty is stimulating as long as it maintains some degree of novelty.

The insignificant. An insignificant object, even if well-crafted, may be cute, pretty, lovely, or decorative, but not startlingly beautiful. The boring is not equivalent to the insignificant. We may be bored by something we hold significant and be attracted by trivial, insignificant objects.

The meaningless. A meaningless object is neither beautiful nor ugly. A meaningless object cannot be beautiful, since one cannot grasp any integration of its parts or be moved by it. A person who is unable to recognize the category within which the particular object falls (and is unable to make sense of it) is unable to appreciate its beauty.

Kitsch. Kitsch consists of beautiful elements, but it is not beautiful in a strict sense. Thomas Kulka holds that a prerequisite of kitsch is that it should employ familiar and well-tested elements that evoke positive responses (1988). Kitsch uses images—such as a bouquet of red roses or a red-roofed hut on the edge of a breathtaking lake—that appeal to many in order to manipulate sentiments and desires for commercial or political purposes. Kitsch is not a failure to create good art; it is, rather, a form of deception that requires "know-how." Seeing kitsch in opposition to beauty suggests that the genuine expe-

Portrait of a Young Man (1487) **by Sandro Botticelli. Tempera on panel.** Theories about the relationship between art and beauty have varied throughout time. Plato saw art as a deception that was a separate concept from beauty, while many contemporary philosophers considered art itself to be beautiful. © NATIONAL GALLERY COLLECTION. REPRODUCED BY KIND PERMISSION OF THE TRUSTEES OF THE NATIONAL GALLERY, LONDON/CORBIS

rience of beauty is sincere, and that it is not constituted by well-tested effective formulae.

The Function of Beauty

According to Kant, beauty has no function beyond the pleasure it generates. As much as this view influenced philosophical discourse, it did not satisfy natural scientists and social and cultural researchers.

Beauty and sexual selection. Charles Darwin (1809–1882) sought to answer the question: how has natural beauty been acquired and what is its purpose? He rejects the idea that beauty in nature is a merely arbitrary outcome of physical forces. Darwin believed that the beautiful colors and diversified patterns we see in butterflies, moths, fish, birds, and other creatures must be beneficial in some way. In *The Descent of Man and Selection in Relation to Sex* (1871), he presents the theory that beauty is a result of accumulative sexual selection. Studying mating rituals among various species, Darwin concludes that the animals' splendid decorations, their pomp and display, could not be inconsequential, and that it is impossible to doubt that the female admires the beauty of her male partner. This contrasts with the traditional view expressed by Burke (1767) that beauty is feminine, while the sublime is masculine.

Kant states that only humans are capable of appreciating beauty. Darwin insists that the origin of the ability to notice beauty (and appreciate it as such) is the same for animals and humans. Yet he agrees that humans' perception of beauty is far more complex than that of animals and involves cultural values and traditions. He examined courting customs in different cultures and confirmed that beauty plays an equally central role in choosing mates, in spite of cultural differences.

Sigmund Freud (1856–1939) concurs with Darwin as to the origin and role of beauty in human life. In *Civilization and Its Discontents* (1930), Freud asserts that there is no doubt that beauty originates in sexual feelings, and that all forms of pleasure are related to sexual love. According to Darwin and Freud, the function of beauty is universal, but the variety of its manifestations coheres with cultural relativism. Tattoos serve as a beautifying means in one culture and are condemned in another. The Makalalo women used to pierce their upper lips and place a ring in it. Piercing, until recently regarded as esoteric in Western culture, is now commonplace in Western society. Facial hair (beard or mustache) is thought to enhance masculine beauty in Western culture. While the American Indians considered facial hair vulgar, they appreciated long hair for men. However, the passion for beauty and the readiness to suffer to achieve it are similar in all cultures.

Naomi Wolf, an active feminist, denies that this is true. She rejects the idea that beauty answers genuine, universal needs. Beauty, according to Wolf, is a myth created during the industrial revolution and used ever since by men to manipulate women for their own interest. Beauty, she holds, is not universal and is not a function of evolution. The readiness of women to suffer in order to achieve the false ideal of beauty indicates the dominance of men and confirms male manipulation. Thus, according to Wolf, the female suffering for beauty is not a genuine product of evolutionary forces (1991). Camille Paglia criticizes this kind of feminist approach for concentrating on images of beauty of the last century and for failing to encompass a broad historical view. Paglia places the origin of beauty in ancient Egypt (1991).

In contrast to Wolf's position, Nancy Etcoff argues that beauty is a powerful and genuine element in everyday life. She agrees with Darwin that beauty influences sexual choice, but she goes on to argue that it influences all aspects of life from early childhood on. Beauty is not the result of political or economical manipulation, but rather the other way around: due to its strong impact, beauty is used as a means of achieving political and economic ends. Beauty, according to Etcoff, is not a product of a certain period in history; its origin, rather, lies in human nature itself (1999).

Beauty and art. Art was traditionally considered a source of beauty; some even argued that natural beauty is subordinated to artistic beauty. Plato, however, separated art and beauty into two independent concepts: real beauty reflects truth, while art is a deceiving imitation of nature. Aristotle, by contrast, held that good art is beautiful and that, therefore, the two are inseparable: a good work of art is a beautiful work. The Aristotelian aesthetic tradition prevailed for centuries, but it was the eighteenth century that gave rise to the idea that creating beauty is the essential purpose of art.

Kant holds that good art is beautiful, although it differs significantly from natural beauty: a good work of art is a beautiful representation. A representation can be beautiful even if its subject matter is not beautiful. Georg Wilhelm Friedrich Hegel (1770–1831) argues that beauty is the essential feature of art, and natural beauty is a reflection of artistic beauty (*Aesthetics*, 1835). In this view, beauty reflects intentional creation, not incidental results of blind, natural forces. The poet Friedrich von Schiller (1759–1805) associates art with freedom and beauty: we arrive at freedom through artistic beauty, since it is a product of intentional, free choice (*Letters on the Aesthetic Education of Man*, 1795). The comparison between artistic and natural beauty led Oscar Wilde (1854–1900) to the observation that life and nature imitate art far more than art imitates life or nature. Art is the creation of beauty; life and nature constitute its raw materials (*The Decay of Lying*, 1894). Benedetto Croce (1866–1952) similarly states that the sense of natural beauty is a derivative of artistic beauty. Beauty of nature cannot be explained unless one regards it as the work of a divine creator. Beauty, according to Croce, is a synonym of intuition and expression, and these refer to the artistic form. The content of the work is beautiful only when wrought into form.

Robin G. Collingwood (1889–1943) defines art as an attempt to achieve beauty (*Outlines of a Philosophy of Art*, 1925). However, his viewpoint did not gain influence in the twentieth century. The prevailing analytical trend preferred, it would seem, clear-cut, definable notions and has not been conducive to the study of the paradoxical nature of beauty, its ambiguous logical status, and the endless disputes over matters of taste. Thus, beauty has been dismissed as a vague and insignificant concept and considered irrelevant to art. Ludwig Wittgenstein (1889–1951) remarks in this analytical vein that beauty is an odd word that is hardly ever used (*Lectures and Conversations on Aesthetics*, 1938). John A. Passmore states that there is something suspicious about the notion of beauty, and that artists seem to get along quite well without it. He associates beauty with kitsch and bourgeois art (1954).

The association of beauty with superficiality and tranquil bourgeois life stood in contrast to the revolutionary spirit of modern art and the general atmosphere between the two world wars and after. Detaching beauty from art became common practice. According to Curt J. Ducasse (1881–1969), there is no essential connection between art and beauty. Art is an attempt to express feelings, and artists may intend to create or express ugliness in their work (*The Philosophy of Art*, 1966). Nelson Goodman (1906–1998) argued that many of the best paintings are, in the most obvious sense, ugly. Beauty, according to Goodman, is a vague and deceptive concept, while art is a kind of language that has no essential bond with beauty (*Languages of Art*, 1968). The influential and much-discussed institutional definition of art presented by George Dickie (1974) similarly bypasses the notion of beauty.

Mary Mothersill strongly criticizes the wide neglect of beauty and its detachment from art. She argues that the idea of beauty is indispensable and taken for granted in art criticism, because although critics do not explicitly refer to beauty, the idea is implicit in their criticism (1984). Mothersill's analysis of beauty reflects a change in approach. By the turn of the century we witness the growth of a renewed interest in various aspects of beauty. Wilfried Van Damme examines the anthropological perspective of beauty (1996). Eddy M. Zemach defends the objectivity of aesthetic properties and their empirical testability (1997). James Kirwan studies the history of the concept in order to illuminate the experience of beauty (1999). Peg Zeglin Brand examines the role and significance of beauty in social life and in relation to gender (2000). Lorand offers a theory of aesthetic order that revives the connection between beauty and art (2000), and Nick Zangwill rethinks the metaphysics of beauty (2001). These and other contemporary studies confirm that beauty is central to human experience in spite of its neglect in the discourse of the last century. The genuine vitality of beauty is bound to intrigue the reflective mind and inspire further investigations of its nature.

See also **Aesthetics; Arts; Emotions; Evolution; Feminism; Imagination; Platonism; Taste; Truth.**

BIBLIOGRAPHY

Arnheim, Rudolf. *Toward a Psychology of Art.* Berkeley: University of California Press, 1966.

Beardsley, Monroe C. "Order and Disorder." In *The Concept of Order,* edited by Paul G. Kuntz. Seattle and London: University of Washington Press, 1968.

Dickie, George. *Art and the Aesthetic: An Institutional Analysis.* Ithaca, N.Y.: Cornell University Press, 1974.

———. *The Century of Taste: The Philosophical Odyssey of Taste in the Eighteenth Century.* Oxford: Oxford University Press, 1996.

Etcoff, Nancy. *Survival of the Prettiest: The Science of Beauty.* New York: Doubleday, 1999.

Eysenck, Hans J. "The Experimental Study of the 'Good Gestalt,' a New Approach." *Psychological Review* 49 (1942): 344–364.

Galton, Francis. "Composite Portraits." *Nature* 18 (1878): 97–100.

Lorand, Ruth. *Aesthetic Order: A Philosophy of Order, Beauty, and Art.* London: Routledge, 2000.

Moles, Abraham. *Information Theory and Esthetic Perception.* Translated by Joel E. Cohen. Urbana: University of Illinois Press, 1966.

Mothersill, Mary. *Beauty Restored.* Oxford: Clarendon, 1984.

Osborne, Harold. "Aesthetics and Other Forms of Order." *British Journal of Aesthetics* 22 (1982): 3–16.

Paglia, Camille. *Sexual Personae: Art and Decadence from Nefertiti to Emily Dickinson.* New York: Vintage, 1991.

Passmore, John A. "The Dreariness of Aesthetics." In *Aesthetics and Language,* edited by William Elton, 36–55. Oxford: B. Blackwell, 1954.

Stolnitz, Jerome. "'Beauty': Some Stages in the History of an Idea." *Journal of the History of Ideas* 22 (1961): 185–204.

Tatarkiewicz, Wladyslaw. *History of Aesthetics.* The Hague: Mouton, 1970–74.

Van Damme, Wilfried. *Beauty in Context.* Leiden, Netherlands, and New York: Brill, 1996.

Wolf, Naomi. *The Beauty Myth.* New York: Anchor, 1992.

Zangwill, Nick. *The Metaphysics of Beauty.* Ithaca, N.Y.: Cornell University Press, 2001.

Zeglin Brand, Peg, ed. *Beauty Matters.* Bloomington: Indiana University Press, 2000.

Zemach, Eddy M. *Real Beauty.* University Park: Pennsylvania State University Press, 1997.

Ruth Lorand

BEHAVIORISM.

Behaviorism is a theoretical approach in psychology that emphasizes the study of behavior—that is, the outwardly observable reactions to a stimulus of an organism, whether animal or human—rather than the content of the mind or the physiological correlates of behavior. Largely centered in the United States, behaviorism had an early stage (1910–1930) that was dominated by the work of the comparative psychologist John B. Watson, and a later stage, neo-behaviorism (1930–1955), defined by the psychologists Edward C. Tolman, Clark Hull, and B. F. Skinner.

Behaviorism has its roots in the work of Ivan Pavlov (1849–1936), a Russian physiologist who studied medicine in St. Petersburg and physiology at the University of Breslau in Germany. Pavlov designed a series of experiments to understand learning, a psychological process, in terms of the physiological process of conditioning, or training, reflex responses. His experimental animal of choice was the dog, though he expected that his results could apply to humans as well. Dogs normally display a salivation reflex at the sight of food. Pavlov's experiment involved ringing a bell at the same moment that the dog was presented with food. After presenting both stimuli in this joint manner, Pavlov simply rang the bell without also presenting the food—and found that the dog salivated. The normal reflex had been conditioned to appear in response to an unconventional stimulus. An organism's innate responses could thus be trained by this conditioning method to be elicited by a range of stimuli that did not normally produce them, and Pavlov used the method to examine the ways in which responses could be excited and inhibited. The method of conditioning reflexes could, according to Pavlov, replace a mentalistic language about what animals see or hear or feel with a physicalistic, materialist language about responses to stimuli. The conditioning method focused on outward, objective observation of animal behavior, rather than on guessing about the content of an animal's mind. In Pavlov's interpretation, seemingly purposeful behavior on the part of the animal could be reduced to the training of reflexes, or the formation and breaking of habits. Such a view bears a strong similarity to that of the behaviorists who followed, but in an important respect Pavlov differed from them. He never abandoned the idea that he was basically a physiologist and that there could be no science of psychology independent of physiology. Pavlov intended that the acts comprising an animal's behavior should eventually be explained in terms of the workings of its brain. He had no patience with the American behaviorists' belief that behavior formed its own autonomous branch of scientific study.

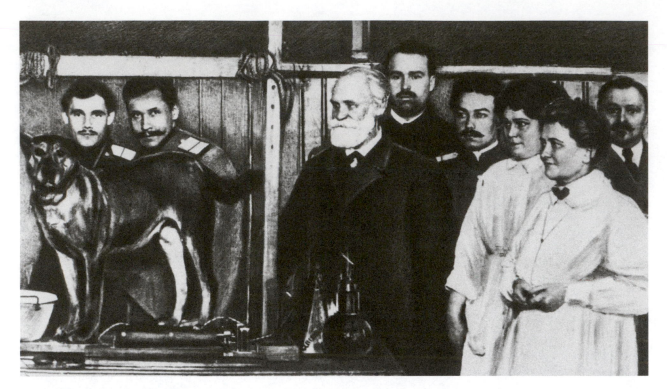

An airbrushed photograph of Russian physiologist Ivan Pavlov and his staff, c. 1925–1936. Pavlov, whose views formed the foundation of Behaviorism, believed that learning consisted of a series of conditioned responses. His experimental animal of choice was the dog, though he expected that his results could apply to humans as well. © BETTMANN/CORBIS

Behaviorism (1910–1930)

Pavlov's experiments in classical conditioning were familiar to Western psychologists from 1906 on and formed the heart of the behaviorist method. In 1913 John B. Watson (1878–1958) systematically and provocatively set out the principles of behaviorism in a manifesto entitled "Psychology As the Behaviorist Views It." Watson was a comparative psychologist interested in making psychology a real science by defining it as the study of outwardly observable behavior, rather than of thought, imagery, consciousness, or mind. In doing so he intended to break psychology's ties with philosophy. As a comparative psychologist with interests also in developmental psychology—the study of how the mind develops in childhood, as well as over the course of evolution—Watson knew that the conventional psychological method of introspection was inapplicable to the subjects of his science. Children and animals could not be asked to introspect, to divulge the contents of their minds, and guessing at what they were thinking Watson judged to be unscientific. Focusing instead on behavior rather than on consciousness was therefore the only way to proceed. Watson also had a practical motivation for his behaviorism— he wanted to make it the science of how people act.

Watson was born in Greenville, South Carolina. He attended college at Furman University and graduate school in the department of philosophy at the University of Chicago, where he was trained in comparative psychology by the neurologist Henry Herbert Donaldson and the psychologist James Rowland Angell. Watson was interested in the work of Jacques

Loeb (1859–1924), a German-trained materialist physiologist at Chicago who studied tropisms, or movements in plants and animals, that he interpreted in solely physico-chemical terms. Donaldson and Angell, however, dissuaded Watson from working with the radical Loeb, and Watson instead wrote his dissertation on the correlation between brain growth and learning ability in rats.

In 1908 Watson became professor of psychology at the Johns Hopkins University, but as a comparative psychologist felt marginalized in the department. In his 1913 manifesto he devised a way to bring comparative psychology to center stage. A truly scientific psychology, he wrote, would abandon talk of mental states or conscious content of minds and instead focus on prediction and control of behavior. By focusing on objectively observable behavior, by getting away from mind, consciousness, and introspection and examining physical variables instead, psychology would become a legitimate science. Like Pavlov, Watson believed in observing and training physical responses to stimuli, making no reference to mind, and thereby treating animal and human behavior on the same level. In his 1919 book, *Psychology From the Standpoint of a Behaviorist,* Watson rejected the concept of mind completely, interpreting even imagery, thought, and language all in terms of behavior accessible to an objective observer.

At Johns Hopkins, Watson was associated with the psychiatrist Adolf Meyer, the head of the Phipps Clinic, where Watson applied behaviorist conditioning methods to children. In a famous series of experiments conducted with his graduate assistant Rosalie Rayner, Watson trained a child by the name of Little Albert (aged 9–13 months) to fear a rat, a response the child then produced in reaction to the sight of any furry creature. Watson's evident success in training even such a deep-seated reaction as fear led him to believe that all of a person's behavior could be altered, any habit could be formed or broken, by the engineering of stimuli—that is, by the control of the person's immediate environment. In his 1924 book *Behaviorism* Watson expressed this environmentalist view in its most extreme terms. But by then Watson had been forced to resign his position at Hopkins because of his involvement in an extramarital love affair with Rayner. He and Rayner moved to New York City, where Watson joined the John Walter Thompson advertising agency, and where both Watson and Rayner became popular authorities on child-rearing according to behaviorist principles. Their *Psychological Care of Infant and Child* appeared in 1928.

Watson was not the only psychologist during the 1910s to advocate behaviorism. At Columbia University Teachers College, Edward L. Thorndike (1874–1949), experimenting with cats learning their way around puzzle-boxes, similarly argued that the study of objectively observable changes in behavior, and their correlation with changes in stimuli, formed the heart of a legitimately scientific psychology. Thorndike formulated the law of effect, which held that pleasure or reward will reinforce a certain behavior, while pain will extinguish it: thus the animal's experience has important consequences for its behavior.

Neobehaviorism (1930–1955)

The second phase of behaviorism, neobehaviorism, was associated with Edward C. Tolman (1886–1959), Clark Hull (1884–1952), and B. F. Skinner (1904–1990). Like Thorndike, Watson, and Pavlov, the neobehaviorists believed that the study of learning and a focus on rigorously objective observational methods were the keys to a scientific psychology. Unlike their predecessors, however, the neobehaviorists were more self-consciously trying to formalize the laws of behavior. They were also influenced by the Vienna Circle of logical positivists, a group of philosophers led by Rudolph Carnap (1891–1970), Otto Neurath (1882–1945), and Herbert Feigl (1902–1988), who argued that meaningful statements about the world had to be cast as statements about physical observations. Anything else was metaphysics or nonsense, not science, and had to be rejected. Knowledge, according to the logical positivists, had to be built on an observational base, and could be verified to the extent that it was in keeping with observation.

A professor of psychology at the University of California at Berkeley, Tolman focused his experimental work largely on white rats learning their way through mazes. He differed from his behaviorist predecessors by taking a more holistic approach to behavior than they had. Rather than talking in terms of atomistic, isolated stimuli and responses, Tolman emphasized their integration with the environment by referring to them as "stimulating agencies" and "behavior acts." In his 1932 *Purposive Behavior in Animals and Men,* Tolman argued that purpose and cognition were essential to behavior and should be

Yvonne Skinner and daughter with experimental psychologist B. F. Skinner's invention, the "baby box," 1945. The "baby box" was a glassed-in playpen in which temperature and humidity were automatically controlled. Skinner's youngest daughter spent her infancy in one. Controversial and misunderstood by the general public, the box was intended by Skinner to serve in the same capacity as a crib, but with an enhanced environment to keep a child safe and healthy. © BETTMANN/CORBIS

interpreted not as mentalistic entities but as outwardly observable features of behavior describable in objective language. He also defined the notion of the intervening variable, a link between stimulus and response that helps to determine behavior. As many as ten intervening variables could exist between a stimulating agency and a rat's decision to move in a certain direction at a choice-point in a maze.

Of the three neobehaviorists, Hull was the most ambitious about constructing a formal theory of behavior. He believed he had found the fundamental law of learning or habit-formation—the law of stimulus generalization—and that this law not only underlay all behavior in animals and humans, but was a principle basic enough to unify all the social sciences. According to the law, a response could be called forth by an unconventional stimulus as long as that stimulus was associated, either temporally or in character, with the stimulus that usually called forth the response. As long as the unconventional stimulus was similar enough to the usual one, it could elicit the response. Pavlov had noted this effect when his dogs salivated at the ringing of a bell. Hull further theorized that learning was continuous—that is, when an animal was trained to respond to a particular positive stimulus (or avoid a negative stimulus), all aspects of that stimulus impinging on the animal's sensorium were gradually associated with that response. Thus the animal learns in an incremental way, not in an all-or-nothing burst, and thus engineering the appearance of stimuli could precisely control the animal's ability to form habits. These laws of behavior explained how all learning took place without resorting to immaterial notions like soul or free will. Hull, who had originally intended to become an engineer, even designed a variety of machines that worked on the principles of conditioning reflexes, in order to demonstrate that learning was a wholly mechanistic process. He expressed his laws of behavior in mathematical terms, filling his 1943 *Principles of Behavior: An Introduction to Behavior Theory* with complex equations.

The rigor for which Hull strove in his science was evident both in his exclusion of any nonmaterial entity and in his formulation of laws. It was also evident in the hypothetico-deductive method by which he believed psychologists must work. Here Hull's inspiration was the certainty of scientific knowledge achieved by the natural philosopher Isaac Newton (1642–1727). In Hull's method, the theorist began with the observation of a certain behavior, derived axioms from that observation, deduced consequences from the axioms, tested the consequences through experiment, and then refined the axioms, ultimately establishing the laws of behavior on a firm observational and experimental footing. In 1929 Hull moved from his teaching position at the University of Wisconsin at Madison to a prestigious post at the Rockefeller Foundation–funded Institute of Human Relations at Yale, where he remained until his death in 1952. Hull's laws of behavior and his rigorous scientific method became central to the Institute's mission to unify the social sciences. Hull's theory of behavior integrated psychology, psychiatry, sociology, and anthropology by describing learning as the forging of connections between stimulus and response, and then envisioning this mechanism as the mediator of all social and cultural activity. The build-up and breakdown of habit was thus interpreted as the key to all behavior. Hull and his work formed the focal points of the Institute of Human Relations, which lasted only as long as Hull lived and was dissolved after his death. His approach was, however, continued by his friend and supporter Kenneth Spence (1907–1967), a psychologist at the University of Iowa.

The Harvard psychologist B. F. Skinner, the third of the important neobehaviorists, rejected Hull's attempts at formal theory building and returned to the Watsonian project of founding a science entirely on the observation of behavior. Skinner devised an experimental set-up, the so-called Skinner box, in which a pigeon or a rat would be rewarded for accomplishing an act, such as raising its head above a certain line, or pressing a lever, by the release of food pellets. In his 1938 *Behavior of Organisms,* Skinner explained that a movement rewarded in this way was reinforced—that is, made more likely to occur—while one that was punished was stamped out. A behavior that was followed by the repetition of that behavior—a movement selected and maintained by its positive consequences—Skinner called the operant. His approach therefore was referred to as operant conditioning. Both animals and people behave the way they do because of the positive consequences produced by past behavior. For Skinner, all learning was a matter of such reinforcement, and his method consisted of recording sequences of movements that revealed the patterns by which behavior was reinforced. He avoided talking about habit formation, and even about stimuli, restricting his science to the observation of these movement patterns.

In his 1953 *Science and Human Behavior,* Skinner explained the principles that underlay his psychology. First, he argued that his science was entirely based in observation, and that theories and hypotheses played a limited role in it: his approach was radically inductivist and empiricist. Second, since psychology was supposed to be restricted to the level of behavioral observation, it had no need of being reduced to or explained in terms of physiology. Physiology was not more fundamental than psychology—it was either unobservable, hence unscientific, or part of behavior itself. Third, for Skinner, mental processes or states were to be interpreted as behavior—memory, knowledge, imagery, and other such mentalistic entities he dismissed as metaphors or fictions. Past consequences of behavior, not mental states, motivated future action. Skinner's 1957 *Verbal Behavior* was his attempt to deal with thought and language in terms of reinforced movements. Finally, Skinner believed that biological adaptation was the ultimate criterion for the persistence of a behavior: if an action aided survival, it persisted.

Skinner argued that behavior could be shaped, or controlled, by controlling the rewards or reinforcements meted out in response to them—that is, by controlling the environment. In the mid 1950s and 1960s, some penal and psychiatric institutions adopted this method of behavior modification to shape the behavior of their inmates. In his 1948 book *Walden Two,* Skinner had prepared the ground for such application of his science by imagining a utopian community led according to behaviorist principles. In his 1971 *Beyond Freedom and Dignity,* Skinner argued that such ethical principles as free will and individual responsibility are simply illusions, and what will make us truly free is the realization that behavior is instead controlled by the past and by the environment.

Neobehaviorism came in for strong criticism in the late 1950s and 1960s. Philosophers of science questioned the claim that any science could be theory-neutral and based solely in observation; observations were themselves seen to be theory-laden. Psychologists questioned the idea that learning was a singular entity that could form the basis for all of psychology. In particular, cognitive psychology, drawing on insights from computer science, redefined mental processes such as problem solving, learning, and memory in terms of information processing, a development that gave a new autonomy and a new respectability to the study of internal mental states. Influenced by this cognitivist turn, the psycholinguist Noam Chomsky (b. 1928) published a scathing review of Skinner's *Verbal Behavior,* arguing that language had to be understood in terms of universal and innate mental structures, not as behavior shaped by the environment. Behaviorism is currently regarded by psychologists as one approach among many; both cognitivism and neuroscience are arguably as influential in understanding mind and behavior.

See also **Biology; Determinism; Education: North America; Psychology and Psychiatry.**

BIBLIOGRAPHY

Amsel, Abram. *Behaviorism, Neobehaviorism, and Cognitivism in Learning Theory: Historical and Contemporary Perspectives.* Hillsdale, N.J.: Erlbaum, 1989.

Boakes, Robert. *From Darwin to Behaviorism: Psychology and the Minds of Animals.* New York: Cambridge University Press, 1984.

Buckley, Kerry. *Mechanical Man: John Broadus Watson and the Beginnings of Behaviorism.* New York: Guilford Press, 1989.

Harris, Benjamin. "Whatever Happened to Little Albert?" *American Psychologist* 34 (1979): 151–160.

Hull, Clark L. *Principles of Behavior: An Introduction to Behavior Theory.* New York: Appleton Century Crofts, 1943.

Mills, John A. *Control: A History of Behavioral Psychology.* New York: New York University Press, 1998.

Morawski, J. G. "Organizing Knowledge and Behavior at Yale's Institute of Human Relations." *Isis* 77 (1986): 219–242.

O'Donnell, John M. *The Origins of Behaviorism: American Psychology, 1870–1920.* New York: New York University Press, 1985.

Pavlov, Ivan P. *Conditioned Reflexes.* Translated by G. Anrep. Oxford: Oxford University Press, 1927.

Samelson, Franz. "Struggle for Scientific Authority: The Reception of Watson's Behaviorism, 1913–1920." *JHBS* 17 (1981): 399–425.

Skinner, B. F. *The Behavior of Organisms.* New York: Appleton Century Crofts, 1938.

Smith, Laurence D. *Behaviorism and Logical Positivism: A Reassessment of the Alliance.* Stanford, Calif.: Stanford University Press, 1986.

Tolman, Edward C. "A New Formula for Behaviorism." *Psychological Review* 29 (1922): 44–53.

Watson, John B. "Psychology as the Behaviorist Views It." *Psychological Review* 20 (1913): 158–178.

Weidman, Nadine M. *Constructing Scientific Psychology: Karl Lashley's Mind-Brain Debates.* New York: Cambridge University Press, 1999.

Nadine Weidman

BELIEF. *See* **Religion.**

BILINGUALISM AND MULTILINGUALISM. A bilingual individual, generally, is someone who speaks two languages. An ideal or balanced bilingual speaks each language as proficiently as an educated native speaker. This is often referred to as an ideal type since few people are regarded as being able to reach this standard. Otherwise, a bilingual may be anywhere on a continuum of skills.

Literacy abilities may be an additional dimension to bilingualism, but they are often referred to separately as *biliteracy*, leaving *bilingualism* to carry the weight of oral language abilities. Bilingualism is a specific case of multilingualism, which has no ceiling on the number of languages a speaker may dominate. The timing and sequence in which one learns each of the languages has led to other distinctions between kinds of multilingualism. Much of the linguistics literature, for example, identifies native language or mother tongue as a first language, ignoring the possibility or diminishing the value of having more than one native language or mother tongue. Such a person is often referred to as a simultaneous bilingual, while someone who acquires the second language after the first one is often referred to as a sequential bilingual ("early" if between early childhood and puberty, and "late" if after puberty). The context of

language acquisition leads naturally to distinguishing between "informal" bilinguals, who acquire their languages outside of formal settings like schools, imitating the natural processes of acquiring the mother tongue, and "formal" bilinguals, who generally learn the language in schools or similar settings.

When these terms apply to groups, one speaks of bilingual or multilingual communities or nations. The aggregate enumeration of the speakers in these groups (also referred to as language diversity or demography) will often profile the number of monolingual and bilingual speakers of each language. For example, there may be a multilingual community in which speakers are monolingual in each of three languages. This would be rare, and the language groups would probably be isolated from each other. More often than not, a multilingual community or nation has multilingual individuals. If the situation involves social or political power, then a language group may be referred to as a language minority (minority-language) group or a language majority (majority-language) group, reflecting the power relationship to other groups in the society or political unit.

Language Diversity

The linguistic diversity of the world has depended on the world population and the number of languages in the world. The world population grew from about 300 million at the time of Christ to an estimated 1 billion in 1804, 2 billion in 1927, and 6 billion at the end of 1999, and is projected to reach 10 billion around 2183. In 1950 there were only four countries with a national population greater than 100 million persons. In 2003 the number of such countries had grown to eleven. The United Nations projects that in 2050 such countries will number eighteen. India, China, and the United States were the top three countries at each of these points in time.

The twentieth century was the highest growth period in the history of humanity, almost quadrupling the world population. The highest rate of growth occurred between 1965 and 1970 (2 percent per annum), and the largest annual increases in population occurred in the late 1980s, with 86 million people added to the world population annually.

One should keep in mind as well that the distribution of the population and its languages around the world is uneven, have changed over time, and are expected to continue such changes, at least into the near future. In 1750, for example, 64 percent of the estimated world population was located in Asia, while 21 percent was in Europe, 13 percent in Africa, and 2 percent in the Americas. By 1950, Asia had lost almost 10 percentage points and Africa about 4 percent; Europe remained steady at 22 percent, but the Americas grew to 14 percent of the total equally between the northern and southern countries. The United Nations Population Division projects that in 2150, Europe and North America will shrink in percentage from 22 percent to 7 percent and from 7 percent to 4 percent, respectively; Asia will remain steady at 60 percent, but Africa will more than double its proportion from 9 percent to 24 percent, and Latin America will increase slightly its portion of the world population from 7 percent to 9 percent. These changing distributions of the human population across

Table 1. Top languages by number of speakers, 2000

(in millions)

Language	Countries		First Language
	Hub	Number	
Chinese (Mandarin)	China	16	874
Hindi	India	17	366
English	United Kingdom	104	341
Spanish	Spain	43	322–358
Bengali	Bangladesh	9	207
Arabic			207
Portuguese	Portugal	33	176
Russian	Russia	30	167
Japanese	Japan	26	125
German	Germany	40	100

SOURCE: Data from McGeveran, pp. 626–627

the world have had and will continue to have an impact on the numbers of speakers of specific languages in those regions, and urbanism and migrations will increase the probability of language contact between speakers of different languages. By the middle of the twentieth century, more than half of the world's population was considered urban. By the end of the twentieth century, about 4 percent of the world's population did not live in their country of birth.

The world's language diversity is only now being better understood and described. The sources of estimating the number of languages in the world vary in the quality of their data and methods, not the least of which is their varying definitions of language. Some authors estimate that somewhere between 30,000 and 500,000 languages have been created and died in the course of human history, indicating that languages usually have a short life span as well as a very high death rate. Only a few (such as Basque, Egyptian, Chinese, Greek, Hebrew, Latin, Persian, Sanskrit, and Tamil) have lasted more than two thousand years.

One of the more widely cited and consistent sources on the number of languages and speakers of those languages estimates that there were approximately 6,800 oral languages in the world at the beginning of the twenty-first century. Some experts argue that the inclusion of manually signed languages would increase the estimate to 12,000 human languages. Chinese Mandarin, English, Hindi, Spanish, and Arabic have been identified as the languages with the greatest number of native speakers in the world in 2000 (see Table 1).

More often than not, the enumeration of speakers through government or organizational surveys only takes into account a single language per person, despite the normative multilingualism around the world. This current multilingualism has been promoted by the greater language contact of the twentieth century, in part the legacy of colonialism and the postcolonial practice of establishing new nation-states with populations that belonged to different ethno-language communities.

In many areas of the imperial colonial language (such as English, French, Spanish, Dutch) was spread as a second or

replacement language among the colonized population, albeit with a wide range in the language proficiencies of these speakers. In some instances, the number of native speakers of these colonial languages is greater outside the metropole of the colonizing nation, and even the second-language speakers of these colonial languages may be larger than the native speakers of the same language. In 1999, for example, English was estimated to have 341 million native speakers around the world and 508 million second-language speakers; Spanish was estimated to have 358 million native speakers globally and 417 million second-language speakers.

In 2000, the enumerated languages were unevenly divided across the world in the various continents. Africa had 30 percent of the oral languages but 13 percent of the world's population; Asia had about 33 percent of the world's languages and 61 percent of the world's population. The Pacific Oceanic area had about 19 percent of the languages, the Americas 15 percent, and Europe had approximately 3 percent of the oral languages and about 12 percent of the world's population. The two most linguistically diverse countries, Papua New Guinea and Indonesia, together had more than 22 percent (1,500) of the world's oral languages, most of which are not spoken in any other country. An overwhelming 83 to 84 percent of the world's languages are spoken in only one country.

The range in the numbers of speakers of a particular language is large, from several hundred to hundreds of millions. The median number of speakers of a language was probably around 5,000 to 6,000 at the turn of the twenty-first century. More than 95 percent of the world's spoken languages have fewer than 1 million native users, while some 5,000 (83 percent) spoken languages have fewer than 100,000 speakers, and more than 3,000 spoken languages have fewer than 10,000 users. About 1,500 spoken languages and most of the sign languages have fewer than 1,000 users. In 1999, some 500 languages had fewer than 100 speakers.

Ranka Bjeljac-Babic proposed that no language could survive unless 100,000 people speak it, and so estimated that at the beginning of the twenty-first century, ten languages were dying each year. Michael Krause projected that 50 to 90 percent of the spoken languages would disappear during the twenty-first century. From one perspective these languages will "wither" by a "voluntary" failure to transmit the language from one generation to another. From another perspective, many of these languages are threatened and "murdered" by repressive nation-state policies and language majoritarian practices, not unlike what has been seen in the past. European colonial conquests, for example, eliminated at least 15 percent of all languages spoken at the outset of the colonial period. According to Bjeljac-Babic, "Over the last 300 years, Europe has lost a dozen [languages], and Australia has only 20 left of the 250 spoken at the outset of the colonial period. According to l, about 540 (three-quarters of the total) have died out since Portuguese colonization began in 1530" (p. 18).

These "heritage" languages will be replaced by another language, adding to the numbers of native speakers of that second language, which may be a regional language or a language of wider communication (an international or world language). If size is a significant factor in the robustness and continuity of a language, then the growth of some of the medium-sized languages with the addition of persons who otherwise would have spoken their heritage language might retard their demise.

It is more difficult to estimate the number of new languages created during any particular period, either from the "splitting" of a natural language into mutually not understandable varieties, the transformation of pidgins (reduced-language contact speech) into elaborated creoles by the acquisition of native speakers who complexify it for all required purposes, or the revival of "dead" languages, such as Hebrew's revival by the new state of Israel, which developed its vocabulary to reflect a modern and more complete range of functions.

Language Diversity in Civil Society

The core sense of "civil" society is generally understood as the societal interaction, organization, and activity that takes place outside of government or the state. From this standpoint, the role of language diversity in civil society has varied across time and settings. Factors such as whether a group of people or a society is primarily rural or urban, sedentary or migratory, will often influence language diversity and individual bilingualism. The social and political relations between groups often determine how it is perceived, treated, or utilized within the society as a resource, problem, or even as a part of the civil and human rights of individuals or groups.

For example, Sue Wright describes the elite in Europe for much of the Middle Ages and the Renaissance as "multicultural and multilingual" because of their need to interact and collaborate with each other despite the different native languages in the region. Acquiring other languages was seen as an expected and normal activity for these mobile elites. Most of the population, however, were sedentary farmers, serfs, or peasants, living in small, monolingual villages and having no contact with or need to learn other languages. They spoke a variety of one of the language "continua" of Romance, Germanic, Celtic, Slavic, or Baltic. The dominant Christian Church operated across kingdoms and "nations" with a common language of wider communication—Latin. In general, villagers attempted to accommodate "others" who did not speak the village language, who were often travelers or soldiers, but otherwise people understood each other from one village to the next, even if their vernaculars were slightly different.

According to Eduardo Ruiz Vietez, three activities caused changes in this situation: the consolidation of national kingdoms, the reformation of the church, and the development of the printing press. The consolidation of kingdoms into more fixed territories meant that the royals governed a multilingual population at the same time that the vernacular language of the capital was promoted as a standard. The first grammar of such a vernacular was presented to the king and queen of Castille, Spain, in 1492, as an instrument of nation building along with the sword and the Bible. The Reformation promoted the translation of the Bible into vernacular languages, establishing a need for literacy and standardization of the text in various lan-

guages. Wright describes the emerging relationship between language and the printing press: "Printers adopted standardised languages with enthusiasm. Print capitalism profited from the standardisation of national languages, because the process delivered bigger markets than the splintered linguistic landscape of the dialect continua" (p. 2).

By the eighteenth and nineteenth centuries in Europe, *nation* was understood in civic terms and in ethnic or cultural terms. Within the civic, fixed territorial states, nation-building pressure was placed on disparate groups. Within the ethnic states, the boundaries were fixed around the single group, with other ethnolinguistic groups often pushed out. Single-language standardization and its association with the state developed a single concept of the nation as a single, unified cultural body, even while in reality, many of these nations contained regional, historically rooted, language minorities (such as the Catalans or Basques), and even migratory or nomadic language groups (such as the Romani) that continue into the early twenty-first century.

For another pattern of language diversity and civil society, one can turn to the Mexican Aztec Empire during the fifteenth century. In the fourteenth and fifteenth centuries, the Aztec Empire was organized into a tributary system, where the Nahuatl language was used in the metropole and throughout the empire. In the subjugated areas of the empire, bilingual administrators, such as "tax" collectors and local governors, were the brokers in local towns and villages and would mediate the tributes and administrative interactions with the central government. Beyond these interactions, the need for Nahuatl was minimal among the local populations, who continued to use their local languages. The language of the empire was highly valued and its value provided an incentive for individual bilingualism among the population, although individual bilingualism was not widespread.

The situation changed after contact with the Spanish and, later, other Europeans. With the imposition of the Spanish colonial structures, Spanish became the "instrument" of empire building, not just nation building. It became the prestige language and was imposed through the process of evangelization and conversion. The libraries of the Aztec Empire were

Table 2. Countries by number of languages, 2000

Country	Languages	Population (2003)
Papua New Guinea	850	5,500,000
Indonesia	670	220,500,000
Nigeria	410	133,900,000
India	380	1,068,600,000
Cameroon	270	15,700,000
Australia	250	19,900,000
Mexico	240	104,900,000
Zaire (Democratic Republic of the Congo)	210	56,600,000
Brazil	210	176,500,000
Philippines	172	81,600,000

SOURCE: Data from Skutnabb-Kangas (2000), p. 34; Population Research Bureau web site

burned and destroyed by the Spanish. Religious leaders, colonial administrators, and indigenous elites, who learned each other's languages, became bilingual and brokered the creation of revised local histories and knowledge. Over time, Spanish was promoted as a single substitute for the indigenous languages, increasing its number of speakers, even while many indigenous languages survive into the early twenty-first century.

In these and other ways, communication in language-diverse settings has been promoted through bilingual brokers. Travelers, soldiers, missionaries, and immigrants often learned new languages to facilitate these communications. Certainly in language contact situations individual bilinguals in the various languages played key roles in the civic interactions between peoples. If the language situation was more complex, involving three languages, a pidgin as "common" language often arose to broker communication between groups.

In the twentieth century, the development of popular schooling in multilingual situations often was organized with bilingual or multilingual instruction. Early primary grades were often taught in the native language of the community, with the regional and/or the national languages added as the student matured. The integration of countries into regional economic, political, and civil societies, such as the European Union, has put social pressures on groups to maintain their national languages at the same time they are to learn other regional languages and some languages for wider communication, such as English. This results in the promotion of at least a trilingualism among the population.

The transnational movement of people (as immigrants, refugees, and international workers) has also created the need for learning the host country's language(s), and for addressing the language needs of their children in schools. When there are substantial numbers of speakers of these (immigrant) languages concentrated in one place over a sufficient time to establish local organizations and institutions, such as local ethnic economy or independent community mother-tongue schools, then there are other local accommodations that often follow, with and without the support of the host society and the dominant language majority.

Government Policies to Accommodate Language Diversity

Official statements or policies about language can be made by governments at any level. These official statements about language may also be made at an institutional level, such as a church, labor union, or school. In general, the statements are about the *status* of a language, designating it as an official or national language; its form or structure (*corpus*), elaborating the language lexicon, or morphology; or its *functions* or use (including domains of use), as in the media of instruction in schools.

Government or official positions regarding language policies may be designed to *promote* a language through its recognition, use, or resource allocation; to *tolerate* the language, by not making any policies with regard to it; to *restrict* it, by conditioning societal benefits, rights, or services on knowledge of

the language; or to *repress* it (sometimes referred to as *linguacide*), by actively prohibiting its use and its transmission from one generation to another. Very often these approaches or designs are influenced by whether the language is seen as a resource (promoting foreign-language learning, for example), a problem, or a right (human or civil). Language policies of promotion and repression may be justified in several ways, sometimes ideologically similar, such as by national unification. Their means, however, are drastically different. These approaches to language policies may favor single or multiple languages. India, for example, has two official languages—Hindi and English—and more than fifteen national languages, reflecting the status of other languages within the component states of the nation.

The juridical concept of human rights has developed over the last hundred-plus years. Language has often been considered an important aspect of these rights. Two international standards are developing: the right to be free from discrimination based on language, and the right to access (acquire and use) one's mother tongue and the languages of the community and state if they are different. In some countries these rights are tied to "individual" freedoms of expression and speech (as in some Western countries); in other countries, they are seen as part of the right to cultural integrity and identity (some socialist countries, for example, recognize clearly identified national minorities as nations with inherent rights and protections).

Evaluation of Language Policies

The success of language policies and planning by governments is not uniform across time and place. Neither is success measured in the same ways. Any such evaluation of language policies would need to take into account the goal, its justification, and the means to achieve it.

L. F. Bosnahan reviewed four cases of language imposition, of which three were successful in seeding and developing the imposed common language of empire—Latin during the Roman Empire, Greek during the Greek Empire, Arabic during the rise of Islam, and Turkish during the Ottoman Empire. The first three cases were successful in having the imposed language become the exclusive or principal speech of the population, replacing the preexisting vernaculars. Bosnahan cites four features he believes made this success possible, if not determinative, where all four cases shared the first two features and were differentiated by the third and fourth: (1) each language was imposed by military authority, resulting in a political unity that increased commercial, political, economic, and/or cultural contact among different sections of the united area; (2) once imposed, it was maintained for at least several centuries by similar authority, allowing the adoption and then transmission of the language across several generations and the spread across the population; (3) the area of language imposition was already multilingual, making the imposed language one for wider communication; and (4) knowledge of the imposed language conferred material advantages and benefits widely recognized among the population, including employment, citizenship and its attendant rights and privileges, acquisition or grants of land, and trade opportunities. Bosnahan identifies another characteristic to which he does not attribute a share of the language imposition but which seems, nonetheless, important: a group that acquires the imposed language more quickly or readily than the rest of the subjugated population becomes an elite or intelligentsia that functions in the first stages of the military invasion and pacification as the interpreters and minor officials of the new authority, and subsequently as the medium through which the new language is transmitted to the subjugated general population.

One can look to other goals or situations, such as group coexistence, democratic pluralism, national integration, or the amelioration of group conflict. Each might require a different type and method of assessment. Some of these might be guided by principles of language diversity that have been borne out by research: (1) language conflict is usually related to other conflicts; (2) individual bilingualism in language contact situations is generally a normal result; (3) language conflict most often arises when one group attempts to impose its language on another; and (4) no two languages will be used by the same group of speakers for all of the same functions at the same time.

Whether there are 6,800 languages in the world, or 3,000, or less than 1,000, globalization is making the globe an ever smaller village. Communication will continue to be humanity's most important task. Addressing language diversity by encouraging individual multilingualism seems to be a continuing, viable strategy for success.

See also **Demography; Language and Linguistics; Language, Linguistics, and Literacy; Population.**

BIBLIOGRAPHY

Andresen, Julie T. *Linguistics in America, 1769–1924: A Critical History.* London: Routledge, 1990.

Bjeljac-Babic, Ranka. "6,000 Languages: An Embattled Heritage." *UNESCO Courier* 53 (April 2000): 18–19.

Brosnahan, L. F. "Some Historical Cases of Language Imposition." In *Varieties of Present-Day English,* edited by Richard W. Bailey and Jay L. Robinson, 40–55. New York: Macmillan, 1973.

Crystal, David. *Cambridge Encyclopedia of Language.* 2nd ed. Cambridge, U.K.: Cambridge University Press, 1997.

Dixon, R. M. W. *The Rise and Fall of Languages.* Cambridge, U.K.: Cambridge University Press, 1997.

Eco, Umberto. *The Search for the Perfect Language.* Oxford: Blackwell, 1995.

Gray, Edward G., and Norman Fiering, eds. *The Language Encounter in the Americas, 1492–1800: A Collection of Essays.* New York: Berghahn, 2000.

Grimes, Barbara, ed. *Languages of the World.* Vol. 1 of *Ethnologue.* 14th ed. Dallas: Summer Institute of Linguistics International, 2000.

Hymes, Dell. "Speech and Language: On the Origins and Foundations of Inequality Among Speakers." Chap. 3 in *Ethnography, Linguistics, Narrative Inequality.* London: Taylor and Francis, 1996.

Krauss, Michael. "The World's Languages in Crisis." *Language* 68, no. 1 (1992): 4–10.

McGeveran, William A. *World Almanac and Book of Facts 2004.* New York: World Almanac Books, 2003.

Phillipson, Robert. *English-Only Europe?: Challenging Language Policy.* London: Routledge, 2003.

Population Research Bureau. *World Population: More than Just Numbers.* Washington, D.C.: Population Research Bureau, 1999. Also available at http://www.prb.org.

Ruiz Vieytez, Eduardo Javier. "The Protection of Linguistic Minorities: A Historical Approach." *MOST Journal on Multicultural Societies* 3, no. 1 (2001). Available at http://www.unesco.org/most/vl31vie.htm.

Skutnabb-Kangas, Tove. "Language Policies and Education: The Role of Education in Destroying or Supporting the World's Linguistic Diversity." Available at http://www.linguapax.org/congres/plenaries/skutnabb.html.

———. *Linguistic Genocide in Education, or Worldwide Diversity and Human Rights?* Mahwah, N.J.: Lawrence Erlbaum, 2000.

Thomason, Sarah. *Language Contact.* Washington, D.C.: Georgetown University Press, 2001.

United Nations Population Division. *The World at Six Billion.* New York: United Nations Population Division, 1999. Also available at http://www.un.org/esa/population/publications/sixbillion/sixbillion.htm.

Wright, Sue. "Language and Power: Background to the Debate on Linguistic Rights." *MOST Journal on Multicultural S ocieties* 3, no. 1 (2001). Available at http://www.unesco.org/most.vl3n1wri.htm.

Reynaldo F. Macías

BIODIVERSITY. *See* **Ecology; Evolution; Nature; Wildlife.**

BIOETHICS. Bioethics as a field is relatively new, emerging only in the late 1960s, though many of the questions it addresses are as old as medicine itself. When Hippocrates wrote his now famous dictum *Primum non nocere* (First, do no harm), he was grappling with one of the core issues still facing human medicine, namely, the role and duty of the physician. With the advent of late-twentieth-century science, an academic field emerged to reflect not only on the important and age-old issues raised by the practice of medicine, but also on the ethical problems generated by rapid progress in technology and science. Forty years after the emergence of this field, bioethics now reflects the profound changes in medicine and the life sciences.

Nature and Scope of Bioethics

Against the backdrop of advances in the life sciences, the field of bioethics has a threefold mission: (1) to raise important questions about the general practice of medicine and the institutions of health care in the United States and other economically advanced nations, (2) to wrestle with the novel bioethical dilemmas constantly being generated by new biomedical technologies, and (3) to challenge the presumptions of international and population-based efforts in public health and the delivery of health care in economically underdeveloped parts of the globe. While attention to the ethical dilemmas accompanying the appearance of new technologies such as stem cell research or nanotechnology can command much of the popular attention devoted to the field, the other missions are of equal importance.

At the core of bioethics are questions about medical professionalism, such as: What are the obligations of physicians to their patients? and What are the virtues of the "good doctor"? Bioethics explores critical issues in clinical and research medicine, including truth telling, informed consent, confidentiality, end-of-life care, conflict of interest, nonabandonment, euthanasia, substituted judgment, rationing of and access to health care, and the withdrawal and withholding of care. Only minimally affected by advances in technology and science, these core bioethical concerns remain the so-called bread-and-butter issues of the field.

The second mission of bioethics is to enable ethical reflection to keep pace with scientific and medical breakthroughs. With each new technology or medical breakthrough, the public finds itself in uncharted ethical terrain it does not know how to navigate. In the twenty-first century—what is very likely to be the "century of biology"—there will be a constant stream of moral quandaries as scientific reach exceeds ethical grasp. As a response to these monumental strides in science and technology, the scope of bioethics has expanded to include the ethical questions raised by the Human Genome Project, stem cell research, artificial reproductive technologies, the genetic engineering of plants and animals, the synthesis of new life-forms, the possibility of successful reproductive cloning, preimplantation genetic diagnosis, nanotechnology, and xenotransplantation—to name only some of the key advances.

Bioethics has also begun to engage with the challenges posed by delivering care in underdeveloped nations. Whose moral standards should govern the conduct of research to find therapies or preventive vaccines useful against malaria, HIV, or Ebola—local standards or Western principles? And to what extent is manipulation or even coercion justified in pursuing such goals as the reduction of risks to health care in children or the advancement of national security? This population-based focus raises new sorts of ethical challenges both for health care providers who seek to improve overall health indicators in populations and for researchers who are trying to conduct research against fatal diseases that are at epidemic levels in some parts of the world.

As no realm of academic or public life remains untouched by pressing bioethical issues, the field of bioethics has broadened to include representation from scholars in disciplines as diverse as philosophy, religion, medicine, law, social science, public policy, disability studies, nursing, and literature.

History of Bioethics

Bioethics as a distinct field of academic study has existed only since the early 1960s, and its history can be traced back to a cluster of scientific and cultural developments in the United States during that decade. The catalysts for the creation of this interdisciplinary field were the extraordinary advances in American medicine during this period coupled simultaneously with radical cultural changes. Organ transplantation, kidney dialysis, respirators, and intensive care units (ICUs) made pos-

sible a level of medical care never before attainable, but these breakthroughs also raised daunting ethical dilemmas the public had never previously been forced to face, such as when to initiate admission to an ICU or when treatments such as dialysis could be withdrawn. The advent of the contraceptive pill and safe techniques for performing abortions added to the ethical quandaries of the "new medicine." At the same time, cultural changes placed a new emphasis on individual autonomy and rights, setting the stage for greater public involvement and control over medical care and treatment. Public debates about abortion, contraceptive freedom, and patient rights were gaining momentum. In response, academics began to write about these thorny issues, and scholars were beginning to view these "applied ethics" questions as the purview of philosophy and theology. "Bioethics"—or, at the time, "medical ethics"—had become a legitimate area of scholarly attention.

In its early years, the study of bioethical questions was undertaken by a handful of scholars whose academic home was traditional university departments of religion or philosophy. These scholars wrote about the problems generated by the new medicine and technologies of the time, but they were not part of a discourse community that could be called an academic field or subject area. Individual scholars, working in isolation, began to legitimize bioethical issues as questions deserving rigorous academic study. But bioethics solidified itself as a field only when it became housed in institutions dedicated to the study of these questions. Academic bioethics was born with the creation of the first "bioethics center."

Ironically, academic bioethics came into existence through the creation of an institution that was not part of the traditional academy. The first institution devoted to the study of bioethical questions was a freestanding bioethics center, purposely removed from the academy with its rigid demarcations of academic study. The institution was the Hastings Center, originally called The Institute of Society, Ethics and the Life Sciences, which opened its doors in September 1970. Its founder, Daniel Callahan, along with the psychiatrist Willard Gaylin, M.D., created the center to be an interdisciplinary institute solely dedicated to the serious study of bioethical questions. Callahan, a recently graduated Ph.D. in philosophy, had been one of the isolated scholars working on an issue in applied ethics, and he had found himself mired in complex questions that took him far afield from the traditional boundaries of philosophy. His topic, abortion, required engagement with the disciplines of law, medicine, and social science, which he felt himself unprepared to navigate. With academic departments functioning as islands within a university, it seemed that truly interdisciplinary work was impossible. The Hastings Center was founded to create an intellectual space for the study of these important questions from multiple perspectives and academic areas.

The second institution that helped solidify the field of bioethics was the Kennedy Institute of Ethics, which opened at Georgetown University in 1971. The founders had similar goals to those of Hastings, though they placed their center inside the traditional academy. While housed outside of any particular academic departments, the Kennedy Institute came to look more like a traditional department, offering degree programs and establishing faculty appointments along a university model.

From these modest beginnings, the field of bioethics exploded, with dozens of universities following suit, creating institutions whose sole function was the study of bioethical issues. Its growth was fueled by the appearance both of new technologies such as the artificial heart and in vitro fertilization and new challenges such as HIV. Bioethics was now permanently on the academic map and central to public discourse.

Institutions of Bioethics

Since the early 1970s, as bioethics has gained legitimacy, there has been an increasing trend of bioethics centers becoming academic departments. Originally modeled on the structure of an independent "think tank," the bioethics centers of the early twenty-first century are often housed within either a medical school or school of arts and sciences, indistinguishable in structure from any other departments in those schools. The professionalization of bioethics has taken it from the academic margins to the center, and with this development has come all of the trappings of traditional academics, such as tenure, degree programs, professional conferences, and academic journals.

Beginning in the 1980s, medical schools began housing bioethics institutes either as departments of medical ethics or departments of medical humanities. Located within an undergraduate medical school, the duties of these departments include the ethics education of the M.D. students. Whereas the original bioethics centers had as their primary focus the production of scholarly research, departments of bioethics have pedagogical obligations and are viewed as institutions designed to serve the narrower educational mission of the school. Bioethics institutions that are instead housed within a school of arts and sciences have the same type of pedagogical obligations, though perhaps serving a different student population, namely, university undergraduates or graduate students. Departments of bioethics, depending on their configuration, offer traditional undergraduate or graduate courses, undergraduate majors or concentrations, graduate degrees (usually master's degrees), undergraduate medical school ethics training, and/or residency ethics training. By the early twenty-first century, there were more than sixty master of bioethics programs in the United States, attracting a diverse student population including recent undergraduates; students pursuing joint J.D., M.D., and Ph.D. degrees; and midcareer professionals from the fields of law, medicine, and public policy whose work requires specialty training in the field of bioethics.

Another result of the professionalization of bioethics was the pressure to publish in traditional scholarly venues, such as academic journals. But the formation of a new academic field of study necessitated the creation of academic journals in which to publish these novel scholarly works. Journals emerged that were designed solely for works in the field of bioethics, including the *Hastings Center Report,* the *Kennedy Institute of Ethics Journal,* the *American Journal of Bioethics,* and *Bioethics.* But the mainstreaming of bioethics into the academy also opened up space within traditional medical and scientific jour-

nals for scholarly works in bioethics. Research in bioethics is now routinely published in the likes of the *Journal of the American Medical Association,* the *New England Journal of Medicine, Science,* and *Nature.*

Perhaps the institution most effectively used within the field of bioethics is the Internet. All major bioethics institutes, centers, and departments (and some journals) have elaborate Web sites, not only offering information about the specific institution, faculty, and degree programs, but also undertaking an educational mission to raise the level of public debate about current bioethical issues. These Web sites offer substantive information for individuals seeking to become better informed about these issues. One of the most developed Web sites is the companion site to the *American Journal of Bioethics* (www .bioethics.net). This Web site not only offers actual scholarly works in the field but also includes a high school bioethics project, job placement information, a "Bioethics for Beginners" section, and a collection of bioethics news stories from the popular press, updated daily, with direct links to the original news articles.

The Methods of Bioethics

The founders of the field of bioethics and its first leaders were largely theologians or philosophers. Reflecting the scholarly conventions of their home disciplines, the first works in bioethics centered on a normative analysis of bioethical issues, arguing for or against the moral permissibility of a particular technology, practice, or policy. Starting in the 1970s, these philosophers and theologians were joined by physicians and lawyers, who too made normative claims about bioethical problems. But by the mid-1990s, bioethics was attracting populations of scholars who had not previously been well represented in the field, namely, social scientists and empirically trained clinicians, both physicians and nurses. With the entry of these new groups of scholars, the "methods" of bioethics began to shift, mirroring the methodologies of the new disciplines becoming central to the field. With this change, bioethics included not only normative analysis but also the empirical study of bioethical questions, what Arthur Caplan has called "empiricized bioethics."

Empiricized bioethics takes one of two forms: either it seeks to collect empirical data needed to shed light on a bioethical problem, or it attempts to stand outside the discipline in order to study the field itself. Projects taking the first form use either qualitative or quantitative social science methodology to collect data needed to make persuasive bioethical arguments. These empirical studies might explore, for example, patient comprehension of medical information, patient and family experience with medical care, the ability of children or incompetent adults to give consent for research participation, or the frequency with which practitioners face particular ethical dilemmas.

Projects taking the second form explore the way in which the field of bioethics is evolving, the influence it has had on policy formation, the methods and strategies it employs, the field's understanding of itself, and its place in public life and contemporary academia. One very prominent contemporary method employing this strategy is narrative bioethics, or what might be called "deconstructionist bioethics." Using the insights of literary criticism, these bioethicists examine the discourse of the field to reveal its biases, conventions, and assumptions, making the field more self-reflective about its motives and goals. Along the same line, the field has seen the development of feminist bioethics and disability bioethics, both of which focus on issues of inclusion and exclusion, voice, and their confluence on particular substantive issues. Altogether, the empirical methods of bioethics have been so well received in the field that by the early twenty-first century, all bioethics centers and departments had representation from the social sciences or clinical medicine, and in many cases the empiricists constituted the majority of center or department membership.

One final methodology that has had a significant presence in medical humanities departments is literary analysis, in which literary texts are used as a vehicle for the ethics education of clinicians in training. These medical humanists use first-person illness narratives or first-person testimonies from clinicians, as well as important works in fiction, to teach health care professionals about the ethical issues involved in being both patient and practitioner.

Current Issues in the Field: Bioethics in the Early Twenty-First Century

The bioethical issues being addressed by the field are too numerous to count, but the flavor of bioethics in the early twenty-first century can be conveyed by an exploration of the bioethical implications of genetic research, health care access reform, and stem cell research, arguably the most pressing issue in the field to date.

Advances in the science of genetics, including the Human Genome Project and the ability to find genetic markers for particular diseases, have raised difficult ethical dilemmas. Two of the most pressing issues are preimplantation genetic diagnosis and the genetic testing of adults. With the technology to identify inherited diseases in the early embryo comes questions about which embryos ought to be implanted, which diseases constitute a legitimate moral reason to discard an embryo or become the criterion for embryo selection, which traits ought parents be allowed to select or test for, and who ought to have access to this technology and on what grounds. For example, while there might be widespread support for testing embryos that might carry the trait for Tay-Sachs disease or cystic fibrosis, there are troubling questions about selecting embryos on the basis of sex, nonlethal trisomes (such as Down's syndrome), or aesthetic or character traits that technology may someday be able to screen for. In adult medicine, genetic tests already exist to detect mutations leading to some forms of inherited breast cancer and to Huntington's disease. Here, questions arise about privacy of health care information, psychological impact, stigmatization, lack of informed consent, health insurance access, and familial disclosure. With the advent of commercial genetic testing centers, patients will soon have easy access to genetic tests independent of the practice of clinical medicine, without the benefit of genetic counseling services, professional psychological support, or adequate, and possibly accurate, clinical information.

The Internet, for example, will likely bring universal access to any genetic test as it becomes available.

Emerging Issues for the Future

As the twenty-first century unfolds, new and expanding areas of research will require increasing attention to their related ethical aspects.

Neuroethics. Knowledge about the human brain holds much promise and offers much needed hope to those who suffer from disorders of the brain and mind. The relative accessibility of the brain through biochemical, electrical, and magnetic stimulation, as well as surgery, makes neurological interventions tempting as knowledge of brain structure, wiring, and chemistry grows. Nevertheless, there has been little systematic analysis of the ethical implications of the revolution in the brain sciences. This revolution raises numerous ethical questions and issues:

- The "essence" of personhood and identity

- The relation between physiological structures and higher functioning ("mind" or "self")

- The ways in which abnormalities in the brain might account for atypical or antisocial human behavior

- The acceptability of using pharmaceuticals, implants, or other interventions to enhance innate traits such as memory, attention span, or musical ability

- The legitimacy of intervening to alter aspects of personality, mood, or emotion; to assess the effectiveness of treatments or incarceration in modifying criminal behavior; or to detect predispositions to both desirable and undesirable behavior in persons who cannot themselves consent

New knowledge of the brain will soon have an enormous impact on the legal and penal systems. How to integrate knowledge of the brain into the practice of forensics, the prosecution of persons accused of crime, and the screening of those seeking parole are all issues likely to become pressing in the not-too-distant future. Equally controversial will be the use of new knowledge about the brain in the detection and prevention of the onset of undesirable behavior in adolescents and children and in trying to improve or enhance their capabilities and skills.

Eugenics. While there has been much attention in bioethics to the mapping of the human genome and to the nuclear transfer techniques used to clone Dolly the sheep and other animals, the most provocative genetics-related issue facing society during the first half of the twenty-first century is likely to be to what extent ought humans design their children. Rudimentary steps toward making eugenics a reality are all around us.

The finalization of a crude map of the human genome and other animal and plant genomes means that medicine will soon have at its disposal a huge amount of information about the contribution genetics makes to a wide variety of traits, behaviors, and phenotypic properties. In addition primitive efforts to introduce genes into the cells of the human body through gene therapy will be refined to the point at which genetic surgeons should be able to introduce targeted genes with specific functions into both somatic cells (cells in a person's body) and germ-line cells such as the stem cells in the testicles that create sperm in a man's body. And the ability to analyze the genetic makeup of sperm, eggs, and embryos has already led to some infertility clinics offering genetic testing for diseases as a part of their standard care for their clients. This means that parents of tomorrow, both infertile and fertile, will increasingly look to medicine to diagnose potential problems and risks before babies and children are created. The issue will not be whether humans should design their children but to what extent and with what if any limits on how far one may go to improve, enhance, and optimize them.

When should a person die? Another fascinating emerging ethical issue is whether humanity should seek to control the time of death. It is one thing to agree that individuals who are dying have the right to withdraw or not initiate medical treatments. It is quite a different matter to say that someone who is not terminally ill but is suffering from a terribly disabling chronic condition, a severely diminished quality of life, or the prospect of decades of life in a state of dementia or extreme frailty should have the right to medical or technological assistance in dying as is already the case in the Netherlands, the state of Oregon, and Colombia. The focus of these debates, however, has been almost exclusively the terminally ill. As the population of the world ages over the course of the twenty-first century, more and more persons may begin to ask or demand the right to control the timing of their death, whether they are deemed terminally ill or not.

See also **Biology; Death; Eugenics; Life; Medicine: Europe and the United States.**

BIBLIOGRAPHY

Callahan, Daniel. "Bioethics as a Discipline." *Hastings Center Studies* 1, no. 1 (1973): 66–73.

Caplan, Arthur L. *Am I My Brother's Keeper? The Ethical Frontiers of Biomedicine.* Bloomington: Indiana University Press, 1997.

Jonsen, Albert R. *The Birth of Bioethics.* New York: Oxford University Press, 1998.

Reich, Warren T. "The Word 'Bioethics': Its Birth and the Legacies of Those Who Shaped Its Meaning." *Kennedy Institute of Ethics Journal* 4, no. 4 (1994): 319–336.

Rothman, David J. *Strangers at the Bedside: A History of How Law and Bioethics Transformed Medical Decision Making.* 2nd ed. New York: Aldine de Gruyter, 2003.

Stevens, M. L. Tina. *Bioethics in America: Origins and Cultural Politics.* Baltimore: Johns Hopkins University Press, 2000.

Arthur Caplan
Autumn Fiester

BIOGRAPHY. One of the oldest genres of literature, biography is a written account of a person's life. It is also known as "life writing," a broader term that encompasses autobiography and other narrative forms such as letters, memoirs, journals, and diaries. The term *biography* derives from the Greek *bios* (life) and *graphein* (to write). Latin and Greek terms for biography were used in antiquity. Before the adoption of the word *biography* into English in the seventeenth century, common terms for biography were *life* and the Latin *biographia*.

Many of the earliest "histories" were biographical accounts of the lives of important historical figures. Biography often has been associated with the field of history (and at times has been considered a branch of it), but distinctions between them were drawn beginning in ancient times. Whereas the writers of histories always have purported to present the truth accurately, biographers more obviously have praised their subjects or have presented them as exemplars for moral or didactic (educational) purposes.

Although formal definitions of biography vary, biographical literature includes such forms as character sketches, single biography, serial biography, literary biography, ethical (or didactic) biography, critical biography, and hagiography (sacred biography). In addition, biography shares many features with other literary genres, including travel writing and epistolary literature (that is, literature based on letters), and certain novelistic forms, such as the biographical novel and the bildungsroman that follows the development of a young character. The mixture of fiction with fact in biography means that it has much in common with imaginative literature. For example, the emergence of the novel as a genre paralleled developments in biography. Many early novels adopted a biographical form. In contemporary literature, a novelized biography may be nearly indistinguishable from a biographical novel.

Some commentators have indicated that biography, as an independent form, has been predominantly a product of Western civilization. In particular, they have pointed to the comparatively greater focus on the individual personality in Western biographical literature. If one follows a narrowly construed definition of biography, and adopts Western forms as standards, then this conclusion may seem plausible. Yet while the development of biography in the West has followed a unique trajectory, the production of biographical literature (and likely the biographical impulse witnessed in oral cultures) appears to be universal. Nevertheless, some differences between Western and non-Western traditions must be considered. In China, for example, biographical literature has been largely contained within a historiographic tradition and has been primarily related to the literature of the art of government. In India, biographical writings (such as fragments regarding the Buddha) have been contained within a larger body of spiritual literature.

Just as it is difficult to find an unbiased historical narrative (and many histories have been written for political purposes), biography long has been written for political, moral, or didactic purposes. The origins of biography in epideictic rhetoric (panegyric, or elaborate praise) means that biographers (whether of kings or revolutionaries) have been more interested in praising their subjects' actions or characters than in presenting historically accurate accounts. For this reason, the genre has lent itself to politicized narratives (including political histories or political romances) and narratives that define personal

New Dictionary of the History of Ideas

identity. Although biography traditionally has centered on rulers, philosophers, or literati, modern biographers have taken a wide variety of persons for their subjects, including women and individuals from underrepresented or persecuted groups.

Ancient Biography

Biographies have evolved from short narratives that commemorate the deeds of illustrious figures to more complex forms that present the life of an individual in considerable detail. The earliest biographical records include the hieroglyphic inscriptions on Egyptian monuments (c. 1300 B.C.E.) and cuneiform inscriptions found in Assyria (c. 720 B.C.E.) and Persia (c. 520 B.C.E.). These quasi-biographical works commemorated the deeds of kings. Similarly, the oldest biographical writings in England were runic inscriptions that related the lives of heroes. Apart from Western quasi-biographical works, the earliest biographies appeared in the second century B.C.E. in China. The *Shih-chih* (Historical records) by Sima Qian (formerly transliterated as Ssu-ma Ch'ien, c. 145–c. 85 B.C.E.) included short character sketches, anecdotes, and dialogue between archetypal subjects. The historian Ban Gu (formerly transliterated as Pan Ku, 31–92 C.E.) continued this tradition in the *Han shu* (History of the former Han dynasty).

While biographical literature existed in the West as early as the fifth century B.C.E., a more defined notion of biography did not appear there until the Hellenistic age. Ion of Chios (c. 490–c. 421 B.C.E.) wrote quasi-biographical character sketches of eminent figures such as Pericles and Sophocles. Xenophon (c. 431–c. 352 B.C.E.) wrote a life of Cyrus (c. 365 B.C.E.) that praised the king. He also commemorated Socrates in the *Memorabilia*. Other quasi-biographical works include Plato's dialogues on Socrates, the *Apology* and the *Phaedo*.

Among the earliest surviving biographies are those contained in *De viris illustribus* (On illustrious men), by Cornelius Nepos (c. 100–c. 25 B.C.E.). This work became a model for subsequent serial biography, a form that consisted of the collected lives of one or more categories of illustrious persons. Plutarch (c. 46–after 119 C.E.) is perhaps the most famous ancient biographer. His *Parallel Lives* comprised forty-six biographies assembled in pairs. This work was an early example of a collection of single, autonomous lives. Plutarch showed a greater interest in revealing a subject's moral character than in documenting historical details, a feature that is typical of panegyric literature. He also praised his subjects in many anecdotes and digressions.

Other early biographers included Cornelius Tacitus (c. 56–c. 120 C.E.) and Suetonius (c. 69–after 122 C.E.). Suetonius presented the life of Julius Caesar and the lives of the first eleven emperors in his *De vita Caesarum* (c. 110 C.E.; English trans. *The Twelve Caesars*, 2003). Following Plutarch, he emphasized the personal lives of the emperors rather than historical details in his collection of single lives. Suetonius also wrote *De viris illustribus* (c. 106–113; On illustrious men), a series of biographies of illustrious figures (philosophers, orators, and literati) that became a model for serial biography.

Diogenes Laertius (3rd century B.C.E.) wrote the *Lives of Eminent Philosophers*, a series of biographies of Greek philosophers. This work is the most complete surviving example of the ancient genre of philosophers' lives (the revival of which in the fifteenth century had a major impact on early modern biography). Diogenes notably indicates in his accounts that the actions and behaviors of the philosophers serve to exemplify their teachings. Although he focused on the private lives of his subjects, he also was known for his meticulous documentation of sources. His serial *Lives* were instructive to later biographers because he arranged them by the relations of masters to disciples and by individuals' contributions in their fields. St. Jerome (c. 347–419 or 420) wrote the exemplary serial biography in late antiquity. His *De viris illustribus* (c. 392; Enlish trans. *On Illustrious Men*, 1999) was an elaboration on Suetonius's notes on the lives of the philosophers. It was widely imitated for three centuries and revived as a model in the twelfth century. He also incorporated elements of classical biography in his lives of saints, which greatly influenced medieval biographers.

Medieval and Renaissance Biography

The works of Plutarch, Suetonius, and St. Jerome remained models for biographers in the medieval and Renaissance periods. The characteristic biographical form of the medieval period was the life of the saint (the sacred life or hagiography). Although many collections of saints' lives or acts (martyrologies) were compiled, there was often little differentiation between the characteristics of individual saints. While medieval hagiographers heavily drew on classic biographies, they focused on praising the spiritual virtues of their subjects and offered evidence for their canonization. Hagiography consequently developed unique conventions, such as the preservation of miracles and the martyrdom of saints. Exemplary lives of this period include Adamnan's *Life of St. Columba* (c. 690), Bede's *Life of St. Cuthbert* (c. 731), Eadmer's *Life of St. Anselm* (c. 1124), and Jean de Joinville's *History of St. Louis* (c. 1309). Other important biographical works include the *Lives of the Fathers* and the *History of the Franks* by Gregory of Tours (538–594), Bede's *Ecclesiastical History of the English People* (c. 731), and later Einhard's *Life of Charlemagne* (c. 829–836; based on Suetonius's *The Twelve Caesars*).

Humanist biographers in the Renaissance were influenced by classical lives and the lives of saints. Petrarch's incomplete *De viris illustribus* (begun c. 1337; On illustrious men) is in the tradition of single biographies of eminent ancient figures (following Suetonius and Plutarch). Giovanni Boccaccio's *Trattatello in laude di Dante* (1354–1355; English trans. *Life of Dante*, 1990) exemplifies the revival of the single life of a subject presented as an ideal. Influenced by Petrarch, Boccaccio assembled two collections of single lives concerning illustrious ancient figures, *De casibus virorum illustrium* (1355–1374; On the fall of illustrious men) and *De claris mulieribus* (1360–1374; On famous women), the first collection of women's lives. Partly in response to Boccaccio's *De claris mulieribus*, Christine de Pisan (1364–c. 1430) wrote her vernacular *Le livre de la cité des dames* (1405; English trans. *The Book of the City of Ladies*, 1998), often considered the first work of feminist literature. Notably, the earliest modern English autobiography is *The Book of Margery Kempe* (c. 1432–1436), by Margery Kempe (c. 1373–c. 1440), a work that largely follows the conventions of medieval sacred biography.

Renaissance biographers borrowed extensively from the works of Diogenes Laertius and St. Jerome, especially in developing new serial lives assembled according to notions of cultural progress. In *De origine civitatis Florentiae et de eiusdem famosis civibus* (c. 1381–1382; On the origins of the Florentine state and her most famous citizens), Filippo Villani presented short sketches of a wide variety of Florentine citizens, including poets, musicians, and painters. Later, Giorgio Vasari wrote his *Lives of the Painters, Sculptors, and Architects* (1550, rev. ed. 1568), following progressive developments in art through a series of biographies that culminated in Michelangelo. In England, William Roper (1496–1578) wrote the *Life of Sir Thomas More* and George Cavendish (1500–1561?) wrote the *Life of Cardinal Wolsey*. Other biographical writings were the *Lives of Famous Ladies* and the *Lives of Famous Men* by Pierre de Bourdeille, seigneur de Brantôme (c. 1540–1614) and Macarius's *Stepennaya Kniga* (1563; Book of degrees) in Russia.

The Seventeenth and Eighteenth Centuries

The English term *biography* was first used by John Dryden in 1683. The seventeenth century and the early eighteenth century witnessed expanded production of many types of life writing, including diaries, letters, and memoirs. Biographies by women appeared in this period, such as *Memoirs of the Life of Colonel Hutchinson* by Lucy Hutchinson (1620–after 1675) and *The Life of William Cavendish* (1667) by Margaret Cavendish (1623–1673). Some important biographical works were the five lives of eminent figures by Izaak Walton (1593–1683), the *Lives of Eminent Men* by John Aubrey (1626–1697), the diary of Samuel Pepys (1633–1703), and Roger North's *Lives of the Norths* (1742–1744). The most influential English biography was James Boswell's *Life of Samuel Johnson* (1791). Boswell adopted the methods of earlier biographers, but artfully combined letters, personal documents, conversation, anecdotes, and his own observations to present a vivid portrait of Johnson. His in-depth treatment had a major impact on biography throughout the world.

The Nineteenth and Twentieth Centuries

Early-nineteenth-century biography was influenced by Boswell's *Life of Samuel Johnson* as well as by the writers within the Romantic movement. The primary biographical form in this period was the Victorian "life and letters" (or "life and times"). It was characterized by relatively great length, sobriety, and concern with social propriety. Some biographies of this period were Thomas Moore's *Life of Sheridan* (1825) and his *Letters and Journals of Lord Byron* (1830), John Lockhart's *Life of Sir Walter Scott* (1837–1838), Elizabeth Gaskell's *Life of Charlotte Brontë* (1857), G. O. Trevelyan's *Life and Letters of Lord Macaulay* (1876), and David Mason's *Life of John Milton: Narrated in Connection with the Political, Ecclesiastical, and Literary History of His Time* (7 vols., London, 1859–1894). Popular literary genres of the later nineteenth and early twentieth centuries that were influenced by biography included the realistic novel and the historical novel.

Biography in the twentieth century reflected the rise of modernism in the arts. There was a reaction against the Victorian style of biography that resulted in shorter, less studious lives. Works of modernist biography include Lytton Strachey's *Eminent Victorians* (1918) and *Queen Victoria* (1921) and the numerous lives by André Maurois (1885–1967). Changes in style also were reflected in biographers' adoption of a scientific outlook. The influence of psychology (especially Freudian and Jungian) eventually led to the development of psychobiography. Experimental forms and methods were explored in works as diverse as Virginia Woolf's mock biography *Orlando* (1928), Lord David Cecil's two-volume work on Lord Melbourne (1939 and 1954), and A. J. A. Symon's *The Quest for Corvo* (1934). Postmodern forms of life writing emerged after World War II. Although more represented in autobiography than biography, postmodern lives have been characterized by further experimentation and the broad use of nontraditional methods. Postmodern biography in many ways reacts against modernist biography but is also an extension of it. It contains elements that are antiheroic, antihistorical, and absurd, or that consciously undermine conventional forms.

There were other major developments in the late twentieth century. One was the widespread appearance of biographies by and about women, and in particular, the establishment of feminist life writing as a literary form. Feminist biography had appeared in the fifteenth century, and feminists' writings had flourished at times, especially in the late eighteenth century (for example, Mary Wollstonecraft's *A Vindication of the Rights of Woman,* 1792). The late twentieth century, however, saw the rise of feminism as a major cultural movement and a rapid increase in feminist life writings. Late-twentieth-century feminist biographies were numerous and included several lives of Woolf. Feminist biographers have drawn inspiration from the works of earlier feminists, including the writings of Charlotte Perkins Gilman (1860–1935) and Woolf's essays *A Room of One's Own* (1929) and *Three Guineas* (1938). In addition to the establishment of feminist biography and the increase in biographies written by women (with women as subjects), lesbian and gay biography also became independent forms in the late twentieth century (such as Elizabeth Mavor's *The Ladies of Llangollen,* 1971).

The late twentieth century witnessed the emergence of traditionally underrepresented groups in biography, both as subjects and as biographers. In the United States, for example, subjects were increasingly African-American, Asian-American, Hispanic, and Native American (or were members of other underrepresented or immigrant groups). Some of these biographies built on earlier traditions (for example, African-American lives range from pre–Civil War slave narratives to Alex Haley's *Roots,* 1976). Biographers working in various postcolonial literatures also produced many lives of subjects from underrepresented groups.

Another major development has been the globalization of biography. As biographical forms have become diffused around the world, they have encompassed subjects from cultures in Africa, the Americas, East and Southeast Asia, Australia, the Middle East, the Indian subcontinent, and other regions. It is notable that while biographical forms have spread worldwide, biographers have continued to draw on forms established in earlier times (both oral and written). In the early twenty-first century, as a result of these trends, biography is an increasingly global art, evidenced by the diversity in its subjects and forms.

See also **Autobiography; Genre; Literature.**

BIBLIOGRAPHY

PRIMARY SOURCES

Ban Gu (Pan Ku). *The History of the Former Han Dynasty.* 3 vols. Translated by Homer H. Dubs. Baltimore, Md.: Waverly Press; and Ithaca, N.Y.: Spoken Language Services, Inc., 1938–1955. Translation of the *Han shu.*

Boccaccio, Giovanni. *Life of Dante.* 1354–1355. Translated by Vincenzo Zin Bollettino. New York: Garland, 1990. Translation of *Trattatello in laude di Dante.*

Boswell, James. *The Life of Johnson.* 1791. Reprint, edited by George Birbeck Hill and L. F. Powell, Oxford: Clarendon, 1971. 4 vols.

Christine de Pisan. *The Book of the City of Ladies.* 1405. Translated by Earl Jeffrey Richards. New York: Persea, 1998. Translation of *Le livre de la cité des dames.*

Jerome, St. *On Illustrious Men.* c. 392. Translated by Thomas P. Halton. Washington, D.C.: Catholic University of America Press, 1999. Translation of *De viris illustribus.*

Nanamoll, Bhikku. *The Life of the Buddha.* Seattle: Buddhist Publication Society, 2001. Translated from the Pali Canon.

Plutarch. *Lives.* Edited by Arthur Hugh Clough and translated by John Dryden. New York: Modern Library, 2001. 2 vols. Clough's 1864 revision of Dryden's 1683 translation.

Sima Quan (Ssu-ma Ch'ien). *The Records of the Grand Historian of China.* 2 vols. Translated by Burton Watson. New York: Columbia University Press, 1961. Translations from the *Shih-chih.*

Strachey, Lytton. *The Eminent Victorians: Cardinal Manning, Florence Nightingale, Dr. Arnold, General Gordon.* 1918. Reprint, London: Continuum, 2002.

Suetonius. *The Twelve Caesars.* c. 110 C.E. Translated by Robert Graves. London: Penguin, 2003.

Sylvester, Richard S., and Davis P. Harding, eds. *Two Early Tudor Lives: "The Life and Death of Cardinal Wolsey," by George Cavendish [and] "The Life of Sir Thomas More," by William Roper.* New Haven, Conn.: Yale University Press, 1962.

Vasari, Giorgio. *Lives of the Painters, Sculptors, and Architects.* Rev. ed. 1568. Translated by Gaston du C. de Vere. New York: Knopf, 1996.

SECONDARY SOURCES

Edel, Leon. *Literary Biography.* Toronto: University of Toronto Press, 1957.

Frederick Liers

BIOLOGY. *Biology* comes from the Greek word for life, *bis,* and the Greek word for thought or reasoning, *logos.* It denotes the science that studies life, the properties and processes that sustain life, the evolutionary history of life, and particular living organisms. It is a science of enormous diversity, breadth, and heterogeneity unified only by the conceptual framework provided by the theory of evolution. Indeed, as famously noted in 1973 by the Russian evolutionary geneticist Theodosius Dobzhansky (1900–1975), "Nothing in biology makes sense except in the light of evolution"—a quote now replicated in so many university-level textbooks that it is almost a dictum in modern biology.

One reason for the diversity of biology comes from the staggering diversity of organisms that can be considered living. These range from viruses, bacteria, and fungi to plants and animals, including humans. Another reason is that life can be studied on various levels in a hierarchy that ranges from the organic-macromolecular level to genes, cells, tissues, organs, and entire organisms. Furthermore, organisms interact in, and can be organized into, families, communities, societies, species, populations, biomes or biota, and perhaps even the global systems (as in the controversial Gaia hypothesis, which postulates that the earth itself is a living organism). To a large extent, biological subdisciplines are organized around each of these levels of activity or organization. Thus, for example, cellular biology, or cytology (coming from the Greek word *cyto* for cell), deals specifically with the study of cells, while ecology (coming from the Greek word *oikos* for habitat) deals with interactions between populations, species, communities, and biomes and the processes that sustain them. Since biology deals immediately with living organisms and processes, it has a large applied component. It touches on medical and health-related areas, pharmacy, agriculture, forestry, and biological oceanography. In contemporary society, the promises and problems associated with applications of biology are staggering. They range from stem-cell research, the development and use of genetically modified organisms, and the use of biological tools as identity markers (as in DNA "fingerprinting") to the possibility of designer babies and human cloning. Whereas the physical sciences and their applications dominated science for much of the history of science, the biological sciences now dominate both popular and scientific discussions, especially after the discovery of the structure of DNA in 1953. Viewing the revolution precipitated by the applications of biology to society at the closing of the twentieth century, many commentators anticipate that the new century will be the century of biology.

The Origins of Biology

Though biology is generally regarded as a modern science with late origins in the early to mid-nineteenth century, it drew on varied traditions, practices, and areas of inquiry beginning in antiquity. Traditional histories of biology generally target two areas that merged into modern biological science: medicine and natural history. The tradition of medicine dates back to the work of ancient Greek medical practitioners such as Hippocrates of Kos (b. 460 B.C.E.) and to figures such as Galen of Pergamum (c. 130–c. 200), who contributed much to early understanding of anatomy and physiology. The tradition of natural history dates back to the work of Aristotle (384–322 B.C.E.). Especially important are his *History of Animals* and other works where he showed naturalist leanings. Also important is the work of Aristotle's student Theophrastus (d. 287 B.C.E.), who contributed to an understanding of plants. Aristotle and Theophrastus contributed not only to zoology and botany, respectively, but also to comparative biology, ecology, and especially taxonomy (the science of classification).

Both natural history and medicine flourished in the middle ages, though work in these areas often proceeded independently. Medicine was especially well studied by Islamic scholars working in the Galenic and Aristotelian traditions, while natural history drew heavily on Aristotelian philosophy, especially in upholding a fixed hierarchy of life. The Roman naturalist Caius Plinius Secundus (23–79), known as Pliny, also had a major influence on natural history during the middle ages, notably through his compendium *Natural History* (later shown to be rife with errors of fact). Without doubt the most outstanding contributor to natural history in the middle ages is Albertus Magnus (1206–1280), recognized for his superb botanical studies and for his work in physiology and zoology. A lesser known figure is Holy Roman Emperor Frederick II (1194–1250), whose treatise *The Art of Falconry* is one of the first serious accounts of ornithology.

Though animals traditionally drew the attention of many naturalists, the study of zoology remained underdeveloped during the middle ages, relying heavily on illustrated books of animals modeled on medieval bestiaries. Botany, on the other hand, flourished in the Renaissance and early modern period. The study of plants was important in medicine, as well as natural history (and in fact constituted one of the few early points of common focus in the two areas), because plants were regarded as *materia medica,* substances with noted medicinal properties. These medicinal properties drew medical attention to plants. Hence it became standard practice to plant gardens next to primary centers of medical instruction, and professors of medicine were very often experts in *materia medica* and served as garden curators. Indeed, noted taxonomists of the early modern period—individuals such as Andrea Cesalpino (1519–1603) and Carl Linnaeus (1707–1778), both of whom are considered fathers of modern botany for their work in reforming taxonomy—were simultaneously physicians and botanists. An exception was John Ray (1627–1705), an English taxonomist who also worked with animals.

Also leading to the growing interest in and need for taxonomy and to an unprecedented development of natural history were the voyages of exploration associated with the establishment of colonies from the late fifteenth century. Largely to meet the demand to classify the collections made by explorers and travelers in order to exploit these natural commodities, gardens and museums of natural history were created in European centers associated with colonial conquests, especially Madrid, Paris, and London. A new period of scientific exploration dawned with the first voyage of Captain James Cook, whose expeditions included not only astronomers and artists but also botanists, such as Joseph Banks (1743–1820). On returning to London, Banks was instrumental in helping to found the Royal Institution of Great Britain, as well as in continuing to expand Kew Garden and the Royal Society. He also encouraged these institutions to serve the interests of both natural history and the expanding British Empire in the late eighteenth and early nineteenth centuries.

While botany and medicine were closely linked, anatomy and physiology followed other trajectories. After Galen, the next major figure in the history of anatomy is Andreas Vesalius (1514–1564) of Belgium. Unlike many anatomists (such as Galen, who relied on dissections of animals such as pigs and Barbary apes), Vesalius drew his knowledge of the human body from detailed dissections on human cadavers. He was unusual for his time in believing that the authority of nature should supercede the authority of ancient texts. His seven-volume atlas of human anatomy, *De Humani Corporis Fabrica* (On the fabric of the human body), covered skeletal and muscular anatomy as well as the major organ systems of the body. Skillfully illustrated by some of the leading Renaissance artists, the atlas was considered a work of art as well as of anatomical science. Although Vesalius challenged many of tenets held by Galen and his numerous commentators, he nonetheless retained some erroneous conventions present in Galen's anatomy, such as the existence of pores in the septum of the heart and "horned" appendages in the uterus (present in the pig uterus but not in the human uterus). Vesalius's work was shortly followed by the work of anatomical specialists such as Bartolomeo Eustachio (1510–1574) and Gabriele Falloppio (1523–1562). Eustachio specialized in the anatomy of the ear, and Falloppio specialized in the female reproductive tract.

Developments in anatomy that turned interest to the parts and organs of the body were accompanied by questions dealing with organ function. In the sixteenth century, physiology, the science that deals specifically with the functioning of living bodies, began to flourish. The major animal physiologist of this period was William Harvey (1578–1657). Harvey performed numerous dissections and vivisections on a range of animals to determine that blood circulates through the body and is not manufactured *de novo,* as Galenic tradition had dictated. Harvey's influence was felt not only in medicine, but also in comparative physiology and comparative biology, since he performed his experiments on diverse animal systems. His experiments and major treatise, *An Anatomical Disputation concerning the Movement of the Heart and Blood in Living Creatures* (1628), are considered one of the first demonstrations of the method of hypothesis testing and experimentation. While Harvey frequently drew analogies between the pumping action of the heart and mechanical pumps, he resisted the idea that the body entirely obeyed mechanistic principles. Unlike his contemporary René Descartes (1596–1650), who held mechanistic theories of the functioning of animal bodies, Harvey maintained that some kind of nonmechanistic special forces, later called "vitalistic," were responsible for the life processes of animate matter.

The mechanical philosophy—the belief that the universe and its constituent parts obeyed mechanical principles that could be understood and determined through reasoned observation and the new scientific method—thus made its way into the history of biology. This engendered a lively discussion between mechanism and vitalism, between the idea that life obeyed mechanistic principles and the idea that life depended on nonmechanistic "vital" principles or somehow acquired "emergent properties." The debate cycled on and off for much of the subsequent history of biology, up to the middle decades of the twentieth century.

During the Renaissance, the mechanical philosophy did gain some proponents in anatomy and physiology, the most notable figure being Giovanni Borelli (1608–1679), who sought to understand muscle action in animal bodies in terms of levers and pulleys. Some early embryologists, as followers of Descartes, espoused the belief that development too followed mechanistic principles. In what came to be known as preformation theory or "emboitement," the seeds of mature but miniaturized mature adult forms or *homunculi* were thought to be embedded entirely intact in mature organisms (as though they were encased in a box within a box, hence the name "emboitement"). Prominent advocates of this view included Marcello Malpighi (1628–1694) and Jan Swammerdam (1637–1680). This stood in contrast to the idea of "epigenesis," the belief dating back to Aristotle and his commentators that development began from initially undifferentiated material (usually the ovum) and then followed an epigenetically determined path of development after fertilization. One of the more prominent proponents of this theory was Pierre Louis Maupertuis (1698–1759), who argued that preformationist theories could not explain why offspring bore characteristics of both parents.

In the seventeenth and eighteenth centuries, theories of embryology and development were superimposed with theories of sexual reproduction, along with a number of theories on the origins of life, most of which upheld the idea of spontaneous generation. During this period debates raged over spontaneous generation, the idea that life was spontaneously created out of inanimate matter. The popular belief that living organisms propagated from mud in streams, dirt and detritus, or environments such as rotting meat was supported by a number of scholars from antiquity on. William Harvey's research into reproduction, published in 1651 as *Exercitationes de Generatione Animalium* (Essays on the generation of animals), began to cast doubt on spontaneous generation. Harvey believed that all life reproduced sexually, a view he pithily stated with his famous dictum *Ex ovo omnia* ("Everything comes from the egg"). In 1668 the Italian physician Francesco Redi (1626–1697) performed a famous experiment that further detracted from the theory of spontaneous generation. By carefully covering rotting meat so that it was not accessible to flies, he showed that maggots did not spontaneously emerge. The idea that sexual reproduction characterized much of life was further reinforced when Nehemiah Grew (1641–1711) demonstrated sexuality in plants in 1682. Later, in 1768, the Italian physiologist Lazzaro Spallanzani (1729–1799) offered additional evidence disproving spontaneous generation, and in 1779 he gave an account of the sexual function of ovum and sperm. Despite this accumulating experimental evidence against spontaneous generation, new developments continued to fuel belief in spontaneous generation. In 1740, for example, Charles Bonnet (1720–1793) discovered parthenogenesis ("virgin birth"—an asexual form of reproduction) in aphids, and in 1748 John Turberville Needham (1731–1781) offered evidence of what he thought were spontaneously generated microbes in a sealed flask of broth (this was later challenged by Pierre-Louis Moreau de Maupertuis [1698–1759]). Finally, the discovery of microbial life supported the idea that living organisms spontaneously emerged from natural environments such as pond water. The seventeenth and eighteenth centuries thus witnessed a number of debates that were only resolved

much later in the late nineteenth century when distinctions were made between the very different processes associated with reproduction, the origins of life, and embryological or developmental unfolding. Belief in spontaneous generation was finally put to rest in 1860 by the celebrated "swan-necked flask" experiments of Louis Pasteur (1822–1895).

Other notable developments in the origins of biology came as the result of new instruments and technologies, the most important of which was the microscope. Developed independently by Robert Hooke (1635–1703) in England and Antony Van Leeuwenhoek (1632–1723) in the Netherlands, the microscope revealed a previously unseen and entirely unimagined universe of life. Robert Hooke first observed repeating units he described as "cells" in his *Micrographia* (1665), while Leeuwenhoek observed varied motile organisms he described as "animalcules." While the microscope opened up cytological and microbiological explorations, it also shattered Aristotle's notion that life is organized along a *scala naturae* (ladder of nature), since new and minute animal forms were not easily located on the ladder of creation. It also fueled the belief in spontaneous generation. Pioneering the use of the microscope and its application to anatomy, Marcello Malphighi (1628–1694), Italian professor of medicine and personal physician to Pope Innocent XII, drawing on the previous work of Andrea Cesalpino and William Harvey, studied the circulatory and respiratory systems of a range of animals (especially insects). He was one of the first to study major organ groups such as the brain, lungs, and kidneys in diverse organisms.

Modern Biology

Though there is some disagreement among historians of biology about the precise origins, the transition to modern biology appears to have occurred from the late eighteenth century to the early nineteenth century. A confluence of developments brought about this transition. In France naturalists reformed taxonomy and began to recognize the extinction of life forms. This progress resulted from the work of natural historians such as the Compte de Buffon (1707–1788), Georges Cuvier (1769–1832), Étienne Geoffroy de Saint Hilaire (1772–1844), and Jean-Baptiste de Lamarck (1744–1829) at institutions such as the Jardin du Roi. New sciences emerged, including comparative anatomy and paleontology, areas in which Cuvier is still recognized as the founding father. French anatomists such as Xavier Bichat (1771–1802) and physiologists such as François Magendie (1783–1855), by experimenting on animal systems (sometimes to questionable excess in the case of Magendie), refined and enhanced understanding of fundamental physiological processes, and thereby revolutionized physiological understanding of life. In Germany the insights of natural philosophers such as Johann Wolfgang von Goethe (1749–1832) and Lorenz Oken (1779–1851) began to generate a serious interest in a unified science of life.

All of this activity was echoed by a number of early references to biology in a number of obscure German contexts beginning in the late eighteenth century. Traditional histories generally pinpoint the first general use of the term *biology* at 1800 in the medical treatise *Prapädeutik zum Studium der gesammten Heilkunst* (Propaedeutic to the study of general medicine) by Karl Friedrich Burdach (1776–1847), who used it mostly for the study of human morphology, physiology, and psychology. It appeared again in 1802 in the work of the German naturalist Gottfried Treviranus (1776–1837) and in the work of Jean-Baptiste de Lamarck, the French botanist and early proponent of transmutationism. Although the word gained some currency by the 1820s, especially in the English language, it was largely through the efforts of August Comte (1798–1857), the French social philosopher, that the term gained its most widespread currency. For Comte, biology, one of the "higher sciences" in his philosophy of positivism, was the discipline of knowledge that organized the study of life and sought the principles of life.

Especially critical to the development of modern biology was the period between 1828, when Friedrich Wöhler (1800–1882) artificially synthesized the organic compound urea in the laboratory (fueling the debate between mechanism and vitalism), and 1866, the year Gregor Mendel (1822–1884) published his theory of heredity. During this time the conceptual foundations of the new science were laid, and many of the defining criteria of nearly all the major subdisciplines of biology were established.

The first areas for which groundwork was laid were cytology (now part of the more general discipline of cell biology) and histology (the study of tissues). Advances in optics in the 1830s by workers such as Giovanni Battista Amici (1784–1863) significantly enhanced the resolving power of the microscope and diminished or entirely eliminated such disruptive phenomena as chromatic aberration. Techniques for selectively dyeing and staining cellular components and enhancements in sectioning that led to thinner and thinner sections further enabled researchers to see more clearly increasingly finer structures. As a result of improvements in microscope technology, a series of plant and animal observations from 1833 led to recognition of a number of cellular structures, beginning with the nucleus, first observed in orchid cells by the English microscopist Robert Brown (1773–1858). Observations on the cells of plants and animals culminated in the establishment of the cell theory in the late 1830s, the recognition that cells were the basic unit of organization in all living tissues. The establishment of the cell theory resulted from observational work by the botanist Matthias Schleiden (1804–1881) and by the animal physiologist Theodor Schwann (1810–1882). Rudolf Virchow (1821–1902) extended this theory in 1840 to include the observation that all cells come from cells, and in 1858, in his *Cellular Pathology*, he provided new foundations for understanding disease in terms of cellular disruption. The germ theory of disease, a theory that Louis Pasteur proposed in the 1860s as a result of his work in microscopy, suggested that microorganisms were the causes of infectious diseases. Advances in microscopy in the nineteenth century thus laid the foundations not only of cytology and histology but also of the new science of microbiology (the study of microbial life), which continued to explore smaller and smaller life forms well into the twentieth century.

Yet another area that drew heavily on microscopy was knowledge of heredity (later designated as the science of genetics), especially in the late nineteenth century after structures such as chromosomes were first observed and cellular reproduction

was understood in terms of meiosis and mitosis. The chromosome theory of heredity, first proposed by Walter Sutton (1877–1916) and Theodor Boveri (1862–1915), largely integrated knowledge of the fine structure and behavior of chromosomes with Mendelian genetics to suggest that chromosomes were the material carriers of heredity. This theory was not articulated until early in the twentieth century, between 1902 and 1903. This development occurred so late because Gregor Mendel's experimental insights into the process of heredity, which had been published in 1866, was not appreciated until its rediscovery in 1900. The modern science of heredity, which William Bateson (1861–1926) designated as genetics, began in the early years of the twentieth century, with initial inquiry determining the extent to which Mendelian principles operated in the natural world. The second area of interest sprung from the pioneering research of the American geneticist Thomas Hunt Morgan (1866–1945) and his laboratory on Mendelian genetics in the fruit fly, *Drosophila melanogaster*. Beginning roughly in the 1910s and peaking in the 1930s, this classic school of genetics worked on the transmission of a number of characteristics by studying mutant forms of *Drosophila*.

Microscopic techniques also played an active role in other important areas of nineteenth-century biology, areas such as embryology, and brought into relief the interplay between heredity, development, cytology, and evolution. By the late nineteenth century, persistent questions of biological development were being tackled with techniques and insights gleaned from cytology and cellular physiology, leading to a renewal of the debate between mechanism and vitalism. Just when figures such as August Weismann (1834–1914) had articulated mechanistic theories linking heredity with development and evolution, leading to movements such as developmental mechanics, individuals such as Hans Driesch (1867–1961) challenged strict mechanism in biology by experimentally demonstrating that almost any part of the cellular constituents of embryonic tissues had the potential to develop into mature forms. Driesch's experimental efforts were rivaled by those of Wilhelm Roux (1850–1924), the leading advocate of developmental mechanics.

The middle decades of the nineteenth century also witnessed improvements in animal physiology, especially through the efforts of the German school associated with Johannes Müller (1801–1858) and later through the pioneering efforts of Hermann von Helmholtz (1821–1894). Increasingly, work in physiology, especially that of Helmholtz, drew heavily on the physical sciences. This research further supported the view that life obeys mechanistic principles and is reducible to such sciences as chemistry and physics. Proponents of this view increasingly dominated physiology, an arch example being Jacques Loeb (1859–1924), the German-American biologist most associated with mechanistic and reductionistic approaches to biology. His essays in *The Mechanistic Conception of Life* (1912) summarized this point of view.

Unquestionably, a major development in the critical early period of modern biology was the articulation and acceptance of evolution as based largely on the mechanistic process of natural selection. Drawing on a number of transmutation theories

---

PROPERTIES OF LIVING ORGANISMS

A capacity for evolution

A capacity for self-replication

A capacity for growth and differentiation via a genetic program

A capacity for self-regulation, to keep the complex system in a steady state (homeostasis, feedback)

A capacity (through perception and sense organs) for response to stimuli from the environment

A capacity for change at the level of phenotype and of genotype

SOURCE: Ernst Mayr, *This is Biology: The Science of the Living World* (1997).

(especially those of Buffon, Lamarck, and Robert Chambers [1802–1871]), Charles Darwin (1809–1882) and Alfred Russel Wallace (1823–1913) independently formulated similar theories of species change through the mechanism of natural selection, jointly publishing their insights in a paper read to the Linnaean Society in 1858. Darwin articulated his theory more fully in his celebrated work *On the Origin of Species by Means of Natural Selection, or the Preservation of Favoured Races in the Struggle for Life* (1859). Though the mechanism of evolutionary change continued to resist full understanding by scientists, the fact that life on earth had had an evolutionary history became widely accepted by the late nineteenth century. Because the mechanism remained uncertain, evolutionary theory remained controversial in the closing decades of the nineteenth century. Suggested alternative mechanisms included neo-Lamarckism, directed evolution, aristogenesis, and mutation theory—an entirely new theoretical formulation that drew on the new experimental science of genetics. The turn of the twentieth century is frequently known as the "eclipse of Darwin," not so much because he fell into disfavor, but because alternatives to his theory of natural selection were being favored instead.

Between 1930 and 1950 scientists became certain about the mechanism of natural selection by integrating insights into heredity from Mendelian genetics with insights from traditional natural-history-oriented areas such as systematics, botany, and paleontology to formulate what has been called the "synthetic theory of evolution." At this time evolutionary biology was organized as a discipline, in order to study the process of evolution from a range of perspectives. This "evolutionary synthesis"—an integration of Darwinian selection theory with the newer Mendelian genetics—is generally recognized as a major event in the history of twentieth-century biology. With the establishment of the synthetic theory of evolution, scientists began to feel that a mature, unified, modern science of biology had emerged. Theodosius Dobzhansky, whose own work in evolutionary genetics served as catalyst for this synthesis, has maintained that evolution went a long way toward unifying biology.

Much of the work of twentieth-century biologists served to integrate biology. In addition, new technologies (such as the first electron microscopes in the 1930s), as well as developments and refinements in existing technologies, led to a staggering range of new discoveries in the twentieth century. In 1895 the Dutch biologist Martinus Beijerinck (1851–1931) designated what is known now as viruses—tiny living aggregations of protein and nucleic acid—as "filterable agents" because they passed through fine filters that could contain bacteria. It was known that these filterable agents could induce disease, but their structure was unknown until 1935, when W. M. Stanley (1904–1981) first crystallized the tobacco mosaic virus. This opened up further inquiry into viruses as disease-causing agents, into proteins and nucleic acids as the sole components of this very simple form of life, and into biochemical techniques instrumental for carrying out this research. By the late 1930s molecular biology and biochemistry were gaining traction. The reductionistic, mechanistic approaches of these sciences further pushed biological thinking about life in those directions. There was acute interest in the molecular structure of important proteins such as insulin, whose structure was determined in 1955 by Frederick Sanger (b. 1918), and in the role played by proteins and nucleic acids in reproduction and genetics.

In 1953 vitalistic approaches and philosophies received two body blows. First, the discovery of the structure of DNA (deoxyribonucleic acid), by Rosalind Franklin (1920–1958), Maurice Wilkins (b. 1916), James D. Watson (b. 1928), and Francis Crick (1916–2004) made the mechanism of the replication of genetic material understandable at the macromolecular level and moved genetics in the direction of molecular genetics. More than any discovery in recent biology, the discovery of the structure of DNA brought forth a revolution in biology, not just because of the theoretical knowledge gleaned, but also because of the potential applications of this knowledge.

EARLY DEFINITIONS OF BIOLOGY

From Lamarck, 1802: Biology: this is one of the three divisions of terrestrial physics; it includes all which pertains to living bodies and particularly to their organization, their developmental processes, the structural complexity resulting from prolonged action of vital movements, the tendency to create special organs and to isolate them by focusing activity in a center, and so on.

From Treviranus, 1802: The objects of our research will be the different forms and phenomena of life, the conditions and laws under which they occur and the causes whereby they are brought into being. The science which concerns itself with these objects we shall designate Biology or the Science of Life.

SOURCE: As translated by William Coleman in *Biology in the Nineteenth Century: Problems of Form, Function, and Transformation* (1971), p. 2.

The second body blow to vitalism was delivered in the same year by news of the celebrated experiment simulating the origins of life under early conditions on earth by Stanley Miller (b. 1930) and Harold C. Urey (1893–1981) at the University of Chicago. Miller and Urey enclosed the constituents of the early atmosphere of earth (methane, ammonia, and hydrogen gas) in a glass vessel and applied a high-energy electrical discharge to it, "sparking" it to simulate lightning. A container of boiling water constantly supplied water vapor and heat. The cooling and condensing water vapor simulated rain. After letting the apparatus run for a number of hours and eventually weeks, Miller and Urey collected a brown-red pastelike substance and chemically analyzed it to reveal a number of amino acids, the building blocks of proteins, and other macromolecules usually associated only with living organisms. The Miller-Urey experiment thus provided evidence that the basic building blocks for life could be generated by the kinds of conditions present in the early atmosphere of the earth. Subsequent experiments simulating conditions on other planets supported the view that life may also have originated in space, on other planets, or wherever similar conditions are found. For this area of study integrating research on the origins of life on earth with research on the existence and specific character of life on other planets, the molecular geneticist Joshua Lederberg (b. 1925) coined the term "exobiology," the biology of organisms outside earth. Its sibling science is esobiology, or earth-based biology.

After World War II, biology boomed, and with it emerged new societies and institutions to organize the growing science. In 1947 the first umbrella organization for the biological sciences, the American Institute of Biological Sciences, was created in the United States. Other institutions, such as the National Science Foundation in the United States, established large divisions (and budgets) to fund research in the biological sciences. Both trends helped shape the direction and character of subsequent biological research. As with many other sciences in the postwar period, the dominant site of activity in the biological sciences had shifted from its older European centers in Germany, France, and England to the United States. At the height of the Cold War, the Soviet launch of the Sputnik satellite drove a panicked U.S. government to offer even stronger support of scientific research. The biological sciences, too, benefited from this turn of events and received generous funding for research and biological instruction. Textbooks such as the popular Biological Sciences Curriculum Study drew on a virtual industry of biologists and educators to produce a series of widely read and influential textbooks for American high school students. Research in the United States continued at specialized research centers such as that at Cold Spring Harbor (in 2004 a center for molecular biology) and more traditional research settings including public and private universities, land-grant colleges, hospitals and medical centers, museums and gardens. In university education, biology as a subject area is considered so vital that it has become a requirement for general education programs. It is rapidly becoming one of the most popular majors for university students not just in the United States but worldwide.

Despite arguments for the unity of the increasingly diverse biological sciences, controversies and debates erupt between biologists about fundamental concepts in the biological sciences. Differences are especially pronounced between more reductionistic, physicalist, laboratory-driven, and experimental sciences such as molecular biology and biochemistry and more integrative, field-oriented, observational, and historical sciences such as evolutionary biology and ecology. In the mid-1960s, university biology departments became divided over differences in conceptual foundations, goals, methodology, philosophy, and scientific style. As a result, at locations such as Harvard University, departments of biology formally divided into departments of molecular biology and organismic biology, an area defined as an integrative approach to the biological sciences that includes a strong historical and ecological component. Roughly at this time ecology—a science of enormous heterogeneity drawing on a range of approaches, practices, and methodologies and rooted in questions pertaining to adaptive responses to varying environments—became integrated with evolutionary approaches and instituted in departments of ecology and evolution. Often located within ecology and evolution departments are systematics and biodiveristy studies, a newer area concerned with biodiversity, including classification and conservation.

In 1961 the evolutionary biologist, historian, and philosopher Ernst Mayr, reflecting on some of these growing differences between biologists, provocatively suggested that biology in fact comprises two sciences. The first is a biology based on proximate causes that answers questions of function (molecular biology, biochemistry, and physiology). The second is a biology based on ultimate causes that seeks historical explanation (evolutionary biology, systematics, and the larger discipline of organismic biology). While the biology of proximate causes is reductionistic and physicalist, the biology of ultimate causes is historical and is characterized by emergent properties. Much of Mayr's reflections on the structure of the biological sciences has formed the backbone of the history and philosophy of biology and has made its way into some textbooks in the biological sciences. While vitalism is no longer tenable in biology, there is considerable support for the belief that complex properties emerge from simpler strata in biology and for the idea that such emergent properties are useful in explaining life.

See also **Evolution; Genetics; Life.**

BIBLIOGRAPHY
Allen, Garland. *Life Science in the Twentieth Century.* New York: Wiley, 1975.
Appel, Toby. *Shaping Biology: The National Science Foundation and American Biological Research, 1945–1975.* Baltimore: Johns Hopkins University Press, 2000.
Caron, Joseph. "'Biology' in the Life Sciences: A Historiographical Contribution." *History of Science* 26 (1988): 223–268.
Coleman, William. *Biology in the Nineteenth Century: Problems of Form, Function, and Transformation.* New York: Wiley, 1971.
Dobzhansky, Theodosius. "Nothing in Biology Makes Sense Except in the Light of Evolution." *American Biology Teacher* 35 (1973): 125–129.
Farley, John. *Gametes and Spores: Ideas about Sexual Reproduction, 1750–1914.* Baltimore: Johns Hopkins University Press, 1982.
———. *The Spontaneous Generation Controversy from Descartes to Oparin.* Baltimore: Johns Hopkins University Press, 1977.
Lenoir, Timothy. *Strategy of Life.* Chicago: University of Chicago Press, 1989.
Loeb, Jacques. *The Mechanistic Conception of Life.* Chicago: University of Chicago Press, 1912.
Lovelock, James. *The Ages of Gaia: A Biography of Our Living Earth.* New York: Norton, 1988.
Mayr, Ernst. "Cause and Effect in Biology." *Science* 134 (1961): 1501–1506.
———. *The Growth of Biological Thought: Diversity, Evolution, and Inheritance.* Cambridge, Mass.: Harvard University Press, 1982.
———. *This Is Biology: The Science of the Living World.* Cambridge, Mass.: Harvard University Press, 1997.
Moore, John A. *Science as a Way of Knowing: The Foundations of Modern Biology.* Cambridge, Mass.: Harvard University Press, 1993.
Morton, A. G. *History of Botanical Science: An Account of the Development of Botany from Ancient Times to the Present Day.* New York: Academic Press, 1981.
Nordenskiöld, Erik. *The History of Biology.* New York: Tudor, 1936.
Nyhart, Lynn. *Biology Takes Form: Animal Morphology and German Universities, 1800–1900.* Chicago: University of Chicago Press, 1995.
Pauly, Philip J. *Biologists and the Promise of American Life.* Princeton, N.J.: Princeton University Press, 2000.
———. *Controlling Life: Jacques Loeb and the Engineering Ideal in Biology.* Berkeley: University of California Press, 1987.
Pinto-Correia, Clara. *The Ovary of Eve: Egg and Sperm and Preformation.* Chicago: University of Chicago Press, 1997.
Richards, Robert J. *The Romantic Conception of Life.* Chicago: University of Chicago Press, 2002.
Smocovitis, Vassilliki Betty. *Unifying Biology: The Evolutionary Synthesis and Evolutionary Biology.* Princeton, N.J.: Princeton University Press, 1996.
Sterelny, Kim, and Paul E. Griffiths. *Sex and Death: An Introduction to the Philosophy of Biology.* Chicago: University of Chicago Press, 1999.
Strick, James E. *Sparks of Life: Darwinism and the Victorian Debates over Spontaneous Generation.* Cambridge, Mass.: Harvard University Press, 2000.

Vassiliki Betty Smocovitis

BIOMETRY. *See* **Evolution.**

BIRTH CONTROL AND ABORTION. *See* **Family Planning.**

BLACK ATLANTIC. In writing *The Black Atlantic: Modernity and Double Consciousness* (1993), Paul Gilroy sought to devise a theoretical approach to understanding race that encompassed three crucial elements. First, the idea of race as fluid and ever-changing, rather than static; second, the idea of race as a transnational and intercultural, rather than strictly national, phenomenon; third, the focus on analyzing resistance to racism as a phenomenon that emerged transnationally and diasporically.

Gilroy seeks to provide a theoretical rendering of race that bridges the hemispheres. To this end he takes the Atlantic as his preferred unit of analysis and uses it to ground his transnational perspective on race. In Gilroy's analysis the black Atlantic represents the history of the movements of people of African descent from Africa to Europe, the Caribbean, and the Americas and provides a lens through which to view the ways that ideas about nationality and identity were formed. Thus, in *Black Atlantic* the focus is on intercontinental trade and travel as well as on processes of conversion and conquest and the resultant forms of creolization and hybridization that occur.

The author maps the Atlantic Ocean as a way to catalogue a whole series of transoceanic transactions and exchanges in the past and in the present and in so doing seeks to move beyond racially essentialist ways of thinking which posit an unvarying, pure, and singular black (or African) culture. In positing the synchretic and hybrid nature of black culture and the deep connections between the formation of modernity and the formation of black culture, Gilroy points to the fact that modernity is itself a profoundly hybrid phenomenon.

The idea of movement is central to Gilroy's argument. Hence, the image of a ship forms a central metaphor in the text. Gilroy describes ships as micropolitical and microsocial systems that focus one's attention on the circulation of ideas as well as identifying them as cultural and political artifacts. Slave ships are particularly central to Gilroy's argument as he posits slavery as a pivotal moment for the emergence of modernity, modern ideas of race, and the *Black Atlantic* as, in his words, "a counterculture of modernity." By a counterculture of modernity, Gilroy refers to the varied ways in which people of African descent responded to and resisted the fact that, in the modern West, racial terror and reason were so deeply connected. It was this yoking together of racism and modernity that led people of African descent across the globe to search for ways to construct oppositional identities, particularly through music, which Gilroy identifies as being the preeminent nontextual form through which African people not only confronted racially repressive social systems but also retained a sense of cultural integrity and forged common cultural memories.

Intellectual Antecedents

Gilroy was not the first scholar to stress the importance of understanding race as a phenomenon that both emerged and was resisted transnationally. Scholars like W. E. B. Du Bois, Eric Williams, and C. L. R. James and Frantz Fanon examined the ways in which slavery and racism were pivotal to the formation of Western modernity. These scholars focused not only on the economic importance of Atlantic slavery to the formation of the West but also on the ways in which blackness was absolutely necessary for the construction of whiteness as an identity. Du Bois and James were also concerned to document the myriad ways in which the black diaspora communities, in their attempts to construct artistic and aesthetic responses to racism, played a critical part in developing the cultural institutions of the West.

Scholars connected with the negritude movement echoed their efforts, focusing on the unique cultural contributions that they attributed to the so-called African personality. Leroi Jones (Amiri Baraka) likewise pioneered the study of the music of the African diaspora, documenting the various ways in which it allowed for the articulation of a complex, albeit nontextual, response to racism. Scholars like Stuart Hall, who brought the insights of Du Bois and Williams to bear on British cultural studies, further developed these ideas. Hall was particularly instrumental in developing an approach to the study of race and culture which sought to understand race as an ideological system which should be analyzed in its political, social, and economic dimensions and black culture as simultaneously heterogeneous and connected.

Intellectual Impact

The concept of the *Black Atlantic* has been enormously influential. Gilroy's focus on the heterogeneous nature of black expressive culture has significantly broadened the field of cultural studies, forcing it beyond its parochial concern with either the cultures of working class Anglo-Saxons or European high culture. The manner in which Gilroy places slavery at the center of Western modernity, racializing and thus fundamentally transforming Georg Wilhelm Friedrich Hegel's rendering of the master-slave dialectic has, likewise, been enormously influential in the field of philosophy.

Gilroy's particular focus on the revolutionary struggles of African-descended peoples has also been enormously influential in the field of labor history, broadening it to examine the histories of the struggles of those other than white European or American working people. His focus on music as a modality through which cultural memories are retained and passed on (in form if not in content) has also been influential in the field of history, opening up new possibilities for uncovering the histories of cultures that place a higher priority on oral, rather than written, forms of communication.

The ideas that underlie the notion of the *Black Atlantic* have also been enormously important in the emerging field of transnational cultural studies. Scholars like Arjun Appadurai, George Lipsitz, and Donna Haraway have furthered Gilroy's emphasis on the intersections between local and global cultural dynamics, examining the global circulation of ideologies, people, technology, capital, and culture. Gilroy's work also played an important role in the emergence of postcolonial studies, much of which took a transnational analysis of the idea of race as its central theoretical concern. Thus, the influence of Gilroy can be seen in the work of scholars like Anne McClintock, David Theo Goldberg, Jean and John Comaroff, Catherine Hall, and Anne Laura Stoler, whose work examines the intertwined histories of colony and metropole and the ways in which ideas about gender, race, and class emerged both transnationally and dialectically. Gilroy has also provided an important challenge to dominant ways of thinking within the field of African-American studies. His critique of essentialist thinking about race has proved to be particularly challenging to devotees of Afrocentrism.

Critiques

Although widely applauded for his intellectual innovations, Gilroy is not without his critics. Some African-Americanists have accused Gilroy of failing to understand the complexities of the African-American experience and, thus, of having underplayed the unique and enduring historical connections between Africans and African-Americans in his effort to highlight flows, indeterminacy, and contingency. The work of feminist scholars has also highlighted the androcentric nature of Gilroy's inquiry; men exemplify the Atlantic experience. Yet, the work of scholars like Vron Ware and Catherine Hall indicates that the women within the abolitionist movement, such as Ida B. Wells Barnett and Charlotte Grimke, were equally important exemplars of precisely those processes of exchange that Gilroy highlights in his text. Gilroy talks about the abolitionist movement as an example of the counterculture of modernity as well as a transnational movement organized around race struggle. Although Gilroy provides many insightful observations about how gender was implicated in the production of both blackness and modernity, these insights are not central to his thesis and oftentimes remain unexplored. Robert Reid-Pharr notes, for example, that Gilroy fails to examine the ways in which thinkers like W. E. B. Du Bois, Martin Delaney, and Frederick Douglass conflated the regeneration of the black nation with the regeneration of the patriarchal black family.

Yet another criticism of Gilroy's work has been that the concept of the *Black Atlantic* is too narrowly focused on the experiences of blacks as minorities in the United States and Great Britain. Thus, the *Black Atlantic* proceeds from the assumption that diasporic black communities are necessarily minority communities. This assumption does not, however, hold true for people in the Caribbean. Furthermore, as Nadi Edwards points out, the ways in which Gilroy makes Afrocentric nationalism (which he opposes) the polar opposite of cultural syncretism (which he celebrates) ignores cultural developments such as negritude, which, although essentialist, also celebrated syncretism and hybridity.

Other scholars have pointed out that a narrow focus on the traffic that occurred across the Atlantic Ocean makes it impossible to understand the totality of the black experience. Françoise Vergès has pointed out that the islands of the Indian Ocean also offer important insights for understanding intercontinental trade and migration, as well as for understanding processes of conquest, conversion, and creolization. The Indian Ocean, like the Atlantic, offers a space for exploring various types of seaborne transactions and exchanges and opens up a space for thinking about the ways in which Africa interfaced not only with the Americas and Europe but also with India and South and East Asia. It also provides an opening for exploring how Africa interacted not only with the Christian, but also with the Islamic, world.

See also **Aesthetics: Africa; Africa, Idea of; African-American Ideas; Afrocentricity; Black Consciousness; Creolization, Caribbean; Diasporas: African Diaspora; Feminism: Africa and African Diaspora; Modernity: Africa; Postcolonial Theory and Literature; Race and Racism.**

BIBLIOGRAPHY

Baraka, Imamu Amiri. *Blues People: Negro Music in White America.* New York: Morrow, 1963.

Comaroff, Jean, and John Comaroff. *Of Revelation and Revolution.* Vol. 1. Chicago: University of Chicago Press, 1993.

Edwards, Nadi. "Roots, and Some Routes Not Taken." *Found Object* 4 (1994): 27–34.

Goldberg, David T. *Racist Culture: Philosophy and the Politics of Meaning.* Oxford: Blackwell, 1993.

Hall, Catherine. *White, Male, and Middle-Class: Explorations in Feminism and History.* London: Routledge, 1992.

Lipsitz, George. *Dangerous Crossroads: Popular Music, Postmodernism, and the Poetics of Place.* London: Verso, 1994.

Reid-Pharr, Robert. "Engendering *The Black Atlantic.*" *Found Object* 4 (1994): 11–16.

Vergès, Françoise. *Monsters and Revolutionaries: Colonial Family Romance and Métissage.* Durham, N.C.: Duke University Press, 1999.

Ware, Vron. *Beyond the Pale: White Women, Racism, and History.* London: Verso, 1992.

Zine Magubane

BLACK CONSCIOUSNESS.

Black consciousness is the name of a black nationalist political movement originating in South Africa during the 1960s and 1970s. It proclaimed the necessity of black South Africans to rely on themselves for liberation and to claim South Africa as an African nation. Black consciousness drew on a tradition of black nationalist thought in South Africa associated with Africanist political movements and emerged during a time when the older antiapartheid movements, especially the African Nationalist Congress and Pan-African Congress, had been driven deep underground by state repression. It also drew on the rhetoric and ideology of black power and black theology coming out of the United States in the 1960s.

Stephen Biko (1946–1977), a former medical student, served as its most important leader and philosophical guide. The movement emphasized black self-reliance in the struggle against the racist apartheid system in South Africa. Many of the participants in the Soweto uprisings of 1976 espoused support for black consciousness. The suppression of that movement and especially Biko's death while in police custody in 1977 weakened the organizational base of the movement. Many of its supporters went into exile, where they mostly joined the larger African National Congress (ANC), the biggest of the movements fighting for majority rule in South Africa. Those that remained in South Africa became active in civic organizations that made up the United Democratic Front during the 1970s and 1980s. Biko himself became an international icon in the struggle against apartheid, and was celebrated in popular music, a best-selling book, and a motion picture. While the movement left little long-term institutional impact, its message of black empowerment helped mobilize the younger generation in the struggle. Its popularity forced the ANC to adopt a more populist approach to the struggle and helped create the basis for the mobilization of the 1980s, which succeeded in forcing the Apartheid regime to free ANC leader Nelson Mandela (b. 1918) and negotiate a relatively peaceful transfer of power. Likewise, the term *black consciousness* entered the lexicon of Pan-African political discourse.

Black consciousness developed out of a long tradition of racial nationalism in South Africa. Liberation movements in South Africa operated within a tension between a liberal and multiracial or nonracial view of the struggle against white domination and a more "Africanist" conception of the struggle. The former emphasized solidarity among all the peoples of South Africa, including progressive whites as well as Asians and "coloreds." The oldest and largest liberation movement, the African National Congress, generally espoused this philosophy even as it became more radically socialist in its politics after World War II. Nonracialism was enshrined in the Freedom Charter of 1955 (along with socialism), giving the movement its alternate name of Charterist. Africanist critiques emerged by the 1920s. They argued that South Africa was an African nation occupied by colonial settlers who had no inherent right to be there. Activists such as Anton Lembede (1914–1947), founder of the Congress Youth League (CYL), often called on the communal traditions of African societies as well as external advocates of black autonomy such as Marcus Garvey (1887–1940) and Booker T. Washington (1856–1915), as their inspirations. The Congress Youth League movement of the ANC in the 1940s brought together young activists who promoted a more Africanist view of the struggle, often pitted against an older ANC leadership that sought allies among liberal whites in South Africa and socialist governments abroad. The CYL movement eventually led to a split in the ANC. One faction, led by Robert Sobukwe, broke off and formed the Pan-African Congress. The rest, led by Nelson Mandela, Walter Sisulu, and Oliver Tambo, gradually took control of the ANC and pushed it to more active resistance in the face of the tightening of Apartheid. They, however, converted to (or remained loyal to) the general Charterist position on nonracialism. The smaller Pan-African Congress (PAC) during the 1950s tried to press for even more direct mobilization against apartheid. The massacre of at least sixty unarmed PAC protesters in 1960 at Sharpeville resulted in the suppression of both the ANC and PAC in South Africa, imprisoning or driving into exile most of the leaders and activists of those organizations.

The early 1960s saw a period of relative quiet in black activism in South Africa. Biko and other black students developed the concept of black consciousness in the later 1960s on the segregated university of campuses of South Africa. By the mid-1960s, the National Union of South African Students (NUSAS) was one of the few national institutions still integrated and engaged in activism for change. However, NUSAS's leaders came primarily from the English-speaking white universities of South Africa and followed a liberal, moderate antiapartheid program. Black students, including students from Indian and coloured campuses, felt the organization was becoming less concerned with political change and more with narrow university issues. In 1967, at a meeting of NUSAS at Rhodes University in Grahamstown, the university administration required the students to use segregated facilities. In response, black students led by Biko, Barney Pityana, and Harry Nengwekulu helped found the all-black South African Students' Organisation (SASO). Biko emerged as the leading spokesman of the group. He was a medical student at the University of Natal Medical School, Black Section.

After 1969, the black consciousness movement called for blacks to liberate themselves psychologically first. It claimed many black people had internalized ideas of inferiority and dependency from the racism of apartheid. Once black people had come to believe that they had the right and power to stand up for themselves, they would then be able to take power in their own hands. One of the principle targets of the movement was the perceived dependence of blacks on white liberals to speak for them. Biko stated, "Merely by describing yourself as black, you have started on a road towards emancipation, you have committed yourself to fight against all forces that seek to use your blackness as a stamp that marks you out as a subservient being." Biko argued that only blacks (and he included the non-African peoples of color in South Africa in this definition) were truly oppressed in South Africa and that white liberals generally sought to play the role of gatekeepers toward blacks. The movement drew to some extent on the ideas of "Africanist" critics of the nonracialism of the ANC such as Sobukwe of the PAC as well as the ideas of black power and the black theology movement in the United States. Like the PAC, the black consciousness movement also criticized the close alignment of the ANC with the South African Communist Party and the Soviet bloc.

After 1969, the black consciousness movement began to gain at least nominal adherents throughout the black population of South Africa. Black consciousness adherents created a number of organizations dedicated to political mobilization and community service. They operated in an environment where the South African government kept a close watch on black organizations and had to be careful about both their words and their actions lest they call down the repressive state apparatus on themselves. In addition to SASO, the Black People's Convention, founded in 1972, created an alliance of over seventy organizations dedicated to black consciousness, including new, often unrecognized, labor unions and the South African Student Movement that included secondary school students. Biko became the head of the organization, and the South African government promptly "banned" him, a sentence that restricted him to his hometown of King William's Town in what is now the Eastern Cape Province and severely limited his ability to remain in contact with other members and organizations in the movement. The University of Natal also expelled him from medical school.

The resonance of black consciousness's call for pride and self-reliance helped create the conditions that led to a wave of antiapartheid unrest by 1976, despite the absence from the active political stage of leaders like Biko. A wave of strikes by black workers swept through the country in 1975 and 1976, and they were often led by "unofficial" unions affiliated with the black consciousness movement. In 1976, the government announced that henceforth it would require the teaching of Afrikaans, the Dutch-based language of white Afrikaners, instead of English in many black schools. Many blacks saw this as an effort to keep them isolated. Students in the township (a suburb designated for blacks only) of Soweto outside Johannesburg began a boycott of classes. Confrontations with the police led to a broader mobilization in favor of school and work stay-aways. Between 16 June and October of 1976, violence spread to townships in many parts of South Africa. Even though the government dropped its requirements on the use of Afrikaans, the movement took on the air of a general uprising. By the end of 1976, the South African government reported over 500 people had died in the violence, a figure many think is much too low to be accurate. Regarded as the guiding light of the uprising, although due to the banning order not particularly involved in its planning, Biko himself was arrested four times during this period, the final time in August

1977. Then, he was beaten repeatedly, suffered head injuries, taken in the back of a Land Rover to Pretoria, and died on 11 September 1977. The government denied responsibility for his death. Only with the work of the postapartheid Truth and Reconciliation Commission in South Africa almost twenty years later was formal responsibility for Biko's death laid at the feet of the police.

Black consciousness organizations and supporters came under extreme pressure after the 1976 uprisings. Many went to prison; many others went into exile. In both places, they began to drift into ANC-led circles. The ANC, for its part, adopted a more populist attitude toward mobilization. In South Africa, organizations affiliated with the black consciousness movement provided the basis for community organizations that continued the struggle against apartheid. Tensions remained between the ANC's commitment to the Freedom Charter, which called for a socialist and nonracial future for South Africa and these organizations and adherents. Some supporters of black consciousness created the Azanian People's Organization (AZAPO), which claims to be the main heir to the black consciousness movement. This movement in the 1980s and political party in the 1990s remained small.

Black consciousness represented a South African response to the conditions of 1960s apartheid. Its leaders drew on a range of ideas from abroad and from the past to shape their version of racial nationalism. Yet the influences of black power and black theology in the United States, the African nationalist movements that brought independence to much of the rest of Africa, revolutionary theorists such as Frantz Fanon (1925–1961) and Amilcar Cabral (1924–1973) merely contributed a language to what was an indigenous development. In its successful mobilization of mass protest, it forced the more widely recognized liberation movements to adopt a more populist and less rigidly ideological approach to the struggle. Likewise, its success at grassroots organizing, which again mirrored the efforts of some black power organizations in the United States, helped change the political landscape of South Africa. The main legacy of the movement remains its mobilization, especially of young people, in the 1970s as a prelude to the struggles of the 1980s that led to the end of apartheid. Nelson Mandela said at the twentieth anniversary of Biko's death, "The driving thrust of black consciousness was to forge pride and unity amongst all the oppressed, to foil the strategy of divide-and-rule, to engender pride amongst the mass of our people and confidence in their ability to throw off their oppression."

See also **Afrocentricity; Apartheid; Authenticity: Africa; Black Atlantic; Internal Colonialism; Nationalism; Pan-Africanism.**

BIBLIOGRAPHY

Biko, Stephen. *Black Consciousness in South Africa.* Edited by Millard Arnold. New York: Vintage, 1979.

———. "The Definition of Black Consciousness." 1971. Available at http://www.azapo.org.za/documents/bcc.htm.

———. *I Write What I Like: A Selection of His Writings.* Edited by Aelred Stubbs. London: Bowerdean Press, 1996.

Frederickson, George M. *Black Liberation: A Comparative History of Black Ideologies in the United States and South Africa.* New York: Oxford University Press, 1995.

Mandela, Nelson. "Address by President Nelson Mandela at the Commemoration of the Twentieth Anniversary of Steve Biko's Death," East London, 12 September 1997. Available at http://www.anc.org.za/ancdocs/history/mandela/1997/sp970912.html.

Mark, Anthony W. *Lessons of the Struggle: South African Internal Opposition, 1960–1990.* New York: Oxford University Press, 1992.

Moodley, Kogila. "The Continued Impact of Black Consciousness in South Africa." *Journal of Modern African Studies* 29, no. 2 (June 1991): 237–252.

Gregory H. Maddox

BLACK ORIENTALISM. *See* **Orientalism: African and Black Orientalism.**

BODY, THE. What is "the body"? If the question seems ridiculous to you, you are undoubtedly not alone. At any given time, in any given culture, most people have an intuitive, if not always easy to articulate, notion of what the body is, and probably regard that notion as shared by all human beings. The fact is, however, that human cultures have not only done an amazing variety of things to human bodies, but have imagined and experienced the nature, limits, and capacities of the human body—and its relation to the self—in extremely diverse ways.

For example, most people living in the early-twenty-first century West believe the body to be a border between the self and the external world, and one that houses only one individual self. Those whose experience departs from this are treated as suffering from a personality disorder. Many non-Western cultures, in contrast, do not regard the skin as an impermeable border between the individual and the natural world, and believe that the physical body may host multiple selves. Another example is the relationship of mind and body. Many cultural systems—Zen Buddhism is one—do not mark a radical distinction between mind and body. In contrast, mind/body dualism has been so thoroughly integrated into the fabric of Western culture that some may have difficulty imagining an experience of the self that does not partake of it.

From the significance of body parts to contemporary theory of the body, different conceptions abound. Neither "race," nor gender, nor sexuality is a universally uniform category. Different cultures imagine different organs as the center of bodily functioning, and privilege different senses; among the Suya of Brazil, for example, hearing is equated with understanding, as seeing is for Europeans and North Americans. And while contemporary biologists attempt to map a basic genetic blueprint, poststructuralists argue that the very notion of a biological body is a human invention.

From a philosophical and anthropological perspective—and to establish limits to an exceedingly broad topic—this article focuses on the intellectual, cultural, and political developments that various disciplines have regarded as landmarks in the history of the idea of the body.

A Brief Tour of Western Dualism from Plato to Plastic Surgery

Despite its familiarity, the notion that human minds or souls are fundamentally different from human bodies is a cultural construction that took many centuries to build. Arguably all human cultures, including prehistoric peoples, have had some concept of spirit residing *in* the body. But this does not yet imply belief in an immaterial substance distinct *from* the body. For many cultures, spirit is simply "aliveness," the vital principle that animates all living things, from plants to humans, and is itself conceived as a kind of material substance. In both Homer and the Hebrew Scriptures, for example, the words *spirit* and *breath* are used interchangeably.

The notion of an immaterial substance that is separable from the body emerges in historical documents first as part of ancient Egyptian and Chinese beliefs in a "dual soul," one aspect of which is joined to the body, while the other travels, after death, to the realm of the ancestors. Greek philosophers visited Egypt and were aware of such notions; their influence is especially striking in Plato (c. 428–347 B.C.E.), who believed that the soul exists both before the birth and after the death of the body. With Plato, however, it is no longer the realm of the ancestors in which the disembodied soul resides, but the world of true knowledge—the Forms. With this innovation, Plato introduces what was to become a central ingredient in later versions of dualism: the elevation of the life of the soul (or mind, or reason, depending upon the system) to the pinnacle of human achievement, with the body imagined as the enemy of its aspirations.

The body as enemy.　For Plato, the body is the enemy of the soul primarily because it apprehends things through the senses—and the senses, notoriously, can lie, can deceive one into mistaking imperfect and transient versions—of love, beauty, and justice—for enduring realities. Reality, for Plato, is composed of eternal, universal Ideas that can only be seen with the mind's eye, and so can only be known by human beings after death (or before life—Plato believed in reincarnation) when they are liberated from their bodily prison. But although Plato mistrusted the body's perceptions, he revered the beauty of the human form and did not view the desires of the body, sexual or otherwise, as sinful. In the *Symposium* (360 B.C.E.), in fact, it is desire for another human being that first touches the philosopher with a passion for beauty, and initiates him into a quest for its timeless essence. The desires of the body, for the Greeks, are only a problem when they are permitted to overrule reason (as they were imagined, for example, to function in women). The Greek ideal was management of the desires of the body in the interests of self-mastery, not, as for Christian thought, denial of the desires of the body in the interests of purity.

Plato's ideas about the body do not constitute a theory but must be patched together from remarks and arguments in various dialogues. For that very reason, however, they could be se-

lectively recruited—and significantly retooled—to serve later systems of Christian thought, where they have exerted a powerful historical influence. Saint Augustine (354–430) was a key architect of such ideas, which have shaped the theory and practice of many strains of Christianity, particularly Catholicism. In Augustine's hands, Plato's prison of the senses becomes the home of "the slimy desires of the flesh," and the judicious management of sexual desire is replaced with the requirement to totally subdue the body's "law of lust." Judaic, African, Eastern, and Greek systems of thought had not viewed sexual desire as an impediment to spirituality, except with regard to an elite, ascetic caste of philosophers or priests, or when indulged in without restraint. Now what had been regarded as a natural human need became, at best, a necessary (to procreation) evil.

The body as machine.　Despite their differences, the dualism of Plato and Augustine shared the ancient view of the living body—and the natural world—as permeated with spirit. René Descartes (1596–1650) was to decisively change that, in a reformulation of mind/body dualism that would herald the birth of modern science. For Descartes, the body is a mechanically functioning system with nothing conscious about it—simply the interaction of fluids, organs, and fleshly matter. Mind, in contrast, became pure consciousness—the famous "I think, therefore I am." This was a separation far more decisive than anything imagined before, as mind and body became defined as mutually exclusive substances.

These abstract reformulations had enormous cultural consequences. For one, the human intellect became elevated to almost God-like status, as it could be imagined as capable—given the right methods of reasoning—of seeing through the illusions of the senses to the underlying reality of things. At the same time, the notion of the body as an intricate but soulless machine made radical experimentation and intervention less troubling to religious-minded scientists and doctors, and liberated human ambitions to explore, dissect, and correct the defects of nature.

In the early-twenty-first century, the body-as-machine is no longer just a guiding metaphysics or metaphor; it has become a material realization. Every day, in hospitals throughout the world, human body parts are being repaired, reconditioned, and replaced, sometimes by the organs of other humans, sometimes by machines. Normally automatic respiratory functioning, the cessation of which used to be a marker of the death of the body, now can be prolonged indefinitely by sophisticated life-support machinery. The domain of cosmetic surgery not only includes the correction of disfiguring accidents and birth defects, but prevention and repair of the physical effects of aging, the rearranging and contouring of face and body to particular beauty ideals, and even—very recently—the promotion of extreme makeovers, composed of multiple surgeries designed to produce wholly new physical selves.

Whatever one's attitude toward such developments, what is clear is arrival of a "cyborg culture." It is not only through the achievements of science that a cyborg culture has been established—or, as others would emphasize, the marriage of medical technology and consumer capitalism—but by virtue of a conception of self for which the body is mere matter to be manipulated at the will of the true "I," the "thinking thing." Such living, historical connections between theory and practice make studying ideas about the body more than a scholarly exercise.

The Mind Embodied

From Plato to Descartes, the body has been imagined as merely attached to—and decidedly inferior to—an idealized intellectual or spiritual essence in which all hope of human accomplishment lies. In the background of this denigration of the body is the virtually obsessive need of Western philosophy and religion, until the nineteenth century, to distinguish "man" from "the animals." Descartes is explicit: Animals have no soul, cannot think, and are mere bundles of instincts, prepackaged by God. The man/animal distinction was already there, however, in remarks strewn throughout philosophy and religion, and (with a few exceptions—for example, Thomas Hobbes and other early materialists) it gathered momentum after Descartes.

In the second half of the nineteenth century, however, the human being begins to be naturalized, imagined more as a complex animal than a potential God unfortunately trapped within a mindlessly craving material body. The foundational contribution to this transformation was Charles Darwin's (1809–1882) theory of evolution, which demoted the human being from a fallen angel to a species that had evolved from other forms of animal life. Evolution not only placed human beings on a continuum with the "mindless" creatures from whom philosophers and theologians had struggled to distinguish them, but suggested that their vaunted, God-like intellect was merely the result of a larger brain, itself the product of environmental contingencies that had allowed certain biological features to "survive" over (that is, outproduce) others.

Not a Darwinian per se, Frederick Nietzsche (1844–1900) insisted forcefully on the instinctual nature of the human being, and far from regarding it as base or evil, viewed it as a force for life and an essential dimension of creativity. He mocked the notion that humans can attain disembodied existence or pure spirit, and mounted a fierce attack on those philosophers and priests who (as Nietzsche viewed it) had made life-denying, ascetic values the standard of human perfection, all the while seeking their own earthly power. For Nietzsche, such "will to power" was a positive thing, so long as it was joyously embraced in oneself and allowed to flourish in others; what he despised about the priestly caste—those "despisers of the body," as he called them—was their professed humility and meekness, even as they dictated the terms of existence for their followers.

With this critique, Nietzsche introduced two themes concerning the body that were to become increasingly prominent in modern and postmodern thought. For many intellectuals, both before and after Nietzsche, the history of philosophy and religion has been imagined as a conversation between disembodied minds (or, more colloquially, talking heads); not only are the class, race, gender, and historical period of participants considered irrelevant to their ideas, but so are emotional attachments, self-interest, and personal history. The seeker of

Truth is supposed to be above all that. Nietzsche was the first to insist that such transcendence of embodied existence is impossible, "The eye that is turned in no particular direction," he wrote, "is an absurdity and a nonsense. . . . There is only a perspectival seeing, only a perspectival knowing" (p. 119). Such notions have played a central role in twentieth-century critiques of Western culture mounted by feminists, deconstructionists, and Foucauldians.

The instinctual body.   The second body theme Nietzsche introduced, which Sigmund Freud (1856–1939), the father of psychoanalysis, was to elaborate and systematize, is the high price human beings have paid in the process of becoming "civilized." For Nietzsche, a decisive historical moment was the banishing of the Dionysian element—ecstatic surrender to the body, the unconscious, and the erotic—from Greek culture. Freud, unlike Nietzsche, viewed the repression of (sexual and aggressive) instinct as necessary to the preservation of human community and order. But he agreed with Nietzsche that the cost of instinctual repression in the interests of civilization was "discontent"—neurosis, depression, phobias, psychosomatic conversions, and just plain "ordinary unhappiness" (as he termed the usual condition of modern man). Much of Freud's writing describes the developmental stages—both in the individual and in the species—that inevitably take the human being from an instinctual existence devoted to "the pleasure principle" through stages of renunciation and accommodation to the demands of reality (which Freud believed were unable to gratify all human needs, even in the most permissive society) and morality (first experienced through parental authority, later internalized as the super-ego).

Freud represents, in many ways, a synthesis of several of the trends outlined in this article so far. In the tradition of Judaic and Greek thought (and unlike Augustine), he did not regard the desires of the body as sinful. Like Darwin, he looked to nature, not God, to understand the design of the human being, and described what he believed he had found with the dedicated detachment of the Cartesian scientist. Like Plato, he believed the "higher" accomplishments of humanity—art, music, literature, philosophy—require the sublimation (or redirection) of the body, from the original aim of sexual fulfillment to the less intense gratifications of art and intellect. But like Nietzsche, he was continually drawn to the exploration of the underside of progress—the unconscious drives and desires, never fully banished from human life, and a constant reminder of the primacy of the body.

The lived body.   Another philosophical spokesperson for the primacy of the body—but with a very different understanding of that primacy than Darwin, Nietzsche, or Freud—was Maurice Merleau-Ponty (1908–1961). Merleau-Ponty, in the tradition of philosophical phenomenology, did not believe the human body could be reduced to a scientific or social object of study. What such perspectives left out, he argued, was what phenomenologists call "the lived body." From the perspective of the lived body, human beings do not *have* bodies (as they might possess hats or coats), they *are* bodies; and as bodies, are more than physically encased minds or collections of instinct. Rather, bodies are the medium of human experience,

Barbette Applying Makeup (1926) by Man Ray. Gender discussions revolving around the body were introduced in the twentieth century. Some researchers believed that the idea of gender based solely on body configuration was illusory. © 2004 MAN RAY TRUST / ARTISTS RIGHTS SOCIETY (ARS), NEW YORK / ADAGP, PARIS / TELIMAGE-2004

through which they engage with their surroundings. Merleau-Ponty, unlike Plato or Descartes, was not concerned with some reality beyond or behind the way things appear, but with the way the world is given to embodied beings. For many twentieth-century continental philosophers, this was the definitive rejection of dualism; by doing away with "two worlds" and concentrating on the world as it appears to us, already saturated with the meaning that bodies give it, Merleau-Ponty reunited mind and body and made them natural allies in the quest for understanding.

Culturally Variable Bodies

Freud drew his conclusions about the inevitable struggle between ego and id from his own psychiatric practice, largely composed of well-to-do Victorians whose problems, arguably, were more the product of the culture they lived in than universal forms of human discontent. The point seems obvious in the early twenty-first century, after half a century of criticism of the many questionable assumptions about gender, class, and sexuality contained in classical Freudian theory. Many people associate such criticism with feminism—and indeed, feminism played a major role in placing Freudian theory in historical perspective. But it was anthropologists who

first called into question the universality, not just of Freudian theory, but of the Western tendency to regard the body—sexuality in particular—as a source of unruly impulses that are fundamentally in tension with the need for human order.

Mead and Mauss. Margaret Mead's (1901–1978) pioneering research in Samoa and New Guinea, for example, was concerned with debunking Western ethnocentrism, including with regard to sexuality. In Samoa, Mead (1928) found that adolescence was not a period of rebellion from parents, nor was adolescent sexuality fraught with the moral constrictions of the West. By revealing the more relaxed child-rearing practices and less rigid sex roles in Samoa and New Guinea, Mead critiqued American patterns and called for their modification.

Marcel Mauss's (1872–1950) reflections on cross-cultural variations in what he called "techniques of the body" constituted another important moment in the development of anthropological thinking about the body. Mauss noted (1934) that while, universally, people successfully hold themselves upright, walk, gesture, talk, and eat, the precise renderings of these activities varies from one society to the next. Later (1938), he formulated the important distinction between the self (*moi*) and the social or culturally constructed person (*la personne*). The former refers to individuals' private, personal sense of themselves; the latter to the cross-culturally variable ways in which societies define the contours of individuals, such as expectations and rights varying by gender and life stage; the degree to which cultural members are perceived to be connected to one another and to nature; and beliefs about the human soul, its essence and location, and how it and the souls of deceased relatives influence the affairs of the living.

Personhood has been the realm of rich sociocultural research, yielding cross-cultural data with myriad implications. For example, in preindustrial societies, where perceptions of the demarcation between nature and culture, and between the living, deceased, and yet-to-be-born, are more gradual than in the postindustrial West, the proper or improper actions of humans are perceived to directly influence the well-being of entire communities (including the spirits of the dead and future generations), and nature's bounty and benevolence as well. A closer connectedness to the suprahuman world is expressed through the greater homage paid to its deceased, to widely varying burial practices centered on the corpse, and to a host of prescriptions and proscriptions concerning the bodies of the bereaved, which vary by gender and kinship status.

Biology and culture. With Mauss, Mead, Bronislaw Malinowski, Ruth Benedict, and others leading the way, anthropologists began to accumulate a storehouse of knowledge concerning the tremendous cultural variation that exists in ideas about the body and their corresponding implications for attitudes toward and practices of sexuality, reproduction, abortion, infanticide, child mortality, breast-feeding, child-raising, pawnship and slavery, and gender roles. It was from such cross-cultural knowledge that anthropology's concept of the body emerged. It is one that sees the corporeal body and its con-

---

THE SOCIAL SKIN

Mary Douglas's work, as well as feminist deconstructions of the meanings contained in representations of the female body, inspired a generation of anthropologists and cultural theorists to explore the human body as a text that can be read to reveal a great deal of cultural information. This symbolic function of the body applies not only to the taboos and rituals described by Douglas, but to parts of the body, to representations of the human body—in artworks, medical texts, racial ideology, and advertisements—and to decorations and modifications of the flesh, from ornaments, hair fashion, cosmetics, masking, costuming, tattooing, piercing, and scarification, to body fattening or thinning, muscular development, and cosmetic surgery. However extreme or seemingly whimsical the practice, it always has meaning, always is shaped by the sociocultural context in and through which people act. Anthropologist Terence Turner called this dimension of the body the "social skin," a concept that applies just as aptly to the nineteenth-century corset and twentieth-century implants as to the traditional neck rings of the Karen peoples of Burma or lip plugs of the Amazonian Kayapo.

A key difference between the body modifications of traditional societies and those of postmodern culture is that the former are dictated by group membership and are nonnegotiable by individuals. The status-significance of the size of Ethiopian lip-plates among brides-to-be is set by custom, as is who may engage in such modification. In contrast, many contemporary body modifications based on traditional practices—piercing, scarification, and tattooing—are freely adopted for their potential to express an individual's choice of alternative values or group identifications. Other contemporary modifications—for example, exercising to change the shape or fat composition of the body, or having one's face lifted to achieve the appearance of youth—are freely engaged in and (in principle) open to members of all social groups, but reflect norms of beauty to which there is considerable pressure to conform. Those who resist or cannot afford to conform pay a stiff price, in lesser access to jobs, mates, and social power.

Whether traditional or contemporary, all body modifications carry meaning, expressing cultural ideals (and anxieties), racial biases, social status, and membership in particular groups. Those meanings may be complex—both female slenderness and male muscularity, for example, are arguably overdetermined to be attractive in the late twentieth and early twenty-first-century context for reasons having to do with anxiety over changing gender roles, the increasing association of bodily discipline with self-control and power, and the moral valuation of leanness in a "super-sized" culture of indulgence (Bordo, 1993, 1999). Bodily meanings are also unstable and highly context-dependent, raising questions about the changing politics of the body: Does hair straightening by blacks, for example, have the same significance in 2004 as it did when "natural" styles were an expression of racial pride? There is no one answer to a question such as this; different analysts will interpret such practices differently. But however controversial or layered, no bodily style can be considered to be "just fashion," the expression of meaningless or arbitrary taste.

---

stituent parts, as well as its movements, gestures, needs, and desires as inextricably both physical and sociocultural. While language, social interaction, eating, drinking, and sexual activity are primary needs for which human bodies contain intrinsically biological capacities, none of these primary needs can be undertaken apart from culture. Thus the physical body is never just a biological organism. It cannot be, because human beings, as Clifford Geertz has observed, "are caught in the webs of significance that they themselves weave" (p. 5).

So, for example, while human differences in skin color, hair texture, and body size and shape have been variably selected by the pressure of different environmental conditions, there is no biological basis for the racial classifications that have been built upon those differences. Such classifications arbitrarily abstract particular phenotypical traits from a human array that is both much more varied and much more continuous than the concept of race allows. Race is not a biological "fact" but an idea—an idea around which an elaborate web of significance, with enormous and destructive consequences for the treatment of human beings, has been woven.

The classification and regulation of sexuality and gender, too, always involve the mediation of meaning, of human ideas, in the physical or biological realm. For example, as Malinowski first showed through his groundbreaking ethnographic research among the Melanesian Trobriand Islanders, ideas about conception affect patterns of sexual control. In matrilineal societies, in which the female is believed to contribute the blood—commonly thought to be the substance that ties lineal descendants to one another—to the fetus, female sexuality is not as strictly controlled as in patrilineal societies, where descent is believed to pass through males. In patrilineal societies, female sexuality tends to be closely monitored to insure that the line remains pure of foreign male intrusion. Depending upon the multitude of ways in which patriliny is interpreted, this monitoring may range from the moral sanction that sexual intercourse be confined to marriage, to the female bodily coverings of Muslim societies, to sharply segregating the sexes, or to various forms of female circumcision that, while often performed as a rite of passage, have the effect of decreasing sexual pleasure.

Research on male same-sex intercourse also highlights how similar physical acts can have widely differing social meanings. In some Latin American cultures, males may perform same-sex acts, but according to machismo ideology, it is only if a male plays the role of the passive partner that he is considered to be a homosexual. Among the Sambia of Papua New Guinea, on the other hand, where the conception of the human body is rooted in bodily fluids, same-sex intercourse isn't even considered sexual but is a ritual of maturation. Within this system, as Gilbert Herdt's research demonstrates, adult men are believed to be created through male elders' constant insemination of boys.

The cross-cultural evidence produced by anthropologists is a powerful argument against the notion that there is a single human body whose blueprint is invariant across history and culture. Evolutionary psychologists may argue that patterns of mate selection, gender differences, and even ideals of beauty are universally inscribed in human genes, but most contemporary biological and social scientists believe that whatever the role of biology—and many consider that role significant—it never manifests itself in pure form, untouched by the guiding, shaping, and disciplining hand of culture. Even such phenotypical results of the genetic code as human height, stature, weight, as well as physiological processes such as sexual orgasm and the onset and cessation of menstruation are more responsive to the socioculturally determined physical environment than was previously thought.

Many psychologists and biologists, too, now believe that genetic determinism does not square with the facts of human physiology. The human brain is extremely large; thus if humans are to squeeze out of their mothers while it is still possible to get through, most of the neural maturation must occur after birth. In the first two years of life, the brain fixes countless synapses it didn't have at birth, while weeding out many others. Which connections are reinforced and which atrophy is the result of the infant's (unavoidably cultural) experience, not inalterable hardwiring that maintains its timeless demands regardless of the particularities of environment and upbringing.

Politics Re-Conceives the Body

Environment and upbringing, of course, include patterns of social inequality. A new attention, not merely to the shaping and disciplining hand of culture, but to the body's role in the maintenance of (and resistance to) the inequalities of gender, race, class, and sexuality was a keynote of the political, social, and intellectual movements of the 1960s and 1970s.

Black Power, Women's Liberation, and the politics of the body. For example, Black Power, a movement that raised consciousness of racist aesthetics and ignited the "Black is Beautiful" philosophy, extended the conception of racial politics to include the body. Until the emergence of Black Power, the struggle for civil rights in the United States had focused on legal obstacles to equality. But Stokely Carmichael and others insisted that this was not sufficient, that blacks must reclaim the cultural heritage and pride that slavery had robbed from them, that they must decolonize their bodies and souls. As people became aware that racism had left its imprints on the body as well as on social institutions, that then-dominant standards of beauty—light skin, blue eyes, straight hair, narrow noses—were as much an expression of white dominance as "whites only" drinking fountains and bathrooms, allowing one's hair to go "natural" began to be seen as a political act.

Taking their cue from Black Power, early second-wave feminists (or women's liberationists, as they were then called) began to redefine the gendered body in political rather than biological terms. The 1950s had been rife with ideology about woman's nature, true femininity, and the horrible consequences of deviance from them. In the late-1960s, these notions, and their bodily accoutrements—speaking softly, moving gracefully, deodorizing, plucking, shaving, and decorating the body to appeal to men—began to be seen as training in subservience and central to the social production of gender. "In our culture," wrote Andrea Dworkin in 1974, "not one part of a woman's body is left untouched, unaltered. No feature or extremity is spared the art, or pain, of improvement." This constant requirement to modify and enhance one's body, she went on to argue, is not merely cosmetic, but disciplinary, as it prescribes "the relationship that an individual will have to her own body . . . her motility, spontaneity, posture, gait, the uses to which she can put her body." Anticipating both Foucault's description of "docile" bodies and later feminist arguments about the "performative" nature of gender, she described "the experience of being a woman" as a "construct" and a "caricature" created not by nature, but arising out of the habitual practices of femininity (pp. 113–114).

This was a pivotal moment in the history of the idea of the body, and hardly confined to Dworkin's work. Plato, Aristotle, and Hobbes had collectively created the metaphor of "the body politic," comparing the state to a human body, with different organs symbolizing different functions, forces, and so on. Authors such as Dworkin, Germaine Greer (whose book *The Female Eunuch* [1970] was the first systematic exploration of the social construction of the female body), Anne Koedt, Shulamith Firestone, Angela Davis, Mary Daly, Barbara Omolade, and Adrienne Rich collectively inverted the metaphor, imagining the female body as itself a politically inscribed entity, its physiology and morphology shaped by histories and practices of containment and control—from foot-binding and corseting to rape and battering to compulsory heterosexuality, forced sterilization, unwanted pregnancy, and the gender-specific abuses of racism and slavery. The "politics of the body" was born.

Gender and the body: from Beauvoir to Butler.

Simone de Beauvoir (1908–1986) was the first philosopher to insert gender into discussions about the body, connecting the social subordination of woman to the cultural associations and practices that tie women to the body, weighed down and imprisoned by her physiology (while men imagine they can transcend their own biology and physicality to commune with pure ideas). The association of woman with nature and body—particularly reproductive processes—became an important theme of early feminist theory throughout the disciplines. Some of the most influential contributions include Susan Griffith's *Woman and Nature* (1978), Dorothy Dinnerstein's *The Mermaid and the Minotaur* (1976), and anthropologist Sherry Ortner's "Is Woman to Man as Nature Is to Culture?" (1974). Ortner argued that menstruation, pregnancy, childbirth, lactation, and breastfeeding are biological processes that everywhere in the world tie women to nature in ways that male biology and physiology do not. Hence cultures everywhere interpret women as closer to nature than men. Because people universally value culture over nature, men are thereby awarded more prestige than women.

Ultimately such notions were challenged in the 1980s and 1990s, as feminist anthropologists turned their attention to the myriad ways that women's (and men's) reproductive biology and physiology have been interpreted through different "webs of significance" (to use Geertz's phrase) throughout the world. Their projects reflected an "anti-essentializing" turn in feminist thought that became a unifying project among postmodern feminist scholars throughout the disciplines, skeptical of generalizations about gender and more attuned to the variable cultural structures and assumptions through which human bodies are perceived, experienced, and socially organized.

"One is not born, but rather becomes, a woman," wrote Simone de Beauvoir in 1952 (p. 301). In retrospect, one can see much of feminist thought since the early 1970s as an elaboration of this idea, from early-second-wave writings on the socialization of Western women—Vivian Gornick and Barbara Moran's path-breaking *Woman in Sexist Society: Studies in Power and Powerlessness* (1971)—to feminist anthropologists' more global perspectives on gender symbolism and sex-role organization, to bell hooks's protests against white-biased assumptions about womanhood, to Iris Young's studies on the phenomenology of female embodiment, to Judith Butler's enormously influential work on the performative nature of gender.

Butler's work was not entirely original. Both Erving Goffman and other feminists had articulated what were essentially performative theories of gender—the notion that there is no stable, essential reality behind the (culturally constructed) acts that constitute gender identities. But by crystallizing, elaborately theorizing, and attaching a set of specific technical terms to ideas that had been in the air for some time, Butler seized a moment that was ripe for being marked as a new turn in feminist and postmodern theory. She also pushed anti-essentialism and social constructionism one step further than others, arguing that not just gender but biological sex has no "core" reality. For Butler, the illusion of such a core—the belief that sexual bodies have a "natural" heterosexual configuration—is itself produced by constant repetition of the bodily gestures and practices that create sexual identity. For Butler, not only are man and woman "made" by cultural discourse and practice, but so, too, is the illusion of their biological reality.

The body as symbol of society: Mary Douglas.

Until the 1960s, philosophers, cultural theorists, and anthropologists had incorporated observations, perspectives on, and ideas about the body in their work. But it is only in the 1960s and 1970s that the body itself became a focus of systematic theorizing. A foundational figure in this development was Mary Douglas, who introduced the notion of the body as a system of "natural symbols" that metaphorically reproduce social categories and concerns—an "image of society" (1970, p. 98). So, for example, when societies are under external attack, the maintenance of rules governing what belongs inside and outside the body becomes especially strict. Or—a different kind of example—"a natural way of investing a social occasion with dignity is to hide organic processes" (1970, p. 12). Hence important social occasions dictate that the body be held stiffly, the limbs and hands under careful control. And in general, manners and etiquette require the conscious withholding of bodily excreta: It is impolite to spit, fart, burp, laugh out loud, or to interrupt conversation with such involuntary expulsions as sneezing, coughing, and runny noses.

Underlying the use of the body as a social metaphor, Douglas argued, is a pan-human need for order, achieved by culturally classifying and systematizing objects, including persons, events, and activities, and by instituting routines. Having established those classifications and routines, people avoid all ambiguous or anomalous objects, states, events, and activities because they interpret them as disorderly and polluting. Douglas coined the phrase, "dirt is matter out of place" to mean that "dirt is a by-product of a systematic ordering and classification of matter" (1966, p. 35). Thus what any human culture considers to be dirt is a function of that culture's particular system and what is considered to be outside and inside its established boundaries.

The theory has broad application, not least of which is to human bodies. An excellent example is the application of her general theory of pollution to the margins of the human body. Douglas argues that everywhere, the boundaries of the body are imbued with heightened metaphorical potency—people react to them intensely; they are "loaded." This includes hair, the bodily lining itself, the skin, as well as all the bodily orifices—the mouth, nose, tear ducts, anus, vagina, and others—and all the bodily wastes that pass through that bodily lining or boundary—such as sweat, tears, saliva, menstrual blood, and semen.

In her earlier work, Douglas concluded that all such bodily marginal phenomena are universally interpreted as defiling. Later (1970) she revised this to a more neutral position, maintaining that they contain enhanced metaphorical potential, but, depending on sociocultural context, they are either heightened to sacred valuation or else denigrated as polluting. It is this latter, more versatile position that has proved most attractive to later anthropologists. For example, feminists later pointed out that the widespread taboos segregating menstruating women may in some cultures be due to an interpretation of menstrual blood as signifying the power of fertility, rather than a polluting substance (see especially Buckley and Gottlieb).

The social management of bodies: Bourdieu and Foucault.

By viewing the body as a text on which societal taboos and values are symbolically inscribed, Douglas's symbolic structuralism focuses on the reproduction of static rules rather than the production of human subjects whose bodies are experienced, trained, and regulated in very particular, practical ways. In the 1970s and 1980s, this emphasis changed, as anthropologist Pierre Bourdieu (1930–2002) and philosopher Michel Foucault (1926–1984), systematizing what in many ways was already implied in feminist body politics, shifted attention to the social "disciplining" of the body.

Bourdieu's emphasis was on what he called "practice"—the everyday habits by means of which the body is inculcated with cultural knowledge. Banally through "the seemingly most insignificant details of dress, bearing, physical and verbal manners," culture is "made body," as Bourdieu puts it—converted into automatic, habitual activity. As such, it is put "beyond the grasp of consciousness," where it exercises "the hidden persuasion of an implicit pedagogy . . . through injunctions as insignificant as 'stand up straight'" (p. 94).

Michel Foucault brought both practice and power onto center stage in contemporary theory. His work on sexuality, gender deviance, madness, and punishment historicizes the changing ways in which people are disciplined to conform to their culture, from the public torture and gallows of the middle ages, to today's largely unconscious self-monitoring and policing of one's own body. Foucault emphasizes that in the modern and postmodern world, people no longer need physical manipulation by centralized authorities in order to create socially disciplined bodies. Rather the spatial and temporal organization of institutions such as prisons, hospitals, and schools, and the practices and categories of knowledge—for example, ideas about what constitutes sickness and health—create norms (gender and sexuality among them) that work on individuals "from below": not chiefly through coercion, but through individual self-surveillance and self-correction. Thus, as Foucault writes, "there is no need for arms, physical violence, material constraints. Just a gaze. An inspecting gaze . . . which each individual under its weight will end by interiorizing to the point where he is his own overseer" (Foucault, 1977, p. 155).

Foucault's model has been influential throughout the disciplines, inspiring many writers to perform their own genealogies of various historical discourses and practices relating to the regulation of sexuality and health. Queer theory has developed, in large part, from his historicization and denaturalization of heterosexual norms. Feminist cultural theorists such as Sandra Bartky and Susan Bordo find Foucault's model of self-surveillance useful for the analysis of femininity, so much of which is reproduced "from below," through self-normalization to cultural ideals of the perfect face and body. For Bordo, Foucault's notion of power was an ally, too, in the development of a model of gender that discards the notion of men as oppressors in favor of an emphasis on systems of power within which people are all enmeshed. This rejection of an oppressor/oppressed model has been salient in the emergence of third-wave feminist theory, as well as recent attention to the male body and masculine acculturation. Postmodern theorists have seized on Foucault's ideas about resistance—"where there is power, there is also resistance," he wrote in his later work (1978, p. 95)—to support studies in the instability of culture and the role of human agency.

The Body in the Early Twenty-First Century

Bodily life in the early twenty-first century is full of contradictions. On the one hand, people appear freer than ever to become individual artisans of the physicality that they present to the world; virtually everything, from the shape of one's noses to one's sexual morphology, can be changed. On the other hand, as Western imagery and surgical technology, deployed throughout the world, makes slender, youthful beauty a global ideal, the choices seem less expressions of individuality than self-correction to standardized (and often racialized) cultural norms.

Increasingly medical technology has become an extension of human bodies, which are now subject to extensive intervention in order to repair malfunctioning organs, to prolong male sexual functioning, to facilitate conception, to determine fetal sex and to avoid genetic defects, to ensure pregnancy to term, and to determine when and how birth and death takes place. The benefits of this technology to alleviate human suffering and extend human choice seem undeniable. However the sweeping dominion of what Foucault called "biopower" has raised questions for which there are not yet clear answers, as many fundamental assumptions about the body are being physically, metaphorically, and ethically challenged.

When adults insist on gender reassignment surgery, are they realizing long-sought-for gendered identities or are they falling victim to the tyranny of genitalia as gender designation? When hearts, livers, and kidneys are implanted in needy persons from brain-dead donors, are some essences of the latter thereby perpetuated? How does such organ transfer influence Western constructions of the body as the sharply bounded sanctuary of the highly individuated self? When a child today can have five parents—genetic mother, surrogate mother, nurturing mother, genetic father and nurturing father—how is kinship relatedness constructed? When bodies can be perpetuated indefinitely on life-support machinery, where and when does life, and by extension one's body, end? The body, clearly, will always be an unfinished concept in the history of ideas.

See also **Biology; Death; Dress; Feminism; Fetishism; Gender; Life; Life Cycle; Person, Idea of the; Sexuality.**

BIBLIOGRAPHY

Augustine, Saint. *The Confessions.* Translated by R S. Pine-Coffin. New York: Penguin, 1991.

Bartky, Sandra. *Femininity and Domination.* New York: Routledge, 1990.

Beauvoir, Simone de. *The Second Sex.* New York: Alfred A. Knopf, 1952. Reprint, New York: Vintage, 1974.

Bordo, Susan. *The Male Body: A New Look at Men in Public and in Private.* New York: Farrar, Straus, and Giroux, 1999.

———. *Unbearable Weight: Feminism, Western Culture, and the Body.* Berkeley: University of California Press, 1993. Reprint, Berkeley: University of California Press, 2003.

Bourdieu, Pierre. *Outline of a Theory of Practice.* Translated by Richard Nice. Cambridge, U.K.: Cambridge University Press, 1977.

Buckley, Thomas, and Alma Gottlieb, eds. *Blood Magic: The Anthropology of Menstruation.* Berkeley: University of California Press, 1988.

Butler, Judith. *Bodies That Matter: On the Discursive Limits of "Sex."* New York: Routledge, 1993.

Darwin, Charles. *The Origin of Species by Means of Natural Selection.* London: John Murray, 1859. Reprint, New York: Penguin, 1968.

Descartes, René. "Meditations." In *The Philosophical Works of Descartes,* edited and translated by Elizabeth Haldane and G. R. T. Ross. 1911. Reprint, London: Cambridge University Press, 1967.

Douglas, Mary. *Natural Symbols: Explorations in Cosmology.* New York: Pantheon, 1970. Reprint, New York: Routledge, 2003.

———. *Purity and Danger: An Analysis of the Concepts of Pollution and Taboo.* New York: Praeger, 1966. Reprint, New York: Routledge, 2002.

Dworkin, Andrea. *Woman-Hating.* New York: Dutton, 1974.

Foucault, Michel. *Discipline and Punish: The Birth of the Prison.* Translated by Alan Sheridan. New York: Vintage, 1977. Reprint, New York: Vintage, 1995.

———. "The Eye of Power." In *Power/Knowledge: Selected Interviews and Other Writings 1972–1977,* edited and translated by Colin Gordo. New York: Pantheon, 1980.

———. *The History of Sexuality.* Vol. 1: *An Introduction.* New York: Vintage, 1978.

Freud, Sigmund. *Civilization and its Discontents.* Translated by James Stranchey. New York: W. W. Norton, 1961.

Geertz, Clifford. *The Interpretation of Cultures.* New York: Basic Books, 1973.

Goffman, Erving. *The Presentation of Self in Everyday Life.* Garden City, N.Y.: Doubleday, 1959.

Gornick, Vivian. *Woman in Sexist Society: Studies in Power and Powerlessness.* New York: Basic Books, 1971.

Herdt, Gilbert, ed. *Ritualized Homosexuality in Melanesia.* Berkeley: University of California Press, 1984.

Laqueur, Thomas. *Making Sex: Body and Gender from the Greeks to Freud.* Cambridge, Mass.; Harvard University Press, 1990.

Malinowski, Bronislaw. *The Sexual Life of Savages in North-western Melanesia.* New York: Eugenics Publishing Company, 1929. Reprint, Boston: Beacon Press, 1987.

Mauss, Marcel. "A Category of the Human Mind: The Notion of Person, the Notion of 'Self.'" In his *Sociology and Psychology: Essays.* Translated by Ben Brewster. London and Boston: Routledge and Kegan Paul, 1979.

Mauss, Marcel. "Techniques of the Body." *Economy and Society* 2 (1973): 70–88.

Mead, Margaret. *Coming of Age in Samoa: A Psychological Study of Primitive Youth for Western Civilisation.* New York: William Morrow, 1928. Reprint, New York: Perennial Classics, 2001.

Merleau-Ponty, Maurice. *Phenomenology of Perception.* London: Routledge and Kegan Paul, 1962.

Nietzsche, Frederick. *The Birth of Tragedy and the Case of Wagner.* Translated with a commentary by Walter Kaufmann. New York: Random House, 1967.

———. *On the Geneology of Morals.* New York: Vintage, 1969.

Omolade, Barbara. "Hearts of Darkness." In *Powers of Desire: The Politics of Sexuality,* edited by Ann Snitow, Christine Stansell, and Sharon Thompson. New York: Monthly Review Press, 1983.

Ortner, Sherry. "Is Female to Male as Nature is to Culture?" In *Woman, Culture and Society,* edited by Michelle Rosaldo and Louise Lamphere. Stanford, Calif.: Stanford University Press, 1974.

Pitts, Victoria. *In the Flesh: The Cultural Politics of Body Modification.* New York: Palgrave Macmillan, 2003.

Plato. *Phaedo. The Dialogues of Plato.* Translated by G. M. A. Grube. Indianapolis: Hackett, 1977.

———. *Symposium.* Translated by Alexander Nehamas and Paul Woodruff. Indianapolis: Hackett, 1989.

Turner, Terence. "The Social Skin." In *Not Work Alone: A Cross-Cultural View of Activities Superfluous to Survival,* edited by Jeremy Cherfas and Roger Levin. Thousand Oaks, Calif.: Sage Publications, 1980.

Young, Iris. *Throwing Like a Girl and Other Essays in Feminist Philosophy and Social Theory.* Bloomington: Indiana University Press, 1990.

Susan Bordo
Monica Udvardy

BORDERS, BORDERLANDS, AND FRONTIERS, GLOBAL.

At first glance the concept of borders, borderlands, or frontiers would seem to be straightforward. A border or boundary is a line on a map delineating a territorial boundary or the limit of a political jurisdiction. Borders are primarily, but far from exclusively, seen as properties of and under the control of states. Nevertheless, this has generally not always been the case. Even in the contemporary world where such an interpretation often does apply, the concept of borders frequently becomes much more complicated.

Complications of a Seemingly Simple Concept

The first complication is semantic. In many European languages, including British English, the term *frontier* is a synonym for border. In the Americas, and especially in the United States, *border* means boundary, between countries, between the states of the United States, or between provinces in Mexico or Canada. *Frontier,* typically but not exclusively, refers to a historical boundary between expanding European settlements and indigenous settlements. Thus in English usage in the United States, frontiers and borders are very different concepts and refer to quite distinct social markers. This usage has often been generalized to any sort of border zone or borderland between different sets of peoples coming into contact. It is frequently extended metaphorically to refer to any boundary between known and unknown, an extension discussed further at the end of this entry.

The second complication is historical. Since the founding of the first states in human history in Mesopotamia some five thousand years ago, boundaries or borders have generally been vague, imprecise zones in which political—and to a lesser extent economic, social, and cultural—control fades away. That is, borders, boundaries, borderlands, and frontiers are zones or regions with some dimension, where there is a shift, more or less gradual, from control by one state to another or to an absence of state control. An important corollary of this complication is that the lack of precision is not necessarily a problem in semantics or conceptualization. Rather, it is often an accurate reflection of an actual fuzziness of boundary zones.

A third complication is that at different times and in different places these concepts have had different meanings, and they have been implemented in different ways. Often a word translated as *border* from one language to another had behind it a different meaning, a different concept of markers, and even different ethical and political implications of what that "border" entailed.

A fourth complication is that the meanings of these terms and how they have been implemented have changed over many millennia. Throughout these changes there have often been disconnects or divergences between their social reality and what various actors (individuals or states) thought they should be.

Finally, there is a problem of scale. Almost any border or boundary zone, when viewed from a sufficient distance, appears as a sharp line. When viewed up close, however, it becomes a zone having some width and often having blurry edges. So from a central capital, a border or frontier may seem precise. Yet from the perspectives of those living on or near the boundary or frontier, or even from the perspectives of those charged with administering or controlling it, it can be quite vague and often contentious.

Defining Borders, Borderlands, and Frontiers

In order to discuss these issues it is useful to present somewhat general definitions of these terms. The following definitions carry two caveats or cautions. First, as with any generalized concepts, they will not be precise for all uses. Second, these terms shift meaning over time and through space. Still, the following are useful for further discussion:

boundary—a demarcation indicating some division in spatial terms

border—an international boundary line; when a border is seen as a zone it is often called a borderland or the borderlands

frontier—a zone of contact with or without a specified boundary line

The term *borderlands* straddles the distinction between frontier and border and is often used as a synonym for frontier as a zone.

The contemporary concept of a border as a sharp, precise line stems from two sources. First is the Peace of Westphalia (1648), which established the modern nation-state system under which a state had full sovereign control of the lands and peoples within its borders. The second source is the development of private property as a concept, in which one individual, or state, had exclusive rights to land or territory. While in the early twenty-first century these conditions are taken as "normal" or "natural," they are neither. Rather, the idea of a border as a precise line grew out of the needs of states to define boundaries. The idea of exclusive control of land developed from the transformation of control of land from a matter of use rights to a concept of land as an economic commodity, that is, something that can be bought and sold. In other words, these contemporary conceptualizations, which are often seen as a part of the process of modernization, were themselves socially constructed under very specific historical, political, and economic conditions.

In premodern times, that is, approximately before the sixteenth century C.E., land was most often thought of as a resource to which individuals, or more typically groups, had rights to use. In many nonstate societies, if the individual or group did not use the land—usually for a considerable time—then they lost their use rights. This is almost always distinctly different, however, from the European concept of *terra nullius,* which means "empty or unused land." For those groups who foraged for a livelihood or who practiced shifting agriculture, "use" of land often included long fallow periods. To groups that practiced intensive agriculture—from classic civilizations to modern states—such fallow land appeared empty, hence unclaimed and available for settlement. These differences in how rights to land are conceptualized have been the source of much conflict over many millennia between agricultural states and nonstate peoples. For example, such conflicting viewpoints are at the root of the myth that the island of Manhattan was "purchased." Dutch occupiers presumed that they were buying a commodity with exclusive rights. Indigenous peoples thought that in consideration for a gift marking friendship they were granting rights to joint use of common lands.

At least two caveats are in order in regard to such conflicts. First, nonstate peoples could and did come into conflict over use of land. Indeed, one of the major mechanisms of the spread of humans derives from such conflicts. Although they were sometimes resolved through fighting, such conflicts were more often resolved by one group moving deeper into unoccupied land, which over time led to the spread of humans over most of the earth. Second, many claims by civilizations or states that land was unused, or was *terra nullius,* were in fact veiled rationalizations for seizing land from peoples who had less complex social or political organization and who did not use the land as intensively.

From the development of the first states some five thousand years ago until the early twenty-first century, though abating somewhat since the Peace of Westphalia (1648), land could be, and often was, seized by conquest. To be ethical, such seizures often needed some sort of justification, such as a "just war," reparation for previous harm done, or evidence of illegitimate use by those from whom the land was seized. Obviously, such claims could, and often were, readily invented and rationalized. Still, states did develop a territorial sense and became concerned with boundaries, borders, borderlands, and frontiers. A primary concern, however, was control, mainly political and economic but sometimes also social and cultural. Even constructed barriers, such as the Great Wall of China or Hadrian's Wall in northern Scotland that marked the edge of the Roman Empire, barriers that did constitute explicit boundaries, were primarily used to control movements of peoples and goods. They were seldom intended as absolute barriers.

Such walls and other barriers were often constructed with military and control functions in mind. They served to regulate interactions between the state or empire and the surrounding groups, whether those were other empires, states, or nonstate peoples. They were constructed to keep members within the state or empire, to keep others out, and to regulate which individuals, groups, or objects could cross the barrier as well as why, when, and under what circumstances such crossings could take place. Such barriers often marked a shift from direct control to indirect control, wherein local leaders controlled the area, but via assorted agreements with the state or empire. In essence, such barriers were not sharp or precise lines but rather the visible centerlines of zones of transition. Some people tried to avoid these controls. Such avoidance is typically defined as "criminal." Thus borders give rise to smuggling and smugglers.

Frontier as Membrane

These sorts of considerations led the historian Richard W. Slatta to describe frontiers as membranes. This is a singularly appropriate metaphor for frontiers and to somewhat lesser extent for borders, borderlands, and boundaries. Membranes are differentially permeable with respect to what may pass through them and what is blocked. Their permeability often is different for opposite directions. That is, some goods are allowed to pass, say horses entering China from the central Asian steppes and silk leaving. Other things, such as armies, are not allowed to pass. Horses came into China but seldom left, unless mounted by soldiers seeking retribution for raids; silk left China but seldom came in. Membranes have thickness. When viewed from a distance they seem thin, almost like lines. When viewed up close they are zones through which objects, people, and ideas may pass.

Borderlands and Frontiers as Zones of Ethnic Change

Because borderlands and frontiers are zones between different human organizations, they are also zones of intense interactions of objects, peoples, and ideas. These interactions can range from very peaceful, mutually beneficial relationships to incessant warfare. Oftentimes, several types of interactions along the range from peaceful to warlike can occur simultaneously. For instance, along the northern frontier of New Spain (what is now the southwestern United States) various indigenous groups would have peaceful trading relationships with some Spanish villages while they were raiding others. This also occurred among various indigenous groups. Indeed, at times these opposite relations were not between different indigenous groups and villages but varied from family group to family group on both sides. In short, frontiers are zones of intense interactions, often of several types at the same time. These interactions can change rapidly with local circumstances. This locally variable volatility is a special characteristic of frontiers and borderlands.

These were and are zones where different products and processes mixed and intermingled, often leading to the development of new products and processes. On frontiers one process of this sort, called ethnogenesis, is especially salient. Ethnogenesis is the formation of a new ethnic group via the amalgamation of two or more previously distinct groups.

With the interactions of different peoples, interbreeding and intermarriage were not rare, even in cases in which one or both sides tried to prevent such mixing. When the mixing became sufficiently regular and frequent, it could give rise to an entirely new group. The Metís in Canada and Genízaros in northern New Spain are examples. The Metís grew from unions between French fur traders—typically males—and indigenous women. These long-term relations were mutually beneficial. French fur traders gained access to furs collected and processed through their wives' groups (such unions were frequently polygynous, with the trader having more than one wife, often from different groups). The indigenous groups gained access to European trade goods acquired through traders who were relatives and hence under considerable kinship obligation to trade fairly. In the early twenty-first century the Metís are still negotiating with the Canadian government for recognition as a people distinct from both indigenous or first nations and from European immigrants.

In northern New Spain there was an active trade in captives, both indigenous peoples captured by Spaniards during fighting and Spaniards captured by indigenous peoples; in both cases, the captives were typically women or children. Indigenous children raised in Spanish communities developed a separate identity that was neither fully Spanish nor fully of their natal indigenous group. If an individual Genízaro or his family rose to prominence, typically as a frontier soldier or sometimes through economic success, he or they could be assimilated into Hispanic society. When the United States annexed the region, the trade in captives rapidly ceased, and the Genízaro population gradually assimilated into either Hispanic or indigenous societies.

The anthropologist Frederick Barth describes another role for boundaries with respect to ethnic identity. Barth argues that ethnicity is not defined by its content but rather by the boundary or boundaries that separate one group from another. This seemingly counterintuitive view developed from studies showing that when individuals or families crossed ethnic boundaries (which may or may not coincide with political boundaries), they often changed identity. Such events are not all that rare in the ethnographic record. Furthermore, some individuals and families made such changes more than once in a single lifetime. Typically, such changes are associated with changes in ecological adaptation. Chinese farmers who moved onto the steppe and became pastoralists typically joined a nomad group and took up that group's culture. If or when they moved back and again took up farming, they again became Chinese. In such cases, not only is the border or frontier a membrane, but it also is a catalyst for identity change. As noted, such ethnic boundaries seem most common where local ecology forces changes in productive strategies. Changes in climate and especially the development of new technologies allow such borders to shift over time.

Recent research by the biologist Mark Pagei and the anthropologist Ruth Mace supports Barth's interpretation. Pagei and Mace argue that boundaries help maintain a sense of group and enhance social solidarity and cooperation, but often at the cost of promoting conflict with other groups. Thus boundaries and borders play an important role in group formation, even while generating conflict between groups.

The Puzzle of Borderlands and Frontiers

These complications give rise to yet another, enduring aspect of borders, borderlands, and frontiers. On first glance they all seem the same or certainly similar. But with closer examination, each border region seems unique. This puzzling aspect of frontiers has fascinated and frustrated scholars who study frontiers comparatively. The sociologist Thomas D. Hall argues that this puzzling quality derives from the complex way in which frontiers are formed. In a nutshell, frontiers are constructed by the interaction of two or more different groups. The location, extent, duration, and changes in any specific frontier zone entail a complex mixture of factors external to the frontier zone and local factors, all mediated by the actions of the peoples who live in the frontier zone.

The broad similarity among frontiers derives from the small number of factors, in the following example numbering five, that shape most frontiers:

- the types of groups that come into interaction (three types: nonstate, tributary [or ancient] states or empires, or capitalist [or modern] states);

- the type of boundary involved (four types: local economic, political or military, long-distance economic, and cultural);

- the types of nonstate groups (three types, such as those conventionally labeled bands, tribes, or chiefdoms);

- the type of frontier (four types: buffer, barrier, internal, or external); and

- the type of ecological environment (four types: steppe, sown, hill, or valley).

These few factors, when divided into only a few basic categories, will generate 576 different types of frontiers. This immense variety—which could easily be expanded with finer categorization—explains why each specific frontier seems unique. The point of this example is *not* the specific list of factors *nor* the number of specific categories into which they are divided. Rather, it is that with only a few factors divided into a small number of categories an immense variety of frontiers or

borderlands can be described. This then "solves" the puzzle of how and why all frontiers seem similar at first glance but on closer examination seem unique. The similarity derives from the small number of factors involved; the uniqueness from the large number of ways they can be combined.

Borders, Borderlands, and Frontiers as Sites of Social Change

Because of the various complex interactions that occur along borders, in borderlands, and on frontiers, such places are very fertile areas for studying how social, political, economic, and cultural changes occur and how individuals and groups both shape and are shaped by those changes. They are zones where the local and the global interact very intensely and hence exhibit processes that are rarely, if ever, seen in more central areas. This is another reason why the study of borderlands and frontiers is often so fascinating to scholars.

Frontiers are often seen as sources of change, as in the famous frontier thesis of the American historian Frederick Jackson Turner (1861–1932): that the frontier zones of the United States shaped the country's national character. Turner has often been criticized for having the causality backwards: It was the central areas that shaped the frontier. The literature of these debates is enormous, even leading some U.S. historians to question the utility of the concept of "the frontier." A major problem here is in the definite article: "the frontier" was in reality many, highly fluid, and changeable frontiers.

One very positive result of these debates has been the development of a growing body of writings on comparative frontiers. By comparing different frontiers, scholars have begun to uncover both common, underlying factors and their various unique constellations. Such studies have done much to further blur the distinctions between history and sociology, anthropology, and geography. A conventional, if caricatured, view of these disciplines is that history is idiographic, concerned with painting detailed pictures, whereas sociology, anthropology, and geography are nomothetic or seeking lawlike regular patterns. This conventional view is flawed in at least two ways. First, it sees the two approaches as opposites or as in conflict rather than complementary. Second, it fails to recognize that there is a vast array of possibilities of combining both types of explanations and descriptions. Studies of frontiers or borderlands, especially comparative studies, must combine both approaches in ways that often render disciplinary distinctions unrecognizable. Phrased alternatively, comparative studies of frontiers are inherently multi- and interdisciplinary. Thus the comparative study of frontiers itself forms a kind of intellectual borderland.

Borderlands and Frontiers as Metaphors

No discussion of borders, borderlands, and frontiers would be complete without some attention to the metaphorical use of these terms. Most readers of English are familiar with such phrases as "the frontiers of medicine," "the frontiers of science," and "space, the final frontier." Behind these metaphors is a state-centered view of borders, borderlands, and frontiers in which such areas mark a zone of transition from well-known territory under control of the state to little-known territory not under control of the state. This metaphor breaks down, however, if pushed too far. Spatial frontiers most often had residents on the other side who were obviously not unknown to themselves. Indeed, at first contact, from each side (and there often are or were borders or frontiers with more than two sides) the other side(s) seemed unknown and were seen as strange or mysterious by the other side(s).

The unknown quality of the "other side of the border or frontier" simultaneously generates curiosity, promise, threat, and fear. It is this combination of reactions brought on by approaching unknown and often uncontrolled territory, peoples, or ideas that is the key difference between frontiers and borderlands on the one hand and a border or boundary in the conventional sense on the other. Presumably with a conventional border, what is on the other side is known but is held separate and distinct by the border. The combination of mystery and danger accompanied by promise and curiosity seems to be at the root of the popularity of the use of frontier (and less frequently borderlands) as a metaphor. In that sense, of course, it is singularly apt for describing or labeling a transition from the known to the unknown.

Thus concepts of borders, borderlands, and frontiers seem at first glance straightforward, simple, and clear. Yet when examined more closely, they are mysterious, complex, and murky. This is why they are often regions of such fascination to scholars and thinkers in many disciplines. Also because of their transitional qualities, they are often excellent sites to study a wide variety of social, cultural, political, and economic change.

See also **Ethnicity and Race; Migration; State, The; World Systems Theory, Latin America.**

BIBLIOGRAPHY

Barth, Frederick, ed. *Ethnic Groups and Boundaries.* Boston: Little, Brown, 1969.

Bentley, Jerry H. *Old World Encounters: Cross-Cultural Contacts and Exchanges in Pre-Modern Times.* Oxford: Oxford University Press, 1993.

Brooks, James F. *Captives and Cousins: Slavery, Kinship, and Community in the Southwest Borderlands.* Chapel Hill: University of North Carolina Press, 2002.

Chase-Dunn, Christopher, and Thomas D. Hall. *Rise and Demise: Comparing World-Systems.* Boulder, Colo.: Westview Press, 1997.

Donnan, Hastings, and Thomas M. Wilson. *Borders: Frontiers of Identity, Nation, and State.* Oxford: Berg, 1999.

Guy, Donna J., and Thomas E. Sheridan, eds. *Contested Ground: Comparative Frontiers on the Northern and Southern Edges of the Spanish Empire.* Tucson: University of Arizona Press, 1998.

Hall, Thomas D. "Frontiers, Ethnogenesis, and World-Systems: Rethinking the Theories." In *A World-Systems Reader: New Perspectives on Gender, Urbanism, Cultures, Indigenous Peoples, and Ecology,* edited by Thomas D. Hall, 237–270. Lanham, Md.: Rowman and Littlefield, 2000.

Hofstadter, Richard, and Seymour Martin Lipset, eds. *Turner and the Sociology of the Frontier.* New York: Basic, 1968.

Lattimore, Owen. *Studies in Frontier History: Collected Papers, 1928–1958.* London: Oxford University Press, 1962.

Mikesell, Marvin W. "Comparative Studies in Frontier History." *Annals of the American Association of Geographers* 50 (1960): 62–74.

Pagei, Mark, and Ruth Mace. "The Cultural Wealth of Nations." *Nature* 428 (March 18, 2004): 275–278.

Slatta, Richard W. *Comparing Cowboys and Frontiers.* Norman: University of Oklahoma Press, 1997.

Taylor, George Rogers, ed. *The Turner Thesis concerning the Role of the Frontier in American History.* 3rd ed. Lexington, Mass.: Heath, 1972.

Weber, David J. *The Spanish Frontier in North America.* New Haven, Conn.: Yale University Press, 1992.

Weber, David J., and Jane M. Rausch, eds. *Where Cultures Meet: Frontiers in Latin American History.* Wilmington, Del.: Scholarly Resources, 1994.

Thomas D. Hall

BRAIN DRAIN. *See* **Migration.**

BUDDHISM

Buddhism, the only truly "world" religion of Asia, was founded in the fifth century B.C.E. in northwest India by a prince named Gautama, who was also called Siddhartha ("He who has reached his goal"), Shakyamuni ("Silent sage of the Shakya clan"), and eventually the Buddha, or "Enlightened One." The religion spread throughout northern India during the next centuries, becoming a major competitor with Hinduism for popular support and royal favor. The traditions of Hinduism and Buddhism mutually influenced each other, sharing many of the same assumptions but also differentiating themselves doctrinally and, to a lesser degree, socially and ritually.

The three major forms of Buddhism—Theravada ("The Speech of the Elders"), Mahayana ("The Great Vehicle"), and Vajrayana ("The Diamond Vehicle")—all were born in India and were given their characteristic stamp in that country. By the end of the first millennium C.E., however, Buddhism was more or less defunct in the land of its origin, in part as a result of invading Muslims who especially targeted Buddhist temples and monasteries and in part because Buddhist doctrines and deities were increasingly assimilated into Hinduism.

Long before it ceased to be a religion of India, however, Buddhism had become a pan-Asian religion. By the middle of the third century B.C.E. the great Mauryan emperor Ashoka consolidated most of the Indian subcontinent under his rule. While Ashoka may or may not have been himself a Buddhist convert, tradition gives him credit for spreading the religion not only throughout India (his "edicts" posted on pillars throughout the subcontinent are often read for their Buddhist or crypto-Buddhist messages) but also into Sri Lanka to the south, where it soon became the state religion. From there Buddhist monks brought the religion to Burma, Thailand, and other parts of Southeast Asia, where it has survived as the predominant faith of that region.

Other monks, starting from points in northern India, followed the trade routes into Central Asia and eventually into China, where Buddhism entered by the first century C.E. Although initially regarded with suspicion as a foreign and "barbarian" faith, over the course of several centuries Buddhism was gradually blended with Chinese culture until it joined Confucianism and Taoism as one of the principal religions of that region. By the middle centuries of the first millennium C.E., Buddhism had become the religion of choice of the newly reunified Chinese empire, and indigenous doctrinal and philosophical schools of Buddhism arose. By the seventh century, Buddhism had converts in China from all strata of society, from the imperial family down to the peasantry, and monasteries flourished throughout the empire. The popularity of Buddhism in China would not last, however, and by the ninth century the religion began to decline.

From China, Buddhism entered Korea by the third century C.E. Missionaries from Korea brought the religion to Japan in the sixth century, where it developed into the dominant religion of that country and exerted a huge influence on Japanese national culture. It was not until the seventh century that Buddhism came from India to remote Tibet where, after a few centuries of ups and downs, it became firmly entrenched by the eleventh century and was the state religion until the Chinese invasions in the 1950s. Tibetan Buddhism was exported to Mongolia originally as a result of the close relations between one of the ruling khans and the first Dalai Lama.

Buddhism has been known in the West since at least the time of Alexander the Great and possibly influenced some forms of Greek philosophy, the Gnostics, and early Christians. In modern times, as a result initially of immigration of Asians to Western countries in the nineteenth and twentieth centuries and increasingly because of interest among Westerners themselves, Buddhism can no longer be regarded as an exclusively Asian religion.

The Buddha and the Fundamental Doctrines of Buddhism

The historical details of the life of the Buddha, like those of the lives of many of the world's religious founders and saints, are probably unrecoverable, buried under layers and layers of mythology and doctrinal revisionism. While there is little doubt that at the origin of Buddhism lies a strong, charismatic founder, the particular contours of the person and life of that founder can only be purely speculative. The oldest Pali and Sanskrit texts do not relay a sustained narrative about the Buddha's life but rather give only snippets and fragmentary references that seem to emphasize his human features. This has led some to argue that Buddhism is fundamentally an "atheistic" religion, although for a variety of reasons this is a distortion of Buddhist belief. There are indications that even in his lifetime Gautama was accorded great respect and veneration and soon after his death was worshipped in the form of relics, pilgrimages to sites of significance in the Buddha's life, and eventually in images that became the centerpieces of devotion.

The first known formal biography or hagiography of Gautama Buddha was the Buddhacarita, written in Sanskrit probably around the first century C.E. by Ashvaghosha. Over subsequent centuries other life stories were produced in India and Sri Lanka incorporating more and more legendary and mythical materials. The later texts in the hagiographical tradition in Buddhism increasingly stress the miraculous and supernatural elements of the founder. Indeed, in many of them Shakyamuni is portrayed as this era's Buddha, the latest in a string of many prior Buddhas and the forerunner of a future Buddha known as Maitreya. By the time of the rise of Mahayana Buddhism in the early centuries C.E. the historical Gautama was wholly eclipsed by a complex "Buddhology" that elevates the Buddha to cosmic and, for most ordinary Buddhists, divine stature.

While there are a variety of understandings of who the Buddha was among the various adherents and sects of Buddhism, all are agreed on the basic outline of his life story. He was supposed to have lived sometime during the period from the sixth to the fourth centuries B.C.E., born into a family of the Kshatriya, or warrior-king, class in the clan called the Shakyas in northeastern India. Many accounts say his birth was attended by miracles and that he was born with signs on his body indicating a destiny either as an enlightened Buddha or as a world-conquering emperor. His parents, preferring the latter career path, kept him isolated from the outside world and educated him to be a prince. Gautama grew up under these pampered circumstances, married, and had a son he named Rahula ("Fetter").

This sheltered life of royal luxury came to an end when the young prince was taken by his charioteer on four excursions outside the confines of the castle. On these trips he saw, for the first time, the suffering nature of a life where sickness, old age, and death are inevitable. On his last tour he also saw a mendicant who was attempting to find an alternative to such a life. These "four sights" provided the impetus for the future Buddha to immediately leave the householder way of life and go in search of the means to liberation from suffering.

The middle centuries B.C.E. in North India were a time of great religious and intellectual ferment and experimentation. Many of the religious assumptions prevailing at that time were integrated into the Buddha's teaching and subsequent Buddhism, including the belief in karma and rebirth, the cyclical nature of time, the pervasiveness of suffering, and the positing of an alternative to suffering and rebirth.

Upon leaving his previous life as a prince, Gautama is said to have joined several of the many different groups of world renouncers living in the wilderness areas of India, including one group of radical ascetics. The future Buddha perfected the methods taught in this group, learning how to live on but a grain of rice a day, until he became skeletal and weak—but not enlightened. According to legend, Gautama abandoned the way of radical asceticism, just as he had early renounced the life of hedonistic pleasure in the castle, and soon discovered a "middle way" between these two extremes. In deep meditation under a "tree of enlightenment," the Buddha reached his own enlightenment and nirvana, the "extinguishing" of ignorance, suffering, and rebirth.

The first sermon or teaching of the newly enlightened Buddha was, according to the legends, given at the Deer Park in Sarnath in northeast India to members of the group of ascetics with whom Gautama had associated earlier. This first "turning of the wheel of dharma" encapsulates the fundamental tenets of all forms of Buddhism and consists of what are called the Four Noble Truths.

The first of these is the universal fact of suffering and dissatisfaction (*duhkha*). A standard formula declares that "birth is suffering, aging is suffering, sickness is suffering, death is suffering; sorrow, lamentation, pain, grief, and despair are suffering; association with what one dislikes is suffering; separation from what one likes is suffering; not getting what one wants is suffering." Such unhappy circumstances are sometimes called "obvious suffering" and are also bound up in another central doctrine of all forms of Buddhism: the insistence that there is no "self" or "essence" to things and beings (*an-atman*). This belief directly contradicts the concept in Hinduism of an *atman,* or fundamental and underlying self (which was not conceived of, however, as the ego or temporary persona that undergoes rebirth). In the Hindu texts known as the Upanishads, realization of one's true nature, one's true self or *atman,* as identical to the ultimate ground of the cosmos (the Brahman), was the end of the mystical pursuit. In contrast, the positing of *an-atman* became one of the distinctive, even unique, features of the Buddhist religion. Suffering occurs in part by grasping and clinging to a self that does not, according to Buddhism, exist.

According to Buddhist doctrine, what we call the "self" is merely a composite of five "aggregates" or "heaps" (*skandhas*). These are "form" (the body in particular and physical and material form in general), feelings (pleasant, unpleasant, and neutral), discrimination (that which processes and categorizes sensory and mental information), karmic predispositions (including, among many other mental factors, will or volition), and consciousness (meaning not only mental awareness but also the "consciousnesses" associated with the five senses). The "self" is but an ever-changing conglomeration of these five aggregates—a process rather than an essential entity.

Another dimension of the first Noble Truth of universal suffering is called the "suffering of change." Even the pleasant things and circumstances of life are not lasting, and when they are lost we suffer. Thus a second central concept of Buddhist metaphysics also tied up with the truth of suffering is that of impermanence, or *anitya*. Buddhism posits the impermanence and changing nature of all caused and compounded or composite things and beings. Suffering occurs when one mistakes impermanence for permanence and, again, becomes ignorantly attached to things and beings in the false belief that they will last.

A third dimension of suffering is sometimes identified: the "pervasive" suffering that accompanies birth in "samsara"—a word that literally means "to wander or pass through a series of states or conditions." Samsara describes the beginningless cycle of cosmic or universal death and rebirth and the fact that phenomenal existence is transient and ever-changing. "Perva-

sive" suffering points to the recurring experience of birth, life, death, and rebirth in such a universe.

The second Noble Truth states that suffering has a cause and is not therefore eternally and hopelessly hard-wired into the nature of things. Suffering, according to Buddhism, is created by our own ignorant and habitual responses to life. The chief cause of suffering is variously identified as "thirst" (*tanha*), "craving" (*trishna*), or the "three poisons": "desire" or "attraction" (*raga*), "aversion" or "hatred" (*pratigha*), and "ignorance" (*avidya*).

Suffering occurs because of a series of interrelated causal factors that are summarized in another important Buddhist doctrine, that of "dependent origination." In essence this doctrine declares "that being, this comes to be; from the arising of that, this arises; that being absent, this is not; from the cessation of that, this ceases" (*Samyuttanikaya* 2.28). In its classical form, dependent origination consists of twelve conditioned and conditioning links: (1) ignorance, (2) formations (the construction of new karma), (3) consciousness, (4) mind and body, (5) the six sense fields, (6) contact of the senses with the sense fields, (7) feeling, (8) craving, (9) grasping, (10) becoming, (11) birth (i.e., rebirth), and (12) aging and death. Each link depends on the one before it. Aging and death (12) depend on birth (11), for if one were not perpetually reborn one would not repeatedly grow old and die. Birth depends on becoming (10, in the sense of the ripening of karma created in the past); becoming depends on grasping or clinging (9), which in turn depends on craving (8). Craving arises due to pleasant and unpleasant feelings (7), which depend on the contact of the senses (6) with the objects or "fields" of the senses (5), which could not exist without a mind and body (4). Mind and body depend on the consciousness of the six sense fields (3, the five senses with the mind as the sixth), which are determined by the volitional forces (2) that come into play due to ignorance (1). When ignorance ceases, karma is no longer produced, and all other links in the chain are stopped, right up through old age and death.

This brings us to the third Noble Truth, which declares that there is an alternative to suffering, the state called *nirvana.* The term literally means an "extinguishing" or "blowing out" and has sometimes been misunderstood as some kind of nihilism. Nirvana is indeed often described in negative terms: the permanent cessation or extinction of suffering and its causes (craving and the three poisons), of the false idea of and attachment to self, of mistaking the impermanent for the permanent, and of rebirth in the world of samsara. But nirvana is also depicted in positive form, as a state of absolute peace, serenity, tranquility, happiness, and bliss. One who achieves such a state is known as an arhat, or "worthy one," and various important milestones along the way are also delineated. One who has had the experience of penetrating into the true nature of reality is called an *arya* (noble one) and a "stream-enterer," for he or she is from that time forward moving inexorably toward nirvana. A "once-returner" has only one more lifetime before achieving the goal, and a "non-returner" will attain nirvana in this lifetime. A distinction is also sometimes made between "nirvana with remainder" (indicating that the person has reached the goal but is still embodied) and "nirvana without remainder," or "final nirvana" (*parinirvana*), which the arhat enters after the death of the body.

The fourth Noble Truth is the declaration that there is a path or method for achieving the state of nirvana. Just as suffering has its causes, so too can the end of suffering be brought about by entering and perfecting the "Eightfold Path," which are sometimes also grouped into what are called the "Three Trainings." The first "training" is in wisdom and covers the first two steps of the Eightfold Path: (1) right view (meaning, among other things, a proper understanding of the Four Noble Truths) and (2) right resolve (the determination to end one's suffering). The second training is in ethics and includes (3) right speech (abstaining from lying, divisive speech, harsh speech, and idle speech), (4) right action (abstaining from killing, stealing, and sexual misconduct), and (5) right livelihood (abstaining from professions that involve harming other beings). The third training is in meditative concentration and covers (6) right effort (persistence in the training of meditation), (7) right mindfulness, and (8) right concentration. Given the crucial importance and centrality of meditation to the Buddhist path, texts go into great detail about the increasingly subtle states of mind associated with right mindfulness and right concentration.

After the first sermon at the Deer Park, the Buddha is said to have traveled and taught in India for many decades. During the Buddha's lifetime, he also apparently inaugurated one of the central institutions of Buddhism, monasticism, the most ancient continuous institution in history. From the earliest period of Buddhism, the community, or *sangha,* consisted of laymen and laywomen on the one hand and monks and nuns on the other. But it was especially the monastics who were encompassed in the term *sangha.* The monastic rules of discipline, or *vinaya,* may go back to the Buddha himself but were in any case codified in a series of councils held after the Buddha's passing away. Being a Buddhist traditionally means that one "takes refuge" in what are called the three jewels—the Buddha, the dharma (i.e., the teachings and the attainments those teachings lead to), and the *sangha* (sometimes meaning exclusively the monastics and sometimes meaning the whole of the Buddhist community).

The Buddha was said to have lived to the age of about eighty, at which time he "passed into his *parinirvana.*" According to the texts, relics from his body were distributed and subsequently buried at the base of distinctively Buddhist places of worship called stupas, which, together with the monasteries and pilgrimage sites, formed the spatial centers of the new religion.

Formation of Theravada Buddhism

According to legend, the first of the Buddhist councils, where monks from all over North India met to collate the Buddha's teachings, occurred just after the Buddha's passing away, and several more were held in the years following. In these councils, the earliest forms of the Buddhist canon were developed. Texts, originally orally recited by monks, were divided into three main divisions or "baskets" (*pitakas*): vinaya (rules for monas-

tics), sutra (discourses), and *abhidharma* (metaphysics). While different traditions have different recensions (in different languages) and even different texts in their canon, all follow this basic division of the sacred scripture into the "three baskets."

It was in the second of these councils, held some one hundred years after the Buddha's *parinirvana,* that sectarian differences led to a division between a group of monks called the "Elders" (Sthaviras) and a breakaway set of groups known collectively as the "Great Assemblists" (Mahasanghikas). While the exact reason for the schism is not known with certainty, it seems as though the Mahasanghikas were the more liberal of the two groups while the Sthaviras were the more conservative, preserving what they regarded as the original purity of the Buddha's teachings. Other schisms and divisions into schools and subschools also occurred, but the Sthaviravadins survived as the "Theravadins" (the Pali name for "teachings of the elders") in South India, especially Sri Lanka, and from there into Southeast Asia.

Prior to the eleventh century, Theravada was but one of the several forms of Buddhism practiced in Sri Lanka. While it, like all other forms of Buddhism, represents itself as "pure" and "original," it is in fact a syncretistic blend of a variety of elements and practices. Various reforms sponsored by royal patrons have attempted to recover the "original purity" of Theravada, and among the monastics movements of conservative "forest monks" have at various times insisted on going back to the meditative base of the tradition. As the form of Buddhism that came to predominate in Sri Lanka and Southeast Asia, Theravada is sometimes also called "southern" Buddhism.

Mahayana Buddhist Doctrines and Traditions

The origins of the second major division within Buddhism are shrouded in uncertainty. What was to be called Mahayana, or the "Great Vehicle," did not originate with any one reforming individual or emerge at any specific time. It at least partially had its roots in a pan-Indian devotional movement (bhakti) that also had a dramatic impact on the Hindu traditions of India around 150 B.C.E. and in the centuries following. Mahayana is also sometimes traced back to the "Great Assemblists," or Mahasanghikas, but it seems that for many years, even centuries, monks who eventually became Mahayana lived and studied in the same monasteries as others. Perhaps the best way to envision Mahayana Buddhism in its earliest years was as a set of new texts that introduced new doctrinal elements into Buddhism. Those who accepted the canonical legitimacy of these new texts were Mahayana.

The doctrines put forward in these new texts were not, however, represented as new. Rather, they too were supposed to originate with the Buddha; they were regarded as "turnings of the wheel of dharma" that taught the deeper meanings of the Buddha's message for disciples who were more capable.

Chief among the distinctive teachings of Mahayana was a new conceptualization of the goal of Buddhism. In early Buddhism as well as in the subsequent Theravada tradition, the attainment of nirvana was theoretically possible for anyone. But Buddhahood itself remained the unique feature of Gautama. The Mahayana Buddhists posited enlightenment and Buddhahood itself as the ultimate goal for all practitioners and regarded nirvana as a lower attainment for those of a "lesser vehicle" (Hinayana).

With this new idea regarding the goal of Buddhism came a radically different understanding of Buddhology. Gautama, for the Mahayana Buddhists, was but one of an innumerable set of Buddhas who populated the cosmos. Each Buddha ruled a region, or "heaven" or "pure land," which was also populated with highly evolved spiritual beings known as Bodhisattvas. These Buddhas and Bodhisattvas were thought to be filled with compassion and with certain abilities and powers to help those who asked for it. One of the chief features of Mahayana Buddhism is its devotional quality, consisting of the worship of and prayers to these celestial Buddhas and Bodhisattvas.

Integral to the new Buddhology that distinguishes the Mahayana is the doctrine of the "three bodies" or "three forms" (rupas) of the Buddha. The first is the "transformation body" (nirmana kaya), which refers to the physical emanations the Buddha sends out to this and other worlds. The historical Buddha, Gautama, was one such emanation according to Mahayana Buddhism—a notion that also assumes that Gautama was always and already enlightened, being merely an earthly incarnation of a previously enlightened cosmic Buddha. Under this conception, Buddhas have the capability of sending out virtually infinite numbers of transformation bodies out of their compassion and urge to help all sentient beings everywhere.

Each Buddha also has what is called an "enjoyment body" (sambhoga kaya), a subtle body of light that appears in that Buddha's heaven or pure land, a paradisiacal world populated with advanced practitioners and Bodhisattvas. Conditions in such a land are highly conducive for the attainment of Buddhahood; one form of Mahayana Buddhist practice is to pray and perform other devotional activities in the hopes that one or another of the Buddhas will admit the devotee into his or her pure land after death.

Finally there is what is called the "dharma body" of the Buddha, which refers to the ultimate nature of the Buddha's mind and to reality itself in its ultimate form. The dharma body includes the omniscience or perfect realization of wisdom in a Buddha's mind. It also includes the ultimate nature of reality itself, its "thusness" or "suchness."

Another innovation in Mahayana Buddhism was the superseding of the Eightfold Path with a new method (leading to a newly reconceived goal). This was what became known as the "Path of the Bodhisattva." The first step on this path was to attain what was termed *bodhicitta,* the "mind of enlightenment" or the motivating wish to attain Buddhahood out of compassion for all sentient beings. A key ingredient to *bodhicitta* and, indeed, a virtue that takes center stage in Mahayana Buddhism, is compassion (*karuna*), which, together with "loving kindness" (*maitri*) and wisdom (*prajna*), form a triad of the distinctive virtues characteristic of the Bodhisattvas ("beings of enlightenment," the ones who have attained *bodhicitta*) and the Buddhas as conceived by Mahayana.

Out of this driving wish for enlightenment, impelled by the altruistic intention to help end the suffering of others, the Mahayana practitioner takes various vows, swearing to live a life guided by compassion, and then engages in the "six perfections," each associated with a progressively higher stage of the Bodhisattva path. The first of these "perfections" (*paramitas*) is generosity, including the giving of material things, protection from fear, and the giving of dharma teachings themselves. In its most advanced form, the perfection of giving includes the willingness of the Bodhisattva to give up his or her own body if necessary. Also included under this perfection is giving in the form of what is known as "transfer of merit" (*parinamana*), the perpetual turning over to the benefit of others any karmic merit done by any meritorious act.

The second perfection is ethics (*shila*) and consists largely of avoidance of the ten basic misdeeds of body, speech, and mind (killing, stealing, sexual misconduct, lying, divisive speech, harsh speech, idle speech, coveting, ill will, and wrong views). Third is the perfection of patience (*kshanti*), specifically combating anger with compassion and loving kindness. The fourth perfection is joyful effort or "vigor" (*virya*), defined as taking joy in doing meritorious and compassionate acts. Fifth comes meditative concentration (*dhyana*) followed by the sixth perfection, wisdom (*prajna*).

The "perfection of wisdom" consists of realizing the truths of the distinctive metaphysics that also defines Mahayana Buddhism. Especially associated with the great philosopher Nagarjuna (c. 150–250 C.E.) is the important doctrine of "emptiness," or *shunyata*. Nagarjuna argued that, as a sort of universal extension of the earlier doctrine of "no-self," all phenomena are "empty" of inherent nature or self-existence. Persons and phenomena exist only dependently, not independently. Emptiness is thus not the ultimate ground of being but rather the insistence that there is no such ultimate, irreducible ground. Emptiness is not some thing but the absence of intrinsic existence to all things. But neither, argued Nagarjuna, does this mean that "nothing exists." Things do exist, but only dependently. The philosophical school associated with Nagarjuna's thought was called the "Middle Way" school (Madhyamika), positing neither nihilism nor eternalism but a median between the two.

Another important philosophical tenet of Mahayana Buddhism is the identity of samsara and nirvana. Liberation is not "outside" or "apart from" a world of suffering; they are not two separate realities. Both are equally "empty" of self-nature and exist, as all things, only dependently.

While other traditions and schools of Buddhism also went from India to China, Korea, and Japan, it was Mahayana Buddhism that flourished and was further developed in those regions. Mahayana is thus sometimes called "northern Buddhism" in contrast to the predominantly Theravada traditions of "southern Buddhism."

Mahayana Buddhism in China was heavily influenced by the preexisting religious philosophies of Confucianism and Taoism and by the presuppositions of a culture already ancient, literate, and sophisticated by the time Buddhism was brought to it in the early centuries C.E. Among the difficulties Buddhism faced in China were monasticism and celibacy, which were understood to be in opposition to the Chinese emphasis on filial piety and ancestor worship. Conversely, the Chinese readily embraced and further elaborated the Mahayana concept of all beings having a "Buddha nature," or the potential to achieve Buddhahood and enlightenment.

By the fifth century C.E. different schools of Buddhism arose in China. Some of these were simply Chinese equivalents of Indian Buddhist schools. San-lun, or the "Three Treatises" school, was the Chinese version of Madhyamika, and Fa-hsiang, or "Characteristics of the Dharma" school, was the equivalent of the Indian philosophical tradition known as Yogacara. But also at about this time, distinctively Chinese schools of Buddhism arose that reflected indigenous cultural and religious emphases. The importance of harmony, for example, produced schools like the T'ien-t'ai ("Heavenly Terrace"; Tendai, in Japan), which placed one text (in this case the Lotus Sutra) above all others and then organized the rest of the diverse Buddhist tradition into a hierarchically ordered synthesis. The T'ien-t'ai philosophy embraced the idea that Buddha nature exists in all things and that the absolute and phenomenal world are not ultimately different. Another school that attempted to harmonize the teachings of Buddhism into a syncretistic whole was the Hua-yan (Kegon, in Japan) school, which elevated the Avatamsaka Sutra to the highest place and oriented the rest of Buddhist texts and teachings around it.

Of special importance, however, were two other schools that arose in China, spread to neighboring regions from there, and survive to the present. The first of these was the "Pure Land" school (Ch'ing-t'u), a devotional and faith-based sect centering on the figure of Amitabha Buddha. Pure Land became the most popular form of the religion in China, Korea, and Japan, especially among the laity. Pure Land promises an easy path to salvation in the guise of rebirth into the heaven or pure land of Amitabha, where one will quickly become enlightened. The principal practice of this form of Buddhism has been to call upon the grace of this Buddha through repeating a formula known as *nien-fo* (*nembutsu* in Japanese). In its more radical forms, Pure Land has insisted that one must rely totally on the "other-power" of the Buddha and not at all on one's own efforts.

The second of the two most important schools that arose initially in China was that known as Ch'an, or Zen as it was termed in Japan. Deriving from a Sanskrit word for "meditation," the Ch'an/Zen tradition offers a stark contrast to the devotionalism of Pure Land. Traced back to an Indian monk-missionary named Bodhidharma, whose radical and uncompromising meditational techniques become legendary, the Ch'an/Zen tradition developed a simple but disciplined and demanding set of methods for directly intuiting one's own Buddha nature and achieving various levels of awakening (*wu*, or *satori* in Japanese). These methods included meditation, the "direct transmission" of wisdom from the mind of the enlightened teacher to that of the student, and the contemplation of riddles known as koans.

Vajrayana or "Tantric" Buddhism

The third major form of Buddhism, like that of Mahayana, was the particular Buddhist expression of a pan-Indian religious movement. Whereas Mahayana became the Buddhist form of the bhakti, or devotional movement, Vajrayana ("Diamond Vehicle") was the Buddhist expression of what has been called Tantrism, an esoteric, sometimes antinomian, and often controversial form of religious belief and practice that became influential throughout India beginning in the middle centuries of the first millennium C.E.

Here too, as with Mahayana, this apparently new form of Buddhism is not represented as new at all. Vajrayana claims to be the secret doctrines and practices taught by the Buddha in his guise as Vajradhara (the "Holder of the diamond") to only his most advanced disciples. It also portrays itself as the quick way to enlightenment in this very lifetime through the attainment of "accomplishments," or powers (*siddhis*), that speed up the process. The tantric master (*mahasiddha*) appropriates to him- or herself the powers of one or another of the Buddhas, who is invoked through the practice of meditative visualizations, symbolic gestures (mudras), and the recitation of sacred words called mantras (indeed, such is the importance of the latter that sometimes this form of Buddhism is called Mantrayana or the "Vehicle of the Mantra").

One key to this form of Buddhism is the emphasis on initiation and the important place of the tantric master, or guru. It is the teacher who is the gateway to the powers of the tantric deity or Buddha and their secret world, or mandala. The techniques and wisdom are to be scrupulously guarded from the uninitiated, and as a result the texts of Vajrayana Buddhism are often encoded in a symbolic or metaphorical language (sometimes called "twilight speech") not easily decipherable by outsiders. Once initiated, the practitioner forms a special connection, even identity, with the tantric deity or Buddha into whose sphere one has entered. By attempting to recognize the union with that deity through meditation and, in more advanced cases, ritual and yogic practices involving a partner of the opposite sex, the practitioner tries to "short-circuit" the mind into a realization of enlightenment and the perception of all things and beings as pure.

Tantric forms of Buddhism perhaps originated among the laity but by the eighth century had been taken up by monastic scholars and brought increasingly into the mainstream of Buddhist thought and practice. By and large the great tantric practitioners who brought this form of Buddhism to Tibet had originally been trained in the monasteries. And while Vajrayana Buddhism spread also to Southeast Asia, Japan, and elsewhere, it was primarily in Tibet and Nepal where this form of Buddhism was preserved after it was extinguished in India.

Later Developments: Modern Buddhism in Asia and Buddhism in the West

Buddhism, like all other religions, has been influenced by the forces of modernity. These forces—including scientific materialism, secularism, technological advances, and the ideologies of democracy, equality, Marxism, and so on—arrived in the traditionally Buddhist Asian countries in the forms of Western imperialism and colonialism and the Christian missionary movement that often accompanied them. In Sri Lanka, Southeast Asia, China, and Japan, the coming of Western influences disrupted the traditional structural alliances between Buddhist monastic institutions and the government. Buddhist revivals in places like Sri Lanka and Thailand resulted in what has been called a new "Protestant" form of Buddhism that emphasizes rationality and deemphasizes the split between monastics and laity. Buddhism also often became associated with cultural and emerging national pride in the battle against the colonial powers and their impact. In Japan and Korea, Buddhist influences combined with modern concepts and in some cases Christian influences to give rise to a slew of new religious movements. And in China and Tibet, where Chinese Communist regimes have not often been favorably disposed to Buddhism, the religion survives in a much-weakened condition in comparison to its earlier influence.

Buddhism in the modern West comprises two very different kinds of groups. On the one hand, it has come to North America and Europe as the religion of Asian immigrants. For these new arrivals, Buddhism provides a sense of cultural community, continuity, and tradition in new and often challenging circumstances. Often over time the Buddhism practiced in these immigrant communities increasingly takes on the shape of Christian church worship, with the introduction of scripture reading, sermons, and youth education ("Sunday school").

The other form of Buddhism in the West is made up of Western converts who are almost always attracted not to the devotional or even the communal element of Buddhist religion as much as to the philosophical and especially meditative component. For these Western lay practitioners (there are at present very few Western Buddhist monastics), the practice of Buddhism means first and foremost meditation, a dimension of the religion formerly in Asian contexts confined almost exclusively to the monastics.

See also **Asceticism: Hindu and Buddhist Asceticism; Chinese Thought; Communication of Ideas: Asia and Its Influence; Consciousness: Chinese Thought; Cosmology: Asia; Daoism; Heaven and Hell (Asian Focus); Hinduism; Meditation, Eastern; Mysticism: Chinese Mysticism; Religion: East and Southeast Asia; Sacred Texts: Asia; Yin and Yang; Zen.**

BIBLIOGRAPHY

Conze, Edward. *A Short History of Buddhism.* London and Boston: Unwin, 1980.

Harvey, Peter. *An Introduction to Buddhism: Teachings, History, and Practices.* Cambridge, U.K., and New York: Cambridge University Press, 1990.

Lopez, Donald S., Jr., ed. *Buddhism in Practice.* Princeton, N.J.: Princeton University Press, 1995.

———, ed. *Buddhist Hermeneutics.* Honolulu: University of Hawaii Press, 1988.

Robinson, Richard H., and Willard L. Johnson. *The Buddhist Religion: A Historical Introduction.* 4th ed. Belmont, Calif.: Wadsworth, 1997.

Strong, John. *The Experience of Buddhism: Sources and Interpretations.* Belmont, Calif.: Wadsworth, 1995.

Takakusu, Junjiro. *The Essentials of Buddhist Philosophy.* 3rd ed. Edited by by Wing-tsit Chan and Charles A. Moore. Honolulu: University of Hawaii Press, 1956.

Tambiah, Stanley J. *World Conqueror and World Renouncer.* Cambridge and New York: Cambridge University Press, 1976.

Walpola, Rahula. *What the Buddha Taught.* Rev. ed. New York: Grove Press, 1974.

Williams, Paul. *Buddhist Thought: A Complete Introduction to the Indian Tradition.* London and New York: Routledge, 2000.

Brian Smith

BUREAUCRACY.

The idea of bureaucracy formally begins with Max Weber (1864–1920); indeed, the *idea* of bureaucracy ends with Weber as well. Prior to Weber's explication of the "ideal type" of rational, efficient organization of public or private business as a bureaucracy, the idea was simply a commonsense, practical method for the organization of economic or government action. While the original idea of bureaucracy was a prescription for social organization for both public and private organizations, the contemporary usage of the term is limited nearly exclusively to public organizations.

The association between Weber and the concept of bureaucracy is readily apparent; however, Weber himself did not explicate a definition of bureaucracy as such. Rather, he simply elaborated on a form of social organization according to specific characteristics and suggested that these were the elements of what would become bureaucracy. It is important to note that Weber was a sociologist committed to explaining the organizational forms within the world around him; bureaucratic forms of social organization were certainly in existence before Weber's ideal typology came to light.

The Practical Form of Social Organization Later Known as Bureaucracy

Prior to the coinage of the term *bureaucracy* in the nineteenth century, organizations that functioned essentially as bureaucracies had long existed throughout the world. As early as the Han Dynasty (206 B.C.E.–220 C.E.), Chinese bureaucracy was taking on the form of a merit-based, centralized administrative apparatus of the state. Other early civilizations, including the Egyptians and the Greeks, included active administrative arms, but unlike the Chinese, were not selected primarily on criteria of merit. The early practice of bureaucracy was nominally a system of individuals employed (often permanently) in court advisership, tax collection, and the implementation of imperial/monarchical policy. This form of bureaucratic social organization dates back to the early Chinese dynasties as well as the early Egyptians, Phoenicians, Romans, Greeks, and other ancient societies, all of whom employed a designated body of loyal officials to implement the various policies of the ruling classes. Throughout the early common era, bureaucracy remained an arm of the ruling powers and the aristocracy; imperial, monarchical, and feudal systems employed bureaucratic-type organizations primarily to implement taxation and land-use policies.

The Middle Ages saw the expansion of another form of public bureaucracy. The ecclesiastic bureaucracy was designed to implement policies and maintain the hierarchy of the Catholic Church. The church was certainly not alone in its use of formal hierarchical structures for the purpose of efficient implementation of policy: early Protestant faiths and the Islamic faith also employed bureaucratized structures for the coordination of their ever-growing populations of clerics and faithful. The bureaucratization of modern life is intimately tied to religion, in Weber's case, Protestantism. The alliance between ecclesiastic and secular bureaucracies would dominate the greater part of the millennium. For example, the Crusades to the Holy Land were in many ways marvels of imperialist-expansionist uses of both bureaucratic structures. The use of the two bureaucratic forms in the foreign occupation and domination of foreign lands would be an important idea in the late-twentieth-century rejection of colonialism. As Rodney argues, the church was also a colonizing force, "[meant] primarily to preserve the social relations of colonialism . . ." (p. 253), and had to be dealt with as a colonizing bureaucratic power.

The key elements of the early practical bureaucracies (from the early Han Dynasty bureaucracy to the nascent Prussian state administration) included significant loyalty to the court, (very) limited policy discretion, frequent abuses of government power for organizational and individual gain, and the erection and maintenance of significant barriers to entry into the public service. The earliest practicing bureaucrats were rightfully accused of coveting and vehemently defending their titles as well as unduly influencing court decisions in favor of maintenance of the bureaucratic structure. This tendency of bureaucratic officials would be a perennial argument against the use of bureaucracy, particularly for the organization of government business. Later, within the early modern era (particularly the time of the prerevolutionary French administration) bureaucracy was used primarily as an aristocratic tool of domination of the many by the few. However, the inefficiencies and graft of rational-legal and formalistic bureaucratic systems are unlikely to be noted as particularly heinous compared to earlier, traditional forms of imperial and aristocratic abuses.

Max Weber and the Idea of Bureaucracy

What is notable about the very idea of bureaucracy is its severe rational modernism. Political modernity and bureaucracy are largely symbiotic; the rise of the state paralleled the rise of the bureaucracy. One of the philosophers of the modern economizing state and the modern bureaucratic idea is Adam Smith (1723–1790), whose defense of the division of labor promoted the bureaucratization of the early Westphalian state. Indeed, Smith's ideas are elemental to Weber's core tenets of bureaucracy: the rigid division of responsibilities and tasks and the economization of organizational forms. Whereas Smith advocated the division of labor in order to promote efficient economic growth, Weber suggests the division of labor for the efficient production of goods or services. Inevitably, bureaucracy was conceived as, and has become, an economizing tool for the rationalization of complex and ambiguous environments.

The rationality of bureaucracy is a central idea within Weber's ideal type. In fact, Weber himself suggests that bureaucracy be a rational-legal form designed to promote the rationalization of organizational tasks and goals. The rational-

izing tendency of bureaucracy, while being one of the elements most open to contemporary criticism, was also its most attractive quality for the architects of Enlightenment-guided governance, who sought alternatives to earlier forms of despotic and aristocratic dominance. The adoption of the bureaucratic form by theorists of liberal government has its roots in the legal protection of natural (rational) rights for all. In fact, embedded in the rationalization structure of bureaucracy is the elimination of particularism—the diminishment of universal individual rights for the sake of traditional forms of class or ethnic domination. Those responsible for the French Revolution pined, within their writings, for the rational nonexceptionalism of the bureaucratic form. Indeed, as Maximilien de Robespierre (1758–1794) and later Alexis de Tocqueville (1805–1859) identified, the *ancien régime* was epitomized by the irrational occupation of power by a centralized bureaucracy of the ruling class.

The products of mid-modern European thought on the liberalizing and economizing role of government produced the context in which Weber penned his essay "Bureaucracy." Within the essay he establishes the criteria elemental to the ideal bureaucracy. Foremost, he recommends that bureaucracy be the instrument of rational-legal authority, which he defines as that manner of authority "resting on a belief in the 'legality' of patterns of normative rules and the right of those elevated to authority under such rules to issue commands" (Scott, p. 44). This supplanted traditional forms of authority such as the sanctity of hereditary rule or charismatic authority such as the leadership of Napoleon. The bureaucratic organization of rational-legal authority involves the following necessary criteria: the specification of jurisdictional areas, the hierarchical organization of roles, a clear and intentionally established system of decision-making rules, the restriction of bureau property to use by the bureau, the compensation by salary (not spoils) of appointed officials, and the professionalization of the bureaucratic role into a tenured lifelong career. The idea of bureaucracy suggests that rules, norms, merit, regulations, and stability are paramount to the operation of government. The rule-bound nature of bureaucracy has been widely critiqued in modern political and sociological analyses; however, the number of alternative forms of organization that have received as much consideration is limited.

Criticism of and Advancements in the Idea of Bureaucracy

Critics primarily attack the practice of bureaucracy, but a few notable scholars attack or enhance the very idea of a bureaucracy and/or a bureaucratic state. Oddly, Georg Wilhelm Friedrich Hegel (1770–1831) was a reformer of the idea of bureaucracy without being an outright critic of the form. The Hegelian notion of the neutral universalizing civil service devoted to the common good contradicts Weber's notion of the bureaucracy that unquestioningly serves the rational-legal authority of the state. Hegel expands the role of bureaucracy beyond simply the implementation of rules to a universalizing and constitutive, productive artifact of modern society. This notion of the constitutive and productive bureaucracy is picked up by later political scientists such as Brian J. Cook. Despite the positive contribution that Hegelian philosophy has upon the idea of bureaucracy, followers of Hegel, such as Karl Marx and

Hannah Arendt, have damned the practice of bureaucracy as a dominating instrument of rationalized capitalist will. However, they have not notably expanded upon the idea of bureaucracy but have rather simply recast the rules already understood to be elemental to the idea and defined them as ills of modernity.

One avenue of expansion upon the idea comes from the criticism that postcolonial and postmodern theorists have directed toward bureaucracy. Weber initially argued for bureaucracy to be a tool for internal organization of offices that served to legitimate the power of the organization's authority through rationalization and rules. What postcolonial and postmodern theorists have charged is that bureaucracy is also designed for domination of the organization by those external to it. Weber's idea was, according to later critics, formed within a social vacuum and neglected the role of environment and context upon bureaucratic behavior. However, Weber likely did not intend to explicate a form of social organization void of social context; rather, he espoused one that could potentially work within a multitude of situations with or without being extensively tailored to individual societies. As such, Weber's original idea is decidedly impersonal and lacks space for exceptionalism. Consequently the organizational form is also ideal for discipline and domination; as an organizational tool within the public, bureaucracy has, as Hegel suspected, a tendency toward projection of a universal standard (of rationality, in this case). As Robert K. Merton suggests, the "formalism, even ritualism [of bureaucracy], ensues with an unchallenged insistence upon punctilious adherence to formalized procedures" (p. 106). The bureaucratic insistence upon rule-based formality codifies conformance, the primary tool of bureaucratic dominance.

Bureaucracies, particularly in modern democratic societies, have significant roles to play as channels of representation. Theorists of representative bureaucracy have expanded upon the idea itself to suggest that the practice be a conduit of effective and well-rounded governance. Similarly, as suggested by Michael Lipsky, lower-level bureaucrats can serve as advocates for citizen needs within their official capacities. Theorists of representative or advocative bureaucracy clearly reject the Weberian characteristic of neutral servants of authority and by doing so expand the idea of bureaucracy from a micro-level instrument of social organization to a macro-level system of social responsibility.

Criticisms of the Practice of Bureaucracy

The speculation that bureaucracy will bear bad fruit within society began with criticisms of government practice across history. These criticisms came from various philosophical schools as well as from the rapidly decolonized nations, particularly following World War II. However, many of the philosophical criticisms of bureaucracy are leveled against the practice rather than the idea. As Charles T. Goodsell notes, there are three broad typologies of antibureaucratic criticism within academia. These are a focus on unacceptable performance, the fear of bureaucracies serving elite interests over the interests of the entire polity, and the fear of bureaucratic oppression through formalism and a general lack of concern for particular needs of clientele. Of these criticisms, the focus on the unacceptable

performance and antihumanitarianism of bureaucracies seems to dominate the majority of the literature. For example, Thorstein Veblen, James Dewey, and D. Warnotte identify ills in bureaucratic practice that include, respectively, "trained incapacity," "occupational psychosis," and "professional deformation" (Merton, p. 104). However, each of these criticisms is lodged against practical states of bureaucratic employment rather than the idea of bureaucracy itself. Additional critical thought on the practice comes largely from contemporary organization theorists who have concerned themselves with the impact of bureaucratic structure on employees' motivation and attitudes. Additionally, theorists of public administration have speculated upon the role of bureaucracy within other organizational forms such as democratic governance. While these criticisms are decidedly useful as a pedagogical tool for understanding the nature of bureaucracy, they represent neither a critical reflection upon nor notable additions to the idea itself.

Goodsell's third typology has been largely taken up by postmodernists, critical theorists, and postcolonial critics of bureaucracy. The use of government bureaucratic domination as well as ecclesiastic bureaucratic domination was highly effective in the overtaking of colonial properties. However, bureaucratization was an ineffective tool for the reformation of decolonized states. Perhaps Weber was correct in his assertion that "bureaucracy, thus understood, is fully developed in political and ecclesiastical communities only in the modern state, and, in the private economy, only in the most advanced institutions of capitalism" (p. 73). The bureaucratization of juridical states and the rise of capitalist economy are inextricably related; the bureaucratic form is unnatural in societies where charismatic or traditional authority still dominates. The modernist preference for rational-legal authority suggests that bureaucracy should be the natural form of organization, but for decolonizing states in a situation of authoritative flux, bureaucracy may be an unnatural and in many cases falsely dominating form of organization.

Another form of critique against the practice of bureaucracy has come from scholars of gender relations. These critiques center primarily upon the rejection of the rationalist-modern form of organization as decidedly male-centered. Feminist scholars have argued that bureaucratic structures privilege male forms of communication, deemphasize intuitive and experiential knowledge, diminish the creative capacities of employees, and encourage conformity with historically male institutions, such as government. Again, while these critiques address some structures of bureaucracy as suggested by Weber, the idea itself is not augmented in the address.

Contrary to the thesis that bureaucratic organizations are consistently dominating is the thesis that bureaucracies (as Hegel supposes) can be neutral civil services devoted to the benefit of all in the society. Particularly because of its rational character and nonparticularistic method of organizing client needs, the bureaucracy can ideally serve all within a given community at an equally efficient level. However, according to some critical theorists, Jürgen Habermas being the most notable, the current conditions of social interaction within society are prohibitive of appreciative discourse between equal parties capable of reaching mutually acceptable and operable conclusions. Whether the bureaucracy offers itself as a neutral public servant or not, the social structure of government in capitalist societies in particular unconsciously promotes unequal dialogue and domination by bureaucracies.

Summary of the History of the Idea of Bureaucracy

The history of the idea of bureaucracy is also marked by changes in the public perception of the term. Prior to Weber's defining the idea of bureaucracy, the practice of rational organization of government services according to neutral merit-based qualifications was viewed as a positive antidote to the nepotism and hereditary domination of traditional monarchical or ethnocentric forms of government. However, across most of the globe, the recent history of the term suggests that it has had a largely negative influence upon society. Indeed, the term *bureaucracy* now evokes epithetical connotations that refer exclusively to perceived inadequacies in government policy implementation.

One final characteristic of the history of the idea of bureaucracy is the multitude of synonyms that have evolved to describe the practice or the idea of bureaucracy in more neutral or passive terms, particularly within the past century. These synonyms include public administration, public management, public service, and governance or policy implementation. In fact, within much of the contemporary literature on bureaucracy, or public administration in particular, the two concepts are used coterminously. This tendency to conflate the idea of bureaucracy with the idea of public service, management, or administration demonstrates that the term has expanded from its original sociological implications. However, this is not to suggest that the idea of bureaucracy as the social organization of complex tasks according to rational-legal authority has lost any of its original appeal. It merely suggests that changing public preferences have altered the disciplinary significance of historical ideas and distorted them to reflect current social contexts, even if it leads to the incorrect hijacking of what once was a neutral academic term.

See also **Democracy; Liberalism; State, The.**

BIBLIOGRAPHY

Arendt, Hannah. *Crises of the Republic.* New York: Harcourt Brace Jovanovitch, 1972.

———. *Eichmann in Jerusalem: A Report on the Banality of Evil.* Rev. and enl. ed. New York: Viking, 1964.

Blau, Peter M. *The Dynamics of Bureaucracy.* 2nd ed. Chicago: University of Chicago Press, 1973.

Cook, Brian J. *Bureaucracy and Self-Government: Reconsidering the Role of Public Administration in American Politics.* Baltimore: Johns Hopkins University Press, 1996.

Creel, H. G. "The Beginnings of Bureaucracy in China: The Origin of the Hsien." *Journal of Asian Studies* 23, no. 2 (1964): 155–184.

Eisenstadt, S. N. *The Political Systems of Empires.* London: Free Press of Glencoe, 1963.

Goodsell, Charles T. *The Case for Bureaucracy: A Public Administration Polemic.* 3rd ed. Chatham, N.J.: Chatham House, 1994.

Habermas, Jürgen. *The Inclusion of the Other: Studies in Political Theory.* Edited by Ciaran Cronin and Pablo de Greiff. Cambridge, Mass.: MIT Press, 1997.

Hegel, G. W. F. *Elements of the Philosophy of Right.* Edited by Allen W. Wood; translated by H. B. Nisbet. Cambridge, U.K., and New York: Cambridge University Press, 1991.

Lipsky, Michael. *Street Level Bureaucracy: Dilemmas of the Individual in Public Services.* New York: Russell Sage Foundation, 1980.

Marx, Karl. *Critique of Hegel's "Philosophy of Right."* Edited by Joseph O'Malley; translated by Annette Jolin and Joseph O'Malley. Cambridge, U.K.: Cambridge University Press, 1970.

———. *Marx's Eighteenth Brumaire: (Post) modern Interpretations.* Edited by Mark Cowling and James Martin. London: Pluto Press, 2002.

Mbembe, Achille. *On the Postcolony.* Berkeley: University of California Press, 2001.

Meier, Kenneth J. "Representative Bureaucracy: An Empirical Analysis." *American Political Science Review* 69, no. 2 (1975): 526–542.

Merton, Robert K. "Bureaucratic Structure and Personality." In his *Social Theory and Social Structure.* Rev. and enl. ed. New York: Free Press, 1957.

Perrow, Charles. "Why Bureaucracy?" In his *Complex Organizations: A Critical Essay.* 3rd ed. New York: McGraw-Hill, 1986.

Reese, Thomas J. *Inside the Vatican: The Politics and Organization of the Catholic Church.* Cambridge, Mass.: Harvard University Press, 1996.

Rodney, Walter. *How Europe Underdeveloped Africa.* Washington, D.C.: Howard University Press, 1981.

Scott, W. Richard. *Organizations: Rational, Natural, and Open Systems.* 5th ed. Upper Saddle River, N.J.: Prentice Hall, 2003.

Skocpol, Theda. *States and Social Revolutions: A Comparative Analysis of France, Russia, and China.* Cambridge, U.K., and New York: Cambridge University Press, 1979.

Smith, Adam. 1776. "Of the Division of Labour." In *Classics of Organization Theory,* edited by Jay M. Schafritz and J. Steven Ott. 5th ed. Fort Worth, Tex.: Harcourt College Publishers, 2001.

Stivers, Camilla. *Bureau Men, Settlement Women: Constructing Public Administration in the Progressive Era.* Lawrence: University of Kansas Press, 2000.

———. *Gender Images in Public Administration: Legitimacy and the Administrative State.* 2nd ed. Thousand Oaks, Calif.: Sage, 2002.

Weber, Max. *From Max Weber: Essays in Sociology.* Edited and translated by H. H. Gerth and C. Wright Mills. Oxford and New York: Oxford University Press, 1946.

Wenke, Robert J. "Egypt: Origins of Complex Societies." *Annual Review of Anthropology* 18 (1989): 129–155.

Wilson, Woodrow. "The Study of Administration." *Political Science Quarterly* 2, no. 2 (1887): 197–222.

Witz, Anne, and Mike Savage, eds. *Gender and Bureaucracy.* Cambridge, Mass.: Blackwell, 1992.

Sara Jordan

BUSHIDO. Literally translated as "way of the warrior," Bushido evolved into a clearly defined ethical system of the *bushi,* or warrior class of Japan, during the seventeenth and eighteenth centuries; the term first appeared in the *Kōyō gunkan* in about 1625. In his 1899 *Bushido: The Soul of Japan,* Nitobe Inazō, the first to articulate the concept in English, enumerated seven essential values of the warrior class: justice, courage, benevolence, politeness, veracity and sincerity, honor, and loyalty. More re-

Samurai warrior, photographed c. 1860 by Felice Beato. Bushido, the samurai code of ethics, was formalized in writing in the sixteenth century and adhered to for some three hundred years. Bushido placed emphasis on certain chivalrous virtues such as loyalty, courage, and courtesy. © HISTORICAL PICTURE ARCHIVE/CORBIS

cently, Bushido has been credited with fueling Japanese atrocities in World War II, through "the unassailable rule that death is preferable to dishonour" (Edwards, p. 5). In fact, neither of these popular conceptions accurately represents the codes of warrior behavior that developed over the course of six centuries.

The Warrior Governments of Japan

In 1192 Minamoto Yoritomo established the first *bakufu*, or "tent government," to counter the growing inability of the imperial family and aristocracy to control the provinces. From that time until the Meiji Restoration of 1868 Japan was governed by its warrior class.

Yoritomo's Kamakura government was later idealized as the warrior's "Golden Age," when "selfless loyalty unto death" characterized relations between warlords and their samurai retainers. Modern scholarship has uncovered a different picture, however. According to Dr. Karl Friday, "From the beginnings of the samurai class and the lord/vassal bond in the eighth century to at least the onset of the early modern age in the seventeenth, the ties between master and retainer were contractual, based on mutual interest and advantage, and were heavily conditioned by the demands of self-interest" (p. 342). There was no single prescriptive code of behavior; instead each warrior clan had its own behavioral norms, sometimes listed in formal "house pre-

cepts," or *kakun,* or in admonitory epistles to a lord's heirs and retainers.

These early warrior documents varied considerably—some had a decidedly Buddhist cast, others insisted on a thorough education in the arts, while still others advised a single-minded focus on strategy and skills for battle. Some were written in a highly stylized Chinese form; others were composed in a more natural Japanese manner. The Chinese-influenced theme of balance between *bun* (literature) and *bu* (martial skills), *bunbu ryōdō,* appears frequently. So do the reciprocal admonitions of loyalty to the lord and benevolence toward retainers. Maintaining martial skills is so important that Shiba Yoshimasa writes, "Insofar as martial arts are concerned, it goes without saying that one should practice . . ." (Hurst, p. 218).

From War to Peace

Prior to the Edo period (1600–1868), the primary function of a warrior was to fight. Writing about how to behave as warriors was of less immediate concern than actual battlefield skills. Tokugawa Ieyasu changed all that, through the unification of the country and his establishment of the third and final bakufu in 1603. Suddenly the *bushi,* who had been engaged in almost continual warfare for one hundred years, were left without any battles to fight. By the eighteenth century, the gap between name and role had widened to the point that the *bushi* experienced a full-fledged identity crisis. The samurai were now primarily administrators and bureaucrats searching for an understanding of their proper role in a warless age.

Unlike their predecessors, who had been writing for fighting men and clan leaders, thinkers such as Yamaga Sokō and his student Daidōji Yūzan wrote about Bushido in an attempt to define and encourage behaviors that would distinguish warriors from the other classes of farmers, artisans, and merchants. Incorporating a more traditional Confucianism than the state-favored Neo-Confucianism, Yamaga argued that the primary duty of the warrior was to serve as an exemplar for the rest of society, through deeply cultivated sincerity of action.

Yamamoto Tsunetomo, in the *Hagakure,* saw a very different purpose for the eighteenth-century warrior—"The Way of the Samurai is found in death" (p. 17). This anachronistic view—warriors had not died in battle for more than a century— is frequently misunderstood. In order to control the armed warriors, Tokugawa Ieyasu established a series of inviolable laws; these at times came into conflict with the warrior's individual loyalties or sense of honor. In particular, both parties in any conflict between samurai were to be punished equally; in this context, Yamamoto urged that if warriors were forced to break the Shogun's law they might as well fight to the death.

Modern Legacy

The values of the *bushi,* both actual and idealized, have permeated all levels of Japanese society. In the Edo period, members of the merchant class deliberately adopted samurai standards of behavior to identify themselves more closely with

---

PRECEPTS OF THE FIGHTING MAN (KAMAKURA, MUROMACHI, AZUCHI-MOMOYAMA PERIODS, 1185–1600)

Rokuhara-dono gokakun (The precepts of the lord of Rokuhara, 1247), by Hōjō Shigetoki

Gokurakuji-dono goshōsoku (The message of the master of Gokurakuji, 1256), by Hōjō Shigetoki

Tōjiin goisho (Last testament from the Tōjiin Temple, 1357), attributed to Ashikaga Takauji

Chikubashō (Bamboo stilt anthology, 1383), by Shiba Yoshimasa

Imagawa kabegaki (Imagawa's wall inscriptions, 1395–1409), by Imagawa Ryōshun

Yoshisadaki (The records of Yoshisada, c. 1338), attributed to Nitta Yoshisada

Jūshichikajō (The seventeen articles, c. 1479), by Asakura Takakage

Nijūikkajō (Twenty-one precepts, c. 1495), by Hōjō Sōun

Soteki waki (The recorded words of Asakura Soteki, c. 1553), by Asakura Soteki

Kyūjūkyū kakun (Ninety-nine precepts, 1558), by Takeda Nobushige; collected in the *Kōyō gunkan*. Redefining the Warrior: the Tokugawa peace (1600–1868)

Kōyō gunkan (A military history of the great men of Kai, c. 1625), compiled by Kōsaka Danjō and Obata Kagenori

Bukyō yōroku (Essentials of military studies, 1656), by Yamaga Sokō

Budō shoshinshū (Introduction to the way of the warrior, 1716), by Daidōji Yūzan

Hagakure (In the shadow of leaves, 1716), by Yamamoto Tsunetomo

---

the ruling class. After the Meiji Restoration, unemployed samurai became doctors and educators, and brought their written codes with them. The *Imagawa kabegaki*, by the fourteenth-century poet-warlord Imagawa Ryōshun, was even used as a textbook in Edo-period schools. During the years prior to the Meiji Restoration, the samurai's spirit of sincerity in action, loyalty, and self-sacrifice allowed them to take leadership in the revolt that would lead to the abolition of their class.

Bushido's most tragic legacy is the warped version ultranationalists used in formulating propaganda to encourage and sustain the Japanese solider before and during World War II. The spirit of the *Hagakure* incited young Japanese men to become kamikaze suicide pilots; death was promoted as preferable to surrender.

In the early twenty-first century the term *Bushido* appeared more frequently in English-language martial arts publications than it ever did in early warrior texts. And even though Nitobe's list of virtues was not directly derived from actual warrior codes, it did reflect romanticized warrior ideals that the rapidly modernized Japanese recognized as noble and found comforting to call their own.

See also **Chinese Warlordism.**

BIBLIOGRAPHY

Edwards, Bernard. *Blood and Bushido: Japanese Atrocities at Sea 1941–1945.* New York: Brick Tower Press, 1991.

Friday, Karl F. "Bushido or Bull? A Medieval Historian's Perspective on the Imperial Army and the Japanese Warrior Tradition." *The History Teacher* 27, no. 3 (1994): 339–349.

Hurst, G. Cameron III. "The Warrior As Ideal for a New Age." In *The Origins of Japan's Medieval World: Courtiers, Clerics, Warriors, and Peasants in the Fourteenth Century,* edited by Jeffrey P. Mass, 209–233. Stanford, Calif.: Stanford University Press, 1997.

Wilson, William Scott, trans. *Ideals of the Samurai: Writings of Japanese Warriors.* Edited by Gregory N. Lee. Burbank, Calif.: Ohara, 1982.

Yamamoto Tsunetomo. *Hagakure: The Book of the Samurai.* Translated by William Scott Wilson. Tokyo and New York: Kodansha International, 1983.

Diane Skoss

C

CALCULATION AND COMPUTATION. Words containing the roots *calcul-* and *comput-* have existed since antiquity. The study of concepts used to indicate actions, professions, and (mental and material) artifacts suggests that *calculation* and *computation* have not been, as canonically assumed, an exclusive concern of modern times. The mere existence of both word clusters throughout the decades (and centuries) prior to World War II also suggests that it may be problematic to assume that the relationship between calculation and computation has been simple—that is, computation existing as an exclusive postwar phenomenon brought about by a technical revolution that left calculation behind. For both Charles Steinmetz (1865–1923) and Vannevar Bush (1890–1974), celebrated pioneers of the prewar and interwar generation of electrical engineering, respectively, both calculation and computation were of constitutional importance to all their technical work. Their writings indicate a belief that the computing revolution started long before the 1940s. Steinmetz and Bush employed both concepts contemporaneously in their pervasive engineering textbooks in order to differentiate between high-skill analysis and low-skill application, between creative mental design and routine manual implementation, between that which was subject to the least and to the most of mechanization.

Steinmetz and Bush perceived themselves as analysts, in the tradition of Gottfried Wilhelm von Leibnitz (1646–1716) and Isaac Newton (1642–1727), the early modern founders of calculus. With the dynamic expansion of the division of labor that has been part and parcel of the expanding capitalist mode of production, the progress of calculation was a prerequisite for the advance of computation. Successful calculation from the top by the well-paid few would, first, routinize the work performed by the multitudes in the base of the pyramid; second, it would minimize the skill required by them; third, it would subject their work to mechanization; and fourth, it would lower their salary expectations. Computation was the job for a low-paid clerk known as the "computer" or "computor." These human computers were usually women, who produced computations for the state and the military, for insurance companies and other businesses, and for analysts within the engineering and scientific community. While human computers worked with a rich variety of artifacts, it was the mass employment of mechanical desktop "calculating machines" that determined their history. By contrast, the engineering graduate, almost exclusively a male, was trying to distance himself from the ranks of the human computers by passionately defending the accuracy of his inexpensive slide rule, which he could own individually and skillfully use to "calculate."

After the 1950s, amid popular expectation that full mechanization had finally arrived, the concept of "computer" connoted a machine rather than a human, thereby signifying the ideological hegemony that pointed to full separation of production from skilled labor, of accumulated (or dead) labor from living labor, and of fixed from variable capital. Instead of disappearing, the dated engineering differentiation between "analysts" and "computors" resurfaced in the system analysts versus coders struggle that marked the emergence of the programmers, computation's new professionals. The difference between computation and calculation resonates throughout the fierce competition between the digital and analog computer (1940s–1950s), followed by the juxtaposition of digital computer hardware to software (1960s–1970s), which, in turn, was succeeded by the contrast between digital computer software operating systems from software for special purposes (i.e., application software) in the 1980s and 1990s.

Premodern, Early Modern, Non-Western

The difference in the meaning of "calculation" and "computation" that are found in Steinmetz and Bush seems to have been built on the precapitalist use of terms formed by the roots *calcul-* and *comput-*, respectively. Historiographically, the late medieval period offers an example when one compares the interest shown in quantifying the heterogeneity of motion by the Merton College theorists known as the "Oxford calculatores" to the practice shown by the ecclesiastical community toward homogenizing the standardization of time through a technique known as *computus*. During the late medieval and early modern period, the attack by the algorists upon the abacists—that is, the promoters of computing who relied upon previous and private memorization of tables of numerical relationships versus the defenders of the ancient tradition who placed emphasis on live calculations performed in public by moving pebbles (that is, *calculi*) along designated lines—compares favorably to the conflict between the digital (programming) and the analog (living labor) of the recent decades.

The physical embodiment of complex numerical relationships through interconnected mechanical parts that were concealed by a case, hence masking the motion of the gears, displayed only the input and output numbers. Some celebrated early modern examples were Blaise Pascal's (1623–1662) adding machine (1642) and Leibniz's adding and multiplication machine (1685). Earlier in the same century (1623), the German mathematician and linguist Wilhelm Schickard (1592–1635) had mechanized the set of numbered sliding rods that John Napier (1550–1617) had devised in 1617 to simplify astronomical calculations. Both Pascal and Leibniz sought to profit selling their machines to merchants and natural philosophers. Galileo Galilei (1564–1642) tried the same with his improved computing dividers. Many of the early modern natural philosophers were heavily involved in calculating innovations. Additional contributions include "calculation by analysis" to the coordinates of René Descartes (1596–1650), by differentiation and integration in the calculus tradition that prefigures in Simon Stevin (1548–1620) and materializes in Newton and Leibniz, and by the analysis of multiplication and division into addition and subtraction through the logarithms that Napier introduced in 1614.

As with the method of algorists, the speed in calculation by logarithms assumed the availability of relevant tables. The transformation of these tables into scales inscribed in, first, circles sharing a fixed center and, soon after, scales that slid beside each other while sharing a fixed framework, found its ultimate presentation in the logarithmic slide rule, configured by William Oughtred (1574–1660) as early as 1621. The interactive proliferation of both tables of logarithms and logarithmic slide rules determined the history of calculation from the early modern period until the very recent decades. The dilemmas of computation in the recent decades have prefigured in the construction and worldwide use of tens (if not hundreds) of millions of slide rules, linear, circular, cylindrical, or hybrid, wooden, metal, or plastic, handmade or mass produced, cheap or expensive, with accessories such as cursors and magnifying glasses to increase the accuracy without increasing the size. The recent debates over special versus general purpose software and over competing software operating systems was long rehearsed in debates over choice of general or special purpose slide rule scales and scale system standards. Moreover, as scales of all sorts slid beside each other or within each other, the logarithmic slide rule turned out to be only one of innumerable versions of slide rules. Material culture scholars see no end to collection of calculation wheels devised to compute phenomena ranging from a menstrual cycle to a baseball season.

The coevolution of logarithmic slide rules and tables of logarithms is no different from the codevelopment of Leibniz's "calculus" and his "calculating machine." Taken together they point to the paired constitution of the scientific and the technical since earlier modernity. If Leibniz sought to sell his machine to merchants, Charles Babbage (1792–1871), a Cambridge mathematics professor, was interested in a calculating engine organized internally according to the symbolic efficiency and rationality of the nascent industrial order emerging within the first half of the nineteenth century in Great Britain. Partially funded by the government, Babbage failed for economic reasons to have his "difference engine" constructed because he was forced to depend on one of the most skillful workers of the period, Joseph Clement (1779–1844), in the workshop of whom the engine to calculate as if powered by "steam" was to be constructed. While the construction of the difference engine encountered the problem of skilled labor, Babbage realized that the use of the engine itself would be limited to special purposes, which would not eliminate calculation's dependence on skilled labor. In 1833, he started drafting sketches of a second engine, the "analytical engine," which he sought to be independent of labor skill. He kept making modifications to the plans until his death in 1871 without ever managing to advance beyond programmatic descriptions of such an engine.

In Babbage's *The Exposition of 1851; or, Views of Industry, the Science and the Government of England,* published in London in 1851 following his review of the panorama of industrial capitalism staged at the Crystal Palace World Fair, he repeatedly touched on the ideal of an engine that would render laborers mere "attendants," unable to influence the production of calculation. Although Babbage's calculating engines matched his promotion of a version of continental analysis that he thought to be more appropriate to a calculation to sustain further industrial growth, he became known for his emphasis on the mechanization rather than the organization of work. The organization of work has been the pursuit of the division-of-labor scheme that the French engineer Gaspard Clair Prony (1755–1839) devised in 1792 to have a new set of logarithmic and trigonometric tables produced as a monument to the new French Republic. Six eminent mathematicians who selected the appropriate equations formed the peak of his pyramid, a layer of ten mathematicians below them advanced the analysis to the point where everything was converted to simple arithmetic, and a group of one hundred humans, recruited even from hairdressers, performed simple operations on a part of a problem before passing it to the next person.

The expansive reproduction of this scheme by setting smaller or larger groups during the nineteenth and the twentieth century, after taking advantage of sources available both within and outside the Western society, resulted in the formation of an army of "computers." By the introduction of commercial calculating machines such as Thomas de Colmar's (1785–1870) Arithmometer, exhibited at the 1855 Paris Exposition, references to "human computers" are found from as near as a British male scientist's environment of female friends and as far as male Indians working in British engineering initiatives in their country. The relative continuity between Leibniz's calculating machine and the Arithmometer—the most widely available calculating machine based on improvements on Leibniz's machine by 1871—is an index of the relative continuity between merchant and industrial capitalism. Leibniz had promoted his machine to a society marked by the dynamic appearance of merchants by stating that "it is unworthy of excellent men to lose hours like slaves in the labor of calculation, which could safely be relegated to anyone else if the machine were used" (Leibniz, quoted in David Eugene Smith, *A Source Book in Mathematics* [1929], pp. 180–181). Babbage's "attendants" were the industrial version of Leibniz's slaves. Babbage wanted his calculating engines used for the production of general and special purpose tables, including tables for the navigational pursuits of the British empire. Batteries of human computers—along with other implements such as calculating machines and slide rules—produced numerous tables and charts for an assortment of military and civilian purposes (scientific, engineering, and commercial).

The lack of a synthesis of scholarly studies limits scholars' ability to compare the modern European experience with calculation and computation to those of non-European societies. What is known about the Inca knotted strings known as *quipu* and the Chinese knotted cords suggests that societies paradigmatic of civilization in other continents relied heavily on what is now identified as calculation and computation. Ongoing historical interpretation of archaeological findings from ancient Mesopotamia point to the few who knew how to connect computations routinely produced by the many to a calculating coefficient that could make the abstract concrete. Projecting Western conceptual demarcations to non-Western societies may prove problematic, especially considering the parallel dead ends from having projected late modern Western demarcations to ancient and early modern histories. Interpretation, for example, of the Hellenistic Antikythera mechanism as "analog," and accordingly, a technically inferior computer, has blocked historians from taking into account the digitalization introduced by the complicated geared structure underneath the disk representing analogically the universe. As a result, the search for how the technical accuracy of the artifact matched with social interests of the period has been replaced by the assumption of limits in the accuracy due to inferiority from belonging to an essentialist inaccurate technical genre. Similarly, a historiography aiming at interpreting the analog motion of the pebbles on ancient and early modern abacuses has been blocked by the late modern emphasis on the resting pebbles—that is, on the perception of pebbles as digits. The tradition of the Chinese and the Western abacus, therefore, has been flatly situated under the "digital," thereby making it impossible to acknowledge differences in the employment of abacus analogies between and within traditions.

Late Modern Period

Abacuses and artifacts from the associated tradition of counting boards with pebbles or beads share the honor of being ancestors of the digital computer along with the various mechanical and electromechanical desktop calculating machines produced from 1850 to 1950. They are joined by an ensemble of mechanical and (later) electromechanical tools and machines used for punching holes into cards, which represent computable variables, for sorting these cards according to the variable to be computed, and for tabulating and printing the results. They are best known as punched card machines, based on the part of the process that was least subjected to mechanization. Going back to the end of the nineteenth century, punched card machines were rented by companies that were ancestors to IBM (International Business Machines) to, first, the United States Census Bureau, and, subsequently, censuses for nations around the world. Calculating and punched card machines were extensively used for filing, accounting, and related activities that involved the processing of large amounts of data in larger enterprises, which have ranged from railroads to insurance companies. The U.S. Social Security Administration also used hundreds of punched card mechanisms and machines to implement a social security system that, in 1935, had to handle information about the wages paid by three million employers to their twenty-six million employees.

In addition to the slide rule, the list of what has been a posteriori placed under analog computers includes calendars, sundials, orreries, astrolabes, planetariums, material models of all kinds (including scale models), mathematical and other

mental models, graphs that could be as complex as the nomograms of Maurice D' Ocagne (1862–1938) and his followers (used from the late nineteenth century until the recent decades), computing linkages, artifacts with mechanical integrators and differentiators, curve tracers and kinematic mechanisms in the tradition of planimeters and associated artifacts, harmonic analyzers and synthesizers like the one that Lord Kelvin had built as a tide predictor, mechanical, electromechanical, and electrical analyzers for general (e.g., Bush's differential analyzer) and special purposes (e.g., Bush's electric power network analyzers), electrolytic tanks, resistive papers and elastic membranes used as models, and countless mechanisms and machines produced and used in fire control (internal, external, and terminal ballistics). Case studies have retrieved the histories of many other cases of unique tools and machines, including those used for crucial tidal calculations in the Netherlands.

Changes in calculating machinery were coupled with changes to make the calculus correspondingly operational. Remembered more as the author of the state-of-the-art calculating machines during the interwar period, Bush was also the author of influential writings on the "operational calculus," which capitalized on a tradition of modifications of the calculus that adjusted it to the ever-changing needs of engineers who thought of themselves as equal to any scientist. In the 1930s and in the 1940s, punched card machines were reconfigured to be useful in scientific calculations. Bush's differential and network analyzers were also used in the scientific calculations of the period immediately before and after World War II. Calculating machines were used in scientific calculations even earlier and so were slide rules.

The various branches of the state have had an organic role in fostering technological change. To the examples of the extensive use of digital punched card machinery by civilian apparatuses such as the census should be added the involvement by the military in purchasing analog fire control mechanisms and machines; of the state's exclusive involvement in cryptography-related calculation and computation even less is known, with the exception of the celebrated Colossus machine during World War II. Using the Colossus machine, a British team that included in its members the mathematician Alan Turing (1912–1954) broke the code produced by a German machine known as the Enigma. The military had actually used hundreds of punched card machines in World War I for materiel inventory and for medical record keeping. Interwar support for military needs changed so remarkably that the computing bombsight and the anti-aircraft director were by World War II extremely complex artifacts with thousands of mechanical, electrical, and electronic parts. The competing development of the computing bombsight, which increased the target reach for a bomber, and the anti-aircraft director, which increased the reach of ground-based fire targeting the bomber itself, has formed a vicious circle that exemplifies the contradiction of modern technology. In the United States, the development of accurate bombsights during World War II was a secret second only to the construction of the atomic bomb. The extreme technological contradiction to date may have been that the most accurate computing bombsight was used to drop the first atomic bomb, a lethal weapon like none before it, the efficient release of which required the least accuracy.

Contemporary Period

The demand for ballistics tables beyond what available human computers could supply in World War II resulted in the construction of ENIAC (Electronic Numerical Integrator and Computer), considered by many to have been the first digital electronic computer. It was constructed by employing 18,000 vacuum tubes between 1943 and 1945 at the Moore School of Pennsylvania by a team led by John Mauchly (1907–1980) and J. Presper Eckert (1919–1995) with funds from the U.S. Army's Ballistics Research Laboratory. Under the direction of Howard Aiken (1900–1973), a physics instructor at Harvard University, IBM completed in 1944 the construction of the Automatic Sequence Controlled Calculator (Harvard Mark I), used to produce the U.S. Navy's ballistic tables. A wealth of detail exists about the 1940s and the 1950s, the period of the heroes of electronic computation, which has attracted the disproportionate attention of historians. At the very least, this attention has made it clear that the electronic computer was a "multiple invention," which means that it came by a social cause, not an individual genius.

The construction of ENIAC was roughly contemporaneous to several other projects. Aiken's efforts at reconfiguring IBM's accounting machines for the purpose of solving nonlinear differential equations went back to 1937. The Bell Labs employee George Stibitz constructed a series of machines based on relays and other telephonic equipment, including the Complex Number Calculator, which was used successfully by the military between 1940 and 1949. In Germany, starting in 1938 and continuing through the war, Conrad Zuse (1910–1995) constructed a series of machines that were also based on electromechanical relays. Iowa State College physics professor John Atanasoff (1903–1995) and his graduate student Clifford Berry (1918–1963) built a special purpose electronic computer, the ABC (Atanasoff-Berry Computer) between 1939 and 1942. Ranging from the big to the gigantic, these machines inaugurated experimentation with correspondence between electronic circuitry and numerical computational relationships, in the decimal or the binary system. Claude Shannon is the most recognizable of those who were arguing for such correspondence theoretically by showing that the design of electronic circuits and the reduction of reasoning to a series of simple algebraic operations (as proposed by the Boolean algebra) could be used to push each other forward.

Having been a participant of the Moore School team, the Princeton mathematician John von Neumann (1903–1957) shaped the following generation of electronic computers by setting the standard of a computer architecture based on an internal division of labor between a control unit that interacted with the memory to check the flow of data between the memory and the arithmetic unit while controlling the input and output. His division between an arithmetic unit, which is where any future calculation was to take place (by taking into account selected past computations from a stock accumulated in the memory) imported the living-dead labor dynamic balance of the whole of the capitalist economy into the

workings of the machine—the balance during the dynamic self-accumulation of past computations in the memory was to be provided by the control unit. The accumulation of data and instructions in the memory unit became known as the "stored program technique." It represented an economy of flexible allocation of resources that was opposite to the brute-force approach of the previous generation of electronic computers. Von Neumann presented his architecture in a 1945 report on EDVAC, a computer to follow ENIAC. The architecture was rehearsed in the construction of the IAS (named after Princeton's Institute for Advanced Study) by a team led by von Neumann at Princeton. It was completed in 1952. Like most experimental computers of the period, IAS was funded by sources such as the military and the Atomic Energy Commission. Similar machines were constructed at seventeen other research centers in the United States and several more in various other countries.

Interested in commercial rather than scientific computers, Eckert and Mauchly tried a series of intermediate computer configurations and business schemes before authorizing the production of the Remington-Rand UNIVAC (Universal Automatic Computer), the first of which was delivered to the Census Bureau in 1951. The first UNIVAC for business use was installed at the General Electric Appliance Division, for payroll computations in 1954. By 1957, the number of UNIVACs sold was up to forty-six. Along with several other manufacturers, IBM entered the electronic computer business in the early 1950s. It started with the 1951 IAS-type Defense Calculator, which was renamed IBM 701. IBM constructed and rented nineteen such machines. By 1960, IBM had dominated the market with machines such as the IBM 650, usually rented to universities under attractive terms, which subsequently tied university computations to IBM. IBM's dominance was solidified by its introduction in the mid-1960s of the standard-setting System/360 family of computers.

By then, the analog-digital debate, which has started in the late 1940s and escalated in the early 1950s, was practically over. The evolution of the MIT Project Whirlwind between 1945 and 1953, under the direction of Jay Forrester, captured the emergence of the analog-digital demarcation. Intended to be used in real-time aircraft flight simulation, it started as an analog machine. Upon learning about the EDVAC, Forrester decided to attempt to construct a digital computer. His costly change was supported, initially, by the U.S. Office of Naval Research with approximately one million dollars per year. When the Navy gave up, the Air Force stepped into the void hoping that the digital Whirlwind computer could lead into a machine suitable to the needs of SAGE (Semi-Automatic Ground Environment), a system to coordinate the detection of and response to the Soviet Union's strategic bombers. The pursuit of SAGE brought about enormous demands for programming, thereby revealing the dependence on computer software. It started to become apparent that the analog-digital contrast was succeeded by a contrast between software and hardware.

There is no record of thinkers who foresaw a market for more than a few mainframes in the 1940s. There is also no record of thinkers who predicted that the future of computation was not in the formation of computer utilities, according to the direction suggested by the time-sharing of mainframes during the 1960s. Patented in 1959 by Jack Kilby of Texas Instruments, the integrated circuit contained all the elements of an electronic circuit in a chip of silicon. The microprocessor appeared a decade later as a general-purpose programmable integrated circuit. The cheapening of the hardware and the miniaturization of electronic components made possible the decrease of the size of the main-frames to that of minicomputers. The potential of reducing the size of the computer further to that of a home appliance was realized in the subsequent decades, resulting in the mass production and use of personal computers during the 1980s and the mass interconnection of personal computers that led to the formation of the Internet and the World Wide Web during the 1990s. In the meantime, microprocessors have been installed everywhere from home appliances to automobiles.

The decrease of the value of hardware accentuated the increase in the value of software. What concluded as a "software crisis" started as a problem of "programmer shortage." Generations of general and special-purpose programming languages, and, by now, software operating systems have yet to provide a stable solution. Attempts at computer-aided programming (machine self-programming) and software engineering (mass production of software) have met with limited success if not complete failure. From eliminating the "programming bugs" that clogged the early electronic computers to blocking the so-called spam that plugs contemporary e-mailing, computation seemed to have increased rather than decreased the dependence on skilled labor. In its absence, all sorts of computer viruses threaten the contemporary world with catastrophe. Many of the world's habitants anxiously anticipated living through the completion of a millennium in the transition from year 1999 to year 2000, which became known as Y2K. Their recollection of the event is marked by the memory of anxiety surrounding Y2K, a concern that stemmed from decades of labor-saving yet short-sighted use of two digits for the purpose of making electronic computations economical.

See also **Computer Science; Mathematics; Technology.**

BIBLIOGRAPHY

Abbate, Janet. *Inventing the Internet.* Cambridge, Mass.: MIT Press, 1999.

Aspray, William. ed. *Computing before Computers.* Ames: Iowa State University Press, 1990.

Beniger, James, R. *The Control Revolution: Technological and Economic Origins of the Information Society.* Cambridge, Mass.: Harvard University Press, 1986.

Black, Edwin. *IBM and the Holocaust: The Strategic Alliance between Nazi Germany and America's Most Powerful Corporation.* New York: Crown, 2001.

Blok, Aad, and Greg Downey, eds. *Uncovering Labour in Information Revolutions, 1750–2000.* Cambridge, U.K., and New York: Cambridge University Press, 2003.

Borst, Arno. *The Ordering of Time: From the Ancient Computus to the Modern Computer.* Translated by Andrew Winnard. Chicago: University of Chicago Press, 1994.

Campbell-Kelly, Martin. *From Airline Reservations to Sonic the Hedgehog: A History of the Software Industry.* Cambridge, Mass.: MIT Press, 2003.

Campbell-Kelly, Martin, et al. *The History of Mathematical Tables: From Sumer to Spreadsheets.* Oxford and New York: Oxford University Press, 2003.

Campbell-Kelly, Martin, and William Aspray. *Computer: A History of the Information Machine.* New York: Basic Books, 1996.

Ceruzzi, Paul. *A History of Modern Computing.* 2nd ed. London and Cambridge, Mass.: MIT Press, 2003.

Cortada, James. *IBM, NCR, Burroughs, and Remington Rand and the Industry They Created, 1865–1956.* Princeton, N.J.: Princeton University Press, 1993.

Edwards, Paul. *The Closed World: Computer and the Politics of Discourse in Cold War America.* Cambridge, Mass.: MIT Press, 1996.

Hopp, Peter M. *Slide Rules: Their History, Models and Makers.* Mendham, N.J.: Astragal Press, 1999.

Jezierski, Dieter von. *Slide Rule: A Journey through the Centuries.* Translated by Rodger Shepherd. Mendham, N.J.: Astragal Press, 2000.

Kline, Ronald. *Steinmetz: Engineer and Socialist.* Baltimore: John Hopkins University Press, 1992.

Lubar, Steven. *InfoCulture: The Smithsonian Book of Information Age Inventions.* Boston, Mass.: Houghton Mifflin, 1993.

MacKenzie, Donald. *Knowing Machines: Essays on Technical Change.* Cambridge, Mass.: MIT Press, 1996.

McFarland, Stephen L. *America's Pursuit of Precision Bombing, 1910–1945.* Washington, D.C.: Smithsonian Institution Press, 1995.

Menninger, Karl. *Number Words and Number Symbols: A Cultural History of Numbers.* Translated by Paul Bronner. Cambridge, Mass.: MIT Press, 1969.

Mindell, David A. *Between Human and Machine: Feedback, Control, and Computing Before Cybernetics.* Baltimore: Johns Hopkins University Press, 2002.

Nebeker, Frederik. *Calculating the Weather: Metrology in the 20th Century.* San Diego, Calif.: Academic Press, 1995.

Small, James S. *The Analogue Alternative: The Electronic Analogue Computer in Britain and the USA, 1930–1975.* London and New York: Routledge, 2001.

Spufford, Francis, and Jenny Uglow, eds. *Cultural Babbage: Technology, Time and Invention.* London: Faber, 1996.

Williams, Michael R. *A History of Computing Technology.* 2nd ed. Los Alamitos, Calif.: IEEE Computer Society, 1997.

Yates, JoAnne. *Control Through Communication: The Rise of American System in Management.* Baltimore: Johns Hopkins University Press, 1989.

Zachary, G. Pascal. *Endless Frontier: Vannevar Bush, Engineer of the American Century.* New York: Free Press, 1997.

Aristotle Tympas

CALENDAR. A calendar is a system of reckoning and ordering time beyond the period of a day in a repetitive, usually annual, cycle. A calendar's primary function is regulating and organizing human activities; the word derives from the Latin *calendarium* or *calendra,* "account book," and *kalendae* or "calends," the new moon and first day of the Roman month, when Romans paid their debts. Calendars may have derived from the human penchant for imposing order; however, the most efficient exploitation of natural resources implies synchronizing productive efforts with nature's cycles. Sensitivity to such cycles is biologically programmed into humans as circadian rhythms, including the twenty-four-hour cycle of sleep and wakefulness and fluctuating body temperature; and in the female menstrual cycle, which approximates a lunar period.

Calendric periodicities are traced ultimately to the Sun and the Moon. The daily apparent rising and setting of the Sun is due to the rotation of the Earth, while the annual cycle of the seasons is related to the revolution of the Earth around the Sun, and the tilt of the Earth relevant to its plane of revolution. The most commonly reckoned calendrical period beyond day and night is the synodical lunar month (the cycle of lunar phases) of 29.5 days. Incommensurability between this period and the seasonal cycle based on the solar year of 365.24 days and the need to process fractions of days in the astronomical cycles with whole-day counts have been among the most difficult challenges for calendar specialists.

Early, Nonliterate, and Folk Calendars

Alexander Marshack sees in the scorings and tally marks on Paleolithic fossils and artifacts the beginnings of time recording. With Neolithic domestication, systematic time reckoning allowed farming practices to fit local moisture and temperature patterns. Such concerns and efforts are suggested at Stonehenge in England, where, beginning about five thousand years ago, massive stones were arranged in geometric patterns. While interpretations of the site vary, its main axis includes an alignment to the June solstice sunrise, the day of longest sunlight.

Small-scale and nonliterate societies such as the Nuer of Africa emphasize a sensitivity and responsiveness to seasonal cycles that E. E. Evans-Pritchard calls "ecological time." Such calendars are characterized by:

1. space-time (the fusing of concepts of time with the space accessed and occupied in that time);

2. fuzzy-bordered seasons (increasing rains gradually transform dry season to wet);

3. "layered" observations of synchronous events at different ecological levels (for example, the bloom of plant species coincident with the movement of fish or game); and

4. diachronic sequences, such as episodic faunal or floral changes or consecutive astronomical observations (for example, advancing stellar positions, changes in the Moon's position and shape, or the movement of the Sun on the horizon).

Calendar Codification and Civilization

Awareness of the astronomical significance behind seasonal phenomena allowed human communities to coordinate their activities seasonally for strategic and productive ends. Once a reliable system of recording such information was devised, calendar refinement and codification were possible. Calendar codification and the enhanced utilization of energy and other resources that this enabled are a significant factor in the process of civilization—a topic deserving additional study. The earliest centers of civilization in Mesopotamia, the Indus and Nile valleys, eastern China, Mesoamerica, and the Andes all have information recording systems and codified calendars, which were probably overseen by high-ranking astronomer-priests who also likely oversaw timely rituals relating human endeavors to cosmic powers.

Varieties of Calendars

The prominence of the Moon in premodern societies with limited lighting and the regularity of its phases resulted in the synodical lunar month being basic to many traditional calendars. In the Muslim calendar, twelve lunar months of twenty-nine or thirty days are reckoned in a year of 354 days, or a leap year of 355, in a thirty-year cycle. The approximately eleven-day difference between such a synodical lunar calendar and the solar year, however, results in a slippage of months through the seasons. In order to maintain synchrony between lunar months and the seasons, an intercalated month is necessary, a strategy employed in the Jewish calendar with influence from Babylonia: seven leap years intersperse with twelve common years in a nineteen-year cycle.

Ancient Egyptians used the annual heliacal rise (predawn reappearance) of Sirius to help coordinate their lunar months with the seasons and solar year. While maintaining this system for religious observance, they later developed a civil year of 365 days comprising twelve fixed months of thirty days with five additional days. The ancient Maya had a similar five-day end-of-year, but divided the other 360 days into eighteen named periods of twenty days. This yearly calendar intermeshed every fifty-two years with a divinatory cycle of 260 days. Maintaining separate calendars for civic and religious (and/or regional and ethnic) functions is a common practice, useful in the twenty-first century for the retention of local traditions amidst the spread of the Gregorian calendar.

The Gregorian Calendar and Globalization

The Gregorian calendar spread through European colonialism and later through international relations, exchange, and commerce. It developed from the first-century B.C.E. Julian calendar, named after Julius Caesar, who commissioned its development and approved the reckoning of months no longer determined by lunar observations in a year that averaged 365.25 days. The Gregorian gets its name from Pope Gregory XIII, by whose election in the year 1572 C.E. the day marking the vernal equinox had strayed ten days from its occurrence. His papal bull in 1582 set out the mechanisms by which:

1. the spring equinox would occur on its actual date;

2. Easter—which depends on calculations from the vernal equinox—would be determined; and

3. a leap year system would be implemented, allowing for prolonged congruency between the calendar and its astronomical underpinnings.

Since the sixteenth century, countries around the world have adopted the Gregorian calendar, including its twelve fixed months, seven-day weeks, and beginning date. However, day and month names usually occur in the vernacular, and traditional reckonings may be kept for local, ethnic, and religious observances.

Through calendars, humans impose culturally significant rhythms on the perception of time. Across human cultures two primary perceptions of the character of time predominate:

1. time as recursive or cyclic, observed in the recurrence of day and night, lunar waxing and waning, and the return of the seasons; and

2. time as linear, an ongoing process, observed in the maturation of vegetation, decay, and the transition of a human life from birth to death.

Specially marked dates and periodicities are the human, cultural cadence in the infinitude of time. While unable to control the passage of time, humans with calendars have increasingly ordered their relationship to and utilization of it.

See also **Astronomy, Pre-Columbian and Latin American; Time.**

BIBLIOGRAPHY

Aveni, Anthony. *Empires of Time: Calendars, Clocks, and Cultures.* Boulder: University Press of Colorado, 2002.

Evans-Pritchard, E. E. *The Nuer: A Description of the Modes of Livelihood and Political Institutions of a Nilotic People.* Oxford: Oxford University Press, 1940. Reprint, 1969.

Fabian, Stephen Michael. *Space-Time of the Bororo of Brazil.* Gainesville: University Press of Florida, 1992.

Marshack, Alexander. *The Roots of Civilization: The Cognitive Beginnings of Man's First Art, Symbol and Notation.* London: Weidenfeld and Nicolson, 1972.

Richards, Edward G. *Mapping Time: The Calendar and Its History.* Oxford: Oxford University Press, 1998.

Westrheim, Margo. *Calendars of the World: A Look at Calendars and the Ways We Celebrate.* Oxford: Oneworld Publications, 1994.

Stephen M. Fabian

CANNIBALISM. The possibility of cannibalism has been an object of thought and imagination in virtually every society. The idea of consuming human body substance as food or for symbolic purposes invokes emotionally charged cultural and psychological concerns with boundaries between self and other, persons and nonpersons, the meanings of food and ingestion, and the limits of a moral community. Many societies, both Western and non-Western, have seen cannibalism as a marker of negative difference between peoples, a quintessential symbol of otherness, savagery, and subhumanity. Others have treated it as a form of exchange or as a mechanism of transformation, regeneration, or reproduction through transactions between ontological categories such as kin and enemy, mortals and deities, human and animal.

In Western thought, two uses of the idea of cannibalism have been recurring themes: as a negative stereotype of exotic "others," and as a metaphor for reflexive questioning, critique, and parody of Western culture. Especially in the politics of colonialism, accusations of cannibalism have been deployed to denigrate non-Western peoples, assert colonizers' moral superiority, and legitimize the takeover of native lives and lands. Only recently have scholars called attention to socially approved cannibal practices in Western history, such as the tradition of using human body substances as medicines, which flourished in Europe until the eighteenth century.

The stigma associated with cannibalism in Western thought makes any assertion that certain people engaged in it politically sensitive. Since the 1970s, especially in the United States, anthropologists and historians have debated where and to what extent cannibalism was an institutionalized, socially accepted practice (as distinguished from its occurrence as an aberrant, individual act motivated by starvation or psychological deviance). These arguments mostly involved historical and retrospective evidence, since under the impact of colonialism and modernity, any former practices of institutionalized flesheating had largely disappeared by the 1970s. Major controversies focused on Michael Harner's and Marvin Harris's interpretation of human sacrifice as a response to dietary shortages among the Aztecs of fifteenth-century Mexico; the role of funerary cannibalism in epidemics of the neurological disease *kuru* in the New Guinea highlands; the ongoing debate between Marshall Sahlins and Gananath Obeyesekere over allegations of cannibalism among South Pacific islanders and after the death of Captain James Cook; and the interpretation of archaeological finds from Europe and the southwestern United States that show dismemberment, mutilation, and cooking of body parts.

A major impetus to debates over the reality of cannibalism came from William Arens's *The Man-Eating Myth* (1979), which examined selected accounts from some non-Western societies. Finding a lack of hard evidence and no credible eyewitness accounts by Western experts, Arens expressed doubt that cannibalism ever existed anywhere as a socially approved practice. He argued that cannibalism is best understood not as a cultural practice but as a projection of Western fantasies, racism, and political propaganda. Although presented as a critique of Orientalist prejudices, the argument reified negative colonial stereotypes with its implicit assumption that the act of ingesting human substance is in all cases repulsive and morally indefensible. Arens's critique of the supposed bias and credulity of those who have written about cannibalism as social practice found some scholarly receptivity, particularly within cultural studies.

In anthropology, Arens's book drew criticism for its methodology, sensational rhetoric, and unreasonable and inconsistent empirical standards. The controversy had the positive effect of stimulating ethnographers and historians to reassess historical and ethnographic evidence. While debates continue over the evidence in specific cases, most anthropologists accept the idea that normative, institutionalized practices of consuming human body substances did occur in some times and places in the past.

Recent anthropological work has sought to contextualize local cultural practices by elucidating their social, symbolic, religious, and ritual significance. A few scholars, such as Eli Sagan and I. M. Lewis, have proposed universal explanations interpreting flesh-eating in all contexts, from warfare to funeral rites, as expressions of similar impulses such as hostility, ambivalence, or desires for dominance. The stronger trend has been to recognize diversity and the many different kinds of practices with distinctive cultural meanings that have been lumped together under the rubric of "cannibalism." Ethnographies from Melanesia and the South Pacific have highlighted how cannibalism, as practice or idea, was linked to cultural ideas about ethnicity and gender, the uses of flesh and food to define spheres of morality and exchange, and human reproduction and the circulation of vital energies or substances contained in the body. Lowland South American ethnography has emphasized cannibalism's role in the production of personhood and alterity and indigenous notions of its role in metaphysical transformations and exchanges between enemies and between the living and the dead, humans and animal, mortals and immortals. There has also been new attention directed to native peoples' images of Europeans or other foreigners and their descendants as "white cannibals." An implicit agenda in much recent scholarship is to undermine negative stereotypes and deexoticize the subject of cannibalism by expanding humanistic understandings of how, within local systems of cultural meaning, some peoples may have felt that consuming human flesh or bones was a positive, morally acceptable thing to do.

Over the past five centuries, numerous writers, from Michel de Montaigne to Jonathan Swift and Ruth Benedict, have used cannibal imagery to express critical perspectives on Western culture and as a rhetorical device for inverting conventional boundaries of civilization and morality. In Brazil in 1928, Oswaldo de Andrade's "Cannibal Manifesto" launched the avant-garde Antropofagia movement, which reclaimed cannibal imagery from native Brazilians' early encounters with Europeans and asserted that the key principle of Brazilian modernity is assimilation of foreign influences. Latin American artists and intellectuals continue to find cannibalism a fertile metaphor for Euro-American culture and exploitative political economic relations.

Since the 1970s, there has been a trend among scholars, artists, and culture critics in the United States and elsewhere to deploy cannibalism as a metaphor for Western civilization itself. Globalization, capitalist consumer culture, and cross-cultural appropriation in tourism, art, media, and museums have been portrayed as forms of cannibalism. Richard King criticizes the Occidentalism in analyses that treat "the West" as a single, undifferentiated entity while perpetuating negative stereotypes, trivializing cannibalism as a real experience and embodied cultural practice, and deflecting attention from its meanings in specific social-historical contexts. As one of the last real taboos in contemporary cosmopolitan society, cannibalism's attention-getting power to shock ensures that it will continue to be a theme and source of fascination in popular culture and scholarship.

See also **Colonialism; Ethnography; Eurocentrism; Occidentalism; Orientalism.**

BIBLIOGRAPHY

Arens, William. *The Man-Eating Myth: Anthropology and Anthropophagy.* Oxford: Oxford University Press, 1979.

Barker, Francis, Peter Hulme, and Margaret Iversen, eds. *Cannibalism and the Colonial World.* New York: Cambridge University Press, 1998.

Brown, Paula, and Donald Tuzin, eds. *The Ethnography of Cannibalism.* Washington, D.C.: Society for Psychological Anthropology, 1983.

Conklin, Beth A. *Consuming Grief: Compassionate Cannibalism in an Amazonian Society.* Austin: University of Texas Press, 2001.

Goldman, Laurence, ed. *The Anthropology of Cannibalism.* Westport, Conn.: Bergin and Garvey, 1999.

Harner, Michael. "The Ecological Basis for Aztec Sacrifice." *American Ethnologist* 4 (1977): 117–135.

Harris, Marvin. "People Eating." In his *The Sacred Cow and the Abominable Pig: Riddles of Food and Culture,* 199–234. New York: Simon and Schuster, 1985.

King, Richard. "The (Mis)Uses of Cannibalism in Contemporary Cultural Critique." *Diacritics* 30, no. 1 (2000): 106–123.

Lestringant, Frank. *Cannibals: The Discovery and Representation of the Cannibal from Columbus to Jules Verne.* Translated by Rosemary Morris. Berkeley: University of California Press, 1997.

Obeyesekere, Gananath. "Cannibal Feasts in Nineteenth-Century Fiji: Seamen's Yarns and the Ethnographic Imagination." In *Cannibalism and the Colonial World,* edited by Francis Barker, Peter Hulme, and Margaret Iverson, 63–86. Cambridge, U.K., and New York: Cambridge University Press.

Sagan, Eli. *Cannibalism: Human Aggression and Cultural Form.* New York: Harper and Row, 1974.

Sahlins, Marshall. *How "Natives" Think: About Captain Cook, for Example.* Chicago: University of Chicago Press, 1995.

Sanday, Peggy Reeves. *Divine Hunger: Cannibalism as a Cultural System.* New York: Cambridge University Press, 1986.

Beth A. Conklin

CAPITALISM.

This entry includes two subentries:

Overview

Africa

OVERVIEW

Capitalism has been the dominant economic system in the West since the nineteenth century and has increasingly spread across the globe. Characterized by unfettered markets in labor and natural resources, commodity production, and the reinvestment of profit, capitalism must be distinguished from other forms of commercial society that existed in early times or outside of the West, in which market-oriented activity remained ultimately subservient to political or moral goals. (Examples of such noncapitalist market society include the so-called mercantilism that preceded full-fledged capitalism in Europe and the city-state empires of the ancient Mediterranean world, which actively engaged in commerce yet did not generate capitalist socioeconomic relations.) Throughout its history—even before it took root—capitalism was a controversial idea that posed serious issues for philosophers, moralists, and social scientists alike.

Early Advocates

Perhaps the best-known and most important early exponent of capitalism was the Scottish economist Adam Smith (1723–1790). Smith employed the term *capital* in technical economic discussions contained in *An Inquiry into the Nature and Causes of the Wealth of Nations* (1776), but he did not describe his economic system as "capitalism." Rather, the latter term seems to have arisen only in the nineteenth century. Smith preferred to speak about natural liberty, by which he meant simply that if everyone acts freely as they see fit in their own interests, then the welfare of the whole society will be best served. For Smith, the system of natural liberty constitutes a sort of automatic or homeostatic mechanism of self-adjustment (which he sometimes calls the "invisible hand"), so that any attempt (on the part of government or some other agent) to interfere in its operation will lead to greater inefficiency and hence less total welfare. The doctrine of natural liberty thus yields the founding principles of capitalism as an economic system. In turn, Smith applied this discovery not only to the operation of the marketplace but also to all aspects of society, including its educational, religious, and judicial institutions. He narrowly confines the role of government to those functions consistent with natural liberty: foreign defense, regulation of criminal activity, and provision of "public goods" too expensive for any single segment of the private economy to undertake.

The sources for Smith's insight about maximized individual liberty, unconstrained by coercive externalities, have been debated. Certainly, an earlier group of French economic theorists, known collectively as the Physiocrats, may have played a role in the formulation of this idea. Perhaps more importantly, as Albert O. Hirschman and others have argued, many influential political and moral theorists writing in the seventeenth and eighteenth centuries had promoted doctrines of human psychology and action that comported well with Smithian natural liberty. So-called heroic virtues were replaced with more mundane values in the writings of a wide range of early modern thinkers, including Niccolò Machiavelli (1469–1527), Thomas Hobbes (1588–1679), François de La Rochefoucauld (1613–1680), Anthony Ashley Cooper, third earl of Shaftesbury (1671–1713), and Bernard Mandeville (c.1670–1733).

The work of Smith inspired a school of thought known broadly as classical political economy. Its leading members in the nineteenth century, such as David Ricardo (1772–1823) and Thomas Malthus (1766–1834), extended and refined Smith's insights, often drawing in addition on the work of the utilitarian philosopher and social reformer Jeremy Bentham (1748–1832). In its most ruthless form, this position was combined with a reading of Darwinian biology to make the argument that capitalism, as a system of the survival of the fittest, was sanctioned by evolution, as in the Social Darwinism of Herbert Spencer (1820–1903). Nor were devotees of unlimited capitalism limited to the earliest stages of capitalist development. The neoclassical school of economic theory, exemplified

by the work of Friedrich von Hayek (1899–1992) and Milton Friedman (b. 1912), continues to exercise considerable influence on all dimensions of social thought into the twenty-first century. The so-called rational choice or public choice economists persist in their belief that the free market relations realized only under capitalism constitute the single legitimate model of all social order.

Foes

Capitalism has by no means lacked for criticism from many different quarters. Communitarians, such as Henri de Saint-Simon (1760–1825), asserted that capitalists' concentration on competition and individual self-interest at the expense of social solidarity would ultimately corrupt and corrode communal order. Utopians, such as Charles Fourier (1772–1837), sought to replace capitalism's exploitation of labor with a free and creative socioeconomic system in which human potential could flourish. The anarchist Pierre-Joseph Proudhon (1809–1865), proclaiming that "private property is theft," denounced the collusion of state and capitalist enterprise and proposed to level the unequal distribution of the material benefits of work and to liberate workers to collaborate freely in their chosen activities. What all of these essentially left-wing responses to capitalism shared was a belief that cooperation rather than competition was the key to the improvement of human society and the amelioration of psychological as well as material misery.

The most famous nineteenth-century opponent of capitalism was Karl Marx (1818–1883), who, with his collaborator Friedrich Engels (1820–1895), offered far-reaching and systematic criticism based on a careful study of the inner operations of the capitalist economy. It is too seldom acknowledged that Marx shared more with the classical political economists than with capitalism's moralistic antagonists. In his unfinished masterwork, *Capital* (volume 1 published in 1867), Marx viewed himself as engaging in the "scientific" analysis of capitalism, borrowing heavily from Smith and his successors, while pointing out the structural weaknesses and limitations that the capitalist apologists had overlooked. In particular, Marx believed that the intense conflicts between capitalists and workers, as well as among capitalists themselves, would produce recurrent and ever-deepening economic, social, and political crises. Eventually the growing body of exploited industrial laborers, whom Marx labeled the proletariat, would recognize the source of its exploitation in the market-engendered condition of "wage slavery" and would revolt against the capitalist system as a whole.

Yet Marx did not dismiss lightly the accomplishments of capitalism. He maintained, instead, that the technological achievement of capitalism in constantly revolutionizing the means of production should be harnessed by any future communist society. Indeed, one of the inherent contradictions of capitalism was its inability to utilize fully its own productive capacity, a situation that would be rectified under communism. In sum, what singled out Marx's criticism of capitalism was its immanent character, in comparison to communitarians, utopians, and anarchists, whose critiques were based on standards external to capitalist economics.

Origins

One of the central issues in the conceptualization of capitalism has been the explanation of its emergence in the first place. Both classical political economists and orthodox Marxists provide essentially materialistic accounts rooted internally in the economic realm, whether arising from technological innovation, class conflict, urbanization, or demographic pressures. In the late nineteenth century, the endogenous position was challenged by the German sociologist Max Weber (1864–1920), who, in a series of studies ultimately published as *The Protestant Ethic and the Spirit of Capitalism,* argued against the validity of all such internal explanations for the growth of capitalism. Rather, Weber proposed that the emergence of a Calvinist version of Reformed Christian theology during the sixteenth and seventeenth centuries constituted the necessary and sufficient condition for capitalism's origins. According to Weber, the Calvinist Protestant was impelled to demonstrate to his community his worthiness for salvation (the certainty of which was by no means earned by external merit, as in Catholicism) by working hard and leading an ascetic life. Such hard work, however, produced economic gains and the temptation for leisure and luxury. What was the Calvinist to do with the deserved profits of his labors? The answer was to rid himself of his riches by investing them in further economic enterprises, which in turn yielded additional wealth. As an unintended consequence of the Calvinist renunciation of worldliness, the circulation of capital was born and with it the pattern of capitalist development. Weber's antimaterialistic explanation of capitalism directly challenged the primacy of the economic realm upheld by classical political economists and Marxists alike.

The response to Weber's thesis was loud and shrill on all sides, and there is good reason to believe that in its initial statement it misrepresents history. Yet the question of why capitalism emerged when and where it did—or indeed at all—remains a widely debated topic. One dimension of this discussion has been a debate raging since the 1940s, centered mainly within differing schools of economic history, concerning the transition from feudalism to capitalism. Scholars such as Paul Sweezy and Immanuel Wallerstein, elaborating on the earlier work of Henri Pirenne (1862–1935), postulated that a commercially stimulated push toward exchange relations, centered in the growing late medieval towns, undermined feudalism and introduced the basic principles of economic rationality. Other historians, such as J. A. Raftis, considering the radical depopulation of Europe at the end of the Middle Ages caused by recurrent and severe plagues, point to purely demographic factors among the laboring masses to account for disruptions in long-established patterns of land tenure that occasioned the decline of feudalism. Still another body of literature, represented by the research of R. H. Hilton and Robert Brenner, places local political factors arising from conflicts between peasant producers and seigneurial appropriators at the center of the transition to capitalist social relations. All of these views, however, share the conviction that material factors endogenous to economic life are adequate to explain the decline of feudalism and the emergence of capitalism.

By contrast, some later scholars, mindful of the pitfalls of the Weberian analysis, have nonetheless sought to proffer an "exogamous" account of the origins of capitalism. For example, Liah Greenfeld has posited a certain version of "nationalism" as the explanatory metric for the spread of the "spirit of capitalism." According to Greenfeld, England in the sixteenth and seventeenth centuries generated a form of nationalism that promoted the common wealth through the pursuit of individual profit, hence leading to the accumulation and circulation of private capital. In turn, the initial success of this nationalism pushed other European countries and regions to pursue similar nationalistic programs, with varied rates of success. As with Weber, Greenfeld maintains that "cultural" or "ideological" factors are required to explain the expansion of the capitalist economy.

Globalization

With the demise of communism as an economic and ideological alternative to capitalism, many thinkers have proclaimed the final and ultimate victory of the capitalist system and its supposedly attendant sociopolitical values of democratic rights and individual liberty. According to Francis Fukuyama, for instance, history has proven that capitalism constitutes the best way of arranging the basic production and distribution of human goods. The global spread of capitalism signals an end to the contention between the fundamentally incommensurable economic ideas and doctrines; all that remains to be done is a fine-tuning of the balance between the private profit economy and those public goods that government is better qualified to provide. The process of capitalist globalization, then, represents nothing less than the civilizing of the human species.

Yet critics of capitalism persist, even in the face of optimism that capitalism will bring prosperity and well-being around the globe "in the long run." (The economist John Maynard Keynes [1883–1946] once famously quipped that "of course, in the long run, we're all dead.") Feminists point out that capitalism has done little to erase the economic and social disparities that exist between men and women. Authors concerned with race relations make a similar point about the market's failure to break down inequalities between people of differing skin colors and ethnicities. Environmentalists charge that capitalism's emphasis on unlimited growth as the only sustainable form of economy has led and will continue to lead to the ruin of the planet and, eventually, to the extinction of the human species. Latter-day communitarians and republicans hold that contempt for legal authority and civic virtue stems from the capitalist-inspired glorification of leisure and luxury. And religious authorities worldwide (including leaders of major Western churches, such as Pope John Paul II) have sternly criticized capitalism for eroding spiritual and moral values in favor of unrestrained accumulation and consumption. Capitalist ideas appear destined to remain controversial even, or perhaps especially, in the age of economic globalization.

See also **Communism; Economics; Marxism.**

BIBLIOGRAPHY

Engelmann, Stephen G. *Imagining Interest in Political Thought: Origins of Economic Rationality.* Durham, N.C.: Duke University Press, 2003.

Fukuyama, Francis. *The End of History and the Last Man.* New York: Free Press, 1992.

Greenfeld, Liah. *The Spirit of Capitalism: Nationalism and Economic Growth.* Cambridge, Mass.: Harvard University Press, 2001.

Hirschman, Albert O. *The Passions and the Interests: Political Arguments for Capitalism before Its Triumph.* Princeton, N.J.: Princeton University Press, 1977.

Holton, Robert J. *Cities, Capitalism, and Civilization.* London and Boston: Allen and Unwin, 1986.

———. *The Transition from Feudalism to Capitalism.* New York: St. Martin's, 1985.

Marx, Karl. *Capital.* Vol. 1. Translated by Samuel Moore and Edward Aveling. London: Lawrence and Wishart, 1974.

Smith, Adam. *An Inquiry into the Nature and Causes of the Wealth of Nations.* Edited by R. H. Campbell and A. S. Skinner. Oxford: Clarendon; New York: Oxford University Press, 1976.

Weber, Max. *The Protestant Ethic and the Spirit of Capitalism.* Translated by Talcott Parsons. New York: Charles Scribner's Sons, 1958.

Wood, Ellen Meiksins. *The Origin of Capitalism: A Longer View.* 2nd ed. London: Verso, 2002.

Cary J. Nederman

AFRICA

Debates over capitalism in Africa revolve around the best means to rescue the continent from a prolonged period of stagnation and decline. Observers agree that the program, in the absence of a socialist alternative, must focus on capitalist development. There is disagreement, however, over the role of the African state in this process, as well as over whether to make raw materials exports or industrialization the main engines of growth. On the one side stand the Bretton Woods Institutions (the World Bank and International Monetary Fund, hereinafter the BWIs), who advocate a neoliberal approach based on freeing up markets for cash crop exports and reducing the state's control over national development. On the other side stand African scholars, mainly those representing the United Nations Economic Commission for Africa (UNECA), who argue for more industrialization and a much stronger role for the state. As the debate has continued, African leaders have moved closer to the BWI position with the establishment of the New Partnership for Africa's Development (NEPAD). Still, NEPAD has its critics, and the debate persists over the relative roles of the state and the market.

The Colonial Legacy and Uneven Capitalist Development

These debates have not unfolded in a vacuum; they are rooted in the colonial legacy and the response to that legacy by the first generation of African leaders. The Atlantic slave trade and colonialism blocked the conditions for the development of capitalism in Africa. In dwarfing all other commerce, the slave trade interrupted the accumulation process necessary for capitalist development. Its abolition reversed this trend by creating an opening for "legitimate" commerce, which African producers pursued by increasing their production of raw materials (such as gum, hides, and palm oil) for expanding European markets. Most of the production, however, was based on noncapitalist

labor regimes such as family and household labor or forced labor of various kinds. Colonialism did not alter this structure appreciably, because the colonial powers tended to block the development of private property and of wage labor—with the exception of migrant labor in the mining and plantation sectors. Although African industries appeared in the major cities, especially after World War II, the absence of land markets and the predominance of migrant labor ensured that capitalism did not develop fully during the colonial period. To make matters worse, the colonial powers discriminated against African capitalists in favor of nonindigenous entrepreneurs, and against women, the main agricultural producers. In sum, capitalism did take root during the colonial era, but its development was uneven, halting, and incomplete.

Independence, State-Led Development, and Import-Substitution Industrialization

Between 1960 and 1975, the new African leaders pursued industrialization in order to overcome the colonial inheritance. Rooted in the anticolonial struggle, some of their programs were socialist (as in Ghana and Algeria), some more explicitly capitalist (as in Kenya). Others, such as that in Ethiopia, were more difficult to define. In practice, however, most African countries shared a commitment to modernization and industrialization. Many followed the model of Import-Substitution Industrialization (ISI), in which governments took control over national industrialization by protecting domestic industries from foreign competition. Rooted in modernization theory, the goal was for the state to mobilize enough investment in domestic industry to achieve the "big push" thought necessary for self-sustaining economic growth. State-led development became the norm in the 1960s.

Ghana and Algeria provide two examples of the socialist variant of ISI, with a high percentage of state-owned enterprises and a professed commitment to labor rather than capital. In Ghana, Kwame Nkrumah implemented a Seven-Year Development Plan (1957–1966) designed to develop domestic industry, infrastructure, and social welfare. Nkrumah mobilized investment capital export taxes, foreign borrowing, and the sale of electricity produced by the new Volta hydroelectric dam. Nkrumah's government took control of the country's major industries as well as the agricultural sector, but he also provided state-sponsored social services such as education and health care. In Algeria, after a nationalist revolution between 1954 and 1962, the country's first leader, Ahmed Ben Bella, pursued an orthodox Marxist program, setting out to smash the middle-class traders and bureaucrats. A military coup in 1965 brought a new leader (Houari Boumédienne), who declared a fusion of socialism, Islam, and Arabic culture. Although Boumédienne left education and cultural matters in the hands of politicians who emphasized Algeria's Islamic heritage, his economic vision was secular, technocratic, and socialist. Between 1966 and 1971, the state nationalized 90 percent of the country's industries, beginning with oil and gas and then extending to industrial production. The idea was to nationalize Algeria's natural resources and use the profits to develop state-owned industrial enterprises. Ultimately this vision failed to achieve its goals, and Boumédienne's socialist program gave way to the increasing "Islamicization" of Algeria.

Kenya and South Africa provide illustrations of a more capitalist road to national development. In Kenya between 1963 and 1978, President Jomo Kenyatta supported the African bourgeoisie with government intervention into agriculture, trade, and production. This program was not uncontested; a number of prominent trade unionists, including Bildad Kaggia and Fred Kubai, argued for a radical socialist alternative. Kenyatta purged these elements from the ruling party (the Kenyan African National Union, or KANU) and pushed ahead with a program of state-managed capitalism, although one of its most famous architects, Tom Mboya, referred to it as "African socialism." While there was an element of redistribution, the core of the Kenyatta-Mboya program is better understood as corporate capitalism, under which the state partnered with labor and capital (domestic and foreign) in the pursuit of capital formation and industrialization. Import-Substitution Industrialization provided the model, with protected home markets for consumer goods and agreements with foreign firms to import essential capital-goods inputs. By the late 1970s, Kenyatta had built up strong agricultural and industrial sectors. South Africa pursued capitalist development through ISI from an early date (the 1940s), with impressive economic results. Industrialization there, however, was racialized, and the post-1948 apartheid state ruthlessly exploited the black population, stripping them of the most basic human and political rights. This strategy worked economically until the 1970s, when the economy faltered and African resistance intensified. International sanctions exacerbated the downward trend in the 1980s, and apartheid finally met its end in 1994, when national elections brought the African National Congress to power under Nelson Mandela. Thirty years after Kenyatta had set out to Africanize the Kenyan economy, South Africa's black majority government faced pressures for similar Africanization, but the state-led option was no longer on the table.

In Ethiopia, the emperor Haile Selassie presided after 1935 over the conversion of feudal lands into private holdings, especially in the southern part of the country. Land sales accelerated between 1960 and 1974, producing concentration in the south, with farms as big as 200,000 acres. Using ISI as a model, the state invested in agricultural commercialization along capitalist lines; in industry the government attempted to develop textile and beverage production. These policies triggered the development of an agrarian bourgeoisie during the 1960s, as well as a small industrial sector, but these were dependent on foreign capital and insignificant in relation to subsistence agriculture, which remained under the domination of the big landlords. Peasant and student resistance to the landlords emerged during the 1970s under the slogan "land to the tiller." Grievances paralleled a wave of army mutinies, resulting in a revolution that swept away the emperor's government in favor of a Soviet-backed regime that ruled between 1974 and 1977. In the end, the ruling military council gave way to an authoritarian regime under Haile Meriam Mengistu, which allied with the Soviets in 1977 and pushed through a collectivization program in the countryside. This program succeeded in revolutionizing the social basis of power in the rural areas, but Mengistu's authoritarianism produced widespread resistance, and the regime finally fell in 1991.

Selassie's state-led development programs produced some significant successes during the 1960s, with growth in gross domestic product and comprehensive social welfare programs. As the decade progressed, however, it became clear that the gains would not be sustainable and that Africa had entered a period of economic stagnation. The oil shocks of 1973 and 1979, and a wave of drought in 1975 and 1976, worsened the crisis considerably. Flagging economic performance fed into a wave of unrest and military coups, including those in Algeria (1965), Ghana (1966), and Ethiopia (1974). As the 1970s progressed, stagnation worsened and African governments became less democratic; the decade witnessed the rise of one-party states presiding over a deteriorating economic climate.

During the 1970s, it seemed that "the African state had not been up to its 'historic mission' of ensuring capitalist accumulation"; as Thandika Mkandwire noted, the question for African analysts was whether this was a temporary phenomenon, which could be solved while retaining Africa's links to the world economy, or a permanent structural problem solvable only by delinking from the global system. In the 1970s several prominent dependency theorists, including Egypt's Samir Amin and Nigeria's Bade Onimode, took up the latter position in arguing for a radical program of African autonomy and self-sufficiency.

In the late 1970s the dependency school lost ground to a more reform-minded version of structuralism, which argued that developing nations could achieve capitalist development while retaining their links to a reformed world economy. UNECA exemplified this stance with its 1976 report entitled the *Revised Framework for the Implementation of the New International Order for Africa*. The *Revised Framework* led to the Lagos Plan of Action (LPA) of 1980, which emphasized external factors—especially the continent's reliance on raw materials exports—as the main causes of Africa's economic stagnation. On this issue the LPA agreed with the dependency argument that declining terms of trade, which reflected the neocolonialist exploitation of the continent, posed a serious threat to African economic development. As a result, the LPA's goals for Africa emphasized regional and continental self-reliance and self-sustaining development, to be achieved through a greater focus on industrialization and economic cooperation. Exports would be pursued, but they would be subordinated to domestic industrial development.

The Lagos Plan of Action also placed gender on the development agenda, arguing that women were central to the development process and that their interests had to be considered in the design and implementation of development programs. This stance provided a welcome corrective to modernization theory, which insisted that women were impediments to development and should be confined to the domestic sphere. This view had been challenged in the 1970s by the Women in Development (WID) paradigm and the proclamation of the UN's International Decade for Women (1975–1985). In 1976, the Association of African Women for Development called for the integration of women into development programs. The LPA took up this call by demanding more support for women in agriculture and industry. Although they praised the LPA's stance as a step in the right direction, critics argued that the plan did little to facilitate a significant shift in African women's economic and political power. This criticism formed part of a larger movement during the 1980s to recognize issues of gender inequality in the design and implementation of development programs. This approach argued that development must address issues such as the sexual division of labor and power over reproduction if African women were to benefit from economic growth.

Neoliberalism, Structural Adjustment, and the African Reaction

African recommendations between 1976 and 1980 set the scene for a protracted debate between African intellectuals and the Bretton Woods Institutions over the terms of capitalist development on the continent. In 1981, the World Bank rejected the LPA in its famous Berg Report (*Towards Accelerated Development in Sub-Saharan Africa*), which attributed economic stagnation to poor government policies rather than external factors. In pursuing Import-Substitution Industrialization, Africa's leaders had turned their backs on the continent's comparative advantage in raw materials, in favor of propping up inefficient domestic industries and a bloated public sector. The Berg Report recommended returning to an outward-oriented program of raw materials exports, to be accomplished by rolling back state intervention and freeing up market forces. Specific recommendations promoted under the rubric of Structural Adjustment Programs (SAPs) included eliminating subsidies and controls (on imports, wages, and prices), devaluing local currencies, and letting the market determine the prices for raw materials exports.

In 1989 UNECA responded to the Berg Report by reaffirming the Lagos Plan through the African Alternative Framework to Structural Adjustment (AAF-SAP). This rejected the outward-oriented, market-based strategy of structural adjustment in favor of an inward-looking, state-led program of African self-reliance. The report also recommended subsidies for exports, bilateral and multilateral trade agreements, and debt forgiveness. Finally, the AAF-SAP stressed the importance of human development, especially the provision of basic social services and education. In short, it advocated a modified version of ISI, with a greater emphasis on the export sector.

The World Bank accepted the need for human-centered development in its 1989 report, *Sub-Saharan Africa: From Crisis to Sustainable Growth*. Citing the LPA and UNECA, this accepted the need to consider human-centered development in creating an environment to enable sustainable economic growth in Africa. The report, however, clung to the bank's commitment to structural adjustment and export-led development. A subsequent bank report emphasized SAPs even more strongly, claiming that "adjustment is working" in countries that followed its prescriptions, in agriculture as well as industry. In 1999, African critics countered once again with a systematic critique of structural adjustment entitled *Our Continent, Our Future: African Perspectives on Structural Adjustment*, which modified earlier calls for African self-reliance by accepting the need to compete in the global economy on the basis of comparative advantage. This was not to be achieved, however, through SAPs and raw materials exports; instead, the study recommended a modified version of ISI in which African governments would nurture high–value-added, labor-intensive industries producing manufactured exports for the world market. Thandika Mkandawire, coeditor of *Our Continent, Our Future*, subsequently argued for the creation of developmental states in Africa—along Asian lines—which he believed could be socially engineered by political actors and civil society within the context of African democratization.

The World Bank has not accepted ISI in the early twenty-first century, but recent bank initiatives have made more concessions to African participation and social development, particularly through the new Comprehensive Development Framework (CDF). This moves beyond structural adjustment to focus on poverty reduction and social development; it also emphasizes local ownership of the development process. African leaders have responded to this shift by creating the New Partnership for Africa's Development (NEPAD), led by Thabo Mbeki of South Africa. NEPAD accepts the BWIs' neoliberal program for capitalist development as well as the need for peace, security, and good governance. To guarantee that Africa will benefit from globalization, however, NEPAD also seeks to reform the rules of globalization to guarantee equity as well as economic growth, by reducing Western protectionism and providing for African social needs. Separating itself from UNECA, the OAU (now reconstituted as the African Union) came out in support of NEPAD in 2001.

Several prominent African scholars have criticized NEPAD for rejecting the programs proposed by UNECA in favor of the neoliberal model of the Bretton Woods Institutions. This acceptance of neoliberalism threatens to reproduce African dependence on Western donors, which is especially dangerous in an age of shrinking Official Development Assistance. African critics of NEPAD argue that any concessions to Western donors must not compromise the principles of the LPA. Some of these critics call for a return of the developmental state. Other African scholars, such as Claude Ake, have tried to find a middle ground between this position and the neoliberal program. Ake proposes a populist alternative, drawing on "the energy of ordinary people" and geared toward the development of smallholder agriculture underwritten by popular democracy. Driven by farmer participation, this approach would increase the efficiency and productivity of small farmers and provide the basis for rural industries such as food processing and packaging. The result would be a bottom-up process of endogenous economic and human development. This process would have to involve African women, who appear to have been left out of the NEPAD blueprint, in what some critics consider a step backward from the LPA on the issue of gender and development.

Claude Ake's work illustrates that the debate over capitalism in Africa in the early 2000s revolves around three poles—the market, the state, and the community—rather than two. It remains an open question, however, which of these will emerge as the preferred trustee over African capitalism in the twenty-first century.

See also **Anticolonialism; Colonialism; Development; Economics; Modernization; Modernization Theory; Neocolonialism; Neoliberalism; Socialisms, African.**

BIBLIOGRAPHY

Ake, Claude. *Democracy and Development in Africa*. Washington, D.C.: Brookings Institution, 1996.

Amin, Samir. *Delinking: Towards a Polycentric World*. London: Zed, 1990.

———. *Neo-colonialism in West Africa*. Harmondsworth, U.K.: Penguin, 1973.

Berman, Bruce, and Colin Leys, eds. *African Capitalists in African Development*. Boulder, Colo.: Lynne Rienner, 1994.

Goldsworthy, David. *Tom Mboya: The Man Kenya Wanted to Forget*. New York: Africana, 1982.

Kennedy, Paul. *African Capitalism: The Struggle for Ascendancy*. Cambridge, U.K., and New York: Cambridge University Press, 1988.

Leys, Colin. *Underdevelopment in Kenya*. London: Heinemann, 1975.

Mkandawire, Thandika. "Thinking about Developmental States in Africa." *Cambridge Journal of Economics* 25 (2001): 289–313.

Mkandiwire, Thandika, and Charles C. Soludo. *Our Continent, Our Future: African Perspectives on Structural Adjustment*. Dakar, Senegal: CODESRIA; Trenton, N.J.: Africa World Press, 1999.

Onimode, Bade. *A Future for Africa: Beyond the Politics of Adjustment*. London: Earthscan, 1992.

———. *Imperialism and Underdevelopment in Nigeria: The Dialectic of Mass Poverty*. London: Zed, 1982.

Organization of African Unity. *Lagos Plan of Action for the Economic Development of Africa, 1980–2000*. Addis Ababa, Ethiopia: OAU; Geneva, Switzerland: International Institute for Labour Studies, 1981.

Owusu, Francis. "Pragmatism and the Gradual Shift from Dependency to Neoliberalism: The World Bank, African Leaders and Development Policy in Africa." *World Development* 31, no 10 (2003): 1655–1672.

Parpart, Jane. *African Women and Development: Gender in the Lagos Plan of Action*. East Lansing: Michigan State University Press, 1985.

Sender, John, and Sheila Smith. *The Development of Capitalism in Africa*. London and New York: Methuen, 1986.

Shenton, Robert W. *The Development of Capitalism in Northern Nigeria*. London: J. Currey; Toronto: University of Toronto Press, 1986.

Women Waging Peace. "African Women Respond: Summary Report on G8 and Nepad Plan and the Impact on Women in Africa." *Women and Developments International Magazine*, no. 58/59 (spring 2003).

World Bank. *Accelerated Development in Sub-Saharan Africa: An Agenda for Action*. Washington, D.C.: World Bank, 1981.

———. *Adjustment in Africa: Reforms, Results, and the Road Ahead*. New York: Oxford University Press, 1994.

Young, Crawford. *Ideology and Development in Africa*. New Haven Conn.: Yale University Press, 1982.

Jeff D. Grischow

CARTESIANISM. When René Descartes died in 1650, his work had already attracted both critics and followers. In 1632 Cartesian philosophy was being taught in the Netherlands by his disciple Henri Reneri (1593–1639), and by the mid-1630s the far more independently minded Henri Regius (1598–1679) was setting out his own version of Cartesianism in a less guarded and more polemical way than had Descartes himself. Indeed it was Regius who attracted the first condemnation of Cartesianism, from the Dutch theologian Gisbert Voetius (1589–1676), in 1641, and in 1642 Voetius turned on Descartes himself, drawing him into a very public controversy. Cartesianism first flourished as a movement in the Netherlands, being established as early as the 1650s at Leiden and Utrecht—where there was a Cartesian club, the College der Savanten—as well as at other Dutch universities. It was through a member of one of these Dutch groups, Johannes Clauberg (1622–1665), that Cartesianism came to be established in Germany: he took up the chair of theology and philosophy at the University of Duisberg in 1651, a new university set up by the cousin of Princess Elizabeth, Descartes's correspondent and staunch defender.

Responses to Descartes

In England there was less enthusiasm. In 1644 Kenelm Digby (1603–1665) set out his own eclectic version of Descartes's philosophy (and invited Descartes to come and live in England), and later in the decade Henry More (1614–1687), the Cambridge Platonist, explored various features of Cartesianism in his correspondence with Descartes. But Cartesianism soon developed a reputation for heterodoxy in England, above all because of his rejection of any aims or ends acting in nature, and his writings were widely attacked in the second half of the seventeenth century. In France, Louis XIV banned the teaching of Cartesian philosophy, and Cartesians were excluded from the Académie des Sciences. While these attacks were directed at the perceived radical nature of Cartesianism, others such as Daniel Huet (1630–1721), a patron of the Jesuits, were charging him with plagiarism: Huet claimed he took his epistemology from the Greek skeptics, the *cogito* from Augustine, and the ontological argument from Anselm.

However, Descartes had disciples in France, including Claude Clerselier (1614–1684), who oversaw the publication of his letters and other hitherto unpublished works (a laborious undertaking, which included retrieving the trunk containing them from the sea and drying them out), establishing a vital resource for scholars all over Europe and in the New World. Moreover, there was a strong French Cartesian movement in natural philosophy, centered on Jacques Rohault (1620–1672) and Pierre-Sylvain Régis (1632–1707), in the second half of the century, and by the 1670s there was a movement applying the Cartesian principle of "clear and distinct ideas" to social and political questions, with radical consequences: François Poulain de la Barre (1647–1723) was defending the equality of the sexes on this basis, and Descartes's niece, Catherine, was proposing Cartesianism as an alternative (with women particularly in mind) to the philosophy of the universities. The peculiar political circumstances in France— Louis in effect brought a delayed Counter-Reformation to France—resulted in a radicalization of Cartesianism in the late seventeenth century. By the early decades of the eighteenth century, there were Cartesians in painting (Charles Le Brun), architecture (the Perrault brothers), and music (Jean-Philippe

Rameau), and Descartes had become almost an establishment figure in France, as the famous attack on him by Voltaire indicates, where he was castigated for being out of date in comparison with developments in English philosophy. Yet by the 1770s he was radicalized again, as the Enlightenment *philosophes* claimed him as a corevolutionary.

Descartes had a deep concern for orthodoxy—even his advocacy of mechanism, in the form of the doctrine of the inertness of nature, can be seen as a response to the heterodox naturalism of the Renaissance, where the powers attributed to nature leave little room for a divine role—and had written his *Principles of Philosophy* with a view to having it adopted as a textbook in Jesuit colleges. Nevertheless, much of his work was bitterly condemned by the Catholic Church after his death. His writings were placed on the *Index of Prohibited Books* in 1663, primarily it would seem because of his heterodox account of transubstantiation, but his view that ours is not the only solar system also elicited explicit condemnations from religious authorities throughout the remainder of the seventeenth century.

Aspects of Cartesianism

In some areas, Descartes's work was accepted as pathbreaking: above all his geometrical optics and his algebra (Isaac Newton learned his advanced mathematics in the first instance from Descartes's *Geometry*). But other areas attracted a more partisan response. We can distinguish three different kinds of concern in the Cartesian corpus in this respect: epistemology and metaphysics, cosmology, and physiology.

Although the *Meditations* is for modern readers the canonical text by Descartes, this focus is really a nineteenth-century development, and the most widely read and discussed of his works in the eighteenth century were the *Discourse on Method, Principles of Philosophy,* and the posthumously published *Treatise on Man.* Moreover, Descartes himself had played down the epistemological and metaphysical concerns that characterize the *Meditations.* Two themes dominate the *Meditations*—a skeptically driven epistemology and the mind/body problem—and the fortunes of these differ radically among later philosophers. Neither Baruch Spinoza (1632–1677) nor Gottfried Wilhelm von Leibniz (1646–1716) could see any value or legitimacy in beginning epistemology by answering radical skeptical problems (and Blaise Pascal [1623–1662] referred to Descartes's philosophy as "useless and uncertain"), and they abandoned the idea of a skeptically driven epistemology. Nicolas Malebranche (1638–1715) was a little closer to Descartes, although still at variance with him on key doctrines, and he was not so dismissive of skeptical beginnings for epistemology, but they work in a rather different way in his philosophy than they do in Descartes. Malebranche's philosophy vied with that of John Locke (1632–1794) at the end of the seventeenth century, and his influence on George Berkeley (1685–1753) and David Hume (1711–1776) was at least as great as that of Locke, putting skeptical issues to the fore. On the mind/body question, no one was satisfied with Cartesian dualism. Spinoza, Malebranche, and Leibniz each saw the question as being the key to success, and each offered their own distinctive solution to the question: neutral monism, occasionalism, and preestablished harmony, respectively. By the eighteenth century,

epistemologically oriented issues of mind had receded from the philosophical arena to some extent, and Cartesianism was less associated with dualism.

Two natural-philosophical topics on which Descartes's views had caused immense controversy were his account of the solar system in book 3 of the *Principles of Philosophy* and his account of the formation of the earth in book 4. Descartes's response to the Copernicanism problem was not to make the sun the center of the cosmos, as Copernicus had done, but to make the sun one of an indefinite (perhaps infinite) number of solar systems, each containing planets like ours that may harbor beings with souls. The idea that our sun was simply one star among many and could not be held to be the center of the cosmos gained credence in the course of the later seventeenth century (for those who held that the universe was infinite there was no issue, of course, since something infinite cannot have a center since every point is equidistant from an infinitely remote boundary). Even more radical was his view of the formation of the earth. The Bible had presented a creation story in which the fabric of the earth, plants, and animals, had a function in a unique, highly designed system. Descartes, by contrast, has a general theory of planet formation: planets derive from stars that have formed a coating of hard matter around their periphery and are squeezed out by surrounding solar systems, in effect becoming massive pieces of refuse that find a home in other solar systems in orbits that depend on their size and speed. No exception is made for the Earth in Descartes's account, which completely robs the formation of earth of any teleology. The account was the first nonmythological treatment of the formation of the earth and was of great influence in the eighteenth century, not least in Georges-Louis Buffon's (1707–1778) account.

More generally, Descartes's cosmology—in which planets were carried around their suns by means of the vortical motion of a swiftly circulating medium in which they were immersed—was taken very seriously, and was the dominant cosmological system before Newton's *Principia.* Indeed, in continental Europe, it was not abandoned in favor of Newtonianism for some time, primarily because it did not involve any appeal to action at a distance, which was universally perceived to be the most problematic general feature of Newton's system. Moreover, Descartes's system was far more comprehensive than Newton's, tying his vortex theory of planetary motion in with phenomena such as magnetism and static electricity.

Descartes's rejection of teleology was also manifest in his account of embryology, set out in the *Treatise on Man* and in more detail in *The Description of the Human Body.* There he insists on a radically mechanistic approach, denying that the fetus strives to realize an end or goal in the development process. The inert and initially undifferentiated matter making up the horse fetus, for example, develops into a horse not because it somehow contains "horseness" or because it is able to shape itself into a horse but because the distinctive mechanical and physio-chemical processes in the womb of a horse cause the matter to develop in a certain way. In this way, Descartes opened up the question of the physiology of fetal development. Embryology is in fact just one topic in Descartes's comprehensive attempt to mechanize physiology, and in the

Treatise on Man a variety of physiological processes are construed in such a way that we need only postulate inert matter being acted upon by mechanical forces. From this derives his infamous doctrine of *bêtes machines* (animal machines), whereby the behavior of animals, who lack minds (in the sense of awareness of their "cognitive" states) in Descartes's account, can be accounted for fully in terms of the mechanically describable interaction between their constituent parts. In 1747 Julien Offray de La Mettrie (1709–1751) published his *Man Machine,* in which he purported to apply the Cartesian theory of animal machines to human beings (actually his materialism was different from Cartesian mechanism), claiming that this could be done successfully, so that it was unnecessary to postulate a human soul to account for human thoughts and behavior. This solidified the image of Descartes as a dangerous materialist, and it was only in the nineteenth century that the idea of Descartes as a dualist was generally revived.

By the twentieth century, interest in Descartes in Anglophone philosophy was largely confined to his skeptically driven epistemology and his dualist account of mind. The revival of interest in empiricist epistemology, helped by the rise of positivism, resulted in skepticism being taken much more seriously as a philosophical problem (for example, in A. J. Ayer). In the philosophy of mind, various alternatives to dualism—such as epiphenomenalism, behaviorism, and materialism—were devised, with the effect that Cartesian dualism was often set up as a straw man by which to contrast one's own theory (as in Gilbert Ryle's defense of behaviorism). By contrast, in French and German philosophy, interest centered rather on Descartes's idea of a self as independent of the world in which it finds itself, as a locus of subjectivity that is given prior to any interactions that it has with other subjects. The ethical and political aspects of this understanding have been explored either in their own right (by Jean-Paul Sartre, for example) or in combination with a Kantian account of ethical autonomy (such as by Jürgen Habermas).

See also **Dualism; Epistemology; Materialism in Eighteenth-Century European Thought; Newtonianism; Philosophy, History of; Skepticism.**

BIBLIOGRAPHY

Balz, Albert G. A. *Cartesian Studies.* New York: Columbia University Press, 1951.

Clarke, Desmond M. *Occult Powers and Hypotheses: Cartesian Natural Philosophy under Louis XIV.* Oxford: Clarendon Press, 1989.

Gaukroger, Stephen, John Schuster, and John Sutton, eds. *Descartes' Natural Philosophy.* London: Routledge, 2000.

Harth, Erica. *Cartesian Women: Versions and Subversions of Rational Discourse in the Old Regime.* Ithaca, N.Y.: Cornell University Press, 1992.

Mouy, Paul. *Le développment de la physique cartésienne, 1646–1712.* Paris: Vrin, 1934. Reprint, New York: Arno, 1981.

Tournadre, Géraud. *L'orientation de la science cartésienne.* Paris: Vrin, 1982.

Verbeek, Theo. *Descartes and the Dutch: Early Reactions to Cartesian Philosophy.* Carbondale: Southern Illinois University Press, 1992.

Stephen Gaukroger

CASUISTRY. From the Latin *casūs* (cases), casuistry is a method of practical reasoning that aims to identify the scope and force of moral obligations in the varied contexts of human action. While the golden era of casuistry belongs to the period 1450–1660, its origins as an intellectual outlook on moral decision-making can be traced back to ancient philosophy and to the legal traditions of medieval Europe. Aristotle, for instance, stressed the importance of an irreducibly practical method of moral reasoning that would be attentive to "the particulars" (*ta kath' hekasta*) of cases. The Stoics also sought to provide detailed reasons as to how universal principles could be applied to particular cases. In addition to this, they bequeathed the idea of a natural law and a set of stock "casuistical examples," such as "Murderer at the Door" and "the Merchant of Rhodes," which would command the attention of European moralists for many centuries.

The development of a casuistical ethics would await the emergence of medieval canon law as set down by Gratian of Bologna (d. before 1159) and his interpreters, as well as the analysis by Scholastic theologians of the problems of human life as they affected the Christian conscience. Alongside canon lawyers, Scholastic thinkers considered cases of conscience (*casūs conscientiae*) that required a sensitive analysis of their conflicting options. The casuistical tendencies inherent in medieval theology and law were further fortified by the stipulation of the Fourth Lateran Council (1215) that all members of the faithful undergo auricular confession before a priest at least once a year. As a result of this development, medieval thought witnessed the advancement of a new genre of theological writing: the *summa confessorum.* These tracts were written for pastors hearing confession and contain detailed recommendations on the types of sin as well as their appropriate penitential tariffs. Well-known fifteenth-century manuals written by Angelo Carletti di Chivasso (1411–1495) and Sylvester Mazzolini (1460–1523) helped to condition the method adopted by later casuistical treatises.

Casuistry came of age in the sixteenth century. Building on the legacy of medieval moral thought, it sought to address the complexities of early modern life by means of restating the verities of the Christian tradition, while developing new theories of moral decision-making. There is a great diversity among the varieties of casuistical writing. On the one hand, there are speculative treatments of the practical problems of natural law and moral theology. An example of this tendency can be witnessed in the writings of Jesuit theologians Gabriel Vásquez (1549 or 1551–1604), Francisco Suárez (1548–1617), and Leonardus Lessius (1554–1623). This, however, might be said to contrast with other types of casuistical writing, where the intention of the author is wholly pastoral. Here the aim was to provide pithy and more accessible treatments of the basic problems of conscience, either for the benefit of those involved in the training of priests—a need that became pressing with the establishment of seminaries after the Council of Trent (1545–1563)—or else for priests engaged in parochial work or missionary activity. Examples of this type of manual can be found in the writings of the Jesuits Franciscus Toletus (1534–1596) and Antonio Escobar y Mendoza (1589–1669).

Probabilism

A distinctive innovation of early modern casuistry was probabilism. Originally advanced by a Dominican theologian, Bartolomé de Medina (1527 or 1528–1580), the theory was later taken up by an assortment of Jesuit theologians. Put briefly, probabilism states that in a case of conscience, provided that both options for a course of action are "probable"—that is, they can be justified by right reason, good argument, and sound authority—and that one alternative is more probable than the other, one is permitted to choose the "least probable" (*minus probabilis*) alternative and is not required to act on the more probable option. Although upheld by many luminaries of early modern Scholastic theology, probabilism failed to convince the vast majority of sixteenth- and seventeenth-century thinkers that it could avoid laxism. Later confections of probabilism, especially those developed by the Cisterican Juan Caramuel Lobkowitz (1606–1682) and the Theatine cleric Antonino Diana (1586–1663), were held to be reprehensible theories that served to endow immoral acts with the token appearance of morality.

The close association of the Jesuit order with probabilism and a residual anti-Jesuit feeling in many quarters of Catholicism and Protestantism conspired to make the terms *Jesuit, probabilist,* and *casuist* synonymous in the European mind from the mid-seventeenth century onward. It was, however, powerful critiques of Jesuit moral theology that did most to alter the fortunes of casuistry and condemn it to years of decline. One of the best-known broadsides was advanced by Blaise Pascal (1623–1662), whose merciless *Les lettres provinciales* (1656–1657) dealt a near fatal blow to casuistry. Pascal's brilliant yet highly rhetorical tirade against the Jesuits sought to expose the putative inconsistencies and errors in their probabilistic method and its application to a wide range of moral questions.

Although Pascal's critique was largely judged to have been a success, it would be wrong to think that the production of works of casuistical ethics or an interest in its issues abruptly terminated after 1657. Even when attacked by an impressive array of detractors, ranging from Dominican supporters of "probabiliorism" (the view that one should always choose the more probable alternative in a case of conscience), Jansensist rigorists, and a hodgepodge of Anglican theologians and Puritan divines to secular moral philosophers, casuistry was still a noticeable feature of the eighteenth-century intellectual landscape, especially in Roman Catholic countries. During a time when European culture and philosophy were being changed as a result of the Enlightenment, the old casuistical methods were similarly refreshed and refashioned by thinkers such as St. Alfonso Maria de' Liguori (1696–1787), who sought to recast theories such as probabilism in order to take account of the preceding century of debate. Liguori's efforts ensured the continuation of vestiges of the casuistical tradition in Roman Catholic moral theology up to the Second Vatican Council (1962–1965).

Decline

While a case-method approach to moral theology can be found in some Anglican writers like Robert Sanderson (1587–1663) and Jeremy Taylor (1613–1667), it is noticeable that most philosophers and theologians in English-speaking countries eschewed probabilism and other theories of Roman Catholic casuistry. Their hostility to these ideas, however, did not prevent them from developing a Christian ethics that addressed its own understanding of cases of conscience. Puritan moralists like William Ames (1576–1633), William Perkins (1558–1602), and Richard Baxter (1615–1691) discussed the vagaries of conscience as they pertained to the practices of piety, while the aforementioned Anglicans, Sanderson and Taylor, and Joseph Hall (1574–1656), were at pains to stress the gulf that separated their treatment of the problems of morality from "papists" and other such undesirables. The effect of these developments was to sideline casuistical ethics within English-speaking moral theology for most of the late seventeenth and eighteenth centuries, with the consequence that it had become invisible by the advent of the nineteenth.

The continuing decline of casuistry can also be witnessed in modern moral philosophy. As they began to express their independence from religion and theology, moral philosophers began to doubt the relevance of a theory of practical conduct indebted to religious values and principles. Further to this, the appeal to authority inherent in a theory like probabilism was now deemed to be authoritarian in an age smitten with ideas of individual autonomy and inalienable rights. For these reasons, traditional casuistry found little favor among philosophers. Thinkers such as Adam Smith (1723–1790) expressed their hostility with aplomb, while Immanuel Kant's (1724–1804) treatment of certain "Casuistical Questions" at the end of his *Metaphysik der Sitten* (1797) reveals the extent of the changes that had occurred within the discussion of casuistry from the mid-seventeenth century onward. For Kant, casuistry could only mean "applied ethics"; the method of the theologians had been debunked and abandoned.

This more neutral sense of casuistry as the "application of moral principles to particular cases" persisted up until the early 2000s, as can be witnessed in the isolated remarks on the subject by William Paley (1743–1805), Henry Sidgwick (1838–1900), and George Edward Moore (1873–1958). Apart from several historical studies that invariably upheld the critique of Pascal, twentieth-century thinkers were rarely inclined to study the claims of the casuistical tradition. This changed, however, with the publication in 1988 of the *Abuse of Casuistry* by Albert Jonsen and Stephen Toulmin. They argued that, notwithstanding its colorful past, the old casuistical methods of the theologians could be transposed with great benefit to ongoing debates in bioethics. Jonsen and Toulmin offered a redescription of casuistry in terms of reasoning about "paradigm cases," a method that they deemed sufficient to fashion a viable notion of moral consensus. If not in moral philosophy, certainly in bioethics their work has been favorably received and continues to stimulate further work on a host of practical issues. Here, "casuistry" is deemed to be an important tool for making decisions of principle while respecting the requirements of particular cases. While Jonsen and Toulmin's portrayal of the casuistical tradition is controversial—not least in its eschewal of probabilism and readiness to concur with the basic ingredients of Pascal's questionable critique—it is interesting that as a new century begins, the much maligned method of the theologians is enjoying something of a modest revival.

See also **Philosophy, Moral; Scholasticism.**

BIBLIOGRAPHY

Jonsen, Albert, and Stephen Toulmin. *The Abuse of Casuistry: A History of Moral Reasoning.* Berkeley: University of California Press, 1988.

Keenan, James F., and Thomas A. Shannon, eds. *The Context of Casuistry.* Washington, D.C.: Georgetown University Press, 1995.

Leites, Edmund, ed. *Conscience and Casuistry in Early Modern Europe.* Cambridge, U.K.: Cambridge University Press, 1988.

Vallance, Edward, and Harald Braun, eds. *Contexts of Conscience in Early Modern Europe, 1500–1700.* London: Palgrave Macmillan, 2004.

M. W. F. Stone

CAUSALITY. The causality debate has been centered on two issues, one metaphysical, the other epistemic. The metaphysical issue concerns the nature of the connection between cause and effect: How and in virtue of what does the cause bring about the effect? The epistemic issue concerns the possibility of causal knowledge: How, if at all, can causal knowledge be obtained?

Aristotle

Aristotle (384–322 B.C.E.) claimed a sharp distinction between understanding the fact and understanding the reason why (*dioti; aitia*). Though both types of understanding proceed via deductive syllogism, only the latter is characteristic of science because only the latter is tied to the knowledge of causes. In his *Posterior Analytics,* Aristotle contrasted the following two instances of deductive syllogism:

A. Planets do not twinkle; what does not twinkle is near; therefore, planets are near.

B. Planets are near; what is near does not twinkle; therefore, planets do not twinkle.

Syllogism A demonstrates the fact that planets are near but does not explain it because it does not state its causes. On the contrary, syllogism B is explanatory because it gives the reason why planets do not twinkle: because they are near. Explanatory syllogisms like B are formally similar to nonexplanatory syllogisms like A. Both are demonstrative arguments of the form: all Fs are Gs; all Gs are Hs; therefore, all Fs are Hs. The difference between them lies in the "middle term" G. In B, but not in A, the middle term states a cause. As Aristotle said: "The middle term is the cause, and in all cases it is the cause that is being sought" (90a5–10). To ask why F is H is to look for a causal link joining F and H. Aristotle's key observation was that, besides being demonstrative, explanatory arguments should also be asymmetric: the asymmetric relation between causes and effects should be reflected in an explanatory asymmetry between the premises and the conclusion of the explanatory arguments—the premises should explain the conclusion and not the other way around.

Aristotle took scientific knowledge to form a tight deductive-axiomatic system whose axioms are first principles, being "true and primary and immediate, and more known than and prior to and causes of the conclusion" (71b20–25). Being an empiricist, he thought that knowledge of causes has experience as its source. But experience on its own cannot lead, through induction, to the first principles: these are universal and necessary and state the ultimate causes. On pain of either circularity or infinite regress, the first principles cannot be demonstrated either. So, something besides experience and demonstration is necessary for the knowledge of first principles. This is a process of abstraction based on intuition, a process that reveals the essences of things—that is, the properties by virtue of which the thing is what it is. In the example B above, it is of the essence of something's being near that it does not twinkle. In the rich Aristotelian ontology, causes are essential properties of their subjects and necessitate their effects. He thought that the logical necessity by which the conclusion follows from the premises of an explanatory argument mirrors the physical necessity by which causes produce their effects.

In his *Physics,* Aristotle distinguishes between four types of causes. The material cause is "that out of which a thing comes to be"; the formal cause is "the definition of its essence"; the efficient cause is "the primary source of the change or rest"; and the final cause is "that for the sake of which a thing is done" (194b23–195a3). For instance, the material cause of a statue is its material; its formal cause is its form or shape; its efficient cause is its maker; and its final cause is the purpose for which the statue was made. Aristotle thought that a complete causal explanation has to cite all four causes: the efficient cause is the active agent that puts the form on matter for a purpose.

Aristotle's Legacy

Most of Aristotle's views were accepted by the Scholastics. Aristotle thought that the chains of efficient causes must stop at some "unmoved movers"—that is, things that are themselves unmoved but produce motion to other things. The Scholastics thought that the only proper efficient cause was God, being the ultimate unmoved mover. Later thinkers revolted against all but efficient causality. Efficient causality, what Aristotle called "the source of motion" (195a10), was taken to be the only type of causality by all those who advocated, in one form or another, the mechanical philosophy: in their hands, efficient causality became tantamount to pushings and pullings. Final causes, in particular, were cast to the winds. Where Aristotle saw goals and purposes in nature, mechanical philosophers either excised purpose from nature (Hobbes, Hume) or placed it firmly in the hands of God (Descartes, Leibniz). The moderns also revolted, to varying degrees, against the rich ontological landscape that Aristotle had painted: essences, substantial forms, activities, and so on. However, two key Aristotelian ideas, that there is necessity in nature and that this necessity is the same as the logical necessity of a demonstrative argument, were to become part of the mainstream philosophical thinking about causality until David Hume (1711–1776) subjected them to severe criticism and undermined them.

Descartes

René Descartes (1596–1650) distinguished all substances into two sorts: thinking things (*res cogitans*) and extended things (*res extensa*). He took the essence of mind to be thought and that of matter extension. Unlike Aristotle, he thought that matter was inert (since its essence is that it occupies space). Yet, there are causal connections between bodies (bits of matter) and between minds and bodies (bits of different substances). So, two big questions emerge within Cartesianism. The first is: how is body-body interaction possible? The second is: how is mind-matter interaction possible? Descartes's answer to the first question is the so-called transference model of causality: when *x* causes *y*, a property of *x* is communicated to *y*. He thought that this view is an obvious consequence of the principle "Nothing comes from nothing." As he put it: "For if we admit that there is something in the effect that was not previously present in the cause, we shall also have to admit that this something was produced by nothing" (vol. 1, p. 97). But Descartes failed to explain how this communication is possible. Indeed, by taking matter to be an inert extended substance, he had to retreat to some external cause of motion and change. Descartes treated forces with suspicion since they did not quite fit within his tight scheme of the two distinct substances and their two essential attributes. So in his *Principles of Philosophy* (1644) he retreated to God, whom he took to be "the efficient cause of all things" (vol. 1, p. 202). But this retreat to God cannot save the transference model. Besides, the transference model of causality makes an answer to the second question above (how do mind and matter interact?) metaphysically impossible. Being distinct substances, they have nothing in common that can be communicated between them. Descartes was a rationalist. He thought that Reason alone can, by a priori reflection, discover the basic casual laws of nature, which, Descartes thought, stem directly from God.

Descartes's Successors

Descartes's successors were divided into two groups: the occasionalists and those who reintroduced activity into nature. Occasionalism is the view that the only real cause of everything is God and that all causal talk that refers to worldly substances is a sham. Nicolas Malebranche (1638–1715) drew a distinction between real causes and natural causes (or occasions). As he put it: "A true cause as I understand it is one such that the mind perceives a necessary connection between it and its effect. Now the mind perceives a necessary connection between the will of an infinite being and its effect. Therefore, it is only God who is the true cause and who truly has the power to move bodies" (1997, p. 450). Natural causes are then merely the occasions on which God causes something to happen. Malebranche pushed Cartesianism to its extremes: since a body's nature is exhausted by its extension, bodies cannot have the power to move anything, and hence to cause anything to happen. What Malebranche also added was that since causality involves a necessary connection between the cause and the effect (a view that Descartes accepted too), and since no such necessary connection is perceived in cases of alleged worldly causality (where, for instance, it is said that a billiard ball causes another one to move), there is no worldly causality: all there is in the world is regular sequences of events, which strictly speaking are not causal. Gottfried Wilhelm Leibniz (1646–1716), on the other hand, aimed to reintroduce forces and active powers into nature. As he said: "activity is the essence of substance" (1981, p. 65). Each substance is sustained by an internal "primitive active force," which causes its subsequent states. Yet, in a rather puzzling move, he also thought that there is no real causality in nature, since Leibnizian substances (what he called "the monads") do not interact. Rather, they are coordinated with each other by God's act of preestablished harmony, which confers on them the natural agreement of exact clocks.

There is an irony to be noted at this point. Most early modern philosophers tried to solve the metaphysical issue of causality. They devised elaborate theories to explain how the cause brings about the effect. But in the end, they excised causality from nature. More mildly put, insofar as there was causality in nature it was taken to be the product of divine impulse (Descartes) or of mysterious primitive forces (Leibniz).

Hume

In his ground-breaking *A Treatise of Human Nature* (1739–1740), David Hume made the scientific hunt for causes possible, by freeing the concept of causality from the metaphysical chains that his predecessors had used to pin it down. For Hume, causality, as it is in the world, is a regular succession of event-types: one thing invariably following another. His famous first definition of causality runs as follows: "We may define a CAUSE to be 'An object precedent and contiguous to another, and where all the objects resembling the former are plac'd in like relations of precedency and contiguity to those objects, that resemble the latter'" (1978 ed., p. 170).

Taking a cue from Malebranche, Hume argued that there was no perception of the supposed necessary connection between the cause and the effect. When a sequence of events that is considered causal is observed—for example, two billiard balls hitting each other and flying apart—there are impressions of the two balls, of their motions, of their collision, and of their flying apart, but there is no impression of any alleged necessity by which the cause brings about the effect. Hume went one step further. He found worthless his predecessors' appeals to the power of God to cause things to happen, since, as he said, such claims give us "no insight into the nature of this power or connection" (p. 249). So, Hume secularized completely the notion of causality. He also found inadequate, because circular, his predecessors' attempts to explain the link between causes and effects in terms of powers, active forces, and so on. As he put it: "[T]he terms *efficacy, agency, power, force, energy, necessity, connexion,* and *productive quality,* are all nearly synonymous; and therefore 'tis an absurdity to employ any of them in defining the rest" (p. 157).

Yet Hume faced a puzzle. According to his empiricist theory of ideas, there are no ideas in the mind unless there were prior impressions (perceptions). He did, however, recognize that the concept of causality involved the idea of necessary connection. Where does this idea come from, if there is no perception of necessity in causal sequences? Hume argued that the source of this idea is the perception of "a new relation betwixt cause and effect": a "constant conjunction" such that "like objects have always been plac'd in like relations of contiguity and succession" (p. 88). The perception of this constant conjunction leads the mind to form a certain habit or custom: to make a "customary transition" from cause to effect. It is this felt determination of the mind that affords us the idea of necessity.

So instead of ascribing the idea of necessity to a feature of the natural world, Hume took it to arise from within the human mind, when the latter is conditioned by the observation of a regularity in nature to form an expectation of the effect, when the cause is present. Indeed, Hume offered a second definition of causality: "A CAUSE is an object precedent and contiguous to another, and so united with it, that the idea of the one determines the mind to form the idea of the other, and the impression of the one to form a more lively idea of the other" (p. 170). Hume thought that he had unpacked the "essence of necessity": it "is something that exists in the mind, not in the objects" (p. 165). He claimed that the supposed objective necessity in nature is spread by the mind onto the world. Hume can be seen as offering an objective theory of causality in the world (since causation amounts to regular succession), which was however accompanied by a mind-dependent view of necessity. This dual aspect of Hume's account of causality is reflected in his two definitions.

Being an empiricist, Hume argued that all causal knowledge stems from experience. He revolted against the traditional view that the necessity that links cause and effect is the same as the logical necessity of a demonstrative argument. He argued that there can be no a priori demonstration of any causal connection, since the cause can be conceived without its effect and conversely. His far-reaching observation was that the alleged necessity of causal connection cannot be proved empirically either. As he famously argued, any attempt to show, based on experience, that a regularity that has held in the past will or must continue to hold in the future will be circular and question-begging. It will presuppose a principle of uniformity of nature. But this principle is not a priori true. Nor can it be proved empirically without circularity. For any attempt to prove it empirically will have to assume what needs to be proved—namely, that since nature has been uniform in the past it will or must continue to be uniform in the future. This Humean challenge to any attempt to establish the necessity of causal connections on empirical grounds has become known as his skepticism about induction. But it should be noted that Hume never doubted that people think and reason inductively. He just took this to be a fundamental psychological fact about human beings that cannot be accommodated within the confines of the traditional conception of Reason. Indeed, Hume went on to describe in detail some basic "rules by which to judge of causes and effects" (p. 173).

Kant

It was Hume's critique of necessity in nature that awoke Immanuel Kant (1724–1804) from his "dogmatic slumber," as he himself famously stated. In his *Critique of Pure Reason* (1787), Kant tried to demonstrate that the principle of causality—namely, "everything that happens, that is, begins to be, presupposes something upon which it follows by rule," (1965 ed., p. 218)—is a precondition for the very possibility of objective experience. He took the principle of causality to be required for the mind to make sense of the temporal irreversibility that there is in certain sequences of impressions. So, whereas we can have the sequence of impressions that correspond to the sides of a house in any order we please, the sequence of impressions that correspond to a ship going downstream cannot be reversed: it exhibits a certain temporal order (or direction). This temporal order by which certain impressions appear can be taken to constitute an objective happening only if the later event is taken to be necessarily determined by the earlier one (i.e., to follow by rule from its cause). For Kant, objective events are not "given": they are constituted by the organizing activity of the mind and in particular by the imposition of the principle of causality on the phenomena. Consequently, the principle of causality is, for Kant, a synthetic a priori principle.

Ingenious though Kant's answer to Hume was, it was ironic in three respects. Firstly, Kant safeguarded the concept of causality but at the price of making it applicable only to the phenomena and not to the unknowable things-in-themselves (noumena). Secondly, recall that Hume argued that the supposed necessity of causal sequences cannot be observed in the sequences themselves, but is projected by the mind onto the world. Kant agreed with all this, but took this projection by the mind onto the world to be presupposed for the distinction between causal and noncausal sequences. Thirdly, Kant identified causality with the rule of natural law: causal sequences of events are lawful sequences of events. This became the main plank of the Humean philosophical tradition. Stripped from objective necessity, natural laws boil down to worldly regularities.

The Regularity View of Causality

Arthur Schopenhauer (1788–1860) charged Kant with showing the absurd result that all sequence is consequence. As he noted, the tones of a musical composition follow each other in a certain objective order and yet it would be absurd to say that they follow each other according to the law of causality. This has also been a major objection to Hume's views. Hume left the metaphysics of causality behind, but like Kant, he ended up with a loose notion of causality. On the one hand, it seems that there can be causality without regularity. This is the case of the so-called singular causality, where one event causes another to happen without this particular (singular) sequence of events falling under a regularity. On the other hand, there can be regularity without causality. There are cases in which events regularly follow each other (like the night always follows the day) without being the cause of each other. Once more, the metaphysical and the epistemological issues of causality come to the fore. We might not be able to know that a sequence of events is causal unless we see it repeat itself many times. But this does not imply that, metaphysically speaking, causality consists in regular sequence. On the Humean view, whether or not a sequence of events is causal depends on things that happen elsewhere and elsewhen in the universe, and in particular on whether or not this particular sequence instantiates a regularity. The Humean view may be entitled the Regularity View of Causality. But an opposite view that became prominent in the twentieth century, due mostly to the work of Curt John Ducasse (1881–1969), is that what makes a sequence of events causal is something that happens there and then: a local tie between the cause and the effect, or an intrinsic feature of the particular sequence. Ducasse's (1968) single-difference account, roughly that an event *c* causes an event *e* if and only if *c* was the last—or, the only—difference in *e*'s environment before *e* occurred, takes causality to link individual events independently of any regular association that there may or may not be between events like the cause and events like the effect. Causality, non-Humeans argue, is essentially singular: a matter of this causing that.

Most advocates of singular causation argue that, contra Hume, causality is observable. A central claim is that causal relations are embodied in language by causal verbs, such as "to bend," "to corrode," "to push," "to break," and so on. So, we are told, when one asserts that, for instance, the vase broke after being struck with a hammer, by the very use of the verb "to break," one makes a causal claim, and one has thereby directly perceived the vase being caused to break. Elizabeth Anscombe (b. 1919) argued that since our language is infested with causal verbs, there is no mystery in the claim that we directly perceive causings: when we learn to report such things as pushings, pullings, breakings, and the like from having observed them, we have thereby learned to report causings from having observed them.

Mill

In his monumental *A System of Logic Ratiocinative and Inductive* (1843), John Stuart Mill (1806–1873) defended the Regularity View of Causality, with the sophisticated addition that in claiming that an effect invariably follows from the cause, the cause should be taken to be the whole conjunction of the conditions that are sufficient and necessary for the effect. For Mill, regular association is not, on its own, enough for causality. A regular association of events is causal only if it is "unconditional"—that is, only if its occurrence does not depend on the presence of further factors which are such that, given their presence, the effect would occur even if its putative cause was not present. A clear case in which unconditionality fails is when the events that are invariably conjoined are effects of a common cause. Ultimately, Mill took to be causal those invariable successions that constitute laws of nature.

Mill is also famous for his methods by which causes can be discovered. These are known as the Method of Agreement and the Method of Difference. According to the first, the cause is the common factor in a number of otherwise different cases in which the effect occurs. According to the second, the cause is the factor that is different in two cases, which are similar except that in the one the effect occurs, while in the other it does not. In effect, Mill's methods encapsulate what is going on in controlled experiments: we find causes by creating circumstances in which the presence (or the absence) of a factor makes the only difference to the production (or the absence) of an effect. Mill, however, was adamant that his methods work only if certain metaphysical assumptions are in place. It must be

the case that: (a) events have causes; (b) events have a limited number of possible causes; and (c) same causes have same effects, and conversely.

Logical Positivism

Bertrand Russell (1872–1970), in his "On the Notion of Cause" (1918), argued that the concept of causality was incoherent. But this was just as well for him, since, as he claimed, physics has stopped looking for causes: for "there are no such things." Here is his famous dictum: "The law of causality, I believe, like much that passes muster among philosophers, is a relic of a bygone age, surviving, like the monarchy, only because it is erroneously supposed to do no harm" (1918, p. 180). His suspicion of the concept of causality was inherited by the movement of logical positivism (the Vienna Circle), which set the agenda for most of the philosophy of science in the twentieth century. They took to heart Hume's critique of the supposed necessary connection between cause and effect. The twist they gave to this critique was based on their verificationist criterion of meaning. As the leader of the Circle, Moritz Schlick (1882–1936), stressed, positing a "linkage" between two events would be tantamount to "committing a kind of nonsense" since all attempts to verify it would be necessarily futile (1979, p. 245). Rudolf Carnap (1891–1970) thought that insofar as the concept of causality is useful to science, it should be understood by reference to the notion of laws of nature. He insisted that the only meaningful content that causal talk can have is when we call "cause" the event, or the physical magnitude, or the physical state, which temporally precedes another one nomologically dependent on the former. The logical positivists took the laws to be exceptionless regularities that are expressed by true universal statements of the form "all Fs are Gs" (e.g., all planets move in ellipses).

Deductive-Nomological Explanation

A central element of the empiricist project was to legitimize—and demystify—the concept of causality by subsuming it under the concept of lawful explanation, which, in turn, was modeled on deductive arguments. This project culminated in Carl Hempel (1905–1977) and Paul Oppenheim's Deductive-Nomological model of explanation. According to this, to offer an explanation of an event *e* is to construct a valid deductive argument of the following form:

Antecedent/Initial Conditions

Statements of Laws

Therefore, *e* (event/fact to be explained)

So, when the claim is made that event *c* causes event *e* (e.g., that the sugar cube dissolved because it was immersed in water), it should be understood as follows: there are relevant laws in virtue of which the occurrence of the antecedent condition *c* (putting the sugar in water) is nomologically sufficient for the occurrence of the event *e* (the dissolving of the sugar). It has been a standard criticism of the Deductive-Nomological (DN) model that, insofar as it aims to offer sufficient and necessary conditions for an argument to count as a bona fide explanation, it fails. For, there are arguments that satisfy the

> There are some philosophers who assert that secondary causes act through their matter, figure, and motion . . . others assert that they do so through a substantial form; others through accidents or qualities, and some through matter and form; of these some through form and accidents, others through certain virtues or faculties different from the above. . . . Philosophers do not even agree about the action by which secondary causes produce their effects. Some of them claim that causality must not be produced, for it is what produces. Others would have them truly act through their action; but they find such great difficulty in explaining precisely what this action is, and there are so many different views on the matter that I cannot bring myself to relate to them.
>
> SOURCE: Nicolas Malebranche, *The Search After Truth (Researche de la Vérité)* (1674–1675), trans. Thomas M. Lennon and Paul J. Olscamp. Cambridge, U.K., and New York: Cambridge University Press, 1997, p. 659.

structure of the DN-model, and yet fail to be bona fide explanations of a certain event. For instance, one can construct a deductive-nomological "explanation" of the height of a flagpole having as premises (a statement of) the length of its shadow and (statements of) relevant laws of optics, but this is not an explanation of why the flagpole has the height it does. In a sense, this counterexample repeats a point that we saw already made by Aristotle—namely, that good explanations are asymmetric: they explain effects in terms of causes and not conversely. Conversely, there are bona fide explanations that fail to instantiate the DN-model. For instance, one can construct an explanation of why there was a car crash (by telling a causal story of how it happened) without referring to any law at all. The joined message of these counterexamples is that the DN-model fails precisely because it ignores the role of causality in explanation. In other words, the moral of the counterexamples is there is more to the concept of causality than what can be captured by DN-explanations.

Laws of Nature

Be that as it may, the Deductive-Nomological model, as well as any attempt to tie causality to laws, faces a rather central conceptual difficulty: the problem of how to characterize the laws of nature. Most Humeans have come to adopt the Regularity View of Laws: laws of nature are regularities. Yet, they have a hurdle to jump: not all regularities are causal. Nor can all regularities be deemed laws of nature. The night always follows the day, but it is not caused by the day. And, though a regularity, it is not a law of nature that all coins in my pocket are euros. So, the Humeans have to draw a distinction between the good regularities (those that constitute the laws of nature) and the bad ones—that is, those that are, as Mill put it, "conjunctions in some sense accidental." Only the former can underpin causality and play a role in explanation. Among the many attempts to distinguish between laws and accidents, the most promising is what may be called the web of laws view. According to this, the regularities that constitute the laws of nature are those that are expressed by the axioms and

theorems of an ideal deductive system of our knowledge of the world, which strikes the best balance between simplicity and strength. Whatever regularity is not part of this best system is merely accidental: it fails to be a genuine law of nature. The gist of this approach, which has been advocated by Mill, Frank Ramsey (1903–1930), and David Lewis (1941–2001), is that no regularity, taken in isolation, can be deemed a law of nature. The regularities that constitute laws of nature are determined in a kind of holistic fashion by being parts of a structure. But despite its many attractions, this view does not offer a purely objective account of laws of nature.

A contrary view that has been defended by David Armstrong (b. 1926) is that lawhood cannot be reduced to regularity. Lawhood is said to be a certain necessitating relation among natural properties. An attraction of this view is that it makes clear how laws can cause anything to happen: they do so because they embody causal relations among properties. But the central concept of nomic necessitation is still not sufficiently clear.

Inus Conditions

Among the more recent attempts to develop more defensible versions of the Regularity View of Causality, J. L. Mackie's (1917–1981) inus-conditions approach stands out. Mackie stressed that effects have, typically, a "plurality of causes" (p. 61). That is, a certain effect can be brought about by a number of distinct clusters of factors. Each cluster is sufficient to bring about the effect, but none of them is necessary. So, he takes the regularities in nature to have a complex form (A&B&C or D&E&F or G&H&I) ↔ E, which should be read as: all (A&B&C or D&E&F or G&H&I) are followed by E, and all E are preceded by (A&B&C or D&E&F or G&H&I). How do we pick out the cause of an event in this setting? Each single factor of A&B&C (e.g., A) is related to the effect E in an important way. It is an *insufficient* but *nonredundant* part of an *unnecessary* but *sufficient* condition for E. Using the first letters of the italicized words, Mackie has called such a factor an inus condition. Causes, then, are inus conditions. So to say that short circuits cause house fires is to say that the short circuit is an inus condition for house fires. It is an insufficient part because it cannot cause the fire on its own (other conditions such as oxygen, inflammable material, etc. should be present). It is, nonetheless, a nonredundant part because, without it, the rest of the conditions are not sufficient for the fire. It is just a part, and not the whole, of a sufficient condition (which includes oxygen, the presence of inflammable material, etc.), but this whole sufficient condition is not necessary, since some other cluster of conditions, for example, an arsonist with gasoline, can produce the fire.

Counterfactual Dependence

In his *Enquiry Concerning Human Understanding* (1748) Hume stated briefly another way to view causality. He said that an object is the cause of another when "if the first object had not been, the second never had existed" (1975 ed., p. 146). This view has been articulated into a theory of causality by David Lewis. Lewis (1986) defined causality in terms of the counterfactual dependence of the effect on the cause: the cause is rendered counterfactually necessary for the effect. For instance, to say that the short-circuit caused the fire is to say that if the short-circuit had not happened, the fire would not have ensued. To be more precise, Lewis defined causality by reference to a *causal chain* of counterfactually dependent events, where a sequence of events ($C, E, E', \ldots$) is a chain of counterfactual dependence if and only if E counterfactually depends on C, E' counterfactually depends on E, and so on. This move is meant to enforce that causation is a transitive relation among events (that is, if C causes E and E causes E', then C causes E'). As Lewis put it: "one event is a cause of another if and only if there exists a causal chain leading from the first to second" (p. 167). Statements such as "if C had happened, then E would have happened" are called counterfactual conditionals (another example, "if this sugar cube had been in water, it would have dissolved") for they state what could or could not have happened, under certain circumstances. But it has been notoriously difficult to specify the conditions under which counterfactual conditionals are true or false. Lewis articulated a rather complicated logic of counterfactual conditionals, which was based on the idea that, besides the actual world, there are also other possible worlds, which can be deemed more or less similar to the actual. A chief but not inviolable criterion for judging the similarity among worlds was taken to be whether the same laws of nature govern the worlds under comparison.

Though it is still one of the main contestants, this view of causality faces important difficulties. A chief among them comes from cases of causal overdetermination, where there are two factors each of which is sufficient to bring about the effect, but none of them is necessary, since even if the one was not present, the other factor would ensure the occurrence of the effect. For instance, two rocks are simultaneously thrown at a bottle and they shatter it. They both caused the shattering, but the effect is not counterfactually dependent on either of them, since if the first rock had missed the bottle, the other would have still shattered it. So there is causality without the cause being counterfactually dependent on the effect.

Here is a billiard-ball lying on the table, and another ball moving towards it with rapidity. They strike; and the ball, which was formerly at rest, now acquires a motion. This is as perfect an instance of the relation of cause and effect as any which we know, either by sensation or by reflection. Let us therefore examine it. 'Tis evident, that the two balls touched one another before the motion was communicated, and that there was no interval betwixt the shock and the motion. *Contiguity* in time and place is therefore a requisite circumstance to the operation of all causes. 'Tis evident likewise, that the motion, which was the cause, is prior to the motion, which was the effect. *Priority* in time, is therefore another requisite circumstance in every cause. But this is not all. Let us try any other balls of the same kind in a like situation, and we shall always find, that the impulse of the one produces motion in the other. Here therefore is a *third* circumstance, viz., that is a constant conjunction betwixt the cause and effect. Every object like the cause, produces always some object like the effect. Beyond these three circumstances of contiguity, priority, and *constant conjunction,* I can discover nothing in this cause. The first ball is in motion; touches the second; immediately the second is in motion: and when I try the experiment with the same or like balls, in the same or like circumstances, I find that upon the motion and touch of the one ball, motion always follows in the other. In whatever shape I turn this matter, and however I examine it, I can find nothing farther. (pp. 649–650)

SOURCE: David Hume, *Abstract to A Treatise of Human Nature*. Published by Hume anonymously in 1739.

Probabilistic Causality

No matter how one thinks about causality, there are certain platitudes that this concept should satisfy. One of them may be called the difference platitude: causes make a difference—namely, things would be different if the causes of some effects were absent. This platitude is normally cast in two ways. We

> [W]e derived the principle that everything that happens has a cause from the condition under which alone a concept of happening in general is objectively possible—namely, by showing that the determination of an event in time, and therefore the event as belonging to experience, would be impossible save as standing under such a dynamical rule.
>
> SOURCE: Immanuel Kant, *Critique of Pure Reason* (1787), trans. Norman Kemp Smith. New York: St. Martin's Press, 1965, p. 624.

have already seen the first, the counterfactual way: if the cause had not been, the effect would not have been either. The other is a probabilistic way: causes raise the chances of their effects—namely, the probability that a certain event happens is higher if we take into account its cause than if we do not. This thought has led to the development of theories of probabilistic causality. We do rightly claim that smoking causes lung cancer, even though there is no regular association (or deterministic connection) between smoking and lung cancer. Some philosophers, most notably Patrick Suppes (1984) and Nancy Cartwright (1983), think that this is already a good argument against the view that causality is connected with invariable sequences or regularities. They then analyze causal claims in terms of probabilistic relations among magnitudes, capitalizing on the intuition that causes (mostly, but not invariably) raise the probabilities of their effects. Some think that there are good empirical reasons to jettison determinism (roughly, that each and every event has a fully sufficient set of causes) in favor of indeterminism (roughly, that there are genuinely chancy events). They then try to show that indeterminism and causality mix well, given the thought that a certain event can be caused to happen even though its cause made only a difference to its chance to happen. Interestingly, these ideas are extended to deterministic causality as well, with the prime thought being that an effect is deterministically caused to happen if its probability, given its cause, is unity.

Causes as Recipes

Another central platitude of the concept of causality may be called the recipe platitude: causes are recipes for producing or preventing their effects. This platitude is normally cast in terms of manipulability: causes can be manipulated to bring about certain effects. G. H. von Wright (1906–2003) developed this thought into a full-blown theory of causality. He took it that what confers on a sequence of events the character of causal connection is "the possibility of subjecting cause-factors to experimental test by interfering with the 'natural' course of events" (1993, p. 117). Since manipulation is a distinctively human action, he concluded that the causal relation is dependent upon the concept of human action. But his views were

taken to be too anthropomorphic. For, do we not think that there would be causal relations, even if there would not be any humans around capable of manipulating anything? Yet, recently, there have been important attempts to give a more objective gloss to the idea of manipulation. James Woodward (2003) introduces a notion of intervention that is not restricted to human action and argues that a relationship among some magnitudes X and Y is causal if, were one to intervene to change the value of X appropriately, the relationship between X and Y would remain invariant but the value of Y would change, as a result of the intervention on X. This interventionist account has been developed by Judea Pearl (2001) into a rather powerful mathematical tool, known as Bayesian probabilistic networks, for discovering and establishing causal relations from relations of probabilistic dependence among variables. An attraction of the interventionist approach is that it is not so much concerned with the metaphysics of causality as with the epistemological and methodological circumstances under which causal facts can be ascertained.

Physical Causality

Lately, there have been a number of attempts to show that there is more to causality than regular succession by positing a physical mechanism that links cause and effect. In his *Scientific Explanation and the Causal Structure of the World* (1984), Wesley Salmon (1925–2001) advanced a mechanistic approach, roughly that an event *c* causes an event *e* if and only if there is a causal process that connects *c* and *e*. Borrowing an idea of Hans Reichenbach's (1956), Salmon characterized "causal" those processes that are capable of transmitting a mark, where a mark is a modification of the structure of a process. Later on, Salmon (1997) and Phil Dowe (2000) took causality to consist in the exchange or transfer of some conserved quantity, such as energy-momentum or charge. Such accounts may be called transference models because they claim that causality consists in the transfer of something (some physical quantity) between the cause and its effect. They claim that causality need not involve regularities or laws. Rather, it consists in a local physical tie between cause and effect. But there is a drawback. Even if it is granted that these models offer neat accounts of causality at the level of physical events or processes, they can be generalized as accounts of causality *simpliciter* only if they are married to strong reductionistic views that all worldly phenomena (be they social or psychological or biological) are, ultimately, reducible to physical phenomena. We saw earlier that Descartes, too, advanced a transference model of causality and that he stumbled on the issue of mental causality: how can the mental cause anything physical to happen, as it manifestly does? The irony is that the very same hurdle might have to be jumped by the advocates of the modern transference models.

Neo-Aristotelianism

Hume found any appeal to causal powers suspect, since he thought there were no impressions of them. Hume's views were dominant until the last quarter of the twentieth century, when there was a resurgence of Aristotelianism. A few contemporary philosophers think that causation should be best understood in terms of causal powers—that is, powers, dispositions, and capacities things have to cause other things to happen. These powers are supposed to stem from the nature or essence of a thing and they determine what a thing is and what it can do. The causal laws that govern the world are supposed to stem from these causal powers. According to Brian Ellis (2001), a chief defender of this view, causal laws state necessary truths about how things are intrinsically disposed to behave. But many philosophers find these views unappealing, not least because they fail to explain the fundamental notion of causal power.

See also **Aristotelianism; Cartesianism; Determinism; Dualism; Empiricism; Neoplatonism; Probability.**

BIBLIOGRAPHY

PRIMARY SOURCES

Anscombe, G. E. M. *Causality and Determination.* London: Cambridge University Press, 1971.

Aristotle. *Physics.* In vol. 1 of *The Complete Works of Aristotle,* 2 vols., edited by Jonathan Barnes. Princeton N.J.: Princeton University Press, 1984.

———. *Posterior Analytics.* 2nd ed. Translated by Jonathan Barnes. Oxford: Clarendon, 1993.

Armstrong, D. M. *What Is a Law of Nature?* Cambridge, U.K., and New York: Cambridge University Press, 1983. Classic defense of the view that natural laws embody necessitating relations among properties.

Carnap, Rudolf. *An Introduction to the Philosophy of Science.* Edited by Martin Gardner. New York: Dover, 1995. A classic late statement of the positivist philosophy of science.

Cartwright, Nancy. *How the Laws of Physics Lie.* Oxford and New York: Clarendon, 1983. A thorough critique of the Regularity Views of Causation and Laws.

Descartes, René. *The Philosophical Writings of Descartes.* 3 vols. Translated by John Cottingham, Robert Stoothoff, and Dugald Murdoch. Cambridge, U.K., and New York: Cambridge University Press, 1985. Vol. 1 includes *Principles of Philosophy* (1644), Descartes's classic presentation of his philosophy of nature.

Dowe, Phil. *Physical Causation.* Cambridge, U.K., and New York: Cambridge University Press, 2000. The standard rendition of the conserved-quantity theory of causation.

Ducasse, C. J. *Causation and the Types of Necessity.* New York: Dover, 1969. Defends singular causation against Hume and Mill.

Ellis, B. D. *Scientific Essentialism.* Cambridge, U.K., and New York: Cambridge University Press, 2001. A thorough defense of neo-Aristotelianism.

Hempel, Carl G. *Aspects of Scientific Explanation, and Other Essays in the Philosophy of Science.* New York: Free Press, 1965.

Hume, David. *An Enquiry Concerning Human Understanding* (1748). Edited by L. A. Selby-Bigge from the posthumous edition of 1777. 3rd ed., edited by P. H. Nidditch, published as *Enquiries Concerning Human Understanding and Concerning the Principles of Morals.* Oxford: Clarendon, 1975. A less skeptical version of Hume's critique of causality.

———. *A Treatise of Human Nature.* 1739. Edited by L. A. Selby-Bigge, 1888. 2nd ed., with text revisions by P. H. Nidditch. Oxford: Clarendon, 1978.

Kant, Immanuel. *Critique of Pure Reason.* 1787. Translated by Norman Kemp Smith. New York: St. Martin's Press, 1965. A classic of Western philosophy.

Leibniz, Gottfried Wilhelm. *New Essays on Human Understanding.* 1765. Translated and edited by Peter Remnant and Jonathan Bennett. Cambridge, U.K., and New York: Cambridge University Press, 1981. Posthumously published defense of rationalism against John Locke's empiricism.

Lewis, David. "Causation." In his *Philosophical Papers,* vol. 2. Oxford: Oxford University Press, 1986.

Mackie, J. L. *The Cement of the Universe: A Study of Causation.* Oxford: Clarendon, 1974. One of the most comprehensive and original books on causality.

Malebranche, Nicolas. *The Search After Truth* (1674–1675). Translated by Thomas M. Lennon and Paul J. Olscamp. Cambridge, U.K., and New York: Cambridge University Press, 1997.

Mill, J. S. *A System of Logic: Ratiocinative and Inductive* (1843). 8th ed. London: Longmans, Green and Co., 1911. Wide-ranging treatment of the methodology of science.

Pearl, Judea. *Causality: Models, Reasoning, and Inference.* Cambridge, U.K.: Cambridge University Press, 2001. Technical but insightful.

Ramsey, F. P. "Universals of Law and of Fact." 1928. In *Foundations: Essays in Philosophy, Logic, Mathematics and Economic,* edited by D. H. Mellor. London: Routledge and Kegan Paul, 1978.

Reichenbach, Hans. *The Direction of Time.* Edited by Maria Reichenbach. Berkeley and Los Angeles: University of California Press, 1956. A defense of the view that the direction of time stems from the direction of causation.

Russell, Bertrand. "On the Notion of Cause." In his *Mysticism and Logic, and Other Essays.* London: George Allen and Unwin, 1932. First published in 1918.

Salmon, Wesley. *Causality and Explanation.* New York: Oxford University Press, 1998.

———. *Scientific Explanation and the Causal Structure of the World.* Princeton, N.J.: Princeton University Press, 1984. The most systematic contemporary mechanistic account of causality.

Schlick, Moritz. "Causation in Everyday Life and in Recent Science." 1932. In *Moritz Schlick Philosophical Papers, Vol. 2 (1925–1936).* Edited by Henk L. Mudler and Barbara F. B. De Velde-Schlick. Dordrecht, Netherlands: D. Reidel, 1979.

Suppes, Patrick. *Probabilistic Metaphysics.* Oxford: Blackwell, 1984.

von Wright, G. H. "On the Logic of the Causal Relations." In *Causation,* edited by Ernst Sosa and Michael Tooley. Oxford: Oxford University Press, 1993.

Woodward, James. *Making Things Happen: A Theory of Causal Explanation.* New York: Oxford University Press, 2003. The standard development of the interventionist approach.

SECONDARY SOURCES

Clatterbaugh, Kenneth. *The Causation Debate in Modern Philosophy, 1637–1739.* New York: Routledge, 1999. Excellent survey of the main theories of causality from Descartes to Hume.

Eells, Ellery. *Probabilistic Causality.* Cambridge, U.K.: Cambridge University Press, 1991. A thorough treatment of theories of probabilistic causality.

Psillos, Stathis. *Causation and Explanation.* Chesham: Acumen and Montreal: McGill-Queens University Press, 2002. Detailed discussion of the main philosophical theories of causality.

Sosa, Ernest, and Michael Tooley, eds. *Causation.* Oxford: Oxford University Press, 1993. A collection of the most influential philosophical papers on causation in the second half of the twentieth century.

Stroud, Barry. *Hume.* London: Routledge and Kegan Paul, 1977. Still the best presentation of Hume's philosophy.

Stathis Psillos

CAUSATION.   Philosophers have theorized about causation since well before Aristotle, who distinguished several types of causation: efficient, material, final, and formal. For example, a wood carving is made by an artist (the efficient cause) by chiseling a piece of wood (the material cause) for the purpose of creating a beautiful object (the final cause), arriving at something that has the properties of a wood carving (the formal cause).

Although Aristotle's typology framed discussions of causation until the scientific revolution and in some circles even until David Hume, the focus settled onto analyzing efficient causation and in particular on understanding the kinds of substances that might interact causally. René Descartes, for example, separated material and mental substances and wrote extensively on how cross-substance causation might happen. Discussions of causation thus became entangled with the metaphysics of substance, and positions ranged all the way from Baruch Spinoza, who claimed there is only one type of substance, to Gottfried Wilhelm Leibniz, who claimed there was an infinity of unique substances, one per monad. Everyone wanted to understand causation as involving some "power" to produce change, and different substances possess different sorts of powers over their own and other substances. For example, the empiricist Bishop George Berkeley argued that our ideas (sensations) cannot be caused by other ideas or matter, because ideas and matter are "inert" and do not have the sort of causal "power" necessary for efficient causation. Only an agent like God or a willful person possesses such power. John Locke, in *An Essay concerning Human Understanding,* wrote voluminously trying to explicate the idea of causal power in empiricist terms. David Hume, the brilliant eighteenth-century Scottish philosopher, finally rejected the notion of causal power as being beyond direct observation, and he recast the problem of understanding the connection between a cause and its effect as another version of the problem of induction. Although causes always seem to be followed by their effects, the bond between them might well be nothing more than a psychological habit we develop as a result of regularly perceiving the idea of one type of object or event (e.g., thunder) just after the idea of another (e.g., lightning). Hume's challenge was to find compelling reasons for believing that when an object similar to one we have seen previously occurs, then the effect must necessarily occur. No one has succeeded in answering Hume's challenge, but his effect on the debate was as powerful as Aristotle's. All modern theories of causation begin with something like Hume's story: there are objects or events that we can group as similar, like the events of walking in the rain with no coat and developing a cold. They all ask what does it mean to assert that the relation between these events is causal.

Modern Theories of Causation

Practically, causation matters. Juries must decide, for example, whether a pregnant mother's refusal to give birth by cesarean section was the cause of the death of one of her twins. Policy makers must decide whether violence on TV causes violence in life. Neither question can be coherently debated without some theory of causation. Fortunately (or not, depending on where one sits), a virtual plethora of theories of causation have been championed in the third of a century between 1970 and 2004.

Before the sketch of a few of the major theories, however, consider what one might want out of a theory of causation. First, although one can agree that causation is a relation, what are the relata? Are causes and effects *objects,* like moving billiard balls? Are they *particular events,* like the *Titanic* hitting an iceberg in 1912? Or are they *kinds of events,* like smoking cigarettes and getting lung cancer? As it turns out, trying to understand causation as a relation between particular objects or events is quite a different task than trying to understand it as relation between *kinds* of occurrences or events.

Second, one wants a theory to clarify, explain, or illuminate those properties of causation that one can agree are central. For example, whatever causation is, it has a direction. Warm weather causes people to wear lighter clothing, but wearing lighter clothing does not cause warm weather. A theory that fails to capture the *asymmetry of causation* will be unsatisfying.

Third, one knows that in many cases one thing can occur regularly *before* another, and thus appear to be related as cause and effect, but is in fact the effect of a common cause, a phenomenon called *spurious causation.* For example, flashes of lightning appear just before and seem to cause the thunderclaps that follow them, but in reality both are effects of a common cause: the superheating of air molecules from the massive static electric discharge between the earth and the atmosphere. A good theory of causation ought to successfully separate cases of real from spurious causation.

The history of thinking on causation from 1970 to 2004 can be organized in many ways, but the one that separates matters best, both temporally and conceptually, is captured eloquently by Clark Glymour:

Philosophical theories come chiefly in two flavors, Socratic and Euclidean. Socratic philosophical theories, whose paradigm is *The Meno,* advance an analysis (sometimes called an "explication"), a set of purportedly necessary and sufficient conditions for some concept, giving its meaning; in justification they consider examples, putative counterexamples, alternative analyses and relations to other concepts. Euclidean philosophical theories, whose paradigm is *The Elements,* advance assumptions, considerations taken to warrant them, and investigate the consequences of the assumptions. Socratic theories have the form of definitions. Analyses of "virtue," "cause," "knowledge," "confirmation," "explanation," are ancient and recent examples. Euclidian theories have the form of formal or informal axiomatic systems and are often essentially mathematical: Euclid's geometry, Frege's

EVENT CAUSATION VERSUS CAUSAL GENERALIZATIONS

Legal cases and accident investigations usually deal with a particular event and ask what caused it. For example, when in February 2003 the space shuttle *Columbia* burned up during reentry, investigators looked for the cause of the disaster. In the end, they concluded that a chunk of foam insulation that had broken off and hit the wing during launch was the cause of a rupture in the insulating tiles, which was the cause of the shuttle's demise during reentry. Philosophers call this *event causation,* or *actual causation,* or *token-causation.*

Policy makers, statisticians, and social scientists usually deal with *kinds* of events, like graduating from college, or becoming a smoker, or playing lots of violent video games. For example, epidemiologists in the 1950s and 1960s looked for the kind of event that was causing a large number of people to get lung cancer, and they identified smoking as a primary cause. Philosophers call this *type-causation,* or *causal generalization,* or *causation among variables.*

The properties of causal relationships are different for actual causation and for causal generalizations. Actual causation is typically considered transitive, antisymmetrical, and irreflexive. If we are willing to say that one event A, say the *Titanic* hitting an iceberg on 12 April 1912,

caused another event B, its hull ripping open below the water line and taking on water moments later, which in turn caused a third event C, its sinking a few hours later, then surely we should be willing to say that event A (hitting the iceberg) caused event C (sinking). So actual causation is transitive. (Plenty of philosophers disagree, for example, see the work of Christopher Hitchcock.) It is antisymmetrical because of how we view time. If a particular event A caused a later event B, then B did not cause A. Finally, single events do not cause themselves, so causation between particular events is irreflexive.

Causal generalizations, however, are usually but not always transitive, definitely not antisymmetrical, and definitely not irreflexive. In some cases causal generalizations *are* symmetrical, for example, confidence causes success, and success causes confidence, but in others they are not, for example, warm weather causes people to wear less clothing, but wearing less clothing does not cause the weather to warm. So causal generalizations are *asymmetrical,* not antisymmetrical, like actual causation. When they are symmetrical, causal generalizations are reflexive. Success breeds more success and so forth.

---

logic, Kolmogorov's probabilities, ... That of course does not mean that Euclidean theories do not also contain definitions, but their definitions are not philosophical analyses of concepts. Nor does it mean that the work of Euclidean theories is confined to theorem proving: axioms may be reformulated to separate and illuminate their contents or to provide justifications (n.p.).

For causation, Socratic-style analyses dominated from approximately 1970 to the mid-1980s. By then, it had become apparent that all such theories either invoked noncausal primitives that were more metaphysically mysterious than causation itself, or were circular, or were simply unable to account for the asymmetry of causation or to separate spurious from real causation. Slowly, Euclidean style theories replaced Socratic ones, and by the early 1990s a rich axiomatic theory of causation had emerged that combined insights from statisticians, computer scientists, philosophers, economists, psychologists, social scientists, biologists, and even epidemiologists.

The 1970s and Early 1980s: The Age of Causal Analyses

Several different analyses of causation were given serious attention in the 1970s. One school gave an account based on counterfactuals, another used Hume's idea of regularity or constant conjunction, still another attempted to reduce causation to probabilistic relations and another to physical processes interacting spatiotemporally, and yet another was founded on the idea of manipulability.

The counterfactual theory. In the late 1960s Robert Stalnaker began the rigorous study of sentences that assert what are called *contrary-to-fact conditionals.* For example, "If the September 11, 2001, terrorist attacks on the United States had not happened, then the United States would not have invaded Afghanistan shortly thereafter." In his classic 1973 book *Counterfactuals,* David Lewis produced what has become the most popular account of such statements. Lewis's theory rests on two ideas: the existence of alternative "possible worlds" and a similarity metric over these worlds. For example, it is intuitive

---

OVERDETERMINATION AND PREEMPTION

A spy, setting out to cross the desert with some key intelligence, fills his canteen with just enough water for the crossing and settles down for a quick nap. While he is asleep, Enemy A sneaks into his tent and pokes a very small hole in the canteen, and a short while later enemy B sneaks in and adds a tasteless poison. The spy awakes, forges ahead into the desert, and when he goes to drink from his canteen discovers it is empty and dies of thirst before he can get water. What was the cause of the spy's death? According to the counterfactual theory, neither enemy's action caused the death. If enemy A had not poked a hole in the canteen, then the spy still would have died by poison. If enemy B had not put poison into the canteen, then he still would have died from thirst. Their actions overdetermined the spy's death, and the pinprick from enemy A preempted the poison from enemy B.

In the beginning of the movie *Magnolia*, a classic causal conundrum is dramatized. A fifteen-year-old boy goes up to the roof of his ten-story apartment building, ponders the abyss, and jumps to his death. Did he commit suicide? It turns out that construction workers had installed netting the day before that would have saved him from the fall, but as he is falling past the fifth story, a gun is shot from inside the building by his mother, and the bullet kills the boy instantly. Did his mother murder her son? As it turns out, his mother fired the family rifle at his drunk stepfather but missed and shot her son by mistake. She fired the gun every week at approximately that time after their horrific regular argument, which the boy cited as his reason for attempting suicide, but the gun was usually not loaded. This week the boy secretly loaded the gun without telling his parents, presumably with the intent of causing the death of his stepfather. Did he, then, in fact commit suicide, albeit unintentionally?

---

that the possible world identical to our own in all details except for the spelling of my wife's middle name ("Anne" instead of "Ann") is closer to the actual world than one in which the asteroid that killed the dinosaurs missed the earth and primates never evolved from mammals.

For Lewis, the meaning and truth of counterfactuals depend on our similarity metric over possible worlds. When we say "if A had not happened, then B would not have happened either," we mean that for each possible world W_1 in which A did not happen and B did happen, there is at least one world W_2 in which A did not happen and B did not happen that is *closer* to the actual world than W_1. Lewis represents counterfactual dependence with the symbol: $\square \rightarrow$, so $P \square \rightarrow Q$ means that, among all the worlds in which P happens, there is a world in which Q also happens that is closer to the actual world than all the worlds in which Q does not.

That there is some connection between counterfactuals and causation seems obvious. We see one event A followed by another B. What do we mean when we say A caused B? We might well mean that if A had not happened, then B would not have happened either. If the *Titanic* had not hit an iceberg, it would not have sunk. Formalizing this intuition in 1973, Lewis analyzed causation as a relation between two events A and B that both occurred such that two counterfactuals hold:

1. $A \square \rightarrow B$, and

2. $\sim A \square \rightarrow \sim B$

Because both A and B already occurred, the first is trivially true, so we need only assess the second in order to assess whether A caused B.

Is this analysis satisfactory? Even if possible worlds and a similarity metric among them are clearer and less metaphysically mysterious than causal claims, which many dispute, there are two major problems with this account of causation. First, in its original version it just misses cases of overdetermination or preemption, that is, cases in which more than one cause was present and could in fact have produced the effect.

Even more importantly, Lewis's counterfactual theory has a very hard time with the asymmetry of causality and only a slightly better time with the problem of spurious causation. Consider a man George who jumps off the Brooklyn Bridge and plunges into the East River. (This example is originally from Horacio Arlo-Costa and is discussed in Hausman, 1998, pp. 116–117.) On Lewis's theory, it is clear that it was jumping that caused George to plunge into the river, because had George not jumped, the world in which he did not plunge is closer to the actual one than any in which he just happened to plunge for some other reason at approximately the same time. Fair enough. But consider the opposite direction: if George had not plunged, then he would not have jumped. Should we assent to this counterfactual? Is a world in which George did not plunge into the river and did not jump closer to the real one than any in which he did not plunge but did jump? Most everyone except Lewis and his followers would say yes. Thus on Lewis's account jumping off the bridge caused George to plunge into the river, but plunging into the river (as distinct from the idea or goal of plunging into the river) also caused George to jump. (Lewis and many others have amended the counterfactual account of causation to handle problems of overdetermination and preemption, but no account has yet satisfactorily handled the asymmetry of causality.)

For the problem of spurious causation, consider Johnny, who gets infected with the measles virus, runs a fever, and shortly thereafter gets a rash. Is it reasonable to assert that if Johnny had not gotten a fever, he would not have gotten a rash? Yes, but it was not the fever that caused the rash, it was the measles virus. Lewis later responded to this problem by prohibiting "backtracking" and to the problem of overdetermination and preemption with an analysis of "influence," but the details are beyond our scope.

Mackie's regularity account.
Where David Lewis tried to base causation on counterfactuals, John Mackie tried to extend Hume's idea that causes and effects are "constantly conjoined" and to use the logical idea of necessary and sufficient conditions to make things clear. In 1974 Mackie published an analysis of causation in some part aimed at solving the problems that plagued Lewis's counterfactual analysis, namely overdetermination and preemption. Mackie realized that *many* factors combine to produce an effect, and it is only our idiosyncratic sense of what is "normal" that draws our attention to one particular feature of the situation, such as hitting the iceberg. It is a set of factors, for example, A: air with sufficient oxygen, B: a dry pile of combustible newspaper and kindling, and C: a lit match that *combine* to cause D: a fire. Together the *set* of factors A, B, and C are *sufficient* for D, but there might be other sets that would work just as well, for example A, B, and F: a bolt of lightning. If there were a fire caused by a lit match, but a bolt of lightning occurred that also would have started the fire, then Lewis's account has trouble saying that the lit match caused the fire, because the fire would have started without the lit match; or put another way, the match was not necessary for starting the fire. Mackie embraces this idea and says that X is a cause of Y just in case X is an Insufficient but Necessary part of an Unnecessary but Sufficient *set* of conditions for Y, that is, an INUS condition. The set of conditions that produced Y need not be the only sufficient set, thus the set is not necessary, but X should be an essential part of a set that is sufficient for Y.

Again, however, the asymmetry of causality and the problem of spurious causation wreak havoc with Mackie's INUS account of causation. Before penicillin, approximately 10 percent of those people who contracted syphilis eventually developed a debilitating disease called paresis, and nothing doctors could measure seemed to tell them anything about which syphilitics developed paresis and which did not. As far as is known, paresis can result only from syphilis, so having paresis is by itself sufficient for having syphilis. Consider applying Mackie's account to this case. Paresis *is* an INUS condition of syphilis, because it is sufficient by itself for having syphilis, but it is surely not a cause of it.

Consider the measles. If we suppose that when people are infected they either show both symptoms (the fever and rash) or their immune system controls it and they show neither, then the INUS theory gets things wrong. The fever is a necessary part of a set that is sufficient for the rash: {fever, infected with measles virus}, and for that matter the rash is a necessary part of a set that is sufficient for fever: {rash, infected with measles virus}. So, unfortunately, on this analysis fever is an INUS cause of rash and rash is also a cause of fever.

Probabilistic causality.
Twentieth-century physics has had a profound effect on a wide range of ideas, including theories of causation. In the years between about 1930 and 1970 the astounding and unabated success of quantum mechanics forced most physicists to accept the idea that, at bedrock, the material universe unfolds probabilistically. Past states of subatomic particles, no matter how finely described, do not determine their future states, they merely determine the probability of such future states. Embracing this brave new world in 1970, Patrick Suppes published a theory of causality that attempted to reduce causation to probability. Whereas electrons have only a propensity, that is, an objective physical probability to be measured at a particular location at a particular time, perhaps macroscopic events like developing lung cancer have only a probability as well. We observe that some events seem to quite dramatically change the probability of other events, however, so perhaps causes *change the probability* of their effects. If $Pr(E)$, the probability of an event E, changes given that another event C has occurred, notated $Pr(E \mid C)$, then we say E and C are *associated*. If not, then we say they are *independent*. Suppes was quite familiar with the problem of asymmetry, and he was well aware that association and independence are perfectly symmetrical, that is, $Pr(E) = Pr(E \mid C) \Leftrightarrow Pr(C) = Pr(C \mid E)$. He was also familiar with the problem of spurious causation and knew that two effects of a common cause could appear associated. To handle asymmetry and spurious causation, he used time and the idea of *conditional* independence. His theory of probabilistic causation is simple and elegant:

1. C is a prima facie cause of E if C occurs before E in time, and C and E are associated, that is, $Pr(E) < Pr(E \mid C)$.

2. C is a *genuine cause* of E if C is a prima facie cause of E, and there is *no* event Z prior to C such that C and E are independent conditional on Z, that is, there is *no* Z such that $Pr(E \mid Z) = Pr(E \mid Z, C)$.

Without doubt, the idea of handling the problem of spurious causation by looking for other events Z that *screen off* C and E, although anticipated by Hans Reichenbach, Irving John Good, and others, was a real breakthrough and remains a key feature of any metaphysical or epistemological account that connects causation to probability. Many other writers have elaborated a probabilistic theory of causation with metaphysical aspirations, for example, Ellery Eells, David Papineau, Brian Skyrms, and Wolfgang Spohn.

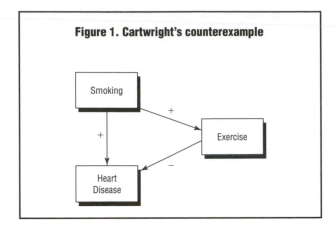

Figure 1. Cartwright's counterexample

SOURCE: Courtesy of the author

Probabilistic accounts have drawn criticism on several fronts. First, defining causation in terms of probability just replaces one mystery with another. Although we have managed to produce a mathematically rigorous theory of probability, the core of which is now widely accepted, we have not managed to produce a reductive metaphysics of probability. It is still as much a mystery as causation. Second, there is something unsatisfying about using time explicitly to handle the asymmetry of causation and at least part of the problem of spurious causation (we can only screen off spurious causes with a Z that is prior in time to C).

Third, as Nancy Cartwright persuasively argued in 1979, we cannot define causation with probabilities alone, we need causal concepts in the definiens (definition) as well as the definiendum (expression being defined). Consider her famous (even if implausible) hypothetical example, shown in Figure 1: smoking might cause more heart disease, but it might also cause exercise, which in turn might cause *less* heart disease. If the negative effect of exercise on heart disease is stronger than the positive effect of smoking and the association between smoking and exercise is high enough, then the probability of heart disease given smoking could be *lower* than the probability of heart disease given not smoking, making it appear as though smoking prevents heart disease instead of causing it.

The two effects could also exactly cancel, making smoking and heart disease look independent. Cartwright's solution is to look at the relationship between smoking and heart disease within groups that are doing the same amount of exercise, that is, to look at the relationship between smoking and heart disease *conditional* on exercise, even though exercise does not in this example come before smoking, as Suppes insists it should. Why does Suppes not allow Zs that are prior to E but after C in time? Because that would allow situations in which although C really does cause E, its influence was entirely mediated by Z, and by conditioning on Z it appears as if C is *not* a genuine cause of E, even though it is (Fig. 2).

In Cartwright's language: Smoking should increase the probability of heart disease in *all causally homogeneous situations* for heart disease. The problem is circularity. By referring to the causally homogeneous situations, we invoke causation in our definition. The moral Cartwright drew, and one that is now widely accepted, is that causation is *connected* to probability but cannot be *defined* in terms of it.

Salmon's physical process theory. A wholly different account of causation comes from Wes Salmon, one of the preeminent philosophers of science in the later half of the twentieth century. In the 1970s Salmon developed a theory of scientific explanation that foundered partly on an asymmetry very similar to the asymmetry of causation. Realizing that causes explain their effects but not vice versa, Salmon made the connection between explanation and causation explicit. He then went on to characterize causation as an interaction between two *physical processes*, not a probabilistic or logical or counterfactual relationship between events. A *causal interaction*, according to Salmon, is the intersection of two *causal processes* and the exchange of some invariant quantity, like momentum. For example, two pool balls that collide each change direction (and perhaps speed), but their total momentum after the collision is (ideally) no different than before. An interaction has taken place, but momentum is conserved. Explaining the features of a causal process is beyond the scope of such a short review article, but Phil Dowe has made them quite accessible and extremely clear in a 2000 review article in the *British Journal for Philosophy of Science*.

It turns out to be very difficult to distinguish real causal processes from psuedo-processes, but even accepting Salmon's and Dowe's criteria, the theory uses time to handle the asymmetry of causation and has big trouble with the problem of spurious causation. Again, see Dowe's excellent review article for details.

Manipulability theories. Perhaps the most tempting strategy for understanding causation is to conceive of it as how the world responds to an intervention or manipulation. Consider a well-insulated, closed room containing two people. The room temperature is 58 degrees Fahrenheit, and each person has a sweater on. Later the room temperature is 78 degrees Fahrenheit and each person has taken his or her sweater off. If we ask whether it was the rise in room temperature that caused the people to peel off their sweaters or the peeling off of sweaters that caused the room temperature to rise, then unless there was some strange signal between the taking off of sweaters and turning up a thermostat somewhere, the answer is obvious. Manipulating the room temperature from 58 to 78 degrees will cause people to take off their sweaters, but manipulating them to take off their sweaters will not make the room heat up.

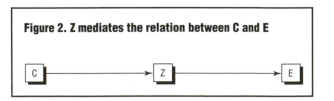

Figure 2. Z mediates the relation between C and E

SOURCE: Courtesy of the author

In general, causes can be used to control their effects, but effects cannot be used to control their causes. Further, there is an invariance between a cause and its effects that does not hold between an effect and its causes. It does not seem to matter *how* we change the temperature in the room from 58 to 78 degrees or from 78 to 58, the co-occurrence between room temperature and sweaters remains. When the temperature is 58, people have sweaters on. When the temperature is 78, they do not. The opposite is not true for the relationship between the effect and its causes. It *does* matter how they come to have their sweaters on. If we let them decide for themselves naturally, then the co-occurrence between sweaters and temperature will remain, but if we intervene to make them take their sweaters off or put them on, then we will annihilate any co-occurrence between wearing sweaters and the room temperature precisely because the room temperature will not *respond* to whether or not people are wearing sweaters. Thus manipulability accounts handle the asymmetry problem.

They do the same for the problem of spurious causation. Tar-stained fingers and lung cancer are both effects of a common cause—smoking. Intervening to remove the stains from one's fingers will not in any way change the probability of getting lung cancer, however.

The philosophical problem with manipulability accounts is circularity, for what is it to "intervene" and "manipulate" other than to "cause"? Intervening to set the thermostat to 78 is just to cause it to be set at 78. Manipulation is causation, so defining causation in terms of manipulation is, at least on the surface of it, circular.

Perhaps we can escape from this circularity by separating human actions from natural ones. Perhaps forming an intention and then acting to execute it *is* special, and *could* be used as a noncausal primitive in a reductive theory of causation. Writers like George Henrik von Wright have pursued this line. Others, like Paul Holland, have gone so far as to say that we have no causation without human manipulation. But is this reasonable or desirable? Virtually all physicists would agree that it is the moon's gravity that causes the tides. Yet we cannot manipulate the moon's position or its gravity. Are we to abandon all instances of causation where human manipulation was not involved? If a painting falls off the wall and hits the thermostat, bumping it up from 58 to 78 degrees, and a half hour later sweaters come off, are we satisfied saying that the sequence: thermostat goes up, room temperature goes up, sweaters come off was not causal?

Because they failed as reductive theories of causation, manipulability theories drew much less attention than perhaps they should have. As James Woodward elegantly puts it:

Philosophical discussion has been unsympathetic to manipulability theories: it is claimed both that they are unilluminatingly circular and that they lead to an implausibly anthropocentric and subjectivist conception of causation. This negative assessment among philosophers contrasts sharply with the widespread view among statisticians, theorists of experimental design, and many social and natural scientists that an appreciation of the

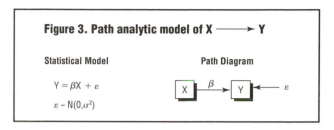

Figure 3. Path analytic model of X ⟶ Y

Statistical Model

$Y = \beta X + \varepsilon$

$\varepsilon \sim N(0, \sigma^2)$

Path Diagram

$X \xrightarrow{\beta} Y \longleftarrow \varepsilon$

SOURCE: Courtesy of the author

connection between causation and manipulation can play an important role in clarifying the meaning of causal claims and understanding their distinctive features. (p. 25)

The Axiomatic and Epistemological Turn: 1985–2004
Although there will always be those unwilling to give up on a reductive analysis of causation, by the mid-1980s it was reasonably clear that such an account was not forthcoming. What has emerged as an alternative, however, is a rich axiomatic theory that clarifies the role of manipulation in much the way Woodward wants and connects rather than reduces causation to probabilistic independence, as Nancy Cartwright insisted. The modern theory of causation is truly interdisciplinary and fundamentally epistemological in focus. That is, it allows a rigorous and systematic investigation of what can and cannot be learned about causation from statistical evidence. Its intellectual beginnings go back to at least the early twentieth century.

Path analysis. Sometime around 1920 the brilliant geneticist Sewall Wright realized that standard statistical tools were too thin to represent the causal mechanisms he wanted to model. He invented "path analysis" to fill the gap. Path analytic models are causal graphs (like those shown in Figs. 1 and 2) that quantify the strength of each arrow, or direct cause, which allowed Wright to quantify and estimate from data the relative strength of two or more mechanisms by which one quantity might affect another. By midcentury prominent economists (e.g., Herbert Simon and Herman Wold) and sociologists (e.g., Hubert Blalock and Otis Dudley Duncan) had adopted this representation. In several instances they made important contributions, either by expanding the representational power of path models or by articulating how one might distinguish one causal model from another with statistical evidence.

Path models, however, did nothing much to help model the asymmetry of causation.

In the simplest possible path model representing that X is a cause of Y (Fig. 3), we write Y as a linear function of X and an "error" term (that represents all other unobserved causes of Y besides X. The real-valued coefficient β quantifies X's effect on Y. Nothing save convention, however, prevents us from inverting the equation and rewriting the statistical model as:

$$X = \alpha Y + \delta, \text{ where } \alpha = 1/\beta \text{ and } \delta = -1/\beta\ \varepsilon$$

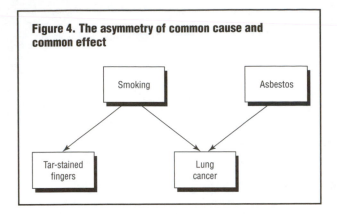

Figure 4. The asymmetry of common cause and common effect

Smoking

Asbestos

Tar-stained fingers

Lung cancer

SOURCE: Courtesy of the author

This algebraically equivalent model makes it appear as if Y is the cause of X instead of vice versa. Equations are symmetrical, but causation is not.

Philosophy. In the early 1980s two philosophers of causation, David Papineau and Daniel Hausman, paying no real attention to path analysis, nevertheless provided major insights into how to incorporate causal asymmetry into path models and probabilistic accounts of causation. Papineau, in a 1985 article titled "Causal Asymmetry," considered the difference between (1) two effects of a common cause and (2) two causes of a common effect (Fig. 4). He argued that two effects of a common cause (tar-stained fingers and lung cancer) are *associated* in virtue of having a common cause (smoking) but that two causes of a common effect (smoking and asbestos) are not associated in virtue of having a common effect (lung cancer). In fact he could have argued that the two effects of a common cause C *are* associated in virtue of C, but are *independent* conditional on C, whereas the two causes of a common effect E *are not* associated in virtue of E but *are associated* conditional on E.

Daniel Hausman, in a 1984 article (and more fully in a 1998 book *Causal Asymmetries*), generalized this insight still further by developing a theory of causal asymmetry based on "causal connection." X and Y are *causally connected* if and only if X is a cause of Y, Y a cause of X, or there is some common cause of both X and Y. Hausman connects causation to probability by assuming that two quantities are associated if they are causally connected and independent if they are not. How does he get the asymmetry of causation? By showing that when X is a cause of Y, anything else causally connected to X is also connected to Y but not vice versa.

Papineau and Hausman handle the asymmetry of causation by considering not just the relationship between the cause and effect but rather by considering the way a cause and effect relate to other quantities in an expanded system. How does this help locate the asymmetry in the path analytic representation of causation? First, consider the apparent symmetry in the statistical model in Figure 3. X and ε are not causally connected and have Y as a common effect. Thus following both Papineau and Hausman, we will assume that X and ε are independent and that in any path model properly representing

a direct causal relation C $\rightarrow$ E, C and the error term for E will be independent. But now consider the equation X = α Y + δ, which we used to make it appear that Y$\rightarrow$ X. Because of the way δ is defined, Y and δ will be associated, except for extremely rare cases.

Statistics and computer science. Path analytic models have two parts, a path diagram and a statistical model. A path diagram is just a directed graph, a mathematical object very familiar to computer scientists and somewhat familiar to statisticians. As we have seen, association and independence are intimately connected to causation, and they happen to be one of the fundamental topics in probability and statistics.

Paying little attention to causation, in the 1970s and early 1980s the statisticians Phil Dawid, David Spiegelhalter, Nanny Wermuth, David Cox, Steffen Lauritzen, and others developed a branch of statistics called *graphical models* that represented the independence relationships among a set of random variables with undirected and directed graphs. Computer scientists interested in studying how robots might learn began to use graphical models to represent and selectively update their uncertainty about the world, especially Judea Pearl and his colleagues at the University of California, Los Angeles (UCLA). By the late 1980s Pearl had developed a very powerful theory of reasoning with uncertainty using Bayesian Networks and the Directed Acyclic Graphs (DAGs) attached to them. Although in 1988 he eschewed interpreting Bayesian Networks causally, Pearl made a major epistemological breakthrough by beginning the study of indistinguishability. He and Thomas Verma characterized when two Bayesian Networks with different DAGs entail the same independencies and are thus empirically indistinguishable on evidence consisting of independence relations.

Philosophy again. In the mid-1980s Peter Spirtes, Clark Glymour, and Richard Scheines (SGS hereafter), philosophers working at Carnegie Mellon, recognized that path analysis was a special case of Pearl's theory of DAGs. Following Hausman, Papineau, Cartwright, and others trying to connect rather than reduce causation to probabilistic independence, they explicitly axiomatized the connection between causation and probabilistic independence in accord with Pearl's theory and work by the statisticians Harry Kiiveri and Terrence Speed. Their theory of causation is explicitly nonreductionist. Instead of trying to define causation in terms of probability, counterfactuals, or some other relation, they are intentionally agnostic about the metaphysics of the subject. Instead, their focus is on the epistemology of causation, in particular on exploring what can and cannot be learned about causal structure from statistics concerning independence and association. SGS formulate several axioms connecting causal structure to probability, but one is central:

Causal Markov Axiom: Every variable is probabilistically independent of all of its noneffects (direct or indirect), conditional on its immediate causes.

The axiom has been the source of a vigorous debate (see the *British Journal for the Philosophy of Science* between 1999

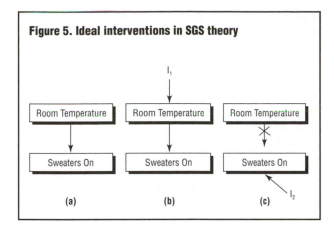

Figure 5. Ideal interventions in SGS theory

(a)　(b)　(c)

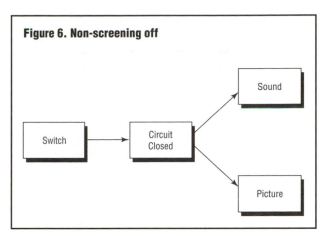

Figure 6. Non-screening off

and 2002), but it is only half of the SGS theory. The second half involves explicitly modeling the idea of a manipulation or intervention. All manipulability theories conceive of interventions as coming from outside the system. SGS model an intervention by adding a new variable external to the system that

1. is a direct cause of exactly the variable it targets and

2. is the effect of no variable in the system

and by assuming that the resulting system still satisfies the Causal Markov Axiom.

If the intervention completely determines the variable it targets, then the intervention is *ideal*. Since an ideal intervention determines its target and thus overrides any influence the variable might have gotten from its other causes, SGS model the intervened system by "x-ing out" the arrows into the variable ideally intervened upon. In Figure 5a, for example, we show the causal graph relating room temperature and wearing sweaters. In Figure 5b we show the system in which we have intervened upon room temperature with I_1 and in Figure 5c the system after an ideal intervention I_2 on sweaters on.

This basic perspective on causation, elaborated powerfully and presented elegantly by Judea Pearl (2000), has also been adopted by other prominent computer scientists (David Heckerman and Greg Cooper), psychologists (Alison Gopnik and Patricia Cheng), economists (David Bessler, Clive Granger, and Kevin Hoover), epidemiologists (Sander Greenland and Jamie Robins), biologists (William Shipley), statisticians (Steffen Lauritzen, Thomas Richardson, and Larry Wasserman), and philosophers (James Woodward and Daniel Hausman).

How is the theory epistemological? Researchers have been able to characterize precisely, for many different sets of assumptions above and beyond the Causal Markov Axiom, the class of causal systems that is empirically indistinguishable, and they have also been able to automate discovery procedures that can efficiently search for such indistinguishable classes of models, including models with hidden common causes. Even in

such cases, we can still sometimes tell just from the independencies and associations among the variables measured that one variable is not a cause of another, that two variables are effects of an unmeasured common cause, or that one variable is a definite cause of another. We even have an algorithm for deciding, from data and the class of models that are indistinguishable on these data, when the effect of an intervention *can* be predicted and when it cannot.

Like anything new, the theory has its detractors. The philosopher Nancy Cartwright, although having herself contributed heavily to the axiomatic theory, has been a vocal critic of its core axiom, the Causal Markov Axiom. Cartwright maintains that common causes do not always screen off their effects. Her chief counterexample involves a chemical factory, but the example is formally identical to another that is easier to understand. Consider a TV with a balky on/off switch. When turned to "on," the switch does not always make the picture and sound come on, but whenever it makes the sound come on, it also makes the picture come on (Fig. 6). The problem is this: knowing the state of the switch does not make the sound and the picture independent. Even having been told that the switch is on, for example, also being told that the sound is on adds information about whether the picture is also on.

The response of SGS and many others (e.g., Hausman and Woodward) is that it only appears as if we do not have screening off because we are not conditioning on *all* the common causes, especially those more proximate to the effects in question. They argue that we must condition on the Circuit Closed, and not just on the Switch, in order to screen off Sound and Picture.

A deeper puzzle along these same lines arises from quantum mechanics. A famous thought experiment, called the Einstein-Podolosky-Rosen experiment, considered a coupled system of quantum particles that are separated gently and allowed to diverge. Each particle is in superposition, that is, it *has no definite spin until it is measured*. J. S. Bell's famous inequality shows that no matter how far apart we allow them to drift, the measurements on one particle will be highly correlated with

THE ASYMMETRY OF CAUSATION THROUGH CAUSAL CONNECTION

Two variables A and B are "causally connected" if either A is a cause of B, B a cause of A, or a third variable causes them both. If causation is transitive, then it turns out that everything causally connected to X is connected to its effects, but not everything connected to Y is connected to its causes. When X → Y, everything causally connected to X is causally connected to Y (Fig. 7a), but something causally connected to Y is *not* necessarily causally connected to X (Fig. 7b).

Figure 7. The asymmetry in the transitivity of causal connection

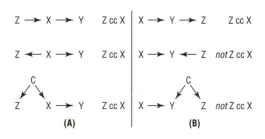

SOURCE: Courtesy of the author

the other, even after we condition on the state of the original coupled system. There are no extra hidden variables (common causes) we could introduce to screen off the measurements of the distant particles. Although the details are quite important and nothing if not controversial, it looks as if the Causal Markov Axiom might not hold in quantum mechanical systems. Why it should hold in macroscopic systems when it might not hold for their constituents is a mystery.

The SGS model of an intervention incorporates many controversial assumptions. In a 2003 tour de force, however, James Woodward works through all the philosophical reasons why the basic model of intervention adopted by the interdisciplinary view is reasonable. For example, Woodward considers why a manipulation must be modeled as a direct cause of only the variable it targets. Not just *any* manipulation of our roomful of sweater-wearing people will settle the question of whether sweater wearing causes the room temperature. If we make people take off their sweaters by blowing super-hot air on them—sufficient to also heat the room—then we have not *independently* manipulated just the sweaters. Similarly, if we are testing to see if confidence improves athletic performance, we cannot intervene to improve confidence with a muscle relaxant that also reduces motor coordination. These manipula-

tions are "fat hand"—they directly cause more than they should.

Woodward covers many issues like this one and develops a rich philosophical theory of intervention that is not reductive but is illuminating and rigorously connects the wide range of ideas that have been associated with causation. For example, the idea of an independent manipulation illuminates and solves the problems we pointed out earlier when discussing the counterfactual theory of causation. Instead of assessing counterfactuals like (1) George would not have plunged into the East River had he not jumped off the Brooklyn Bridge and (2) George would not have jumped off the bridge had he not plunged into the East River, we should assess counterfactuals about manipulations: (1′) George would not have plunged into the East River had he been independently manipulated to not jump off the Brooklyn Bridge and (2′) George would not have jumped off the bridge had he been independently manipulated not to have plunged into the East River. The difference is in how we interpret "independently manipulated." In the case of 2′ we mean if we assign George to not plunging but leave everything else as it was, for example, if we catch George just before he dunks. In this way of conceiving of the counterfactual, George *would* have jumped off the bridge, and so we can recover the asymmetry of causation once we augment the counterfactual theory with the idea of an independent manipulation, as Woodward argues.

Conclusion

Although the whirlwind tour in this short article is woefully inadequate, the references below (and especially their bibliographies) should be sufficient to point interested readers to the voluminous literature on causation produced in the late twentieth century and early twenty-first century. Although the literature is vast and somewhat inchoate, it is safe to say that no reductive analysis of causation has emerged still afloat and basically seaworthy. What has been described here as the interdisciplinary theory of causation takes direct causation as a primitive, defines intervention from direct causation, and then connects causal systems to probabilities and statistical evidence through axioms, including the Causal Markov Axiom. Although it provides little comfort for those hoping to analyze causation Socratically, the theory does open the topic of causal epistemology in a way that has affected statistical and scientific practice, hopefully for the better. Surely that is some progress.

See also **Empiricism; Epistemology; Logic; Quantum; Rationalism.**

BIBLIOGRAPHY

Bell, J. "On the Einstein-Podolsky-Rosen Paradox." *Physics* 1 (1964): 195–200.

Cartwright, Nancy. "Against Modularity, the Causal Markov Condition, and Any Link between the Two." *British Journal for Philosophy of Science* 53 (2002): 411–453.

———. "Causal Laws and Effective Strategies." *Noûs* 13 (1979).

———. *How the Laws of Physics Lie.* New York: Oxford University Press. 1983.

———. *Nature's Capacities and Their Measurement.* New York: Oxford University Press, 1989.

Dowe, Phil. "Causality and Explanation." *British Journal for Philosophy of Science* 51 (2000): 165–174.

Glymour, Clark. "Review of James Woodward, *Making Things Happen: A Theory of Causal Explanation.*" *British Journal for Philosophy of Science.* Forthcoming.

Hausman, Daniel. *Causal Asymmetries.* New York: Cambridge University Press, 1998.

———. "Causal Priority." *Noûs* 18 (1984): 261–279.

Halpern, J., and Judea Pearl. "Actual Causality." *IJCAI Proceedings.* 2002.

Hitchcock, C. "The Intransitivity of Causation Revealed in Equations and Graphs." *Journal of Philosophy* 98 (2001): 273–299.

———. "Of Humean Bondage." *British Journal for Philosophy of Science* 54 (2003): 1–25.

Holland, Paul. "Statistics and Causal Inference." *Journal of the American Statistical Association* 81 (1986): 945–960.

Kiiveri, H., and T. Speed. "Structural Analysis of Multivariate Data: A Review." In *Sociological Methodology,* edited by S. Leinhardt. San Francisco: Jossey-Bass, 1982.

Lauritzen, Steffen. *Graphical Models.* New York: Oxford University Press, 1996.

Lewis, David. "Causation as Influence." *Journal of Philosophy* 97 (2000): 182–197.

———. *Counterfactuals.* Cambridge, Mass.: Harvard University Press, 1973.

Mackie, John. *The Cement of the Universe.* New York: Oxford University Press, 1974.

McKim, S., and S. Turner. *Causality in Crisis? Statistical Methods and the Search for Causal Knowledge in the Social Sciences.* Notre Dame, Ind.: University of Notre Dame Press, 1997.

Meek, C., and C. Glymour. "Conditioning and Intervening." *British Journal for Philosophy of Science* 45 (1994): 1001–1021.

Papineau, David. "Causal Asymmetry." *British Journal for Philosophy of Science* 36 (1985): 273–289.

Pearl, Judea. *Causality: Models, Reasoning, and Inference.* New York: Cambridge University Press, 2000.

———. *Probabilistic Reasoning in Intelligent Systems.* San Mateo, Calif.: Morgan and Kaufman, 1988.

Reichenbach, Hans. *The Direction of Time.* Berkeley: University of California Press, 1956.

Salmon, Wes. *Scientific Explanation and the Causal Structure of the World.* Princeton, N.J.: Princeton University Press, 1984.

Simon, Herbert. "Spurious Correlation: A Causal Interpretation." *JASA* 49 (1954): 467–479.

Spirtes, Peter, Clark Glymour, and Richard Scheines. *Causation, Prediction, and Search.* 2nd ed. Cambridge, Mass.: MIT Press, 2000.

Spohn, Wolfgang. "Deterministic and Probabilistic Reasons and Causes." *Erkenntnis* 19 (1983): 371–396.

Suppes, Patrick. *A Probabilistic Theory of Causality.* Amsterdam: North-Holland, 1970.

Woodward, James. *Making Things Happen: A Theory of Causal Explanation.* Oxford: Oxford University Press, 2003.

Wright, Sewall. "The Method of Path Coefficients." *Annals of Mathematical Statistics* 5 (1934): 161–215.

Richard Scheines

CAUSATION IN EAST ASIAN AND SOUTHEAST ASIAN PHILOSOPHY.

Causation is defined most commonly as a relationship between two events or two states of affairs in which the first brings about the second. The idea of causation has long existed among the peoples in South and East Asia, but as a historical notion, it has taken different forms of expression in these regions.

The Influence of Buddhism in South Asia

In South Asia, where the belief in reincarnation constituted an important philosophical base for both Hinduism and Buddhism, the concept of causation played a vital role in shaping one's outlook on life and history. According to Buddhism, all forms of existence are related one way or another in an infinite and endless causal web. Thus the creation theory, which is crucial to some religions, finds no place in Buddhism. Drawing on the incarnation belief, Buddhism also connects the life of this world to the next, in which the rise or fall of one's status leading to either salvation or condemnation is dependent on the karma one accumulates in this life. Ironically, however, this causal connection between this world and the next is not necessarily conducive to the development of historical consciousness because it dwells on the mutability, fluidity, and temporality of life, which breeds an extreme relativism that negates the meaning of life itself. Indeed, while Buddhism urges one to improve one's karma in life, it also stresses, extending the broad-based belief in eschatology in South Asia, that life is merely a fleeting bubble and that the world is extinguishable ablaze. Moreover, because everything is causally related in an infinite and endless web, nothing is constant or specifically consequential to anything else. Explanation for change also becomes unnecessary.

In its later development, however, Buddhism began to value life and history, which in turn translated its idea of causation into an important contribution to the development of historical thinking. In Theravada Buddhism, hagiological need led to the development of a scholastic trend. The same need also gave rise to a new concept of time, in which the birth of Buddha became a watershed in the otherwise completely cyclical flow of time. More important, the appearance of Buddha was not considered an accidental event, but a result of the work of an inexorable, omnipresent rule or norm. All this renders the Buddhist theory of causation germane to the study of history. Buddhists continue to situate the change of history in an infinite causal relation, or an "iron chain of causality," which leads them to a multilateral and simultaneous consideration of historical causation. In the meantime, they also seek to identify the specific causes for each event. They argue that even if the result is the same, the causal relation between the result and its causes remains unique. Historical change thus is regarded as an outcome of the concatenation of a number of divergent factors coming together in a unique circumstance and relationship.

The Influence of Confucianism in East Asia

In East Asia, the conception of causation was also characterized by relativism, or by a correlative way of thinking that, in both ontology and cosmology, took what Joseph Needham called "an organistic" approach to describing the relationship between humans and their environment. This correlative thought originated from speculations on the possible impact of what happened in nature, or in Heaven, on human lives on Earth. But in its later development, particularly in the theoretical formations of yin and yang and the Five Elements/Phases (*wuxing*), it exerted a fundamental and pervasive influence on shaping the notion of causality in ancient China. Instead of searching for a linear, particulate cause, ancient Chinese approached causation in a circumambient (all-encompassing) manner, which allowed them to note an organic web of causal connection.

Out of its worldly interest and moral concerns, Confucianism appears more assertive in defining causal relations in human affairs, although it was by no means immune to the idea of a Heaven–humanity correlation in developing historical explanations. Confucius (551–479 B.C.E.), for example, believed that the rise and fall of political powers depended on the Mandate of Heaven. But dismayed by the decline of central government of his time, he nevertheless set out, after seeing the unicorn that to him suggested a mission charged by Heaven, to revise the *Spring and Autumn Annals,* hoping to bring about a punitive consequence for the unruly behaviors of officials and princes. Mencius (c. 371–c. 289 B.C.E.), devout follower of Confucius, claimed that Confucius's effort was not in vain, indicating a belief in historical causation among the Confucians in that immoral behavior is to be condemned through the course of history. Throughout early imperial China, the idea of a Heaven–humanity correlation represented a major expression of historical causation, subscribed to by Dong Zhongshu (c. 194–c. 114 B.C.E.), a political theorist, as well as by Sima Qian (c. 145–86 B.C.E.), a court historian. Dong used it to forge a theory on dynastic succession for legitimizing the reigning Han dynasty (206 B.C.E.–220 C.E.), whereas Sima used it to help structure his interpretative framework of history. While a main framework, the correlative idea did not stop Sima from searching for other temporal and coincidental causes in explaining historical change. In fact, Sima was both commended and chided for demonstrating great curiosity for the "wonders" of history in his *Shiji* (The records of history). By comparison, Ban Gu (32–92 C.E.), also a Han historian, was narrower in his interest and more rigid in his method in seeking causal explanations for history, focusing on the bond between morality and history.

Diversifying Tradition in Post-Han Era

After the fall of the Han dynasty, China's cultural tradition diversified as a result of the entrance of Buddhism, which gave rise to the expansion of Daoism and the resurgence of Confucianism. The theories of historical causation also flourished. Yet a general tendency remained identifiable, marked by the decline of the notion of a Heaven–humanity correlation. This decline was shown in the tradition, established in the seventh century, of writing official dynastic histories, which, following Ban Gu's model, purported to draw analogies from the history of previous dynasties for the benefit of the reigning dynasty. Hence the writing of dynastic historiography amounted to a serious effort to find specific causal relations in history, rather than to apply the mysterious and superstitious correlative idea. In his *Zizhi tongjian* (A comprehensive mirror of aid for government), Sima Guang (1019–1086) made a valiant at-

tempt to generalize the causes for the successes and failures of the previous rulers. Of the important ones identified by him, few were attributed to the will of Heaven.

Yet the notion of Heaven remained important. Influenced by the metaphysics of Buddhism, the Neo-Confucians of the Song period (960–1279), such as Zhu Xi (1130–1200), averred that *li* (principle), or *tianli* (heavenly principle), was the ultimate cause for the change of history, commanding the ebb and flow of good and evil times. At the same time, they searched for *tianli*'s various worldly manifestations in order to demonstrate and explain the mutability and temporality of life and history. This effort was continued by Wang Fuzhi (1619–1692) in late imperial China and Arai Hakuseki (1657–1725) of Tokugawa Japan (1603–1867). Wang and Arai discussed the concept *shi* (circumstance), which they used to underscore the uniqueness of the causal relations of historical events, an emphasis also readily identifiable in the Buddhist construction of historical causation.

See also **Buddhism; Causation; Confucianism; Hinduism.**

BIBLIOGRAPHY
Gokhale, B. G. "The Theravada-Buddhist View of History." *Journal of the American Oriental Society* 85, no. 3 (1965): 354–360.
Needham, Joseph. *History of Scientific Thought.* Vol. 2 of *Science and Civilisation in China.* Cambridge, U.K.: Cambridge University Press, 1956.
Wu, Huaiqi. *Zhongguo shixue sixiangshi.* Hefei, China: Anhui renmin chubanshe, 1996.

Q. Edward Wang

CENSORSHIP. Censorship comprises many methods of preventing the publication or dissemination of speech, printed matter, art, theater, music, electronic media, or other forms of expression. The most common subjects that are censored are religion, politics, and sex. The usual justification is that such expression is subversive, blasphemous, heretical, obscene, pornographic, or otherwise offensive or harmful. Censorship can take place before publication, known as prior restraint, in the form of requirements such as licensing and prior review. It can also take place after publication in such forms as banning, burning, or boycotting of the published product and fining, imprisonment, or the death penalty for the author or publisher.

The English term is derived from the ancient Roman institution of the censors, two elected magistrates responsible for overseeing the morals of the Roman people and who could warn or ban certain people or behavior at will. In later times censorship has often been carried out by individuals or committees appointed by religious or political authorities, but it can also be carried out by self-appointed vigilantes. The term has been expanded to include self-censorship, in which one does not express something for fear of the consequences, and market censorship, in which suppression of a publication is caused by the refusal of advertisers to advertise in it or of the public to buy it.

The political ideology of modern liberalism is generally against censorship on the ground that it limits freedom unnecessarily. By far the largest body of reflection on censorship has been written by its opponents. Those who are in a position to impose censorship have usually done it without articulating their reasons in any depth. Communitarian and autocratic ideologies such as socialism, national socialism, communism, absolute monarchism, and theocracy have generally done little more than assert that censorship protects the community and its leaders against perceived threats. In the late twentieth and early twenty-first centuries, there has been an upsurge in articulation of justifications for censorship. Radical feminists and spokespersons for ethnic, religious, or formerly colonized groups have supported censorship of pornography, "hate speech," and criticism of themselves, pointing to the harm that uncensored expression can do.

Sex has been the target of much censorship. Objectionable sexual material is variously labeled obscene, pornographic, indecent, or degrading. Obscenity has been defined as having a tendency to deprave or corrupt; as appealing to prurient interest; or as being offensive to prevailing moral standards. Pornography has been defined as explicit depiction of sexual behavior intended to cause arousal. Censorship of these matters is sometimes limited to shielding younger age-groups, and it is sometimes claimed that this type of censorship should only be applied if there is no redeeming scientific, artistic, or political value to sexual materials. Since the 1980s, censorship has been justified by the argument that pornography is equivalent to rape.

Almost no one believes in absolute freedom of expression. Libel, slander, and defamation are prohibited by nearly every legal code. These prohibitions are not usually considered to be censorship, but rather a part of tort law.

It is widely accepted that prior restraint is more effective at preventing expression than postpublication censorship. The requirement to submit items for approval may intimidate someone into not submitting something that might actually be approved or that might not attract negative attention if it were published. Postpublication punishment is rarely fully effective: the censors might miss a few items entirely, and when books or recordings that have already been published are destroyed, a few copies can often be saved surreptitiously.

Blasphemy, Heresy, and Atheism

Socrates (c. 470–399 B.C.E.) was put to death in ancient Greece for introducing new gods, among other charges. Later, the main religions introduced doctrines of blasphemy and heresy as justifications for censorship. For the Jews blasphemy meant insult to God and was closely related to idolatry. The Christians expanded the meaning to include insult to Christ, and they tended to confuse blasphemy with heresy, or theological error. There is little evidence that blasphemy was a major concern in early Islam, but in 1989 a *fatwa* in Iran called for the death penalty against the author Salman Rushdie (1947–) for blasphemy. The same year, Hindu fundamentalists issued a death threat against the historian M. M. Kalburgi for blasphemy.

In the widest meaning of heresy, the beliefs of every sect are heresies to every other sect, but it is usually the dominant orthodoxy that gets to define the heretical for practical purposes. Censorship of heresies can begin with prohibition of expression and develop through excommunication and punishment up to the death penalty. Atheism is a heresy to most religions and is sometimes considered worse than mere adherence to a mistaken religion. In ancient Greece, Anaxagoras (c. 500–c. 428 B.C.E.) was prosecuted for denying the existence of the gods.

The Catholic Church developed the most sophisticated early censoring apparatus in the form of the Inquisitions and *Index*. In 1231 the Dominican and Franciscan orders were charged with inquiry into the spread of heresy, an undertaking later known as the Inquisition. The Spanish Inquisition was instituted in 1478, and after various experiments with local inquisitions, a centralized Roman Inquisition was set up in 1542 to root out heresy. Lists of banned books were published in Paris (1544), Lucca (1545), Louvain (1546), and Venice (1549). In 1559 the first *Index of Prohibited Books* was issued at the Council of Trent, and a separate papal Congregation of the Index, set up in 1571, continued to issue an *Index* every few decades until it was abolished in 1966. Enforcement of such efforts at censorship depends in part on the climate of public opinion: in the eighteenth century, for example, sale of the *Index* was banned in Austria because people were buying it to use as a guide to reading.

Political Subversion

Because his pupils were closely allied to the oligarchy, it is arguable that the real reason for the persecution of Socrates was his political stance. Plato's *Laws* (c. 350 B.C.E.) makes the case for wide powers of censorship in order to prevent innovation: If no new songs and books are allowed and few people are allowed to travel, there will be no new ideas and no pressure for harmful political change.

In the Roman Empire, censorship of writers was often provoked by political satires of the emperors. In later times, political authorities have often censored expressions that they perceived to be threatening to their power and social stability, even claiming that any opposition to their persons or policies is treason.

The Netherlands and England

The first two countries to have substantial freedom from censorship were the Netherlands and England. At the time of the Dutch Revolt (1568–1648), the chaos of civil war, an extreme federalism consisting of numerous jurisdictions, and the growing economic importance of the commercial book market meant that the Dutch civil authorities were too exhausted to initiate effective censorship, that what was banned in one jurisdiction could be published in another, and that economic interests opposed censorship in the Netherlands. Protestant criticism of the Catholic Inquisition and *Index* also made it difficult to justify Protestant censorship. Similar reasons encouraged effective limits on censorship during the English Civil War and Commonwealth (1642–1660).

Postal Censorship Office in England, 1939. During World Wars I and II, mail in the participating countries was frequently censored to ensure that specifics about military strengths or weaknesses were not being leaked or that propaganda was not being spread. © HULTON-DEUTSCH COLLECTION/CORBIS

The English philosopher Thomas Hobbes articulated the case for censorship in his *Leviathan* (1651). A philosophical nominalist, Hobbes believed very much in the importance of words and even claimed that the English Civil War was caused by too much reading of ancient republican authors. Therefore, he argued, the prince should have control over all forms of expression, a position frequently emulated by political authorities elsewhere. But even Hobbes did not articulate a full case for censorship with no exceptions. He warned princes against wasting valuable power trying to control people's minds when unnecessary.

The first major articulation of opposition to censorship was John Milton's (1608–1674) *Areopagitica* of 1644. He associated licensing with the infamous Inquisition of the Catholic Church and argued that knowledge of errors helps confirm the truth. Also among his arguments were that books cannot be suppressed without great harm to learning, and most people do not learn their evil ways from books. The censors

are not infallible, he said, and the attempt to regulate all forms of expression would be both exhausting and futile. Furthermore, he said, criticism of magistrates helps keep them informed. As usual, there were limits to Milton's tolerance: he approved of suppression of Catholics and the impious as threats to society. In the same period, Henry Robinson argued in *Liberty of Conscience* (1644) for liberty of the press on the ground that it was good for business.

The Dutch writer Benedictus de Spinoza (1632–1677) wrote provocative historical criticism of the Bible in his *Theological-Political Treatise* (1670), which also called for the freedom of every person to think what he wanted and to say what he thought. Spinoza's posthumously published *Ethics* (1677) argued for materialism, which was widely interpreted as atheism, and also asserted that part of the definition of a free man is one who can say what he thinks. Even though he wrote in Latin to avoid attention from anybody but the most educated, Spinoza's work was widely banned, and his followers were persecuted and censored throughout the following century.

Charles Blount (1654–1693) published *A Just Vindication of Learning* in 1679, and in *Miracles, No Violation of the Laws of Nature* (1683), he offered the first translation of part of Spinoza's work into English. His *Reasons Humbly Offered for the Liberty of Unlicens'd Printing* (1693) retailed Milton's reasoning and may have influenced Parliament's decision not to renew the Licensing Act in 1695. Like Milton, the English philosopher John Locke (1632–1704) opposed toleration of atheists and Catholics, and he also wrote several memoranda in the 1690s against the renewal of the Licensing Act. "I know not why a man should not have liberty to print what ever he would speake, and to be answerable for the one just as he is for the other if he transgresses the law in either," he wrote. When the Licensing Act expired in 1695 without renewal, England had de facto press freedom.

The deist John Toland (1670–1722) was responsible for the widespread distribution of Milton's *Areopagitica* in his 1698 edition of Milton's complete works, and he attacked censorship in several later publications. Other English deists from Anthony Collins to Matthew Tindal also defended freedom of expression. Both Spinoza and the deists are examples of radical philosophers in opposition to censorship.

James Mill (1773–1836) and his son John Stuart Mill (1806–1873) updated many of the arguments against censorship that had circulated in English, French, and German before them. James Mill argued that true statements about individuals should never be censored and that only direct obstruction of government operations should be censored, not general objections to policy. John Stuart Mill insisted that we do not really know anything unless we have considered the alternatives to it and that there is some truth in every opinion.

From Bayle to Constant

In the francophone world, the Huguenot refugee Pierre Bayle (1647–1706) penned the first general justification of the publication of obscenity. His "An Explanation Concerning Obscenities" (1702) argued that outright recommendation of lewdness and debauchery should be punished, but anything less than that should be left to the people to judge for themselves. The works of great authors such as Giovanni Boccaccio are protected by a "right" of the republic of letters, he argued, and even the Bible contains accounts of lewdness. Finally, he said that historians can report obscene things as mere facts of history, and no one is forced to read them. Bayle also wrote against censorship of atheists.

In 1747 Elie Luzac (1723–1796) published the atheistic *Man a Machine* by J. O. de La Mettrie, which resulted in much scandal. He was forced to turn over most copies for burning. Luzac then wrote his *Essay on Freedom of Expression* (1749) in order to defend freedom of the press. He relied on the tradition of natural law and claimed that the expression of ideas can never be harmful to society: false ideas will be refuted, and even true ideas will not be fully convincing unless we have seen the false alternatives. Luzac also pointed out that prohibited books will circulate underground anyway. He was no social or political radical, and his work demonstrates that conservatives can oppose censorship.

When her work was attacked in the press, Germaine de Staël (1766–1817) wrote in favor of censorship. Her intellectual companion, Benjamin Constant (1767–1830), countered with the case against censorship in many writings, including *Principles of Government Applicable to All Representative Governments* (1815). He agreed that writers who preach murder, theft, and pillage should be punished, but he argued that most pamphlets are harmless.

From Schmidt to Bahrdt

In the German-speaking world, substantial freedom of the press emerged from the multiple jurisdictions in the region, but authors were still imprisoned for their publications. Johann Lorenz Schmidt's (1702–1749) rationalist translation of the Bible in 1735 was outlawed in 1737, and he was imprisoned but escaped. The introduction to his German translation (1741) of Matthew Tindal's *Christianity as Old as the Creation* included a 130-page prefatory essay on freedom of the press, which may have been the first extended critique of censorship in German. Schmidt also translated Spinoza's *Ethics* into German in 1744.

Joseph II (1741–1790) relaxed press controls in the Habsburg Empire, and Frederick II of Prussia (1712–1786) generally limited censorship to political matters, not attacks on religion. In the decades of ferment after about 1770, many German writers called for press freedom. Christoph Martin Wieland's periodical *German Mercury* called press freedom the palladium of humanity in 1784; August Ludwig von Schlözer's *Letters to Eichstädt in Vindication of Publicity* (1785) rejected a bishop's censorship; and Johannes Kern's *Letters on Freedom of Thought, Belief, Speech, and the Press* (1786) based such freedoms on the social nature of mankind. The philosopher Immanuel Kant (1724–1804) elevated press freedom into the transcendental principle of public law.

Carl Friedrich Bahrdt's *On Freedom of the Press and Its Limits* (1787) consolidated much of the foregoing German material into an extended critique of censorship. He labeled freedom of the press a human right and argued that people only really believe truths they have found for ourselves. He opposed suppression of atheism and claimed that all human progress depends on mutual communication. Bahrdt was willing to condone censorship of state secrets and private matters and spelled out what later became known as the public figure doctrine. His satire of the Prussian king Frederick William II, *The Edict of Religion* (1788), landed him in prison for more than a year.

Pushkin and Solzhenitsyn

In the nineteenth and twentieth centuries, two Russian writers penned brilliant critiques of censorship. Aleksandr Pushkin's (1799–1837) long poems "Epistle to the Censor" (1822) and "Second Epistle to the Censor" (1824) could not be published in his lifetime. They described censors as gloomy, "meddling eunuchs." Aleksandr Solzhenitsyn's (1918–) "Letter to the Fourth Writers Congress" (1967) called censorship a survival from the Middle Ages and complained about the power of ignorant censors over literature.

Legal Declarations

In 1767 Sweden became the first country in the world to declare official freedom of the press, although a number of countries already had de facto freedom from censorship by then. However, Sweden's law specifically excepted matters of religion, one of the most common matters censored. In 1770 Denmark became the first to end censorship of all subjects. The decree was the work of Prime Minister Johann Friedrich Struensee (1737–1772), whose publications had been censored in Hamburg a decade before. He was overthrown and executed in 1772, but prior restraint of the press was not reimposed.

The fledgling United States was the site of several declarations of freedom of the press. The Virginia Declaration of Rights (1776) asserted that freedom of the press is one of the bulwarks of freedom itself, and declarations and constitutions in Pennsylvania (1776), Delaware (1776), North Carolina (1776), Vermont (1777), South Carolina (1778), and other states contained similar provisions. These provisions were precedents for the First Amendment to the United States Constitution (1791), which holds that "Congress shall make no law . . . abridging the freedom of speech, or of the press." How these words would be interpreted, of course, would have a great effect on censorship in the United States. Thomas Jefferson, for example, was highly in favor of freedom of the press until he became president, when he prosecuted newspapers that criticized his policies.

Article 11 of the French Declaration of the Rights of Man of 1789 provided that "Every citizen may freely speak, write, and print, subject to accountability for abuse of this freedom."

Many European constitutions of the nineteenth century abolished censorship. Article 19 of the United Nations Universal Declaration of Human Rights (1948) provides that "Everyone has the right to freedom of opinion and expression; this right includes freedom to . . . seek, receive and impart information and ideas through any media."

Sites of Censorship

Public libraries, museums, and schools are common sites of efforts to censor. The financing of libraries and museums by the public is alleged to confer a different standard than the open market, and protection of children from harmful materials is the usual justification for censorship of schoolbooks.

The development of each new medium of communication has brought with it efforts to censor that medium. Internet censorship is the latest in that line, with authorities around the world trying more or less effectively to limit access to certain Web sites and information.

Another late-twentieth-century phenomenon is the spread of "hate speech" codes on academic campuses. Intended to protect the vulnerable against speech that is alleged to express hate, the codes are open to wide-ranging interpretation and amount to imposition of judgments by whomever controls the censoring apparatus. Wherever anyone alleges that the expressions of others are insulting, offensive, or degrading, presumably those others could assert that the former's allegations are insulting, offensive, or degrading to them.

China has been a particularly active site for censorship and protests against it since the 1990s, but few observers from other countries can indulge in complacency. Derek Jones's *Censorship* (2001) details numerous cases of censorship of writers, directors, and artists on every continent and in almost every country in the twentieth century.

Censorship is not always an unmitigated bane for writers, artists, and publishers. One advantage is that it draws attention to works and causes. Authors have actively sought book burnings for the publicity value, and some books that have been taken off prohibited lists have seen their sales drop. Artistic careers have been made from the martyr value of censorship.

See also **Arts; Democracy; Liberty; Power.**

BIBLIOGRAPHY

PRIMARY SOURCES

Bahrdt, Carl Friedrich. *On Freedom of the Press and Its Limits.* In *Early French and German Defenses of Freedom of the Press,* edited by John Christian Laursen and Johan van der Zande. Leiden, Netherlands: Brill, 2003. Originally published in 1787.

Bayle, Pierre. "An Explanation Concerning Obscenities." In *Bayle: Political Writings,* edited by Sally L. Jenkinson. Cambridge, U.K., and New York: Cambridge University Press, 2000.

Locke, John. "Appendix: Documents Relating to the Termination of the Licensing Act, 1695." In *The Correspondence of John Locke,* edited by E. S. De Beer. Vol. 8. Oxford: Clarendon, 1979.

Luzac, Elie. *Essay on Freedom of Expression.* In *Early French and German Defenses of Freedom of the Press,* edited by John Christian Laursen and Johan van der Zande. Leiden, Netherlands: Brill, 2003. Originally published in 1749.

Milton, John. *Areopagitica.* In *Areopagitica, and Other Political Writings of John Milton,* edited by John Alvis. Indianapolis: Liberty Fund, 1999. Originally published in 1644.

Spinoza, Benedictus de [Baruch]. *Theological-Political Treatise.* Translated by Samuel Shirley. 2nd ed. Indianapolis: Hackett, 2001. Originally published in 1670.

SECONDARY SOURCES

Coetzee, J. M. *Giving Offense: Essays on Censorship.* Chicago: University of Chicago Press, 1996.

Foerstel, Herbert N. *Free Expression and Censorship in America: An Encyclopedia.* Westport, Conn.: Greenwood, 1997.

Goldstein, Robert Justin, ed. *The War for the Public Mind: Political Censorship in Nineteenth-Century Europe.* Westport, Conn.: Praeger, 2000.

Harrison, Nicholas. *Circles of Censorship: Censorship and its Metaphors in French History, Literature, and Theory.* Oxford: Clarendon, 1995.

Index on Censorship (spring 1972–). Quarterly magazine.

Israel, Jonathan. "The Intellectual Debate about Toleration in the Dutch Republic." In *The Emergence of Tolerance in the Dutch Republic,* edited by C. Berkvens-Stevelinck, J. Israel, and G. H. M. Posthumus Meyjes. Leiden, Netherlands: Brill, 1997.

Jones, Derek, ed. *Censorship: A World Encyclopedia.* 4 vols. London and Chicago: Fitzroy Dearborn, 2001.

Spalding, Paul. *Seize the Book, Jail the Author: Johann Lorenz Schmidt and Censorship in Eighteenth-Century Germany.* West Lafayette, Ind.: Purdue University Press, 1998.

John Christian Laursen

CELL THEORY. See **Biology; Genetics: History of; Science, History of.**

CHAIN OF BEING. See **Hierarchy and Order.**

CHANGE. "Cold things warm up, the hot cools off, wet becomes dry, dry becomes wet," observes Heracleitus (fr. 126), as if to state an obvious fact. Yet this fact became highly troublesome to early philosophers.

Antiquity
Although his predecessors had theories to account for natural changes, Heracleitus (c. 540–c. 480 b.c.e.) seems to be the first Western thinker to raise philosophical questions about change itself. According to Plato, Heracleitus held that (1) all things are changing, and (2) comparing life to a river, he claimed that one could not step twice into the same river (Cratylus 402a). On the basis of these two theses Plato draws the conclusion that (3) Heracleitus maintained that contradictory propositions were true (Theaetetus 182–183). In fact, Heracleitus seems to have held a more defensible, if still radical, view. Plato probably derives (1) and (2) directly from Heracleitus fr. 12: "On those stepping into the same rivers, other and other waters flow." Instead of saying the rivers are different, Heracleitus says they are the same—in contrast to the waters that comprise them. From this and other fragments we can extract a theory that although there is constant change in the materials of the world, stable structures supervene on them. Indeed, Heracleitus seems to imply that if there were not constant exchanges of matter, the structures would not exist; for instance, if the water ceased to flow, the river would cease to be.

The Eleatic challenge. In contrast to Heracleitus, Parmenides (b. c. 515 B.C.E.) of Elea (possibly reacting to Heracleitus, though this is controversial) denies the possibility of change. Rejecting the way "that it is not" because what-is-not could not be uttered (fr. 2), Parmenides rules out whatever properties rely on not-being. Since coming to be or perishing presuppose a time when something is not, they are not allowed, and similarly motion (in place?) is to be rejected (fr. 8). Parmenides enumerates several kinds of change: "coming to be and perishing, being and not being, changing place and exchanging bright color" (fr. 8.40–41). He seems to reject all of these as impossible. Parmenides' argument presents a problem often called the "Eleatic challenge": how can what-is come from what-is-not? The challenge poses a direct threat to cosmogony, the standard kind of pre-Socratic theory. After Parmenides, most cosmological theories posited the existence of a plurality of continuing materials that were individually supposed to be everlasting, for instance the four elements of

Empedocles (c. 490–c. 430 B.C.E.): earth, water, air, and fire. Thus cosmologists could claim that they did not allow coming to be or perishing of the ultimate realities, but only a harmless rearrangement of them. Nonetheless, Parmenides' argument seems to rule out not only coming to be and perishing, but all other kinds of change as well, and also to preclude a plurality of existences. Reinforced and sharpened by Zeno of Elea (c. 495–c. 430 B.C.E.) and Melissus of Samos (5th c. B.C.E.), the Eleatic challenge seems to have gone unanswered for more than a century.

Plato's response. Perhaps influenced by the lectures of Cratylus (a follower of Heracleitus), Plato (c. 428–348 or 347 B.C.E.) attributes a radical flux to the world of sensible things: they are always changing and never completely stable. If sensible things were the only existing things, knowledge and even discourse about the world would be impossible. But there is another world of changeless realities, the Forms, which provide a stable structure for sensible things, referents for language, and objects for knowledge. Forms, such as Justice and Equality, and perhaps Bed, have Parmenidean properties but no Heracleitean properties. Thus Plato creates a two-world theory, in which Heracleitean change of sensible things is tempered by Parmenidean constancy of ideal things. In his later work, Plato even posits a Form of Motion and another of Rest as ultimate kinds in which all sensible things participate (Sophist 254d). Unfortunately, a Form of Motion does not allow for any analysis of different kinds of motion or of different stages within a motion. Plato claims that the ultimate source of orderly motion is soul, which is immortal and self-moving (Phaedrus 245c–e).

Aristotle. Aristotle (384–322 B.C.E.) provides the first systematic study of change. He maintains that only primary substances can survive a change of one property to its opposite, implying that changes are variations in properties over time (Categories 5). He distinguishes several types of change by the kind of entity involved: coming-to-be and its opposite perishing (change in the category of substance), alteration (change of quality), increase and decrease (change of quantity), and locomotion (change of place) (ibid. 14). In Physics I, he sets out to answer the Eleatic challenge. Observing that changes always involve a subject changing from one opposite state to another, he generalizes this scheme to the most problematic case: that of change in substance. Even in this case there is some continuing subject for a change from one state to its opposite, as in the case of bronze, which goes from being unformed to being formed (in a statue). Similarly, there is some continuing substratum for something going from being not-human to human; the substratum for substantial change can be called matter (e.g., bronze), the negative state the privation (e.g., not-formed), the positive state the form (e.g., formed). On this model, though the final object comes from what-is-not, it does not come from nothing: the negative state is not nonexistence, but characterizes something that is, e.g., the bronze. "What-is-not" is seen to pick out not-*F*, and to presuppose a matter *m*, and not to refer to nothing at all. The Eleatic challenge rests on a mistake.

Aristotle sets out the circumstances of change as follows: a cause of motion *M* causes an object *O* to change from condition (place, property, etc.) C_1 to C_2 between times t_1 and t_2 (*Physics* V 1). In those cases in which O does not come to be or perish (undergo change of substance), the change is a *motion*. We may identify the circumstances with identity conditions: two changes are the same just in case they have the same mover, object, initial and final conditions, and beginning and ending times.

Not satisfied with a general definition and defense of change, Aristotle seeks to identify its place in the cosmos. Some things are always in motion (e.g., the heavenly bodies), some always at rest (e.g., the earth), and some things are at different times in motion and at rest (e.g., animals). Because there can be no beginning of time, but time is only the measure of regular motion, there must always have been cosmic motion. The only kind of motion that can be everlasting is locomotion in a circle (seen in the heavenly bodies). Such everlasting motion is only possible if there is some unmoved entity that causes the motion (*Physics* VIII). This is the first unmoved mover, which acts as a final cause, so that the heavenly bodies try to imitate its perfect (but motionless) actuality. Aristotle assumes that motion needs some sort of explanation, and everlasting motion needs an everlasting cause.

Christian Platonism.

Throughout late antiquity and the Middle Ages, Platonic and Aristotelian concepts of change continued to provide the standard account. There is, however, one important departure from classical theories that early Christian thinkers made: beginning in the second century C.E. they began to claim that God created the world ex nihilo (out of nothing), contrary to the classical notion expressed by Parmenides that what-is could not come from what-is-not. The Creation was a miraculous event caused by an omnipotent God.

Later Platonists interpreted Plato as saying that there was a simple and perfect One from which Mind (including the Platonic Forms) emanated; from Mind, Soul emanated, and from Soul, matter. Emanation was a kind of ontological overflowing according to which one being gave of its fullness to produce a lower-level being; the lower being proceeds from the higher in a timeless way such that the lower is always in existence, but dependent on the higher. Temporal distinctions are found only in the lower beings, so that the One and Mind are not in time and hence not subject to change.

In Christian Platonism, both ex nihilo creation and a changeless deity are combined with a historical account of God's interaction with the world, as in St. Augustine of Hippo's (354–430) *City of God*. Paradoxically, a changeless God interacts with changeable mortals to produce the drama of human salvation.

Modern Era

In the modern era a fundamental reorientation in the theory of motion occurred when the principle of inertia was recognized. Put forth first by René Descartes (1596–1650) and Pierre Gassendi (1592–1655), and canonized by Isaac Newton (1642–1727) as his first law, the principle stated that a body in uniform straight motion tends to stay in motion, and a body at rest tends to stay at rest. Thus the physicist did not need to explain continued motion. Moreover, since Newton's law of gravity could account for elliptical motions of satellites around a massive body, there was no longer any need for an unmoved mover to maintain the cosmic order. The kind of kinetic change that needed to be explained was acceleration, which depended on the application of a force to the moving body. John Locke (1632–1704) identified motion and rest as primary qualities whose ideas resembled the originals; colors and the like were secondary qualities whose ideas did not resemble the originals. Increasingly, motion in place came to be seen as the fundamental kind of change, which accounted for all other kinds.

History and physics.

Up until the nineteenth century, the study of history had been of little interest to philosophers. Aristotle had said that history was less philosophical than poetry, because it dealt with the particular rather than the universal. But when Georg Wilhelm Friedrich Hegel (1770–1831) explained the development of consciousness as a dialectical progression leading to ever more comprehensive concepts, he made history vitally important to philosophy. In particular the history of thought seemed to reflect the growth of spirit, exemplifying the realization of freedom and self-consciousness. An understanding of the development of culture and human institutions was now indispensable for philosophy. Historical change was essential to human self-realization. Becoming was the fulfillment of the concepts of *being* and *not-being*.

Although the historicist idealism launched by Hegel was highly influential, it eventually occasioned a strong reaction in England. One of the leading critics of idealism, Bertrand Russell (1872–1970), argued against "internal relations" by which every event was necessarily connected with every other. Instead, he proposed that the world consisted of a set of independent facts. Change itself could be defined in terms of propositions: "Change is the difference, in respect of truth or falsehood, between a proposition concerning an entity and a time T, and a proposition concerning the same entity and another time $T\prime$, provided that the two propositions differ only by the fact that T occurs in one where $T\prime$ occurs in the other" (sec. 442). Thus if "Socrates is literate at T" is false and "Socrates is literate at $T\prime$" is true for the times 465 B.C.E. and 450 B.C.E., respectively, we can infer a change. Against Russell, John M. E. M'Taggart (1866–1925) has argued that we should distinguish between an "A series" of events ordered with respect to past, present, and future, and a "B series" ordered with respect to before and after; only the former entails the existence (the flow) of time, since the latter involves only a fixed sequence of determinate events. But the A series produces contradiction, since every event is allegedly past, present, and future, that is, has incompatible predicates. Thus the A series is incoherent, and consequently there is no time and hence no change. Yet one can reply that the B series provides an adequate basis for time and change, and that the predicates *past, present,* and *future* are no more incompatible than *taller* and *shorter:* they are incomplete predicates, which, when properly completed for a given subject, would not produce a contradiction: "past with respect to time T_3 [or event E_3, etc.]," "present with respect to T_2," "future with respect to T_1." The kinds of changes described by Russell's and M'Taggart's accounts (sometimes called "Cambridge changes") have been criticized as too weak: a statement about a subject can change truth value with the subject's undergoing any alteration. For instance, I become shorter than my son when he grows taller than I, even though my stature does not change. Russell could reply that his account is meant only to identify some change in the world, not to analyze the subject of that change. In any case, we seem to need a richer account than Russell's to analyze the structure of change itself.

Advances in physics have affected views of the place of change in the world. Whereas Newtonian physics saw motion and rest as interchangeable phenomena seen from different frames of reference, the Theory of Relativity puts a limit on speed (the speed of light) and makes time a fourth dimension on a par with the three dimensions of space. Space, time, and mass all became relative quantities, and acceleration ceased to provide a necessary condition of change. At a quantum level, some particles have properties of both bodies and waves, and subatomic particles seem to be packets of energy. New theories such as String Theory suggest that subatomic particles are states of multidimensional strings of energy. Alfred North Whitehead (1861–1947) drew on early-twentieth-century physics to develop a speculative metaphysics positing processes rather than things as the ultimate realities. His style of philosophy, however, has gone out of favor, and in the late twentieth century philosophers tended to study change in trying to specify identity conditions for events.

See also **Cycles; History, Idea of; Physics; Relativity; Time.**

BIBLIOGRAPHY

Gill, Mary Louise, and James G. Lennox, eds. *Self-Motion: From Aristotle to Newton.* Princeton, N.J.: Princeton University Press, 1994.

Lombard, Lawrence Brian. *Events: A Metaphysical Study.* London: Routledge and Kegan Paul, 1986.

McTaggart, John McTaggart Ellis. *The Nature of Existence.* 2 vols. Edited by C. D. Broad. Cambridge, U.K.: Cambridge University Press, 1921–1927.

Russell, Bertrand. *The Principles of Mathematics.* 2nd ed. London: Allen and Unwin, 1937.

Sorabji, Richard. *Matter, Space, and Motion: Theories in Antiquity and Their Sequel.* Ithaca, N.Y.: Cornell University Press, 1988.

Waterlow, Sarah. *Nature, Change, and Agency in Aristotle's Physics: A Philosophical Study.* Oxford: Clarendon, 1982.

Whitehead, Alfred North. *Process and Reality: An Essay in Cosmology.* New York: Macmillan, 1929.

Daniel W. Graham

CHARACTER. The word *character,* when applied to persons, has two sources, distinguished lexically in ancient Greek by the terms *êthos* and *charaktêr. Êthos,* originally referring to a disposition or custom, from Aristotle on refers to the stable dispositions that guide a person's actions and that are suitable objects of moral praise and blame. The earliest uses of *charaktêr* in Greek, like the earliest uses of *character* in English, refer to an impression such as would be carved or stamped onto a coin or tablet; metaphorically, "characters" are signs (actions, facial features, social positions) that reveal something about a person's soul. Dur-

ing the seventeenth century, the sense of "character" in English came to include a person's psychological traits themselves.

Aristotle and Virtue Ethics

The fourth-century B.C.E. philosopher Aristotle, in *Nicomachean Ethics,* understands character (*êthos;* or *hexis êthikê,* "moral disposition") to be a disposition of the appetitive and emotional faculties, which leads its possessor to act and feel in particular ways. This disposition is acquired through habituation, a process that develops the intellectual as well as the appetitive and emotional faculties. Aristotelian virtues are such dispositions informed by practical wisdom—a capacity for judgment developed through experience and reflection, which guides conduct where technical knowledge cannot. This is one point of convergence between Aristotle's ethics and the thinking of contemporary virtue theorists, for as Aristotle rejects the claims of his teacher Plato (c. 428–348 or 347 B.C.E.) and Sophists such as Protagoras (c. 485–410 B.C.E.) that there is some art or science that can guide conduct, contemporary virtue theorists reject the claims of deontological ethics that conduct is well-guided by rules, such as "maximize utility" or "act only upon a maxim you could without contradiction will to be a universal maxim." Aristotle and contemporary virtue theorists also share the view that characters are appropriate objects of moral praise and blame; Aristotle reasons that this requires that our characters be voluntary, and argues that this is so on the grounds that our actions are voluntary and our characters are the products of our actions.

Aristotle's *Ethics* focuses on the cultivation (or acquisition or promotion in others) of virtuous character. When Aristotle describes the courageous or liberal person, he does so from the inside, showing us the person's concerns so that we see how, given the person's values, it makes sense for him to do as he does. But Aristotle's *Rhetoric* uses characterization to dispose audiences to trust a speaker, and his *Poetics,* to effect an appropriate fit between a person and his words and deeds; here, words and actions are signs by which we may know someone's character. Subsequently, Aristotle's student Theophrastus (c. 372–c. 287 B.C.E.) sketched representative vicious types by enumerating their typical words and deeds, in a work that came to be known as the *Êthikoi Charaktêres* (English trans. *Characters of Theophrastus,* or Moral signs), which was much imitated in English literature from the seventeenth century on. In *Characters of Vertues and Vices* (1608), by the English prelate Joseph Hall (1574–1656), "character" for the first time refers to a type of person, rather than just to the signs that reveal that type. A "character" genre evolved in various directions in the seventeenth and eighteenth centuries, adding to moral types, types of men and women in various stations of life (perhaps influenced by the Stoic notion that human beings are given *personae,* or roles to play in this world), and using their sketches to satirize individuals and societies. Although this literature interacts richly with popular ideas about character, it has generally not been taken up in philosophical ethics.

Kantian Ethics

An ancient tradition in natural philosophy, and particularly medicine, sought to explain an individual's character (*ēthos*) in terms of the four humors, or bodily fluids—namely the melancholy, phlegmatic, sanguine, and choleric. In his *Anthropology from a Pragmatic Point of View,* the eighteenth-century philosopher Immanuel Kant (1724–1804) sweeps such speculation to one side by distinguishing character from temperament: Temperament is given one by nature or habituation. People may vary in their temperaments, and indeed be classified by their dominant humors; however, character, which one either has or lacks, is the property of the will by which one binds oneself to self-prescribed rational practical principles. Kant's most influential ethical work, *The Groundwork for the Metaphysics of Morals,* identifies character with the good will, a will motivated solely by duty or principles of practical reason that it legislates to itself; Kant gives character the role of making use of such qualities as courage, resolution, and perseverance—which belong to temperament and might be bad if not in the control of a good will, the only thing good without qualification. In the *Metaphysics of Morals,* Kant likewise describes virtue as self-constraint, a power to withstand those of our inclinations that oppose morality—not merely some habit of morally good actions, virtue requires acting on "considered, firm and continually purified principles."

Neo-Aristotelian critics have charged that Kant's emphasis on acting on principle results in his neglecting the roles character and virtue play in both a good ethical life and morally praiseworthy action, and Kantian defenders often reply by pointing to Kant's doctrine of virtue. But the criticism can be raised anew with respect to Kant's conception of character and virtue itself, for these replace appropriate feeling and the sensitivity it affords with a commitment to acting on principle. One source of apparent disagreement between Kant and Aristotle is terminological: Aristotle defines moral character as a disposition of appetite and emotion, but he insists that it cannot exist without practical wisdom. So Aristotle does not consider an act or person guided solely by appetite and emotion, however well trained these may be, to be virtuous or praiseworthy. For Aristotle, practical wisdom is necessary for appetitive and emotional dispositions to be good (this is what distinguishes virtue proper from natural virtue), just as for Kant, the good will is necessary for courage, resolution, and perseverance to be good. Still, principle is not practical wisdom, and Kant has less faith in the ability of developed capacities of judgment and feeling to result in right action, and more faith in the ability of principles to do so, than does Aristotle. This may be one reason for Kant's restriction of character to one's commitment to the ends that practical reason prescribes itself; presumably another is that, to the extent that character is the appropriate object of praise and blame, it ought to be voluntary, and Kant takes only our resolutions, but not our natural and habituated inclinations, to be voluntary.

Utilitarianism

Not himself a utilitarian, the eighteenth-century philosopher David Hume (1711–1776) characterizes virtuous character traits as those that tend to the good, of mankind or at least of their possessor, and vicious ones as those that tend to the bad. Hume thus shares with utilitarians the view that the moral value of a character trait depends on its nonmoral value for people. Given its first widely influential formulation by Jeremy Bentham (1748–1832) in the nineteenth century in *The Principles of Morals and Legislation,* utilitarianism focuses on the rightness or wrongness of actions: the principle of utility deems that action right that, of the available alternatives in any given situation, tends to maximize the happiness of those affected. Utilitarianism's critics fault it for being insensitive to the importance of character evaluation for moral evaluation, but John Stuart Mill (1806–1873), a second-generation utilitarian, already stresses that acts ought to be evaluated for their consequences on character and character formation and includes as ingredients of happiness or utility such diverse intrinsic goods as friendship and virtue. A utilitarian may also subject character-traits and rules, and not only acts, to utilitarian assessment.

Challenges

In the twentieth and twenty-first centuries, questions have been raised about whether there is such a thing as character at all. The existentialist philosopher Jean-Paul Sartre (1905–1980) charged that to explain a person's (one's own or someone else's) action in terms of his or her character is to assimilate the action to an event in the natural world (for which the character is an ad hoc explanation), denying the person's freedom and refusing the rational understanding that human action demands. In a separate development, a research tradition in experimental social psychology, "situationism," holds that people's behavior is not distinctive or consistent across a range of situations. These criticisms may apply more to the conception of character as revealed in signs than to the conception put forth in philosophical ethics.

See also **Aristotelianism; Good; Kantianism; Moral Sense; Person, Idea of the; Utilitarianism; Virtue Ethics.**

BIBLIOGRAPHY

Aristotle. *Nicomachean Ethics.* Translated by Christopher Rowe. Oxford and New York: Oxford University Press, 2002.

Bentham, Jeremy. *The Principles of Morals and Legislation.* Buffalo, N.Y.: Prometheus, 1988.

Boyce, Benjamin. *The Theophrastan Character in England to 1642.* Cambridge, Mass.: Harvard University Press, 1947.

Hume, David. *A Treatise of Human Nature.* Edited by L. A. Selby-Bigge. 2nd ed. Oxford: Clarendon; New York: Oxford University Press, 1978.

Kant, Immanuel. *Anthropology from a Pragmatic Point of View.* Translated by Mary J. Gregor. The Hague, Netherlands: M. Nijhoff, 1974.

———. *Practical Philosophy.* Translated by Mary J. Gregor. Cambridge, U.K., and New York: Cambridge University Press, 1996. Includes *Metaphysics of Morals* and *Groundwork for the Metaphysics of Morals.*

Klibansky, Raymond, Erwin Panofsky, and Fritz Saxl. *Saturn and Melancholy: Studies in the History of Natural Philosophy, Religion, and Art.* New York: Basic Books, 1964.

Liddell, Henry George, and Robert Scott, comps. *Greek-English Lexicon.* Oxford: Clarendon; New York: Oxford University Press, 1996.

Mill, John Stuart. *Essays on Politics and Culture.* Edited by Gertrude Himmelfarb. Garden City, N.Y.: Doubleday, 1962.

———. *Utilitarianism.* Edited by George Sher. Indianapolis: Hackett, 1979.

Railton, Peter. "How Thinking about Character and Utilitarianism Might Lead to Rethinking the Character of Utilitarianism." *Midwest Studies in Philosophy* 13 (1988): 398–416.

Ross, Lee, and Richard E. Nisbett. *The Person and the Situation: Perspectives of Social Psychology.* Philadelphia: Temple University Press, 1991.

Sartre, Jean-Paul. *Anti-Semite and Jew.* Translated by George J. Becker. New York: Schocken, 1948.

Theophrastus. *The Characters of Theophrastus: An English Translation from a Revised Text.* Translated by J. E. Sandys. London: Macmillan, 1909.

Rachana Kamtekar

CHEMISTRY. Where and when did chemistry originate? Some chemists would identify ancient Egypt as the birthplace of chemistry because of that culture's glassworks, cosmetics, and mummification techniques. Advocates of this theory might also refer to a possible etymology of the word *chemistry* from the Egyptian word for *black.* Other historians place the origins of chemistry amid ancient Greek theories of matter that formulated the basic concepts—principles, elements, and atoms—for understanding the individuality of material substances and their transformations. Others would argue that chemistry emerged in medieval alchemy: alchemists invented the laboratory that is still the site for the production of chemical knowledge, and they established and transmitted techniques and instruments that are still at work in many chemical processes. Meanwhile, historians of institutional life would assert that chemistry emerged in seventeenth-century Europe when public lectures and chairs of chemistry were created.

The variety of answers to the question of origins points to the multiple identities of chemistry. A posteriori it seems natural to consider chemistry as an autonomous academic science with technological applications in a variety of domains. However, this is only one face of chemistry. Whether we consider chemistry as a set of technological practices—such as metal reduction, dyeing, glass-making—or as a theory of matter transformations, or as a teachable and public knowledge enjoying an academic status, the chronological marks change dramatically.

The question of origin cannot be settled not only because chemistry is multifaceted, but also because the answer depends heavily on the image of chemistry one wants to convey. For instance, eighteenth-century chemists strongly denied any connection between chemistry and alchemy. The kind of useful and reliable discipline they wanted to promote on the academic stage was contrasted with the obscurity and fraudulent practices of alchemists, although this is a discontinuity seriously questioned by historians of alchemy at the turn of the twenty-first century.

Alchemy in the Scientific Revolution

First, historians of alchemy note that there was no linguistic distinction between chemistry and alchemy in the seventeenth century—both disciplines being named "chymistry." Second,

Eighteenth-century illustration depicting Antoine-Laurent Lavoisier in his laboratory, by P. Fouche. Regarded as the founder of modern chemistry, Lavoisier (1743–1794) conducted groundbreaking quantitative experiments that led to the formulation of the law of the conservation of matter. © LEONARD DE SELVA/CORBIS

against the popular view of alchemy as a spiritual quest based on religious symbolism, historians such as Lawrence Principe and William Newman claim that "chymists" did actually manipulate and transform matter. While the religious interpretation of alchemy served to distance it from chemistry, they emphasize the continuity and argue that medieval alchemists already had developed experimental methods often considered as chief characteristics of modern science. They established a number of tests to identify substances; they used analysis and synthesis in order to demonstrate the similarity between substances extracted from nature and substances artificially produced in the laboratory; and they used weight measurements and the balance-sheet method traditionally credited to Antoine-Laurent de Lavoisier (1743–1794) to determine the identity of substances.

Early modern "chymistry" also questions the grand narrative of the scientific revolution, with Galileo Galilei's (1564–1642) and Robert Boyle's (1627–1691) mechanical philosophy whisking away the alchemical tradition. Boyle's view of material phenomena as being produced by the interaction of small particles that have only primary qualities (size, shape, and motion) by no means implied a rejection of the alchemical tradition. Since Jabir ibn Hayyan (c. 721–c. 851), whose work was spread and discussed in the West in the thirteenth century, the discipline of alchemy had fostered a corpuscular view of matter that was later developed by Daniel Sennert (1572–1657), an early seventeenth-century chemist. Sennert managed to reconfigure the Aristotelian theory of matter by combining the four principles with Democritean atomism. In order to provide experimental demonstration that matter at the microlevel is made by the juxtaposition of atoms, he performed a *reductio in pristinum statum* (reduction into the pristine state). Although Boyle positioned himself as a "natural philosopher" against "chymical philosophers, he was in debt to Sennert, since he tacitly used his experiments and his theoretical framework in his early essays as well as in *The Sceptical Chymist* (1680).

In addition, Boyle's skepticism did not apply to alchemical transmutations. Until his death, he kept seeking the philosopher's stone, using the knowledge he had learned in his youth from the American chymist George Starkey (1627–1665), who also initiated Sir Isaac Newton (1642–1727). Boyle, the advocate of public knowledge at the Royal Society, concealed his transmutational processes in secret language.

Thus, two of the celebrated founding fathers of modern science, Boyle and Newton, were dedicated believers in alchemical transmutation. Since Betty Dobbs's 1975 work, *The Foundations of Newton's Alchemy: or, "The Hunting of the Greene Lyon,"* historians of chemistry have reconsidered the impact of Newton's bold chemical hypothesis at the end of his *Opticks* (1704). In the famous Query 31, Newton ventured an interpretation of chemical reactions in terms of attraction between the smallest particles of matter. A uniform attractive force allowed the smallest particles to cohere and form aggregates whose "virtue" gradually decreased as the aggregates became bigger and bigger. Whereas this hypothesis has been read as an extrapolation of gravitational physics to chemistry, it is possible to view it as a way to rationalize chemical practices that was impossible in Cartesian mechanism. Newton allowed chemists to understand and measure affinities in purely chemical terms.

Eighteenth-Century Cultures of Chemistry

Such was the program initiated by Etienne-François Geoffroy (Geoffroy the Elder; 1672–1731), who published a "Table des rapports" (table of affinities) in 1718. The substance at the head of a column is followed by all the substances that could combine with it in order of decreasing affinity—the degree of affinity being indicated by the place in the column. A substance C that displaces B from a combination AB to form AC will be located above B in the column because of its stronger affinity for A. Displacement reactions thus provided a qualitative measure of affinities and allowed predicting the outcome of reactions. Thus, chemistry came to be seen as a predictive and useful science in the eighteenth century.

It is important to stress that long before Lavoisier, chemistry had conquered the status of an autonomous academic discipline. A chemistry class had been established at the Paris Academy of Science in the late seventeenth century, whereas the physics class was only created in 1785. The chemistry class conducted systematic research programs in plant analysis and mineralogy. Not only were chemistry chairs established in a number of European universities, but also innumerable public and private courses of chemistry opened up with experimental demonstrations. They were attended by a variety of audiences: pharmacists, metallurgists, as well as gentlemen and "philosophes" who practiced chemistry as enlightened amateurs. Chemistry was promoted alongside Enlightenment values as a rational and useful knowledge that would be of benefit to economy and society. A key strategy for winning political support was the introduction of the distinction between "pure" and "applied" chemistry by Johan Gottschalk Wallerius (1709–1785), who took the chair of chemistry in Uppsala in 1753. This distinction asserted the dignity of pure chemistry while transforming the chronological priority of chemical arts into a logical dependence upon "pure" knowledge. Chemistry could thus be perceived as a legitimate academic discipline in university curricula and highly valued for its usefulness in various applications. At the same time in France, chemistry was celebrated in the context of the *Encyclopédie* as a model science based on empirical data rather than on a priori speculations, a science requiring craft and labor, cultivated by skilled "artists" working hard in their laboratories unlike those lazy philosophers who never took off the academic gown.

However, chemistry was more than a fashionable science. So decisive was the success of Lavoisier's revolution in the 1780s that most chemists and historians of science, according to Frederic Holmes, "viewed eighteenth-century chemistry as the stage on which the drama of the chemical revolution was performed" (Holmes, 1989, p. 3). They once described it as an obscure and inconsistent set of practical rules based on the erroneous phlogiston theory. This theory, shaped by Georg-Ernst Stahl in the early eighteenth century, explained a number of phenomena such as combustion, as well as properties such as metals or acids, by the action of an invisible principle or fire named phlogistan (from the Greek term for "burnt"). The canonical story thus culminated in Lavoisier's questioning the existence of phlogiston and its alleged presence in metals, in acids, in combustion and respiration, and consequently overthrowing the old paradigm.

When historians resist the temptation to read eighteenth-century chemistry backward, waiting for Lavoisier to arrive on the stage, they quickly realize that this standard picture was only one aspect among numerous diverse cultures of chemistry in the eighteenth century, many of which were extremely innovative. In workshops and firms, the invention of continuous processes led to what historians of industry described as "the chemical revolution." In more academic spaces, laboratory practices were also deeply changed by the study of salt solutions when wet analysis was added to the traditional fire analysis and color indicators were systematically applied to acids and alkalis. This change, especially visible in the research program conducted at the Paris Academy of Science on plant and mineral analysis, had a theoretical impact: chemists gave up the old concept of salt as a universal principle, in favor of the notion of middle salt—a substance resulting from the combination of volatile and nonvolatile salts or of alkali and acid. This redefinition subverted the traditional notion of principles as material entities as bearers of properties. Substances could present similar properties and belong to the same class despite their different constituent principles. The idea of interchangeability was reinforced by the displacement reactions that allowed the construction of affinity tables. Affinity tables favored the view that the behavior of a "mixt" (compound) depends less upon the nature of its constituent principles than on its relations with other substances. The relational identity of chemical substances minimized the importance of principles—whether they be three, four, or five—that chemists used to oppose to the mechanistic view of a "catholic matter." Moreover in a number of eighteenth-century chemistry courses—for instance in Hermann Boerhaave's (1668–1738) textbook and Guillaume-François Rouelle's (1703–1770) lectures—elements were often redefined as "agents" of chemical reactions rather than as constituent principles. Elements were consequently presented as "natural instruments" together with "artificial instruments" such as laboratory vessels, furnaces, and alembics. This pragmatic notion of elements accompanied their redefinition in operational terms as substances that could not be further decomposed by available analytic techniques.

From Phlogiston to Oxygen

In addition, the phlogiston theory was neither an overarching nor a rigid framework. The notion, which was first forged by Georg Ernst Stahl (c. 1660–1734) around 1700, was most often mixed either with Newton's views of matter that inspired salt and affinity chemistry or with various notions inspired by local mining or pharmaceutical traditions. It is therefore difficult to identify a unitary phlogiston theory that would define eighteenth-century chemistry. Rather, two distinct phlogiston theories prevailed in two different contexts. In mid-eighteenth-century France, Stahl was considered as the founder of chemistry when Rouelle and his pupils redefined Stahl's "inflammable earth" as fire. The fire principle, always invisible because it circulated from one combination to another one, imparted combustibility or metallic properties when it was "fixed." It was released during combustion and metals calcination. Indeed, there was a difficulty here: if phlogiston was released when metals calcinated, how would one explain their increase of weight? The anomaly had been known for decades and had not prevented the success of this powerful theoretical framework since, as Immanuel Kant and Lavoisier himself acknowledged, it was Stahl's merit to realize that combustion and reduction were two inverse reactions and that calcination and combustion were one and the same process despite their phenomenological dissimilarities. Lavoisier cast doubts on phlogiston when he addressed the question of weight increase in 1772. After conducting experiments of combustion of phosphorus and lead calcination with careful weighing of each ingredient and each piece of apparatus before and after the reaction took place, he concluded that the weight gain could be due to a combination with part of the air contained under the flask. Although Lavoisier was convinced that his discovery was about to cause a revolutionary change in physics and chemistry, he could not yet refute that combustion released phlogiston. Unsurprisingly many contemporary chemists adopted a compromise between the two interpretations, and Pierre-Joseph Macquer (1718–1784) redefined phlogiston as the principle of light distinct from heat. Meanwhile an "English phlogiston" emerged from pneumatic studies that gained a sound phenomenological reality through its assimilation with hydrogen.

The study of gases so much changed the landscape of chemistry in the 1770s that some contemporary chemists used the phrase "the pneumatic revolution." Although air had been considered as one of the four elements, it was considered as a mechanical agent rather than as a chemical reactant until Stephen Hales (1677–1761), a British plant physiologist, built a "pneumatic chest" for collecting gases released by physiological processes. With this apparatus chemists were able to collect the gases given off by chemical reactions, to measure their volume, and to submit them to various tests. Joseph Black (1728–1799) identified "fixed air" (carbon dioxide) in 1756; in 1766, Henry Cavendish (1731–1810) isolated "inflammable air" (hydrogen); in 1772 Joseph Priestley (1733–1804) described a dozen new airs in his *Experiments and Observations on Different Kinds of Air*. In 1774 Karl Wilhelm Scheele (1742–1786), a Swedish pharmacist, isolated and described a new air that made a candle flame brighter and facilitated respiration. By the same time, Priestley had also produced a similar air by the reduction of the "red precipitate of mercury," a result that he communicated to Lavoisier when he visited him in Paris in October 1774.

Lavoisier was a latecomer in the crowd of chemists "hunting" airs, his earlier interest in chemistry being related to geology. His attention was drawn to the mechanisms of fixation and release of gases when he discovered the role of air in combustion. He consequently became aware of the British works—with the help of his wife Marie-Anne-Pierrette Paulze-Lavoisier (1758–1836), who translated foreign publications for him. He conducted systematic experiments on "elastic fluids" that were published in his *Opuscules physiques et chymiques* in 1774. He repeated Priestley's reduction of the red precipitate of mercury and performed the reverse operation of calcining mercury. Whereas Priestley characterized the gas released as "dephlogisticated air" Lavoisier concluded in 1778 that this gas was "the purest part of the air."

Two alternative views of gases were in competition. For the British pneumatists, the various gases isolated were composed of one single air differentiated according to the proportion of phlogiston they contained. In other terms, they fit nicely into the phlogiston paradigm. They even reinforced it because a pneumatic science, whose unquestioned leader was Priestly and which allowed a better understanding of physiological processes in plants and animals as well as medical applications, emerged. By contrast, Lavoisier came to see atmospheric air as a compound and developed a theory of gaseous state. All solid or liquid substances could be in a gaseous state depending on the quantity of caloric (or heat) they fix. Thanks to his caloric theory of gases, Lavoisier was in a better position to refute the phlogiston theory of combustion. He could account for the release of heat once he admitted that combustion consisted in a combination with a portion of atmospheric air that released its caloric. This portion of air that he first named "vital air"—later renamed oxygen—would play a key role in Lavoisier's chemistry. Not only did it explain combustion and calcinations but it was also the principle of acidity. Therefore, during the controversy that followed, Lavoisier's theory was referred to as "oxygen theory" or sometimes "antiphlogistic theory." Phlogiston was condemned as a useless chimerical entity, only to be replaced by another enigmatic principle of heat, "caloric," while the omnipresent element oxygen's being a bearer of properties was an echo of the older chemistry.

Revolution or Foundation?

Lavoisier's revolution did not condemn the old notion of elements common to all substances, although he destroyed three of the traditional four elements, fire, air, and water. The demonstration that water was not an element but a compound of two gases was made in a solemn experiment of analysis and synthesis of water set up in February 1785. It required heavy and expensive equipment designed with the help of a military engineer and with the support of an academic Commission of Study for the Improvement of Balloons. With this spectacular experiment Lavoisier won his first allies. Together they were able to take advantage of the opportunity to reform the chemical language as outlined by Louis Bernard Guyton de Morveau (1737–1816) and build up a new "Method of Chymical Nomenclature" that reflected Lavoisier's theory and eliminated phlogiston. The new system, published in 1777, was seen as a coup d'état and sparkled a fierce controversy. The anti-phlogisticians mobilized all resources, including the creation of a new journal, *Annales de chimie,* in order to convince European chemists. Moreover, to defeat the last and attractive British version of phlogiston as inflammable air (hydrogen), which was articulated by Richard Kirwan (1732–1812), Madame Lavoisier translated into French his *Essai sur le phlogistique* (1788; Essay on phlogiston), while the anti-phlogisticians criticized the author's view in footnotes. Beyond the issue of phlogiston, numerous objections to the new language were raised by contemporary chemists concerning the choice of terms, such as "oxygen" (an acid generator according to Lavoisier's theory of acids) and "azote" (improper for animal life and a property of many other gases). Although the French "nomenclators" did not change any term, their system was finally adopted throughout Europe by 1800. But this victory did not always mean conversion to all facets of Lavoisier's chemistry. The reform of language fulfilled a long-felt need among the chemical community and it came at the right moment: textbooks were needed to train pharmacists as well as chemists for burgeoning industries. The new systematic language and Lavoisier's *Elements of Chemistry* (1789) facilitated the teaching of chemistry.

In the context of the French Revolution, which resulted in Lavoisier's death on the guillotine and the creation of a new educational system, Lavoisier's revolution has been perceived as the destruction of premodern chemistry and the foundation of modern chemistry on a tabula rasa. However, the celebration of the founding hero overemphasizes the impact of his contribution to chemistry. Lavoisier did not overthrow the whole of chemistry. The tradition of salt and affinity chemistry remained untouched. Rather, the latter was revised and integrated in a grandiose "Newtonian dream" by Claude-Louis Berthollet (1748–1822) in his *Essai de statique chimique* (1803). Lavoisier invented neither the "law of conservation of matter"—a kind of axiomatic principle tacitly assumed by all natural scientists long before him—nor the laws of chemical proportions that inspired the chemical atomism developed by the next generation of chemists.

Nineteenth-Century Chemical Atoms

Nineteenth-century chemistry has often been described as a smooth sequence of discoveries that gradually established modern chemistry. Positivist historians were content with reporting landmark events such as John Dalton's atomic theory, Amedeo Avogadro's law, Dmitry Ivanovich Mendeleev's periodic system, and so on. In thus conveying a cumulative process, they not only distorted history but also tended to deprive past scientists of inner consistency because they failed to accept many of these "great discoveries."

One major feature of nineteenth-century chemistry is that the history of ideas did not follow the pathway that seems logical from a present-day perspective. For instance, the laws of chemical proportions did not follow from Lavoisier's program. Instead, they emerged from salt chemistry, more precisely from attempts to determine the weight or ponderous quantity of a base that could neutralize a definite quantity of acid. While the chemical revolution was drawing all attention toward Paris, two German chemists, Karl Friedrich Wenzel (1740–1793) and Jeremias Richter (1762–1807), were initiating a quantitative chemistry that they named *stöichiometrie* or stoichiometry (from the Greek *stoicheion,* or element). The main assumption that the properties of any substance depend upon the nature and proportion of its constituent elements opened up a research program for chemists whose key words were *analysis* and *quantification* (titration or dosage).

The field of stoichiometry was extended in 1802 when Joseph Louis Proust (1754–1826) applied Richter's notion of "equivalent," so far limited to reactions between acids and bases, to all combinations and formulated a general law: the relationships of the masses according to which two or several elements combine are fixed and not susceptible of continuous variations. While Berthollet questioned the generality of Proust's law of definite proportions, John Dalton (1766–1844), a professor at Manchester, made it the basis for his atomic hypothesis. He assumed that chemical combinations take place unit by unit, or atom by atom. He added a law of multiple proportions: when two elements form more than one compound, the weight proportions of the element that combines with a fixed proportion of another one are in a simple numerical ratio. Dalton's hypothesis rested on the assumption that atoms were solid and indivisible, that they were surrounded by an atmosphere of heat, that there were as many kinds of atoms as there were elements. Dalton's atoms were not the uniform and minute discrete units that structured all material bodies of ancient atomism. Rather, they were minimum and discrete units of chemical combination. And Dalton assumed that atoms would combine in the simplest way, that is, two atoms formed a binary compound. The main advantage of Dalton's hypothesis was that it allowed simple formulas. Instead of determining the composition of a body by percentages, chemists could express it in terms of constituent atoms thanks to the determination of atomic weights. Of course it was impossible to weigh individual atoms. Since Dalton could not determine this weight by using the neutrality of the compound like Richter, he elected a conventional standard. He chose hydrogen as the unit of reference. For instance, hydrogen and oxygen were known to form water, whose analysis gave the ratio 87.4 parts by weight of oxygen for 12.6 of hydrogen. If hydrogen has a weight equal to 1, the relative atomic weight of an atom of oxygen will be roughly 7. Shortly after Dalton's *New System of Chemical Philosophy* (1808), Joseph Gay-Lussac (1778–1850) announced that volumes of gas that combine with each other were in direct proportion and that the volume of the compound thus formed was also in direct proportion with the volume of the constituent gases. The volumetric proportions thus seemed to confirm Dalton's weight ratios.

To explain the convergence, both Amedeo Avogadro (1776–1856) in 1811 and André-Marie Ampère (1775–1836) in 1814 suggested that in the same conditions of temperature and pressure, equal volumes of gases contain the same number of molecules. In order to admit this simple hypothesis, however, both men had to admit a second hypothesis: that when two gases joined to form a compound, the integrating molecules should divide into two parts.

From a modern perspective this hypothesis was a big step forward because it suggested the distinction between atoms and molecules. Why, then, was it rejected in the 1830s and for several decades afterward by the most prominent chemists? The rejection of Avogadro's law is a classical topos for illustrating the opposition between presentist and historicist approaches. The alleged "blindness" of nineteenth-century chemists appears as a perfectly consistent attitude once one considers that Avogadro's hypothesis of molecules formed of two atoms of the same element stood in contradiction to the theoretical framework of chemical atomism. In Dalton's theory, such diatomic molecules were physically impossible because of the repulsion between the atmospheres of heat of two identical atoms, and they were theoretically impossible in the new electrochemical paradigm set up by Jöns Jacob Berzelius (1779–1848) on the basis of his experiments on electrolytic decomposition. Elements were defined by their electric polarity, and the intensity of the positive or negative charge determined the affinity between them. Molecules of two atoms of the same element were impossible because of the repulsion between two identical electrical charges.

The distinction between atom and molecule did not directly follow from Avogadro's law. Rather it was formulated by a young chemist, Auguste Laurent (1807–1853), trained in mineralogy and crystallography. He challenged Berzelius's electrochemical view. For Berzelius all compounds resulted from the electric attraction between two elements. This dualistic view was extended to organic compounds thanks to the notion of radical—for instance the benzoyl radical discovered by Leibig—a group of atoms that, like elements, persisted through reactions. In the 1830s Jean-Baptiste-André Dumas (1800–1884) prepared trichloracetic acid by the substitution of three atoms of chlorine to three atoms of hydrogen in acetic acid. His student Laurent noticed the similarity of properties between the two acids. Electronegative atoms of chlorine could replace electropositive atoms of hydrogen without changing the properties too much. He consequently developed a unitary theory that Dumas called "type theory" in 1838: in organic compounds there exist types that persist when elements are changed. This suggested that the properties of compounds depended more on the architecture of molecules than on the nature of constituent atoms. Type theory applied to the increasing crowd of organic compounds while inorganic chemistry was still ruled by dualism.

Charles Frédéric Gerhardt (1816–1856) attempted to reunify chemistry by extending the type theory to all compounds, using analogy as a guide. Although he admitted that we do not know anything about the actual arrangement of atoms in a molecule, he defined three types—hydrogen, water, and ammonia—as an ideal taxonomic scheme. According to Gerhardt, all compounds derived from these three types.

The theory of type implicitly indicated that atoms of different elements had different combining powers or valences. Hydrogen, for example, has a valence of one, while oxygen has two and nitrogen three. It is worth emphasizing that although nineteenth-century organic chemists such as Gerhardt and August Kekulé (1829–1896) did not believe in the actual existence of atoms and molecules, they were able to invent structural formulas that allowed them to predict and create new compounds.

The Construction of the Periodic System

Gerhardt's unitary perspective also provided the foundation for the construction of the periodic system. Dmitry Ivanovich Mendeleev (1834–1907) was certainly not the first chemist who tried to classify elements on the basis of atomic weights. Van Spronsen reasonably argued that the periodic system was codiscovered by six chemists in the 1860s. However, Mendeleev adopted a different strategy. He pointed to the Karlsruhe Conference, held in 1860, as the first step toward the periodic law. This first international meeting of chemists adopted atomic weights based on Avogadro's and Gerhardt's views. From the general agreement on the distinction between atoms and molecules, Mendeleev derived another crucial distinction, between simple body and element. Since Lavoisier's famous definition of elements as nondecomposed bodies, most chemists did not distinguish between the two terms. Mendeleev, on the contrary, stressed the difference between the simple substances, empirical residues of decomposition characterized by their physical properties and molecular weights, and the abstract element defined as an invisible ingredient and characterized by its atomic weight. Mendeleev chose to classify elements rather than simple bodies because he considered them as responsible for the properties of simple and compound substances. Mendeleev was thus the first chemist who really worried about a clear definition of what was to be classified. Although abstract and unobservable, Mendeleev's elements were material entities and true individuals. Mendeleev was a staunch opponent of the hypothesis formulated by William Prout (1785–1850), which asserted that the multitude of simple substances derived from one single primary element, usually identified as hydrogen. Throughout the nineteenth century this reductionist mainstream stimulated attempts at classifying elements. Classifications were mainly aimed at tracing genealogical relations or families by grouping analogous elements in triads or families according to the numerical ratios of their atomic weights. Starting from the assumption that elements would never be divided or transmuted into one another, Mendeleev took an opposite direction. He sought unity in a natural law ruling the multiple elements, rather than in matter itself. He compared the most dissimilar elements and firmly relied on the order of increasing atomic weights. Whereas grouping elements on the basis of valences always faced the difficulty of multiple valences, Mendeleev strictly relied on the order of increasing atomic weight, which he regarded as the constant criterion of the individuality of chemical elements.

Indeed, this criterion revealed some deficiencies. It sometimes blurred strong chemical analogies (for instance between Li and Mg, Be and Al, B and Si) or induced unexpected proximities (for example, in Mendeleev's eighth group). Mendeleev struggled with these difficulties and published thirty different tables in order to better suit his system with chemical analogies. However, his abstract notion of elements allowed predictions of unknown elements. Many of these elements were confirmed during Mendeleev's lifetime and served to validate his system while guarding it from further challenges. The discovery of a dozen rare earth elements in the late nineteenth century created difficulties because they lack individual properties and have strong mutual analogies. The inert gases were not welcomed either, first, because they had not been predicted, but mainly because they did not exhibit chemical properties. The atomic weights determined by William Ramsay (1852–1916) and Lord Rayleigh (John William Strutt; 1842–1919) for helium (4) and argon (40) would result in the placement of the latter between potassium and calcium according to its atomic weight. This was impossible, and the whole periodic system was in danger to collapse. Mendeleev raised doubts about the elemental nature of argon. Thanks to their sound belief in the periodic law, Ramsey and Rayleigh found a place for them at the cost of a new reversal of increasing atomic weight values and a new prediction of an intermediate element between neon and argon. A zero group was opened up that first undermined Mendeleev's notion of individual elements defined by their atomic weight. A second blow came from the discovery of electrons and radioactivity. Mendeleev desperately tried to explain this apparent anomaly with the hypothesis of confused movements of ether around heavy atoms. In this grandiose attempt to unify mechanics and chemistry, Mendeleev admitted ether in the periodic system in the 0 group. This error is instructive because it reveals the intellectual roots of Mendeleev's system. It is thus impossible to consider Mendeleev's system as a kind of precursor of quantum chemistry. Mendeleev dealt with elements and not with atoms.

Chemistry and Quantum Theory

The periodic system nevertheless served as a guide in the emergence of atomic physics, especially for Niels Bohr's (1885–1962) quantum model of the atom. Atoms of successive elements in the periodic system present an additional electron on the outermost shell. When a shell becomes full, a new shell begins to fill. Exceptions to this rule are reflected in the uneven length of periods in the periodic system.

The autonomy of chemistry thus seemed to be deeply questioned in the mid-twentieth century. If individual properties of chemical elements can be deduced from quantum theory, the theoretical foundations of chemistry lie in physics. Chemistry would be a reduced science. Many chemistry teachers struggle against these reductionist tendencies and claim that all the properties of chemical elements and compounds cannot be predicted by quantum calculus, even with the help of computer simulation. The bottom-up approach that prevails in recent materials chemistry and pharmaceutical research places great expectations in the control of individual atoms. However, those nanotechnologies also reveal that the chemist's ability to synthesize new products relies on a good deal of know-how and astute rules as much as on the fundamental laws of nature. Furthermore, recent synthetic strategies are more and more inspired by living organisms. For instance, supramolecular chemistry aims to design chemical processes that mimic the selectivity of biological processes to obtain molecular recognition without the help of genetic code. Thus, chemistry is renewing its old alliance with life science.

See also **Alchemy; Physics; Science, History of; Quantum.**

BIBLIOGRAPHY

Bensaude-Vincent, Bernadette. *Lavoisier: Mémoires d'une révolution.* Paris: Flammarion, 1993.

———. "L'éther, élément chimique: Un essai malheureux de Mendeleev en 1904." *British Journal for the History of Science* 15 (1982): 183–187.

———. "Mendeleev's Periodic System of Chemical Elements." *British Journal for the History of Science* 19 (1986): 3–17.

Bensaude-Vincent Bernadette, and Isabelle Stengers. *A History of Chemistry.* Translated by Deborah van Dam. Cambridge, Mass., and London: Harvard University Press, 1996.

Bensaude-Vincent, Bernadette, and Ferdinando Abbri, eds. *Lavoisier in European Context: Negotiating a New Language for Chemistry.* Canton, Mass.: Science History Publications/USA, 1995.

Beretta, Marco. *The Enlightenment of Matter: The Definition of Chemistry from Agricola to Lavoisier.* Canton, Mass.: Science History Publications/USA, 1993.

Brock, William H. *The Fontana History of Chemistry.* London: Fontana Press, 1992. Also published as *The Norton History of Chemistry.* New York: Norton, 1994.

Donovan, Arthur. *Antoine Lavoisier: Science, Administration, and Revolution.* Cambridge, Mass., and Oxford: Blackwell, 1993.

———, ed. *The Chemical Revolution: Essays in Reinterpretation. Osiris,* 2nd ser. 4 (1988). A special issue of the journal *Osiris.*

Holmes, Frederic Lawrence. *Antoine Lavoisier: The Next Crucial Year, or the Sources of His Quantitative Method in Chemistry.* Princeton, N.J.: Princeton University Press, 1998.

———. *Eighteenth-Century Chemistry as an Investigative Enterprise.* Berkeley: Office for the History of Science and Technology, University of California at Berkeley, 1989.

———. *Lavoisier and the Chemistry of Life: An Exploration of Scientific Creativity.* Madison: University of Wisconsin Press, 1985.

Knight, David M. *Ideas in Chemistry: A History of the Science.* New Brunswick, N.J.: Rutgers University Press, 1992.

Levere, Trevor H. *Transforming Matter: A History of Chemistry from Alchemy to the Buckyball.* Baltimore: Johns Hopkins University Press, 2001.

Newman, William R., and Lawrence M. Principe. *Alchemy Tried in the Fire: Starkey, Boyle, and the Fate of Helmontian Chymistry.* Chicago: University of Chicago Press, 2002.

Nye, Mary Jo. *Before Big Science: The Pursuit of Modern Chemistry and Physics, 1800–1940.* New York and London: Twayne, 1996.

———. *From Chemical Philosophy to Theoretical Chemistry: Dynamics of Matter and Dynamics of Disciplines, 1800–1950.* Berkeley and London: University of California Press, 1993.

Principe, Lawrence M. *The Aspiring Adept: Robert Boyle and His Alchemical Quest.* Princeton, N.J.: Princeton University Press, 1998.

Rocke, Alan J. *Chemical Atomism in the Nineteenth Century: From Dalton to Cannizzaro.* Columbus: Ohio State University Press, 1984.

———. *The Quiet Revolution: Hermann Kolbe and the Science of Organic Chemistry.* Berkeley and London: University of California Press, 1993.

Van Spronsen, J. W. *The Periodic System of the Chemical Elements: A History of the First Hundred Years.* Amsterdam, London, and New York: Elsevier, 1969.

Bernadette Bensaude-Vincent

CHICANO MOVEMENT. Between 1966 and 1977, members of the Mexican-American community engaged in a period of widespread political activism akin to other civil rights and antiwar movements of the 1960s. The resulting challenges and concurrent mentalities became the Chicano movement, or as it is now known in recognition of the equally important participation of Chicanas, the Chicana/o movement. During this period large-scale political organizing occurred among the Mexican-American community with a hitherto unprecedented urban energy. For those involved in the Chicana/o movement, the experience was characterized by a remarkable intensity at the personal and local collective levels. This rise in political engagement was the consequence of an interaction between a specific cultural context and contending, contentious social efforts, civic events, and ideological beliefs. It challenged the ineffectiveness of liberalism and the increasing economic and human cost of an armed interventionist foreign policy in the third world and this, combined with urban youth dissidence and ethnic protests, encouraged growing social and political militancy among Mexican-Americans.

A series of changes and continuities took place across Mexamerica in regard to the position and status of Mexican-Americans. Even though Mexicans slowly entered the skilled labor market, larger numbers remained poor due to discrimination and exploitation, and their social and educational possibilities were inhibited by social controls and economic immobility. At the same time, a very modest, educated, and political middle class burgeoned. During the 1950s and 1960s, the number of Mexican-Americans elected to office slowly increased, but electoral underrepresentation remained the rule. In comparison with the preceding periods, the number of Mexican-American union participants slightly increased in industries accessible to unions. However, far more people were barred from, rather than included in, these unions. Basic workers and farm laborers remained the most visibly excluded.

While explicit anti-Mexican discrimination receded in some areas of employment and housing, overall discrimination continued. Mexicans held the least desirable and worst-paying jobs in the economy and lagged behind the income and schooling levels of both Anglos and blacks. Despite this, the Mexican community grew numerically, including both citizens and immigrants, and this was reflected in the increase of Mexican high school and college graduates. Growth continued into the following decades. Women's participative access to heretofore enclosed social and economic sectors was particularly noticeable, yet some exclusion persisted. The number of Mexican female college graduates increased relative to years past, as did female business ownership. Still, most Mexican women did not attend college and continued to figure prominently in the minimum-wage labor sectors. They were variously oppressed by diverse institutions including the state, their neighborhoods, and their family circles. Immigrant single mothers were most vulnerable to forms of brutality and violence, which included forced sterilizations. These multiple oppressions continued to limit the opportunities for Mexican women, as well as Mexican men and children, over generations.

Selecting chronological dates is always an arguable procedure, but there are two events that, because of their public resonance, could be used to chart the rise and decline of the national Chicana/o movement. The 1966 farmworkers' march to Sacramento, California, is often acknowledged as a visible sign of rising, proactive Mexican-American public sentiment. This could be considered the beginning of notable political ferment. Ten years or so later, the 1977 San Antonio, Texas, Immigrant Rights Conference, which was prefaced by growing anti-Mexican outlooks, signaled an acknowledged decline of Chicano militant effectiveness since the attempt at coordinated pro-immigrant rights failed on this occasion. This was soon followed by the anti–affirmative action backlash stimulated by the Supreme Court's "reverse discrimination" decision in *Bakke v. Regents of the University of California* (1978).

The view of some Chicana/o activists from the mid-1960s to the mid-1970s was that civic matters compelled a reevaluation of earlier ideological tenets (a trend emphasizing gradualism known as Mexican-Americanism), and required the development of a new "in your face" style of politics. There was much insistence upon democratic rights, and high-volume addresses were full of heightened cultural and ethnic references. These trends were effectively legitimated by relatively wide mobilizations. Advocacy reform practices previously local became increasingly regional and tentatively national. In short, the Chicana/o movement flourished as an ethnic revivalist movement of the 1960s and 1970s and was anchored in new, specifically charged politics. It involved thousands and spread from Galveston to Chicago, from Seattle to Brownsville.

Contents

Central to the movement phenomena, ad hoc organizations that focused on specific local crises or sector needs sprang up across the Southwest and Midwest. These groups centered on issues such as education reforms, service inequities, undesired urban changes, biases in war on poverty programs, drug impact, welfare rights, child care and ex-felon needs. Title II of the Economic Opportunity Act of 1964, which stipulates participation by the "client" (that is, the poor), encouraged local group mobilization either through a positive outreach facilitating participation or as a consequence of negative reactions to the perceived malfunctioning or exclusivity of certain programs. Self-help organizations advocating individual determination developed in many localities and placed stress on individual rights and access to services, particularly for women and children. Many urban Mexican-Americans increasingly came to participate in public civic activities that involved direct interaction with officials and program personnel. The youth and women stepped forward as the primary participants in these efforts. Although Chicana/o politics in the early 1960s remained overwhelmingly liberal and reformist in content, more radical currents insisted on civic equities and plural participation within areas often controlled by electoral or patronage cliques. However, the dynamic leadership initiators often voiced a distrust of known older electoral *políticos*. By the late 1960s, certain currents encompassed procommunity autonomy and pluralist tendencies vis-à-vis constituted civic arrangements that were perceived as exclusionary and manipulated. Importantly, movement spokespersons established relations with groups, organizations, educational institutions, and political leaders not only across the Mexican border but also in other countries.

Cultural Context

At times, Chicana/o political energy flowed from cultural circumstances. On other occasions, political conditions encouraged cultural happenings. Culture, history, and arts resonated in every discourse. Community affairs became increasingly varied and complex, reflecting nearly all hues of the social spectrum from center to left. To oppose the movement, its cultural rhetoric, professed priorities, or stressed styles could be interpreted as a confession of rightist sympathies. To be sure, older organizations and electoral politics continued as the new politics emerged. The origins of this energized cultural ideological activity lie in the demographic and material circumstances of the early 1960s as well as in subjective conditions. Certainly, contrasting opinions on politics and history—of complacency versus insurgency—contributed to ideological growth. Mexicans were increasingly recognized by the media as the nation's second-largest minority, but their protest movement was not defined in the way that those of white and black dissidents were, and the media did not actively shape their leadership and rhetoric. The widespread social and economic conditions of laboring people heightened the political consciousness of Chicana/o activists. The movement drew inspirational and ideological reinforcements from a variety of sources, including those common to other social movements. But it also uniquely derived many of its beliefs from the historical heritage of Mexican-Americans themselves and in particular the ideological legacy of Mexico and Latin America. Significantly, Chicana/o activists also explored and deployed nativist Mesoamerican heritages, and this was particularly evident in the arts. After politicized arts hammered on doors, commercially expressive cultural activities eventually flowed to the public domain.

Sharing the upheaval that grew out of changes in the ideological climate and material conditions of the early 1960s, individuals of Mexican descent engaged in a variegated burst of activity loosely identified as the "Chicano movement." Among the seminal organizing and strategic forces were student organizations, defense groups, and artists' coalitions; the United Farm Workers Union; the Alianza Federal de Mercedes, or land rights movement; the Crusade for Justice, a political rights organization; and eventually, La Raza Unida Party. These were followed by church associations and women's and immigrants' rights organizations. Most of these forces were comprised of working-class people, and women often provided the membership base. The movement had a range of concurrent fronts, which were noticeably secured in local bases where individuals chose priorities and the levels of their participation. Whatever the particular goals and methods of the political activism, the underlying motivation was always a general dissatisfaction over the Mexican's political, economic, and social status in an Anglo-dominated society. Focus was increasingly placed on questions of exploitation, repression, exclusion, alienation, ethnicity, identity, class, gender, and chauvinism. History was privileged, perhaps more than in other social movements. Understanding the dynamics of the Mexican-American experience became a paramount motif, a voiced ideological necessity in the struggle to assess the present and envision a future for Mexican-Americans. These particular issues were sharply expressed in the arts; poets and muralists served as ideologues.

Ideology

Although *Chicanismo* often seemed a loosely expressed concept, in specific situations it could translate as a radical political and affirmative ethnic populism. The issue of identity linked to political demands jumped to the forefront. The term *Chicano* itself, used among the youth in particular regions, denoted the person and the group. *Chicanismo* referred to a set of beliefs and, more importantly, to a political practice. Its emphasis on dignity, self-worth, pride, uniqueness, and a feeling of cultural rebirth made the term attractive to many people of Mexican origin, as well as some of Latin American descent, in a way that cut across class, gender, regional, and generational lines. Negative past experiences regarding the denial of cultural heritage increased the appeal of *Chicanismo,* which emphasized Mexican cultural consciousness and social and linguistic tradition as well as economic and occupational opportunities. The Chicana/o movement became a challenge to the assumptions, politics, and principles of the established systems within and outside the community. However, even though it marked a progressive step in the struggle for identity by denying the grosser aspects of deculturalization, the designation also became a subterfuge for avoiding a critique of identity and Mexican "singularity." The widespread appeal of *Chicanismo* without explicit ideological class content shows, in large part, how often heterogeneous political elements could identify with the "Chicano movement." In practice, people expressed *Chicanismo* in a variety of ways.

In hindsight, one can ask whether *Chicanismo,* if seen through a militant conceptualization and in the context of its identity and ideological notions, was not simply one more effort to subsume Mexican identity and all of its implications in a dominant social context of covert anti-Mexicanism. Indeed, the term was a necessary referent for a distinct social group that could be differentiated from others in the United States by virtue of its ethnic and national roots. Other designations continued to be used, and the tension between *Chicano* and *Mexican* evolved rather than disappeared. In the initial cultural and political discourse, *Chicano* was clearly an abbreviated form for Mexicans north of the Rio Bravo, and *Chicanismo* meant a politically asserted *Mexicanidad.* Curiously, many middle-class people rejected the term as pejorative, while the lower classes preferred the appellation of *Mexicano.* Yet, to many of the young, *Chicano* was *the* term; for activists it was *the* litmus test for a political frame of mind. Furthermore, the *Chicano* denotation not only emphasized an unconventional "lifestyle" stressing *Chicanismo* but also stressed the more widely noted features of emphatic public cultural practices and radical personal values of the late 1960s embodied in the attitude, *"Soy Chicano y qué!"* (*"I am Chicano and what of it!"*).

Gender

The gender issue was sharply raised by individuals, organizations, and community activists in several Chicana/o movement areas starting in the late 1960s. Particularly noticeable were matters related to women in community settings and youth and student circles and on the perceived subordination of women and gender issues within the movement itself. Nonetheless, women obviously participated in all efforts associated with the Chicano movement. Any reference to its subsumed activities objectively implied female participation even as some pointed out that traditional gender roles were enforced, meaning that women could only occasionally assume leadership roles in many movement organizations. Inspired by militant women, Chicanas integrated Mexican and Latin American feminist heritages and drew from the contemporary radical feminist programs. Increasingly, women's organizations grew out of community actions, political campaigns, union groups, campus activities, and inmate and ex-felon concerns. The late 1960s and the 1970s witnessed an increasing emphasis on full female participation in all aspects of community civic efforts as well as on the development of activities specific to women. At the same time, movement newspapers and journals increased their coverage on issues pertinent to gender issues.

Chicanas believed in Chicana solutions to Chicana problems the same way that Chicanos upheld Chicano solutions to Chicano problems. The initial impetus was for a critique of stereotypes impeding gender equality. This thrust grew organizationally, and its edge reflected the internal dynamics within movement organizations. Eventually a view of Chicanas as the victims of multiple oppressions (as women, ethnics, and workers) evolved. Female activity remained strongest in community arenas such as those of unionization and public services. The majority of Chicana activists participated in organizations that were not exclusively female, but gender issues arose in all groups and circumstances and were dealt with in one way or another. Over time Chicana/o organizations have had prominent female members. In fact, MALDEF (Mexican American Legal Defense and Educational Fund), a highly visible civil rights organization, has had two long-term national women leaders. Women in higher education circles had advantaged access to forums from the 1980s onward and publicized their views and priorities. Despite resistance and controversy, veteran militants did not ultimately defer the feminist concerns, and eventually a persistent strain of efforts addressed the needs and concerns of lesbian and bisexual women.

Universalism

From the late 1960s through the 1970s, the tendencies of utopian indigenismo, cultural nationalism, and Saul Alinsky–style civil rights activism seemingly spread. These spoke only partially to the more structurally oriented economic critiques of the Mexican-American reality being raised. These criticisms were condensed into a modestly growing Marxist current within the Mexican-American community containing many of the various Marxist tendencies found in the United States. For some Marxism remained an intellectual fad, and a few considered it a philosophical critique of the capitalist society and capitalist "hegemonic culture" in particular. For others Marxism became a conceptual framework for examining the Mexican experience in a more specific and extensive manner, particularly as related to labor and gender. And some took it as an ideology combining analysis and guidance in political action and organizational structure. In this renovation, members of the 1960s and 1970s generations joined Marxists from the 1940s and 1950s. Despite the Chicana/o left wing's ideological commonality, this sector's social makeup was varied. Moreover, a substantial part of the Mexican Left had no specific organizational allegiance. And the part that did drew a distinction between those groups stemming from the community, such as CASA (Court Appointed Special Advocates), and those outside of it.

Problems and Achievements

As the events of the 1960s and 1970s unfolded, a presently unmeasurable element impacted political development, organization, and leadership. Police surveillance presumably occurred throughout the Southwest among Chicana/o efforts. Targets were determined, strategies devised, and tactics conducted to weaken militancy and political organizations of all types. This covert procedure was concurrent with the more visible and understood overt activities of incitements, arrests, and beatings. Police provocation to commit violent acts and, more frequently, display counterproductive behavior, was a fact. This of course led to dissension within or between groups, as well as among individuals. Police control remained constant throughout the 1970s, perhaps negatively affecting achievements.

By stressing self-determination, pride, and even aggression, the spokespersons of the Chicana/o movement achieved reasonable successes during the 1960s and 1970s: they made the larger social majority acknowledge the discrepancy between the democratic stance professed by the state and the reality in the barrios. Moreover, leaders undertook the strong actions needed to enable the more moderate elements to enter governmental, academic, and labor institutions. Significantly, several movement thrusts continued: unionization, Chicano studies, civil rights litigation, and immigrant rights are some examples.

Clear limitations stand out when reviewing the accomplishments of the movement. Token reforms, limited representation, and personal mobility were often achieved. But Chicano self-determination, though espoused, was not accomplished. The problems confronting the movement were several: the lack of a coherent, broad, radical program for a convinced constituency; a lack of adequate material resources; and a lack of structured disciplined organizations with stable leadership mechanisms.

Conclusion

The Chicana/o movement reflected a broad and deep range of activities, most of which proved seminal to the debates, issues, and forms of later years. By the late 1970s, activists and goals diffused, and priorities and means were transformed. The intensity of the movement's momentum diminished somewhat, and activism too often became a consciously delimited activity for individuals. Mexican-American political players were no longer easily identifiable as stemming from two or three sectors within the community, nor did they share the same ethnic fervor or radical perspective as the militant Chicanas/os who had first created the context and opportunity for empowerment. Rather, spokespersons and leaders, women and men, became a complex amalgam of backgrounds, interests, ways, and goals. A growing number of professional politicians surfaced from a variety of Mexican communities, each of them espousing the concerns of a unique political constituency, and were increasingly acknowledged or tolerated as public "leadership." Many young Mexicans had explored the forbearance of the establishment and, in every way accessible, pursued what the system offered and accepted pragmatic ways of achieving reformist results. Almost bereft of resources, activists transmuted their energy into assets for their community. In that turnabout, young Chicanas/os motivated a large percentage of their community leaders to exhibit a stronger public image. In effect, they demanded that society at large receive a new message about what it meant to be of Mexican descent. They also generated support for educational, political, and economic advancements.

Public officials began addressing issues of concern to Mexican-Americans in a more considerate manner. Finally, and perhaps most importantly, the Chicana/o movement forced certain concessions from the Anglo institutional mainstream, and some of these concessions—voting and representational rights, partial bilingual education, meagerly funded Chicano studies programs and unenthusiastic affirmative-action employment practices—created a setting from which a viable Mexican middle class could expand to local prominence. The 1960s and 1970s activists also laid the groundwork for a series of economic advancements, so that by the 1980s a Mexican middle class had indeed effectively consolidated within the community. The short-term occupational gains of the 1970s were perhaps magnified by the economic setbacks of the 1980s and the consequences of 1990s globalism. Mexican-Americans suffered the effects of drastic federal policy changes lessening government support for affirmative action and civil rights affirmations. But as with other U.S. constituencies, some Mexican-American

analysts in the late 1980s totaled the score card. The score was short but the game was still on.

In retrospect, the late twentieth century looms as a time of cultural revitalization within the community. This was evident in the energies directed toward education, unions, the arts, the media, and religious institutions, as well as in a period of increased efforts at social integration. In a whip of that cultural whirlwind, the Chicana/o community remains tempered by a uniquely Mexican-American concern for both cultural continuity and political affirmation while testing how pluralistic the allegedly diverse system is. In the 1990s, dominant social elites put forth two overarching responses: promulgate the belief that civil rights gains had consolidated, and propagandize the notion that Mexican aliens subverted the society by their presence. In this context, the master narrative of the Chicana/o movement is still being elaborated.

See also **Bilingualism and Multilingualism; Ethnohistory, U.S.; Feminism: Chicana Feminisms; Indigenismo; Political Protest, U.S.**

BIBLIOGRAPHY

Acuña, Rodolfo. *A Community under Siege: A Chronicle of Chicanos East of the Los Angeles River, 1945–1975.* Los Angeles: Chicano Studies Research Center, University of California, Los Angeles, 1984.

———. *Occupied America: A History of the Chicanos.* 5th ed. New York: Pearson Longman, 2004.

Chavez, Ernesto. *Mi Raza Primero! (My people first!): Nationalism, Identity, and Insurgency in the Chicano Movement in Los Angeles.* Berkeley: University of California Press, 2002.

Delgado Bernal, Dolores. *Chicana School Resistance.* Ph.D. dissertation, University of California, Los Angeles, 1999.

Garcia, Alma M., ed. *Chicana Feminist Thought: The Basic Historical Writings.* New York: Routledge, 1997.

Garciá, Ignacio. *United We Win: The Rise and Fall of La Raza Unida Party.* Tucson: University of Arizona Press, 1989.

Gómez-Quinones, Juan. *Mexican Students Por La Raza: The Chicano Student Movement in Southern California, 1967–1977.* Santa Barbara, Calif.: Editorial La Causa, 1978.

Gonzales Berry, Erlinda, and David Maciel, eds. *The Contested Homeland: A Chicano History of New Mexico.* Albuquerque: University of New Mexico Press, 2001.

Gutierrez, Jose Angel. *The Making of a Chicano Militant.* Madison: University of Wisconsin Press, 1998.

Mora, Magdalena, and Adelaida del Castillo, eds. *Mexican Women in the United States: Struggles Past and Present.* Los Angeles: Chicano Studies Research Center, University of California, Los Angeles, 1980.

Muñoz, Carlos. *Youth, Identity, Power: The Chicano Movement.* London and New York: Verso, 1989.

Navarro, Armando. *Mexican American Youth Organization: Avant-Garde of the Chicano Movement in Texas.* Austin: University of Texas Press, 1985.

Rosales, Francisco Arturo. *Chicano! The History of the Mexican American Civil Rights Movement.* Houston: Arte Público Press, 1996.

Sanchez, David. *Expedition through Aztlan.* Los Angeles: Perspectiva Press, 1996.

Vigil, Ernesto. *The Crusade for Justice: Chicano Militancy and the Government's War on Dissent.* Madison: University of Wisconsin Press, 1969.

Juan Gómez-Quiñones
Irene Vasquez Morris

CHILDHOOD AND CHILD REARING.

During the last two centuries, even amid poverty and war, more children have had the opportunity for successful lives than ever before. The modern concern for child health, education, and well-being, however, emerged only after long millennia in which children's welfare was subordinated to the needs and goals of caretakers and communities—a pattern also encountered today in developing regions of the world. In recent decades, scholars have gained considerable understanding of the experience of children, as well as attitudes toward childhood in the premodern world.

The Child-Centered Modern Age

Since the nineteenth century, scholars, scientists, and writers, along with lawyers, statesmen, and philanthropists, have concerned themselves with the nature and welfare of the child as at no previous time. Triggering that interest were the ideas of John Locke (1632–1704), Jean-Jacques Rousseau (1712–1778), and later authors of the Romantic movement.

Elaborated in his *Essay on Human Understanding* (1690), Locke's notion that the human infant's brain is a tabula rasa, free of innate ideas but subject to the formative stresses of the environment, made the earliest stage of human development seem critical. In his *Émile* (1762), Rousseau understood the child as a noble savage, best able to gather knowledge as he pursued his natural interests and instincts long before he needed to master the artificial skills of the schoolroom. Soon afterwards, Romantic writers and artists idealized childhood innocence and empathized with childhood experience, as did William Blake (1757–1827) in his *Songs of Innocence* (1789) and William Wordsworth (1770–1850) in his *Ode: Intimations of Immortality from Recollections of Early Childhood* (1807).

The exploration of childhood proceeded as new "social sciences" of the human condition developed. Charles Darwin's (1809–1882) theory of evolution by the process of natural selection, described in his seminal works *The Origin of Species* (1859) and *The Descent of Man* (1871), envisioned the creation of new species as the product of individual acts of procreation by millions of genetically privileged individuals—a vision of biological change, that is, centered on the birth of new infant generations. In a series of works published from the 1890s through the 1930s, the Austrian psychoanalyst Sigmund Freud (1856–1939) explored the role of childhood trauma on later adulthood and mapped the struggles toward autonomy of the developing infant personality. In *The School and Society* (1899), among other works, the American philosopher John Dewey (1859–1952) redefined the purpose of education: its aim was not to instill the accumulation of adult learning but to prepare future citizens and workers.

Practitioners of the new science of anthropology traveled the globe to study pre-state human societies, including their child-rearing concepts and practices, an interest exhibited in, among others, Margaret Mead's (1901–1978) *Coming of Age in Samoa* (1928). Sociologists investigated the situation of youth in modern societies, looking at peer groups, youth gangs, adolescent drug use, and teen pregnancy, among many other topics. Psychologists explored early childhood learning and development, a topic they share more recently with biologists, philosophers, and linguists in the interdisciplinary pursuit of "cognitive science."

Social reformers, philanthropists, and journalists, meanwhile, took up the cause of child welfare, as did Danish-born Jacob Riis (1849–1914) and Lewis Hine (1874–1940), for instance, who depicted in photographs and prose the condition of "street Arabs" and child workers at the turn of the twentieth century in America. While advocating women's civil rights, the early feminist movement highlighted women's maternal capacities and duties, an orientation that culminated in the publication in 1900 of the Swedish feminist Ellen Key's (1849–1926) influential book, *The Century of the Child*.

In the twentieth century, both communist and fascist governments targeted the child. Soviet Communism promoted collective childcare so as to free women to become workers, while Italian Fascists and German Nazis adopted maternalist and pro-natalist policies. Totalitarian states of both persuasions promoted youth societies that indoctrinated adolescents in official ideology. Reeling from the slaughter of World War I, meanwhile, democratic states instituted welfare policies that supported mothers, families, and children. Among the free and the unfree, twentieth century wars and genocidal projects resulted in the slaughter, starvation, displacement, and militarization of children. The United Nations Convention on the Rights of the Child (1989) addresses these, among other abuses of children that have survived in the modern world.

At the same time, the twentieth century has also seen great progress in the medical care of the child. The modern practice of childbirth put traditional midwives out of business by about 1900. Whereas vaccination for smallpox had been known since the eighteenth century, the twentieth century brought new vaccinations against diseases dangerous specifically for children, such as diphtheria. In addition, the availability of pasteurization, refrigeration, and devices for artificial feeding dramatically improved survival rates of abandoned and orphaned children. Funded by public and private monies, social workers tended to the needs of the children of the poor and immigrant populations. Experts on child rearing flooded the market with advice books for middle-class readers, a flood epitomized by the popular work of Dr. Benjamin Spock (1903–1998), whose *Common Sense Book of Baby and Child Care,* first published in 1946, reached its seventh edition before the author's death in 1998.

A generation before Spock's death, however, a new book appeared in France that shook the scholarly world: Philippe Ariès's *Centuries of Childhood* (1960; English trans., 1962). So careful of children had citizens of the modern West become that they had forgotten the lost world of not so very long ago:

The Virgin and Child Before a Firescreen by Robert Campin, c. 1430. Oil on wood. The many artistic depictions of Mary and the baby Jesus created throughout the centuries have served to focus attention on the symbiotic relationship that exists between mother and child. © THE ART ARCHIVE / NATIONAL GALLERY LONDON / EILEEN TWEEDY

the premodern world, where children perhaps counted not so much as in the present era, or at least not in the same way.

The Historicity of Childhood

Centuries of Childhood presents the thesis that the "concept of childhood" itself is modern: a creation of the seventeenth and eighteenth centuries. This thesis has been disputed and defended by later scholars. As a product of that controversy, the historicity of childhood has been established indisputably. The concept of childhood, along with childhood itself, is subject to change in changing historical circumstances.

In earlier times, Ariès argued, children were perceived as participants in adult society. They shared the same amusements as adults and did not have distinctive occupations or adornments. Even at school, children, adolescents, and adults intermingled, without distinction of age. The important boundary was not between child and elder, but dependent and master. Sentimental relations between parents and children were weakened, moreover, by the frequency of child death. Attitudes began to shift in the seventeenth century as smaller, coherent family groups supported the experience of individual children. Literary works evinced a newfound affection for children, while families willingly invested in child accessories and

education and grieved at child deaths. Ariès based his arguments mainly on literary texts and artistic representations, mostly from France and England between 1500 and 1750.

Ariès's work evoked responses that critiqued and confirmed his hypotheses. In 1965 the British historian Peter Laslett published *The World We Have Lost* echoing some of Ariès's conclusions. Laslett was reporting on the project of empirical research on the history of the family centered at Cambridge University, which studied such archival sources as baptismal records for evidence of family structure, ages of baptism, marriage, and death. Using different sources, Laslett, like Ariès, concluded that the experience of past childhood was unlike that in the modern age: such children lived in a world we have lost.

Also affirming Ariès's hypothesis, Lawrence Stone's massive *Family, Sex, and Marriage in England, 1500–1800* (1977) focused on elite households and utilized literary evidence such as diaries, autobiographies, and letters. Over three stages of development ranging from large, authoritarian households to smaller, more egalitarian ones, the family became increasingly "affective," Stone argued, characterized by strong sentimental ties and abundant investment in child welfare.

The American psychohistorian Lloyd de Mause, agreeing with Ariès and Stone on the greater importance of the child in modern times, proposed a model of the history of childhood that unfolded in five stages from the horrors of antiquity to the enlightened childrearing practices of the present day. Declaring in his seminal 1973 essay "The Evolution of Childhood" that the history of childhood was a "nightmare from which we have just begun to awaken," de Mause credited modern psychoanalytic theory with persuading adults to abandon age-old practices of abuse and consciously to further the child's autonomy and creativity. Also highlighting recent shifts in child-rearing attitudes, Edward Shorter's *Making of the Modern Family* (1975) argued that warmer, sentimental relations between men and women encouraged a stronger bond between mother and child.

Historians of the Italian Renaissance, examining a period (principally the fifteenth century) well before the kind of turning point in perceptions of children identified by Ariès, Stone, de Mause, or Shorter, found a trove of empirical data that permitted the mapping of household structures of Florence and its surrounding countryside. The work of David Herlihy and Christiane Klapisch-Zuber, first published in 1978, yielded important insights about family size and ethos in different social groups. In essays collected and republished in 1993, Richard Trexler further explored both the dependency of children in Florence and their capacity as innocents as agents of salvation. Turning from Florence, Margaret King studied childhood death and adult bereavement in a noble Venetian family (1994).

While not aligning themselves as supporters or opponents of Ariès, Renaissance historians added to the evidence pointing to the difference between modern and past childhoods. In the wake of Stone's study, however, historians of England plunged into the controversy, generally to defend past parents and childhoods. Clarissa Atkinson's study of medieval motherhood, and Barbara Hanawalt's of children in fourteenth-century London, pointed to the complexity of past family relationships in contradiction to Ariès's notion of a premodern "indifference." More heatedly, Linda Pollock plowed through hundreds of diaries (mostly seventeenth century) to support her claim that parents cared deeply about their children. Alan Macfarlane, in studies of the origins of English individualism (1978) and of love and marriage in the early modern era (1986), proposed that familial relationships in England had long exhibited supposedly "modern" qualities of profound sentiment.

Examining Puritan communities in England and colonial Anglo-America, John Sommerville and John Demos each found attitudes toward children that were surprisingly modern. Examining family documents from Reformation-era Germany in several studies between 1983 and 2001, Steven Ozment argued (as had Macfarlane for England) that modern sentiments of family intimacy were well-established long before the modern age. Historians of ancient Greece and Rome such as Mark Golden and Suzanne Dixon, similarly, did not detect, as Ariès had suggested, any lack of a "concept" of childhood. Anthropologists note that in the Americas, early documents about the Aztec and Inca civilizations reveal a very structured picture of the life course, in which phases of childhood play an important role; in tribal societies of Africa and the Americas, too, initiation rituals divide a life into discrete phases associated with childhood, adolescence, parenthood, and grandparenthood. Hugh Cunningham, finally, focusing on children in the industrial era, placed the break between older and modern perceptions of children not in the early modern era, as had Ariès and Stone, but in the nineteenth century.

This brief overview shows that Ariès's pioneering hypothesis did not win universal acceptance from scholars. On one point agreement has been general: childhood is not the unchanging phenomenon contemporary experts often assume it is, but it varies according to time, setting, social context, gender, and culture. Ariès's great achievement was to establish the historicity of childhood as something no longer capable of refutation.

That established, it is clear that scholars have moved beyond the issues of the Ariès debate to explore a broader range of issues. These include issues concerning the child in the context of the mother-child relationship; those concerning the child in the context of the father-headed household; and those related to the training and education of children. This survey concludes with a consideration of the impact of industrialization on childhood, ushering us into the modern world.

Mother and Child: The First Dyad

Women alone give birth to children, although in the simplest band-level societies, child rearing is a more collective enterprise than among later agriculturalists, and even among agricultural peoples, social structures such as kin groups (clans and lineages) and polygynous marriages often lead to families in which children acknowledge multiple adults who raise them, and adults correspondingly recognize their responsibilities to-

Eskimo mother and child, c. 1915, photographed by H. G. Kaiser. The ultimate human bond has long been believed to be that between mother and child, and many cultures possess myths and legends centering on avenging mothers and mother goddesses. NATIONAL ARCHIVES AND RECORDS ADMINISTRATION

ward children other than their own birth children. In history, those children who survived were reared by mothers or mother surrogates. Even in advanced societies, the most powerful of human bonds has been that between mother and child, and the metaphor of motherhood is often used by other adults in expressing their bond with a child, as Gracia Clark has shown in her studies of West African motherhood. The dependency of the child on the mother, and the implication of the mother in the life of the child, is expressed in artistic representations of the mother-child dyad that appear in many different cultural settings—most famously, for Western civilization, in the image of Mary, the virgin mother, and the child Jesus. In recent years, however, African-American and Chicana scholars, while emphasizing the significance of motherhood within their cultural traditions, have used concepts such as "Othermothering" to underscore that mothering is typically a task shared among kinswomen, in contrast to the isolated white mother of the middle-class Euro-American nuclear family.

The importance of motherhood is further expressed in mythologies and cult objects: mother goddesses, fierce and gentle, the consorts of their sons, the guarantors of the fertility of the fields or of safety in childbirth, conspirators at times against the power of men. The fantasies of maternal power are also expressed in fantasies of matriarchal societies—although scholars now generally agree that there were none truly such—such as that of the Amazons.

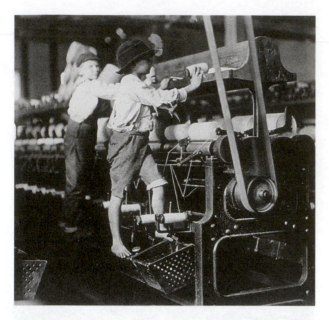

Children working in a textile mill. During the early years of the industrial era, children were frequently employed to work long hours under dangerous conditions in factories and mills. By the end of the nineteenth century, inquests into child safety resulted in protective laws being passed. THE LIBRARY OF CONGRESS

Although anthropologists, linguists, and literary critics have been the primary observers of the ancient figure of the mother, real and mythic, historians have also examined the circles of women who surround the mother. These were the women who, across cultures, gathered to assist mothers in childbirth—female kin, friends, servants, and neighbors—while the skilled expert among them, the midwife, took charge. (Male physicians retained control of the theoretical literature about childbirth until the eighteenth century, when they took on the obstetrical role as well.) The same communities of women gathered to mourn the dead, or to provide advice at times of crisis and illness. John Riddle has shown in his works on abortion and herbalism that these informal women's groups wordlessly transmitted medical and physiological information across generations.

In some societies, such female communities lived in physical isolation within larger households, as in the *gynaeceum* of the ancient Greeks, or the "inner quarters" of elite Chinese families. Here children of both sexes were raised until about age seven, and girls remained until they were wed. The harems of the Chinese emperors and Ottoman sultans constituted more formalized versions of such female communities. In these separate worlds, women gave birth, raised children, tended the sick, spun thread, and mourned the dead.

Supported by female networks, mothers faced that first essential task after childbirth itself: breastfeeding. The health and survival chances of all children before modern times depended on the availability of a lactating mother or mother-surrogate, as Valerie Fildes has shown in her comprehensive history of nursing. The alternatives that were attempted, including arti-

ficial feeding of nonhuman milk and nursing from animal teats, often resulted in infant death. In societies such as ancient Rome and the Americas, slave nurses nourished and reared the children of their masters. In the premodern West and later colonial and postcolonial settings, paid wetnurses were hired to feed the children of the nobility, and later of urban, colonial, and racial elites. Gilberto Freye's classic psychosocial analysis of Brazilian society, *The Masters and the Slaves* (English trans., 1947), dissects the effects of this infantile closeness with the black female body, and concomitant distance from the white mother, on the sexual development of Brazil's upper classes. This practice was commonplace in premodern Europe despite the universal advice of expert physicians, theologians, and philosophers. In the West, as in China and the Islamic world, injunctions to mothers to nurse their children account for a large part of all advice literature pertaining to children.

Mothers regularly experienced the deaths of their offspring in childbirth, in infancy, and in early childhood, an experience that is still common today for the world's poor, as documented in Nancy Scheper-Hughes's penetrating analysis of motherhood in urban Brazil, *Death without Weeping* (1992). The toll of infant death prior to modernization was in the range of 20 to 50 percent of live births, statistics that remain all too common in impoverished areas of the developing world. In the near-absence of birth control, fertility was high, and women commonly gave birth to many children, with totals of more than twenty not uncommon; yet mothers often saw only a few children reach adulthood. The high rate of infant and child mortality is the single most important fact to be culled from the history of childhood; as Scheper-Hughes documents, childhood signifies differently when few children reach adulthood.

Most babies died of disease or malnutrition, from which perils their mothers could not protect them, as they still cannot today. Others died also from accidents, neglect, or infanticide, the last of these an act most often perpetrated by mothers—and sometimes by salaried or servile nurses. Impoverished mothers, often servants, slaves, or prostitutes, or others whose conception and parturition was deemed "illegitimate," were often, and disproportionately, infanticidal. Enslaved Africans and American Indian mothers often chose to terminate their infants' lives rather than see them grow up under the tragic circumstances in which their mothers lived; for slave women, this horror was compounded by the knowledge that the children belonged to the master, and not to their own parents.

Mothering varies, of course, according to economic status. Among working families, the labor of absent mothers earning cash to support their children counted as material symbols of maternal love, whereas in middle-class, mid-twentieth-century American families, it was the presence of the mother inside the home rather than in the workplace that demonstrated her commitment to her children. In wealthy households, mothers are often freed from the constant demands of children by the services provided by hired help—nannies, babysitters, and tutors. In contemporary American and European societies, this labor is provided by immigrant women whose own children are often a continent away, cared for by grandparents or other female kin.

In Western society, the profound detestation of maternal, and more broadly female, endangerment of children is witnessed by the condemnation and, sporadically, prosecution of abortion and infanticide. The idea of the evil mother appears to have triggered profound passions expressed in the fantasies of the evil deeds done by witches (in Europe, especially the fifteenth to seventeenth centuries); by Christians (as perceived by the Romans during the late-ancient era of persecution); or by Jews (as perceived by Christians during anti-Semitic outbursts). All of these persecuted malefactors were believed to have sickened, killed, and cannibalized children.

The vulnerability of children was thus a source of great anxiety to the adults who, nevertheless, sacrificed children to divine forces in a practice that was once nearly universal—as Martin Bergmann, among others, informs us. Although mothers were not the only agents of child sacrifice, the connection already seen of women with death and mourning, with the often fatal event of childbirth, and with frequent child death, indicates that connection.

Successful mothers of child survivors were, in addition, the primary educators of children. Modern social science has established that mothers and mother substitutes are the first teachers of language—in the Western world, a fact reflected in the term used for the natal language as the "mother tongue" (*lingua materna, Muttersprache*). In the United States, the notion of "mother language" took on special poignancy for the young children of immigrants. Warm childhood memories of the smells and sounds of their monolingual mother's kitchens contrasted with life at school and workplaces, where they struggled to master the language and customs of an alien and sometimes racially and ethnically hostile world. Throughout history, male suspicion of mothers and nurses as shapers of language also testifies to their important role: the ancient Roman statesman and author Cato the Elder (234–149 B.C.E.) would not have his children spoken to by nurses, and the Dutch humanist Desiderius Erasmus (1466?–1536) disdained the linguistic environment of the nursery and urged the swift conveyance of the child to a qualified tutor. In contrast, Chinese theorists celebrated those heroic mothers who prepared their sons from infancy to study for the civil service examinations.

The maternal role was probably more potent than these experts feared. Before written texts, the values and traditions of a culture were probably transmitted in story and, even more likely, in song, sung by mothers and nurses to generations of infants. In more developed societies, mothers and mother-surrogates were the first agents of religious instruction, a powerful welder of civilizational loyalties.

The Household: The Father's Domain

In premodern times, a child's chances of survival depended on her mother's availability to nurture; but so, too, on her father's benevolence. For once human beings joined together in sedentary communities to engage in agricultural production, the father-headed household made an appearance. Fathers were the gatekeepers of households, and the guardians of the children he admitted to them. Those fortunate children were generally the offspring of approved women: those considered to be "legitimate." A bright line divided the spheres of legitimacy and illegitimacy, with great consequence for the lives of children (even though, in many societies, the illegitimate children of concubines lived under the same roof as their preferred half-siblings).

In Greek and Roman society, the master of the household had the power to welcome or reject a newborn child. Children not so welcomed would be "exposed," or placed outside the household in a place where they might perhaps perish, or possibly be retrieved by other families seeking a servant or by slavedealers interested in exploiting the child as a laborer or prostitute. As John Boswell carefully noted, exposure was not necessarily coterminous with infanticide; but certainly, a child's destiny was more assured if he remained in the household into which he was born.

The "exposure," abandonment, or killing of unwanted infants was commonplace in ancient civilizations, including China as well as those of the Mediterranean world. The aim was to limit population and conserve household resources, purposes achieved in modern times by contraception and abortion. Another form of abandonment practiced in medieval Europe, which may also have been caused by demographic factors, had at least superficially a religious motivation as well. Children given to a monastery, as "oblates" (offerings), would not only disburden a family of too many children, but would enhance their parents' chances of salvation. Yet the oblation of a child had ancient roots as well and approaches the phenomenon of child sacrifice as much as that of abandonment.

When fathers kept or exposed children, gender issues came into play. Boys were generally preferred to girls, as skewed sex ratios in different communities of the ancient world inform us; indeed, they still do so inform us, as sex preference by abortion is widely practiced today in Asia. When girls were raised in the household, the status of males remained higher. In ancient Rome, for instance, when boys received distinctive personal names at birth, girls bore their fathers' name with a feminine ending: the daughter of Julius, for instance, was Julia. In Italian Renaissance genealogies, daughters were often anonymous, designated only as "filia" (daughter). In contrast, in some pre-state societies, such as those of the American Iroquois or Hopi, the birth of a female child was celebrated.

In Western and Asian civilizations, boys were generally preferred to girls as heirs, whether they were valued as the keepers of the family rites, as in China and Rome, or as the inheritors of property, as they were nearly everywhere. The dowry was a common device—prevalent among the Hebrews and Babylonians, the Chinese and Indians, the Greeks and Romans, and premodern Europeans—used to give a limited portion of a patrimony to daughters upon marriage (or entry to a convent, in Christendom) so that the bulk of it was preserved for one or more sons.

The concern with inheritance, resulting in the devaluation of daughters relative to sons, characterizes societies organized by father-dominated households. The organization of those households, however, varies enormously according to region, era, and social rank. In China, India, and Islamic society, the young tended to marry early and remain within or closely related to the bridegroom's male kin. In Islam, endogamous marriage, principally to first cousins, was and remains common, and polygamy, although never universal, is permitted. In China, young brides often suffered under the hand of their powerful mothers-in-law.

European society, in a pattern especially characteristic of northwestern Europe, tended toward late marriage and the establishment of autonomous households, and truly nuclear families, by the newly married. As Alan Macfarlane has argued (1978, and again in 1985), the latter pattern, which prevailed in England, was conducive to the development of behavioral autonomy and the sense of individualism that was to manifest itself in the theoretical products of the Renaissance and Enlightenment. Certainly, in monogamous, nuclear families, it may be assumed that individual children received greater parental attention, with a consequent enhancement of their life chances.

The iron reality of high mortality meant that, whether the family was more or less extended, all children in premodern times experienced a different type of household than is common in contemporary society. Women generally gave birth to children over the whole span of their fertile years. Their first-born children might be twenty or more years older than their last. Sibling relationships would be greatly complicated by this fact: late-born children would find themselves subject to the authority of early children, if those remained at home; or early-born children might be ejected early from the household in favor of late-born dependents. As women's lives were often cut short by death in childbirth, moreover, husbands tended to remarry, and more than once. Their second and subsequent wives continued to bear children, who were half-children of the first wife, occasioning even more intense sibling rivalries and the often-hostile presence of the stepmother.

When the father of the household died, patterns of widow remarriage differed. In China, India, and the West, the preference was that they should not remarry—and in traditional India, some widows died on their husbands' funeral pyres, in the Hindu custom of suttee. In Europe, although chaste widowhood was theoretically preferred, widow remarriage was common. Young widows who remarried might surrender their children to their husband's kin. Widows who did not remarry might continue to rear their children in the households of their husbands, or form one of the few woman-headed households.

A child's life chances in history depended even more than today on the nature of her mother, her father, and her household. So too did the kind of training or education that children received.

Training and Education: The Circulation of Children
Maternal rearing lasted until the age of seven, approximately, in most societies. Thereafter, although some girls continued under their mothers' care until marriage, most children learned

the tasks of adulthood elsewhere: from tutors, at work, in school, or by apprenticeship.

Almost universally, the age of seven (sometimes six or eight) is the point at which children were thought to reach an age of competence. At that point, they could perform tasks responsibly, understand religious instruction, or begin formal education. At this point, too, boys were generally transferred from maternal to paternal oversight. In some tribal societies, as in such settings as ancient Sparta, the Ottoman Janissary Corps, and the nineteenth-century English public school, boys have been removed from the care of their mothers at an early age and raised in exclusively male groups—a kind of collective extension of paternal care.

If there was general agreement on the approximate age of seven as demarcating a stage of childhood, other demarcations were variable. Weaning (around eighteen months to two years was typical in the Western world) marked for some the boundary between infancy and early childhood. Later childhood was often seen to begin somewhere after age ten, when children were seen working outside the home, although some did so as early as age eight or nine as well. Some societies, like the Jews and the Romans, ritually marked the entry of boys into adulthood at age thirteen or fourteen. Minimum ages of marriage for girls clustered around age twelve.

No consensus, therefore, existed on the stages of childhood after age seven, or about the length of childhood. The child who was trained to peasant labor, or apprenticed to a master, or sent into service, or swept up in the experience of war, had only a brief childhood. In those peasant societies where household structures were extended, as in China, sons lived in the natal household even after marriage, still subordinate to paternal authority, while girls often married young, to be raised by the parents of their young husbands. In Western society, where it was common for young couples to begin their own separate households, adulthood began with marriage.

After regional and cultural factors, the boundaries of childhood depended most on the social standing of the child. In Western society, many children were in a process of circulation from ages as young as eight or nine. The poor were sent from home to labor as servants; nobles to acquire the skills of knighthood (if male) or household management (if female); those of artisan origin to apprenticeships lasting five, seven, or even ten years. Children circulated for purposes other than work or training. Wealthy households took in the surplus or orphaned children of their kin, while the children of an unwed or widowed mother would follow her on a tedious journey in search of shelter or employment.

In contrast, those children privileged enough to remain at home, supported by their bourgeois or aristocratic parents, were the real prototype of modern children. Dressed in special clothing, and endowed with specialized objects—known to us as toys—to enhance their play, they would be perceived as uniquely innocent. They would be protected from exposure to adult sexuality and violence; they would be tended in illness and mourned in death; and they might be given tutors and teachers and provided a liberal education. An interesting comparison is provided by Bronislaw Malinowski's famous description of childhood in the Trobriand Islands off the coast of Papua New Guinea, where children spent their days in a separate "nation of children," similarly freed from adult responsibility, but also from adult supervision to a degree unthinkable in the upper- and middle-class West.

Until recent times, schooling has been an opportunity limited to the fortunate few. One of the hallmarks of civilization, literacy was initially the property of an esoteric elite of priests and scribes. In Mesopotamia, Egypt, and China, writing consisted of numerous and intricate characters that were learned with difficulty and reproduced slowly. That pattern persisted in imperial China, where the literary arts were highly esteemed, and families sacrificed so that their sons could be educated and compete, and sometimes qualify for office, in strenuous state-run examinations. In tribal societies, sex-specific education could last for years, but usually took place in sex-segregated contexts and depended upon the oral and ritual transmission of knowledge.

Alphabetic writing systems made literacy easier to achieve. As merchants and artisans gained access to writing skills, schooling became more generalized. In Greek, Hellenistic, and Roman society, literacy was relatively widespread among urban elites. Islamic civilization, as well, esteemed literacy. Significant numbers of Muslims from the straits of Gibraltar into south Asia and Oceania learned to read Arabic, the language of the Koran.

In the wake of the Germanic invasions of the fifth and sixth centuries, the level of civilization in Europe dropped dramatically from Roman days. For centuries, literacy was limited to members of the Christian church hierarchy: priests and monks. Schools were appendages of monasteries and cathedrals, their prime purpose to supply the minimal knowledge of Latin necessary to perform the liturgy. As scholastic (school-based) learning developed in the twelfth and thirteenth century, stimulated by the incorporation of ancient Greek (especially Aristotelian) texts, universities took form. In these institutions of higher learning—the world's first—students in their teens and twenties gained degrees in philosophy, theology, medicine, and law. In the Americas, Aztec and Inca noble youth entered priest-run schools where they received education in the forms of knowledge; only among the Maya, however, would this include literacy in the Western sense.

The humanists of the Italian Renaissance created a form of schooling beyond the church-based system, whose purpose was to enlighten and develop the individual rather than to instill specific systems of knowledge. The Protestant and Catholic Reformations each adopted the Renaissance notion of elementary and secondary schools that now proliferated, serving to prepare not only a priestly class, but male elites from the middle classes and the nobility, and even girls at elementary levels. These educational initiatives, together with revolutions in economics and science that made backward Europe the dominant world power, greatly enhanced the chances children would have for their own advancement.

Schooling came at a cost for young students—the cost of corporal punishment. From antiquity, the symbol of a teacher was the rod that he wielded to "correct" the unruly or unresponsive student. In medieval Europe, it was understood that Latin was literally to be beaten into the young. Although humanist pedagogues deplored the use of the rod, corporal punishment remained a feature of the schoolroom into modern times. Such abuse was only an extension of norms outside the classroom. Those with power could visit physical chastisement on their dependents: masters over apprentices, householders over servants, the state over malefactors, and fathers over children. Perhaps the world has seen, over the last century, along with those consumed by Holocaust, world war, and state-sponsored famine, the first children to escape the rod.

The Advent of Modernity: School and Work

The twin processes of Enlightenment and industrialization mark the division between premodern and modern for childhood and concepts of childhood. Whereas the Enlightenment introduced the ideas with which this article began, leading to the modern disciplines that specialize in the condition and care of the child, industrialization introduced new forms of exploitation of children, but also, in time, new opportunities for family life as standards of living eventually rose. In the two areas of work and schooling, the lives of children changed most dramatically during the industrial era.

Industrialization meant, above all, the factory organization of labor. Children, notoriously, labored in the early factories, to the great detriment of their health and well-being. As industrialization progressed, an inquest into the welfare of children workers resulted in Britain's Factory Act of 1833, which set hour limits for child workdays. Following suit, most advanced nations introduced the regulation of child labor, beginning with France in 1841, and culminating in the first decades of the next century with Japan, Russia, and the United States. Today, child labor is found in developing regions of the world and is the subject of investigation and censure by many activists and policy-makers in the developed world.

As policy-makers, employers, and parents came to understand that children must not spend their lives in factory labor, they established instead the goal of sending all children to school. Beginning with France by 1878 and Britain by 1891, secular, free, and compulsory mass public education was the norm for the wealthiest nations of Europe and the Americas, as well as rapidly modernized Japan. At the same time, the kindergarten movement created by central European pedagogical theorists Johann Heinrich Pestalozzi (1746–1827) and Friedrich W. A. Froebel (1782–1852) swept the Western world, encouraging the establishment of kindergartens supported by fee-paying elite parents and charitable institutions. In the early twentieth century, Maria Montessori (1870–1952) introduced the concept of a nursery school for the very young, featuring child-friendly spaces and materials and a structured but individualized and child-appropriate curriculum. In the more privileged countries, these opportunities for young children have become increasingly commonplace. In poor countries, in contrast, even children over age seven, especially girls, lack the opportunity for a basic education.

New Dictionary of the History of Ideas

Laslett's depiction of *The World We Have Lost* poignantly alerted modern readers to the unbridgeable distance between their own reality and that of children of premodern times. More recently, we have learned that the distance is not so very great. In the developing nations of the modern world, millions of children live in conditions strikingly like those of the times we thought we had left behind: among them, continual maternal childbearing without possibility of contraception; high rates of infant and child mortality; abandonment, infanticide, and abuse; absent or tyrannical fathers; child labor; and the cataclysm of war.

See also **Education; Family; Motherhood and Maternity.**

BIBLIOGRAPHY

Ariès, Philippe. *Centuries of Childhood: A Social History of Family Life.* Translated by Robert Baldick. New York: Vintage, 1962.

Atkinson, Clarissa W. *The Oldest Vocation: Christian Motherhood in the Middle Ages.* Ithaca, N.Y.: Cornell University Press, 1991.

Bergmann, Martin S. *In the Shadow of Moloch: The Sacrifice of Children and Its Impact on Western Religions.* New York: Columbia University Press, 1992.

Boswell, John Eastburn. *The Kindness of Strangers: The Abandonment of Children in Western Europe from Late Antiquity to the Renaissance.* New York: Pantheon, 1988.

Clark, Gracia. *Onions Are My Husband: Survival and Accumulation by West African Market Women.* Chicago: University of Chicago Press, 1994.

Cunningham, Hugh. *Children and Childhood in Western Society since 1500.* London: Longman, 1995.

Demos, John. *A Little Commonwealth: Family Life in Plymouth Colony.* Oxford and New York: Oxford University Press, 1970.

Dixon, Suzanne. *The Roman Family.* Baltimore: Johns Hopkins University Press, 1992.

Ebrey, Patricia Buckley. *The Inner Quarters: Marriage and the Lives of Chinese Women in the Sung Period.* Berkeley: University of California Press, 1993.

Fildes, Valerie A. *Breasts, Bottles and Babies: A History of Infant Feeding.* Edinburgh: Edinburgh University Press, 1986.

Freyre, Gilberto. *The Masters and the Slaves (Casa-grande & Senzala): A Study in the Development of Brazilian Civilization.* Translated by Samuel Putnam. New York: Knopf, 1947.

Golden, Mark. *Children and Childhood in Classical Athens.* Baltimore: Johns Hopkins University Press, 1990.

Goody, Jack. *The Development of the Family and Marriage in Europe.* Cambridge, U.K., and New York: Cambridge University Press, 1983.

Grendler, Paul. *Schooling in Renaissance Italy: Literacy and Learning, 1300–1600.* Baltimore: Johns Hopkins University Press, 1989.

Hanawalt, Barbara A. *Growing Up in Medieval London: The Experience of Childhood in History.* Oxford and New York: Oxford University Press, 1993.

Herlihy, David. *Medieval Households.* Cambridge, Mass.: Harvard University Press, 1985.

Herlihy, David, and Christiane Klapisch-Zuber. *Tuscans and Their Families: The Florentine Catasto of 1427.* Abridged translation. New Haven, Conn.: Yale University Press, 1985.

Hoffer, Peter C., and N. E. H. Hull. *Murdering Mothers: Infanticide in England and New England, 1558–1803.* New York: New York University Press, 1981.

King, Margaret. *The Death of the Child Valerio Marcello.* Chicago: University of Chicago Press, 1994.

Klapisch-Zuber, Christiane. *Women, Family and Ritual in Renaissance Italy.* Translated by Lydia Cochrane. Chicago: Chicago University Press, 1985.

Laslett, Peter. *The World We Have Lost.* New York: Scribners, 1965.

Macfarlane, Alan. *Marriage and Love in England: Modes of Reproduction, 1300–1840.* Oxford, and New York: Blackwell, 1985.

———. *The Origins of English Individualism: The Family, Property, and Social Transition.* Oxford: Blackwell, 1978.

de Mause, Lloyd. "The Evolution of Childhood." In *The History of Childhood,* edited by Lloyd de Mause. New York: Psychohistory Press, 1976.

Mitterauer, Michael. *A History of Youth.* Oxford and New York: Blackwell, 1992.

Ozment, Steven. *Ancestors: The Loving Family in Old Europe.* Cambridge, Mass.: Harvard University Press, 2001.

Pollock, Linda. *Forgotten Children: Parent-Child Relations from 1500 to 1900.* Cambridge, U.K., and New York: Cambridge University Press, 1983.

Riddle, John M. *Eve's Herbs: A History of Contraception and Abortion in the West.* Cambridge, Mass.: Harvard University Press, 1997.

Scheper-Hughes, Nancy. *Death without Weeping: The Violence of Everyday Life in Brazil.* Berkeley: University of California Press, 1992.

Sommerville, C. John. *The Discovery of Childhood in Puritan England.* Athens: University of Georgia Press, 1992.

Stone, Lawrence. *The Family, Sex, and Marriage in England, 1500–1800.* London and New York: Weidenfeld and Nicolson, 1977.

Trexler, Richard C. *Power and Dependence in Renaissance Florence.* Vol. 1, *The Children of Florence.* Binghamton: State University of New York Press, 1993.

Zelizer, Viviana A. *Pricing the Priceless Child: The Changing Social Value of Children.* Reprint, Princeton, N.J.: Princeton University Press, 1994.

Margaret L. King

CHINESE THOUGHT. *Chinese thought* is a generic term, referring to the ideas produced, expanded, and transmitted in the history of China. First, these ideas are not simply general opinions, but the philosophical views of the world, life, and society that have been commonly accepted as concepts or systematic theories. These ideas or theories are the end-products of logical reasoning—in Chinese, the two characters *si xiang* (thought) both contain a radical *xin* (heart/mind), the faculty of which is defined as "thinking" (Mengzi, 6A:15, p. 168). Secondly, these concepts or theories are primarily transmitted through words or writings, conveyable to and understandable by the people of later generations, although other means can also be used to pass on ideas; for example, symbolic form and structure of excavated artifacts and architectures have been correctly "understood" or interpreted as the meaningful ideas that underlie, and are integrated with, the history and culture of China. Thirdly, these concepts or theories are "typical" of the Chinese, who have employed them as tools to explore the inner and the external world, and to recapture the interaction between human activities and the natural and/or the supernatural realms. What is meant by "typical" here is in practice the formalization of philosophical opinions characteristic of the process of thinking by major Chinese philosophers.

The Origin

There is no consensus among modern scholars as to when Chinese thought started and whether or not the philosophical ideas of Chinese people originated from a single source. According to traditional beliefs, Chinese culture started with the invention of the diagrams or ideographical symbols by a legendary figure Fu Xi, and was continually shaped through the working of cultural heroes and legendary sage kings, particularly the Yellow Emperor (Huang di), Yao, Shun, and Yu, who are believed to have been the leaders of China in the fourth to third millennia B.C.E. It is traditionally believed that the period of cultural heroes was followed by the three dynasties—Xia (c. 2205–c. 1600 B.C.E.), Shang (c. 1600–c. 1045 B.C.E.), and Zhou (c. 1045–256 B.C.E.)—in which a reasonably comprehensive system of thought about the philosophical foundation of the world developed and that the earliest writings discovered so far as presented in "oracle bone inscriptions," recording royal divinations and major natural and political events in the early part of the Shang dynasty, mark the beginning of systematic thinking concerning political, religious, and philosophical matters. Modern scholarship on ancient China and new findings of regional centers of civilization, however, have challenged the traditional convictions about the actual existence and functioning of the Xia dynasty and about a single line of development in early Chinese thought. Symbols and preliminary pictographs on potteries and jades discovered in East and South China (Longshan culture), and jade wares and bronze figures and masks found in Southwest China (Shu culture), have shed a new light on the multioriginal sources of Chinese thought, and on the ways these sources were integrated into a single culture through a long and gradual process. Archaeological excavations of houses, cities, and sacrificial sites dated to the prehistoric period also prove that well before using characters to record their thinking of the world and life, the people who lived in the land of China had started to reflect on the physical and the metaphysical world, search for the harmonious interaction between the spiritual and the mundane, and implement these ideas in construction, decoration, and in a variety of economic, political, and religious activities.

The Rise of Rational Thinking

Having said this, we are fully aware of the importance of written language, without which it would be impossible to form abstract concepts, and to preserve and transmit systematic ideas. The ideas as presented in the oracle bones inscriptions of the Shang and the bronze inscriptions of the early Zhou represented an attempt to rationalize, albeit in a preliminary way, the Chinese understanding about cosmic change, the nature and function of social institutions, life and death, and so on. These ideas were later reflected and expanded upon in the *Book of Documents* (*Shu*), the *Book of Poetry* (*Shi*), and the *Book of Changes* (*Yi*), part of which can be dated to the western Zhou dynasty (1045?–771 B.C.E.). However, the rationalization of Chinese thought did not come into full play until

the Spring and Autumn period (770–476 B.C.E.), when the early theological view of the world was challenged, modified, and transformed by new thinkers. Since the moving of the capital to Luoyang in 770 B.C.E., the Zhou kings gradually lost control over the states, while the lords of large states became powerful and competed with each other for the domination of the smaller ones. Natural disasters and administrative abuses had fundamentally shaken the political and economic foundation of the feudal system, and society experienced dramatic change and transformation. Substantially weakened were the force of the beliefs that the power of the Zhou king was endowed in the name of the Mandate of Heaven (*tian ming*) and that the ritual (*li*) binding people and states to the king was part of the cosmic order. The official ideology under the royal patronage and control was gradually torn apart: "The arts of the Way in time comes to be rent and torn apart by the world" (Zhuangzi, p. 364), and Chinese thought came to the stage where several distinct ways of thinking were pioneered as responses to the social and political reality, either negatively deconstructing or positively reconstructing. These thinking streams led to the final formation of a number of major schools, the so-called "a hundred schools" (*bai jia*), during the Warring States period (475–221 B.C.E.), whose rational calling found representative voices in Confucianism (*Ru*), Daoism (*Dao*), Mohism (*Mo*), Legalism (*Fa*), Logicians (*Ming*), Yin-yang School, School of Military Strategies (*Bing*), School of Agriculture (*Nong*), and so on. The competition and mutual criticism between these schools was substantial and productive, in which they developed and extended the boundaries of their own thought. Of these schools Confucianism, Daoism, Mohism, and Legalism were of the greatest significance for the formation and development of Chinese thought.

Confucianism. The early *ru* tradition became a school of thought that bears the name of Confucianism in the West today, mainly through the educational efforts of Confucius (Kong fuzi, 551–479 B.C.E.), who, although claiming only to be a transmitter of ancient culture, attempted to rectify political chaos and social disruption by transmitting and transforming the ritual and learning of the past. Employing "controlling one's selfish desires" (*ke ji*) and "re-establishing the ethical codes of conduct" (*fu li*) as two major tools, Confucius was devoted to the realization of a humane and righteous society in which people followed the good example of rulers and treated each other in accord with the rules of propriety or moral codes. Confucius trained his students to become conscious moral agents or "gentlemen" (*jun zi*), who sincerely upheld the Way (*dao*), were grounded firmly on virtues (*de*), behaved in accord with humaneness (*ren*), and took recreation in the arts (Confucius 7:6, p. 86). In practice he required them to be filial to their parents, respectful to the elders in community, earnest in action and trustful in words, and to love all the people, have the friendship of the good, and cultivate themselves through studying traditional culture (Confucius 1:6, pp. 59–60). The ideas and ideals Confucius illustrated in his conversations that were later compiled into a book entitled *Lun yu* (*The Analects*) and were further expanded by his followers during the Warring States period, among whom Mengzi (372?–289? B.C.E.) and Xunzi (330?–227? B.C.E.) took a lead. Mengzi believed in the religious, ethical, and political vision contained in the Confucian classics, and developed the Confucian doctrine in a religio-ethical direction, while Xunzi was inclined toward the naturalistic and ritualistic vision, and cultivated it in the spirit of humanistic rationalism. Both honored Confucius and believed that everybody was able to attain the ideal—that is, to become a sage (*sheng*) through learning and practicing—but Mengzi and Xunzi differed dramatically in their views of Heaven (*tian*) and human nature (*xing*): while the former held that Heaven is the supreme moral authority and humans are born with a good nature, the latter argued that Heaven is natural and human instincts would lead to evil and chaos if not checked by rituals, moral rules, and sagely teachings. New discoveries of writings on bamboo strips at Guodian and other parts of south China dating to about 300 B.C.E. provided certain evidence that between Confucius and Mengzi there were active a number of Confucian "sub-schools" that developed Confucius's thinking about the Way of Heaven, human nature, and moral and political applications.

Daoism. In contrast to Confucian ideals, many Daoist ideas were propagated as an alternative route to social harmony, as evidenced in the following passage: "Exterminate the sage, discard the wise; and the people will benefit a hundredfold; exterminate benevolence, discard rectitude, and the people again will be filial" (Laozi, 1963 p. 75). A variety of sources have been identified showing the rise of the Daoist thought during the end of the Spring and Autumn period and the beginning of the Warring States period, but no definitive dates for the Daoist masters Laozi (traditional dates c. 571–c. 480 B.C.E.) and Zhuangzi (360?–280? B.C.E.) have been agreed on. The majority of modern scholars have refuted the traditional beliefs, arguing that the two most important Daoist philosophical books, *Daode jing* (or *Laozi*) and *Zhuangzi*, might not have come into existence until the fourth to third centuries B.C.E. However, the two silk texts of the *Laozi* discovered in 1973 at a Han tomb in Mawangdui dated to 168 B.C.E. and the bamboo version of part of the *Laozi* excavated in 1993 from a Chu tomb at Guodian were testimony that this Daoist work had already had different lines of textual transmission by the fourth century B.C.E. It is clear that the *Laozi* and the *Zhuangzi* were representative of the way of life for those people who withdrew themselves from social and political controversies. Central to them are the concepts of *dao*, the Way, and *de*, its power. As the mystic origin and principle of the world, we are told, *dao* cannot be known unless we have reduced our sensational experience and knowledge to the minimum, which is described either as a process of "polishing the mystic mirror" (Laozi, 1963, p. 66) and/or as "driving out perception and intellect" and "doing away with understanding" (*Zhuangzi*, p. 90). To live peacefully in a chaotic society, we are advised to take water as our guide: staying lower, withdrawing from politics, and not contending with others. In defining the nature of Dao as *yin* or yielding, the *Laozi* openly opted for a "feministic approach" and took "the mystic female" as the model for humanity. Withdrawing from the corrupted and chaotic society, the Daoist masters propagated a natural way of life in which there was no competition and purposeful action (*wu wei*). Apart from these philosophical collections, other strings of Daoist ideas and practices, such as the so-called Learning of Huang (the Yellow Emperor)-Lao (Laozi), also played an important part in the formation of Daoism.

Mohism. Mohism (also spelled Moism) was virtually created in the activities and thought of Mo Di or Mozi (Master Mo, 468?–376? B.C.E.). Differing from Confucians who presented a humanistic system that defined and redefined the moral-political-religious code by way of a "virtue ethic," Mohists went for a utilitarian way to improve people's material welfare, maintaining that a theory was good only if it was able to bring benefits to the people, order to society, and an increase in population to the state. For Mozi, what brought the greatest harm to the world was partiality (*bie*) that caused people to love their own parents, families, and states while hating and attacking the parents, families, and states of others. He called for the abandonment of partiality and replaced it with universal love (*jian ai*), regarding the states of others as our own, and loving the families of others as our own. By this, it was claimed, the ideal society of the great unity would be realized. Based on utilitarian principles, Mozi was strongly against all activities that did not contribute to the material welfare of the people, and called for the abandonment of Confucian ritual and music. Unlike Daoists who simply withdrew themselves, Mohists were constantly on peace missions, strongly condemning aggressive wars and selflessly aiding the defense of the state attacked. Against the tide of pragmatism, rationalism, and agnosticism, Mozi and his followers reconfirmed the authority of the spirits and spiritual powers, arguing that the righteous way we must follow was to worship Heaven above, to provide services to the spirits in the middle realm, and to bring benefits to the people below. In politics they called for "honoring the worthies"—namely, selecting and promoting the most qualified to governmental posts. In order to increase the welfare of the state and the people, they put forward as important policies "identifying with the superior" and exercising the control of thought as the tool for social order. Having a particular appeal to artisans, merchants, and small property owners, Mohism occupied a distinguished and influential position in the philosophical arena during that time, which can be seen from the fact that Mengzi listed the school of Mo as one of the two most dangerous rivals (Menzi, 3B:9, p. 114), while Han Fei (280?–233 B.C.E.), a Legalist thinker, described Mohism as one of the two most important schools (Han Fei, p. 118). After the death of Master Mo, however, Mohists disintegrated into three sub-schools, each claiming to be "true Mohism" and accusing others of being "false Mohism." They developed Mohist thought in the areas of epistemology and formal logics, which together with many of earlier Mohist ideas and ideals had a lasting effect on the development of Chinese thought, although Mohism as a school had died out by the time of the Han dynasty.

Legalism. Listed under "Legalism" (*fa jia*) by later historians or catalogs are such politicians and thinkers as Guang Zhong or Guanzi (d. c. 645 B.C.E.), Shang Yang (390?–338 B.C.E.), Shen Buhai (401?–337 B.C.E.), Shen Dao (350?–275? B.C.E.), and Han Fei (280?–233 B.C.E.). According to the authors of *Han shu* (History of the former Han dynasty), Legalists originated with administrative officials (*li guan*), who put into practice realizable codes of rewards and penalties in order to support rites and institutions (Ban Gu, p. 1736). However, the formation of the so-called Legalism school followed a route quite different from that of other schools, since these men were not united by loyalty to a master, nor by an organization, nor through their commitment to specific books. They were grouped together as a single school on the grounds that they all asserted that the only way to save the world from collapse and to strengthen the power of the state was to govern it by penal codes and restrain it with clearly defined law (*fa*). All Legalists attempted to justify the universality of law, and to identify law not only with the codes of punishment, but also with the "standardized" patterns of behavior, including administrative and military planning and statecraft. Taking law as the most important tool for governance, some Legalists deliberately associated law (*fa*) with the arts of rulership (*shu*) and the authoritative power (*shi*). Entwined with administrative techniques, Legalism demonstrated a tendency toward ideological authoritarianism, encouraging the ruler of the state to exercise control over people's thinking, constantly disciplining as well as stimulating individuals to avoid punishment and to seek benefits. Differing from the other schools of the time that engaged in scholarly debates and argument as the way to prevail, some Legalists held a negative attitude towards the so-called "useless and harmful" philosophies and encouraged the ruler to suppress them if at all possible. Hostile to Confucians who took the past as the moral and political model for today, Legalists argued that the times had changed and the past must not be used to guide today's activities, and some went even further to attack the so-called sage kings as the culprits of an immoral society. Despising the reclusive Daoists who refrained from engaging in politics, Legalists positively took part in the state administration; also, ignoring Mohists who opposed aggressive war and championed for peace, Legalists took war as a necessary tool to strengthen the power of the ruler, expand the state, and make the people strong, disciplined, and submissive. Effective means as many Legalist ideas were in increasing the power and wealth of a state, Legalism virtually elevated the state of Qin in West China above all other states and was instrumental to the final establishment of a unified empire in 221 B.C.E.

Heaven and Humans

Divergent as these schools are in terms of metaphysical views and political vision, they developed their ideas and theories around a certain number of key themes, such as Heaven and humans, the Way and changes, the past and today, knowledge and the criteria of truth, the internal and the external realms, and so on. Of these themes the relation between Heaven and humans stands at the center, underlying almost all the important ideas and ideals propagated by the major thinkers, and functioning as the core of Chinese thought in later history. Heaven is a convenient translation of *tian,* which, originally meaning "sky" above us, contains multidimensional meanings, such as the natural order, the religious ultimate (the Lord of Heaven), the source of the political order (the Mandate of Heaven), and the moral order. In search of the Way of Heaven and its relation to the way of humans, Chinese thinkers of the Axial era (800–200 B.C.E.) raised a number of questions such as whether or not Heaven or the Will of Heaven could be known, whether or not Heaven would intervene in human affairs, and what attitude humans should have toward Heaven.

The majority of the early philosophers came to the understanding that harmonious interaction between Heaven and humans was the key to the solving of all social, political, and philosophical problems.

In its metaphysical and physical connotation, Heaven refers to the cosmos, the material world, the Natural Law, or simply Nature, in which humans live, act, and regenerate, and to which humans conform. When asked why he did not speak, Confucius pointed out that silent Heaven ran its course by its law rather than by its words: "What does Heaven ever say? Yet there are the four seasons going round and there are the hundred things coming into being" (Confucius 17:19, p. 146). Major Daoist masters took Dao (the Way) as the original substance of Heaven, and regarded the returning to Heaven as a necessary step for the unity with Dao: "Humans follow the way of Earth; Earth follows the way of Heaven; Heaven follows Dao, and Dao follows its own nature" (*Laozi,* chapter 25; see Laozi, 1963, p. 82). Xunzi understood Heaven as the natural order operating according to unchanging principles, arguing that Heaven ran its courses constantly and did not change along with the events in the human society. Against the religious and moralist teaching that Heaven would bless the good and punish evil, Xunzi believed that Heaven did not intervene in human affairs but provided the environment in which all living things exist. Differing from the ideas that humans could do nothing in relation to the natural order, however, Xunzi defends the position of humans in the world that while performing their duties in accord with seasonal changes, humans should not simply glorify and obey Heaven, but rather must "regulate what Heaven has mandated and use it" (*Xunzi,* vol. 3, p. 21). The texts of *The Book of Changes* (*Yi jing*) provided many insights into the nature and function of the universal order (Heaven and Earth) that underlies the myriad phenomena and defines the natural law of Heaven as the foundation of human existence. Represented by the sage, humans are equipped with the power and intelligence to stay in tune with the natural order.

Applied in the spiritual realm, Heaven signifies an anthropomorphic Lord (*huang tian*) who presides above, and rules over or governs directly, the spiritual and material worlds, by which humans fulfill their destiny. In the Confucian classics, particularly the *Book of Poetry,* the *Book of Documents,* and the *Book of Rites,* Heaven and humans are locked in a mandate giver and receiver relation: while the king rules the world by the Mandate of Heaven (*tian ming*), he must be responsible to Heaven above him. It is a fundamental belief that as the spiritual power, Heaven awards virtuous people with the right to govern and punishes those who depart from the Way, which will definitively lead to the collapse of the dynasty. Succeeding to this tradition, Confucius claimed that "Heaven alone is great!" (Confucius 8:19, p. 94), believing that whether or not the Way prevailed in the world was predetermined by Heaven, and that his mission to transmit the ancient culture was endowed by the power of Heaven. However, Confucius admitted that it was not easy for ordinary people to understand the will of Heaven, and that the only path to this kind of knowledge was through learning and practice (Confucius 2:4, p. 63). This theme is further illustrated in the *Mengzi,* where humans are required to know their heart/mind first: by extending the heart/mind, we are able to know the will of Heaven and to serve Heaven (*Mencius* 7 A:1, p. 182). The spiritual relationship between Heaven and humans is clearly explained in Mohism: Heaven is like the watchdog above us and nobody would be able to evade Heaven's eyes. For Mozi, Heaven desires righteousness and hates unrighteousness, and if we devote ourselves to righteousness then we are doing what Heaven desires, and if we disobey the will of Heaven then we are bringing misfortune and calamity upon ourselves (Mozi, p. 79).

For a majority of Confucian followers, Heaven is the source of virtues, the prototype of the moral order that guides humans in their social life, and the supreme sanction of human behavior. Confucius claimed that "Heaven has given birth to virtues that are in me" (Confucius 7:23, p. 89). Mengzi believed that there are two kinds of honors, the honors bestowed by Heaven (for example, humaneness, righteousness, sincerity, and the like) and the honors bestowed by humans (for example, positions and ranks in the government). He believed that the former should be sought after first and the latter would follow as a matter of course (Mengzi 6A:16, pp. 168–169). Even Xunzi, who attempted to separate the natural order and the moral order, defining the three roots of rituals as serving Heaven above and Earth below, paying honor to one's forebears and exalting rulers and teachers, drew much from the moral significance of Heaven (Xunzi, vol. 3, p. 58). Later Confucians in general took Heaven and Earth as the model of moral rules and principles; for example, just as Heaven is above and the earth below, so too the sovereign is placed over his ministers and subjects, parents over their children, and a husband over his wife. Although other schools did not emphasize as much the moral nature of Heaven as the Confucians did, they argued from different perspectives that the Way of Heaven was the foundation of moral virtues. Mozi drew upon his understanding that Heaven has its will, and argued that humans must follow Heaven's will, devoting themselves to the good fortune and prosperity of the people (Mozi, p. 79). Regarding Heaven as a natural process revolving ceaselessly, the *Zhuangzi* nevertheless requires the virtue of emperors and kings to take Heaven and Earth as its ancestor, the Way and its virtue as its master, and to take nonaction as its constant rule (Zhuangzi, p. 144). Han Fei believed that the Way was the beginning of all beings and the measures of right and wrong, although under Daoist influence he argued that only by being empty and still could the ruler hold fast to the Way (Han Fei, p. 16).

Syncretic Philosophies

The so-called philosophical schools were never clear-cut in their heritages and boundaries. It has been argued that diverse as they were, these schools actually sprang from the unified tradition of an earlier time and shared a common root in their teachings. The commonality in theoretical deliberation and the practical needs for communication between different schools paved the way for a philosophical syncretism. Toward the end of the Warring States period syncretic writings became dominant, in which mutual accommodation between seemingly divergent theories and inter-philosophical dialogue were enthusiastically engaged. Qin (221–206 B.C.E.) and Han (206

B.C.E.–220 C.E.) thinkers went even further by drawing upon a variety of cultural and literary lineages, and constructed or reconstructed a grand philosophy of cosmological, religious, political, and ethical theories, which is evidenced in such eclectic collections as *The Spring and Autumn Annals of Mr. Lü, The Book of Guan Zhong,* and *The Book of Master Huainan.* Yin-yang, the Five Elements or Five Agents (*wu xing*), the Way, Heaven, the spiritual realm and the mundane world, political ideals, and ethical norms were all woven into a structure in which Heaven, Earth, and humanity stood as the three interrelated pillars of the universe, and resonances between human society, government administration, and natural processes were intensively sought after. In the powerful current of syncretism, the earlier teachings of the philosophical schools were transformed and regenerated, and became constituent elements of a new phase in the development of Chinese thought.

Confucian ethics and the Confucian orthodoxy. Confucian thinkers and politicians led the way of syncretism and pushed the boundaries of their own teachings far beyond the recognition of early Confucian masters. Confucian ethics and the Confucian political blueprint were replanted in the rich soil of syncretic ideas and values, embodied in such popular texts as *Xiao jing* (The book of filial piety), as well as *Da xue* (The great learning), *Zhong yong* (The doctrine of the mean) and *Li yun* (The evolution of rites), three of the essays on ritual and rites in an anthology entitled *Li ji* (The book of rites). The transmission of the mainstream Confucian learning was focused on the commentary lineages of *Chun qiu* (The spring and autumn annals), a work believed to be composed by Confucius himself. Dong Zhongshu (195?–105? B.C.E.), a leading thinker of the Han period, drew upon the earlier resources, Confucian, Daoist, Legalist, and particularly that of Yin-yang and the Five Elements, and constructed Confucian doctrines in line with the new thinking of the Han. He reinterpreted the relationship between Heaven and humans into the backbone of a new integrated system of ethics, politics, religion, and education. Eclectic as he was in the book attributed to him, *The Luxurious Dews of the Spring and Autumn Annals* (*Chunqiu Fanlu*), Dong was nevertheless faithful to Confucian ideals, according to which harmony between the three realms, Heaven, Earth, and humans, is central to the peace of the world, while the king or emperor is described as the agent of Heaven who ruled over the world by the mandate from above. In holding the vital and immense responsibility for the moral guidance of the people, the ruler's authority must be spiritually disciplined and practically based on the advice of the enlightened scholar-officials and support by the people. It was this kind of Confucian thought that was eventually elevated to be the state orthodoxy during the reign of Emperor Wu (r. 141–87 B.C.E.), to which all other schools of thought were required to conform.

Daoist religion and Neo-Daoist philosophy. The wisdom in Lao-Zhuang Daoism was particularly appealing to thinkers with a creative mind, and its leaning to the concepts of *xuan* (mystery), *wu wei* (nonaction or no purposeful action), *wu* (nothingness), *kong* (emptiness), and *jing* (tranquility) opened up the imaginary vision of philosophers and religious practitioners as well. The other branch of the broadly defined Daoism, the teachings of the Yellow Emperor and Laozi (Huang-Lao) was also particularly popular at the time and penetrated all layers of social life through medical and shamanic practices that, extended and put into political practices, underlay the imperial policies during the first few decades of the Han dynasty. Through synthesizing Confucian ethics, Lao-Zhuang philosophy, and Huang-Lao teaching, Daoism developed in two directions: religio-political movements aimed at purifying the world, prolonging the life, and overthrowing the Han dynasty, and a kind of Mysterious Learning (*xuan xue*) emerging during the Wei-Jing period (256–420 C.E.). In the former, Dao was mystified as the divine source and Laozi the philosopher as the Savior of the world, while in the latter the heavily politicized relation between Heaven and humans was reinterpreted as that between social norms and human naturalness, and the philosophers Confucius and Laozi were transformed into the moral ideals who had embodied Dao and had reached very high stages in self-cultivation. Religious Daoism and Neo-Daoist philosophy were combined and integrated into the Daoist tradition that exercised a powerful influence over the way of life in Chinese history.

Buddhism and the interaction of "the three teachings." By the first century of the common era, if not earlier, Buddhism had been introduced to China via Central Asia. Different but innovative, Buddhist teachings on ignorance, suffering, and Buddhahood were met both with enthusiasm and suspicion, welcomed by those who were preoccupied with issues of longevity, metaphysical speculation, and superhuman achievements, while resisted by those who attempted to secure the integrity of Chinese culture in relation to the state and family. In debates with Confucians and Daoists, Buddhists skillfully accommodated their teachings to the cultural requirements and spiritual needs of Chinese society, soon seizing the minds of the people and becoming powerful in the reshaping of the political and religious landscape. Based on the study of particular texts and the synthesis of Indian and Chinese understandings, distinguished Buddhist thinkers and their followers created various schools of Buddhist doctrine, of which Tiantai, Huayan, Chan, and Pure Land were particularly important and influential. In search of harmony and unity between the three teachings, Confucian, Daoist, and Buddhist theorists and practitioners consciously explored and justified the rationality of the one body of the three teachings (*san jiao yi ti*). Confucius, Laozi, and the Buddha were recognized as the fountainheads of three religio-ethical traditions, distinctive from each other and yet being the same in essence. It was held that in their mutual supplementation, the three teachings were all needed to meet the political, ethical, personal, social, and spiritual needs of the society. The interaction between Confucianism, Daoism, and Buddhism became the major subject matter and the mainstream current in the later development of Chinese thought.

Neo-Confucianism. Well embedded in the integral development of the "three traditions," the Confucians of the Song (906–1279) and Ming (1368–1644) dynasties revived the traditional Confucian teachings in response to the challenges

from a variety of philosophical lineages, particularly those of Buddhism and Daoism. Their works or commentaries on earlier Confucian texts revealed new horizons for Confucian philosophy, innovating its ethical understandings, and placing moral and political principles on the ground of metaphysical and metaethical rethinking about the Supreme Ultimate (*Tai ji*), Heaven (*tian*), Principles of Heaven (*Tian li*), material force (*qi*), and the heart/mind (*xin*). Of the seminal thinkers of this period, Cheng Yi (1033–1107) and Zhu Xi (1130–1200) led the way to a rational reasoning about the reality of Confucian principles and norms, while Lu Jiuyuan (1139–1193) and Wang Shouren (1472–1523) preferred an idealistic identification between human heart/mind and social virtues and between knowledge and action. Common to both types of Confucian learning, however, was the emphasis on humanity and self-cultivation, pointing to the direction of the attainability of sagehood by all. Reshaped as the new learning of the Confucian Way, known as Neo-Confucianism in the West, Confucian thought became the state ideology and the philosophical basis of Chinese life and thinking until the beginning of the nineteenth century.

However, Neo-Confucianism did not go without significant challenges. Dissatisfied with the stereotypes of Zhu Xi's authoritarian scholarship, a number of independent thinkers in the Qing dynasty (1644–1911) branded Song scholars as "unfaithful followers" of the Confucian Way, proposing to return to the learning of the Han dynasty (*Han Xue*) and to take studies of Confucian classics rather than philosophical reinterpretations as the path to Confucian values. Other scholars engaged in "evidential studies" of ancient texts and commentaries (*Kao Zheng Xue*) against speculations, and explored new ways by which Confucian learning could be used to improve people's lives and to strengthen the state. Although these currents did not change the overall landscape of Qing learning, they in one way or another prepared Confucian intellectuals for a new stage that was looming large with the incoming of "Western learning" (*Xi Xue*), in which the further development of Chinese thought would be fundamentally influenced by the conflict and interaction between the Chinese and the Western cultures.

See also ***Confucianism; Consciousness: Chinese Thought; Daoism; Humanism: Chinese Conception of; Justice: Justice in East Asian Thought; Legalism, Ancient China; Maoism; Mohism; Mysticism: Chinese Mysticism; Religion: East and Southeast Asia; Time: China.***

BIBLIOGRAPHY

PRIMARY SOURCES

Ban Gu. *Han Shu.* 12 vols. Hong Kong: Zhonghua Shuju, 1970.
Confucius. *The Analects.* Translated with an introduction by D. C. Lau. Harmondsworth, U.K., and New York: Penguin, 1979.
Han Fei. *Han Fei Tzu Basic Writings.* Translated by Burton Watson. New York: Columbia University Press, 1964.
Laozi. *The Classic of the Way and Virtue: A New Translation of the Tao-te Ching of Laozi As Interpreted by Wang Bi.* Translated by Richard John Lynn. New York: Columbia University Press, 1999.

———. *Lao Tzu: Tao Te Ching.* Translated with an introduction by D. C. Lau. Harmondsworth, U.K.: Penguin, 1963.

———. *Lau Tzu's Tao Te Ching—A Translation of the Startling New Documents Found at Guodian.* Translated by Robert G. Henricks. New York: Columbia University Press, 2000.

Lau, D. C., trans. *Mencius.* Harmondsworth, U.K.: Penguin, 1970.

Mozi. *Mo Tzu Basic Writings.* Translated by Burton Watson. New York: Columbia University Press, 1963.

Shang Yang. *The Book of Lord Shang: A Classic of the Chinese School of Law.* Translated by J. J. L. Duyvendak. London: Arthur Probsthain, 1928.

Xunzi. *Xunzi: A Translation and Study of the Complete Works.* Translated by John Knoblock, 3 vols. Stanford, Calif.: Stanford University Press, 1988–1994.

Zhuangzi. *The Complete Words of Chuang Tzu.* Translated by Burton Watson. New York: Columbia University Press, 1968.

SECONDARY SOURCES

Bloom, Irene, and Wm. Theodore de Bary, eds. *Principle and Practicality: Essays in Neo-Confucianism and Practical Learning.* New York: Columbia University Press, 1979.

Chan, Wing-tsit, ed. *Chu Hsi and Neo-Confucianism.* Honolulu: University of Hawaii Press, 1986.

De Bary, Wm. Theodore. *The Message of the Mind in Neo-Confucianism.* New York: Columbia University Press, 1989.

De Bary, Wm. Theodore, and Irene Bloom, comps. *Sources of Chinese Tradition,* vol. 1. 2nd ed. New York: Columbia University Press, 1999.

Eno, Robert. *The Confucian Creation of Heaven: Philosophy and the Defense of Ritual Mastery.* Albany: State University of New York, 1989.

Graham, A. C. *Disputers of the Tao: Philosophical Argument in Ancient China.* La Salle, Ill.: Open Court, 1989.

Hall, David L., and Roger T. Ames. *Thinking from the Han: Self, Truth, and Transcendence in Chinese and Western Culture.* Albany: State University of New York Press, 1998.

Hansen, Chad. *A Daoist Theory of Chinese Thought: A Philosophical Interpretation.* New York and Oxford: Oxford University Press, 1992.

Kohn, Livia. *Daoism and Chinese Culture.* Cambridge, Mass: Three Pines Press, 2001.

———. *Laughing at the Tao: Debates among Buddhists and Taoists in Medieval China.* Princeton, N.J.: Princeton University Press, 1995.

Loewe, Michael, and Edward L. Shaughnessy, eds. *The Cambridge History of Ancient China.* Cambridge, U.K., and New York: Cambridge University Press, 1999.

Queen, Sarah A. *From Chronicle to Canon—The Hermeneutics of the Spring and Autumn according to Tung Chung-shu.* Cambridge, U.K., and New York: Cambridge University Press, 1996.

Schwartz, Benjamin I. *The World of Thought in Ancient China.* Cambridge, Mass.: Belknap Press of Harvard University, 1985.

Yao, Xinzhong. *An Introduction to Confucianism.* New York: Cambridge University Press, 2000.

Zhang, Dainian. *Key Concepts in Chinese Philosophy.* Translated and edited by Edmund Ryden. New Haven, Conn., and London: Yale University Press, 2002.

Xinzhong Yao

CHINESE WARLORDISM.

The term *junfa* became part of the Chinese vocabulary in the 1910s and gained popularity in the 1920s to describe the phenomenon of militarism that dominated the Chinese political scene between 1916 and 1928. While both characters, *jun* (military) and *fa* (as in *menfa*, prominent lineage), are ancient Chinese words, it was in Japan that *fa* as a suffix was paired with other words to mean "a clique of" or "a faction of." *Zaibatsu,* for example, means financial combines (*caifa* in Chinese); and *gunbatsu,* meaning military clique, helped the Chinese define the emerging situation of militarism in China.

Before *junfa,* there were other Chinese terms to refer to individual military governors. *Zongdu*—viceroy, for example—was used in the Qing text. In the early twentieth century, the character *du,* "to supervise," appeared in such compounds as *dudu, dujun,* and *duban*—all referring to a military governor.

Junfa, or its English equivalents *warlords* and *warlordism,* when used in the context of Chinese polity and society during the first part of the twentieth century, are pejorative expressions, evoking brutality, chaos, and the plundering of the civilian population. The warlord era was marked by constant warfare, thrusting China into perpetual economic and political instability. Typically, modern warlordism in China applies to the years between 1916 and 1928, but its impact and legacy, with its residual influence, lasted well into the 1940s. Official history in Beijing and Taipei denounces warlords and characterizes the era as reactionary to China's endeavor toward national unity and progress. Both Chinese and English scholarship describe the warlords as regional militarists, possessing personal armies that they constantly strove to expand and heavily relied on to advance their own interests in power and money. Backed by their military power, they maintained virtual territorial autonomy over the regions under their control. They relied heavily on taxes of the local population for revenue. While petty warlords depended more on local sources, including the domestic opium traffic, more significant ones had established ties with the foreign powers present in China from whom they gained financial and military support.

However, it would be a mistake to think of warlords as being under the thumb of the foreign powers. Between 1916 and 1928, when the warlords held sway in China, they numbered in the hundreds if not in the thousands. Their strengths varied tremendously, from a force composed of no more than a handful of men to well-armed troops of several hundred thousand strong. Numerous as they were, there were fewer than a dozen major factions, among which were three infamous cliques in North China. The Anhui clique (Wan) was headed by Duan Qirui, the premier of the Beijing government between 1912 and 1920. The Zhili (Zhi) faction was commanded by Feng Guozhang, who, after his death, was succeeded by Cao Kun. The Fengtian (Feng) clique was led by Zhang Zuolin. Members of all warlord coalitions, big and small, shifted their allegiance constantly as was the nature of the warlord alliances; but the three northern factions stood out and commanded more attention than the southern warlord groupings because they fought for national power represented by the Beijing government.

Warlordism in modern China had its origin in the last decades of the nineteenth century, when the Qing government was losing control of the empire under the pressure of domestic unrest and foreign intervention. Though not the hereditary descendants of the regionally originated Xiang and Huai armies that aided the imperial government in defeating the Taiping rebels in the mid-1800s, the later warlord troops were nourished by the same political crisis that had challenged the Qing's power. A more immediate model followed by the twentieth-century warlord system was the New Army that the Qing established in the 1890s as part of its attempt to revamp the imperial power. Unfortunately for the central government, the reform effort failed, and the New Army, comparatively modern in training and equipment, acquired the quality of a personal army loyal to its commander, Yuan Shikai.

With this army at his command, Yuan emerged as a power to be reckoned with at a time when China was undergoing its most fundamental historical transformation. Oscillating between the Qing and the anti-Qing forces, but finally leaning toward the latter, Yuan used his military power to gain the highest political position in the new government, becoming the first president of the Republic of China in 1912. During his reign, Yuan more than once resorted to force in implementing his policies. His opponents also turned to military power in their effort to block and defeat Yuan's political agenda, as in the anti-monarchical war in 1915, touched off by Yuan's scheme of putting himself on the dragon throne. Military force, thus politicized and empowered by political leaders, established its legitimate authority in political struggles.

China was well on the road toward rule by the gun during Yuan's presidency. But his regime was not a military regime; it represented a central authority supported by provincial leaders, a structure not fundamentally different from the Qing bureaucracy. However, more than the Qing monarchy, Yuan's government was plagued by the perennial tension between centralization and local autonomy. Yuan's death in 1916 left the weak and antiquated civil institutions in the hands of his less capable successors, plunging the country into complete fragmentation.

What also contributed to the rise of the system of warlords was the absence of an institutional passage to power. The civil service examination had long channeled the talented and ambitious to the service of the imperial bureaucracy. No longer in use, it left one with nothing to follow but one's own ability to survive. Consequently, military power became the assurance of success in a society without a clearly defined code of conduct.

Instead of an aberration, twentieth-century warlordism was a manifestation of a recurrent theme in Chinese history—a history that alternated between political integration and fragmentation and a history filled with struggles of local powers challenging the central authority. During times of disintegration, soldiers dominated politics. The backgrounds of the modern warlords were diverse: some were bandits with little education; others had training in Confucianist classics. A few may even have received some Western education. While many deserved the reputation of being a breed of gross and unscrupulous men, there were also those who succeeded in presenting themselves as men of idealism and altruism, steeped in Confucianist morality and Christian benevolence. Provincial warlords such as those in Sichuan were notoriously corrupt and cruel; Yan Xishan, who overlorded Shanxi, was mostly noted for his effective control of the province. Nationally known figures such as Wu Peifu and Feng Yuxiang, on the other hand, maintained a façade of being honest and high-minded. Though some of them displayed modern attitudes and used rhetoric of patriotic nationalism, and in fact many of them adopted modern organization and technology to their forces, they were not men of ideology. Their political and military maneuvering at various levels, confusing and conflicting but ultimately in accordance with their own interests, only prolonged and deepened China's political crisis.

Though the warlords dominated Chinese politics during the early years of the Republic of China, they did not come to power suddenly in the wake of the fall of the Qing dynasty. The system evolved over a period of time. In contrast, the end of the warlords' rule came rather suddenly. After two years between 1926 and 1928, the Northern Expedition claimed victory over the warlords when its troops entered Beijing, signifying the reunification of the whole of China. The defeat of the warlords was more than a military victory. Built on the rising nationalistic desire for a strong and unified China and a strong antiwarlordist sentiment, the nationalist government was finally able to wage a successful war against the warlords.

However, this was not a complete victory, as political and military expediency forced the newly established nationalist government to negotiate with some of the warlords, allowing their troops to be absorbed en masse into its own army in exchange for their allegiance. These "residual warlords" continued to contest the central power and made China's unification only a nominal reality. The Communist victory in 1949 ultimately put an end to the influence of the warlords who had survived throughout the Republican era.

See also **Bushido.**

BIBLIOGRAPHY

Ch'i, Hsi-sheng. *Warlord Politics in China, 1916–1928.* Stanford, Calif.: Stanford University Press, 1976. A classic, offering a comprehensive analysis of warlord politics.

Lary, Diana. *Warlord Soldiers: Chinese Common Soldiers, 1911–1937.* Cambridge, U.K.: Cambridge University Press, 1985. An extraordinary study of common soldiers in warlord troops.

McCord, Edward A. *The Power of the Gun: The Emergence of Modern Chinese Warlordism.* Berkeley and Los Angeles: University of California Press, 1993. An in-depth study of the origins of warlords in two provinces of Hunan and Hubei.

Wou, Odoric Y. K. *Militarism in Modern China: The Career of Wu P'ei-fu, 1916–1939.* Folkestone, U.K.: Dawson, 1978. An example of many studies on individual warlords.

Yu Shen

CHRISTIANITY.

This entry includes two subentries:

Overview
Asia

OVERVIEW

According to the writers of the Gospels, Jesus of Nazareth gathered a small group of disciples and went about for three years in first century Galilee, preaching a message of hope to the poor and healing the sick. John the "Baptist" had gone before him, calling people to repent and be baptized, promising the imminent coming of the Kingdom of Heaven. He recognized in Jesus a far greater preacher than himself, sent from God. Jesus and his disciples eventually set out for Jerusalem. He threw out those who were trading in the temple precincts. He prophesied that the temple would be destroyed. The Jewish leaders pressed for his punishment and the Roman authorities authorized his crucifixion, with a mocking title nailed to the Cross: "Jesus of Nazareth, King of the Jews." Three days after Jesus's body was buried it was discovered to be missing from the tomb where it had been laid. Some of the disciples said they had seen and spoken to the Risen Lord and later that they had seen him ascend into heaven. They began to declare him to be the Son of God.

The spread of Christianity toward the West, through the Roman Empire and eventually the whole world, began with the conversion of the Saul of Tarsus, known after his conversion as Paul. He had been determined to eradicate this new sect until he had a vision on the road to Damascus that took him from an energetic Judaism to missionary zeal for Christianity. It was he who persuaded Peter and the other disciples that it was God's will that they should preach the gospel of Jesus to everyone and not just the Jews.

Jesus wrote nothing, and the lack of contemporary accounts of his ministry makes the "historical Jesus" hard to be sure of. The Holy Scriptures of the Christian faith were composed after his death. The four Gospels, accounts of the life of Jesus, the Acts of the Apostles (a history of the early church), a series of pastoral letters to young churches by Paul and others, and an Apocalypse describing the end of all things came to be accepted by the end of the fourth century as a divinely inspired "New Testament" to be added to the Old Testament of the Jewish Scriptures to form the Bible. The Bible has always been used as authority, taken literally by fundamentalists but in most centuries figuratively interpreted as a means of resolving apparent contradictions within it and using it to answer questions it does not directly address.

Christianity and Secular Thought

A series of Christian authors during the first centuries C.E., later known as "the Fathers," defended the faith to contemporary philosophers. Roman imperial religion was syncretistic. Apart from the Christians only the Jews refused to mingle their God with the gods of the pagans. Christians claimed that Jesus of Nazareth was the Son of God and had promised to send the Holy Spirit, or Paraclete, into the world to be "with" his people. Contemporary philosophy described a Trinity in descending order: a Supreme Being, a Logos, a "Soul of the World." Christians insisted that the three "Persons" in one God in their Trinity were equal and coeternal. There were long-running debates about the manner in which God could have "become man." The definitive creed of the council of the whole church held at Nicaea in 325 provided an "official" statement of the approved faith.

With the fall of the Roman Empire, the arena of debate changed. In the Eastern, Greek-speaking half of the old Roman Empire, Christian learning survived in deeply conservative monasteries and focused on a mystical spirituality colored by late Platonism. Christian thought and learning in the West moved into the new Christian monasteries, the cathedral schools, and eventually, from the end of the twelfth century, into the newly created universities. Islamic scholarship had preserved and developed Greek thought and was absorbed in its turn by the Christian scholars of the thirteenth century.

Thinkers of the Middle Ages such as Peter Lombard (c. 1095–1160) and Thomas Aquinas (c. 1224–1274) worked out a "systematic theology" covering the existence and nature of God, Unity, and Trinity; the way in which God became man and why; a doctrine of the church and the sacraments; and the relationship of human free will to the foreknowledge and predestination and grace of an omniscient and omnipotent God. For most of fifteen hundred years in the West the church dominated intellectual endeavor to the point where philosophy and science were subsumed in theology.

Division

Christians, despite their schismatic tendencies, always put a premium on unity of faith. Yet the Christological debates of the third to fifth centuries ultimately led to the separation of the Monophysite Churches after the Council of Chalcedon (451). In 1054 the Orthodox Church and the Western Roman Church divided, partly over the Western addition to the creed of the assertion that the Holy Spirit proceeded from both the Father and the Son.

The Reformation of the sixteenth century in western Europe divided the Roman Catholic Church from the Lutherans, Calvinists, Anglicans, and other "reforming" communities. In dispute at this period were the claims of the institutional church to provide the only route to salvation and the reformers' claim that the individual needed only a justifying faith and the Bible to read, and the grace of the Holy Spirit would do the rest. In the eighteenth century the Methodist Church separated from the Church of England (Anglican) over the validity of its ministry and in due course itself became a worldwide "communion."

Ecumenism

From the second half of the twentieth century there have been serious attempts to restore Christian unity. From 1948, the World Council of Churches, which influenced the whole of the twentieth century with its work on "faith and order" as well as on "peace and justice," excluded the Roman Catholic Church. The Second Vatican Council of the early 1960s put the Roman Catholic Church's stamp of approval on the modern ecumenical movement and allowed it to enter into bilateral and multilateral dialogues with other Christian communities.

Christianity and Modern Thought

The eighteenth-century Age of Enlightenment returned to "natural" religion, those "truths" that can be arrived at by rational observation of the "created world." This was a first step in allowing changes of fashion in modern secular philosophy and political assumption to drive new thinking in Christian theology. Theologians were prompted to fresh thinking by philosophers such as Immanuel Kant. Friedrich Schleiermacher continued the challenge into the nineteenth century. Søren Kierkegaard called for a move away from believing "propositions" to living the Christian life. Charles Darwin's work on the *Origin of Species* forced Christians to think radically about the story of the Creation told in Genesis. Karl Barth, Rudolf Bultmann, Dietrich Bonhoeffer, Reinhold Niebuhr, Paul Tillich, and Karl Rahner are leading theologians of the twentieth century who have attempted modern restatements of the faith that allow for the changed philosophical infrastructure. "Process theology" (Alfred Whitehead and Charles Hartshorne) postulated that God is changeable and challengeable—a process, not a substance. Don Cupitt and others have experimented with the idea of the "death" of God. Postmodernism, a multiple and shapeless movement emerging after World War II, and the "deconstruction" of language and forms (Michel Foucault and Jacques Derrida) have undermined old certainties.

Christianity and Secular Politics

The Gospels say that Jesus taught his disciples to be compliant citizens, "rendering to Caesar" what the law required. The Roman Empire became officially Christian with the conversion of the emperor Constantine the Great in the early fourth century. Modern manifestations of the resulting long-term tension in relations of church and state include liberation theology in South America in the late twentieth century, which pressed for recognition of the dignity of the poor. Liberal feminism, especially vigorous in the United States in the late twentieth century, called for inclusiveness of language and an end to the assumption that God is a "he." Women are ordained to the Anglican, though not the Roman Catholic or Orthodox, priesthood and episcopate in the early twenty-first century. The old debate about the relationship of science and religion has moved partly into the political arena and is now preoccupied with the ethics of the mapping of the human genome, genetically modified food, and the means now available to achieve live births of human children not conceived by ordinary sexual intercourse.

Mission and Interfaith Relations

The Gospels relate that Jesus charged his disciples with spreading the Gospel, and the first generations took it throughout the Roman Empire. Gregory the Great sent a mis-

sion of Augustine of Canterbury to England in 597, and from there Boniface in the eighth century took missions into continental Europe. Christianity was still spreading east and north in the tenth and eleventh centuries. The crusading period from the late eleventh to the thirteenth century brought Christianity into contact with Islam in the Middle East and the first translation of the Koran was made in the West in the mid-twelfth century. With world explorations and discovery of the Americas in the sixteenth century it was carried to the New World. There the Roman Catholic tradition dominated Latin America and the colonies established by the Spanish and French in North America, with the future United States predominantly colonized by Protestant exiles from Northern Europe. The nineteenth century saw a somewhat "imperialist" spreading of the faith into the Far East and Africa and the Pacific. Much of this later missionary endeavor has been "denominational"; American Baptist missionaries entered Orthodox Russia after the fall of communism. Throughout the Middle Ages and early modern period the Jews had lived in Europe alongside the Christian communities. During World War II the Roman Catholic Church did not protest about the Holocaust, and Pope John Paul II eventually apologized for the silence of the Church. Interfaith dialogue in the early twenty-first century seeks to establish a basis of mutual respect on which adherents of different faiths may live.

Conclusion

Christianity remains numerically probably the largest world religion, with Islam close behind. About a third of the population of the world was Christian in the 1990s, and the majority of the non-Christian population knew of Christianity or had some opportunity of contact with it. The largest number of Christians resided in Latin America, with Europe second and Africa third, then North America, then South Asia. Postcolonialism and globalization pose major challenges as to how far the faith can absorb local culture without itself being essentially changed. But paradoxically the loss of heritage makes for conservatism. The fastest-growing Christian community is in Africa, where the intellectual history of the patristic and medieval West is often unfamiliar. Conservative fundamentalism is making the ordination of homosexuals as priests and bishops in the West a church-dividing matter in parts of Africa. The altered balance of the Christian populations worldwide has begun to throw into question the continuance of an intellectual tradition now culturally remote from many Christians while it continues to privilege the Bible as the foundation text and ultimate authority.

See also **Christianity: Asia; Free Will, Determinism, and Predestination; Heaven and Hell; Heresy and Apostasy; Philosophy and Religion in Western Thought; Philosophy of Religion; Pietism; Puritanism; Religion and Science; Religion and the State; Ritual: Religion; Sacred and Profane.**

BIBLIOGRAPHY

Evans, G. R., ed. *The Early Christian Theologians*. Oxford: Blackwell, 2004.

———, ed. *The Medieval Theologians*. Oxford: Blackwell, 2001.

Ford, David, ed. *The Modern Theologians*. 2nd ed. Oxford: Blackwell, 1997.

Gascoigne, Bamber. *A Brief History of Christianity*. London: Robinson, 2003.

Lindberg, Carter, ed. *The Reformation Theologians*. Oxford: Blackwell, 2002.

McBrien, Richard P. *Catholicism*. 3rd ed. London: Geoffrey Chapman, 1994.

Piepkorn, Arthur Carl. *Profiles in Belief: The Religious Bodies of the United States and Canada*. 4 vols. New York: Harper and Row, 1977–1979. Covers all the main Christian denominations with an account of their differences.

Sanders, E. P. *The Historical Figure of Jesus*. London: Penguin, 1995.

———. *Paul*. Oxford: Oxford University Press, 1991.

Ward, Keith. *Christianity: A Short Introduction*. Oxford: Oneworld, 2000.

Ware, Timothy. *The Orthodox Church*. New ed. London: Penguin, 1993.

G. R. Evans

ASIA

Since the 1970s, the study of Christianity in Asia has been transformed by new approaches in which the scholarly perspective has become less Eurocentric and more Asian. Particularly in regard to China, Western missionary sources have given way to Chinese sources while the meaning of Christianity has been broadened beyond a narrow religious content to include Asian cultural elements.

The history of Christianity in Asia begins with the unconfirmed legend that St. Thomas, one of the original Twelve Disciples, carried the teaching as a missionary to the southwest coast of India. By the third century, Nestorian Christians of the Syrian church were well established in the Malabar Coast region of India. When the Portuguese began landing in India in 1498, they encountered a group of approximately 100,000 St. Thomas Christians.

Christianity in East Asia dates from the arrival of the missionary Aluoben in the Tang capital of Changan in 635. This Nestorian church in China grew with imperial support until it peaked in 781 and then was destroyed in the anti-Buddhist persecution of 845. The period of continuous and sustained development of Christianity in China dates from the entry of Jesuit missionaries in 1580. It was the result of European global voyages, Catholic Reformation fervor, and Chinese receptivity in the syncretic cultural atmosphere of the Ming dynasty (1368–1644).

Jesuit Accommodation

The newly formed Society of Jesus led the way in missionizing Asia in the early modern period. The Jesuits cultivated regional Asian elites in an effort to accommodate Christianity with indigenous cultural elements. While Jesuit accommodation was criticized by other missionaries, it is clear that some process of inculturation (assimilation) was necessary for the long-term viability of Christianity in Asia.

In China, led by the pioneering Father Matteo Ricci (1552–1610), the Jesuits developed a mission strategy focusing on the scholar-officials. A number of prominent literati were converted in the early seventeenth century, including the famous Three Pillars of the Early Christian Church: Xu Guangqi (1562–1633), Li Zhizao (1565–1630), and Yang Tingyun (1557–1627). Instead of syncretizing the traditional Three Teachings (Buddhism, Confucianism, and Daoism), Xu proposed to "supplement Confucianism and displace Buddhism" by blending Confucianism and Christianity. This formula influenced later literati, such as Shang Huqing (b. 1619) and Zhang Xingyao (b. 1633). However, with the Manchu conquest of 1644, Chinese culture became more conservative and less open to creative synthesizing, causing the literati converts to decrease both in numbers and eminence.

In south India, a Jesuit named Robert de Nobili (1577–1656) studied the languages of ancient India (Sanskrit and classical Tamil) to develop a new and fruitful approach to inculturating Christianity into Tamil culture in the years 1605–1656. However, the Hindu and Muslim cultures of this region resisted Christianity, making South Asia far less fertile territory than East Asia. In southeast Asia, Buddhist cultures resisted the penetration of Christianity, with the notable exception of Vietnam. The French Jesuit Alexandre de Rhodes (1593–1660) developed a remarkably effective missionary method by creating a Vietnamese group of catechists who were trained in basic medicine and who lived as a celibate brotherhood. This led to the creation of a thriving Catholic Church. In more recent times, evangelical Protestants in Vietnam have grown to an estimated 700,000 in number.

In Japan, missionaries met with striking initial success followed by rejection. The Jesuit Francis Xavier arrived in 1549 while Japan was emerging from a period of warring feudal chaos, which provided a brief window of opportunity for the missionaries. Within sixty-five years, there were 300,000 Christians in a Japanese population of twenty million. However, fears of subversion by this foreign religion led to a harsh persecution of Christians that culminated in the death of 3,125 Christian martyrs in the years 1597–1660. Christianity was exterminated in Japan, except for a small group of underground Christians in the area of Nagasaki. Christianity never again rekindled the interest that it had in the late sixteenth century in spite of the extensive investment of American missionaries and church funds made in Japan in the aftermath of World War II.

The isolation of Korea, which was controlled by China, delayed the development of Christianity by denying access to missionaries. However, Jesuit publications in Chinese did reach China and these stimulated a young Korean named Lee Sunghun (1751–1801) to travel to Beijing and be baptized in 1784. Lee returned to Korea and converted other Koreans. The first Protestant missionaries entered Korea in 1885 and in the twentieth century, Korea became a leading area of Christian growth in Asia.

The entire population of the Philippines was converted within one century after the arrival of Spanish missionaries in

1565. Protestant missionaries first entered the Philippines when the Americans replaced the Spaniards as colonizers in 1898. The Philippines remain today the only Asian country where Christianity is a majority religion, although there has been rapid growth in China, Indonesia, Singapore, and South Korea.

Asian Inculturation

In China, the acceptance of Christianity was made more difficult by the Rites Controversy and related Eurocentric rulings from Rome that were inflexible in dealing with rites to ancestors and to Confucius. This produced an untenable situation in which conversion to Christianity forced one to be unfilial to one's ancestors. Rome later reversed these rulings in 1939 in a case involving Japanese Shinto rites. With the Jesuits losing favor at the court in Beijing, most of the conversions made in the late seventeenth and eighteenth centuries were made by non-Jesuit missionaries working in the provincial cities and rural areas of China. Although magistrates were increasingly harsh in their treatment of Christians, the Catholic rural converts remained faithful.

The first Protestant missionary to work in China was Robert Morrison (1782–1834) of the London Missionary Society who served in Macau and Canton from 1807 to 1834. The missionaries working out of Canton distributed religious tracts that were instrumental in stimulating mystical visions in a frustrated examination candidate named Hong Xiuquan who became convinced that he was the younger brother of Jesus. The result was a powerful blending of Christian and native Chinese folk beliefs in a Taiping movement that nearly toppled the Qing dynasty in 1853–1864. Whereas Catholics emphasized the development of Chinese catechisms, Protestants concentrated on translating the Bible into Chinese. The Delegates Version appeared in 1852–1854 and the Union Version in 1919.

After the Treaty of Nanjing (1842), other treaty ports were opened up to Christian missionaries. However, the missionaries were tainted in the eyes of many Chinese by their association with foreign imperialist pressures. When the Communists took over in 1949 and expelled both the imperialists and the missionaries, there were three million Catholics and 1.5 million Protestants. Because the Chinese communist government and the Vatican refused to normalize relations, Catholic churches split into those registered with the government (Chinese Catholic Patriotic Association) and underground Catholic churches loyal to Rome. Distrust of the government caused a similar split of Protestants into registered churches (Three-Self Patriotic Movement) and unregistered house churches.

Many observers believed that Christian churches were nearly exterminated in China during the antireligious activities of the Cultural Revolution (1966–1976). Actually, religious persecution and in more recent times, the spiritual thirst generated by a rapidly changing society, have fostered strong growth in the numbers of Christians, particularly in native Chinese churches. The emergence of these indigenous movements indicates that Christianity is taking root in China, although it is likely to remain, like Buddhism, a minority religion. Estimates today place the number of Catholics at ten million and the number of Protestants at thirty million. This would mean that 3 percent of the Chinese population is Christian. Of the three billion people in Asia today, 8 percent are estimated to be Christians.

See also **Confucianism; Religion: East and Southeast Asia.**

BIBLIOGRAPHY

Eber, Irene, Sze-kar Wan, and Knut Wulf, eds. *Bible in Modern China: The Literary and Intellectual Impact.* Nettetal, Germany: Steyler, 1999.
Elison, George. *Deus Destroyed: the Image of Christianity in Early Modern Japan.* Cambridge, Mass.: Harvard University Press, 1974.
Gernet, Jacques. *China and the Christian Impact: A Conflict of Cultures.* Translated by Janet Lloyd. Cambridge, U.K., and New York: Cambridge University Press, 1985.
Mungello, D. E. *The Spirit and the Flesh in Shandong, 1650–1785.* Lanham, Md.: Rowman and Littlefield, 2001.
Neill, Stephen. *A History of Christian Missions.* Hammondsworth, U.K.: Penguin, 1964. Revised 2nd ed., 1986.
Ricci, Matteo, S.J. *The True Meaning of the Lord of Heaven (T'ien-chu Shih-i).* Translated by Douglas Lancashire and Peter Hu Kuo-chen, S.J. St. Louis: Institute of Jesuit Sources, 1985.
Spence, Jonathan. *God's Chinese Son: The Taiping Heavenly Kingdom of Hong Xiuquan.* New York: Norton, 1996.
Standaert, Nicolas, ed. *Handbook of Christianity in China.* Vol. 1, 635–1800. Leiden, Netherlands: Brill, 2001.

D. E. Mungello

CHURCH AND STATE. *See* **Religion and the State.**

CINEMA.

The latter half of the twentieth century witnessed a swift decline in the popularity and significance of cinemagoing in the West, associated with suburbanization and the rise of competitor media like rock and roll and television. From the 1990s, cinema release was repositioned as a cornerstone of multimedia-themed product lines, including alternative forms of distribution and exhibition (in-flight entertainment, video, broadcast, DVD, and Webstreaming) and spin-offs such as soundtrack albums, novelizations, comic books, franchised toys, board and computer games, and fast-food branding. Moribund profit centers like celebrity gossip magazines were revivified, and new ones like product placement inaugurated. Integration of print, TV, theme parks, and Internet companies into massive corporations allowed for an increasing cross-marketing of products in cycles of which film was only one instance. In this transition from mass spectacle to integrated media product, it might have been difficult to retain respect for cinema as "the seventh art." Nonetheless, during this period and into the early twenty-first century, there has been vigorous interest in the medium of film.

The Language of Cinema

As a broad generalization, the development of cinema studies since 1970 has been shaped by a debate between the search for a medium-specific "language" of cinema and inquiries into the ways cinema reflects, reproduces, or otherwise expresses

THE LORD OF THE RINGS

Ian McKellen as Gandalf in *Lord of the Rings: The Fellowship of the Ring* **(2001).** The massive production of the *Lord of the Rings* trilogy was aided by shooting outside the U.S. to take advantage of cheaper labor costs and flexible working arrangements. THE KOBAL COLLECTION

The Lord of the Rings: The Fellowship of the Ring, directed by Peter Jackson, New Line/Wingnut, New Zealand/USA, 2001, 178 mins.

The Lord of the Rings: The Two Towers, directed by Peter Jackson, New Line/Wingnut, New Zealand/USA, 2002, 179 mins.

The Lord of the Rings: The Return of the King, directed by Peter Jackson, New Line/Wingnut, New Zealand/USA, 2003, 201 mins.

Based on the best-selling novel of the twentieth century, the first major blockbuster of the twenty-first could base its innovations on a significant preexisting fan base. The trilogy format, already opened up as a possibility by the highly successful 1999 release of *The Matrix,* differed from the better established "franchise" model of comic-book superhero and horror cycles in the 1980s and 1990s by promising to tell a complete narrative, rather than an open-ended series of discrete tales. Though large, the production budget

was comparable to similarly ambitious blockbuster films of the period. The risk of spending such budgets on fantasy, a genre notoriously difficult to sell to mass audiences, was spread across the fame of the original "property," J. R. R. Tolkien's novel, the use of overseas labor, and an innovative marketing campaign.

The Lord of the Rings, though frequently marketed as a triumph of the New Zealand film industry, is an example of a "runaway" production—that is, a Hollywood project filmed in a foreign territory to benefit not only from location scenery but from tax breaks offered by national governments to entice high-spending studio productions, cheaper labor costs than the highly unionized U.S. industry, and flexible working arrangements often unavailable in the United States. Unusually for a big-budget production, the film employed relatively unknown actors at cheaper rates, concentrating spending instead on props, stunts, locations, and digital effects. Without a star, the film then needed to be sold on its look and its story. (The 1977 blockbuster *Star Wars* is a comparable example.)

During the 1990s, a low-budget student film achieved significant box-office success through judicious use of word-of-mouth advertising on the then-new Worldwide Web. The marketing of *The Lord of the Rings,* while also using the familiar channels for preselling blockbusters, used carefully leaked and later carefully timed releases of teasers, interviews, backstage footage, trailers, stills, and production details to fan sites, even inviting fan Webmasters to attend significant film festivals and to report on them. In contrast to the Disney Company, which had set lawyers onto fans running Harry Potter sites, New Line, the AOL–Time-Warner branch company responsible for the film, used the fans as a medium for publicity before, during, and after the release of the films.

The trilogy extended and systematized a number of developments in the blockbuster film

(continued on the next page)

THE LORD OF THE RINGS

(continued from previous page)

that may now be referred to as event movies. The theatrical release of the film is the trigger for a raft of related products including books, toys, computer games, soundtrack albums, and, very significantly, DVD release. Unusually, *The Lord of the Rings* could not benefit from the lucrative market in "product placement" (the sale of screen time within the film to automobile, computer, hotel and food companies, among others). Instead it capitalized on the very authenticity of a fantastic world without commercial products. The international touring exhibition of props from the films helped build this aura of authenticity. The planning and filming of substantial extra scenes so that the theatrical release of the film could be supplemented with up to an hour of extra storytime on the extended DVD release allowed an innovative release pattern for the films stretching over a five- to six-year period. This in turn required a loyal fan base, whose interest could be maintained over the extended period of the release strategy.

The films' budget also required that the movies, like *The Matrix* and *Crouching Tiger, Hidden Dragon* (2000), should be especially palatable to East Asian audiences. Action sequences quoting both Hong Kong fight films and Japanese anime graphic style have become key components in large-budget films destined for a cosmopolitan marketplace. Cinema theory now needs to undertake explorations of such global cultural phenomena, their relationship with both the United States and the country of production, and the future status of cultural specificity in the global circulation of audiovisual materials.

---

the cultures it derives from or seeks to change. Initial work of the later 1960s emphasized the linguistic structures that appeared to govern cinema. In the later 1970s, two backlashes came in the form first of a film-specific criticism antipathetic to the idea that "bourgeois" forms like the novel and the feature film shared similar structures, and second, of a move away from "theory" toward more traditional forms of humanistic and sociological scholarship. The 1980s witnessed a powerful burst of interest in the cultural dimensions of cinema as an expression of macro- and microcultures—African-American, queer, and third cinema theories privileging the role of cinema as communicator of distinct and differentiated cultural values. In the 1990s, additional emphases were placed on ostensibly marginalized techniques like sound and animation, while the struggle over theory was renewed in the arrival of new theoretical paradigms, notably from phenomenology and the philosophy of desire.

Earlier criticism (commonly referred to as "classical film theory") often celebrated cinema's capacity for realism (see Andrew, 1976). After 1968 the French journal *Cahiers du cinéma,* in common with much of French culture, was rapidly and radically politicized and began to critique the illusion of reality in cinema. In the person of Christian Metz, the new criticism articulated an influential mix of Marxism, psychoanalysis, and semiotics, the "science of signs." In the 1970s, critics associated with the U.K. journal *Screen* began to translate much of this work, and to develop an indigenous theoretical practice, today often referred to as *Screen* theory. The addition of a powerful strand of feminist criticism was the most significant new development, especially as presented in Laura Mulvey's 1975 essay "Visual Pleasure and Narrative Cinema" and in the work of Stephen Heath, while Paul Willemen added political commitment and polemic. Rejecting the realist proposals of André Bazin and Siegfried Kracauer, the *Screen* critics proposed that cinema acted as an ideological apparatus, a term borrowed in part from the French Communist Party's leading philosopher of the day, Louis Althusser. Rather than transmitting ideological messages, as earlier political critics had assumed, cinema's technical apparatus of camera and projector lenses and screens recreated a model in which the audience member was constructed as the subject of ideology. Interpellated (or "hailed") by the apparatus and positioned by it, the cinematic subject became a willing participant in the construction of illusion. (It is interesting to note that the two leading political theorists of working-class collusion in their own oppression, Louis Althusser and Antonio Gramsci, were both translated by editors of *Screen.*)

In Mulvey's version, this process recapitulated the mirror phase of early childhood development proposed by the French psychoanalyst Jacques Lacan. For Lacan, the child's first recognition of itself in the mirror was both a traumatic discovery of separation from the maternal body and the first identification with an ideal version of itself—more distinct, more capable than it feels itself to be. This dialectic between the loss and idealization of the self Mulvey holds to be the origin of identification with human figures on screen, a fundamental identification that is then articulated with the differing representations of men and women (the one typically looking, the other typically being looked at) to produce the effect of gendered subjectivity in the cinema apparatus. *Screen* critics prized especially the works

PRINCESS MONONOKE

Princess Mononoke (Mononoke-hime, 1997). A product of the Japanese animation industry, *Princess Mononoke* depicts the struggle between the natural world and technology. REUTERS NEWMEDIA INC./CORBIS

Princess Mononoke, directed by Hayao Miyazake, Tokuma Shoten/Nippon Television Network/ Dentsu/Studio Ghibli/Miramax, Japan, 1999 (U.S. version), 128 mins.

Hayao Miyazake's *Mononoke-hime* (1997; released in the United States in 1999 as *Princess Mononoke*), the sixth feature film for his Studio Ghibli, built on the success of his child-oriented anime, extending back more than a decade. The Japanese animation industry, powered in part by its close relations with the export of television shows for children and the toys and games crazes of the 1980s, had turned in the late 1980s to themes more suited to young adults. The international success of Katsuhiro Otomo's *Akira* in 1988 and Mamoru Oshii and Masamune Shirow's *Ghost in the Shell* of 1995 had paved the way for higher production values, the assimilation of digital technologies into traditional hand-painted cel animation, and increasingly convoluted narrative lines.

Immensely successful in Japan, where it was only outgrossed by *Titanic,* the film raises special challenges for the theory of cinema. The animation form has traditionally been seen as childish and has received proportionately little critical attention, while Japanese product aimed at television sales had acquired a reputation for shoddy technique, often due to the practice of farming large proportions of the handcraft out to overseas animation factories, notably in Thailand. Miyazake's film is extremely well crafted throughout, essential if the film was to succeed on the big screen. Several innovations helped, including the use of specially-written software to make three-dimensional digital animation look more like traditional cartoons.

Princess Mononoke's themes of struggle between environmental and mechanistic forces at a formative moment in Japanese history seem not only to have chimed with audiences, but to have echoed in the cartoon form the dialectics of technology and nature. Evoking the environmental ethics of first peoples, the film seeks to reconcile

(continued on the next page)

PRINCESS MONONOKE

(continued from previous page)

technological progress with a mystical understanding of the forest as stronghold of nature. The very unnaturalness of the medium, including the necessity to invent sounds for the various cartoon creatures that inhabit the film, give the movie a greater depth and deeper conflicts than the wishful ending would suggest. And the success of the film challenges cinema theory to address two of its major weaknesses: the first being the audio component of audiovisual media and its articulation with the visual; the second, the distance between photographic and graphic depiction.

Digital theorist Lev Manovich observes that the rise of digital cinema makes contemporary audiences aware that cinematography is a brief excursion in the history of animated pictures. From such specialized formal analyses, cinema studies can hope to derive new paradigms for understanding relations between recording, inventing, representing, and communicating in an increasingly global media society.

---

of the avant-garde, deploying the semiotic theory of signs to advance the theory that avant-garde cinema freed signifiers (the materials of light and shade for example) from their bondage to the signified (to the illusory representation of an always already ideological reality). At the same time, they sought out more popular films that exemplified the contradictory and dialectical tendencies within the dominant ideology, such as the 1950s melodramas of Douglas Sirk with their clash of wealthy lifestyles and emotional catastrophe. Technical work in film semiotics continues with the work of Warren Buckland, and *Screen* theory has retained its position since the 1970s, especially among feminist critics like Kaja Silverman, but it has never been uncontroversial.

The Specificity of Cinema

The most influential critic of the *Screen* agenda has been David Bordwell. Accusing the *Screen* critics of blindness to the specificity of film, Bordwell and his co-author Kristin Thompson developed a "neoformalist" analysis. Combining inspiration from Russian formalism with cognitive psychology, they proposed a rigorous film scholarship grounded in archive work and extensive as well as intensive film viewing. They also argued for what appeared to be a more commonsense approach to audience activity. Using cognitive theories, Bordwell argued that audiences were actively engaged in constructing meaning, guessing what will happen next, forming hypotheses and mental maps, and piecing together the action of the plot from the fragments of edited film narration. Criticized for their normative and apolitical account of the cinema experience, and despite the sometimes strident protestations of their later work, Thompson and Bordwell have been influential in establishing close analysis of filmic technique and high levels of historical scholarship as necessary prerequisites of film study.

New historicism (rather confusingly referred to as "revisionist" in some accounts) has been especially effective in the renewal of film studies, focusing attention on the specificity of film's evolution as technology, industry, and culture. In the 1980s and 1990s scholars such as Barry Salt, Tom Gunning, Roberta Pearson, Janet Staiger, Miriam Hansen, Kevin Brownlow, and Robert Allen and Douglas Gomery on U.S. cinema; Michael Chanan, Pam Cook, Andrew Higson, John Hill, and Robert Murphy on the United Kingdom; Thomas Elsaesser on Germany; Richard Abel on France; Yuri Tsivian on Russia; and others have radically rewritten the glib accounts of journalistic film history. The new cinema historicism diminishes the importance of individuals and denies the apparent linear progress from silent to sound, monochrome to color. Instead the new historicists emphasize the importance of institutional forces and economic trends in the innovation and dissemination of technologies and techniques, seeking reasons why certain promising technologies are delayed or abandoned, assessing the reactions of audiences and exhibitors to emerging technologies, focusing on the institutional histories of studios and government agencies, and tracing links between cinema and cognate industries. In the process some key beliefs of even recent film criticism have been undermined, as when Rick Altman argued, on evidence from D. W. Griffith's involvement with the stage, that melodrama was a formative component of classical Hollywood, thus critiquing both the belief that U.S. cinema was realist in essence and that melodrama was an effective antidote to its dominance.

Since the 1990s film historians have turned to oral history and documentary accounts of audience activity in the cinema. A major element of television studies throughout its life, audience studies have had a weaker position in film studies, perhaps because of the relative difficulty and social impropriety of staring at audience members in the dark. Early accounts from the 1930s by participants in the British Mass Observation project, even Hugo Münsterberg's pioneering psychological study of 1916, failed to establish a strong tradition of reception studies. Distinguishing themselves from market

THE RULES OF THE GAME

Scene from *La Règle du jeu* (*The Rules of the Game*), 1939. France has produced many films that have proven to possess cross-cultural appeal. One of these is Jean Renoir's classic *La Régle du jeu*. The original negative was damaged during the German occupation of World War II but was restored in 1956. NOUVELLE EDITION FRANCAISE / THE KOBAL COLLECTION

La Règle du jeu, directed by Jean Renoir, Nouvelle Editions Françaises, France, 1939, 110 mins.

Hated or ignored on its release in 1939, Jean Renoir's *La Règle du jeu* is one of the most consistently admired of all films. An ensemble cast in an upstairs-downstairs country weekend enact the rituals of a dying civilization on the brink of war. With its deep staging and deep-focus cinematography, its long takes, and a fluid camera that seems to track the actors (rather than construct the action for the camera), the film became a touchstone of realist criticism.

In a widely read essay, "*S/Z* and *Rules of the Game*" (in the film journal *Jump Cut,* nos. 12–13, winter 1976–1977, pp. 45–51), Julia Lesage argued that in fact the film was constructed through the types of code identified by Roland Barthes and that its realism was merely the effect of cinematic and narrative technique. This formalist analysis would also inspire readings by, among others, Kristin Thompson, for whom the film is an elaborately constructed artifice. That Renoir appears in the film as the character Octave, caught between the aristocrats and the servants, inspired a number of *auteur* critics to single out the film as an account of the artist's role in society and in cinema. In his 1990s *His-*

(continued on the next page)

THE RULES OF THE GAME

(continued from previous page)

toire du cinéma, the cinéaste Jean-Luc Godard returns many times to *The Rules of the Game* as if to an exemplary combination of formal innovation and political commitment.

Phenomenological and psychoanalytic critics have focused on the role of illusion in the film, the series of mistaken identities that propel the plot, and the ethos of "keeping up appearances" that leads to the final tragedy. Still baffling for textual analysts is the charm and the comedy that have kept the film popular not only with critics but with film buffs for more than sixty years. Compellingly humanist in outlook—Renoir's direction rarely if ever seems to dislike his characters—the film's narrative nonetheless enacts a damning satire on a rigidly stratified society that prides itself on the appearances through which it lies to itself. This paradox of a realist cinema portraying an unreal society maintains the film's interest long after that society has faded away.

---

research by their interest in emotional, inventive, ironic, and resistant attitudes, and in the extremities of fan culture, such studies of necessity emphasize the depth rather than the breadth of their findings, giving more attention to highly specific audiences than to the standard aggregate measure of film audience, box-office returns. At least one international project attempted to do both deep and broad research, investigating cross-cultural meanings of fantasy though an Internet-based survey of responses to the twenty-first century blockbuster *The Lord of the Rings.* Both historical and contemporary reception studies focus on the cultural construction of audiences, the determinations of race, class, gender, and other formations on the ways audiences read and react to movies, disputing both the *Screen* concept of an apparatus that determines response, and Bordwell's idea of the audience's work of textual reconstruction.

Cultures and Economies of Cinema

Cross-cultural dimensions of cinema, initially discussed mostly in terms of the textual properties and ideological concerns of national cinemas, are now the object of much work in reception, political economy, and postcolonial research. Summed up in Ella Shohat and Robert Stam's 1994 title "Unthinking Eurocentrism," cross-cultural studies result in several kinds of work that dispute the normative tendency of neoformalism and the blindness to cultural difference of the apparatus theory espoused by the *Screen* critics. Some scholars have been at pains to emphasize the creativity or political significance of previously marginalized cinemas and directors. Others apply rigorous theoretical critique to such art house favorites as the Chinese fifth-generation filmmakers. Still more radical was the movement in filmmaking and film theory known as *third cinema,* after an influential 1976 essay by Cuban cinéastes Fernando Solanas and Octavio Gettino, which argued that the first and second cinemas—mass entertainment and bourgeois psychodramas, respectively—had failed the revolution and that a third cinema based in popular forms and addressing popular struggles was the best way forward. This spirit was echoed across the world, in the films of Haile Gerima

in Ethiopa, Sembene Ousmane in Senegal, and Anand Patwardhan in India, and in the critical writings of Teshome Gabriel, Trinh Minh-Ha, and others (for example, Jim Pines, Paul Willemen, Coco Fusco, and John Downing). Since a central tenet of third cinema was that cultural specificity was integral to a cinema that was genuinely popular in the sense of belonging to and acting with the people, the term acted as an umbrella for a wide range of practice. Another early Cuban proponent, Julio Garcia Espinoza, called for an imperfect cinema; in Brazil, Glauber Rocha called for a cinema of hunger. For some proponents, the third cinema demanded a break with the technical wealth as well as the techniques of the first and second cinemas, while for others the resultant formally challenging films were merely reversions to the self-important antics of art house cinema and of no interest or use to the oppressed. This debate became especially vibrant in North America and in Europe where a new and intensely articulate generation of filmmakers and critics from African- and Hispanic-American, black British, and British-Asian backgrounds began to give voice to their artistic and political demands.

A second effect of this global consciousness has been a reappraisal of the old Marxist political economy espoused by *Screen* theory, updating the analysis to take account of globalization on the film business, its working practices, and its use of international free trade agreements to maintain and develop monopolistic corporate cartels. Janet Wasko, Andrew Higson, and Richard Maltby, among others, have addressed the impact of information technologies and the increasing integration of entertainment industries in guiding the development of new industrial practices as well as strategic policy on global media flows, intellectual property rights legislation, and the potential impacts of North American dominance of film distribution on the cultural lives of smaller nations. Increasingly, studies of auteurs are articulating the creative process with the industrial, and the best of them are also informed by theoretical paradigms that explain the dependence of creation in film on industrial and technical processes over which an individual director has little control.

Such studies of the development of film industries merge with analytical concerns in the study of cinema's relationships with modernity. A number of scholars, among them Anne Friedberg and Friedrich Kittler, trace cinema's roots back to related developments of the late nineteenth century such as department stores, electric streetlights, railways, and advertising, and argue forward to the digital era that cinema has always integrated with a range of other media into a broad process of modernization. In this context the study of entertainment has developed rapidly, with increasing awareness of the cross-media appeal of stardom, movie soundtracks, and animation. Film sound has benefited especially from the work of Michel Chion, Rick Altman, and Philip Brophy, who listen not only to music but to sound effects, to the construction of off-screen space, thematic constructions of gender and race, and the shifting hierarchy of recorded sound and recorded image. Like stardom, which is governed by a dialectical relation between on-screen presence and real absence, the study of film sound reveals complex interactions of space and time, sometimes reinforcing and sometimes undermining the coherence of a film's imaginary world. The sense of modernity as a complex process of homogenization and fragmentation is also common to studies of popular genres like horror, action movies, and science fiction, genres that frequently evoke both utopian and dystopian alternatives to dominant conceptions of embodiment, agency, and the necessity of current social arrangements.

Technologies of Cinema

The arrival of digital technologies in cinema has provoked debate over the degree of continuity between this process of modernization in the predigital cinema and the potential postmodernity of digital film. Critics like Lev Manovich believe in the continuity of the two, and in cinema's powerful determination of such key factors of digital media as the use of screens. Others derive from digital media new paradigms for reviewing the historical data, rediscovering such typically digital techniques as motion capture in the pre-cinematic chronophotography of Étienne-Jules Marey, or digital compositing of layers in the trompe-l'oeil sets of Georges Méliès' early fantasy films. Scholars of special effects, such as Vivian Sobchack, Scott Bukatman, and Timothy Murray, have begun to analyze the diminishing dependence of cinema on what can be enacted in front of a camera, tracing, in Michelle Pearson's work, a transition from spectacle for its own sake to a more embedded expectation of near-photographic illusion seamlessly wedded to cinematographic imagery, as in James Cameron's *Titanic* (1997), a case argued by Angela Ndalianis, for whom spectacle is, if anything, a more significant element of contemporary entertainment than at any time since the Baroque.

At certain points, this discussion of the transition from photo-mechanical to electronic cinema replicates the long-running debate between culturalist and medium-specific accounts of film. If such vast currents as modernity or globalization run through the transition to digital, then there will be continuity. But if the deep-seated alterations to cinematic technique take precedence, then the experience of cinema, and to some extent of cultural activity at large, can be expected to change equally. This hypothesis has been tested especially by a generation of phenomenological critics like Vivian Sobchack and Laura U. Marks, for whom the object of inquiry is the physical embodiment of the spectator and the ways this relates to the richness of the felt experience of cinema. This type of work, instigated by Dudley Andrew, is extended in Marks's work into a consideration of the emulation of touching in certain modes of cinema practice. The theme of embodiment also runs through the rapid rise of interest in Gilles Deleuze's two-volume analysis of cinema, remarkable for its espousal of a philosophy of desire grounded in Henri Bergson (rather than the ubiquitous Heideggerianism, in themes of loss, lack, and the fading of reality, of poststructural criticism) and for its meticulous readings of individual films. Deleuze envisages a shift from the "movement-image" pre-1945 toward a "direct time image" in postwar cinema. Informed by the semiotic pragmatism of Charles Sanders Peirce, Deleuze deploys an idiosyncratic vocabulary to argue for cinema's gradual liberation from a mechanistic dependence on the image of the human body toward a more metaphysical engagement with the pure dimensionality of time and its flows.

Challenges of Cinema

The tumultuous history of cinema studies since the mid twentieth century has concentrated several core debates in the history of ideas. Should the study of film deploy traditional hermeneutic and humanistic techniques, or should it abandon them for a more rigorous analysis grounded in linguistics? Or was such grappling with continental theory an alibi for a failure to address the realities of political economy, actual rather than textually determined readers, and the operations of oppression and exploitation disguised or denied by filmic representations? Or was cinema in any case an entirely symbolic activity, a simulacrum with no relation to any reality, physical or social? In institutions where cinema has been taught, there have been the additional claims that the analysis of film is mere carping, all too often negative and destructive, and of no use to those who wish to move into filmmaking as a career. Such claims have led to the rise of major literatures in script analysis and structure, in the technical aspects of filmmaking, and in elements of creative industries literature devoted to film financing, marketing, and policy, many of which have been subsumed into the canon of cinema studies teaching.

Looking to cinema's specific contributions to the history of ideas, among the most significant has been its meticulous attention to the specificities of cultural difference and the contemporaneous splitting and differentiation of subjectivity, in the admission of transcultural cinemas and in queer cinema, for example. At its best, the affirmation of camp, for example in Richard Dyer's work on queer cinema, is valuable not only for film studies but for better understanding of the rich emotional life of the culture.

Indeed, if anything distinguishes the cinema theory among media studies, it is its readiness to engage with the emotional life. Alongside the cool analysis of finance, technique, and box office, it is difficult to sidestep the intense emotive power of film, from haunting abstraction to political passion, and in physiological reactions of tears, shrieks, and laughter. While some advances have been made in the study of the erotic (by Linda Williams) and the horrific (by Barbara Creed), both comedy and tearjerkers have resisted analysis and remain in many ways the most difficult emotional technologies to account for, partially because they are among the least esteemed in intellectual circles.

There is too the contradictory fascination of cinema captured in the phrase *the dream factory*. Flagship of the consciousness industries, cinema figures as both escape and utopia, flight from oppression or flight toward its alternative. It is both a device for replenishing the exhausted with meaningless entertainment and a technology for demanding the impossible. Its illusions may be seen as lies and ideology, or as evocations of emotional and spiritual satisfactions denied and destroyed by consumerism. Its darkness, serried ranks of seating, and clockwork rhythms of projection can appear as both a continuation of factory discipline into leisure time and as an expression of solidarity, community, and sociability.

Meanwhile, despite (and, in some resistant political sense, perhaps because of) the dominance of Hollywood on world screens, cinema has proved remarkably successful at translating cultural difference across the world: one thinks of the mix of kung fu, spaghetti western, and U.S. gangster in Perry Henzell's Jamaican *The Harder They Come* (1973). The films of Rainer Werner Fassbinder, John Woo, Akira Kurosawa, and Satyajit Ray have reached far more people than equivalent literary or even musical creations. Nonetheless, there remain huge difficulties in securing distribution for non-Hollywood films, a challenge that film studies shows signs of addressing in the early twenty-first century, along with the issues of cross-cultural transmission, emotion, and identification, and the utopian as well as the industrial capabilities of the medium.

See also **Media, History of; Third Cinema; Visual Culture.**

BIBLIOGRAPHY
Andrew, J. Dudley. *Concepts in Film Theory.* Oxford and New York: Oxford University Press, 1984.
————. *The Major Film Theories: An Introduction.* London and New York: Oxford University Press, 1976.
Gledhill, Christine, and Linda Williams, eds. *Reinventing Film Studies.* London: Arnold, 2000.
Metz, Christian. *Film Language: A Semiotics of the Cinema.* Translated by Michael Taylor. New York: Oxford University Press, 1974.
————. *The Imaginary Signifier: Psychoanalysis and Cinema.* Translated by Celia Britton et al. Bloomington: Indiana University Press, 1982.
————. *Language and Cinema.* Translated by Donna Jean Umiker-Seboek. The Hague: Mouton, 1974.
Miller, Toby, and Robert Stam, eds. *A Companion to Film Theory.* Malden, Mass.: Blackwell, 1999.
Mulvey, Laura. "Visual Pleasure and Narrative Cinema." *Screen* 16, no. 3 (autumn 1975): 6–18. Reprinted in her *Visual and Other Pleasures.* Bloomington: Indiana University Press, 1989.
Nichols, Bill, ed. *Movies and Methods.* 2 vols. Berkeley: University of California Press, 1976–1985.
Shohat, Ella. and Robert Stam. *Unthinking Eurocentrism: Multiculturalism and the Media.* London and New York: Routledge, 1994.
Solanas, Fernando, and Octavio Getino. "Towards a Third Cinema." In *Movies and Methods,* Vol. 1, edited by Bill Nichols. Berkeley: University of California Press, 1976. Revised translation in *25 Years of Latin American Cinema,* edited by Michael Chanan. London: BFI/Channel 4, 1984.
Stam, Robert, and Toby Miller, eds. *Film and Theory: An Anthology.* Malden, Mass.: Blackwell, 2000.

Sean Cubitt

CITIZENSHIP.

This entry includes three subentries:

Overview
Cultural Citizenship
Naturalization

OVERVIEW

Citizenship consists in sharing a political community, and enjoying the benefits and assuming the political responsibilities that give effect to this experience of shared political community. If the purpose of political philosophy is to provide a principled account of the nature and appropriate boundaries of political community, then it makes sense to say that the tradition of political philosophy from Aristotle to the present is more or less defined by a tradition of reflection on the normative foundations of citizenship. In an important sense, then, the whole history of political philosophy offers a continuing reflection on and dialogue about the nature of citizenship, and it is not clear that one can give a full report on the history of reflection about citizenship with anything less than a thorough and comprehensive account of the history of political philosophy in its totality. This is impossible here, and therefore a short summary of basic themes in the tradition of political philosophy, and its relation to thinking concerning the meaning of citizenship, will have to suffice.

Citizenship in the History of Political Philosophy

Book three of *The Politics* by Aristotle (384–322 B.C.E.) is the first treatise on citizenship, and it remains an essential reference point for all subsequent reflection on what it means to be a citizen: "The citizen in an unqualified sense is defined by no other thing so much as by sharing in decision and office. . . . Whoever is entitled to participate in an office involving deliberation or decision is . . . a citizen in this city; and the city is the multitude of such persons that is adequate with a view to a self-sufficient life" (p. 87). Aristotle's definition of citizenship sounds modest enough, but in fact it encapsulates an awesomely ambitious account of what is required in order for human nature truly to flourish. Aristotle's account of what it means to be a citizen is intended to be a conceptualization of the experience of free, native-born males in the polis as a unique site for the development of properly human capacities. What the definition affirms is that only a very small number of human beings in the history of humankind (and only a minority of the inhabitants of Athens even during the age of the polis) have been in a position to realize their full humanity because they happen to be members of the kind of political community that uniquely gives play to their properly human (political or polis-based) capacities.

In republican Rome the idea of citizen virtue was detached from the robust theory of moral development offered by Aristotle, and saw its crowning ideal in a practice of courageous military heroism in defense of the free state. Still, the Roman drive for glory, honor, and power to defend the liberties of collective, aristocratic self-rule was regarded as double-edged by one of the great Christian fathers, St. Augustine of Hippo (354–430). While praising the Romans in his *City of God* for such a long-lasting and glorious state, Augustine called upon Christian believers (and those who felt themselves to be future citizens of heaven) to recognize the pride residing in these Roman ideals of citizenship, and to see the ultimate futility of all earthly ambitions. Christians, as pilgrims in this world, should adopt a stance of submission, disengaging themselves from the ideals of active participation. Augustine saw in the ultimate failure of human enterprises an opportunity to cultivate humility and acceptance of God's will.

It has long been thought that, following Augustine, the ideals of citizenship were largely absent from medieval thinking and only reappeared in the Western tradition in the Italian Renaissance. However, more recent research has shown the deep historical roots of the links between the language of citizenship and the struggle for communal independence throughout Europe (see Höfert). The lingering presence of Roman law, along with the emergence of a class of burghers who sought new forms of political influence, gave rise to political struggles in which the language of citizenship became, once again, salient.

Niccolò Machiavelli (1469–1527), particularly in his *Discourses on Livy,* is regarded as the most famous—as well as the most controversial—defender of citizen liberties. Inspired by the ideal of civic virtue as practiced by the Romans, he called for a new ethos of devotion to the political community sealed by a practice of collective self-rule and self-defense. Needless to say, Machiavelli's conception of the citizen-body remains emphatically patriarchal, as is the case, with rare exceptions, for the entire political theory tradition until recent times. Understanding of the internal and external challenges to the survival of the free state led him to recognize that the duties of successful leadership of a free state would necessitate actions that would, at times, contravene the precepts of conventional morality. Nonetheless, he praised republics over principalities, for it was only through collective self-rule that the greatest number could guarantee their personal autonomy and independence and thereby achieve a more lasting and glorious state.

Post-Reformation religious struggles in Europe gave rise to new accounts of the proper relation between rulers and their peoples, especially in matters of religious practice. While these debates were initially more relevant to individuals as subjects of absolute rulers, they brought about broader reflection on the concept of natural individual rights, which would later become a powerful tool in the struggle against absolutist rule. *The Second Treatise of Government,* by John Locke (1632–1704), is the best-known account, harnessing the idea of individual rights to a notion of collective sovereignty even though Locke does not reject monarchy. Still, with the advent of commercial society, the possibility of fusing the promotion of individual liberties with a form of government that would require very limited participation on the part of all citizens was increasingly regarded as an attractive alternative. It has meant that in the modern era the quality of citizenship has often been judged more by the accountability of liberal democratic governments toward their citizenry than by the actual forms and degrees of popular participation. But this new synthesis has not been without its critics: modern theorists, notably Jean-Jacques Rousseau (1712–1778), have drawn on more ancient accounts of citizen virtue to decry the lack of active participation in collective self-rule as an ongoing assault upon true popular liberties.

On the Social Contract, by Rousseau, and *The Philosophy of Right,* by Georg Wilhelm Friedrich Hegel (1770–1831), remain the two most important modern treatises on citizenship. At the core of Rousseau's political philosophy is the idea that modern human beings should be judged by the (suitably high) standard of the ancient experience of citizenship. When Rousseau claims, in a note to *Social Contract* (Book one, chap. 6), that modern men know only what it means to be bourgeois and have no notion of what it means to be a *citoyen* (citizen), he makes perfectly clear how deficient he regards modern human beings in relation to this standard. This celebration (mythicization?) of ancient citizenship has of course not gone uncontested within modern political thought: just as Rousseau challenged the Lockean synthesis outlined above, so Rousseau's account of citizenship in turn was challenged vigorously by subsequent liberals. Hence it has been one of the chief theoretical purposes defining liberal political theory going back to Charles de Montesquieu (1689–1755)—or perhaps going back to Thomas Hobbes (1588–1679) if one considers Hobbes part of the liberal tradition—precisely to challenge the normative superiority of classical republicanism. This has been nicely summarized by J. G. A. Pocock: "[Thinkers such as Montesquieu, David Hume (1711–1776), and Adam Smith (1723–1790)] argued that the virtuous man of antiquity was obliged by the lack of a free market to live off the labour of slaves who worked his land and gave him the leisure to serve the republic. His 'virtue' made him harsh and barbaric; even his moral personality was impoverished by his inability to exchange goods with his fellows. . . . [With the development of the market, the] rigid and fragile virtue of antique man was replaced by the greater flexibility of 'manners'" (Pocock, p. xxi). Hegel, with his huge debt to the vindication of modernity contained in the classical political economy tradition (see Plant), represents perhaps the crowning expression of the thought that citizenship in the modern liberal state cannot be exhausted by the notion of citizens unwaveringly committed to the exertions of civic virtue. Hegel, in common with other liberals, believed that consciousness of rightful membership in the modern state must incorporate a clear acknowledgment of the legitimacy and, indeed, moral necessity of the energies that individuals invest in their private lives.

Reading Rousseau gives one the impression that the most powerful theorizing about citizenship is located outside of, and in polemical opposition to, the liberal tradition. But students of the history of political philosophy should never forget that there is at the same time a decisively important tradition of reflection about citizenship and civic virtue *within* liberalism. Alexis de Tocqueville (1805–1859) and John Stuart Mill (1806–1873) are two great exemplars of civic theorizing within the liberal tradition. For all Mill's apprehensions about an unrestricted franchise, and for all Tocqueville's anxieties about the unwelcome consequences of the culture of democracy, both of them were strongly committed to enhancing the civic dimension of liberalism, and in that sense, both are important modern theorists of citizenship.

Citizenship in Contemporary Debates

Not surprisingly, the problem of citizenship has continued to shape contemporary debates in political philosophy. Communitarianism, at least as expressed in the work of Charles Taylor and Michael Sandel, presented itself as a new vocabulary for articulating an old complaint about the attenuated character of liberal citizenship. (This is emphatically not the case with the communitarianism of Alasdair MacIntyre, who fundamentally rejects modern nation-state-based citizenship as a site for moral community.) In the case of Sandel, for example, the more he has continued to develop his theoretical concerns, the clearer it has become that his real concern is not with community per se, but rather with the eclipse of richer possibilities of civic engagement and civic identity in an age dominated by liberal-proceduralist conceptions of politics. This basically civic-republican critique of liberalism should be set within a broader resurgence of civic-republican theorizing. Civic republicanism has surged back to life, philosophically, in the influential work of Hannah Arendt and, in a more historical vein, in the work of John Pocock, Quentin Skinner, and Philip Pettit.

More recently, new challenges to liberal citizenship have arisen in the debates about feminism and multiculturalism. As regards the latter, important arguments have been mounted to the effect that civic norms defined within the horizon of liberalism cannot do justice to the profound forms of cultural diversity ("deep diversity") that characterize virtually all political communities today. The basic multiculturalist idea is that liberal societies cannot fully honor the citizenship of their members if essential aspects of the identity of those members are slighted or treated as irrelevant to citizenship. Like any doctrine in political theory, multiculturalism comes in strikingly different versions. In Iris Young's view, liberal citizenship must be radically reconstructed so as to acknowledge an emphatic "politics of difference." In Will Kymlicka's more moderate view, accommodations to cultural difference are themselves required by liberal justice, rightly understood. According to the latter view, multiculturalism is merely a more effective (and more just) vehicle for the integration of minorities into a liberal civic regime, whereas according to the former view, the liberal vision of citizenship is intrinsically flawed, since liberal universalism is simply a mask for the hegemony of a majority culture.

At the same time, one can say that the powerful challenges to liberal understandings of citizenship generated by communitarian, civic-republican, and multiculturalist theorists have provoked, in response, more robust and more philosophical theories of citizenship from the liberal side. Jürgen Habermas's theory of communicative action can be interpreted as a new liberal (or post-liberal) doctrine of citizenship, and John Rawls's ambitious meditation on the notion of "public reason" in the latter phase of his intellectual career offers another such doctrine. The fundamental issue is posed by Rawls in relation to what he calls "civic humanism" ("classical republicanism" he regards as a more modest doctrine): "[Civic humanists believe that] the activity in which human beings achieve their fullest realization, their greatest good, is in the activities of political life. . . . [Liberal justice as Rawls understands it] rejects any such declaration; and to make the good of civil society subordinate to that of public life it views as mistaken" (Rawls, pp. 420–421; cf. pp. 205–206).

The opposing side is represented by Hannah Arendt when, at the conclusion of *On Revolution,* she endorses the ancient Greek solution to the problem, posed by Sophocles, of how "to bear life's burden": "It was the polis, the space of men's free deeds and living words, which could endow life with splendor" (Arendt, p. 285). The issue here, as it was originally in Aristotle's doctrine of citizenship, is whether civic life constitutes a privileged location for the expression of our proper humanity, or whether it ought merely to furnish a procedural framework for more diverse, privately defined activities in which we express our humanity. So we see that one of the core debates that has animated political philosophy throughout its history—for instance, in the argument between Rousseau, with his uncompromising republicanism, and his liberal critics such as Adam Smith (see Ignatieff) and Benjamin Constant (1767–1830)—continues to be a living question in contemporary thought.

See also **Civil Society; Democracy; Nation; Political, The; Social Contract.**

BIBLIOGRAPHY

Arendt, Hannah. *On Revolution.* New York: Viking, 1965.

Aristotle. *The Politics.* Translated by Carnes Lord. Chicago: University of Chicago Press, 1984.

Beiner, Ronald, ed. *Theorizing Citizenship.* Albany: State University of New York Press, 1995.

Hegel, G. W. F. *Elements of the Philosophy of Right.* Edited by Allen W. Wood. Translated by H. B. Nisbet. Cambridge, U.K.: Cambridge University Press, 1991.

Höfert, Almut. "States, Cities, and Citizens in the Later Middle Ages." In *States and Citizens: History, Theory, Prospects,* edited by Quentin Skinner and Bo Stråth, 63–75. Cambridge, U.K.: Cambridge University Press, 2003.

Ignatieff, Michael. *The Needs of Strangers: An Essay on Privacy, Solidarity, and the Politics of Being Human.* New York: Viking, 1984. See chapter four.

Machiavelli, Niccolò. *Discourses on Livy.* Translated by Harvey C. Mansfield and Nathan Tarcov. Chicago: University of Chicago Press, 1996.

Juan Gómez-Quiñones

Born of Mexican parents in 1940 in Parral, Chihuahua, Juan Gómez-Quiñones has been active in the articulation and political negotiation of cultural citizenship since the 1960s. His experience in the United States' Chicano civil rights movement led to his authoring of foundational papers on the history and identity of Chicano peoples of the southwestern United States. Soon after, he expressed the importance of and developed an epistemology for Chicano studies as a new interdisciplinary field. Such efforts helped to establish Chicano studies in institutions of higher education throughout the nation. Among his published works are *Chicano Politics: Reality and Promise, 1940–1990* (1990); *Mexican American Labor, 1790–1990* (1994); and *Roots of Chicano Politics, 1600–1940* (1994). In 1971 he helped found *Aztlan: International Journal of Chicano Studies Research,* the United States' premier journal of Chicana and Chicano studies. He is professor of history at the University of California at Los Angeles (UCLA) and lives with his family in Santa Monica, California. In 2003 UCLA presented him with the Rosenfield Distinguished Community Partnership Prize for community service.

Plant, Raymond. "Hegel and Political Economy." *New Left Review* no. 103 (May/June 1977) and no. 104 (July/August 1977).

Pocock, J. G. A. "Introduction." In Edmund Burke, *Reflections on the Revolution in France.* Indianapolis: Hackett, 1987.

Rawls, John. *Political Liberalism.* New York: Columbia University Press, 1993.

Riesenberg, Peter. *Citizenship in the Western Tradition: Plato to Rousseau.* Chapel Hill: University of North Carolina Press, 1992.

Rousseau, Jean-Jacques. *On the Social Contract.* Edited by Roger D. Masters. Translated by Judith R. Masters. New York: St. Martin's, 1978.

Ronald Beiner
Rebecca Kingston

CULTURAL CITIZENSHIP

Cultural citizenship has been part of a broader discussion on cultural pluralism that began in the United States at the beginning of the twentieth century. Since then pluralism has undergone at least three noteworthy transformations, beginning with, during the first quarter of the twentieth century, attempts to preserve primarily European immigrant cultures vis-à-vis the state, followed by the integrationist civil rights movements of the 1960s and 1970s, and lastly, the mainstreaming of "difference" and a multiculturalism that began in the 1980s. Never intended to destabilize the authority of the nation-state or its ideology, these "politics of difference" have helped give voice to American democratic citizenship.

Cultural Citizenship and Latinos

The notion of cultural citizenship initially developed in the 1980s, in part to bring greater multicultural emphasis to discourses of race in the United States that stressed black and white dichotomies. It is both a theoretical perspective and methodological approach with which to examine the sociocultural identity, political will, and cultural creation of primarily Latino populations in the United States. Theoretically, the notion acknowledges the cultural resiliency, social reproduction (the class, cultural, and linguistic knowledge and skills that establish the cultural capital of social groups), and rights-claiming agency of ethnic communities and other marginalized groups as viable and worthy outcomes of social injustice and alienation. Methodologically, cultural citizenship requires that social scientists approach their studies from the perspective of subordinate groups in order to understand the latter's goals, perceptions, and purposes. The term appears to have been coined by the anthropologist Renato Rosaldo, who first used it in the late 1980s to make a case for the democratization of institutions of higher education through diversity in the classroom, curricula, decision making, and society at large; a call not unlike that made by Chicano civil rights leaders of a generation before. In the 1980s and 1990s a Latino cohort of social scientists, among them Rosaldo, used the concept to examine Latino civic participation in the voicing, claiming, and negotiating of cultural space. Importantly, these studies speak to cultural phenomena as the aesthetic and force behind the empowerment of groups to civic action. As such, cultural citizenship examines the colloquial meanings of alienation and belonging as they apply to marginalized groups with respect to the national community. In this context, claims to rights made against the state by subordinate communities arise as a consequence of degradation and exclusion in their daily environments but may also result from acts of self-definition, representation, affirmation, sensibility, and aesthetics. Specifically, these may be expressed as desires and aspirations for equality, respect, and dignity. In the early years of the twenty-first century, cultural citizenship has been applied to modernizing efforts in an international context.

Sociocultural Agents of Citizenship

It is clear from the literature on cultural citizenship that cultural phenomena and issues of identity are privileged over theoretical considerations having to do with membership in the polity, except for its emphasis on the group. Unlike traditional concepts of citizenship in which the individual is the rights holder, the agents and subjects of cultural citizenship are undeniably the group. In concert with the literature on cultural pluralism, cultural citizenship too presents rights claiming as the prerogative of the group and, as such, calls attention to an ongoing broader debate between cultural pluralism and universal citizenship in the nation-state.

For much of the studies on Latino cultural citizenship, membership in the nation-state is implicitly ambiguous as if yet to be determined or in the process of becoming, as must be the case for illegal immigrant populations in the nation-state. Others describe a kind of citizenship practiced by Latino communities before the nation-state as "social citizenship," specifically using T. H. Marshal's meaning of *social* as entitlement to benefits deriving from the largesse of the welfare state. Similarly, social rights to citizenship have been used to describe a "citizenship without consent" practiced by communities of Mexican illegal immigrants in a postnational context inclusive of as well as beyond the nation-state.

Group-differentiated citizenship has been criticized on several counts, among them its reverting to premodern ways of using religious, ethnic, or class membership to determine the political status of people; its discouraging the integration of ethnoracial groups into mainstream society; and its undermining of a greater fraternity between all Americans and a common sense of purpose. The historian David Hollinger argues that group-differentiated citizenship is provincial and given to insularity when the need is for cosmopolitanism and "freedom of affiliation" embodied by the exceptional growth (compared with other nations) of mixed-raced people in the United States.

In response, cultural pluralists point out that citizenship rights as originally conceived by the nation's founding fathers are oblivious to the needs and differences of multicultural groups. Indeed, the philosopher Iris M. Young argues, the American liberal concept of equal citizenship plays no part in the notion of universal citizenship, nor is it meant to, since the latter assumes and upholds a homogeneous collective community at the expense and suppression of group difference. For this reason, Juan Gómez-Quiñones believes, Chicano/Latino cultural identity is vital to membership in a political community precisely because citizenship rights and responsibilities do not encompass multicultural rights. "Though there has been a great stress on voting qua voting as a measure of political achievement and influence," he writes, "the act of voting does not promise the achievement of full equities, much less direct and full democracy" (p. 211).

Defenders of differentiated group representation believe that citizenship should recognize and accommodate sociocultural difference to compensate for past injustices. For Young, any conception of equal citizenship must include historically excluded groups in the political community both as individuals and as members of the group. Young questions an ideal that in practice reinforces the power of the privileged in "this unified public" (of universal citizenship) while marginalizing others. An alternative approach to membership in the polity is "differentiated citizenship," which allows for group-based claims or distinct group rights for what Young calls "social-cultural" groups but which the philosopher Will Kymlicka distinguishes as national and ethnic minorities and underrepresented groups. According to Kymlicka, some form of differentiated group rights for the latter comprise part of citizenship rights in most, if not all, modern democracies.

See also **Assimilation; Citizenship: Naturalization; Identity, Multiple; Nation.**

BIBLIOGRAPHY

Flores, William V. "Citizens vs. Citizenry: Undocumented Immigrants and Latino Cultural Citizenship." In *Latino Cultural Citizenship: Claiming Identity, Space, and Rights,* edited by William V. Flores and Rina Benmayor. Boston: Beacon Press, 1997.

Gómez-Quiñones, Juan. *Chicano Politics: Reality and Promise, 1940–1990.* Albuquerque: University of New Mexico Press, 1990.

Hollinger, David A. *Postethnic America: Beyond Multiculturalism.* New York: Basic Books, 1995.

Kymlicka, Will. *Multicultural Citizenship: A Liberal Theory of Minority Rights.* Oxford: Clarendon; New York: Oxford University Press, 1995.

Rosaldo, Renato. "Cultural Citizenship, Inequality, and Multiculturalism." In *Race, Identity, and Citizenship: A Reader,* edited by Rodolfo D. Torres, Louis F. Mirón, and Jonathan X. Inda. Malden, Mass.: Blackwell, 1999.

———. *Culture and Truth: The Remaking of Social Analysis.* Rev. ed. Boston: Beacon Press, 1993.

Rosaldo, Renato, ed. *Cultural Citizenship in Island Southeast Asia: Nation and Belonging in the Hinterlands.* Berkeley: University of California Press, 2003.

Walzer, Michael. "Pluralism: A Political Perspective." In *Harvard Encyclopedia of American Ethnic Groups,* edited by Stephan Thernstrom. Cambridge, Mass.: Belknap Press of Harvard University, 1980.

Young, Iris M. "Polity and Group Difference: A Critique of the Ideal of Universal Citizenship." In *Theorizing Citizenship,* edited by Ronald Beiner. Albany: State University of New York Press, 1995.

Adelaida R. Del Castillo

NATURALIZATION

Citizenship rests with territory at the heart of the definition of *nation-state.* If territory determines the geographical limits of state sovereignty, citizenship determines a state's population. Beyond these limits one finds foreign land, foreign sovereignty, and foreigners. Drawing the boundary within which some human beings are included and others excluded as foreigners, permitting some of them to acquire citizenship with certain conditions and others to lose citizenship, is a state prerogative that requires legal tools. In citizenship law, the two most important legal tools traditionally used to determine citizenship are:

1. *Birthplace,* or jus soli, the fact of being born in a territory over which the state maintains, has maintained, or wishes to extend its sovereignty.

2. *Bloodline,* or jus sanguinis, citizenship as a result of the nationality of one parent or of other, more distant ancestors.

All nations use jus soli and jus sanguinis in defining attribution of citizenship at birth. However, two other tools are used in citizenship law, attributing citizenship after birth through naturalization:

1. *Marital status,* in that marriage to a citizen of another country can lead to the acquisition of the spouse's citizenship.

2. Past, present, or future *residence* within the country's past, present, future, or intended borders (including colonial borders).

In eighteenth-century Europe, jus soli was the dominant criterion of nationality in the two most powerful kingdoms: France and the United Kingdom. The state simply inherited feudal tradition: human beings were linked to the lord who held the land where they were born. The French Revolution broke with this feudal tradition. Against Napoléon Bonaparte's wish, the new civil code of 1804 granted French nationality at birth only to a child born to a French father, either in France or abroad. This policy of jus sanguinis, representing a modern innovation, was not ethnically motivated; it simply reflected the fact that individual rights and family had become more important than subjecthood and state power. This French innovation was borrowed extensively and became the law in Austria (1811), Belgium (1831), Spain (1837), Prussia (1842), Russia (1864), Italy (1865), Netherlands (1888), Norway (1892), and Sweden (1894).

The British tradition of jus soli, on the contrary, was transplanted, unamended and unbroken, to Britain's colonies in North America (the United States and Canada), Europe (Ireland), Africa (South Africa), and Australia. It also influenced Portugal and Denmark until the Nordic countries adopted a common nationality regime in the 1920s.

Were a population and territory to match one another exactly, attributing citizenship on the basis of jus sanguinis, jus soli or residence would not make any difference. Citizenship law would concern the same population and would have the same juridical effects. Further, naturalization would be irrelevant. It is the case, of course, that the population and territory of a nation-state do not coincide. People migrate and, with respect to migration, one can distinguish broadly between two different types of countries:

1. "Countries of emigration" are countries where part of the core population resides outside the national boundaries, a characteristic applying to the majority of European countries before World War II (with the exception of France), and Mexico since the 1930s.

2. "Countries of immigration" are those in which the majority of citizens are immigrants or descendents of immigrants, or whose foreign populations have settled as permanent residents alongside a majority population that is perceived to have existed since time immemorial and is not descended from immigrants. The United States, Canada, and Australia and countries of South America are examples of the former, while the latter category includes France since the mid-nineteenth century and all other western European countries since World War II.

The legal traditions of jus soli and jus sanguinis were maintained with consistency and relative ease in the majority of these different countries until World War II. In countries of immigration such as the United States, jus soli allows the children of immigrants to acquire citizenship automatically. For continental European countries that were countries of emigration, jus sanguinis allowed citizens abroad to maintain links until their descendants lost touch.

Since World War II, however, citizenship laws have converged across all democratic states, due to the large increase in the scale of migrations across the world. In many continental European states, large-scale postwar immigration led to legislative changes so as to permit increasingly large segments of the population born in their territories, namely second- and third-generation immigrants, to access citizenship more easily. Elements of jus soli have been included in their jus sanguinis tradition that extends citizenship automatically at birth to third-generation immigrants (France since 1889, the Netherlands since 1953, Spain since 1990, and Belgium since 1992). For the second generation, in many countries, children born to immigrants on national territory are entitled to citizenship if the child (Belgium, Denmark, Finland, France, Italy, Netherlands, Spain, Sweden) or one of the child's parents (Germany) has lawfully resided there for a period of years.

Countries with nationality laws based upon automatic jus soli often attracted a number of immigrants into their territory, encouraging these countries to become more restrictive. For example, the United Kingdom's imperial and expansive conception of territory, combined with its jus soli tradition, involuntarily encouraged immigration. Just after World War II, all subjects of the British Empire had access to British citizenship simply by residing in the territory of the United Kingdom proper. Since that time, British legislation on nationality has undergone a swift and silent revolution away from the extended and automatic jus soli to a 1981 law that attributes citizenship only to children born in U.K. territory to parents with legal residence status. The legal residence of parents has also been included as a requirement in the Portuguese and South African laws.

The trend toward convergence in nationality laws concerns almost all advanced industrial countries, insofar as they share three basic characteristics: democratic values, stable borders, and a self-perception as countries of immigration rather than of emigration. The importance of these three conditions is confirmed when considering exceptions to this rule, such as Israel and Russia. In both countries, there is a dominant perception that many of their citizens reside outside their borders, and that the borders—indispensable for the definition of the soli—are not stable. Jus sanguinis thus remains at the center of both of their citizenship laws. But for all countries, regardless of their situation concerning migration or their level of development, there are two distinct lines of convergence in nationality laws. First, there has been a notable trend since the mid-twentieth century toward repealing provisions for the automatic acquisition of citizenship through marriage, a move motivated at the same time by the development of equal rights between men and women in nationality laws and by worries about fraudulent marriages with illegal aliens. Second, equal rights between men and women to transmit their citizenship to their children has produced the development of dual citizenship and more toleration of this phenomenon in many countries that formerly refused it (for example, Switzerland since 1990). What remains divergent are the rules for naturalization; that is, the processes by which foreign residents of the first generation access citizenship in a host country. States generally require a period of residence and knowledge of the language, and take into account a criminal record, but the details of these requirements still vary greatly, both in the formal requirements of nationality laws and in the practices through which these laws are enforced.

See also **Americanization, U.S.; Citizenship: Cultural Citizenship.**

BIBLIOGRAPHY

Aleinikoff, T. Alexander, and Douglas Klusmeyer. *Citizenship Policies for an Age of Migration.* Washington, D.C.: Carnegie Endowment for International Peace, 2002.

Aleinikoff, T. Alexander, and Douglas Klusmeyer, eds. *Citizenship Today: Global Perspectives and Practices.* Washington, D.C.: Carnegie Endowment for International Peace, 2001.

Hansen, Randall, and Patrick Weil, eds. *Dual Nationality, Social Rights, and Federal Citizenship in the U.S. and Europe: The Reinvention of Citizenship.* New York: Berghan, 2002.

———. *Towards a European Nationality: Citizenship, Immigration and Nationality Law in the EU.* Houndsmills, U.K., and New York: Palgrave, 2001.

Weil, Patrick. *Qu'est ce qu'un français? Histoire de la nationalité française depuis la Révolution.* Paris: Grasset, 2002.

Patrick Weil

CITY, THE.

This entry includes four subentries.

THE CITY AS CULTURAL CENTER

In the modern conception of the word *city*—characterized by the size, the aggregation of housing, differentiated division of labor, and the density of interaction—the first cities appeared in Mesopotamia around 10,000 B.C.E. and most clearly by 3,000 B.C.E. The great city of Babylon marked the coming of age of civilization, characterized by an urban culture that highlighted sophisticated arts and crafts, rare products, a multiplicity of material objects introduced through trade, the emergence of new ideas and modes of domination, and a more complex social structure.

From the early days of urbanization, several often competing conceptions of cities were evident:

- the material city of walls, squares, houses, roads, light, utilities, buildings, waste, and physical infrastructure;

- the cultural city in terms of imaginations, differences, representations, ideas, symbols, arts, texts, senses, religion, aesthetics;

- the politics and policies of the city in terms of domination, power, government, mobilization, public policies, welfare, education;

- the social city of riots, ethnic, economic, or gender inequalities, everyday life, and social movements;

- the economy of the city: division of labor, scale, production, consumption, and trade.

As a unit of analysis the city is often characterized through the emphasis on diversity, fragmentation, strangeness, encounters with strangers, the mosaic of variety, contingent interactions, moving borders, everyday life and events, and the multitude of interactions. However, another perspective focuses upon integration, domination, assimilation, social order, control, inequalities, unity, models, patterns of economic development, structures, and systems. From Babylon, Athens, Rome, and later Florence, to the present era's so-called global cities comes the idea that cities are places where culture flourishes, where civilization reaches its highest point of complexity and sophistication The density and diversity of interactions are supposed to stimulate innovations in all sorts of ways, to free urban inhabitants from traditional cultural constraint. Cities are therefore presented by social scientists, historians, and writers in a progressive way as centers of innovation and culture even if civilizations first developed without or beyond cities, as, for instance, in the case of Egypt. By contrast, the city is also portrayed as the place of darkness, chaos, violence, riots, exploitation, marginal life and deviance, destruction, and oppression.

Those categories were for the most part derived from the division of labor between disciplines put forward at the end of the nineteenth century. The study of the city as a cultural center evoked passionate debates at the start of the twentieth century when the German sociologists Max Weber, Werner Sombart, and Georg Simmel discussed the relationship between cities, culture, arts, technological developments, and domination. They asked questions about the influence of a particular set of structural social, economic, political, and cultural conditions such as capitalism on the effect of cities or on individual and collective behavior, modes of thinking, ways of life, cultural creation, and imagination.

The City as an Integrated Political and Social Structure

In the Western world, cities emerged at the turn of the first millennium, insinuating themselves into the gaps of the feudal system. In a section titled "The City" in his 1925 study, *Economy and Society,* Max Weber portrays the medieval Western city as having the following characteristic features: fortifications, a market, and a specifically urban economy of consumption, exchange, and production; a court of law and the ability to ordain a set of rules and laws; rules relating to landed property (since cities were not subject to the taxes and constraints of feudalism); a structure based on associations of guilds; and—at least partial—political autonomy, expressed in particular through the existence of an administrative body and the participation of the burghers in local government, and sometimes even through the existence of an army and an actual policy of foreign expansion; and a citizenship with relative freedom often associated with affiliation to a guild.

The medieval city was the crucible of European society, a place in which new cultural and political models developed, along with new social relations and cultural and organizational innovations, furthered by interactions between the various populations thus promoting mechanisms for learning a collective way of life, for innovation and spreading innovation, rapid accumulation, transformation of behaviors, interplay of competition and cooperation, and processes of social differentiation engendered by proximity. The Europe of cities was not just the Europe of early capitalism and of merchants, but also the Europe of intellectuals, universities, and culture that launched the Renaissance.

In analytical terms, this sketches out a research perspective in terms of local societies and governance that is crucial for the analysis of contemporary cities, in Europe in particular. The city is conceived as an integrated local society (most of

the time, incomplete), and as a complex social formation, sometimes a local society. Cities may be more or less structured in their economic and cultural exchanges, and the different actors may be related to each other in the same local context with long-term strategies, investing their resources in a coordinated way and adding to the social capital riches. In this case the urban society appears as well structured and visible, and one can detect forms of (relative) integration. If not, the city reveals itself as less structured and as such no longer a significant subject for study: somewhere where decisions are made externally by separate actors. Such an analysis examines the interplay and conflicts of social groups, interests, and institutions, and the way in which, to some extent, regulations have been put in place through conflicts and the logics of integration. Cities do not develop solely according to interactions and contingencies: groups, actors, and organizations oppose one another, enter into conflict, coordinate, produce representations in order to institutionalize collective forms of action, implement policies, structure inequalities, and defend their interests. This perspective on cities highlights the informal economy, the dynamism of localized family relations, the interplay of associations, reciprocity, culture and ways of life, the density of localized horizontal relations, and local social formations.

The Industrial City

The industrial revolution led to a new wave of urbanization. Concentration in great metropolises and large industrial areas lent a different dynamic to cities, changing them both socially and physically: a new type of industrial city emerged in the nineteenth century—most often around coal mining, textiles, or iron and steel, then later chemicals, electricity, and mechanical engineering—enjoying an extraordinarily rapid growth fueled by immigration and leading to the formation of dense industrial regions and centers as in Britain, the German Ruhr, or the northeast of France—"Coketowns" as Lewis Mumford put it. The "tyranny of fixed cost" (transport) also supported the rise of industrial ports and the pace of concentration in large industrial cities such as Calcutta and, most decisively, in large U.S. cities of the Northeast and Midwest—New York and Chicago in particular. Cities became places

***Ideal City,* c. 1470, by Piero della Francesca.** Although cities are almost inevitably prone to incidents of violence and oppression, they have also historically been centers of progress and innovation where diversity, knowledge, and culture are celebrated concepts. © ARTE & IMMAGINI SRL/CORBIS

where capital was tied up in major fixed assets, with labor forces that varied in composition and size, and with a high level of internal diversity.

The industrial city is first and foremost a place of social conflicts, inequalities, urban poverty, social segregation, and speculation. Karl Marx and his followers sketched a view of the city organized by capitalism, a place of class struggle determined to a large extent by the economy. The Marxist analysis was "urbanized" by David Harvey, who stressed the role of land and property for capital accumulation, investment together with the contradictions of capitalism in cities. He underlined both the role of the built environment in capitalism and the social struggle of social groups to prevent the disinvestment in industrial cities, which fed the dynamics of deindustrialization and urban crisis. Others have developed the role of class struggle to analyze the dynamics and culture of cities in different parts of the world. Changing forms of capitalism after 1945 gave rise to the analysis of the "Fordist city"—that is, the city organized around and for the needs of the large industry.

Industrial cities are characterized by their social structure and by their form and organization. Although U.S. cities had large firms and major entrepreneurs, they were above all workers' cities, sites of immense poverty and exploitation, and crucibles for working-class organization. The industrial city took the form of this combination of industries, workers' housing (slums, social housing, suburban houses), minimal communal amenities, transportation infrastructure, and, later, social democratic forms of urban government. Overpopulated working-class districts mixed with factories in city centers, driving out the bourgeoisie (in a configuration that reversed that of the old European cities, where industrial activities and working populations had most often been pushed out to the periphery) into what became the suburbs. Social surveys were initiated in Britain, France, and Germany to assess poverty and the terrible conditions of public health. Working-class culture was organized around work, clubs, cafés, dances, and sport, although with considerable variations from one city to another. Even beyond the structural opposition between the bourgeoisie and the newly forming working class, these industrial cities were socially diverse places: artisans continued to exist and to develop, and the number of shops increased, if only to feed the abundant populations of vagrants, prostitutes, and white-collar office workers.

After the 1960s, the most industrialized cities declined in the United States and Western Europe, leading to a postindustrial landscape, a mix of derelict land and buildings and new cultural or housing activities. By contrast, other cities in the world—for instance, in rapidly urbanizing China—have become the new workshops of the world, comprising a high concentration of the working class in the manufacturing sector.

The Rise of the Metropolis: Centers of Experiment for Modern Social Life

For observers of the late nineteenth and early twentieth century (Simmel in particular), the development of the large metropolis is a major phenomenon, both in Europe and in the United States.

Capital cities benefited from the consolidation of states, the shift of political life onto the national level, and the strengthening of the states'—and therefore the bureaucracies' (including the army's)—capacity for control, as well as from industrial development and colonization. These major cities absorbed a large part of the flow of migration, thus providing sizeable reserves of labor. They were the first beneficiaries of the transport revolution, from tramways to road and rail networks. Open to the world in an era that saw increasing numbers of different kinds of exchanges, discoveries, and technical innovations, they established their role by organizing universal exhibitions and great fairs. Concerned with public health and safety, governments organized major improvement works, created wide avenues, and constructed new public buildings: stations, squares, and monuments that symbolized their dynamism and technical progress. These cities were also places of speculation, of public and private investment in housing, and of financial capital. Their cultural influence changed scale because of more rapid diffusion, transports, and colonial empires. In particular, London, Paris, Berlin, and Vienna were the theaters of extraordinary physical and cultural transformations. As university cities and cultural centers, they were the focus of unrest and the sites of the political and social revolts that punctuated the nineteenth century. The great metropolis became the site of consumption, of department stores and wide avenues, of overstimulation that changed the urban cultural experience. This led also to physical transformation with the ever-increasing diffusion of urbanization around those large metropolises, hence the rise of suburbs, either working-class ones such as the red belt in Paris or bourgeois suburbs where the middle class abandoned the center.

The rise of the large metropolis became an American feature: New York and Chicago and later Los Angeles in particular gradually replaced European cities in the urban imagination of the modernist metropolis. They grew thanks to stunning economic development and massive immigration. In the 1920s both the American and European metropolis became a place of strong inequalities, anti-Semitism, violence against foreigners, racism, anticommunist movements, and flamboyant cultural creativity. The U.S. model is constructed around the industrial city with its low-income neighborhoods linked to manufacturing districts and close to commercial cores and its middle-income neighborhoods beyond. Out of the suburban migration of the middle classes accentuated after World War II emerged the prototypical metropolis with its central city ringed by suburban enclaves. In the best case, the commercial core became dominant. In the worst cases it, along with the manufacturing district, was in decline. The dynamics of development was horizontal, with activities deconcentrated and decentralized.

The metropolis and the neighborhood are associated with the Chicago school of urban sociology, which for several decades developed ethnographic studies on different ethnic communities and neighborhoods, and also—in research such as that by Robert Ezra Park, Ernest W. Burgess, and Roderick D. McKenzie—on groups such as hobos, gangs, and the like. Such work concentrates on interaction and on the density of interactions within the city, leading to an ecological model of the urban process based upon the dynamics of competition and conflict between different groups and their evolution in terms of social and spatial mobility. The city is the place of dense interaction, of mobility, within a context of rapid social change, industrialization, and immigration, a "social laboratory" of modernity where more classic social structures are eroded.

The issue of immigration and the presence of ghettos became central, and racism was quickly established as the leading cultural divide within cities. The question of race and relations between ethnic groups, particularly in U.S. cities, became the cornerstone of American sociology and urban sociology. Ghetto formation, competition between ethnic and racial groups, and assimilation remain the main lenses through which cities are analyzed.

Related debates concerning the integration of diverse ethnic groups took place in European cities during the period of mass migration to industrial cities in the 1960s and 1970s, and the urban-ethnic issue also became central in the political and social dynamics of cities: suburbanization and the rise of xenophobic organizations.

Cities of Difference: Globalization in Progress

Urbanization was reaching new highs in the contemporary world with the rise of mega cities whose greater metropolitan populations exceeded 15 million, such as Calcutta, Cairo, Tokyo, Bombay, and Seoul. Beyond the modern metropolis, researchers try to make sense of those large urban areas with terms such as "postmetropolis," "global cities," and "global city-regions." The processes of globalization, including transnational migration, architecture, financial transactions, transport flux, and dissemination of technological innovations contribute to the rise of mega cities in different parts of the globe.

In contrast to the modernist view of the metropolis, cities have been a major subject of the cultural turn in the social sciences suggesting that culture orients our behavior and shapes what we are able to know about the world. According to cultural studies that have taken place within cities, the question of identity and culture has become a central paradigm. Immigration and the pluralization of identity pave the way for the image of the city as fragmented mosaics. The city is about "the other," and the risks associated with diversity.

The first impact of the cultural turn is about the questioning of classic Western categories such as cities, gender, ethnic, militarism, surveillance, and colonialism. A body of research has made visible issues of sexual, racial, age, religious, gender, and ethnic minorities, together with class, stressing the fluidity of cities, the role of informal organizations and social movements in social conflicts; it has raised issues of justice and the pluralization of identity formation beyond the state. The city is therefore analyzed through representation, discourse, objects, arts. Cultural studies scholars now take up goods as texts that signal the important social processes of their time and context. They look at cities as worked out through perception, memories, and imagination, everyday life and practices, interactions and events, a space simultaneously real and imagined,

material and metaphorical, ordered and disordered: from gay enclaves to fortress cities and postcolonial environments. The city is seen as a fluid process, constantly reshaped, chaotic and indeterminate, subject to rival and contradictory claims.

Culture is now a major determinant of migration and the dynamics of cities. From the studios of Los Angeles and Hong Kong to the old neighborhood of Istanbul or Bombay and the cultural clusters of Florence and Prague, all places have culture industries from museums to choirs, county fairs to religious buildings, galleries to theaters. Each city is unique, and its uniqueness relies both upon the interactions within the city, a place for spectacles, and upon interactions with other cities. Tourism, migration, economic development, and urban regeneration seem to rely now, at least in part, upon culture.

"Fantasy cities" are on the rise (as documented by John Hannigan) and one exemplar, Las Vegas, is the fastest growing city in the United States. Surveillance technologies, marketing, standardized entertainment, and culture give a new boost to cities as places of cultural consumption under strict surveillance, at the expense of local groups, social conflicts, and local culture.

The traditional ideas of the city, the modern metropolis or the industrial city, are now associated or replaced by contradictory images of those mega cities where one either emphasizes cultural diversity and the infinite range of interactions or the strength of control and capital accumulation by dominant groups. The rise of mobility and transnational flux within more globalized capitalist cities raise new issues about assimilation, social order, politics, and culture in cities. Cities are reshaped by local groups and culture interacting, adapting, or protesting against globalized flows.

See also **Civil Society; Cultural History; Globalization; Social Capital.**

BIBLIOGRAPHY

Bagnasco, Arnaldo, and Patrick Le Galès, eds. *Cities in Contemporary Europe.* Cambridge, U.K., and New York: Cambridge University Press, 2000.

Briggs, Asa. *Victorian Cities.* London: Penguin, 1962.

Davis, Mike. *City of Quartz: Excavating the Future in Los Angeles.* London and New York: Verso, 1990.

Eade, John, and Christopher Mele, eds. *Understanding the City, Contemporary and Future Perspectives.* Oxford and Malden, Mass.: Blackwell, 2002.

Fincher, Ruth, and Jane M. Jacobs, eds. *Cities of Difference.* New York: Guilford Press, 1998.

Hannigan, John. *Fantasy City: Pleasure and Profit in the Postmodern Metropolis.* London and New York: Routledge, 1998.

Harvey, David. *The Urbanization of Capital: Studies in the History and Theory of Capital Urbanization.* Baltimore: Johns Hopkins University Press, 1985.

King, Anthony D., ed. *Re-presenting the City: Ethnicity, Capital, and Cultural in the Twenty-first-Century Metropolis.* New York: New York University Press, 1996.

Logan, John R., ed. *The New Chinese City: Globalization and Market Reform.* Oxford: Blackwell, 2002.

Massey, Douglas S., and Nancy Denton. *American Apartheid: Segregation and the Making of the Underclass.* Cambridge, Mass.: Harvard University Press, 1993.

Mingione, Enzo, ed. *Urban Poverty and the Underclass.* Oxford and Cambridge, Mass.: Blackwell, 1996.

Mumford, Lewis. *The City in History: Its Origin, Its Transformations, and Its Prospects.* New York: Harcourt, Brace and World, 1961.

Park, Robert Ezra, Ernest W. Burgess, and Roderick D. McKenzie. *The City.* Chicago: University of Chicago Press, 1967.

Sassen, Saskia. *The Global City: London, New York, Tokyo.* Princeton, N.J.: Princeton University Press, 2001.

Scott, Allen J., and Edward W. Soja, eds. *The City: Los Angeles and Urban Theory at the End of the Twentieth Century.* Berkeley: University of California Press, 1996.

Sennett, Richard. *The Conscience of the Eye: The Design and Social Life of Cities.* New York: Knopf, 1990.

Smith, Michael Peter. *Transnational Urbanism: Locating Globalization.* Oxford: Blackwell, 2001.

Storper, Michael. *The Regional World: Territorial Development in a Global Economy.* New York: Guilford Press, 1997.

Walton, John, and David Seldon. *Free Markets and Food Riots: The Politics of Global Adjustment.* Oxford: Blackwell, 1994.

Weber, Max. *Economy and Society: An Outline of Interpretive Sociology,* 2 vols., edited by Guenther Roth and Claus Wittich. Berkeley: University of California Press, 1978. Originally published as *Wirtschaft und gesellschaft,* 1925.

Zukin, Sharon. *The Cultures of Cities.* Oxford: Blackwell, 1995.

Patrick Le Galès

THE CITY AS POLITICAL CENTER

In Western political thought, ideas about cities, citizenship, and democracy have always been inextricably linked. Since Socrates suggested in *The Republic* that his interlocutors help him to create a city in speech, the city has functioned as a real and metaphorical center for struggles over what it means to be political. Ideas about civilization and barbarism, egalitarianism and exclusion, virtue and vice, civic participation and social unrest, all find expression in discussions of the city. Yet the city is and has always been an ambiguous achievement; its success (or failure) as a form of political organization rests on its citizens' dubious abilities to govern themselves, deliberate with strangers, act on principles beyond narrow self-interest, and collectively determine their future. Thus the state of a nation's cities is often used as a barometer to judge the quality of its political life.

City as Democratic Ideal

In its most utopian incarnations, the city is common ground, a space where the democratic values of equality, heterogeneity, public life, and creative expression might be freely lived. In the United States the roots of its democratic heritage are routinely traced to ancient Greece, where in Athens in the fifth century B.C.E. the vision of the "good life" was concomitant with city life. As Pericles famously argued:

Our constitution is called a democracy because power is in the hands not of a minority but of the whole people.

When it is a question of settling private disputes, everyone is equal before the law. . . . [J]ust as our political life is free and open, so is our day-to-day life in our relations with each other. We do not get in a state with our next door neighbor if he enjoys himself in his own way. . . . We are free and tolerant in our private lives, but in public affairs we keep to the law. . . . Here each individual is interested not only in his own affairs but in the affairs of the state as well: even those who are mostly occupied with their own business are extremely well-informed on general politics—this is a peculiarity of ours: we do not say that a man who takes no interest in politics is a man who minds his own business; we say that he has no business here at all. (Pericles' Funeral Oration, in Thucydides, pp. 145–147)

Equality before the law, tolerance of difference, and civic participation—these are the qualities of city life that are found desirable and worthy of imitation.

In the modern context, the ideal of metropolitan democracy is grounded in the potential found in these three aspects of city life originally articulated in Pericles' speech. First, as Max Weber argued, modern city life—as characterized by economic and bureaucratic rationalization and autonomous law and administration—disrupted feudal and paternalistic forms of governance. Traditional and often immutable hierarchies (such as tribe, religion, or kinship) thus were replaced by more egalitarian political associations.

Second, democratic urbanists exalt the city's inherent heterogeneity as democracy's greatest good. The city is a place where citizens are required to negotiate many different axes of identity and difference (for example, race, class, gender, and sexual orientation), so city life cultivates an appreciation of diverse groups without necessarily assuming either assimilation or exclusion. While in ancient Athens the boundaries for demarcating "citizen" and "other" were considerably narrower than they are in the early twenty-first century, the principles of toleration and noninterference are cornerstones of democratic urbanism. The city functions as a place where persons unknown to each other and often without shared familial, religious, ethnic, or cultural ties have the opportunity to act in concert to achieve mutual good; a certain kind of cosmopolitanism (or an ability to "move comfortably in diversity") is intrinsic to discussions of democratic urbanism (Sennett, p. 17).

Third, because political life is not based on private relationships but on the whole body of citizens deliberating among themselves (the public's business is everyone's business), the presence of truly public spaces—boulevards, parks, and plazas—is a requirement for collective action. In fact such places serve as stages for political activity, facilitating interaction among diverse groups with different interests and creating the necessary conditions for collective decision-making. This very material public sphere both presupposes and cultivates political imagination by encouraging citizens to think and act in ways that transcend their particular experiences.

The City as Democratic Menace

From its inception, however, the city's equality and diversity have also signified its instability—the threat it poses to moral, social, and political order. The city has been regarded as the site of sinful excess and moral turpitude, where upstanding citizens may risk succumbing to the depravity of the mob. Despite (or because of) its status as the rationalized center of Western political and economic life, the city has also been the site of its revolutions; from Europe in 1848 to the United States and Paris in 1968, cities have been recognized as the epicenters of democratic upheaval.

Attempts to secure the city as a political and cultural center have historically often sought to contain, control, or eliminate many of the very elements urban democrats find so promising. Efforts to create meaningful, modern urban life have varied greatly, ranging from the reinvention of Paris by Baron Georges-Eugène Haussmann (1809–1891), the Garden City of Ebenezer Howard (1850–1928), the City Beautiful of Daniel Burnham (1846–1912), and the Radiant City of Le Corbusier (1887–1965), to numerous public housing projects across the United States and Europe. But as Elizabeth Wilson notes, what these efforts have in common is the desire to replace chaos with order, heterogeneity with uniformity, and the noise and commotion inevitable in lively public places with placidity and good behavior.

Contemporary Challenges to the City's Democratic Potential

One of the widely debated issues regarding cities in the early twenty-first century is how their democratic possibilities might be realized in practice. While (at least implicitly) remaining sympathetic to the ideal of the city as a democratic space, important contributions in critical urban thought examine the inequalities woven into the urban fabric that delimit the amount and quality of freedom allowed to citizens, especially through residential segregation and the privatization of public space.

Residential segregation is caused by any number of factors. In the American context, typical examples of these include the use of racially restrictive covenants and redlining up through the 1960s; the priority placed on the federal highway system rather than public transit; federal tax incentives offered to homeowners (via deductions for mortgage interest) rather than to renters; and the use of local property taxes to fund public schools. These practices are not accidental but institutional and political, and they work to create, sustain, and embed economic and racial inequalities in the urban landscape. All result in widely divergent experiences for living, working, and pursuing educational opportunities in the context of modern city life.

As a result of these practices the inner city and inner-ring suburban areas are increasingly racially segregated and economically isolated. The results of this are myriad. First, the economically privileged have less and less contact with working-class and poor people, especially persons of color. Second, geographic segregation often produces serious spatial mismatches, where jobs and workers move in opposite directions; as more companies move to areas outside the central city, low-wage workers have more difficulty finding jobs and then commuting to them, since they often cannot afford to work, live, and find child care in the same areas. Finally, residents in poor and working-class neighborhoods often pay more for basic goods and services, such as groceries (Dreier et al., pp. 41–77).

These costs are not only directed at the economically underprivileged, however. Instead, what is commonly referred to as "urban sprawl" (low-density development at the edges of an existing city) is the other side of concentrated poverty and has its own burdens: complete car dependency and longer commutes, shrinking green space and loss of farmland, increased pollution and flooding, and higher taxes to support new infrastructure (roads, schools, water and sewer, and power lines). Furthermore, these sprawling, redundant netherworlds between city and suburb defy Kevin Lynch's (1960) aesthetic prescriptions for memorable, livable cities: a legible city, he suggested, would be one whose physical features and landmarks are easily identifiable. As a result of sprawl, urban peripheries look more and more similar (freeways and off-ramps, chain stores and traffic), while also looking less and less like traditional urban centers.

Intensifying residential segregation finds its apotheosis in gated communities, which not only include elite suburban housing developments but also increasingly many inner-city, middle-income apartment buildings. While scholars stress numerous reasons for Americans' affinity for living behind walls (ranging from fear of falling property values to craving privacy, security, and/or like-minded neighbors), they generally agree that such arrangements inhibit, rather than promote, democracy. In gated communities, typically public spaces such as streets, sidewalks, and green spaces are walled off and "forted up" (in Blakely and Snyder's evocative phrase), privatizing not only individual residences but community space as well. Gated communities also are often racially homogenous. According to the U.S. Census Bureau's 2001 American housing survey, while the white and Hispanic middle classes are embracing gated communities in greater numbers, African Americans are much less likely to live in such areas. Although gated communities take a variety of forms and serve myriad functions (from retirement communities to inner-city security zones), spaces that promote homogeneity and exclusivity can only have a chilling effect on democracy. Their net result, then, is division rather than diversification, thus "undermin[ing] the very concept of civitas, organized community life" (Blakely and Snyder in Ellin, ed., p. 85). Residential segregation—especially as exemplified in gated communities—thus undermines the city's potential to foster tolerance of and political alliances across class and racial differences.

In part gated communities are symptomatic of the second challenge to urban democracy: the rapid privatization of public space. In *City of Quartz*, Mike Davis observes that "the American city . . . is being systematically turned inside out— or, rather, outside in. The valorized spaces of the new megastructures and super-malls are concentrated in the center, street frontage is denuded, public activity is sorted into strictly functional compartments, and circulation is internalized in corridors under the gaze of private police" (p. 226). Boundaries between public and private spaces are consciously constructed through the use of walls, landscapes, and police or private security guards, but they are also marked through less tangible (though no less real) obstructions: commodities some cannot purchase, real estate that some cannot afford, a history and traditions that are not commonly shared. Davis argues that while architectural critics (often members of the dominant racial group and economic class) are often oblivious to these sorts of spatial segregation, marginalized groups recognize these borders immediately (p. 226).

This is all to say that urban space is no longer exemplified by truly public places. Instead, urban space at the millennium is increasingly contained, sanitized, monitored and defended; its goal is not to promote democracy (as in the Athenian polis) but rather to provide safe spaces for (predominantly white) middle-class suburbanites to work, shop, and play (Davis, p. 227).

Whither the City Center?

Many predictions for the future of urban democracy are dire. As Elizabeth Wilson plainly states, "The result is that today in many cities we have the worst of all worlds: danger without pleasure, safety without stimulation, consumerism without choice, monumentality without diversity. At the same time, larger and larger numbers of people inhabit zones that are no longer really either town or countryside" (p. 9).

These indeterminate zones that are not "town or countryside" indicate a final challenge for the city as political center: a new kind of urbanism typified by exurbs or edge cities that are no longer economically dependent on an urban center and defy the "core-periphery" model of the twentieth-century city. In fact, some would argue, casting the "city as political center" at the new millennium is entirely misguided. Rather, as Robert Fishman contends, "the true centre of this new city is not in some downtown business district but in each residential unit. From that central starting point, the members of the household create their own city from the multitude of destinations that are within suitable driving distance" (p. 185).

The "city" as it exists for most people, then, no longer matches the traditional picture of centrally concentrated economic and cultural life but rather comprises travel routes and endpoints, transportation and communications networks that together form weblike metropolitan regions that often include more than one urban center and frequently span several states. Edge cities and exurbs, some commentators assert, are almost entirely disconnected from their nearest urban centers, containing within themselves all the necessities of life: opportunities not only to live (as in traditional suburbs) but also for commerce and leisure, functions previously delegated to cities. Faced with the dilution of urban public life, the "city on a hill" is replaced by the "dream home" as the site of utopian possibilities.

The diminishment of the city as political center raises the question of whether or not the city has declined in importance as an economic center. Some theorists of the global city argue that industrial restructuring and the development of sophisticated communications networks have rendered city space less crucial than what Manuel Castells calls "the space of flows," or the continual movement of people, goods, technology, and information over large distances, and the material infrastructure

that makes this movement possible. For Castells, what is important is no longer centers but networks, which allows real-time interaction between dispersed actors. Others, most notably Saskia Sassen, contend that the past few decades have seen the emergence of truly global cities, which provide an immense telecommunications, design, and service infrastructure for transnational corporations. This has created an unprecedented concentration of wealth and labor power in these cities while at the same time forging even greater disparities of wealth.

Throughout history people have staked claims to better lives in better cities, knowing that this particular spatial form of organization carries with it the potential both for hegemony and equality, disenfranchisement and deliberation. The question for advocates of urban democracy is how to correct some of the egregious inequalities rendered by twenty-first-century urban planning practices and globalization and how to best modify governance systems to take into account the changing shape of metropolitan democracy. The shapes presently given to cities and towns, the lines drawn with concrete and steel or building codes and zoning ordinances—or the connections forged with digital communications networks—enable citizens to make material their ideas about assimilation, stratification, and segregation. Uncritically adopting the city as a normative ideal, however, ignores the ways in which the built environment can legitimate and perpetuate exclusion, inequality, and even disenfranchisement from the ranks of proper citizenship.

See also **City, The: The City as a Cultural Center; Democracy; Public Sphere.**

BIBLIOGRAPHY

Blakely, Edward J., and Mary Gail Snyder. "Divided We Fall: Gated and Walled Communities in the United States." In *Architecture of Fear*, edited by Nan Ellin, 85–99. New York: Princeton Architectural Press, 1997.

Blakely, Edward J. and Mary Gail Snyder. *Fortress America: Gated Communities in the United States*. Washington, D.C.: Brookings Institution, 1997.

Castells, Manuel. *The Informational City*. Oxford: Blackwell, 1989.

Davis, Mike. *City of Quartz: Excavating the Future in Los Angeles*. London: Verso, 1990.

Dreier, Peter, John Mollenkopf, and Todd Swanstrom. *Place Matters: Metropolitics for the Twenty-first Century*. Lawrence: University Press of Kansas, 2001.

Fishman, Robert. *Bourgeois Utopias: The Rise and Fall of Suburbia*. New York: Basic Books, 1987.

Jacobs, Jane. *The Death and Life of Great American Cities*. 1961. Reprint, New York: Vintage, 1993.

Lynch, Kevin. *The Image of the City*. Cambridge, Mass.: Technology Press, 1960.

Plato. *The Republic*. Translated by Allan Bloom. 2nd ed. 1968. Reprint, New York: Basic Books, 1991.

Sassen, Saskia. *The Global City: New York, London, Tokyo*. 2nd ed. 1991. Reprint, Princeton, N.J.: Princeton University Press, 2001.

Sennett, Richard. *The Fall of Public Man*. 1974. Reprint, New York: Norton, 1992.

Thucydides. *The Peloponnesian War*. Harmondsworth, U.K.: Penguin, 1972.

Weber, Max. *Economy and Society: An Outline of Interpretive Sociology.* 1921. Reprint, Berkeley and Los Angeles: University of California Press, 1978.

Wilson, Elizabeth. *The Sphinx in the City: Urban Life, the Control of Disorder, and Women.* Berkeley: University of California Press, 1991.

Young, Iris Marion. *Justice and the Politics of Difference.* Princeton, N.J.: Princeton University Press, 1990.

Margaret E. Farrar

THE ISLAMIC AND BYZANTINE CITY

Islam first developed and spread in a region of the world where urban civilizations had originated. Caravan routes crisscrossed the Fertile Crescent and the Arabian peninsula several millennia prior to the birth of Christianity, linking the urban-centered civilizations of Mesopotamia, the Nile Valley, and the Indian subcontinent. Overland routes were supplemented by water transit via the Red Sea and the Persian (Arab) Gulf, with transshipping ports in what is now Yemen. Arabia was then more fertile than it is in the early 2000s, and its products (including frankincense and myrrh) were in much demand.

The lands through which the desert caravans passed were divided into the territories of seminomadic tribes that controlled and protected passage. The islands in the narrow gulfs harbored "pirates" who could block passage, pillage, and even sink sailing dhows. If there was not to be a war of all against all, the neighboring communities, whether urban, transhumant, or nomadic, had to develop rules of trust, hospitality, and fair exchange of goods. And there needed to be centers of safety in which members of diverse tribes and communities could mingle without fear.

Mecca: A Place of Safety

Long before the message of Muhammad initiated the religion of Islam, the thriving city of Mecca was just such a place of safety. It was considered "sacred;" its Ka'ba (an enormous, cubicle black stone) was endowed with holy significance (Esin). In much the same way that the polytheism of Greek mythology derived from the unification of various city-states, each with its own deity, so the Ka'ba was host to the gods of various tribes and peoples who, at least there, could coexist. In this context, "sacred" meant safe. As early as the first millennium B.C.E., Mecca had been established as a place of pilgrimage, where traders could meet without fear. Greco-Roman influences and the monotheistic cults of Judaism and, later, Christianity, were already present in Mecca when Muhammad was born in Arabia in about 570 C.E. He eventually settled in Mecca where he lived with his first wife, Khadijah, serving as commercial agent for her long-distance caravan trade. When he was about forty years old, revelations began to appear to him, in which the text of the Koran was revealed in a series of retreats.

Thus began the formulation of a new monotheism called Islam, considered seditious by the residents of Mecca. In 622, when Muhammad was fifty-three and in declining health, he

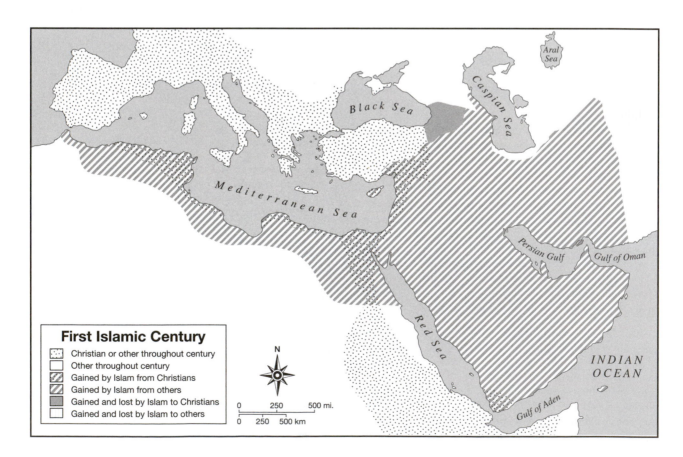

First Islamic Century
- Christian or other throughout century
- Other throughout century
- Gained by Islam from Christians
- Gained by Islam from others
- Gained and lost by Islam to Christians
- Gained and lost by Islam to others

N

0   250   500 mi.
0 250 500 km

was forced to escape with his followers to the city of Yathrib (later renamed Al-Medina, meaning "The City") and gained the support of the local tribe there and his first converts to the new religion. The date of the Hegira (flight to Yathrib) is accepted as the founding date of Islam and the first year in the Muslim calendar. The first mosque, a simple unroofed walled square with the prayer direction oriented toward the Ka'ba in Mecca, was built in the desert outside Medina, to which followers were summoned to gather five times per day by a call to communal prayer. Resisting recurring attacks from Meccans, Muhammad finally returned to Mecca in 630 at the head of a powerful army of his followers, accepted the keys to the Ka'ba, destroyed the idols and other signs of polytheism, and dedicated the structure (and the city) to the worship of one God and as the destination of prayer and pilgrimage. Two years later the Messenger of God was dead.

The Rapid Spread of the New Religion

Within one century of the death of the Prophet, Islam had spread to a vast area that included, in addition to the Arabian peninsula, Sassanid Persia as far north as the Caucasus and including Mesopotamia, the Fertile Crescent, and a thin coastal layer along North Africa that stretched from northern Egypt up the Nile to Cairo and had reached the westernmost tip of Morocco. The Byzantine Empire, defenders of Orthodox Christianity, controlled much of the northern edge of the Mediterranean, from its base in Anatolia and its capital, the New Rome, in Constantinople. While it is impossible to estimate what proportion of the populations in these two juxtaposed "empires" actually lived in urban centers (and that would depend upon the demographic definition of a city one accepted), it must be acknowledged that, for its time, the region was, along with the Indian subcontinent and China, certainly one of the most "urbanized" in the world.

Over the ensuing centuries, the Arab Conquest increased the levels of urbanization in three ways: by establishing temporary encampments for its troops and their accompanying dependents, by founding new "princely" cities for the successive ruling dynasties that came to power in various subregions of western Islam, and by occupying preexisting cities that would grow larger under conditions of increased prosperity.

The New Garrison Towns

The early days of expansion saw the founding of armed camps, often outside existing settlements, where troops were quartered, mosques were constructed, captive populations administered, and conversions encouraged. Basra and Kufa were the first "garrison towns" (*amsar*) set up by the Arab conquerors in the Persian-ruled region of lower Mesopotamia. *Fustat,* which means "tent city," was an army camp set up beyond the limits of an existing Greco-Roman bishopric seat of Babylon, near present-day Cairo, by the Arab general who in 640 C.E. conquered Egypt. Another variety was the *ribat* or fort. Rabat in Morocco began as just such a walled fortress in which the ruler and his troops were quartered. "The term Amsar . . . as later used . . . to designate those fustats and ribats that were selected as centers to manage the conquered territories and as bases from which further military campaigns could be launched" (Al-

Sayyad, p. 45). Their regular gridiron arrangements revealed their military origins, just as the bastide towns in Gaul revealed their origins in the Roman conquests. Gradually, as the lines between conquerors and converts grew more permeable, these army camps blended with existing settlements and were transformed into cities endowed with schools and mosques, palaces, and offices of the rulers, and took on unified commercial functions.

New Princely Capitals for Dynasties

Although fewer in number and developed later, these served significant symbolic purposes, since the "royal cities" established in the emerging Islamic world were often accompanied by regime changes: the movement of the caliphate or shifts between Sunni and Shiite sects. Two notable examples were the planned princely cities of Baghdad (properly Madinat al-Salam, the "City of Peace," or Madinat al-Mansur, the "City of the [Caliph] Mansur") founded during the second half of the eighth century by the Abbasids who displaced the Umayyad caliphate, formerly located in Damascus, and Cairo (Al-Qahirah, "the Victorious"), founded in 969 by the Fatimids, a Shiite dynasty coming from Tunisia that displaced the former Sunni rulers. Both were new cities, located on level and well-irrigated land some distance from existing settlements; they were carefully designed as walled protected enclaves for new rulers. But they differed radically in terms of conceptions and plans.

The royal city of Baghdad was a circular city on the opposite bank of the Tigris from the village of Baghdad, intended to house the newly victorious Abbasid caliphate. Surrounded by a pair of formidable walls and a moat, with entry restricted to four gateways and commoners forbidden admittance, the round city held at its center the palace of the caliph with its attached cathedral mosque. Around this most protected focus were the palaces for the princes and their armed defenders. Inside the peripheral walls were arranged governmental offices to administer the empire. Gradually, population gathered on the outskirts of this city, of which only archaeological traces remain. Within a short time Baghdad had grown into a large capital in which Islamic learning and scientific and intellectual development reached a medieval peak—at least until it was sacked by the Mongols in 1258.

Cairo, in contrast, would eventually grow from imperial enclave into the greatest capital in the Islamic world until Ottoman times, filled with architectural and artistic treasures, many of which are preserved to this day. Laid out in the form of a walled rectangle with a regular street pattern of two major streets intersecting at right angles and leading to four impressive gateways, it contained the palaces of Mu'izz al-Din, the newly installed Fatimid caliph, the major mosque, and quarters assigned to various ethnic groups that made up his army. The ordinary citizens of Fustat, by then grown into a prosperous commercial city to its south, were at first enjoined from entering. Only after Fustat was burned (in 1169) to protect the princely city from invading Crusaders, were the gates to Al-Qahirah opened to the "masses." But this marked the rise of Salah al-Din Yusuf al-Ayyub (Saladin; 1137/8–1193), the demise of the Fatimids, and the establishment of the Ayyubid dynasty. Thereafter, the history of the city's development approximated that of the third category.

Conversions of Existing Cities into Cities of the Dar al-Islam

Constantinople, the Christian capital of Byzantium until its conquest by Muslim forces in 1453 (officially renamed Istanbul in 1930), and the Roman-patterned cities of Aleppo and Damascus in Syria and of Tunis in North Africa, are noteworthy examples of existing cities whose plans were transformed by Islamic occupation. These walled cities had inherited from the pre-Islamic period regular streets and processionals, churches, covered markets, and a clear division, according to principles of Roman property law, between public (both secular and religious) and private space. Over time, the major changes were to create, from those regular divisions, the narrow labyrinthian paths and dead-ends that are associated with the Islamic city.

Sauvaget, in his pathbreaking studies of the transformation of Damascus (1934) and Aleppo (1941), traced these changes, attributing them to the substitution of Islamic law for Roman law, a theory more fully explicated by Hakim (1986), who examined Islamic legal precedents as they developed primarily in the Maghreb (western North Africa). In Islamic property law, responsibilities to one's neighbors, including the protection of their visual privacy, took precedence over a priori protection of the public way. As a result, buildings began to infringe on the streets, unless neighbors objected in the courts, and the residential neighborhoods became honeycombed into cells of semipublic space. Given the greater segregation between male and female space in Islamic codes of modesty, markets and residential zones became more spatially differentiated, with markets, courts, mosques, and industrial districts more specialized. These changes, which occurred over time in both preexisting "Christian" cities and in formally planned army camps and princely towns, gave rise to many of the characteristics now associated with the Islamic city.

Relation of Islam to the Idea of the City

This brief history is sufficient to establish several principles of Islamic expansion and its urban and social roots.

1. First, cities and commerce were central to the new religion, and many of the developments in Islamic law and jurisprudence dealt with densely settled urban places.

2. Islam was initially tolerant of other religions but welcoming to converts, extending to them equality in the *umma* (community of believers).

3. Property laws differed substantially from Roman law.

4. The religion stressed rules to police business practices and ensure trust and credit in trade.

5. Laws reformed social relations, regularizing and liberalizing relations between masters and slaves, husbands and wives, albeit while increasing gender separation.

6. Religious duties were encumbent on all members of the community of believers, including declaring belief in one God (Allah), accepting the prophetic message of Muhammad, praying five times daily, tithing to charity and sharing wealth with the poor, observing the dawn to dusk fast during the month of Ramadan, and make the pilgrimage to Mecca.

Common Consequences of these Distinguishing Features

The *amsar,* the *ribat*s, the converted Greco-Roman settlements, and the new princely capitals, while differing in origins and original plans, eventually evolved into communities that had much in common. Most were walled. The center of the city usually contained the main mosque, next to which were linear market streets specializing in books, candles, and other religious items. Nearby were the hostels for long-distance merchants and high value, low bulk items such as gold, other precious metals and minerals, and the officer whose duties included policing honest trade in the markets. Another main thoroughfare held the workshops of artisans and their shops, other mosques, hospitals, and schools, with the judicial courts and other government offices nearby. Outside or just inside the major gates to the walls were the markets for live animals and bulk agricultural products, on which taxes were imposed. But what was particularly noticeable in developed towns of Islam, attributable to Islamic property law, was the tendency of regular plans to be transformed into cellular structures of what might be called "defensible space." Religious charitable endowments (called *awaqf,* sing., *waqf*) and the largesse of rulers provided material support for many of the "public" functions, such as hospitals, schools, mosques, and water fountains, that Westerners associate with municipal government. Unlike the West, however, private users were held collectively responsible for cleaning, sprinkling, and lighting the streets in their own neighborhoods, as well as for protecting the safety of their residents. It was a workable system of governance so long as the empires remained prosperous but, as in all cities, in times of economic, political, and epidemic troubles, urban decay could set in.

The Consequences of Ottoman Rule and Subsequent Colonialism

The conquest by the Ottoman Turks of Constantinople in the mid-fifteenth century and the expansion of the Ottoman Empire to the Arab provinces in the Fertile Crescent and North Africa in the sixteenth century led to a period when the wealth of empire was concentrated in their capital Konstantiniyee (Constantinople), known by its popular Turkish name as Istanbul. Istanbul grew to become one of the largest cities in the world, whereas former major metropolitan centers such as Cairo were demoted to mere provincial capitals, losing population and economic vigor. Severely weakened, province after province fell victim to European colonial incursions in the course of the nineteenth century, and the remaining remnants of the Ottoman Empire, with the exception of Anatolia, were lost to the victorious Allies after World War I.

While twentieth-century decolonization movements, with few exceptions, succeeded in liberating the countries of western Islam, the region was fragmented into many small states, in contrast to the unities in religion and law the region had enjoyed during the heights of earlier empires, and the poor economic conditions due to subservience to the industrialized West left a heritage of underdevelopment. Although urban populations increased, from both higher rates of natural increase and immigration from the countryside (Istanbul in the early 2000s has a population of eleven million and the greater Cairo region houses perhaps sixteen million), economic development lagged behind, creating conditions typical in Third World cities. In most countries, although Islam remains the official religion, governing laws mostly derive from the Napoleonic Code. Many of the older forms of urban property law, charity, and personal behavior no longer sustain vital urban functions.

See also **Law, Islamic; Religion and the State: Middle East.**

BIBLIOGRAPHY
Abu-Lughod, Janet L. *Cairo: 1001 Years of the City Victorious.* Princeton, N.J.: Princeton University Press, 1971.
———. "The Islamic City—The Historic Myth, Islamic Essence and Contemporary Relevance." *International Journal of Middle East Studies* 19, no. 2 (May 1987): 155–176.
———. *Rabat: Urban Apartheid in Morocco.* Princeton, N.J.: Princeton University Press, 1980.
AlSayyad, Nezar. *Cities and Caliphs: On the Genesis of Arab Muslim Urbanism.* New York: Greenwood Press, 1991.
Celik, Zeynep. *The Remaking of Istanbul: Portrait of an Ottoman City in the Nineteenth Century.* Seattle and London: University of Washington Press, 1986.
Esin, Emil. *Mecca the Blessed/Medina the Radiant.* New York: Crown; Novaro, Italy: Paul Elek Ltd., 1963.
Hakim, Besim Selim. *Arabic-Islamic Cities: Building and Planning Principles.* London and New York: KPI, 1986.
Hitti, Philip K. *Capital Cities of Arab Islam.* Minneapolis: University of Minnesota Press, 1973.
Sauvaget, Jean. *Alep: Essai sur le developpment d'une grande ville Syrienne.* Paris: Librairie Orientaliste, 1941.
———. "Esquisse d'une histoire de la ville de Damas." *Revue Etudes Islamiques* 3 (1934): 421–480.

Janet L. Abu-Lughod

LATIN AMERICA

The history of the city in Latin America stretches over three thousand years and a vast geographic area. The cities vary considerably over space and time. Prior to the coming of the Spaniards, many pre-Columbian cities are thought to have been cosmograms or cosmologically conceived—the cities' buildings and plans emulated the cosmos as their leaders conceived of it. After the conquest, the Spanish Crown sought to impose order on the new lands in its possession and based planning on a grid that had a centrally located church fronting on a plaza. The checkerboard grid plan persisted throughout the colonial period. After independence from Spain, Latin-American countries sought out new forms of city planning in Europe, especially France, that would make visible their status as newly formed republics.

Ancient Indigenous America: Mesoamerican and Andean Civilization

Ancient indigenous cities in the Western Hemisphere were prominent, complex centers of economic, cultural, political, and religious power and authority. As administrative centers, cities functioned variously as city-states, centers of regional states, and centers of empire. Political life and religious life were intertwined and overseen by divine and semidivine rulers or the ruling elite. At the heart of most cities were palaces, monumental civic-religious structures, and the ceremonial plazas where public rituals took place. Cities were also frequently cosmopolitan, with enclaves of resident foreigners who are identified as such by cultural practices and material goods consistent with their culture of origin.

The city as cosmogram. City plans are many and varied; in some regions, such as the central Mexican urban center at Teotihuacan, planners imposed a consistent grid plan on every structure, from central temples and palaces to small outlying barrios. In contrast, the Chimu capital of Chan Chan in Peru was comprised of large walled palatial compounds that loosely shared the same orientation. Elsewhere, notably in the clusters of buildings and temples organized around plazas among the Maya and the capital city of Cuzco (Peru), site plans are irregular in shape, their form dictated by the local topography and inherent processes of agglutination, yet still organized according to an internal logic, albeit a more organic one. The organizing plan of Cuzco has been the subject of lively debate, with some scholars suggesting that it represents a puma, while others note its grid plan tempered by topographic irregularities. Of particular interest are the forty-two sacred *ceque* (pathways) radiating from a central node outward, linking the sacred city to all corners of the Inka empire.

Regardless of these differences, common shared features among these pre-Columbian centers include the cosmological alignment of major buildings and of the city itself with the passage of the Sun, the movement of significant planets and stars, and the cardinal directions; the alignment of buildings with significant features of the surrounding topography such as sacred places, caves, and mountains; built statements of politico-religious power and authority such as large pyramids and walled precincts; as well as the pragmatic concerns of dense, urban life (workshops, urban housing of workers, water, food, and disposal of waste, for example). The indigenous city harmonized with its environment even as it shaped that environment and gave focus and significance to elements of the environment that were held to be important. Natural features of the landscape, such as the rivers at Teotihuacan and Cuzco, were even made to conform to the planning principles employed. As symbolic texts, indigenous cities gave visible form to collective belief and shared identity. Through the powerful intersection of cosmological time and space, the city functioned as both axis mundi and cosmogram.

Colonial Spanish America

From its inception, Spanish urban planning in the Western hemisphere was based on the grid plan, with its characteristic large central plaza dominated by a church. The earliest royal instructions (1513) and government decrees indicated that a geometric grid was to be used, but not until 1573 did King Philip II's ordinances explicitly direct that the grid be used in city planning, thereby codifying practices long in effect. Scholars have cited gridded prototypes ranging from indigenous city planning; the Roman *castrum;* the French *bastide;* the ideal city of the Renaissance architectural theorist, Leon Battista Alberti; Santa Fe (1491), the military encampment of Ferdinand and Isabella at the siege of Granada; and the apocalyptic New Jerusalem in the Book of Revelation. It is probable that some or all of these multiple indigenous and European urban sources were precursors to the colonial Spanish-American urban grid and converged to serve complementary economic, social, political, and religious goals.

The ordered city. In Mexico, the typical grid plan came into being in urban developments in the 1520s and 1530s as new towns were built and the destroyed Aztec capital Tenochtitlan, an indigenous gridded city, was rebuilt as the administrative capital of New Spain. These geometrically ordered, regularized towns met the needs of the army, church, and state bureaucracy as they provided a framework for administrative efficiency, political control, and Christian indoctrination. The urban landscape was radically altered as the multiple cultural expressions of preconquest cities were supplanted by the uniformity of the grid extended across space and time in what had become Spanish America. The grid physically and symbolically established and confirmed the desired social order and clearly marked both the land and its people as being under the well-ordered, administrative, and Christian control of the Spanish.

Republican and Contemporary Latin America

Latin-American countries, with the exception of Cuba and Puerto Rico, won their political independence from Spain and Portugal between 1808 and 1826. As newly independent countries, they sought to express national identity, progress, and modernity and take their place among the metropolises of the Western world. To do so and to refashion its capital cities, Latin America looked to Paris, which was itself undergoing modern transformation under the direction of Georges-Eugène Haussmann. France's economic connections to Latin America and its position as a champion of independence and republicanism and a center of the arts and urbanity made it a natural model for the new Latin-American republics. Large public parks and grand, tree-lined, diagonal boulevards (such as the Paseo de la Reforma in Mexico City) followed the Haussmann model and reshaped Latin-American cities, freeing them from the colonial grid.

From metropolis to megalopolis. In the second half of the nineteenth century and the beginning of the twentieth, many urban populations grew exponentially as foreign investments and overseas immigrants poured into Latin America. Capitals were enlarged to accommodate their growing populations, and the ideas of the early-twentieth-century Swiss architect and planner, Charles-Édouard Jeanneret, known as Le Corbusier, and his followers in the Congrès International d'Architecture Mod-

erne (CIAM) became influential. Le Corbusier's ideas focused on high-rise buildings to increase living density and relieve overcrowding, new highways to relieve traffic congestion, and urban space zoned according to function; in short, an attempt to bring order and efficiency to cities that had grown rapidly. Although Brasília, the new, disembedded capital city of Brazil planned by Lúcio Costa and inaugurated in 1960, incorporated some of Le Corbusier's ideas, his urban plans and those of his followers were rarely implemented. Le Corbusier's legacy is more clearly to be seen in high-rise buildings of cement, glass, and steel and in the peripheral highways encircling many of Latin America's major cities.

See also **City, The: The City as Cultural Center; City, The: The City as Political Center.**

BIBLIOGRAPHY

Almandoz, Arturo, ed. *Planning Latin America's Capital Cities, 1850–1950.* New York and London: Routledge, 2002.

Fraser, Valerie. *Building the New World: Studies in the Modern Architecture of Latin America, 1930–1960.* London: Verso, 2000.

Hardoy, Jorge E. "Theory and Practice of Urban Planning in Europe, 1850–1930: Its Transfer to Latin America." In *Rethinking the Latin American City,* edited by Richard M. Morse and Jorge E. Hardoy, 20–49. Washington, D.C.: Woodrow Wilson Center Press, 1992.

Schaedel, Richard P., Jorge E. Hardoy, and Nora Scott Kinzer, eds. *Urbanization in the Americas from Its Beginnings to the Present.* The Hague, Netherlands: Mouton, 1978.

Smith, Monica L., ed. *The Social Construction of Ancient Cities.* Washington, D.C.: Smithsonian Institution Press, 2003.

Townsend, Richard F., ed. *Ancient Americas: Art from Sacred Landscapes.* Chicago: Art Institute of Chicago, 1992.

Ellen T. Baird

CIVIL DISOBEDIENCE. Civil disobedience is an illegal act performed publicly in contravention of a law or laws of the government for the short-term purpose of bringing about a change in the law or laws and for the long-term purpose of improving society as a whole. It is a political act because its underlying principles are the principles of political justice that regulate the state and its institutions, and not those of private conduct. The act is called "civil" because it is courteous in the manner of its performance, not criminal in its methods or revolutionary in its effects. It presupposes the legitimacy of the state and the constitutional order, and its aim is the preservation of an improved state, not its overthrow.

Civil disobedience may be carried out by individuals or by masses of people. Its acts may be symbolic, as in the case of fasts, vigils, the burning of official documents, and so forth, or they may be substantial, as in the case of boycotts, strikes, marches, mass meetings, withdrawal of cooperation with the government and its institutions, sit-ins, occupation of public buildings, and the like.

In the late twentieth century, the idea of civil disobedience acquired a legal standing in international jurisprudence thanks especially to the Nuremberg trials. The latter established the legal norm according to which individuals may be held responsible for not disobeying domestic laws that grossly violate fundamental human rights.

The History of the Concept

The concept of civil disobedience has evolved over a long period of time. Ideas drawn from different periods of history and from different cultures have contributed to its evolution. The idea that there is a law that transcends the laws of the state is found in Socrates (c. 470–399 B.C.E.), in some of the classical Greek tragedies, and in the Indian concept of dharma (duty). In these traditions, should the higher law and the laws of the state come into conflict, the individual had the obligation to disobey the laws of the state. In the Middle Ages, St. Thomas Aquinas (1225–1274) defended the natural-law view that unjust laws did not bind the citizen in conscience. John Locke (1632–1704) taught that the government derived its authority from the people, that one of the purposes of the government was the protection of the natural rights of the people, and that the people had the right to alter the government should it fail to discharge its fundamental duties.

Thoreau. The writer who made the theory famous, put it into practice, and gave the practice the name "civil disobedience" was Henry David Thoreau (1817–1862). His ideas on the subject are found in the celebrated lecture that he delivered in 1848 to the Concord Lyceum in Massachusetts, under the title "On the Relation of the Individual to the State." It was first published in printed form in 1849 under a different title, "Resistance to Civil Government," in *Aesthetic Papers,* a volume edited by Elizabeth Peabody. It first appeared under the title "Civil Disobedience" only in 1866, four years after Thoreau's death, in a volume of his writings entitled *A Yankee in Canada with Anti-Slavery and Reform Papers.*

Two principles underlie Thoreau's conception of civil disobedience. The first is that the authority of the government depends on the consent of the governed. The second is that justice is superior to the laws enacted by the government, and the individual has the right to judge whether a given law reflects or flouts justice. In the latter case the individual has the duty to disobey the law and accept the consequences of the disobedience nonviolently. In Thoreau's case, he judged that the laws upholding slavery and supporting the Mexican War (1846–1848) were unjust. He chose to spend a night in jail rather than submit to the unjust laws.

Gandhi. Mahatma Gandhi (1869–1948) broadened the scope of civil disobedience and internationalized its practice. Gandhian civil disobedience originated in 1906, in South Africa, as part of his campaign for the defense of the civil rights of the disenfranchised Indian immigrants. On his return to India in 1915, he made civil disobedience the primary moral force behind his leadership of the Indian nationalist movement.

His idea of civil disobedience drew from a wide variety of intellectual sources. Plato's *Apology of Socrates* was one of them. In 1908 he published a paraphrase of it under the title *The Story of a Soldier of Truth.* The Sermon on the Mount had a profound influence on him, especially as interpreted by Leo Tolstoy in his *The Kingdom of God Is within You* (1893). Patanjali's *Yogasutra* and the *Bhagavad Gita* also guided the development of his thoughts on nonviolence as it applied to civil disobedience.

When in 1906 he started the civil rights campaign in South Africa, Gandhi did not know what term to use to describe it. (He read Thoreau only in 1907). Some called the new campaign passive resistance, in comparison with the British Passive Resistance Movement against the Education Act of 1902. But he was unhappy with the comparison for two reasons. The first was that British passive resistance did not forbid violence as a means of achieving its goal; the second was that it did not require that its practitioners be free from hatred of their political opponents.

Gandhi called his practice "satyagraha," a Gujarati word meaning "firmness in adhering to truth." Satyagraha, free of the defects of passive resistance, introduced six elements into the theory and practice of civil disobedience:

- First, its moral basis was grounded in truth, a basis much deeper than that provided by the theory of consent. To be binding, laws had to be truthful. All untruthful laws had to be resisted, though civilly—that is, by truthful means.

- Second, civil disobedience presupposed the obligation to obey the state: only those had the right to practice civil disobedience who knew "how to offer voluntary and deliberate obedience" to the laws of the state.

- Third, commitment to nonviolence was an essential component of civil disobedience. The commitment in question could be either moral or tactical, depending on the moral aptitude of the practitioner.

- Fourth, the practice of civil disobedience required a minimum degree of moral fitness, to be acquired by the exercise of such virtues as truthfulness, nonviolence, temperance, courage, fearlessness, and freedom from greed.

- Fifth, a practitioner of civil disobedience had to accept the punishment consequent to the disobedience voluntarily, and without complaint.

- Finally, engagement in civil disobedience had to be complemented by engagement in organized social work.

For Gandhi, it was not enough to seek to improve the state; it was equally necessary to seek to improve civil society. To assist Indians to combine civil disobedience with voluntary social work, he wrote *Constructive Programme* (1941, revised in 1945). It identified the major social evils prevalent in Indian society, such as religious intolerance, caste violence, and discrimination against the untouchables, minorities, and women. The removal of these social evils by voluntary work was as important as the removal of unjust laws by civil disobedience. According to

Gandhi, "civil disobedience without the constructive program will be like a paralyzed hand attempting to lift a spoon."

Martin Luther King Jr. The third major figure who contributed greatly to the development of the practice of civil disobedience was Martin Luther King Jr. (1929–1968). He made civil disobedience the distinguishing feature of the civil rights movement in the United States. In this he was deeply influenced by Gandhi's methods. But he was also influenced by Christian humanism, as is evident in his "Letter from Birmingham Jail" (1963). The letter has been called the most widely read and discussed manifesto on civil disobedience since Thoreau's essay. Addressed to his fellow African-American clergymen, it explained why immediate, direct, nonviolent action was a duty incumbent upon every American who wished to rid the nation of segregationist laws. Here King faced a dilemma. On the one hand, the law had by 1954 declared segregation to be unconstitutional, yet on the other it also tolerated segregationist practices in certain states. How then could one advocate breaking some laws while obeying others?

One could do both, he contended, because one had the right to judge each law on its own merit. And the criterion he recommended for making such judgement was drawn from Christian humanism. According to St. Augustine of Hippo (354–430), an unjust law was no law at all. And according to Aquinas, an unjust law was a human law that was not rooted in eternal and natural law. Just laws uplifted human beings, while unjust ones degraded them. The segregationist laws were unjust and dehumanizing and therefore had to be disobeyed. King contributed greatly to making civil disobedience a respected tradition of American politics. In this he marks an advance on Thoreau, who seemed to appeal, hitherto, mostly to New England intellectuals. King actualized the potential that was in Thoreau.

In the late twentieth century, civil disobedience became a tactic adopted by various protest movements worldwide. The anti-nuclear weapons movement, the green movement, and the movement against globalization have adopted it with varying degrees of enthusiasm.

Philosophic Status Today

Thoreau, Gandhi, and King were primarily practitioners rather than philosophers of civil disobedience. Even though a philosophy did underlie their practice, they themselves did not elaborate it in any systematic fashion. From the last quarter of the twentieth century onward, however, philosophers and political theorists have taken a keen interest in the philosophic aspects of civil disobedience. The most significant of these philosophers is John Rawls (1921–2002). His *Theory of Justice* (1971) integrates civil disobedience into the liberal-contractarian philosophy of justice. It grounds civil disobedience in the two principles of Rawlsian justice—namely, those of equal basic liberty of the citizens and equality of opportunity. However, a society built on these principles is not a "perfectly just society," but only "a nearly just society." Though it is a well-ordered society, "serious violations" of justice can and do occur in it. This imperfect character of the justice of the liberal society places the citizen in a moral quandary. There is on the one

hand the obligation to obey laws enacted under an agreed upon constitution, yet on the other there is the duty to oppose the injustices of particular laws and the right to defend the basic liberty of citizens. That is to say, the obligation to obey in a liberal society is relative, not absolute—relative to the prior right to defend one's basic liberty and the duty to oppose injustice.

It is here that civil disobedience comes to the rescue of the embattled citizen. It permits the citizen to disobey an unjust law, but only within the bounds of fidelity to the constitutional order. In this way civil disobedience helps test the moral basis of liberal democracy. It also points to the limits of the majority principle. If the majority fails to respect the basic liberty of citizens and equality of opportunity, the grieved citizen or citizens have the right to disobey the law, irrespective of the position of the majority.

However, for Rawls, civil disobedience may not be violent in its methods; it has to be nonviolent for two reasons. First, in a liberal democratic society civil disobedience is a mode of appealing to the latent sense of fundamental justice that the majority is presumed to possess. This appeal can succeed only if the means of civil disobedience remains nonviolent. The civilly disobedient may warn and admonish, but not threaten. Second, nonviolence is a method of expressing disobedience within the limits of fidelity to the constitutional order, and of accepting voluntarily the legal consequences of disobedience. Thus, though contrary to a given law, civil disobedience is a morally correct way of maintaining the constitutional order in an admittedly imperfect society. It becomes part of free government. It gives stability to the constitutional order and helps actualize the capacity for self-correction.

Rawls's theory has the merit of explaining why civil disobedience works only in certain societies and not in others. It works in societies whose contending members can agree on what constitutes justice. Because of this they are able to compose their differences. Civil disobedience tests the solidity of this consensus. In societies whose contending members cannot agree on what constitutes justice, there is no room for civil disobedience, but only for civil war or something close to it. Thus, Rawls's theory can also explain why civil disobedience succeeded the way it did in unjust colonial societies such as South Africa and India. It succeeded because, paradoxically, the higher colonial administration and the civilly disobedient citizens were able to agree on the basic principles of liberal justice.

There is one major difference, however, between Rawls's theory and that of Gandhi and King. Rawls grounds his theory in the principles of liberty and equality, without asking whether they need grounding in some other principle. Gandhi and King ground their conceptions of liberty and equality in the higher principle of the spiritual personality of human beings—atman (the spiritual self) in the case of Gandhi and the immortal soul in that of King. It is because humans have a spiritual personality that they ought to be free and equal in society. Their theory of disobedience has deeper roots than does Rawls's. The latter operates within the limits of European Enlightenment, whereas the other two operate within a broader framework.

Disputed Questions

Although the theory of civil disobedience has achieved philosophic maturity, there are two questions that still remain unresolved. One has to do with the place of violence in civil disobedience. Theorists such as Christian Bay do not rule out the use of limited physical violence. The problem here is where to draw the line between limited physical violence and revolutionary violence. The other question has to do with the acceptance of punishment due to civil disobedience. Some, including Rawls, accept it for prudential reasons, while others such as Gandhi do so for moral reasons. Gandhi believes that the suffering of the innocent victim has a unique moral force, which civil disobedience should integrate into its moral theory.

See also **Protest, Political; Reform; Resistance and Accommodation; Revolution.**

BIBLIOGRAPHY

Bass, Jonathan, S. *Blessed Are the Peacemakers: Martin Luther King Jr., Eight White Religious Leaders, and the "Letter From Birmingham Jail."* Baton Rouge: Louisiana State University Press, 2001.

Bay, Christian, and Charles C. Walker. *Civil Disobedience: Theory and Practice.* Montreal: Black Rose, 1975.

Bedau, H. A., comp. *Civil Disobedience: Theory and Practice.* Indianapolis: Pegasus, 1969.

Gandhi, Mahatma. *Hind Swaraj and Other Writings.* Edited by Anthony J. Parel. Cambridge, U.K.: Cambridge University Press, 1997.

———. *Satyagraha in South Africa.* Ahmedabad: Navajivan, 1972.

Gans, Chaim. *Philosophical Anarchism and Political Disobedience.* Cambridge, U.K.: Cambridge University Press, 1992.

Haksar, Vinit. *Rights, Communities, and Disobedience: Liberalism and Gandhi.* New York: Oxford University Press, 2001.

Rawls, John. *A Theory of Justice.* Cambridge, Mass.: Harvard University Press, 1971.

Thoreau, Henry David. *Political Writings.* Edited by Nancy L. Rosenblum. New York: Cambridge University Press, 1996.

Anthony Parel

CIVIL SOCIETY.

This entry includes two subentries:

Europe and the United States
Responses in Africa and the Middle East

EUROPE AND THE UNITED STATES

An ancient term of Western political and social theory, *civil society* has enjoyed enormous popularity in recent years and has outstripped its geographic origins to spread all over the world. Public leaders, newspaper writers, religious figures, social theorists, political activists, and commentators from many different perspectives now use the term on a regular basis. The term's meaning has shifted dramatically over the centuries, and different historical periods have understood it in distinct ways.

Three distinct usages can be delineated. *Civil society* first appears in classical Greek and Roman thought, which considered it to be synonymous with a politically organized commonwealth—a view that was modified by the medieval church's distaste for purely political categories and came to describe a society organized around the primacy of religion. As powerful markets and centralized states began to erode medieval institutions, a second, and characteristically modern, liberal understanding arose that conceived of civil society as the arena of economic relations and institutions. Frightened by the consequences of the French Revolution and the advent of mass political activity, a third conception developed during the middle of the nineteenth century to describe civil society as a sphere of voluntary intermediate organizations that stand between the state and the citizen. Pioneered by Alexis de Tocqueville (1805–1859), this is the way *civil society* is understood in contemporary usage. Although chronologically distinct, each of these understandings contributes important insights to political and social life and sheds light on contemporary issues of democracy and equality.

Political and Religious Commonwealths

When Cicero (106–43 B.C.E.) equated civil society with a politically constituted commonwealth, he expressed a powerful tendency to understand "civility" as the requirements of citizenship. His effort represented the most complete development of classical thinking about civil society. Plato (c. 428–348 or 347 B.C.E.) had attempted to articulate an invariant ethical center for public life, an effort that Aristotle (c. 384–322 B.C.E.) tried to correct by recognizing that people live their lives in different spheres and in multiple associations. Aristotle's respect for variation and distinction underlay a political theory that understood civil society as a moral-political association that improved the life of its citizens, but the Roman recognition of a legally protected private realm made it possible to equate civil society with republican virtues and political life. Imperial collapse led to St. Augustine of Hippo's (354–430 C.E.) devastating attack on the classical tradition's effort to organize a self-reliant public sphere, but Christian insistence that civil society could be understood only in terms of the requirements of faith and church made it difficult to organize human affairs with such depraved material as fallen man. St. Thomas Aquinas (c. 1224–1274) was more willing than Augustine to recognize that politics could sustain a measure of moral action and constitute civil society, but the corrosive effects of markets and the pressure of centralizing kings brought the first period of theorizing to a halt.

Markets, Individuals, and Interests

Niccolò Machiavelli's (1469–1527) rediscovery of classical republicanism and Thomas Hobbes's (1588–1679) insistence that only a single point of sovereign power could protect the calculating individual and his interests pointed the way toward a fully modern conception of civil society. It was not long before those interests became expressed as property, production, and acquisition. John Locke's (1632–1704) civil society was made possible by the sovereign power of states, but it was really the pursuit of private interest that made political liberty worthwhile. Locke's clear preference for economic activity anchored many later conceptions, and Adam Smith (1723–1790) articulated the first fully bourgeois theory of civil society as a sphere of production and competition that was driven by the self-interested calculations of isolated individuals. The state played an organizing and protecting role, but Smith's conviction that economic processes could organize social life expressed liberalism's suspicion of centralized political power and its assumption that civil society is constituted by the market. Jean-Jacques Rousseau (1712–1778), Immanuel Kant (1724–1804), and Georg Wilhelm Friedrich Hegel (1770–1831) would try to infuse civil society—now equated with "civilization"—with solidarity and moral purpose, but it was plain that this tradition of thought understood civil society as a law-governed sphere where property, civil liberties, and political equality would enable self-serving individuals to make private decisions in conditions of freedom and security. If the classical view of civil society had been shaped by the ancient traditions of civil republicanism and came to an end with the fall of the Roman Empire, the second view was clearly related to the early framework of capitalism. Karl Marx's (1818–1883) desire to overcome civil society's foundation in the class relations of bourgeois society looked to a socialist state to democratize civil society itself and seemed to recapture a moment of the classical heritage. It also shed light on an important weakness in liberal theory by calling for democratic supervision of civil society's chaos and instability.

Intermediate Associations and the State

Drawing on Aristotle, Cicero, and Machiavelli for the theory of the mixed constitution, Baron de Montesquieu (1689–1755) located intermediate bodies at the heart of his aristocratic theory of civil society. His fear of royal power fed Edmund Burke's (1729–1797) defense of local privilege against the leveling and centralizing French Revolution, but it was Tocqueville's claim that voluntary activity connected individualistic, self-serving Americans to the common good that proved particularly powerful. Tocqueville's insight has fed most of the contemporary interest in civil society, in large measure because of his desire to limit the thrust of the democratic state by preserving local freedom, protecting pockets of local privilege, and nurturing traditions of self-organization. His assumption of widespread equality of condition meant that he did not have to examine how inequality and voluntary activity might reinforce one another—a matter that has become vitally important, given contemporary economic and political trends. Nevertheless, powerful American traditions of suspicion of the state and a history of local volunteerism have all but guaranteed that Tocqueville finds a ready audience in this country—particularly in politically conservative periods.

Contemporary Issues

Interest in civil society was largely confined to academic circles until the early 1980s, when dissident Polish intellectuals and journalists began talking of "the rebellion of civil society against the state." It wasn't long before an influential body of Eastern European thought began to understand civil society as constitutional republics and intermediate associations. As Soviet-style socialism continued to be hostile to almost all spontaneous social initiatives, it made sense that dissidents would be interested in limiting state power and would be indifferent to the market's threat to freedom and equality. But their sunny optimism would soon fade away. As the East European civic forums, underground newspapers, student leagues, "flying universities," and other groupings began to yield to the logic of economics and the imperatives of politics, it became practically and theoretically imperative to understand how civil society can serve democracy in conditions of powerful markets and bureaucratized states. Voluntary organizations and social movements have contributed to freedom and equality in important ways, but the naive assumption that they constitute a democratic sphere of action in their own right has begun to yield to more sober questions of how local voluntary activity can serve democracy in an environment that is constituted by widening inequality and dominated by large, powerful institutions. It is important to understand how the local and the small can serve freedom and democracy with, not against, the universal and the large. Further intellectual and practical activity will be compelled to investigate how inequality and bureaucracy affect the ability to organize on the one hand, and how local activity can mitigate the effects of inequality and hold political structures to account on the other.

See also **Citizenship; Democracy; Equality; Society.**

BIBLIOGRAPHY

Eberly, Don E., ed. *The Essential Civil Society Reader: Classic Essays in the American Civil Society Debate.* Lanham, Md.: Rowman and Littlefield, 2000.

Ehrenberg, John. *Civil Society: The Critical History of an Idea.* New York: New York University Press, 1999.

Putnam, Robert D. *Bowling Alone: The Collapse and Revival of American Community.* New York: Simon and Schuster, 2000.

Seligman, Adam. *The Idea of Civil Society.* Princeton, N.J.: Princeton University Press, 1995.

Skocpol, Theda, and Morris P. Fiorina, eds. *Civic Engagement in American Democracy.* Washington, D.C.: Brookings Institution Press, 1999.Verba, Sidney, Kay Lehman Schlozman, and Henry E. Brady. *Voice and Equality: Civic Voluntarism in American Politics.* Cambridge, Mass.: Harvard University Press, 1995.

John Ehrenberg

RESPONSES IN AFRICA AND THE MIDDLE EAST

"All vogue words tend to share a similar fate," observes Zygmunt Bauman. "The more experiences they pretend to make apparent, the more they themselves become opaque. The more numerous are the orthodox truths they elbow out and supplant, the faster they turn into no-questions-asked canons" (p. 1). Bauman's specific subject was globalization, but he may well have been alluding to civil society. Ever since it made a blazing entry into mainstream political theory in the mid 1980s, *civil society* has had a quite remarkable career as a buzzword, both in policy and scholarly circles. Rare is that academic without a perspective on civil society. For all this analytic intensity however, civil society continues to evade the critical gaze, and seemingly definitive statements about its meaning or origin have merely given rise to even knottier dilemmas.

Ironically, history has been of little help. In most cases, historical excursion has only complicated the riddle, for civil society has not one but many genealogies. Its complex story traces back to a tangle of understandings, and scholars generally tend to privilege whatever genealogy best suits their purposes.

Apparently, many of the hurdles encountered in grappling with the idea of civil society could be scaled easily. One is the problem of definition, which, Iris Marion Young contends, has persisted simply because many scholars stubbornly hanker after a one-sentence definition. The implicit suggestion here is that deeper understanding of civil society might be gained if the inquirer were to take for granted its conceptual diversity. This may not be the vehicle that transports one to definitional nirvana, but there is at least the precognition of the inherent plurality of the subject. A second problem is the popular conflation of civil society as an idea, an ideal, and a device for the attainment of a vaguely defined "good society." Again, as Michael Edwards suggests, the problem comes not from this trifurcation, but rather from imagining that civil society cannot be all three at the same time.

Different Understandings

This definitional problem is not new, and one way of illustrating this is to briefly explore some of the several ways in which civil society has been historically understood. We deal with a dense and richly conflicted narrative, and the distinctions made here are, of necessity, a guide. The first understanding is that of civil society as the opposite of the state of nature. In this view, civil society points to a condition of refinement, a departure from a state in which humanity was slave to its instincts and passions, to one in which it is governed by reason and rationality. This is a mere prototype of course, as many who have sadly contemplated the horrors of the past century might readily attest, but it should help in underscoring the point that most times, civil society is merely that to which groups or peoples aspire. Even more important, implicit in this definition is an undeniable gender bias, especially given that women were often described as being closer to a state of nature than men. Therefore, civil society, at least within the framework of this understanding, is profoundly patriarchal. However, scholars like Adam Seligman have provided a more historically rooted picture. For him, the state of nature could be taken as the immediate post-Enlightenment seventeenth- and eighteenth-century Europe in which there was a clear need to tame the demon of unfeeling individuation, which had been an unexpected concomitant of the new era of rapid industrialization. According to this account, the accent on rationality as opposed to feelings that was the immediate by-product of the European Enlightenment, and the emergence of the market as the arena where the new individual could realize his newly found "freedom" had to be checked by something much larger than the private individual himself, hence "civil" society; a society, in Keith Tester's words, of "less barbarous manners." If nothing at all, it is this "civil" or "polite" society that defines and imposes the parameters of social conduct, "reestablishing some public (and perforce communal) space to mediate what are seen as the adverse effects of the ideology of individualism" (p. 28).

A second understanding is the envisioning of civil society as connoting the possession of certain values (privacy, individualism, and the market, say) that are present in and actually define the West but are, alas, in short supply or completely absent from other societies. Scholars generally trace the intellectual pedigree of this controversial formulation to Adam Ferguson (1723–1816) and Georg Wilhelm Friedrich Hegel (1770–1831), but its most forceful affirmation could be seen in the writings of Ernest Gellner. According to this view, civil society is what his "Atlantic society" has that "others" do not; "others" here signifies either other cultures or sociopolitical systems, or a combination of both. Thus, civil society becomes, "like human rights, what authoritarian regimes lack by definition. It is what the Greeks, the Enlightenment and we today have; it is what despotic governments, whether in the past or the present, the here or the elsewhere, do not have" (Goody, p. 150).

Other conceptualizations certainly exist, and admittedly, it is well nigh impossible to scour the fastnesses of the history of political thought and philosophy for every analysis of the subject of civil society. One of the more influential formulations, in reality a conceptual first, has been the Hegelian delineation of civil society as that which is separate from the state. Drawing partly on the work of the Scottish chaplain Adam Ferguson, Hegel defines civil society as "the realm of difference, intermediate between the family and the state." His conception of civil society makes clearer sense within the ambit of his rather abstruse philosophy of history, which, mindful of the risks inherent in simplification, can be articulated thus: History is the evolution of consciousness and the modern world is the highest demonstration of that evolution. For Hegel then, civil society is "the achievement of modernity," one *moment* (the other two being the family and the state), in which the movement of the objective spirit (*Geist*) can be analyzed (Schecter, 2000). Even though in sharp contrast to Ferguson he insisted on the ontological integrity of the state as having a "concrete existence" (Schecter, p. 38) of its own, Hegel shared Ferguson's derision for the state-of-nature construct. His case for its rejection is based on his appreciation of historical developments, particularly in the economic sphere. While the dichotomy that the state of nature/state of civilization presumed might have possibly made some sense at a historical moment, Hegel believed that profound changes in the economic realm had made this binary otiose, or useless. The indelible consequences of this economic revolution, he thought, were to be seen in the specific transformation of what was regarded as the private sphere. More specifically, the expansion of the economy, Hegel argued, had incorporated and dominated civil society, leaving the state to emerge more clearly as a "separate political sphere." The family, for its own part, is relegated to what is left of the by now "emaciated" public sphere.

Skeptics usually seize on this extensive mesh of meanings and nuances to assert that civil society is nothing more than a "plastic concept," one whose shelf life will come to an abrupt halt sooner rather than later. Optimists disagree. Indeed, they argue that the hermeneutic elasticity of civil society is good both for the subject and for the various political projects in whose cause it is usually invoked. Mary Kaldor, for example, thinks that the changing meaning arises from several factors: "the changing content and coverage of the term—what it was not; the tension between normative and descriptive, idealistic and empiricist, subjective and objective implications of the concept; and the relative emphasis on the private and the public or the individual and the social" (p. 16).

Be that as it may, policy and scholarly infatuation with civil society has shown little sign of waning. To be sure, the immediate backcloth for the contemporary revival was lent by events in former Eastern Europe, where the idea inspired dissident groups intent on rolling back the authoritarian communist state. In this specific context, civil society was the social culture, one framed by the rule of law and an institutional civility that was lacking from the social system that the dissidents sought to destabilize and disestablish. Particular inspiration for the dissidents' challenge to the state had come from the prison writings of Antonio Gramsci (1891–1937), the atypical Italian Marxist who posited, contra Karl Marx, that civil society, being the sphere of culture, ideology, and associations, is equally that of contestation. While Marx reduces civil society to the market economy, arguing that it is basically a bourgeois lie, Gramsci contends that it (that is, civil society) "offers the popular classes an opportunity to deny the ruling classes hegemony in the realm of ideas, values and culture, as a basis for the ultimate seizure of power and the transformation of capitalist property relations and the state" (quoted in Bangura, pp. 45–46). This, together with the work of Alexis de Tocqueville (1805–1859), who had speculated on the bountiful social capital accruing from Americans' "habit of association," had informed the quite successful invocation of the idea in Eastern Europe.

From Eastern Europe, the idea diffused to the rest of the world, where, fortuitously, it fed into the existing disenchantment with the welfare state across the Western world, the search for an ethical force in the wake of the perceived global slide into moral decay, the explosion in the number of NGOs (nongovernmental organizations), and the anticipation of greater civility amid the rampant surge of religious and other kinds of fundamentalism. Outside the West, particularly in the developing countries, the idea of civil society emerged in the thick of the struggle for democratic liberalization and social inclusion for marginalized groups. To be sure, this idea of civil society as a useful tool in the resistance to hegemony by dispossessed groups owes much to early feminist and suffragist movements in Britain. These movements drew heavily on the postulations of John Stuart Mill (among others) regarding civil society, while at the same time seeking to make the concept more inclusive. Across Africa in the late 1980s and early 1990s, the association of civil society with democracy, or at least the possibility of its achievement, was common indeed. Many freely conflated the two, and the popular media treated them as though they were synonyms.

Alternative Genealogies

The embrace of the idea of civil society in non-Western contexts was always going to be difficult. First, there was the problem posed by the specifically Western origin of the idea, one that automatically generated the poser: Is civil society applicable or "thinkable" outside its specific Western cultural and geographic provenance, and might it be compatible with societies denounced by Gellner as "non-modular," "ritual-

pervaded," and "segmentary"? Second, if civil society actually exists outside the West, in places like Africa, Asia, and the Middle East, what might it mean, and with what unit will scholars analyze it? Contrary to general belief, these dilemmas have not been raised by scholars in the West alone. Both Africans and Africanists, like Mahmood Mamdani, Peter Ekeh, Emmanuel Gyimah-Boadi, Eboe Hutchful, Thomas Callaghy, and Stephen Orvis, have expressed deep skepticism about the usefulness of the idea of civil society ("a vague, often confusing and ever-shifting concept") in explicating non-Western or, specifically African, realities; although in the process they have generated insights that have enriched the relevant literature considerably. This has also been the case in the Middle East and Asia, where thinkers like Sudipta Kaviraj, Sunil Khilnani, Neera Chandhoke, Farhad Kazemi, and Masoud Kamali have picked up the gauntlet.

As a result, issues surrounding the so-called alien nativity of civil society have led to the emergence of a critical and fascinating oeuvre. So powerful and diverse is this emergent corpus that Jude Howell and Jenny Pearce think that it forms the core of what might well be called an "alternative genealogy" of civil society. But what are its arguments? The first is to stress the crucial fact that, its Western origins notwithstanding, civil society has over the past decade become a useful tool in the resistance to hegemony by dispossessed groups. Howell and Pearce note that if there is a common thread in the non-Western application of civil society, it is its use to legitimize citizens' right to resist the prevailing development paradigm, thus showing how truly contested the liberal meanings of the concept are. In the process, "civil society has enabled critical voices to occupy an intellectual space where an alternative set of values and propositions on how societies ought to develop and change can be put forward, challenging those that would otherwise dominate" (Howell and Pearce, p. 36).

A second argument of the emergent alternative genealogy is to say that it does not serve any purpose to lay emphasis on the rash of possible meanings of civil society outside the West, especially as even in the West itself, it is impossible to point to a single coherent narrative of civil society. This position has been seemingly corroborated by the plethora of meanings of civil society advanced by different Western scholars. Examples are the imagination of civil society as: "the natural condition of freedom" (Keane); "a condition of education, refinement and sophistication as opposed to a condition of barbarism" (Tester); a "point of refuge from the dangerous totalising systems of state and economy that threatened the life-world" (Habermas); a "metaphor for Western liberalism" (Seckinelgin), and "the anchorage of liberty" (Dahrendorf).

Afro-Arab Discourses

For obvious reasons, the debate on the possibility and meanings of civil society outside the West has elicited a more spirited discourse in Africa and the Islamic world. Gellner, we recall, had vilified Islamic societies for "exemplifying a social order which seems to lack much capacity to provide political countervailing institutions, which is atomised without much individualism, and operates effectively without pluralism"

(p. 29). The denial of civil society in Africa is inspired by a similar characterization.

In both cases, the challenge has been to postulate a theory of civil society that simultaneously recognizes the idea's Western origin and usefulness to the Afro-Arab world. This cannot be done without redefining the term, a cause that has been helped by its unique lack of a commonly agreed definition. Thus, formulating civil society as the "values of mutual support and solidarity [which] exist in the history of human sociability" (Howell and Pearce, p. 36), scholars in Africa and the Middle East argue that civil society has always existed in different forms in other societies. Not surprisingly, a wealth of literature has emerged on African and Islamic civil societies.

One outcome of these attempts, coupled with the ever-increasing policy focus on civil society is the emergence of the idea in a form that is not "civilizationally circumscribed" (Hefner, p. 221). There may be some residual skepticism about the applicability of civil society outside the West, but at least nobody seems to be saying that anymore. The global "professionalization of the third sector," to borrow the words of Michael Edwards, has led to the increased popularity of civil society, and these days the international aid industry seems to be more bothered about empowering civil society than defining it. While this ought to give cause for a pause, it seems more important to observe that in tandem with the "professionalization" of civil society, different local meanings are being created around the concept as part of an increasingly universal negotiation between citizens, states, and markets. This is the real future of the idea, and it would seem to be the next subject for scholarly research.

See also **Civil Society: Europe and the United States; Democracy; Third World.**

BIBLIOGRAPHY

Bangura, Yusuf. "Authoritarian Rule and Democracy in Africa: A Theoretical Discourse." In *Authoritarianism, Democracy, and Adjustment: The Politics of Economic Reform in Africa,* edited by Peter Gibbon, Yusuf Bangura, and Arve Ofstad. Uppsala: Scandinavian Institute of African Studies, 1992.

Bauman, Zygmunt. *Globalization: The Human Consequences.* New York: Columbia University Press, 1998.

Dahrendorf, Ralf. *Reflections on the Revolution in Europe: In a Letter Intended to Have Been Sent to a Gentleman in Warsaw.* London: Chatto and Windus, 1990.

Edwards, Michael. *Civil Society.* Malden, Mass.: Polity, 2004.

Gellner, Ernest. *Conditions of Liberty: Civil Society and Its Rivals.* New York: Lane, 1994.

Goody, J. R. "Civil Society in an Extra-European Perspective." In *Civil Society History and Possibilities,* edited by Sudipta Kaviraj and Sunil Khilnani. Cambridge, U.K.: Cambridge University Press, 2001.

Habermas, Jürgen. *Between Facts and Norms: Contributions to a Discourse Theory of Law and Democracy.* Translated by William Rehg. Cambridge, Mass.: MIT Press, 1996.

Hefner, Robert W. *Civil Islam: Muslims and Democratization in Indonesia.* Princeton, N.J.: Princeton University Press, 2000.

Howell, Jude, and Jenny Pearce. *Civil Society and Development: A Critical Exploration.* Boulder, Colo.: Lynne Rienner, 2001.

Kaldor, Mary. *Global Civil Society: An Answer to War.* Cambridge, U.K.: Polity, 2003.

Keane, John. *Civil Society: Old Images, New Visions.* Stanford, Calif.: Stanford University Press, 1998.

Lewis, David. "Civil Society in African Contexts: Reflections on the Usefulness of a Concept." *Development and Change* 33, no. 4 (2002): 569–586.

Seckinelgin, Hakan. *Civil Society as a Metaphor for Western Liberalism.* London: London School of Economics and Political Science, 2002.

Seligman, Adam B. *The Idea of Civil Society.* New York: Free Press, 1992

Schecter, Darrow. *Sovereign States or Political Communities?: Civil Society and Contemporary Politics.* Manchester, U.K.: Manchester University Press, 2000.

Tester, Keith. *Civil Society.* London and New York: Routledge, 1992.

Ebenezer Obadare

CLASS. The term *class* is used in a wide range of intellectual discourses, including logic, the natural sciences, and pedagogy. At its Latin origins, however, *classis* was first and foremost a social term, denoting the division of the Roman people attributed to King Servius Tullius (r. 578–534 B.C.E.). In early Rome, class connoted a distinction in rank between those who paid tribute (property tax) and those who did not, as well as the system of divisions between types of military service. In particular, *classis* often seems to have been reserved to describe citizens on the lower social and economic rungs. Only after the principate of Augustus (31 B.C.E.–14 A.D.) did *classis* come to be employed in a more general sense to mean a division of all sorts of things into groups.

Early Histories

The Latin genesis of class nomenclature does not mean that the idea behind it (in either a social or general sense) did not exist prior to the rise of the Roman Republic. Aristotle's *Organon* proposed a logical system of classification of natural and linguistic types into genus and species according to categorical criteria. For the ancient Greeks, the Few and the Many constituted a central measure of division within the social order. Both Plato and Aristotle divided social groups into functional classes whose status and power was graded according to the contributions each made to the purposes of the civil community as a whole. Plato's *Republic* famously identified within the city three parts—rulers, soldiers, and laborers—while Aristotle distinguished six socioeconomic classes—soldiers, priests, judges, farmers, artisans, and traders—of whom only the first three were deemed fully qualified to exercise the rights associated with citizenship, at least in the best political system.

Class thus has generally been associated with systems of social exclusion. Indeed, elaborate mythologies have been generated to support or justify class divisions. The tale of Noah's curse on the descendents of his son Ham, in Genesis 9:20–27, has been taken as an explanation for class inequality. Likewise, the Koran (Sura 43:31) declares that social differentiation arises from Allah's will that the inferior should be subjected to the superior. The caste system that long governed social organization and relations in India and elsewhere in Asia purported to reflect the disparate origins of the various groups as described in the Vedas: the Brahmans from the lips of Brahma, the Kshatriya from the shoulders, the Vaisya from the thighs, and the Sudra from the feet.

During the European Middle Ages, the idea behind class distinctions was popularly captured by various forms of organic unities. Many medieval thinkers, quite possibly under the indirect influence of Plato, divided society into the three-fold functional ordering of those who fight, those who work, and those who pray. In the High Middle Ages, this was gradually replaced by the more developed organic doctrine of the body politic, the most influential exponent of which was John of Salisbury (1115 or 1120–1180). His *Policraticus* (completed 1159) contained an extensive account of how each of the organs and limbs of the human body—from the head to the toes—had a direct counterpart in society, from the king, his advisors, soldiers, and diverse magistrates all the way down to the peasants and artisans. Class divisions were natural and necessary in order to maintain justice and the common good. Essentially this view enjoyed wide currency in Europe well into early modern times.

The Renewal of Class

For the first millennium and more of European history, the term *class* was not invoked in order to describe the distinctions between and identities of social groups. Rather, *class* was invoked through what we might call "status language," such as *gradus* in Latin, *état* in French, *Stand* in German, and "orders" or "estates" in English. At the end of the eighteenth century, however, a notable linguistic shift that renewed the nomenclature of class appeared in most major European languages. This change seems to have accompanied the transformations wrought by the industrial revolution and the rise of political economy: class conveyed an essential economic overtone that was not fully captured by the status language of earlier times. The work of authors such as Thomas Malthus (1766–1834) and David Ricardo (1772–1823) did much to disseminate class discourse, and especially phrases such as "the laboring classes" and "the working class."

The nineteenth century was the heyday of discussions about class in this updated economic sense. Class divisions were upheld by classical political economy on the grounds that the division of labor and the competition implied therein were necessary for the efficient use of productive resources. Critics of capitalism, whether communitarians such as Claude-Henri de Rouvroy, comte de Saint-Simon (1760–1825) or utopians such as Charles Fourier (1772–1837) or anarchists such as Pierre-Joseph Proudhon (1809–1865), remained convinced that the sources of exploitation were not inherent in class divisions per se so much as in unequal distribution of property or wages or the material benefits of work. Differentiation in the contributions made by laborers thus did not excuse their subordination in economic, political, or social standing.

The Marxist Transformation

Without doubt, the most famous promulgator of the idea of class in the modern world was also its most profound critic: Karl Marx (1818–1883). Marx treated class distinction as a universal characteristic of human history from the earliest times of social organization until his own day. For Marx, classes were economic groups constituted by differential access to the means of production—that is, the technologies and natural resources necessary for human beings to reproduce their physical existence. In every social formation, there were two essential and contending classes: a working class, which used, but did not directly own or control, the means of production; and an appropriating class, which lived directly or indirectly from the labor of workers. In different economic systems, the type and nature of technology, and of the social relationships employed in organizing labor and maintaining domination over it, might vary considerably. Hence, tribal societies met the physical and extraphysical needs of their members differently than did subsequent ancient slave or feudal systems. But the fundamental clash of interests between workers and appropriators was a permanent feature of history up to the present day.

In previous social systems, Marx held, the struggle between the classes had wound up with the replacement of one exploitative mode of production (the material and social elements of the economy) with another, culminating in capitalism. On the one hand, capitalism, with its veneer of freedom and equality, produced the most intense exploitation of the worker ever achieved. Yet, on the other hand, just because the condition of the capitalist working class, termed the proletariat, was so degraded, Marx believed that it formed a "universal class," capable of releasing and realizing all of the untapped potential of a truly liberated humanity. For this reason, Marx held that the proletariat, once it became conscious of its own circumstances and the source of its immiseration, would revolt against its capitalist oppressors and would generate a qualitatively different kind of society. The future society, which Marx called communism, would be classless, since the proletariat, as the most completely exploited class in history, would have no remaining object to exploit. Communism would see the end of human history as a dynamic series of class struggles and would instead herald a new beginning of history in which each and every individual as a full human being would have the opportunity to pursue and attain his or her freely chosen needs.

The Weberian Reply

The primary response to Marx's conception of class was proposed by the German sociological thinker Max Weber (1864–1920). Weber's main insight was to recognize the empirical faults of an exclusive emphasis on class as an economic phenomenon. Rather, Weber saw society—in particular, in the modern world—as far too complex in its stratification to fit into the straightjacket of economic determinism. It should be noted that Weber's critique was directed not just at Marx and other radical critics of capitalism, but also at the classical political economists, who shared with Marxism a stridently economistic orientation.

In one sense, Weber does adopt an economic conception of *class*; it is the term he employs to designate social differentiation based on occupation and function as defined by the market. But class is simply one form of distinction. Equally important are status and power. Status denotes the factors of honor and reputation that attach to specific ways of life and are accorded deference by others. Thus, individuals of certain status (say, from a landed nobility) may enjoy greater repute than those of a given class who are wealthier but whose sources of income (say, commerce) are generally held to be debased or ignoble. Power applies to the capability of a group to impose its collective will on others, even in the face of their resistance. Weber points out how, in the modern world, those with the greatest class position or status often do not occupy the positions of administrative or bureaucratic authority. In turn, bureaucrats can and do enact policies that run contrary to the real or perceived interests of economic and reputational elites. This demonstrates that their social position depends on a source—power—that cannot be entirely assimilated to class or status.

Later social scientists have extended and enlarged the factors that influence social differentiation well beyond Weber's original triad. Such elements as kinship, occupation, race and ethnicity, and education have been added to the basic dimensions of class, status, and power. But it seems safe to say that the dominant perspective on social stratification both normatively and empirically during the last century remained Weberian in orientation.

Marxist Rejoinders

Somewhat ironically, many of the fiercest critics of the classical Marxist doctrine of class would consider themselves to fall into the Marxist camp. The failure of the proletariat to rise up against and to crush capitalism even as the conditions of its exploitation worsened led some Marxists, especially in Western Europe, to revisit Marx's conception of class struggle. The so-called Frankfurt School of Critical Social Theory renounced the crass economism of classical Marxism in favor of an analysis that emphasized the cultural sources of working-class conservatism, including the mass media, out-group scapegoating (anti-Semitism and other forms of ethnic and racial hatred), and the predominance of so-called technological rationality. Members of the Frankfurt School embraced, alternately, pessimism about the possibility of successful class struggle (as in the work of Max Horkheimer [1895–1973] and Theodor W. Adorno [1903–1969]) or optimism that other marginalized groups, such as racial minorities, students, denizens of Third World nations, women, and environmentalists, might become the bearers of the revolutionary subjectivity of Marx's proletariat (as Herbert Marcuse [1898–1979] asserted). In either instance, traditional Marxian class analysis leading to proletarian revolution was set aside as an unrealistic and unrealizable expectation.

Another school of Marxist thought, drawing upon the rigorous methodological principles of modern economics and the other social sciences, sought to wed so-called rational choice doctrines of economic behavior to a radical worldview. Authors such as Jon Elster (b. 1940) and John Roemer (b. 1938) argue that class should be reinterpreted according to the standards of methodological individualism, so that a class is not greater than the sum of its parts, but a coordinated body of similarly positioned individual agents. Known as "rational choice" or "analytical" Marxism, this approach attempts to strip class of perceived metaphysical accretions—for example, the holism criticized by Sir Karl Popper (1902–1994)—without eliminating it as a workable foundation for a viable theory of economic exploitation.

Still other thinkers within a Marxist vein have set out to restore the "political" dimension to Marx's conception of class struggle. Historians such as Robert Brenner (b. 1943) and political theorists such as Ellen Meiksins Wood (b. 1939) stress the contingency of class relations depending on political context, and thus they foreground local juridical-coercive institutions in understanding the constitution of class identities. This perspective insists on the wholly illusory nature of the supposed separation of the economic and the political under capitalism. Political power shapes class conflict, and thus the state itself is the prime site for class struggle and opposition.

Beyond Class

An important trend in the late twentieth and early twenty-first century has been to resist both Marxian and Weberian theories of social differentiation in favor of other fundamental sources of division among human beings. Feminism provides an example of one such line of reasoning. Feminist theory claims that gender, rather than class, constitutes the defining division in human historical dynamics. Broadly stated, feminists assert that reproduction trumps production as the organizing principle around which human social institutions are fixed. Thus, it is the gender divide, emerging from the male oppression of women, that drives social processes throughout history. Patriarchalism, not classism, constitutes the major division among human beings, and the obsession with class is itself a patriarchal trick to divert attention from the fundamental struggle between the sexes.

Class-oriented conceptions of social power and dynamic have also come under attack from proponents of critical race theory. The orientation of critical race theory raises questions quite similar to those of traditional Marxism concerning the ways in which state power (in its legal-juridical and coercive applications) reinscribes and reinforces racial divides. Thus, just as gender is foregrounded in feminist analysis, so race becomes the central focus of analysis among proponents of the critical race school.

The Future of Class?

Class has become anathema in political discourse in the West. Politicians are able to silence their opponents with the mere assertion that "class war" is being invoked. Liberalism—democracy's insistence that equality constitutes the salient feature of social life—even in spite of the evident social, economic, racial, and political disparities that exist in liberal-democratic regimes—suggests that class is effectively dead as a category of social analysis and critique. Yet the discourse of class seems to reappear regularly among the intellectual categories with which

Sandro Botticelli's *Birth of Venus* **(1482). Tempera on canvas.** Botticelli painted his masterpiece during the Renaissance, the period in which classicism bloomed. A member of Lorenzo de' Medici's intellectual circle, Botticelli strove to reconcile Christian beliefs with classical concerns in his work. GALLERIA DEGLI UFFIZI, FLORENCE, ITALY. © THE ART ARCHIVE/DAGLI ORTI

social thinkers, and social movements, narrate their self-understandings. May class yet outlive those whose interests prescribe its obsolescence?

See also **Communism; Critical Race Theory; Marxism; Power.**

BIBLIOGRAPHY

Brennan, Catherine. *Max Weber on Power and Social Stratification: An Introduction and Critique.* Aldershot, U.K.: Ashgate, 1997.

Brown, Donald E. *Hierarchy, History, and Human Nature: The Social Origins of Historical Consciousness.* Tucson: University of Arizona Press, 1988.

Calvert, Peter. *The Concept of Class: An Historical Introduction.* New York: St. Martin's, 1982.

Carling, Alan H. *Social Division.* London: Verso, 1991.

Clark, Terry Nichols, and Seymour Martin Lipset, eds. *The Breakdown of Class Politics: A Debate on Post-Industrial Stratification.* Baltimore: Johns Hopkins University Press, 2001.

Crenshaw, Kimberlé, ed. *Critical Race Theory: The Key Writings That Formed the Movement.* New York: Norton, 1995.

Horkheimer, Max, and Theodor W. Adorno. *Dialectic of Enlightenment.* Translated by John Cumming. New York: Herder and Herder, 1972.

Horowitz, Maryanne C., ed. *Race, Class, and Gender in Nineteenth-Century Culture.* Rochester, N.Y.: University of Rochester Press, 1991.

Marcuse, Herbert. *An Essay on Liberation.* Boston: Beacon, 1969.

McNall, Scott G., Rhonda F. Levine, and Rick Fantasia, eds. *Bringing Class Back in Contemporary and Historical Perspectives.* Boulder, Colo.: Westview, 1991.

Moravcsik, J. M. E., ed. *Aristotle: A Collection of Critical Essays.* London: Macmillan, 1968.

Roemer, John, ed. *Analytical Marxism.* Cambridge, U.K.: Cambridge University Press, 1986.

Russ, Joanna. *What Are We Fighting For? Sex, Race, Class, and the Future of Feminism.* New York: St. Martin's, 1998.

Skeggs, Beverley. *Formations of Class and Gender: Becoming Respectable.* London: Sage, 1997.

Wood, Ellen Meiksins. *Democracy against Capitalism: Renewing Historical Materialism.* Cambridge, U.K., Cambridge University Press, 1995.

Cary J. Nederman

CLASSICISM. Classicism has two dominant meanings in the West. The first concerns the Greeks of the sixth and fifth centuries B.C.E. and their influence, first on the Romans and then on Western cultures from the Renaissance on. The second meaning, evolved from the first, concerns the quality of a work—its style, its structure, and to some extent its content, always with the quality of the Greek models in mind. The *Oxford English Dictionary* definition, "The principles of classic literature or art; adherence to . . . a classical style," comprehends both meanings. The word *classicism* has become a common term since its first use in the nineteenth century. Classicism spread across Europe from Italy to Germany, to France, to Russia, to England, with the place and the time of its usage shading its meaning. It remains a useful term, with contextual clues indicating its intended meaning.

The intellectual and aesthetic outflow of the Greeks was prodigious and the extant aesthetic, philosophical, historical, and political writings have had a phenomenal impact on Western culture. Homer's epics (c. 800 B.C.E.), the poetry of Sappho (seventh century B.C.E.) and Pindar (sixth century B.C.E.); the dramas of Aeschylus, Sophocles, Euripedes, and Aristophanes (fifth century B.C.E.); the sculptures of Phidias; the oratory of Pericles and the writings of Plato and Aristotle (fifth and fourth centuries B.C.E.) are but some of the most prominent Greek contributions to Western culture. In the works of these and other Greeks, future generations have found what has come to be understood as the features of classicism: beauty, balance, proportion, formal structure, intellectual vigor and depth, rational content supported by symmetrical form, often accompanied by a sense of humor and skillful satire. All of these characteristics are manifested in a humanist context. Unfortunately, much of our knowledge of this great outpouring comes to us secondhand because the originals no longer exist, although we have some fragments of the writings—a few poems of Sappho and some works of Aristotle, for example—and some remains of aesthetic works, such as the Elgin Marbles, the sculpture of Hera, friezes of the battle of the centurians, and drawings on pottery. These remains have been studied for centuries.

Much of what we know of Greek contributions comes from two sources: writings about them and copies of them. Aristotle in his *Poetics* analyzed and commented on Greek drama, vastly amplifying the evidence from the few extant dramas. Longinus illuminated the style and purpose of art. Much of what we know of Greek sculpture comes from Roman copies, and much of what we know of Greek and Roman architecture comes from Vitruvius, the Roman architect who wrote about architecture in *De re architectura* (first century C.E.), the manuscript of which was found in the fifteenth century and translated into many languages.

The Romans and Medieval Europe

The Romans, conscious of Greek art and thought, intentionally copied the Greeks. The first neoclassical age was really the Roman one between about the first century C.E. and the fifth century C.E. A good deal of what we now call classicism is a Roman continuation and expansion of Greek thought and aesthetic ideas and values. Fortunately, most of the Roman works are extant, and the writings of the poets Horace, Ovid, and Virgil, as well as the orators and prose writers including Cicero, Cato, Pliny the Elder, and Quintilian, have greatly enriched the classical tradition. Latin had a vigorous life all through the medieval period. It was the lingua franca not only

Queen's House, Greenwich, England, constructed in 1616. Architect Inigo Jones drew upon the work of the celebrated Andrea Palladio in his design for Queen's House. The spare, symmetrical appearance of the structure recalls ancient Greek architecture. EDIFICE/CORBIS

of the church but of the universities, which started in the twelfth and thirteenth centuries, as well as most serious writing.

The Renaissance

The next neoclassical period, which we call the Renaissance, exploded in Italy under the patronage of such personages as the Medicis and Pope Leo X. The Renaissance with its focus on secular life, fortified by the availability of the important literary works of the Romans and by translations of the Greeks into Latin, sometimes via Arabic, and then by the study of Greek, enabling educated people to read Greek originals, created the great flowering of classicism. Fortified by copious commentary on the ancients from such scholars as Pico della Mirandola and Ficino and stimulated by such scholars as the humanist Erasmus, educated people across Europe talked about classical language, art, architecture, and ideas. Petrarch wrote sonnets in the vernacular. Botticelli painted the beautiful *Birth of Venus*. Great works of poetry, painting, architecture, and sculpture appeared first in Italy in the mid-fourteenth century, and then surged across Europe, into France, Germany, the Netherlands, England, and elsewhere.

An excellent illustration of this sweep of classicism across Europe and into America is in architecture. Andrea Palladio (1508–1580), probably the most influential architect in Western history, rejected the medieval Gothic structures, turning instead to classical antiquity for models. He not only created beautiful classical buildings in northern Italy, but he published his ideas, complete with goals, models, dimensions, materials, and methods of construction. Designers such as the English architect Inigo Jones read Palladio's books and went to see his buildings, then went back home to construct Palladian architecture, the most famous being the classic Queen's House in Greenwich (1616). Its simple, clean, symmetrical elegance contrasted strongly with Tudor architecture. Over a century later, Alexander Pope wrote a 204-line poem on English architecture ("Moral Essays: Epistle IV, Of the Use of Riches," 1734), praising the good taste of Lord Burlington, who discriminately applied Palladian ideas, and satirizing noblemen who built expensive mansions lacking in harmony and proportion. Palladian architecture moved across Europe, into parts of Asia, and especially to the Americas, dominating colonial architecture in the United States. Buildings across the world illustrate Palladio's influence: symmetrical structures with balanced vertical and horizontal lines, grand staircases, Greek pillars and Roman arches, porticoes and frescoes, pediments and loggias, statues in the Greek style. In each building, every part contributes to a harmonious, unified whole.

Neoclassicism

As with architecture, almost all fields were affected by classicism, especially literature. The rich collection of Greek and Roman writings, the theories of Aristotle and Longinus, and the considerable body of accumulating Italian and French literary criticism inspired many to write in imitation (mimesis) of the ancients, observing the "rules" they thought inherent in the ancient writings. The flourishing literary criticism included, for example, long discussions of the unities of time, place, and action, of decorum, and of high moral quality. France for a time became the artistic center of this new neoclassicism. Although Racine, Corneille, Molière, Boileau, and others were successful in espousing and observing the rules of classicism, an individual genius elevated their writing. The rules were followed less successfully in Joseph Addison's correct and popular, though stiff Cato, but Dryden and Pope in England, and Goethe and Schiller in Germany wrote many inspired classical works.

In the twenty-first century we speak of many creators prior to the early nineteenth century as being classical or neoclassical. Classicism has a recognizable core of ideas that draws creators and critics to it again and again. Behind classicism is the innate desire to make accessible the civilizing influence of great art, music, literature, and architecture. The painters Jacques-Louis David in France (1748–1825) and Joshua Reynolds in Britain (1723–1792) were influential classicists who not only painted but also put their theories into print. Even music, which has no extant models from the ancients, produced classicists: The music of Haydn, Mozart, and the early Beethoven has a strong, clear structure. Their dominant sonata form—orderly, complete, balanced—gives shape and purpose to the chaos of sound.

By the late eighteenth century the neoclassical movement began to burn itself out as artists turned elsewhere for inspiration. In a sense, classicism is an ideal not a reality, since humans almost compulsively veer into irregularities or even rebel against ideals. Classicism tried to give answers, but multitudinous questions remained. Hence countermovements arose, which critics have termed Romantic, with its concern for self-expression, and baroque, with its intentional rejection of balance and harmony. Classicism's closed form, with its completeness, balanced proportion, solid repose, and clean structure, often became a more open form, with restless parts and unstressed edges. The classical *The Ambassadors* (1533) of Hans Holbein (1497–1543), for example, has a symmetrical structure with clear, distinct figures. In contrast, in the baroque *Christ Washing the Feet of His Disciples* (1556) of Tintoretto (Jacopo Robusti, 1518–1594), Christ at the center right of the picture is smaller than the figures on the left, and the colors and shapes blend into one another.

Though theoretically classicism aspires to produce the best art, in reality much of the best art veers from the classical or outright rebels against it. The classical critic Samuel Johnson has pointed out the many deviations from classicism of William Shakespeare's plays but still recognized their greatness. Much art has elements of classicism. Mary Cassatt's (1844–1926) many paintings, for example, have classical beauty, balance, and repose, but contiguous mothers and daughters blend. The much-admired works of Paul Klee (1879–1940) or Jackson Pollock (1912–1956) demonstrate rejection of classicism. Note the restless parts and unstressed edges of Klee's *Remembrance of a Garden* or Pollock's *Moon Woman*.

Conclusion

Still, during the many centuries of admiring and imitating the Greeks, the term *classicism* has evolved to describe an ideal, a set of aspirations that humans keep returning to. The style of classicism tends to be clear, elegant, precise, rational; the structure, to be formal, balanced, cohesive, closed; the content, to be uplifting, idealized, humanist. Classicism does not have as strong a pull as it used to, in part because it can be pushed into absolutism, and humans are increasingly seeing the world in relative terms. Classical artists from the past—Phidias, Virgil, Raphael, Michelangelo, Titian—will always be with us. But there are also modern exponents of classicism ranging from poets such as T. S. Eliot and W. H. Auden to literary critics including Irving Babbitt and Jacques Barzun, from artists such as Paul Cézanne and William Bailey to musicians like Sergey Prokofiev, Igor Stravinsky, and Béla Bartók. So ingrained is the term *classicism* that many critics use it to describe contemporary forms of art, such as jazz, or even cuisine. It implies a standard of excellence only rarely achieved. Postmodernism saw an almost total rejection of classicism in the late twentieth century, but reaction might well lead to a revival of classicism in some form or another.

See also **Aesthetics; Arts; Periodization of the Arts.**

BIBLIOGRAPHY

Aristotle. *Poetics.* Translated by George Whalley. Edited by John Baxter and Patrick Atherton. Montreal: McGill-Queen's University Press, 1997.

Avery, Catherine B., ed. *The New Century Italian Renaissance Encyclopedia.* New York: Appleton-Century-Crofts, 1972.

Eliot, T. S. *What Is a Classic? An Address Delivered before the Virgil Society on the 16th of October 1944.* London: Faber and Faber, 1946.

Fletcher, Banister. *A History of Architecture on the Comparative Method.* Rev. by R. A. Cordingley. 17th ed. rev. New York: Scribners, 1975.

Hornblower, Simon, and Antony Spawforth, eds. *The Oxford Classical Dictionary.* 3rd ed. Oxford and New York: Oxford University Press, 1996.

Murphy, Bruce, ed. *Benet's Reader's Encyclopedia.* 4th ed. New York: HarperCollins, 1996.

Preminger, Alex, ed. *Princeton Encyclopedia of Poetry and Poetics.* Enl. ed. Princeton, N.J.: Princeton University Press, 1974.

Rosen, Charles. *The Classical Style: Haydn, Mozart, Beethoven.* New York: Viking, 1971.

Sadie, Stanley, ed. *The New Grove Dictionary of Music and Musicians.* 20 vols. London: Macmillan; Washington, D.C.: Groves Dictionaries of Music, 1980.

Secrétan, Dominique. *Classicism.* London: Methuen, 1973.

Speake, Graham, ed. *Encyclopedia of Greece and the Hellenic Tradition.* 2 vols. London and Chicago: Fitzroy Dearborn, 2000.

Summerson, John. *The Classical Language of Architecture.* Cambridge, Mass.: MIT Press, 1980.

Turner, Jane, ed. *The Dictionary of Art.* 34 vols. New York: Grove, 1996.

Wellek, René. "Classicism in Literature." In *Dictionary of the History of Ideas; Studies of Selected Pivotal Ideas,* edited by Philip P. Wiener. 5 vols. New York: Scribners, 1973–1974.

Wölfflin, Heinrich. *Principles of Art History: The Problem of the Development of Style in Later Art.* Translated by M. D. Hottinger. 7th ed. New York: Dover, 1950.

Gwen W. Brewer

CLASSIFICATION OF ARTS AND SCIENCES, EARLY MODERN.

The concept of *classification* seems obvious and benign. To classify is to arrange or distribute according to a system or method, a sense of the word that has not altered since its inception in antiquity. The significance of classification lies not in what it means, but in how it is applied. How people classify—according to what principles—has evolved and altered over time as their understanding of the world has altered. How people classify also bears directly on important issues in metaphysics. Does the world come "precarved" into natural kinds, or is classification merely an arbitrary exercise of human volition? If natural kinds exist, then classification reveals truths about the external world. The development of ideas about classification (and the things classified) has paralleled both scientific and artistic developments in the early modern period.

Aristotelian Background

To understand the concept of classification in the early modern period, it is necessary to first understand the conceptual framework the early moderns inherited from their predecessors. The world prior to 1600 was still largely Aristotelian. Aristotle (384–322 B.C.E.) provided a classification scheme based on matching a basic kind (species) with a set of distinguishing characteristics (differentia) in order to sort things in the world. Thus a human individual is a rational animal. That is, a human is of the kind "animal" but is distinguished from all other animals by rationality. This example reveals an underlying assumption of Aristotle's system: genuine classification provides definitions. When a thing is properly classified, it is defined. Definition, in turn, relies on the concept of essences. An essence is a property

> I do not deny but nature, in the constant production of particular beings, makes them not always new and various, but very much alike and of kin one to another. But I think it nevertheless true, that the boundaries of the species whereby men sort them, are made by men; since the essences of the species, distinguished by different names, are, as has been proved, of man's making, and seldom adequate to the internal nature of the things they are taken from. So that we may truly say, such a manner of sorting things is the workmanship of men.
>
> SOURCE: John Locke, *An Essay concerning Human Understanding,* III.6.37, p. 462.

a thing must have to be what it is. Thus one might say that being rational is essential to being human; an individual thing is simply not a human if it lacks rationality.

In Aristotle is also found the first division between the arts and sciences. The distinction is modeled on the natural/artificial divide. *Scientia* concerns demonstrable and certain knowledge derived from nature. In nature, things develop according to natural internal principles of change (entelechies). Something is artificial if it changes because of an external source—like some clay becoming a sculpture because of a craftsman's work. Sculptures are artificial because they do not possess internal principles of change. They are what they are because someone or something else altered them. This distinction led Aristotle to characterize science as an enterprise whose goal is to account for the internal causes or explanatory principles we find in nature. Since this goal is reached by definition (asserting the essences of things), one discovers that appropriate classification is in fact *the* scientific enterprise—the process of acquiring knowledge. (See *Posterior Analytics,* in *Complete Works,* book 2, especially 93a1–10).

Medieval Academia

Building on this Aristotelian foundation, medieval thinkers developed the core distinction between nature and artifice into an academic edifice. The sciences concerned nature. Since God is the author of nature, it follows that not only should people study nature, they also should expect to find regular order and well-defined kinds within it, as would be consonant with the perfection of the deity. Science is the practice of proper classification by definition. The arts more properly concern skills, whether mental or physical. The Latin root *artes* refers to the technical skills needed to produce something, a fact more apparent in the Greek root *techne,* as in the word "technology." For the medieval period there is no sense of the "fine

> I do not know why you and your associates always want to make virtues, truths and species depend upon our opinion as knowledge. They are present in nature, whether or not we know it or like it.
>
> SOURCE: Gottfried Wilhelm Leibniz, *New Essays on Human Understanding*, p. 327.

arts." All art is craft. A painter or sculptor is as much a craftsman as a carpenter or shipwright. The goal of the artist is the technical perfection of their work or trade.

Although the sciences were broadly treated and classified in the same way, some innovation occurred in the classification of the arts. In the medieval period is seen the division of the arts into those that are "liberal" (meaning that they are suitable for free citizens) and those that are "servile" (work that was typically manual and done by slaves). Hence a liberal arts curriculum is first found in the early universities. Students who completed courses of study in grammar, rhetoric, logic, arithmetic, geometry, music, and astronomy were awarded a bachelor of arts. This already implies a division in the arts, since these fields were thought to have redeeming features, whether beauty or intellectual stimulation. Interestingly, many of the fields now routinely called arts were excluded. Poetry and the visual arts, for instance, were not considered suitable subjects for inclusion. Unlike the other fields, these (and others) were not judged to be intellectual arts; competences in these areas were thought to depend on the practice of bodily skills and not on the deepening of mental skills.

Early Modern Context

In many ways the early moderns were still in the grips of the Aristotelian worldview. René Descartes (1596–1650), like the Cartesians who followed him, assumed that knowledge is a mathematical mapping of the system or structure of nature. As humanity comes to grips with the order of nature and learns to sort it into kinds, it gains knowledge about nature.

Descartes and most of the early moderns preserve the traditional distinction between the arts and the sciences. Science is acquired by the mind; art is a bodily aptitude appropriate to craftsmen. Thus Descartes notes that oratory and poetry are "gifts of the mind" and hence not properly arts at all (*Philosophical Writings,* vol. 1, p. 114). It was not until the eighteenth century that a robust separation between the fine and useful arts emerged. Parallel with this core difference between conceptions of science and art, classification within each underwent an increasingly divergent development. This development occurred although one key characteristic of early modern theory of art is that art possesses an essentially intellectual character. Perhaps in response to Cartesian and me-

dieval thinking, advocates sought to establish a place for the arts within the mental realm.

This new development generated some interesting thinking about classification. In both the arts and sciences, classification frequently depended on subject matter. Descartes did not like this method for the sciences, since it emphasized material particularity over mental universality. Thus one finds a significant point of departure for classification in the arts and sciences. Genuine knowledge comes from the application of a unified methodology. Hence Descartes argues that it is inappropriate to separate the sciences on the basis of subject matter, since quality scientists should be applying a single method of thought in all scientific matters. The arts, however, comprise separate and distinct skills. As a result, the arts should be distinguished, studied and mastered individually. Skilled craftsmen specialize; skilled intellects universalize. The arts are those intellectual enterprises that also require a practical component, but the latter should not diminish the fact of the former.

Yet as the eighteenth century unfolds there occurs a startling series of innovations in both the arts and the sciences. As the sciences mature, an understanding of what it means to classify comes into focus. The arts develop an independent character, and theories of art push thinking about the nature of classification in the arts in new directions.

Early Modern Classification in the Arts

A number of transformations in the arts took place during the early modern period. What constitutes art, how one ought to classify its various subfields, and even how one ought to judge works of art all underwent bold revisions. The nature and number of the changes is considerable, but it is worth sampling some of the more significant developments.

The concept of invention in art (in the sense of a creative process) altered in the period and would ultimately change how people think about what constitutes art. The old view (even espoused by Leon Battista Alberti, an important Italian theorist of art, as late as the fifteenth century) is that an inventive artist is one that preserves tradition, communal values, and accepted ways of thinking. By the eighteenth century, however, the artist as a solitary figure committed to breaking or superseding traditional norms and artistic methodologies was firmly entrenched. Thus a new intellectual tool developed for categorizing within art and for what counts as art. As the humanist movement took root, artists increasingly redefined their discipline and the standards of quality within their work.

How one identifies and classifies beauty also underwent substantial change as the early modern period unfolded. Prior to the eighteenth century beauty was an objective feature of things in the world. For the followers of Plato beauty was a transcendental property, a "Form" in which beautiful things participated. For others beauty was more immanent and empirical but nonetheless present *in a thing*. Thus classifying things as beautiful depended on isolating features in the objective world. In this sense, classifying objects in the world of art was similar to classifying things in the sciences. The world comes pre-jointed, and peoples' task as aesthetes is to learn to recognize those divisions.

Beauty is no quality in things themselves: It exists merely in the mind which contemplates them; and each mind perceives a different beauty. One person may even perceive deformity, where another is sensible of beauty; and every individual ought to acquiesce in his own sentiment, without pretending to regulate those of others. To seek the real beauty, or real deformity, is as fruitless an enquiry, as to pretend to ascertain the real sweet or real bitter.

SOURCE: David Hume, *Essays Moral . . .* section 23, "Of the Standard of Taste."

Starting with the work of Francis Hutcheson (1694–1746) in the early 1700s and best displayed in the work of David Hume (1711–1776) later in the century, theorists of art shifted the concept of beauty away from an external objective standard to an internal standard. This shift did not necessarily signal the abandonment of objectivity in beauty, but it moved the focus of attention away from the natural world to the person making aesthetic judgments. Both Hutcheson and Hume developed theories of "taste," theories of artistic sensibilities that classify on the basis of perceiving subjects and not objects.

In a similar vein, the concept of the sublime became elevated as an independent kind of experience. The sublime (roughly a lofty, elated feeling), especially in the work of Edmund Burke (1729–1797), now becomes a separate class quite distinct from beauty. Interestingly, earlier seventeenth-century discussions of the sublime apply the concept only to certain arts such as rhetoric and poetry; no mention is made of the sublime with respect to the visual arts. Jonathan Richardson (1665–1745) was one of the first to apply sublimity explicitly to the visual arts, marking yet another important step in the increasing stratification and complication of artistic categories.

In general the middle of the eighteenth century witnessed the birth of modern theory of art. In 1750 Alexander Baumgarten (1714–1762) published *Aesthetica* and established aesthetics as an independent field studying sensual cognition. Later in the same decade Denis Diderot began publishing his biennial critical reviews of the salons, effectively launching serious art criticism. With criticism comes classification, not only of quality but of many other features. It should thus be expected that during this time there would be a conceptual explosion of classification in the arts to support all of this innovation in theory of art. The expectation is not disappointed.

Perhaps the most prominent example of this classificatory explosion is seen in the work of Gérard de Lairesse (1641–1711), a Dutch painter and author who published several lengthy volumes at the inception of the eighteenth century about the visual arts. After distinguishing art (a production of the mind) from manner (a manual execution of a skill), he divides the arts into various kinds. Though divisions based on the content of what is painted had been already present for centuries, Lairesse is important because he shifted his classificatory scheme from content to modes of representation. Instead of sorting paintings and painters by their pictorial genres (landscapes, still lifes, portraits, and so forth), he advocated a system based on how the artist seeks to represent the content of the work. Kinds of brush strokes and implicit symbolizations became at least as important as the superficial object depicted. Even still lifes could have allegorical meaning, thus altering how the nature and kind of the work ought to be viewed.

Early Modern Classification in the Sciences

The core problem for the sciences regarding classification during the period concerned was how to carve the world into kinds. For instance, while natural philosophers were engaged in debates over how to classify organisms, metaphysicians asked more foundational questions, such as whether there were natural kinds. Did nature come predivided into kinds? If so, then the task of science was merely to reveal these ultimate classes. And how might this task best be done? Was it even possible to ascertain nature's "joints"? Alternatively, if nature does not come already divided, what are the implications for the sciences? Independently of whether there are natural kinds, there remains the question as to whether there is an ideal system for sorting individuals. In the history of science are found the key foundational theories for the contemporary system of scientific nomenclature being developed in this period.

The problem of natural kinds remains in the early twenty-first century. The philosopher John Locke (1632–1704), an antirealist about species (he did not believe that the world came antecedently divided into distinct species/kinds), argued that in principle one can have no access to the "real essences" of things and as a result cannot ever hope to know how reality is "really" divided. Instead, the most for which one can hope is to develop an empirical system of classification based on nominal essences—the names or appearances of things: "the sorting of things is the workmanship of the understanding" (*Essay*, p. 415). A particular lump of matter is classified as gold because it appears to have the set of properties that have been assigned to the concept of the kind gold. This view was deeply unsatisfying to many, Wilhelm Leibniz (1646–1716) in particular. Leibniz argued that nature *had* to come prepackaged into kinds and furthermore that there existed some empirical (perhaps even a priori) evidence as to what those kinds in fact are. What is important about this debate is not its resolution—philosophers continue to argue whether there is one yet—but its impact on thinking about classification generally. This debate helped to liberate scientific thinking from the Aristotelian view of classification as definition. It was no longer deemed sufficient to classify the world by simply positing one or several definitions. How the world may be classified into scientific kinds has to obey certain empirical and analytical restrictions.

Much of the work came in response to the practical issue of how best to classify in the emerging sciences. A great deal of urgency was attached to developing coherent systems of classification, especially as human knowledge about the natural world and the variety therein continued to grow. Early modern scientific systems tended to be either artificial (classifying on the basis of convenience for identification) or natural (classifying according to natural kinds). Most of the classification systems in biology during the period were by the "habit" of the kind. So plants were categorized by whether they flower or whether they produce fruit. Animals were classified by whether they lay eggs or are nocturnal, and so on. The most important development, however, was the application of new rational systems of naming kinds. Carolus Linnaeus (1707–1778), a Swedish botanist, devised the precursor to the present system of nomenclature in the eighteenth century (although there were some, such as Jean Bauhin in the sixteenth century, who anticipated this system). His system of binomial nomenclature relied on the division between male and female as one of its fundamental kind distinctions (which is no longer used), but his basic methodology has been adopted as the standard for classification in the biological sciences.

Robert Boyle (1627–1691) is an exemplar of early modern thinkers who helped define "scientific" theories as rational and ordered methodologies. Boyle, now famous for his development of early chemical theories, argued passionately that chemical kinds had to be subject to empirical experimentation. The old chemical categories were deficient precisely because they were not subject to verifiable tests. Boyle further developed the distinction between primary and secondary qualities (though he coined the terms, the concepts can be traced back at least to Galileo), thus preparing the ground for additional scientific inquiry based on a classification of things in nature that were in principle subject to empirical testing. Thus in the debate over how to carve up nature into kinds, new meta-insights emerged that provided constraints on what sorts of classificatory schemes were acceptable. Even if one cannot know whether the particular details about the kinds one picks out in the world are accurate, there nonetheless emerges a theory of classification that indicates that how one classifies is not purely arbitrary.

It is worth noting an issue not addressed by the early moderns but that was fast approaching. All of the reasoning about classification in this period was pre-Darwinian. Phylogenetic systems of classification (those that classify according to evolutionary sequences) did not emerge until later and hence there was no pressure to suppose that there are deep connections *between* the kinds that are picked out in nature. Thus one of the constraints that would appear after the development of the theory of evolution (that species-kinds might be interrelated in definable ways) was not yet present. But one might speculate that the innovations in theory of classification in the previous century were part of what made evolutionary theory possible. That there are constraints on what could count as a good system of classification prepares one for additional deep connections in certain fields of inquiry.

Emerging into the Nineteenth Century

By the end of the eighteenth century one can detect a clear separation between theorizing about classification in the arts and in the sciences. Thinkers preserved in the sciences the ideal of external objectivity but grappled with whether this ideal could be achieved. Most importantly, the scientific community developed theories that preserved the ideal in the face of epistemological shortcomings by positing meta-constraints on what could count as a satisfactory theory of kinds. In the arts, classification shifted away from external objectivity to more subjective and intersubjective forms of classification. This shift was facilitated by the distinction between the fine arts and useful arts and more generally by the development of new and separate theories of art. Aesthetics emerged as an independent field of inquiry with its own set of kinds and categories. The early modern period witnessed the development of separate and new ways of classifying in the arts distinct from the sciences.

By the nineteenth century the arts and the sciences were conceived of as separate disciplines with distinct classificatory systems. And as such a new question arose: How is it determined whether some activity or thing should be classified as science or as art, as scientific or as artistic? Separating art and science by how they classify does not entail that they use different conceptions of what it means more broadly to classify at all. In fact, this article has assumed the contrary. Furthermore, separating art and science does not imply that the two domains are utterly distinct. As Leo Tolstoy wrote at the close of the nineteenth century, "Science and art are as closely bound together as the lungs and the heart, so that if the one organ is vitiated the other cannot act rightly" (p. 277).

See also **Aesthetics; Arts; Science, History of.**

BIBLIOGRAPHY

PRIMARY SOURCES

Aristotle. *The Complete Works of Aristotle.* Edited by Jonathan Barnes. Princeton, N.J.: Princeton University Press, 1984.

Baumgarten, Alexander. *Aesthetica.* 1750. Hildesheim, Germany: G. Olms, 1961.

Boyle, Robert. *Selected Philosophical Papers of Robert Boyle.* Edited by M. A. Stewart. Manchester, U.K.: Manchester University Press, 1979.

Burke, Edmund. *A Philosophical Enquiry into the Origin of Our Ideas of the Sublime and Beautiful.* Edited by James T. Boulton. London: Routledge and Kegan Paul, 1958.

Descartes, René. *The Philosophical Writings of Descartes.* Translated by John Cottingham et al. 3 vols. New York: Cambridge University Press, 1985–1991.

Hume, David. *Essays Moral, Political and Literary.* Edited by Eugene F. Miller. Indianapolis: Liberty Classics, 1985.

Hutcheson, Francis. *An Inquiry concerning Beauty, Order, Harmony, Design.* Edited by Peter Kivy. The Hague: Martinus Nijhoff, 1973.

Kant, Immanuel. *Critique of Judgment.* Translated by Werner S. Pluhar. Indianapolis: Hackett, 1987.

Leibniz, Gottfried Wilhelm. *New Essays on Human Understanding.* Translated and edited by Peter Remnant and Jonathan Bennett. Cambridge, U.K., and New York: Cambridge University Press, 1981.

Locke, John. *An Essay concerning Human Understanding.* Edited by Peter H. Nidditch. New York: Oxford University Press, 1975.

Tolstoy, Leo. *What Is Art?* Translated by Aylmer Maude. London: Oxford University Press, 1930.

SECONDARY SOURCES

Barasch, Moshe. *Modern Theories of Art.* Vol. 1: *From Winckelmann to Baudelaire.* New York: New York University Press, 1990. Excellent historical approach to developments in theory of art.

Gaut, Berys, and Lopes, Dominic, eds. *The Routledge Companion to Aesthetics.* London and New York: Routledge, 2001. Excellent general resource, including separate articles on key historical figures in the philosophy of art.

Lawrence, George. *Taxonomy of Vascular Plants.* New York: Macmillan, 1951. Although dated, this text contains an excellent history of classificatory systems in the sciences.

Wittkower, Rudolf, and Margot Wittkower. *Born under Saturn.* New York: Norton, 1963. A history of artists and how they have been viewed from antiquity to the end of the early modern period.

Marc A. Hight

CLEANLINESS.   *See* Hygiene.

COGNITIVE SCIENCE.   *See* Philosophy of Mind.

COLONIALISM.

This entry includes three subentries:

Africa
Latin America
Southeast Asia

AFRICA

Conceptions and characterizations of colonialism vary considerably among scholars of Africa. Differences and debates center on four sets of interrelated issues: first, the place and importance of the colonial period in African history; second, the nature of the colonial encounter and its driving force; third, the typologies of African colonialism; and fourth, the legacies of colonialism for postcolonial Africa. These questions have been addressed from a wide variety of disciplinary and analytical traditions. In general, the historiography of colonialism in Africa has been dominated at different moments by four paradigms: the imperialist, nationalist, radical, and postcolonial.

Imperialist approaches, which prevailed in the early twentieth century, emphasized the civilizing mission and impact of colonialism. Critiques against this tradition, combined with nationalist struggles that led to decolonization, culminated in the rise of nationalist historiography, which emphasized African activities and agency. From the 1970s, influenced by a growing sense of pessimism about the developmental and democratic capacities of the postcolonial state and the rise of militant ide-

ologies and social movements, "radical" approaches emerged, centered on dependency and Marxist ideas that highlighted the economic depredations and effects of colonialism. In the 1990s, following the demise of socialist regimes and ideologies and the spread of poststructuralism and postmodernism, postcolonial perspectives were increasingly used to reinterpret the cultural and discursive dynamics and complexities of colonialism. Additional paradigms on colonialism arose, most critically those informed by feminist and environmental studies, which stress the role of gender and ecology in the construction of colonial identities, societies, and political economies.

Colonialism in African History

Imperialist and nationalist historiographies represent almost diametrically opposed views of the place and impact of colonialism in African history, with one regarding it as a decisive moment, the other, as a parenthesis. To the imperialists, colonialism in fact brought Africa into history, for in their view, Africa "proper," to use Hegel's moniker—from which North Africa was excised—was the land of the "Unhistorical, Undeveloped Spirit," exhibiting "the natural man in his completely wild and untamed state" (pp. 91, 93). European colonialism, therefore, was depicted as a civilizing mission undertaken to historicize and humanize Africans.

Consequently, imperialist historians mostly discussed in positive light the policies of colonial governments and the activities of colonial auxiliaries, from European merchants to missionaries. When their narratives mentioned Africans, it was to condemn their societies and cultures or to chronicle their Westernization or modernization. Those who resisted colonial conquest or colonial rule were depicted as atavistic, while those who collaborated or accepted the colonial regime were praised for their foresight and wisdom. In fact, in-depth study of African societies was largely left to anthropology, which, with its functionalist-positivist paradigms and ethnographic present, exonerated, if not extolled, colonialism.

Nationalist historians offered an ideological and methodological revolt against imperialist historiography. Using new sources, including oral tradition, historical linguistics, and historical anthropology, together with written and archaeological sources, they chronicled the histories of African states and societies before the European colonial conquest and celebrated the growth and eventual triumph of nationalism during the colonial era. They sought to unravel painstakingly African activity, adaptations, choice, and initiative. Led by J. F. Ade Ajayi (1968) in Anglophone Africa and Cheikh Anta Diop (1974) in Francophone Africa, they emphasized continuity in Africa's long history and reduced colonialism to a parenthesis, an episode, a digression, a footnote that had altered African cultures and societies only slightly. In this narrative, independence marked a moment of historical recovery in which the agency of the precolonial past was restored and reconnected to the postcolonial future. The linear and celebratory tales of nationalist historiography were later found wanting by numerous critics.

While both the dependency and the Marxist scholars focused on the exploitative economic structures and processes of colonialism, the former were more interested in explaining the external forces that produced and reproduced Africa's underdevelopment; the latter preferred to concentrate on the internal dynamics. To the *dependentistas*, colonialism marked a second stage in Africa's incorporation into an unequal world capitalist system that was ushered in during the fifteenth century with the onset of the Atlantic slave trade. Marxist scholars sought to transcend the ubiquitous and homogeneous capitalism of dependency theory. Colonialism, they argued, entails the articulation of modes of production whereby precapitalist modes are articulated in their diverse relations with the capitalist mode. Hence the introduction of capitalism by colonialism does not eliminate the precapitalist modes but reshapes them; the latter are progressively subordinated to capital through a contradictory process of destruction, preservation, and transformation.

Unlike the nationalists, the imperialist, dependency, and Marxist historians share the view that the colonial period was decisive in African history. But they differ in their characterization and conceptualization of the place and impact of colonialism. Like the nationalists and unlike the imperialists, the *dependentistas* and Marxists see colonialism as an intrusive moment in the *longue durée* of African history. Insofar as dependency analyses concentrate on the external determinations of underdevelopment, they diminish African agency and echo imperialist accounts of African history, whereas the Marxist focus on internal production processes and social relations resonates with nationalist historiography.

The nationalist periodization of African history, in which the colonial moment occupies limited space, was sanctified in the Cambridge (*History of Africa,* 1977–1985) and UNESCO (*General History of Africa,* 1981–1993) histories, each in eight thick volumes, only two of which were on the colonial and postcolonial periods. Yet far more African historians currently work on the colonial period than on the precolonial period.

The Nature of the Colonial Encounter

Colonialism in Africa entailed an encounter between the continent and Europe. This encounter encompassed multiple spheres (from politics, economy, and culture to sexuality, psychology, and representations), spatial scales (from local and individual colonial territories to subregions and the continent as a whole), and social groups and inscriptions (from the colonizers and colonized to class, gender, and generation). Analyzing the nature of the colonial encounter, therefore, has proved exceedingly complex and contentious, given the range of possible analytical categories and conceptions of what indeed "Europe" and "Africa" mean. Different readings informed by disparate disciplinary or theoretical orientations emphasize the political, economic, cultural, or representational import of the colonial encounter.

Overall, some regard this encounter as essentially antagonistic while others depict it as ambivalent or even accommodative. Until recently, especially before the rise of postcolonial theory, colonialism was largely conceived in antagonistic terms as a series of encounters between the seemingly enduring and impermeable binaries of colonizer and colonized, Western and non-Western, domination and resistance, modernity and tradition, destruction and preservation, and universal and local. Post-

colonialists insist on the ambivalent nature of colonialism, its contingency and decenteredness, and the hybridities and pluralities of the identities it produced. If colonialism is primarily viewed as a political encounter among imperialist and nationalist scholars and as an economic one among the radicals, the postcolonialists emphasize its cultural and discursive dimensions.

The Bifurcated Colonial State

Studies on colonialism as politics and the politics of colonialism have tended to focus on two main issues: the nature of the colonial state and African resistance. Discussion and debate on the colonial state have centered on its specificities and construction, how to classify African colonial states and administrations, the dynamics of colonial power and civil society, and the demise or reconstitution of the colonial state into the postcolonial state. Crawford Young has argued quite forcefully that the African colonial state derives its peculiarity from the fact that it enjoyed only some of the crucial attributes of the modern state (territory, population, sovereignty, power, law, and the state as nation, an international actor, and an idea) and could not exercise some of its imperatives (hegemony, autonomy, security, legitimacy, revenue, and accumulation).

This is because the colonial state in Africa was created in the late nineteenth century, long after both the modern metropolitan state and the generic colonial state had been formed, which allowed for no experimentation. Also, as a conquest state imposed by force, its hegemony was excessively coercive, so that it enjoyed little legitimacy. Moreover, its territoriality was ambiguous, its sovereignty and institutions of rule were extraverted and resided in the imperial metropole, and its revenue base was weak. Charged with the onerous tasks of consolidating colonial rule, linking the colony to the metropole, and establishing or promoting colonial capitalism, the result was that the colonial state was both interventionist and fragile, authoritarian and weak, and exercised domination without hegemony, all of which ensured its eventual downfall.

All colonial states, irrespective of their ideologies and administrative systems, justified themselves in the names of civilization and pacification. Economic motivations of colonialism were assiduously downplayed. Moreover, all colonial powers used African intermediaries in their administrative systems because they lacked personnel and local knowledge and in order to minimize African resistance and administrative costs. They also used chartered companies in some of their colonies in the early years.

In imperialist historiography, colonial power was portrayed as unassailable because it was for Africa's good. For the opposite reason it was decried in nationalist historiography, which stressed its oppressiveness and incapacity to withstand the full might of nationalist struggle. Dependency writers tended to disregard the importance of politics because they believed that neither the colonial state nor African resistance could stop the ineluctable juggernaut of the world capitalist system, while Marxists subsumed colonial politics to either local class struggles (waged by the numerically small working classes, and only reluctantly and later were struggles by the much larger peasantries considered) or anti-imperialist struggles mediated by communist parties in the imperial metropoles themselves or the Soviet Union. Many of the early studies failed to examine the ways that colonial power was specifically deployed, engaged, contested, deflected, or appropriated.

It was not until Peter Ekeh published his influential essay "Colonialism and the Two Publics in Africa" that colonial civil society began to receive serious scholarly attention. He argued that colonialism created two publics that he called the primordial and civic publics, whose dialectical relationships accounted for the political problems of postcolonial Africa. The first public is associated with primordial groupings, sentiments, and activities; the second is associated with the colonial administration and is amoral, lacking the generalized moral imperatives operative in the private realm and in the primordial public. The two publics emerged because colonial ideologies of legitimation denigrated African societies and cultures and glorified European colonial rule, while African bourgeois ideologies of legitimation accepted colonial ideas and principles to justify the leadership of the elites in the fight against colonialism and the inheritance of the postcolonial state. Both ideologies envisaged and sought to separate the indigenous and colonial publics, in which different conceptions of citizenship, morality, and material expectations prevailed. Thus colonial civil society was characterized by the bifurcation of the public realm, which accounts for the centrality of ethnicity in African politics and the disjunction between the state and society that has bedeviled postcolonial Africa.

Others saw the bifurcation and ethnicization of colonial civil society differently. In his award-winning book *Citizen and Subject,* Mahmood Mamdani argued that the bifurcation of power in Africa results from the continent's distinctive colonial experience. The configuration of colonial rule in Africa led first to the institutionalization of two systems of power under a single authority: one urban, based on civil power and rights, excluding the colonized on the basis of race, the other rural, where tradition and culture incorporated the colonized into the rule of custom. Second, colonial rule in Africa led to the privileging of state-ordained and state-enforced traditions that had least historical depth and were monarchical, authoritarian, and patriarchal, so that customary power and law became an integral part of a decentralized despotism. Finally, with custom becoming the language of force, colonial rule led to rationalizing the appropriation and management of land and the mobilization of labor under the colonial rubric.

This bifurcated state power, civil and customary, first crystallized in equatorial Africa—as "indirect rule" in British colonies and "association" in French colonies—and later spread to older colonies to the north and south, including South Africa, where apartheid represented the last attempt at reorganizing the state structure to incorporate the "native" population in a world of enforced tradition. The challenges confronting African countries in the struggles for independence and after were to democratize the state and particularly customary power, deracialize civil society, and restructure unequal external relations of dependency.

Dependent Colonial Capitalism

To many scholars, economics, not politics, is central to the colonial project. In the 1970s systematic studies began to appear on African colonial economies. Three dominant approaches emerged. The first was rooted in neoclassical economic theory and focused largely on market processes and the problems of resource allocation. Anthony Hopkins has provided the most famous neoclassical treatment of African economic history. Using vent-for-plus theory (that colonialism provided a "vent," or an "opening"), he argues that colonialism inaugurated an "open economy" of increased market opportunities, which West Africans seized with alacrity by mobilizing previously underutilized resources. Hopkins's economic history walked a fine line between the imperialist approaches that stressed the modernizing impact of colonialism and the nationalist emphasis on African initiatives.

The second approach was dependency, which was born out of dissatisfaction with prevailing neoclassical descriptions, analyses, and prescriptions for Third World development. Using the concepts of "incorporation," "unequal exchange," "development of underdevelopment," and "center-periphery," dependency writers emphasized external economic linkages and exchange relations, often at the expense of internal and production processes. Walter Rodney's influential text *How Europe Underdeveloped Africa* portrayed colonialism simply as a new stage in Africa's unrelenting slide into structural internal underdevelopment and external dependency.

Marxist scholars attacked both neoclassical and dependency writers for alleged theoretical inadequacies, empirical shortcomings, and ideological biases. They sought to employ concepts of dialectical and historical materialism—which seek to examine how specific systems originate, develop, function, and change in given historical epochs—to unravel Africa's historical realities. For the precolonial era, it proved difficult to fit Africa into the traditional Marxian modes or to construct specific African ones. As far as the colonial economy was concerned, many Marxists found the concept of the articulation of modes of production useful and produced interesting studies on labor and workers, agriculture and peasants, and the changing structures of Africa's incorporation into the world economy.

Despite the different emphases of the three approaches, it is possible to outline the common features shared by African colonial economies: they were all expected to provide raw materials and markets for the imperial economies and to be financially self-supporting. The colonial economy was characteristically export-oriented and monocultural and suffered from uneven productivity between sectors and outside domination in terms of markets, technology, and capital. It developed in three phases: first, the period up to World War I, when coercion—forced labor, cultivation, and taxation—predominated; second, the interwar years, characterized by regulation of the colonial economy and the disruptions of the Great Depression, which exposed its vulnerabilities and fostered new economic policies of development planning; and third, the post–World War II period, when "colonial development and welfare" policies took hold, characterized by increased state intervention and investment in "economic development."

Typologies of Colonialism

A key challenge in analyzing African colonial economies, as with other spheres of colonialism, is their sheer diversity. The temporal division between precolonial and colonial economies and polities and their spatial development during the colonial period were manifested quite unevenly. The growth and structure of colonial economies, for example, were determined by the level of development of the precolonial economies themselves, the nature of precolonial relations with Europe, the modes of conquest and resistance, the level of development of the colonizing powers, the resource endowment of each territory, and the presence or absence of European settlers.

Several attempts have been made to construct typologies of African economies and colonialism more broadly. Three can be identified. First is the renowned tripartite division of Africa developed by Samir Amin (1972): the Africa of the labor reserves (Algeria, Kenya, and much of southern Africa), where Africans were primarily expected to provide labor for European colonial enterprises; the Africa of trade (West Africa, Uganda, Morocco, and Tunisia), where Africa produced the bulk of commodities traded by colonial companies; and the Africa of concession companies (central and equatorial Africa and the Portuguese colonies), where chartered companies enjoyed economic and administrative control over African labor and produce. Second is Thandika Mkandawire's typology distinguishing between rentier and merchant economies, in which surpluses are extracted from rents from mining and trade and taxes from agriculture, respectively. Third is the distinction often drawn between settler and peasant economies or modes of production.

The concept of peasants has a rich and controversial literature in African studies. Debate has focused on the historical origins of African peasantries, their relations with capital and the state, internal differentiations, the changing organization of peasant work—especially its complex articulations with gender and generational relations and divisions—the impact of environmental conditions and changes, the complex patterns of rural cultural construction, peasant knowledge systems, and the intricacies of peasant politics and struggles at various levels, from the household and the local community to the national and global system. In this context, not only did colonialism alter the lives of African peasantries, but the latter also profoundly shaped the terrain of colonialism in Africa.

The concept of the settler mode of production sought to capture the specificities of settler colonies. Settler colonialism was characterized by several features: the exclusion of competition (settler control of key economic resources, including land, allocation of infrastructure, banking, and marketing, at the expense of the indigenous people); the predominance of the migrant labor system (which allowed the costs of reproducing labor power to be borne in the rural reserves); generalized repression whereby direct and brutal force was used regularly; and the close intersection of race and class.

Linked to the concept of settler colonialism is the concept of internal colonialism, in which the colonizing "nation" or "race" occupies the same territory as the colonized people. This concept found favor among some academics and liberation movements in South Africa who saw the hierarchical, exploitative, and separatist structures of segregation and apartheid as analogous to the relationship of domination and subjection between an imperialist state and its racialized colonies. Harold Wolpe attacked the concept for positing an unexplained autonomy of racial, ethnic, and cultural groups and obscuring the relationships between them, akin to the theory of plural society widely used by liberal scholars to describe South African society.

The Ambivalences of Colonial Society

The pluralist approach was widely applied by social anthropologies to explain many other African colonial societies, which were depicted as "plural societies" in which different ethnic groups and races lived in close proximity; colonial social change was attributed to "culture contact" and "acculturation." To the pluralists, colonialism provided an arena for the acculturation of African ethnic groups to European culture and values, and so they were preoccupied with recording the patterns of what they called "detribalization" as indicated by changes in clothes, occupations, education, family forms, and leisure activities.

Marxist critics such as Bernard Magubane attacked the indices used by the pluralists and the fact that the specifics of European life and culture in Africa and their own "acculturation" or "Africanization" were ignored. Above all, in their view, the pluralists mystified the real social relations for they failed to place colonial social change in the context of colonialism as a global system of economic relations. The Marxists demonstrated that behind the processes of "acculturation" lay widespread practices of resistance. For example, the leisure activities of workers, as exhibited in work songs, often articulated African popular resistance against colonial rule. Similarly, it was demonstrated that transformations of cultural practices in the rural areas reflected peasant attempts to resist and remake the colonial situation. The Marxists maintained that religious conversions, whether to Christianity or Islam, represented not simply "acculturation" and the renunciation of the old religions but also translations of the old religions into new terms as filtered through the complex mediations of class and social consciousness.

Preoccupied as they were to show African agency, nationalist scholars were perhaps the loudest in refusing to see the processes of colonial social and cultural change simply as a product of "Westernization." In a famous essay on the invention of tradition in colonial Africa, Terence Ranger insisted that social and cultural traditions were invented and manipulated by both Europeans and Africans to serve their own interests. Specifically, elders, men, ruling aristocracies, and indigenous people appealed to "tradition." The elders did so in order to defend their dominance over the rural means of production against challenges from the youth; men wanted to retain control against women, who were playing an increasingly important role in the rural areas, especially in regions dominated by male migrant labor; ruling aristocracies sought to maintain or extend their control over their subjects; and indigenous people were anxious to ensure that migrants who settled among them did not achieve political or economic rights. This model became popular for analyzing the contexts in which various cultural and social practices in colonial Africa developed—from music and dance to law and marriage.

This constructivist approach was to be fully developed by postcolonial scholars, for whom colonialism was a regime of material and cultural relations as well as discursive and symbolic representations that affected both Africans and Europeans profoundly, although in different ways. The postcolonialists sought to dismantle the image of colonialism as a coherent and monolithic process, to transcend the dichotomy of colonizer and colonized by problematizing, differentiating, and pluralizing each group and mapping out their complex and shifting relations, and to specify the cultural configurations and discourses fashioned out of their changing identities, consciousness, interactions, and negotiations.

Postcolonialists brought into sharper focus issues previously ignored or misconstrued in structuralist and social scientific analyses of colonialism, especially those concerning sexuality, subjectivity, psychology, and language. Besides the textual notions and readings of colonial culture, analyses have increasingly come to stress the nonverbal, tactile dimensions of social practice and the corporeal regimes of bodies, clothing, and performances. Particularly influential have been Frantz Fanon's acclaimed work on the psychology of colonialism and his crucial insights that "blackness" and "whiteness" were mutually constitutive ideological constructions. Building on Fanon's insights, scholars of Africa have highlighted the construction of colonial mentalities, madness, and medicine as mechanisms for inscribing and policing racial and sexual boundaries. Kwame Appiah has shown how the ideas of race in Africa were socially constructed and how colonial and anticolonial discourses reinforced each other to fix racial essences on bodies.

The Feminist Intervention

Many of the approaches used to analyze African colonial politics, economies, societies, and cultures were often gender-blind and tended to ignore women's lives, experiences, contributions, voices, perceptions, representations, and struggles. This began to change following the rise of the feminist movement, which emerged out of both localized and transnational trajectories and intellectual and political struggles within and outside the academy. While the struggles to mainstream women and gender are far from over, African women have become increasingly more visible in histories of colonialism, which has disrupted the binaries and chronologies that tend to frame colonialism in Africa.

As the field of women's studies has expanded, African women have become more differentiated in terms of class, culture, and status, and their complex engagements, encounters, and negotiations with and contestations against the wide range of forces described as colonial are now clearer. From the large and diverse body of theoretical, methodological, and pedagogical literature that has been generated in the last three decades, vigorous debates are evident. One of the most intriguing is on the validity of the term *gender* itself, with writ-

ers such as Ifi Amadiume stressing the relative flexibility of sex/gender relations in precolonial Africa, and Oyèrónké Oyewùmí denying the existence of gender categories altogether.

In the early twenty-first century it has become well established that colonialism had a contradictory impact on different groups of women, although the dominant tendency was to undermine the position of women as a whole. Colonialism combined European and African patriarchal ideologies to create new practices, relations, and ideologies. Earlier work on colonial gender regimes focused on women in productive and commercial activities in the rural and urban areas and the acute tensions in gender relations that were created, to which the colonial state responded by tightening already restrictive customary law, leading to important changes in family structure and new forms of patriarchal power. The topic that attracted by far the most attention was that of women's resistance to colonial rule. Studies ranged from those that examined specific activists and events to general analyses of women's involvement in nationalist struggles in various countries that demonstrated conclusively women's political engagements and contributions.

More recent work has focused on issues of sexuality, constructions of gender identities, and colonial representations. According to Zine Magubane, African sexuality and its control and representations were central to ideologies of colonial domination. In colonial discourse, female bodies symbolized Africa as the conquered land, and the alleged hyperfecundity and sexual profligacy of African men and women made Africa an object of colonial desire and derision, a wild space of pornographic pleasures in need of sexual policing. Sexuality was implicated in all forms of colonial rule as an intimate encounter that could be used simultaneously to maintain and to erode racial difference and as a process essential for the reproduction of human labor power for the colonial economy, both of which demanded close surveillance and control, especially of African female sexuality.

Feminist studies on the construction of gender identities and relations have helped spawn a growing literature on the creation and transformation of colonial masculinities. Writing on Southern Africa, Robert Morrell argues that the colonial divisions of class and race produced different masculinities, some of which were dominant and hegemonic, and others, subordinate and subversive, although the latter received a patriarchal dividend over women of their class and race. These masculinities were produced and performed in different institutional contexts, each with its own gender regime and power relations, from the state, church, and school to the workplace and the home. Needless to say, masculinities changed over time and manifested themselves differently in rural and urban areas, where different gender and associational systems existed and patterns of political, social, and political change took place.

The Demise of Colonialism

Conceptions and analyses of colonialism in Africa have been affected quite considerably by how the demise of colonialism is understood. This in turn has centered on how two processes are examined—namely, decolonization, and African nationalism or resistance—and the connections between the two. Nationalist historians contend that nationalism was primarily responsible for the dismantling of the colonial empires, while to imperialist historians decolonization was largely a product of metropolitan policy and planning. Others seek to place decolonization in the context of changes in the international relations system. Clearly, a process as complex as decolonization was a product of many factors. It involved a complex interplay of the prevailing international situation, the policies of the colonial powers, and the nature and strength of the nationalist movements, which in turn reflected internal conditions both in the metropoles and the colonies and the ideologies and visions of the postcolonial world. There were also variations in the patterns of decolonization among regions and colonies, conditioned by the way in which these factors coalesced and manifested themselves. Furthermore, decolonization was affected by the relative presence and power of European settlers and the perceived geopolitical strategic importance of each colony.

Similarly, the nature and dynamics of African nationalism were exceedingly complex. Not only were the spatial locus and social referent of the "nation" imagined by the nationalists fluid (they could be ethnic, national, regional, and continental), but multiple secular and religious visions of the postcolonial state vied for supremacy. Moreover, nationalism was articulated and fought on many fronts (political, economic, social, cultural, religious, and artistic) through different organizational forms (from political and civic organizations to cultural and religious movements) and in different terrains (rural and urban). The development and impact of nationalism also varied between different colonies even among those under the same imperial power, depending on such factors as the way the colony had been acquired and was administered, the presence or absence of settlers, the traditions of resistance, and the social composition of the nationalist movement and its type of leadership.

Two key questions dominate African scholarship on decolonization and nationalism. The first is the social content and composition of anticolonial resistance. By the 1980s the old accounts of elite politics and heroic resistance had been abandoned in favor of analyses of resistance by peasants, workers, and women, and from the early 1990s more attention was paid to everyday forms of resistance by various subaltern groups, including youth. In short, the challenge was to write resistance with a small "r" rather than a capital "R" without losing, as Frederick Cooper (1994) insisted, the connections between the subaltern resistances and the larger and fluid constructs of colonialism. The second question centers on the continuities and discontinuities marked by decolonization. In the 1960s, nationalist scholars were inclined to see decolonization as ushering a radical break with colonialism. From the 1970s, the revolutionary pessimism of Fanon, who had pronounced decolonization false in his searing treatise of 1963, *The Wretched of the Earth,* gained adherents among radical scholars who stressed the structural continuities of colonialism. For their part, the postcolonialists, with their fixation on colonialism, recentered colonialism in African history.

See also **Africa, Idea of; Anticolonialism: Africa; Empire and Imperialism; Internal Colonialism; Nationalism.**

BIBLIOGRAPHY

Ajayi, J. F. Ade. "The Continuity of African Institutions under Colonialism." In *Emerging Themes of African History: Proceedings,* edited by T. O. Ranger, 189–200. Nairobi, Kenya: East African Publishing House, 1968.

Allman, Jean, Susan Geiger, and Nakanyike Musisi, eds. *Women in African Colonial Histories.* Bloomington: Indiana University Press, 2002.

Amadiume, Ifi. *Male Daughters, Female Husbands.* London and Atlantic Highlands, N.J.: Zed Books, 1987.

Amin, Samir. "Underdevelopment and Dependence in Black Africa: Historical Origins." *Journal of Modern African Studies* 10, no. 4 (1972): 503–524.

Appiah, Kwame Anthony. *In My Father's House: Africa in the Philosophy of Culture.* New York: Oxford University Press, 1992.

Cooper, Frederick. "Conflict and Colonialism: Rethinking Colonial African History." *American Historical Review* 99, no. 5 (1994): 1516–1545.

Cooper, Frederick, and Ann Laura Stoler. *Tensions of Empire: Colonial Cultures in a Bourgeois World.* Berkeley: University of California Press, 1997.

Diop, Cheikh Anta. *The African Origin of Civilization: Myth or Reality.* Translated by Mercer Cook. New York: L. Hill, 1974.

Diouf, Mamadou. *Historians and Histories: What For? African Historiography between State and the Communities.* Amsterdam and Calcutta: Sephis and CSSSC, 2003.

Ekeh, Peter P. "Colonialism and the Two Publics in Africa: A Theoretical Statement." *Comparative Studies in Society and History* 17, no. 1 (1975): 91–112.

Fanon, Frantz. *The Wretched of the Earth.* Preface by Jean-Paul Sartre. Translated by Constance Farrington. New York: Grove, 1963.

Hegel, G. W. F. *The Philosophy of History.* Translated by J. Sibree with a new introduction by C. J. Friedrich. New York: Dover Publications, 1956.

Hopkins, Anthony G. *An Economic History of West Africa.* London: Longman, 1973.

Jewsiewicki, Bogumil. "African Historical Studies: Academic Knowledge as 'Usable Past' and Radical Scholarship." *African Studies Review* 32, no. 3 (1989): 1–76.

Loomba, Ania. *Colonialism/Postcolonialism.* London and New York: Routledge, 1998.

Magubane, Bernard. "A Critical Look at Indices in the Study of Social Change in Colonial Africa." *Current Anthropology* 12, nos. 4/5 (1971): 419–445.

Magubane, Zine. *Bringing the Empire Home: Race, Class, and Gender in Britain and Colonial South Africa.* Chicago: University of Chicago Press, 2004.

Mamdani, Mahmood. *Citizen and Subject: Contemporary Africa and the Legacy of Late Colonialism.* Princeton, N.J.: Princeton University Press, 1996.

Mazrui, A. A., ed., and C. Wondji, assistant. ed. *Africa Since 1935.* Vol. 8 of *General History of Africa,* UNESCO International Scientific Committee for the Drafting of a General History of Africa. Berkeley: University of California Press, 1993.

McClintock, Anne. *Imperial Leather: Race, Gender, and Sexuality in the Colonial Contest.* New York: Routledge, 1995.

Mkandawire, Thandika. "The State and Agriculture in Africa: Introductory Remarks." In *The State and Agriculture in Africa,* edited by Naceur Bourenane and Thandika Mkandawire. Dakar, Senegal: Codesria, 1987.

Morrell, Robert. "Of Boys and Men: Masculinity and Gender in Southern African Studies." *Journal of Southern African Studies* 24, no. 4 (1998): 605–630.

Oyewùmí, Oyèrónké. *The Invention of Women: Making an African Sense of Western Gender Discourses.* Minneapolis: University of Minnesota Press, 1997.

Ranger, Terence O. "The Invention of Tradition in Colonial Africa." In *The Invention of Tradition,* edited by Eric Hobsbawm and Terence Ranger. Cambridge, U.K., and New York: Cambridge University Press, 1983.

Rodney, Walter. *How Europe Underdeveloped Africa.* Rev. ed. Postscript by A. M. Babu. Washington, D.C.: Howard University Press, 1981.

Wolpe, Harold. "The Theory of Internal Colonialism: The South African Case." In *Beyond the Sociology of Development: Economy and Society in Latin America and Africa,* edited by Ivar Oxaal, Tony Barnett, and David Booth, 229–252. London and Boston: Routledge and Kegan Paul, 1975.

Young, Crawford. *The African Colonial State in Comparative Perspective.* New Haven, Conn.: Yale University Press, 1994.

Zeleza, Paul Tiyambe. *Manufacturing African Studies and Crises.* Dakar, Senegal: Codesria, 1997.

Paul Tiyambe Zeleza

LATIN AMERICA

Colonialism is all about the exercise of power and its consequences. Theoretically, the exercise of power entails the interaction of at least two parties negotiating (by various means or practices) their wills on one or more issues, as shown by their various actions or statements. This definition holds for interactions of both individuals and institutions. The imposition of one state's will over another is the essence of colonialism. This phenomenon can be observed in a formal sense, when, for example, a mother country dominates a colony, as Spain and Portugal controlled their kingdoms in the Americas. It can also be seen in an informal sense, when the British government pressured Argentine representatives to repay the Baring Brothers' loan in the nineteenth century.

The history of colonialism, which has been a ubiquitous part of the history of the Americas for centuries, can be divided into four parts: pre-Colombian native imperialism; early modern European colonialism; new colonialism (in the nineteenth and early twentieth centuries); and neocolonialism, which came to dominate especially after World War II. Archaeologists and historians have described two major pre-Columbian empires in this hemisphere. In the first, the Nahuatl-speaking people, who called themselves the Mexica, dominated the far-flung "Aztec" empire, which was akin to a loose confederation of city-states under one dominant power. The second great indigenous imperial regime was that of the Inca in South America. Because the Inca required all peoples newly incorporated into the empire to add the Inca Sun god to their religious hierarchy, to learn to communicate in the Quechua language, and to serve the Inca state as requested, they established an empire that was more unified and homogeneous than their counterparts in Mexico.

The age of modern colonialism began in the fifteenth century with the rise of modern nation-states and the beginning of European exploration and discovery. Both of the pre-Columbian empires of the Americas were subsequently conquered and colonized by the Spanish. Representatives of the Spanish crown quickly reorganized the indigenous population to facilitate their rule. To anchor Spaniards in place, colonial authorities—beginning with Hernando Cortez in North America and Francisco Pizarro in South America—gave to their followers grants of native peoples and the rights to their labor—called *encomiendas.* Thus imperial fiat created a new Spanish elite. The grantees or *encomenderos* ruled the native population at will until reports of misuse, exploitation, and the attendant demographic catastrophe motivated the king to establish a government to implement his law and will.

In Spain, the Council of the Indies (Consejo de Indias) was created to study and make policy for the New World, advise the king, and settle important court cases on appeal. The crown created the House of Trade (Casa de la Contratación) in Seville to regulate commerce, collect taxes, and license immigrants. In America, viceroys represented the monarch's person. Supreme courts (*real audiencias*) and treasury departments (*real haciendas*) were also established. Local representation of the king was entrusted to district governors, or *corregidores.* Each Spanish city had a town council (*cabildo*) that was entrusted with overseeing the urban population, planning and growth, sanitation, and law and order. Because the overseas state remained relatively unelaborated and weak under the Habsburgs, the Spanish king relied on the church to help rule. The church provided education to a select few; kept the baptismal, marriage, and burial records; served as a source of capital; provided the moral underpinnings of order; oversaw charity; and proved a ready channel of communication for royal mandates.

Under the Habsburg kings, the colonies provided the mother country with agricultural commodities, precious metals, and exotic products, and proved a ready and profitable market for manufactured goods, which were increasingly made elsewhere in Europe but shipped in Spanish ships in exchange for Spanish civilization and culture (language, religion, and lifeways), manufactured goods, and law and governance. Because Habsburg bureaucratic jurisdictions remained blurred and overlapping, this partnership between church and state resulted in a flexible and long-lasting system of rule that, because of the distances and difficulties in communication, gave many American districts a measure of local autonomy.

In 1700, the Bourbons inherited the Spanish kingdoms. They realized that Spain's global power had waned since the late sixteenth century and that the American kingdoms were deficient in supplying the mother country with sufficient revenues to justify their new designation as colonies. Therefore the Bourbons set about reforming the colonial structure and its personnel (1) to defend the overseas kingdoms from the encroachment of the Dutch, the French, and the British, who all wanted footholds in the Americas and access to their raw materials and markets; (2) to rationalize the administration of the New World kingdoms; and (3) to maximize the revenues flowing into the royal treasury of Spain. The Bourbons did this in stages—working on the reforms first at home in the peninsula, then in the Caribbean, next in New Spain, and finally in Peru. Among the reforms were (1) the expulsion of the Jesuit order on charges of disloyalty and sedition (teaching new and prohibited treasonous ideas associated with Enlightenment philosophers such as Locke and Montesquieu); (2) the creation of the two new viceroyalties of New Granada (1717, 1739) and La Plata (1776) from the viceroyalty of Peru, ostensibly to bring justice closer to the settlers; (3) the replacement of the creole *corregidor* system of local administration with that of an *intendente* system of peninsular-born royal officials who enjoyed higher status and broader jurisdiction; (4) the renewal of the tax system to increase some levies (e.g., the sales tax) and create new ones (e.g., the tobacco monopoly); (5) the creation of the first true military organization (for defense); (6) the promotion of new technology (for example, pumps and the Born process to increase the productivity of the mines); and (7) the passage of legislation opening up trade.

These reforms alienated (1) the church, because of the monarch's growing anticlericalism; (2) creole families, because the Jesuits had been the favored educators of elite sons; (3) creole *corregidores,* who were replaced with peninsular-born *intendentes;* (4) people of mixed blood (i.e., the *castas*), who were particularly hard hit by increasing taxes; (5) creole militiamen, who resented the fact that the new military organization allowed persons of mixed blood to join; (6) miners, who wondered why it had taken the crown so long to send them the pump that could solve their flooding problems; (7) large wholesale merchants, who lost their monopoly on import supply; and (8) provincial towns that lost the business from overland traffic of mule teams and llama caravans in the Andes as new seaports were opened up for freer trade.

In the short run, the reforms did improve security, administrative expediency, and tax revenues. But in the long run, the imposition of the will of the mother country stifled local autonomy and was interpreted as a threat to the sociopolitical and economic interests of the creoles, causing enough resentment to heighten the desire for independence. Independence, which split the Spanish-American colonies into more than twenty separate countries in the first three decades of the nineteenth century, ended the formal unequal exchange between Spain and its American colonies.

Portuguese colonization followed the same general outlines, with some notable differences. The Portuguese overseas government in Brazil was established in the middle of the sixteenth century in part to prevent the French and other foreign interlopers from taking control of selected areas. The flight of the royal family and its court from Napoleon in 1807 and arrival in Brazil in 1808 and the presence of the royal family in the early nineteenth century resulted in a controlled independence and rule by members of the royal family, Pedro I and Pedro II, as kings of a separate Portuguese kingdom. Pedro II ruled in a relatively enlightened way, but resentment mounted nonetheless, culminating with the issuance in 1888 of the "Golden Law," freeing the slaves, that fatally undermined support for his rule and led to his exile in 1889.

Independence, which foreshadowed the age of new imperialism, however, did not bring the new republican governments total control over their own affairs. The new nations were politically independent but became subject to foreign invasions and state-to-state pressures over debts and the maintenance of law and order. Europe's industries were eager to find sources of raw materials and new markets. Investors willingly exported capital. As mentioned above, the Argentine government defaulted on its first loan, subjecting it to years of informal British diplomatic pressure for repayment. Further north, Mexico, Central America, and the Caribbean nations faced invasion to collect similar debts, as when the Spanish, French, and British governments sent troops into Mexico during the rule of the constitutionally elected presidency of Benito Juárez to collect overdue moneys.

In the twentieth century, the term "neocolonialism" referred to informal economic ties and the growing predominance of the cultures and values of the former colonial powers by which they continued to influence the cultures and outlooks of Latin-American states. Unequal terms of trade exacerbated Latin America's relations with the rest of the world as more and more products (such as bananas, coffee, sugar, and tin) were needed to buy the same or equivalent imported products. Resentment at this situation stimulated a rich intellectual life across the continent in the twentieth century; in fields as varied as economics, political philosophy, literature, and art, antiimperialism was a hallmark of a distinctively Latin American form of modernism.

Deteriorating terms of trade and dependency on other world powers have split the populations of the various countries. The elites support the foreign loans, aid, and close trading relations because they are importers and exporters who profit from such relations or the bankers, lawyers, and politicians who negotiate the loans, write the contracts, and collect the fees for their efforts. Nationalists, in contrast, are against such dealings, arguing that their nations export low-priced products to buy relatively high-cost manufactured goods that are often inappropriate technologically to the needs of the majority of their people. These nations also pay out more in principal, interest, fees, and patent and licensing costs than they take in, thus exacerbating inequality between countries and within their own nations, perpetuating their subordinate status, inequality, and poverty.

In addition, nationalists claim that the ruling elites colonize their own compatriots, in that provincial producers sell their local products—be it oranges or potatoes—at low prices and buy high-priced manufactured goods in return. In addition, the provinces send taxes to the capital and get much less back in the form of public works and services (such as schools)—a form of internal colonialism.

Such unequal relations have left a legacy of inequality and growing suspicion of and covert and overt resistance to the rule-makers at home and abroad. Under the Habsburgs, colonial populations resisted, saying, "*obedesco pero no cumplo*" (I obey but will not comply), implying that they recognized that the king had the right to issue the law but that if he had been better informed, he would not have done so. While they informed him of their circumstances and the reasons why the decree is not wise, it was not locally enforced. Increasingly this practice has been replaced by the attitude summarized as "*hecho la ley, hecho la trampa*" (a law passed is a law bypassed [by cheating, trickery, cleverness, or deceit]). This shows the growing cynicism and intolerance of the general population to their governments, international agencies, and unequal relations with the more developed world.

At the beginning of the twenty-first century, the picture is mixed. The fall of the Soviet Union has undermined the sense of any alternative to U.S. capitalism; at the same time, however, the disastrous economic situation that has resulted from neoliberal reforms—the latest set of policies imposed by international creditors on Latin-American nations—has fueled a new sense of resentment. At the same time, a militant desire for functioning democracy, transparency, and an end to corruption has fostered the growth of a wide variety of grassroots political movements. But for many, the only solution is to migrate, legally or illegally, north—into what a previous generation of anticolonialist Latin Americans called "the belly of the beast."

See also **Anticolonialism: Latin America; Empire and Imperialism: Americas.**

BIBLIOGRAPHY

Bernecker, Walther L., and Hans Werner Tobler, eds. *Development and Underdevelopment in America: Contrasts of Economic Growth in North and Latin America in Historical Perspective.* New York: Walter de Gruyter, 1993.

Felix, David, ed. *Debt and Transfiguration? Prospects for Latin America's Economic Revival.* Armonk, N.Y.: M. E. Sharpe, 1990.

Frank, Andre Gunder. *Latin America: Underdevelopment or Revolution: Essays on the Development of Underdevelopment and the Immediate Enemy.* New York: Monthly Review Press, 1969.

Galeano, Eduardo. *Open Veins of Latin America: Five Centuries of the Pillage of a Continent.* Translated by Cedric Belfrage. New York: Monthly Review Press, 1973.

Johnson, John J. *Latin America in Caricature.* Austin: University of Texas Press, 1980.

Keen, Benjamin. *A History of Latin America.* 4th edition. 2 vols. Boston: Houghton Mifflin, 1991.

Susan Elizabeth Ramirez

SOUTHEAST ASIA

Studies detailing the nature of colonial policy and practice in Southeast Asia have all acknowledged its disparate nature and overwhelming range of characteristics. While many European powers shared the desire to establish colonies overseas, the manner in which this was accomplished was more random than regular. Factors contributing to this variance include differing philosophies of administrative governance, differing levels of indigenous resistance, and differing periods of influence in the region. For instance, Spanish colonial projects in Southeast Asia began in the 1560s, nearly two hundred years earlier than the efforts of the British, French, and Dutch, resulting

in a much longer and more enduring history of colonialism in the Philippines (originally a Spanish colony) than in Malaya (a British colony). The Dutch employed a more indirectly ruled system (using indigenous elites to initiate their policies) than the British, who in Burma, for example, deposed the sitting monarchy in favor of ruling more directly through an impersonal civil service administration. In French Vietnam, there was a mixture of both systems, resulting in corresponding levels of resistance in areas more intensively encroached upon by colonial authorities. In general, polities that had achieved sophisticated levels of cultural, political, and economic integration tended to resist European powers more vigorously than polities in more decentralized areas. Some polities in insular Southeast Asia, whose political relations were more tenuous because of geographical constraints, competitive economies, and personal ties, offered less sustained, organized, or intensive resistance than in the mainland kingdoms whose populations were linked by common religious, economic, and historical worldviews. Simply put, the shape of colonialism in Southeast Asia was in large part determined by the nature of precolonial regional dynamics and the ability of the local communities to interact and respond to the differing policies, attractions, and challenges of colonial governance. Yet the idea of colonialism in Southeast Asia has also been understood and considered through approaches suggested by scholars of both Southeast Asian and colonial studies. This entry, after first providing a brief historical overview of colonialism in the region, discusses the ways in which Southeast Asian studies was constructed and shaped by scholars who were writing about or reacting to colonialism, producing works that revealed the complexities of that encounter as well as the epistemological links between the two branches of study.

Historical Overview

While this article is not concerned with the history of the colonialism in Southeast Asia per se, a brief overview highlighting some of its key points is necessary. The history of Southeast Asia's encounter with Europe begins as early as the first decades of the sixteenth century, an occurrence that is indeed one of the earliest episodes in the history of colonialism as a global phenomenon. In many respects, some of the "classical" features of colonialism—such as territorial conquest; the intervention and disruption of local socioeconomic networks; and the introduction of new cultural regimes and models through various missionary and educational activity—first came into play in Southeast Asia before they appeared later elsewhere. All major colonial European powers (as well as, later, the United States and Japan) took part in the long history of colonialism in the region: In the twentieth century the Netherlands was in control of Indonesia; Portugal, of East Timor; the United States, of the Philippines (taken from Spain after 1898); France, of Vietnam, Laos, and Cambodia (so-called French Indochina); and Great Britain, of Malaya and Myanmar (Burma). The region also provides the unique example of Thailand (Siam), which was never colonized, though institutional and cultural changes were significantly connected to European diplomatic pressures along its borders. During World War II most of these territories were occupied by Japan, whose imperial designs, cultural sensibilities, and economic initiatives disconnected Europe and America's hold on the region, which indirectly contributed to the tensions of a nationalist sentiment and Cold War competitions within the former colonies. Most of the European powers, weakened by the war, would lose their colonies after the war, though attempts were made (in varying degrees) to regain their original foothold within the region.

As the cases of the Mayla Emergency, the Indonesian Revolution, the Indochinese War, and, later, the Vietnam War show, the response to colonialism in Southeast Asia continued in the form of anticolonial resistance movements, though external observers tended to regard these wars in the context of the Cold War.

Trends in the Study of Colonialism

The story of Southeast Asia's encounter with Europe spans several centuries, leaving a long and complex record of exchange, negotiation, and domination. Colonialism in Southeast Asia might be considered one important chapter in that much larger story of global interaction. Within the region's early colonial historiography, colonialism pertained to the transformation of "traditionally" defined polities into dependent states modeled along European definitions of organization and administration. Because this approach to colonialism was significantly linked to the perspective of those who were immersed within the colonial service, it was no surprise that this understanding of colonialism was expressed through studies of administrative changes and their effects on local societies, economies, and cultures. Equally important was the overarching representation of the colonial encounter in binary terms: all that was "modern" was inherently European and became the standard to which Southeast Asian culture and history would be measured. Interestingly enough, these studies formed the foundations for the area studies disciplines, as many of the earliest doyens in the fields were from the ranks of the scholar-administrator. Early linguists, anthropologists, and historians, working within the colonial administrations, set the paradigms and agendas that later scholars would either confirm or contest, creating important but imposing discussions that would dominate the course of scholarship. Their views of the peoples and cultures they encountered set into motion a whole genealogy of scholarship that responded in various ways to their findings. For example, reports that discussed the despotic nature of Southeast Asian leadership not only reveal the way in which colonial agendas colored early documentation, they also identify why writing about "Southeast Asian kingship" was important in the first place. While these early writings relate something about Southeast Asia, they also reveal important insight into how colonialism was perceived by those working within it. Thus, the propagation of colonialism in Southeast Asia by these officials was partially responsible for the emergence of Southeast Asian studies as a field of study.

Thematically, colonialism has come to refer to a variety of processes that contributed to a fundamental change in identity, worldview, and consciousness. These institutional and cultural transformations were initiated at different levels and in varying intensities by many groups within the European com-

munity, indigenous elites, and rural populations. The complicated and complex nature of this interaction has been decoded by a variety of interpretations, affecting the many understandings and forms of colonialism. Colonial administrator-scholars referred to colonialism in terms of its policies and practices that contributed to the administrative formation of the colonies, whereas nationalist historians treated the subject as the processes of interaction, subjugation, and control that enabled the peoples and societies of Southeast Asia to come under colonial authority. Another manifestation of colonialism took its shape (although indirectly) through studies of indigenous forms of resistance and protest, whereas others explored colonialism through the multitude of indigenous social institutions it encountered and affected. More recent trends position colonialism through its relationship to the nation and the forming of national cultures; criminality, counterinsurgency, and prisons; and its forms of knowledge and various modes of representation. In addition, it has also been illustrated through technology, literature, and film. In short, the shape of colonialism has been fashioned through a variety of approaches, reflecting trends in the study of colonialism as a thematic category and through the interdisciplinary guilds within area studies.

Colonialism since 1970

Conceptions of colonialism in Southeast Asia have developed significantly since 1970, though scholarship began widening its historical gaze of the region's history and colonialism's place in it nearly a decade earlier. In response to colonial and nationalist-oriented histories of the colonial past, in which the attention was directed toward colonial administrators, policies, and interests in the region, scholars began shifting their focus, creating histories that told the same stories from internal, local, or indigenous perspectives. One of the most significant interventions was offered by John Smail, who saw a lingering problem in the historiography of modern Southeast Asian history. He concluded that both colonial and nationalist scholarship seemed to privilege the same European contexts, events, and narratives about the "colonial period" even when their political sympathies tended to diverge in analysis. In addition, the very conception of "modernity" in the region's history was automatically being associated with the trends, institutions, and ideas that emerged during the colonial period. According to Smail, modern history tended to focus on colonial narratives, concerns, and priorities that signaled a deep disjuncture with the precolonial past, whose own narratives, cultural forms, and terminology were being neglected by the grand narratives of empire, development, and modernity. In order to challenge the prevailing fixtures of colonial and nationalist historiography, Smail called for a writing and periodization of modern Southeast Asian history that applied indigenous categories of analysis, reconstituting the way in which modernity and colonialism would be defined, interpreted, and chronicled. Identifying these cultural forms that could structure the writing of an "autonomous" history of Southeast Asia during this period of intense Eurasian exchange became the overarching paradigm for scholars of the late 1960s and 1970s. This approach aimed to address the imbalance in scholarship, which had tended strongly toward European-oriented histories (which emphasize fundamental changes in society), by favoring histories that engaged the possibility of regional cultural continuities. To Smail, colonialism would no longer mark the arrival of modernity; it would merely mark a stage within the long-term patterns and processes of the region's history.

These adjustments lifted the idea of colonialism from the confines of European studies and placed it within the framework of Southeast Asian studies, which shifted attention that previously privileged the study of history through colonial categories to studies that investigated the nature of indigenous culture during the colonial encounter. While early studies might have explored the ways in which ideas of leadership, agriculture patterns, community organization, and kinship relations were affected by colonial policies and practices, the new interest in an "autonomous" perspective urged scholars to prioritize local institutions, patterns, and terms as the main subject of inquiry, so that the study of colonialism would become integrated into the cultural history and anthropology of Southeast Asia. One example could be found in the work of Emanuel Sarkisyanz, who demonstrated through his study of Burmese Buddhism that Southeast Asians reacted and responded to colonialism through local terms and concepts inherent to their worldview. The dismantling of the monarchy, subsequent rebellions, and nationalism were all considered through the prism of Buddhism in Burma, suggesting that it was possible to view the colonial period from a more Southeast Asian perspective. At the same time, effort was directed toward the ways in which global, regional, and local forces bound and interacted with peasant societies outside state or religious institutions, shifting the terms of engagement of colonialism to everyday life and practices. Seminal works such as James C. Scott's *The Moral Economy of the Peasant* directed attention to the ways in which global market economies affected the everyday life of the peasant in Southeast Asia, fundamentally challenging local conceptions of legitimacy, economy, and authority. In addition, such approaches stretched the legacy of precolonial traditions, which were often labeled as "traditional," into an epistemological space that previously scholarship had neglected to consider. Indigenous religion, ritual, and customary laws, and other modes of the precolonial conceptual world, became categories of analysis that were now used to study the role and nature of colonialism in Southeast Asia.

Colonial Dichotomies

While the terms of the colonial encounter were being reconfigured and though scholars were seemingly decolonizing the epistemology of Southeast Asia, others began to question the direction the field had taken and the perspective in which colonialism was being discussed. Smail's "autonomous" history had fundamentally edged the scholarship toward a fresh course of research, but there were still some lingering issues that needed to be resolved. The field's leanings toward supposed indigenous categories as modes of analyses might have fallen a bit short in providing a total picture of colonialism in Southeast Asia by underestimating the impact of colonial influences on society. Scholars had merely swung the pendulum from one

end of the spectrum to the other, extending a little too much enthusiasm for the continuities and unchanging nature of Southeast Asian cultural forms.

Following the important arguments in Edward Said's *Orientalism,* scholars such as Ann Laura Stoler questioned the essential nature of these categories while at the same time challenging the "European versus Southeast Asian" perspective upon which studies of colonialism continued to rest. Although important writers such as Franz Fanon and Albert Memmi had developed their seminal arguments about those who lay between the "colonized" and "colonizer," applying these types of questions to the study of colonial society in Southeast Asia remained in its infancy. With these new callings, the study of "mixed-bloods" in Dutch Indonesia, the "métisse" in French Vietnam, "mestizos" in the Spanish Philippines, and "Eurasians" became an important challenge to the idea that colonial society and its study could be divided into simple binary categories of analysis. These studies also suggested that colonialism in Southeast Asia (and beyond) was much more complex than previously imagined, pointing to a variety of situations and scenarios in which ideas, institutions, and technology were exchanged in different and often complicated ways. Colonialism in Southeast Asia could no longer be viewed as a neat and simple process, the colonial encounter could no longer be approached through binary framings, and it became clear that the categories that had been considered intrinsically "European" or "Southeast Asian" were no longer tenable.

The realization that colonialism was a much more complicated process that occurred at different intensities, at different times, and in different places also inspired scholars to look at other domains in Southeast Asia where such mixing and blurring of ideas might occur. Many scholars had been pondering this idea for some time, outside the contours of colonial studies but within the framework of Asian nationalism. Benedict Anderson's seminal *Imagined Communities* set the agenda by demonstrating that the nation-state was articulated through cultural forms that enabled peoples to bridge the conceptual gap between kin and citizen. Many of these forms of community bonding were those introduced by colonial authorities, adopted by urban nationalists, and localized by grassroots leaders. These patterns of exchange were shown to have occurred at every level of society, and consequently colonialism's shape became influenced by the concerns and mechanics of nationalism.

Colonialism's relationship to Southeast Asian nationalism developed significantly following the important insights of Anderson. One of his students, Thongchai Winichakul, extended the connections between colonial statecraft and nationalist identity by demonstrating the influence of map-making and the creation of Thai identity in his exceptional work, *Siam Mapped.* Though his emphasis was on the notion of "Thainess" and its relationship to boundaries, Winichakul's study reinforced the idea that colonial notions of space, measurement, ethnicity, and history were being actively engaged by Southeast Asian elites—even from those who were not formally colonized. Colonial knowledge was not something that was strictly part of the European conceptual world, it was constantly being reshaped, modified, and localized to fit the needs of Southeast Asians, who in many cases used these new ideas to emulate as well as resist European hegemony. Along the same lines, Maurizio Peleggi's *Lords of Things* demonstrates how the Thai monarchy embraced different forms of European material culture in an effort to redefine itself in the style of European monarchies, changing its public image through colonial ideas of modernization. Studies exploring the nature and origins of Southeast Asian nationalism indirectly contributed to the changing understanding of colonialism by continuing to challenge the terms and situations that characterized that encounter. Writing against the pervasive grain that had kept Southeast Asians locked in their temporal and spatial limbo, scholars began to investigate the ways in which technologies were disseminated and more often appropriated to transform the Southeast Asian conceptual world. Print culture, education, social engineering, and advancements in communication were actively being adopted to fit the needs of new and old elites alike, while at the same time these modes of colonialism were also being used to reify and remake "traditional" forms of Southeast Asian culture.

Trends in the Late 1990s and Early 2000s

Scholarship from the late 1990s and early 2000s has made provocative connections between the history of colonialism and the production of knowledge in Southeast Asia. Many of the categories and approaches used to conceptualize the region's contours—its cultures, institutions, languages, ethnicities, and histories—have been shown to be largely conceived, organized, and textualized by colonial administrator-scholars seeking to make legible the vast territories, societies, and peoples that had come under their authority. This legacy has not always been recognized, though active measures were taken by scholars in the 1960s and 1970s hoping to decolonize the epistemology of Southeast Asia by referring to categories and terms thought to be "autonomous" to the region. Although this scholarship produced the bulk of Southeast Asian knowledge, research from the late 1990s and beyond is noticing that some of these studies relied on categories and perspectives that emerged through colonial understandings of Southeast Asia. Turning to indigenous language sources or traditional perspectives was not enough—the evidence for what was considered traditional, indigenous, or autonomous was often based on the documents of officials who wrote into these sources their own agendas, concerns, and priorities.

One such example might be found in Laurie J. Sears's pathbreaking study *Shadows of Empire,* which reconstructs the way in which Dutch views of traditional *wayang kulit* (shadow-puppet theater) were adopted by scholars and Javanese alike. Not only is the role of the Dutch in the "inventing" of tradition explored, but Sears also charts the way in which the meanings of these cultural symbols were contested by officials, scholars, and performers throughout history. This approach recast the way in which colonialism was being considered: Elements thought to be distinctly Southeast Asian were now being reevaluated as products of colonialism, revealing the unsettled nature of "traditional" culture and revisiting European influence on the epistemological landscape of the region.

The picture of colonialism was that its reach was far more penetrating than once held and that through the study of more benign forms of authority, the actual extent of that influence might be perceived. Leading scholars such as Vicente L. Rafael, author of *White Love and Other Events in Filipino History,* and Rudolf Mrázek, author of *Engineers of Happy Land,* have revealed how colonial photography, roads, language policy, architecture, electricity, and travel literature reflect the relationship between colonial technology, knowledge, and power. Moreover, Mrázek's work employs an important and provocative approach by suggesting that it is possible to "read" colonial society and its forms like a text. In a sense, his unique "translation" of Dutch buildings, roads, and magazines applies approaches to colonial society that are usually reserved for studying Southeast Asia's deep past. Panivong Norindr's *Phantasmatic Indochina* addresses the ways in which French colonial ideology can be gleaned from its films, exhibitions, and architecture. More importantly, the studies contained within this work address how the very idea of "Indochine" was a concept that was invented, reified, and articulated to justify political-economic policies on the one hand and how cultural forms contributed to that imagining on the other. Ironically, colonial studies has gone from one end of the spectrum to the other; while early colonial administrators tried hard to textualize the boundaries and contents of their imagined colony, scholars today are disassembling those constructs by relying on the very sources those early officials produced.

Finally, advancement in gender and identity studies has also reworked the manner in which scholars have approached the relationship between colonialism and social policies. Just as the categories of colonizer and colonized were once problematized to reveal those communities lying "in-between," approaching colonialism through gender-inspired scholars to consider how European notions of womanhood transformed sexual relations and expectations of "native" women within colonial communities. These studies have explored the role and symbol of European motherhood in the colony and the manner in which this image affected policy toward the maintenance of white communities. By doing so, they have directly confronted the image of the colony as a site for "unfettered economic and sexual opportunity" through policies that attempted to curb men from racial intermixing and "going native."

Conclusion

Scholars continue to add to this discursive body of colonial knowledge, which has only recently and sporadically been problematized. Exploring the contexts in which much of this knowledge was produced has led to new questions about what is actually known about the region and new perspectives in which the scholarly understanding of colonialism in Southeast Asia might be expanded. These sentiments suggest that colonialism and colonial society can be studied from colonialism's cultural forms—its institutions, languages, ideas, economies, and literary representations—to reveal new perspectives about the processes of change and continuity. Proponents for this anthropology of colonialism suggest that by understanding how Southeast Asia was made through "scholarship," one can get a sense of colonialism and the effects of that encounter with the peoples and cultures of the region.

At the same time, considerable effort has been spent on delineating the actual conditions on the ground, which were much more complicated than perhaps official documents or earlier studies attempted to convey. Scholars have shifted their emphasis on rebellions as the sole sign of protest to show that resistance, subversion, and circumvention was occurring in an everyday fashion in everyday settings. Inconsistent policies toward Southeast Asians in rural and urban settings intensified incoherency, mismanagement, and competition among colonial officials while exacerbating tensions between metropole (European capitals) and colonial capitals. It is with this last trend where the idea of colonialism has taken its most current shape. Scholars within Southeast Asian studies are beginning to examine how competing interests, agendas, and concerns within colonial communities produced different boundaries in colonial society, while the contestation of categories has led to the understanding that the differences between European and Southeast Asian were created, defined, and maintained. Hybridity has not hidden the scholarly reemphasis on European colonialism within a Southeast Asian world, but if historiography repeats itself as much as history seems to, one can anticipate further studies of "Southeast Asian" hybridity in the colonial setting to emerge in the future.

See also **Anticolonialism: Southeast Asia; Empire and Imperialism: Asia; Westernization: Southeast Asia.**

BIBLIOGRAPHY

Anderson, Benedict. *Imagined Communities: Reflections on the Origin and Spread of Nationalism.* Rev. ed. London: Verso, 1991.

Cohn, Bernard S. *Colonialism and Its Forms of Knowledge: The British in India.* Princeton, N.J.: Princeton University Press, 1996.

Cooper, Frederick, and Ann Laura Stoler, eds. *Tensions of Empire: Colonial Cultures in a Bourgeois World.* Berkeley and Los Angeles: University of California Press, 1997.

Dirks, Nicholas B., ed. *Colonialism and Culture.* Ann Arbor: University of Michigan Press, 1992.

McHale, Shawn Frederick. *Print and Power: Confucianism, Communism, and Buddhism in the Making of Modern Vietnam.* Honolulu: University of Hawaii Press, 2004.

Mrázek, Rudolf. *Engineers of Happy Land: Technology and Nationalism in a Colony.* Princeton, N.J.: Princeton University Press, 2002.

Norindr, Panivong. *Phantasmatic Indochina: French Colonial Ideology in Architecture, Film, and Literature.* Durham, N.C.: Duke University Press, 1996.

Peleggi, Maurizio. *Lords of Things: The Fashioning of the Siamese Monarchy's Modern Image.* Honolulu: University of Hawaii Press, 2002.

Rafael, Vicente L. *White Love and Other Events in Filipino History.* Durham, N.C.: Duke University Press, 2000.

Reid, Anthony. *Southeast Asia in the Age of Commerce, 1450–1680,* Vol. 1: *The Lands below the Winds.* New Haven, Conn.: Yale University Press, 1988.

———. *Southeast Asia in the Age of Commerce, 1450–1680,* Vol. 2: *Expansion and Crisis.* New Haven, Conn.: Yale University Press, 1993.

Sears, Laurie J. *Shadows of Empire: Colonial Discourse and Javanese Tales.* Durham, N.C.: Duke University Press, 1996.

Stoler, Ann Laura. *Capitalism and Confrontation in Sumatra's Plantation Belt, 1870–1979.* 2nd ed. Ann Arbor: University of Michigan Press, 1995.

Tarling, Nicholas, ed. *The Cambridge History of Southeast Asia,* Vol. 2: *The Nineteenth and Twentieth Centuries.* Cambridge, U.K.: Cambridge University Press, 1992.

Thongchai Winichakul. *Siam Mapped: A History of the Geo-body of a Nation.* Honolulu: University of Hawaii Press, 1994.

Zinoman, Peter. *The Colonial Bastille: A History of Imprisonment in Vietnam, 1862–1940.* Berkeley and Los Angeles: University of California Press, 2001.

Maitrii Aung-Thwin

COMEDY. *See* **Humor; Tragedy and Comedy.**

COMMON SENSE.

The common-sense philosophers of the Scottish school—including Thomas Reid, Dugald Stewart, James Beattie, George Campbell, and James Oswald—argued against George Berkeley and David Hume that ordinary human perception and moral judgment need not be defended against skeptical inquiry but ought to be taken as self-evident. As Campbell put it, "to maintain propositions the reverse of the primary truths of common sense, doth not imply a contradiction, it only implies insanity" (*The Philosophy of Rhetoric,* 1776). The common-sense school was criticized by Immanuel Kant for its "appeal to the opinion of the multitude" (*Prolegomena,* 1783); Joseph Priestley, for example, wrote in his "examination" of Reid, Beattie, and Oswald (1774) that common sense is for persons of "middling" capacities. Nevertheless, their ideas enjoyed immense influence, not only in Great Britain but also in Germany and elsewhere. The idea that ordinary language can express principles of common sense, emphasized in the works of the Scottish school and also present in the work of the Italian jurist Giambattista Vico, led to interest in common sense on the part of later philosophers, including Henry Sidgwick, G. E. Moore, Hans-Georg Gadamer, J. L. Austin, and Hannah Arendt.

While most members of the Scottish school are read today primarily for historical interest, the work of the Presbyterian minister and professor of moral philosophy, Thomas Reid, has undergone a revival in recent years. Reid began his career at Marischal College in Aberdeen, where he founded the Aberdeen Philosophical Society, or "Wise Club." The group concentrated much of its energy on the work of fellow Scot David Hume. While the poet, zealous Christian, and anti-Humean polemicist, James Beattie, joined the society some nine years after its founding, most of its members were more concerned with establishing an empirical foundation for British learning than with combating potential heresy. Hume called Beattie's *Essay on the Nature and Immutability of Truth* (1770) "a horrible large lie in octavo"; though Hume disagreed with Reid's criticism of his work and once suggested in a letter to a mutual friend that pastors ought to stick to "worrying" each other and leave the philosophers to their arguments, he generally treated Reid with respect.

Hume's work was of great interest to the Aberdeen philosophers—and to members of the Scottish common-sense school in general—because it brings Cartesian skepticism to conclusions that, for them, are so contrary to ordinary human experience that they demonstrate the futility of all such philosophizing. In his *Inquiry* (1764), Reid writes that "since we cannot get rid of the vulgar notion and belief of an external world, [we ought] to reconcile our reason to it as well we can." Half a century earlier, Anthony Ashley Cooper, third earl of Shaftesbury, had argued in a commonsensical vein that it would be easier to imagine half of mankind mad than to deny the conclusions of "natural knowledge, fundamental reason, and common sense" ("Sensus Communis," 1710). For Shaftesbury, human beings have a natural faculty of moral sense.

One difficulty with tracing the influence of the idea of common sense is the variety of meanings attached to it even by thinkers in close geographical and historical proximity. Reid's commonsense access to moral judgment is much more like reasoned appeal to a self-evident principle than Shaftesbury's combination of feeling and thinking, and Francis Hutcheson's use of the term "moral sense" implies still less reason and still more immediate sensation than Shaftesbury's. Reid's realism is starkly opposed to Berkeleyan idealism, yet both authors appeal directly to the authority of common sense.

These difficulties aside, however, it is possible to specify several important views that set the Scottish common-sense school apart. First, common-sense philosophy criticized both moral and epistemological skepticism from the point of view of ordinary reason. This argument sometimes took the form of ad hominem attack on Hume: "Even the author of the *Treatise of human nature,* though he saw no reason for this belief [in hardness of bodies in nature], but many against it, could hardly conquer it in his speculative and solitary moments; at other times he fairly yielded to it, and confesses that he found it necessary to do so" (Reid, *Inquiry,* 1764).

Second, philosophy takes its starting point from the self-evident principles of common sense. For Oswald, these self-evident principles included many Christian religious doctrines, and indeed a good bit of the common-sense school's subsequent popularity lay in its claim to defend the religious views of ordinary British citizens from the perceived incursions of system-building philosophers. Reid's position on religion and self-evidence is more complex and interesting; for example, he argues that it makes no sense to deny the validity of perception while accepting that of reason because both faculties "come out of the same shop."

Third, not only does common sense furnish pragmatic certainty about the evidence of our senses and the existence of our selves, but it also provides natural insight into moral questions. Along with commonsense views of right and wrong comes the conviction of one's own human agency. Reid developed this idea into what contemporary philosophers would call an in-

compatibilist defense of freedom: for Reid, free human agents begin causal chains of events independent of natural causes.

The German reception of the Scottish common-sense philosophers is frequently described by commentators as a "misreception." Generally, while German readers were enthusiastic about the contributions of the Scots, they tended to empty the idea of "common sense" of the moral and social elements present in Reid's and others' work. The "popular philosophy" movement of the mid-eighteenth century in Germany shared the commonsense zeal of the Scottish school, and members of both groups criticized the absurdities of academic philosophizing. As Christian Garve put it (writing, in 1798, his observations on the most common principles of ethics), common sense is not "common because it is contemptible, but because it is, or should be, the common property of all human beings" Unlike the popular philosophers, Kant was highly critical of the Scottish common-sense school and its reading of Hume in his *Prolegomena* (1783); however, he took the concept of common sense itself seriously in his *Critique of Judgment* (1790). There Kant distinguished between "*sensus communis,*" considered as an idea of a comparative sense, and "common human understanding," which includes qualities exhibited by all normal human reason.

Of course Kant, unlike the Scottish school, denies that either *sensus communis* or common sense frees us from the need to justify our sensations and beliefs. However, Kant did provide some intriguing suggestions about both concepts' functions; each, in a different way, serves to replace unavailable certainty in judgment with an approximation of collective judgment. This aspect of Kant's treatment of common sense inspired Hannah Arendt's interesting independent reflections on the topic, which include the suggestion that when it comes to choosing between moral approbation and disapprobation, the "criterion . . . is communicability, and the standard of deciding about it is common sense."

See also **Enlightenment; Knowledge; Moral Sense; Skepticism.**

BIBLIOGRAPHY

Arendt, Hannah. *Lectures on Kant's Political Philosophy,* edited by Ronald Beiner. Chicago: University of Chicago Press, 1982.

Beattie, James. *An Essay on the Nature and Immutability of Truth: In Opposition to Sophistry and Skepticism.* 1770. Reprint, Bristol: Thoemmes Press, 1999.

Broadie, Alexander, ed. *The Cambridge Companion to the Scottish Enlightenment.* Cambridge, U.K.: Cambridge University Press, 2003.

Campbell, George. *The Philosophy of Rhetoric.* 1776. Reprint, edited by Lloyd F. Bitzer. Carbondale: Southern Illinois University Press, 1988.

Garve, Christian. *Einige Betrachtungen über die allgemeinsten Grundsätze der Sittenlehre.* Wroclaw, Poland: W. G. Korn, 1798.

Kant, Immanuel. *Prolegomena to Any Future Metaphysics.* 1783. Rev. ed., translated and edited by Gary Hatfield. Cambridge, U.K.: Cambridge University Press, 2004.

Oz-Salzberger, Fania. *Translating the Enlightenment: Scottish Civic Discourse in Eighteenth-Century Germany.* Oxford: Clarendon, 1995.

Priestley, Joseph. *An Examination of Dr. Reid's Inquiry into the Human Mind on the Principles of Common Sense, Dr. Beattie's Essay on the Nature and Immutability of Truth, and Dr. Oswald's Appeal to Common Sense in Behalf of Religion.* London: J. Johnson, 1774.

Reid, Thomas. *An Inquiry into the Human Mind: On the Principles of Common Sense,* edited by Derek Brookes. University Park: Pennsylvania State University Press, 1997. Authoritative, new critical edition.

Shaftesbury, Anthony Ashley Cooper, Earl of. "Sensus Communis, an Essay on the Freedom of Wit and Humour in a Letter to a Friend." 1710. Reprinted in Shaftesbury, *Characteristics of Men, Manners, Opinions, Times,* edited by Lawrence E. Klein. Cambridge, U.K.: Cambridge University Press, 1999.

Yaffe, Gideon. *Manifest Activity: Thomas Reid's Theory of Action.* Oxford: Clarendon, 2004.

Elisabeth Ellis